HANDBOOKS IN OPERATIONS RESEARCH
AND MANAGEMENT SCIENCE
VOLUME 9

Handbooks in Operations Research and Management Science

Editors

G.L. Nemhauser
Georgia Institute of Technology

A.H.G. Rinnooy Kan
Erasmus University Rotterdam

Volume 9

ELSEVIER
Amsterdam – Lausanne – New York – Oxford – Shannon – Tokyo

Finance

Edited by

R.A. Jarrow
Cornell University

V. Maksimovic
University of Maryland

W.T. Ziemba
University of British Columbia

ELSEVIER
Amsterdam – Lausanne – New York – Oxford – Shannon – Singapore – Tokyo

ELSEVIER SCIENCE B.V.
Sara Burgerhartstraat 25
P.O. Box 211, 1000 AE Amsterdam, The Netherlands

First edition: 1995
Second impression: 1998

ISBN: 0 444 89084 X

This book is printed on acid-free paper.

Printed in The Netherlands.

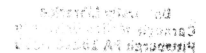

Preface

The Handbook of Finance is a primary reference work for financial economics and financial modeling students, faculty and practitioners. The expository treatments are suitable for masters and PhD students with discussions leading from first principles to current research with reference to important research works in the area. This handbook is intended to be a synopsis of the current state of various aspects of the theory of financial economics and its application to important financial problems. The coverage consists of thirty-three chapters written by leading experts in the field. The contributions are in two broad categories: capital markets and corporate finance. The chapters are tutorial and survey-like in nature with expositions that vary from discussion of important results of the area in great detail to general treatments to more cursory presentation of key results with reference to where to find their development in their original presentation.

Financial economics has undergone a very rapid development in the past thirty years. While this handbook is in the Operations Research/Management Science series, the treatment is in most cases in the mainstream of financial economics theory and empirical measurement. It is noteworthy that the three Nobel Laureates in Financial Economics, Professors Harry M. Markowitz, Merton H. Miller and William F. Sharpe all began their careers with strong operations research/management science backgrounds and used this knowledge and techniques throughout their careers. Some of their work is discussed in this handbook.

While this volume is a large one comprising over 1100 pages and the treatment of topics is thorough, the vastness of the subject matter of finance preludes the possibility of an exhaustive survey. We have chosen to include what we think are the key topics of the theory with strong emphasis on empirical work and practice. Hopefully the background in these thirty-three chapters will lay the foundations for further study of leading journals, books and other research materials.

Capital Markets

Portfolio theory is the analysis of the real world phenomenon of diversification. Chapter 1 by Constantinides and Malliaris exposits this theory in its historical evolution, from the early work on static mean-variance mathematics to its generalization of dynamic consumption and portfolio rules. In its intellectual development, portfolio theory has benefited from empirical work which came from capital asset pricing tests and from statistical investigations of the distribution of asset prices. Furthermore, as more powerful techniques were developed, such as stochastic calculus, portfolio theory became dynamic and many results were generalized. The modification of the theoretical results of portfolio theory due to transaction costs is also presented.

In Chapter 2, Naik presents key results in securities market models and arbitrage. The material in this fundamental chapter underlies the arbitrage-free pricing methodology used in modern option pricing theory [see Chapters 8, 9 and 11 below]. Naik studies finite state securities market models on a finite horizon. This setting facilitates mathematical analysis as well as the economic intuition. In this chapter, the concept of no arbitrage is first defined, and characterized under frictionless markets, i.e., no transaction costs nor trading constraints. This frictionless setting is then relaxed, and a characterization of no arbitrage is given under various types of market frictions.

In Chapter 3, Hakansson and Ziemba review the theory of capital growth, in particular the growth-optimal investment strategy, its properties, its uses, and its links to betting and other investment models. This strategy, also known as the geometric mean model and the Kelly criterion, implies, and is implied by, a logarithmic utility function. The strategy has many very desirable properties such as maximizing the long-run growth of capital asymptotically — even though the optimal policy is myopic. Among the less appealing properties are the fact the growth-optimal strategy does not maximize expected utility for non-log utility functions, and that it is more risk-tolerant than the average investor. This suggests trading off growth for security of wealth using fractional Kelly strategies, for example. Hakansson and Ziemba derive the conditions for optimal capital growth, relate the model to other investment strategies, show its role in inter temporal investment/consumption models and review various applications.

Connor and Korajczyk survey the multi-factor arbitrage pricing theory of Ross and extensions of that theory in Chapter 4. The basic insight is that a linear factor model of asset returns, in an economy with a large number of assets implies that the idiosyncratic risk is diversifiable and that the equilibrium prices of securities will be approximately linear in their factor exposures. They discuss theoretical results, econometric testing and applications of the APT to problems in investments and corporate finance. The model assumes that the random return of each security is a linear combination of a small number of common factors plus asset specific random variables. The vector random process can be divided to separate the nondiversifiable from the diversifiable components of risk as in the CAPM (discussed in Chapter 5 by Ferson). The authors carefully consider the testability of the APT using equilibrium-based derivations of the pricing relationships well diversified portfolio approximations to the latter, via competitive equilibrium models, and with models assuming an infinite number of assets.

The CAPM holds if the market portfolio (a particular linear combination of factor portfolios) is mean-variance efficient. The CAPM requires observations of the market portfolio returns whereas the APT requires observation of the factors or factor-mimicking portfolios. Whether or not one of the models outperforms the other is difficult to ascertain since neither is a restricted (nested) version of the other. However, in the cases in which the APT is compared to implementation of the CAPM, the APT better explains the cross section in asset returns and explains some pricing anomalies not explained by the CAPM, and it generally has lower pricing errors. The discussion of empirical tests of the APT discusses a variety of applications such as the US and international modeling, portfolio performance evaluation, cost of capital estimation, and event studies.

Ferson, in Chapter 5, integrates the major asset pricing models such as those related to the CAPM, consumption and production based models and ARCH-GARCH using a self contained discussion based on simple first principles. He then reviews empirical tests of the models with a unified framework using the generalized method of moments due to Hansen. This allows the estimation and testing of models, termed conditional asset pricing models, where the expected returns and risks of the assets may change over time with the arrival of new information. Ferson concludes by reviewing cross-sectional regression methods. The role of conditioning information in these models represents significant challenges for future theoretical and empirical research on asset pricing.

In Chapter 6, Stultz reviews international portfolio choice theories using a common framework based on the international capital asset pricing model, assesses their empirical tests and discusses their relevance to the field of international finance. If investment and consumption opportunity sets do not differ across countries then currencies have no significant effect on portfolio choice and asset pricing. Traditional approaches to portfolio choice and asset pricing, as discussed in earlier chapters by Constantinides and Mallarios and Ferson, respectively, do not accurately predict asset holdings across countries, in particular, the home bias for investments. However, they are useful in explaining the cross sectional variation in conditional expected returns across countries. Stultz then shows how the predictions of these models change if there are differences in consumption and investment opportunity sets.

In Chapter 7, Carr and Jarrow review the literature in the area of options and futures. This is an immense body of work, spanning more than twenty years of investigation. This chapter studies this literature by synthesizing the existing results as special cases of a more general valuation model based on the evolution of a term structure of futures prices. This general valuation approach is consistent with current research perspectives and is based on the methodology of Chapter 2. The setting is a discrete time, binomial model. Extensions are discussed.

Jarrow, in Chapter 8 summaries the recent literature in the area of interest rate options. A discrete time model illustrates the application of the no arbitrage techniques of Chapter 2 to the pricing of interest rate options. A theoretical perspective is taken where different models in the literature are presented as special cases of a more general formulation. Some of the models included in this analysis are those of Black, Derman and Toy, Hull and White, Ho and Lee, and Heath, Jarrow, and Morton. This review provides an integrative exposition of the various models currently available.

Chapter 9 by Marsh applies the techniques presented in Chapter 8 on interest rate options and the equilibrium pricing methodologies underlying Chapter 1 to the pricing of fixed income claims and bonds. The paper first reviews the pricing models, then applies them to default-free bond valuation. Calibration issues, estimation, and stochastic process specification issues are discussed.

Stock index futures and program trading are among the most important financial market innovations of the 1980's. In Chapter 10, Canina and Figlewski survey the literature and provide an overview of the somewhat controversial area of index arbitrage. They begin with a description of how index futures work, how they should be priced in equilibrium according to the 'cost of carry' model, and how index arbitrage works to enforce the theoretical pricing relationship. In theory, index arbitrage is riskless, but they describe how it is affected in practice by transactions costs, execution risk, capital and short sales constraints, and the possibility of unwinding profitable trades before futures expiration. They conclude with a discussion of the impact of index futures and arbitrage on the volatility of the underlying stock market.

Torous, in Chapter 11, applies the arbitrage pricing theory of Chapter 2 to the valuation of mortgage backed securities. The paper begins with a categorization of the different types of mortgages. It then discusses mortgage pass-through securities and the different types of collateralized mortgage obligations. In valuing these claims, the most difficult component to analyze is the prepayment risk. A general class of prepayment models is provided, and the valuation of mortgage backed securities is illustrated.

In Chapter 12, Easley and O'Hara review the area of market microstructure, an alternative approach to Chapter 1 for understanding the pricing of securities. Market microstructure studies the interaction of the institutional trading rules with the information and trading preferences of investors to obtain the price process. This paper reviews the literature, beginning with a study of the rational expectations paradigm. Included are analyses of the models of Kyle, and the models of Easley and O'Hara, among others.

In Chapter 13, DeBondt and Thaler provide a selected review of recent work in behavioral finance. They observe that financial economics is, perhaps, the least behavioral of the various subdisciplines of economics in that the standard paradigm does not consider what people actually do but rather what they should do. In financial economics, as surveyed in many of the chapters in this volume, it is assumed that investors optimize their actions subject to rational economic models without error. Several contributions in the volume, particularly chapters 16–18, utilize results along the lines discussed by DeBondt and Thaler that consider behavioral aspects, non-optimal behavior and various imperfections. The authors begin by discussing concepts such as overconfidence, non-Bayesian forecasting, loss aversion, framing, mental accounting, fashions and fads, regret, responsibility and prudence. They then consider investor psychology and market prices in general with discussions of the effects of trading volumes, contrarian investment strategies, investor sentiment, closed-end mutual fund discounts and premiums, the equity premium puzzle, dividend policy, earnings management, and corporate expansion and decline. The ideas point to problems with the ability of many existing theories to explain observed market behavior and to possible ways to improve these theories.

In Chapter 14, Le Roy and Steigerwald use Monte Carlo methods to compaı the power of volatility and returns tests of the present-value model of stock prices against the alternative that stock prices contain a white noise component. The variances of the price dividends ratio and rate of return are assumed constant and, in the case of the model-based volatility test, dividends are specified to follow a geometric random walk. These assumptions were assumed satisfied in the Monte Carlo runs as well. They find that a model-free volatility test has greater power than the benchmark returns test and that a model-based volatility test constructed on the assumption that dividends follow a geometric random walk has far greater explanatory power than the benchmark returns test. These results are due to low sample variability as the sample variances of the ex-post rational price dividends ratio, the actual price dividends ratio and the rate of return are highly correlated. The superiority of the volatility tests demonstrated by the Monte Carlo results reflects the fact that the volatility tests require stronger assumptions than the returns tests.

Asset allocation choices are the most important investment decisions for long-term investors. Chapter 15, by Mulvey and Ziemba, describes a range of practical techniques for modeling the allocation mix over time. Starting with the static Markowitz mean-variance model, they show that additional realistic issues can be handled via multi-stage stochastic programming models. The advantages of integrating assets, liabilities, and investment goals using discrete probability scenarios to model the uncertainty over time are discussed. The role of global investing is emphasized in the context of optimal diversification strategies. The authors review various practical applications of asset-liability management modeling systems for pension plans, insurance companies, and individual investors.

In Chapter 16, Kleidon studies stock market crashes focusing on whether particular large decreases in investor wealth in short periods are consistent with rational individual behavior. He first outlines evidence from experimental security markets in settings when individuals do not completely aggregate their private information to yield fully revealing prices. The laboratory results suggest that crashes are more likely to occur when there is an absence of common information about preferences or beliefs of other traders and a lack of market experience in the market setting. These results are consistent with the economics of information aggregation. Kleidon then examines alternative explanations of the October 1987 crash. This includes an examination of models that contain new *internal* information about fundamentals operating within a framework of rational expectations. A crash may occur even without new identifiable external news but rather from the aggregation of diverse information already known to various individuals. Changes in *external* information about fundamentals can explain some crashes such as October 1989. However, the crashes of 1929 and 1987 require changes in internal information about fundamentals revealed through the trading process to be consistent with rational economic models. This chapter concludes with a discussion of various responses to crashes such as the Brady Commission's proposals for a single regulatory authority to oversee the stock, futures and options market, unified margin requirements and circuit breakers, as well as sunshine trading, securities transactions costs and the responses of monetary authorities to crashes.

In Chapter 17, Hawawini and Keim examine empirical findings concerned with the predictability of stock prices in US and worldwide equity markets. They survey numerous findings that document persistent cross section and time series patterns in returns that are not predicted by asset pricing models such as those discussed in chapters 4 and 5. The authors do not focus on tests of market inefficiency which would be joint tests of particular equilibrium models with the possible market inefficiency. Rather they concentrate on a presentation of the evidence. This consists of cross sectional predictability in the relationship of returns with fundamental variables such as size, earnings to price and price to book ratios. They also document evidence concerning in time series returns such as return autocorrelations and seasonal return patterns. The latter focuses on anomalous return distributions such as the January turn-of-the-year, turn-of-the-month, holiday and day-of-the-week effects.

Sports and lottery betting markets are well suited for testing market efficiency and bettor rationality. Vast price and fundamental data is available, and technical and fundamental systems abound that utilize this information. Each bet has a specified termination point when its final asset value (possibly zero) is determined. For rationality tests this latter property has an advantage over most security markets where current value depends upon future events and current expectations of future values. Since the expected return in these betting markets is negative there is a search for systems that provide winning strategies. Such technical systems exist in a number of circumstances such as in blackjack by card counting, in horseracing by using price information in simple markets to fairly price wagers in more complex markets, and in lotteries by wagering on unpopular numbers. In Chapter 18, Hausch and Ziemba survey this literature. They discuss the level of gambling in the US. They then focus on racetrack efficiency in various markets such as win, place, show, exotics and cross tracks. They describe how efficiencies might be exploited using the capital growth methods discussed by Hakansson and Ziemba in Chapter 3. They conclude by discussing efficiency of football, basketball and lottery betting markets.

Institutional investors manage trillions of dollars in equity portfolios. Together with individual investors, they are the market. Grinblatt and Titman, in Chapter 19, study performance evaluation of managers and seek to develop theories that will evaluate the economic worth of portfolio managers. They begin with the basic premise that mean returns are positively related to risk. The performance measures studied adjust returns for priced risk and, in some cases, for diversification. They compare active management returns with benchmark passive buy and hold portfolios with the same level of risk. They consider two classes of measures, namely, those that require the observation of the returns of the evaluated portfolio plus those of one or more benchmark portfolios and a risk-free asset; and those with information about the composition of the evaluated portfolio but not necessarily any benchmark portfolios. They utilize strong stationary assumptions for both classes, with normality required for some in the first class. They attempt to address the Roll critique concerning the choice of the passive portfolio benchmark and joint test problems. Measures in the first class include Treynor's ratio, Jensen's alpha and the Treynor–Black appraisal ratio. Measures in the second class include the event study measure used by Copeland and Mayers to study the Value Line rankings and measures devised by Grinblatt and Titman. They conclude that there is little evidence that mutual funds can time the market but that some mutual funds consistently achieve abnormal returns through their stock selection procedures.

In Chapter 20, Cherian and Jarrow study the impact of relaxing the competitive market assumption in Chapter 1 on security pricing theory. This impact is analyzed from the perspective of market manipulation, which (roughly defined) is the strategic manipulation of prices to one's advantage. This is a new area of financial economic theory. This chapter reviews this literature via a general model where the existing theories can be classified as special cases.

Corporate Finance

Chapters 21–33 deal with various aspects of corporate finance theory and empirical testing of these theories.

In Chapter 21, Sick summaries the basic techniques for analyzing real options. Such options arise from the flexibility a manager has to choose the time to commence a project, to abandon a project and to adjust production levels within an operating project. The ideas are related to those of the financial option literature. However, the early exercise decision is more important in real options analysis. Also, the underlying risk often cannot easily be summarized by the price changes of a traded financial asset, so greater flexibility in modeling project value is needed. The ability to formulate useful and understandable models is more important than precise estimates of option values. This Chapter relates real option analysis to the classic capital budgeting techniques of cost of-capital and present-value analysis. Sick also relates asset pricing to state-space pricing, martingale pricing and consumption asset pricing theory; develops a tax adjustment to the riskless bond return for a real options analysis; develops the intuition behind the fundamental partial differential equations that are used to price options and futures; and shows how to use futures markets to impute convenience dividends, which are necessary for real options analysis. Additive and lognormal diffusions as well as two mean-reverting models are discussed. Sick discusses how to build tree-like lattice structures to value these options. The chapter concludes by discussing other work from the real options literature.

Financial economists have devoted considerable attention to contracts between different classes of investors and between the firm and its managers. These contracts are important because they determine the incentives of both the firm's equity holders and its managers, thereby affecting the firm's conduct.

The traditional approach to analysis of the firm's contractual arrangements has been to take as given the existence of commonly observed contractual arrangements, such as debt and equity, and to trace out the effects on incentives of changing the levels of these instruments. An advantage of this approach is that it often yields tractable models. However, because the form of the contracts is exogenous in these models, the question whether the firms being modeled would optimally chose this set of contracts is not discussed.

Another strand of the literature, examined by Allen and Winton in Chapter 22, explicitly derives optimal financial contracts as responses to conflicts of interest between different agents in the corporation.

One of the most significant conflicts of interest within the firm is that between the firm's insiders (owners and managers) and potential new investors. In many cases the firm's insiders have better access to information about the firm than potential investors. As a result, investors attempt to infer the insiders' information from the firm's decisions to issue securities and its choice of securities to issue. As Myers and Majluf (1984) showed, these responses to the informational asymmetry by investors may induce insiders to deviate from investment decisions that maximize firm value.

Several important recent contributions to the theory corporate finance have extended the argument in Myers and Majluf to argue that the firm's principal financial decisions, such as its dividend policy and the timing of the initiation of investment projects, can act as signals that convey information that mitigates the problems identified by Myers and Majluf. As pointed out in the literature, attempts to communicate with investors in this way themselves introduce costly distortions in the firm's optimal financial and investment policies.

The signaling role of each of these financial decisions has typically been considered in isolation. As a result, it is not clear if the financial signals considered in the literature induce equivalent policy distortions, and if not, how their costs compare. In Chapter 23, Daniel and Titman provide a unified framework for analyzing a large class of signals proposed in the literature. They show that many of these signals impose costs that are equivalent to money burning. They further show how the dissipative costs of different signals is affected by the nature of the information asymmetry.

In the last thirty years numerous contributions in the financial economics literature have explored how the tax system affects the choice of securities that firms issue. Systematic differences in the tax treatment of income from different classes of securities suggest that taxes may be an important determinant of firms' financing choices. However, because the effective marginal tax rates on income differs across investors, a full understanding of how taxes affect financing choices requires considerations of the entire tax system.

In Chapter 24, Swoboda and Zechner present a framework for analyzing the capital structure equilibria for the tax systems in the principal developed economies. The framework enables them to exhibit clearly how the finer features of the tax system, such as the priority in bankruptcy of tax payments, principal repayments and interest payments, may affect the existence of optimal financing choices for firms. They also describe how the insights from single country tax models can be extended to analyze financing choices in a multinational setting.

Decisions on dividends are among the most visible components of a corporation's financial policy and dividend policy has received a great deal of attention by researchers. As a result of a large body of empirical work, we have made a great deal of progress in characterizing the dividend policies of American firms.

As pointed out by Allen and Michaely in Chapter 25, the challenge to financial economists has been to explain the empirically observed dividend policies by models based on optimizing behavior of firms and investors. Unfortunately, this has proved more difficult to accomplish than might have been expected. Several important observations have been difficult to explain satisfactorily. In particular, the fact that corporations pay dividends even though share repurchases offer substantial tax advantages has puzzled financial economists (Black (1976)) and has provoked a great many attempts to explain it.

Allen and Michaely begin their review of the theoretical literature by discussing Miller and Modigliani (1961). Modigliani and Miller exhibit conditions under which the firm's dividend policy does not affect its value. Allen and Michaely use this model as a benchmark against which they evaluate the assumptions of subsequent models that attempt to justify dividend policy in terms of value maximization. They conclude that the theoretical literature has identified several potential "imperfections" — taxes, informational asymmetries, institutional constraints, transactions costs and incomplete contracts — that may induce value maximizing firms to adopt specific dividend policies. However, as they point out, financial economists are not yet in a position to convert these insights into specific policy advice.

In Chapter 26, Hirshleifer studies strategic and informational issues in takeovers (both mergers and acquisitions). Leaving aside whether takeovers have positive, neutral or negative economic value, he focuses on the decision making relevant to takeovers. There are many conflicts of interest and informational differences among parties to takeovers: bidding shareholders may only want an acquisition if the price of the target is not too high compared to underlying value; bidding management may seek self-aggrandizement through takeover; target shareholders may wish to obtain a price that fully reflects any possible takeover improvements; target management may wish to retain private benefits of control; and potential competing bidders must decide whether to make their own offers. In some cases, the decisions of a few shareholders are pivotal. Hirshleifer describes the relationships between different models of the takeover process and integrates major trends in the literature. He focuses on models of tender offers which examine the decisions of individual shareholders whether to tender (sell) their shares to a bidder; models of competition among multiple bidders; and models that examine the voting power of target managers who own shares. He considers the impact of asymmetric information, bid revision, regulations, means of payment, and how pivotal a shareholder is (concentration of ownership).

Corporate finance is largely concerned with the effect of financial and capital budgeting policies on the choice and the value of exogenously given projects. Relatively little attention has been paid to the firm's product market environment. As a result, less is known about how the structure of the firm's financial contracts affects its ability to compete with rival firms and to contract with customers. However, recently, several means by which financial structure affects value in product markets have been identified in the literature.

In Chapter 27, Maksimovic reviews recent contributions that have attempted to characterize possible links between the firm's product market strategy and its financing choices. The links considered are: the effect of investment choices of other firms in the industry on the interaction between the firm's financial structure and its investment incentives; the effect of debt on a firm's ability to enter into advantageous implicit and explicit contracts with competitors or customers; the effects of changes in leverage on firms' incentives and on industry equilibrium in oligopolies; and the exploitation by competitors of conflicts of interest caused by the firm's need to finance its investments externally.

This chapter also reviews several attempts to empirically test models of financial-product market interactions. Empirical testing is still at an early stage. The range of interactions that have to be quantified is greater than that in typical financial models and the product-market data is usually more difficult to obtain. Moreover, the predictions of the models frequently depend on values of specific parameters. Despite these difficulties considerable progress has been made in empirically testing several of the models.

A key question in the corporate finance literature is whether insolvent firms are efficiently reorganized and the assets of unproductive firms are effectively redeployed. In the United States, the legal framework for the resolution of impaired contractual claims held against the firm is provided by the Bankruptcy Act of 1978. In Chapter 28, Senbet and Seward discuss the economic implications of the main provisions of the Act and, more generally, the incentives of the firm's stakeholders when the firm is in financial distress.

As Senbet and Seward show, financial economists have made important strides in the analysis of financial distress and bankruptcy. One of the primary contributions has been to clarify the distinction between economic distress, which results from the inability of the firm to meet the demands of the marketplace, and financial distress, which results from the difficulty in meeting its financial obligations. This distinction is important because the resolution of the two problems often differs: a reorganization of the firm's operations is required in the former case, whereas a restructuring of its financial claims may be appropriate in the latter case. Once the distinction is understood, then the direct and indirect costs of financial distress can be identified and attempts in the literature to measure them empirically can be evaluated. Senbet and Seward also review the literature on financial distress and incentives. Financial distress frequently alters the incentives of the firm's stakeholders — owners, managers, workers, customers and others whose well-being depends on the firm's performance. If invoked, the Bankruptcy Act itself changes the bargaining power of the stakeholders in economically significant ways. These effects on incentives are important because they affect the likelihood of an efficient resolution of financial distress. They are also interesting from a research perspective, because the heightened conflicts between the stakeholders provide an excellent setting in which to observe the effects of incentives on the behavior of agents, the consequences of asymmetries of information between the firm's insiders and investors and the effect of financial structure on the firm's product market behavior. These issues are discussed in the chapters by Allen and Winton [22], Daniel and Titman [23], and Maksimovic [27], respectively.

A primary empirical research methodology in empirical corporate finance is the use of financial market reactions to corporate events to test hypotheses about the process by which the firm creates value. While most empirical researchers in corporate finance use this research design, known as event study methodology, there has not existed a unified analysis and evaluation of these methods. In Chapter 29, Thompson provides a systematic treatment of the empirical methods used in event studies and a guide to practitioners. As described by Thompson, in an event study the researcher first postulates a link between a specific event of interest (e.g., the disclosure of a takeover attempt) and the value of traded securities issued by the corporation. The researcher then attempts to estimate the difference between the value of the traded security conditional on the event occurring and the value of the security conditional on the event not occurring. Inferences about the validity of the initial hypotheses are based on these estimates.

The appropriate estimator of the differences of the conditional valuations depends in general on the specifics of the event being examined. Thompson introduces a general framework that encompasses many of the existing empirical studies and discusses specific methods appropriate to several important estimation problems faced in practice. He also addresses several conceptual problems that arise in the application of event-study methodology. In particular, any methodology that relies on market reactions to corporate events as a measure of value may be affected by the market's prior expectations of the event. As Thompson points out, this may have implications about the hypotheses that can be tested by event-study methods.

Initial public offerings (IPOs) have received considerable attention in the corporate finance literature. Much interest has been generated by the fact that researchers have identified several interesting empirical facts about IPOs that have not been successfully explained by theory. Thus, there have been no wholly satisfactory explanations for the fact that new issues tend, on the average, to be underpriced, that there appear to be cycles in the magnitude of this underpricing and that, in the long-run, new issues appear to underperform the market. Equally perplexing, some entrepreneurs appear to be pleased when the after-market price of their shares exceeds the offer price, allowing the initial purchasers of their shares to realize a quick gain.

Researchers have sought to explain these anomalies as rational outcomes in a market with significant asymmetries of information. As discussed in the chapters by Allen and Winton [22] and Daniel and Titman [23], such asymmetries may generate seemingly perverse incentives and market failures. Since IPOs frequently involve small, risky firms exploiting untried technologies, these problems are likely to be particularly severe in the market for new issues. The conjunction of anomalous observations, together with the conviction that these observations can be explained by adverse selection or moral hazard, has produced several very creative theoretical explanations. Ibbotson and Ritter begin their chapter on IPOs by examining the three IPO empirical anomalies noted above and by discussing the principal proposed explanations. They then discuss the IPO as an event in the firm's life-cycle. Finally, they briefly review some of the mechanisms by which firms go public.

In Chapter 31, Eckbo and Masulis survey research on seasoned equity offerings. Seasoned equity offerings are important, both in their own right, and because firms' choices while making a seasoned offering (e.g., choices of flotation method, timing and issue size) provide investors with information about their financial standing. By analyzing these choices and the stock market's reactions to them, researchers have gained insights into the asymmetries of information that exist between issuing firms and investors. Eckbo and Masulis begin by examining the empirical evidence on the frequency of seasoned offerings and the differences in costs of alternative floatation methods. They relate the empirical findings to models of flotation choice that explicitly allow for asymmetries of information between issuing firms and investors. In their concluding sections they focus on the decision to issue, and review research on the relationship between issue activity and the business cycle. In their examination of secondary offerings, Eckbo and Masulis address some of the most fundamental theoretical issues in corporate finance. In particular, their chapter is closely related to Daniel and Titman's chapter on the theory of financing investment under asymmetric information. The two chapters complement each other: Daniel and Titman systematically explore a specific theoretical paradigm while Eckbo and Masulis review the empirical evidence on an important class of transactions and draw a broader set of theoretical arguments as required.

In recent years there has been dramatic innovation in the services offered by financial intermediaries. There has also been corresponding progress in techniques for valuing these services and analyzing the economic benefits they provide for sellers and buyers. In Chapter 32, Thakor provides an overview of the principal services provided by intermediaries and illustrates how tools from information economics can be used in evaluating them. Thakor classifies the services provided by intermediaries into two categories: brokerage services and qualitative asset transformations. A brokerage service is provided when an intermediary facilitates a financial transaction without affecting the payoffs either party receives from the traded contract. A qualitative asset transformation occurs when the intermediary's participation affects the payoffs of the claims being traded. For each of these types of services, Thakor identifies the potential value added by an intermediary and discusses the role of diversification. Issues in qualitative asset transformation are illustrated by extended consideration two examples: loan commitments and interest rate swaps.

Certain types of qualitative asset transformation may require that intermediaries take on risks. In Chapter 32, Thakor argues that because it is difficult to monitor the amount of risk that intermediaries take on, they may have an incentive to engage in excessive risk-taking. Pyle's Chapter 33 on the U.S. Savings and Loan Crisis illustrates both the risks of qualitative asset transformation and the incentives for opportunistic behavior that accompanied it. The crisis that engulfed the U.S. savings and loans industry was of major proportions. As Pyle notes, over 1100 insolvent S&Ls were closed down by government agencies. The final cost of the debacle is in excess of two hundred billion dollars. In the period leading up to the crisis S&Ls were heavily engaged in a specific asset transformation: their assets were principally long-term fixed rate mortgages while their liabilities were short-term deposits. Pyle shows how this imbalance, when combined with dysfunctional governmental regulations and deposit guarantees that provided perverse incentives, created the conditions for the crisis. One of the few heartening aspects of this account is Pyle's demonstration of how the tools of financial analysis can be used to analyze the incentives of depositors and the S&Ls in the period before the crisis.

Robert Jarrow
Vojislav Maksimovic
William T. Ziemba

May 1995

Contents

R. Jarrow et al., Eds., *Handbooks in OR & MS, Vol. 9*

Chapter 1

Portfolio Theory

G.M. Constantinides
Graduate School of Business, University of Chicago, 1101 East 58th Street, Chicago, IL 60637, U.S.A.; and NBER

A.G. Malliaris
School of Business Administration, Loyola University of Chicago, 820 North Michigan Avenue, Chicago, IL 60611, U.S.A.

1. Introduction

Consider a consumer with a given amount of income. Such a consumer typically faces two important economic decisions. First, how to allocate his or her current consumption among goods and services. Second, how to invest among various assets. These two interrelated consumer or household problems are known as the consumption-saving decision and the portfolio selection decision.

Beginning with Adam Smith, economists have systematically studied the first decision. Arguing that a consumer will choose commodities and services that offer the greatest marginal utility relative to price, a theory of value was developed that combines subjective notions from consumer utility with objective notions from the production theory of the firm. By the beginning of the twentieth century, neoclassical economists had developed a static theory of consumer behavior as part of an analysis of market pricing under conditions of perfect competition and certainty.

The asset allocation decision was not adequately addressed by neoclassical economists, probably because they treated savings as the supply of loanable funds in developing a theory of interest rate determination instead of portfolio selection. More importantly, however, these two decisions, although closely interrelated, require substantially different methodologies. The methodology of deterministic calculus is adequate for the decision of maximizing a consumer's utility subject to a budget constraint. Portfolio selection involves making a decision under uncertainty. The probabilistic notions of expected return and risk become very important. Neoclassical economists did not have such a methodology available to them and despite some very early attempts by probabilists, like Bernoulli [1738] to define and measure risk, or Irving Fisher [1906] to describe asset returns in terms of a probability distribution, the twin concepts of expected return and risk had not yet been fully integrated. An early and important attempt to do that was made by

Marschak [1938] who expressed preferences for investment by indifference curves in the mean–variance space.[1]

The methodological breakthrough of treating axiomatically the theory of choice under uncertainty was offered by von Neumann & Morgenstern [1947] and it was only a few years later that Markowitz [1952, 1959] and Tobin [1958], used this theory to formulate and solve the portfolio selection problem.

In this essay we plan to exposit portfolio theory with a special emphasis on its historical evolution and methodological foundations. In Section 2, we describe the early work of Markowitz [1952, 1959] and Tobin [1958] to illustrate the individual contributions of these authors. Following these general remarks about the early beginning of portfolio theory, we define and solve the mean–variance portfolio problem in Section 3 and relate it to its most famous intellectual first fruits, namely the two-fund separation and the capital asset pricing theory of Sharpe [1964] and Lintner [1965] in Sections 4, 5 and 6. In particular, a portion of Section 6 is devoted to the presentation of Roll's [1977] critique of the asset pricing theory's tests and the interplay of analysis and empirical testing. This leads to an analysis of the foundational assumptions of portfolio theory with respect to investor preferences and asset return distributions, both reviewed in Section 7. The contrast of methodologies is illustrated in Sections 8 and 9 where stochastic calculus and stochastic control techniques are used to generalize the consumption-investment problem to an arbitrary number of periods. Market imperfections are addressed in Section 10. The last section identifies several extensions and refers the reader to several articles, some included in this volume. It also contains our summary and conclusions.

2. The early contributions

Markowitz [1952] marks the beginning of modern portfolio theory, where for the first time, the problem of portfolio selection is clearly formulated and solved. Earlier contributions of Keynes [1936], Marschak [1938] and others only tangentially analyze investment decisions. Markowitz's focus is the explanation of the phenomenon of portfolio diversification.

Before Markowitz could propose the "expected returns–variance of returns" rule, he first had to discredit the then widely accepted principle that an investor chooses a portfolio by selecting securities that maximize discounted expected returns.[2] Markowitz points out that if an investor follows this rule, his or her

[1] Marschak [1938, p. 312] recognizes that "the unsatisfactory state of Monetary Theory as compared with General Economics is due to the fact that the principle of determinateness so well established by Walras and Pareto for the world of perishable consumption goods and labor services has never been applied with much consistency to durable goods and, still less, to claims (securities, loans, cash)". In our modern terminology we could replace the names Monetary Theory and General Economics with Financial Economics and Microeconomic Theory, respectively.

[2] Markowitz refers the reader to a standard investments textbook by Williams [1938] that elaborates the notion that portfolio choice is guided by the rule of maximizing the discounted

portfolio will consist of only one stock, namely the one that has the highest discounted expected return which is contrary to the observed phenomenon of diversification. Therefore a rule of investor behavior which does not yield portfolio diversification must be rejected. Furthermore, the rejection of this rule holds no matter how expectations of future returns are formed and how discount rates are selected. Markowitz then proposes the expected mean returns–variance of returns M–V rule. He concludes that the M–V rule not only implies diversification, it actually implies the right kind of diversification for the right reason. In trying to reduce the portfolio variance, it is not enough to just invest in many securities. It is important to diversify across securities with low return covariances. In 1959, Markowitz published a monograph on the same topic. In the last part (consisting of four chapters) and in an appendix, portfolio selection is grounded firmly as rational choice under uncertainty.

In contrast to Markowitz's contributions which may be viewed as microeconomic, Tobin [1958] addresses a standard Keynesian macroeconomic problem, namely liquidity preference. Keynes [1936] used the concept of liquidity preference to describe an inverse relationship between the demand for cash balances and the rate of interest. This aggregative function was postulated by Keynes without a formal derivation. Tobin derives the economy's liquidity preference by developing a theory that explains the behavior of the decision-making units of the economy.[3]

Numerous contributions followed. To mention just a few, Sharpe [1970], Merton [1972], Gonzalez-Gaverra [1973], Fama [1976] and Roll [1977], are important references. Ziemba & Vickson [1975] have collected numerous classic articles on both static and dynamic models of portfolio selection. The recent books by Ingersoll [1987], Huang & Litzenberger [1988], and Jarrow [1988] also contain a useful analysis of the mean–variance portfolio theory. Our exposition relies heavily on Roll [1977].

value of future returns. It is not correct to deduce that earlier economists completely ignored the notion of risk. They simply were unsuccessful in developing a precise microeconomic theory of investor behavior under conditions of risk. The typical way risk was accounted for in Keynes' [1936] marginal efficiency of investment or Hicks' [1939] development of the investment decisions of a firm was by letting expected future returns include an allowance for risk or by adding a risk premium to discount rates.

[3] One may wonder what is the connection between liquidity preference and portfolio theory. You may recall that Keynes identified three motives for holding cash balances: transactions, precautionary and speculative. Furthermore, while the transactions and precautionary motives were determined by income, the amount of cash balances held for speculative purposes was influenced by the rate of interest. Tobin analyzes this speculative motive of investors to offer a theoretically sound foundation of the interest elasticity of the liquidity preference. Because he wishes to explain the demand for cash, he considers an investor whose portfolio selection includes only two assets: cash and consoles. Of course, the yield of cash is zero while the yield of consoles is positive. Tobin posits and solves a two-asset portfolio selection problem using a quadratic expected utility function. He justifies his choice of a quadratic utility function by arguing that the investor considers two parameters in his or her portfolio selection: expected return and risk (measured by the standard deviation of the portfolio return). Finally, having developed his portfolio selection theory, he applies it to show that changes in real interest rates affect inversely the demand for cash, which is what Keynes had conjectured without offering a proof.

3. Mean–variance portfolio selection

In the formulation of the mean–variance portfolio we use the following notation: $\boldsymbol{x}$ is an n-column vector whose components $x_1, \ldots x_n$ denote the weight or proportion of the investor's wealth allocated to the ith asset in the portfolio with $i = 1, 2, \ldots n$. Obviously the sum of weights is equal to 1, i.e. $\sum_1^n x_i = 1$; $\mathbf{1}$ is an n-column vector of ones and superscript T denotes the transpose of a vector or a matrix. $\boldsymbol{R}$ is an n-column vector of mean returns $R_1, \ldots, R_n$ of the n assets, where it is assumed that not all elements of $\boldsymbol{R}$ are equal, and $\mathbf{V}$ is the $n \times n$ covariance matrix with entries σ_{ij}, $i, j = 1, 2, \ldots n$. We assume that $\mathbf{V}$ is nonsingular. This essentially requires that none of the asset returns is perfectly correlated with the return of a portfolio made up of the remaining assets; and that none of the assets or portfolios of the assets is riskless. The case where one of the assets is riskless will be treated separately at a later stage. Observe that $\mathbf{V}$ is symmetric and positive definite being a covariance matrix. We say that an $n \times n$ matrix $\mathbf{V}$ is *positive definite*, if for any nonzero n-vector $\boldsymbol{x}$, it follows that $\boldsymbol{x}^{\mathrm{T}}\mathbf{V}\boldsymbol{x} > 0$. In our case the property of positive definiteness of $\mathbf{V}$ follows from the fact that variances of risky portfolios are strictly positive. The mean returns and covariance matrix of the assets are assumed to be known. We do not specify if n denotes the entire population or just a sample of assets. Finally, for a given portfolio p, its variance, denoted by σ_p^2, is given by $\boldsymbol{x}^{\mathrm{T}}\mathbf{V}\boldsymbol{x}$, while the portfolio mean, denoted by R_p, is given by $R_p = \boldsymbol{x}^{\mathrm{T}}\boldsymbol{R}$.

Much in the spirit of Markowitz's [1952] formulation[4] the portfolio selection problem can be stated as

$$\begin{aligned} \text{minimize} \quad & \sigma_p^2 = \boldsymbol{x}^{\mathrm{T}}\mathbf{V}\boldsymbol{x} \\ \text{subject to} \quad & \boldsymbol{x}^{\mathrm{T}}\mathbf{1} = 1 \\ & \boldsymbol{x}^{\mathrm{T}}\boldsymbol{R} = R_p. \end{aligned} \tag{3.1}$$

In problem (3.1) we minimize the portfolio variance σ_p^2 subject to two constraints: first, the portfolio weights must sum to unity, which means that all the wealth is invested, and second the portfolio must earn an expected rate of return equal to R_p. Technically, we minimize a convex function subject to linear constraints. Observe that $\boldsymbol{x}^{\mathrm{T}}\mathbf{V}\boldsymbol{x}$ is convex because $\mathbf{V}$ is positive definite and also note that the two linear constraints define a convex set. Therefore, the problem has a unique solution and we only need to obtain the first-order conditions.

Two remarks are appropriate. First, the investor's preferences, as represented by a utility function, do not enter explicitly in (3.1). We only assume that a utility function exists which is defined over the mean and variance of the portfolio return and which has the further property of favoring higher mean and smaller variance. Second, unlike Tobin who explicitly considers cash in his portfolio selection

[4] Markowitz [1952] considers only three securities because he solves the same problem as (3.1) using geometric methods. He does not allow short sales in order to simplify the analysis. In (3.1) short sales are permitted, which means that portfolio weights are allowed to be negative.

problem, (3.1) does not include a riskless asset. A riskless asset will be included in Section 5.

Form the Lagrangian function

$$L = \boldsymbol{x}^{\mathrm{T}}\mathbf{V}\boldsymbol{x} - \lambda_1(\boldsymbol{x}^{\mathrm{T}}\boldsymbol{R} - R_p) - \lambda_2(\boldsymbol{x}^{\mathrm{T}}\mathbf{1} - 1). \tag{3.2}$$

The first-order conditions are

$$\frac{\partial L}{\partial \boldsymbol{x}} = 2\mathbf{V}\boldsymbol{x} - \lambda_1\boldsymbol{R} - \lambda_2\mathbf{1} = \mathbf{0}, \tag{3.3}$$

where $\mathbf{0}$ in (3.3) is an n-vector of zeros, and

$$\frac{\partial L}{\partial \lambda_1} = R_p - \boldsymbol{x}^{\mathrm{T}}\boldsymbol{R} = 0, \tag{3.4}$$

$$\frac{\partial L}{\partial \lambda_2} = 1 - \boldsymbol{x}^{\mathrm{T}}\mathbf{1} = 0. \tag{3.5}$$

From equation (3.3) we obtain

$$\boldsymbol{x} = \frac{1}{2}\mathbf{V}^{-1}(\lambda_1\boldsymbol{R} + \lambda_2\mathbf{1}) = \frac{1}{2}\mathbf{V}^{-1}[\boldsymbol{R}\ \ \mathbf{1}]\begin{bmatrix}\lambda_1\\ \lambda_2\end{bmatrix}. \tag{3.6}$$

In this last equation the term $\lambda_1\boldsymbol{R} + \lambda_2\mathbf{1}$ is written in a matrix form because we will use (3.4) and (3.5) to solve for $\begin{bmatrix}\lambda_1\\ \lambda_2\end{bmatrix}$. Doing this we write (3.4) and (3.5) as

$$[\boldsymbol{R}\ \ \mathbf{1}]^{\mathrm{T}}\boldsymbol{x} = \begin{bmatrix}R_p\\ 1\end{bmatrix}. \tag{3.7}$$

Premultiply both sides of (3.6) by $[\boldsymbol{R}\ \ \boldsymbol{1}]^{\mathrm{T}}$ and use (3.7) to obtain

$$[\boldsymbol{R}\ \ \mathbf{1}]^{\mathrm{T}}\boldsymbol{x} = \frac{1}{2}[\boldsymbol{R}\ \ \mathbf{1}]^{\mathrm{T}}\mathbf{V}^{-1}[\boldsymbol{R}\ \ \mathbf{1}]\begin{bmatrix}\lambda_1\\ \lambda_2\end{bmatrix} = \begin{bmatrix}R_p\\ 1\end{bmatrix}. \tag{3.8}$$

For notational convenience denote by

$$\mathbf{A} \equiv [\boldsymbol{R}\ \ \mathbf{1}]^{\mathrm{T}}\mathbf{V}^{-1}[\boldsymbol{R}\ \ \mathbf{1}] \tag{3.9}$$

the 2×2 symmetric matrix with entries

$$\begin{bmatrix}a & b\\ b & c\end{bmatrix} = \begin{bmatrix}\boldsymbol{R}^{\mathrm{T}}\mathbf{V}^{-1}\boldsymbol{R} & \boldsymbol{R}^{\mathrm{T}}\mathbf{V}^{-1}\mathbf{1}\\ \boldsymbol{R}^{\mathrm{T}}\mathbf{V}^{-1}\mathbf{1} & \mathbf{1}^{\mathrm{T}}\mathbf{V}^{-1}\mathbf{1}\end{bmatrix}. \tag{3.10}$$

We need to establish that $\mathbf{A}$ is positive definite. For any y_1, y_2 such that at least one of the elements y_1, y_2 is nonzero, observe that

$$[\boldsymbol{R}\ \ \mathbf{1}]\begin{bmatrix}y_1\\ y_2\end{bmatrix} = [y_1\boldsymbol{R} + y_2\mathbf{1}]$$

is a nonzero n-vector because, by assumption, the elements of $\boldsymbol{R}$ are not all equal.

Then $\mathbf{A}$ is positive definite because

$$[y_1 \;\; y_2]\mathbf{A}\begin{bmatrix} y_1 \\ y_2 \end{bmatrix} = [y_1 \;\; y_2][\boldsymbol{R} \;\; \mathbf{1}]^{\mathrm{T}}\mathbf{V}^{-1}[\boldsymbol{R} \;\; \mathbf{1}]\begin{bmatrix} y_1 \\ y_2 \end{bmatrix}$$
$$= [y_1\boldsymbol{R} + y_2\mathbf{1}]^{\mathrm{T}}\mathbf{V}^{-1}[y_1\boldsymbol{R} + y_2\mathbf{1}] > 0$$

by the positive definiteness of $\mathbf{V}^{-1}$.

Substitute the newly defined $\mathbf{A}$ in (3.9) to get

$$\frac{1}{2}\mathbf{A}\begin{bmatrix} \lambda_1 \\ \lambda_2 \end{bmatrix} = \begin{bmatrix} R_p \\ 1 \end{bmatrix}$$

from which we can immediately solve for the multipliers since $\mathbf{A}$ is nonsingular and its inverse exists. Thus

$$\frac{1}{2}\begin{bmatrix} \lambda_1 \\ \lambda_2 \end{bmatrix} = \mathbf{A}^{-1}\begin{bmatrix} R_p \\ 1 \end{bmatrix}. \tag{3.11}$$

From these manipulations we obtain the desired result using (3.11) and (3.6). Thus, the n-vector of portfolio weights $\boldsymbol{x}$ that minimizes portfolio variance for a given mean return is

$$\boldsymbol{x} = \frac{1}{2}\mathbf{V}^{-1}[\boldsymbol{R} \;\; \mathbf{1}]\begin{bmatrix} \lambda_1 \\ \lambda_2 \end{bmatrix} = \mathbf{V}^{-1}[\boldsymbol{R} \;\; \mathbf{1}]\mathbf{A}^{-1}\begin{bmatrix} R_p \\ 1 \end{bmatrix}. \tag{3.12}$$

The result of this analysis can be stated as:

Theorem 3.1 (Mean–variance portfolio selection). *Let* $\mathbf{V}$ *be the* $n \times n$ *positive definite covariance matrix and* $\boldsymbol{R}$ *be the n-column vector of mean returns of the n assets where it is assumed that not all elements of* $\boldsymbol{R}$ *are equal. Then the minimum variance portfolio with given mean return* R_p *is unique and its weights are given by (3.12).*

Let us compute the variance of any minimum variance portfolio with a given mean R_p. Using the definitions of the variance σ_p^2, matrix $\mathbf{A}$ in (3.9) and the solution of weights in (3.12), calculate

$$\begin{aligned}
\sigma_p^2 &= \boldsymbol{x}^{\mathrm{T}}\mathbf{V}\boldsymbol{x} = [R_p \;\; 1]\mathbf{A}^{-1}[\boldsymbol{R} \;\; \mathbf{1}]^{\mathrm{T}}\mathbf{V}^{-1}\mathbf{V}\mathbf{V}^{-1}[\boldsymbol{R} \;\; \mathbf{1}]\mathbf{A}^{-1}\begin{bmatrix} R_p \\ 1 \end{bmatrix} \\
&= [R_p \;\; 1]\mathbf{A}^{-1}\begin{bmatrix} R_p \\ 1 \end{bmatrix} \\
&= [R_p \;\; 1]\frac{1}{(ac - b^2)}\begin{bmatrix} c & -b \\ -b & a \end{bmatrix}\begin{bmatrix} R_p \\ 1 \end{bmatrix} \\
&= \frac{a - 2bR_p + cR_p^2}{(ac - b^2)}.
\end{aligned} \tag{3.13}$$

In (3.13) the relation between the variance of the minimum variance portfolio σ_p^2 for any given mean R_p is expressed as a parabola and is called the *minimum variance portfolio frontier* or *locus*. In mean–standard-deviation space the relation is expressed as a hyperbola.

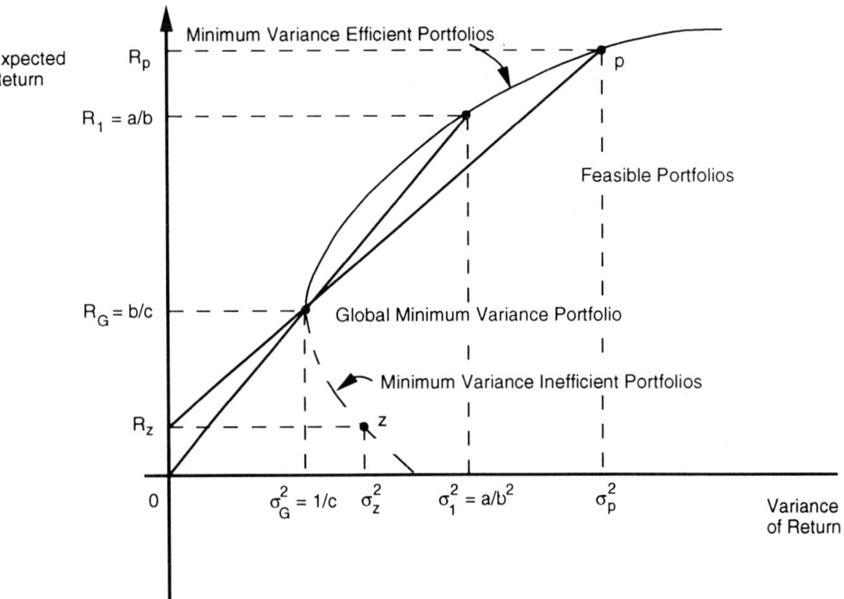

Fig. 1. Portfolios of n risky assets.

Figure 1 graphs equation (3.13) and distinguishes between the upper half (solid curve) and the bottom half (broken curve). The upper half of the minimum variance portfolio frontier identifies the set of portfolios having the highest return for a given variance; these are called mean–variance *efficient portfolios*. The portfolios on the bottom half are called *inefficient portfolios*. The mean–variance efficient portfolios are a subset of the minimum variance portfolios. Portfolios to the right of the parabola are called *feasible*. For a given variance the mean return of a feasible portfolio is less than the mean return of an efficient portfolio and higher than the mean return of an inefficient one, both having the same variance.

Figure 1 also identifies the *global minimum variance portfolio*. This is the portfolio with the smallest possible variance for any mean return. Its mean, denoted by R_{G} is obtained by minimizing (3.13) with respect to R_p, to yield

$$R_{\mathrm{G}} = \frac{b}{c} \tag{3.14}$$

and its variance, denoted by σ_{G}^2, is calculated by inserting (3.14) into the general equation (3.13) to obtain

$$\sigma_{\mathrm{G}}^2 = \frac{a - 2bR_{\mathrm{G}} + cR_{\mathrm{G}}^2}{ac - b^2} = \frac{a - 2b(b/c) + c(b/c)^2}{ac - b^2} = \frac{1}{c}. \tag{3.15}$$

Similarly, by inserting R_G from (3.14) into (3.12) we find the weights of the global minimum variance portfolio, denoted by $\boldsymbol{x}_{\mathrm{G}}$,

$$\boldsymbol{x}_{\mathrm{G}} = \mathbf{V}^{-1}[\boldsymbol{R}\ \mathbf{1}]\mathbf{A}^{-1}\begin{bmatrix} R_{\mathrm{G}} \\ 1 \end{bmatrix} = \frac{\mathbf{V}^{-1}[\boldsymbol{R}\ \mathbf{1}]\begin{bmatrix} c & -b \\ -b & a \end{bmatrix}\begin{bmatrix} b/c \\ 1 \end{bmatrix}}{(ac-b^2)} = \frac{\mathbf{V}^{-1}\ \mathbf{1}}{c}. \tag{3.16}$$

An additional notion that will be used later in this section and which is illustrated in Figure 1 also, is the concept of an orthogonal portfolio. We say that two minimum variance portfolios $\boldsymbol{x}_p$ and $\boldsymbol{x}_z$ are *orthogonal* if their covariance is zero, that is,

$$\boldsymbol{x}_z^{\mathrm{T}}\mathbf{V}\boldsymbol{x}_p = 0. \tag{3.17}$$

We want to show that for every minimum variance portfolio, except the global minimum variance portfolio, we can find a unique orthogonal minimum variance portfolio. Furthermore, if the first portfolio has mean R_p, its orthogonal one has mean R_z with

$$R_z = \frac{a - bR_p}{b - cR_p}. \tag{3.18}$$

To establish (3.18), let first p and z be two arbitrary minimum variance portfolios with weights $\boldsymbol{x}_p$ given by (3.12) and $\boldsymbol{x}_z$ given by

$$\boldsymbol{x}_z = \mathbf{V}^{-1}[\boldsymbol{R}\ \mathbf{1}]\mathbf{A}^{-1}\begin{bmatrix} R_z \\ 1 \end{bmatrix}. \tag{3.19}$$

The covariance between portfolios p and z, being zero implies

$$0 = \boldsymbol{x}_z^{\mathrm{T}}\mathbf{V}\boldsymbol{x}_p = \begin{bmatrix} R_z & 1 \end{bmatrix}\mathbf{A}^{-1}\begin{bmatrix} R_p \\ 1 \end{bmatrix}, \tag{3.20}$$

from which (3.18) follows.

In Figure 1, we also illustrate the geometry of orthogonal portfolios. Given an arbitrary efficient portfolio p on the efficient portfolio frontier, the line passing between p and the global minimum variance portfolio can be shown to intersect the expected return axis at R_z. Once R_z is known, then the orthogonal portfolio z can be uniquely identified on the minimum variance portfolio frontier. Note that if a portfolio p is efficient and therefore lies on the positively sloped segment of the portfolio frontier, as in Figure 1, then its orthogonal portfolio z is inefficient and lies on the negatively sloped segment. In general, orthogonal portfolios lie on opposite-sloped segments of the portfolio frontier.

4. Two-fund separation

We now present the important property of two-fund separation. The mathematics of this property is straightforward; its economic implications however are significant because the following theorem establishes that the minimum variance portfolio frontier can be generated by any two distinct frontier portfolios.

Theorem 4.1 (Two-fund separation). *Let $\boldsymbol{x}_a$ and $\boldsymbol{x}_b$ be two minimum variance portfolios with mean returns R_a and R_b respectively, such that $R_a \neq R_b$.*

(a) Then every minimum variance portfolio $\boldsymbol{x}_c$ is a linear combination of $\boldsymbol{x}_a$ and $\boldsymbol{x}_b$.

(b) Conversely, every portfolio which is a linear combination of $\boldsymbol{x}_a$ and $\boldsymbol{x}_b$, i.e, $\alpha\boldsymbol{x}_a + (1-\alpha)\boldsymbol{x}_b$, is a minimum variance portfolio.

(c) In particular, if $\boldsymbol{x}_a$ and $\boldsymbol{x}_b$ are minimum variance efficient portfolios, then $\alpha\boldsymbol{x}_a + (1-\alpha)\boldsymbol{x}_b$ is a minimum variance efficient portfolio for $0 \leq \alpha \leq 1$.

Proof. (a) Let R_c denote the mean return of the given minimum variance portfolio $\boldsymbol{x}_c$. Choose parameter α such that

$$R_c = \alpha R_a + (1-\alpha) R_b \tag{4.1}$$

that is, choose α given by

$$\alpha = \frac{R_c - R_b}{R_a - R_b}. \tag{4.2}$$

Note that α exists and is unique because by hypothesis $R_a \neq R_b$.

We claim that

$$\boldsymbol{x}_c = \alpha\boldsymbol{x}_a + (1-\alpha)\boldsymbol{x}_b. \tag{4.3}$$

To establish (4.3) use first (3.12) and next (4.1) to write

$$\begin{aligned}
\boldsymbol{x}_c &= \mathbf{V}^{-1}[\boldsymbol{R}\ \mathbf{1}]\mathbf{A}^{-1}\begin{bmatrix} R_c \\ 1 \end{bmatrix} \\
&= \mathbf{V}^{-1}[\boldsymbol{R}\ \mathbf{1}]\mathbf{A}^{-1}\begin{bmatrix} \alpha R_a + (1-\alpha) R_b \\ \alpha + (1-\alpha) \end{bmatrix} \\
&= \alpha\mathbf{V}^{-1}[\boldsymbol{R}\ \mathbf{1}]\mathbf{A}^{-1}\begin{bmatrix} R_a \\ 1 \end{bmatrix} + (1-\alpha)\mathbf{V}^{-1}[\boldsymbol{R}\ \mathbf{1}]\mathbf{A}^{-1}\begin{bmatrix} R_b \\ 1 \end{bmatrix} \\
&= \alpha\boldsymbol{x}_a + (1-\alpha)\boldsymbol{x}_b.
\end{aligned} \tag{4.4}$$

(b) Consider portfolio $\boldsymbol{x}_c$ which is a linear combination of $\boldsymbol{x}_a$ and $\boldsymbol{x}_b$ as in (4.3). Then

$$\begin{aligned}
\boldsymbol{x}_c &= \alpha\boldsymbol{x}_a + (1-\alpha)\boldsymbol{x}_b \\
&= \alpha\mathbf{V}^{-1}[\boldsymbol{R}\ \mathbf{1}]\mathbf{A}^{-1}\begin{bmatrix} R_a \\ 1 \end{bmatrix} + (1-\alpha)\mathbf{V}^{-1}[\boldsymbol{R}\ \mathbf{1}]\mathbf{A}^{-1}\begin{bmatrix} R_b \\ 1 \end{bmatrix} \\
&= \mathbf{V}^{-1}[\boldsymbol{R}\ \mathbf{1}]\mathbf{A}^{-1}\begin{bmatrix} \alpha R_a + (1-\alpha) R_b \\ 1 \end{bmatrix}
\end{aligned}$$

By (3.12) we conclude that $\boldsymbol{x}_c$ is the minimum variance portfolio with expected return $\alpha R_a + (1-\alpha) R_b$.

(c) This is proved as in (b) noting that the restriction $0 \leq \alpha \leq 1$ implies, $R_a \leq \alpha R_a + (1-\alpha) R_b \leq R_b$, if $R_a \leq R_b$.

This completes the proof. □

It is of historical interest that this fact was discovered by Tobin [1958]. Tobin uses only two assets (riskless cash and a risky consol), and demonstrates that nothing essential is changed if there are many risky assets. He argues that the risky assets can be viewed as a single composite asset (mutual fund) and investors find it optimal to combine their cash with a specific portfolio of risky assets. In particular, Theorem 4.1 shows that any mean variance efficient portfolio can be generated by two arbitrary distinct mean–variance efficient portfolios. In other words, if an investor wishes to invest in a mean–variance efficient portfolio with a given expected return and variance, he or she can achieve this goal by investing in an appropriate linear combination of any two mutual funds which are also mean–variance efficient. Practically this means that the n original assets can be purchased by only two mutual funds and investors then can just choose to allocate their wealth, not in the original n assets directly but in these two mutual funds in such a way that the investment results (mean–variance) of the two actions (portfolios) would be identical.

There is, however, an additional implication from part (c) of the two-fund separation theorem. Suppose that utility functions are restricted so that all investors choose to invest in mean–variance efficient portfolios and choose $\boldsymbol{x}_a$ and $\boldsymbol{x}_b$ to be the investment proportions of two distinct mean–variance efficient portfolios that generate all the others. In particular $\boldsymbol{x}_a$ and $\boldsymbol{x}_b$ can be used to generate the *market portfolio*, that is, the wealth weighted sum of the portfolio holdings of all investors.[5] This implies that the market portfolio is also mean–variance efficient. Black [1972] employs this result in deriving the capital asset pricing model.

Having shown that any two distinct portfolios can generate all other portfolios, it is of practical interest to select two portfolios whose means and variances are easy to compute. One such portfolio is the global minimum variance portfolio with R_{G}, σ_{G}^2 and $\boldsymbol{x}_{\mathrm{G}}$ given in the previous section. The other one is identified in Figure 1, with $R_1 = a/b$, $\sigma_1^2 = a/b^2$, and

$$\boldsymbol{x}_1 = \frac{\mathbf{V}^{-1}\boldsymbol{R}}{b}. \tag{4.5}$$

[5] To clarify the concept of market portfolio, it is helpful to proceed inductively. Suppose that investors 1 and 2 have wealth w_1 and w_2 invested in minimum variance efficient portfolios with weights $\boldsymbol{x}_1$ and $\boldsymbol{x}_2$. Then the sum of their holdings is a portfolio with wealth $\mathrm{w}_1 + w_2$ and portfolio weights $\alpha\boldsymbol{x}_1 + (1-\alpha)\boldsymbol{x}_2$ where $\alpha = w_1/(w_1+w_2)$. Since $0 \leq \alpha \leq 1$, from Theorem 4.1(c), the sum total of their holdings is also an efficient portfolio. Next suppose that the wealth w_n of n investors is invested in an efficient portfolio with weights $\boldsymbol{x}_n$ and investor $n+1$ has wealth w_{n+1} invested in an efficient portfolio with weights $\boldsymbol{x}_{n+1}$. Again from Theorem 4.1(c) the sum total of the holdings of all $n+1$ investors is an efficient portfolio. Proceeding in this manner we conclude that the sum total of all the investors' portfolios is an efficient portfolio. By definition, however, this is the market portfolio. Thus we conclude that the market portfolio is efficient.

Observe from Figure 1 that this second portfolio's orthogonal portfolio has an expected return of zero. Theorem 4.2 below uses these two portfolios x_G and x_1.

We state a theorem about the relation of individual asset parameters which will be useful in the analysis of the capital asset pricing model.

Theorem 4.2. *For a given portfolio x_p, the covariance vector of individual assets with respect to portfolio p is linear in the vector of mean returns R if and only if p is a minimum variance portfolio.*

Proof. Let x_p be the weights of a minimum variance portfolio which can be written as (3.12). The vector of covariances between individual assets and x_p is given by

$$\mathbf{V}x_p = \mathbf{V}\mathbf{V}^{-1}[\boldsymbol{R}\ \ \mathbf{1}]\mathbf{A}^{-1}\begin{bmatrix} R_p \\ 1 \end{bmatrix} = [\boldsymbol{R}\ \ \mathbf{1}]\mathbf{A}^{-1}\begin{bmatrix} R_p \\ 1 \end{bmatrix} \tag{4.6}$$

which verifies the linearity between the covariance vector and the vector of expected returns, $\boldsymbol{R}$.

Conversely, let the vector of covariances with an arbitrary portfolio x_p be expressed linearly as

$$\mathbf{V}x_p = g\boldsymbol{R} + h\mathbf{1} \tag{4.7}$$

where g and h are arbitrary constants. From (4.7), solving for x_p we get

$$x_p = g\mathbf{V}^{-1}\boldsymbol{R} + \mathbf{V}^{-1}\mathbf{1} = gbx_1 + hcx_G. \tag{4.8}$$

Note that in this last equation x_p is generated by two distinct efficient portfolios x_1 and x_G. Recall that x_G is the vector of investment proportions of the global minimum variance portfolio and x_1 is the vector of investment proportions described in (4.5). Since both x_G and x_1 are investment proportions, they satisfy $x_G^T\mathbf{1} = x_1^T\mathbf{1} = 1$ which combined with the property that $x_p^T\mathbf{1} = 1$ allows us to conclude that $gb + hc = 1$. Thus we conclude from Theorem 4.1 that x_p is a minimum variance portfolio. This completes the proof. □

We close this section by expressing (4.6) in a way that will be useful in the discussion of the capital asset pricing model in Section 6. From (4.6) write

$$\begin{aligned} \operatorname{cov}(R_i, R_p) &= [0\ \dots\ 1\ \dots\ 0]\mathbf{V}x_p \\ &= [0\ \dots\ 1\ \dots\ 0][\boldsymbol{R}\ \ \mathbf{1}]\mathbf{A}^{-1}\begin{bmatrix} R_p \\ 1 \end{bmatrix} \\ &= [R_i\ \ 1]\mathbf{A}^{-1}\begin{bmatrix} R_p \\ 1 \end{bmatrix}, \end{aligned} \tag{4.9}$$

where the 1 in the row vector is placed in the position of the ith asset. Let x_z be orthogonal to x_p and calculate their covariance as in (3.20). Subtract (3.20) from (4.9) to get

$$\operatorname{cov}(R_i, R_p) = [r_i\ \ 0]\mathbf{A}^{-1}\begin{bmatrix} R_p \\ 1 \end{bmatrix} = \gamma r_i \tag{4.10}$$

where the two new variables r_i and γ are defined as

$$r_i = R_i - R_z, \tag{4.11}$$

and

$$\gamma = \frac{cR_p - b}{ac - b^2}. \tag{4.12}$$

Observe that (4.10) holds for each i and must therefore hold for all assets, i.e.

$$\text{cov}\,(R_p, R_p) = \sigma_p^2 = \gamma r_p, \tag{4.13}$$

where r_p expresses the excess mean return of portfolio p from its orthogonal z. From this last equation obtain $\gamma = \sigma_p^2/r_p$ and substitute in (4.10) to conclude that

$$r_i = \frac{\text{cov}\,(R_i, R_p)}{\sigma_p^2} r_p = \beta_i r_p \tag{4.14}$$

which expresses the excess mean return of the ith asset as a proportion of its beta, β_i, with respect to portfolio p, where

$$\beta_i = \frac{\text{cov}\,(R_i, R_p)}{\sigma_p^2}. \tag{4.15}$$

These mathematical manipulations show that (4.14), which has a capital asset pricing appearance, holds true for any minimum variance portfolio, in general, and for any minimum variance efficient portfolio, in particular.

5. Mean–variance portfolio with a riskless asset

The previous two sections presented and solved the portfolio selection problem for n risky assets, and then established the two fund separation theorem. We now return to Tobin's original idea of introducing a riskless asset. The portfolio selection problem with n risky assets and one riskless, i.e. a total of $(n + 1)$ assets can easily be formulated and solved. Let there be $n + 1$ assets, $i = 0, 1, 2, \ldots, n$, where 0 denotes the riskless asset with return R_0. The vector of expected excess returns has elements defined as $r_i = R_i - R_0$, $i = 1, 2, \ldots, n$, and is denoted by $\boldsymbol{r}$. Wealth is now allocated among $(n + 1)$ assets with weights $w_0, w_1, \ldots, w_n$. In the various calculations we denote the vector of weights $w_1, \ldots, w_n$ as $\boldsymbol{w}$ and write $w_0 = 1 - \boldsymbol{w}^{\mathrm{T}}\mathbf{1}$.

For a given portfolio p, the mean excess return is

$$r_p = \boldsymbol{w}^{\mathrm{T}}\boldsymbol{R} + (1 - \boldsymbol{w}^{\mathrm{T}}\mathbf{1})R_0 - R_0 = \boldsymbol{w}^{\mathrm{T}}\boldsymbol{r}. \tag{5.1}$$

The variance of p is

$$\sigma_p^2 = \boldsymbol{w}^{\mathrm{T}}\mathbf{V}\boldsymbol{w}, \tag{5.2}$$

where in (5.1) and (5.2), $\boldsymbol{R}$ and $\mathbf{V}$ are as in Section 3. Note that in (5.2) the riskless asset does not contribute to the variance.

The mean–variance portfolio selection problem with a riskless asset can be stated as

$$\begin{aligned} &\text{minimize} \quad \boldsymbol{w}^{\mathrm{T}}\mathbf{V}\boldsymbol{w} \\ &\text{subject to} \quad \boldsymbol{w}^{\mathrm{T}}\boldsymbol{r} = r_p. \end{aligned} \tag{5.3}$$

In (5.3), the variance of the n-risky assets is minimized subject to a given excess return r_p. Note that $\boldsymbol{w}^{\mathrm{T}}\mathbf{1} = 1$ is not a constraint because the wealth need not all be allocated to the n-risky assets; some may be held in the riskless asset.

Following the method of (3.1) one obtains the solution

$$\boldsymbol{w} = \left(\frac{r_p}{\boldsymbol{r}^{\mathrm{T}}\mathbf{V}^{-1}\boldsymbol{r}}\right)\mathbf{V}^{-1}\boldsymbol{r} \tag{5.4}$$

which gives the variance of the minimum-variance portfolio with excess mean r_p as

$$\begin{aligned} \sigma_p^2 &= \boldsymbol{w}^{\mathrm{T}}\mathbf{V}\boldsymbol{w} \\ &= \left(\frac{r_p}{\boldsymbol{r}^{\mathrm{T}}\mathbf{V}^{-1}\boldsymbol{r}}\right)^2 \boldsymbol{r}^{\mathrm{T}}\mathbf{V}^{-1}\mathbf{V}\mathbf{V}^{-1}\boldsymbol{r} \\ &= \frac{r_p^2}{\boldsymbol{r}^{\mathrm{T}}\mathbf{V}^{-1}\boldsymbol{r}}. \end{aligned} \tag{5.5}$$

The Sharpe's measure of portfolio p, defined as the ratio of its excess mean return to the standard deviation of its return, is obtained from (5.5) as

$$\frac{r_p}{\sigma_p} = \left\{ \begin{array}{ll} (\boldsymbol{r}^{\mathrm{T}}\mathbf{V}^{-1}\boldsymbol{r})^{1/2}, & \text{if } r_p \geq 0 \\ -(\boldsymbol{r}^{\mathrm{T}}\mathbf{V}^{-1}\boldsymbol{r})^{1/2}, & \text{if } r_p < 0 \end{array} \right\}. \tag{5.6}$$

The tangency portfolio T is the minimum-variance portfolio for which

$$\mathbf{1}^{\mathrm{T}}\boldsymbol{w}_{\mathrm{T}} = 1. \tag{5.7}$$

Combining equations (5.4) and (5.7) we obtain

$$r_{\mathrm{T}} = \frac{\boldsymbol{r}^{\mathrm{T}}\mathbf{V}^{-1}\boldsymbol{r}}{\mathbf{1}^{\mathrm{T}}\mathbf{V}^{-1}\boldsymbol{r}} \gtrless 0. \tag{5.8}$$

It is economically plausible to assert that the riskless return is lower than the mean return of the global minimum variance portfolio of the risky assets, that is, $R_0 < R_{\mathrm{G}}$. We may then prove that $\mathbf{1}^{\mathrm{T}}\mathbf{V}^{-1}\boldsymbol{r} > 0$. Also $\boldsymbol{r}^{\mathrm{T}}\mathbf{V}^{-1}\boldsymbol{r} > 0$ by the positive definiteness of the matrix $\mathbf{V}$. It then follows that $r_{\mathrm{T}} > 0$ and the slope of the tangency line in Figure 2 is positive. This positively-sloped line is the capital market line and defines the set of minimum variance efficient portfolios. For an actual calculation of Figure 2, see Ziemba, Parkan & Brooks-Hill [1974].

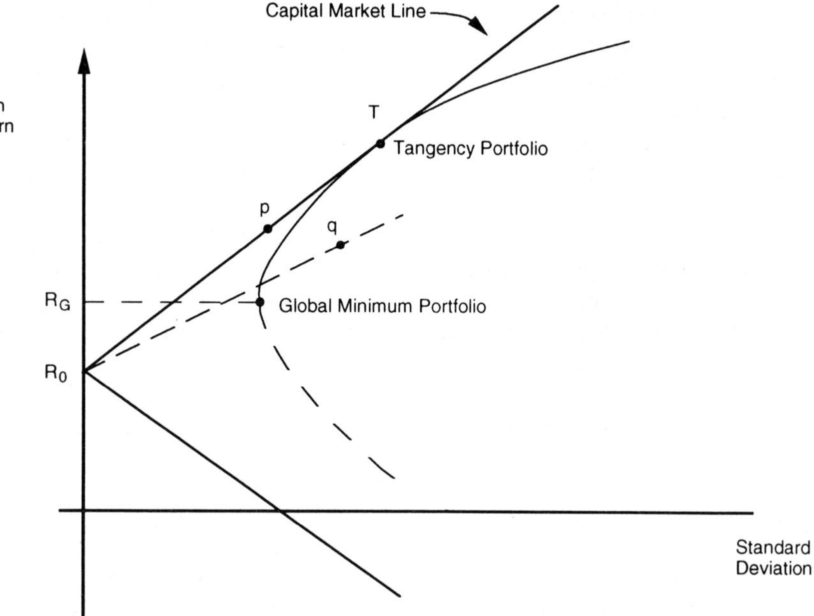

Fig. 2. Portfolios of n-risky assets and a riskless asset.

The correlation coefficient of the return of any portfolio q, with weights $\boldsymbol{w}_q$, and any portfolio p on the efficient segment of the minimum-variance frontier is

$$\begin{aligned}\rho(p,q) &= \frac{\boldsymbol{w}_q^{\mathrm{T}}\mathbf{V}\boldsymbol{w}_p}{\sigma_q\sigma_p} \\ &= \frac{r_p r_q}{(\boldsymbol{r}^{\mathrm{T}}\mathbf{V}^{-1}\boldsymbol{r})\sigma_q\sigma_p} \\ &= \frac{r_q/\sigma_q}{r_p/\sigma_p} \\ &= \frac{\text{Sharpe's measure of portfolio } q}{\text{Sharpe's measure of portfolio } p}\end{aligned} \tag{5.9}$$

Referring to Figure 2, the correlation $\rho(p, q)$ is the ratio of the slope of the line from R_0 to q to the slope of the efficient frontier.

6. The capital asset pricing model

Markowitz's approach to portfolio selection may be characterized as normative. The analysis of Sections 3, 4 and 5 concentrates on a typical investor and by making several simplifying assumptions, solves the investor's portfolio selection problem. Recall the assumptions: (i) the investor considers only the first two moments of the probability distribution of returns; (ii) given the mean portfolio return, the investor chooses a portfolio with the lowest variance of returns; and (iii) the investment horizon is one period. There are also a few additional assumptions that are implicit: (i) the investor's individual decisions do not affect market prices; (ii) fractional shares may be purchased (i.e. investments are infinitely divisible); (iii) transaction costs and taxes do not exist, and (iv) investors can sell assets short.

It is historically worth observing that six years had to elapse before the normative results of portfolio selection could be generalized into a positive theory of capital markets. Brennan [1989] claims that "[t]he reason for delay was undoubtedly the boldness of the assumption required for progress, namely that all investors hold the same beliefs about the joint distribution of a security[6]". Indeed, Sharpe [1964] emphasizes that in order to obtain equilibrium conditions in the capital market the *homogeneity of investor expectations*[7] assumption must be made.

Under these assumptions we have demonstrated that all investors hold mean–variance efficient portfolios. With the added homogeneity assumption, Theorem 4.1 shows that a portfolio which consists of two (or more) mean–variance efficient portfolios is mean variance efficient. Therefore the market portfolio is mean variance efficient. Therefore, the mean asset returns are linear in their covariance with the market return as shown in Theorem 4.2. This simple, yet powerful argument due to Black [1972] does not rely on the existence of a riskless asset, unlike the original derivation of the Capital Asset Pricing Model (CAPM) by Sharpe [1964]. From equation (4.14) we may write the CAPM as

$$R_i - R_z = \beta_i (R_{\mathrm{M}} - R_z) \tag{6.1}$$

where R_{M} is the mean return of the market portfolio, β_i is $\mathrm{cov}(R_i, R_{\mathrm{M}})/\mathrm{var}(R_{\mathrm{M}})$ and R_z is the mean return of a minimum variance portfolio which is orthogonal to the market portfolio. In the special case that a riskless asset exists, R_z must equal the riskless rate of return. Ferson [1994] surveys in this volume both the theory and testing of the capital asset pricing model.

Fama [1976] and Roll [1977] pointed out that testing the capital asset pricing model is equivalent to testing the market's mean–variance efficiency. If the only testable hypothesis of the capital asset pricing theory is that the market portfolio is mean–variance efficient, then such testing is infeasible. The infeasibility is due to our ignorance of the exact composition of the true market portfolio. In other words, the capital asset pricing theory is not testable unless all individual assets are included in the market. Using a proxy for the true market portfolio does not solve the problem for two reasons: first, the proxy itself may be mean–variance

[6] See Brennan [1989, p. 93].

[7] Two brief remarks are in order. First, Sharpe attributes the term of homogeneity of investor expectations to one of the referees of his paper. Second, he acknowledges that this assumption is highly restrictive and unrealistic but defends it because of its implication, i.e. attainment of equilibrium. See also Lintner [1965] and Mossin [1966]. Numerous papers have appeared which have relaxed some of the stated assumptions. For example see Levy & Samuelson [1992]

efficient even when the true market portfolio is not; second, the chosen proxy may be inefficient even though the true market portfolio is actually efficient.

We conclude this section by pointing out that the empirical methodologies of testing for the mean–variance efficiency of a given portfolio may be applied in testing a broad class of asset pricing models. Absence of arbitrage among n assets with returns represented by the random variables, $\tilde{R}_i$ $i = 1, \ldots, n$, implies the existence of a strictly positive pricing kernel represented by the random variable $\tilde{m}$ such that

$$E\left[\tilde{m} \ \tilde{R}_i\right] = 1, \qquad i = 1, \ldots, n. \tag{6.2}$$

For example, in the consumption asset pricing model, $\tilde{m}$ stands for the marginal rate of substitution in consumption between the beginning and end of the period.

Let $\boldsymbol{x}$ denote the weights of a portfolio of n assets which has return maximally correlated with the pricing operator $\tilde{m}$. Then we can write $\tilde{m}$ as

$$\tilde{m} = \alpha \sum_{j=1}^{n} x_j \tilde{R}_j + \tilde{\varepsilon} \tag{6.3}$$

where α is a constant. The property of maximal correlation implies that $\mathrm{cov}(\tilde{\varepsilon}, \tilde{R}_j) = 0$, $j = 1, \ldots, n$. Combining equations (6.2) and (6.3) we obtain

$$1 = E\left[\tilde{m} \ \tilde{R}_i\right] = E\left[\tilde{m}\right]E\left[\tilde{R}_i\right] + \alpha \,\mathrm{cov}\left(\sum_{j=1}^{n} x_j \tilde{R}_j, \tilde{R}_i\right), \qquad i = 1, \ldots, n. \tag{6.4}$$

This implies that the n assets' covariances with the portfolio $\boldsymbol{x}$ are linear in their mean returns. By Theorem 4.2 we conclude that the portfolio $\boldsymbol{x}$ must lie on the minimum-variance frontier of the n assets, a property which can be tested by the methodologies which test for the efficiency of a given portfolio. For further discussion of these issues see the papers of Hansen & Jagannathan [1991] and Ferson [1995].

7. Theoretical justification of mean–variance analysis, mutual fund separation and the CAPM

In this section we first address the following question: what set of assumptions is needed on the investor's utility function or distribution of asset returns so that the investor chooses a mean–variance efficient portfolio?

Tobin [1958] uses a quadratic utility function represented by

$$u(c) = c - B\frac{c^2}{2}, \qquad B > 0 \tag{7.1}$$

and defined only for $c \leq 1/B$, where c denotes consumption. Arrow [1971] has remarked that quadratic utility exhibits increasing absolute risk aversion which implies that risky assets are inferior goods in the context of the portfolio selection problem. It can be easily shown that utility is increasing in the mean and decreasing in the variance, and that moments higher than the variance do not matter. Therefore only mean–variance efficient portfolios will be selected by expected quadratic utility maximizing investors.

Next note that multivariate normality is a special distribution of asset returns for which mean–variance analysis is consistent with expected utility maximization without assuming quadratic utility. To show this recall that the distribution of any portfolio is completely specified by its mean and variance. This follows from the basic property that any linear combination of multivariate normally distributed variables has a distribution in the same family.

Chamberlain [1983a] shows that the most general class of distributions that allow investors to rank portfolios based on the first two generalized moments is the family of *elliptical distributions*. A vector $\boldsymbol{x}$ of n random variables is said to be elliptically distributed if its density function is of the form

$$f(x) = |\boldsymbol{\Omega}|^{-1/2} g[(\boldsymbol{x} - \boldsymbol{\mu})^{\mathrm{T}} \boldsymbol{\Omega}^{-1} (\boldsymbol{x} - \boldsymbol{\mu}); \boldsymbol{x}] \tag{7.2}$$

where $\boldsymbol{\Omega}$ is an $n \times n$ positive definite dispersion matrix and $\boldsymbol{\mu}$ is the vector of medians. From (7.1) Ingersoll [1987] obtains as special cases both the multivariate normal and the multivariate Student-t distributions.

Having presented a theoretical justification for mean–variance analysis[8] we can now ask a second and broader question: which is the class of utility functions that imply two-fund separation? Without assuming the existence of a riskless asset, Cass & Stiglitz [1970] prove that a necessary and sufficient condition for two-fund separation is that preferences are either quadratic or of the constant-relative-risk-aversion family, $u(c) = (1 - A)^{-1} c^{1-A}$, $A > 0$, $A \neq 1$ (with $u(c) = \ln c$ corresponding to the case $A = 1$). Actually constant relative risk aversion implies the stronger property of one-fund separation. If a riskless asset is assumed to exist, the necessary and sufficient condition for two-fund separation is either quadratic preferences or HARA preferences defined as $u(c) = (1 - A)^{-1}(c - \hat{c})^{1-A}$, $A > 0$, $A \neq 1$ (with $u(c) = \ln(c - \hat{c})$ corresponding to the case $A = 1$). Their main conclusion is that utility-based conditions under which separation holds are very restrictive. But more to the point, utility-based two-fund separation, with the exception of quadratic utility, does not imply mean–variance choice and does not imply the CAPM.

Ross [1978] establishes the necessary and sufficient conditions on the stochastic structure of asset returns such that two-fund portfolio separation would obtain for any increasing and concave von Neumann–Morgenstern utility function. More specifically, a vector of asset returns $\boldsymbol{R}$ is said to exhibit two-fund separability if

[8] Ingersoll [1975] and Kraus & Litzenberger [1976] address the interesting question of how portfolios are formed when either the utility function or the distribution of returns are not of the type that imply mean–variance analysis. In particular, Kraus & Litzenberger [1976] extend the portfolio selection problem to include the effect of skewness. The rate of return on the investor's portfolio is assumed to be nonsymmetrically distributed and the investor's utility function considers the first three moments of such a distribution. See also Ziemba [1994], Ohlson & Ziemba [1976], and Kallberg & Ziemba [1983].

there are two mutual funds α and β of n assets such that for any portfolio q there exists a portfolio weight λ such that

$$E[u(\lambda R_\alpha + (1-\lambda)R_\beta)] \geq E[u(R_q)] \tag{7.3}$$

for each monotone increasing and concave utility functions $u(\cdot)$. Observe that (7.3) captures analytically the intuitive notion that portfolios generated by the two funds are preferred to arbitrary portfolios. There is an extensive literature that deals with this important issue of comparing portfolios for a class of investor preferences known as *stochastic dominance*. Ingersoll [1987] or Huang & Litzenberger [1988] give a general overview of these ideas and Rothschild & Stiglitz [1970] offer a detailed analysis.

From the above definition, Ross [1978, p. 267] proves that two-fund separability is equivalent to the following conditions: there exist random variables $\tilde{R}$, $\tilde{Y}$ and $\tilde{\varepsilon}$ and weights x_i, x_i^{M} and x_i^z, $i = 1, 2, \ldots, n$, such that

$$\tilde{R}_i = \tilde{R} + b_i\tilde{Y} + \tilde{\varepsilon}_i \qquad \text{for all } i \tag{7.4}$$

$$E[\tilde{\varepsilon}_i \mid \tilde{R} + \xi\tilde{Y}] = 0 \qquad \text{for all } i,\ \xi \tag{7.5}$$

$$\sum_i w_i^{\mathrm{M}} = 1, \qquad \sum_i w_i^z = 1 \tag{7.6}$$

$$\sum_i w_i^{\mathrm{M}}\tilde{\varepsilon}_i = 0, \qquad \sum_i w_i^z\tilde{\varepsilon}_i = 0 \tag{7.7}$$

$$\text{and either } b_i = b \text{ for all } i, \text{ or } \sum_i w_i^{\mathrm{M}} b_i \neq \sum_i w_i^z b_i. \tag{7.8}$$

Observe that conditions (7.4)–(7.8) represent the most general form of distribution of returns which permits two-fund separation. In particular, Ross [1978, p. 273] shows that all multivariate normally distributed random variables satisfy condition (7.7). But, more to the point Ross shows that, if asset returns are drawn from the family of two-fund separating distributions, and if asset variances are finite, then the CAPM holds.

Having reviewed the assumptions needed on asset distributions for mean–variance portfolio theory and two-fund separation to hold, we close with a brief evaluation of these assumptions. Osborne [1959], Mandelbrot [1963], Fama [1965a, b], Boness, Chen & Jatusipitak [1974] and numerous other studies have shown that there are substantial deviations from normality in the distribution of actual stock prices. Although actual returns are not normally distributed and the use of quadratic utility cannot be supported empirically, the mean–variance portfolio theory remains theoretically useful and empirically relevant. Actually, portfolio theory is a prime example of Milton Friedman's assertion that a theory should not be judged by the relevance of its assumptions, but rather, by the realism of its predictions.[9]

[9] Stiglitz [1989] evaluates the various assumptions placed on investor preferences, and Markowitz [1991] in his Nobel Lecture supports the appropriateness of the approximation. See also Levy & Markowitz [1979] and Markowitz [1987].

8. Consumption and portfolio selection in continuous time

Mean–variance portfolio theory addresses the investor's asset selection problem for an investment horizon of one period. Progress in portfolio theory came as financial economists relaxed this restrictive assumption. In so doing, however, they were faced with the twin decisions discussed in the introduction: consumption-saving and portfolio selection. The relaxation of the single-period assumption proceeded along two lines: first, in discrete time multiperiod models by Samuelson [1969], Hakansson [1970], Fama [1970], Rubinstein [1976], Long [1974] and others, and second, in continuous time models by Merton [1969, 1971, 1973], Breeden [1979, 1986], Cox, Ingersoll & Ross [1985a, b], and others. Ingersoll [1987] presents a detailed overview of discrete time models. Here, we follow Merton [1973] to develop and solve a continuous-time intertemporal portfolio selection problem.[10]

Assume that there exist continuously trading markets for all $n+1$ assets and that prices per share $P_i(t)$ are generated by Itô processes, i.e.

$$\frac{\mathrm{d}P_i}{P_i} = \alpha_i(x,t)\,\mathrm{d}t + \sigma_i(x,t)\,\mathrm{d}z_i(t), \qquad i = 1, \ldots, n+1 \tag{8.1}$$

where α_i is the conditional arithmetic expected rate of return and $\sigma_i^2\,\mathrm{d}t$ is the conditional variance of the rate of return of asset i. We either assume zero dividends on the stock or, more plausibly, we assume that the dividends are continuously reinvested in the stock and P_i represents the price of one share plus the value of the reinvested dividends. The random variable $z_i(t)$ is a Wiener process. The variance of the increment of the Wiener process is $\mathrm{d}t$. The processes $z_i(t)$ and $z_j(t)$ have correlated increments and we denote

$$\mathrm{cov}\left[\sigma_i \mathrm{d}z_i(t), \sigma_j \mathrm{d}z_j(t)\right] = \sigma_{ij}\mathrm{d}t.$$

In the particular case (not assumed hereafter) where α_i and σ_i are constants, the price $P_i(t)$ is lognormally distributed.

The conditional mean and variance of the rate of return are functions of the random variable $x(t)$, assumed here to be a scalar solely for expositional ease. The random variable $x(t)$, referred to here as the *state variable*, is an Itô process

$$\mathrm{d}x = m(x,t)\mathrm{d}t + s(x,t)s\mathrm{d}\hat{z}(t). \tag{8.2}$$

The covariance $\mathrm{cov}[s\mathrm{d}\hat{z}(t), \sigma_i \mathrm{d}z_i(t)]$ is denoted by $\sigma_{ix}\mathrm{d}t$.

[10] The appropriateness of the continuous-time approach to the intertemporal portfolio selection problem in particular, and to problems of financial economics in general, is skillfully evaluated in Merton [1975, 1982]. He argues that the use of stochastic calculus methods in finance allows the financial theorist to obtain important generalizations by making realistic assumptions about trading and the evolution of uncertainty. These methods are briefly exposited in Ingersoll [1987] or more extensively in Malliaris & Brock [1982]. The remainder of this paper assumes some familiarity with these techniques.

An investor has wealth $W(t)$ at time t. The investor consumes $C(t)\mathrm{d}t$ over $[t, t+\mathrm{d}t]$ and invests fraction $w_i(t)$ of the wealth in asset i, $i = 1, \ldots, n, n+1$. The budget constraint, or wealth dynamics, is

$$\mathrm{d}W(t) = \mathrm{d}y(t) - C\mathrm{d}t + \sum_{i=1}^{n+1} w_i \frac{\mathrm{d}P_i}{P_i} W \tag{8.3}$$

where $\mathrm{d}y(t)$ is the labor income, or generally the exogenous endowment income over the infinitesimal interval $[t, t+\mathrm{d}t]$.

For expositional simplicity we assume that the labor income is zero. We also assume that the $(n+1)$st asset is riskless, i.e. $\sigma_{n+1} = 0$ and we denote α_{n+1} by r, the instantaneously riskless rate of interest. Then the wealth dynamics equation simplifies to

$$\begin{aligned} \mathrm{d}W &= -C\mathrm{d}t + rW(1 - \sum_{i=1}^{n} w_i)\mathrm{d}t + \sum_{i=1}^{n} w_i W(\alpha_i \mathrm{d}t + \sigma_i \mathrm{d}z_i) \\ &= -C\mathrm{d}t + rW\mathrm{d}t + \sum_{i=1}^{n} w_i W[(\alpha_i - r)\mathrm{d}t + \sigma_i \mathrm{d}z_i]\,. \end{aligned} \tag{8.4}$$

We assume that the investor makes sequential consumption and investment decisions with the objective to maximize the von Neumann–Morgenstern expected utility i.e.

$$\max E_0 \left[\int_0^\infty u(C, x, t)\, \mathrm{d}t \right] \tag{8.5}$$

where u is monotone increasing and concave in the consumption flow C. Note that in the above representation of preferences utility is time-separable but nonstate separable since preferences depend on x. The case of nontime-separable preferences is discussed in Sundaresan [1989], Constantinides [1990], and Detemple & Zapatero [1991].

To derive the optimal consumption and investment policies we define

$$J(W, x, t) = \max_{\{C, w\}} E_t \left[\int_t^\infty u(C, x, \tau)\, \mathrm{d}\tau \right].$$

Assuming sufficient regularity conditions as presented in Fleming & Richel [1975], so that a solution exists, the derived utility of wealth, J, satisfies the equation derived by Merton [1971, 1973]

$$\begin{aligned} 0 = \max_{\{C, w\}} \Bigg[& u(C, x, t) + \left\{ -C + rW + W \sum_{i=1}^{n} w_i(\alpha_i - r) \right\} J_W + mJ_x + J_t + \\ & + \frac{1}{2} W^2 J_{WW} \sum_{i=1}^{n} \sum_{j=1}^{n} w_i w_j \sigma_{ij} + W J_{Wx} \sum_{i=1}^{n} w_i \sigma_{ix} + \frac{s^2}{2} J_{xx} \Bigg]. \end{aligned} \tag{8.6}$$

The first-order conditions with respect to C and w_i are

$$u_C - J_W = 0 \tag{8.7}$$

and

$$W(\alpha_i - r)J_W + W^2 J_{WW} \sum_{j=1}^{n} w_j \sigma_{ij} + W J_{Wx} \sigma_{ix} = 0, \quad i = 1, \dots, n. \tag{8.8}$$

The concavity of the utility function implies that J is concave in W; hence the second-order conditions are satisfied.

Under appropriate regularity conditions which are not discussed here a verification theorem can be stated to the effect that the solution of the partial differential equation is unique, and therefore is the solution of the original optimal consumption and investment problem.

Since the topic of this essay is the portfolio problem we focus on the first-order conditions (8.8) implied by optimal investment which we write in matrix notation as

$$(\boldsymbol{\alpha} - r\mathbf{1})J_W + W J_{WW} \mathbf{w}^{\mathrm{T}} \mathbf{V} + J_{Wx} \boldsymbol{\sigma}_x = 0, \tag{8.9}$$

where $\mathbf{V}$ is the $n \times n$ covariance matrix with $i \times j$ element σ_{ij} and $\boldsymbol{\sigma}_x$ is a vector with ith element σ_{ix}. Solving for the optimal portfolio weights we obtain

$$\mathbf{w} = \left(\frac{-J_W}{W J_{WW}}\right) \mathbf{V}^{-1}(\boldsymbol{\alpha} - r\mathbf{1}) - \frac{J_{Wx}}{W J_{WW}} \mathbf{V}^{-1} \boldsymbol{\sigma}_x. \tag{8.10}$$

Before we analyze the optimal portfolio decision in its full generality, consider first the important special case where the term $[J_{Wx}/(W J_{WW})]\mathbf{V}^{-1}\boldsymbol{\sigma}_x$ is a vector of zeros. We will shortly discuss three cases where this occurs. Then we may write equation (8.10) as

$$\mathbf{w} = \left(\frac{-J_W}{W J_{WW}}\right) \left[\mathbf{1}^{\mathrm{T}} \mathbf{V}^{-1} (\boldsymbol{\alpha} - r\mathbf{1})\right] \mathbf{w}_{\mathrm{T}} \tag{8.11}$$

where

$$\mathbf{w}_{\mathrm{T}} = \frac{\mathbf{V}^{-1}(\boldsymbol{\alpha} - r\mathbf{1})}{\mathbf{1}^{\mathrm{T}} \mathbf{V}^{-1} (\boldsymbol{\alpha} - r\mathbf{1})}. \tag{8.12}$$

From our discussion in Section 5, we recognize $\mathbf{w}_{\mathrm{T}}$ as the vector of portfolio weights of the tangency portfolio on the frontier of minimum variance portfolios generated by the n risky assets. We also interpret $(-J_W/W J_{WW})^{-1}$ as the relative risk aversion (RRA) coefficient of the investor. Then equation (8.11) states that the investor invests in just two portfolios, namely the riskless asset and the tangency portfolio. The extent of the investment in the tangency portfolio depends on the investor's RRA coefficient. Thus we have proved that there is two-fund separation with the two funds being the riskless asset and the tangency portfolio. From here it is a small step, outlined in Section 9, to show that the CAPM holds.

We present three sets of conditions each of which implies two-fund separation and the CAPM:

(a) Logarithmic utility. Then we may show that the derived utility $J(W, x)$ is the sum of a function of W and a function of x. Hence the cross-derivative J_{Wx} equals zero and the second term in equation (8.10) becomes a vector of zeros.

(b) All assets' returns are uncorrelated with the change in x, i.e. $\sigma_{ix} = 0$, $i = 1, \ldots, n$.

(c) All assets have distributions of returns which are independent of x, i.e. α_i, σ_i are independent of x for $i = 1, \ldots, n$.

We now return to the general case where none of the assumptions (a)–(c) hold and the term $[J_{Wx}/(WJ_{WW})]\mathbf{V}^{-1}\boldsymbol{\sigma}_x$ is not a vector of zeros. Define by $\boldsymbol{w}_{\mathrm{H}}$ the weights of a portfolio

$$\boldsymbol{w}_{\mathrm{H}} = \frac{\mathbf{V}^{-1}\boldsymbol{\sigma}_x}{\mathbf{1}^{\mathrm{T}}\mathbf{V}^{-1}\boldsymbol{\sigma}_x}.$$

Then we may write equation (8.10) as

$$\boldsymbol{w} = \left(\frac{-J_W}{WJ_{WW}}\right)\left[\mathbf{1}^{\mathrm{T}}V^{-1}(\alpha - r\mathbf{1})\right]\boldsymbol{w}_{\mathrm{T}} + \left(\frac{-J_{Wx}}{WJ_{WW}}\right)\left[\mathbf{1}^{\mathrm{T}}V^{-1}\boldsymbol{\sigma}_x\right]\boldsymbol{w}_{\mathrm{H}}. \quad (8.13)$$

We observe that three-fund portfolio separation obtains: The investor invests in the riskless asset, the tangency portfolio $\boldsymbol{w}_{\mathrm{T}}$ and the hedging portfolio $\boldsymbol{w}_{\mathrm{H}}$. The weights which the investor assigns to each portfolio depend on his/her preferences and are, therefore, investor-specific.

We may further interpret the hedging portfolio by solving the following maximization problem: Choose vector $\boldsymbol{y}$ such that $\mathbf{1}^{\mathrm{T}}\boldsymbol{y} = 1$ (i.e. $\boldsymbol{y}$ is the vector of a portfolio's weights) to maximize the correlation of $\mathrm{d}x$ and $\sum_{i=1}^{n} y_i(\mathrm{d}P_i/P_i)$. The solution to this problem is easily shown to be $\boldsymbol{y} = \boldsymbol{w}_{\mathrm{H}}$. That is, the hedging portfolio is the portfolio of the risky assets with returns maximally correlated with the change in the state variable x.

Note that x enters into the decision problem through α_i and σ_i, that is, it causes changes in the investment opportunity set and through the utility of consumption, $u(C, x, t)$, that is, it causes shifts in tastes. We may interpret the three fund separation result as follows: The investor invests in the riskless asset and in the tangency portfolio, as in the mean–variance case, but modifies his or her portfolio investing in (or selling short) a third portfolio which has returns maximally correlated with changes in the variable x which represents shifts in the investment opportunity set and tastes.

As we stated earlier we have chosen x to be a scalar solely for expositional ease. If instead, $\boldsymbol{x}$ is a vector with m elements we obtain $(m + 2)$-fund separation where the investor invests in the riskless asset, the tangency portfolio and the m hedging portfolios.

In evaluating Merton's [1971, 1973] intertemporal continuous-time portfolio theory at least two important contributions need to be identified: first, its generalization of the static mean–variance theory is achieved by considering both the consumption and portfolio selection over time and by dropping the quadratic utility assumption; and second, its realism and tractability compared to the discrete-time portfolio theories which assume normally distributed asset prices implying a nonzero probability of negative asset prices. By replacing the assumption of normally distributed asset prices with the assumption that prices follow (8.1), the continuous-time portfolio theory becomes more realistic as well as more tractable in view of the extensive mathematical literature on diffusion processes.

Merton's work was extended in several directions. Among them, Breeden [1979] and Cox, Ingersoll & Ross [1985a, b] consider a generalization of the intertemporal continuous-time portfolio theory in a general equilibrium model with production. Another contribution was made by Breeden [1979] who shows that Merton's [1973] multi-beta pricing model can be expressed with a single beta measured with respect to changes in aggregate consumption assuming that consumption preferences are time separable. One interesting result of Breeden's work is that, in an intertemporal economy, the portfolio that has the highest correlation of returns with aggregate real consumption changes is mean–variance efficient.

Several authors have considered equation (8.1) which is the most significant assumption of continuous-time portfolio theory and have asked the question: under what conditions is a price system representable by Itô processes such as (8.1)? Huang [1985a, b] shows that when the information structure is a Brownian filtration then any arbitrage-free price system is an Itô process. The arbitrage-free concept is analyzed in Harrison & Kreps [1979] and Harrison & Pliska [1981] who make a connection to a martingale representation theorem. The role of information is analyzed in Duffie & Huang [1986].

Finally, in contrast to the stochastic dynamic programming approach to the continuous time consumption and portfolio problem, Pliska [1986] and Cox & Huang [1989], among others have used the martingale representation methodology. In the martingale approach, first, the dynamic consumption and portfolio problem is transformed and solved as a static utility maximization problem to find the optimal consumption and, second, the martingale representation theorem is applied to determine the portfolio trading strategy which is consistent with the optimal consumption. It is usually assumed that markets are dynamically complete which allows for the determination of a budget constraint and the solution of the static utility maximization. The case when markets are dynamically incomplete with the dimension of the Brownian motion driving the security prices being greater than the number of risky securities is presented in He & Pearson [1991].

9. The Intertemporal Asset Pricing Model (ICAPM) and the Arbitrage Pricing Theory (APT)

In the last section we solved for the optimal weights of the portfolio of risky assets held by an investor with given preferences. If all consumers in the economy have identical preferences and endowments then the above optimal portfolio may be identified as the market portfolio of risky assets. The condition that consumers have identical preferences and endowments may be relaxed under conditions which imply demand aggregation as in Rubinstein [1974] and Constantinides [1980] or under complete markets as in Constantinides [1982]. Hereafter we assume that either through demand aggregation or through complete markets we can claim that the optimal portfolio in (8.10) is indeed the market portfolio of risky assets. We denote the weights of this portfolio by $\boldsymbol{w}^{\mathrm{M}}$ and its return by

$$\frac{\mathrm{d}P_{\mathrm{M}}}{P_{\mathrm{M}}} = \sum_{i=1}^{n} w_i^{\mathrm{M}} \frac{\mathrm{d}P_i}{P_i}$$

We should stress that, in general, the market portfolio does not coincide with the tangency portfolio. In the last section we discussed conditions under which the two portfolios coincide but these conditions will not be imposed here.

To derive the intertemporal capital asset pricing model (ICAPM), we rewrite equation (8.8) as

$$\begin{aligned} \alpha_i - r &= \left(-\frac{W J_{WW}}{J_W}\right) \sum_{j=1}^{n} w_j^{\mathrm{M}} \sigma_{ij} + \left(-\frac{J_{Wx}}{J_W}\right) \sigma_{ix} \\ &= \lambda_{\mathrm{M}} \beta_{iM} + \lambda_x \beta_{ix} \qquad i = 1, \ldots, n. \end{aligned} \tag{9.1}$$

where

$$\beta_{iM} = \frac{\operatorname{cov}(\mathrm{d}P_i/P_i, \mathrm{d}P_{\mathrm{M}}/P_{\mathrm{M}})}{\operatorname{var}(\mathrm{d}P_{\mathrm{M}}/P_{\mathrm{M}})}$$

$$\lambda_{\mathrm{M}} = -\frac{W J_{WW}}{J_W} \frac{\operatorname{var}(\mathrm{d}P_{\mathrm{M}}/P_{\mathrm{M}})}{\mathrm{d}t}$$

$$\beta_{ix} = \frac{\operatorname{cov}(\mathrm{d}P_i/P_i, \mathrm{d}x)}{\operatorname{var}(\mathrm{d}x)}$$

and

$$\lambda_x = -\frac{J_{Wx}}{J_W} \frac{\operatorname{var}(\mathrm{d}x)}{\mathrm{d}t}.$$

This result generalizes in a routine fashion to the case where the state variable is a vector.

We conclude this section by discussing the empirically testable implications of the theory, along with the arbitrage pricing theory of Ross [1976a, b]. The common starting point of both the ICAPM and the APT is a linear multivariate regression of the $n \times 1$ vector of asset returns, $\tilde{\boldsymbol{R}}$, on a $k \times 1$ vector of state variables (in the ICAPM) or factors (in the APT), $\tilde{f}$:

$$\tilde{\boldsymbol{R}} = \boldsymbol{R} + B(\tilde{f} - f) + \tilde{\varepsilon} \tag{9.2}$$

where $R \equiv E[\tilde{\boldsymbol{R}}]$, $f \equiv E[\tilde{f}]$ and $E[\tilde{\varepsilon}] = 0$. In both theories the elements of $\tilde{f}$ are assumed to have finite variance. The covariance matrix $\Omega \equiv E[\tilde{\varepsilon}\tilde{\varepsilon}^{\mathrm{T}}]$ is assumed to have finite elements. Furthermore, in the APT the elements of $\tilde{f}$ are assumed to be factors in the sense that the largest eigenvalue of Ω remains bounded as $n \to \infty$ [see Chamberlain, 1983b].

The pricing restriction implied by the ICAPM is that there exist a constant, λ_0, and a $k \times 1$ vector of risk "premia", $\boldsymbol{\lambda}$, such that

$$\boldsymbol{R} = \lambda_0 \mathbf{1} + B\boldsymbol{\lambda} \tag{9.3}$$

where $\mathbf{1}$ is the $n \times 1$ vector of ones as before. The pricing restriction implied by the APT is

$$\lim_{n \to \infty} (\boldsymbol{R} - \lambda_0 \mathbf{1} - B\boldsymbol{\lambda})^{\mathrm{T}} (\boldsymbol{R} - \lambda_0 \mathbf{1} - B\boldsymbol{\lambda}) = A, \qquad A < \infty \tag{9.4}$$

which, in empirical work (where n is finite), is interpreted to imply (9.3).

If the proxies for state variables in the ICAPM or factors in the APT are portfolios of the n assets, the ICAPM or APT pricing restrictions, (9.3), state that there exists a portfolio of these proxy portfolios which has mean and variance on the mean–variance, minimum-variance frontier. See Jobson & Korkie [1985], Grinblatt & Titman [1987] and Huberman, Kandel & Stambaugh [1987]. Therefore the econometric methods for testing that a given portfolio lies on the minimum-variance frontier may be extended to test the ICAPM and the APT. See Kandel & Stambaugh [1989] and the Connor & Korajczyk [1995] essay in this volume.

10. Market imperfections

Market imperfections were suppressed in our earlier discussion by implicitly assuming that (i) transaction costs are zero, (ii) the capital gains tax is zero (or, capital gains and losses are realized and taxed in every period), and (iii) the assets may be sold short with full use of the proceeds which, in the case of a riskless asset, implies that the borrowing rate equals the lending rate. How sensitive are our conclusions on portfolio selection and equilibrium asset pricing to the presence of these imperfections? Whereas a comprehensive discussion of these issues is beyond the scope of this essay, we discuss briefly one instance of market imperfections.

Consider first the discrete-time intertemporal investment and consumption problem with proportional transaction costs. The agent maximizes the expectation of a time-separable utility function where the period utility is of the convenient power form. The agent consumes in every period and invests the remaining wealth in only two assets. The agent enters period t with x_t units of account of the first asset and y_t units of account of the second asset. If the agent buys (or, sells) v_t units of account of the second asset, the holding of the first asset becomes $x_t - v_t - \max[k_1 v_t, -k_2 v_t]$, net of transaction costs where the constants k_1, k_2 satisfy $0 \le k_1 \le 1$ and $0 \le k_2 \le 1$. The optimal investment policy, described in terms of two parameters $\underline{\alpha}_t$ and $\overline{\alpha}_t$, $\underline{\alpha}_t \le \overline{\alpha}_t$, is to refrain from transacting as long as the portfolio proportions, x_t/y_t, lie within the interval $[\underline{\alpha}_t, \overline{\alpha}_t]$; and transact to the closer boundary, $\underline{\alpha}_t$ or $\overline{\alpha}_t$, of the region of no transactions whenever the portfolio proportions lie outside this interval (provided, of course, that this is feasible). The parameters $(\underline{\alpha}_t, \overline{\alpha}_t)$ are functions of time and of the state variables which define the conditional distribution of the assets' return. This general form of the optimal portfolio policy also holds in a model with continuous trading under additional assumptions on the distribution of asset returns. See Kamin [1975], Constantinides [1979], Taksar, Klass & Assaf [1988] and Davis & Norman [1990].

In numerical solutions of the portfolio problem with even small proportional transaction costs one finds that the region of no transactions is wide. We conclude from these examples and extrapolate in more general cases with transaction costs that even small transaction costs distort significantly the optimal portfolio policy which is optimal in the absence of transaction costs. See Constantinides [1986], Dumas & Luciano [1991], Fleming, Grossman, Vila & Zariphopoulou [1990] and Gennotte & Jung [1991]. An encouraging finding, however, is that transaction costs have only a second-order effect on equilibrium asset returns: investors accommodate large transaction costs by drastically reducing the frequency and volume of trade. It turns out that the agent's utility is insensitive to deviations of the asset proportions from those proportions which are optimal in the absence of transaction costs. Therefore, a small liquidity premium is sufficient to compensate an agent for deviating significantly from the target portfolio proportions. These results need to be qualified as they apply to the case where the only motive for trade is portfolio rebalancing. Transaction costs may have a first-order effect on equilibrium asset returns in cases where the investors receive exogenous income or trade on the basis of inside information.

11. Concluding remarks

Portfolio theory is the analysis of the real world phenomenon of diversification. This paper has exposited this theory in its historical evolution, from the early work on static mean–variance mathematics to its generalization of dynamic consumption and portfolio rules. In its intellectual development portfolio theory has benefitted from empirical work which came from capital asset pricing tests and from statistical investigations of the distributions of asset prices. Furthermore, as more powerful techniques were developed, such as stochastic calculus, portfolio theory became dynamic and many results were generalized.

Because the topic of our paper is theoretical, we have not mentioned any issues related to real world portfolio management. Interested readers can find such topics in standard graduate textbooks such as Lee, Finnerty & Wort [1990] or papers in this volume on performance evaluation by Grinblatt & Titman [1995], on market microstructure by Easley & O'Hara [1995], and on world wide security market regularities by Hawawini & Keim [1995], among others. Although our topic was on portfolio theory, numerous important theoretical developments are not mentioned. Fortunately again, some are treated in this volume such as futures and options markets by Carr & Jarrow [1995], market volatility by LeRoy

& Steigerwald [1995], and the extension of portfolio theory from national to international markets by Stulz [1995]. A useful companion survey is presented in Constantinides [1989], where theoretical issues of financial valuation are presented in a unified way.

Acknowledgements

We thank Wayne Ferson, Brian Kennedy and Bill Ziemba for several useful comments.

References

Arrow, K.J. (1971). *Essays on the Theory of Risk-Bearing*, Markham, Chicago.

Bernoulli, D. (1738). Exposition of a new theory of the measurement of risk, translated by L. Sommer and published in 1954 in *Econometrica* 22, 23–36.

Black, F. (1972). Capital market equilibrium with restricted borrowing. *J. Bus.* 45, 444–455.

Boness, A.J., A. Chen and S. Jatusipitak (1974). Investigations on nonstationarity in prices. *J. Bus.* 47, 518–537.

Breeden, D.T. (1979). An intertemporal asset pricing model with stochastic consumption and investment opportunities. *J. Financ. Econ.* 7, 265–296.

Breeden, D.T. (1986). Consumption, production, inflation, and interest rates: A synthesis. *J. Financ. Econ.* 16, 3–39.

Brennan, M.J. (1989). Capital asset pricing model, in: J. Eatwell, M. Milgate and P. Newman (eds.), *The New Palgrave Dictionary of Economics*, Stockton Press, New York, NY.

Carr, P., and R.A. Jarrow (1995). A discrete time synthesis of derivative security valuation using a term structure of futures prices, in: R. Jarrow, V. Maksimovic and W.T. Ziemba (eds.), *Finance*, Elsevier, Amsterdam, pp. (this volume).

Cass, D., and J. Stiglitz (1970). The structure of investor preferences and asset returns, and separability in portfolio selection: A contribution to the pure theory of mutual funds. *J. Econ. Theory* 2, 122–160.

Chamberlain, G. (1983a). A characterization of the distributions that imply mean–variance utility functions. *J. Econ. Theory* 29, 185–201.

Chamberlain, G. (1983b). Funds, factors, and diversification in arbitrage pricing models. *Econometrica* 51, 1305–1323.

Connor, G, and R. Korajczyk (1995). The arbitrage pricing theory, and multifactor models of asset returns, in: R. Jarrow, V. Maksimovic and W.T. Ziemba (eds.), *Finance*, Elsevier, Amsterdam, pp. 65–122 (this volume).

Constantinides, G.M. (1979). Multiperiod consumption and investment behavior with convex transaction costs. *Manage. Sci.* 25, 1127–1137.

Constantinides, G.M. (1980). Admissible uncertainty in the intertemporal asset pricing model. *J. Financ. Econ.* 8, 71–86.

Constantinides, G.M. (1982). Intertemporal asset pricing with heterogeneous consumers and without demand aggregation. *J. Bus.* 55, 253–267.

Constantinides, G.M. (1986). Capital market equilibrium with transaction costs. *J. Polit. Econ.* 94, 842–862.

Constantinides, G.M. (1989). Theory of valuation: Overview and recent developments, in: S. Bhattacharya and G.M. Constantinides (eds.), *Theory of Valuation*, Rowman & Littlefield, Totowa, NJ.

Constantinides, G.M. (1990). Habit formation: A resolution of the equity premium puzzle. *J. Polit. Econ.* 98, 519–543.

Cox, J.C, and C.F. Huang (1989). Optimal consumption and portfolio policies when asset prices follow a diffusion process. *J. Econ. Theory* 49, 33–83.

Cox, J.C., J.E. Ingersoll, and S.A. Ross (1985a). A theory of the term structure of interest rates. *Econometrica* 53, 385–407.

Cox, J.C., J.E. Ingersoll, and S.A. Ross (1985b). An intertemporal general equilibrium model of asset prices. *Econometrica* 53, 363–384.

Davis, M.H.A., and A.R. Norman (1990). Portfolio selection with transactions costs. *Math. Oper. Res.* 15, 676–713.

Detemple, J.B., and F. Zapatero (1991). Asset prices in an exchange economy with habit formation. *Econometrica* 59, 1633–1657.

Dumas, B., and E. Luciano (1991). An exact solution to a dynamic portfolio choice problem under transactions costs. *J. Finance* 46, 577–595.

Duffie, D, and C. Huang (1986). Multiperiod securities markets with differential information: Martingales and resolution times. *J. Math. Econ.* 15, 283–303.

Easley, M, and M. O'Hara (1995). Market microstructure, in: R. Jarrow, V. Maksimovic and W.T. Ziemba (eds.), *Finance*, Elsevier, Amsterdam, pp. 357–384 (this volume).

Fama, E.F. (1965a). Portfolio analysis in a stable Paretian market. *Manage. Sci.* 11, 409–419.

Fama, E.F. (1965b). The behavior of stock market prices. *J. Bus.* 38, 34–105.

Fama, E.F. (1970). Multiperiod consumption-investment decisions. *Am. Econ. Rev.* 60, 163–174.

Fama, E.F. (1976). *Foundations of Finance*, Basic Books, New York, NY.

Ferson, W. (1995). Theory and empirical testing of asset pricing models, in: R. Jarrow, V. Maksimovic and W.T. Ziemba (eds.), *Finance*, Elsevier, Amsterdam, pp. 145–200 (this volume).

Fisher, I. (1906). *The Nature of Capital and Income*, Macmillan, New York, NY.

Fleming, W, and R. Richel (1975). *Deterministic and Stochastic Optimal Control*, Springer-Verlag, New York, NY.

Fleming, W.H.S., S.G. Grossman, J.L. Vila, and T. Zariphopoulou (1990). Optimal portfolio rebalancing with transactions costs. Working paper, Brown University.

Gennotte, G, and A. Jung (1991). Investment strategies under transaction costs: The finite horizon case. Working paper, University of California at Berkeley.

Gonzalez-Gaverra, N. (1973). Inflation and capital asset market prices: Theory and tests. Unpublished PhD Dissertation, Stanford University.

Grinblatt, M, and S. Titman (1987). The relation between mean–variance efficiency and arbitrage pricing. *J. Bus.* 60, 97–112.

Grinblatt, M, and S. Titman (1995). Performance evaluation, in: R. Jarrow, V. Maksimovic and W.T. Ziemba (eds.), *Finance*, Elsevier, Amsterdam, pp. 581–610 (this volume).

Hakansson, N. (1970). Optimal investment and consumption strategies under risk for a class of utility functions. *Econometrica* 38, 587–607.

Hakansson, N. (1974). Convergence in multiperiod portfolio choice. *J. Financ. Econ.* 1, 201–224.

Hansen, L.P, and R. Jagannathan (1991). Implications of security market data for models of dynamic economies. *J. Polit. Econ.* 99, 225–262.

Harrison, M, and D. Kreps (1979). Martingales and arbitrage in multiperiod securities markets. *J. Econ. Theory* 20, 381–408.

Harrison, M, and S. Pliska (1981). Martingales and stochastic integrals in the theory of continuous trading. *Stoch. Process Appl.* 11, 215–260.

Hawawini, G, and D. Keim (1995). On the predictability of common stock returns: world-wide evidence, in: R. Jarrow, V. Maksimovic and W.T. Ziemba (eds.), *Finance*, Elsevier, Amsterdam, pp. (this volume).

He, H, and N.D. Pearson (1991). Consumption and portfolio policies with incomplete markets and short-sale constraints: The infinite dimensional case. *J. Econ. Theory* 54, 259–304.

Hicks, J.R. (1939). *Value and Capital*, Oxford University Press, New York, NY.

Huang, C. (1985a). Information structure and equilibrium asset prices. *J. Econ. Theory* 35, 33–71.

Huang, C. (1985b). Information structure and viable price systems. *J. Math. Econ.* 14, 215–240.

Huang, C.F, and R.H. Litzenberger (1988). *Foundations for Financial Economics*, North Holland, Amsterdam.

Huberman G., S. Kandel, and R.F. Stambaugh (1987). Mimicking portfolios and exact arbitrage pricing. *J. Finance* 42, 1–9.

Ingersoll, Jr., J.E. (1975). Multidimensional security pricing. *J. Financ. Quant. Anal.* 10, 785–798.

Ingersoll, Jr., J.E. (1987). *Theory of Financial Decision Making*, Rowman and Littlefield, Totowa, NJ.

Jarrow, R.A. (1988). *Finance Theory*, Prentice Hall, Englewood Cliffs, NJ.

Jobson, J.D., and B. Korkie (1985). Some tests of linear asset pricing with multivariate normality. *Can. J. Adm. Sci.* 2, 114–138.

Kallberg, J.G, and W.T. Ziemba (1983). Comparison of alternative utility functions in portfolio selection problems. *Manage. Sci.* 29, 1257–1276.

Kamin, J. (1975). Optimal portfolio revision with a proportional transactions cost. *Manage. Sci.* 21, 1263–1271.

Kandel, S., and R.F. Stambaugh (1989). A mean–variance framework for tests of asset pricing models. *Rev. Financ. Studies* 2, 125–156.

Keynes, J.L. (1936). *The General Theory of Employment, Interest and Money*, Harcourt Brace and Company, New York, NY.

Kraus, A, and R. Litzenberger (1976). Skewness preference and the valuation of risk assets. *J. Finance* 31, 1085–1100.

Lee, C.F., J.E. Finnerty and D.H. Wort (1990). *Security Analysis and Portfolio Management*, Scott, Foresman and Company, Glenview, IL.

LeRoy, S, and D. Steigerwald (1995). Volatility, in: R. Jarrow, V. Maksimovic and W.T. Ziemba (eds.), *Finance*, Elsevier, Amsterdam, pp. 411–434 (this volume).

Levy, H, and H.M. Markowitz (1979). Approximating expected utility by a function of mean and variance. *Am. Econ. Rev.* 69, 308–317.

Levy, H, and P.A. Samuelson (1992) The capital asset pricing model with diverse holding periods. *Manage. Sci.* 38, 1529–1542.

Lintner, J. (1965). The valuation of risk assets and the selection of risky investments in stock portfolios and capital assets. *Rev. Econ. Stat.* 47, 13–37.

Long, J.B. (1974). Stock prices, inflation, and the term structure of interest rates. *J. Financ. Econ.* 2, 131–170.

Malliaris, A.G, and W.A. Brock (1982). *Stochastic Methods in Economics and Finance*, North Holland, Amsterdam.

Mandelbrot, B. (1963). The variation of certain speculative prices. *J. Bus.* 36, 394–419.

Markowitz, H. (1952). Portfolio selection. *J. Finance* 7, 77–91.

Markowitz, H. (1959). *Portfolio Selection: Efficient Diversification of Investments*, Wiley, New York, NY.

Markowitz, H.M. (1987). *Mean–Variance Analysis in Portfolio Choice and Capital Markets*, Basil Blackwell, Oxford.

Markowitz, H.M. (1991). Foundations of portfolio theory. *J. Finance* 46, 469–477.

Marschak, J. (1938). Money and the theory of assets. *Econometrica* 6, 311–325.

Merton, R.C. (1969). Lifetime portfolio selection under uncertainty: The continuous time case. *Rev. Econ. Stat.* 51, 247–257.

Merton, R.C. (1971). Optimum consumption and portfolio rules in a continuous time model. *J. Econ. Theory* 3, 373–413.

Merton, R.C. (1972). An analytical derivation of the efficient portfolio frontier. *J. Financ. Quant. Anal.* 7, 1851–1872.

Merton, R.C. (1973). An intertemporal capital asset pricing model. *Econometrica* 41, 867–887.

Merton, R.C. (1975). Theory of finance from the perspective of continuous time. *J. Financ. Quant. Anal.* 10, 659–674.

Merton, R.C. (1980). On estimating the expected return on the market: An explanatory investigation. *J. Financ. Econ.* 8, 323–361.

Merton, R.C. (1982). On the mathematics and economics assumptions of continuous-time models, in: W.F. Sharpe and C.M. Cootner (eds.), *Financial Economics: Essays in Honor of Paul Cootner*, Prentice Hall, Englewood Cliffs, NJ.

Mossin, J. (1966). Equilibrium in a capital asset market. *Econometrica* 35, 768–783.

Mossin, J. (1969). Optimal multiperiod portfolio policies. *J. Bus.* 41, 215–229.

Ohlson, J.A, and W.T. Ziemba (1976). Portfolio selection in a lognormal market when the investor has a power utility function. *J. Financ. Quant. Anal.* 11, 393–401.

Osborne, M.F.M. (1959). Brownian motion in the stock market. *Oper. Res.* 7, 145–173.

Pliska, S. (1986). A stochastic calculus model of continuous trading: Optimal portfolios. *Math. Oper. Res.* 11, 371–382.

Roll, R. (1977). A critique of the asset pricing theory's tests: Part I. *J. Financ. Econ.* 4, 129–176.

Rothschild, M, and J. Stiglitz (1970). Increasing risk. I. A definition. *J. Econ. Theory* 2, 225–243.

Ross, S.A. (1976a). Return, risk and arbitrage, in: I. Friend and J. Bicksler (eds.), *Risk and Return in Finance*, Ballinger, Cambridge, MA.

Ross, S.A. (1976b). The arbitrage theory of capital asset pricing. *J. Econ. Theory* 13, 341–360.

Ross, S.A. (1978). Mutual fund separation in financial theory — The separating distributions. *J. Econ. Theory* 17, 254–286.

Rubinstein, M. (1974). An aggregation theorem for security markets. *J. Financ. Econ.* 1, 225–244.

Rubinstein, M. (1976). The valuation of uncertain income streams and the pricing of options. *Bell J. Econ. Manage. Sci.* 7, 407–425.

Samuelson, P. (1969). Lifetime portfolio selection by dynamic stochastic programming. *Rev. Econ. Stat.* 57, 239–246.

Sharpe, W.F. (1964). Capital asset prices: A theory of market equilibrium under conditions of risk. *J. Finance* 19, 425–442.

Sharpe, W.F. (1970). *Portfolio Theory and Capital Markets*, McGraw-Hill, New York, NY.

Stiglitz, J.E. (1989). Discussion: Mutual funds, capital structure, and economic efficiency, in: S. Bhattacharya and G.M. Constantinides (eds.), *Theory of Valuation*, Rowman & Littlefield Publishers, Totowa, NJ.

Stulz, R. (1995). International portfolio choice and asset pricing: an integrative survey, in: R. Jarrow, V. Maksimovic and W.T. Ziemba (eds.), *Finance*, Elsevier, Amsterdam, pp. 201–224 (this volume).

Sundaresan, S.M. (1989). Intertemporal dependent preferences and the volatility of consumption and wealth. *Rev. Financ. Studies* 2, 73–90.

Taksar, M., M. Klass, and D. Assaf (1988). A diffusion model for optimal portfolio selection in the presence of brokerage fees. *Math. Oper. Res.* 13, 277–294.

Tobin, J. (1958). Liquidity preference as behavior toward risk. *Rev. Econ. Studies* 25, 65–86.

Von Neumann, J, and O. Morgenstern (1947). *Theory of Games and Economic Behavior*, 2nd edition, Princeton University Press, Princeton.

Williams J.B. (1938). *The Theory of Investment Value*, Harvard University Press, Cambridge, MA.

Ziemba W.T., C. Parkan and R. Brooks-Hill (1974). Calculation of investment portfolios with risk free borrowing and lending. *Manage. Sci.* 21, 209–222.

Ziemba, W.T. (1974). Choosing investment portfolios when returns have stable distributions, in: P.L. Hammer and G. Zoutendijk (eds.), *Mathematical Programming in Theory and Practice*, North-Holland, Amsterdam, pp. 443–482.

Ziemba, W.T, and R.G. Vickson, editors (1975). *Stochastic Optimization Models in Finance*, Academic Press, New York, NY.

R. Jarrow et al., Eds., *Handbooks in OR & MS, Vol. 9*

Chapter 2

Finite State Securities Market Models and Arbitrage

Vasant Naik

University of British Columbia, Faculty of Commerce and Business Administration, 2053 Main Mall, Vancouver, B.C., V6T1Z2, Canada.

1. Introduction

A fundamental characteristic of security prices in a competitive securities market is that they do not permit arbitrage opportunities. The theory of arbitrage-based asset pricing is concerned with the implications of the lack of arbitrage opportunities. There are two basic questions that this theory addresses. The first is what restrictions can be placed on security price behavior if no arbitrage opportunities exist. The second question of interest is the converse of the first one; that is, what restrictions are needed to ensure that a given security price process is free of arbitrage opportunities. The resolution of these questions is of basic importance in financial economics. This is because, in the presence of investors who strictly prefer more wealth to less, a set of prices that permits arbitrage cannot possibly be sustained as an equilibrium. Not surprisingly then, the questions raised above have been the subject of intensive research in the last two decades. In this chapter we present the key results of this research.

In our analysis we assume that the number of states in the economy is finite. This allows for a simple and elegant characterization of arbitrage-free security prices. Not only is the finite state model an elegant theoretical construct, it also leads to very useful practical applications. For example, the celebrated binomial model of option pricing is an application of the finite state model of security prices.[1]

We provide an analysis of three topics related to the theory of arbitrage. Firstly, we analyze how one can characterize arbitrage-free prices in a frictionless securities market. To this end, we prove the fundamental theorem of asset pricing which links the lack of arbitrage opportunities to the existence of a risk-neutral probability measure. We also discuss the issue of dynamic completeness. We show how any contingent claim can be replicated by trading in existing securities in a dynamically complete market and, therefore, valued by arbitrage considerations alone.

[1] The binomial model was first presented by Sharpe [1978] and was fully developed in Cox, Ross & Rubinstein [1979] and Rendleman & Bartter [1979].

Secondly, we analyze how to characterize arbitrage-free asset prices in a market where there are costs of trading securities. Here we show how the fundamental theorem of asset pricing needs to be generalized to take account of market frictions. The questions of replicating state-contingent payoffs in the presence of transactions costs and market incompleteness are also analyzed. We show that if one's objective is to replicate a given payoff, it might be cheaper to replicate a payoff greater than the one originally targeted. We also show how the problem of minimum-cost replication of state-contingent payoffs can be formulated and solved when transaction costs are present.

The two questions mentioned above relate to the behavior of security prices and contingent claims valuation. We also discuss the question of optimal portfolio choice in a complete or incomplete market, with or without transactions costs. The focus here is on the optimal portfolio choice behavior of an individual investor who takes as given an arbitrage-free process for asset prices. This question is typically analyzed using the dynamic programming approach, as shown, for example, in Hakansson [1970] & Merton [1971]. Recently, another approach has been devised to solve the portfolio choice problem which reduces the dynamic problem to a static one using the properties of arbitrage free security prices.[2] The static approach leads to an elegant characterization of the optimal portfolio choice problem. Moreover, it is easier to apply than the dynamic programming approach in some cases. Our analysis of the portfolio problem is based on the static approach. Again it is seen that the finite state framework is quite useful in bringing forward important economic insights related to the portfolio choice question.

This chapter builds on several excellent articles that analyze the connection between arbitrage and security prices in a finite state model. We now mention some of these articles, noting, however, that the objective here is not to conduct an exhaustive survey. Our analysis is based on Ross [1976, 1978], Dybvig & Ross [1986], Huang & Litzenberger [1988] and Kreps [1979]. The articles by Ross, and Dybvig and Ross present an analysis of the fundamental theorem of asset pricing in a two date economy. An extension of this theorem to a multi-period set-up can be found in Chapter 8 of Huang and Litzenberger. However, in the interest of simplicity of analysis, Huang and Litzenberger assume that preferences of investors are given by time additive expected utility. The case of securities markets with frictions is also not considered in these articles. The analysis in the presence of transactions costs and other market frictions is presented in Garman & Ohlson [1981], Prisman [1986], Dammon & Green [1987] and Ross [1987]. Finally, we draw on the work of Kreps [1979] where a definitive analysis of dynamic completeness and its welfare implications is carried out in a finite state model.

This chapter is organized as follows. Section 2 contains a description of the finite state securities market model that is used in our analysis. Section 3 discusses arbitrage and security prices in frictionless markets. Section 4 considers the case

[2] For a derivation of this approach, see Cox & Leland [1982], Cox & Huang [1989], He & Pearson [1991a, b], Karatzas, Lehoczky & Shreve [1987] and Karatzas, Lehoczky, Shreve & Xu [1991].

of markets with transactions costs. The problem of optimal portfolio choice is analyzed in Section 5 and Section 6 presents concluding remarks.

2. The model

We need a model of the securities market to analyze rigorously the portfolio choice decision of investors and the behavior of security prices. In this section, we describe the basic elements of such a model.

2.1. The information structure

There are $T + 1$ dates, $0, \ldots, T$, on which economic activity takes place in our model of the economy. The uncertainty in the economy stems from the fact that the state of the world that will prevail at date T could be any one of K $(K < \infty)$ possible states. The set of possible states is denoted Ω and its generic element is denoted ω.

New information arrives in the market at every date and this may cause the investors' portfolios and asset prices to change. To model the arrival of information, we take as given a family of increasingly finer partitions of Ω, denoted $\{\mathcal{F}_t, t = 0, \ldots, T\}$.[3] The partition $\mathcal{F}_t$ contains the information available to investors at date t. For every t, $\mathcal{F}_t$ is a collection of disjoint subsets of Ω such that their union equals Ω. We assume that $\mathcal{F}_0 = \Omega$ and $\mathcal{F}_T = \{\{\omega\},\ \omega \in \Omega\}$. The above assumptions imply that: (i) no information has arrived at time zero, (ii) as time progresses, investors come to know about gradually decreasing subsets of Ω which contain the true state of the world and (iii) the state of the world is fully revealed at date T. As shown in Figure 1, such information arrival can be illustrated by an event tree of a 3-date economy. In this event tree, $T = 2$, $\Omega \equiv \{\omega_i,\ i = 1, 6\} \equiv \{uu, um, ud, du, dm, dd\}$, $\mathcal{F}_0 = \{\Omega\}$, $\mathcal{F}_1 = \{u, d\}$ with $u = \{uu, um, ud\}$ and $d = \{du, dm, dd\}$, and $\mathcal{F}_2 = \{\{\omega\},\ \omega \in \Omega\}$.

Given the information structure described above, a stochastic process $\{y(t),\ t = 1, \ldots, T\}$ is $\mathcal{F}_t$-adapted if, for each t, $y(t)$ is measurable with respect to the σ-algebra generated by the elements of $\mathcal{F}_t$. Let $\mathcal{X}$ denote the set of all $\mathcal{F}_t$-adapted stochastic processes defined on Ω.[4] The adaptability requirement implies that $y(t)$ can take only $N(t)$ different values where $N(t)$ denotes the number of elements in $\mathcal{F}_t$, for $t = 1, \ldots, T$. Hence, an element of $\mathcal{X}$ can be identified with a point in $\prod_{t=1}^{T} \Re^{N(t)}$.

2.2. Securities

There are $N + 1$ securities available for trading in this economy. There is one good in the economy which serves as the numeraire. The securities are indexed

[3] That is, $\mathcal{F}_t \subset \mathcal{F}_{t+1}$ for $t = 0, \ldots, T - 1$.

[4] The elements of $\mathcal{X}$ are adapted stochastic processes that start at $t = 1$.

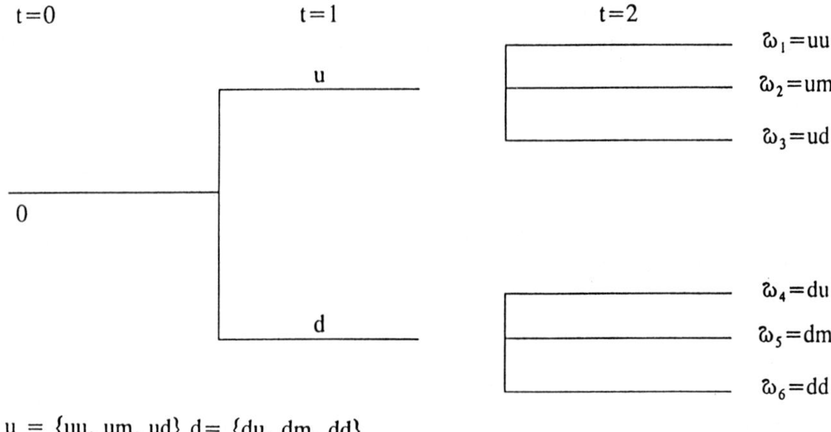

Fig. 1.

from 0 to N. Trading in these securities takes place at every $t = 0, \ldots, T$. The payoffs on the securities occur only at date T and they are in terms of the consumption good. The payoff on security i at time T is given by an $\mathcal{F}_T$ measurable random variable, $d_i(T)$, for $i = 0, \ldots, N$. The prices of traded securities from date 1 onwards are given by an $(N+1)$ dimensional $\mathcal{F}_t$-adapted stochastic process defined on Ω. Security prices at $t = 0$ are elements of $\Re$. The price process is $S \equiv \{S(t),\ t = 0, \ldots, T\}$ with $S_i(T) \equiv d_i(T) \forall i$ and with $S \in \Re \times \mathcal{X}$. It is also assumed that the 0th security is a riskless bond paying off one unit of the numeraire at time T in all possible states. The price process, S, is determined in a competitive equilibrium.

2.3 Investors

There are M investors who can consume at any date between 0 and T. For $j = 1, \ldots, M$, agent j is characterized by her consumption set $\mathcal{X}_j \subset \Re \times \mathcal{X}$, over which her preferences for consumption are defined. A typical element of $\mathcal{X}_j$ is (x, y) where x denotes consumption at $t = 0$ and y denotes the stochastic stream of consumption from $t = 1$ onwards. We believe that only positive consumption is meaningful and therefore we take the consumption set of each agent to be $\Re_+ \times \mathcal{X}_+$.[5] Every agent has an endowed cash flow stream which is assumed to be positive. A typical endowment stream is denoted by $e \equiv \{e(t),\ t = 0, \ldots, T\} \in \Re_+ \times \mathcal{X}_+$. The jth investor's preference for consumption is given by a strictly increasing preference relation $\succeq_j$ defined on $\Re_+ \times \mathcal{X}_+$.[6] The decision problem of the investors is to choose an optimal consumption plan subject to feasibility constraints.

[5] Here, $\Re_+$ is the set of positive reals and $\mathcal{X}_+ \equiv \{x \in \mathcal{X} \mid x \geq 0\}$.

[6] For a characterization of arbitrage-free asset prices in an economy where investors' preferences satisfy the additional condition of risk aversion, see Green & Srivastava [1985].

The purpose of a securities market in our model is to enable investors to alter the risk and time profile of their endowments to satisfy their risk and time preferences in the best possible way. The choice variable of every investor is a portfolio strategy. A portfolio strategy specifies the number of shares of each traded asset to be held at each date. A typical portfolio strategy, $\{\theta(t),\ t = 1, \ldots, T\}$, is an $(N + 1)$ dimensional stochastic process defined on Ω. For $t = 1, \ldots, T$, $\theta(t)$ denotes the number of shares of every traded asset that are held from time $t - 1$ to t before trading takes place at t. Every trading strategy, $\theta \equiv \{\theta(t),\ t = 1, \ldots, T\}$, results in a cash flow stream $c_\theta \in \Re \times \mathcal{X}$, where $c_\theta \equiv \{c_\theta(t),\ t = 0, \ldots, T\}$ is defined by:

$$c_\theta(0) = -\theta^{\mathrm{T}}(1)S(0)$$

$$c_\theta(t) = [\theta^{\mathrm{T}}(t) - \theta^{\mathrm{T}}(t+1)]S(t), \quad t = 1, \ldots, T-1,$$

and

$$c_\theta(T) = \theta^{\mathrm{T}}(T)d(T) \tag{1}$$

where $\theta^{\mathrm{T}}(.)$ denotes the transpose of $\theta(.)$. Thus, $c_\theta(0)$ is the initial investment and $\{c_\theta(t),\ t = 1, \ldots, T\}$ is the cash flow stream that the strategy θ generates.

The consumption plan of an agent with endowment e and trading strategy θ is given by $e + c_\theta \in \Re_+ \times \mathcal{X}_+$. The investors choose a feasible trading strategy that yields a consumption plan which maximizes their utility. A trading strategy is feasible if it satisfies the following two conditions. First, it must be predictable. That is, $\theta(t)$ must be $\mathcal{F}_{t-1}$ measurable for $t = 1, \ldots, T$. This is an informational constraint on the investors. It ensures that the portfolio with which they enter time t is determined by information available up to time $t - 1$. The absence of this constraint would allow investors to buy at $t - 1$ those assets whose prices will go up at t and sell those whose prices go down at t. This would clearly be unacceptable in any reasonable model of a competitive securities market. The second condition for feasibility of a trading strategy is that the consumption plan that it generates should lie in the consumption set of the agent. Given that investors can only consume positive amounts, this condition ensures that the trading strategy that an investor follows is within her budget.

The set of feasible consumption plans for an agent with endowment e given prices S is given by

$$B(e, S) \equiv \{y \in \Re_+ \times \mathcal{X}_+ \mid \exists\, \theta \in \Theta, \text{ such that } y = c_\theta + e\}$$

where Θ denotes the set of all predictable processes defined on Ω. Then, the decision problem of agent j with endowments e described above is also that of choosing a consumption plan y that is $\succeq_j$-maximal on $B(e, S)$.

For the discussion in the following sections it is convenient to define the set of marketed cash flows. If, for a given $x \in \mathcal{X}$, there exists a θ such that $x(t) = c_\theta(t)$ for $t = 1, \ldots, T$, then we say that the stream $\{x(t),\ t = 1, \ldots, T\}$ is generated by trading strategy θ with initial investment $\theta^{\mathrm{T}}(1)S(0) = -c_\theta(0)$. The elements of $\mathcal{X}$ which are generated by some $\theta \in \Theta$ are said to be marketed cash flows.

3. Arbitrage and security prices in a frictionless market

We now have the set-up to define what is meant by arbitrage and to discuss the connection between arbitrage and security prices in our model of the securities market. An arbitrage opportunity is a trading strategy that generates a strictly positive cash flow between 0 and T in at least one state and does not require an outflow of funds at any date. An arbitrage opportunity, thus, is a trading strategy that produces something from nothing. We do not expect such strategies to exist in a well-functioning securities market.

In this section, we characterize a set of security prices that do not permit arbitrage. We assume that the securities market is frictionless. That is, there are no restrictions on trading and no transactions costs. The main results of this section are what Dybvig & Ross [1986] term the fundamental theorem of asset pricing and the pricing rule representation theorem. We discuss these theorems below.

To state the fundamental theorem of asset pricing, we first provide a formal definition of an arbitrage opportunity. Given a price process S, an arbitrage opportunity is said to exist if there exists a predictable process, θ, such that the cash flow stream generated by it, c_θ, is in $\Re_+ \times \mathcal{X}_+$ and $c_\theta \neq 0$. Equivalently, an arbitrage opportunity exists if a strictly positive consumption stream can be obtained by an agent with no endowments. In a securities market without trading restrictions, investors can execute an arbitrage strategy at an arbitrary scale and make an arbitrarily large profit without any risk. Clearly, any reasonable model of asset prices should not permit such arbitrage strategies. The fundamental theorem of asset pricing provides conditions on a set of asset prices that are equivalent to the absence of arbitrage opportunities given those prices.

The following is the statement of the fundamental theorem of asset pricing in the present set-up with a finite state space and a frictionless securities market.

Theorem 1 (The fundamental theorem of asset pricing). *The following statements are equivalent in the economy described above:*

(1) There exist no arbitrage opportunities in the securities market.

(2) There exists an equivalent martingale measure for security prices. That is, there exists a probability measure Q on Ω, with $Q(\omega) > 0$, $\forall \omega \in \Omega$, such that for $t = 0, \dots, T$ and for $i = 0, \dots, N$

$$S_0(t) E_t^Q d_i(T) = S_i(t)$$

where we recall that the 0th security is a riskless bond maturing at T and with face value 1.[7]

(3) There exists a consistent, positive and linear pricing rule on $\mathcal{X}$. That is, there exists a function $\pi : \mathcal{X} \to \Re$ such that (i) $\pi(ax + by) = a\pi(x) + b\pi(y)$ (linearity),

[7] A probability measure satisfying the condition mentioned in (2) is also known as a risk-neutral probability measure. Any such measure, Q, is known as a martingale measure because under Q, $s_i(t)/s_0(t)$ is an θ_t–martingale for $i = 0, \dots, N$.

(ii) $\pi(x) \geq 0$ *if* $x \geq 0$ *and* $\pi(x) > 0$ *if* $x > 0$ *(positivity)*[8] *and (iii) if* $x \equiv \{x(t),\ t = 1, \ldots, T\}$ *is generated by a strategy* $\theta \in \Theta$*, then* $\pi(x) = \theta^{\mathrm{T}}(1)S(0)$ *(consistency).*

(4) There exists an increasing preference relation $\succeq$ *and an endowment process, e, such that the utility maximization problem of an agent with preferences* $\succeq$ *and endowments e has a solution.*

Proof. To prove the theorem, we show that *(1)* $\Rightarrow$ (2) $\Rightarrow$ *(3)* $\Rightarrow$ *(1)* and *(1)* $\Leftrightarrow$ *(4)*. We first show the easy implications (2) $\Rightarrow$ *(3)* $\Rightarrow$ *(1)* and *(4)* $\Rightarrow$ *(1)*. Then, we provide the proof of the implication *(1)* $\Rightarrow$ (2). The proof of the implication *(1)* $\Rightarrow$ *(4)* is in Section 5.

1. (2) $\Rightarrow$ *(3)*. Suppose that there exists an equivalent martingale measure Q. For $x \equiv \{x(t),\ t = 1, \ldots, T\} \in \mathcal{X}$, define

$$\pi(x) = S_0(0)E_0^Q \sum_{t=1}^{T} \frac{x(t)}{S_0(t)}. \tag{2}$$

The function $\pi : \mathcal{X} \to \Re$ is linear and strictly positive since $S_0(t) > 0$ and $Q(\omega) > 0,\ \forall\, \omega \in \Omega$. To show that $\pi(.)$ is consistent in the sense mentioned above, use the fact that, under Q, the security prices (expressed in terms of the riskless bond) are martingales. Consider an $x \in \mathcal{X}$ that is financed by a $\theta \in \Theta$. Then, for $t = 1, \ldots, T$

$$x(t) = c_\theta(t) = [\theta(t) - \theta(t+1)]^{\mathrm{T}} S(t)$$

where, by convention, $\theta(T+1) \equiv 0$. Letting $S^*(t) = 1/S_0(t) \times S(t)$ for $t = 1, \ldots, T$, yields

$$E_0^Q \sum_{t=1}^{T} \frac{x(t)}{S_0(t)} = E_0^Q \sum_{t=1}^{T} [\theta(t) - \theta(t+1)]^{\mathrm{T}} S^*(t).$$

which also equals

$$E_0^Q \theta^{\mathrm{T}}(1) S^*(1) + E_0^Q \sum_{t=2}^{T+1} \theta^{\mathrm{T}}(t)[S^*(t-1) - S^*(t)] \tag{3}$$

Since $S^*(t)$ is a martingale under Q, and $\theta(t)$ is $\mathcal{F}_{t-1}$ measurable, the second term in (3) is equal to zero and the first term equals $\theta^{\mathrm{T}}(1)S^*(0)$. This implies that $S_0(0)E_0^Q \sum_{t=1}^{T} x(t)/S_0(t) = \theta^{\mathrm{T}}(1)S(0)$. This shows that $\pi(.)$, defined in (2), is indeed consistent.

2. *(3)* $\Rightarrow$ *(1)*. Suppose that there exist a positive, consistent and linear pricing rule on $\mathcal{X}$. Suppose also that there exists an arbitrage opportunity. We will derive a contradiction. The existence of an arbitrage opportunity implies there exists a $\theta \in \Theta$ such that $c_\theta \geq 0$ and $c_\theta \neq 0$. Let $x \in \mathcal{X}$ be defined as follows: $\{x(t) = c_\theta(t),\ t = 1, \ldots, T\}$. Then, either $x > 0$ and $c_\theta(0) \geq 0$ or $x \geq 0$ and

[8] For a vector x, $x \geq 0$ if all elements of x are nonnegative, $x > 0$ if $x \geq 0$ and $x \neq 0$ and $x \gg 0$ if all elements of x are strictly positive.

$c_\theta(0) > 0$. If $x > 0$, we must have $\pi(x) = -c_\theta(0) > 0$ from the positivity and consistency of $\pi(.)$. This contradicts the fact that $c_\theta(0) \geq 0$. Alternatively, if $x \geq 0$ then the consistency and positivity of $\pi(.)$ imply that $\pi(x) = -c_\theta(0) \geq 0$ but that contradicts the fact that $c_\theta(0) > 0$. This means that if there exists a strictly positive linear and consistent pricing rule on $\mathcal{X}$, then there cannot exist any arbitrage opportunities.

3. *(4)* $\Rightarrow$ *(1)*. Suppose that there exist an arbitrage opportunity generated by a trading strategy, θ. Suppose that the utility maximization problem of an agent with preferences $\succeq$ is solved by a cash flow plan c_{θ^*} generated by a trading strategy θ^*. Then, $\theta_* + \theta$ is also budget feasible for the agent and generates a consumption plan that is strictly greater than c_{θ^*} in at least one state. Since $\succeq$ is strictly increasing, θ_* could not solve the utility maximization problem of the agent.

4. *(1)* $\Rightarrow$ *(2)*. We prove this implication the case of a three date economy with 2 assets whose information structure is depicted in Figure 1. The proof for the general case can be constructed similarly. In the case shown in Figure 1, a trading strategy θ is a vector in $\Re^6$, with $\theta \equiv \{\theta_0(0), \theta_1(0), \theta_0(u), \theta_1(u), \theta_0(d), \theta_1(d)\}^{\mathrm{T}}$ where, for $j = 0, 1$ and $a = 0, u, d$, $\theta_j(a)$ denotes the number of shares of the jth traded asset held in the strategy at node a.

Suppose that no arbitrage opportunities exist. This means that there does not exist a trading strategy $\theta \in \Re^6$, such that the following inequalities hold (with at least one inequality holding strictly)[9]:

1. $-[\theta_0(0)S_0(0) + \theta_1(0)S_1(0)] \geq 0.$
2. $[\theta_0(0) - \theta_0(u)]S_0(u) + [\theta_1(0) - \theta_1(u)]S_1(u) \geq 0$
3. $[\theta_0(0) - \theta_0(d)]S_0(d) + [\theta_1(0) - \theta_1(d)]S_1(d) \geq 0$
4. $\theta_0(u)S_0(j) + \theta_1(u)S_1(j) \geq 0, \quad$ for $j = uu,\ um,\ ud.$
5. $\theta_0(d)S_0(j) + \theta_1(d)S_1(j) \geq 0, \quad$ for $j = du,\ dm,\ dd.$

In matrix notation, the above conditions imply that there does not exist $\theta \equiv \{\theta_0(0), \theta_1(0), \theta_0(u), \theta_1(u), \theta_0(d), \theta_1(d)\}^{\mathrm{T}} \in \Re^6$ such that $A\theta > 0$ where

$$A \equiv \begin{bmatrix} -S_0(0) & -S_1(0) & 0 & 0 & 0 & 0 \\ S_0(u) & S_1(u) & -S_0(u) & -S_1(u) & 0 & 0 \\ S_0(u) & S_1(u) & 0 & 0 & -S_0(d) & -S_1(d) \\ 0 & 0 & 1 & S_1(uu) & 0 & 0 \\ 0 & 0 & 1 & S_1(um) & 0 & 0 \\ 0 & 0 & 1 & S_1(ud) & 0 & 0 \\ 0 & 0 & 0 & 0 & 1 & S_1(du) \\ 0 & 0 & 0 & 0 & 1 & S_1(dm) \\ 0 & 0 & 0 & 0 & 1 & S_1(dd) \end{bmatrix}.$$

[9] Here, $S_j(a)$ denotes the price of jth asset in event a, for $j = 1, 2$ and $a \in \mathcal{F}_t,\ t = 0, \ldots, 2.$

However, this implies from Steimke's lemma [Mangasarian, 1969] that there exists $y \gg 0 \in \Re^9$ such that $y^T A = 0$. Writing out this condition for each column of A and defining $Q(\omega_k) = (y_{3+k}/S_0(0)y_1)$, $k = 1, \ldots, 6$, shows that Q is an equivalent martingale measure for the above securities market. This finishes the proof of Theorem 1. □

The main conclusions of Theorem 1 can be understood as follows. In an economy with risk-neutral investors, security prices are equal to their expected payoffs discounted at the riskless rate. However, when the investors are risk averse, this property cannot hold. Theorem 1 states that, in an economy possibly with risk averse investors, the above property must hold after a change of the probability measure if (and only if) no arbitrage opportunities exist. The following example shows a simple application of the above theorem.

Example 1. Suppose that in a 3 date economy the information structure is given as in Figure 1. There are two assets available for trading in this economy, a risky stock and a riskless bond. The terminal dividends of these assets and their price processes are as given in Figure 2. The question to which we can apply the results of Theorem 1 is whether any arbitrage opportunities exist in this market. Define a probability measure on Ω as follows: $Q(uu) = 0.35$, $Q(um) = 0.28$, $Q(ud) = 0.07$, $Q(du) = 0.15$, $Q(dm) = 0.12$, $Q(dd) = 0.03$. This gives the unconditional probability of different states. Using this measure, we can also compute the

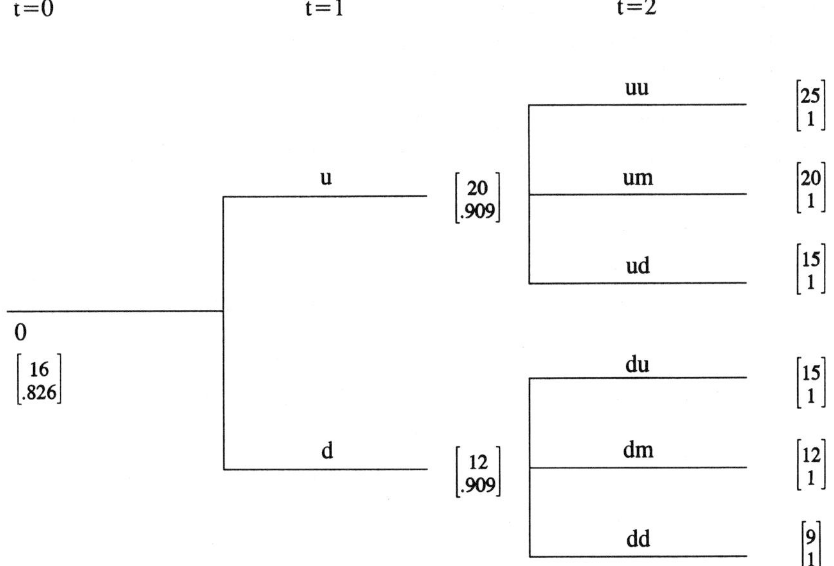

Fig. 2. The first element of the security price vector at any node denotes the price of the risky stock at that node. The second element of the price vector at a given node denotes the price of a riskless bond that matures at t=2 and has a face value of 1.

conditional probability of any state given the information at time 1. This is defined as follows: for any $a \in \mathcal{F}_1$ $Q(\omega \mid a) = Q(\omega)/Q(a)$, if $\omega \in a$ and 0 otherwise where $Q(a) = \sum_{\omega \in a} Q(\omega)$. Thus, for example, $Q(u) = 0.7$ and $Q(d) = 0.3$ and $Q(uu \mid u) = 0.5$.

If we compute the expected value (discounted at the riskless rate) of $S_1(T)$ at time 1 at node u and d using the above probabilities, we obtain the current values of the stock. Similarly for the bond. This and the fact that $Q \gg 0$ means that the measure Q constructed above is an equivalent martingale measure. Theorem 1 then implies that there exist no arbitrage opportunities in the above market.

The measure Q constructed above is not the only equivalent martingale measure in the above economy. It can be checked that any Q constructed as follows is an equivalent martingale measure:

1. For any $p \in (0.4, 0.7)$, set $Q(uu \mid u) = p$, $Q(um \mid u) = 1.4 - 2p$ and $Q(ud \mid u) = p - 0.4$.
2. Set $Q(du \mid d) = Q(uu \mid u)$, $Q(dm \mid d) = Q(um \mid u)$ and $Q(dd \mid d) = Q(ud \mid d)$.
3. Set $Q(u) = 0.7$ and $Q(d) = 0.3$.
4. Set $Q(\omega)$ using the rule that $Q(\omega) = Q(\omega \mid a) \times Q(a)$ for $\omega \in a$ and $a \in \mathcal{F}_1$.

Thus, there are several risk-neutral probability measures in this market. As shown below, this is related to the fact that the above market is incomplete, that is, there are too few traded securities relative to the amount of uncertainty in the economy.

3.1. Dynamic trading and dynamic completeness

In the above discussion we have not assumed that state contingent claims for each state are available for trading. Thus, the fundamental theorem of asset pricing does not require complete securities markets. We now discuss what is meant by complete markets in a dynamic setting, how the availability of trading can expand the span of the securities market and what can be said about arbitrage and security prices in a complete market.

A securities market is said to be complete if, at $t = 0$, investors in the market can trade in state contingent claims for every time and event pair that can occur. Thus, our securities market would be complete if, for $a \in \mathcal{F}_t$, and $t = 0, \ldots, T$, there are securities available for trading in the market at $t = 0$ that yield a cash flow of 1 unit of the numeraire at time t if and only if event a is realized at time t. Denote the cash flow stream of a state contingent security for a given time–event pair (a_0, t_0) as $\mathbf{1}_{a_0,t_0} = \{\mathbf{1}_{a_0,t_0}(t), t = 0, \ldots, T\}$ with

$$\mathbf{1}_{a_0,t_0}(t) \equiv \begin{cases} 1, & \text{if } t = t_0 \text{ and } a(t_0) = a_0 \\ 0. & \text{otherwise} \end{cases}$$

where $a(t_0)$ denotes the event realized at t_0. State contingent securities are also known as Arrow–Debreu securities. For notational convenience, the payoff stream

$\mathbf{1}_{\{\omega\},T}$ is denoted simply as $\mathbf{1}_{\omega}$, for all $\omega \in \Omega$. This payoff equals 1 at time T if and only if the state ω is realized at that time and zero otherwise.

It is well known that complete markets allow for optimal risk sharing in the economy and lead to Pareto optimal consumption allocations. However, even in a multi-period economy with a very simple information structure, the number of Arrow–Debreu securities needed to complete the markets would increase exponentially with the number of trading dates. Thus, completing markets by allowing investors to form portfolios of Arrow–Debreu securities would seem to be an impractical idea. At the same time, we expect intuitively that a financial market that is open for trading at all times should also allow for a better allocation of risk than that possible in an economy where trading can take place only once. Therefore, it is of interest to examine to what extent risk sharing can be improved by increasing trading opportunities in the economy. Kreps [1979] uses the finite state securities market model of the type described in Section 1 to analyze this question definitively. Kreps' analysis shows that we could indirectly complete a securities market by allowing trading in only a few long lived securities. It is not the total number of states that is important in determining how many securities are needed to obtain a complete market in the economy, but the nature of uncertainty resolution or information arrival in the financial markets.

We say that a securities market is *dynamically* complete given prices S, if the cash flow on every state contingent claim can be financed by some trading strategy in Θ. The following example illustrates the results of Kreps [1979].

Example 2. Consider an economy in which there are 3 dates in the economy, $\{0, 1, 2\}$. At date 1 the economy can be in state u or state d. From state u, the economy can transit to state uu or state ud at time 2. From state d, the transition can be to state du or dd. Thus, to be statically complete this market would need 6 securities.[10]

Suppose, however, that there are two assets in this economy: a riskless bond which pays off 1 unit of the consumption good at time 2 in all states, and a risky stock which pays off a risky terminal dividend at time 2 given by: $S_1(uu) = 25$, $S_1(ud) = 15$, $S_1(du) = 15$ and $S_1(dd) = 9$. The price processes of the stock and the bond are given as shown in Figure 3. Assume that the one period riskless rate is constant at 10%.

Observe that, at every node, there are as many securities with linearly independent payoffs in the successor nodes as there are branches out of that node. As a result, we can synthetically create a state contingent payoff for any possible state by dynamic trading in the stock and the bond. To see this, consider the payoff on an Arrow–Debreu security that pays off 1 unit of the numeraire at time 2 in state uu and 0 at all other times and in all other states. To find the dynamic strategy that generates this cash flow, let us make the following computations:

[10] If the economy had T periods and the information arrival at each date was similar to that depicted in Figure 3 (that is, only two branches emanated from every node), the economy would need 2^T securities for static completeness.

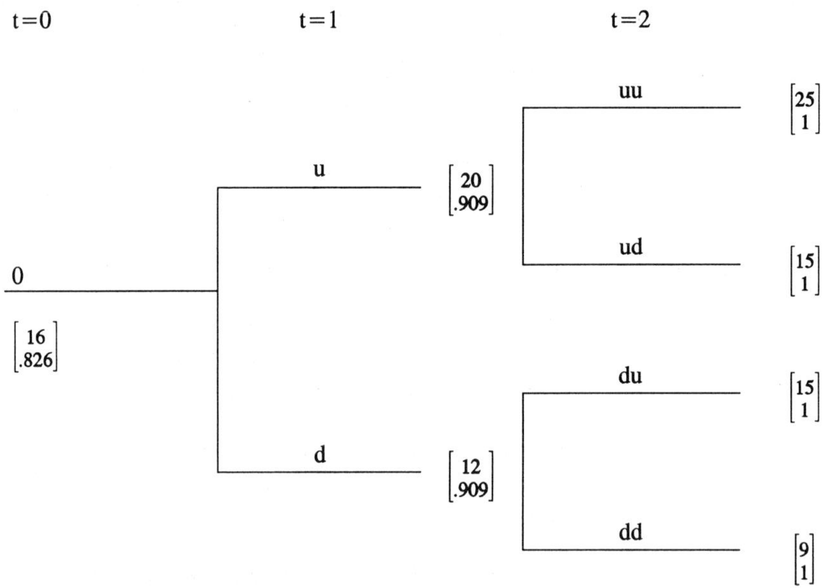

Fig. 3. The first element of the security price vector at any node denotes the price of the risky stock at that node. The second element of the price vector at a given node denotes the price of a riskless bond that matures at t=2 and has a face value of 1.

1. Suppose that we are at node u at $t = 1$. Find which portfolio of the stock and the bond yields a payoff of 1 in state uu and 0 in state ud. The required portfolio consists of x shares of the stock and y units of the bond where

$$\begin{aligned} 25x + y &= 1 \\ 15x + y &= 0 \end{aligned} \tag{4}$$

This means that $x = 0.1$ and $y = -1.5$. This is said to be the replicating portfolio of the desired payoff. At $t = 1$ at node u, the cost of this portfolio is $0.1 \times 20 - 1.5 \times 0.909 = 0.636363$.

2. From node d onwards, the Arrow–Debreu security that we are trying to duplicate has a zero payoff. Thus, its replicating portfolio at this node consists of zero shares of the stock and zero bonds. The cost of this portfolio at $t = 1$ is zero.

3. Find the portfolio of the stock and the bond at $t = 0$ that is worth 0.636363 if event u occurs at $t = 1$ and zero otherwise. This portfolio consists of 0.079545 units of the stock and -1.05 units of the bond. The cost of this portfolio at $t = 0$ is 0.405.

We have now computed a trading strategy that will yield a payoff exactly equal to the payoff on the Arrow–Debreu security for node uu. This strategy consists of (i) buying 0.079545 units of the stock and shorting 1.05 units of the bond at $t = 0$, (ii) if state u is observed at $t = 1$, selling the portfolio purchased at $t = 0$ and buying 0.1 units of the stock and shorting 1.5 units of the bond, and (iii) doing nothing at node d. The consequence of these trades is that, at time $t = 2$, the portfolio will be worth 1 in state uu and 0 otherwise. Note also that the trades prescribed above are feasible because the values of the portfolios that we enter nodes u and d with are the same as the ones that we buy at those nodes.

Thus, if at every node of the event tree, there are as many securities with linearly independent payoffs available for trading as the number of the successor nodes, then we can find the strategy that duplicates the payoff on any Arrow–Debreu security. Thus, the securities market of this example is dynamically complete. Whether or not the market is complete depends on the given process for asset prices. Since prices are endogenously determined in an economic model, the property of dynamic completeness is also an endogenously determined property.

The fact that the number of linearly independent securities and the number of branches at any node are the same also implies that the equivalent martingale measure in the above market is unique. As documented in the following proposition, this is a defining property of dynamically complete markets.

Proposition 1. *Suppose that there are no arbitrage opportunities in a securities market model. The equivalent martingale measure in such a model is unique if and only if the market is dynamically complete.*

Proof. We first provide the proof of the 'if' part of this proposition. Suppose that Q and Q' are two equivalent martingale measures in the model. Then, by the definition of an expectation, $Q(\omega) = E^Q \mathbf{1}_\omega(T)$ for $\omega \in \Omega$ where $\mathbf{1}_\omega(T)$ denotes a random variable that is realized at T and takes value 1 if state ω is realized at T and 0 otherwise. Similarly, $Q'(\omega) = E^{Q'} \mathbf{1}_\omega(T)$. However, since Q and Q' are equivalent martingale measures, the arguments mentioned in part 1 of the proof of Theorem 1 imply that, for all $\omega \in \Omega$, $E^Q \mathbf{1}_\omega(T)$ and $E^{Q'} \mathbf{1}_\omega(T)$ both equal $\theta_\omega^T(1)S(0)/S_0(0)$ where $\{\theta_\omega^T(t), t = 1, \ldots, T\}$ denotes a trading strategy that replicates the payoff $\mathbf{1}_\omega(T)$. Such a strategy exists for all ω in Ω because the market is dynamically complete. Thus, we have that for $\omega \in \Omega$,

$$Q(\omega) = Q'(\omega) = \frac{\theta_\omega^T(1)S(0)}{S_0(0)}. \tag{5}$$

This proves that the equivalent martingale measure is unique.

The 'only if' part of this proposition can be proven using the fact that there are as many linearly independent securities as there are branches out of a node. We provide a slightly different proof in the appendix. □

As a simple application of the above proposition, note that in the economy described in Example 2, there is a unique risk-neutral probability measure given by $Q(uu) = 0.49$, $Q(ud) = Q(du) = 0.21$ and $Q(dd) = 0.09$. This implies and is implied by the fact that the markets are dynamically complete in this example.

3.2. Valuation of contingent claims in dynamically complete markets

In a dynamically complete market, one can replicate all possible Arrow–Debreu securities. Since all cash flows can be expressed as a combination of Arrow–

Debreu securities, this means that any payoff can be replicated by dynamic trading in the stock and the bond. This implies that all securities other than those whose prices are given, are redundant. The absence of arbitrage, then, guarantees that the price of the replicating portfolio of a cash flow and price of a security paying off that cash flow should be identical. In Example 3, for instance, the price at $t = 0$ of Arrow–Debreu security of state uu (if it were traded) would have to be .405 units of the numeraire.

The above simple observation has been used to derive powerful results regarding the pricing of derivative securities. To see how this result can be used to value a contingent claim, consider the following example.

Example 3. Suppose that a European call option with exercise price 10 and maturity $t = 2$ is available for trading in the above market. The payoff on the option at $t = 2$ is given by $\max[S_1(2) - 10, 0]$. Calculations similar to ones shown in Example 2 imply that the following trading strategy replicates the cash flow on the call: (i) at $t = 0$, hold 0.96591 units of the stock and short 9.25 units of the bond, (ii) at $t = 1$ if event u is observed, trade the portfolio purchased at $t = 0$ for a portfolio consisting of 1 share of the stock and 10 units of the bond short, and (iii) at $t = 1$ if event d is observed, trade the portfolio purchased at $t = 0$ for a portfolio consisting of 0.83333 units of the stock and 7.5 units of the bond short. The trades prescribed at $t = 1$ are all feasible because the value of the portfolio that one enters date $t = 1$ with and the value of the new portfolio at that date are the same. The lack of arbitrage opportunities now implies that the price of the option at time 0 must be equal to $0.96591 \times 16 - 9.25 \times .826 = 7.81$. Similarly, the price of the option at time 1 must be 10.91 in event u and 3.1818 in event d.

The fact that the equivalent martingale measure is unique in complete markets could also have been used to value the above option. As noted earlier, the unique equivalent martingale measure is given by $Q(uu) = .49$, $Q(ud) = Q(du) = 0.21$ and $Q(dd) = 0.09$. Theorem 1 then implies that the price of the call at $t = 0$ is

$$S_0(0) \sum_{\omega \in \Omega} Q(\omega) \max[S_1(2, \omega) - 10, 0] =$$
$$= 0.826 \times \{0.49 \times 15 + 0.42 \times 5\} = 7.81$$

as expected. This concludes Example 3.

The above is a numerical example of the celebrated Cox, Ross & Rubinstein [1979] binomial option pricing formula. This model assumes a securities market with two assets-a risky stock and a riskless bond. The price of the stock is assumed to evolve according to:

$$S_1(t+1) = S_1(t)\epsilon(t+1) \tag{6}$$

for $t = 0, \ldots, T-1$ where for each t, $\epsilon(t) \in \{u, d\}$. The bond price is assumed to evolve according to

$$S_0(t+1) = S_0(t)(1+r)$$

with $S_0(0) = (1+r)^{-T}$. The condition that ensures lack of arbitrage opportunities is $u > (1+r) > d$. With this condition, a probability measure that assigns the probability of an up move from any node to be $\pi(u) = (1+r-d)/(u-d)$ and the probability of a down move from any node to be $\pi(d) = (u - r - 1/u - d)$ is the unique equivalent martingale measure. The price at $t = 0$ of a claim that pays off $g[S(T)]$ at time T is then

$$S_0(0) \sum_{j=0}^{T} B(T, j) \pi(u)^j \pi^{T-j}(d) g\left[S_1(0)\, u^j\, d^{T-j}\right]$$

where $B(T, j) = T!/[j!(T-j)!]$. The Cox, Ross & Rubinstein [1979] binomial model has been extensively used for valuing claims contingent on stock prices, stock market indices and the exchange rate. Ho & Lee [1986] develop a binomial model for valuing term structure contingent claim. Carr & Jarrow [1995] provide a finite state model for valuing claims contingent on the term structure of futures prices.

3.3. Replicating payoffs in an incomplete market

The above discussion shows that in dynamically complete markets, we can replicate any given payoff stream. This makes arbitrage-based valuation possible for an arbitrary contingent claim in complete markets. In incomplete markets, we cannot replicate certain contingent claims. Yet, in such a market we can ask how can one replicate a payoff that is equal to or *greater than* a given payoff in the cheapest possible way. The trading strategy that accomplishes this can be termed the minimum cost strategy for the given payoff. For any $y \equiv \{y(t),\ t = 1, \ldots, T\} \in \mathcal{X}$, the minimum cost strategy can be obtained by solving the following linear programming problem, $\mathbf{P}(y)$:

$$\min_{\{\theta(t),\ t=1,\ldots,T\}} \quad \theta^{\mathrm{T}}(1) S(0)$$

subject to

$$\left[\theta^{\mathrm{T}}(t) - \theta^{\mathrm{T}}(t+1)\right] S(t) \geq y(t), \qquad t = 1, \ldots, T-1,$$

and

$$\theta^{\mathrm{T}}(T) d(T) \geq y(T).$$

Let $C(y) = \mathrm{val}[\mathbf{P}(y)]$ for $y \in \mathcal{X}$. We term this functional the minimum cost functional.

The functional $C(.)$ defined above can be interpreted as a bound on prices of contingent claims as follows. Consider a market in which $N+1$ assets *and* a claim with payoff stream y are traded. Suppose that the prices of the first $N+1$ assets are given by the $(N+1)$-dimensional process $\{S(t),\ t = 0, \ldots, T\}$. To avoid arbitrage, it must be the case that the price of the claim y is less than or equal to $C(y)$. Similarly, it must be the case that the price of the claim y is greater than or equal to $-C(-y)$.

The following example demonstrates the computation of the minimum cost hedging strategy in an incomplete market.

Example 4. Consider the economy described in Example 1. There are two assets: a stock and a riskless bond with price processes given in Figure 2. Suppose that we want to replicate the payoff on a call option on the stock with exercise price of 12. Then, the solution of the linear programming problem **P**(.) for the payoff on the call implies that the minimum cost hedging strategy for this payoff is: (i) 0.898 shares of the stock long and 9.75 units of the riskless bond (maturing at $t = 2$ and face value of 1) short at $t = 0$ (ii) 1 share of stock long and 12 units of the bond short at node u and (iii) 0.5 shares of the stock long and 4.5 units of the bond short at node d. The initial cost of implementing this strategy (or the value of the function $C(.)$ for this call) is 6.306. The minimum cost trading strategy generates a surplus cash flow at node dm. Indeed, the minimum cost replicating strategy for convex payoffs will always exactly replicate the cash flows in the extreme branches emanating from any node and may generate a slack at the middle branches. Further results on replication in incomplete markets can be found in Ritchken & Kuo [1988]. Naik & Uppal [1994] analyze the case of minimum cost hedging in the presence of leverage constraints.

We can also use the function $C(.)$ to obtain a characterization of complete markets. This is shown in the following remark.

Remark 1. Suppose that there are no arbitrage opportunities in a securities market model. Then, the securities market is complete if and only if the function $C(y)$ defined above is linear.

Proof. Suppose that $C(y)$ is linear and the securities market is incomplete. We show that this leads to a contradiction. Market incompleteness implies the existence of t_0 and $a_0 \in \mathcal{F}_{t_0}$ such that $\mathbf{1}_{a_0,t_0}$ is not financed by any trading strategy in Θ. Consider the trading strategy that solves $\mathbf{P}(\mathbf{1}_{a_0,t_0})$. Let this be denoted $\hat{\theta}$ and let the cash flow stream generated by it be denoted $c_{\hat{\theta}}$. We know that $c_{\hat{\theta}} \geq \mathbf{1}_{a_0,t_0}$, with a strict inequality at some (a_t, t). Let $\epsilon \equiv \{\epsilon(t) = c_{\hat{\theta}}(t) - \mathbf{1}_{a_0,t_0}(t),\ t = 1, \ldots, T\}$. Then,

$$\begin{aligned}\hat{\theta}^{\mathrm{T}}(1)S(0) &= C(c_{\hat{\theta}}) = C(\mathbf{1}_{a_0,t_0} + \epsilon) = C(\mathbf{1}_{a_0,t_0}) + C(\epsilon) \\ &= \hat{\theta}^{\mathrm{T}}(1)S(0) + C(\epsilon).\end{aligned} \tag{7}$$

In (7), the first equality follows from the fact that $c_{\hat{\theta}}$ is financed by $\hat{\theta}$, the second equality follows from the definition of ϵ, the third equality follows from the hypothesis that $C(.)$ is linear and the fourth equality follows from the fact that $\hat{\theta}^{\mathrm{T}}(1)S(0)$ is the minimum cost of obtaining a payoff that is at least equal to $\mathbf{1}_{a_0,t_0}$. However, (7) cannot be true since $\epsilon > 0$ which implies that $C(\epsilon) > 0$ from the positivity of $C(.)$ ensured by the lack of arbitrage opportunities. This proves that if $C(.)$ is linear, then markets cannot be incomplete. This finishes the proof of the 'if' part of Remark 1. The proof of the 'only if' part of this remark is in the appendix. □

The minimum cost functional $C(.)$ can also be used to form the budget constraint in the optimal portfolio choice problem of an investor in an incomplete market. This is shown in Section 5.

4. Arbitrage and security prices in a model with transactions costs

In our discussion so far, we have assumed that the securities market is frictionless. This assumption is implicit in the fact that there was no distinction made between the price for buying a security and the price for selling it. Moreover, it was assumed that there are no restrictions on trading. In practice, the buying and selling prices of many securities are separated by the bid–ask spread. In addition, investors face other kinds of transactions costs and trading restrictions. These restrictions could be in the form of margin requirements, constraints on short selling, lot size restrictions and position limits. We now show how the fundamental theorem of asset pricing needs to be modified in the presence of transactions costs.

To incorporate transactions costs, we allow the buying prices of the traded securities to be different from their selling prices. Denote the ask price by $S_a(t)$ and the bid price by $S_b(t)$. We shall also make the following simplifying assumption:

Assumption A. There are no transaction costs at time T and the payoff on the ith security at time T continue to be given by the random variable $d_i(T)$, for $i = 0, \ldots, N$. In addition, it is assumed that there are no transactions costs on the riskless asset and $S_{a0}(t) = S_{b0}(t) = S_0(t)$.

Since the buying and selling prices of securities are different, we need to specify trading strategies slightly differently. The formal definition of an arbitrage opportunity also needs to be modified. In the previous section, a trading strategy $\theta \equiv \{\theta(t),\ t = 1, \ldots, T\}$ was an $N+1$ dimensional predictable process, with each component of $\theta(t)$ denoting the net position of the investor in a particular security at time t. There was no distinction between a long or a short position. Now, we shall find it convenient to keep track of the short and long positions in different securities separately because buying and selling takes place at different prices. Thus, an investor's trading strategy is denoted (θ_l, θ_s) now. The ith component of $\theta_l(t)$ denotes the cumulative number of shares of the ith security that the investor has bought until time t. Similarly, the ith component of $\theta_s(t)$ denotes the cumulative number of shares of the ith security that the investor has sold until time t. Both θ_l and θ_s are required to be $N+1$-dimensional predictable and nondecreasing processes.[11] The cash flow stream generated by a trading strategy

[11] We need to restrict θ_l and θ_s to be nondecreasing processes because otherwise their definition as cumulative number of shares bought and sold would not be sensible.

is given by:

$$c_\theta(0) = \theta_s^T(1)S_b(0) - \theta_l^T(1)S_a(0)$$

$$c_\theta(t) = [\theta_l^T(t) - \theta_l^T(t+1)]S_a(t) - [\theta_s^T(t) - \theta_s^T(t+1)]S_b(t), \quad t = 1, \ldots, T-1,$$

and

$$c_\theta(T) = [\theta_l^T(T) - \theta_s^T(T)]d(T).$$

An arbitrage opportunity is a trading strategy that does not require any investment at time 0 (after accounting for transactions costs) and produces a positive cash flow on or before date T in at least one state and never produces a negative cash flow. Formally, an arbitrage opportunity is said to exist if there exist predictable and nondecreasing processes (θ_l, θ_s) such that the cash flow c_θ that it generates (defined above) lies in $\Re_+ \times \mathcal{X}_+$ and $c_\theta \neq 0$. Equivalently, an arbitrage opportunity exists if there exist a trading strategy that generates a positive and nonzero consumption plan which is budget feasible for an investor with no endowments.

To account for transactions costs, the minimum cost functional introduced in the last section needs to be redefined. Denote the minimum cost functional in the presence of transaction costs as $C_1 : \mathcal{X} \to \Re$. For $y \equiv \{y(t),\ t = 1, \ldots, T\}$, we define the minimum cost functional $C_1(y) = \text{val}[\mathbf{P}_1(y)]$ where val[.] denotes the value of a given optimization problem and $\mathbf{P}_1(y)$ denotes the following linear programming problem:

$$\min_{(\theta_l, \theta_s) \in \Theta \times \Theta} \theta_l^T(1)S_a(0) - \theta_s^T(1)S_b(0)$$

subject to

$$[\theta_l^T(t) - \theta_l^T(t+1)]S_a(t) - [\theta_s^T(t) - \theta_s^T(t+1)]S_b(t) \geq y(t), \quad t = 1, \ldots, T-1,$$

$$[\theta_l^T(T) - \theta_s^T(T)]d(T) \geq y(T),$$

$$\theta_l(t+1) \geq \theta_l(t), \qquad \theta_s(t+1) \geq \theta_s(t), \qquad t = 1, \ldots, T-1,$$

and

$$\theta_l(1) \geq 0, \qquad \theta_s(1) \geq 0.$$

The first two constraints in the above problem ensure that the chosen trading strategy generates a cash flow that is greater than or equal to y and the last two constraints ensure that the chosen strategy is a nonnegative and nondecreasing process.

Before stating the fundamental theorem of asset pricing in the presence of transactions costs, we need to document the following results.

Proposition 2. *For any* $y \equiv \{y(t),\ t = 1, \ldots, T\} \in \mathcal{X}$*, the dual of* $\mathbf{P}_1(y)$ *is the following linear programming problem,* $\mathbf{D}_1(y)$*:*

$$\max_{Q \in \mathcal{Q}} \quad S_0(0) E^Q \sum_{t=1}^{T} \frac{y(t)}{S_0(t)}$$

where $\mathcal{Q}$ *is the set of probability measures, (with generic element* Q*) on* Ω *under which the following condition is satisfied:*

$$S_{ai}(t) \leq S_0(t) E_t^Q d_i(T) \leq S_{bi}(t)$$

for $i = 0, \ldots, N$ *and for* $t = 0, \ldots, T$.

Proof. The above result follows from explicitly writing out the primal problem and its dual. □

We also need to document some properties of $C_1(.)$ which are required in our subsequent discussion. It can be shown that $C_1(.)$ is subadditive and finite-valued on $\mathcal{X}$. To prove the subadditivity of $C_1(.)$ take x and y in $\mathcal{X}$. Let Q_x denote a solution to the problem $\mathbf{D}_1(x)$ and Q_y be a solution to the problem $\mathbf{D}_1(y)$. Let $z = x + y$ and let Q_z be a solution to the problem $\mathbf{D}_1(z)$. Then,

$$C_1(z) = S_0(0) E^{Q_z} \sum_{t=1}^{T} \frac{z(t)}{S_0(t)} = S_0(0) E^{Q_z} \sum_{t=1}^{T} \frac{x(t)}{S_0(t)} + S_0(0) E^{Q_z} \sum_{t=1}^{T} \frac{y(t)}{S_0(t)}.$$

But $E^{Q_z} \sum_{t=1}^{T} x(t)/S_0(t)$ is less than or equal to $E^{Q_x} \sum_{t=1}^{T} x(t)/S_0(t)$ because the Q_z is feasible in the problem $\mathbf{D}_1(x)$. The constraint set in $\mathbf{D}_1(x)$ is independent of x. Applying a similar argument to y and Q_y, yields that $C_1(z) \leq C_1(x) + C_1(y)$. Thus, $C_1(.)$ is subadditive. It is also true that $C_1(.)$ is positively homogeneous of degree one, that is, it satisfies $C_1(\beta y) = \beta C_1(y)$ for $\beta > 0$. The properties of positive homogeneity and subadditivity imply that $C_1(.)$ is convex.[12] The fact that $C_1(.)$ is finite valued on $\mathcal{X}$ follows from the fact that $C_1(y)$ is always less than $S_0(0) \times \sum_{t=1}^{T} F(t)$ where $F(t)$ is the deterministic process defined by $\max_{a \in \mathcal{F}_t} \{y(a, t)/S_0(a, t)\}$ for $t = 1, \ldots, T$. In addition, $C_1(y)$ is greater than or equal to $S_0(0) \times \sum_{t=1}^{T} G(t)$ where $G(t)$ is the deterministic process defined by $\min_{a \in \mathcal{F}_t} \{y(a, t)/S_0(a, t)\}$ for $t = 1, \ldots, T$. By Corollary 5.2.2.1 (p. 98) of Bank, Guddat, Klatte, Kummer & Tammer [1983], the convexity and finiteness of $C_1(.)$ imply that it is continuous on $\mathcal{X}$.

We can now state the fundamental theorem of asset pricing with transactions costs.

Theorem 2 (The fundamental theorem of asset pricing with transactions costs). *Maintain Assumption A. Then, the following statements are equivalent in a dynamic economy with transaction costs described above:*

[12] See Theorem 4.7 of Rockafellar [1970].

(1) No arbitrage opportunities exist.

(2) There exists a probability measure Q on Ω with $Q(\omega) > 0$, $\forall \omega \in \Omega$ such that

$$S_{ai}(t) \leq S_0(t) E_t^Q d_i(T) \leq S_{bi}(t)$$

for $i = 0, \ldots, N$ and for $t = 0, \ldots, T$.

(3) The function $C_1 : \mathcal{X} \to \Re$ (defined earlier) is positive. That is $C_1(y) \geq 0$ if $y \geq 0$ and $C_1(y) > 0$ if $y > 0$.

(4) There exists an increasing preference relation $\succeq$ and endowments e such that the utility maximization problem of an agent with preferences $\succeq$ and endowments e has a solution.

Proof. To prove the theorem, we show that *(1)* $\Rightarrow$ (2) $\Rightarrow$ (3) $\Rightarrow$ *(1)* and *(1)* $\Leftrightarrow$ *(4)*.

1. (2) $\Rightarrow$ (3). Denote the measure satisfying the condition noted in (2) by Q_0. Then, (2) $\Rightarrow$ (3) follows from the fact that

$$C_1(y) = \text{val}[\mathbf{P}_1(y)] = \text{val}[\mathbf{D}_1(y)] \geq S_0(0) E^{Q_0} \sum_{t=1}^{T} \frac{y(t)}{S_0(t)}$$

and the fact that the fourth term in the above equation is strictly positive if $y > 0$ and is positive if $y \geq 0$ because $Q_0 \gg 0$ and $S_0(t) > 0$, $t = 0, \ldots, T$. That the value of dual and primal problems are equal follows because (i) the primal is always feasible under the assumption of the existence whose price is strictly positive at all times,[13] and (ii) if Q_0 with the above property exists then $\mathbf{D}_1(y)$ is also feasible. The feasibility of both the dual and the primal implies that the optimal solutions to both exist and that the values of the two problems are the same.

2. *(3)* $\Rightarrow$ *(1)*. To prove this implication, suppose that *(3)* holds and there exists an arbitrage opportunity. Then, there exists a nondecreasing and predictable process $\theta \equiv (\theta_l, \theta_s)$, such that either (i) $c_\theta(0) > 0$ and $c_\theta(t) \geq 0$, $t = 1, \ldots, T$ or (ii) $c_\theta(0) \geq 0$ and $c_\theta(t) > 0$, $t = 1, T$ Let $y = \{y(t),\ t = 1, \ldots, T\} = \{c_\theta(t),\ t = 1, T\}$. Consider case (i) first. If statement *(3)* above is true then $C_1(y)$ must be positive. However, by the definition of $C_1(y)$ we know that $C_1(y) \leq -c_\theta(0)$. But, if case (i) holds then $c_\theta(0) > 0$. This yields a contradiction. The proof for case (ii) is similar.

3. The proof of *(4)* $\Rightarrow$ *(1)* is identical to the proof of this statement in Theorem 1. The proof of the implication *(1)* $\Rightarrow$ *(4)* is provided in the next section.

4. *(1)* $\Rightarrow$ (2). As before, we prove this implication for the case of a 3-date economy with two securities and the information structure given in Example 1. In this case, a trading strategy θ is an element of $\Re^{12}$ and $\theta \equiv \{\theta_l(0), \theta_s(0), \theta_l(u), \theta_s(u), \theta_l(d), \theta_s(d)\}$ with $\theta_k(a) = \{\theta_{0k}(a), \theta_{1k}(a)\}$ for $a = 0, u, d$ and for $k = l, s$. Thus, $\theta_l(a)$ gives the number of shares of various assets held long by the trading strategy at node a, for $a = 0, u, d$. Similarly, $\theta_s(a)$ denotes the number of shares of various assets held short by the strategy at node a.

[13] In our model, the riskless bond is such an asset.

As in the proof of Theorem 1, one can show that the absence of arbitrage opportunities implies that there does not exist $\theta \in \Re^{12}$ (as defined above) such that $A\theta > 0$ and $B\theta \geq 0$ where the matrix $A = [A_1, A_u, A_d]$ with[14]:

$$A_1 \equiv \begin{bmatrix} -S_0(0) & -S_{1a}(0) & S_0(0) & S_{1b}(0) \\ S_0(u) & S_{1a}(u) & -S_0(u) & -S_{1b}(u) \\ S_0(d) & S_{1a}(d) & -S_0(d) & -S_{1b}(d) \\ 0 & 0 & 0 & 0 \\ 0 & 0 & 0 & 0 \\ 0 & 0 & 0 & 0 \\ 0 & 0 & 0 & 0 \\ 0 & 0 & 0 & 0 \\ 0 & 0 & 0 & 0 \end{bmatrix}$$

$$A_u \equiv \begin{bmatrix} 0 & 0 & 0 & 0 \\ -S_0(u) & -S_{1a}(u) & S_0(u) & S_{1b}(u) \\ 0 & 0 & 0 & 0 \\ 1 & S_1(uu) & -1 & -S_1(uu) \\ 1 & S_1(um) & -1 & -S_1(um) \\ 1 & S_1(ud) & -1 & -S_1(ud) \\ 0 & 0 & 0 & 0 \\ 0 & 0 & 0 & 0 \\ 0 & 0 & 0 & 0 \end{bmatrix}$$

$$A_d \equiv \begin{bmatrix} 0 & 0 & 0 & 0 \\ 0 & 0 & 0 & 0 \\ -S_0(d) & -S_{1a}(d)) & S_0(d) & S_{1b}(d) \\ 0 & 0 & 0 & 0 \\ 0 & 0 & 0 & 0 \\ 0 & 0 & 0 & 0 \\ 1 & S_1(du) & -1 & -S_1(du) \\ 1 & S_1(dm) & -1 & -S_1(dm) \\ 1 & S_1(dd) & -1 & -S_1(dd) \end{bmatrix}$$

[14] Here, $S_{1a}(a)$ ($S_{1b}(a)$) denotes the ask (bid) price of the stock at event a for $a \in \mathcal{F}_t,\ t = 0, 1, 2$.

and

$$B \equiv \begin{bmatrix} -\mathbf{I} & \mathbf{I} & \mathbf{0} \\ -\mathbf{I} & \mathbf{0} & \mathbf{I} \\ \mathbf{I} & \mathbf{0} & \mathbf{0} \end{bmatrix}$$

where $\mathbf{I}$ is a 4×4 identity matrix and $\mathbf{0}$ is a 4×4 matrix of zeros. The condition $A\theta > 0$ is the usual definition of an arbitrage opportunity and $B\theta \geq 0$ ensures that θ is a nonnegative and nondecreasing process. Now we can apply Tucker's theorem to obtain that there exist $y \in \Re^9$ and $h \in \Re^{12}$ with $y \gg 0$ and $h \geq 0$ such that $y^{\mathrm{T}} A + h^{\mathrm{T}} B = 0$.[15] Statement *(2)* of the theorem now follows from defining $Q(\omega_k) = y_{3+k}/[y_0 S_0(0)]$, $k = 1, \ldots, 6$ and writing out the condition $y^{\mathrm{T}} A + h^{\mathrm{T}} B = 0$ explicitly. The proof of the implication *(1)* $\Rightarrow$ *(2)* for the general case can be constructed similarly. This finishes the proof of Theorem 2.

The main conclusion of Theorem 2 and the relation of this theorem with Theorem 1 can be understood as follows. When there are no transactions costs, Theorem 1 states that the absence of arbitrage is equivalent to the existence of a probability measure under which security prices *equal* their expected payoffs discounted at the riskless rate. When there are transactions costs, the absence of arbitrage cannot restrict security prices to this extent. Now, one can only derive an inequality result and not an equality. As Theorem 2 shows, with trading costs the absence of arbitrage implies that there is a probability measure such that discounted expected payoffs under that measure lie between the bid and the ask prices of various securities.

4.1. Replication of state contingent payoffs with market imperfections

We now turn to the question of replicating and valuing state-contingent payoffs in the presence of transactions costs. We provide an example of how the function $C_1(.)$ and the solution to the problem $\mathbf{P}_1(.)$ can be used in this analysis.

Example 5. This example is taken from Edirisinghe, Naik & Uppal [1993]. The information structure of the economy is given by a binomial tree. There are two assets, a risky stock and a riskless discount bond with maturity T and face value 1. For $t = 1, \ldots, T-1$, $S_{1a}(t) = S_1(t)(1+\theta)$ and $S_{1b}(t) = S_1(t)(1-\theta)$. For $t = 0$ and $t = T$, $S_{1a}(t) = S_{1b}(t) = S_1(t)$. Moreover, $S_1(t)$ evolves according to (6) with $u = 1.01$, $d = 1/u$. Also, $T = 3$, $S_1(0) = 1$, $\theta = 0.01$. The price of the bond is assumed to equal 1 at all dates.

Suppose that we want to find the minimum-cost self financing strategy that yields at least the payoff to a European call option with strike price, $K = 1$, and maturity $T = 3$. We solve the problem $\mathbf{P}_1(.)$ for the option payoff. With these parameters, the minimum cost of replication (or the value of $C_1(.)$ for the call) is 0.01245 dollars. The function $C_1(.)$ can be used to place bounds on the prices of

[15] For a statement of Tucker's theorem, see Mangasarian [1969].

contingent claims in the presence of trading costs. If the call option is traded and the prices of the stock and the bond are as given in the example, the price of the call must be less than the value of $C_1(.)$ derived above to avoid arbitrage.

It is also of interest to examine the minimum cost trading strategy for the above option. This strategy is:

- At $t = 0$: buy 0.5056 shares and short sell 0.4931 bonds.
- At $t = 1$, if event u occurs (stock price goes up): revise the portfolio holdings to 0.7537 shares long and 0.7463 bonds short.
- At $t = 1$, if event d occurs (stock price goes down): revise the portfolio holdings to 0.2537 shares long and 0.2463 bonds short.
- Do not trade at $t = 2$.

Note that it is optimal to dominate the required cash flows at maturity, instead of matching them exactly. For example, at node[16] udu where the stock price is 1.01, the cash generated is 0.0149 while only 0.01 is required. Similarly, at node dud no cash flow is required but 0.0049 dollars are generated. Also, the replicating strategy is path dependent, that is, the stock and bond positions at event ud and du are not identical, though the stock prices at these events are the same. Both these features are in contrast to the case without transactions costs. In the presence of transactions costs path-independent strategies will typically be suboptimal. For a detailed analysis of the above problem of replication of payoffs with transactions costs and trading restrictions, see Bensaid, Lesne, Pages & Scheinkman [1992] and Edirisinghe, Naik & Uppal [1993]. Also see Boyle & Vorst [1992], Shen [1990] and Merton [1989].

5. Optimal portfolio choice in a finite state model: the static optimization approach

We now use the results derived earlier to solve an important problem of financial economics. This is the optimal portfolio choice problem of an investor who maximizes expected utility of her lifetime consumption. We will not use the traditional dynamic programming approach to characterize a solution to this problem but reduce the dynamic problem to a static optimization problem using the concepts and results developed in the previous sections. This results in an elegant characterization of the optimal portfolio choice of the investor and makes the proofs of existence and uniqueness of optimal solutions very simple. Also, taking account of nonnegativity constraints on consumption is easier with the static approach.

5.1. Optimal portfolio choice in a complete market

We first define the portfolio choice problem of an investor in a dynamically complete market without transaction costs. Suppose that an investor starts out with

[16] The node udu is the one reached by the stock price at $t = 3$ after it has moved up at $t = 1$, moved down at $t = 2$ and moved up at $t = 3$. The symbols for other nodes are similarly defined.

an initial endowment of $e(0)$. She wants to find a portfolio strategy that generates the consumption plan that maximizes her lifetime, time-additive expected utility of consumption. We assume that she receives no endowments after date 0, i.e. $e(t) = 0,\ t = 1, \ldots, T$. We assume that the investor's preferences for consumption over time can be represented by a time additive expected utility function. Thus, the utility of a consumption stream $\{x(t),\ t = 0, \ldots, T\}$ is given by

$$U(x(0), 0) + E\sum_{t=1}^{T} U(x(t), t)$$

where $U(., t)$ is continuous, differentiable, strictly concave and strictly increasing, for $t = 0, \ldots, T$. We assume that the agent's probability assessments are given by a probability measure P. The portfolio choice problem of the above investor, $\mathbf{P}_{\mathrm{A}}$ is then

$$\text{Max}_{\ x(0)\in\Re_+,\ x\in\mathcal{X}_+}\ U(x(0), 0) + E\sum_{t=1}^{T} U(x(t), t)$$

subject to

$$x(0) + \theta_x^{\mathrm{T}}(1)S(0) \leq e(0)$$

where $\theta_x \in \Theta$ denotes a predictable trading strategy that generates the cash flow plan x. In other words, $\theta_x = \theta \in \Theta$ such that $c_\theta(t) = x(t),\ t = 1, \ldots, T$ where c_θ is defined in (1). There are three types of constraints implicit in the above formulation. First, we are constraining the chosen consumption stream to be positive. Secondly, we require that the chosen consumption stream should satisfy the initial wealth constraint. Thirdly, the chosen consumption plan, x must be financed by the chosen trading strategy θ_x. This constraint is really a sequence of constraints that relate consumption at any date to the changes in the portfolio at that date using (1). Because of these sequential constraints and the recursive nature of the objective function, the usual way to solve this problem is to introduce the investor's current wealth as a state variable and then use the principles of dynamic programming.

Here we use another approach that reduces the above problem to static concave optimization problem. This approach originates from the work of Cox & Leland [1982] and Cox & Huang [1989]. The following proposition documents a static optimization problem that is equivalent to the above problem.

Proposition 3. *Suppose that there are no arbitrage opportunities in the securities market. In addition, suppose that the markets are dynamically complete. Denote the unique equivalent martingale measure in the market as Q_0. The following problem, $\mathbf{P}_{\mathrm{B}}$ is equivalent to the above problem:*

$$\text{Max}_{\ x(0)\in\Re_+,\ x\in\mathcal{X}_+}\ U(x(0), 0) + E\sum_{t=1}^{T} U(x(t), t)$$

subject to

$$x(0) + S_0(0)E^{Q_0}\sum_{t=1}^{T}\frac{x(t)}{S_0(t)} \le e(0).$$

Proof. To prove the result it is sufficient to show that the set

$$F_A \equiv \{(x(0), y) \in \Re \times \mathcal{X} \mid (x(0), y) \text{ feasible in } \mathbf{P}_\mathrm{A}\}$$

is equal to the set

$$F_B \equiv \{(x(0), y) \in \Re \times \mathcal{X} \mid (x(0), y) \text{ feasible in } \mathbf{P}_\mathrm{B}\}.$$

Consider an element (x, y) of F_A. We know that it is positive. Since there are no arbitrage opportunities and the market is complete, we also know that if y is financed by θ_y then $\theta_y^\mathrm{T}(1)S(0) = S_0(0)E^{Q_0}\sum_{t=1}^{T} y(t)/S_0(t)$. This implies that $(x, y) \in F_B$. On the other hand take an element $(x, y) \in F_B$. We know that y is financed by some trading strategy in $\theta_y \in \Theta$ since markets are complete. Moreover, lack of arbitrage opportunities implies that

$$x(0) + \theta_y^\mathrm{T}(1)S(0) = x(0) + S_0(0)E^{Q_0}\sum_{t=1}^{T}\frac{y(t)}{S_0(t)}$$

Thus, $(x, y) \in F_A$. Thus, $F_A = F_B$.

The problem $\mathbf{P}_\mathrm{B}$ is a standard concave programming problem subject to non-negativity constraints and subject to a single linear budget constraint. These facts are sufficient to imply that if there exists a solution to the above problem, then it is unique. It is shown later in a more general setting that the feasible set is compact. Since the objective function is continuous, the existence of a solution is also guaranteed. This finishes the proof of Proposition 3. This also proves the implication *(1)* $\Rightarrow$ *(4)* in Theorem 1. □

The solution of the problem described in Proposition 3 can be obtained from its first order conditions. Assuming that $U_1(0, t) = \infty$, $U_1(\infty, t) = 0$ for $t = 0, \ldots, T$, and denoting the Lagrange multiplier for the budget constraint by λ, we can state the first order conditions as follows.[17] For all $a \in \mathcal{F}_t$, $t = 0, \ldots, T$,

$$P(a)U_1(x^*(a, t), t) = \lambda Q_0(a)\frac{S_0(0)}{S_0(a, t)}$$

where $P(.)$ denotes the probability that the agent assigns to event a, $x^*(.)$ denotes the optimal consumption in various states, $Q_0(a)$ is the probability of event a under the unique risk-neutral probability measure and $S_0(a, t)$ is the price of the riskless bond in event a at time t. Letting $f(., t)$ be the inverse of $U_1(., t)$, we have that $x^*(a, t) = f(\xi(a, t), t)$ where $\xi(a, t) = \lambda[Q_0(a)/P(a)][S_0(0)/S_0(a, t)]$

[17] Here, $U_1(., t)$ denotes derivative of $U(., .)$ with respect to its first argument.

and $\lambda > 0$ is the unique solution to the following equation:

$$f(\lambda, 0) + S_0(0) \sum_{t=1}^{T} \sum_{a \in \mathcal{F}_t} \frac{Q_0(a)}{S_0(a,t)} f\left(\lambda \frac{Q_0(a)}{P(a)} \frac{S_0(0)}{S_0(a,t)}, t\right) = e(0)$$

The above equation is obtained by substituting the expression for the optimal consumption plan in the budget constraint of the utility maximization problem.

We now consider a numerical example of the static approach to solving the portfolio choice problem.

Example 6. Consider the securities market of Example 2. Suppose that there is an investor who starts out with initial endowments of $e(0) = 10$ and wants to choose a portfolio strategy that maximizes her lifetime consumption. Let the investor's probability beliefs be given by: $P(uu) = P(ud) = P(du) = P(dd) = 0.25$. Suppose that her utility function is:

$$\log[x(0)] + \sum_{j \in \Omega} P(j) \log[x(j)].$$

This market is dynamically complete and the unique equivalent martingale measure is given by: $Q(uu) = 0.49$, $Q(ud) = 0.21$ $Q(du) = 0.21$ and $Q(dd) = 0.09$. Let $\pi(j) = S_0(0)Q(j)$ for $j = uu, ud, du, dd$. The static version of the investor's portfolio choice problem can then be written as follows:

$$\max_{x(0)\geq 0,\ \{x(j)\geq 0,\ j\in\Omega\}} \log[x(0)] + \sum_{j \in \Omega} P(j) \log[x(j)]$$

subject to

$$x(0) + \pi(uu)x(uu) + \pi(ud)x(ud) + \pi(du)x(du) + \pi(dd)x(dd) \leq 10$$

Manipulating the standard first order condition of this problem, we obtain the following consumption plan, $\{x^*(j), j = 0, uu, ud, du, dd\}$ as the optimal choice: (i) $x^*(0) = e(0)/2$ and (ii) $x^*(j) = [P(j)/\pi(j)]x^*(0)$, $j \in \Omega$. Thus, the optimal consumption plan is $x^*(0) = 5$, $x^*(uu) = 3.08675$, $x^*(ud) = 7.2024$, $x^*(du) = 7.2024$, and $x^*(dd) = 16.80555$. The agent chooses to consume more in states with lower prices of the stock because for these states, the ratio of the probability of the state to the price of the state-contingent securities is larger. Therefore, intuitively speaking, one gets most value per dollar spent by consuming in these states.

Once the optimal consumption plan is in hand, the optimal portfolio policy is just the one that replicates the optimal plan. The following trading strategy generates the optimal consumption plan: (i) at $t = 0$ buy 18.726 bonds and short 0.6547608 shares of the stock (ii) at $t = 1$ if event u is observed, trade the $t = 0$ portfolio for a portfolio consisting of 13.377 bonds and 0.411565 shares of the stock short, and (iii) at $t = 1$ if event d is observed, trade the $t = 0$ portfolio for a portfolio consisting of 31.213 bonds and 1.601 shares of the stock short. This finishes Example 6.

5.2. Optimal portfolio choice with incomplete markets and transactions costs

The above discussion shows that the problem of optimal portfolio selection in complete markets without transaction costs can be written as a concave optimization problem subject to one linear budget constraint. This result makes use of the fact that in complete markets there exists a unique equivalent martingale measure. In incomplete markets and markets with transactions costs, the equivalent martingale measures are not unique. Therefore, one needs a generalization of the above approach to solve the problem of portfolio choice in incomplete markets and in markets with transactions costs. This is discussed below.[18] Our analysis here draws on the work of He & Pearson [1991a].

We first formulate the general portfolio choice problem of an investor without assuming dynamic completeness. This problem, denoted $\mathbf{P}_{\mathrm{G}}$, is the following:

$$\max_{x(0)\in\Re_+,\ x\in\mathcal{X}_+} U(x(0),0) + E\sum_{t=1}^{T} U(x(t),t)$$

subject to the constraint that there exist predictable, nonnegative and nondecreasing processes $(\theta_{x\mathrm{l}}, \theta_{x\mathrm{s}})$ that generate the consumption plan x and such that

$$x(0) + \theta_{x\mathrm{l}}^{\mathrm{T}}(1)S_{\mathrm{a}}(0) - \theta_{x\mathrm{s}}^{\mathrm{T}}(1)S_{\mathrm{b}}(0) \leq e(0).$$

The definition of a trading strategy that generates a given consumption plan in the presence of transactions costs is given Section 4.

This problem is similar to problem $\mathbf{P}_{\mathrm{A}}$ defined above except for the fact that buying and selling prices of securities may not be the same because of transactions costs. We now discuss how to reduce the above problem to a static concave optimization problem without assuming market completeness. For this purpose, we use the minimum cost functional introduced in the previous sections. Recall that $C_1(y)$ is defined to be minimum cost of generating a cash flow that is at least equal to y for any $y \in \mathcal{X}$. In the presence of transactions costs it is given as the value of the linear program $\mathbf{P}_1(.)$ [or $\mathbf{D}_1(.)$] defined in Section 4. Then we have the following result.

Proposition 4. Consider the following problem, denoted $\mathbf{P}_{\mathrm{H}}$:

$$\text{Max}_{\ x(0)\in\Re_+,y\in\mathcal{X}_+} U(x(0),0) + E\sum_{t=1}^{T} U(y(t),t)$$

subject to the constraint that

$$x(0) + C_1(y) \leq e(0).$$

[18] For an analysis of the portfolio choice problem with transactions cost in a finite state economy using the dynamic programming approach, see Gennotte & Jung [1994] and Boyle & Lin [1994]. For an analysis of optimal portfolio choice with transactions costs in a continuous time economy, see Constantinides [1986] and Davis & Norman [1990].

If there exist no arbitrage opportunities then there exists a unique solution to $\mathbf{P}_{\mathrm{H}}$. *The consumption plan that solves* $\mathbf{P}_{\mathrm{H}}$ *also solves* $\mathbf{P}_{\mathrm{G}}$.

Proof. Denote the set of feasible consumption plans in $\mathbf{P}_{\mathrm{H}}$ as F_H. We first prove the uniqueness of the solution to $\mathbf{P}_{\mathrm{H}}$. Note that $C_1(y)$ is a convex function as shown in the previous section. As a result, F_H is a convex subset of $\mathcal{X}$. The objective function is assumed to be strictly concave. This implies that if a solution to $\mathbf{P}_{\mathrm{H}}$ exists it must be unique. To prove the existence of a solution to $\mathbf{P}_{\mathrm{H}}$ note that the objective function is assumed to be continuous. It is sufficient to show, therefore, that F_H is compact. The feasible set is the intersection of the positive orthant of $\mathcal{X}$ and the set $A = \{(x, y) \mid x + C_1(y) \le e(0)\}$. The set A is closed because $C_1(y)$ is continuous. Therefore, it only remains to show the boundedness of F_H. Recall that (x, y) can be identified with a vector in $\Re \times \prod_{t=1}^{T} \Re^{N(t)}$. We claim that if $(x, y) \in F_H$ then every component of (x, y) is less than or equal to $e(0)/0.5\epsilon$ where $\epsilon = \min\{1, \delta\}$ and

$$\delta \equiv \min_{a\in\mathcal{F}_t,\ t=1,\ldots,T} C_1(\mathbf{1}_{a,t})$$

and $C_1(\mathbf{1}_{a,t})$ denotes the minimum cost of obtaining a cash flow stream that is at least equal to the cash flow on the Arrow–Debreu security for time–event pair (a, t). The lack of arbitrage opportunities implies that $\epsilon > 0$.

To prove the above claim, we suppose that it is not true and derive a contradiction. If the above claim is not true then, there exist $(x, y) \in F_H$ for which either $x > e(0)/0.5\epsilon$ or there is a time–event pair (a_0, t_0), $t_0 \ge 1$ such that $y(t_0) > e(0)/0.5\epsilon$ in the event a_0. This means that either (i) $x > e(0)/0.5\epsilon$ and $y \ge 0$ or (ii) $x \ge 0$ and $y > e(0)/0.5\epsilon\mathbf{1}_{a_0,t_0}$. Here we have used the fact that $(x, y) \in F_H$ implies that $(x, y) \ge 0$. In case (i),

$$x + C_1(y) \ge \frac{e(0)}{0.5\epsilon} \ge e(0)$$

because $C_1(y) \ge 0$ and $\epsilon \le 1$. In case (ii),

$$x + C_1(y) \ge C_1\left(\frac{e(0)}{0.5\epsilon}\mathbf{1}_{a_0,t_0}\right) = \frac{e(0)}{0.5\epsilon} C_1(\mathbf{1}_{a_0,t_0}) > e(0). \tag{8}$$

The equality in (8) follows from the positive homogeneity of $C_1(.)$ and the last inequality follows from the above-mentioned definition of ϵ. This means that (x, y) could not be in F_H. Thus, we have proved that F_H is bounded.

We now prove the statement that the plan that solves $\mathbf{P}_{\mathrm{H}}$ also solves $\mathbf{P}_{\mathrm{G}}$. To prove this, note that val[$\mathbf{P}_{\mathrm{H}}$] $\ge$ val[$\mathbf{P}_{\mathrm{G}}$] because any consumption plan that is feasible in $\mathbf{P}_{\mathrm{G}}$ is also feasible in $\mathbf{P}_{\mathrm{H}}$. On the other hand, for any consumption plan feasible in $\mathbf{P}_{\mathrm{H}}$, say (x, y), there exists another consumption plan $(\hat{x}, \hat{y})$ that is feasible in $\mathbf{P}_{\mathrm{G}}$ and is such that $(\hat{x}, \hat{y}) \ge (x, y)$. Take $\hat{x} = x$ and $\hat{y}$ to equal the consumption plan generated by the trading strategy that solves the problem $\mathbf{P}_1(y)$. Since the utility functions are increasing, this implies that val[$\mathbf{P}_{\mathrm{H}}$] $\le$ val[$\mathbf{P}_{\mathrm{G}}$]. Thus, val[$\mathbf{P}_{\mathrm{H}}$] $=$ val[$\mathbf{P}_{\mathrm{G}}$]. However, we know that the maximum in $\mathbf{P}_{\mathrm{H}}$ is attained and uniquely so. Therefore, the unique solution to $\mathbf{P}_{\mathrm{H}}$ is also a solution to $\mathbf{P}_{\mathrm{G}}$. This finishes the proof of Proposition 4. This also proves the implication *(1)* $\Rightarrow$ *(4)* in Theorem 2. □

He & Pearson [1991a] characterize the budget constraint of an investor maximizing her utility in an incomplete market in terms to the extreme points of the constraint set of the problem $\mathbf{D}_1(.)$. The above approach is equivalent to theirs.

The solution of the problem mentioned in Proposition 4 can also be characterized using its first order conditions. However, the situation is more complex here because the budget constraint is nonlinear and nondifferentiable. We refer the readers to He & Pearson [1991a] for greater detail.

Below, we provide an example to illustrate the conclusions of Proposition 4.

Example 7. Consider the following 3 date securities market model. There are two assets: one risky stock and a riskless bond. The price process of these assets is given as follows:

$$S_1(t+1) = S_1(t)[\mu + \sigma(t)\epsilon(t+1)]$$

where $\epsilon(t) \in \{+1, -1\}$ for $t = 1, 2$, $\mu = 1.12$ and $\sigma(0) = 0.1$. At $t = 1$, $\sigma(1)$ can either be 0.1 or 0.125. The riskless rate of interest is assumed to be constant at 10% per period. We also assume that there are no transactions costs. The information structure and the price processes for this example are as in Figure 4.

The above is a simple example of an incomplete market. The incompleteness arises because of stochastic changes in the volatility of stock return and the fact that there are only two assets available for trading. Consider an investor who seeks to maximize her expected utility of consumption at date 2. Suppose that her utility function $U(c) = (1/\gamma)c^{\gamma}$ with $\gamma = 0.5$. Her initial endowments equal 10 and she assigns equal probability to each state in Ω. Let us use the above construction to solve the optimal portfolio choice problem of this investor by reducing it to a static optimization problem.

Let $y \equiv \{y(j),\ j \in \Omega\}$ be a cash flow which occurs at time 2.[19] It can be shown that the function, $C_1(y)$ is given by: $0.5\max[J(u_{\mathrm{a}}),\ J(u_{\mathrm{b}})] + 0.5\max[J(d_{\mathrm{a}}),\ J(d_{\mathrm{b}})]$ where $J(a) = 0.5y(au) + 0.5y(ad)$ for $a = u_{\mathrm{a}}, u_{\mathrm{b}}, d_{\mathrm{a}}, d_{\mathrm{b}}$.

Then, according to Proposition 4, the optimal portfolio choice problem of the investor is equivalent to the problem:

$$\max_{\{y(j)\geq 0,\ j\in\Omega\}} \sum_{j\in\Omega} P(j)\frac{[y(j)]^{\gamma}}{\gamma}$$

subject to

$$0.5\max[J(u_{\mathrm{a}}),\ J(u_{\mathrm{b}})] + 0.5\max[J(d_{\mathrm{a}}),\ J(d_{\mathrm{b}})] \leq e(0)$$

where $J(.)$ is defined above.

[19] In this example, $\Omega = \{u_{\mathrm{a}}u, u_{\mathrm{a}}d, u_{\mathrm{b}}u, u_{\mathrm{b}}d, d_{\mathrm{a}}u, d_{\mathrm{a}}d, d_{\mathrm{b}}u, d_{\mathrm{b}}d\}$.

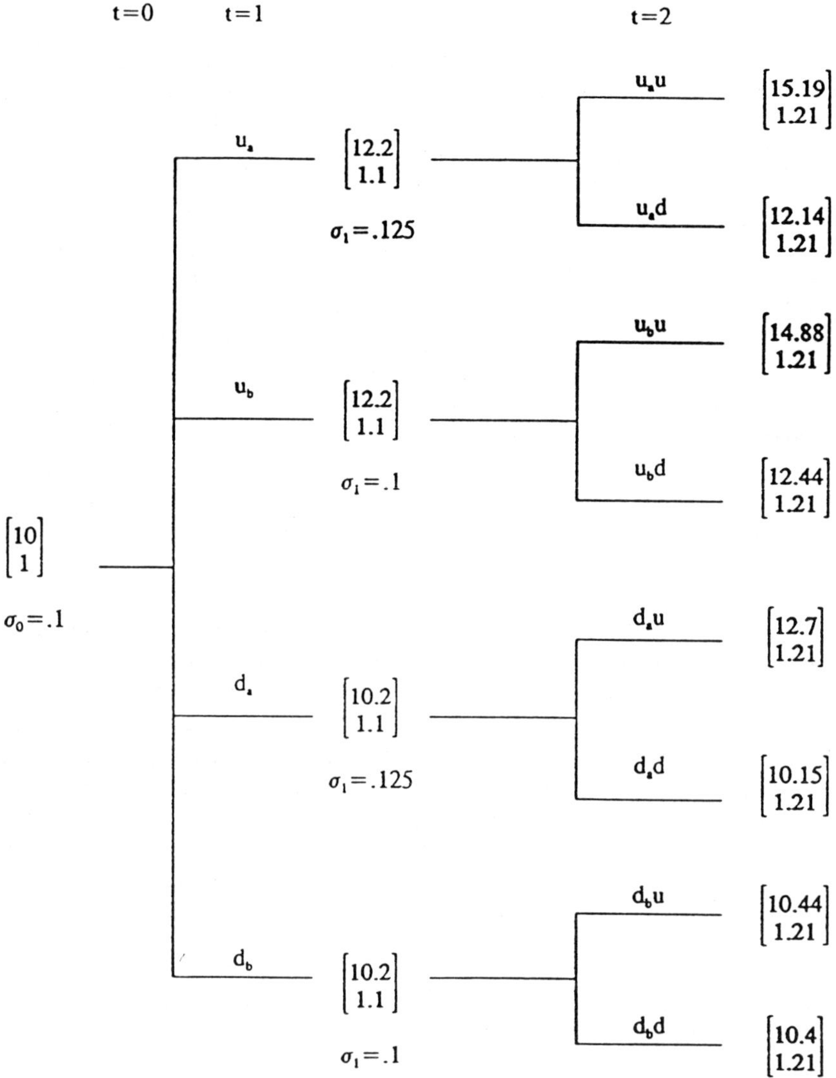

Fig. 4. The first element of the security price vector at any node denotes the price of the risky stock at that node. The second element of the price vector at a given node denotes the value at that node of a dollar invested in the riskless bond at t=0.

The consumption plan that solves the above problem is given by y^* with $y^*(u_a u) = 25.0643$, $y^*(u_a d) = 13.1431$, $y^*(d_a u) = 11.1397$, $y^*(d_a d) = 5.8414$, $y^*(u_b u) = 27.225$, $y^*(u_b d) = 12.1$, $y^*(d_b u) = 12.1$, $y^*(d_b d) = 5.378$. The process for optimally invested wealth, $w^*(t)$ is: $w^*(0) = e(0)$, $w^*(u_a) = w^*(u_b) = 16.5$, $w^*(d_a) = w^*(d_b) = 7.333$ and $w^*(a) = y^*(a)$ for $a \in \mathcal{F}_2$. Since $w^*(.)$ at $t = 1$ does not differ according to the volatility state, it is easy to verify that the consumption plan given here is marketed, as it must be.

6. Concluding remarks

This chapter presents the key results that characterize the behavior of security prices in a finite state economy that does not permit any arbitrage opportunities. The assumption of a finite number of states leads to a simple yet powerful model for analyzing security price behavior in a competitive economy. The main result that one is able to derive in a finite state model is the fundamental theorem of asset pricing. In the case of a frictionless securities market, this theorem asserts (among other facts) the equivalence of a risk-neutral probability measure and the lack of arbitrage opportunities. The analysis illustrates how, in a model of arbitrage free security prices, we can (i) value contingent claims in a perfect securities market, (ii) place bounds on the values of contingent claims when these cannot be exactly valued because of the presence of market frictions and (iii) solve the dynamic portfolio choice problem in a securities market with or without imperfections using a static optimization approach.

In closing, we note that the assumption of a finite number of states simplifies the analysis considerably because it implies that the investors have only a finite number of trading opportunities. When an infinite number of states is possible, the situation is substantially more complex. As Back & Pliska [1991] show, one can no longer prove the fundamental theorem of asset pricing in the form stated here. We mention just one complication that arises with an infinite number of states. The existence of a risk-neutral probability measure is not sufficient to rule out arbitrage opportunities. This is because of the presence of 'doubling' strategies that can be executed if one could trade an infinite number of times. Then, to rule out arbitrage, one requires the additional assumption that trading strategies that lead to nonnegative wealth are not admissible. The literature on the properties of arbitrage-free asset prices in an infinite state economy with or without market imperfections is extensive and deserves a separate survey. However, as a starting point we refer the readers who are interested in this important topic to the work of Back and Pliska, Duffie [1992, Chapter 6], Dybvig & Huang [1988], Harrison & Kreps [1979], Harrison & Pliska [1981] and Kreps [1981]. Other papers of interest in this area include those by Clark [1993], Duffie & Huang [1986], Delang, Morton & Willinger [1990], Delbaen [1992], Jouini & Kallal [1991], Kallal [1992], Hindy [1995], Huang [1985] and Lakner [1993].

Appendix

A.1. The proof of the 'only if' part of Proposition 1

In this proof, we need the following result.

Remark 2. For any $y \equiv \{y(t),\ t = 1, \ldots, T\} \in \mathcal{X}$, the dual of $\mathbf{P}(y)$ is the following linear programming problem, $\mathbf{D}(y)$:

$$\max_{Q \in \mathcal{Q}} S_0(0) E^Q \sum_{t=1}^{T} \frac{y(t)}{S_0(t)}$$

where $\mathcal{Q}$ is the set of probability measures, (with generic element Q) on Ω under which the following condition is satisfied:

$$S_0(t)E_t^Q d_i(T) = S_i(t)$$

for $i = 0, \ldots, N$ and for $t = 0, \ldots, T$.

The proof of Remark 2 follows from explicitly writing out the dual problem. Using Remark 2, the proof of the only if part of Proposition 1 can be stated as follows. Suppose that there exists a unique equivalent martingale measure, denoted Q_0. This means that for any y the linear programming problem, $\mathbf{D}(y)$, has only one feasible point. To show this, suppose that there exist another point $Q' \neq Q_0$ which is feasible in $\mathbf{D}(y)$ for any given y. This would mean that $\exists \lambda \in (0, 1)$ such that $\lambda Q_0 + (1 - \lambda)Q'$ is also feasible in $\mathbf{D}(y)$ and is strictly positive. This contradicts the uniqueness of Q_0. If Q_0 is the only feasible point in $D(y)$ for any y, then

$$\text{val}\,[\mathbf{D}(y)] = S_0(0)E^{Q_0}\sum_{t=1}^{T}\frac{y(t)}{S_0(t)} = \text{val}\,[\mathbf{P}(y)] = C(y).$$

As a result, $C(y)$ must be linear which implies the completeness of the securities market as shown in the proof of the 'if' part of Remark 1.

A.2. The proof of the 'only if' part of Remark 1

This follows from the fact that if the market is complete then there is a unique equivalent martingale measure, as shown in the 'if' part of Proposition 1. This implies that $C(.)$ must be linear as argued above.

Acknowledgements

Financial support for this work was provided by the Social Sciences and Humanities Research Council of Canada. I thank Murray Carlson, Mary Kelly, Burton Hollifield, Patrick Savaria, Raman Uppal and William Ziemba for useful comments.

References

Back, K., and S. Pliska (1991). On the fundamental theorem of asset pricing with an infinite state space. *J. Math. Econ.* 20, 1–18.

Bank, B., J. Guddat, D. Klatte, B. Kummer and K. Tammer (1983). *Non-linear Parametric Optimization*, Birkhauser Verlag, Boston.

Bensaid, B., J. Lesne, H. Pages and J. Scheinkman (1992). Derivative asset pricing with transaction costs. *Math. Finance* 2, 63–86.

Boyle, P., and X. Lin (1994). Optimal portfolio selection with transactions costs, Working Paper, University of Waterloo.

Boyle, P., and T. Vorst (1992). Option pricing in discrete time with transaction costs. *J. Finance* 47, 271–293.

Carr, P., and R. Jarrow (1995). A discrete time synthesis of derivative security valuation using a term structure of futures price, in: R. Jarrow, V. Maksimovic and W.T. Ziemba (eds.), *Finance*, Elsevier, Amsterdam, pp. 225–250 (this volume).

Clark, S. (1993). The valuation problem in arbitrage pricing theory, *J. Math. Econ.* 22, 5, 463–478.

Constantinides, G. (1986). Capital market equilibrium with transactions costs. *J. Polit. Econ.* 94, 842–862.

Cox, J., and C. Huang (1989). Optimal consumption and portfolio policies when asset prices follow a diffusion process. *J. Econ. Theory* 49, 33–83.

Cox, J., and H. Leland (1982). Notes on inter-temporal investment policies, Working Paper, Stanford University.

Cox, J., S. Ross and M. Rubinstein (1979). Option pricing: A simplified approach. *J. Financ. Econ.* 7, 229–263.

Dammon, R., and R. Green (1987). Tax arbitrage and the existence of equilibrium prices for financial assets. *J. Finance* 42, 5, 1143–1166.

Davis M., and A. Norman (1990). Portfolio selection with transactions costs. *Math. Oper. Res.* 15.4, 676–713.

Delang, R., A. Morton and W. Willinger (1990). Equivalent martingale measures and no-arbitrage in stochastic securities market models. *Stochast. Stochast. Rep.* 29, 185–201.

Delbaen, F. (1992). Representing martingale measures when asset prices are continuous and bounded. *Math. Finance* 2, 107–130.

Duffie, D. (1992). *Dynamic Asset Pricing Theory*, Princeton University Press, Princeton, NJ.

Duffie, D., and C. Huang (1986). Multiperiod security markets with differential information. *J. Math. Econ.* 15, 283–303.

Dybvig, P., and C. Huang (1988). Non-negative wealth, absence of arbitrage, and feasible consumption plans. *Rev. Financ. Studies* 1, 377–401.

Dybvig, P., and S. Ross (1986). Arbitrage, in: J. Eatwell, M. Milgate and P. Newman (eds.), *The New Palgrave: A Dictionary of Economics*, Vol. 1, MacMillan, London, pp. 100–106.

Edirisinghe, C., V. Naik and R. Uppal (1993). Optimal replication of options with transactions costs and trading restrictions. *J. Financ. Quant. Anal.* 28, 117–138.

Garman M., and J. Ohlson (1981). Valuation of risky assets in arbitrage free economies with transactions costs. *J. Financ. Econ.* 9, 271–280.

Gennotte, G., and A. Jung (1994). Investment strategies under transactions costs: The finite horizon case, *Mgmt. Sci.* 40, 3, 385–404.

Green, R., and S. Srivastava (1985). Risk aversion and arbitrage. *J. Finance* 40, 1, 257–268.

Hakansson, N. (1970). Optimal investment and consumption strategies under risk for a class of utility functions. *Econometrica* 38, 587–607.

Harrison, J., and D. Kreps (1979). Martingale and arbitrage in multi-period securities markets. *J. Econ. Theory* 20, 381–408.

Harrison, J., and S. Pliska (1981). Martingales and stochastic integrals in the theory of continuous trading. *Stochast. Processes Appl.* 11, 215–260.

He, H., and N. Pearson (1991a). Consumption and portfolio policies with incomplete markets and short-sale constraints: The finite-dimensional case. *Math. Finance* 1, 3, 1–10.

He, H., and N. Pearson (1991b). Consumption and portfolio policies with incomplete markets and short-sale constraints: The infinite dimensional case. *J. Econ. Theory* 54, 259–304.

Hindy, A. (1995). Viable prices in financial markets with solvency constraints, *J. Math. Econ.* 24, 105–135.

Ho, T., and S. Lee (1986). Term structure movements and pricing interest rate contingent claims. *J. Finance* 41, 1011–1029.

Huang, C. (1985). Information structures and equilibrium asset prices. *J. Econ. Theory* 31, 33–71.

Huang, C., and R.H. Litzenberger (1988). *Foundations of Financial Economics*, North-Holland, New York, NY.

Jouini, E., and H. Kallal (1991). Martingale, arbitrage and equilibrium in security markets with transactions costs (forthcoming).

Kallal, H. (1992). Arbitrage and equilibrium in securities markets with shortsale constraints, Working Paper, New York University.

Karatzas, J. Lehoczky and S. Shreve (1987). Optimal portfolio and consumption decisions for a small investor on a finite horizon. *SIAM J. Control Optim.* 25, 1557–1586.

Karatzas, J. Lehoczky, S. Shreve and G. Xu (1991). Martingale and duality methods for utility maximization in incomplete markets. *SIAM J. Control Optim.* 29, 702–730.

Kreps, D. (1979). Multi-period securities and efficient allocation of risk, in: J.J. McCall (ed.), *The Economics of Uncertainty and Information*, University of Chicago Press, Chicago, pp. 203–232.

Kreps, D. (1981). Arbitrage and equilibrium in economies with infinitely many commodities. *J. Math. Econ.* 8, 15–35.

Lakner, P. (1993). Martingale measures for a class of right-continuous processes. *Math. Finance* 3, 1, 43–53.

Mangasarian, O.L. (1969). *Non-linear Programming*, McGraw-Hill, New York, NY.

Merton, R. (1971). Optimal consumption and portfolio rules in a continuous time model. *J. Econ. Theory* 3, 373–413.

Merton, R.C. (1989). On the application of the continuous time theory of finance to financial intermediation and insurance. in: *The Geneva Papers on Risk and Insurance* pp. 225–261.

Naik, V., and R. Uppal (1994). Leverage constraints and the optimal hedging of stock and bond options. *J. Financ. Quant. Anal.* 29, 2 (199–222.

Prisman. E. (1986). Valuation of risky asset in arbitrage free economies with frictions. *J. Finance* 41, 3, 545–557.

Rendleman R., and B. Bartter (1979). Two-state option pricing. *J. Finance* 34, 5, 1093–1110.

Ritchken, P.H., and S. Kuo (1988). Option bounds with finite revision opportunities. *J. Finance* 43, 301–308.

Rockafellar, R. (1970). *Convex Analysis*, Princeton University Press, Princeton, NJ.

Ross, S. (1976). Risk, return and arbitrage, in: I. Friend and J. Bicksler (eds.), *Risk and Return in Finance*, Ballinger Press, Cambridge.

Ross, S. (1978). A simple approach to the valuation of risky streams. *J. Bus.* 51, 453–475.

Ross, S. (1987). Arbitrage and martingales with taxation. *J. Polit. Econ.* 95, 371–393.

Sharpe, W. (1978). *Investments*, 1st edition, Prentice-Hall, Englewood Cliffs, NJ.

Shen, Q. (1990). Bid–ask prices for call options with transaction costs, Working Paper, Wharton School.

R. Jarrow et al., Eds., *Handbooks in OR & MS, Vol. 9*

Chapter 3

Capital Growth Theory

Nils H. Hakansson
Walter A. Haas School of Business, University of California, Berkeley, CA 94720, U.S.A.

William T. Ziemba
Faculty of Commerce and Business Administration, University of British Columbia, Vancouver, B.C. V6T 1Y8, Canada

1. Introduction

Even casual observation strongly suggests that capital growth is not just a catch-phrase but something which many actively strive to achieve. It is therefore rather surprising that capital growth *theory* is a relatively obscure subject. For example, the great bulk of today's MBA's have had little or no exposure to the subject, having had their attention focussed almost exclusively on the single-period mean–variance model of portfolio choice. The purpose of this essay is to review the theory of capital growth, in particular the so-called growth-optimal investment strategy, its properties, its uses, and its links to betting and other investment models. We also discuss several applications that have tended to refine the basic theory.

The central feature of the growth-optimal investment strategy, also known as the geometric mean model and the Kelly criterion, is the logarithmic shape of the objective function. But the power and durability of the model is due to a remarkable set of properties. Some of these are unique to the growth-optimal strategy and the others are shared by all the members of the (remarkable) small family to which the growth optimal strategy belongs.

Investment over time is multiplicative, not additive, due to the compounding nature of the process itself. This makes a number of results in dynamic investment theory appear nonintuitive. For example, in the single-period portfolio problem, the optimal investment policy is very sensitive to the utility function being used; the set of policies that are inadmissible or dominated across all utility functions is relatively small. The same observation holds in the dynamic case when the number of periods is not large. But as the number of periods does become large, the set of investment policies that are optimal for *current* investment tends to shrink drastically, at least in the basic reinvestment case without transaction costs. As we will see, many strikingly different investors will, in essence, invest the same way when the horizon is distant and will only begin to part company as their horizons near.

It is tempting to conjecture that all long-run investment policies to which risk-averse investors with monotone increasing utility functions will flock, under a favorable return structure, insure growth of capital with a very high probability. Such a conjecture is false; many investors will, even in this case, converge on investment policies which almost surely risk ruin in the long run, in effect ignoring feasible policies which almost surely lead to capital growth. Similarly, the relationship between the behavior of capital over time and the behavior of the expected utility of that same capital over time often appears strikingly nonintuitive.

Section 2 reviews the origins of the capital growth model while Section 3 contains a derivation and identifies its key properties. The conditions for capital growth are examined in Section 4. The model's relationship to other long-run investment models is studied in Section 5 and Section 6 contains its role in intertemporal investment/consumption models. Section 7 adds various constraints for accomplishing tradeoffs between growth and security, while Section 8 reviews various applications. A concluding summary is given in Section 9.

2. Origins of the model

The approach to investment commonly known as the growth-optimal investment strategy has a number of apparently independent origins. In particular, Williams [1936], Kelly [1956], Latane [1959], and Breiman [1960, 1961] seem to have been unaware of each other's papers. But one can also argue that Bernoulli (1738) unwittingly stumbled on it in 1738 in his resolution of the St. Petersburg Paradox — see the 1954 translation — and Samuelson's survey [1977].

Samuelson [1971] appears to be the earliest to have related the geometric mean criterion to utility theory — and to find it wanting. The growth optimal strategy's inviolability in the larger consumption–investment context when preferences for consumption are logarithmic was first noted by Hakansson [1970]. Finally, models considering tradeoffs between capital growth and security appear to have been pioneered by MacLean & Ziemba [1986].

3. The model and its basic properties

The following notation and basic assumptions will be employed:

w_t = amount of investment capital at decision point t (the end of the tth period);

M_t = the number of investment opportunities available in period t, where $M_t \leq M$;

S_t = the subset of investment opportunities which it is possible to sell short in period t;

r_{1t} = rate of interest in period t;

r_{it} = return per unit of capital invested in opportunity i, where $i = 2, \ldots, M_t$, in the tth period (random variable). That is, if we invest an amount θ in i at the beginning of the period, we will obtain $(1 + r_{it})\theta$ at the end of that period;

z_{1t} = amount lent in period t (negative z_{1t} indicate borrowing) (decision variable);

z_{it} = amount invested in opportunity $i, i = 2, \ldots, M_t$ at the beginning of the tth period (decision variable);

$F_t(y_2, y_3, \ldots, y_{M_t}) \equiv \Pr\{r_{2t} \le y_2, r_{3t} \le y_3, \ldots, r_{M_t t} \le y_{M_t}\}$;

$z_t \equiv (z_{2t}, \ldots, z_{M_t t})$;

$x_{it} \equiv \dfrac{z_{it}}{w_{t-1}}, \qquad i = 1, \ldots, M_t$;

$x_t \equiv x_{2t}, \ldots, x_{M_t t}$;

$\langle x_t \rangle \equiv x_1, \ldots, x_t$.

The capital market will generally be assumed to be perfect, i.e. that there are no transaction costs or taxes, that the investor has no influence on prices or returns, that the amount invested can be any real number, and that the investor has full use of the proceeds from any short sale.

The following basic properties of returns will be assumed:

$$r_{1t} \ge 0, \qquad t = 1, 2, \ldots \tag{1}$$

$$E[r_{it}] \ge \delta + r_{lt}, \qquad \delta > 0, \qquad \text{some } i, t = 1, 2, \ldots \tag{2}$$

$$E[r_{it}] \le K, \qquad \text{all } i, t. \tag{3}$$

These assumptions imply that the financial market provides a 'favorable game.'

We also assume that the (nonstationary) return distributions F_t are either independent from period to period or obey a Markov process and they also satisfy the 'no-easy-money condition'

$$\mathrm{P}\left\{\sum_{i=2}^{M_t}(r_{it} - r_{1t})\theta_i < \delta_1\right\} > \delta_2 \text{ for all } t \text{ and all } \theta_i \text{ such that } \sum_{i=2}^{M_t}|\theta_i| = 1, \text{ and } \theta_i \ge 0 \text{ for all } i \notin S_t, \tag{4}$$

where $\delta_1 < 0$, $\delta_2 > 0$.

Condition (4) is equivalent to what is often referred to as the no-arbitrage condition. It is generally a necessary condition for the portfolio problem to have a solution.

We also assume that the investor must remain solvent in each period, i.e., that he or she must satisfy the solvency constraints

$$\Pr\{w_t \ge 0\} = 1, \qquad t = 1, 2, \ldots. \tag{5}$$

The amount invested at time $t-1$ is

$$\sum_{i=1}^{M_t} z_{it} = w_{t-1}$$

and the value of the investment at time t, broken down between its risky and riskfree components, is

$$w_t = \sum_{i=2}^{M_t}(1+r_{it})z_{it} + (1+r_{1t})\Big(1-\sum_{i=2}^{M_t} z_{it}\Big),$$

which together yield the basic difference equation

$$\begin{aligned} w_t &= \sum_{i=2}^{M_t}(r_{it}-r_{1t})z_{it} + w_{t-1}(1+r_{1t}), \qquad t=1,2,\ldots \\ &= w_{t-1}R_t(x_t) = w_0 R_1(x_1)\ldots R_t(x_t), \qquad t=1,2,\ldots \end{aligned} \tag{6}$$

where

$$R_t(x_t) \equiv \sum_{i=2}^{M_t}(r_{it}-r_{1t})x_{it} + 1 + r_{1t}. \tag{7}$$

Let us now turn to the basic reinvestment problem which (ignores capital infusions and distributions and) simply revises the portfolio at discrete points in time. In view of (5), (6) may be written

$$w_t = w_0 \exp\Big\{\sum_{n=1}^{t} \ln R_n(x_n)\Big\}, \qquad t=1,2,\ldots. \tag{8}$$

Defining

$$G_t(\langle x_t\rangle) \equiv \frac{\Big[\sum_{n=1}^{t} \ln R_n(x_n)\Big]}{t}, \tag{9}$$

(8) becomes

$$\begin{aligned} w_t &= w_0[\exp\{G_t(\langle x_t\rangle)\}]^t \\ &= w_0(1+g_t)^t, \end{aligned} \tag{10}$$

where $g_t = \exp G_t(\langle x_t\rangle) - 1$ is the compound growth rate of capital over the first t periods.

By the law of large numbers,

$$G_t(\langle x_t\rangle) \to E[G_t(\langle x_t\rangle)]$$

under mild conditions. Thus, it is evident that for large T,

$$w_t \to 0 \text{ if } E[G_t] \le \delta < 0, \quad t \ge T, \tag{11}$$

$$w_t \to \infty \text{ if } E[G_t] \geq \delta > 0, \quad t \geq T \tag{12}$$

$$g_t \to \exp E[G_t] - 1. \tag{13}$$

Under stationary returns and policies$\langle x_t \rangle$, (11) and (12) simplify to

$$\begin{aligned} w_t &\to 0 \ \text{ if } E[\ln R_n(x_n)] < 0 \\ w_t &\to \infty \text{ if } E[\ln R_n(x_n)] > 0 \end{aligned} \quad \text{any } n.$$

There is nothing intuitive that would suggest that the sign of $E[\ln R_n(x_n)]$ is the determinant of whether our capital will decline or grow in the (stationary) simple reinvestment problem. What *is* evident is that the *expected* return on capital, $E[R_n] - 1$, is *not* what matters. As (6) reminds us, capital growth (positive or negative) is a multiplicative, not an additive process.

To illustrate the point, consider the case of only two assets, one riskfree yielding 5% per period, and the other returning either −60% or +100% with equal probabilities in each period. Always putting all of our capital in the riskfree asset clearly gives a 5% growth rate of capital. The *expected* return on the risky asset is 20% per period. Yet placing all of our funds in the risky asset at the beginning of each period results in a capital growth rate that converges to −10.55%! It is easy to see this. We will double our money to 200% roughly half of the time. But we will also lose 60% (bringing the 200% to 80%) of our beginning-of-period capital about half the time, for a 'two-period return' of −20% on average, or −10.55% per period. *Expected* capital $E[w_t]$, on the other hand, has a growth rate of 20% per period.

What this simple example demonstrates is that there are many investment strategies for which, as $t \to \infty$,

$$\begin{aligned} &E[w_t] \to \infty \\ &\text{Median}\,[w_t] \to 0 \\ &\text{Mode}\,[w_t] \to 0 \\ &\Pr\{w_t < \$1\} \to 1. \end{aligned}$$

The coexistence of the above four measures results when $E[G_t] \leq \delta < 0$ for $t \geq T$ and a long (but thin) upper tail is generated as w_t moves forward in time.

In view of (7), (9) and (10), we observe that to 'maximize' the long-run growth rate g_t, it is necessary and sufficient to maximize $E[G_t(\langle x_t \rangle)]$, or

$$\text{Max}\,\{E[\ln R_1(x_1)] + E[\ln R_2(x_2)] + \ldots\} \tag{14}$$

Whenever returns are independent from period to period or the economy obeys a Markov process [1], it is necessary and sufficient to accomplish (14) to

$$\underset{x_t}{\text{Max}}\ E[\ln R_t(x_t)] \text{ sequentially at each } t - 1. \tag{15}$$

[1] Algoet & Cover [1988] show formally that the growth-optimal strategy maintains its basic properties under arbitrary returns processes.

Since the geometric mean of $R_t(x_t) = \exp\{E[\ln R_t(x_t)]\}$, we observe that (15) is also equivalent to maximizing the geometric mean of principal plus return at each point in time.

3.1. *Properties of the growth-optimal investment strategy*

Since the solution $\langle x_t^* \rangle$ to (15), in view of (10) and (13), *almost surely* leads to more capital in the long run than any other investment policy which does not converge to it, $\langle x_t^* \rangle$ is referred to as the growth-optimal investment strategy. Existence is assured by the no-easy-money condition (4), the bounds on expected returns (1)–(3), and the solvency constraint (5). The strict concavity of the objective function in (15) implies that the optimal payoff distribution $R_t(x_t^*)$ is unique; the optimal policy x_t^* itself will be unique only if, for any security i, there is no portfolio of the other assets which can replicate the return pattern r_{it}.

It is probably not surprising that the growth-optimal strategy never risks ruin, i.e.

$$\Pr\{R_t(x_t^*) = 0\} = 0$$

— because to grow you have to survive. But this need not mean that the solvency constraint is not binding: $E[\ln R_t(x_t)]$ may exist even when R_t touches 0 as long as the lower tail is very thin. The conditions (1)–(3) imply that positive growth is feasible. Another dimension of the consistency between short-term and long-term performance was observed by Bell & Cover [1988].

As shown by Breiman [1961], the growth-optimal strategy also has the property that it asymptotically minimizes the expected time to reach a given level of capital. This is not surprising in view of the characteristics noted in the previous two paragraphs.

It is also evident from (15) that the growth-optimal strategy is *myopic* even when returns obey a Markov process (Hakansson 1971c). This property is clearly of great practical significance since it means that the investor only needs to estimate the coming period's (joint) return structure in order to behave optimally in a long-run sense; future periods' return structures have no influence on the current period's optimal decision. *No* other dynamic investment model has this property in a Markov economy; only a small set of other families have it when returns are independent from period to period (see Section 5).

The growth-optimal strategy implies, and is implied by, logarithmic utility of wealth at the end of each period. This is because at each $t-1$

$$\begin{aligned}
&\operatorname*{Max}_{x_t} E[\ln R_t(x_t)] \\
&\sim \operatorname*{Max}_{x_t} \{E[\ln R_t(x_t) + \ln w_{t-1}]\} \\
&= \operatorname*{Max}_{x_t} E[\ln(w_{t-1} R_t(x_t))] = \operatorname*{Max}_{z_t} E[\ln w_t(z_t)].
\end{aligned}$$

Since every utility function is unique (up to a positive linear transformation), it also follows that the growth-optimal strategy is *not* consistent with any other end-of-period utility function (more on this in the next subsection).

The relative risk aversion function

$$q(w) \equiv -\frac{wu''(w)}{u'(w)}$$

equals 1 when $u(w) = \ln(w)$ (it is 0 for a risk-neutral investor). Thus, we observe that to do 'the best' in the long run in terms of capital growth, it is not only necessary to be risk averse in each period. We must also display the 'right' amount of risk aversion. The long-run growth rate of capital will be lower either if one invests in a way which is *more* risk averse than the logarithmic function or relies on an objective function which is *less* risk averse.

The growth-optimal investment strategy is not only linear in beginning-of-period wealth but proportional as well since definitionally

$$z_t^* = w_{t-1}x_t^*.$$

Both of these properties are shared by only a small family of investment models.

Since the growth-optimal strategy is consistent with a logarithmic end-of-period utility function only, it is clearly *not* consistent with the mean–variance approach to portfolio choice — which in turn is consistent with quadratic utility for arbitrary security return structures, and, for normally distributed returns, with those utility functions whose expected utilities exist when integrated with the normal distribution, plus a few other cases, as shown by Ziemba & Vickson [1975] and Chamberlain [1983]. This incompatibility is easy to understand; in solving for the growth-optimal strategy, *all* of the moments of the return distributions matter, with positive skewness being particularly favored. When the returns on the risky assets are normally distributed, no matter how favorable the means and variances are, the growth-optimal strategy cooly places 100% of the investable funds in the riskfree asset.

The preceding does not imply that the growth-optimal portfolio necessarily is far from the mean–variance efficient frontier (although this *may* be the case [see e.g. Hakansson, 1971a]). It will generally be close to the MV-efficient frontier, especially when returns are fairly symmetric. And as shown in Section 8, the mean–variance model can in some cases be used to (sequentially) generate a close approximation to the growth-optimal portfolios.

Other properties of the Kelly criterion can be found in MacLean, Ziemba & Blazenko [1992, table 1].

3.2. Capital growth vs. expected utility

Based on (10), the uniqueness properties implied by (15), and the law of large numbers, it is undisputable, as noted in the previous subsection, that the growth-optimal strategy almost surely generates more capital (under basic reinvestment) in the long run than any other strategy which does not converge to it. At the same time, however, we observed that the growth-optimal strategy is consistent with logarithmic end-of-period utility of wealth *only*. This clearly implies that there must be 'reasonable' utility functions which value almost surely less capital in the long run more than they value the distribution generated by the Kelly criterion.

Consider the family

$$u(w) = \frac{1}{\gamma} w^{\gamma}, \qquad \gamma < 1, \tag{16}$$

to which $u(w) = \ln(w)$ belongs via $\gamma = 0$, and let $\langle x_t(\gamma)\rangle$ be the optimal portfolio sequence generated by solving

$$\operatorname*{Max}_{x_t} E\left[\frac{1}{\gamma} w_t^{\gamma}\right] \text{ at each } t-1.$$

For simplicity, consider the case of stationary returns. Since $x_t(\gamma) \neq x_t(0) = x_t^*$, it is evident that

$$\operatorname{Max} E\left[\frac{1}{\gamma} w_t(\langle x_t(\gamma)\rangle)^{\gamma}\right] > E\left[\frac{1}{\gamma} w_t(\langle x_t^*\rangle)^{\gamma}\right], \quad \gamma \neq 0 \tag{17}$$

even though there exist numbers $a > 1$ and $T(\epsilon)$ such that

$$\Pr\{w_t(\langle x_t(\gamma)\rangle) < w_0 a^t < w_t(\langle x_t^*\rangle)\} \geq 1-\epsilon, \quad t > T(\epsilon) \tag{18}$$

for every $(1 >)\ \epsilon > 0$.

Many a student of investment has stubbed his toe by interpreting (18) to mean that $\langle x_t^*\rangle$ generates higher expected utility than, say, $\langle x_t(\gamma)\rangle$. (17) and (18) may seem like a paradox but clearly implies that the geometric mean criterion *does not* give rise to a 'universally best' investment strategy.

The intuition behind this truth is as follows. For $\gamma < 0$ in (16), (17) and (18) occur because, despite the fact that the wealth distribution for $\langle x_t(\gamma)\rangle$ lies almost entirely to the *left* of the wealth distribution for $\langle x_t^*\rangle$, the lower tail of the distribution for $\langle x_t(\gamma)\rangle$ is shorter and (imperceptibly) thinner than the (bounded) left tail of the growth-optimal distribution. Thus, for negative powers, very small adverse changes in the lower tail overpower the value of almost surely ending up with a higher compound return. Conversely, for $\gamma > 0$, it is the *longer* (though admittedly very thin) upper tail that gives rise to (17) in the presence of (18) even though, again, the wealth distribution for $\langle x_t(\gamma)\rangle$ lies almost entirely to the *left* of the wealth distribution for $\langle x_t^*\rangle$.

4. Conditions for capital growth

As already noted, the determinants of whether capital will grow or decline (almost surely) in the long run are given by (12) and (11). Conditions (1)–(2) insure that (12) is feasible; in the absence of (1)–(2), positive growth may be infeasible. If a positive long-run growth rate (bounded away from zero) is achievable, then the growth-optimal strategy will find it. Thus we can state:

Theorem. *In the absence of (1) and (2), a necessary and sufficient condition for long-run capital growth to be feasible is that the growth-optimal strategy achieves a positive growth rate, i.e. that for some* $\epsilon > 0$ *and large* T

$$E[\ln R_t(x_t^*)] \geq \epsilon, \quad t \geq T \tag{19}$$

For $\gamma < 0$, the objective functions in (16) attain long-run growth rates of capital between those of the risk-free asset and of the growth-optimal strategy. But for $\gamma > 0$, the long run growth-rate may be negative. Consider for a moment the utility function $u(w) = w^{1/2}$, one of the most frequently cited examples of 'substantial' risk aversion since Bernoulli's time. Even this venerable function may, however, lead to (almost sure) ruin in the long-run: suppose, for example, that the riskfree asset yields 2% per period and that there is only one risky asset, which gives either a loss of 8.2% with probability 0.9, or a gain of 206% with probability 0.1. The optimal policy then calls for investing the fraction 1.5792 in the risky asset (by borrowing the fraction 0.5792 of current wealth to complete the financing) in each period. But the average compound growth rate g_t in (10) will now tend to -0.00756, or $-3/4\%$. Thus, expected utility 'grows' as capital itself almost surely vanishes.

What this example illustrates is that risk aversion plus a favorable return structure [see (1)–(3)] are *not* sufficient to insure capital growth in the basic reinvestment case.

5. Relationship to other long-run investment models

As shown in Section 3, the growth-optimal investment strategy has its traditional origin in arguments concerning capital growth and the law of large numbers. But it can also be derived strictly from an expected utility perspective — but only as a member of a small family.

Let n be the number of periods left to a terminal horizon point at time 0. Assume that wealth at that point, w_0, has utility $U_0(w_0)$, where $U_0' > 0$ everywhere and $U_0'' < 0$ for large w_0. Then, with one period to go, we have the single-period portfolio problem

$$U_1(w_1) \equiv \underset{z_1|w_1}{\text{Max}}\ E[U_0(w_0(z_1))]$$

where $U_1(w_1)$ is the induced, or derived, utility of wealth w_1 at time 1 and the difference equation (6) has been trivially modified to

$$w_{n-1} = \sum_{i=2}^{M_n}(1 + r_{in})z_{in} + w_n(1 + r_{1n}), \quad n = 1, 2, \ldots. \tag{20}$$

Thus, with n periods to go, we obtain

$$U_n(w_n) \equiv \underset{z_n|w_n}{\text{Max}}\ E[U_{n-1}(w_{n-1}(z_n))], \quad n = 1, 2, \ldots \tag{21}$$

where (21) is a standard recursive equation.

The induced utility of current wealth, $U_n(w_n)$, of course, generally depends on all the inputs to the problem, that is the utility of terminal wealth U_0, the joint distribution functions of future returns $F_n, \ldots, F_1$, and the future interest rates $r_{1n}, \ldots, r_{11}$. But there are two rather interesting special cases. The first is the case in which the induced utility functions $U_n(w_n)$ depend *only* on the terminal utility function U_0. This occurs when the returns are independent from period to period and $U_0(w_0)$ is isoelastic, i.e.

$$U_0(w_0) = \frac{1}{\gamma} w_0^\gamma, \text{ some } \gamma < 1.$$

As first shown by Mossin [1968], (21) now gives

$$\begin{aligned} U_n(w_n) &= a_n U_0(w_n) + b_n \\ &\sim U_0(w_n) \end{aligned}$$

(where $\sim$ means equivalent to) since a_n and b_n are constraints with a_n positive. The optimal investment policy is both myopic and proportional, i.e.

$$z_{in}^*(w_n) = x_{in}(\gamma) w_n, \text{ all } i$$

where the $x_{in}(\gamma)$ are constants.

The second special case obtains when returns are independent from period to period, interest rates are deterministic, and the terminal utility function reflects hyperbolic absolute risk aversion, that is (Hakansson 1971c)

$$U_0(w_0) = \begin{cases} \dfrac{1}{\gamma}(w_0 + \phi)^\gamma, & \gamma < 1, \\ \text{or} & \\ (\phi - w_0)^\gamma, & \gamma > 1, \ \phi \text{ large;} \\ \text{or} & \\ -\exp\{-\phi w_0\} & \phi > 0. \end{cases} \tag{22}$$

In the first subcase

$$U_n(w_n) = \frac{1}{\gamma}\left(w_n + \frac{\phi}{(1+r_1)\ldots(1+r_{1n})}\right)^\gamma \tag{23}$$

where (23) holds globally for $\phi \leq 0$ and locally for $\phi > 0$, i.e. for $w_n \geq L_n > 0$. The optimal investment policy is

$$z_{in}^*(w_n) = x_{in}(\gamma)\left(w_n + \frac{\phi}{(1+r_{11})\ldots(1+r_{1n})}\right), \quad i \geq 2.$$

In the other two subcases, a closed form solution holds only locally.

But the most interesting result associated with (21) is surprisingly general. Under mild conditions on $U_0(w_0)$, and independent (but nonstationary) returns from period to period, we obtain [Hakansson, 1974; see also Leland, 1972; Ross,

1974; Huberman and Ross 1983]:

$$u_n(w_n) \to \frac{1}{\gamma} w_n^\gamma \tag{24}$$

and, if returns are stationary,

$$z_{in}^*(w_n) \to x_{in}^*(\gamma) w_n. \tag{25}$$

Thus, the class of utility functions

$$u(w) = \frac{1}{\gamma} w^\gamma, \quad \gamma < 1, \tag{16}$$

the only family with constant relative risk aversion (ranging from 0 to infinity) and exhibiting myopic and proportional investment policies, is evidently applicable to a *large* class of long-run investors. The optimal policies above are not mean–variance efficient, but for reasonably symmetric return distributions, they come close to MV efficiency.

Since $\gamma = 0$ in (24) corresponds to logarithmic utility of wealth, the growth-optimal strategy is clearly a member of this elite family of long-run oriented investors. In other words, the geometric mean investment strategy has a solid foundation in utility theory as well.

6. Relationship to intertemporal consumption–investment models

Up to this point, we have examined the basic dynamic investment problem, i.e. without reference to cash inflows or outflows. Under some conditions, the inclusion of these factors is straightforward and does not materially affect the optimal investment policy. But a realistic model incorporating noncapital in- and outflows typically complicates the model substantially.

The basic dynamic consumption–investment model incorporates consumption and a labor income into the dynamic reinvestment model. Following Fisher [1936], wealth is viewed as a means to an end, namely consumption.

The basic difference equation (6) now becomes

$$w_t = \sum_{i=2}^{M_t} (r_{it} - r_{1t}) z_{it} + (1 + r_{1t})(w_{t-1} - c_t) + y_t, \quad t = 1, \ldots, T, \tag{26}$$

where c_t is the amount consumed in period t (set aside at the beginning of the period) and y_t is the labor income received at the end of period t.

Consistent with the foregoing, the individual's objective becomes

$$\text{Max } E[U(c_1, \ldots, c_T)]$$

subject to

$$c_t \geq 0, \text{ all } t$$

where U is assumed to be monotone, strictly concave, and to reflect impatience, i.e. considering the two consumption streams

$$(a,\ b,\ c_3, \ldots, c_T)$$
$$(b,\ a,\ c_3, \ldots, c_T), \quad a > b$$

the first is preferred to the second.

In order to attain tractability, several strong assumptions are usually imposed:

1) the individual's lifetime (horizon) is known,
2) interest rates are viewed as deterministic,
3) the labor income y_t is deterministic; its present value is thus

$$Y_{t-1} \equiv \frac{y_t}{r_{1t}} + \ldots + \frac{y_T}{(1+r_{1t})\ldots(1+r_{1T})},$$

4) the utility function is assumed to be additive, i.e.

$$U(c_1, \ldots, c_T) = u_1(c_1) + \alpha_1 u_2(c_2) + \ldots + \alpha_1 \ldots \alpha_{T-1} u_T(c_T), \tag{27}$$

where $u_t' > 0$, $u_t'' < 0$, and typically $\alpha_t < 1$, for all t, which implies that preferences are independent of past consumption.

Let

$$f_{t-1}(w_{t-1}) \ = \ \text{maximum expected utility at } t-1 \text{ given } w_{t-1}.$$

This gives

$$f_{t-1}(w_{t-1}) = \operatorname*{Max}_{c_t, z_t} \{u_t(c_t) + \alpha_t E[f_t(w_t)]\}, \quad t = 1, \ldots, T, \tag{28}$$

where $f_T(w_T) \equiv 0$ or $b_T(w_T)$

$$\text{subject to} \quad c_t \geq 0 \tag{29}$$
$$\Pr\{w_t \geq -Y_t\} = 1 \tag{30}$$
$$z_{it} \geq 0, \quad i \notin S_t \tag{31}$$

for each t, where $b_T(w_T)$ represents a possible bequest motive. It is apparent that $f_{t-1}(w_{t-1})$ represents the utility of wealth and that it is *induced* or *derived*; it clearly depends on everything in the model. Solving (28) recursively, it is evident that, under our assumptions concerning labor income and interest rates, Y_t can be exchanged for cash in the solution.

Suppose that in (27)

$$u_t(c_t) = \frac{1}{\gamma} c_t^{\gamma}, \quad \gamma < 1,\ t = 1, \ldots, T. \tag{32}$$

Then [Hakansson, 1970]

$$f_{t-1}(w_{t-1}) = A_{t-1}(w_{t-1} + Y_{t-1})^{\gamma} + B_{t-1},$$
$$c_t^*(w_{t-1}) = C_t(w_{t-1} + Y_{t-1}),$$

$$z_{it}^*(w_{t-1}) = (1 - C_t)x_{it\gamma}^*(w_{t-1} + Y_{t-1}), \quad i \geq 2,$$

and

$$z_{1t}^*(w_{t-1}) = w_{t-1} - c_t^* - \sum_{i=2}^{M_t} z_{it}^*(w_{t-1}),$$

where the A_t, B_t, and C_t are constants. Thus, the optimal consumption and investment policies are again proportional, not to w_{t-1} but to $w_{t-1} + Y_{t-1}$. The latter quantity is sometimes referred to as permanent income.

Note that when $\gamma = 0$ in (32), the consumer-investor does indeed employ the growth-optimal strategy to invested funds.

Finally, the model (28)–(31) has been extended in a number of directions, to incorporate a random lifetime, life insurance, a subsistence level constraint on consumption, a Markov process for the economy, and an uncertain income stream from labor — with limited success [see Hakansson 1969, 1971b, 1972; Miller, 1974]. In general, closed-form solutions do not exist when income streams, payment obligations, and interest rates are stochastic. In such cases, multi-stage stochastic programming models are helpful [see e.g. Mulvey & Ziemba, 1995].

7. Growth vs. security

Empirical evidence suggests that the average investor is more risk averse than the growth-optimal investor, with a risk-tolerance corresponding to $\gamma \approx -3$ in (16) [see e.g. Blume & Friend, 1975]. While real-world investors exhibit a wide range of attitudes towards risk, this means that the majority of investors are in effect willing to sacrifice a certain amount of growth in favor of less variability, or greater 'security'.

7.1 The discrete-time case

In view of the convergence results (24) and (25), it is evident that repeated employment of (16) for any $\gamma < 0$ attains an efficient tradeoff between growth and security, as defined above, for the long-run investor. The concept of 'efficiency' is thus employed in a sense analogous to that used in mean–variance analysis.

A number of more direct measures of the sacrifice of growth for security have also been examined. In particular, MacLean, Ziemba & Blazenko [1992] analyzed the tradeoffs based on three growth and three security measures. The three growth measures are:

1. $E(w_t(\langle x_t \rangle))]$, the expected wealth level after t periods;
2. $E[g_t]$, the mean compound growth rate over the first t periods;
3. $E[t : w_t(\langle x_t \rangle) \geq y]$, the mean first passage time to reach wealth level y;

while the three security measures are:

4. $\Pr\{w_t(\langle x_t \rangle) \geq y\}$, the probability that wealth level y will be reached in t periods;

5. $\Pr\{w_t(\langle x_t \rangle) \geq b_t,\ t = 1, 2, \ldots\}$, the probability that the investor's wealth is on or above a specified path;

6. $\Pr\{w_t(\langle x_t \rangle) \geq y$ before $w_t(\langle x_t \rangle) \leq b$, where $b < w_0 < y\}$, which includes the probability of doubling before halving.

Tradeoffs were generated via fractional Kelly strategies, i.e. strategies involving (stationary) mixtures of cash and the growth-optimal investment portfolio. Applied to a stationary environment, these strategies were shown to produce effective tradeoffs in that as growth declines, security increases. However, these tradeoffs, while easily computable, are generally not efficient, i.e. do not maximize security for a given (minimum) level of growth. Other comparisons involving the growth-optimal strategy and half Kelly or other strategies may be found in Ziemba & Hausch [1986], Rubinstein [1991], and Aucamp [1993].

7.2. *The continuous-time case*

Since transaction costs are zero under the perfect market assumption, it is natural to consider shorter and shorter periods between reinvestment decisions. In the limit, reinvestment takes place continuously. Assuming that the returns on risky assets can be described by diffusion processes, we obtain that optimal portfolios are mean–variance efficient in that the instantaneous variance is minimized for a given instantaneous expected return. The intuitive reason for this is that as the trading interval is shortened, the first two moments of the security's return become more and more dominant [see Samuelson, 1970]. The optimal portfolios also exhibit the separation property — as if returns over very short periods were normally distributed. Over any fixed interval, however, payoff distributions are, due to the compounding effect, usually lognormal. In other words, all investors with the same probability assessments, but regardless of risk attitude, invest in only two mutual funds, one of which is riskfree [Merton, 1971]. See also Karatzas, Lehoczky, Sethi and Shreve [1986] and Sethi and Taksar [1988].

In view of the above, it is evident that the tradeoff between growth and security generated by the fractional Kelly strategies in the continuous-time model when the wealth process is lognormal is efficient in a mean–variance sense. Li [1993] has addressed the growth vs. security question for the two asset case while Li & Ziemba [1992] and Dohi, Tanaka, Kaio & Osaki [1994] have done so when there are n risky assets that are jointly lognormally distributed.

8. Applications

8.1. *Asset allocation*

In view of the myopic property of the optimal investment policy in the dynamic reinvestment problem [see (24) and (25)], it is natural to apply (15) for different values of γ to the problem of choosing investment portfolios over time. In particular, the choice of broad asset categories, also known as the asset allocation problem, lends itself especially well to such treatment. Thus, to implement the growth-optimal strategy, for example, we merely solve (15) subject to relevant constraints (on borrowing when available and on short positions) at the beginning of each period.

To implement the model, it is necessary to estimate the joint distribution function for next period's returns. Since all moments and comoments matter, one way to do this is to employ the joint empirical distribution for the previous n periods. This approach provides a simple and realistic means of generating nonstationary scenarios of the possible outcomes over time. The raw distribution may of course may be modified in any number of ways, for example via Stein estimators [Jorion, 1985, 1986, 1991; Grauer & Hakansson, 1995], an inflation adapter [Hakansson, 1989], or some other method.

Grauer and Hakansson applied the dynamic reinvestment model in a number of settings with up to 16 different risk attitudes γ under both quarterly and annual portfolio revision. In the domestic setting [Grauer & Hakansson, 1982, 1985, 1986], the model was employed to construct and rebalance portfolios composed of U.S. stocks, corporate bonds, government bonds, and a riskfree asset. Borrowing was ruled out in the first article while margin purchases were permitted in the other two. The third article also included small stocks as a separate investment vehicle. On the whole, the growth-optimal strategy lived up to its reputation. On the basis of the empirical probability assessment approach, quarterly rebalancing, and a 32-quarter estimating period applied to 1934–1992, the growth-optimal strategy outperformed all the others — with borrowing permitted, it earned an average annual compound return of nearly 15%.

In Grauer & Hakansson [1987], the model was applied to a global environment by including in the universe the four principal U.S. asset categories and up to fourteen non-U.S. equity and bond categories. The results showed that the gains from including non-U.S. asset classes in the universe were remarkably large (in some cases statistically significant), especially for the highly risk-averse strategies. With leverage permitted and quarterly rebalancing, the geometric mean strategy again came out on top, generating an annual compound return of 27% over the 1970–1986 period. A different study examined the impact from adding three separate real estate investment categories to the universe of available categories [Grauer & Hakansson, 1994b]. Finally, Grauer, Hakansson & Shen [1990] examined the asset allocation problem when the universe of risky assets was composed of twelve equal- and value-weighted industry components of the U.S. stock market.

Mulvey [1993] developed a multi-period model of asset allocation which incorporates transaction costs, including price impact. The objective function is a general concave utility function. A computational version developed by Mulvey & Vladimirou [1992] focused on the isoelastic class of functions in which the objective was to maximize the expected utility of wealth at the end of the planning horizon. This model, like those based on the empirical distribution approach, can handle assets possessing skewed returns, such as options and other derivatives, and can be extended to include liabilities [see Mulvey & Ziemba, 1995]. Based on historical data over the period 1979 to 1988, this research, based on multi-stage stochastic programming, showed that efficiencies could be gained vis-à-vis myopic models in the presence of transaction costs by taking advantage of the network or linear structure of the problem.

Mean–variance approximations. A number of authors have argued that, in the single period case, power function policies can be well approximated by MV policies, e.g. Levy & Markowitz [1979], Pulley [1981, 1983], Kallberg & Ziemba [1979, 1983], and Kroll, Levy & Markowitz [1984]. However, there is an opposing intuition which suggests that the power functions' strong aversion to low returns and bankruptcy will lead them to select portfolios that are not MV-efficient, e.g. Hakansson [1971a] and Grauer [1981, 1986]. It is therefore of interest to know whether the power policies differ from the corresponding MV and quadratic policies when returns are compounded over many periods.

Let μ_{it} be the expected rate of return on security i at time t and σ_{ijt} be the covariance between the returns on securities i and j at time t. Then the MV investment problem is

$$\max_{x_t} \{T(1+\mu_t) - \tfrac{1}{2}\sigma_t^2\},$$

subject to the usual constraints. The MV approximation to the power functions in (16) are obtained [Ohlson, 1975; Pulley, 1981] when

$$T = \frac{1}{1-\gamma}.$$

Under certain conditions this result holds exactly in continuous time [see Merton, 1973, 1980].

With quarterly revision, the MV model was found to approximate the exact power function model very well [Grauer & Hakansson, 1993]. But with annual revision, the portfolio compositions and returns earned by the more risk averse power function strategies bore little resemblance to those of the corresponding MV approximations. Quadratic approximations proved even less satisfactory in this case. These results contrast somewhat with those of Kallberg & Ziemba [1983], who in the quadratic case with smaller variances obtained good approximations for horizons up to a whole year [see also MacLean, Ziemba & Blazenko, 1992].

8.2. *Growth–security tradeoffs*

The growth vs. security model has been applied to four well-known gambling-investment problems: blackjack, horse race wagering, lotto games, and commodity trading with stock index futures. In at least the first three cases, the basic investment situation is unfavorable for the average player. However, systems have been developed that yield a positive expected return. The various applications use a variety of growth and security measures that appear to model each situation well. The size of the optimal investment gamble also varies greatly, from over half to less than one millionth of one's fortune.

Blackjack. By wagering more in favorable situations and less or nothing when the deck is unfavorable, an average weighted edge is about 2%. An approximation to provide insight into the long-run behavior of a player's fortune is to assume that the game is a Bernoulli trial with a probability of success equal to 0.51. With a 2% edge, the optimal wager is also 2% of one's fortune. Professional blackjack teams often use a fractional Kelly wagering strategy with the fraction drawn from the interval 0.2 to 0.8. For further discussion, see Gottlieb [1985] and Maclean, Ziemba & Blazenko [1992].

Horseracing. There is considerable evidence supporting the proposition that it is possible to identify races where there is a substantial edge in the bettor's favor (see the survey by Hausch & Ziemba [1995] in this volume). At thoroughbred racetracks, one can find about 2–4 profitable wagers with an edge of 10% or more on an average day. These opportunities arise because (1) the public has a distaste for the high probability–low payoff wagers, and (2) the public is unable to properly evaluate the worth of multiple horse place and show and exotic wagers because of their complexity; for example, in a ten-horse race there are 120 possible show finishes, each with a different payoff and chance of occurrence. In this situation, interesting tradeoffs between growth and security arise as well.

The Kentucky Derby represents an interesting special case because of the long distance (1 1/4 miles), the fact that the horses have not previously run this distance, and the fame of the race. Hausch, Bain & Ziemba [1995] tabulated the results from Kelly and half Kelly wagers using the system in Ziemba & Hausch [1987] over the 61-year period 1934–1994. They also report the results from using a filter rule based on the horse's breeding.

Lotto games. Lotteries tend to have very low expected payoffs, typically on the order of 40 to 50%. One way to 'beat' parimutuel games is to wager on unpopular numbers — see Hausch & Ziemba [1995] for a survey. But even when the odds are 'turned' favorable, the optimal Kelly wagers are extremely small and it may take a very long time to reach substantial profits with high probability. Often an initial wealth level in the seven figures is required to justify the purchase of even a single $1 ticket. Comparisons between fractional and full Kelly strategies can be found in MacLean, Ziemba & Blazenko [1992].

Commodity trading. Repeated investments in commodity trades can be modeled as a capital growth problem via suitable modifications for margin requirements, daily mark-to-the-market procedures, and other practical details. An interesting example is the turn-of-the-year effect exhibited by U.S. small stocks in January.

One way to benefit from this anomaly is to take long positions in a small stock index and short positions in large stock indices, because the transaction costs (commissions plus market impact) are less than a tenth of what they would be by transacting in the corresponding basket of securities. Using data from 1976 through January 1987, Clark & Ziemba [1987] calculated that the growth-optimal strategy would invest 74% of one's capital in this opportunity. Hence fractional Kelly strategies are suggested. See also Ziemba [1994].

9. Summary

Capital growth theory is useful in the analysis of many dynamic investment situations, with many attractive properties. In the basic reinvestment case, the growth-optimal investment strategy, also known as the Kelly criterion, almost surely leads to more capital in the long run than any other investment policy which does not converge to it. It never risks ruin, and also has the appealing property that it asymptotically minimizes the expected time to reach a given level of capital. The Kelly criterion implies, and is implied by, logarithmic utility of wealth (only) at the end of each period; thus, its relative risk aversion equals 1, which makes it more risk-tolerant than the average investor. As a result, tradeoffs between growth and security have found application in a rich set of circumstances.

The fact that the growth-optimal investment strategy is proportional to beginning-of-period wealth is of great practical value. But perhaps the most significant property of the Kelly criterion is that it is myopic not only when returns are nonstationary and independent but also when they obey a Markov process. In the dynamic investment model with a given terminal objective function, the growth-optimal strategy is a member of the set to which the optimal policy converges as the horizon becomes more distant. Finally, the Kelly criterion is optimal in many environments in which consumption, noncapital income, and payment obligations are present.

References

Algoet, P.H., and T.M. Cover (1988). Asymptotic optimality and asymtotic equipartition properties at log-optimum investment. *Ann. Prob.*, 16, 876–898.

Aucamp, D. (1993). On the extensive number of plays to achieve superior performance with the geometric mean strategy. *Manage. Sci.* 39, 1163–1172.

Bell, R.M., and T.M. Cover (1980). Competitive optimality of logarithmic investment. *Math. Oper. Res.* 5, 161–166.

Bell, R., and T.M. Cover (1988). Game-theoretic optimal portfolios. *Manage. Sci.* 34, 724–733.

Bernoulli, D. (1738/1954). Exposition of a new theory on the measurement of risk (translation Louise Summer). *Econometrica*, 22, 23–36.

Blume, M.E., and I. Friend (1975). The asset structure of individual portfolios and some implications for utility functions. *J. Finance* 30, 585–603.

Breiman, L. (1960). Investment policies for expanding business optimal in a long-run sense. *Nav. Res. Logist. Q.* 7, 647–651.

Breiman, L. (1961). Optimal gambling system for favorable games, in: *Proc. 4th Berkeley Symp. on Mathematics, Statistics and Probability* 1, 63–68.

Chamberlain, G. (1983). A characterization of the distributions that imply mean–variance utility functions. *J. Econ. Theory* 29, 185–201.

Chernoff, H. (1980/1981). An analysis of the Massachusetts Numbers Game, Tech. Rep. No. 23, MIT Department of Mathematics, Massachusetts Institute of Technology, Cambridge, MA.,

1980; shortened version published in *Math. Intell.* 3, 166–172.

Clark, R., and W.T. Ziemba (1987). Playing the turn of the year with index futures. *Oper. Res.* 35, 799–813.

Dohi, T., H. Tanaka, N. Kaio and S. Osaki (1994). Alternative Growth Versus Security in Continuous Dynamic Trading. *Eur. J. Oper. Res.*, in press.

Efron, B., and C. Morris (1973). Stein's estimation rule and its competitors — An empirical Bayes approach. *J. Am. Stat. Assoc.* 68, 117–130.

Efron, B., and C. Morris (1975). Data analysis using Stein's estimator and its generalizations. *J. Am. Stat. Assoc.* 70, 311–319.

Efron, B., and C. Morris (1977). Stein's paradox in statistics. *Sci. Am.* 236, 119–127.

Epstein, R.A. (1977). *The Theory of Gambling and Statistical Logic*, 2nd edition, Academic Press, New York, NY.

Ethier, S.N. (1987). The Proportional Bettor's Fortune, in: *Proc. 7th Int. Conf. on Gambling and Risk Taking*, Department of Economics, University of Nevada, Reno, NV.

Ethier, S.N., and S. Tavare (1983). The proportional bettor's return on investment. *J. Appl. Probab.* 20, 563–573.

Feller, W. (1962). *An Introduction to Probability Theory and Its Applications*, 1, 2nd edition, John Wiley & Sons, New York, NY.

Ferguson, T.S. (1965). Betting systems which minimize the probability of ruin. *J. Soc. Appl. Math.* 13, 795–818.

Finkelstein, M., and R. Whitley (1981). Optimal strategies for repeated games. *Adv. Appl. Prob.* 13, 415–428.

Fisher, I. (1930). *The Theory of Interest*, New York, MacMillan, reprinted Augustus Kelley, 1965.

Friedman, J. (1982). Using the Kelly criterion to select optimal blackjack bets, Mimeo, Stanford University.

Goldman, B. (1974). A negative report on the 'near optimality' of the max-expected log policy as applied to bounded utilities for long-lived programs. *J. Financ. Econ.* 1, 97–103.

Gottlieb, G. (1984). An optimal betting strategy for repeated games, Mimeo, New York University.

Gottlieb, G. (1985). An analystic derivation of blackjack win rates. *Oper. Res.* 33, 971–988.

Grauer, R.R. (1981). A comparison of growth optimal and mean variance investment policies. *J. Financ. Quant. Anal.* 16, 1–21.

Grauer, R.R. (1986). Normality, Solvency and Portfolio Choice, *J. Financ. Quant. Anal.* 21, 265–278.

Grauer, R.R., and N.H. Hakansson (1982). Higher return, lower risk: Historical returns on long-run, actively managed portfolios of stocks, bonds and bills, 1936–1978. *Financ. Anal. J.* 38, 39–53.

Grauer, R.R., and N.H. Hakansson (1985). Returns on levered, actively managed long-run portfolios of stocks, bonds and bills, 1934–1984. *Financ. Anal. J.* 41, 24–43.

Grauer, R.R., and N.H. Hakansson (1986). A half-century of returns on levered and unlevered portfolios of stocks, bonds, and bills, with and without small stocks. *J. Bus.* 59, 287–318.

Grauer, R.R., and N.H. Hakansson (1987). Gains from international diversification: 1968–85 returns on portfolios of stocks and bonds. *J. Finance* 42, 721–739.

Grauer, R.R., and N.H. Hakansson (1993). On the use of mean–variance and quadratic approximations in implementing dynamic investment strategies: A comparison of returns and investment policies. *Manage. Sci.* 39, 856–871.

Grauer, R.R., and N.H. Hakansson (1994a). On timing the market: The empirical probability approach with an inflation adapter, Manuscript.

Grauer, R.R., and N.H. Hakansson (1994b). Gains from diversifying into real estate: Three decades of portfolio returns based on the dynamic investment model, *Real Estate Economics* 23, 119–159.

Grauer, R.R., and N.H. Hakansson (1995). Stein and CAPM estimators of the means in asset allocation, Working Paper (forthcoming)

Grauer, R.R., N.H. Hakansson and F.C. Shen (1990). Industry rotation in the U.S. stock market: 1934-1986 returns on passive, semi-passive, and active strategies. *J. Banking Finance* 14, 513–535.

Griffin, P. (1985). Different measures of win rate for optimal proportional betting. *Manage. Sci.* 30, 1540–1547.

Hakansson, N. (1969). Optimal investment and consumption strategies under risk, an uncertain lifetime, and insurance. *Int. Econ. Rev.* 10, 443–466.

Hakansson, N. (1970). Optimal investment and consumption strategies under risk for a class of utility functions. *Econometrica* 38, 587–607.

Hakansson, N. (1971a). Capital growth and the mean–variance approach to portfolio selection. *J. Financ. Quant. Anal.* 6, 517–557.

Hakansson, N. (1971b). Optimal entrepreneurial decisions in a completely stochastic environment. *Manage. Sci., Theory* 17, 427–449.

Hakansson, N. (1971c). On optimal myopic portfolio policies, with and without serial correlation of yields. *J. Bus.* 44, 324–234.

Hakansson, N. (1972). Sequential investment–consumption strategies for individuals and endowment funds with lexicographic preferences, in: J. Bicksler (ed.), *Methodology in Finance — Investments*, D.C. Heath & Company, Lexington, MA, pp. 175–203.

Hakansson, N. (1974). Convergence to isoelastic utility and policy in multiperiod portfolio choice. *J. Financ. Econ.* 1, 201–224.

Hakansson, N. (1979). A characterization of optimal multiperiod portfolio policies, in: E. Elton and M. Gruber (eds.), *Portfolio Theory, 25 Years Later*, Amsterdam, North Holland, pp. 169–177.

Hakansson, N. (1989). On the value of adapting to inflation in sequential portfolio decisions, in: B. Fridman and L. Ostman (eds.), *Accounting Development — Some Perspectives*, The Economic Research Institute, Stockholm School of Economics, pp. 151–185.

Hakansson, N., and B. Miller (1975). Compound-return mean–variance efficient portfolios never risk ruin. *Manage. Sci.* 22, 391–400.

Hausch, D., and W.T. Ziemba (1985). Transactions costs, extent of inefficiencies, entries and multiple wagers in a racetrack betting model. *Manage. Sci.* 31, 381–392.

Hausch, D., and W.T. Ziemba (1990). Arbitrage strategies for cross-track betting on major horse races. *J. Bus.* 63, 61–78.

Hausch, D., and W.T. Ziemba (1995). Efficiency of sports and lottery betting markets, in: R. Jarrow, V. Maksimovic and W.T. Ziemba (eds.), *Finance*, Handbooks in Operations Research and Management Science, Vol 9, Elsevier, Amsterdam, pp. 545–580 (this volume).

Hausch, D., W.T. Ziemba and M. Rubinstein (1981). Efficiency of the market for racetrack betting. *Manage. Sci.* 27, 1435–1452.

Hausch, D., R. Bain and W.T. Ziemba (1995). Wagering on the Kentucky Derby, 1934–1994, Mimeo, University of British Columbia.

Huberman, G., and S. Ross (1983). Portfolio turnpike theorems, risk aversion and regularly varying utility functions. *Econometrica* 51, 1345–1361.

Ibbotson Associates, Inc. (1986). *Stocks, Bonds, Bills and Inflation: Market Results for 1926–1985*, Ibbotson Associates, Inc., Chicago.

Ibbotson Associates, Inc. (1988). *Stocks, Bonds, Bills and Inflation: 1987 Yearbook*, Ibbotson Associates, Inc., Chicago.

James, W., and C. Stein (1961). Estimation with quadratic loss, in: *Proc. 4th Berkeley Symp. on Probability and Statistics I*, Berkeley, University of California Press, pp. 361–379.

Jobson, J.D., and B. Korkie (1981). Putting Markowitz theory to work. *J. Portfolio Manag.* 7, 70–74.

Jobson, J.D., B. Korkie and V. Ratti (1979). Improved estimation for Markowitz portfolios using James–Stein type estimators. in: *Proc. American Statistical Association*, Business and Economics Statistics Section 41, 279–284.

Jorion, P. (1985). International portfolio diversification with estimation risk. *J. Bus.* 58, 259–278.

Jorion, P. (1986). Bayes–Stein estimation for portfolio analysis. *J. Financ. Quant. Anal.* 21, 279–292.

Jorion, P (1991). Bayesian and CAPM estimators of the means: Implications for portfolio selection. *J. Banking Finance* 15, 717–727.

Kalymon, B. (1971). Estimation risk in the portfolio selection model. *J. Financ. Quant. Anal.* 6, 559–582.

Kallberg, J.G., and W.T. Ziemba (1979). On the robustness of the Arrow–Pratt risk aversion measure. *Econ. Lett.* 2, 21–26.

Kallberg, J.G., and W.T. Ziemba (1983). Comparison of alternative utility functions in portfolio selection problems. *Manage. Sci.* 9, 1257–1276.

Karatzas, I., J. Lehoczky, S.P. Sethi and S.F. Shreve (1986). Explicit Solution of a General Consumption/Investment Problem. *Math. Oper. Res.* 11, 261–294.

Kelly, J.L., Jr. (1956). A new interpretation of information rate. *Bell Syst. Tech. J.* 35 917–926.

Kroll, Y., H. Levy and H. Markowitz (1984). Mean–variance versus direct utility maximization. *J. Finance* 39, 47–75.

Latane, H. (1959). Criteria for choice among risky ventures. *J. Polit. Econ.* 67, 144–145.

Leland, H. (1972). On turnpike portfolios, in: K. Shell and G.P. Szego (eds.), *Mathematical Methods in Investment and Finance*, Amsterdam, North-Holland.

Levy, H., and H. Markowitz (1979). Approximating expected utility by a function of mean and variance. *Am. Econ. Rev.* 69, 308–317.

Li, Y. (1993). Growth–security investment strategy for long and short runs. *Manage. Sci.* 39, 915–934.

Li, Y., and W.T. Ziemba (1992). Security aspects of optimal growth models with minimum expected time criteria, Mimeo, University of British Columbia, Canada.

Loistl, O. (1976). The erroneous approximation of expected utility by means of a Taylor's series expansion: Analytic and computational results. *Am. Econ. Rev.* 66, 904–910.

MacLean, L.C., and W.T. Ziemba (1986). Growth versus security in a risky investment model, in: F. Archetti, G. DiPillo and M. Lucertini (eds.), *Stochastic Programming*, Springer Verlag, pp. 78–87.

MacLean, L.C., and W.T. Ziemba (1990). Growth–security profiles in capital accumulation under risk. *Ann. Oper. Res.* 31, 501–509.

MacLean, L.C., and W.T. Ziemba (1994). Capital growth and proportional investment strategies, Mimeo, Dalhousie University.

MacLean, L.C., W.T. Ziemba and G. Blazenko (1992). Growth versus security in dynamic investment analysis. *Manage. Sci.* 38, 1562–1585.

Markowitz, H.M. (1959). *Portfolio Selection: Efficient Diversification of Investments*. John Wiley & Sons, Inc., New York, NY.

Markowitz, H. (1976). Investment for the long run: New evidence for an old rule. *J. Finance* 31, 1273–1286.

Merton, R.C. (1971). Optimal consumption and portfolio rules in a continuous-time model. *J. Econ. Theory* 3, 373–413.

Merton, R.C. (1973). An intertemporal capital asset pricing model. *Econometrica* 41, 867–887.

Merton, R.C. (1980). On estimating the expected return on the market: An exploratory investigation. *J. Financ. Econ.* 8, 323–361.

Miller, B.L. (1974). Optimal consumption with a stochastic income stream. *Econometrica* 42, 253–266.

Mossin, J. (1968). Optimal multiperiod portfolio policies. *J. Bus.* 41, 215–229.

Mulvey, J.M. (1993). Incorporating transaction costs in models for asset allocation, in: *Financial Optimization*, S. Zenios (ed.) Cambridge University Press.

Mulvey, J.M., and H. Vladimirou (1992). Stochastic network programming for financial planning problems. *Manage. Sci.* 38, 1642–1664.

Mulvey, J.M., and W.T. Ziemba (1995). Asset and liability allocation in a global environment. in: R. Jarrow, V. Maksimovic and W.T. Ziemba (eds.), *Finance*, Handbooks in Operations Research and Management Science, Vol 9, Elsevier, Amsterdam, pp. 435–464 (this volume).

Ohlson, J.A. (1975). The asymptotic validity of quadratic utility as the trading interval approaches zero, in: W.T. Ziemba and R.G. Vickson (eds.), *Stochastic Optimization Models in Finance*, Academic Press, New York, NY.

Pulley, L.B. (1981). A general mean–variance approximation to expected utility for short holding periods. *J. Financ. Quant. Anal.* 16, 361–373.

Pulley, L.B. (1983). Mean–variance approximation to expected logarithmic utility. *Oper. Res.* 31, 685–696.

Ritter, J.R. (1988). The buying and selling behavior of individual investors at the turn of the year: Evidence of price pressure effects. *J. Finance* 43, 701–719.

Roll, R. (1983). Was ist das? The turn of the year effect and the return premia of small firms. *J. Portfolio Manag.* 10, 18–28.

Ross, S. (1974). Portfolio turnpike theorems for constant policies. *J. Financ. Econ.* 1, 171–198.

Rotando, L.M., and E.O. Thorp (1992). The Kelly criterion and the stock market. *Am. Math. Mon.* December, 922–931.

Rubinstein, M. (1977). The strong case for log as the premier model for financial modeling, in: H. Levy and M. Sarnat (eds.), *Financial Decisions Under Uncertainty*, Academic Press, New York, NY.

Rubinstein, M. (1991). Continuously rebalanced investment strategies. *J. Portfolio Manage.* 17, 78–81.

Samuelson, P.A. (1970). The fundamental approximation theorem of portfolio analysis in terms of means, variances, and higher moments. *Rev. Econ. Studies* 36, 537–542.

Samuelson, P.A. (1971). The 'fallacy' of maximizing the geometric mean in long sequences of investing or gambling. *Proc. Nat. Acad. Sci.* 68, 2493–2496.

Samuelson, P.A. (1977). St. Petersburg paradoxes: Defanged, dissected, and historically described. *J. Econ. Lit.* XV, 24–55.

Sethi, S.P. and M.I. Taksar (1988). A Note on Merton's Optimum Consumption and Portfolio Rules in a Continuous-Time Model. *J. Econ. Theory* 46, 395–401.

Stein, C. (1955). Inadmissibility of the usual estimator for the mean of a multivariate normal distribution, in: *Proc. 3rd Berkeley Symp. on Probability and Statistics I*, University of California Press, Berkeley, CA, pp. 197–206.

Thorp, E.O. (1966). *Beat the Dealer*, 2nd edition, Random House, New York, NY.

Thorp, E.O. (1975). Portfolio choice and the Kelly criterion, in: W.T. Ziemba and R.G. Vickson (eds.), *Stochastic Optimization Models in Finance*, Academic Press, New York, NY.

Williams, J. (1936). Speculation and carryover. *Q. J. Econ.* L, 436–455.

Wu, M.G.H., and W.T. Ziemba (1990). Growth versus security tradeoffs in dynamic investment analysis, Mimeo, University of British Columbia, B.C.

Ziemba, W.T. (1994). Investing in the turn of the year effect in the U.S. futures markets. *Interfaces* 24, 46–61.

Ziemba, W.T., and D.B. Hausch (1986). *Betting at the Racetrack*, Dr. Z Investments, Inc., Los Angeles and Vancouver.

Ziemba, W.T., and D.B. Hausch (1987). *Dr. Z's Beat the Racetrack*, William Morrow, New York (revised and expanded second edition of Ziemba–Hausch, *Beat the Racetrack*, Harcourt, Brace and Jovanovich, 1984).

Ziemba, W.T., C. Parkan and R. Brooks-Hill (1974). Calculation of investment portfolios with risk-free borrowing and lending. *Manage. Sci.* 21, 209–222.

Ziemba, W.T., S.L. Brumelle, A. Gautier and S.L. Schwartz (1986). *Dr. Z's 6/49 Lotto Guidebook*, Dr. Z Investments, Inc., Los Angeles and Vancouver.

Ziemba, W.T. and R.G. Vickson (eds.) (1975). Stochastic Optimization Models in Finance, Academic Press, New York, N.Y.

R. Jarrow et al., Eds., *Handbooks in OR & MS, Vol. 9*

Chapter 4

The Arbitrage Pricing Theory and Multifactor Models of Asset Returns

Gregory Connor
BARRA International Ltd, 1 Whittington Ave, London EC3V1LE, United Kingdom

Robert A. Korajczyk
Kellogg Graduate School of Management, Northwestern University, 2001 Sheridan Road, Evanston, IL 60208-2006, U.S.A.

1. Introduction

The Arbitrage Pricing Theory (APT) of Ross [1976, 1977], and extensions of that theory, constitute an important branch of asset pricing theory and one of the primary alternatives to the Capital Asset Pricing Model (CAPM). In this chapter we survey the theoretical underpinnings, econometric testing, and applications of the APT. We aim for variety in viewpoint without attempting to be all-inclusive. Where necessary, we refer the reader to the primary literature for more complete treatments of the various research areas we discuss.

In Section 2 we discuss factor modelling of asset returns. The APT relies fundamentally on a factor model of asset returns. Section 3 describes theoretical derivations of the APT pricing restriction. Section 4 surveys the evidence from estimates and tests of the APT. In Section 5 we discuss several additional empirical topics in applying multifactor models of asset returns. We survey applications of the APT to problems in investments and corporate finance in Section 6. We provide some concluding comments in Section 7.

2. Strict and approximate factor models

Stock and bond returns are characterized by a very large cross-sectional sample (in excess of 10,000 simultaneous return observations in some studies) with strong comovements. The fundamental sources of these comovements are not always obvious and are not easily measured. Such a statistical system, where a few unobservable sources of system-wide variation affect many random variables, lends itself naturally to factor modelling. The APT begins by assuming that asset returns follow a factor model.

In a factor model, the random return of each security is a linear combination of a small number of common, or pervasive, factors, plus an asset-specific random variable. Let n denote the number of assets and k the number of factors. Let f denote the k-vector of random factors, B the $n \times k$ matrix of linear coefficients representing assets' sensitivities to movements in the factors (called factor betas or factor loadings), and ε the n-vector of asset-specific random variables (called the idiosyncratic returns). We can write the n-vector of returns, r, as expected returns plus the sum of two sources of random return, factor return and idiosyncratic return:

$$r = E[r] + Bf + \varepsilon, \tag{1}$$

where $E[f] = 0$, $E[\varepsilon] = 0$, and $E[f\varepsilon'] = 0$. The beta matrix, B, is defined by the standard linear projection, $B = E[(r - E[r])f'](E[ff'])^{-1}$. Given a vector of returns, r, and a vector of zero-mean variates, f, the standard linear projection divides the returns into expected returns, k linear components correlated with f, and zero-mean idiosyncratic returns uncorrelated with f. The standard linear projection imposes no structure on the returns or factors besides requiring that the variances and expected returns exist. In Sections 2.1 and 2.3 below, we provide enough additional structure on (1) so that the idiosyncratic returns are diversifiable risk and the factor risks are not.

2.1. *Strict factor models*

Since the factors and idiosyncratic risks in (1) are uncorrelated, the covariance matrix of asset returns, $\Sigma = E[(r - E[r])(r - E[r])']$, can be written as the sum of two matrices, the covariance matrix of each security's factor risk and the covariance matrix of idiosyncratic risks:

$$\Sigma = BE[ff']B' + V \tag{2}$$

where $V = E[\varepsilon\varepsilon']$. In a strict factor model, the idiosyncratic returns are assumed to be uncorrelated with one another. This means that the covariance matrix of idiosyncratic risks, V, is a diagonal matrix. This captures the essential feature of a strict factor model: the covariance matrix of securities can be decomposed as the sum of a matrix of rank k and a diagonal matrix of rank n. This imposes restrictions on the covariance matrix as long as k is less than n.

A strict factor model divides a vector random process into k common sources of randomness (each with linear impact across assets) and n asset-specific sources of randomness. One of Ross's insights was to see that this model could be employed to separate the nondiversifiable and diversifiable components of portfolio risk. Suppose that there are many available assets (i.e., n is large). The idiosyncratic variance of a portfolio with portfolio proportions equal to ω is:

$$\omega' V \omega = \sum_{i=1}^{n} \omega_i^2 \sigma_i^2 \le (\max_i \sigma_i^2) \sum_{i=1}^{n} \omega_i^2.$$

Since the portfolio weights sum to one, the average portfolio weight is $1/n$. If the holdings are spread widely over the n assets (so that all the portfolio weights are close to $1/n$) then the sum of squared portfolio weights approaches zero as n goes to infinity. As long as there is an upper bound on the idiosyncratic variances of the individual assets, the idiosyncratic variance of any well-spread portfolio will be near zero. Therefore, given a strict factor model and many assets, the idiosyncratic returns contain only diversifiable risk.

2.2. Choice of rotation

There is a rotational indeterminacy in the definition of the factors and the betas in equation (1). Given B and f, consider any nonsingular $k \times k$ matrix L and construct $B^* = BL$ and $f^* = L^{-1}f$. Replacing B and f with B^* and f^* yields an observationally equivalent return generating model. There are various approaches to choosing which of the infinite set of (B,f) pairs to use. Often the analyst chooses to simplify (2), without loss of generality, by letting $E[ff'] = I_k$. Another common choice of rotation is the eigenvector decomposition. Given a strict factor model, define the square root inverse matrix of V, $V^{-1/2}$, in the obvious way: $(V^{-1/2})_{ii} = (V_{ii})^{-1/2}$ and $(V^{-1/2})_{ij} = 0$ for $i \neq j$. Scale the covariance matrix of returns by pre- and post-multiplying by $V^{-1/2}$: $\Sigma^* = V^{-1/2}\,\Sigma\,V^{-1/2}$. (Note that if we scale each asset return by its idiosyncratic standard deviation then Σ^* is the covariance matrix of the rescaled returns). Using (2) we can write:

$$\Sigma^* = J\,\Lambda\,J' + I_k$$

where J is the $n \times k$ matrix of the first[1] k eigenvectors of Σ^* and Λ is a $k \times k$ diagonal matrix of the associated eigenvalues squared [see Chamberlain & Rothschild, 1983]. One choice of rotation is to set $B = J$. This choice is often used in econometric work since there are well-known techniques for calculating the dominant eigenvectors of a matrix.

The factors underlying the comovements in security returns presumably come from economy-wide shocks to expected cash flows and required returns. Suppose that we can exactly identify the economic shocks giving rise to the comovements; let g denote the k-vector of these observable economic shocks. The statistical factors, f, and economic shocks, g, are equivalent if $g = L^{-1}f$ for a nonrandom $k \times k$ matrix L. In this case, the obvious choice of rotation is $f^* = g$. More realistically, the statistical factors in security returns and any set of observed economic shocks will be imperfectly correlated. There are various statistical techniques used to rotate the factors to be 'as close as possible' to the observed economic shocks [see, for example, Burmeister & McElroy, 1988].

Suppose for now that the economic shocks and statistical factors are equivalent and consider the obvious rotation $f^* = g$. Rewriting (1) using this rotation gives:

$$r = E[r] + B^*g + \varepsilon. \tag{3}$$

[1] The 'first k' eigenvectors are the k eigenvectors associated with the k largest eigenvalues. That is, we order the eigenvalues by descending size, and then use the induced ordering on the eigenvectors.

A model using economically interpretable factors, as in (3), has notable advantages over (1). Since the factors are observed economic shocks, we can interpret the beta coefficients B^* in economically meaningful ways. After estimation, we can make statements such as 'asset i has a high inflation risk'. Contrast this with the betas estimated using the eigenvector rotation. Here we can only make statements such as 'asset i has a high sensitivity to eigenvector 2 risk'. Since the eigenvectors are statistical artifacts, the betas from them provide little interpretable information. Most APT researchers would agree that, other things being equal, an economically meaningful rotation, as in (3), is preferable to (1). From an empirical viewpoint, other things are not equal. Models with statistically generated factors fit the returns data better than ones with economic shocks as proxies for the factors, in the sense that the fraction of time series variance explained is higher. This is distinct from the question of which set of factors perform better in terms of explaining cross-sectional differences in asset returns.

As the number of securities grows large, the de-meaned returns to well-diversified portfolio returns approximate a linear combination of the factors. That is, any portfolio ω such that $\omega'\varepsilon \approx 0$ has de-meaned return [from equation (1)] approximately equal to a linear combination of the factors. That is, $r_\omega - E[r_\omega] \approx b_\omega f$, where $b_\omega = \omega' B$ is the $1 \times k$ vector of factor betas for this portfolio. Thus, any set of k well-diversified and linearly independent portfolios has de-meaned returns approximately equivalent to a rotation of the factors [see Admati & Pfleiderer, 1985]. We will call such portfolios factor representing or factor-mimicking portfolios.

2.3. *Approximate factor models*

In order for a strict factor model to have empirical content, k must be less than n. For stock market return data, k is usually taken to be much less than n. A typical empirical study with U.S. equity returns will have k in the range of one to fifteen, whereas n, the number of available U.S. equity returns, is from one thousand to six thousand (depending upon the selection criteria). A strict factor model imposes too severe a restriction on the covariance matrix of returns when n/k is this large.

Ross uses the factor model assumption to show that idiosyncratic risks can be diversified away in a many-asset portfolio. The strict diagonality of V is sufficient for Ross's diversification argument, but not necessary. Chamberlain [1983] and Chamberlain & Rothschild [1983] develop an asymptotic statistical model for asset returns data called an *approximate factor model*. This model preserves the diversifiability of idiosyncratic returns but weakens the diagonality condition on V. It also imposes a condition which ensures that the factor risks are *not* diversifiable.

An approximate factor model relies on limiting conditions as the number of assets grows large. We start with an infinite sequence of random asset returns, r_i, $i = 1, 2, \ldots$, with finite means and variances. We treat the observed assets as the first n assets from this infinite sequence, and impose limiting conditions as n goes to infinity.

Let f denote a k-vector of mean-zero random variates with finite variances. We can always express asset returns using the standard linear projection (1): expected returns plus a beta matrix multiplied by the factors plus idiosyncratic return where the factors and idiosyncratic returns are uncorrelated. Therefore, we can always describe the covariance matrix of asset returns using (2): $\Sigma = BE[ff']B' + V$. We seek conditions on Σ to ensure that the idiosyncratic returns are diversifiable and the factor risks are not. We say that ε is *diversifiable risk* if $\lim_{n\to\infty} \omega^{n\prime}\omega^n = 0$ implies $\lim_{n\to\infty} E[(\omega^{n\prime}\varepsilon)^2] = 0$, where ω^n is the $n \times 1$ vector of portfolio weights for a portfolio formed from the first n assets. This means that all well-diversified portfolios have idiosyncratic variance near zero. A converse condition is imposed on factor risks. Let z^j denote an n-vector with a one in the jth component and zeros elsewhere. The factors, f, are *pervasive risk* if for each z^j, $j = 1, \ldots, k$, there exists an ω^n such that $\lim_{n\to\infty} \omega^{n\prime}\omega^n = 0$ and $\omega^{n\prime}B = z^j$ for all n. This condition guarantees that each factor risk affects many assets in the economy.

Chamberlain and Rothschild define an *approximate factor structure* as a factor decomposition where the ε's are diversifiable and the f's are pervasive. They show that the diversifiable risk condition is equivalent to a finite upper bound on the maximum eigenvalue of V^n as n goes to infinity and that the pervasiveness condition is equivalent to the minimum eigenvalue of $B^{n\prime}B^n$ going to infinity with n.

Note that the covariance matrix of returns is the sum of two components, $B^n\mathrm{B}^{n\prime}$ and V^n. In an approximate factor model, $B^nB^{n\prime}$ has all of its eigenvalues going to infinity, whereas V^n has a bound on all its eigenvalues. Chamberlain and Rothschild show that these bounds carry over to the covariance matrix. In an approximate factor model, the k largest eigenvalues of the covariance matrix go to infinity with n, and the $k+1$st largest eigenvalue is bounded for all n. They prove that this is a sufficient condition as well. Consider a countable infinity of assets whose sequence of covariance matrices has exactly k unbounded eigenvalues. Then the asset returns necessarily follow an approximate k-factor model. So the conditions on the sequence of eigenvalues (kth unbounded, $k+1$st bounded) characterize an approximate k-factor model.

An intuitive example of an approximate factor model is a sector and industry model of risk. Suppose that there is a large number (n) of assets each representing the common shares of one firm. Each firm belongs to one of a large number (m) of industries each with a small number (h, with h approximately equal to n/m) of firms. Idiosyncratic returns are correlated within industries but uncorrelated across industries. In this case, the covariance matrix of idiosyncratic returns consists of a series of $h \times h$ submatrices along the diagonal and zeros elsewhere, when assets are ordered by industry grouping. The submatrices are the within-industry covariance matrices. Holding h constant and letting n and m increase, this series of covariance matrices has bounded eigenvalues.[2]

[2] The maximum eigenvalue of this matrix is equal to the maximum eigenvalue of the within-industry covariance matrices. This eigenvalue is less than or equal to h times the maximum idiosyncratic variance of an asset in the industry.

On the other hand, suppose that there is a small number, k, of sectors, each containing n/k firms. All firms within sector j are subject to sector shock f_j with unit betas (for simplicity). Firms in sector j are unaffected by the shocks of other sectors. Given these assumptions, the sector shocks constitute pervasive risk.[3] Note the clear distinction between industries (a small proportion of the firms are in each industry) versus sectors (a substantial proportion of the firms are in each sector).

Connor & Korajczyk [1993] suggest that, for econometric work, imposing a mixing condition on the sequence of idiosyncratic returns is more useful than the bounded eigenvalue condition alone. The cross-sectional sequence of idiosyncratic returns, ε_i, $i = 1, \ldots$, is called a mixing process if the probability distribution of ε_{i+m}, conditional on ε_i, approaches its unconditional distribution as m goes to infinity. (See White & Domowitz [1984] for a discussion of mixing processes and their applications). The idiosyncratic return of an asset may be strongly related to those of a few other 'close' assets, but it must have asymptotically zero relationship to most assets. The mixing condition differs from the bound on eigenvalues in that it restricts the entire conditional probability distribution rather than only the covariance matrix. In many estimation problems, restrictions on the covariances alone are not enough to derive asymptotic distributions of test statistics.

2.4. *Conditional factor models*

There is clear empirical support for time-varying means and variances in asset returns, and this has led to some recent work on time-varying (or dynamic) factor models of returns. Dropping the assumption that returns are independently and identically distributed through time, and rewriting (1) with an explicit time subscript, gives:

$$r_t = E_{t-1}[r_t] + B_{t-1} f_t + \varepsilon_t.$$

Let B_{t-1} be chosen by the conditional projection of r_t on f_t [i.e., $B_{t-1} = E_{t-1}[(r_t - E_{t-1}[r_t]) f_t'](E_{t-1}[f_t f_t'])^{-1}$] so that $E_{t-1}[\varepsilon_t' f_t] = 0$. The conditional covariance matrix can be written as:

$$\Sigma_{t-1} = B_{t-1}\Omega_{t-1}B_{t-1}' + V_{t-1},$$

where $\Omega_{t-1} = E_{t-1}[f_t f_t']$ and $V_{t-1} = E_{t-1}[\varepsilon_t \varepsilon_t']$. Even if we impose that V_{t-1} is diagonal for all t, the system is not statistically identified in this general form. Suppose that we observe the returns on n securities for T periods. For each date, t, we must estimate the n elements of V_{t-1}, the nk elements of B_{t-1}, and the k^2 elements of Ω_{t-1}. This gives a total of $T(n + nk + k^2)$ parameters to be estimated from nT return observations. Obviously we must impose more structure to get an identified model.

[3] It is easy to show that $B'B = (n/k)I_k$ where I_k is the $k \times k$ identity matrix. The k eigenvalues of this matrix all equal n/k, which goes to infinity with n.

Moving to dynamic models can eliminate some rotational indeterminacies of static models but some indeterminacies remain. For example, time variation in $B_{t-1}\Omega_{t-1}B'_{t-1}$ could be caused by time variation in the factor betas, B_{t-1}, with homoscedastic factors (i.e., $\Omega_{t-1} = \Omega$); by heteroscedastic factors with constant factor betas; or by time variation in both B_{t-1} and Ω_{t-1}. The structure imposed on B_{t-1} and Ω_{t-1} for identifiability is related to the assumed nature of the dynamic influence. Suppose that the analyst assumed that $\Omega_{t-1} = I_k$ for all t, so that the factors are homoscedastic. Then, all of the dynamics are due to time variation in B_t. Alternatively the analyst can assume that $B_{t-1} = B$ for all t, in which case any time-variation in the factor model appears in Ω_{t-1} [for example, see Engle, Ng & Rothschild, 1990].

Conditional on the assumed source of time variation in the factor model (B_{t-1} or Ω_{t-1}) and the assumed time-series properties of the dynamics (e.g., Engle, Ng & Rothschild [1990] assume that the factors follow GARCH[4] processes), the dynamic structure can eliminate some of the standard rotational indeterminacy found in static factor models [Sentana, 1992].

Some recent papers in this area also allow for time variation in expected returns, so that $E_{t-1}[r_t]$ is not constant [see, for example, Engle, Ng & Rothschild, 1990].

3. Derivation of the pricing restriction

Now we will use the factor model of returns to derive the APT pricing result:

$$E[r] \approx \iota^n \lambda_0 + B\lambda \tag{4}$$

where λ_0 is a constant, λ is a k-vector of factor risk premia, and ι^n is an n-vector of ones. The approximate equality sign '$\approx$' in (4) reflects the fact that the APT holds only approximately, requiring that the economy has a large number of traded assets in order to be an accurate pricing model, on average.

3.1. Exact pricing in a noiseless factor model

We begin with a *noiseless* factor model (one with no idiosyncratic risk), where $r = E[r] + Bf$. This is much too strong a restriction on asset returns but is useful for the intuition it provides. In this case, an exact arbitrage argument is sufficient for the APT. Here we do not need a large number of assets, and there is no approximation error in the APT pricing restriction. The result comes from Ross [1977]. To derive the APT in this case, project $E[r]$ on ι^n and B to get projection coefficients λ_0 and λ and a projection residual vector η:

$$E[r] = \lambda_0 \iota^n + B\lambda + \eta. \tag{5}$$

By the property of projection residuals we have $\eta' B = 0$ and $\eta' \iota^n = 0$. Consider the n-vector, η, viewed as a portfolio of asset purchases and sales. This portfolio

[4] See Bollerslev [1986] for a detailed analysis of GARCH models.

has zero cost since $\eta' \iota^n = 0$ and no randomness since $\eta' B = 0$. If this portfolio had a positive expected return, it would represent an arbitrage opportunity, that is, a zero-cost portfolio with a strictly positive expected payoff and no chance of a negative payoff. The existence of an arbitrage opportunity is inconsistent with even the weakest type of pricing equilibrium. The expected payoff of the portfolio under consideration is $\eta' E[r] = \eta' \eta$. This can only be zero if $\eta = 0$. So the APT pricing model (4) holds with equality in the absence of arbitrage opportunities.

We can combine the noiseless factor model, $r = E[r] + Bf$, with the APT pricing result, $E[r] = \iota^n \lambda_0 + B\lambda$, to show that $r = \iota^n \lambda_0 + B(f + \lambda)$. A unit-cost portfolio is any collection of assets such that $\omega' \iota^n = 1$. The payoff to a unit-cost portfolio is a portfolio return. A unit cost portfolio with $\omega' B = 0$ (no factor risk) has a risk-free return equal to λ_0. As long as the $(k+1) \times n$ matrix $[\iota^n, B]$ has rank $k+1$, we can construct such a portfolio,[5] and identify λ_0 as the risk-free return. A unit cost portfolio with a unit sensitivity to factor j and zero sensitivity to the other factors has expected return $\lambda_0 + \lambda_j$. Hence, the k-vector λ measures the risk premia (expected returns above the risk-free return) per beta-unit of each factor risk. These risk premia are dependent on the factor rotation, which affects the scales of the betas.

3.2. *Approximate nonarbitrage*

The argument used for the noiseless factor model can be extended to a strict or approximate factor model. In this case, we get a pricing relation which holds approximately in an economy with many assets. For generality we work with the case of an approximate factor model. We combine the original formulation of Ross [1976] with some refinements of Huberman [1982]. Consider the orthogonal price deviations η defined by (5), as in the noiseless case. Define a sequence of portfolios as follows: the nth portfolio consists of holdings of the first n assets in proportion to their price deviations, scaled by the sum of squares of these deviations:

$$\omega^n = \frac{\eta^n}{(\eta^{n\prime} \eta^n)}.$$

Using the same steps as in the noiseless case, one can show that the cost of each of these portfolios is zero, the expected payoff of each is 1, and the variance is $(\eta^{n\prime} \eta^n)^{-2} \eta^{n\prime} V^n \eta^n$. Using the property of the maximum eigenvalue, we have $\eta^{n\prime} V^n \eta^n \leq (\eta^{n\prime} \eta^n) \| V^n \|$, where $\| V^n \|$ denotes the maximum eigenvalue of V^n. Therefore the portfolio variance is less than or equal to $(\eta^{n\prime} \eta^n)^{-1} \| V^n \|$.

[5] If ι^n and B are linearly dependent, then the $k+1 \times n$ matrix $[\iota^n, B]$ has rank k. In this case, there is a rotation of the factors under which every asset in the economy has unit betas against (at least) one factor. Thus, there is no way to construct a zero-beta portfolio with unit cost (since any asset combination with unit cost also has a beta of unity with respect to the above factor). This situation creates an ambiguity in the definition of λ_0 since there is no well-defined risk-free return. If a risk-free asset exists separately from the factor model (this assumption is often made), then the ambiguity disappears.

Since $\|V^n\|$ is bounded (by the definition of an approximate factor model), the variance of this sequence of portfolios goes to zero as n increases if $\eta^{n\prime}\eta^n$ is not bounded above. This would constitute a sequence of 'approximate arbitrage portfolios'. These portfolios have zero cost, unit expected payoff, and variance approaching zero, as the number of assets in the economy increases. Ross [1976], Huberman [1982], Ingersoll [1984], and Jarrow [1988] show that approximate arbitrage portfolios will not exist in a well-functioning capital market. If we rule out approximate arbitrage portfolios, then $\eta^{n\prime}\eta^n$ must be bounded for all n.

The bound on the sum of squared pricing errors has the following interpretation. Although the APT can substantially misprice any one asset (or any limited collection of assets), the prices of most assets in a many-asset economy must be closely approximated. Let c denote the upper bound on $\eta^{n\prime}\eta^n$. The average squared pricing error is less than c/n and, for any $\xi > 0$, only c/ξ assets have squared pricing errors greater than or equal to ξ. The proportion of assets with squared pricing errors greater than ξ goes to zero as n increases.

The approximate nature of the APT pricing relation in (4) causes important problems for tests of the APT. With a finite set of assets, the sum of squared pricing errors must be finite, so we cannot directly test whether $\eta^{n\prime}\eta^n$ is bounded. Shanken [1982] argues that the weakness of this price approximation renders the APT untestable. He shows that this pricing bound is not invariant to 'repackaging' the assets into an equivalent set of n unit-cost portfolios [Gilles & LeRoy [1991] make a similar argument]. Shanken argues that only equilibrium-based derivations of the APT (which can provide an exact pricing approximation) are truly testable. The equilibrium-based derivations involve additional assumptions besides those needed to derive (4), and are discussed below. Ingersoll [1984] notes that the APT pricing approximation will be close for all well-diversified portfolios (since the pricing errors diversify away). He argues that the pricing of these portfolios should be of more concern to the economist than the pricing of individual assets, and therefore the weakness of the pricing approximation for individual assets is not crucial. A well-diversified factor-mimicking portfolio will have an expected excess return close to the factor risk premium. Heston [1991] builds on Ingersoll's analysis to show that the weakness of the pricing approximation does not affect some statistical tests based on large cross-sections of assets.

Reisman [1992b] expands on Shanken's argument. He proves that the approximate-arbitrage pricing bound is unaffected by measurement error in the factors. If there are k true factors, then *any* set of k or more random variables which are correlated with the factors can be used as proxies. For example, almost *any* set of k or more individual assets returns (as long as they have differing beta coefficients) can be used as factors. The finite bound on the sum of squared APT pricing errors absorbs the additional pricing error generated by any mismeasurement of the factors or overestimate of the number of factors [also see Shanken, 1992b].

So far we have considered an economy with a large, but finite, number of assets. Chamberlain [1983] extends the APT to an economy with an infinite number of assets. To accomplish this, he expands the space of portfolio returns to include infinite-dimensional linear combinations of asset returns. Let r^n denote the n-

vector of the first n of the infinite set of assets. We define a limit portfolio return as the limit of the returns to n-asset portfolios as n goes to infinity:

$$r_\omega = \lim_{n\to\infty} \omega^{n\prime} r^n. \tag{6}$$

The limit in (6) is usually taken with respect to the second-moment norm $\|r_\omega\| = E[r_\omega^2]$. A simple example of a convergent sequence of portfolios is $\omega^n = (1/n, 1/n, \ldots, 1/n)$. Note that, element-by-element, this sequence of portfolio weights converges to a zero vector. Yet the limit portfolio of this sequence has a well-defined, nonzero return in most cases.[6] Limit portfolio returns can be perfectly diversified, that is, have idiosyncratic variance of exactly zero.

Ross [1978b] and Kreps [1981] develop an exact nonarbitrage pricing theory (this is not the same as the APT). In the absence of exact arbitrage opportunities, there must exist a positive, linear pricing operator over state-contingent payoffs. Chamberlain & Rothschild [1983] show that in an infinite-asset model the approximate-arbitrage APT is an extension of the Ross–Kreps exact nonarbitrage pricing theory. In the absence of approximate arbitrage, the positive linear pricing operator defined by Ross and Kreps must be continuous with respect to the second moment norm. Given an approximate factor model for asset returns, this continuity condition implies the same bound on APT pricing errors described above. Reisman [1988] extends the Chamberlain–Rothschild result to general normed linear spaces. He shows that the APT can be reduced to an application of the Hahn–Banach theorem using two assumptions: one, the nonexistence of approximate arbitrage opportunities for limit portfolios, and two, the approximate factor model assumption on the countably infinite set of asset returns.

Stambaugh [1983] extends the APT to an economy in which investors have heterogeneous information and/or the econometrician has less information than investors. Unconditional asset returns must obey a factor model, but the conditional asset returns (as perceived by an investor with special information) need not obey a factor model. In the absence of approximate arbitrage (for an informed or uninformed investor, or both) the APT pricing restriction holds using the unconditional betas.

3.3. Competitive equilibrium derivations of the APT

There are advantages to the approximate-arbitrage proof of the APT, since the nonexistence of approximate arbitrage opportunities is such a weak assumption. One drawback is the weakness of the pricing approximation. As an alternative to the approximate arbitrage approach, one can derive the APT by imposing competitive equilibrium. This gives a stronger pricing approximation, and links the APT with other equilibrium-based pricing models.

Consider an investor with a risk-averse utility function $u(\cdot)$ for end-of-period wealth. Suppose that returns obey an approximate factor model, with the additional

[6] If the asset returns are independent and identically distributed with finite mean and variance, then the return to this portfolio is the expected return of the assets.

assumption that idiosyncratic risks are conditionally mean zero given the factors:

$$E[\varepsilon \mid f] = 0.$$

Let W_0 denote the investor's wealth at time 0. In competitive equilibrium, a first-order portfolio optimization condition must hold for every investor:

$$E[u'(W_0\omega' r)r] = \iota^n \gamma, \tag{7}$$

for some positive scalar γ. For notational simplicity, let $W_0 = 1$. Inserting (1) into (7), separating the three additive terms and bringing constants outside the expectations operator gives:

$$E'[r] = \iota^n \lambda_0 + B\lambda + \frac{E[u'(\omega' r)\varepsilon]}{E[u'(\omega' r)]} \tag{8}$$

where $\lambda_0 = \gamma / E[u'(\omega' r)]$ and $\lambda = -E[u'(\omega' r) f]/E[u'(\omega' r)]$. The competitive equilibrium derivations of the APT assume a sufficient set of conditions so that the last term in (8) is approximately a vector of zeros. Note that this last term is the vector of risk premia the investor assigns to the idiosyncratic returns. So proving the equilibrium APT amounts to showing that, in competitive equilibrium, investors will assign a zero or near-zero risk premium to each idiosyncratic return.

Chen & Ingersoll [1983] assume that in competitive equilibrium some investor has a portfolio return with no idiosyncratic risk. Let r_N denote this portfolio return where $r_N = E[r_N] + bf$ for some k-vector b. Using $E[\varepsilon \mid f] = 0$, we have $E[u'(r_N)\varepsilon] = E\big[E[u'(r_N)\varepsilon \mid f]\big] = 0$. So in the Chen & Ingersoll [1983] model, the APT holds exactly.

Consider again the optimality condition (7), but assume that the chosen portfolio is well-diversified (with idiosyncratic variance near zero) but not perfectly diversified. Consider an exact first-order Taylor expansion of $u'(\omega' r) = u'(\omega' E[r] + \omega' Bf + \omega' \varepsilon)$ around $\omega' E[r] + \omega' Bf$:

$$u'(\omega' r) = u'(\omega' E[r] + \omega' Bf) + (\omega' \varepsilon) u''(\omega' E[r] + \omega' Bf + \delta),$$

where δ is the Taylor residual term. Therefore,

$$\begin{aligned} E[\varepsilon u'(\omega' r)] = {} & E[\varepsilon u'(\omega' E[r] + \omega' Bf)] + \\ & + E[\varepsilon(\omega' \varepsilon) u''(\omega' E[r] + \omega' Bf + \delta)]. \end{aligned} \tag{9}$$

The first vector term of (9) is exactly zero, as noted above. Under reasonable assumptions, every component of the second vector term is near zero if the chosen portfolio is well-diversified. For simplicity, suppose the investor has quadratic utility, so that u'' is a constant. Then $E[\varepsilon(\omega' \varepsilon) u''(\omega' Bf + \delta)] = E[\varepsilon \omega \varepsilon'] u'' = E[\varepsilon \varepsilon'] \omega u''$. Consider an arbitrary term of this n$-$vector (the ith term) and note that $(E[\varepsilon \varepsilon'] \omega u'')_i \leq \|V\| \omega' \omega u''$, which goes to zero as $\omega' \omega$ goes to zero. With nonquadratic utility, the proof that this term approaches zero is messier than, but not fundamentally different from, the quadratic utility case (see, for example, Dybvig [1983] or Grinblatt & Titman [1983]).

The model above has the shortcoming that it assumes a particular form for the equilibrium portfolio returns of investors. It is preferable in economic modelling to derive the properties of endogenous equilibrium variables (such as portfolio returns) rather than to impose assumptions on them. Dybvig [1983] develops a simple and elegant equilibrium version of the APT which accomplishes this. Dybvig assumes that all investors have constant relative risk aversion and that the security market is effectively complete. That is, all welfare-increasing trading opportunities are available [see Ingersoll [1987, ch. 8] for a discussion of effectively complete markets]. When the security market is effectively complete, one can construct a representative investor for the economy. By definition, the representative investor finds it optimal, conditional on budget constraints, to hold the market portfolio. Dybvig assumes that the market portfolio is well-diversified (which is an assumption common to all equilibrium derivations of the APT[7]). Dybvig considers the optimality condition (7) for the representative investor who holds the market portfolio, and derives the utility function for this investor (it is a linear combination of the constant relative risk aversion functions of the investors). He shows that the Taylor residual in expression (9) converges to zero for each asset, given this utility function. Connor [1982] and Grinblatt & Titman [1983] develop models broadly similar to Dybvig's, though differing in details.

The equilibrium version of the APT can also be derived using Chamberlain's infinite-asset techniques. Connor [1984] requires that the market portfolio return is a perfectly diversified limit portfolio return. He allows investors to hold limit portfolios in equilibrium. He then shows (along the lines of Chen & Ingersoll [1983] discussed above) that in competitive equilibrium all investors choose to hold perfectly diversified portfolios and the APT pricing relation holds exactly for every asset.

Milne [1988] adds a real investment side to the equilibrium APT. Each corporation owns a capital investment function which produces random profits. The firms are purely equity financed. The model is static; each firm issues equity and invests the proceeds in its investment technology, which produces a random profit at the end of the period. Recall that the equilibrium version of the APT requires that the market portfolio is well-diversified. With production, the relative supplies of the various assets are endogenous to the model since the issuance of equity depends upon the capital investment decisions of firms. The pricing theory requires that the capital investment plans chosen by corporations must be such that the market portfolio is well-diversified after the firms make their decisions [also see Brock, 1982].

3.4 Mean–variance efficiency and exact factor pricing

Mean–variance efficiency mathematics can be employed to restate the APT pricing restriction. This restatement is particularly useful for econometric modelling.

[7] This assumption does not appear explicitly in Chen & Ingersoll [1983] because they make an exogenous assumption about equilibrium portfolios.

Consider the set of unit-cost portfolios obtainable as linear combinations of an n-vector of asset returns, r. Note that for any portfolio return, r_ω, we can define the one-factor projection equation:

$$r = E[r] + bf + \varepsilon \tag{10}$$

where $f = r_\omega - E[r_\omega]$. A single-beta pricing model holds with respect to (10) if:

$$E[r] = \iota^n \lambda_0 + b\lambda \tag{11}$$

for some scalars λ_0 and λ. Define a mean–variance efficient portfolio as a unit-cost portfolio which minimizes variance subject to $E[\omega' r] = c$ for some c. One can show[8] that (11) is the necessary and sufficient condition for the mean–variance efficiency of ω. Therefore, proving that (11) holds is equivalent to proving that ω is mean–variance efficient. Note that this is *not* a pricing theory; it is a mathematical equivalence between the pricing restriction (11) and the mean–variance efficiency of ω. If ω is the market portfolio, then (11) is the conventional statement of the CAPM. We can equivalently restate the CAPM as 'the market portfolio is mean–variance efficient'.

The relationship between mean–variance efficiency and beta pricing carries over to a multi-beta model. Given an n-vector of returns r, consider any set of k portfolio returns $r_{\omega 1}, r_{\omega 2}, \ldots, r_{\omega k}$ and the projection equation:

$$r = E[r] + Bf + \varepsilon,$$

where $f_j = r_{\omega j} - E[r_{\omega j}]$ for $j = 1, \ldots, k$. Hypothesize linear pricing with respect to these factor-mimicking portfolios as in equation (11)

$$E[r] = \iota^n \lambda_0 + B\lambda. \tag{12}$$

Grinblatt & Titman [1987] show that (12) holds if and only if some linear combination of the portfolios $\omega_1, \ldots, \omega_k$ is mean–variance efficient. Chamberlain [1983] derives this same result for large-n and infinite-n models. Chamberlain shows that if a linear combination of factor portfolios converges to a mean–variance efficient portfolio as n goes to infinity, then the deviations from APT pricing go to zero. He gives explicit bounds on the speed of convergence of the sum of squared pricing errors to zero. In an infinite-asset economy, if a linear combination of factor portfolios is mean–variance efficient, then the APT holds exactly.

The Grinblatt–Titman and Chamberlain analysis is not an independent pricing theory, but rather a useful reinterpretation of the APT pricing formula. The mean–variance efficiency criteria restates the mathematical relationship between expected returns and betas given by (12). That is, we can restate the APT pricing restriction as 'a linear combination of factor portfolios is mean–variance efficient'. This alternative characterization proves very useful for econometric modelling;

[8] The first-order condition for the mean–variance efficiency of ω is $\Sigma\omega = E[r]\gamma_1 + \iota^n \gamma_2$, where γ_1 and γ_2 are proportional to Lagrange multipliers for the constrained optimization problem. Rearranging this first-order condition gives (11). See Grinblatt & Titman [1987] for more details.

see Shanken [1987a] and Kandel & Stambaugh [1989] for the derivation of APT test statistics based on this approach. Most econometric analyses of the APT along these lines have relied on the exact finite-n model of Grinblatt and Titman. Given the interesting cross-sectional asymptotic analysis of Heston [1991], Reisman [1992b], and Mei [1993], it might be useful to extend this econometric framework to encompass the large-n asymptotic mean–variance efficiency described by Chamberlain [1983].

The equivalence between the mean–variance efficiency of factor portfolios and exact APT pricing also sheds light on the relationship between the CAPM and APT. Assume that the market portfolio is perfectly diversified (it has zero idiosyncratic variance). Some variation on this assumption is necessary if we are to derive the APT using an equilibrium argument, and it is widely accepted as a natural assumption even when the model is derived via approximate arbitrage [see, e.g., Ingersoll, 1984, and Dybvig & Ross, 1985]. This assumption implies that the return to the market portfolio is a linear combination of factor portfolio returns. The APT holds if any linear combination of factor portfolios is mean–variance efficient. The CAPM holds if the market portfolio (a *particular* linear combination of factor portfolios) is mean–variance efficient. Note that the CAPM requires observation of the market portfolio returns whereas the APT needs observations of the factors or factor-mimicking portfolios. Analysts differ on which is easier to observe [e.g., Shanken, 1982, 1985, and Dybvig & Ross, 1985].

Wei [1988] constructs a model which combines features of the CAPM and APT. He assumes that asset returns obey an approximate factor model, and that the idiosyncratic returns obey a mutual fund separating condition. (The simplest case is that the idiosyncratic returns are independent of the factors and multivariate normal.) He shows that in competitive equilibrium, an exact $k+1$-factor pricing model holds. Consider the projection equation linking the market portfolio return and the factors:

$$r_q = E[r_q] + h'f + \varepsilon_q.$$

Wei calls the random variable ε_q the 'residual market factor'. He shows that there exists a k-vector λ and scalar λ_q such that

$$E[r] = \iota^n\lambda_0 + B\lambda + \beta\lambda_q,$$

where $\beta = \mathrm{cov}(r, \varepsilon_q)/\mathrm{var}(\varepsilon_q)$. If the market portfolio is well-diversified, then the $k+1$st factor premium is redundant (since β is a linear combination of B) and the pricing equation holds with only k factors.

3.5. Pricing dynamics

Dynamic versions of the APT generally specify an exogenous factor model for the cash flows (dividends) paid by firms and derive the factor model for the prices of securities endogenously. Discrete time dynamic models are derived in Jagannathan & Viswanathan [1988], Bossaerts & Green [1989], Connor &

Korajczyk [1989], and Hollifield [1993]. Even if the factor loadings (betas) for the cash flow process are time invariant, the betas of asset returns (relative to factor-mimicking portfolios) will be functions of the current information set. In the static APT we can replicate the priced payoff from a security with the riskless asset and factor-mimicking portfolios. Jagannathan & Viswanathan [1988] show that in a multiperiod economy there is, in general, a different riskless asset for every maturity (i.e., a discount bond with that maturity). Thus, even though the risky components of assets' payoffs are driven by, for example, a one-factor model, asset returns may follow an infinite factor structure (corresponding to a portfolio mimicking the single factor, plus the returns on discount bonds for every maturity).

Connor & Korajczyk [1989] develop a multiperiod model in which they assume that per-share dividends, rather than asset returns, obey an approximate factor model. They show that expected returns obey the exact APT pricing restriction at each date. However, the general version of their model is not statistically identified since the beta coefficients and factor risk premia vary through time. They describe additional conditions on preferences and the stochastic process for dividends which give a statistically identified model. The stochastic process for dividends is such that the infinite number of term structure factors in the general formulation of Jagannathan & Viswanathan [1988] are replaced by the return on a single consol bond.

Bossaerts & Green [1989] develop an alternative with a more explicit description of the time-varying risk premia. They treat the special case of a one-factor model for dividends, but it is straightforward to generalize much of their analysis to a multi-factor model. The return on a consol bond plays an important role in their model. They give explicit, testable expressions for the time-variation in asset betas and the factor risk premia by substituting observable quantities (returns on a reference portfolio and the relative prices of assets) for the unobservable return on the consol bond.

Engle, Ng & Rothschild [1990] also develop a multi-period equilibrium version of the APT. They begin along the lines of Chen & Ingersoll [1983] by assuming that the marginal utility of consumption for a representative investor can be described as a function of k random factors. They also assume that returns at each date follow an approximate factor model with conditionally mean zero idiosyncratic returns. The standard first-order condition for a budget-constrained optimal portfolio [i.e., equation (7)] gives an exact version of the APT.

Bansal & Viswanathan [1993] also rely on an assumption that the marginal utility of consumption of a representative investor can be described by a (potentially nonlinear) function of k random factors. They do not assume that all assets have returns given by an approximate factor model. In any competitive equilibrium, all assets, even those not obeying an approximate factor model, must have expected returns given by the Ross–Kreps positive linear state space pricing function. The contribution of Bansal and Viswanathan is to note that this state pricing function can be described as a function of the k random factors which explain the representative investor's marginal utility. This gives rise to a *nonlinear* k-factor pricing model (see Latham [1989] for a related model).

Reisman [1992a], building on earlier work by Ohlson & Garman [1980], extends the APT to a continuous-time economy. He assumes that there are a large number of assets, each paying a liquidating dividend at the terminal date T. From time 0 to T asset prices are continuously set so as to exclude approximate arbitrage. He assumes that the continuous-time information flow about the vector of terminal dividends follows a continuous-time approximate factor model. He shows that instantaneous expected returns obey the APT with bounded pricing errors, almost surely.

Chamberlain [1988] develops an intertemporal equilibrium asset pricing model which integrates the APT with Merton's [1973] Intertemporal Capital Asset Pricing Model (ICAPM). In Chamberlain's model, trading lasts from 0 to T and investors can trade continuously during that time. There exists a countably infinite set of assets; the vector of random asset payoffs at time T, conditioned at any time, t, between 0 and T, follows a continuous-time approximate factor model. Chamberlain assumes that the market portfolio is well-diversified. He proves that, at each time t, asset prices obey the APT formula, *and* that this formula is identical to the CAPM pricing formula (if k equals one) or the ICAPM formula (if k is greater than or equal to one). Constantinides [1989] gives an alternative proof in a slightly different framework.

Chamberlain's model is an important contribution for the way it rigorously unifies the APT and ICAPM. In his framework, these two pricing models are not testably distinct. Connor & Korajczyk [1989] argue that the APT and ICAPM should be separated by econometric and empirical considerations rather than theoretical ones. The ICAPM stresses the role of state variables as the fundamental determinants of asset risk premia, whereas the APT stresses the pervasive factors in random returns as the key determinants. Chamberlain's model shows that these two categories are not always distinct: the set of state variables of the ICAPM can be identical to the set of pervasive factors of the APT.

4. Empirical analysis of the APT

Analyses of the factor structure of asset returns actually predate the APT. Rather than being motivated by the pricing implications of the APT, this strand of the literature was primarily motivated by a desire to describe, in a parsimonious manner, the covariance structure of asset returns, Σ. The covariance matrix of asset returns is, of course, a major component of a portfolio optimization problem. Estimation of the unrestricted covariance matrix of n securities requires the estimation of $n \times (n+1)/2$ distinct elements. The single index, or diagonal, model of Sharpe [1963] postulated that all of the common elements of returns were due to assets' relations with the index. Thus, only $3 \times n$ parameters needed to be estimated: n 'betas' relative to the index, n unique variances, and n intercept terms. This approach reduced much of the noise in the estimate of Σ. One could view the single-index model as a strict one-factor model with a prespecified factor. In practice, the single index did not describe all of the common movements across assets (i.e., the residual matrix is not diagonal) so there seemed to be some additional benefit from using a multifactor model. With k factors there are still only $n \times (k+2)$ parameters to estimate ($n \times k$ betas, n intercepts or means, and n unique variances). Some studies in this area are Farrar [1962], King [1966], Cohen & Pogue [1967], and Elton & Gruber [1973].

Our primary interest, however, is the evidence regarding the pricing implications of the APT. As discussed in Section 3, the main implication of the APT is that expected returns on assets are approximately linear in their sensitivities to the factors [equation (4)]:

$$E[r] \approx \iota^n \lambda_0 + B\lambda.$$

With additional restrictions used in some competitive equilibrium derivations of the APT (Section 3.3), it is possible to obtain the pricing relation as an equality. Since standard statistical methods are not amenable to testing approximations, most empirical tests actually evaluate whether (4) holds as an equality. Thus the tests are joint tests of the APT plus any ancillary assumptions required to obtain the exact pricing relation [Shanken, 1985]:

$$E[r] = \iota^n \lambda_0 + B\lambda. \tag{13}$$

Once the relevant factors have been identified or estimated, approaches to analyzing and testing the APT have, to a large extent, mirrored developments in analyzing and testing other asset pricing models, such as the CAPM (see Ferson [1995] for a review of tests of asset pricing models). Various aspects of (13) have been investigated. Some authors have focussed on evidence regarding the size and significance of the factor risk premia vector, λ. One testable restriction of the model is that the implied risk premia are the same across subsets of assets. That is, if we partition the return vector, r, into components, $r^1, r^2, \ldots, r^s$, with B^i representing the same partitioning of B, and investigate the subset pricing relations

$$E[r^i] = \iota^n \lambda_0^i + B^i \lambda^i \qquad i = 1, 2, \ldots, s, \tag{14}$$

then $\lambda_0^i = \lambda_0$ and $\lambda^i = \lambda$ for all i. Another restriction implied by the pricing model is that variables in the agents' information set should not allow us to predict expected returns which differ from the relation in (13). These restrictions form the basis for testing the APT.

The exact pricing relation (13), along with the factor model for the return generating process (1), imply that the n-vector of returns at time t, r_t, is given by:

$$r_t = \iota^n \lambda_{0,t-1} + B(\lambda_{t-1} + f_t) + \varepsilon_t. \tag{15}$$

The riskless rate of return, $\lambda_{0,t-1}$, and the risk premia, λ_{t-1}, have a time $t-1$ subscript since they are determined by expectations conditional on information at time $t-1$. If we observe the return on the riskless asset, $\lambda_{0,t-1}$, we get an equivalent relation between returns in *excess* of the riskless rate $R_t = r_t - \iota^n \lambda_{0,t-1}$,

B, and the factor returns, $\lambda_{t-1} + f_t$:

$$R_t = B(\lambda_{t-1} + f_t) + \varepsilon_t. \tag{16}$$

All empirical analyses of the APT involve analysis of a panel of asset return data in which we observe a time series of returns ($t = 1, 2, \ldots, T$) on a cross-sectional sample of assets or portfolios (the n different assets in r_t or R_t). Even though all empirical studies combine cross-sectional and time-series data, it is common to classify them as cross-sectional or time-series studies on the basis of the approach used in the final, testing stage of the analysis. That is, conditional on B, (15) and (16) can be thought of as cross-sectional regressions in which the parameters being estimated are $\lambda_{0,t-1}$ and $(\lambda_{t-1} + f_t)$. Conversely, conditional on $\lambda_{0,t-1}$ and $(\lambda_{t-1} + f_t)$, (15) and (16) can be thought of as time-series regressions in which the parameters being estimated are the elements of B. Some studies, such as McElroy & Burmeister [1988], jointly estimate the model in one step. We will first consider a sample of cross-sectional tests of the APT and then describe some time-series tests.

4.1. Cross-sectional tests of the APT

For the moment, assume that we observe the $n \times k$ matrix B, representing the assets' sensitivity to the factors. Then (15) and (16) can be viewed as cross-sectional regressions of r_t and R_t, respectively, on a constant and the matrix k factor sensitivities, B.

$$r_t = \iota^n F_{0,t-1} + BF_t + \varepsilon_t \tag{17}$$

$$R_t = \iota^n F_{0,t-1} + BF_t + \varepsilon_t \tag{18}$$

The parameters to be estimated are an intercept, $F_{0,t-1}$, and the k-vector of slope coefficients, F_t. The parameters can be estimated by a variety of methods, including ordinary least squares (OLS), weighted least squares (WLS), and generalized least squares (GLS). Under standard conditions, the estimates are unbiased and consistent. That is, as the cross-sectional sample size, n, approaches infinity, $\hat{F}_{0,t-1}$ should be equal to $\lambda_{0,t-1}$ in (17) and zero in (18) and $\hat{F}_t$ should be equal to the vector of factor realizations, $\lambda_{t-1} + f_t$ (where ^ denotes the estimate of the parameter).

In a given period, we cannot disentangle from $\hat{F}_t$ the risk premia λ_{t-1} and the unexpected factor shocks f_t. However, given a time series of returns r_t ($t = 1, 2, \ldots, T$), we can estimate a cross-sectional regression for each period, yielding a time series of estimates $\hat{F}_1, \hat{F}_2, \ldots, \hat{F}_T$ (as well as $\hat{F}_{0,0}, \hat{F}_{0,1}, \ldots, \hat{F}_{0,T}$). Since the unexpected factor shocks are conditionally mean zero (otherwise they would not be unexpected), we can learn about the risk premium vector by investigating the time-series average of the estimates, $\bar{F} = (\hat{F}_1 + \hat{F}_2 + \ldots + \hat{F}_T)/\mathrm{T}$ and $\bar{F}_0 = (\hat{F}_{0,0} + \hat{F}_{0,1} + \ldots + \hat{F}_{0,T})/\mathrm{T}$. If the risk premium vector is stationary, with mean λ, then $\bar{F}$ should converge to λ since the average of the f_t will converge to zero.[9] The precision of our estimate of λ, $\bar{F}$, can be estimated by the time-series variability of $\hat{F}_t$.

[9] A special case of this is when λ_t is assumed to be constant through time, although the theory does not require this.

We can also test the predictions of the exact APT by augmenting the cross-sectional regressions in (17) and (18) with a $n \times j$ matrix of firm-specific instruments, Z_{t-1}, observable at the beginning of the period:[10]

$$r_t = \iota^n F_{0,t-1} + BF_t + Z_{t-1}\delta + \varepsilon_t \tag{19}$$

$$R_t = \iota^n F_{0,t-1} + BF_t + Z_{t-1}\delta + \varepsilon_t \tag{20}$$

where δ is an j-vector of parameters. If the model is correct, cross-sectional differences in expected returns should only be due to differences in factor sensitivities, B, and not due to other variables such as the instruments, Z_{t-1}. Therefore, values of δ different from zero are inconsistent with the model.

In the raw return regression (17), the estimate $\hat{F}_{0,t-1}$ represents a unit investment portfolio with zero exposure to factor risk (or market risk in the CAPM) and should converge to the riskless rate of interest. The estimate $\hat{F}_t$ represents a set of k zero-investment (arbitrage) portfolios, with portfolio j having a sensitivity of unity to the jth factor and a sensitivity of zero to the remaining factors [see Fama, 1976, ch. 9]. Thus the vector $\hat{F}_t$ represents a set of excess returns to factor-mimicking portfolios.

This cross-sectional approach is used by Fama & MacBeth [1973] to test the CAPM. Unlike the assumption we made above, however, we are not generally endowed with the true matrix of factor sensitivities, B. Fama & MacBeth [1973] propose using, in an initial stage, time-series regressions of asset returns on a proxy for the market portfolio to obtain estimates of the sensitivities, or betas. The second-stage cross-sectional regressions then use these estimates as the independent variables. Fama & MacBeth [1973] also include as instruments [our Z_{t-1} in (19) and (20)] the squared values of beta and the asset-specific, or residual, risk as measured by the standard deviation of the error from the first-stage time-series regressions.

Given that the cross-sectional regressions use estimates of B instead of the true value, the regressions suffer from an errors-in-variables (EIV) problem. Since the betas of portfolios are more precisely measured than the betas of individual assets, Fama & MacBeth use portfolios of assets in the cross-sectional regressions instead of individual assets. This reduces the EIV problem. The portfolios are formed in a manner designed to maintain cross-sectional dispersion in the independent variable, beta [see Fama & MacBeth, 1973, or Fama, 1976, ch. 9, for details]. A multiple-factor analog of this two-pass, cross-sectional regression procedure forms the basis of many tests of the APT.[11] The two-pass procedure is analyzed and extended in Shanken [1992a].

The first step in the Fama–MacBeth procedure is to obtain an estimate of the matrix of asset sensitivities to the factors, B. If we observe the factors, f, directly,

[10] Equations (19) and (20) assume that the instruments Z_{t-1} are predetermined relative to r_t and F_t. Not all studies use instruments that are strictly predetermined.

[11] In some cases there are multiple passes in which the $\hat{F}_t$ from a cross-sectional regression is used to reestimate betas in additional time-series regressions. These new betas are then used to reestimate $\hat{F}_t$ via cross-sectional regressions [see Connor & Uhlaner, 1989].

then B, $E[r]$, and V in (1) and (2) can be estimated through standard time-series regression procedures as is done in Fama & MacBeth [1973] using the returns on a market portfolio proxy. This approach forces us to choose the factors ex ante. An alternative approach to estimating B that relies only on the assumed strict factor model is factor analysis [see, for example, Morrison, 1976, ch. 9, or Anderson, 1984, ch. 14]. Let us assume that returns follow a strict factor model, have a multivariate normal distribution cross-sectionally, and are independently and identically distributed through time. Let $\hat{\Sigma}$ denote the sample covariance matrix of returns, estimated using T time-series observations of n securities, with $T > n$. Under these conditions, the $n \times n$ matrix, $\hat{\Sigma}$, has a Wishart distribution. The parameters of the distribution are the $n \times k$ matrix of factor betas, B, and the n idiosyncratic variances V_{ii}, $i = 1, \ldots, n$. (Note that the off-diagonal elements of V equal zero by assumption.) The maximum likelihood estimates $\hat{B}$ and $\hat{V}$ are those which maximize the likelihood of observing $\hat{\Sigma}$ given $B = \hat{B}$ and $V = \hat{V}$. Various numerical techniques have been suggested for solving the maximum likelihood problem. The first-order conditions for a maximum can be written as follows:

$$\operatorname{diag}[\hat{B}\hat{B}' + \hat{V}] = \operatorname{diag}[\hat{\Sigma}]$$

$$\hat{\Sigma}\hat{V}^{-1}\hat{B} = \hat{B}(I + \hat{B}'\hat{V}^{-1}\hat{B}).$$

The first-order conditions are necessary but not sufficient. They do not encompass the restriction that the diagonal elements of V must be nonnegative.[12] Also, the matrix B is only identified up to an orthogonal transformation. This is known as rotational indeterminacy (see Section 2.2 above). The computational complexity of this maximum likelihood problem increases dramatically with n. This has led some analysts to use small cross-sectional samples. Alternative computational algorithms have been developed to alleviate these problems. These issues will be discussed in the context of particular empirical studies below.

To our knowledge, the first empirical analysis of the APT is by Gehr [1978], who uses a variant of the cross-sectional approach. This study applies factor analysis to a set of 41 individual company returns (chosen from different industries) to obtain an initial set of factor-mimicking portfolios, $\hat{F}_t$, in two steps. In step one, factor analysis is applied to the sample covariance matrix in order to obtain an estimate of the assets' matrix of factor sensitivities, B (called factor loadings in the factor analysis literature). In step two, a cross-sectional regression of asset returns on $\hat{B}$ [as in (17)] gives an initial estimate of the factor-mimicking portfolios, $\hat{F}_t$ (called factor scores in the factor analysis literature). For a second set of assets (24 industry portfolios), the matrix of betas is then estimated by a time-series regression of asset returns on the returns of either one, two, or three initial factor-mimicking portfolios. Finally, the average premium vector, $\bar{F}$, is estimated from a cross-sectional regression of average returns of the 24 industry portfolios, $\bar{r}$, on their estimated betas.

[12] Solutions to the first-order equations with negative V_{ii} (negative idiosyncratic variances) are called Heywood cases (see Anderson [1984] for proposals for dealing with them).

In our description of the cross-sectional regression approach above, we estimated $\hat{F}_t$ for each period and then averaged these estimates to get $\bar{F}$ In Gehr [1978] the returns are averaged first and then regressed on the beta matrix. If the beta matrix is held constant over the period, these two approaches will lead to *identical* point estimates. However, the standard errors calculated from the time series of the $\hat{F}_t$ will be different than the OLS standard errors from the single regression of average returns on betas. The time-series standard errors should be preferable since they incorporate cross-sectional dependence and heteroscedasticity that is ignored in the OLS standard errors. Shanken [1992a] suggests additional adjustments to the time-series standard errors to account for the EIV problem in the betas.

Gehr [1978] uses 30 years of monthly data to estimate the vector of average risk premia, $\bar{F}$. His focus is on whether the premia are significantly different from zero, and therefore no explicit tests of the model's over-identifying restrictions are performed in the study. Over the 30-year period only one of the three factors, the third factor, has a significant premium. Over the three 10-year subintervals there were one, none, and two factors, respectively, with significant premia.

Roll & Ross [1980] estimate factor risk premia and test the APT restrictions with a sample of daily returns on 1260 firms over the period from July 1962 to December 1972. Due to computational considerations, they divide the cross-sectional sample into 42 groups of thirty firms each and perform an analysis on each group. For a five factor model they use maximum likelihood factor analysis to estimate B, the matrix of assets' sensitivities to the factors. Given this estimate of B, $\hat{B}$, they perform cross-sectional regressions of asset returns on $\hat{B}$, as in (17). They also perform cross-sectional regressions of asset excess returns (i.e., returns in excess of an assumed riskless rate, λ_0, of 6% per annum) on $\hat{B}$, as in (18). As in Fama & MacBeth [1973], the cross-sectional regressions are estimated each period and the risk premia are measured by the time-series average of the estimates, $\bar{F}$. Roll & Ross [1980] use generalized least squares in the cross-sectional regressions rather than OLS. The relevant covariance matrix for the GLS weighting is obtained from the inputs to the factor analysis step. The results indicate that as many as four factors have significant risk premia.

Roll & Ross [1980] test the APT by including the sample standard deviation of the asset as an instrument in cross-sectional regressions such as (19) and (20). In their tests, the estimate of the standard deviation is not predetermined. In one version of this test (their Table IV), the sample standard deviation, estimated beta matrix, $\hat{B}$, and asset returns are from the same sample. In this case, the test strongly rejects the APT because of the apparent significant relation between mean returns and standard deviation, even after controlling for factor risk. As Roll & Ross [1980] point out, the use of the same sample to estimate the dependent and independent variables in the regressions may lead to spurious significance of the parameter δ in (19) and (20). This could be caused by correlation in the sampling errors of mean returns and sample standard deviations (this problem is also discussed in Miller & Scholes [1972] and Lehmann [1990]). To overcome this problem, Roll & Ross [1980] perform the tests using disjoint subsets of the data to estimate the inputs. That is, they use observations 3, 9, 15, etc. to get the estimated factor sensitivities, $\hat{B}$; use observations 5, 11, 17, etc. to estimate the standard deviation; and use the returns for observations 1, 7, 13, etc. to estimate the cross-sectional regression (19). The use of disjoint subsets to estimate the inputs should reduce the potential for spurious significance. In this case, three of the forty-two groups of assets have a statistically significant value of δ. They argue that there is little evidence against the hypothesis that an asset's own standard deviation has no incremental power over the asset's factor sensitivities in explaining mean returns.

An additional implication of the model, shown in (14), is that the implied zero-beta (or riskless) return, λ_0, and the implied risk premia, λ, should be the same across subsets of assets. Because of the standard rotational indeterminacy of the estimate, $\hat{B}$, from factor analysis, Roll & Ross [1980] cannot compare λ^i to λ^j (where i and j denote different subgroups of assets) because the rotations across the subgroups may be different. However, they can compare λ_0^i and λ_0^j. In a final test they use a Hotelling T^2 test to test the equality of the mean zero-beta return across 38 of the 42 groups (four groups were excluded because of lack of time-series data). They could not reject the hypothesis that the mean zero-beta returns were the same across groups.

One of the advantages of using daily data, as in Roll & Ross [1980], is the large number of time-series observations available for estimation. This is particularly important when the sample is to be subdivided to estimate factor sensitivities, standard deviations, and mean returns over separate observations. However, the use of daily data causes some problems in terms of estimating the matrix of factor sensitivities, B. The main input into factor analysis is the sample covariance matrix of asset returns. The standard sample covariance assumes that we have returns that are synchronous (i.e., observed over the same period). In a given observation period (in this case, a day) the returns on one asset are actually measured over a different time interval than the returns on another asset, in general. This is due to the fact that returns are calculated from the percentage change in closing prices (adjusted for any distributions on that day). The closing prices are usually the price of the last trade of the day. This last trade might have occurred at the close of the day for some assets but earlier in the day for others. The usual pairwise sample covariance will tend to underestimate the true covariance because it is only measuring the comovement over the typical daily common observation period across assets. The nonsynchroneity also induces lead and lagged cross-correlations. The extent of the bias in the covariance estimates depends on the severity of the nonsynchroneity.

This bias is not restricted to daily data; it is present at any observation frequency. However, the bias is a function of the amount of nonsynchroneity, as a fraction of the observation period. This will be much larger for daily observations than for monthly observations, for example. The equivalent problem occurs in applications of the CAPM or event studies that need to adjust for cross-sectional differences in sensitivities to a market index. Scholes & Williams [1977], Cohen, Hawawini, Maier, Schwartz & Whitcomb [1983], and Andersen [1989] propose estimators for beta which correct for the bias in the standard OLS estimate of beta. The estimators consist of the sum of lead, contemporaneous, and lagged betas, adjusted for the serial correlation in the market.

Shanken [1987b] recognizes that the same type of synchroneity problem arises in the use of factor analysis to obtain first stage estimates of B. He proposes a covariance matrix estimator based on the methods of Cohen, et al [1983] for use in the factor analysis stage. Shanken [1987b] applies this approach to a set of assets chosen to be comparable to the sample in Roll & Ross [1980]. Empirically, he finds that the average estimate of pairwise covariance, adjusted for nonsynchronous trading, is twice as large as the average unadjusted sample covariance. In fact, almost all (97%) of the adjusted estimates are larger than the unadjusted estimates. He also finds that factor-mimicking portfolios constructed from $\hat{B}$'s adjusted for nonsynchroneity have small correlations with portfolios constructed from unadjusted B's. This implies that using unadjusted covariance matrices in the factor analysis stage is not just an innocuous choice of a different rotation of the same factors. The evidence in Shanken [1987b] indicates that nonsynchronous trading may induce significant biases when applying factor analysis to high frequency data. Therefore, if one wishes to use daily data in order to increase the size of the time-series sample, some adjustment for nonsynchroneity should be considered.

Brown & Weinstein [1983], using a data set and time period chosen to be the same as those chosen by Roll & Ross [1980], test the equality of the risk premia across subgroups of assets [i.e., they test $\lambda_0^i = \lambda_0$ and $\lambda^i = \lambda$ in (14)].[13] Rather than performing the analysis on 42 groups of thirty stocks each, they use twenty-one groups of sixty stocks each. Each group of sixty assets is divided into two subgroups of thirty assets. For each group of sixty securities, maximum likelihood factor analysis is used to get an estimate, $\hat{B}$, of the matrix of factor sensitivities as well as estimates for the two subgroups, $\hat{B}^1$ and $\hat{B}^2$. Let $\hat{B}_\text{u}$ be the unrestricted factor beta matrix formed by stacking $\hat{B}^1$ and $\hat{B}^2$ (i.e., $\hat{B}'_\text{u} = [\hat{B}^{1'} : \hat{B}^{2'}]$). An unrestricted form of the model is estimated by a cross-sectional GLS regression of the form (19) in which returns are regressed on ι^{60}, $\hat{B}_\text{u}$, and Z. The top $30 \times (k+1)$ submatrix of instruments, Z, is a matrix of zeros and the bottom $30 \times (k+1)$ submatrix of Z is equal to $[\iota^{30} : B^2]$. A restricted form of the model is estimated by a cross-sectional GLS regression of the form (17) in which returns are regressed on ι^{60} and $\hat{B}$. The test statistic is formed from the diagonal elements of the restricted and unrestricted residual covariance matrices.[14] The test is equivalent to a test for a shift in the regression parameters (sometimes referred to as a Chow test). The law of one price implies that the price of

[13] The tests of $\lambda_0^i = \lambda_0$ and $\lambda^i = \lambda$ in (14) can be viewed as tests of the law of one price (i.e., that the price of risk is the same across subgroups), *conditional* on an estimated factor model. Chen & Knez [1992] propose a test of consistent pricing across subsets of assets that does not require a first-stage estimation of a factor model.

[14] An alternative approach would be to estimate only the restricted factor sensitivity matrix, $\hat{B}$, and regress returns on ι^{60}, $\hat{B}$, and Z, as in (19) and (20). The top $30 \times (k+1)$ submatrix of Z is a matrix of zeros and the bottom $30 \times (k+1)$ submatrix of Z is equal to $[\iota^{30} : B^2]$ where $\hat{B}^2$ is defined as the last 30 rows of $\hat{B}$. Then a test of $\delta = 0$ is a test of consistent pricing across subgroups.

risk should be the same across subgroups. Brown & Weinstein [1983] test the hypothesis of equal price of risk across subgroups for three, five, and seven factor models. They find that the restrictions are rejected at standard levels of statistical significance but argue that this may be an artifact of the large number of observations available. That is, holding the size of the test (i.e., the probability of type I error) constant, the probability of a type II error approaches zero as the number of observations increases. Brown & Weinstein [1983] propose using a posterior odds ratio approach to alter the size of the test to reflect the large sample. After this adjustment, the tests still reject the hypothesis of equal prices of risk approximately fifty percent of the time.

Early factor-analytic-based empirical analyses of the APT tended to focus on small subgroups of securities (between 24 and 60 assets per group in the studies discussed above) because of the computational problems associated with performing factor analysis of large-scale covariance matrices. Much subsequent research has been devoted to developing methods that can accommodate large cross-sectional samples. One such method is proposed in Chen [1983]. He analyzes daily stock return data over the 16-year period from 1963 through 1978, divided into four four-year subperiods. The number of assets analyzed in the subperiods is 1064, 1562, 1580, and 1378, respectively. He chooses the first 180 stocks (alphabetically) in each subperiod and uses factor analysis to estimate the factor sensitivities for a ten factor model. Factor-mimicking portfolios for a five factor model are then formed from these same 180 stocks by a mathematical programming algorithm that imposes a penalty for choosing portfolio weights very different from $1/n$ and which also disallows short positions. The factor sensitivities of the remaining n-180 assets are estimated from their covariances with the factor-mimicking portfolios [see Chen, 1983, equation A1]. Cross-sectional regressions of the form (17) are estimated for the five factor APT and the CAPM (where the S&P 500, equal-weighted CRSP portfolio, and value-weighted CRSP portfolio are used as proxies for the market portfolio). The asset returns on even days are used as dependent variables while the factor sensitivities, $\hat{B}$, and CAPM betas are estimated with data from odd days. Chen [1983] finds that the vector of average factor risk premia, $\bar{F}$, is significantly different from the zero vector.

Many studies focus only on the question of whether the restrictions implied by the APT can be rejected. A more important question is whether the model outperforms or underperforms alternative asset pricing models. This is a difficult problem because the competing hypotheses (e.g., the APT versus the CAPM) are not nested. That is, one hypothesis is not a restricted version of the other hypothesis. Chen [1983] addresses this issue by applying methods of testing nonnested hypotheses [see Davidson & Mackinnon, 1981]. Let $\hat{r}_{i,t,\mathrm{APT}}$ denote the fitted value for $r_{i,t}$ from the regression (17) when the estimated factor sensitivities are used to form $\hat{B}$, and let $\hat{r}_{i,t,\mathrm{CAPM}}$ denote the fitted value for $r_{i,t}$ from the regression (17) when the estimated market betas are used to form $\hat{B}$. Consider the cross-sectional regression

$$r_{i,t} = \alpha_t \hat{r}_{i,t,\,\mathrm{APT}} + (1 - \alpha_t)\hat{r}_{i,t,\,\mathrm{CAPM}} + e_{it}. \tag{21}$$

The time series of α_t can be used to calculate the mean value $\bar{\alpha}$, and the standard error of $\bar{\alpha}$. If the APT is the appropriate model of asset returns then one would expect $\bar{\alpha}$ to equal 1.0, while one would expect $\bar{\alpha}$ to equal zero if the CAPM is the appropriate model. Chen finds that, across the four subperiods and across various market portfolio proxies, he can often reject both the hypothesis that $\alpha = 0$ and the hypothesis that $\alpha = 1$. However, the point estimates are all very close to one. That is, $\bar{\alpha}$ is between 0.938 and 1.006. Also, Chen [1983] finds that the residuals from the CAPM cross-sectional regression (17) can be explained by the factor sensitivities while the residuals from the APT cross-sectional regression are not explained by assets' betas relative to the market portfolio. Thus, the data seem to support the APT as a better model of asset returns.

Chen [1983] also compares the returns on a portfolio of high variance stocks to the returns on a portfolio of low variance stocks constructed to have the same estimated factor sensitivities. If the APT is correct, these two portfolios should have the same expected returns (since they have the same factor sensitivities, B). There is no significant difference in returns. The same procedure is applied to portfolios of large capitalization and small capitalization stocks. Chen finds that, while all of the point estimates indicate that large firms had lower returns than small firms with the same factor risk, the difference is statistically significant in only one of the four subperiods. He concludes that the size anomaly is explained by differences in factor risk.

Reinganum [1981] uses the same method of factor beta estimation as Chen [1983] to compare ten portfolios formed on the basis of market value of equity. The returns on these portfolios are compared to control portfolios constructed to have the same sensitivity to the factors. This is done for three, four, and five factor models. Unlike Chen [1983], Reinganum [1981] concludes that the size anomaly is not explained by the APT.

The above studies use factor analysis, or some variant, to estimate assets' factor betas. An alternative approach is taken by Chen, Roll & Ross [1986] who specify, ex ante, a set of observable variables as proxies for the systematic 'state variables' or factors in the economy. The prespecified factors are (i) the monthly percentage change in industrial production (lead by one period)[15]; (ii) a measure of unexpected inflation; (iii) the change in expected inflation[16]; (iv) the difference in returns on low-grade (Baa and under) corporate bonds and long-term government bonds; and (v) the difference in returns on long-term government bonds and short-term Treasury bills.

Sixty months of time-series observations are used to estimate assets' betas relative to these prespecified factors. Given these estimates of the factor sensitivities, $\hat{B}$, cross-sectional regressions of returns on $\hat{B}$ [as in (17)] are estimated in order

[15] In some specifications, the annual percentage change in industrial production is also included, but is not found to be statistically significant.

[16] The unexpected inflation and change in expected inflation variables require a model of expected inflation. Chen, Roll & Ross [1986] use the approach to measuring expected inflation developed by Fama & Gibbons [1984].

to get estimates of the returns on factor-mimicking portfolios, $\hat{F}_t$. As in Fama & MacBeth [1973], portfolios rather than individual assets are used in these second-stage regressions in order to reduce the EIV problem caused by the use of $\hat{B}$ rather than B. Chen, Roll & Ross [1986] form twenty portfolios on the basis of firm size (market capitalization of equity) at the beginning of the particular test period. The average risk premia are estimated for the full sample period, January 1958 to December 1984, as well as three subperiods.

The average factor risk premia, $\bar{F}$, are statistically significant over the entire sample period for the industrial production, unexpected inflation, and low-grade bond factors, and is marginally significant for the term-spread factor (v). To check how robust the results are to changes in the prespecified factors, Chen, Roll & Ross [1986] perform the above exercise with the change in industrial production factor replaced by several alternative factors. One can view this as estimating (19) with the extra instruments, Z_{t-1}, being the betas on the extra factors. If the specified model is adequate, then δ should be equal to zero.

In the CAPM, the appropriate measure of risk is an asset's beta with respect to a market portfolio. Therefore, one logical alternative candidate as a factor would be a market portfolio proxy. The above analysis is conducted with the annual industrial production factor replaced by a market portfolio factor (either the equal-weighted or the value-weighted NYSE portfolio). They find that the risk premia on the market factors are not statistically significant when the other factors are included in the regression (17).

Consumption-based asset pricing models [e.g., Lucas, 1978, and Breeden, 1979] imply that risk premia are determined by assets' covariance with agents' intertemporal marginal rate of substitution in consumption. This can be approximated by assets' covariance with changes in consumption. The growth rate in per capita real consumption is added as a factor (to replace the market portfolios). This growth rate is actually lead by one period to reflect the fact that there are lags in data collection. The risk premium on the consumption factor is not significant when the other five prespecified factors are included.

The last alternative factor analyzed by Chen, Roll & Ross [1986] is the percentage change in the price of oil. The same analysis as above is performed with the beta of assets' returns with respect to changes in oil prices replacing the other alternative factors. The estimated risk premium associated with oil price shocks is statistically insignificant for the full period and for two of the three subperiods. The subperiod in which the premium is statistically significant is the 1958–1967 period.

Chen, Roll & Ross [1986] conclude that the five prespecified factors provide a reasonable specification of the sources of systematic and priced risk in the economy. This is based largely on their results which suggest that, after controlling for factor risk, other measures of risk (such as market betas or consumption betas) do not seem to be priced.

Chan, Chen & Hsieh [1985] use the same set of factors as Chen, Roll & Ross [1986] in order to determine whether cross-sectional differences in factor risk are enough to explain the size anomaly evident in the CAPM literature and in some previous APT studies [e.g., Reinganum, 1981]. For each test year from 1958 to 1977, an estimation period is defined as the previous five year interval (i.e, 1953–1957 is the estimation period for 1958, 1954–1958 is the estimation period for 1959, etc.). The sample consists of all NYSE firms that exist at the beginning of the estimation period and have price data at the end of the estimation period. Firm size is defined as the market capitalization of the firm's equity at the end of the estimation period. Each firm is ranked by firm size and assigned to one of twenty portfolios.

Chan, Chen & Hsieh [1985] estimate the factor sensitivities of the twenty size-based portfolios relative to the prespecified factors and the equal-weighted NYSE portfolio over the estimation period. In the subsequent test year, cross-sectional regressions, such as (17), of portfolio returns on the estimated factor sensitivities, $\hat{B}$, are run each month. This is repeated for each test year and yields a monthly time series of returns on factor-mimicking portfolios from January 1958 to December 1977.

If the risk premia from the factor model explain the size anomaly, then the time-series averages of the residuals from (17) should be zero. Chan, Chen & Hsieh [1985] use paired t tests and the Hotelling T^2 test to determine if the residuals have the same means across different size portfolios.[17] These tests are equivalent to estimating (19) where Z_{t-1} represent various combinations of portfolio dummy variables and testing whether the elements of the vector δ are equal to each other.

Chan, Chen & Hsieh [1985] find that the risk premium for the equal-weighted market portfolio is positive in each subperiod, but is not statistically significant. Over the entire period they find significant premia for the industrial production factor, the unexpected inflation factor, and the low-grade bond spread factor. They find that the average residuals are not significantly different across portfolios and that the difference in the average residuals between the portfolio of smallest firms and the portfolio of largest firms, while positive, is not significantly different from zero. The average difference in monthly returns between these two portfolios is 0.956%; 0.453% is due to the low-grade bond risk premium, 0.352% is due to the NYSE market risk premium, 0.204% is due to the industrial production risk premium, and 0.120% is left unexplained.

Chan, Chen, and Hsieh also run regressions such as (19) in which the instrument, Z_{t-1}, is the logarithm of firm size. When the $\hat{B}$ matrix includes the betas for the prespecified factors and the equal-weighted NYSE portfolio, then the coefficient on firm size, δ, is statistically significant. When $\hat{B}$ only contains betas for the prespecified factors, then δ is insignificant. They conclude that the multifactor model explains the size anomaly.

Shanken & Weinstein [1990] reevaluate the evidence on the risk premia associated with the prespecified factors used in Chan, Chen & Hsieh [1985] and Chen, Roll & Ross [1986]. While Shanken & Weinstein [1990] use the same set of five prespecified factors and time periods similar to those in Chan, Chen & Hsieh [1985] and Chen, Roll & Ross [1986], they make several changes in the

[17] This is a slightly weaker test than testing whether the mean residuals are zero.

procedures. One adjustment is an EIV correction for the time-series standard errors of $\bar{F}$, which is derived in Shanken [1992a]. This correction tends to increase the standard errors and, hence, decrease the reported test statistics.

A second change involves the manner in which the size-based portfolios are formed for the estimation of the matrix of factor sensitivities of those portfolios. Chan, Chen & Hsieh [1985] and Chen, Roll & Ross [1986] form the size-based portfolios on the basis of the market capitalization of the firms at the *end* of the estimation period. For example, betas are estimated by Chan, Chen & Hsieh [1985] over the period 1953–1957 for twenty size-based portfolios formed on the basis of market capitalization at the end of December 1957. Given these estimates, cross-sectional regressions are run for the twelve months of 1958. While this approach does not induce bias in the portfolio returns for 1958, it may induce correlation between the estimation error in betas, $\hat{B} - B$, and the allocation of firms to portfolios. For example, some of the firms allocated to the small firm portfolios in December 1957 will have had poor performance over the period 1953–1957, while the opposite is true for the firms allocated to the large firm portfolios. However, if the current beta is related to past performance, then the historical betas calculated over 1953–1957 will systematically misstate the current level of beta. For example, leverage effects could lead to a negative relation between beta and performance (i.e., increases in beta for poor performers and decreases in beta for good performers). This type of effect will cause the historical estimate of beta (as an estimate of beta for the *next year*) to be too small for the small firm portfolios and too large for the large firm portfolios. Shanken & Weinstein [1990] argue that this decrease in dispersion of betas would lead to an upward bias in the estimated risk premia from the cross-sectional regressions (assuming the premia are nonzero in the first place). This bias could lead to spurious significance in the estimated risk premia.

The alternative portfolio formation procedure used by Shanken & Weinstein [1990] is to form size portfolios at the beginning of each year and use asset returns over the subsequent year to estimate betas. For example, for the 1953–1957 estimation period, form portfolios at the end of December 1952 to calculate returns in 1953, form portfolios at the end of December 1953 to calculate returns in 1954, and so on. This procedure does not induce correlation between beta estimation errors and portfolio groupings since the allocation to groups is chosen ex ante.

Shanken & Weinstein [1990] estimate cross-sectional regressions (18) using betas estimated from the prior five-year period as well as betas estimated over the same period as the cross-sectional regressions. They check the sensitivity of the results to the number of portfolios used by estimating the cross-sectional regressions with 20, 60, and 120 portfolios (using WLS). They also estimate restricted versions of the cross-sectional regressions that take advantage of the fact that some of the prespecified factors are excess returns on financial assets. $\bar{F}_j$, the jth element of $\bar{F}$, is the excess return on a portfolio that mimics factor j. If factor j is an asset excess return then it mimics itself without error, so we can impose the restriction that $\bar{F}_j$ is equal to the time-series mean of the factor. The sample period of 1958–1983 is divided into three subperiods, 1958–1967, 1968–1977, and 1978–1983. With a design similar to that used by Chan, Chen & Hsieh [1985] and Chen, Roll & Ross [1986] (using the prior period betas, 20 portfolios, and without the above restrictions imposed) none of the factor risk premia are statistically significant (at the 5% level) in the three subperiods. Only the industrial production factor premium is significant over the entire sample period. Using a larger number of cross-sections increases the evidence for a significant price of risk for this factor and provides some evidence for a significant risk premium associated with the low-grade bond factor in the first subperiod.

The use of contemporaneously estimated betas does not seem to influence the results greatly. The restricted estimates described above tend to decrease the significance of the low-grade bond factor and increase the significance of the industrial production and term-structure factors.

Similar to Chan, Chen & Hsieh [1985], Shanken & Weinstein [1990] use the Hotelling T^2 statistic[18] to test whether the portfolio residuals from (18) have a mean of zero. The T^2 tests do not reject the hypothesis that the residuals have a mean of zero for both the unrestricted and restricted estimators. They also test whether the price of risk is equal across small and large firms. This is done in the framework of (20) where the instrument, Z_{t-1}, is the product of $\hat{B}$ and a dummy variable. The dummy variable is equal to one if the portfolio is one of the first $n/2$ size-based portfolios (where n is the total number of portfolios) and is equal to zero otherwise. If the price of risk is the same across subgroups, then δ should be zero. There is little evidence of differential pricing of risk for both the unrestricted and restricted estimators.

As in the previous studies, Shanken & Weinstein [1990] check the specification of the prespecified factor by including betas relative to a market portfolio proxy (the value-weighted CRSP index) in the cross-sectional regressions. Using the design of Chan, Chen & Hsieh [1985] and Chen, Roll & Ross [1986], the estimated market risk premium is not significant. Using the restricted model or the unrestricted model with contemporaneous betas, Shanken and Weinstein find that the estimated risk premium on the market proxy is statistically significant.

The results of Shanken & Weinstein [1990] suggest that the previous significance of the prespecified factor risk premia and the ability of those factors to render the market risk premium insignificant may be sensitive to the portfolio formation strategy and to whether or not one uses the EIV adjustment. The results also suggest that the choice of the number of assets or portfolios used in estimating the parameters in the cross-sectional regressions [equations (17)–(20)] may have an important influence on the precision of the estimates.

A related issue regarding the portfolio formation process's influence on the power of statistical tests is raised in Warga [1989]. He argues that the manner in which portfolios are chosen will tend to maximize the cross-sectional dispersion of assets' sensitivities to some factors but will yield low dispersion of assets' sensitivities to other factors. Dispersion in betas is important for the precision

[18] The statistic is adjusted by the EIV correction from Shanken [1992a].

of the estimates in the cross-sectional regressions. The typical methods will then give precise estimates of the premia for some factors and imprecise estimates for others. He provides evidence that the size-based stratification will yield dispersion in assets' sensitivities to the low-grade bond factor but will yield low dispersion in assets' sensitivities to the market portfolio proxy. This implies low power against the hypothesis that the market risk premium is zero and may be an additional reason why Chan, Chen & Hsieh [1985] and Chen, Roll & Ross [1986] found that market risk was insignificant. The larger number of portfolios in some of the tests in Shanken & Weinstein [1990] will increase dispersion in the betas and lead to more precise estimates.

Studies which test the APT in ways similar to Chan, Chen & Hsieh [1985] and Chen, Roll & Ross [1986] include Burmeister & Wall [1986], Berry, Burmeister & McElroy [1988b], Connor & Uhlaner [1988], Ferson and Harvey [1991a,1991b], Wei, Lee & Chen [1991], and Cragg & Donald [1992].

4.2. Time-series tests of the APT

Now, rather than assuming we observe the matrix of factor betas, B, let us assume that we observe $\lambda_{0,t-1}$, and $\lambda_{t-1} + f_t$, which represent the return on a zero-beta asset and the vector of excess returns (i.e., returns in excess of the zero-beta return) of k portfolios which are perfectly correlated with the factors.[19] We can then view (15) and (16) as restricted versions of time-series regressions of asset excess returns on the factor portfolio returns $(\lambda_{t-1} + f_t)$ in which the parameters to be estimated are the entries in the factor beta matrix, B. For example, let F_t denote $\lambda_{t-1} + f_t$, assume that B is constant over time, and consider the time-series system of regressions:

$$R_t = \alpha + BF_t + \varepsilon_t \tag{22}$$

where α is an $n \times 1$ vector of intercept coefficients. A testable restriction implied by the pricing model is that $\alpha = 0$. This approach to testing the specification of asset pricing models is used by Black, Jensen & Scholes [1972] to test the CAPM where F_t represents the excess return on a market portfolio proxy (the equal-weighted NYSE portfolio in their case). Jobson [1982] discusses this approach in an APT context. A variant of this approach applies when the riskless or zero-beta return is not observed. Let F_t^* denote $\lambda_{0,t-1}\iota^k + F_t$, the 'raw' returns (i.e., not in excess of the zero-beta return) on a set of k factor-mimicking portfolios, and consider the time-series regression:

$$r_t = \alpha + BF_t^* + \varepsilon_t. \tag{23}$$

Under the assumption that $\lambda_{0,t-1}$ is constant through time and equal to λ_0, the asset pricing model implies the restriction:

$$\alpha = (\iota^n - B\iota^k)\lambda_0.$$

[19] We will assume that such portfolios exist.

This approach is used in a CAPM context in Gibbons [1982] with F_t^* being the equal-weighted NYSE portfolio.

The pricing restrictions that we have seen so far are equivalent to having some linear combination of factor-mimicking portfolios on the mean/variance efficient frontier of asset returns (as discussed in Section 3.4). A stronger condition is that the factor-mimicking portfolios span the entire mean/variance efficient frontier. Spanning would imply the restrictions that $\alpha = 0$, or equivalently $B\iota^k = \iota^n$, in (23) [see Huberman & Kandel, 1987].

Lehmann & Modest [1988] perform time-series based tests of the APT restriction, $\alpha = 0$ in (22) and (23). They divide the period from 1963 to 1982 into four five-year subperiods. Firms traded on the NYSE and AMEX that do not have missing daily data over a subperiod comprise the sample. For each subperiod, 750 of these firms are selected at random and their daily returns are used to estimate the covariance matrix of returns. Factor analysis is applied to the covariance matrix of returns in order to estimate the factor sensitivities of the assets. Lehmann & Modest [1988] use the *EM* algorithm [see Dempster, Laird & Rubin, 1977] to factor analyze the full 750×750 return covariance matrix.[20] This eliminates the need to analyze many small subsets of data, as was done previously by many authors. The ability to use large numbers of individual assets to form factor-mimicking portfolios is an important improvement because it allows us to form well-diversified portfolios without inadvertently masking important characteristics of the data.

Given the $n \times k$ matrix of estimated factor sensitivities, $\hat{B}$, and an estimate of the idiosyncratic covariance matrix, $\hat{V}$ (assumed to be diagonal), Lehmann and Modest form k factor-mimicking portfolios and a zero-beta mimicking portfolio by minimizing the idiosyncratic risk of the portfolio subject to the constraint that the portfolio only has sensitivity to one factor. That is, the n-vector of portfolio weights for the jth factor-mimicking portfolio, w_j, is chosen to solve:

$$\begin{aligned} &\min_{\omega_j} \omega_j' \hat{V} \omega_j \\ \text{such that} \quad &\omega_j' \hat{B}_{.,s} = 0 \qquad \text{for all } s \neq j \\ &\omega_j' \iota^n \quad = 1 \end{aligned} \tag{24}$$

where $\hat{B}_{.,s}$ denotes the sth column of $\hat{B}$. The zero-beta portfolio is formed in the same way except that $\omega j' \hat{B}_{.,s} = 0$ for all s [see Lehmann & Modest, 1985, 1988, for details]. Given these portfolio weights, they calculate weekly returns on factor-mimicking portfolios for models with five, ten, and fifteen factors. Excess returns of these factor-mimicking portfolios are used as F_t in the regressions (22) and raw returns are used as F_t^* in the regressions (23).

Lehmann & Modest [1988] calculate several sets of weekly returns to be used as R_t and r_t. All NYSE and AMEX firms that meet the data requirements are

[20] Stroyny [1992] suggests a modification to the *EM* algorithm that substantially improves its rate of convergence.

allocated to quintile and ventile portfolios. Two sets of sized-based portfolios are formed by ranking firms by market capitalization at the beginning of the test period and forming five and twenty equally-weighted portfolios, respectively. Two sets of dividend yield-based portfolios are formed by ranking firms by dividend yield in the year before the test period. The first portfolio in each set contains all firms with a zero dividend yield. The remaining assets are allocated equally to the other four or nineteen portfolios (depending on whether there are five or twenty portfolios in R_t). Finally, two sets of variance-based portfolios are formed by ranking firms by their sample variances in the year before the test period (using daily data) and forming five and twenty equally-weighted portfolios, respectively. The various sets of weekly portfolio returns are regressed on the raw or excess returns on the factor-mimicking portfolios in a standard multivariate regression analysis. Similar regressions are run with single-index market portfolio proxies, the CRSP equal-weighted and value-weighted portfolios.

Using the five size-based quintile portfolios, Lehmann & Modest [1988] reject the hypothesis (at p-values less than 5%) that $\alpha = 0$ in (22) and (23) for both of the CRSP indices and the 5, 10, and 15 factor models (their table 1). Using the twenty size ventile portfolios, the single-index models are rejected while the APT models are generally not rejected. Given that the models are rejected with the quintile portfolios, Lehmann & Modest [1988] argue that the failure to reject the models with the ventile portfolios may be due to lower power in that specification.

Using the five dividend quintile portfolios the single-index models are rejected while only the single-index model using the equal-weighted portfolio is rejected using the twenty yield portfolios. The APT models are not rejected using either the quintile or ventile portfolios (their table 4). The results for the variance-based portfolios are similar to the results for the dividend yield portfolios (their table 5).

As discussed above, if the factor portfolios span the mean/variance efficient frontier, then there is a testable restriction on the factor sensitivities, $B\iota^k = \iota^n$ in the regression (23). Lehmann & Modest [1988, table 8] test this restriction which is overwhelmingly rejected.

Lehmann & Modest [1988] conclude that, while the APT is rejected on the basis of the regressions with size-based portfolios, its apparent ability to explain the dividend yield and variance effects that are unexplained by the CAPM (with standard proxies for the market portfolio) make it a good alternative model of asset pricing.

Connor & Korajczyk [1988a] also use a large number of individual assets to form factor-mimicking portfolios. They use the asymptotic principal components procedure derived in Connor & Korajczyk [1986]. The asymptotic principal components procedure provides a computationally feasible method of estimating factor-mimicking portfolios from very large cross-sections. Let R denote the $n \times T$ matrix of excess returns on assets, assume that asset returns follow an approximate k-factor model, and define Ω to be equal to $R'R/n$. Connor & Korajczyk [1986] show that the first k eigenvectors of the matrix Ω converge to excess returns on factor-mimicking portfolios (subject to the typical rotational indeterminacy). Note that Ω is a $T \times T$ matrix so that one only needs to perform eigenvector decompositions of a $T \times T$ matrix, regardless of the size of the cross-sectional sample. Factor analytic approaches require the decomposition of an $n \times n$ matrix followed by a portfolio formation procedure such as (24) or cross-sectional regressions. For large n and moderate T the computational burden of asymptotic principal components is much smaller than factor analytic procedures. Also, the procedure does not require that T be larger than n, only that T be larger than k, the number of factors. Some studies have used asymptotic principal components with cross-sectional samples in excess of 11,000.

Connor & Korajczyk [1988a] use monthly data on NYSE and AMEX firms over the twenty year period from 1964 to 1983. The sample period is divided into four 5-year subperiods. In each subperiod, the asymptotic principal components technique is applied to the returns, in excess of the one-month Treasury bill return, for all firms without any missing monthly returns over the subinterval. This yields excess returns on factor-mimicking portfolios constructed from samples of 1487, 1720, 1734, and 1745 firms in the respective subperiods. These portfolio excess returns are used as F_t in (22) to test five-factor and ten-factor versions of the APT.

There are two sets of test assets used as R_t in (22). The first is a set of ten size-based portfolios. Firms are ranked on the basis of market capitalization at the beginning of the five year subperiod and are allocated to ten equal-weighted size decile portfolios. This is similar to the portfolio formation strategy of Lehmann & Modest [1988] except that there are ten rather than five or twenty portfolios. The second set of test assets is the entire sample of individual assets for each subperiod. The statistics used to test the hypothesis that $\alpha = 0$ require a decomposition of the idiosyncratic covariance matrix, $\hat{V}$. The tests of Lehmann & Modest [1988] and Connor & Korajczyk [1988a] when portfolios are used as R_t do not place any restrictions on the specific form (such as diagonality) of $\hat{V}$.[21] However, when using individual assets, an unrestricted $\hat{V}$ is not feasible (if for no other reason than that there are more parameters to estimate than observations in the data). The approach taken by Connor & Korajczyk [1988a] in this case is to assume that V is block diagonal by industry, where industry is defined by 3-digit SIC codes. That is, within a 3-digit industry V is unrestricted but $V_{i,j}$ is assumed to be zero if firms i and j are in different industries. Connor & Korajczyk [1988a] also estimate an alternative regression which includes instruments, Z_{t-1}:

$$R_t = \alpha + BF_t + \delta Z_{t-1} + \varepsilon_t \tag{25}$$

where Z_{t-1} is a January dummy variable, equal to 1 if month t is January and zero otherwise. This is the time-series equivalent of (20) and the asset pricing model implies that $\alpha = 0$ and $\delta = 0$. The choice of a January dummy variable for Z is motivated by the inability of the CAPM to explain seasonality in asset returns [Keim, 1983].

The test statistics in Connor & Korajczyk [1988a] are modified likelihood ratio statistics [see Rao, 1973, pp. 554–556] which have an exact small sample distribu-

[21] Note that the restriction that V be diagonal is not required by the APT. In approximate factor models, V may be nondiagonal, but this correlation across assets needs to be weak.

tion under the null hypothesis that the idiosyncratic returns, ε_t, are multivariate normal. The modified statistic is used because the standard asymptotic tests seem to have poor small sample properties [Binder, 1985, and Shanken, 1985].

Using the size portfolios as test assets, Connor & Korajczyk [1988a] reject (at the 5% level) $\alpha = 0$ in (22) for the value-weighted CAPM as well as the APT with five and ten factors, while the CAPM using the equal-weighted CRSP proxy is not rejected. Using the seasonal instruments as in (25), the hypothesis that $\delta = 0$ is strongly rejected for the market portfolio proxies but not for the APT models, while the hypothesis that $\alpha = 0$ is rejected for the APT but not for the market proxies.

The test statistics seem to indicate that the APT models do a better job of explaining the seasonality in size portfolio returns but a worse job of explaining the nonseasonal size anomaly, relative to the single index CAPM-like models. However, given that the models are not nested, a direct comparison of the test statistics can be misleading. That is, a larger and therefore 'more significant' test statistic for one model versus another does not necessarily mean that the former model fits the data less well. As an analogy, consider testing $\alpha_i = 0$ for a single portfolio or asset i in (22), with F_t either being a vector of five factors or a single market portfolio. This test is a simple t-test, defined as the estimate, $\hat{\alpha}_i$, divided by its standard error. The t-statistic can be larger for a given model either because $\hat{\alpha}_i$ is larger or because the standard error is smaller (i.e., $\hat{\alpha}_i$ is measured with less error). Using multiple factors tends to increase the R^2 of the regression and, consequently, the precision of the estimates of α_i increases. Thus, we can have smaller deviations from the null hypothesis, $\alpha_i = 0$, in an economic sense that are more significant in the statistical sense. As an informal check for this, Connor & Korajczyk [1988a] plot the estimates of α_i and δ_i for the size portfolios. The plots bear out the indication that the APT models perform better in terms of explaining the seasonal effects. There is a pronounced size pattern in δ_i for the CAPM models but no pattern for the APT models. However, in contrast to the impression that might be given by the test statistics, there is no clear-cut difference in the magnitude of α_i between the APT models and the single-index models. The stronger rejections of the restriction that $\alpha = 0$ in (25) seem to be due to greater precision of the estimate of α for the APT relative to the CAPM.[22]

In Connor & Korajczyk [1988a], the tests using individual assets rather than the size based portfolios do not provide much power to discriminate between models. For most subperiods and hypotheses [i.e., $\alpha = 0$ in (22), $\alpha = 0$ in (25), and $\delta = 0$ in (25)] the tests either reject all models or fail to reject all models. For a few of the tests the statistics lead to rejection of the CAPM and fail to reject the APT, while there are no cases of the reverse happening. Finally, they test whether the estimates α_i and δ_i are related to market capitalization of the firm using a large-sample approximation to a posterior odds ratio. The CAPM is rejected in

[22] The fact that the R^2 value for the typical regressions in (22) and (25) is around 98% for the APT models and 75% for the CAPM models gives some indication of the greater precision of the estimated α vector in the former case.

almost every subperiod while the APT models tend to reject the hypothesis that α is not related to size but fail to reject that δ is not related to size. This is consistent with the pattern of pricing errors for the size-based portfolios described above.

Just as some authors have specified, ex ante, certain macroeconomic series as being the pervasive factors [e.g., Chen, Roll & Ross, 1986], other authors have specified, ex ante, sets of portfolios whose returns are assumed to be maximally correlated with the pervasive factors. When macroeconomic series are used, a second step is required to form factor-mimicking portfolios (generally through cross-sectional regressions of asset returns on estimated betas). When ex-ante specified portfolios are used, one can avoid the second step since the factors are asset returns which contain the appropriate risk premia. Huberman & Kandel [1987] specify the factors to be three size-based portfolios. Fama & French [1993] specify the factors to be five portfolio excess returns: (i) the return on a value-weighted market portfolio (in excess of the one-month Treasury bill return); (ii) the difference in returns on a small-firm portfolio and a large firm portfolio; (iii) the difference in returns on a portfolio of firms with high book-to-market equity (i.e., book value of equity relative to market value of equity) and a portfolio of firms with low book-to-market equity; (iv) the difference in the return on a long-term government bond portfolio and the return on the one-month Treasury bill; and (v) the difference in the return on a long-term corporate bond portfolio and the return on a long-term government bond portfolio.

Huberman & Kandel [1987] and Fama & French [1993] find that the multi-factor models do a much better job in explaining asset returns (i.e., values of α close to zero) than do standard single-index models.

McElroy & Burmeister [1988] postulate macroeconomic variables as observable factors and use nonlinear time-series regression to estimate the parameters of the factor model. Their approach allows joint estimation of the parameters of the model in one step rather than the two step procedures common to many of the previous studies. The pricing restrictions of the APT imply cross-equation restrictions on the statistical model. They use monthly returns on 70 individual stocks (from January 1972 through December 1982) as the set of test assets and five prespecified factors that are similar to the factors used by Chen, Roll & Ross [1986]. The five factors are: (i) the difference in returns of long-term corporate bonds and long-term government bonds plus a constant;[23] (ii) the difference in returns on long-term government bonds and short-term Treasury bills; (iii) a measure of unexpected deflation (the negative of unexpected inflation); (iv) a measure of unexpected growth in sales; and (v) either a return on market index (the S &P 500 portfolio) or a 'residual market factor' equal to the residuals from a regression of the market index on the other four factors.

Assuming that the prespecified factors correspond to the factor innovation, f_t, that the factor risk premia are constant through time ($\lambda_{t-1} = \lambda$ for all t), and that

[23] The constant is chosen to make the sample mean of the factor, from 1926 to 1981, equal to zero.

the exact pricing model holds, we can rewrite (16) as the multivariate time-series regression:

$$R_t = B\lambda + Bf_t + \varepsilon_t \tag{26}$$

where the parameters to be estimated are B and λ. The $n - k$ nonlinear cross-equation restrictions implied by the model are requirements that the intercept in (26) be equal to $B\lambda$. McElroy & Burmeister [1988] present an error components motivation for including either the return on a well-diversified portfolio or the residuals from a regression of the return on that portfolio on the other macroeconomic factors (the 'residual market factor') as one of the factors. In either case the model implies testable restrictions of the same form as above. They estimate (26) using iterated nonlinear seemingly unrelated regression (INLSUR)[24] and find that the estimated risk premia $\hat{\lambda}$ are significantly different from zero (at the 5% level) for each factor except the unexpected deflation factor. The overidentifying cross-equation restrictions are not rejected, leading McElroy and Burmeister to conclude that the multifactor model used here is a 'useful empirical framework' for linking macroeconomic innovations to expected asset returns.

Bossaerts & Green [1989] and Hollifield [1993] test dynamic versions of the APT. They find that static, constant parameter models are rejected, while the dynamic models perform well. Bansal & Viswanathan [1993] implement their nonlinear APT by noting that the return on the aggregate wealth portfolio and yields on default free bonds are free of idiosyncratic risk. The value-weighted NYSE portfolio is used as an aggregate wealth proxy while the yield on one-month Treasury bills and the yield spread between six and nine month Treasury bills are used as the idiosyncratic risk free yields. Some agent's intertemporal marginal rate of substitution is postulated to be an unknown nonlinear function of these three idiosyncratic risk free variables. Bansal & Viswanathan [1993] use semi-nonparametric techniques to estimate the intertemporal marginal rate of substitution or state pricing function. They find that linear versions of the model are rejected in favor of nonlinear versions, using their choice of factors. They also find that a one-factor (the NYSE portfolio) nonlinear model is rejected in favor of a two-factor (the NYSE portfolio and the one-month Treasury bill) nonlinear model. There is not much support for adding a third factor (the yield spread). While there is some evidence indicating that the nonlinear APT does not completely price assets and dynamic trading strategies, Bansal & Viswanathan [1993] argue that the nonlinear models perform better than linear versions of their model.

As noted above, the results of classical significance tests can be difficult to interpret. For example, the causes or economic implications of rejecting or failing to reject a model are often not addressed [see McCloskey, 1985]. Do we reject a model because it is a poor description of the data or because we have a huge amount of data? Do we fail to reject a model because it is a good description of

[24] See McElroy & Burmeister [1988] or Gallant [1987, ch. 5] for a discussion of the estimation methods.

the data or because the tests have no power? What is an economically significant departure from the model?

McCulloch & Rossi [1990, 1991] provide Bayesian analyses of time-series implementations of the APT which explicitly incorporate an evaluation of the informativeness of the data and measures of economic significance, in addition to statistical significance. McCulloch & Rossi [1991] evaluate the performance of the APT by calculating posterior odds ratios. They use the same sample and factor-mimicking portfolio formation methods as Connor & Korajczyk [1988a] and investigate the null hypothesis that $\alpha = 0$ in (22). The posterior odds ratio, K, for the null hypothesis versus the alternative that $\alpha \neq 0$ is given by:

$$K = \frac{p(D \mid \alpha = 0)}{p(D \mid \alpha \neq 0)} \times \frac{p(\alpha = 0)}{p(\alpha \neq 0)} \tag{27}$$

where D represents the sample data, $p(\alpha = 0)/p(\alpha \neq 0)$ is the prior odds ratio, and $p(D \mid \alpha = 0)/p(D \mid \alpha \neq 0)$ is a ratio of predictive densities. The odds ratio explicitly takes into account the informativeness of the data. An odds ratio greater than 1 : 1 favors the null hypothesis while an odds ratio less than 1 : 1 favors the alternative hypothesis.

For a one-factor model McCulloch & Rossi [1991] find that the odds ratio favors the alternative hypothesis ($\alpha \neq 0$), except for the case when the prior distribution is relatively uninformative. For a five-factor model they find that the odds ratio favors the null hypothesis ($\alpha = 0$), except for the case when the prior distribution is relatively informative. The sensitivity of the odds ratio to the specification of the prior distribution leads McCulloch and Rossi to conclude that the data are relatively uninformative about the model.

McCulloch & Rossi [1990] derive utility-based metrics to assess the economic significance of deviations from the exact APT pricing restrictions. McCulloch & Rossi [1990] construct weekly returns on all NYSE and AMEX firms from January 1, 1963 to December 31, 1987. They construct weekly excess returns on factor-mimicking portfolios using the asymptotic principal components procedure of Connor & Korajczyk [1988b] and construct weekly returns on ten size-based portfolios with monthly rebalancing. The ten size-based portfolios are the test assets whose vector of pricing errors, α, should be zero.

McCulloch & Rossi [1990] begin by evaluating the posterior distribution of α in (22) using a diffuse prior. They find evidence against the APT in the sense that the mass of the posterior distribution of α is often far from the null hypothesis of zero. McCulloch & Rossi [1990] wish to determine whether these deviations from the null hypothesis are economically significant. A reasonable metric is how much utility one would lose by assuming the null hypothesis is true. To determine this they investigate the posterior distribution of the difference in certainty equivalents between two utility-maximizing investors; one choosing portfolios assuming $\alpha \neq 0$ and the other choosing portfolios assuming $\alpha = 0$. A negative exponential utility function is postulated and normality of asset returns is assumed. The hypothetical investors choose to allocate their portfolios across the ten size-based portfolios and the riskless asset.

McCulloch & Rossi [1990] find that the dispersion on the posterior distribution of the certainty equivalents is quite large when the analysis is performed over five-year subintervals, thus confirming the odds ratio results indicating that the data are relatively uninformative. Over the full sample, however, the posterior distribution of the certainty equivalents is much tighter and closer to zero, the value implied by the null hypothesis. The predictive distribution of returns, with and without the restriction that $\alpha = 0$, is used to derive efficient frontiers. McCulloch & Rossi [1990] conclude that there is an economically significant difference between the unrestricted and restricted frontiers, but that the high level of parameter uncertainty makes definitive statements about the validity of the APT difficult.

Geweke & Zhou [1993] evaluate the posterior distribution of the average squared pricing deviations (the cross-sectional average of α_i^2, $i = 1, 2, \ldots, n$) from the APT. They use industry and size-decile portfolios to estimate the posterior mean of the average squared pricing deviations. They argue that a one factor model explains most of the variation in expected returns with the remaining variation being economically negligible.

4.3. *Summary of tests of the APT*

The tests often reject the overidentifying restrictions of the APT. However, this by itself is not as useful as a direct comparison of the APT to competing models of asset returns. This type of comparison is made difficult by the fact that the models are not, in general, nested models. In the cases in which the APT is compared to implementations of the CAPM, the APT seems to fare well in the sense that it does a better job of explaining cross-sectional differences in asset returns (e.g., the nonnested hypothesis tests of Chen [1983]), it seems to explain some pricing anomalies relative to the CAPM (e.g., the dividend yield anomaly seems to be eliminated by the APT in Lehmann & Modest [1988] while there are mixed results about the APT's ability to explain the size anomaly), and it generally has smaller pricing errors than the CAPM (e.g., the absolute size of α seems to be smaller for the APT, see Connor & Korajczyk [1988a, figs. 1–6]).

On the other hand, there is evidence which suggests that the asset pricing models are not providing much information about unconditional cross-sectional differences in expected returns. In standard tests of the models, this is evident through the frequent inability of researchers to find significant risk premia for market risk or factor risk. The lack of information provided by the models is also evident in the sensitivity of the posterior odds ratios to changes in prior distributions [McCulloch & Rossi, 1991] and in the large dispersion in the posterior distributions of the difference in certainty equivalents in the utility-based approach of McCulloch & Rossi [1990]. These difficulties are essentially all related to the fact that, given the inherent variability in asset returns, it is difficult to measure unconditional mean return with much precision. This problem is one shared by all models of unconditional asset pricing and is not specific to the APT.

5. Other empirical topics

The APT does not provide an a priori specification of the appropriate number of priced factors. The choice of the appropriate number of factors is complicated by the fact that, with a finite number of assets, alternative rotations of the factors can change the apparent factor structure [Shanken, 1982]. In Section 5.1 we survey the literature on testing for the appropriate number of factors. In Section 5.2 we discuss alternative methods of forming factor-mimicking portfolios that have not been discussed above and Section 5.3 contains a survey of international applications of the APT.

5.1. Tests for the appropriate number of factors

Estimates and tests of the APT require, as a maintained hypothesis, that returns follow a factor model with a prespecified number of factors. Roll & Ross [1980] use a likelihood ratio test of the hypothesis that k factors are sufficient to characterize U.S. stock market returns. The data set and empirical estimation methodology of their paper have been discussed in Section 4.1 above. The likelihood ratio test comes from the factor analysis literature [e.g., see Morrison, 1976, section 9.5] and is given by:

$$\left[T - 1 - \frac{2n+5}{6} - \frac{2k}{3}\right] \ln\left[\frac{\hat{\Sigma}_k}{\hat{\Sigma}}\right]$$

where $\hat{\Sigma}_k$ is the maximum likelihood estimate of the $n \times n$ covariance matrix of returns, Σ, under the constraint that returns follow a strict k-factor model; $\hat{\Sigma}$ is the unconstrained maximum likelihood estimate of Σ; T is the size of the time-series sample; and n is the number of assets in the cross-section. If asset returns follow a strict k-factor model and have a multivariate normal distribution, then the test statistic has an asymptotic distribution that is χ^2 with degrees of freedom equal to $[(n-k)^2 - n - k]/2$ (where asymptotic means large T and fixed n). Roll and Ross apply the likelihood ratio test to 42 groups of 30 stocks each (sorted alphabetically). They find that, for most groups, five factors seems sufficient. In 32 of the 42 groups, the p-values of the test statistics (for the hypothesis that five factors were sufficient) were less that 0.50. Roll and Ross stress the tentative nature of their statistical tests; their paper is the first full-scale estimation and testing of the APT.

Dhrymes, Friend & Gultekin [1984] increase the number of securities in each estimation group from 30 (the number used in Roll & Ross [1980]), to 60, 120, and 180. They repeat the likelihood ratio test for the number of factors on these larger cross-sectional sample sizes. They find that as the number of securities covered in the test increases, the number of statistically significant factors also increases. The Dhrymes, Friend & Gultekin result is confirmed on British stock market returns data by Diacogiannis [1986].

There are at least two reasons why one might find that the number of significant factors increases as the number of assets increases. First, the likelihood ratio statistics are only asymptotically χ^2. Conway & Reinganum [1988] demonstrate that there is a pronounced tendency to find *too many* factors in small samples (i.e., small time-series samples). If we hold the size of the time series fixed at T, and increase the number of cross-sections, n, then the effective size of the sample decreases and the small sample bias in favor of finding extra factors increases [also see Raveh, 1985].

Secondly, the likelihood ratio test assumes a strict factor model. Suppose instead that returns obey an *approximate* factor model with, say, five factors. In addition to the five pervasive factors, there are within-industry effects and other sources of cross-firm correlations which are not strong enough to qualify as pervasive sources of risk. Using groups of thirty securities chosen randomly, the analyst is unlikely to identify these second-order sources of correlations as factors. As the number of securities in the test increases, these 'unimportant' factors may become statistically significant [Roll & Ross, 1984b]. The Dhrymes, Friend & Gultekin [1984] findings highlight the weakness of the exact (as opposed to approximate) factor model assumption for security market returns data.

A separate issue regarding the Roll & Ross [1980] test for the number of factors is related to the adjustments for nonsynchroneity in Shanken [1987b]. As discussed in Section 4.1 above, Shanken adjusts the daily return covariance estimates for the presence of nonsynchronous trading. He applies the likelihood ratio test to the adjusted covariance matrix, with different results. Following Roll & Ross [1980] by using alphabetically-sorted groups of 30 securities each, Shanken finds at least a 99% chance of greater than ten factors in all cases.

The work of Chamberlain & Rothschild [1983] on approximate factor models has led to a search for alternative tests for the number of factors that are robust to the existence of an approximate, rather than a strict, factor model. Recall from Section 2.3 above that an approximate k-factor model is equivalent to exactly k eigenvalues of the covariance matrix of returns going to infinity as the number of cross-sections, n, increases to infinity. If we can observe the sequence of covariance matrices (with increasing n) then we can look for the number of eigenvalues which grow unboundedly with n. Note that this type of test relies only on an approximate, not a strict, factor model, a substantial advantage for equity market returns data. Luedecke [1984] and Trzcinka [1986] provide the first statistical analysis along these lines. The problem, as they both note, is that the sampling properties of n-asymptotic (as opposed to T-asymptotic) eigenvalues are unknown, and so their work is exploratory. They find that the first eigenvalue of the sample covariance matrix is much larger than the others, and that all of the eigenvalues increase as n increases. By one possible standard (dominant eigenvalues), the empirical evidence indicates a single-factor model, whereas by another possible standard (increasing eigenvalues with n), the evidence points to a many-factor model.

Brown [1989] analyzes the behavior of the eigenvalues of the sample covariance matrix, $\hat{\Sigma}$, through simulations. The simulated asset returns follow a four-factor model. Brown [1989] analytically derives the behavior, as n increases, of the eigenvalues of the population covariance matrix, Σ. The first four population eigenvalues grow with n while the remaining eigenvalues are constant. Brown then investigates the behavior of the sample eigenvalues through simulation. He applies the Luedecke–Trzcinka test to a simulated sample with the same dimensions (n and T) as that of Trzcinka. He finds that the first eigenvalue dominates (as in Luedecke and Trzcinka) and that *all* the other eigenvalues increase with n (again, as in Luedecke and Trzcinka). It is clear from Brown's simulations that we cannot infer the behavior, as n increases, of population eigenvalues, from the behavior, as n increases but with *T held constant*, of the sample eigenvalues. The problem is not the total number of return observations, but the *relative* size of the cross-sectional and time-series samples. This issue is also discussed in Connor & Korajczyk [1993].

Korajczyk & Viallet [1989] suggest a test for the number of factors which relies on the fact that well-diversified portfolios have no idiosyncratic risk (in the limit, as n approaches infinity). Assume that asset returns follow an approximate k-factor model, but that a $k+1$-factor model is estimated, where the $k+1$st factor is just picking up some idiosyncratic cross-correlations. In a time-series regression of a well-diversified portfolio's returns on the $k+1$ factors the coefficients should be statistically significant for the k pervasive factors and zero for factor $k+1$. Korajczyk & Viallet [1989] use the equal-weighted market portfolio (i.e., the portfolio weights are $1/n$) as a proxy for a well-diversified portfolio. They find that this test identifies a large number of significant factors. This might be due to the fact that there are a large number of factors *or* due to the fact that the equal-weighted portfolio is, strictly speaking, only well-diversified when n is equal to infinity. Thus, the test may be finding factors due to the idiosyncratic risk left in the portfolio. This test is generalized in Heston [1991, example 5] to the case where the limiting portfolios are well-diversified, but need not have equal weights.

Connor & Korajczyk [1993] provide a different test for the number of factors in an approximate factor model. They analyze the decrease in cross-sectional average idiosyncratic variance in moving from a k factor model to a $k+1$ factor model. If returns are generated by a k factor model, then the expected decrease is zero, and Connor and Korajczyk provide a test statistic for a significant decrease. They find that the data suggest between one and six statistically significant factors.

The inferences from alternative tests for the number of factors tend to be bi-modal. There is a group of tests that indicates a very large number of factors and a group of tests that indicates a rather small number of factors. At this stage, there does not seem to be a general consensus on this point. A common approach taken by authors, in the face of this uncertainty about the appropriate number of factors, is to perform their analyses with various numbers of factors to determine whether the results are sensitive to the addition of factors.

5.2. Alternative factor-mimicking portfolio estimation methods

In Section 4 we discussed several methods of constructing sets of factor-mimicking portfolios for use in testing the APT and estimating the risk premium associated with factor risk. The most frequently used approach is the cross-sectional regression of asset returns on some estimate of factor sensitivities, $\hat{B}$, as in (17) and (18). The estimate of B may come from a time-series regression of asset returns on prespecified factors or from factor analysis if the factors are not prespecified. An alternative approach is to prespecify the matrix of factor sensitivities directly. That is, assume that certain observable, firm specific, variables are equal to the factor sensitivities (or at least that they are equal to some linear combination of the factor sensitivities).

For example, assume that we can observe k attributes for each of the n firms (such as firm size, earnings/price ratios, etc.). Call the $n \times k$ matrix of attributes X. If we are willing to assume that $X = BL$ where L is some $k \times k$ nonsingular matrix, then cross-sectional regressions of returns on X will yield factor-mimicking portfolios that span the same space as portfolios created by regressing returns on B. The most important assumption is, of course, that $X = BL$. This is not very different from the implicit assumption used in studies that prespecify the factors to be particular macroeconomic innovations (i.e., that the macroeconomic variables are $L^{-1}F$ where L is a $k \times k$ nonsingular matrix and F is the $k \times T$ matrix of true factors).

This type of procedure is discussed by Rosenberg [1974] and used by Kale, Hakansson & Platt [1991] who chose the firm attributes to include book value-to-price ratios, firm size, dividend yield, fraction of sales in various industries, and several other attributes.

Fama & French [1992] investigate the power of several firm attributes (size, book value/market value, leverage, earnings/price and market beta) to explain cross-sectional differences in asset returns. They use Fama–MacBeth cross-sectional regressions to estimate the excess returns on portfolios with unit average levels of each attribute (and zero average level of the other attributes). Fama & French [1992] find that the attributes of size and book/market ratios absorb the effects of the other attributes and that the market beta has no explanatory power. They conclude that there are multidimensional aspects of risk that are proxied by size and book/market ratios but not by betas relative to a market proxy. One possible interpretation of the results is that a multifactor asset pricing model is being used to price assets and that size and book/market ratios are good proxies for assets' sensitivities to the factors.

Mei [1993] suggests an alternative approach to estimating factor-mimicking portfolios. He uses cross-sectional regressions to estimate the returns on factor-mimicking portfolios, but instead of using $\hat{B}$ as the set of independent variables, he uses realized returns from a prior period. The intuition for this can be most easily seen if we consider a noiseless factor model as described in Section 3.1 [i.e., $\varepsilon = 0$ in (1)]. In this case the excess returns from the prior period are proportional to B since $R_t = B(\lambda_{t-1} + f_t)$ as in (16). Thus, if B is constant through time, the cross-sectional regression of excess returns on past excess returns is the same as a regression of returns on B [up to a scale transformation which is a function of the prior period factors, $(\lambda_{t-1} + f_t)$]. Mei [1993] suggests an instrumental variable approach to account for the fact that the return generating process does have an idiosyncratic return component.

5.3. Tests of international models

The empirical work described above uses data on assets in the United States exclusively. There have been a number of papers that perform the same or similar tests on the assets of other countries individually. There have also been a number of papers that use the APT to analyze asset returns across two or more countries.

Examples of single-economy applications of the APT are Chan & Beenstock [1984] and Abeysekera & Mahajan [1987] for the United Kingdom; Dumontier [1986] for France; Hamao [1988] and Brown & Otsuki [1990] for Japan; Hughes [1984] for Canada; and Winkelmann [1984] for Germany. Generally these papers have yielded similar inferences for these economies as the papers dealing with data from the United States. We will not describe these papers in detail here.

International versions of the APT are derived in Ross & Walsh [1983], Solnik [1983], and Levine [1989]. Under the assumption that the exchange rate follows the same factor model as asset returns, Ross & Walsh [1983] and Solnik [1983] show that the same basic linear pricing result holds. If the exchange rate is spanned by the factors (i.e., it has no idiosyncratic risk) then we can change numeraires without changing the factor structure. On the other hand, if the exchange rate has idiosyncratic risk, then changing numeraires will entail introducing an additional, but unpriced, factor (see, for example, Clyman, Edelson & Hiller, 1991].

Integration across national markets would require that common sources of risk be priced in a consistent manner across countries. A number of authors have used international versions of the APT to assess the severity of capital controls, or barriers to market integration. Also, the assumption that exchange rates follow the same type of factor structure and are priced in a manner consistent with other assets has implications for the pricing of forward positions in currencies.

Cho, Eun & Senbet [1986] use a variant of factor analysis, inter-battery factor analysis [see Cho, 1984], to estimate the factor sensitivity matrix, B, for factors common across pairs of countries. Inter-battery factor analysis is computationally less burdensome than standard factor analysis since it estimates factor sensitivities only for common factors. A drawback to the technique is that it cannot estimate country-specific factors, which are not ruled out, a priori, by the international APT. Cho, Eun & Senbet [1986] then test for consistent pricing across countries [as in (14), where a subset is defined as the assets of one country] in a manner similar to that of Brown & Weinstein [1983].

Their sample consists of returns on 349 stocks from eleven countries from January 1973 through December 1983. The tests are performed separately for each possible pair of countries. Three hypotheses are investigated. The first is that $\lambda_0^i = \lambda_0$ in (14), the second is that $\lambda^i = \lambda$ in (14), and the third is that both $\lambda_0^i = \lambda_0$ and $\lambda^i = \lambda$. Since inter-battery factor analysis picks out only common factors, the second hypothesis alone is strictly implied by the exact version of the APT. The values of λ_0^i may differ across countries since they could incorporate the risk premia for factors specific to that country which are still not globally diversifiable.[25] They reject (at the 5% level) the hypothesis that $\lambda_0^i = \lambda_0$ in three of the 55 country pairs. The hypothesis that $\lambda^i = \lambda$ is rejected in 30 of the 55 cases and the joint hypothesis that $\lambda_0^i = \lambda_0$ and $\lambda^i = \lambda$ is rejected in 32 of the 55 pairs. Although the tests are not independent, the large fraction of rejections lead Cho, Eun & Senbet [1986] to conclude that the second and third hypotheses are not supported by the data. They suggest that this rejection may be due to lack of integration of capital markets or possibly to differential tax effects across countries.

Berges-Lobera (undated) tests for equality of factor risk premia across common stocks traded in the United States, Canada, the United Kingdom, and Spain. Monthly data from 1955 through 1980 are used for 100 firms each in the U.S. and U.K., 82 firms in Canada, and 62 firms in Spain. The hypothesis that pricing across markets is consistent is not rejected for the United States and Canada but is rejected for the United Kingdom/United States and United Kingdom/Canada pairs. The estimated risk premia for Spain are not precise enough to draw firm conclusions.

Korajczyk & Viallet [1989] perform time-series tests, as in (22) and (25), of single-economy and international versions of the CAPM and APT. They use monthly stock return data from France, Japan, the United States, and the United Kingdom over the period from January 1969 to December 1983. The number of firms with return data available ranges from 4211 to 6692. The asymptotic principal components technique is used to estimate the returns on factor-mimicking portfolios, F_t. The test assets that make up R_t are sets of size based decile portfolios. For the single-economy versions, the factor portfolios and size portfolios are estimated using assets from one country (e.g., single-economy models for Japan would use Japanese stocks to estimate F_t and form R_t). In the international versions, all of the assets are used to estimate F_t and form the size portfolios R_t. In the international versions of the model, tests of the restriction $\alpha = 0$ in (22) are implicitly tests of equal prices of risk across countries [$\lambda_0^i = \lambda_0$ and $\lambda^i = \lambda$ in (14)]. This is due to the fact that the method of forming factor-mimicking portfolios assumes consistent factor pricing across assets. Any differences in the pricing of factor risk across countries is then picked up in the intercept, α, of the time-series regression. Over the full sample, the statistical tests provide some evidence against all of the models (CAPM and APT in single-economy and international versions). The APT seems to perform better than the CAPM, in terms of the magnitudes of α. An analysis of the size of the α across models does not yield a clear advantage to either single-economy or international versions of the models.

The sample period used in this study includes several important changes in international capital markets. There is a trend toward the relaxation of capital

[25] Financial market integration does not imply or require that the countries be engaged in producing the same goods. Therefore, financially integrated countries might still have assets that are subject to country-specific productivity shocks. A country-specific, but priced, factor could occur if the country in question is not small relative to the world economy.

controls, which should lead to greater integration of markets. Also, the period includes a switch from fixed to floating exchange rates. Korajczyk & Viallet [1989] identify two periods, 1974 and 1979, as being particularly important periods of change. Estimates of α which allow for these periods to be isolated indicate that the rejections of the hypothesis that $\alpha = 0$ seem to be due to the earliest period (before February 1974). Since this corresponds to the period with the most severe barriers to international capital movements, the results are consistent with important pricing effects of capital controls.

Gultekin, Gultekin & Penati [1989] use the APT to investigate the effect of a particular change in capital controls, a revision of Japan's Foreign Exchange and Foreign Trade Control Law (FEFTCL), which took effect in December 1980 [see Suzuki, 1987]. The revision of the FEFTCL amounted to a change from a regime with many barriers to capital flows to a regime with essentially no barriers to capital flows.

Gultekin, Gultekin & Penati [1989] argue that while barriers to capital movements before the revision might lead to differential pricing of factor risk between Japan and other economies, the lack of barriers after the revision should lead to consistent pricing of factor risk [$\lambda_0^i = \lambda_0$ and $\lambda^i = \lambda$ in (14) where i denotes the ith country].

Weekly common stock returns on 110 stocks traded in Japan and 110 stocks traded in the United States over the period 1977–1984 are used for the tests. The capital control period is 1977–1980 and the integrated period is 1981–1984. Gultekin, Gultekin & Penati [1989] use both prespecified factors and factor analysis to estimate the assets' factor sensitivities, B. They find that they are able to reject the hypothesis of equal prices of risk across countries in the 1977–1980 period but are not able to reject the hypothesis in the 1981–1984 period. They interpret the results as indicating capital market segregation before the revision in the FEFTCL and integration afterward. There is also some evidence that the risk premia are estimated less precisely in the 1981–1984 period, which might mean that the failure to reject in that period is due to the test having low power.

Another implication of the international versions of the APT is that the risk premia on forward positions in currencies should be explained by the currencies' sensitivities to the pervasive factors. There exists a substantial literature indicating time-varying returns on forward currency positions [e.g., Bilson, 1981; Fama, 1984; Korajczyk, 1985; and Hodrick, 1987] which has been interpreted by some as a market inefficiency and by others as evidence of time-varying risk premia in the forward currency market. Korajczyk and Viallet [1992] test whether the observed premia can be explained by an international version of the APT. They form factor-mimicking portfolios from data on monthly common stock returns for 23,587 firms from Australia, France, Japan, the United States, and the United Kingdom over the period from January 1974 to December 1988. The number of firms, with return data available in a given month, ranges from 8,010 to 11,659. The asymptotic principal components technique is used to estimate the returns on factor-mimicking portfolios, F_t. The test asset returns, R_t, are the excess returns on forward positions in eight foreign currencies (the exchange rates are all relative to the U.S. dollar and are from Canada, France, Germany, Italy, Japan, the Netherlands, Switzerland, and the United Kingdom). They estimate time-series regressions such as (25) in which the instrument, Z_{t-1}, is the differential between the forward and spot exchange rates at the end of the previous month. If this implementation of the APT is successful in pricing currency returns, then α and δ in (25) should be zero.

Korajczyk & Viallet [1992] find that the factor model explains a large part of the risk premia in currency returns. However, they are able to reject the joint hypothesis that $\alpha = 0$ and $\delta = 0$ for the forward currency positions. Thus, the model does not provide a complete characterization of forward currency risk premia.

Heston, Rouwenhorst & Wessels [1992] test for capital market integration between the United States and twelve European markets. They use monthly common stock returns on 4,490 stocks in the United States and 1,863 stocks on European markets, over the period 1978 through 1990, to estimate excess returns on factor-mimicking portfolios, F_t. The asymptotic principal components procedure is applied to the entire cross-sectional sample to estimate international factors and is applied to each country's assets to estimate domestic factor-mimicking portfolios.

Capital market integration is tested through time-series regressions of the form (22). The factors, F_t, are the excess returns on the international factor-mimicking portfolios. There are several sets of test assets. The first set of test asset excess returns, R_t, is composed of the equal-weighted market portfolios for each of the thirteen countries. The second set of test asset returns is composed of the value-weighted market portfolios for each of the thirteen countries. Then there are thirteen sets of test asset returns, one for each country, which are the first five domestic factor-mimicking portfolios. The null hypothesis, that $\alpha = 0$ in (22), finds mixed support. The null hypothesis is generally not rejected using the equal-weighted market portfolios or the domestic factor-mimicking portfolios, but is rejected using the value-weighted market portfolios as test assets.

Heston, Rouwenhorst & Wessels [1992] also test whether forward currency returns are explained by the international factor-mimicking portfolios by estimating (22) and testing whether $\alpha = 0$ for the forward returns. This is similar to the tests of Korajczyk & Viallet [1992] except that Korajczyk and Viallet also include lagged instruments in the tests [as in (25)]. The results reject the hypothesis that $\alpha = 0$ for the forward currency returns.

Bansal, Hsieh & Viswanathan [1993] apply the nonlinear APT of Bansal & Viswanathan [1993] to the pricing of international equity indices (from Germany, Japan, the United Kingdom, and the United States), short-term bonds (U.S. Treasury bills and Eurodollar deposits), and forward currency contracts. They use weekly returns data from January 1975 through December 1990. They find that a nonlinear single-factor model (with a world equity index as the factor) is not rejected, while linear single-factor models are rejected.

6. Applications

Asset pricing models have uses in a variety of applications in investments and corporate finance. The APT has been used as an alternative to other asset pricing models for many applied problems, a few of which we discuss here.

6.1. Portfolio performance evaluation

A standard application of asset pricing models is the evaluation of the performance of professionally managed portfolios. If the APT is the appropriate model of the risk/return tradeoff for securities, then all individual assets and portfolios formed on the basis of public information should have values of α in (22) equal to zero. This corresponds to the case where all expected returns above the riskless rate are due to factor risk premia. On the other hand, if a portfolio manager has superior ability in choosing assets, then one would expect that the manager's portfolio would earn higher rates of return than is warranted by its level of risk. That is, superior ability should lead to values of α greater than zero. Conversely, large transactions costs caused by excessive turnover should lead to negative values for α. Thus, α is one metric of risk-adjusted portfolio performance. This measure has been used extensively in the context of the CAPM and has come to be known as Jensen's measure of portfolio performance [see Jensen, 1968, 1969]. Given the excess returns on factor-mimicking portfolios, F_t, α, in (22) is simply the multi-factor, APT analog of Jensen's measure.

Lehmann & Modest [1987] provide an extensive comparison of APT-based and CAPM-based portfolio performance measures. The equal-weighted and value-weighted NYSE portfolios are used as proxies for the market portfolio. A variety of alternative implementations of the APT are used by Lehmann & Modest [1987]. For each estimation method, they estimate a version of the APT that assumes the existence of a riskless asset (the riskless rate version) and a version that does not make this assumption (the zero-beta version). The matrix of factor sensitivities, B, is estimated by four alternative methods: (i) maximum likelihood factor analysis; (ii) restricted maximum likelihood factor analysis [where the restriction is that $E(r_t)$ is given by (13)]; (iii) principal components; and (iv) instrumental variables factor analysis [see Madansky, 1964]. Given the estimate, $\hat{B}$, factor-mimicking portfolios are formed using the minimum idiosyncratic risk procedure described above [see (24)].

The sample used to estimate F_t is essentially the same as the sample in Lehmann & Modest [1988]. The returns used for R_t are the monthly returns on 130 mutual funds over the period from January 1968 to December 1982. Lehmann & Modest [1987] find that the rankings of mutual funds and the average size of Jensen's measure is sensitive to whether the APT or CAPM benchmarks are used and to the type of factor estimation procedure used. The measured performance using the APT benchmarks was not sensitive to the number of factors beyond five factors. The CAPM-based performance measures were more highly related to simple average returns without risk adjustment than to the APT-based measures. The average Jensen measure, across funds, was consistently negative.

Connor & Korajczyk [1991] evaluate the performance of the same set of mutual funds used in Lehmann & Modest [1987] using a hybrid approach to constructing the factor-mimicking portfolios. The asymptotic principal components procedure is used to estimate excess returns on factor-mimicking portfolios. Then, linear combinations of these portfolios are formed so that they are maximally correlated with a set of macroeconomic factors, similar to those chosen by Chen, Roll & Ross [1986]. This combines the advantages of statistical estimation of the factors with the advantage of interpretability of the macroeconomic factors. As in Lehmann & Modest [1987], Connor & Korajczyk [1991] find that the average APT-based estimates of Jensen's measure for various portfolio classes (e.g., income, growth, maximum capital gain, etc.) are consistently negative as well as being different from the CAPM-based measures using the value-weighted NYSE/AMEX portfolio. Lehmann & Modest [1987] and Connor & Korajczyk [1991] also address some issues related to the effects of market timing activities on the part of portfolio managers on Jensen's measure. We will not address those issues here [see also Admati, Bhattacharya, Pfleiderer & Ross, 1986]. Rubio [1992] applies similar methods to a sample of Spanish mutual funds. He also finds negative fund performance, on average.

The negative average performance of mutual funds might be related to the size anomaly. Mutual funds tend to hold high capitalization stocks which have underperformed low capitalization stocks, on average.

Sharpe [1988, 1992] suggests a multifactor model of returns for portfolio evaluation where the factors are defined to be various asset classes. He adds the constraint that the factor benchmarks, against which the portfolios are compared, do not have short positions in assets. Other empirical studies of mutual fund performance using the APT include Chang & Lewellen [1985], Berry, Burmeister & McElroy [1988a], and Frohlich [1991].

6.2. Cost of capital estimation

Another major use of asset pricing models is the estimation of costs of capital for use in capital budgeting problems. As in the portfolio performance evaluation literature, the CAPM has traditionally been the workhorse of risk adjustment in corporate finance texts. However, the APT is becoming a more common alternative to the CAPM [e.g., see Copeland & Weston, 1988; Copeland, Koller & Murrin, 1990; Brealey & Myers, 1991; and Ross, Westerfield & Jaffe, 1993]. To the extent that one believes that the APT provides a better description of the risk/return tradeoff demanded by the capital market, the argument can be made for the use of the APT instead of the CAPM for cost of capital estimation.

The empirical literature on testing the APT, discussed in Section 4, and the extensive empirical literature on the CAPM, provide the most extensive set of information on the performance of the models. However, many studies investigate only one of the models, so that making cross-model comparisons is sometimes difficult.

On a more pragmatic level, it is certainly of some interest to determine if costs of capital implied by the CAPM and APT are very different. Copeland, Koller & Murrin [1990, exhibit 6.7] and Brealey & Myers [1991, table 8–2] provide some comparisons for various industries, while Roll & Ross [1983] and Bower, Bower & Logue [1984] provide estimates for utilities. While the CAPM and APT estimated costs of capital can be quite close to each other for some industries, they can be quite different for others. Thus, the choice of the appropriate model can be a substantive issue.

6.3. Event studies

Single index models are used extensively in studies of market reaction to firm-specific or industry-specific events. This method was originally developed by Fama, Fisher, Jensen & Roll [1969].[26] The notion is that firm-specific news should be reflected in the idiosyncratic component of returns, ε, in (1). If we wish to study the market's reaction to a firm-specific (or at least nonpervasive) announcement,[27] then ε_t provides a less noisy estimate of the reaction than r_t. If including multiple factors reduces the variability of ε_t attributable to news other than the event in question, then using multiple factors might increase the accuracy of the estimated effect and the power of any related hypothesis tests. Merely adding factors, however, does not guarantee more precise estimates of ε_t, since the variance of $\hat{\varepsilon}_t$ is determined by the population variance of ε_t *and* the sampling error of $\hat{B}$. Adding factors would decrease the population variance but could increase or decrease the sampling variance. Thus, the use of multifactor models in event studies does not necessarily lead to unambiguous improvement. Brown & Weinstein [1985] and Chen, Copeland & Mayers [1987] compare single and multiple factor approaches to estimating the valuation effects of news.

Brown & Weinstein [1985] simulate abnormal returns in a manner similar to that of Brown & Warner [1980, 1985] and tabulate the size and power of single and multiple factor models for detecting these abnormal returns. They find that there is not an appreciable difference between single and multiple factor results. The multiple factor models seem to perform marginally better in their simulations.

Chen, Copeland & Mayers [1987] apply single factor and multiple factor models to portfolios formed on the basis of assets' ranking of forecasted performance by *Value Line* and on the basis of firm size. They find that neither procedure has a particular bias. In terms of the variance of the estimate $\hat{\varepsilon}_t$, they find that single factor models tend to perform better when the test portfolio return, r_t, is poorly diversified, while multiple factor models tend to perform better when the test portfolio is diversified. This is due to the fact that diversification of the portfolio leads to lower estimation error in $\hat{B}$, which in turn leads to a smaller variance in $\hat{\varepsilon}_t$.

[26] Brown & Warner [1980, 1985] analyze the properties of various alternative approaches to estimating the asset-specific reaction to news.

[27] Examples of primarily firm-specific news are announcements related to stock splits, corporate earnings, dividend declarations, and equity issues.

The applications of multifactor models to event studies are somewhat peripheral to the question of whether the APT, the CAPM, or some other model is a better model for assets' expected returns. This is due to the fact that the event study applications rarely impose the restrictions implied by the various pricing models. This strand of the literature is more in the spirit of the early studies on the factor structure of asset returns, which were primarily interested in a parsimonious description of the primary variables influencing returns.

7. Conclusion

The APT is based on a simple and intuitive concept. Ross's basic insight was that a linear factor model of asset returns, in an economy with a large number of available assets, implies that idiosyncratic risk is diversifiable and that the equilibrium prices of securities will be approximately linear in their factor exposures. This idea has spawned a literature which has pushed the scientific frontiers in several directions. It has led to new work in mathematical economics on infinite-dimensional vector spaces as models of many-asset portfolio returns, and the properties of continuous pricing operators on these vector spaces. It has led to econometric insights about what constitutes a factor model, and how to efficiently estimate factor models with large cross-sectional data sets. It has underpinned an enormous body of empirical research on asset pricing relationships, and on related topics such as performance measurement and cost of capital estimation.

Lack of arbitrage opportunities implies that assets can be priced by a single random variable, variously referred to in the literature as the pricing kernel, stochastic discount factor, intertemporal marginal rate of substitution, or state price density [see Ross, 1978; Dybvig & Ross, 1989; Ferson, 1995]. One might wonder, then, what the advantage would be to using a multiple factor model. Particular asset pricing models differ in their specification of the stochastic discount factor. If there is an advantage to using multifactor models, it must be that the multifactor models provide a closer approximation to the stochastic discount factor than alternative approaches. To date, the empirical literature has tended to emphasize tests of the restrictions of a single model rather than emphasize comparisons across models. When comparisons across models have been made, the APT has tended to do well against the competing models. More of these cross-model comparisons are needed to assess relative performance across models. Many studies have rejected the strict restrictions of various asset pricing models, including the APT. The persistence and size of these asset pricing anomalies may not be total explicable within the paradigm of frictionless markets [MacKinlay, 1993]. The existence of frictions in asset markets has potential for explaining some of the observed failures of existing models [e.g., see Luttmer, 1993].

As Fama [1991] stresses, one cannot expect any particular asset pricing model to completely describe reality; an asset pricing model is a success if it improves our understanding of security market returns. By this standard, the APT is a success. The APT does have weaknesses and gaps. Current statistical methods are not amenable to testing an approximate pricing relation. As a result, our tests of the exact multifactor pricing relation are joint tests of the APT and additional assumptions necessary to obtain exact pricing. The empirical work on identifying the factor structure in security returns has had mixed success, and the econometric techniques in this area are insufficiently developed, particularly with respect to incorporating conditioning information. The APT would be a better model if we could relate the factors more closely to identifiable sources of economic risk. Understanding the relationship between return factors and economic risks requires more work in asset pricing theory, macroeconomics, and econometrics. The APT will continue to evolve and may eventually be changed beyond recognition. Yet whatever changes occur, Ross's creative insight will endure as a fundamental building block in asset pricing theory.

Acknowledgements

The size of the literature related to arbitrage pricing theory precludes us from summarizing all relevant contributions and we apologize in advance to those whose work has not been discussed here. We have received helpful comments from many colleagues. We owe particular thanks to Torben Andersen, Denis Gromb, Ravi Jagannathan, Jack Treynor, and Mark Weinstein. We also thank Mary Korajczyk for editorial assistance.

References

Abeysekera, S.P., and A. Mahajan (1987). A test of the APT in pricing UK stocks. *J. Bus. Finance Account.* 14, 377–391.

Admati, A.R., S. Bhattacharya, P. Pfleiderer and S.A. Ross (1986). On timing and selectivity. *J. Finance* 41, 715–730.

Admati, A.R., and P. Pfleiderer (1985). Interpreting the factor risk premia in the arbitrage pricing theory. *J. Econ. Theory* 35, 191–195.

Andersen, T.G. (1989). Estimation of systematic risk in the presence of non-trading: Comments and extensions, Working paper, Yale University.

Anderson, T.W. (1984). *An Introduction to Multivariate Statistical Analysis*, 2nd edition, Wiley, New York, NY.

Bansal, R., D.A. Hsieh and S. Viswanathan (1993). A new approach to international arbitrage pricing. *J. Finan.* 48, 1719–1747.

Bansal, R., and S. Viswanathan (1993). No arbitrage and arbitrage pricing: A new approach. *J. Finan.* 48, 1231–1262.

Berges-Lobera, A. (undated). An empirical study on international asset pricing models and capital market integration, Working paper, Universidad Autonoma de Madrid.

Berry, M.A., E. Burmeister and M.B. McElroy (1988a). A practical perspective on evaluating mutual fund risk. *Investment Manage. Rev.* 2, 78–86.

Berry, M.A., E. Burmeister and M.B. McElroy (1988b). Sorting out risks using known APT factors. *Financ. Anal. J.* 44, 29–42.

Bilson, J.F.O. (1981). The 'speculative efficiency' hypothesis. *J. Bus.* 54, 435–452.

Binder, J.J. (1985). On the use of the multivariate regression model in event studies. *J. Account. Res.* 23, 370–383.

Black, F., M.C. Jensen and M. Scholes (1972). The capital asset pricing model: Some empirical tests, in: Michael C. Jensen (ed.), *Studies in the Theory of Capital Markets*, Praeger, New York, NY.

Bollerslev, T. (1986). Generalized autoregressive conditional heteroscedasticity. *J. Econometr.* 31, 307–327.

Bossaerts, P., and R.C. Green (1989). A general equilibrium model of changing risk premia: Theory and tests. *Rev. Financ. Studies* 2, 467–493.

Bower, D.H., R.S. Bower and D.E. Logue (1984). Arbitrage pricing theory and utility stock returns. *J. Finance* 39, 1041–1054.

Brealey, R.A., and S.C. Myers (1991). *Principles of Corporate Finance*, 4th edition, McGraw-Hill, New York, NY.

Breeden, D.T. (1979). An intertemporal asset pricing model with stochastic consumption and investment opportunities. *J. Financ. Econ.* 7, 265–296.

Brennan, M.J. (1971). Capital asset pricing and the structure of security returns, Working paper, University of British Columbia.

Brock, W.A. (1982). Asset prices in a production economy, in: John J. McCall (ed.). *The Economics of Information and Uncertainty*, University of Chicago Press, Chicago.

Brown, S.J. (1989). The number of factors in security returns. *J. Finance* 44, 1247–1262.

Brown, S.J., and T. Otsuki (1990). Macroeconomic factors and the japanese equity markets: The CAPMD project, in: Edwin J. Elton and Martin J. Gruber (eds.), *Japanese Capital Markets*, Harper & Row, New York, NY.

Brown, S.J., and J.B. Warner (1980). Measuring security price performance. *J. Financ. Econ.* 8, 205–258.

Brown, S.J., and J.B. Warner (1985). Using daily stock returns: The case of event studies. *J. Financ. Econ.* 14, 3–31.

Brown, S.J., and M.I. Weinstein (1983). A new approach to asset pricing models: The bilinear paradigm. *J. Finance* 38, 711–743.

Brown, S.J., and M.I. Weinstein (1985). Derived factors in event studies. *J. Financ. Econ.* 14, 491–495.

Burmeister, E., and M.B. McElroy (1988). Joint estimation of factor sensitivities and risk premia for the arbitrage pricing theory. *J. Finance* 43, 721–733.

Burmeister, E., and K.D. Wall (1986). The arbitrage pricing theory and macroeconomic factor measures. *The Financ. Rev.* 21, 1–20.

Chamberlain, G. (1983). Funds, factors and diversification in arbitrage pricing models. *Econometrica* 51, 1305–1323.

Chamberlain, G. (1988). Asset pricing in multiperiod securities markets. *Econometrica* 51, 1283–1300.

Chamberlain, G., and M. Rothschild (1983). Arbitrage and mean variance analysis on large asset markets. *Econometrica* 51, 1281–1304.

Chan, K.-F., and M. Beenstock (1984). Testing the arbitrage pricing theory in the U.K. 1961–1982, in: *Proc. 11th Annu. Meet. of the European Finance Association*, Manchester.

Chan, K.C., N.-f. Chen and D. Hsieh (1985). An exploratory investigation of the firm size effect. *J. Financ. Econ.* 14, 451–471.

Chang, E.C., and W.G. Lewellen (1985). An arbitrage pricing approach to evaluating mutual fund perfomance. *J. Financ. Res.* 8, 15–30.

Chen, N.-f. (1983). Some empirical tests of the theory of arbitrage pricing. *J. Finance* 38, 1393–1414.

Chen, N.-f., T.E. Copeland and D. Mayers (1987). A comparison of single and multifactor portfolio performance methodologies. *J. Financ. Quant. Anal.* 22, 401–417.

Chen, Z., and P.J. Knez (1992). A pricing operator-based testing foundation for the arbitrage pricing theory, Working paper, University of Wisconsin.

Chen, N.-f., and J.E. Ingersoll, Jr. (1983). Exact pricing in linear factor models with finitely many assets: A note. *J. Finance* 38, 985–988.

Chen, N.-f., R. Roll and S.A. Ross (1986). Economic forces and the stock market. *J. Bus.* 59, 383–403.

Cho, D.C. (1984). On testing the arbitrage pricing theory: Inter-battery factor analysis. *J. Finance* 39, 1485–1502.

Cho, D.C., E.J. Elton and M.J. Gruber (1984). On the robustness of the Roll and Ross arbitrage pricing theory. *J. Financ. Quant. Anal.* 19, 1–10.

Cho, D.C., Ch.S. Eun and L.W. Senbet (1986). International arbitrage pricing theory: An empirical investigation. *J. Finance* 41, 313–329.

Clyman, D.R., M.E. Edelson and R.S. Hiller (1991). International arbitrage pricing, risk premia and exchange rate drift, Working paper 92-019, Harvard Business School, Boston, MA.

Cohen, K.J., G.A. Hawawini, S.F. Maier, Robert A. Schwartz and David K. Whitcomb (1983). Friction in the trading process and the estimation of systematic risk. *J. Financ. Econ.* 12, 263–278.

Cohen, K.J., and J.A. Pogue (1967). An empirical evaluation of alternative portfolio-selection models. *J. Bus.* 40, 166–193.

Connor, G. (1982). Asset pricing theory in factor economies, Ph.D. dissertation, Yale University, New Haven, CT.

Connor, G. (1984). A unified beta pricing theory. *J. Econ. Theory* 34, 13–31.

Connor, G. (1989). Notes on the arbitrage pricing theory, in: Sudipto Bhattacharya and George M. Constantinides (eds.), *Theory of Valuation: Frontiers of Modern Financial Theory*, Vol. 1, Rowman & Littlefield, Totowa, NJ.

Connor, G., and R.A. Korajczyk (1986). Performance measurement with the arbitrage pricing theory: A new framework for analysis. *J. Financ. Econ.* 15, 373–394.

Connor, G., and R.A. Korajczyk (1988a). Risk and return in an equilibrium APT: Application of a new test methodology. *J. Financ. Econ.* 21, 255–289.

Connor, G., and R.A. Korajczyk (1988b). Estimating pervasive economic factors with missing observations, Working paper 34, Department of Finance, Northwestern University, Evanston, IL.

Connor, G., and R.A. Korajczyk (1989). An intertemporal equilibrium beta pricing model. *Rev. Financ. Studies* 2, 373–392.

Connor, G., and R.A. Korajczyk (1991). The attributes, behavior, and performance of U.S. mutual funds. *Rev. Quant. Finance Account.* 1, 5–26.

Connor, G., and R.A. Korajczyk (1993). A test for the number of factors in an approximate factor model. *J. Finan.* 48, 1263–1291.

Connor, G., and R. Uhlaner (1988). New cross-sectional regression tests of beta pricing models, Working paper, School of Business Administration, University of California, Berkeley, CA.

Connor, G., and R. Uhlaner (1989). A synthesis of two approaches to factor estimation, Working paper, School of Business Administration, University of California, Berkeley, CA.

Constantinides, G.M. (1989). Theory of valuation: Overview and recent developments, in: Sudipto Bhattacharya and George M. Constantinides (eds.), *Theory of Valuation: Frontiers of Modern Financial Theory*, Vol. 1, Rowman & Littlefield, Totowa, NJ.

Conway, D.A., and M.R. Reinganum (1988). Stable factors in security returns: Identification through cross validation. *J. Bus. Econ. Stat.* 6, 1–15.

Copeland, Th.E., and J.F. Weston (1988). *Financial Theory and Corporate Policy*, 3rd edition, Addison-Wesley, Reading.

Copeland, T., T. Koller and J. Murrin (1990). *Valuation: Measuring and Managing the Value of Companies*, Wiley, New York, NY.

Cragg, J.G., and S.G. Donald (1992). Testing and determining arbitrage pricing structure from regressions on macro variables, Working paper, University of British Columbia, Vancouver, BC.

Cragg, J.G., and B.G. Malkiel (1982). *Expectations and the Structure of Share Prices*, University of Chicago Press, Chicago.

Davidson, R., and J.G. Mackinnon (1981). Several tests for model specification in the presence of alternative hypotheses. *Econometrica* 49, 781–793.

Dempster, A.P., N.M. Laird and D.B. Rubin (1977). Maximum likelihood from incomplete data via the *EM* algorithm. *J. R. Stat. Soc., Ser. B* 39, 1–22.

Dhrymes, P.J., I. Friend and N.B. Gultekin (1984). A critical reexamination of the empirical evidence on the arbitrage pricing theory. *J. Finance* 39, 323–346.

Diacogiannis, G.P. (1986). Arbitrage pricing model: A critical examination of its empirical applicability for the London stock exchange. *J. Bus. Finance Account.* 13, 489–504.

Dumontier, P. (1986). Le modèle d'évaluation par arbitrage des actifs financiers: Une étude sur le marché financier parisien. *Finance* 7, 7–21.

Dybvig, P.H. (1983). An explicit bound on deviations from APT pricing in a finite economy. *J. Financ. Econ.* 12, 483–496.

Dybvig, P.H., and S.A. Ross (1985). Yes, the APT is testable. *J. Finance* 40, 1173–1188.

Dybvig, P.H., and S.A. Ross (1989). Arbitrage, in: J. Eatwell, M. Milgate and P. Newman (eds.), *The New Palgrave: Finance*, Norton, New York, NY.

Elton, E.J., and M.J. Gruber (1973). Estimating the dependence structure of share prices — implications for portfolio selection. *J. Finance* 28, 1203–1232.

Engle, R.F., V.K. Ng and M. Rothschild (1990). Asset pricing with a factor-ARCH covariance structure: Empirical estimates for treasury bills. *J. Econometr.* 45, 213–237.

Fama, E.F. (1976). *Foundations of Finance*, Basic Books, New York, NY.

Fama, E.F. (1984). Forward and spot exchange rates. *J. Monetary Econ.* 14, 319–338.

Fama, E.F. (1991). Efficient capital markets: II. *J. Finance* 46, 1575–1617.

Fama, E.F., L. Fisher, M.C. Jensen and R. Roll (1969). The adjustment of stock prices to new information. *Int. Econ. Rev.* 10, 1–21.

Fama, E.F., and K.R. French (1992). The cross-section of expected stock returns. *J. Finance* 47, 427–465.

Fama, E.F., and K.R. French (1993). Common risk factors in the returns on stocks and bonds. *J. Financ. Econ.* 33, 3–56.

Fama, E.F., and M.R. Gibbons (1984). A comparison of inflation forecasts. *J. Monetary Econ.* 13, 327–348.

Fama, E.F., and J.D. MacBeth (1973). Risk, return, and equilibrium: Empirical tests. *J. Polit. Econ.* 71, 607–636.

Farrar, D.E. (1962). *The Investment Decision under Uncertainy*, Prentice-Hall, Englewood Cliffs, NJ.

Ferson, W.E. (1992). Asset pricing models, Working paper 351, Center for Research in Security Prices, University of Chicago, Forthcoming, in: Douglas Greenwald (ed.), *The Encyclopedia of Economics*, McGraw-Hill, New York, NY.

Ferson, W.E. (1995). Theory and empirical testing of asset pricing models, in: R. Jarrow, V. Maksimovic and W.T. Ziemba (eds.), *Finance*, Handbooks in Operations Research and Management Science, Vol. 9, North-Holland, Amsterdam, pp. 145–200 (this volume).

Ferson, W.E., and C.R. Harvey (1991a). The variation of economic risk premiums. *J. Polit. Econ.* 99, 385–415.

Ferson, W.E., and C.R. Harvey (1991b). Sources of predictability in portfolio returns. *Financ. Anal. J.* 47, 49–56.

Ferson, W.E., and R.A. Korajczyk (1995). Do arbitrage pricing models explain the predictability of stock returns? *J. Business* 68, 309–349.

Frohlich, C.J. (1991). A performance measure for mutual funds using the Connor–Korajczyk methodology: An empirical study. *Rev. Quant. Finance Account.* 1, 427–434.

Gallant, A.R. 1987. *Nonlinear Statistical Models*, Wiley, New York, NY.

Gehr, A., Jr. (1978). Some tests of the arbitrage pricing theory. *J. Midwest Finance Assoc.* 7, 91–106.

Geweke, J., and G. Zhou (1993). Measuring the pricing error of the arbitrage pricing theory, Working paper, University of Minnesota, Minneapolis, MN.

Gibbons, M.R. (1982). Multivariate tests of financial models: A new approach. *J. Financ. Econ.* 10, 3–27.

Gibbons, M.R. (1986). Empirical examination of the return generating process of the arbitrage pricing theory, Research paper 881, Graduate School of Business, Stanford University.

Gilles, Ch., and S.F. LeRoy (1990). The arbitrage pricing theory: A geometric interpretation, Working paper, Carleton University, Ottawa, Ont.

Gilles, Ch., and S.F. LeRoy (1991). On the arbitrage pricing theory. *Econ. Theory* 1, 213–229.

Grinblatt, M., and S. Titman (1983). Factor pricing in a finite economy. *J. Financ. Econ.* 12, 497–507.

Grinblatt, M., and S. Titman (1985). Approximate factor structures: Interpretations and implications for empirical tests. *J. Finance* 40, 1367–1373.

Grinblatt, M., and S. Titman (1987). The relation between mean–variance efficiency and arbitrage pricing. *J. Bus.* 60, 97–112.

Gultekin, M.N., N.B. Gultekin and A. Penati (1989). Capital controls and international capital market segmentation: The evidence from the Japanese and American stock markets. *J. Finance* 44, 849–869.

Hamao, Y. (1988). An empirical examination of the arbitrage pricing theory: Using japanese data. *Jpn World Econ.* 1, 45–61.

Hansen, L.P., and R. Jagannathan (1991a). Implications of security market data for models of dynamic economies. *J. Polit. Econ.* 99, 225–262.

Hansen, L.P., and R. Jagannathan (1991b). Assessing specification errors in stochastic discount factor models, Working paper, University of Chicago, Chicago, IL.

Harrington, D.R. (1987). *Modern Portfolio Theory, The Capital Asset Pricing Model & Arbitrage Pricing Theory: A User's Guide*, 2nd edition, Prentice-Hall, Englewood Cliffs, NJ.

Harrison, J.M., and D.M. Kreps (1979). Martingales and arbitrage in multiperiod securities markets. *J. Econ. Theory* 20, 381–408.

Heston, S. (1991). Testing approximate linear asset pricing models, Working paper, Yale University, New Haven, CT.

Heston, S.L., K.G. Rouwenhorst and R.O E. Wessels (1992). The structure of international stock returns and the integration of capital markets, Working paper, Yale University, New Haven, CT.

Hodrick, R.J. (1987). *The Empirical Evidence on the Efficiency of Forward and Futures Foreign Exchange Markets*, Harwood Academic Publishers.

Hollifield, B. (1993). Linear asset pricing with time-varying betas and risk premia, Working paper, University of British Columbia, Vancouver, BC.

Huberman, G. (1982). A simple approach to arbitrage pricing. *J. Econ. Theory* 28, 183–191.

Huberman, G. (1989). Arbitrage pricing theory, in: J. Eatwell, M. Milgate and P. Newman (eds.). *The New Palgrave: Finance*, Norton, New York, NY.

Huberman, G., and S. Kandel (1987). Mean–variance spanning. *J. Finance* 42, 873–888.

Huberman, G., S. Kandel and G.A. Karolyi (1987). Size and industry related covariations of stock returns, Working paper 202, CRSP, University of Chicago, Chicago, IL.

Huberman, G., S. Kandel and R.F. Stambaugh (1987). Mimicking portfolios and exact asset pricing. *J. Finance* 42, 1–9.

Hughes, P.J. (1984). A test of the arbitrage pricing theory using Canadian security returns. *Can. J. Adm. Sci.* 1, 195–214.

Ingersoll, J.E., Jr. (1984). Some results in the theory of arbitrage pricing. *J. Finance* 39, 1021–1039.

Ingersoll, J.E., Jr. (1987). *Theory of Financial Decision Making*, Rowman & Littlefield, Totowa, NJ.

Jagannathan, R., and S. Viswanathan (1988). Linear factor pricing, term structure of interest rates and the small firm anomaly, Working paper 57, Department of Finance, Northwestern University, Evanston, IL.

Jarrow, R.A. (1988). Preferences, continuity, and the arbitrage pricing theory. *Rev. Financ. Studies* 1, 159–172.

Jensen, M.C. (1968). The performance of mutual funds in the period 1945–1964. *J. Finance* 23, 389–419.

Jensen, M.C. (1969). Risk, the pricing of capital assets, and the evaluation of investment portfolios. *J. Bus.* 42, 167–247.

Jobson, J.D. (1982). A multivariate linear regression test of the arbitrage pricing theory. *J. Finance* 37, 1037–1042.

Kale, J.K., Nils H. Hakansson and G.W. Platt (1991). Industry vs. other factors in risk prediction, Finance working paper 201, University of California, Berkeley, CA.

Kandel, S., and R.F. Stambaugh (1989). A mean–variance framework for tests of asset pricing models. *Rev. Financ. Studies* 2, 125–156.

Keim, D.B. (1983). Size-related anomalies and stock return seasonality: Further empirical evidence. *J. Financ. Econ.* 12, 13–32.

Ketterer, J. (1987). Asset pricing with differential information, Working paper, Department of Finance, Northwestern University, Evanston, IL.

King, B.F. (1966). Market and industry factors in stock price behavior. *J. Bus.* 39, 139–190.

Korajczyk, R.A. (1985). The pricing of forward contracts for foreign exchange. *J. Political Economy* 93, 346–368.

Korajczyk, R.A., and C.J. Viallet (1989). An empirical investigation of international asset pricing. *Rev. Financ. Studies* 2, 553–585.

Korajczyk, R.A., and C.J. Viallet (1992). Equity risk premia and the pricing of foreign exchange risk. *J. Int. Econ.* 33, 199–219.

Kreps, D.M. (1981). Arbitrage and equilibrium in economies with infinitely many commodities. *J. Math. Econ.* 8, 15–35.

Kritzman, M. (1993). What practitioners need to know about factor methods. *Financ. Anal. J.* 49, 12–15.

Latham, M. (1989). The arbitrage pricing theory and supershares. *J. Finance* 44, 263–281.

Lehmann, B.N. (1990). Residual risk revisited. *J. Econometr.* 45, 71–97.

Lehmann, B.N. (1992). Notes on dynamic factor pricing models. *Rev. Quant. Finance Account.* 2, 69–87.

Lehmann, B.N., and David M. Modest (1985). The empirical foundations of the arbitrage pricing theory II: The optimal construction of basis portfolio, Working paper 292, Department of Economics, Columbia University, New York, NY.

Lehmann, B.N., and David M. Modest (1987). Mutual fund performance evaluation: A comparison and benchmarks and benchmark comparisons. *J. Finance* 42, 233–265.

Lehmann, B.N., and David M. Modest (1988). The empirical foundations of the arbitrage pricing theory. *J. Financ. Econ.* 21, 213–254.

Levine, R. (1989). An international arbitrage pricing model with PPP deviations. *Econ. Inquiry* 27, 87–599.

Litterman, R., and J. Scheinkman (1991). Common factors affecting bond returns. *J. Fixed Income* 1, 54–61.

Long, J.B. (1974). Stock prices, inflation and the term structure of interest rates. *J. Financ. Econ.* 1, 131–170.

Lucas, R.E., Jr. (1978). Asset prices in an exchange economy. *Econometrica* 46, 1429–1445.

Luedecke, B.P. (1984). An empirical investigation into arbitrage and approximate K-factor structure on large asset markets, Doctoral dissertation, Department of Economics, University of Wisconsin, Madison, WI.

Luttmer, E.G.J. (1993). Asset pricing in economies with frictions, Working paper 151, Department of Finance, Northwestern University, Evanston, IL.

MacKinlay, A.C. (1993). Multifactor models do not explain deviations from the CAPM, Working paper, University of Pennsylvania, Philadelphia, PA.

Madansky, A. (1964). Instrumental variables in factor analysis. *Psychometrica* 29, 105–113.

McCloskey, D.N. (1985). The loss function has been mislaid: The rhetoric of significance tests. *Am. Econ. Rev.* 75, 201–205.

McCulloch, R., and P.E. Rossi (1990). Posterior, predictive, and utility-based approaches to testing the arbitrage pricing theory. *J. Financ. Econ.* 28, 7–38.

McCulloch, R., and P.E. Rossi (1991). A Bayesian approach to testing the arbitrage pricing theory. *J. Econometr.* 49, 141–168.

McElroy, M.B., and E. Burmeister (1988). Arbitrage pricing theory as a restricted nonlinear multivariate regression model. *J. Bus. Econ. Stat.* 6, 29–42.

Mei, J. (1993). A semi-autoregression approach to the arbitrage pricing theory. *J. Finance* 48, 599–620.

Merton, R.C. (1973). An intertemporal capital asset pricing model. *Econometrica* 41, 867–887.

Merton, R.C. (1977). A reexamination of the capital asset pricing model, in: I. Friend and J. Bicksler (eds.), *Risk and Return in Finance*, Ballinger, Cambridge, MA.

Miller, M.H., and M. Scholes (1972). Rates of return in relation to risk: A re-examination of some recent findings, in: M.C. Jensen (ed.), *Studies in the Theory of Capital Markets*, Praeger, New York, NY.

Milne, F. (1988). Arbitrage and diversification in a general equilibrium asset economy. *Econometrica* 56, 815–840.

Morrison, D.F. (1976). *Multivariate Statistical Methods*, 2nd edition, McGraw-Hill, New York, NY.

Ng, V.R. Engle, and M. Rothschild (1992). A multi-dynamic-factor model for stock returns. *J. Econometr.* 52, 245–266.

Ohlson, J.A., and M.B. Garman (1980). A dynamic equilibrium for the Ross arbitrage model. *J. Finance* 35, 675–684.

Raveh, A. (1985). A note on factor analysis and arbitrage pricing theory. *J. Banking Finance* 9, 317–321.

Rao, C.R. (1973). *Linear Statistical Inference and its Applications,* 2nd edition, Wiley, New York, NY.

Reinganum, M.R. (1981). The arbitrage pricing theory: Some simple tests. *J. Finance* 36, 313–322.

Reisman, H. (1988). A general approach to the arbitrage pricing theory (APT). *Econometrica* 56, 473–476.

Reisman, H. (1992a). Intertemporal arbitrage pricing theory. *Rev. Financ. Studies* 5, 105–122.

Reisman, H. (1992b). Reference variables, factor structure, and the approximate multibeta representation. *J. Finance* 47, 1303–1314.

Reisman, H. (1992c). The APT with proxies, Working paper, Technion, Haifa.

Roll, R., and S.A. Ross (1980). An empirical investigation of the arbitrage pricing theory. *J. Finance* 35, 1073–1103.

Roll, R., and S.A. Ross (1983). Regulation, the capital asset pricing model, and the arbitrage pricing theory. *Public Util. Fortn.* 111, 22–28.

Roll, R., and S.A. Ross (1984a). The arbitrage pricing theory approach to strategic portfolio planning. *Financ. Anal. J.* 14–26.

Roll, R., and S.A. Ross (1984b). A critical reexamination of the empirical evidence on the arbitrage pricing theory: A reply. *J. Finance* 39, 347–350.

Rosenberg, B. (1974). Extra-market components of covariance in security returns. *J. Financ. Quant. Anal.* 9, 263–274.

Ross, S.A. (1976). The arbitrage theory of capital asset pricing. *J. Econ. Theory* 13, 341–360.

Ross, S.A. (1977). Return, risk and arbitrage, in: I. Friend and J. Bicksler (ed.), *Risk and Return in Finance*, Ballinger, Cambridge, MA.

Ross, S.A. (1978a). The current status of the capital asset pricing model (CAPM). *J. Finance* 33, 885–901.

Ross, S.A. (1978b). A simple approach to the valuation of risky streams. *J. Bus.* 51, 453–475.

Ross, S.A. (1982). On the general validity of the mean–variance approach in large markets, in: W.F. Sharpe and C.M. Cootner (eds.), *Financial Economics: Essays in Honor of Paul Cootner*, Prentice-Hall, Englewood Cliffs, NJ.

Ross, S.A. (1990). Arbitrage and the APT: Some new results, Working paper, School of Management, Yale University, New Haven, CT.

Ross, S.A., and M.M. Walsh (1983). A simple approach to the pricing of risky assets with uncertain exchange rates. *Res. Int. Bus. Finance* 3, 39–54.

Ross, S.A., R.W. Westerfield and J.F. Jaffe (1993). *Corporate Finance*, 3rd edition, Irwin, Homewood.

Rothschild, M. (1986). Asset pricing theories, in: W.P. Heller, R.M. Starr and D.A. Starrett (eds.), *Uncertainty, Information, and Communication: Essays in Honor of Kennth J. Arrow*, Vol. III, Cambridge University Press, Cambridge.

Rubio, G. (1992). Further evidence on performance evaluation: Portfolio holdings, recommendations, and turnover costs, Finance working paper 222, University of California, Berkeley, CA.

Scholes, M., and J. Williams (1977). Estimating betas from nonsynchronous data. *J. Financ. Econ.* 5, 309–327.

Sentana, E. (1992). Identification of multivariate conditionally heteroskedastic factor models, Discussion paper 139, London School of Economics, London.

Shanken, J. (1982). The arbitrage pricing theory: Is it testable? *J. Finance* 37, 1129–1140.

Shanken, J. (1985). Multi-beta CAPM or equilibrium APT: A reply. *J. Finance* 40, 1189–1196.

Shanken, J. (1987a). Multivariate proxies and asset pricing relations: Living with Roll critique. *J. Financ. Econ.* 18, 91–110.

Shanken, J. (1987b). Nonsynchronous data and the covariance-factor structure of returns. *J. Finance* 42, 221–231.

Shanken, J. (1990). Intertemporal asset pricing: An empirical investigation. *J. Econometr.* 45, 99–120.

Shanken, J. (1992a). On the estimation of beta-pricing models. *Rev. Financ. Studies* 5, 1–33.

Shanken, J. (1992b). The current state of the arbitrage pricing theory. *J. Finance* 47, 1569–1574.

Shanken, J., and M.I. Weinstein (1990). Macroeconomic variables and asset pricing: Estimation and tests, Working paper, University of Rochester, Rochester, NY.

Sharpe, W.F. (1963). A simplified model for portfolio analysis. *Manage. Sci.* 9, 277–293.

Sharpe, W.F. (1977). The capital asset pricing model: A multi-beta interpretation, in: H. Levy and M. Sarnat (eds.), *Financial Decision Making under Uncertainty*, Academic Press, New York, NY.

Sharpe, W.F. (1982). Some factors in New York Stock Exchange security returns (1931–1979). *J. Portfolio Manage.* 8, 5–19.

Sharpe, W.F. (1984). Factor models, CAPMs, and the APT. *J. Portfolio Manage.* 11, 21–25.

Sharpe, W.F. (1988). Determining a fund's effective asset mix. *Investment Manage. Rev.* 2, 59–69.

Sharpe, W.F. (1992). Asset allocation: Management style and performance measurement. *J. Portfolio Manage.* 18, 7–19.

Solnik, B. (1983). International arbitrage pricing theory. *J. Finance* 38, 449–457.

Stambaugh, R.F. (1983). Arbitrage pricing with information. *J. Financ. Econ.* 12, 357–69.

Stroyny, A.L. (1992). Still more on *EM* factor analysis, Working paper, University of Wisconsin, Milwaukee, WI.

Suzuki, Y., editor (1987). *The Japanese Financial System*, Clarendon Press, Oxford.

Trzcinka, Ch. (1986). On the number of factors in the arbitrage pricing model. *J. Finance* 41, 347–368.

Warga, A. (1989). Experimental design in tests of linear factor models. *J. Bus. Econ. Stat.* 7, 191–198.

Wei, K.C.J. (1988). An asset pricing theory unifying the CAPM and APT. *J. Finance* 43, 881–892.

Wei, K.C.J., C.-f. Lee and A.H. Chen (1991). Multivariate regression tests of the arbitrage pricing theory: The instrumental variables approach. *Rev. Quant. Finance Account.* 1, 191–208.

White, H., and I. Domowitz (1984). Nonlinear regression with dependent observations. *Econometrica* 52, 143–161.

Winkelmann, M. (1984). Testing APT for the German stock market, in: *Proc. 11th Annu. Meet. of the European Finance Association*, Manchester.

Young, S.D., M.A. Berry, D.W. Harvey and J.R. Page (1987). Systematic risk and accounting information under the arbitrage pricing theory. *Financ. Anal. J.* 43, 73–76.

R. Jarrow et al., Eds., *Handbooks in OR & MS, Vol. 9*

Chapter 5

Theory and Empirical Testing of Asset Pricing Models

Wayne E. Ferson

University of Washington, Department of Finance and Business Economics, DJ10, Seattle, WA 90195, U.S.A.

1. Introduction

This chapter concentrates on selected advances in financial asset pricing over approximately the last decade. There are two main objectives. The first is to integrate the major asset pricing models in a self contained discussion using simple first principles. The second is to review empirical tests of the models within a unified framework. One cost of this approach is that some of the subtle distinctions between the theories is not addressed. More recent or accessible references are often used instead of carefully attributing the ideas to the original authors, but this provides a trail which the serious student can follow back to the original works.

The theory of financial asset pricing as it existed in 1993 while this was being written, was essentially in place a decade before. Advances on the theoretical front have mainly involved finer articulation of the models and an improved understanding of the relations among them. The review of theory in Section 2 of this chapter reflects this state of affairs. For maximum simplicity the models and their tests are presented in discrete time.[1] Section 2 begins by setting up a general framework, which is then specialized to review various models. Emphasis is given to some recent theoretical refinements which have been the subject of empirical tests. The choice of refinements is selective, reflecting the author's tastes and interests. Nonseparable preference models and production-based asset pricing are two areas that receive special attention.

While the theory of financial asset pricing has essentially been in place for more than a decade, there have been major advances in empirical methods over the same period. These methods are the subject of Section 3. The introduction of Hansen's [1982] Generalized Method of Moments (GMM) into the tool kit of the financial econometrician is perhaps the most important methodological innovation of the decade. As many empirical methods are special cases of the GMM, the approach is used here to unify the discussion of empirical methods.

[1] See Constantinides & Malliaris [1995 (chapter 1 of this volume)] for a review of continuous time portfolio theory with applications to financial asset pricing.

Significant progress has been made over the last decade, toward modelling expected returns and risks of assets that may change over time with economic information. Models which incorporate this feature, which we call *conditional asset pricing models* are a major focus of this chapter. Finally, Section 3 concludes with a review of cross-sectional regression methods. Such methods have traditionally been a mainstay of empirical work on asset pricing and may continue to be useful for estimating and testing dynamic models.

2. Asset pricing models: a selective review and integration

2.1. General asset pricing expressions

Virtually all financial asset pricing models imply that the return of any asset i, $R_{i,t+1}$, multiplied by a market-wide random variable, m_{t+1}, has a constant conditional expectation:

$$E_t\{m_{t+1}R_{i,t+1}\} = 1, \quad \text{all } i = 1, \ldots, N. \tag{1}$$

The gross return $R_{i,t+1}$ is defined as $(P_{i,t+1} + D_{i,t+1})/P_{i,t}$, where $P_{i,t}$ is the price of the asset i at time t and $D_{i,t+1}$ is the amount of any dividends, interest or other payments received at time $t+1$. In special cases, m_{t+1} is known as a stochastic discount factor, an equivalent martingale measure, a Radon-Nicodym derivative, or an intertemporal marginal rate of substitution. This chapter will refer to equation (1) as the *canonical asset pricing equation*, and to an m_{t+1} which satisfies (1) as a *benchmark pricing variable*. The notation $E_t\{.\}$ will be used to denote the conditional expectation, given a 'market-wide' information set. Sometimes it will be convenient to refer to expectations conditional on a subset, Z_t, of the market information, which are denoted as $E(. \mid Z_t)$. When Z_t is the null information set, the unconditional expectation is denoted as $E(.)$. Taking the expected values of equation (1), it follows that versions of (1) must hold for the expectations $E(. \mid Z_t)$ and $E(.)$.

Repeated substitution in equation (1), assuming that the limiting expression is finite produces:

$$P_t = E_t\Big\{\sum_{j>0}\Big[\prod_{k=1,\ldots,j} m_{t+k}\Big]D_{t+j}\Big\}. \tag{2}$$

Equation (2) is the *present value model*, which equates price to the expected discounted value of future cash flows. In early work m_{t+j} was taken to be a fixed *discount factor* $[m_{t+j} = (1+r)^{-j})]$, possibly adjusted for risk in ad hoc ways. More recently, the present value model has been used to study the relation between the variance of stock prices and dividends.[2]

[2] See LeRoy & Porter [1981], Shiller [1981], Kleidon [1986], Campbell & Shiller [1987] and Cochrane [1992]. Campbell [1991] and Campbell & Mei [1993] employ linearizations of equation (2) that allow for changing expected returns. See Cochrane [1991b] and Gilles & LeRoy [1991] for recent reviews.

You don't have to say much about m_{t+1} to give equation (1) economic content. The existence of an m_{t+1} that satisfies (1) says that all assets with the same payoffs have the same price (sometimes referred to as the law of one price). With the restriction that m_{t+1} is a strictly positive random variable, equation (1) becomes equivalent to a *no-arbitrage* condition. The condition is that all portfolios of assets with payoffs that can never be negative but are positive with positive probability, must have positive prices. The no-arbitrage condition does not uniquely identify m_{t+1} unless markets are complete. In that case, m_{t+1} is equal to primitive state prices divided by state probabilities.[3]

Without more structure equation (1) has little empirical content because it is easy to find some random variable m_{t+1} for which the equation holds.[4] It is the specific form of m_{t+1} implied by a model that gives the equation further empirical content. Empirical tests of asset pricing models often work directly with equation (1) and the relevant definition of m_{t+1}.

In an equilibrium asset pricing model equation (1) arises as a first order condition for a consumer-investor's optimization problem, and a benchmark variable is defined by the model. The agent maximizes a lifetime utility function of consumption (including possibly a bequest to heirs). Denote this function by $V(.)$. If the allocation of resources to consumption and investment assets is optimal, it is not possible to obtain higher utility by changing the allocation. Suppose an investor considers reducing consumption at time t to purchase more of (any) asset. The utility cost at time t of the foregone consumption is the marginal utility of consumption expenditures C_t, denoted by $MU_t = (\partial V/\partial C_t) > 0$, multiplied by the price $P_{i,t}$ of the asset, measured in the same units as the consumption expenditures. The expected utility gain of selling the share and consuming the proceeds at time $t+1$ is $E_t\{(P_{i,t+1} + D_{i,t+1})MU_{t+1}\}$. If the allocation maximizes expected utility, the following must hold: $P_{i,t}E_t\{(\partial V/\partial C_t)\} = E_t\{(P_{i,t+1} + D_{i,t+1})(\partial V/\partial C_{t+1})\}$, which is equivalent to equation (1), with

$$m_{t+1} = \frac{\partial V/\partial C_{t+1}}{E_t\{(\partial V/\partial C_t)\}}. \tag{3}$$

The m_{t+1} in equation (3) is the *intertemporal marginal rate of substitution* (IMRS) of the consumer. When equation (3) defines m_{t+1}, equation (1) is the consumer's intertemporal *Euler equation*. The Euler equation is a necessary condition for an individual consumer's optimization problem.

[3] Write equation (1) as $P_{it} = E_t\{m_{t+1}X_{i,t+1}\}$, where $X_{i,t+1}$ is the payoff of asset i at time $t+1$, and $R_{i,t+1} = X_{i,t+1}/P_{it}$. In a discrete-state setting, $P_{it} = \sum_s \pi_s X_{i,s} = \sum_s q_s(\pi_s/q_s)X_{i,s}$, where π_s is the state price, equal to the value at time t of one unit of the numeraire to be paid at time $t+1$ if state s occurs at time $t+1$, and $X_{i,s}$ is the value of security i at time $t+1$ if state s occurs. Comparing this expression with equation (1) shows that $m_s = \pi_s/q_s$ is the value of the benchmark pricing variable in state s. See Marsh [1995 (chapter 9 of this volume)] for applications to interest dependent contingent claims. See also Beja [1971], Rubinstein [1976], Ross [1977], Harrison & Kreps [1979] and Hansen & Richard [1987].

[4] For example, take a sample of assets with a nonsingular covariance matrix and let m_{t+1} be $[\underline{1}'(E_t\{R_{t+1}R'_{t+1}\})^{-1}]R_{t+1}$, where R_{t+1} is the $N \times 1$ vector of asset returns and $\underline{1}$ is an $N \times 1$ vector of ones. We will use this particular representation again in section 3.

Asset pricing models typically focus on the relation of security returns to aggregate quantities. It is therefore necessary to aggregate the Euler equations of individuals to obtain equilibrium expressions in terms of aggregate quantities. Theoretical conditions which justify the use of aggregate quantities are discussed by Gorman [1953], Wilson [1968], Rubinstein [1974], Constantinides [1982], and recently by Lewbel [1989] and Luttmer [1993].

To interpret the Euler equation as an asset pricing model, the approach is to take the IMRS as given. The objective is to use the IMRS to 'explain' asset returns through equation (1). Macroeconomists frequently take an opposite, but complementary approach. Taking asset returns as given, the Euler equation becomes a model for aggregate consumption behavior, as in modern 'permanent income' models [e.g. Hall, 1978].

Empirical implications

Typically, empirical work focusses on expressions for expected returns and excess rates of return. The expected excess returns are modelled in relation to risk and therefore denoted as *expected risk premiums*. Consider any asset return $R_{i,t+1}$ and a reference asset return, $R_{0,t+1}$. Define the excess return of asset i, relative to the reference asset as $r_{i,t+1} = R_{i,t+1} - R_{0,t+1}$. If equation (1) holds for both assets it implies:

$$E_t\{m_{t+1} r_{i,t+1}\} = 0, \quad \text{for all } i. \tag{4}$$

Use the definition of covariance to expand equation (4) into the product of expectations plus the covariance, obtaining:

$$E_t\{r_{i,t+1}\} = \frac{\operatorname{Cov}_t(r_{i,t+1}; -m_{t+1})}{E_t\{m_{t+1}\}}, \quad \text{for all } i, \tag{5}$$

where $\operatorname{Cov}_t(.;.)$ is the conditional covariance. Given a benchmark pricing variable, the conditional covariance of the return of asset i with m_{t+1} is a general measure of *systematic risk* of asset i. The risk is systematic in the sense that it is related to an economy-wide benchmark variable. If the conditional covariance is zero for a particular asset, the expected excess return of that asset should be zero.[5] Consider the case where m_{t+1} is an aggregate IMRS. The equation (5) says that a security will earn a positive risk premium if its return is negatively correlated with the aggregate IMRS. Negative correlation means that the asset is likely to return more than expected when the marginal utility in the future period $t + 1$, relative to the current period t, is lower than expected. The more negative is the covariance with the IMRS the less desirable is the distribution of the random return, and the larger must be the expected compensation for holding the asset.

[5] At this level of generality we can think of the returns and of the m_{t+1} as being either 'real' or 'nominal'. Any common unit of measurement is legitimate.

Conditional expected risk premiums should differ across assets in proportion to their conditional covariances with the IMRS.

Equation (5) is weaker than equation (1), since equation (5) is equivalent to $E_t\{m_{t+1}R_{i,t+1}\} = \Delta_t$, all i, where Δ_t is a constant across assets, while equation (1) restricts $\Delta_t = 1$. Therefore, empirical tests based on equation (5) do not exploit all of the restrictions implied by a model that may be stated in the form of equation (1).

Empirical work on asset pricing models typically relies on *rational expectations*, which is the assumption that the expectation terms in the model are mathematical conditional expectations.[6] Rational expectations implies that the difference between observed realizations and the expectations in the model should be unrelated to the information that the expectations in the model are conditioned on. For example, equation (1) says that the conditional expectation of the product of m_{t+1} and $R_{i,t+1}$ is the constant, 1.0. Therefore, $1 - m_{t+1}R_{i,t+1}$ should not be predictably different from zero using any information available at time t. If there is variation over time in a return $R_{i,t+1}$ that is predictable using instruments Z_t, the model implies that the predictability is removed when $R_{i,t+1}$ is multiplied by the correct m_{t+1}. This is the sense in which conditional asset pricing models are asked to 'explain' any predictable variation in asset returns. This generalizes the older 'random walk' model of stock values, which states that stock returns should be completely unpredictable. That model is a special case which can be motivated by risk neutrality. Under risk neutrality the IMRS is a constant. Therefore, the return $R_{i,t+1}$ should not differ predictably from a constant.

2.2. Time-separable, consumption-based asset pricing models

Theory

If the representative consumer's lifetime utility function is time-separable, $(\partial V/\partial C_t)$ depends only on variables dated at time t. Breeden [1979] derived a consumption-based asset pricing model in continuous time, assuming that the preferences are time-additive: $V = \sum_t \beta^t u(C_t)$, where β is a time preference parameter and $u(.)$ is increasing and concave in current consumption, C_t. Breeden's model is a linearization of equation (1) which follows from the assumption that asset values and consumption follow diffusion processes [see also Bhattacharya, 1981 and Grossman & Shiller, 1982]. The most widely-studied version of the consumption-based model is in discrete-time and follows Lucas [1978], assuming a power function:

$$u(C) = \frac{C^{1-\alpha} - 1}{1 - \alpha}. \tag{6}$$

[6] Rational expectations is used when the expected value in equation (1) is treated as a mathematical conditional expectation to obtain expressions for $E(. \mid Z)$ and $E(.)$.

In equation (6), $\alpha > 0$ is the concavity parameter of the period utility function. This function displays constant relative risk aversion[7] equal to α. Using (6) the IMRS in equation (3) becomes:

$$m_{t+1} = \beta \left(\frac{C_{t+1}}{C_t} \right)^{-\alpha} \tag{7}$$

The time-additive constant relative risk aversion consumption model has been the subject of numerous empirical tests using the Euler equation (1), equation (7) and data on aggregate consumption and real asset returns.

Implications for the level of interest rates also follow from equations (1) and (6). Let RF_t be a real rate of return for the t to $t+1$ period, assumed to be riskless in the sense that it is known at time t. The model implies:

$$RF_t = \frac{1}{E_t\{m_{t+1}\}} = \left[E_t \left\{ \beta \left(\frac{C_{t+1}}{C_t} \right)^{-\alpha} \right\} \right]^{-1} \tag{8}$$

Real interest rates should be related to the expected growth rates of consumption in this model.[8]

Empirical evidence

Hansen & Singleton [1982, 1984] and others empirically test the time-separable consumption-based asset pricing model with constant relative risk aversion and observe that the model is rejected. Singleton [1990] reviews this literature. Mehra & Prescott [1985] construct a model economy based on the same Euler equation. They assumed that equity is a claim to the aggregate consumption stream, which is given exogenously. They conclude that the volatility of aggregate consumption growth in the U.S. is too low for their model to match both an average short term U.S. Treasury bill return and an average equity return, without resorting to values of α larger than 10.[9] Dunn & Singleton [1986] found a similar result. They examined fitted values of equation (5) and found that the covariances of Treasury

[7] *Relative risk aversion* in consumption is defined as $-Cu''(C)/u'(C)$. Absolute risk aversion is $-u''(C)/u'(C)$. Ferson [1983] studies a consumption-based asset pricing model with constant absolute risk aversion.

[8] Equation (8) can be linearized by assuming lognormality of consumption or using a Taylor series to obtain:

$$\ln(RF_t) = -\ln\beta + \alpha E_t \left\{ \ln \left(\frac{C_{t+1}}{C_t} \right) \right\} - \phi_t,$$

where ϕ_t depends on the conditional second moments. Linearized versions of the model are studied by Hansen & Singleton [1983], Ferson [1983], Grossman, Melino & Shiller [1987], Ferson & Merrick [1987], Harvey [1988], Chan [1994], Ferson & Harvey [1993], Evans & Wachtel [1992] and others.

[9] Refinements and extensions of the Mehra & Prescott [1985] exercise include Reitz [1988] who considered rare but extreme consumption declines, Mankiw [1986] and Telmer [1991] who studied heterogeneous consumers who do not efficiently pool risks, Kocherlakota [1990] who allowed $\beta > 1$, Kandel & Stambaugh [1989] who examined $\alpha \gg 10$, and others.

bills with the IMRS for consumption do not differ enough relative to the average return differences.

Miron [1986] and Ferson & Harvey [1992] emphasize that as such results are based on seasonally-adjusted consumption data, they could potentially be an artifact of data smoothing.[10] They extend the model to incorporate seasonal effects and they use not seasonally adjusted consumption data. Ferson & Harvey [1992] find that seasonal adjustment does not explain the poor fit of the model to asset return data. They also find that the variation over time in conditional expected risk premiums is large relative to the variation over time in the conditional covariances of excess returns with the measures of consumption. Thus, a pattern similar to the equity premium puzzle exists as a dynamic phenomenon. The time-separable consumption model with small values of α does not appear to deliver enough time-series variation in m_{t+1} and its covariances with assets to control the predictable variation in asset returns over time.[11] Such results motivate the study of more general models.

2.3. Nonseparable preference models

Theory

Dunn & Singleton [1986] and Eichenbaum, Hansen & Singleton [1988], among others, incorporate consumption expenditures that may be durable in nature in their models. Durability introduces nonseparability over time, since the flow of services depends on past consumption expenditures. The consumer optimizes over the expenditures C_t, and durability implies that $(\partial V/\partial C_t)$ depends on variables dated other than date t. Current expenditures increase the consumer's future utility if the expenditures are durable.

Another form of time nonseparability arises if the utility function exhibits habit persistence. Habit persistence means that consumption at two points in time are complements. For example, the utility of current consumption is evaluated relative to what was consumed in the past. Such models are studied in Ryder & Heal [1973], Sundaresan [1989], Constantinides [1990], and Detemple & Zapatero [1991], among others. Constantinides [1990] studied a model in which the representative agent's utility function is of the form: $V = (1 - \alpha)^{-1} \sum_t \beta^t (C_t - hX_t)^{1-\alpha}$, $0 \leq h < 1$. hX_t is a subsistence level and X_t is assumed to be an exponentially weighted average of past consumptions C_{t-k}, $k > 0$.

A key attribute of the habit persistence model is that it allows the concepts of risk aversion and intertemporal substitution to be disentangled. In the time-

[10] Mehra and Prescott used annual data which are five-year moving averages (from Kuznets) prior to 1929, and are therefore smoothed in a different way. Even monthly data are smoothed relative to the theory. The theory relates to consumption and returns at specific points in time, while the available consumption data measure average expenditures over a period. This problem of *time-aggregation* of the consumption data is studied by Grossman, Melino & Shiller [1987], Breeden, Gibbons & Litzenberger [1989], Ermini [1991] and Heaton [1991].

[11] However, Kandel & Stambaugh [1989] show that with large values of α a model economy with time-separable preferences can mimic many of the dynamic properties of asset returns.

separable model with constant relative risk aversion α, the two are inversely related. Risk aversion is related to a consumer's attitudes toward variation across states of the world at a point in time. Intertemporal substitution is related to variation in consumption over time, and may be defined in the absence of risk. Lucas [1978] and Hall [1988] point out that the intertemporal elasticity of consumption in the time-additive power utility model is $1/\alpha$.

Constantinides [1990] argues that in a dynamic model risk aversion should be measured in terms of wealth [12], and he defines the elasticity of consumption as the partial derivative of expected consumption growth with respect to a given interest rate. In a time separable model, the product of the two is 1.0. With habit persistence, the relative risk aversion is not changed much over a range of values for the parameter h, while the elasticity of consumption is drastically reduced as h is increased.

Ferson & Constantinides [1991] model both the durability of consumption expenditures and habit persistence. They show that the two combine as opposing effects. They consider an example in which the effect is truncated at a single lag. The derived utility of expenditures for a (possibly durable) good is:

$$V = (1-\alpha)^{-1} \sum_t \beta^t (C_t + bC_{t-1})^{1-\alpha}, \tag{9}$$

The IMRS is obtained by using equation (3) with:

$$\frac{\partial V}{\partial C_t} = \beta^t (C_t + bC_{t-1})^{-\alpha} + \beta^{t+1} b E_t \left\{ (C_{t+1} + bC_t)^{-\alpha} \right\}. \tag{10}$$

The coefficient b is positive and measures the rate of depreciation if the good is durable and there is no habit persistence ($h = 0$). If habit persistence is present and the good is nondurable it implies that the lagged expenditures enter with a negative effect ($b < 0$).

Heaton [1991] and Ferson & Harvey [1992] consider a form of time nonseparability which emphasizes seasonality. The utility function is $(1-\alpha)^{-1} \sum_t \beta^t (C_t + bC_{t-4})^{1-\alpha}$, where the consumption expenditure decisions are assumed to be quarterly. The subsistence level (in the case of habit persistence) or the flow of services (in the case of durability) is assumed to depend only on the consumption expenditure in the same quarter of the previous year.

Abel [1990] studies an alternative form of habit persistence in which the consumer evaluates current consumption relative to the aggregate consumption in the previous period, which he or she takes as exogenous. The idea is that people care about 'keeping up with the Joneses'. In equilibrium, the aggregate IMRS becomes: $m_{t+1} = \beta(C_{t+1}/C_t)^{-\alpha}(C_{t-1}/C_t)^{\alpha-1}$ in Abel's model.

Another version of non time-separable consumption-based asset pricing model is studied by Epstein & Zin [1989, 1991] and others. The expected utility model is generalized to a class of recursive preferences which can be written

[12] Relative risk aversion is $-WJ_{ww}/J_w$, where J is the indirect utility of wealth, W, and subscripts denote partial derivatives.

as: $V_t = F(C_t, CEQ_t(V_{t+1}))$. $CEQ_t(.)$ is a time t 'certainty equivalent' for the future lifetime utility V_{t+1}. The function $F(., CEQ_t(.))$ may be different from the expected utility of lifetime consumption. The model is not time-separable when $\partial V/\partial C_t$ depends on variables other than those at time t. Recursive preferences have some advantages and some disadvantages over the expected utility model. As it is more general, a recursive preference model allows for behavioral attributes that cannot be captured by expected utility. In particular, it is possible to capture preferences for the timing of the resolution of uncertainty, to which expected utility is indifferent [Kreps & Porteus, 1978]. It allows a separation of the concepts of risk aversion and intertemporal substitution. Unlike the non time-separable expected utility models, this can be accomplished without carrying past consumption as a state variable, a feature which aids analytical tractability in some cases. However, recursive preferences are difficult to aggregate across consumers, so the representative agent paradigm is more difficult to justify than with expected utility. In the time-separable expected utility model, it is possible to justify empirical work using components of aggregate consumption expenditures (e.g., nondurable goods) by assuming that the utility is additively separable across the components. A similar argument does not go through with recursive preferences. Epstein [1990] provides a more comprehensive review and discussion of these issues.

Epstein & Zin [1989] study a special case of the recursive preference model in which the preferences are:

$$V_t = \left[(1-\beta)C_t^p + \beta E_t(V_{t+1}^{1-\alpha})^{p/(1-\alpha)}\right]^{1/p}. \tag{11}$$

They show that the IMRS for a representative agent becomes (when $p \neq 0$, $1-\alpha \neq 0$):

$$m_{t+1} = \left[\beta\left(\frac{C_{t+1}}{C_t}\right)^{p-1}\right]^{(1-\alpha)/p} R_{m,t+1}^{(1-\alpha-p)/p}, \tag{12}$$

where $R_{m,t+1}$ is the market portfolio return. The coefficient of relative risk aversion for timeless consumption gambles is α and the elasticity of substitution for deterministic consumption is $(1-p)^{-1}$. If $\alpha = 1-p$ the model reduces to the time-separable, constant relative risk aversion model, as (12) reduces to equation (7). If $\alpha = 1$ the log utility model of Rubinstein [1976] is obtained, where $m_{t+1} = 1/R_{m,t+1}$.

Recent theoretical work on consumption-based asset pricing has focused on refinements and extensions of the basic models. He & Modest [1992] and Luttmer [1993] incorporate market frictions, such as transaction costs, short-selling restrictions and bid–ask spreads. Constantinides & Duffie [1992] extend previous work which models consumer heterogeneity and incomplete markets. They show how uninsurable and persistent income shocks can result in Euler equations, stated in terms of aggregate quantities, which imply very different parameter values than in a representative agent model. Consumption-based asset pricing will probably continue to be an active area of research for some time.

Empirical evidence

Using monthly U.S. data, studies such as Dunn & Singleton [1986] and Eichenbaum, Hansen & Singleton [1988] have found mixed evidence for the importance of durability in consumption-based asset pricing models. Allowing nonseparability seems to improve goodness-of-fit tests of the model, but in some cases the coefficients on the lagged expenditures are negative, which is the 'wrong' sign for durability. Durability in expenditures reduces the volatility of the flow of services relative to the expenditures, and therefore reduces the volatility of the implied marginal utility of the services. In the equity premium puzzle, Mehra & Prescott [1985] found that the volatility of the implied marginal utility is too low in a model without durability. Therefore, durability has the wrong implication for the volatility of marginal utility.

With habit persistence, the implied IMRS is more volatile than it is in a time separable model or a model with durability, based on the same expenditure data. Habit persistence reduces the volatility of the optimal expenditures, since a consumer will optimally smooth consumption more than in a time-separable model. Constantinides [1990] found that habit persistence allows the model to successfully match certain sample moments of consumption and returns which Mehra & Prescott [1985] were unable to match in a time-separable model. Ferson & Constantinides [1991] found that evidence of durability, based on the parameter estimates in U.S. monthly data is not robust, while habit persistence dominates durability in U.S. quarterly and annual data. Ferson & Constantinides [1991] and Ferson & Harvey [1992] find that models incorporating strong habit persistence fare better in goodness-of-fit tests using U.S. data than do models with durability or time-separability. Braun, Constantinides & Ferson [1993] extend this evidence to quarterly data for several other countries.

Despite this positive evidence, there is also evidence that the habit persistence model using consumption does not provide a fully satisfactory empirical explanation of asset returns. Ferson & Constantinides [1991] find that although they did not reject the habit model when their tests focus on the dynamic properties of returns, the model does not explain the first moment of the equity premium puzzle. That is, when the tests emphasize the cross sectional structure of average returns the models can be rejected. They interpret these results as consistent with the theoretical effects of habit persistence on risk aversion and intertemporal substitution. Allen [1991] finds that failure to reject the model in some cases is attributed in part to the higher volatility of the IMRS under habit persistence, which results in less precise estimates of the moments that are used to form the test statistics. Telmer [1991] and Ni [1991] come to similar conclusions using different approaches.

Mankiw & Shapiro [1986] tested linearized versions of the Euler equation with the IMRS given by the recursive preference model (12). They found that introducing the market return improved the ability of the model to explain a cross-section of average returns. Kandel & Stambaugh [1991] find that a model economy with recursive preferences can match some of the dynamic properties of asset returns. However, Weil [1989] finds in a calibration exercise similar to Mehra & Prescott [1985], that a recursive preference model does not resolve the equity premium puzzle. Epstein & Zin [1991] formally test recursive preference models. They reject the hypothesis that $\alpha = 1 - p$. However, they conclude that their tests do not provide much support for the more general model.

2.4. Beta pricing models

Theory

The vast majority of the empirical work on asset pricing models has involved expressions for expected returns, stated in terms of *beta coefficients* relative to one or more portfolios. The beta is the regression coefficient of the asset return on the portfolio. The concept of a *minimum variance portfolio* is central in this literature. The portfolio $R_{p,t+1}$ is a minimum variance portfolio if it has the smallest variance of any portfolio with the same expected return. Roll [1977] and others have shown that the portfolio $R_{p,t+1}$ is a conditional minimum variance portfolio if and only if a *beta pricing model* holds for all assets in the portfolio:[13]

$$E_t\{R_{i,t+1} - R_{pz,t+1}\} = \beta_{ipt} E_t\{R_{p,t+1} - R_{pz,t+1}\}, \quad \text{all } i;$$
$$\beta_{ipt} = \left[\frac{\mathrm{Cov}_t(R_{i,t+1}; R_{p,t+1})}{\mathrm{Var}_t(R_{p,t+1})}\right]. \tag{13}$$

In equation (13), β_{ipt} is the *conditional beta* of $R_{i,t+1}$ relative to $R_{p,t+1}$. $R_{pz,t+1}$ is a *zero beta* asset relative to $R_{p,t+1}$. A zero beta asset satisfies $\mathrm{Cov}_t(R_{pz,t+1}; R_{p,t+1}) = 0$.

Equation (13) first appeared as an asset pricing model in the famous Capital Asset Pricing Model (CAPM) of Sharpe [1964], Lintner [1965], and Black [1972]. The CAPM is equivalent to the statement that the *market portfolio* $R_{m,t+1}$ is *mean–variance efficient*. The market portfolio is the portfolio of all marketed assets, weighted according to their relative total values. A portfolio is mean–variance efficient if it satisfies equation (13), and if it is also on the positively-sloped portion of the minimum variance boundary of all asset returns, so that $E_t(R_{m,t+1} - R_{mz,t+1}) > 0$.

The canonical asset pricing expression (1) relates directly to minimum variance portfolios and beta pricing. Equation (1) implies that a portfolio which maximizes squared correlation with m_{t+1} is a minimum variance portfolio. To see this consider a projection of m_{t+1} on the vector of returns R_{t+1}. Define the portfolio return $R_{p,t+1} = (w_t/w_t'\underline{1})'R_{t+1}$, using the minimum-distance weights $w_t' = \underline{1}'(E_t(R_{t+1}R_{t+1}')^{-1})$ [the expression for the weights uses equation (1)]. The

[13] See Constantinides & Malliaris [1995 (chapter 1 of this volume)] for proofs and a review of the mean–variance analysis of portfolios. It is assumed that the portfolio $R_{p,t+1}$ is not the global minimum variance portfolio in (13).

projection can be written as $m_{t+1} = (w_t'\underline{1})R_{p,t+1} + \epsilon_{t+1}$. The error term ϵ_{t+1} is conditionally uncorrelated with $R_{i,t+1}$ for all i, and therefore with $R_{p,t+1}$. Therefore, the fitted values of the projection maximize the squared correlation and will have the same pricing implications as m_{t+1}. That is, $m^*_{t+1} = (w_t'\underline{1})R_{p,t+1}$ can replace m_{t+1} in equation (1).[14] Performing this same substitution in equation (5) produces:

$$E_t\{r_{i,t+1}\} = \left[\frac{\text{Cov}_t(r_{i,t+1}; R_{p,t+1})}{\text{Cov}_t(r_{p,t+1}; R_{p,t+1})}\right] E_t\{r_{p,t+1}\}, \quad \text{all } i, \tag{14}$$

where $r_{i,t+1}$ and $r_{p,t+1}$ are excess returns and where the scale factor $-(w_t'\underline{1})$ has been cancelled from both the numerator and denominator. If the reference asset for the excess returns is $R_{pz,t+1}$, a zero beta asset for $R_{p,t+1}$, then equation (13) follows directly from (14). Since equation (13) holds if and only if $R_{p,t+1}$ is a conditional minimum variance portfolio, we have shown equation (1) implies that if $R_{p,t+1}$ maximizes (squared) correlation with m_{t+1}, then $R_{p,t+1}$ is a minimum variance portfolio.

Empirical work often focusses on models with more than one risk factor and more than one beta for each asset. Two broad classes of asset pricing models with multiple sources of risk lead to expressions for expected returns with multiple beta coefficients. One is based on arbitrage arguments, such as the Arbitrage Pricing Theory (APT) and the other is based on investor optimization and equilibrium.[15] Both of these approaches lead to models with the following form:

$$E_t(R_{i,t+1}) = \lambda_{0t} + \sum_{j=1}^{K} b_{ijt}\lambda_{jt}, \quad \text{for all } i. \tag{15}$$

The $b_{i1t}, \ldots, b_{iKt}$ are the time t conditional betas of asset i relative to K risk factors. The λ_{jt}, $j = 1, \ldots, K$ are market-wide expected risk premiums, which represent increments to the expected return per unit of type-j beta. The premiums are market wide because they do not depend on the specific security i, but apply to all securities in the market. λ_{0t} is the expected *zero-beta rate*. This is the expected return of any security that is conditionally uncorrelated with each of the K sources of risk in the model (i.e., $b_{0jt} = 0$, $j = 1, \ldots, K$). If there is a risk-free asset, then λ_{0t} is the return of this asset.

[14] Note that when the covariance matrix of asset returns is nonsingular, m^*_{t+1} is the unique benchmark variable (i.e. satisfies (1)) which is also an asset return. A benchmark which satisfies (1) is not in general an asset return, nor is it unique, unless markets are complete. If markets are complete, m^*_{t+1} is perfectly correlated with m_{t+1} [Hansen & Richard, 1987].

[15] The multiple-beta equilibrium model was developed in continuous time by Merton [1973], Breeden [1979] and Cox, Ingersoll & Ross [1985]. The APT was developed by Ross [1976] and has been refined by Huberman [1982], Chamberlain & Rothschild [1983], Ingersoll [1984], Reisman [1992] and others. Long [1974], Sharpe [1977], Cragg & Malkiel [1982], Connor [1984], Dybvig [1983], Grinblatt & Titman [1983] and Shanken [1987] provide multibeta interpretations of equilibrium models in discrete time.

The conditional betas are the multiple regression coefficients of the assets on some *risk factors* $F_{j,t+1}$, $j = 1, .., K$, which may be described by a *factor model* regression:

$$R_{i,t+1} = a_{it} + \sum_{j=1}^{K} b_{ijt} F_{jt+1} + u_{it+1}, \quad \text{for all } i, \tag{16}$$

where $E_t(u_{i,t+1} F_{j,t+1}) = E_t(u_{i,t+1}) = 0$ for all i and j.

The APT assumes that the factors $F_{j,t+1}$ represent the important comovements in the asset returns. This would be the case, for example, if $\mathrm{Cov}_t(u_{i,t+1}; u_{j,t+1}) = 0$ for $i \neq j$. Then the factors would capture all of the covariance of asset returns. It is easy to see that the $u_{i,t+1}$ are diversifiable risks in large portfolios, in such a case.[16] Weaker conditions are sufficient, however, to derive equation (15). Chamberlain & Rothschild [1983] assume that the eigenvalues of the $N \times N$ conditional covariance matrix of the errors u_{it+1}, are bounded, while the eigenvalues of the $N \times N$ matrix of the betas bb' are exploding. A no-arbitrage argument is applied asymptotically as N, the number of assets, becomes infinite and equation (15) is obtained as an approximation. Empirical proxies for the risk factors can then be obtained using factor analysis or principal components methods [Roll & Ross, 1980; Connor & Korajczyk, 1986, 1988]. The APT approach is reviewed by Connor & Korajczyk [1995 (chapter 3 of this volume)].

An alternative development of (15) uses the canonical asset pricing expression (1), assuming that the factors capture economic risk in the sense that the error terms in (16) are uncorrelated with m_{t+1}: $E_t(u_{i,t+1}, m_{t+1}) = 0$. Consider equation (5), where $R_{0,t+1}$ is chosen to be a zero beta portfolio, conditionally uncorrelated with m_{t+1}. We see that equation (1) implies:

$$E_t(R_{i,t+1}) = \lambda_{0t} + \frac{\mathrm{Cov}_t(R_{i,t+1}; -m_{t+1})}{E_t(m_{t+1})}, \tag{17}$$

where λ_{0t} is the expected return on a zero beta portfolio to m_{t+1}. Substituting the factor model (16) into the right hand side of (17) and assuming that $\mathrm{Cov}_t(u_{i,t+1}; m_{t+1}) = 0$ implies:

$$E_t(R_{i,t+1}) = \lambda_{0t} + \sum_{j=1,\ldots K} b_{ijt} \left[\frac{\mathrm{Cov}_t\{F_{j,t+1}, -m_{t+1}\}}{E_t(m_{t+1})} \right], \tag{18}$$

which is the same as equation (15). The market-wide risk premium per unit of beta is $\lambda_{jt} = [\mathrm{Cov}_t\{F_{j,t+1}, -m_{t+1}\}/E_t(m_{t+1})]$. In the special case where the factor is a traded asset return, equation (17) implies that $\lambda_{jt} = E_t(F_{j,t+1}) - \lambda_{0t}$; the expected risk premium equals the factor portfolio's expected excess return.

Equation (18) provides economic intuition about the signs and magnitudes of expected risk premiums for particular factors. If a risk factor $F_{j,t+1}$ is negatively-correlated with an IMRS m_{t+1}, the model implies a positive risk premium. A

[16] Consider an equally-weighted portfolio of N assets. The variance attributable to the error terms is $\mathrm{Var}_t(\sum_i u_{i,t+1}/N) = s^2/N \to 0$, where s^2 is the average of the $\mathrm{Var}_t(u_{i,t+1})$ across the assets, i.

factor that is positively-related to marginal utility should have a negative risk premium. Expected risk premiums for a factor should change over time if the conditional covariances with the scaled marginal utility $[m_{t+1}/E_t(m_{t+1})]$ vary over time.

If the factors are not traded asset returns, then it is typically necessary to estimate the expected risk premiums λ_{jt}, which are the conditional expected excess returns on *factor-mimicking portfolios*. A factor-mimicking portfolio is defined as a portfolio whose return can be used in place of the factors, both in the factor model (16) and to identify the expected risk premiums in (15) or (18). A mimicking portfolio for a non-asset risk factor can be obtained as the fitted value of a (conditional) regression function of the factor on the vector of all asset returns. The portfolio of the assets determined by the fitted values is the mimicking portfolio.[17]

When mimicking portfolios are used equation (15) is equivalent to the statement that a combination of the portfolios is minimum variance and therefore satisfies equation (13) [Grinblatt & Titman, 1987; Huberman, Kandel & Stambaugh, 1987]. Therefore, tests of multiple beta asset pricing models like (15) are tests that combinations of particular portfolios are minimum variance portfolios.

The role of conditioning information[18]

Our discussion of beta pricing models has referred to the expected returns and betas, conditional on the information at time t. This follows the interpretation of the models by their original authors. However, empirical tests of beta pricing models have traditionally examined unconditional expected returns and betas, or have used instruments which are a subset of the information available at time t. Therefore, empirical work has examined whether particular portfolios are unconditionally minimum variance, or minimum variance conditional on a subset of the information. It is therefore of interest to examine the relation between conditional and unconditional minimum variance portfolios.

Recall that the variance of a random variable is the expected value of the square less the square of the expected value. A particular portfolio R_{p^*} is therefore of conditional minimum variance in a set of available portfolio returns (*CMV*) if it satisfies the definition:[19]

$$CMV \text{ iff } E_t(R_{p^*}^2) \leq E_t(R_p^2) \text{ for all } R_p \text{ with } E_t(R_p) = E_t(R_{p^*}). \tag{19}$$

Similarly, a portfolio is of unconditional minimum variance in the set of available portfolio returns (*UMV*) if it satisfies the definition:

[17] Breeden [1979, footnote 7] provides a proof of this result. Grinblatt & Titman [1987], Lehmann & Modest [1988], and Huberman, Kandel & Stambaugh [1987] provide further characterizations of mimicking portfolios.

[18] This discussion simplifies some of the results in Hansen & Richard [1987]. See that paper for more rigorous discussions.

[19] If R_{t+1} is the vector of underlying asset returns, the *set of available portfolio returns* is the set of all $R_{p,t+1} = w_t' R_{t+1}$, where w_t is in the conditioning information set at time t. It is assumed that all second moments, both conditional and unconditional, are finite.

$$UMV \text{ iff } E(R_{p^*}^2) \leq E(R_p^2) \text{ for all } R_p \text{ with } E(R_p) = E(R_{p^*}). \tag{20}$$

The relation between the two properties is one of inclusion. The set of conditionally minimum variance portfolios is (weakly) larger than the set of unconditionally minimum variance portfolios, for the same set of available portfolio returns.

Theorem. *If a portfolio is UMV, then it must be CMV, but if it is CMV that does not imply that it is UMV.*

Proof. To prove that $UMV \rightarrow CMV$ assume the contrary. Then there exists a *UMV* portfolio R_{p^*} that is not *CMV*; that is, it can be shown [e.g. Hansen and Richard, 1987, p. 597] there is some R_p with $E_t(R_p) = E_t(R_{p^*})$ and $E_t(R_{p^*}^2) - E_t(R_p^2) \equiv \pi_t > 0$. Taking the unconditional expected values implies $E(R_p) = E(R_{p^*})$ and $E(R_{p^*}^2) - E(R_p^2) = E(\pi_t) > 0$, which contradicts that R_{p^*} is *UMV*. To prove that *CMV* and *UMV* are not equivalent, it is only necessary to find a *CMV* portfolio that is not *UMV*. Consider an example in which at time t there is a risk-free asset with return RF_t. Let the risk-free rate be the conditioning information. Then a portfolio with weight of 1.0 in the risk-free asset and zero on all other assets is *CMV*. Consider a portfolio of the risky returns, R^* where $\text{Cov}(R^*; RF_t) = 0$ and $E(R^*) > E(RF_t)$. If a fixed-weight combination of R^* and RF is *UMV*, where w is the weight on R^* and $(1 - w)$ is the weight on RF, it implies that the following first order condition is satisfied: $w\{\text{Var}(R^*) + \text{Var}(RF)\} - \text{Var}(RF) = \lambda E(R^* - RF)$, for some $\lambda \geq 0$. If RF is *UMV*, the first order condition must hold at $w = 0$, which can only be true in the trivial cases where either $\text{Var}(RF) = 0$, or $E(RF)$ is the highest expected return available. We therefore have shown that RF is *CMV* but not *UMV*. □

Discussion. The arguments in the theorem go through if the expectations $E(. \mid Z)$ replace $E_t(.)$ or if the $E(. \mid Z)$ replace the $E(.)$. Therefore, the collection of minimum variance portfolios, conditional on the market information set [i.e., using the $E_t(.)$] includes the minimum variance portfolios conditional on Z, which in turn includes the unconditional minimum variance portfolios, for a given set of available portfolio returns.

The theorem has important implications for tests of conditional asset pricing models. In principle, we can reject the hypothesis that a portfolio is unconditional minimum variance or is minimum variance conditional on some observed instruments, but we cannot test if it is conditionally minimum variance given all available information, which is generally unobserved. If we interpret asset pricing models as statements about which portfolios are conditionally minimum variance given an unobserved market information set, then we have a problem testing the models. Even if we reject that a portfolio is *UMV*, we cannot infer it is not *CMV*. This is similar to the Roll [1977] critique of tests of the CAPM. Roll pointed out that since the market portfolio of the CAPM cannot be measured, the CAPM cannot be tested without making assumptions about the unobserved market return. The theorem says that even if we could measure the true market portfolio return, we cannot test the CAPM because the full information set is not observed, unless we make assumptions about the unobserved information set.

When tests are based on equation (1) for some specified m_{t+1}, then it is possible to test the model without observing the complete information set. If m_{t+1} is an observable function of the data and model parameters, then equation (1) implies that $E(m_{t+1}R_{t+1} \mid Z_t) = 1$, so tests may proceed using the observed instruments Z_t.

Equation (1) implies that certain portfolios are both *CMV* and *UMV*. We showed above that the maximum squared correlation portfolio to m_{t+1}, denoted by m^*_{t+1}, also satisfies equation (1) and is therefore *CMV*. By iterated expectations, $E(m^*_{t+1}R_{t+1}) = 1$, and it follows that m^*_{t+1} is also *UMV*. However, m^*_{t+1} is found from a conditional regression function of m_{t+1} onto the set of available portfolio returns, and thus depends on the conditioning information. Therefore, m^*_{t+1} is in general a function of an unobserved information set.

In some applications, there may be interest in portfolios that are *UMV* in a set of available portfolio returns which does not depend on the conditioning information. For example, an investor cannot form portfolios whose weights depend on information that he does not have. If a portfolio is *UMV* (or *CMV*) in a set of available returns, then it must be *UMV* (or *CMV*) in a subset of those returns. However, if a portfolio is *UMV* in a subset of returns, that does not imply that it is *UMV* (or *CMV*) in a larger set of available returns.

Empirical evidence

A beta pricing model has no empirical content until the factors are specified, since there will always be a minimum variance portfolio which satisfies (13). The minimum variance portfolio can serve as a single factor in (15). Therefore, the empirical content of the model is the discipline imposed in selecting the factors. There have been three main approaches to specifying empirical factors for multiple-beta asset pricing models. One approach is to use factor analytic or principal components methods. This approach is motivated by the APT, as described above. In a second approach the risk factors are chosen economic variables or portfolios [e.g., Chen, Roll & Ross, 1986; Cochrane, 1992; Fama & French, 1992, 1993]. A third approach, used primarily by investment practitioners to date, uses cross-sectional regressions of stock returns on firm attributes to estimate the factors. This approach is described in Section 3.7. The literature which empirically examines beta pricing models is vast. A comprehensive review would warrant its own chapter. Fama [1991] and Connor & Korajczyk [1995 (chapter 3 of this volume)] provide recent selective reviews.

2.5. *Production-based asset pricing*

In a basic economics course, students are exposed to the simple Fisher diagram, and learn that optimizing consumers equate their marginal rates of substitution for consumption at two dates, to market interest rates. The canonical asset pricing equation, when m_{t+1} is an IMRS, becomes an Euler equation which is the stochastic generalization of this principle. Basic investment theory states that firms should invest to equate their marginal rates of transformation to market interest rates. Profit maximizing firms in a stochastic model imply an Euler equation, which states that the expected marginal cost of investment should equal the expected marginal value of the future proceeds. These conditions link optimal production and investment to optimal consumption and asset returns. The analysis of optimal production decisions therefore has the potential to better explain the links between macroeconomic aggregates and security returns than does a narrow focus on the consumer's optimization problem.

A firm's Euler equation, like a consumers, can be used in two different ways. Taking the asset market returns as given, it becomes a theory of investment. This is analogous to using the consumer's Euler equation in modern 'permanent income' models of consumption. To interpret the firm's Euler equation as a production-based asset pricing model, the idea is to take the production side as given, using it to 'explain' asset returns. The problem is that the firm's Euler equation refers to the market value of its output, and a benchmark pricing variable is needed to calculate the market value. It is therefore difficult to separate the firm's Euler equation from the consumers'.

A central concept in production-based asset pricing models is the *investment return*, denoted by $R_{\mathrm{I},t+1}$. The investment return to capital is the rate at which a firm can transform time t consumption into time $t+1$ consumption, through marginal investment changes. To illustrate, suppose a firm hypothetically diverts one unit of its output at time t to increased capital investment, producing more output at time $t+1$, while leaving its capital stock and future output unchanged for dates $t+\tau$, $\tau > 1$. The marginal rate of transformation is the investment return. The investment return depends on the parameters of the production and cost functions faced by the firm. For example, consider a firm facing a profit function $\pi_t(K_t, .)$, assume that capital K_t depreciates exponentially at rate δ, and assume that the marginal cost of investing one unit of consumption in the capital stock is 1.0. Then the gross investment return to capital is: $R_{I,t+1} = (1-\delta)\partial\pi_{t+1}/\partial K_{t+1}$. Cochrane [1991a, b, 1992], Sharathchandra [1991] and Braun [1993] derive the investment return for production functions which allow adjustment costs for physical investment. (A similar analysis could also be conducted for investment in labor, or human capital.)

The nascent literature on production-based asset pricing has proceeded in one of two ways to obtain testable models. Braun [1993] examines Euler equations of the form: $E_t\{m_{t+1}R_{I,t+1}\} = 1$, for specified choices of the IMRS, m_{t+1}. This essentially asks whether physical investment returns are priced like financial asset returns. Cochrane [1991a] and Sharathchandra [1991] assume that consumers have log utility functions and that the aggregate investment return is the return on aggregate wealth. In this case, $m_{t+1} = R_{I,t+1}^{-1}$, and the Euler equations imply $E_t\{R_{I,t+1}^{-1}R_{i,t+1}\} = 1$, for all financial assets i. Cochrane [1992] assumes that m_{t+1} can be described using a factor model, similar to the discussion in Section 2.4, in which investment returns are the factors. Such production-based asset pricing models can be empirically tested just like the consumption-based models described above. So far, this literature has failed to produce a model of m_{t+1} that is preference free, and which can therefore be used as the basis of a true production-based asset pricing model.

Empirical evidence

Cochrane [1992] and Braun [1993] find that investment returns are highly correlated with the growth rates of the aggregate investment series used, for all of the adjustment cost and production functions they examine. Cochrane [1991a] finds that conditional expectations of future stock returns, estimated by regressing stock returns on lagged variables, behave similar to expected investment returns. He also finds that expected future GNP growth, conditioned on lagged investment returns, are similar to those conditioned on lagged stock market returns. Braun [1993] rejects the hypothesis that investment returns are priced through the Euler equation (1) when m_{t+1} is the inverse of the return on aggregate wealth, using a number of proxies for aggregate wealth. Sharathchandra [1991] rejects the same hypothesis for a simpler production function, in which the investment return is a fixed linear function of the output-to-capital ratio. However, Cochrane [1992] finds that investment returns are useful factors in a multiple beta asset pricing model, in the sense that they work about as well as the factors proposed by Chen, Roll & Ross [1986], and better than a simple consumption model.

3. Methodology and tests of asset pricing models

This section starts with the general and moves to more specific tests of asset pricing models. First, inequality restrictions that are implied by the canonical asset pricing expression (1) for any model of m_{t+1} are discussed and related to the traditional mean–variance analysis. The method of moments is then reviewed as a general way to test models based on equation (1). This general framework is then specialized to discuss various tests of asset pricing models.

3.1. Moment inequality restrictions

Hansen & Jagannathan [1991] showed how the canonical asset pricing equation (1) places restrictions on the mean and variance of m_{t+1}. These restrictions depend only on the sample of assets, and provide a diagnostic tool for comparing different models of m_{t+1}. For the purposes of this discussion the model of m_{t+1} includes the choice of any parameters on which it depends. This allows us to defer the estimation problem until later.

Equation (1) implies that for any excess return r_i, $E(mr_i) = 0$, where the time subscripts are suppressed. It is convenient to assume that the returns are in excess of a hypothetical unconditionally risk-free rate RF, in which case the mean of r_i is shifted relative to the raw return but the variance is not affected by measuring excess returns. The existence of such an asset is a strong assumption, and is not required for the Hansen–Jagannathan analysis. We use it only to simplify the present discussion. Since $E(mRF) = 1$, then choosing a value for RF amounts to choosing an unconditional mean for a prospective canonical pricing variable, $E(m)$. For different hypothetical values of RF, we can trace out the possible variances of m that are consistent with a set of asset returns.

The expectation of a product is the product of the expectations plus the covariance. Therefore, $E(m)E(r_i) = \text{cov}(-m, r_i) = \rho(-m, r_i)\sigma(m)\sigma(r_i)$, and (as the correlation is less than or equal to 1.0),

$$\frac{\sigma(m)}{E(m)} \geq \frac{E(r_i)}{\sigma(r_i)}, \quad \text{for all } i, \tag{21}$$

which implies

$$\frac{\sigma(m)}{E(m)} \geq \operatorname*{Max}_i \left|\frac{E(r_i)}{\sigma(r_i)}\right| = \left|\frac{E(r^*)}{\sigma(r^*)}\right|. \tag{22}$$

Equation (22) defines a mean–standard deviation boundary which must restrict any canonical pricing variable, m_{t+1}. The bounds depend only on the sample of asset returns, through the right-hand side of (22). The right-hand side of equation (22) is recognized as the 'Sharpe ratio'. The Sharpe ratio is the slope of a line drawn from the risk-free rate RF, and tangent to the traditional minimum-variance boundary at the mean–variance efficient portfolio r^*. This is illustrated in Figure 1. Both the tangent portfolio r^* and the Sharpe ratio depend on the given value of RF. We therefore denote the Sharpe ratio as $S(RF)$ in Figure 1. As we vary RF we move the tangent point around the minimum variance boundary.[20]

The Hansen & Jagannathan [1991] region for $\{E(m), \sigma(m)\}$ is given by equation (22). The boundary of this region corresponds to the minimum value of $\sigma(m)$ for each value of $E(m)$. An example is illustrated in Figure 2. As we vary $E(m)$ in Figure 2 we move around the $\{E(m), \sigma(m)\}$ boundary.

There is a simple correspondence between the Hansen–Jagannathan boundary in Figure 2 and the traditional minimum variance boundary for the assets in Figure 1. Since $E(m) = RF^{-1}$, equation (22) implies: $\sigma(m) \geq RF^{-1}\{E(r^*)/\sigma(r^*)\} = RF^{-1}|S(RF)|$, where the absolute value is taken to allow for cases where $S(RF) < 0$.

Figure 2 was drawn using the moments from a given sample of asset returns and the above relation.[21] For each point on the boundary in Figure 1 there is a unique pair $\{RF, S(RF)\}$, and a corresponding point on the boundary of Figure 2, which is $\{|S(RF)|/RF, 1/RF\}$. The two figures therefore reflect exactly the same information. They depend only on the means variances, and covariances of the assets. The appeal of Figure 2 is that alternative models for m_{t+1} can be visually compared with the Hansen–Jagannathan bounds by superimposing estimates of

[20] Note that if RF exceeds the gross expected return on the global minimum variance portfolio, then r^* is on the lower half of the minimum variance boundary in Figure 1 and is not mean–variance efficient, although it is of minimum variance given its expected return.

[21] Monthly data on ten size-decile portfolios of common stocks for 1926–1989 was used.

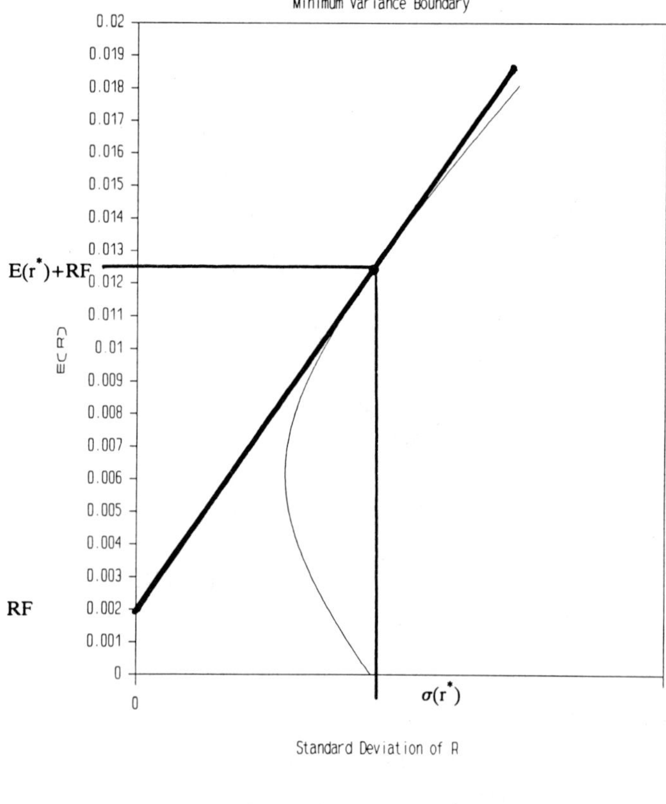

S(RF)=E(r*)/σ(r*)

Fig. 1.

their means and standard deviations on the graph, to see if they lie within the bounds.

It is useful to show how to compute the boundary of Figure 2 directly. Using equation (1), write $E(mR') = \underline{1}'$, where $\underline{1}'$ is a row vector of ones. A benchmark pricing variable can be formed as a linear combination of the assets: $m^*_{t+1} = [\underline{1}'\{E(R_{t+1}R'_{t+1})\}^{-1}]R_{t+1}$ so that $E(m^*R') = \underline{1}'$. The benchmark m^*_{t+1} satisfies $m_{t+1} = m^*_{t+1} + \epsilon_{t+1}$, where ϵ_{t+1} is a projection error uncorrelated with R_{t+1} and m^*_{t+1}. Therefore:

$$\begin{aligned} \operatorname{var}(m) &\geq \operatorname{var}(m^*) \\ &= \underline{1}'[E(RR')^{-1}]V(R)[E(RR')^{-1}]'\underline{1}, \end{aligned} \tag{23}$$

where $V(R)$ is the covariance matrix of returns. Using the definition of the covariance and the fact that $E(mR') = \underline{1}'$ we have:

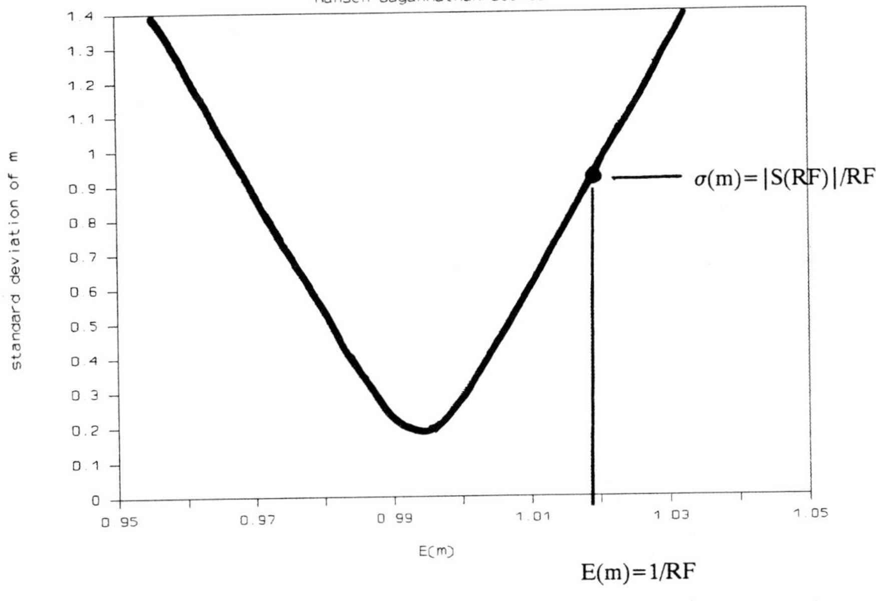

Fig. 2.

$$
\begin{aligned}
1' - E(m)E(R') &= \operatorname{cov}(m, R) \\
&= \operatorname{cov}(m^*, R) \\
&= \underline{1}'[E(RR')^{-1}]V(R)
\end{aligned}
\tag{24}
$$

Substituting from equation (24) into the right hand side of equation (23) implies:

$$
\begin{aligned}
\operatorname{var}(m) &\geq [\underline{1}' - E(m)E(R')][E(RR')^{-1}]\underline{1} \\
&= [\underline{1}' - E(m)E(R')]\{V(R)^{-1}\}[\underline{1}' - E(m)E(R')]'.
\end{aligned}
\tag{25}
$$

For a given sample of returns which determine $E(R)$ and $V(R)$, equation (25) provides a lower bound for the variance of m_{t+1} as a function of the mean of m_{t+1}. The square root of equation (25) determines the boundary of Figure 2.[22]

The bound in (25) is not the sharpest lower bound on $\sigma(m)$ that can be derived. Hansen & Jagannathan [1991] show how imposing that m_{t+1} is a strictly positive random variable can sharpen the bound. Computing the bounds imposing positivity requires a numerical search procedure. For their sample of assets, Hansen and Jagannathan find that the bounds imposing positivity are nearly coincident with the simpler bounds in the portion of the parabola where the standard deviation is low, and differ much from the simpler bounds when the standard deviation is relatively high. For a given value of $E(m)$ the bounds are

[22] Note that the existence of an unconditionally risk-free asset is not assumed in (25).

stricter when the Sharpe ratio is higher, as can be seen from (22). When the standard deviation of m is large relative to its mean, the probability of extreme values is high. In such cases imposing that m is positive has more impact.

The above analysis is based on the unconditional moments, which obviously is leaving out information. In principle, everything above could have been stated for conditional means and variances. Hansen & Jagannathan [1991] describe a clever way to extend the analysis to partially exploit the information in a set of instruments, Z_t. Equation (4) implies that for any set of instruments and for any fixed function $f(.)$, $E\{m_{t+1}r_{i,t+1}f(Z_t) \mid Z_t\} = 0$, and therefore $E\{m_{t+1}r_{i,t+1}f(Z_t)\} = 0$. If we view $\{r_{i,t+1}f(Z_t)\}$ as the returns to an augmented set of portfolio strategies where $f(.)$ is the trading rule, the above analysis goes through essentially unchanged.[23] Cochrane [1992] studies such scaled returns and also takes an alternative view. Cochrane uses the original returns, but views $m_{t+1}f(Z_t)$ as a new benchmark variable.

Multiplying the excess returns or the factors by given functions of Z_t only partially exploits the information in Z_t if unconditional moments are used. If we study the implications of $E\{m_{t+1}r_{i,t+1}f(Z_t)\} = 0$, then the additional information in the conditional expectations implied by $E\{m_{t+1}r_{i,t+1}f(Z_t) \mid Z_t\} = 0$ is not used. Gallant, Hansen & Tauchen [1990] take the Hansen–Jagannathan analysis one step further by estimating these conditional expectations.

The time-nonseparable models discussed in Section 2.2 complicate the Hansen–Jagannathan analysis. The Euler equations in such models imply that the IMRS in the canonical asset pricing equation can be written in the form $m_{t+1} = m_{1,t+1}/E_t(m_{2,t+1})$, where m_1 and m_2 are functions of current and future consumption and the model parameters [see equations (3) and (10)]. When it is desired to exploit the information in the conditional moments the models are more complex than the time-separable models, because the conditional expectation in the denominator must be estimated. However, Ferson & Harvey [1992] show that these complications are avoided if only unconditional moments are used. They show that one can simply divide $m_{1,t+1}$ by the sample mean of $m_{2,t+1}$ and proceed with the analysis as before.

The Hansen–Jagannathan analysis only restricts the mean and variance of m_{t+1} and therefore does not exhaust the implications of equation (1) for a given model of m_{t+1}, even if conditional moments are used. Snow [1991] extends the analysis to study bounds on the δth moment of m_{t+1} for δ's other than 2. For a given δ let $1/\delta + 1/q = 1$. Then, by Holder's inequality:

$$1 = E(mR) \leq E(m^{\delta})^{1/\delta}E(R^{q})^{1/q}. \tag{26}$$

The analysis of Hansen and Jagannathan is a special case, where $\delta = q = 2$. Snow notes that for δ's close to 1.0, q is large and his bounds depend on higher moments of asset returns. Among other things, such bounds will be more sensitive to outliers. We showed above how the bounds of Hansen and Jagannathan are

[23] The trading rule is to hold, at time t, $f(Z_t)$ units of the asset whose return is $R_{i,t+1}$ long and $f(Z_t)$ units of the zero-th asset short.

related to minimum variance portfolios. Snow shows that his bounds are related to portfolios which minimize $E(R^q)$ for a given mean return.

If m_{t+1} satisfies (1), then $m_{t+1} + \epsilon$ does too, for any random variable ϵ with $E_t\{\epsilon R_{t+1}\} = 0$. Hence, it may be possible to 'find' candidate IMRS's which satisfy the Hansen–Jagannathan bounds by virtue of being 'noisy'. Cochrane & Hansen [1992] therefore extend the analysis to consider the correlation of m_{t+1} with asset returns and the variation in the conditional mean of m_{t+1}.

Additional extensions of the Hansen–Jagannathan bounds have been developed and more are likely to follow. For example, Luttmer [1993], He & Modest [1992] and Cochrane & Hansen [1992] incorporate transaction costs. Cochrane & Hansen [1992] extend the analysis to study the cross moments of asset returns. Hansen & Jagannathan [1994] analyze pricing errors for assets and provide measures for specification errors, when a particular candidate for m_{t+1} is examined. A number of studies have recently addressed the problem of accounting for sampling error, to see if a candidate model for m_{t+1} is significantly far away from the Hansen–Jagannathan region, and to test related hypotheses.[24] This work moves the approach closer to a formal testing procedure.

The moment inequality restrictions of Hansen & Jagannathan [1991], Snow [1991], and their extensions do not exhaust the implications of equation (1) for a model of m_{t+1}. Satisfying the bounds is a necessary condition for equation (1) to hold; however, even if a candidate for m_{t+1} satisfies the bounds it may fail to explain asset returns. This motivates more explicit tests which use more information.

3.2. *The generalized method of moments approach*

Let x_{t+1} be a vector of observable variables. Given a model which specifies $m_{t+1} = m(\theta, x_{t+1})$, estimation of the parameters θ and tests of the model can proceed under weak assumptions, using the Generalized Method of Moments (GMM), as developed by Hansen [1982]. Define the model error term:

$$u_{i,t+1} = m(\theta, x_{t+1})R_{i,t+1} - 1. \tag{27}$$

Suppose that we have a sample of N assets and T time periods. Combine the error terms from (27) into a $T \times N$ matrix $\mathbf{u}$, with typical row u'_{t+1}. Equation (1) and the model for m_{t+1} imply that $E(u_{i,t+1} \mid Z_t) = 0$ for all i and t, and therefore $E(u_{t+1}Z_t) = 0$ for all t. The condition $E(u_{t+1}Z_t) = 0$ says that u_{t+1} is orthogonal to Z_t, and is therefore called an *orthogonality condition*. Define an $N \times L$ matrix of sample mean orthogonality conditions: $G = (\mathbf{u}'Z/T)$ and let $g = \text{vec}(G)$, where Z is a $T \times L$ matrix of observed instruments with typical row Z'_t, a subset of the available information at time t.[25] The vectorization of the

[24] See, for examples, Hansen & Jagannathan [1994], Burnside [1993], Cochrane & Hansen [1992], Cecchetti, Lam & Mark [1992], and Luttmer [1993].

[25] This section assumes that the same instruments are used for each of the asset equations. In general, each asset equation could use a different set of instruments, which complicates the notation.

matrix by the vec(.) operator means partition G into row vectors, each of length L: $(\underline{h}_1, \underline{h}_2, \ldots, \underline{h}_N)$. Then stack the h's into a vector, g, with length equal to the number of orthogonality conditions, NL. Hansen's [1982] GMM estimates of θ are obtained as follows. An algorithm searches for parameter values that make g close to zero by minimizing a quadratic form $g'Wg$.[26] Hansen [1982] shows that the estimators of θ that minimize $g'Wg$ are consistent and asymptotically normal, for any fixed W. If the $NL \times NL$ weighting matrix W is chosen to be the inverse of a consistent estimate of the covariance matrix of the orthogonality conditions, 9, the estimators are asymptotically efficient in the class of estimators that minimize $g'Wg$ for fixed W's. The asymptotic variance matrix of the GMM estimator of the parameter vector is given as:

$$\hat{\mathrm{C}}\mathrm{ov}\,(\theta) \approx \left[T\left(\frac{\partial g}{\partial \theta}\right)' W \left(\frac{\partial g}{\partial \theta}\right)\right]^{-1}. \tag{28}$$

where $\partial g/\partial \theta$ is an $NL \times \dim(\theta)$ matrix of derivatives. Hansen [1982] also shows that $Tg'Wg$ is asymptotically chi-square distributed, with degrees of freedom equal to the difference between the number of orthogonality conditions NL and the number of parameters, $\dim(\theta)$. T times the minimized quadratic form thus serves as a goodness-of-fit statistic for the model. Several choices for the weighting matrix W are available. A simple one is given by Hansen [1982] as $W = \hat{\mathrm{C}}\mathrm{ov}(g)^{-1}$, where:

$$\hat{\mathrm{C}}\mathrm{ov}\,(g) = \left[\left(\frac{1}{T}\right)\sum_t (u_{t+1}u'_{t+1}) \otimes (Z_t Z'_t)\right], \tag{29}$$

and $\otimes$ denotes the Kronecker product.

Equation (29) assumes that the error terms u_t are serially uncorrelated. However, in some cases the error terms may be serially correlated. Such cases arise when asset returns are measured more frequently than the length of the holding period and the data are overlapping. For example monthly observations of annual returns would induce autocorrelation of the first eleven lags, and the covariance matrix should be adjusted for this autocorrelation. Richardson & Smith [1991] go one step further, using the GMM to estimate the autocorrelations, assuming homoskedasticity to simplify the problem. Hodrick [1991] provides further analysis of serial correlation and multiple horizon returns. Serial correlation can also arise from time nonseparability in the model for m_{t+1}. For example, in a time-separable consumption-based asset pricing model using (10), u_t is a function of the variables R_t, C_{t-1}, and C_t, which are known at time t. Since u_t is in the consumer's information set at time t, the Euler equations imply that $E[u_{t+j} \mid u_t] = 0$, $j > 0$, and $E[u_{t+j}u_t] = 0$ for any j not equal to zero. The error terms are not serially correlated. The covariance matrix in equation (29) is a consistent estimate of

[26] The appendix, Section 5 of this chapter, provides a sample program for the GMM written in the matrix programming language Gauss™. This program may be easily modified for specific problems and translated into other programming languages.

$\mathrm{Cov}(g)$ in this case. However, in the time-nonseparable model of equations (12) and (13), u_t is a function of C_{t+1} as well as R_t, C_{t-1}, and C_t. Since u_t is not known at time t, the Euler equation does not imply that $E[u_{t+1} \mid u_t] = 0$, but it does imply that $E[u_{t+j} \mid u_t] = 0$, $j > 1$. In this model, u_t follows a first order moving average process and the covariance matrix should be adjusted to account for the moving average terms. A consistent estimator for $\mathrm{Cov}(g)$ when there are τ moving average terms is given by Newey & West [1987a] as:

$$\hat{\mathrm{Cov}}(g) = \left[\left(\frac{1}{T}\right)\sum_{t}\sum_{j=-\tau,\ldots,\tau}\left\{1 - \frac{|j|}{\tau+1}\right\}(u_{t+1}u'_{t-j+1}) \otimes (Z_t Z'_{t-j})\right], \tag{30}$$

Hansen [1982] discusses the case where the weights $\{1 - |j|/(\tau + 1)\}$ are set equal to 1.0, $j = -\tau, \ldots, \tau$.

Hansen & Singleton [1982] suggest subtracting the sample means from the elements of g in computing the weighting matrix. While the asymptotic distribution of estimators and test statistics are unaffected, they suggested that this procedure may result in more power against some alternative hypotheses. The idea is that under the alternative hypothesis the mean of g is not zero, so the second moment matrix of the sample orthogonality conditions, as used above, will be larger than the sample covariance matrix of the orthogonality conditions. A smaller estimate of the covariance matrix of g leads to a larger value of the test statistic, and therefore to more power, given the alternative.

An important issue in using the GMM to estimate and test asset pricing models is the selection of the instruments, Z_t. The instruments affect the efficiency of the estimators and the power of the tests. Hansen [1985] and Tauchen [1986] describe a lower bound for the asymptotic variance of GMM estimators, and suggest that the choice of instruments should attempt to get close to the bound. Unfortunately, the lower bound depends both on the information set on which the expectations in the model are conditioned, which is not observed, and on the true values of the model parameters. Hansen & Singelton [1988] study optimal instrument selection in linear models where the information set is known. Section 3.4 reviews the choices of instruments that have been made in the empirical literature.

There are two standard tests based on the GMM that are often used in the literature testing asset pricing models. The first is a generalization of the Wald test, the second is analogous to a likelihood ratio test statistic. Additional model specification tests based on the GMM are reviewed by Newey [1985] and Newey & West [1987b].. For the Wald test, consider the hypothesis to be tested expressed as the M-vector valued function $H(\theta) = 0$, where $M < \dim(\theta)$. The GMM estimates of θ are asymptotically normal with mean θ and variance matrix $\hat{\mathrm{Cov}}(\theta)$. Given standard regularity conditions, it follows by Taylor series expansion that the estimates $\hat{H}$ are asymptotically normal with mean zero and variance matrix $\hat{H}_\theta \hat{\mathrm{Cov}}(\theta)\hat{H}'_\theta$, where subscripts denote partial derivatives, and that the quadratic form $T\hat{H}'[\hat{H}_\theta \hat{\mathrm{Cov}}(\theta)\hat{H}'_\theta]^{-1}\hat{H}$ is asymptotically chi-square distributed [e.g. Newey & West, 1987b].

A likelihood ratio type test is described by Newey & West [1987b], Eichenbaum, Hansen & Singleton [1988, appendix C] and Gallant [1987]. Assume that the null hypothesis implies the orthogonality conditions $E(g^*) = 0$ hold while under the alternative a subset $E(g) = 0$ hold. For example, $g^* = (g, v)$, where $E(v) \neq 0$ under the alternative and v is of length M. Estimating the model under the null hypothesis the quadratic form $g^{*\prime}W^*g^*$ is minimized. Let W_{11}^* be the inverse of the upper left block of W^{*-1}. Holding this matrix fixed the model is estimated under the alternative by minimizing $g'W_{11}^*g$. The difference of the two quadratic forms $T[g^{*\prime}W^*g^* - g'W_{11}^*g]$ is asymptotically chi-square with degrees of freedom equal to M if the null hypothesis is true. Newey and West call this the D test.

Finite sample properties

Hansen & Singleton [1982], in their widely-cited implementation of the GMM, describe a two-step approach. In the first step, the identity matrix is substituted for W to obtain initial estimates of the parameters. These parameters are then used to form an estimate of W. The estimate of W is used in the quadratic form, $g'Wg$, to obtain second-stage estimates of the parameters. The second stage parameters are used to form a second stage estimate of the weighting matrix and the quadratic form. Call this a '2-stage GMM' approach. However, simulation studies have found that in practice it may be desirable to iterate, repeatedly updating the weighting matrix until the procedure converges according to some prespecified criterion. Such an *'iterated GMM'* approach is found to have better finite sample properties [Ferson & Foerster, 1994].

Simulation studies find that the asymptotic standard errors given by equation (28) are likely to be understated in small samples [Kocherlakota, 1990; Flesaker, 1993; Richardson & Smith, 1991; Ferson & Foerster, 1994; Smith, 1994]. In practice, it may be desirable to adjust the standard errors in small samples. One example is analogous to the usual adjustment of the maximum likelihood estimate of a covariance matrix [e.g., Hinkley, 1977]. Multiply the asymptotic variance by the adjustment factor $[T/(T-P)]$, where P is the number of model parameters. Ferson & Foerster [1994] evaluate the traditional adjustment and an alternative adjustment given by $[(N+L)T/((N+L)T-Q)]$, where N is the number of assets and Q is the number of model parameters plus the number of unique elements in the GMM weighting matrix: $Q = P + ((NL)^2 + NL)/2$. They find that the alternative adjustment performs the better in the context of the latent variables models discussed in Section 3.5.

Smith [1994] and Koh [1992] examine the size and power of the likelihood ratio type test and of the Wald test described above, in the context of a model with Epstein–Zin preferences as in equation (12). They find that the D test is well specified in samples as small as 90 observations.

3.3. Examples: tests of beta pricing models

Any test of a beta pricing model is equivalent to a test that some portfolio or combination of portfolios is a minimum variance portfolio. Early tests of the CAPM focussed on the unconditional mean–variance efficiency of empirical proxies for the market portfolio $R_{m,t+1}$. They therefore focused on equation (8), stated for the unconditional mean returns and market betas. Early tests relied on the two-pass, cross-sectional regression methods which are the subject of Section 3.7. Gibbons [1982] and Stambaugh [1982] showed how to test the unconditional CAPM as a set of cross-equation restrictions on the multivariate regression model:

$$R_{i,t+1} = a_i + b_{im} R_{m,t+1} + u_{i,t+1}, \quad \text{all } i, t = 1, \ldots, T. \tag{31}$$

where b_{im} is the unconditional beta of asset i on the market portfolio proxy. The restrictions on the parameters of the *market model regression* (31) are $a_i = \lambda_0(1 - b_{im})$ for all i, where the parameter λ_0 is $E(R_{zm,t+1})$, the expected return of a zero beta portfolio to $R_{m,t+1}$. Gibbons [1982] and Stambaugh [1982] tested the model in a normal likelihood framework, using standard likelihood ratio and Lagrange multiplier test statistics. Their tests assumed that the error terms are independent and identically distributed. MacKinlay [1987], Gibbons, Ross & Shanken [1989], Shanken [1985, 1986], Roll [1985], Kandel [1984, 1986] and Kandel & Stambaugh [1989] provide further analysis and interpretation of test statistics for this case. See also Shanken [1992] for a recent synthesis.

Unconditional tests of the CAPM can be formulated in the GMM framework by defining:

$$u_{i,t+1} = R_{i,t+1} - \lambda_0(1 - b_{im}) - b_{im} R_{m,t+1}, \quad \text{all } i, t = 1, \ldots, T. \tag{32}$$

The model implies that $E(u'Z) = 0$, where the instrument matrix Z is a $T \times 2$ matrix consisting of a vector of ones and the elements of $R_{m,t+1}$. MacKinlay & Richardson [1991] study such tests using the GMM.

Gibbons [1982] and others showed how the multivariate regression tests are extended to examine multiple beta models [equation (15)], when the risk factors are specified mimicking portfolios $R_{j,t+1}$, $j = 1, \ldots, K$. The regression is:

$$R_{i,t+1} = a_i + \sum_{j=1,\ldots,K} b_{ij} R_{j,t+1} + u_{i,t+1}, \quad \text{all } i, t = 1, \ldots, T. \tag{33}$$

The intercept restriction implied by equation (15) is: $a_i = \lambda_0(1 - \sum_{j=1,\ldots,K} b_{ij})$. Huberman and Kandel [1987] show that this restriction on (33) is equivalent to *mean–variance intersection*, which means that the minimum variance boundaries of the sample of all of the asset returns and of the mimicking portfolios intersect at one point. That is, there is a combination of the mimicking portfolios which lies on the minimum variance boundary for all of the assets, including the portfolios.

By the principle of portfolio separation, two points on a minimum variance boundary can be combined to generate the entire boundary. The boundaries for a sample of assets and a subset of those assets (the mimicking portfolios) can lie one inside the other, intersect at one point, or intersect at more than one point. In the latter case the two boundaries are coincident, which Huberman & Kandel [1987] denote as *mean–variance spanning*. They show that the following restrictions on the regression system (33) are equivalent to mean–variance spanning: $a_i = 0$, $\sum_{j=1,\ldots,K} b_{ij} = 1$ for all i.

Huberman & Kandel [1987] conduct tests of unconditional mean–variance spanning and intersection, assuming that the error terms are independent and normally distributed over time, with a fixed covariance matrix. They study an exact F test and a likelihood ratio test statistic. Using equation (33) to define the error terms, Ferson, Foerster & Keim [1993] conduct GMM tests of both conditional and unconditional mean–variance spanning. These tests are more general than the tests of Huberman & Kandel [1987], as the GMM does not require normality or IID error terms.

Further intuition can be obtained by relating the tests of mean–variance spanning and intersection to the canonical asset pricing equation (1). We established in Section 2.4 that a portfolio $R_{p,t+1}$ is a minimum variance portfolio if it is proportional to a projection of a benchmark pricing variable m_{t+1} onto the vector of all asset returns R_{t+1}. Multiple beta pricing therefore says that such a portfolio is a combination of K mimicking portfolios for the risk factors. Therefore, the projection of m_{t+1} onto the vector of returns R_{t+1} can be expressed as a combination of the K mimicking portfolios. Let $\mathbf{R}$ be the $T \times N$ matrix of asset returns where a subset R_1 are hypothesized to be mimicking portfolios that can be used to price the remaining assets R_2. That is, the portfolio R_p can be formed as a combination of the returns in R_1. Partition the vector of expected returns as $E(R) = (\mu_1, \mu_2)$ and partition the covariance matrix $\mathrm{Cov}(\mathbf{R}) = \Sigma$ conformably. Hansen & Jagannathan [1991] consider a projection of a benchmark pricing variable m on the full set of asset returns:

$$m = E(m) + [R - E(R)]\beta + \epsilon \tag{34}$$

where $\beta = \Sigma^{-1}\mathrm{Cov}(R, m)$ is the regression coefficient. The fitted values are a benchmark pricing variable, as $m^* = E(m) + [R - E(R)]\beta$ satisfies $E(m^* R) = 1$. Cochrane [1992] and De Santis [1993] conduct tests of the hypothesis that a benchmark pricing variable can be formed using only R_1, in which case it should be possible to set $\beta_2 = 0$, were $\beta = (\beta_1, \beta_2)$.[27] One way to do conduct such a test is to multiply right hand side of equation (34) by R and subtract one to obtain an error term that should have mean zero. The parameters to be estimated are $E(m)$ and β. Tests of the zero restrictions on β can be conducted using either Wald-type tests or the difference in quadratic forms test, as described in Section 3.2.

When unconditional moments are used, the restrictions on β in the tests of Cochrane and De Santis are equivalent to the tests of Huberman & Kandel [1987]. To see this, use a standard expression for the inverse of a partitioned matrix:

$$\begin{aligned}\beta_2 = &-(\Sigma_{22} - \Sigma_{21}\Sigma_{11}^{-1}\Sigma_{12})^{-1}\Sigma_{21}\Sigma_{11}^{-1}(\underline{1} - \mu_1 E(m)) + \\ &+ (\Sigma_{22} - \Sigma_{21}\Sigma_{11}^{-1}\Sigma_{12})^{-1}(\underline{1} - \mu_2 E(m)),\end{aligned} \tag{35}$$

[27] Alternative formulations of the projection equation may be preferred for statistical efficiency. See De Santis [1993] for more discussion.

which is equal to zero if and only if:

$$\Sigma_{21}\Sigma_{11}^{-1}(\underline{1} - \mu_1 E(m)) = (\underline{1} - \mu_2 E(m)). \tag{36}$$

Mean–variance intersection says that there is only one value of $E(m) = \lambda_0^{-1}$ at which the two frontiers coincide. Substituting $E(m) = \lambda_0^{-1}$ in equation (36), it can be seen that the restriction is *exactly* the same as the one proposed by Huberman & Kandel [1987]. Mean variance spanning says that the two minimum variance boundaries are coincident, which means that equation (36) holds for all possible values of $E(m)$. Equation (36) holds for all values of $E(m)$ if and only if:

$$\Sigma_{21}\Sigma_{11}^{-1}\underline{1} = \underline{1} \quad \text{and} \quad \Sigma_{21}\Sigma_{11}^{-1}\mu_1 = \mu_2, \tag{37}$$

which are the restrictions for mean–variance spanning proposed by Huberman & Kandel [1987].

Harvey [1989] conducts simple GMM tests of the conditional CAPM, which allow for changing betas and expected risk premiums. Given a model for the conditional expected excess market return, say $E(r_{m,t+1} \mid Z_t\} = f_m(\delta_m, Z_t)$, then:

$$u_{m,t+1} = r_{m,t+1} - \gamma_1\{r_{m,t+1} - f_m(\delta_m, Z_t)\}^2$$

is an error term with $E(u_{m,t+1} \mid Z_t) = 0$. The parameter γ_1 is the conditional expected excess return to variance ratio for the market portfolio.[28] Note that if $E(r_{m,t+1} \mid Z_t)$ is linear in Z_t and if γ_1 is fixed, then the conditional covariance, which is the conditional expectation of {the term in brackets}, is implicitly assumed to be a linear function of Z_t.

If the market portfolio is conditionally mean–variance efficient given Z_t and γ_1 is a constant, it implies that $E(r_{i,t+1} \mid Z_t) = \gamma_1 \mathrm{Cov}(r_{i,t+1}; r_{m,t+1} \mid Z_t)$ for all assets i. The following error term should then be conditionally mean zero for each excess return:

$$u_{i,t+1} = r_{i,t+1} - \gamma_1\{r_{i,t+1}(r_{m,t+1} - f_m(\delta_m, Z_t))\}.$$

Harvey [1989] uses the GMM to estimate several conditional CAPM models. In one case, the expected excess return to variance ratio is the fixed parameter γ_1 and the expected excess market return is a linear function of the instruments. He rejects this model, concluding that the ratio of expected excess return to variance should be allowed to vary over time. A second formulation allows γ_1 to be time-varying, by adding the assumption that $E(r_{i,t+1} \mid Z_t) = \delta_i' Z_t$. Harvey considers the error term:

$$\epsilon_{i,t+1} = (u_{m,t+1})^2 \delta_i' Z_t - (u_{i,t+1} u_{m,t+1})\delta_m' Z_t, \; E(\epsilon_{i,t+1} \mid Z_t) = 0,$$

where the $u_{i,t+1}$ and $u_{m,t+1}$ are the innovations in the linear models for $E(r_{i,t+1} \mid Z_t)$ and $E(r_{m,t+1} \mid Z_t)$. Note that in this formulation the conditional beta of asset i is: $E(u_{i,t+1}u_{m,t+1} \mid Z_t)/E(u_{m,t+1}^2)$, which is implicitly assumed to be a ratio of linear functions of Z_t.

[28] In the model of Merton [1980], γ_1 is the coefficient of relative risk aversion, which is a constant parameter.

3.4. Instruments for time-varying expected returns

A number of predetermined instruments have been shown to be useful in forecasting the future returns and excess returns of stocks and bonds, measured over various holding periods. The predictive ability of these variables has been a major stimulus to the development of tests of conditional asset pricing models. Some of the more prominent predictor variables used as the Z_t are now briefly described. Hawawini & Keim [1995 (chapter 17 of this volume)] provide a more comprehensive review of the empirical evidence.

Many early empirical studies of 'market efficiency' focussed explicitly or implicitly on lagged returns as predictors of future returns. That is, they studied the autocorrelation structure of returns. Fama [1970] reviews this early literature. Fama & French [1988b] examine the autocorrelations in multiple horizon rates of return on stock portfolios and find weak evidence for negative autocorrelation in the multi-year returns. Negative autocorrelation suggests that returns have a tendency to revert to some long run mean value. Lo & MacKinlay [1988], Conrad, Gultekin & Kaul [1991] and others examine shorter horizon (e.g. weekly) returns and find evidence for positive autocorrelation. Such positive autocorrelation in returns could arise if expected returns are positively autocorrelated over time. However, the statistical significance of the evidence for nonzero autocorrelation in returns is controversial [Richardson & Smith, 1991; Richardson, 1990], and the economic significance is not clear either. Less controversial is the evidence that other lagged variables can predict stock and bond returns to some extent.

Short term interest rates are prominent instruments in a number of studies. Fama & Schwert [1977] and others show that future stock returns are negatively related to the levels of U.S. Treasury bill rates. Campbell [1987], Ferson [1989] and Schwert [1989] find that bill rates are related to the conditional second moments of asset returns. As bill rates may be closely related to expected inflation, Fama and Schwert interpreted their results as evidence that expected stock returns are negatively correlated with expected inflation. This stimulated an active literature on the relation of stock returns to inflation, aggregate output and money [e.g. Fama, 1981; Fama & Gibbons, 1982; Geske & Roll, 1983; Kaul, 1987; Marshall, 1991]. Short term interest rates are important instruments in tests of asset pricing models, as their relation to consumption, production and returns appears to challenge the predictions of the models in several dimensions.

Fama & French [1988b, 1989], Campbell & Shiller [1988], Poterba & Summers [1988] and others study the predictive ability of dividend yields and find that they are positively related to the future returns of long term bonds and stocks. The dividend yield is measured as the price level of a stock index divided into the previous year's dividend payments for the index. This removes the strong seasonality of dividend payments and results in a series with high autocorrelation. The Federal Reserve computes dividend yields for the Standard and Poors 500 stock index in this way.

Keim & Stambaugh [1986] document the ability of a related variable, inverse stock price levels, to predict future returns in both the bond and the stock markets.

It is found that when prices are relatively low, it is more likely that future returns will be high. The price level is detrended by the following simple procedure in a number of studies. The average level of a stock price index over the past twelve months is divided by level of the index at the end of the current month.

Measures of the slope of the term structure of interest rates are used to predict bond and stock returns in a number of studies. Campbell [1987] used short term interest rate spreads, while Fama & French [1989] and Fama [1990] used a longer maturity spread. An example used by Ferson & Korajczyk [1995] is the difference between the yields-to-maturity of corporate bonds in the composite bond index with more than 15 years to maturity, less the yield of bonds with 5 to 15 years to maturity.

A yield spread associated with borrower quality differences in the corporate bond market is used to predict returns by Keim & Stambaugh [1986], Fama & French [1989], Fama [1990] and others. An example is the yield to maturity of Baa rated bonds, less the yield of Aaa rated bonds. Such a yield spread is generally found to be positively related to future returns on stocks and long term bonds. Schwert [1989] finds that a spread is also related to stock market volatility.

A default-related yield spread can be understood by reference to first principles, using equation (2). Consider two pure discount bonds. The first bond A is default-free, and will pay off one unit at time $T > t$. The second bond B has default risk, so it will pay the random amount $(1-\epsilon)$, $0 < \epsilon < 1$ at time T. Let $n_{t,t+T} = \prod_{j=0,T} m_{t+j}$, then equation (2) implies that the continuously-compounded yields are:

$$y_{t,A} = -\left(\frac{1}{T}\right) \ln E_t(n_{t,t+T})$$

$$y_{t,B} = -\left(\frac{1}{T}\right) \ln E_t(n_{t,t+T}(1-\epsilon))$$

and the yield spread is

$$y_{t,B} - y_{t,A} = -\left(\frac{1}{T}\right) \ln\left[E_t(1-\epsilon) - \frac{\text{Cov}_t(\epsilon; n_{t,t+T})}{E_t(n_{t,t+T})}\right].$$

The yield spread depends on two terms. The first is the expected default loss on the risky bond and the second is a risk premium which depends on second moments. The yield spread should fluctuate over time as either of these expectations changes with economic conditions.

A short term spread between commercial paper and Treasury bill yields is studied by Bernanke [1990]. The spread is found to be negatively related to future economic output. Bernanke [1990] argues that fluctuations in the spread reflect fluctuations in monetary policy and bank lending costs which produce changes in the supply of commercial paper as a substitute for bank financing. Bernanke & Gertler [1989] argue that when more commercial paper is used relative to bank debt, then asymmetric information costs between borrowers and lenders are increased, which costs are a negative effect on real activity.

Keim [1983] studies the ability of a dummy variable for the month of January to predict the returns of common stock portfolios formed from firms with different market capitalizations. The well-known January effect in small stocks is the observation that the return of small stocks is likely to be larger in January than at other times.

Empirical work on the predictable variation in bond and stock returns and of the predictive ability of lagged instruments continues to build at a rapid pace. The relation of conditional asset pricing theories to the patterns of predictable variation will therefore be a question of continuing interest.

3.5. Latent variable models

Formulation

Although the consumption-based asset pricing literature has allowed for time-varying expected returns since the early 1980s [e.g. Hansen & Singleton, 1982], the first asset pricing tests which focussed directly on changing expected returns were the so-called *latent variable models*. These models were introduced to financial economists by Hansen & Hodrick [1983] and Gibbons & Ferson [1985]. The methodology is further refined and extended in Campbell [1987], Harvey [1989], Ferson [1990] and Ferson, Foerster & Keim [1993]. This review describes a simple example.

Consider a set of asset returns R_{it}, $i = 1, \dots, N$, regressed on a vector of predetermined variables, $\mathbf{Z}_{t-1}$. The projections $\delta_i' \mathbf{Z}_{t-1}$ are used to model the conditional expected returns. Latent variable models study cross-equation restrictions on the coefficients of the projections, δ_i. The tests detect reduced dimensionality across assets in the time-variation of expected returns. Such tests can be motivated from conditional beta pricing models when the models are specialized by assuming that the betas are fixed parameters over time. The unobserved mimicking portfolios' expected returns are treated as the latent variables.

For notational convenience, drop the time subscript in equation (15) and define the $T \times N$ matrix $\mathbf{r}$, with typical element $r_{it} = R_{it} - R_{0t}$, were R_{0t} is the return of an arbitrarily chosen zero-th asset and r_{it} is the excess return. Define the $T \times K$ matrix of expected risk premiums as $\lambda(Z)$, where Z is the $T \times L$ matrix of Z_{t-1}'s. Equation (15) implies the following expression for the expected excess returns:

$$E(\mathbf{r} \mid Z) = \lambda(Z)\beta, \tag{38}$$

where β is the $K \times N$ matrix of conditional betas for the excess returns ($\beta_{ij} = b_{ij} - b_{0j}$) and $E(r \mid Z)$ is the $T \times N$ matrix of the $E(\mathbf{r}_t \mid \mathbf{Z}_{t-1})$, $t = 1, \dots T$.

Partition the excess returns as $\mathbf{r}=(\mathbf{r}_1, \mathbf{r}_2)$, where $\mathbf{r}_1$ is a $T \times K$ matrix of reference assets and $\mathbf{r}_2$ is a $T \times (N - K)$ matrix of test assets. Partition the matrix of betas as $\beta = (\beta_1, \beta_2)$. The reference assets are chosen so that the $K \times K$ matrix β_1 is nonsingular. From the partitioned equation (38), solve for the risk premiums, $\lambda(Z)$, in terms of the expected excess returns of the reference assets, and substitute the resulting expression, $\lambda(Z) = E(r_1 \mid Z)\beta_1^{-1}$, to obtain the following restrictions:

$$E(r_2 \mid Z) = E(r_1 \mid Z)C, \tag{39}$$

where C is a $K \times (N - K)$ matrix equal to $\beta_1^{-1}\beta_2$.

Assume that the C coefficients in equation (39) are fixed parameters; i.e., the relative betas do not change over time, and that the conditional expected excess returns of the reference assets are linear regression functions of the instruments. These assumptions imply the restricted regression system:

$$\begin{aligned} \mathbf{r}_1 &= Z\delta_1 + u_1 \\ \mathbf{r}_2 &= Z\delta_1 C + u_2, \end{aligned} \tag{40}$$

where Z includes a constant term, δ_1 is an $L \times K$ matrix of regression coefficients and $E(u_1 \mid Z) = E(u_2 \mid Z) = 0$.

The system (40) says that if there are K common factors which describe expected excess returns over time, then the regression functions which predict the excess returns of K reference assets are sufficient to capture the predictable variation. The expected excess returns of the remaining $N - K$ assets can be formed as linear combinations of these K regression functions. Consider for example, a special case of model where $K = 1$ and the expected excess return for each asset is given by the product of a constant beta coefficient and a single market-wide, time-varying risk premium. In this case all of the regression coefficient vectors δ_i are proportional to a common vector δ_1, and C is a vector of the proportionality coefficients for the $N - 1$ test assets.

Latent variable models can be estimated and tested using a number of econometric techniques. A natural approach is to estimate equation (40) by the GMM as described in Section 3.2. It can be shown that the value of the GMM test statistic is invariant to which of the assets are chosen as the reference assets, r_1.[29]

Campbell [1987] and Campbell & Clarida [1987] emphasize that tests of the cross-equation restrictions may be viewed simply as data description. Given a sample of returns and instrumental variables, a researcher might wish to characterize the variation in expected returns that is captured by the sample. This might be done as a prelude to an examination of more structured asset pricing hypotheses, as in Ferson [1990].

[29] To see this, let $u = r - Z[\delta^{\sim}\delta C]$, where $^{\sim}$ indicates concatenation by column, and the initial choice of reference assets is the first K columns of the $T \times N$ matrix r. Let $g = \text{vec}(u'Z)$ and assume that $g'Wg$ is minimized at $[\delta^{\sim}\delta C]$, where W is the inverse of the covariance matrix of g. We show that there is a matrix of parameters $[\delta^* C^{*\sim}\delta^*]$, where $u^* \equiv r - Z[\delta^* C^{*\sim}\delta^*] = u$, and without loss of generality, the last K assets are chosen as the reference assets. This implies that the sample value of the test statistic is invariant to the choice of reference assets. A sufficient assumption is that each choice of reference assets has a conditional mean function with full column rank, so that $(\delta^{*\prime}\delta^*)$ and $(\delta'\delta)$ are nonsingular. The proof is by construction. Let $C = [C_1{}^{\sim}C_2]$, where C_1 is the first $N - 2K$ columns of C. The nonsingularity assumption implies that the $K \times K$ matrix C_2 is nonsingular. Let $C^* = [C_1^{*\sim}C_2^*]$, where C_1^* is $K \times K$, and choose $\delta^* = \delta C_2$, $C_1^* = (\delta^{*\prime}\delta^*) - 1(\delta^{*\prime}\delta)$, and $C_2^* = C_1^* C_1$. Substitution shows that $[\delta^* C^{*\sim}\delta^*]$ is equal to $[\delta^{\sim}\delta C]$.

When tests of the cross equation restrictions are interpreted as tests of asset pricing models, there is a joint hypothesis involved. The joint hypothesis may be characterized as consisting of two parts: a statement about asset pricing and 'statistical' assumptions. The asset pricing part of the hypothesis, as always, is a specification of benchmark portfolios. The statistical assumptions involve the properties of the means and second moments which are parameterized in the model.

Different combinations of asset pricing theories and statistical assumptions can imply the same latent variable model. One example which implies a single-premium model [$K = 1$ in equation (40)] is a conditional version of the CAPM with constant conditional betas. This is the example that Gibbons & Ferson [1985] use to motivate the latent variable tests. A second example hypothesizes that asset prices are consistent with investor optimization, so that conditional expected excess returns are proportional to the conditional covariances of assets with an investor's marginal utility, as in equation (5). If the conditional covariances with marginal utility are constant or move over time proportionally, a single latent variable model is implied. This example is studied by Ferson [1989]. A third example exploits Roll's [1977] observation that in any sample there will almost always be a (conditionally) minimum variance portfolio. If the expected return of any such portfolio is linearly related to the predetermined variables Z_{t-1}, and if ratios of the assets' excess return betas with respect to this portfolio are fixed parameters, then a single latent variable model is implied. This example is discussed by Wheatley [1989].

These examples illustrate that a given latent variable model is implied by a *class of hypotheses* about asset pricing, combined with statistical assumptions. If the model is rejected, then *every member* of this class is rejected. If we do not reject a latent variable model the cross-equation restrictions identify the coefficients C, that implicitly measure systematic risk. In a single factor model for example, an asset with a larger C coefficient has a larger beta on the single factor. Fama & French [1989] apply this logic informally to the corporate bond market and Chang & Huang [1990] test the corresponding latent variable model.

Empirical evidence

The original latent variable asset pricing studies of Hansen & Hodrick [1983] and Gibbons & Ferson [1985] did not reject models with a single risk premium for their samples of currency premiums and the Dow Jones 30 common stocks, respectively. Using extended samples, Hodrick & Srivastava [1984] and Ferson, Foerster & Keim [1993] show that single factor models can be rejected in these contexts. Other studies reject single latent variable models for a variety of samples of bonds, stocks and other assets.[30] Typically the tests indicate that the number of

[30] Chan [1988] and Foerster [1987] examined stock returns, while Stambaugh [1988] and Chang & Huang [1990] examined bond returns. Campbell [1987] and Ferson [1989, 1990] studied both stock and bond returns. Forward currency premiums are further examined by Cumby [1987, 1988], Campbell & Clarida [1987], Jorion & Giovannini [1987], Bekaert & Hodrick [1990], Cumby &

latent variables is small, usually no more than 2 or 3. This suggests that expected returns can be modelled using a small number of common factors. Alternatively, the tests could have low power. This would not be surprising, given that the fraction of the variance in asset returns that is explained by lagged instrumental variables is usually small. Latent variable models rely on this predictable variation for their power. For example, if assets' excess returns are independent and identically distributed over time then the only predetermined variable that would enter into a predictive regression would be a constant term. A single-premium latent variable model would trivially hold, and the approach would have no power. Wheatley [1989] argues that latent variable tests can have low power as tests of asset pricing models, as the statistical assumptions in the joint hypothesis are difficult to verify. Ferson & Foerster [1994,1995] provide simulation evidence on the power of latent variables tests which are implemented using the GMM.

3.6. Time-varying second moments

Motivation

If conditional asset pricing models are being examined, it can be argued virtually from first principles that the conditional second moments should be allowed to be time-varying. The following argument [adapted from Ferson, 1989] provides a general motivation for empirical modelling of time-varying second moments. Any benchmark pricing variable 'explains' expected returns, as in equation (5). Take the expected value of equation (1) given instruments Z_t which include the current Treasury bill rate RF_t, and interpret the returns as nominal returns. It follows that $E(m_{t+1} \mid Z_t) = RF_t^{-1}$ for any such Z_t. Equation (5) and rational expectations implies the following regression equation:

$$R_{i,t+1} - RF_t = C_{it}(RF_t) + u_{i,t+1}, \tag{41}$$

where $u_{i,t+1}$ is a forecast error with conditional mean zero given Z_t and $C_{it} = \mathrm{Cov}(-m_{t+1}; R_{i,t+1} \mid Z_t)$. If there is a benchmark variable m_{t+1} for which the conditional covariances are constant parameters over time ($C_{it} = C_i$), then, a time-series regression of excess returns on the riskless interest rate ($RF_t - 1$) and a constant, should have slopes and intercepts both equal to C_i.

Fama & Schwert [1977] regressed asset returns on the Treasury bill rate. They found large, negative slope coefficients and positive intercepts for common stocks, using 1953–1971 data. Ferson [1989] uses more recent data and other assets. These results imply that C_{it} cannot be a constant. Therefore, a model should allow the conditional covariances of returns with a benchmark pricing variable to change as the level of the interest rate changes.

Possibly, the conditional covariances vary with interest rates in a simple way so that conditional betas with respect to a minimum variance portfolio can be

Huizinga [1991] and others. International equities are examined by Campbell & Hamao [1992], Harvey [1991], Chang, Pinegar & Ravichandran [1991], Bekaert & Hodrick [1991], Cumby & Huizinga [1991] and others. Bessembinder & Chan [1991] examine commodity futures and common stocks.

modelled as fixed parameters. However from equation (13) this implies that a single latent variable model holds, an hypothesis that is rejected by a number of studies. Therefore, assets' conditional covariances and betas with a single benchmark pricing variable cannot be fixed parameters over time.[31] This provides a strong motivation for modelling the conditional covariances of asset returns in a way that allows them to vary over time as a function of changes in interest rates. Campbell [1987] and Schwert [1989] provide direct evidence that stock market volatility is related to the level of interest rates.

A general model

Various approaches for empirically modelling time-varying second moments have been used in the asset pricing literature. One approach is to assume that the conditional second moments have a specific functional relation to the lagged instruments. Another approach uses lagged values of the squares and products of the innovations in returns to model the time series of conditional second moments, in a manner analogous to ARIMA models [e.g. Box & Jenkins, 1980] for the levels of time series. The first approach can be illustrated using the GMM as follows. Assume that the conditional expectation $E(R_{t+1} \mid Z_t)$ is given by some function $f(\delta, Z_t)$, where δ is a vector of parameters. A linear regression function is an example: $f(\delta, Z_t) = \delta' Z_t$. The conditional covariance is by definition $\mathrm{Cov}(R_{i,t+1}; R_{j,t+1} \mid Z_t) = E\{(R_{i,t+1} - f_i(\delta_i, Z_t))(R_{j,t+1} - f_j(\delta_j, Z_t)) \mid Z_t\}$. Assuming a functional form for the conditional covariance, say $s_{ij}(\theta, Z_t)$, then the following moment conditions can be estimated using the GMM,

$$
\begin{aligned}
&R_{i,t+1} - f_i(\delta_i, Z_t) = u_{i,t+1} \\
&R_{j,t+1} - f_j(\delta_j, Z_t) = u_{j,t+1} \\
&(R_{i,t+1} - f_i(\delta_i, Z_t))(R_{j,t+1} - f_j(\delta_j, Z_t)) - s_{ij}(\theta, Z_t) = v_{t+1}
\end{aligned}
\tag{42}
$$

where $E\{(u_{i,t+1} u_{j,t+1} v_{t+1}) \mid Z_t\} = 0$. When system (42) is exactly identified and the functions $f(.)$ and $s_{ij}(.)$ are linear in Z with unique coefficients, then a two-step OLS technique of first regressing returns on the instruments and then regressing the products of the fitted residuals on the instruments produces consistent estimates of the coefficients. The GMM standard errors given in Section 3.2 are asymptotically correct (See Newey [1985] for further analysis). This approach can be easily modified to estimate other conditional moments. Tests of asset pricing models can be conducted by examining restrictions between the mean functions $f(.)$ and the second moment functions $s_{ij}(.)$.

ARCH-type models

A large and growing number of empirical studies in finance have applied Autoregressive Conditional Heteroskedasticity (ARCH, see Engle [1982], Generalized ARCH (or GARCH, see Bollerslev [1986]) and related models to the study of security returns. The ARCH-type models posit a simple functional relation

[31] This does not imply that a multiple beta model must have time-varying betas.

between the conditional second moments at time-t and the lagged innovations of the variable. GARCH extends the specification to include the lagged conditional second moments as well, in a manner analogous to ARIMA models. A number of variations on the ARCH-type models have been developed, each with its own clever acronym. Examples include EGARCH [Nelson, 1991], MARCH TARCH [Gourieroux and Monfort, 1992], and others. See Engle & Rothschild [1992] for an overview. Pagan & Schwert [1990] compare the performance of a few alternative models. Bollerslev, Chou & Kroner [1992] provide a more comprehensive review and finance applications.

A special class of ARCH-type models have been of particular interest in asset pricing. Asset pricing theories imply restrictions between the conditional first and second moments of returns. Such restrictions are a central feature of the ARCH-M model proposed by Engle, Lilien & Robbins [1987], and extended to include both lagged conditional variances and squared innovations (GARCH-M) in subsequent studies. The bulk of the empirical work on GARCH-M models of asset pricing has focussed on the conditional mean–variance efficiency of a standard stock market index (MVE).[32] There is also limited work on asset pricing with consumption and with multiple risk factors, using GARCH.[33]

A simple example of a GARCH-M model is the following:

$$\begin{aligned} r_{m,t+1} &= \gamma_0 + \gamma_1 \sigma^2_{m,t} + u_{m,t+1} \\ \sigma^2_{m,t+1} &= a_{0m} + a_{1m}\sigma^2_{m,t} + a_{2m}u^2_{m,t+1}, \end{aligned} \tag{43}$$

where $r_{m,t+1}$ is the *excess* return of a benchmark asset (e.g. a market portfolio). The symbol σ^2_{mt} represents the conditional variance of $r_{m,t+1}$ based on the information at time t. The error term $u_{m,t+1}$ represents the innovation to the market excess return, $r_{m,t+1} - E(r_{m,t+1} \mid Z_t)$. The information Z_t in this model consists of the lagged innovations of the returns. However, it is possible to include additional instruments, such as lagged interest rates, as additional regressors in the equations. The second equation of (43) states that the conditional variance of the return follows a GARCH(1,1) model. The nomenclature is analogous to an ARMA(p, q), where $p = 1$ indicates there is one lagged squared innovation in the model and $q = 1$ indicates there is one lagged conditional variance. The first equation of (43) embodies the mean restriction

$$E\{r_{m,t+1} \mid Z_t\} = \gamma_0 + \gamma_1 \sigma^2_{m,t}, \tag{44}$$

which states that the conditional mean excess return of the market is linearly related to the conditional variance. Such a restriction for a market index return

[32] Examples include Bodurtha & Mark [1991], Ng [1991], Mark [1988], Jorion & Giovannini [1987], Bollerslev, Engle & Wooldridge [1988], Engel & Rodrigues [1989], Attanasio & Edey [1987], and Giovannini & Jorion [1989].

[33] For work on consumption models with GARCH see Nanisetty [1991], Kandel & Stambaugh [1990], Attanasio [1991] and Lewis [1990]. For multiple factor asset pricing models using GARCH type models see Engle, Ng & Rothschild [1992], and Buse, Korkie & Turtle [1994].

is motivated by the model of Merton [1980], in which $\gamma_0 = 0$ and γ_1 equals the coefficient of relative risk aversion. This model is investigated empirically by French, Schwert & Stambaugh [1987] and Harvey [1989], among others. The nonzero intercept term γ_0 is included by French, Schwert and Stambaugh as an ad hoc alternative hypothesis.

3.7. Cross-sectional regression methods

Cross-sectional regressions of asset returns on the measured attributes of portfolios of common stocks have long been a staple of empirical financial economics. Early studies of the CAPM, for example, regressed portfolio returns on the portfolio's betas. The coefficients served as estimates of the market premium. Later, returns were regressed on several betas [e.g. Chen, Roll & Ross, 1986]. The multivariate regression model approach of Gibbons [1982], Stambaugh [1982] and others may be viewed as a system of cross-sectional regressions for each of the months, where the betas are constrained to be the same in each of the cross-sectional regressions, and the premium is constrained to equal the measured market return. Typically, the focus of such studies has been the relation of average returns to betas; that is, the unconditional moments are examined. Shanken [1992] provides a recent review and synthesis of these approaches.

Cross-sectional regression approaches have also been used to estimate and test conditional asset pricing models. This section begins by interpreting cross-sectional regressions of stock returns on the attributes of firms. The discussion draws from Fama [1976].[34] The ideas are first illustrated using a single attribute and then extended to a multiple-beta pricing context.

Consider a cross-sectional regression of a set of portfolio or asset returns $R_{i,t}$ on predetermined measures of the firm's attributes:

$$R_{it} = \gamma_{0t} + \gamma_{1t}(\mathrm{P/E})_{i,t-1} + u_{it}, \qquad i = 1, \ldots, N. \tag{45}$$

The attribute *price/earnings ratio*, denoted by (P/E) is used as an example. The attribute is assumed to be known at time $t-1$, while the returns are not realized until time t. Firms are indexed by i and the γ 's are regression coefficients. Regression (45) is therefore a predictive regression. It is an attempt to use differences in the (P/E)'s across firms at time $t-1$ to predict differences in their future returns.[35] The regression is assumed to be well-specified in the sense that $E_{t-1}(u_{it}) = 0$.

Suppose that regression (45) is estimated several times, once for each date t, resulting in a sequence of the coefficients γ_{1t}, $t = 1, \ldots, T$. In general, a regression coefficient estimate is a linear combination of the observations on the

[34] Especially pp. 323–337.

[35] In practice, the attributes are often 'studentized'; that is, the average of the (P/E)'s at time $t-1$ is subtracted from the $(\mathrm{P/E})_{i,t-1}$ for each firm i and the difference is divided by the cross-sectional standard deviation of the (P/E)'s at time $t-1$. See Rosenberg, Reid & Lanstein [1985], for example.

dependent variable.[36] In this case, the estimate of γ_{1t} is a linear combination of the R_{it}'s with weights $x_{i,t-1}$, and may be interpreted as a portfolio return:

$$\hat{\gamma}_{1t} = \sum x_{i,t-1} R_{it} = \left(\sum x_{i,t-1}\right) \gamma_{0t} + \\ + \gamma_{1t} \left(\sum x_{i,t-1} (\mathrm{P/E})_{i,t-1}\right) + \left(\sum x_{i,t-1} u_{it}\right), \quad (46)$$

One important attribute of a regression estimator for γ_{1t} is that it be unbiased. That is, the expected value of the estimator should be equal to γ_{1t}. From equation (46), an unbiased estimator for γ_{1t} must have:

$$\sum x_{i,t-1} = 0; \quad \text{i.e. the portfolio is a 'zero net investment' or 'arbitrage portfolio,' and} \\ \sum x_{i,t-1}(P/E)_{i,t-1} = 1; \quad \text{i.e., the portfolio's weighted average (P/E) ratio is 1.0.}^{37} \quad (47)$$

A second important attribute of a regression coefficient is efficiency. If the estimator is best linear unbiased, it has the smallest variance among all unbiased portfolio (i.e. linear) estimators. To find such an estimator one solves a portfolio optimization problem. The objective is:

$$\underset{\{x_{i,t-1}\}_i}{\text{minimize}} \ \mathrm{Var}\,(\hat{\gamma}_{1t}) = \mathrm{Var}\left(\sum x_{i,t-1} R_{it}\right) \quad (48)$$

subject to the constraints given by equations (47). Notice that minimizing variance subject to these constraints is equivalent to minimizing residual variance, $\mathrm{Var}(\sum x_{i,t-1} u_{it})$, subject to the same constraints.

Given the above facts about the cross-sectional regression estimates, they can now be interpreted in an asset pricing context. To illustrate, assume a conditional version of the Capital Asset Pricing Model (CAPM) as the theoretical model for expected returns:

$$E_{t-1}(R_{it}) = \lambda_{0,t-1} + \beta_{im,t-1} E_{t-1}(R_{mt} - \lambda_{0,t-1}), \quad (49)$$

where R_{mt} is the market portfolio return, $\beta_{im,t-1}$ is the conditional market beta and $\lambda_{0,t-1}$ is the expected 'zero beta' return. Take the expected value of regression (45), given information at time $t-1$ to obtain:

$$E_{t-1}(R_{it}) = E_{t-1}(\gamma_{0t}) + E_{t-1}(\gamma_{1t})(\mathrm{P/E})_{i,t-1}. \quad (50)$$

The theoretical model, equation (49) implies that the only thing that differs across assets i in the expression for expected returns is the beta, $\beta_{im,t-1}$. Therefore, if some attribute like $(\mathrm{P/E})_{i,t-1}$ enters with a nonzero coefficient in

[36] For example consider the OLS estimate of the slope b in the usual equation $y = a + bx + u$. The estimate of b is $\sum(x_i y_i)/\sum(x_i^2) = \sum\{x_i/(\sum x_i^2)\} y_i$, where the x_i's and y_i's are demeaned. The estimate of b is a linear combination of the y_i's. The weight for y_i is $\{x_i/(\sum x_i^2)\}$.

[37] With studentized (P/E)'s this implies that the portfolio's (P/E) is one standard deviation above the average of the (P/E)'s across all firms.

a regression like (45), the theory implies that it must be a proxy for the beta. Equating the right hand sides of (49) and (50) implies that there is a linear cross-sectional relation between the (P/E)'s and the betas, which we can write as:

$$\beta_{im,t-1} = a_t + b_t(\mathrm{P/E})_{i,t-1}, \tag{51}$$

where the values of a_t and b_t do not depend on the asset i. The coefficients a_t and b_t can be interpreted as follows:

$$\begin{aligned}
&\sum x_{i,t-1}(\mathrm{P/E})_{i,t-1} = 1 = \sum x_{i,t-1}\left\{\frac{\beta_{im,t-1} - a_t}{b_t}\right\}\\
&\Rightarrow b_t = \sum x_{i,t-1}(\beta_{im,t-1} - a_t)\\
&\quad = \sum x_{i,t-1}\beta_{im,t-1}, \quad \text{since } \left(\sum x_{i,t-1}\right) = 0.
\end{aligned}$$

This shows that the coefficient b_t is the conditional market beta of the portfolio $\hat{\gamma}_{1t}$.

Using a similar argument it is straightforward to interpret the intercept in the cross-sectional regression. $\hat{\gamma}_{0t}$ is a minimum variance portfolio with weights that sum to 1.0 and with weighted average studentized (P/E) ratio of zero. The conditional market beta of $\hat{\gamma}_{0t}$ is the a_t coefficient in equation (51). Equations (49) and (50) also imply that the conditional expected values of the cross-sectional coefficients γ_{0t} and γ_{1t} are related to the expected market premium and the zero-beta rate.[38] Such coefficients have been used by practitioners as 'factors' in applied factor models.

All of this extends easily to a multiple regression context. Assume that the beta pricing model of equation (15) describes expected returns, and that we are given a time series of the 'true' conditional betas, $\{\beta_{ijt}\}$, to use as attributes in the regressions.[39] The cross-sectional regression for month t is:

$$r_{it} = \gamma_{0t} + \sum_{j=1}^{K} \gamma_{jt}\beta_{ij,t-1} + \epsilon_{it}; \quad i = 1, \ldots, N, \tag{52}$$

where r_{it} is the return in excess of a Treasury bill. A slope coefficient in this regression, γ_{jt}, $j = 1, \ldots, K$ is a portfolio excess return, observed in month t,

[38] Let $\gamma = (E_t\{\gamma_{0t}\}, E_t\{\gamma_{1t}\})'$, $\lambda = (\lambda_{0,t}, E_t\{R_{m,t+1} - \lambda_{0t}\})'$, $B = (1, \beta_t)'$, and $P = (1, P/E_t)'$, where the betas and P/E ratios at time t are stacked up across the firms. The equations imply that $\lambda = \gamma PB(BB')^{-1}$.

[39] The most common approach for obtaining instruments for the betas, $\beta_{ij,t-1}$, is to regress the excess returns on the specified risk factors, using the time series for months $t-60$ to $t-1$. The slope coefficients in the time series regressions provide the estimates of betas. Fama & MacBeth [1973], Choi & Jen [1991] and Ferson & Harvey [1991] use these coefficients as instruments for the *conditional* betas given information available at month $t-1$. Braun, Nelson & Sunier [1991] provide evidence that such betas are similar to ARCH models of conditional betas. One advantage of such an approach is that the conditional betas are allowed to vary over time in a flexible way. A disadvantage is that measurement errors in the betas imply problems in the cross-sectional regressions.

whose conditional expected value at time $t-1$ is an estimate of the risk premium, λ_{jt-1}, for the risk factor j.[40] The risk factors are said to be 'priced' if the expected premiums differ from zero; that is, if expected returns differ across the assets, depending on their conditional betas with respect to the risk factors.

Ferson & Harvey [1991] note that the cross-sectional regression (52) provides a decomposition of each excess return for each month, which can be used to analyze the sources of predictability in returns. The first component, $\sum_{j=1}^{K} \gamma_{jt}\beta_{ij,t-1}$, is the part of the return of asset i that is related to the measures of risk, and which may be predictable to the extent that conditional betas and expected risk premiums move over time. The remaining component for month t, $\gamma_{0t} + \epsilon_{it}$, is the part of the asset return that is uncorrelated with the measures of risk, and which should not be predictable, according to the model. Equation (15) implies that γ_{0t} is zero and $E(\epsilon_{it} \mid Z_{t-1}) = 0$, assuming that the correct conditional betas of the excess returns are used in the regressions.

Cross-sectional regression approaches raise a number of econometric issues. Even if the 'true' conditional betas were known the cross-sectional regressions are complicated because security returns are correlated and heteroskedastic. Conclusions based on the usual standard errors for the cross-sectional regressions are known to be unreliable. Fama & MacBeth [1973] suggest using the time series of the coefficient estimates $\hat{\gamma}_{jt}$ to compute a standard error for the mean. This standard error is useful for testing the hypothesis that the unconditional expected risk premium is zero. Shanken [1992] provides an asymptotic correction factor for Fama & MacBeth's [1973] standard errors under the assumption that a time series of length $T \to \infty$ is used to estimate a fixed beta coefficient for each asset. In this case the true unconditional betas are known as the number of time-series observations is increased. Amsler & Schmidt [1985] provide evidence on the small-sample properties of cross-sectional regression estimators in an unconditional asset pricing context.

Measurement errors may be especially important in some cross-sectional regression applications. Even if the betas or firm attributes are themselves unbiased estimates, estimation error creates an errors-in-variables bias in the cross-sectional regressions. The errors-in-variables bias has been extensively analyzed in an unconditional asset pricing context and is reviewed in Shanken [1992]. Connor & Uhlaner [1989] show that an iterated version of the cross-sectional regression methodology can deliver consistent estimates of the risk premiums under assumptions similar to Shanken's [1992]. They assume that there is a factor structure in the returns with fixed loadings (betas), but they allow for time-varying risk premiums. Their approach iterates back and forth between a time series regression of the asset returns on the mimicking portfolio estimators and cross-sectional regressions of the returns on the resulting betas. The effects of measurement errors

[40] To see this note that the slope coefficient estimator has conditional beta on factor j equal to 1.0, conditional betas on the other factors equal to 0.0, and minimizes conditional variance subject to those restrictions. The portfolio therefore maximizes correlation with the risk factor j subject to the restrictions.

on cross-sectional regressions using conditional betas remains an open question, and little is known about the asymptotic properties of these approaches in a conditional asset pricing context.

4. Conclusions

This chapter has reviewed some of the main asset pricing theories in finance, attempting to tie the models together using a simple, unifying framework. The models are viewed as special cases of a canonical pricing equation. The canonical expression provides simple testable restrictions on the models. It can also be estimated and tested directly once the form of the pricing variable, implied by a particular model, is specified. The generalized method of moments provides a unifying econometric framework for discussing recent advances in formulating and testing asset pricing models. This chapter has placed special emphasis on models in which expected returns and measures of risk are conditioned on, and may vary with economic information. It is the author's view that understanding the role of conditioning information in asset pricing models represents one of the greatest challenges and opportunities for asset pricing research, both theoretical and empirical. I look forward to working with you toward this goal.

Acknowledgements

The author is grateful to Mark Chockalingam, John Cochrane, George Constantinides, Johhny Liew, Anthony Lynch, Giorgio De Santis, Mike Hendrickson, Ravi Jagannathan, Robert Korajczyk, Yasuhiku Tanigawa, Simon Wheatley and Chu Zhang for helpful comments. Part of this chapter was written while the author was at the University of Chicago, Graduate School of Business. Presentations at Arizona State, the Eastern Finance Association, the 1994 Osaka Finance Conference and the University of Oklahama were helpful. The author acknowledges financial support from the Pigott-PACCAR professorship at the University of Washington.

Appendix: Gauss™ code for the GMM

```
#lineson;

@ ****************************************************************************
        GMM.PRG
****************************************************************************  @
        output file=temp.out reset;
@ ****************************************************************************
    Load data below here. The matrix of returns should be called r.
    The matrix of instruments should be called z.
****************************************************************************  @
n=rows(r);
```

```
@ ******************************************************************************
     INITIALIZATION
****************************************************************************** @
"Do you want to view the detailed iteration output? (1=yes, 2=no)";
rview=con(1,1);
maxweigh=50;                       @ --- max number of stages --- @
" maximum number of stages is";; (maxweigh);

"enter 1 for Newey-West, 2 for Hansen matrix"; mtype=con(1,1);
"Using linesearch for optimal stepsize at each iteration (see optstp)";
"using numerical derivatives (see formgd)";

mterms=2;
"NUMBER OF MOVING AVERAGE TERMS IN WEIGHING MATRIX IS";; mterms;

noz=cols(z);                       @ number of instruments @
obj=1000.0;                        @ initial objective value @
tol=0.0001;                        @ convergence criterion @
neq=cols(r);                       @ number of assets @
north=neq*noz;                     @ number of orthogonality conditions @
g=zeros(north,1);
maxit=50;                          @ max no. iterations each stage @

K=;
coeff=zeros(K,1);                  @ initial cofficients here, K their number @

w=eye(north);                      @ initial weighting matrix @
stage=1;
begtime=hsec;
oldsbj=obj;
  if stage>=2; goto stage2; endif;
  if rview==1;" ***** Stage 1: forming initial g,w *****"; endif;
  goto iterate;
stage2: if rview==1; "***** Stage 2 Iterations *****"; endif;

MULSTAGE:
oldsbj=obj;

ITERATE:
delob=1.0;
dc=1.0;
if stage==1; noconv=1; c=coeff;


     gosub formg;
     gosub optw; stage=stage+1; goto stage2;
     endif;

if stage>=2; noconv=maxit; endif;

iter=1;
do until abs(dc) < tol or abs(delob) < tol or iter > noconv;
     oldobj=obj;
```

```
      clear stp,gd,obj,gdwgd,gdwg;
      c=coeff;
      gosub formg;
      gosub formgd;
      gdwgd=gd'w*gd;
      gosub formg;
      gdwg=gd'w*g;
      obj=g'w*g;
      direc=solpd(gdwg,gdwgd);
      gosub optstp;
      coeff=coeff-direc*stp;
      iter=iter+1;
      c=coeff;
      gosub formg;
      obj=g'w*g;
      delob=obj-oldobj;
      dc=g'w*gd*invpd(gd'w*gd)*gd'w*g;

   if rview==1;
      "end of iter=";; iter;; "stage=";;stage;;"obj=";; obj;
      format 10,6;
   endif;

endo;                                  @ iterations for this stage loop here @

clear w;
gosub optw;
vc=invpd(gdwgd);

stage=stage+1;
   stderr=sqrt(diag(vc));
   t=coeff./stderr;

if rview==1;
   format 3,2;
   "        *********************************";
   "        ** GMM Results, Stage ";; stage-1;; " **";
   "        *********************************";
   "  ";
   "Coe ff Value Std Err T-stat";
   j=1;
     do while j < =k;
        format 3,2; "coeff";; j;;
        format 14,6; (c[j,1]);; (stderr[j,1]);; (t[j,1]);
        j=j+1;
     endo;
   endif;
format;

obj=g'w*g;                             @ quad form with new weighing matrix @

   dfchi=north-k;
```

```
  if dfchi;
    probchi=cdfchic(obj,dfchi);

if rview==1;
    "Chi-square=";; obj;
    "right-tail p-value=";; probchi;
    "df=";;dfchi;
  endif;

  endif;

if stage <=2; goto mulstage; endif;
if stage > maxweigh; goto qstage; endif;
if abs(oldsbj-obj) <=tol; goto qstage; endif;
goto mulstage;

qstage:                          @ final output here @

  format 3,2;
  "      **************************************************";
  "      FINAL GMM Results at Stage ";; stage-1;; " ";
  "      **************************************************";
  "   ";
  "Coeff Value Std Err T-stat";
j=1;
  do while j <=k;
    format 3,2; "coeff";; j;;
    format 14,6; (c[j,1]);; (stderr[j,1]);; (t[j,1]);
    j=j+1;
  endo;

  dfchi=north-k;
  if dfchi;
    probchi=cdfchic(obj,dfchi);
    "Chi-square=";; obj;
    "right-tail p-value=";; probchi;
    "df=";;dfchi;
  endif;

endtime=hsec;
tottime=endtime-begtime;
format 10,2;
"Time to execute: ";; tottime/100;; " seconds";
end;

@ ---------------------------------------------------------------------- @
@   Subroutines                                                          @
@ ---------------------------------------------------------------------- @

@ ---------------------------------------------------------------------- @
@   This subroutine computes g, the vector of sample orthogonality conditions.  @
@ ---------------------------------------------------------------------- @
```

```
formg:

theta=c;                          @ current coefficient vector @

@ ***************************************************************************
     form mstar here as a function of the model parameters theta and the data
 ************************************************************************** @

mstar=;
u=mstar.* (r+1)-ones(rows(r),cols(r));
g=reshape( u'z,north,1);
return;

@ ------------------------------------------------------------------------- @
@    This subroutine computes gd, the north by k matrix of numerical derivatives @
@ ------------------------------------------------------------------------- @

formgd:
dh=1e-6;                          @set precision@
e=eye(k);
fn bv(c0,aa,i)=c0+aa*e[.,i]*dh;   @ c is the coefficient vector kx1 @
gd=zeros(north,k);
i=1; c0=c;
do until i > k;
  c=bv(c0,1,i); gosub formg; gplus=g;
  c=bv(c0,-1,i); gosub formg; gminus=g;
  gd[.,i]=(gplus-gminus)./(2*dh);
  i=i+1;
endo;
c=c0;
clear dh,e,c0;
return;

@ ------------------------------------------------------------------------- @
     This subroutine computes the optimal stepsize using a linesearch
@ ------------------------------------------------------------------------- @

optstp:
stp=.01;
coeff0=c;
     fcn0=obj;
     try=stp;
     c=coeff-try*direc;
     gosub formg;
     fcn1=g'w*g;
     if fcn1 >=fcn0; goto backs; endif;
     chang=fcn0-fcn1;
  do while chang >=0;
     fcn0=fcn1;
     stp=try;
     try=try*2.0;
     c=coeff-try*direc;
```

```
      gosub formg;
      fcn1=g'w*g;
      chang=fcn0-fcn1;
   endo;
   c=coeff0;
clear coeff0,fcn0,try,fcn1,chang;
   return;
   backs:
      iters=0;
      do while fcn1 > fcn0 and iters < 10;
         iters=iters +1;
         try=try*0.5;
         c=coeff-try*direc;
         gosub formg;
         fcn1=g'w*g;
      endo;
   if fcn1 >=fcn0; stp=0.0; else; stp=try; endif;
   c=coeff0;
   clear iters,try,fcn0,fcn1;
return;

@ -------------------------------------------------------------------------- @
@    Subroutine finds the weighting matrix                                  @
@ -------------------------------------------------------------------------- @

optw:
s=zeros(north,north);
j=0;
do while j < mterms +1;          @ form SJ for each mavg lag @
   SJ=zeros(north,north);
   i=j+1;
   do while i < n+1;
      dum1=u[i,.]'u[i-j,.];
      dum2=z[i,.]'z[i-j,.];
      SJ=SJ +dum1.*. dum2;
      i=i+1;
   endo;
   if j==0; s=SJ; endif;
   if j > 0 and mtype==2; s=s +( SJ +SJ' ); endif;
   if j > 0 and mtype==1; s=s +( sj +sj')*( 1- j/(mterms +1)); endif;
   j=j+1;
endo;
clear sj,dum1,dum2;
w=invpd(s);
return;
```

References

Abel, A.B. (1990). Asset prices under habit formation and catching up with the Joneses. *Am. Econ. Rev.* 80, 38–42.

Allen, E.R. (1991). Evaluating consumption-based models of asset pricing, unpublised Ph.D. dissertation, University of Chicago.

Affleck-Graves, J., and W. MacDonald (1990). Multivariate tests of asset pricing: the comparative power of alternative statistics. *J. Financ. Quant. Anal.* 25, 163–185.

Amsler, C., and P. Schmidt (1985). A monte carlo investigation of the accuracy of multivariate CAPM tests. *J. Financ. Econ.* 14, 359–375.

Attanasio, O.P. (1991). Risk, time-varying second moments and market efficiency. *Rev. Econ. Studies* 58, 479–494.

Attanasio, O.P. and M. Edey (1987). Time-varying volatility and Foreign Exchange Risks, manuscript, London School of Economics.

Bekaert, G., and R.J. Hodrick (1991). Characterizing predictable components in excess returns on equity and foreign exchange markets, working paper, Northwestern University.

Beja, A. (1971). The structure of the cost of capital under uncertainty. *Rev. Econ. Studies* 4, 359–369.

Bernanke, B. (1990). On the predictive power of interest rates and interest rate spreads, NBER working paper no. 3486.

Bernanke, B., and M. Gertler (1989). Agency costs, net worth and Business fluctuations. *Am. Econ. Rev.* 79, 14–31.

Bessembinder, H., and K. Chan (1991). Forecastability of futures returns, working paper, Arizona State University.

Bhattacharya, S. (1981). Notes on multiperiod valuation and the pricing of options. *J. Finance* 36, 163–180.

Boudoukh, J., M. Richardson and T. Smith (1992). Testing inequality restrictions implied from conditional asset pricing models, working paper, New York University.

Black, F. (1972). Capital market equilibrium with restricted borrowing. *J. Bus.* 45, 444–454.

Bodurtha, J.N., and N.C. Mark (1991). Testing the CAPM with time-varying risks and returns. *J. Finance* 46, 1485–1506.

Bollerslev, T. (1986). Generalized autoregressive conditional heteroskedasticity. *J. Econometr.* 31, 307–327.

Bollerslev, T., R. Chou and K.F. Kroner (1992). ARCH modelling in finance: a review of theory and empirical evidence. *J. Econometr.* 52, 5–60.

Bollerslev, T., R.F. Engle and J.M. Wooldridge (1988). A captial asset pricing model with time-varying covariances. *J. Polit. Econ.* 96, 116–131.

Box, G.E.P., and G.M. Jenkins (1980). *Time series analysis: Forecasting and control*, Holden-Day Inc., San Fransisco, CA.

Braun, P.A. (1993). Asset pricing and capital investment: theory and evidence, unpublished Ph.D. dissertation, University of Chicago.

Braun, P., G.M. Constantinides and W.E. Ferson (1993). Time Nonseparability in Aggregate Consumption: International Evidence. *Eur. Econ. Rev.* 37, 897–920.

Braun, P., D. Nelson and A. Sunier (1991). Good news, bad news, volatility and betas, working paper, University of Chicago.

Breeden, D. (1979). An intertemporal asset pricing model with stochastic consumption and investment opportunities. *J. Financ. Econ.* 7, 265–296.

Breeden, D.T., M.R. Gibbons and R.H. Litzenberger (1989). Empirical tests of the consumption-oriented CAPM. *J. Finance* 44, 231–62.

Burnside, A.C. (1993). Hansen–Jagannathan bounds as classical tests of asset pricing models, working paper, University of Pittsburgh.

Buse, A., R. Korkie and H. Turtle (1994). Tests of a conditional asset pricing model with time-varying moments and risk prices. *J. Financ. Quant. Anal.* 29, 15–29.

Campbell, J.Y. (1987). Stock returns and the term structure. *J. Financ. Econ.* 18, 373–399.

Campbell, J.Y. (1993). Intertemporal asset pricing without consumption data. *Am. Econ. Rev.* 83, 487–512.

Campbell, J.Y., and R.H. Clarida (1987). The term structure of Euromarket interest rates: An empirical investigation. *J. Monetary Econ.* 19, 25–44.

Campbell, J.Y., and Y. Hamao (1992). Predictable bond and stock returns in the United States and Japan: A study of long-term capital market integration. *J. Finance* 47, 43–70.

Campbell, J.Y., and J.P. Mei (1993). Where do betas come from? *Rev. Financ. Studies* 6, 567–592.

Campbell, J.Y., and R.J. Shiller (1987). Cointegration and tests of present value models. *J. Polit. Econ.* 95, 1062–1088.

Campbell, J.Y., and R.J. Shiller (1988). The dividend price ratio and expectations of future dividends and discount factors. *Rev. Financ. Studies* 1, 195–228.

Cecchetti. S.G., P.-S. Lam and N. Mark (1990). Mean reversion in equilibrium asset prices. *Am. Econ. Rev.* 80, 398–418.

Cecchetti, S.G., P.-S. Lam and N. Mark (1992). Testing volatility restrictions on intertemporal marginal rates of substitution implied by Euler equations of asset returns, working paper, Ohio State University.

Chamberlain, G. (1983). Funds, factors and diversification in arbitrage pricing models. *Econometrica* 51, 1305–1324.

Chamberlain, G., and A.S. Goldberger (1990). Latent variables in econometrics. *J. Econ. Perspect.* 4, 125–152.

Chamberlain, G., and M. Rothschild (1983). Arbitrage, factor structure and mean variance analysis on large asset markets. *Econometrica* 51, 1281–1304.

Chan, K.C. (1988). Autocorrelation of stock returns and market efficiency, working paper, Ohio State University.

Chan, L.K.C. (1994). Consumption, inflation, risk and real interest rates: An empirical analysis. *J. Business* 67, 69–96.

Chang, E.C., and R. Huang (1990). Time-varying return and risk in the corporate bond market. *J. Financ. Quant. Anal.* 25, 323–340.

Chang, E.C., J.M. Pinegar and R. Ravichandran (1990). Latent variable tests of the integration of European equity markets, working paper, University of Maryland.

Chan, K.C., N.-f. Chen and D. Hsieh (1985). An exploratory investigation of the firm size effect. *J. Financ. Econ.* 14, 451–472.

Chen, N.-f. (1991). Financial investment opportunities and the real economy. *J. Finance* 46, 529–554.

Chen, N.-f., R. Roll and S. Ross (1986). Economic forces and the stock market. *J. Bus.* 59, 383–403.

Choi, D., and F.C. Jen (1991). The relation between stock returns and short term interest rates. *Rev. Quant. Finance Account.* 1, 75–90.

Cochrane, J.H. (1991a). Production-based asset pricing and the link between stock returns and economic fluctuations. *J. Finance* 46, 207.234.

Cochrane, J.H. (1991b). Volatility tests and market efficiency: a review essay. *J. Monetary Econ.* 27, 463–485.

Cochrane, J.H. (1992). A cross-sectional test of a production based asset pricing model, working paper, University of Chicago.

Cochrane, J., and L. Hansen (1992). Asset pricing lessons for macroeconomics, in: O. Blanchard and S. Fisher (eds.), *The Macroeconomics Annual*, MIT Press, Cambridge.

Connor, G. (1984). A Unified beta pricing Theory. *J. Econ. Theory* 34, 13–31.

Connor G., and R.A. Korajczyk (1986). Performance measurement with the arbitrage pricing theory: A new framework for analysis. *J. Financ. Econ.* 15, 373–394.

Connor, G., and R. Korajczyck (1988). Risk and return in an equilibrium APT: Application of a new test methodology. *J. Financ. Econ.* 21, 255–290.

Connor, G., and R. Korajczyk (1995). Arbitrage pricing theory, in: R. Jarrow, V. Maksimovic and W.T. Ziemba (eds.), *Finance*, Handbooks in Operations Research and Management Science, Vol. 9., North-Holland, Amsterdam, pp. 87–144 (this volume).

Connor, G., and R. Uhlaner (1989). A synthesis of two approaches to factor estimation, working paper, University of California at Berkeley.

Conrad, J., M. Gultekin and G. Kaul (1991). Asymmetric predictability of conditional variances. *Rev. Financ. Studies* 4, 597–622.

Constantinides, G.M. (1982). Intertemporal Asset Pricing with heterogeneous consumers and without demand Aggregation. *J. Bus.* 55, 253–267.

Constantinides, G.M. (1990). Habit formation: a resolution of the equity premium puzzle. *J. Polit. Econ.* 98, 519–543.

Constantinides, G.M., and D. Duffie (1992). Asset pricing with heterogeneous consumers, working paper, University of Chicago and Stanford University.

Constantinides, G.M., and A.G. Malliaris (1992). Portfolio theory, in: R. Jarrow, V. Maksimovic and W.T. Ziemba (eds.). *Finance*, Handbooks in Operations Research and Management Science, Vol. 9., North-Holland, Amsterdam, pp. 1–30 (this volume).

Cox, J.C., J.E. Ingersoll, and S.A. Ross (1985). A theory of the term structure of interest rates. *Econometrica* 53, 385–408.

Cragg, J.G., and B.G. Malkiel (1982). *Expectations and the Structure of Share Prices*. University of Chicago Press, Chicago, IL.

Cumby. R.E. (1987). Consumption risk and international asset returns: Some empirical evidence, working paper, National Bureau of Economic Research, #2383

Cumby, R.E. (1988). Is it risk? Explaining deviations from uncovered interest parity. *J. Monetary Econ.* 22, 279–299.

Cumby, R.E. and J. Huizinga (1991). Investigating the correlation of unobserved expectations: Expected returns in equity and foreign exchange markets and other examples, working paper, New University.

Detemple, J.B., and F. Zapatero (1991). Asset prices in an exchange economy with habit formation. *Econometrica* 59, 1633–1657.

De Santis, G. (1993). Volatility bounds for stochastic discount factors: Tests and implications from international stock returns, working paper, University of Southern California.

Dunn, K.B., and K.J. Singleton (1986). Modelling the term structure of interest rates under non-separable utility and durability of goods. *J. Financ. Econ.* 17, 27–55.

Dybvig, P.H. (1983). An explicit bound on individual assets' deviations from APT pricing in a finite economy. *J. Financ. Econ.* 12, 483–496.

Efron, B. (1982). *The jackknife, the bootstrap, and other resampling plans*, Society for Industrial and Applied Mathematics, Philadelphia, PA.

Eichenbaum, M.S., L.P. Hansen, and K.J. Singleton (1988). A time series analysis of representative agent models of consumption and leisure choices under uncertainty. *Q. J. Econ.* 103, 51–78.

Engel, Ch., and A. Rodrigues (1989). Tests of international CAPM with time-varying covariances. *J. Appl. Econometr.* 4, 119–138.

Engle, R.F. (1982). Autoregressive conditional heteroskedasticity with estimates of the variance of United Kingdom Inflation. *Econometrica* 50, 975–986.

Engle, R.F., D. Lilien and R.P. Robins (1987). Estimating time-varying risk premia in the term structure: The ARCH-M model. *Econometrica* 55, 391–408.

Engle, R.F., V. Ng and M. Rothschild (1992). A multi-dynamic factor model for stock returns. *J. Econometr.* 52, 245–266.

Engle, R.F., and M. Rothschild (1992). Editors' introduction: statistical models for financial volatility. *J. Econometr.* 52, 1–4.

Ermini, L. (1991). Reinterpreting a temporally-aggregated consumption CAP model. *J. Bus. Econ. Stat.* 9, 325–328.

Epstein, L.G. (1990). Behavior under risk: Recent developments in theory and applications, working paper, University of Toronto, Department of Economics.

Epstein, L.G., and S.E. Zin (1991). Substitution, risk aversion and the temporal behavior of asset returns. *J. Polit. Econ.* 99, 263–286.

Epstein, L.G., and S.E. Zin (1989). Substitution, risk aversion and the temporal behavior of asset returns: A theoretical approach. *Econometrica* 57, 937–970.

Evans, M.D.D. (1992). Expected returns, time-varying risk and risk premia, working paper, New York University.

Evans, M., and P. Wachtel (1992). Interpreting the Movements in short term interest rates, working paper, New York University.

Fama, E.F. (1970). Efficient capital markets: A review of theory and empirical work, *J. Finance* 25, 383–417.

Fama, E.F. (1976). *Foundations of Finance*, Basic Books, New York, NY.

Fama, E.F. (1981). Stock returns, real activity, inflation and money. *Am. Econ. Rev.* 71, 545–565.

Fama, E.F. (1990). Stock returns, expected returns and real activity. *J. Finance* 45, 1089–1108.

Fama, E.F. (1991). Efficient capital markets II. *J. Finance* 46, 1575–1617.

Fama, E., and K. French (1988a). Permanent and temporary components of stock prices. *J. Polit. Econ.* 96, 246–73.

Fama, E.F., and K.R. French (1988b). Dividend yields and expected stock returns. *J. Financ. Econ.* 22, 3–25.

Fama, E.F., and K.R. French (1989). Business conditions and expected stock returns. *J. Financ. Econ.* 25, 23–50.

Fama, E.F. and K.R. French (1992). The cross-section of expected stock return. *J. Finance* 47, 427–466.

Fama, E.F. and K.R. French (1993). Common risk factors in the returns on stocks and bonds. *J. Financ. Econ.* 23, 3–56.

Fama, E.F., and M.R. Gibbons (1982). Inflation, real returns and capital investment. *J. Monetary Econ.* 9, 297–323.

Fama, E.F., and J.D. MacBeth (1973). Risk, return and equilibrium: Empirical tests. *J. Polit. Econ.* 81, 607–36.

Fama, E.F., and G.W. Schwert (1977). Asset returns and inflation. *J. Financ. Econ.* 5, 115–146.

Ferson, W.E. (1983). Expectations of real interest rates and aggregate consumption: Empirical tests. *J. Financ. Quant.Anal.* 18, 477–497.

Ferson, W.E. (1989). Changes in expected security returns, risk, and the level of interest rates. *J. Finance* 44, 1191–1217.

Ferson, W.E. (1990). Are the latent variables in time-varying expected returns compensation for consumption risk? *J. Finance* 45, 397–430.

Ferson, W.E., and G.M. Constantinides (1991). Habit persistence and durability in aggregate consumption: empirical tests. *J. Financ. Econ.* 29, 199–240.

Ferson, W.E., and S.R. Foerster (1994). Small sample properties of the Generalized method of moments in tests of conditional asset pricing models. *J. Financ. Econ.* 36, 29–36.

Ferson, W.E and S.R. Foerster (1995). Further results on the small-sample properties of the Generalized Method of Moments: Tests of Latent Variable Models, in *Res. Finance* 13, JAI press (forthcoming).

Ferson, W.E., S.R. Foerster, and D.B. Keim (1993). General tests of latent variable models and mean variance spanning. *J. Finance* 48, 131–156.

Ferson, W.E., and C.R. Harvey (1991). The variation of economic risk premiums. *J. Polit. Econ.* 99, 385–415.

Ferson, W.E., and C.R. Harvey (1992). Seasonality and Consumption based Asset Pricing Models. *J. Finance* 47, 511–552.

Ferson, W.E. and C.R. Harvey (1993). Seasonality and Heteroskedasticity in Consumption-based Asset Princing: An analysis of linear models, in *Res. Finance* 11, 1–35. JAI Press.

Ferson, W.E., S.A. Kandel and R.F. Stambaugh (1987). Tests of asset pricing with time-varying expected risk premiums and market betas. *J. Finance* 62, 201–220.

Ferson, W.E., and R.A. Korajczyk (1995). Do arbitrage pricing models explain the predictability of stock returns? *J. Business* (forthcoming).

Ferson, W.E., and J.J. Merrick (1987). Non-stationarity and stage of the business cycle effects in consumption-based asset pricing relations. *J. Financ. Econ.* 18, 127–146.

Flesaker, B. (1993). Testing of the Heath–Jarrow–Morton HO-LCC model of interest rate contingent claims pricing. *J. Financ. Quant. Anal.* 28, 483–496.

Foerster, S.R. (1987). Asset pricing models with changing expectations: An empirical study, unpublished Ph.D. dissertation, The Wharton School, University of Pennsylvania, Philadelphia, PA.

French, K.R., G.W. Schwert and R.F. Stambaugh (1987). Expected stock returns and volatility. *J. Financ. Econ.* (19). 3–30.

Gallant, R. (1987). *Nonlinear Statistical Models*, Wiley and Sons, New York, NY.

Gallant, R.A., L.P. Hansen and G. Tauchen (1990). Using the conditional moments of asset payoffs to infer the volatility of intertemporal marginal rates of substitution. *J. Econometr.* 45, 141–179.

Gallant, R.A., and G. Tauchen (1989). Seminonparametric estimation of conditionally constrained heterogeneous processes: Asset pricing applications. *Econometrica* 57, 1091–1120.

Geske, R., and R. Roll (1983). The fiscal and monetary linkage between stock returns and inflation. *J. Finance* 38, 1–34.

Ghysels, E., and A. Hall (1990). Are consumption-based asset pricing models structural? *J. Econometr.* 45, 121–139.

Gibbons, M.R. (1982). Multivariate tests of financial models. *J. Financ. Econ.* 10, 3–27.

Gibbons, M.R., and W.E. Ferson (1985). Testing asset pricing models with changing expectations and an unobservable market portfolio. *J. Financ. Econ.* 14, 217–236.

Gibbons, M.R., S.A. Ross and J. Shanken (1989). A test of the efficiency of a given portfolio. *Econometrica* 57, 1121–1152.

Gilles, C., and S.F. Leroy (1991). Econometric aspects of variance bounds tests: a survey. *Rev. Financ. Studies* 4, 953–791.

Giovannini, A., and P. Jorion (1989). The time-variation of risk and return in the Foreign exchange and stock markets. *J. Finance* 44, 307–325.

Grinblatt, M., and S. Titman (1983). Factor pricing in a finite economy. *J. Financ. Econ.* 12, 497–508.

Grinblatt, M., and S. Titman (1987). The relation between mean–variance efficiency and arbitrage pricing. *J. Bus.* 60, 97–112.

Gorman, W.M. (1953). Community preference fields. *Econometrica* 21, 63–80.

Gourieroux, C., and A. Monfort (1992). Qualitative threshold ARCH models. *J. Econometr.* 52, 159–200.

Grossman, S., and R.J. Shiller (1982). Consumption correlatedness and risk measurement in economies with nontraded assets and heterogeneous information. *J. Financ. Econ.* 10, 195–210.

Grossman. S., A. Melino and R.J. Shiller (1987). Estimation of the continuous-time consumption-based asset pricing model. *J. Bus. Econ. Stat.* 5, 315–327.

Hall, R.E. (1978). Stockastic implications of the life cycle permanent income hypothesis: theory and evidence. *J. Polit. Econ.* 86, 971–987.

Hall, R.E. (1988). Intertemporal substitution in consumption. *J. Polit. Econ.* 96, 339–357.

Hansen, L.P. (1982). Large sample properties of the generalized method of moments estimators. *Econometrica* 50, 1029–1054.

Hansen, L.P. (1985). A method for calculating bounds on the asymptotic covariance matrices of Generalized Method of Moments Estimators. *J. Econometrics* 30, 203–238.

Hansen, L.P., and R.J. Hodrick (1983). Risk averse speculation in the forward foreign exchange market: An econometric analysis of linear models, in: J. Frenkel (ed.), *Exchange Rates and International Macroeconomics*, University of Chicago Press, Chicago, IL.

Hansen, L.P., and R. Jagannathan (1994). Assesing specification errors in stochastic discount factor models, working paper, University of Minnesota.

Hansen, L.P., and R. Jagannathan (1991). Implications of security market data for models of dynamic economies. *J.Polit. Econ.* 99, 225–262.

Hansen, L.P., and S.F.R. Richard (1987). The role of conditioning information in deducing testable restrictions implied by dynamic asset pricing models. *Econometrica* 55, 587–613.

Hansen, L.P., and K. Singleton (1982). Generalized instrumental variables estimation of nonlinear rational expectations models. *Econometrica* 50, 1269–1285.

Hansen, L.P., and K.J. Singleton (1983). Stochastic consumption, risk aversion and the temporal behavior of asset returns. *J. Polit. Econ.* 91, 249–266.

Hansen, L.P., and K.J. Singleton (1984). Errata. *Econometrica* 52, 267–268.

Hansen, L.P. and K.J. Singleton (1988). Efficient estimation of linear asset pricing models with moving average errors, working paper, Stanford University.

Harrison M., and D. Kreps (1979). Martingales and arbitrage in multi-period securities markets. *J. Econ. Theory* 20, 381–408.

Harvey, C.R. (1991). The world price of covariance risk. *J.Finance* 46, 111–158.

Harvey, C.R. (1988). The real term structure and consumption growth. *J. Financ. Econ.* 22, 305–314.

Harvey, C.R. (1989). Time-varying conditional covariances in tests of asset pricing models. *J. Financ. Econ.*,24, 289–318.

Hawawini, G., and D.B. Keim (1995). On the predictability of common stock returns: World-wide evidence, in: R. Jarrow, V. Maksimovic and W.T. Ziemba (eds.), *Finance*, Handbooks in Operations Research and Management Science, Vol. 9., North Holland, Amsterdam, pp. 497–544 (this volume).

He, H., and D.M. Modest (1992). Market frictions and consumption-based asset pricing, working paper, University of California at Berkeley.

Heaton, J. (1991). An empirical investigation of asset pricing with temporally dependent preferences, working paper, MIT, Sloan School of Management.

Hinkley, D.V. (1977). Jackknifing in unbalanced situations. *Technometrics* 19, 285–292.

Hodrick, R. (1991). Dividend Yields and expected stock returns: Alternative procedures for inference and measurement, working paper, Northwestern University.

Hodrick, R., and S. Srivastava (1984). An investigation of risk and return in forward foreign exchange. *J. Int. Money Finance* 3, 5–29.

Huang, R.D. (1989). An analysis of intertemporal pricing for forward foreign exchange contracts. *J. Finance* 44, 183–194.

Huberman, G. (1982). A simple approach to arbitrage pricing theory. *J. Econ. Theory* 28, 183–191.

Huberman, G. and S.A. Kandel (1987). Mean-variance spanning. *J. Finance* 42, 383–388.

Huberman, G., S.A. Kandel and R.F. Stambaugh (1987). Mimicking portfolios and exact arbitrage pricing. *J. Finance* 42, 1–10.

Ingersoll, J.E. (1984). Some results in the theory of arbitrage pricing. *J. Finance* 39, 1021–1039.

Jobson, J.D., and R. Korkie (1982). Potential performance and tests of portfolio efficiency. *J. Financ. Econ.* 10, 433–466.

Jobson, J.D., and R. Korkie (1985). Some tests of asset pricing with multivariate normality. *Can. J. Adm. Sci.* 2, 114–138.

Jorion, Ph., and A. Giovannini (1987). Interest rates and risk premia in the stock market and in the foreign exchange market. *J. Int. Money Finance* 6, 107–123.

Kandel, S.A. (1984). The likelihood ratio test statistic of mean variance efficiency without a riskless asset. *J. Financ. Econ.* 13, 575–592.

Kandel, S.A. (1986). The geometry of the maximum likelihood estimator of the zero beta return. *J. Finance* 31, 339–346.

Kandel, S., and R.F. Stambaugh (1989). A mean variance framework for tests of asset pricing models. *Rev. Financ.Studies* 2, 125–156.

Kandel, S., and R.F. Stambaugh (1990). Expectations and volatility of consumption and asset returns. *Rev. Financ. Studies* 3, 207–232.

Kandel, S., and R.F. Stambaugh (1991). Asset returns and intertemporal preferences. *J. Monetary Econ.* 27, 39–71.

Kaul, G. (1987). Stock returns and inflation: The role of the monetary sector. *J. Financ. Econ.* 18, 253–276.

Keim, D.B. (1983). Size-related anomalies and stock return seasonality: Further empirical evidence. *J. Financ. Econ.* 12, 13–32.

Keim, D.B., and R.F. Stambaugh (1986). Predicting returns in the bond and stock markets. *J. Financ. Econ.* 17, 357–90.

Kleidon, A.W. (1986). Variance bounds tests and stock price valuation models. *J. Polit. Econ.* 94, 953–1001.

Kocherlakota, N. (1990). On tests of representative consumer asset pricing models. *J. Monetary Econ.* 26, 285–304.

Koh, S.-K. (1992). Finite sample properties of the generalized method of moments in a non expected utility framework, working paper, national university of Singapore.

Kreps, D.M., and E.L. Porteus (1978). Temporal resolution of uncertainty and dynamic choice theory. *Econometrica* 46, 185–200.

Lehmann, B.N., and D.M. Modest (1988). The empirical foundations of the arbitrage pricing theory. *J. Financ. Econ.* 21, 213–254.

LeRoy, S.F., and R.D. Porter (1981). The present value relation: tests based on implied variance bounds. *Econometrica* 49, 555–574.

Lewbel, A. (1989). Exact aggregation and a representative consumer. *Q. J. Econ.* 104(3), 621–633.

Lewis, K. (1990). The behavior of Eurocurrency returns across different holding period returns and monetary regimes. *J. Finance* 45, 1211–1236.

Li, Y. (1991). Intertemporal asset pricing without consumption: Empirical tests, working paper, University of Chicago.

Lo, A. and A.C. MacKinlay (1988). Stock prices do not follow random walks: Evidence from a simple specification test. *Rev. Financ. Studies* 1, 41–66.

Long, J. (1974). Stock prices, inflation, and the term structure of interest rates. *J. Financ. Econ.* 1, 131–170.

Lintner, J. (1965). The valuation of risk assets and the selection of risky investments in stock portfolios and capital budgets. *Rev. Econ. Stat.* 47, 13–37.

Lucas, R.E., Jr. (1978). Asset prices in an exchange economy. *Econometrica* 46, 1429–1445.

Luttmer, E.G.J. (1993). Asset pricing in economies with frictions, working paper, Northwestern University.

MacKinlay, A.C. (1987). On multivariate tests of the CAPM. *J. Financ. Econ.* 18, 341–371.

MacKinlay, A.C., and M.P. Richardson (1991). Using the generalized method of moments to test mean–variance efficiency. *J. Finance* 46, 511–528.

Mankiw, N.G. (1986). The equity premium and the concentration of aggregate shocks. *J. Financ. Econ.* 17, 211–219.

Mankiw, N.G., and M.D. Shapiro (1986). Risk and return: Consumption beta versus market beta. *Rev. Econ. Stat.* 68, 452–459.

Mao, C.-S. (1991). Hypothesis testing and finite sample properties of generalized method of moments estimators: a monte carlo study, working paper, Federal Reserve Bank of Richmond, Va.

Mark, N.C. (1988). Time-varying betas and risk premia in the pricing of forward foreign exchange contracts. *J. Financ. Econ.* 22, 335–354.

Marsh, T.A. (1995). Term structure of interest rates and the pricing of fixed income claims and bonds, in: R. Jarrow, V. Maksimovic and W.T. Ziemba (eds.), *Finance*, Handbooks in Operations Research and Management Science, Vol. 9., North Holland, Amsterdam, pp. 273–314 (this volume).

Marshall, D.A. (1991). Inflation and asset returns in a monetary economy, working paper, Northwestern University.

Mehra, R., and E. Prescott (1985). The equity premium: a Puzzle. *J. Monetary Econ.* 15, 145–162.

Merton, R.C. (1973). An intertemporal capital asset pricing model. *Econometrica* 41, 867–87.

Merton, R.C. (1980). On estimating the expected return on the market: An exploratory investigation. *J. Financ. Econ.* 8, 323–362.

Miron, J.A. (1986). Seasonal fluctuations in the life cycle-permanent income model of consumption. *J. Polit. Econ.* 94, 1258–1279.

Nelson, D. (1991). Conditional heteroskedasticity in asset returns: A new approach. *Econometrica* 59, 347–370.

Newey, W. (1985). Generalized method of moments specification testing. *J. Econometr.* 29, 199–256.

Newey. W., and K.D. West (1987a). A simple, positive definite, heteroskedasticity and autocorrelation consistent covariance matrix. *Econometrica* 55, 703–708.

Newey, W., and K.D. West (1987b). Hypothesis tesing with efficient method of moments estimators. *Int. Econ. Rev.* 28, 777–787.

Nanisetty, P. (1991). The effect of time-varying covariances on asset risk premia: A test of an intertemporal CAPM, working paper, Indiana University.

Ng. L. (1991). Tests of the CAPM with time-varying covariances: A multivariate GARCH approach. *J. Finance* 46, 1507–1522.

Ni, X. (1991). Scaling factors and the equity premium puzzle, working paper, University of Missouri, Columbia.

Pagan, A.R. and G.W. Schwert (1990). Alternative Models for conditional stock volatility. *J. Econometrics* 45, 267–290.

Poterba, J.M., and L.H. Summers (1988). Mean reversion in stock prices: Evidence and implications. *J. Financ. Econ.* 22, 27–60.

Reisman, H. (1992). Reference variables, factor structure, and the approximate multibeta representation. *J. Finance* 47, 1303–1314.

Reitz, T.A. (1988). The equity premium puzzle: a solution. *J. Monetary Econ.* 22, 117–131.

Richardson, M. (1990). Temporary components of stock prices: a skeptic's view, working paper, the University of Pennsylvania.

Richardson, M., and T. Smith (1991). Tests of financial models in the presence of overlapping observations. *Rev. Econ. Studies* 4, 227–454.

Roll, R. (1977). A critique of the asset pricing theory's tests — part 1: On past and potential testability of the theory. *J. Financ. Econ.* 4, 129–176.

Roll, R.R. (1985). A note on the geometry of Shanken's CSR T^2 test for mean/variance efficiency. *J. Financ. Econ.* 14, 349–357.

Roll, R.R., and S.A. Ross (1980). An empirical examination of the arbitrage pricing theory. *J. Finance* 35, 1073–1103.

Rosenberg, B., K. Reid and R. Lanstein (1985). Persuasive evidence of market inefficiency. *J. Portfolio Manage.* 3, 9–17.

Ross, S.A. (1976). The arbitrage pricing theory of capital asset pricing. *J. Econ. Theory* 13, 341–60.

Ross, S. (1977). Risk, return and arbitrage, in: I. Friend and J. Bicksler (eds.), *Risk and Return in Finance*, Ballinger, Cambridge, MA.

Rubinstein, M. (1974). An aggregation theorem for securities markets. *J. Financ. Econ.* 1, 225–244.

Rubinstein, M. (1976). The valuation of uncertain income streams and the pricing of options. *Bell J. Econ. Manage. Sci.* 7, 407–425.

Ryder, H.E., Jr., and G.M. Heal (1973). Optimal growth with intertemporally dependent preferences. *Rev. Econ. Studies* 40, 1–31.

Schwert, G.W. (1989). Why does stock market volatility change over time? *J. Finance* 44, 1115–1154.

Schwert, G.W. (1990). *Business Cycles, Financial Crises and Stock Volatility*, Carnegie-Rochester conference series.

Schwert, G.W., and P.J. Seguin (1990). Heteroskedasticity in stock returns. *J. Finance* 45, 1129–1156.

Shanken, J. (1985). Multivariate tests of portfolio efficiency when the zero beta rate is unknown. *J. Financ. Econ.* 14, 327–348.

Shanken, J. (1986). Testing portfolio efficiency when the zero beta rate is unknown: a note. *J. Finance* 41, 269–276.

Shanken, J. (1987). Multivariate proxies and asset pricing relations: Living with the Roll critique. *J. Financ. Econ.* 18, 91–110.

Shanken, J. (1992). On the estimation of beta pricing models. *Rev. Financ. Studies* 5, 1–34.

Shanken, J., and M.I. Weinstein (1990). Macroeconomic variables and asset pricing: Estimation and tests, working paper, University of Rochester.

Sharathchandra, G. (1991). An asset pricing model with production: Theory and empirical tests, working paper, Southern Methodist University.
Sharpe, W.F. (1964). Capital asset prices: A theory of market equilibrium under conditions of risk. *J. Finance* (19). 425–442.
Sharpe, W.F. (1977). The capital asset pricing model: A muti-beta interpretation, in: H. Levy and M. Sarnat (eds.), *Financial Decision Making under Uncertainty*, Academic Press, New York, NY.
Sharpe, W.F. (1984). Factor models, CAPM's and the APT. *J.Portfolio Manage.* 11, 21–25.
Sharpe, W.F. (1991). Capital asset prices with and without negative holdings. *J. Finance* 46, 489–510.
Shiller, R.J. (1981). Do stock prices move too much to be justified by subsequent changes in dividends? *Am. Econ. Review* 7, 521–536.
Singleton, K. (1990). Specification and estimation of intertemporal asset pricing models, in: B. Freidman and F. Hahn (eds.), *Handbook of Monetary Economics*, North Holland, Amsterdam.
Smith, D.C. (1994). Finite sample properties of the Epstein–Zin Asset Pricing Model, working paper, Norwegian School of Management.
Snow, K.N. (1991). Diagnosing asset pricing models using the distribution of asset returns. *J. Finance* 46, 955–983.
Stambaugh, R.F. (1982). On the exclusion of assets from tests of the two-parameter model: a sensitivity analysis. *J. Financ. Econ.* 10, 237–268.
Stambaugh, R.F. (1988). The information in forward rates: Implications for models of the term structure. *J. Financ. Econ.* 21, 41–70.
Sundaresan, S.M. (1989). Intertemporally dependent preferences and the volatility of consumption and wealth. *Rev. Financ. Studies* 2, 73–89.
Tauchen, G. (1986). Statistical properties of generalized method-of-moment estimators of structural parameters obtained from financial market data. *J. Bus. Econ. Stat.* 4, 397–425.
Telmer, C.I. (1991). Asset pricing puzzles in incomplete markets, working paper, Queens University.
Wheatley, S. (1988). Some tests of equity market integration. *J. Financ. Econ.* 21, 177–212.
Wheatley, S. (1989). A critique of latent variable tests of asset pricing models. *J. Financ. Econ.* 23, 325–338.
Weil, Ph. (1989). The equity premium puzzle and the risk-free rate puzzle. *J. Monetary Econ.* 24, 401–421.
White, H. (1980). A heteroskedasticity-consistent covariance matrix estimator and a direct test for heteroskedasticity. *Econometrica* 48, 817–838.
Wilson, R.B. (1968). The theory of syndicates. *Econometrica* 36, 119–131.

R. Jarrow et al., Eds., *Handbooks in OR & MS, Vol. 9*

Chapter 6

International Portfolio Choice and Asset Pricing: An Integrative Survey

René M. Stulz

Kurtz Chair in Finance, The Ohio State University, 1775 College Road, Columbus, OH 43210, U.S.A.

1. Introduction

In general, theories of portfolio choice and asset pricing let investors differ at most with respect to their preferences, their wealth and, possibly, their information sets. If there are multiple countries, however, the investment and consumption opportunity sets of investors depend on their country of residence. International portfolio choice and asset pricing theories attempt to understand how the existence of country-specific investment and consumption opportunity sets affect the portfolios held by investors and the expected returns of assets. In this paper, we review these theories within a common framework, discuss how they fare in empirical tests, and assess their relevance for the field of international finance.

At a point in time, an investor's consumption opportunity set is composed of the goods that the investor can consume and their relative prices. Consumption opportunity sets differ across countries when the relative prices of goods depend on where goods are located. An investor's investment opportunity set is described by the distributions of wealth available to that investor for each future date. If two investors who differ in their country of residence can obtain the same distributions of wealth for all future dates in terms of the same arbitrary numeraire, they have the same investment opportunity sets. Investment opportunity sets differ across countries when investment barriers introduce a wedge between returns on assets for residents and for nonresidents.

In this paper, we first show that if investment and consumption opportunity sets do not differ across countries, the fact that countries use different currencies has no significant implications for portfolio choice and asset pricing. In this special case, the traditional approaches to portfolio choice and asset pricing apply. Whereas these models perform poorly in predicting asset holdings across countries, they have some success in explaining the cross-sectional variation in conditional expected returns across countries. We then show how the predictions of the traditional models are affected if one allows for differences in consumption opportunity sets and discuss the empirical relevance of such an extension of traditional models. Finally, we allow for differences in investment opportunity sets. We conclude by focusing on the weaknesses of this literature and suggest directions for future research.

Whereas this paper reviews the existing literature on portfolio choice and international asset pricing, it makes no attempt to discuss every paper in this literature. As the reader will certainly notice, we neglect to talk about some important papers so that we can focus better on our main themes.

2. The case of no differences in consumption and investment opportunity sets

We consider a world where asset prices and exchange rates are jointly lognormally distributed. There is only one consumption good. Trading in the consumption good and in financial claims is continuous and costless. Markets are perfect. There are no transaction costs, no transportation costs, no tariffs, no taxes, no restrictions on short-sales, no barriers to international investment. Each investor is a price-taker, has the same information, and is risk-averse.

Formally, we assume that the price of the ith financial claim in country j, I_{ij}, changes according to:

$$\frac{\mathrm{d}I_{ij}}{I_{ij}} = \mu_{ij}\mathrm{d}t + \sigma_{ij}\mathrm{d}z_{ij} \tag{1}$$

where $\mathrm{d}z_{ij}$ is the instantaneous increment to a standard Wiener process, μ_{ij} is the instantaneous expected return per unit of time, and σ_{ij} is the instantaneous standard deviation of the return per unit of time.

When forming a portfolio, an investor from country j is concerned about the real return of financial assets rather than their nominal return in currency j. With a single consumption good trading on perfect markets, it must be the case that the price of the good is the same in currency j, for all j's, irrespective of the country in which it is bought. In the literature on foreign exchange rate determination, this result is usually called the law of one price. More formally, if p_j is the price of the consumption good in country j and e_{ij} is the price of currency j in country i, the price of the consumption good in country i is $p_i = e_{ij}p_j$.

With our assumptions, there are no differences in investment opportunity sets across countries, meaning that an investor in country h, for all h's, would have the same wealth at each future date if he had the investment opportunities of an investor in country j, for all j's.

If investors have identical consumption and investment opportunity sets, there is no loss of generality in assuming that all investors compute the returns of assets using the same numeraire to form their portfolios. We could use any numeraire, but if we use a currency as the numeraire, each investor's indirect utility depends on his consumption expenditures in that currency as well as on the price of the consumption good in that currency. In contrast, if we use the consumption good as the numeraire and assume, as we do here, that the joint distribution of returns is constant, the utility of an investor depends only on the number of units of the consumption good he consumes and his portfolio decisions depend only on the mean and variance of the real rate of return on his portfolio. For simplicity, we therefore assume that all investors use the consumption good as the numeraire. To obtain real returns, we need to specify the dynamics of the price of the consumption good. We assume that the price of the consumption good in currency j, p_j, follows:

$$\frac{\mathrm{d}p_j}{p_j} = \mu_{p_j}\mathrm{d}t + \sigma_{p_j}\mathrm{d}z_{p_j} \tag{2}$$

for all j's. Using the dynamics for p_j and for the return of the ith asset from country j, we can obtain the return of that asset in terms of the price of the consumption good:

$$\frac{\mathrm{d}(I_{ij}/p_j)}{I_{ij}/p_j} = (\mu_{ij} - \mu_{p_j} - \sigma_{ij,p_j} + \sigma_{p_j}^2)\mathrm{d}t + \sigma_{ij}\mathrm{d}z_{ij} - \sigma_{p_j}\mathrm{d}z_{p_j} \tag{3}$$

where σ_{ij,p_j} is the instantaneous covariance between the return of the ith asset of country j and the rate of change of the price of the consumption good in terms of currency j.

We now assume that investors can freely lend and borrow at the instantaneous rate r per unit of time in units of the consumption good. With this additional assumption, we now have a model in which we can completely ignore the existence of multiple countries and simply focus on the asset demands of investors in terms of the numeraire. With our assumptions, the joint distribution of real returns (i.e., returns in terms of the consumption good) is constant. This means that all the results of mean–variance portfolio choice theory apply in this case.[1] In particular, all risk-averse investors, irrespective of their preferences, hold their wealth in the risk-free asset and in one portfolio of risky assets that is common to all investors. Since the portfolio of risky assets is common to all investors, it must be the market portfolio of risky assets. A world where all investors hold the same portfolio of risky assets is the world of the Sharpe–Lintner capital asset pricing model.

In this world, the expected real excess return of an asset, namely the expected real return of the asset in excess of the real risk-free rate, obeys the following formula:

$$\mu_{ij} - \mu_{p_j} - \sigma_{ij,p_j} + \sigma_{p_j}^2 - r = \beta_{ij}[\mu_{\mathrm{w}} - r] \tag{4}$$

where β_{ij} is the instantaneous covariance between the real return of asset ij and the real return of the world market portfolio divided by the instantaneous variance of the real return of the world market portfolio, and μ_{w} is the instantaneous expected real return per unit of time of the world market portfolio. The world market portfolio is a portfolio that comprises all securities in the world in proportion to their capitalization relative to world wealth using a consumption good as the numeraire to measure world wealth and each security's capitalization.

[1] See Huang & Litzenberger [1988] for a review of these results.

We call the model that yields equation (4) the international capital asset pricing model (ICAPM).

The ICAPM can be used to compute the expected real excess return of a nominal default-free bond in country i over a nominal default-free bond in country j and hence makes it possible to value currency-dependent claims. Define R_i to be the instantaneous nominal return on a bond whose return is certain in currency i. With this notation, the real return on a bond of country i minus the real return on a bond of country j is:

$$\begin{aligned}\left(R_i \mathrm{d}t - \frac{\mathrm{d}p_i}{p_i} + \sigma^2_{p_i}\mathrm{d}t\right) - \left(R_j \mathrm{d}t - \frac{\mathrm{d}p_j}{p_j} + \sigma^2_{p_j}\mathrm{d}t\right) = \\ = R_i \mathrm{d}t + \frac{\mathrm{d}e_{ij}}{e_{ij}} - \sigma^2_{e_{ij}}\mathrm{d}t - \sigma_{e_{ij},p_i}\mathrm{d}t - R_j\mathrm{d}t\end{aligned} \tag{5}$$

where e_{ij} is the price in currency j of currency i and where we use the fact that the law of one price implies $p_j = e_{ij}p_i$. Applying equation (4), we can obtain the expected real return on a long position in the bond of country i financed by a short position in the bond of country j:

$$R_i + \mu_{e_{ij}} - \sigma^2_{e_{ij}} - \sigma_{e_{ij},p_i} - R_j = \beta_{e_{ij}}[\mu_{\mathrm{w}} - r] \tag{6}$$

where $\beta_{e_{ij}}$ is the ratio of the instantaneous covariance of the rate of change of the exchange rate with the real return on the world market portfolio and of the instantaneous variance of the real return on the world market portfolio. The pricing relation implies that a portfolio with a long position in a nominal bond of country i and a short position in a nominal bond of country j has a positive expected real return if the rate of change of the price of currency i in country j has a positive covariance with the real return of the world market portfolio. This is because, in this model, adding an asset whose real return has a positive covariance with the return of the world market portfolio to the portfolio of risky assets held by investors forces them to bear more risk. If this asset does not yield a risk premium, investors hold it short to decrease the risk of their portfolios and there is an excess supply of that asset.

The pricing relation can be looked at in a different way that is also useful. A well-established relation in international finance is the interest rate parity theorem, which here states that the instantaneous forward premium per unit of time on currency i in terms of currency j, f_{ij}, is equal to $R_j - R_i$, so that equation (6) becomes:

$$\mu_{e_{ij}} - f_{ij} - \sigma^2_{e_{ij}} - \sigma_{e_{ij},p_i} = \beta_{e_{ij}}[\mu_{\mathrm{w}} - r] \tag{7}$$

Hence, the pricing equation can also be used to obtain the relation between the forward premium and the expected rate of growth of the exchange rate. It immediately follows from the pricing equation that the expected spot exchange rate exceeds the forward exchange rate if the covariance of the growth rate of the exchange rate with the world market portfolio is sufficiently large. This is because, in this case, the holder of a long forward contract bears risk and has to be rewarded for doing so by a positive expected payoff from the position. In the model of this section, a long position in a foreign currency yields a risk premium only to the extent that the risk of that position is not diversifiable.

An important implication of equation (7) is that the expected excess real return on a forward contract differs from zero if the exchange rate has a β equal to zero. In this case, the instantaneous forward premium must satisfy:

$$\mu_{e_{ij}} - f_{ij} = \sigma^2_{e_{ij}} + \sigma_{e_{ij},p_i} \tag{8}$$

Equation (8) implies that the diversifiability of exchange rate risk is not a sufficient condition for the forward premium to equal the expected rate of change of the spot exchange rate. In addition, it must be the case that the instantaneous variance of the rate of change of the exchange rate is equal to minus the instantaneous covariance of the rate of change of the exchange rate with the rate of change of the price of the consumption good in currency i. Equation (5) makes this result easily understandable. Investors care about the real return of the forward position. This real return is the payoff of the forward position divided by the price of the consumption good. The expected real payoff is therefore $E[(e - F)/P]$, where e is the end-of-period exchange rate, F is the (nonstochastic) forward rate, and P is the end-of-period price of the consumption good. This expression is not equal to zero if $E(e) - F$ equals zero because the end-of-period price of the consumption good is a random variable, so that $E[(e - F)/P]$ is not equal to $E(e - F)/E(P)$. Note that this result holds also if β risk is not priced because investors are risk-neutral. In this section, all investors look at asset returns in the same way, so that the expected real return on forward contracts is the same for all investors in the world.

So far, we have formulated the pricing equation of the ICAPM using the consumption good as the numeraire. If (A) the asset in country j with an instantaneous risk-free nominal return in currency j has a beta equal to zero in terms of the pricing equation (4), and (B) the rate of growth of the price of the consumption good in currency j is uncorrelated with nominal asset returns in that currency, then the ICAPM can be formulated using nominal returns in currency j. To see this, note that with our assumptions, the excess return of the ith asset in country j in terms of the price of the consumption good is:

$$\begin{aligned}
\frac{\mathrm{d}(I_{ij}/p_j)}{I_{ij}/p_j} - r\mathrm{d}t &= (\mu_{ij} - \mu_{p_j} - \sigma_{ij,p_j} + \sigma^2_{p_j} - r)\mathrm{d}t + \sigma_{ij}\mathrm{d}z_{ij} - \sigma_{p_j}\mathrm{d}z_{p_j} \\
&= (\mu_{ij} - R_j + R_j - \mu_{p_j} + \sigma^2_{p_j} - r)\mathrm{d}t + \sigma_{ij}\mathrm{d}z_{ij} - \sigma_{p_j}\mathrm{d}z_{p_j} \\
&= (\mu_{ij}\mathrm{d}t + \sigma_{ij}\mathrm{d}z_{ij} - R_j\mathrm{d}t) + \\
&\quad + (R_j\mathrm{d}t - \mu_{p_j}\mathrm{d}t - \sigma_{p_j}\mathrm{d}z_{p_j} + \sigma^2_{p_j}\mathrm{d}t - r\mathrm{d}t) \\
&= \left(\frac{\mathrm{d}I_{ij}}{I_{ij}} - R_j\mathrm{d}t\right) + \left(R_j\mathrm{d}t - \frac{\mathrm{d}p_j}{p_j} + \sigma^2_{p_j}\mathrm{d}t - r\mathrm{d}t\right)
\end{aligned} \tag{9}$$

where we take into account assumption (B) that the rate of growth of p_j is uncorrelated with nominal asset returns in currency j, i.e., $\sigma_{ij,p_j} = 0$, when going from the first line to the second line of equation (9). This assumption makes it possible to decompose the excess real return of security ij into a nominal excess return which does not depend on the dynamics of the consumption good price and a real excess return which does not depend on the dynamics of the asset price. Without this assumption, the last line of equation (9) would depend on the instantaneous covariance between the nominal return of asset ij and the rate of change of the price of the consumption good in currency j. This covariance plays no role in nominal CAPMs. With assumption (A), the β of the excess return of the nominal bond is zero. Consequently, the β of asset ij computed using excess real returns equals the β of the same asset computed using nominal excess returns in currency j. Further, the expected real excess return of asset ij equals its nominal expected excess return. Since this result holds for any asset ij, it also holds for the world market portfolio. Hence, we have shown that with our assumptions:

$$\mu_{ij} - R_j = \beta_{ij}[\mu_{\mathrm{w}j} - R_j] \tag{10}$$

where the β can be computed using nominal or real excess returns and where $\mu_{\mathrm{w}j}$ is the nominal expected return of the world market portfolio in currency j.

In general, nominal excess returns cannot be substituted for real excess returns, but there may be countries for which approximating real excess returns by nominal excess returns turns out to be harmless. Hence, if the ICAPM in real excess returns holds, it may be that an empiricist could reject it using nominal excess returns in one currency and could not reject it using nominal excess returns in another currency. One would be more comfortable using the nominal excess return approximation in countries where inflation has little systematic risk. It should be noted that tests of the CAPM that use only assets of one country are generally formulated using nominal excess returns; if such a practice makes sense for a particular country, then it makes equal sense to test the ICAPM in nominal excess returns from the perspective of that country.

How well does the ICAPM perform in an international setting? A number of papers provide unconditional tests of the ICAPM. Stehle [1977] uses monthly returns on U.S. securities and eight foreign indices to investigate whether U.S. assets are priced internationally, in the sense that risks that are diversifiable internationally but not domestically are not priced. He finds evidence in favor of this hypothesis, but the return for the zero-beta portfolio is too high to be consistent with the model. Korajczyk & Viallet [1989] provide evidence using a large number of securities from the U.S. and three foreign countries that the ICAPM outperforms the domestic CAPM in the sense that the average mispricing is smaller; however, in their various tests, they also find that the model leads to large pricing errors for small stocks, that the average mispricings are significantly different from zero for at least one market in all their specifications and that the performance of the ICAPM is better for more recent sample periods. Cumby & Glen [1990] and Harvey [1991] cannot reject the hypothesis that the world portfolio of the Morgan Stanley/Capital International indices is efficient in a setting where the portfolios on the efficient frontier are formed from national indices.

A number of recent studies investigate the model assuming that it holds period per period, allowing the joint distribution of asset returns to change over time and, for some studies, also allowing the price of risk to change over time. Merton [1973] shows that the CAPM holds period per period with changing investment opportunities either if investors have logarithmic utility functions or if they cannot use financial assets to hedge against changes in investment opportunities. It seems implausible that there are no assets whose return is correlated with changes in the distribution of asset returns. This means that the theoretical underpinnings of these studies are strongest for the case where investors all have logarithmic utility functions. Unfortunately, in that case, the price of risk is constant.

Mark [1988], Giovannini & Jorion [1989] and McCurdy & Morgan [1991] use the model to investigate the risk premium incorporated in forward contracts. Whereas the model has some success in explaining conditional risk premia, it does not explain why conditional risk premia are so large for forward contracts.[2] Harvey [1991] uses the model to examine the expected excess returns of the Morgan Stanley/Capital International monthly indices allowing for both changes in the betas of individual indices and changes in the price of risk. He finds that the model is useful to understand differences in conditional expected excess returns across countries; the model does not predict well the conditional expected excess returns of some countries, however, suggesting that these countries are not well-integrated in world capital markets or that the model does not capture some priced risks in addition to the ICAPM systematic risk. Finally, Chan, Karolyi & Stulz [1992] test some implications of the model using daily data for the 1980s. They cannot reject the ICAPM in a model with a domestic and a foreign portfolio at a conventional significance level. However, they find that a two-beta model where each portfolio is a source of risk performs better than the single-beta model.

Several papers investigate the APT in an international context assuming identical consumption and investment opportunity sets across countries. The APT in this context relies on different assumptions about asset price and exchange rate dynamics than those we made in this section — namely, with the APT, the dynamics of asset and currency prices depend on multiple sources of risk. Solnik [1983] shows that if the exchange rates follow the same factor structure as stock prices, the APT holds internationally. In this case, the currency of denomination of returns becomes irrelevant and the priced factors can be obtained from the universe of stock returns. Hence, with Solnik's assumptions, the relation between the international APT and the domestic APT is the same as the relation between the ICAPM and the domestic CAPM.[3] Cho, Eun & Senbet [1986] are the first to provide tests of the international APT and reject the joint hypothesis that markets are integrated and the APT is valid; however, their evidence is consistent with integration for subsets of countries. Gultekin, Gultekin & Penati [1989] and Korajczyk & Viallet [1989] show that the performance of the international APT depends on the

[2] See Backus, Gregory & Telmer [1993] for a discussion of this problem.

[3] Ikeda [1991] shows how the model changes if Solnik's key assumption is relaxed.

regime for barriers to international investment. Korajczyk and Viallet find that the APT performs better than the CAPM with a value-weighted market portfolio but not than the CAPM with an equally-weighted portfolio. Somewhat surprisingly, they find that the domestic APT outperforms the international APT. Korajczyk & Viallet [1992] explore the joint returns of stocks and forward contracts in an APT setting with time-varying betas. They find that changes in the risk premia of factors derived from the equity markets do not span changes in risk premia on forward contracts. A possible explanation of this finding is that there are some priced risks in forward contracts that are not present in equities.

Whereas the ICAPM's performance for predicting conditional expected excess returns is good enough to lend some credibility to the model, the model fails dramatically in another dimension. The model predicts that investors hold the world market portfolio of risky assets irrespective of their country of residence. Yet, empirically, investors have a strong preference for the assets of their home country.[4] This preference of investors is the major empirical motivation for much of the literature on international portfolio choice and asset pricing. Theoretically, this literature proceeds from changing two assumptions that are crucial to the derivation of the ICAPM. The first assumption is that investors all have the same consumption investment opportunity set. Empirically, deviations from the law of one price resulting from the existence of costs to goods arbitrage are well-documented and are consistent with the considerable variation in real exchange rates documented in the literature.[5] The second assumption is that the investment opportunity set is the same for all investors.

3. The implications of differences in consumption opportunity sets

Consider now a world with many different goods whose relative prices change over time and may differ across countries and where investors' preferences over goods can differ according to their country of residence. Differences in preferences across countries imply that purchasing power parity does not hold since changes in relative prices have differential effects on the price of the consumption basket consumed by investors in different countries. Purchasing power parity also fails if investors have the same preferences but relative prices of goods differ across countries. Deviations from the law of one price could arise, for instance, because goods arbitrage involves transportation costs as modeled by Dumas [1992]. If purchasing power parity does not hold, investors hold different portfolios across countries if they choose to hedge against unanticipated changes in the cost of their consumption basket since that cost evolves differentially across countries. Changes in the relative costs of consumption baskets affect asset demands and hence expected returns. This means that, in general, one would expect the investment

[4] See French & Poterba [1991], Cooper & Kaplanis [1990] and Tesar & Werner [1993] for evidence.

[5] See, for instance, Cumby & Obstfeld [1984] for evidence and references to the literature.

opportunity set to change randomly over time if relative costs of consumption baskets change randomly over time.

To understand the asset demands implied by this extended model better,[6] define $\ln \boldsymbol{P}$ to be the $P \times 1$ vector of logarithms of goods prices in currency i. If the law of one price holds for a good, the location of the good is not a relevant attribute of the good; in contrast, however, if the law of one price does not hold for a good, then its location is a priced attribute of the good. Hence, in the vector of goods prices, the goods for which the law of one price does not hold have to be treated as different goods if their location differs whereas location is irrelevant for the goods for which the law of one price holds.

With the formulation of the vector of goods prices used here, all investors can use the same currency to compute their optimal consumption and portfolio policies. This formulation of the investor's optimization problem is sufficiently general that it encompasses the case where the consumption opportunity sets of investors have no goods in common and the case where the consumption opportunity sets of investors are the same. We assume that the state of investment opportunities is characterized by a vector of S states variables, $\boldsymbol{S}$. The first P state variables are the logarithms of the consumption good prices.

Using currency i as the numeraire, define $J(W, \boldsymbol{S}, t)$ as the indirect utility of wealth for an investor, where W is his wealth in the currency of country i:

$$J(W, \boldsymbol{S}, t) = E_t \left[\operatorname{Max} \int_{\theta=0}^{\theta=\infty} U(C(\theta), \ln \boldsymbol{P}(\theta), \theta)\, \mathrm{d}\theta \right]$$

where $U(C(\theta), \ln \boldsymbol{P}(\theta), \theta)$ is the indirect utility of consumption (i.e., the utility obtained by the investor by maximizing his utility function defined over goods, given expenditures $C(\theta)$ and prices of goods $\boldsymbol{P}(\theta)$). It follows from Stulz [1981a] that for this investor, the $n \times 1$ vector of risky asset holdings $\boldsymbol{w}$, where n is the number of risky assets in currency i, is:

$$\boldsymbol{w} = \left(\frac{-J_W}{J_{WW} W} \right) V^{-1} \mu_x - \left(\frac{J'_{WS}}{J_{WW} W} \right) V^{-1} V_S \tag{11}$$

where J_W is the partial derivative of the indirect utility of wealth with respect to wealth, J_{WW} is the partial derivative of J_W with respect to W, J_{WS} denotes the $S \times 1$ vector of partial derivatives of J_W with respect to S, a prime denotes a transpose, μ_x is the $n \times 1$ vector of expected excess returns, V is the $n \times n$ variance–covariance matrix of the returns of risky assets in currency i in excess of the risk-free rate in currency i, V_S is the $n \times S$ covariance matrix of excess returns with the rates of change of the state variables. Note that if we change the currency of denomination of returns, the asset with a nonstochastic return in currency i has a stochastic return in the new currency of denomination of returns.

By inspection of equation (11), it follows that the investor's wealth can be decomposed into holdings of $S + 1$ mutual funds, where S is the number of goods.

[6] The analysis of this section makes extensive use of Stulz [1981a].

The first fund, with holdings proportional to $V^{-1}\mu_x$, is the portfolio of risky assets held by an investor who has logarithmic utility, since, for such an investor, the vector of partial derivatives of J_W with respect to the state variables has only zeroes and the coefficient of relative risk aversion of the indirect utility function of wealth, $-J_W/J_{WW}$, is equal to one. The next S funds are optimal hedges against unanticipated changes in goods prices. With our formulation, the partial derivative of J_W with respect to the price of goods the investor does not consume is zero, so that S is the highest number of hedge portfolios an investor could take positions in. The matrix product $V^{-1}V_S$ yields S vectors that correspond to the investments in risky assets of portfolios that are minimum-variance hedges for state variable changes; whereas the elements of these vectors do not sum to one, borrowing or lending at the risk-free rate can be used to form portfolios.

The asset demands given by equation (11) are general enough that the asset demands of existing international asset pricing models with constant and identical investment opportunities across countries are special cases. The asset demands of the existing models can be obtained from equation (11) as follows:

(A) Solnik [1974a]. Solnik's model is one that focuses on consumption basket differences across countries; in his model, the price of the consumption basket consumed by investors of country j is constant in the currency of that country, so that exchange rates are relative prices of consumption baskets. To obtain Solnik's model, assume that (1) for each country there is a good whose price is constant in the currency of that country, (2) there are as many goods as there are countries, (3) investors consume only the good that has zero inflation in their country, and (4) the investment opportunity set is constant. In addition, Solnik makes the assumption that stock returns in their own currency are uncorrelated with exchange rates; this assumption was subsequently relaxed in an insightful paper by Sercu [1980]. In this model, the return on default-free bonds of a foreign country is perfectly correlated with the growth rate of the exchange rate of that country. Hence, an investor of country i can hold an asset that has a risk-free return in terms of his consumption basket, namely the bond of his country. This means that if asset demands in the model are computed in the same currency for all investors, each investor has a perfect hedge in terms of equation (11). If investors of country i want to be long in the bond of their country, however, investors of foreign countries must be short that bond when the bond is in zero net supply; hence, the portfolio that is common to all investors must include short positions in the bonds held long for hedging purposes by some investors. In the following, we call the Solnik–Sercu model the SS-IAPM.

(B) Grauer, Litzenberger & Stehle [1976]. These authors, together with Kouri [1976] and Fama & Farber [1979], consider models where purchasing power parity holds and the investment opportunity set is constant. The model of Grauer, Litzenberger and Stehle is similar to the one of Section 2. They assume that there are multiple goods. However, in their model, investors consume the same goods and hence face the same consumption opportunity set. With constant expenditure shares, there is no loss of generality in assuming that investors consume a single good which is the same for all investors. One can therefore use that good as

numeraire to obtain the ICAPM of Section 2. The Fama & Farber [1979] model assumes that investors derive benefits from holding their domestic currency. This leads to different demands for bonds across investors from different countries because a short position in a country's risk-free nominal bond can be used to hedge a long position in cash balances from this country. Stockman [1980] goes further and assumes that investors hold currencies from all countries from which they import consumption goods.

(C) Stulz [1981a] *and Adler & Dumas* [1983]. These models allow for both stochastic inflation in each country and deviations from purchasing power parity. Whereas Adler & Dumas [1983] assume a constant investment opportunity set, Stulz [1981a] does not. In these models, a domestic bond is risky in real terms for domestic investors. This means that investors who want to hold a risk-free real asset cannot do so, but instead can only hold a portfolio that has the lowest volatility in real terms. Since investors consume different consumption baskets across countries, the portfolio with lowest volatility of real returns differs across investors. Whereas Adler & Dumas [1983] posit dynamics for price levels in each country, Stulz [1981a] posits dynamics for goods prices so that the model encompasses the case where the law of one price holds for all goods but price indices differ across countries because of differences in tastes and the case where there are goods for which the law of one price does not hold, possibly because they are not traded internationally.

(D) Kouri & DeMacedo [1978]. They assume a constant investment opportunity set. In their model, each country has one good whose price is constant in the currency of that country, so that the exchange rate corresponds to a relative price. In this case, investors with constant expenditure shares can form a riskless portfolio by investing in each country's bond in proportion to the expenditure share of the good of that country. Krugman [1981] shows that the implications of this case for asset demands depend on the investors' degree of relative risk aversion, in the sense that investors with a relative risk aversion coefficient smaller than one will choose not to hedge against changes in relative prices; Stulz [1983] shows that this result holds generally only if investors have constant expenditure shares and derives results that do not rely on the assumption of constant expenditure shares.

Whereas the composition of the hedge portfolios depends on the assumptions made about exchange rate dynamics, their relevance for how investors allocate their wealth is a function of the degree of risk-aversion of investors. If investors have logarithmic utility, they take no positions in assets to hedge against changes in prices. It can be shown that if investors all have logarithmic utility, they all hold the same portfolio, which has to be the world market portfolio irrespective of how they allocate their consumption expenditures across goods. If consumption baskets differ across investors with relative risk-tolerance coefficients different from one, one can still view them as holding the portfolio they would hold if they had logarithmic utility plus positions in S hedge portfolios. However, in that case, there is no reason for the world market portfolio to be efficient for each investor since investors compute their returns differently. To see this, suppose that there is a security that has a riskless return in terms of the consumption basket of a particular investor. Obviously, this security will be an efficient portfolio for that investor. Hence, for this investor, the efficient frontier can be formed by taking combinations of that security and the portfolio the investor would hold if he had logarithmic utility. Consider now a second investor whose consumption basket is such that no risk-free security exists for that individual. For this second investor, the risk-free security of the first investor will not be an efficient portfolio and hence the efficient frontiers of the two investors differ. If there are only these two investors in the world, the world market portfolio is a weighted average of the portfolios they hold and hence is on neither efficient frontier.

The asset demands of equation (11) can be aggregated across all investors. In equilibrium, the aggregate demand for assets must equal their supply. This equilibrium condition implies that expected excess returns must satisfy the following equation:

$$V\left[w^{\mathrm{S}}H\right]' M^{-1}\left[\mu_{\mathrm{W}}\mu_{\mathrm{H}}\right] = \mu_{x} \tag{12}$$

where w^{S} is the world market portfolio, H is $V^{-1}VS$, M is $[w^{\mathrm{S}}H]'V[Hw^{\mathrm{S}}]$, μ_{W} is the expected excess return on the world market portfolio, and μ_{H} is the vector of expected excess returns on the portfolios that hedge investors against state variable risks. In this model, if investors actively hedge against state variable risks, assets that help all investors to hedge have lower expected excess returns since such assets have a higher demand than in the ICAPM. By construction, the asset pricing model derived here subsumes the various other models presented in the literature which differ with respect to their assumptions concerning the dynamics of the consumption opportunity sets of investors that reside in different countries and the dynamics of the investment opportunity set.

As with the ICAPM, the forward rate is a biased predictor of the future spot exchange rate even if there is no risk premium. However, the approach in this section makes it clear that the expected real return on forward contracts is not the same for all investors if investors have different consumption opportunity sets or different preferences for goods. For instance, Solnik's model implies that if uncovered interest rate parity holds between countries j and i from the perspective of investors from country j, a forward contract to buy currency j has a positive expected excess return for investors from country i since $E(e - F) = 0 < E(1/e - 1/F)$ from Jensen's inequality. Hence, in his model, investors in country j want to be long currency i if there is no risk premium; investors of country i are willing to be short currency i (long currency j), only if they get a positive expected excess return on the long currency j position. Black [1991] shows that this implies that in this class of models investors have long positions in foreign currencies, so that their equity holdings in foreign countries are not completely hedged against exchange rate risk.[7]

In the SS-IAPM, the hedge portfolios are the foreign currency bonds. It turns out that, in that model, one can obtain an ICAPM that can be used to price all

[7] See Adler & Prasad [1992] for a critique and elaboration of Black's approach.

risky assets except the foreign currency bonds. In that version of the model, the excess returns are the excess returns of zero investment portfolios of stocks hedged against exchange rate risk rather than the excess returns in a common numeraire used in the model presented in Section 2.[8] If the hedge portfolios are foreign currency bonds, the SS-IAPM discussed here may differ little empirically from the ICAPM discussed in the first section. To see this, note that unconditionally the two models differ because in the SS-IAPM the expected excess return on risky assets depends on their exposure to foreign currencies and hence is affected by the risk premium associated with bearing that exposure. However, unconditionally, the risk premium on positions in foreign currencies is generally not statistically different from zero.[9] Hence, in unconditional tests, the SS-IAPM and the ICAPM are unlikely to be distinguishable if one focuses on the additional risk premia associated with the SS-IAPM. Conditionally, the expected return on forward positions is not zero, so that the models can be distinguished empirically using conditional tests. Whereas the ICAPM can be interpreted as holding period by period under the assumption of logarithmic utility, the SS-IAPM collapses into the ICAPM when investors have logarithmic utility because, in that case, investors' portfolios do not depend on the numeraire. Hence, the theoretical underpinnings of conditional tests of the SS-IAPM are unclear.

An important difference between the model of Section 2 and the model of this section is that the ICAPM predicts that all investors hold the same portfolio of risky assets, whereas the model of this section (which we call the IAPM) does not. With the ICAPM, there are no risk-free nominal assets outstanding if all nominal assets are in zero net supply, since all investors would want to have identical positions in these assets. In contrast, with the model of this section, investors have positions in nominal assets that depend on their country of residence. For instance, in the SS-IAPM, investors have demands for foreign bonds which are in zero net supply.[10] In the presence of differential demands for bonds, the logarithmic portfolio includes positions in bonds. Hence, the portfolio held by a logarithmic investor differs in its composition depending on which model holds. There is evidence in Stambaugh [1982] that, in a domestic context, the inclusion of bonds in a portfolio has little impact on tests of whether that portfolio is mean–variance efficient; such evidence makes it unlikely that unconditional empirical tests could determine whether the logarithmic portfolio includes positions in foreign bonds that have negligible unconditional expected excess returns. However, whereas the

[8] Empirically, positions in foreign indices financed through foreign borrowings are generally hedged against foreign exchange risk. See, for instance, Adler & Simon [1986] and Bailey, Ng & Stulz [1992] for evidence.

[9] See Hodrick [1987] for a review of the literature on the pricing of foreign exchange risk in forward contracts.

[10] Frankel [1979] derives related asset pricing results assuming that nominal bonds are outside assets, in which case they belong to the market portfolio. In this case, the risk premium on forward contracts depends on the supplies of nominal assets. In Frankel [1982] and other papers he provides evidence that the asset demands implied by the ex post risk premia on foreign exchange do not correspond to the existing supplies of nominal assets in the context of his model.

tangency portfolio of the ICAPM is a priori observable in the sense that if one knows the asset supplies, one knows that portfolio, the same is not true for the tangency portfolio of the IAPM since knowing the asset supplies does not yield the tangency portfolio.

Whereas many models assume a constant investment opportunity set, equation (12) is consistent with an investment opportunity set which changes stochastically. Allowing the investment opportunity set to change stochastically seems important given the evidence that conditional risk premia on foreign exchange are significant and variable.[11] Such an extension implies that investors not only hedge against unanticipated changes in relative prices, but also against unanticipated changes in the joint distribution of asset returns. Hence, equation (12) incorporates additional hedge portfolios. Empirically, we therefore end up with a model where the tangency portfolio is not observable and tests of that model are misspecified if hedge portfolios are omitted. This suggests that it is better to focus on an alternative representation of expected returns that exploits the condition that the expected product of the payoffs of assets and marginal utility has to be the same for all assets to insure that expected utility is maximized. Exploiting this condition in a continuous-time model leads to a pricing equation where the risk of assets is measured in terms of the covariance of their return with respect to consumption growth. Assuming constant expenditure shares so that there is a well-defined price index, we can write that:

$$\mu_i - r = \beta_i[\mu_c - r] \tag{13}$$

where the left-hand side is the expected excess real return on asset i, β_i is the beta of the real return of asset i with respect to the real return of the portfolio whose real return is the most highly correlated with consumption growth, and μ_c is the expected real rate of return on that portfolio. In equilibrium, this equation holds for any country and hence can be implemented using the price index of just one country. It could be the case, however, that the equation holds for one country and not another simply because the first has access to all securities without barriers to international investment whereas the other does not. Hence, a test of whether markets are internationally integrated is whether the equation holds in terms of world consumption. The consumption beta model has the advantage of holding irrespective of the assumptions made about exchange rate dynamics, so that financial economists do not need to commit themselves to a specific model of exchange rate dynamics to investigate the pricing of risky assets across countries. Since it allows for changes in the investment opportunity set, it is generally consistent with general equilibrium models. In contrast, the IAPMs with constant investment opportunity sets are unlikely to be supported by general equilibrium models because, since optimal portfolios differ across countries if investors do not have logarithmic utility, relative wealth is not constant across countries. Changes

[11] It is possible for the investment opportunity set to change over time and for all investors to have the same constant, identical consumption opportunity set. Hodrick [1981] presents such a model in an international setting.

in relative wealth imply changes in asset demands and hence in risk premia which are inconsistent with a model with a constant investment opportunity set. If investors have logarithmic utility, investors' wealth will be perfectly correlated even if their consumption opportunity sets and their consumption preferences can differ across countries as shown in Stulz [1987] for a model with money and nontraded goods.

The IAPMs that imply that hedging portfolios are foreign bonds have not been tested extensively. Solnik [1974b] tests his model using stock returns from nine countries. He finds that there is substantial evidence for the presence of national factors in the pricing of common stocks. However, his sample covers the period of March 1966 to April 1971, which is a period where one would expect substantial barriers to international investment to be in place. Roll & Solnik [1977] test the model for the pricing of forward contracts and find supportive evidence. Recently, Chan, Karolyi & Stulz [1992] provide a test of the Solnik model allowing for time-varying variances and covariances for the excess returns of the S&P 500 and of the Nikkei 225 (which is assumed to proxy for the market portfolio of non-U.S. assets). With their dataset, they can reject neither the ICAPM nor the Solnik model. Dumas & Solnik [1995] provide conditional tests of the SS-IAPM; their results indicate that exposure to exchange rates significantly affects expected returns, but mostly in explaining the expected returns of short-term bonds.[12]

Recent papers emphasize the importance of allowing expected returns to change over time. Ferson & Harvey [1993], Campbell & Hamao [1992] and Bekaert & Hodrick [1992] show that expected returns of individual countries are forecastable and that the cross-sectional variation of expected returns is related to the variables that explain how expected returns vary over time.[13] These papers also suggest that the cross-sectional variation in expected returns can be understood better using additional measures of risk besides systematic risk. For instance, Ferson & Harvey [1993] show that a multi-beta model performs better than the ICAPM of Section 2. Whereas these papers indicate that time-variation in expected returns is important, they cannot be viewed as formal tests of equation (12) since they show either that more than one latent variable is needed to characterize changes in expected returns or that expected returns are related to exposure to pre-specified factors. In contrast, however, the consumption-beta model has been tested and seems to do reasonably well at explaining the cross-sectional distribution of returns across countries [Wheatley, 1988, and Cumby, 1990] and at explaining the returns on forward contracts [Cumby, 1988]. In Wheatley's case, the model does poorly for a few countries that may not be well-integrated in international asset markets, whereas in Cumby's case the model does much better for the 1980s than for a longer sample period. Although the theoretical case for the consumption ICAPM

[12] See also Lewis [1988]. She tests a model that is similar to the Adler and Dumas model for currencies, implicitly assuming that currency returns are uncorrelated with stock returns. Her results are generally negative.

[13] Solnik [1993] also provides evidence that expected returns are forecastable, but his work focuses on the implications of forecastability for portfolio choice rather than for asset pricing.

is strong, testing of the model suffers from the deficiencies of the consumption data which limit the power of tests.

The usefulness of international asset pricing models can be investigated by considering their implications for asset demands as well as their implications for expected excess returns. The SS-IAPM model predicts that investors hold identical common stock portfolios and hence cannot explain the home-bias in portfolio holdings. The Adler and Dumas model does not make the same prediction, but they argue that empirically it is likely to yield the same conclusion as the SS-IAPM because there is little variability in inflation rates and, for a particular investor, the hedge portfolio is most likely to be composed of the default-free bonds from his country. In contrast, there is no a priori reason why the consumption asset pricing model cannot explain asset holdings across countries since it allows relative stock holdings to differ across countries. In principle, any bias in equity holdings can be consistent with the consumption asset pricing model; however, the literature has failed either empirically or theoretically to provide convincing evidence that the bias results from differences in consumption preferences and opportunity sets. For instance, Uppal [1993] builds on the model of departures from the law of one price of Dumas [1992] and finds the paradoxical results that, in his model, if investors choose to hedge against deviations from the law of one price, the home-bias will be exhibited by investors with a relative risk-aversion coefficient below one. Hence, in his model, investors exhibit a home-bias only if their degree of risk-aversion is low. On the empirical front, Cooper & Kaplanis [1994] provide some evidence that the magnitude of the home-bias cannot be explained by a model with deviations from purchasing power parity such as the Adler and Dumas model.

4. Barriers to international investment

Existing evidence on the ICAPM and on the international consumption asset pricing model shows that the models do not work well for some countries. Viewed more broadly, tests of these models against a null hypothesis that the relationships posited by these models do not hold are not very powerful against alternative hypotheses that there are some barriers to international investment. To understand this, note that if there are barriers to international investment that imply that returns in a country differ from those predicted by the ICAPM or consumption-based model, but the abnormal returns implied by the barriers are small, empirical tests will not be able to find evidence of these abnormal returns. Yet, for the central question of why investors prefer home-country assets, relatively small abnormal returns due to barriers to international investment can have a big impact on asset holdings and can explain the home-country bias. To seek evidence on barriers to international investment, the lack of power of asset pricing tests with unspecified null hypotheses has led to two approaches. First, models that explicitly specify the impact of barriers to international investment have been developed and tested. Second, authors have focused on cases where more direct approaches permit more precise measurement of barriers to international investment. We discuss these two literatures in turn.

To understand the impact of barriers to international investment on asset demands, consider again the asset demands developed in Section 3, but now allow for the existence of barriers to international investment whereby a domestic investor holding asset ij long must pay a tax per unit invested of δ_{lij}. A domestic investor holding the same asset short must pay a tax per unit invested of δ_{sij}. In this case, a straightforward extension of Stulz [1981b] shows that asset demands can be written:

$$\begin{aligned} &V^{-1}\left[\left(\frac{-J_W}{J_{WW}W}\right)[\mu_{\mathrm{w}}-\delta_l]-\frac{\mu}{J_{WW}W}\right]+V^{-1}V_S\left(\frac{-J_{WS}}{J_{WW}W}\right)-s\geq l \\ &V^{-1}\left[\left(\frac{-J_W}{J_{WW}W}\right)[\mu_{\mathrm{w}}-\delta_s]-\frac{\omega}{J_{WW}W}\right]+V^{-1}V_S\left(\frac{-J_{WS}}{J_{WW}W}\right)-l\leq s \end{aligned} \tag{14}$$

where δ_l and δ_s are the vectors of tax rates on long and short positions respectively, μ and ω are the vectors of Lagrangean multipliers associated with the constraints that long positions and short positions must be positive. l and s are respectively the long and short positions of investors expressed as fractions of their wealth. Since the tax rates differ for long and short positions, we now have two sets of asset demands. These asset demands are formulated using inequalities because it is possible for an investor to neither want a long nor a short position in an asset. In other words, in this model it is possible for some assets to be nontraded. Intuitively, barriers to international investment lower the expected excess return on foreign assets for domestic investors. For an investor to still be willing to take a position in the asset, it must be that the diversification or hedging benefits that come from this asset must be large enough to offset its lower return. Not surprisingly, the barriers to international investment considered here reduce holdings of foreign assets because, being nonstochastic, they do not affect the variance of the return of a portfolio held without barriers, but decrease its expected excess return.

The asset demands given in equation (14) are the canonical asset demands of models with investment barriers, since these models can be obtained from equation (14) by making the following assumptions:

(A) Black [1974]. Black's model assumes that investors face different tax rates depending on their country of residence and that investment and consumption opportunity sets are constant. These taxes are imposed on the absolute amount invested in a country and hence are not taxes on income. The model has no short-sale restrictions. Since the tax rate is assumed to be the same on short and long positions, investors pay negative taxes on short positions since taxes paid are the tax rate times the size of the position. Further, the investment opportunity set is constant and identical for all investors. Since there are no short-sale restrictions, his model can be obtained by setting $\delta_{lij} = \delta_{sij}$ for all assets, in which case the distinction between short and long positions becomes irrelevant, and by assuming that relative prices are constant. With this model, the asset demands differ across countries because tax rates differ across countries.

(B) Stulz [1981b]. The interest of the Black model is largely that the tax rates can proxy for costs of international diversification. With this interpretation, the tax rates can proxy for per period pecuniary or nonpecuniary costs of holding foreign assets. The Black model implies, however, that short positions in foreign assets are subsidized since they have negative tax payments. The Stulz [1981b] model assumes that investors pay a positive per-period tax whether they are long or short in a foreign asset and otherwise makes the same assumptions as those required by the Black model. A direct implication of this positive tax assumption is that some domestic assets are held only by domestic investors because they do not provide diversification benefits large enough to overcome the tax.

(C) Errunza & Losq [1985] *and Eun & Janakiramanan* [1986]. These papers assume that some securities are not available internationally, which amounts to assuming that the tax rate is infinite for some securities in the Stulz model. The Errunza & Losq [1985] paper considers the case where securities from a country are not available to foreign investors, but investors from that country can invest abroad. In contrast, in the Eun & Janakiramanan [1986] paper, the country with restrictions makes some securities available, but possibly only to a limited extent.

There exist a number of empirical tests of these models with barriers. Wheatley [1988] uses the Stulz [1981b] model as the alternative to the international consumption pricing model discussed in the previous section and finds evidence of significant barriers to international investment for some countries. Errunza and Losq provide empirical evidence supportive of their model. Hietala [1989] tests a model similar to the Eun & Janakiramanan [1986] model using Finland as the country with restricted shares and finds supportive evidence.

The problem with using asset pricing models to test for the existence of barriers to international investment is that such tests typically lack power. The estimates are sufficiently imprecise that tests that use market integration as the null hypothesis cannot reject the existence of economically significant barriers. To wit, a barrier that reduces the return on foreign securities by 200 basis points a year would be economically significant. For instance, such a barrier would be sufficient to explain much of the home-bias in portfolio holdings [see Cooper & Kaplanis, 1994]. However, asset pricing tests typically cannot reject the hypothesis that such a barrier exists when they fail to reject market integration. An alternative approach to studying barriers to international investment is to examine whether the law of one price holds for securities. This approach compares prices of identical securities that trade in different countries. The most common tests of the law of one price on security markets focus on the interest rate parity theorem. Recently, however, a number of papers have investigated the pricing of similar securities on different markets.

Much attention has been given to the Euromarkets in this research because of the often made claim by corporate treasurers that they can borrow more cheaply on these markets than on domestic markets. There is some limited evidence of profitable arbitrage transactions where corporations could borrow more cheaply on the Eurobond markets than the U.S. Treasury could in the U.S. markets at the same time. There is also substantial evidence that issuing securities offshore could increase shareholder wealth relative to issuing in domestic markets when foreign holders of bonds issued in the U.S. had to pay a withholding tax.[14] Whereas this evidence focuses on corporate bonds, there is also some related evidence on equities. In particular, there is substantial evidence that stocks that differ only because of their availability to foreign investors sell for different prices and that the more widely available stocks sell for a relatively higher price [see, for instance, Hietala, 1989, and Stulz & Wasserfallen, 1995].

5. An assessment of the current state of international finance

At this point, the international finance literature has a number of theoretical models that are consistent with the most salient facts about international capital markets. The empirical work has progressed dramatically during the 1980s with the greater availability of data. The main conclusion of this empirical work seems to be that when one focuses on indices across countries, much of the evidence is consistent with market integration. The problem with most existing empirical work, though, is that the tests seem to have limited power in assessing the importance of barriers to international investment. Further, if the home-bias is the outcome of investors' optimization, existing tests of international asset pricing models do not have enough power to provide support for this view. Finally, the models seem to fare poorly when tests investigate the returns of individuals stocks and/or bonds.[15]

A more fundamental criticism can be directed at much of the existing literature reviewed in this paper, though. Neither the ICAPM nor the IAPM are specifically international models. Though these models allow for differences in inflation rates across countries, they could as well be used to characterize asset demands within the U.S. Why should the differences in consumption opportunities between Paris and Geneva be more important than differences in consumption opportunities between Anchorage and Key West? Though some argue that departures from PPP make asset pricing models truly international, would somebody be willing to argue that the law of one price holds better between Anchorage and Key West than it does between Paris and Geneva? There is a fundamental difference between Paris and Geneva which does not exist between Anchorage and Key West. Paris and Geneva belong to different countries. Governments affect saving and investment decisions of investors in crucial ways:

(i) They define the rights and obligations of the holders of financial assets issued within a country and can change these definitions. This power allows them to discriminate against or in favor of foreign investors.

(ii) They define the rights and obligations of the residents of a country. In

[14] See Kim & Stulz [1989] for evidence and references to other papers studying the Euromarkets.

[15] In a recent study, Bansal, Hsieh & Viswanathan [1993 (p. 1742)] write that 'The challenge in international asset pricing is in explaining forward contracts and bond returns and not stock index returns'.

particular, they determine how income is taxed, how assets are traded and how residents can invest abroad.

(iii) They define legal tender within the country. Hence, they make it necessary for investors to hold the currency of the country, in contrast to many models of international asset pricing where the location of an investor is irrelevant in his portfolio decisions.

The fact that the existence of countries has implications for the saving and investment decisions of investors is the foundation of international finance and makes international finance a field that is distinct from domestic finance. Hopefully, much of future research in international finance will focus on questions that would not arise if there was only one country.

A less ambitious but more clearly defined research agenda for the field of international finance should include the following avenues of research:

1. One approach to obtain more powerful tests of international asset pricing models is to use more securities. Most existing empirical work uses indices; work that uses large numbers of securities for different countries seems to be primarily devoted to studying the relation between asset returns in two countries rather than to testing international asset pricing models.[16]

2. Most empirical work tests the hypothesis of market integration against an unidentified alternative hypothesis. Since there exist well-specified models with barriers to international investment, tests could gain more power by searching for pricing patterns that are consistent with specific types of barriers to international investment.

3. Whereas taxation regimes differ across countries, we have little understanding of how these differences affect portfolio decisions, expected returns, asset supplies and the growth of markets.

4. It is now clear that holdings of foreign securities, and hence the extent of the home bias, change over time. A challenge for both theoretical and empirical work is to explain these changes and to construct models that are consistent with such changes. Presumably, one reason for such changes is that barriers to international investment change over time, but we have little in the way of theory that explains why such barriers exist or why they change over time.

5. Most models reviewed in this paper take exchange rate dynamics as given. Models which describe more explicitly the determinants of exchange rate changes should provide more testable restrictions on asset prices and make clearer which dynamics for asset prices are consistent with existing theories of exchange rate determination.[17]

[16] For instance, Jorion & Schwartz [1986] investigate jointly the U.S. and Canadian stock markets and find evidence against integration. More recently, Mittoo [1992] finds that interlisted stocks seem priced in an integrated market, whereas Canadian stocks trading only in Canada only do not.

[17] See Uppal [1993] for work that attempts to use the Dumas [1992] model to address this issue. Models without frictions in commodity markets include Stockman [1980], Stulz [1984, 1987] and Svensson [1987].

Acknowledgements

I am grateful to Warren Bailey, Lee Riddick, Piet Sercu and Bruno Solnik for useful comments.

References

Adler, M., and B. Dumas (1983). International portfolio choice and corporation finance: A synthesis. *J. Finance* 38, 925–984.

Adler, M., and B. Prasad (1992). On universal currency hedges, *J. Financ. Quant. Anal.* 27, 19–38.

Adler, M., and D. Simon (1986). Exchange risk suprises in international portfolios. *J. Portfolio Manage.* 12, 44–53.

Backus, D.K.G., A.W. Gregory and C.I. Telmer (1993). Accounting for forward rates in markets for foreign currency. *J. Finance* 48, 1887–1909.

Bansal, R., D.A. Hsieh, and S. Viswanathan (1993). A new approach to international arbitrage pricing. *J. Finance* 48, 1719–1749.

Bailey, W., E. Ng and R.M. Stulz (1992). Optimal hedging of stock portfolios against foreign exchange risk: The case of the Nikkei 225, *Global Finance J.* 3, 97–114.

Bekaert, G., and R.J. Hodrick (1992). Characterizing predictable components in excess returns on equity and foreign exchange markets. *J. Finance* 47, 467–510.

Black, F. (1974). International capital market equilibrium with investment barriers. *J. Financ. Econ.* 1, 337–352.

Black, F. (1991). Equilibrium exchange rate hedging. *J. Finance* 45, 899–909.

Campbell, J.Y., and Y. Hamao (1992). Predictable stock returns in the United States and Japan: A study of long-term capital market integration. *J. Finance* 47, 43–69.

Chan, K.C., G.A. Karolyi and R.M. Stulz (1992). Global financial markets and the risk premium on U.S. equity. *J. Financ. Econ.* 32, 137–167.

Chen, N.-F., R.R. Roll and S.A. Ross (1986). Economic forces and the stock market. *J. Bus.* 59, 383–403.

Cho, D.C., Eun, C.S., and L.W. Senbet (1986). International arbitrage pricing theory: An empirical investigation. *J. Finance* 41, 313–329.

Cooper, I.A., and E. Kaplanis (1994). What explains the home bias in portfolio investment, *Rev. Financ. Studies* 7, 45–60.

Cumby, R.E. (1988). Is it risk? Explaining deviations from uncovered interest rate parity. *J. Monetary Econ.* 22, 279–299.

Cumby, R.E. (1990). Consumption risk and international equity returns: Some empirical evidence. *J. Int. Money Finance* 9, 182–192.

Cumby, R.E., and J.D. Glen (1990). Evaluating the performance of international mutual funds. *J. Finance* 45, 497–522.

Cumby, R.E., and M. Obstfeld (1984). International interest rate and price level linkages under floating exchanges: A review of recent evidence, in: J.F.O. Bilson and R. Marston (eds.), *Exchange Rate Theory and Practice*, University of Chicago Press, Chicago, IL.

Dumas, B. (1992). Dynamic equilibrium and the real exchange rate in a spatially separated world. *Rev. Financ. Studies* 5, 153–180.

Dumas, B., and B. Solnik (1995). The world price of exchange rate risk, *J. Finance* 50, 445–479.

Errunza, V., and E. Losq (1985). International asset pricing under mild segmentation: Theory and tests. *J. Finance* 40, 105–124.

Eun, C.S., and B.G. Resnick (1988). Exchange rate uncertainty, forward contracts, and international portfolio selection. *J. Finance* 43, 197–216.

Eun. C.S., and S. Janakiramanan (1986). A model of international asset pricing with a constraint on the foreign equity ownership. *J. Finance* 44, 1025–1038.

Fama, E.F., and A. Farber (1979). Money, bonds and foreign exchange. *Am. Econ. Rev.* 69, 639–649.

Ferson, W.E., and C.R. Harvey (1993). The risk and predictability of international equity returns. *Rev. Financ. Studies* 6, 527–567.

Frankel, J. (1979). The diversifiability of exchange risk. *J. Int. Econ.* 9, 379–394.

Frankel, J. (1982). In search of the exchange-risk premium: A six-currency test assuming mean–variance optimization. *J. Int. Money Finance* 1, 255–274.

French, K.R., and J.M. Poterba (1991). Investor diversification and international equity markets. *Am. Econ. Rev.*, Pap. Proc., pp. 222–226.

Giovannini, A., and P. Jorion (1989). The time variation of risk and return in the foreign exchange and stock markets. *J. Finance* 44, 307–325.

Grauer, F.L.A., R.H. Litzenberger and R.S. Stehle (1976). Sharing rules and equilibrium in an international capital market under uncertainty. *J. Financ. Econ.* 3, 233–256.

Gultekin N.M., N.B. Gultekin and A. Penati (1989). Capital controls and international capital market segmentation: The evidence from the Japanese and American stock markets. *J. Finance* 44, 849–869.

Harvey, C.R. (1991). The world price of covariance risk. *J. Finance* 46, 111–157.

Hietala, P.K. (1989). Asset pricing in partially segmented markets. *J. Finance* 44, 697–715.

Hodrick, R. (1981). International asset pricing with time-varying risk premia. *J. Int. Econ.* 11, 573–575.

Hodrick, R.J. (1987). *The Empirical Evidence on the Efficiency of Forward and Futures Markets*, Harwood Academic Publishers, London.

Huang, C.-F., and R.H. Litzenberger (1988). *Foundations for Financial Economics*, North-Holland, New York.

Ikeda, S. (1991). Arbitrage asset pricing under exchange risk. *J. Finance* 46, 447–455.

Jorion, P., and E. Schwartz (1986). Integration versus segmentation in the Canadian stock market. *J. Finance* 41, 603–613.

Kim, Y.C., and R.M. Stulz (1989). The Eurobond market and corporate financial policy: A test of the clientele hypothesis. *J. Financ. Econ.* 22, 189–225.

Korajczyk, R.A., and C.J. Viallet (1989). An empirical investigation of international asset pricing. *Rev. Financ. Studies* 2, 553–585.

Korajczyk, R.A., and C.J. Viallet (1993). Equity risk premia and the pricing of foreign exchange risk. *J. Int. Econ.* 33, 199–228.

Kouri, P. (1976). The determinants of the forward premium, IIES Seminar Paper 62, University of Stockholm, Stockholm, Sweden.

Kouri, P., and B. De Macedo (1978). Exchange rates and the international adjustment process, Brookings Papers on Economic Activity, pp. 111–150.

Krugman, P. (1981). Consumption preferences, asset demands, and the distribution effects in international financial markets, Working Paper No. 651, National Bureau of Economic Research, Boston, MA.

Lewis, K.K. (1988). Inflation risk and asset market disturbances: The mean–variance model revisited. *J. Int. Money Finance* 7, 273–288.

Mark, N.C. (1988). Time-varying betas and risk premia in the pricing of forward foreign exchange contracts. *J. Financ. Econ.* 22, 3–18.

McCurdy, T.H., and I.G. Morgan (1991). Tests for a systematic risk component in deviations from uncovered interest rate parity. *Rev. Econ. Studies* 58, 587–602.

Merton, R.C. (1973). An intertemporal capital asset pricing model, *Econometrica* 41, 867–888.

Mittoo, U.R. (1992). Additional evidence on integration in the Canadian stock market. *J. Finance* 47, 2035–2054.

Roll, R., and B. Solnik (1977). A pure foreign exchange asset pricing model. *J. Int. Econ.* 7, 161–179.

Sercu, P. (1980). A generalization of the international asset pricing model. *Rev. Assoc. Fr. Finance* 1, 91–135.

Solnik, B.H. (1974a). An equilibrium model of the international capital market. *J. Econ. Theory* 8, 500–524.

Solnik, B.H. (1974b). The international pricing of risk: An empirical investigation of the world capital market structure. *J. Finance* 29, 48–54.

Solnik, B.H. (1983). International arbitrage pricing theory. *J. Finance* 38, 449–457.

Solnik, B.H. (1993). The performance of international asset allocation strategies using conditioning information. *J. Empirical Finance* 1, 33–55.

Stambaugh, R.F. (1982). On the exclusion of assets from tests of the two-parameter model: A sensitivity analysis. *J. Financ. Econ.* 10, 235–237.

Stehle, R. (1977). An empirical test of the alternative hypotheses of national and international pricing of risky assets. *J. Finance* 32, 493–502.

Stockman, A.C. (1980). A theory of exchange rate determination. *J. Polit. Econ.* 88, 673–698.

Stulz, R.M. (1981a). A model of international asset pricing. *J. Financ. Econ.* 9, 383–406.

Stulz, R.M. (1981b). On the effects of barriers to international investment. *J. Finance* 36, 923–934.

Stulz, R.M. (1983). The demand for foreign bonds. *J. Int. Econ.*, 383–406.

Stulz, R.M. (1984). Currency preferences, purchasing power risks and the determination of exchange rates. *J. Money, Credit Banking* 16, 302–316.

Stulz, R.M. (1987). An equilibrium model of exchange rate determination and asset pricing with nontraded goods and imperfect information. *J. Polit. Econ.* 95, 1024–1041.

Stulz, R.M., and W. Wasserfallen (1995). Foreign equity investment restrictions: Theory and evidence, *Rev. Financ. Studies* (forthcoming).

Svensson, L. (1987). Currency prices, terms of trade and interest rates: A general equilibrium asset-pricing, cash-in-advance approach. *J. Int. Econ.* 18, 17–41.

Tesar, L., and I.M. Werner (1993). Home bias and the globalization of securities markets, unpublished working paper, Stanford University.

Uppal, R. (1993). A general equilibrium model of international portfolio choice, *J. Finance* 48, 529–553.

Wheatley, S. (1988). Some tests of international equity integration. *J. Financ. Econ.* 21, 177–212.

R. Jarrow et al., Eds., *Handbooks in OR & MS, Vol. 9*

Chapter 7

A Discrete Time Synthesis of Derivative Security Valuation Using a Term Structure of Futures Prices

Peter P. Carr and Robert A. Jarrow

Johnson Graduate School of Management, Cornell University, Ithaca, NY 14853, U.S.A.

1. Introduction

> Because options are specialized and relatively unimportant financial securities, the amount of time and space devoted to the development of a pricing theory might be questioned. One justification is that ...

The above quote is taken from Robert C. Merton's classic article [1973] 'Theory of Rational Option Pricing'. Apparently, the justification given by the author was persuasive; as of April 1994, this paper had 543 citations. The classic paper by Black & Scholes [1973] 'The Pricing of Options and Corporate Liabilities' had 955 citations. In his entry entitled 'Finance' in the New Palgrave Dictionary of Economics and Finance, Ross [1992] writes:

> when judged by its ability to explain the empirical data, option-pricing theory is the most successful theory not only in finance, but in all of economics. It is now widely employed by the financial industry and its impact on economics has been far-ranging.

Although Ross eloquently surveys the entire field of finance in about 15 pages, we feel that an attempt to survey the voluminous futures and option pricing literature would be impossible. We have instead opted to provide an analytic synthesis of the literature in the text, and to briefly describe several surveys, texts, anthologies, and journals on the subject in this introduction. Since we may have omitted several important references in our brief review, we would like to issue an apology to our slighted readers.

The progression of academic thought on the subject of futures and option pricing theory is easily discerned by scanning the large number of surveys on the subject. An early survey by Smith [1976] stresses the analytic point of view prevalent in the early to mid 70s. A later survey [Smith, 1979] by the same author emphasizes applications in corporate finance, as does the even later survey by Mason & Merton [1985]. More recent introductory surveys are contained in Merton [1990], Rubinstein [1987], and Van Hulle [1988]. Entries relating to Option Pricing Theory in the New Palgrave Dictionary of Economics include those by Babbs & Selby [1992], Finnerty [1992], Ingersoll [1992b], Jarrow [1992], Merton [1992], and Ross [1992]. Empirical validation of option pricing models is ably summarized in Galai [1983] and Geske & Trautmann [1986]. Alternative stochastic processes for the price of the underlying asset are emphasized in Cox & Rubinstein [1983] and Jarrow & Wiggins [1989]. Similarly, alternative contractual structures are valued in a review of exotic options by Rubinstein & Reiner [1992]. The survey by Cox & Huang [1989] is excellent for understanding the early literature in the context of the modern martingale technology. Finally, the surveys by Jarrow [1995, this volume], Jarrow & Turnbull [1992] and by Clewlow, Hodges, Selby, Strickland & Xu [1992] discuss term structure models and serve as excellent companion readings for the current paper.

Textbooks on the subject of futures and option pricing theory are usually aimed at either master's students, practitioners, or doctoral students. The early texts by Cox & Rubinstein [1985] and Jarrow & Rudd [1983] were aimed at master's level students and practitioners. Several later books appeal to both undergraduates and master's students including those by Chance [1989], Figlewski, Silber & Subrahmanyam [1990], Hull [1991], Ritchken [1987], and Stoll & Whaley [1993]. Books by Bookstaber [1987], Gastineau [1988], Hull [1992], and McMillan [1993], appeal to practitioners. Books primarily oriented towards futures contracts include those by Duffie [1989] and Kolb [1991]. Several doctoral level books contain useful chapters on option pricing theory, including those by Duffie [1992], Dothan [1990], Huang & Litzenberger [1988], Ingersoll [1987], Shimko [1991], and Wilmott, DeWynne & Howison [1993]. Anthologies which wholly or mainly consist of articles on option pricing include those edited by Brenner [1983], Bhattacharya & Constantinides [1989], Chance & Trippi [1993], Fabozzi [1991], Field, Jaycolbs & Tompkins [1992], Hodges [1990], Kolb [1992], Merton [1990], Smith & Smithson [1990], and Whaley [1992]. Two forthcoming books intended to be of general interest are Carr, Reiner & Rubinstein on exotic options and Jarrow on interest rate derivatives.

Most of the widely cited articles on option pricing theory have appeared in journals of general interest to finance academics. However, several journals exist which are either exclusively oriented towards derivative securities or have an emphasis on derivatives. These include Journal of Applied Mathematical Finance, Journal of Derivatives, Review of Derivatives Research, Journal of Financial Engineering, Journal of Fixed Income, Journal of Futures Markets, Review of Futures Markets, and Mathematical Finance.

In the remainder of the paper, we present an analytic synthesis of the discrete-time option pricing literature. Our motivation for focussing on discrete-time models lies in the inherent simplicity of this approach. In the next section, we present a general model which posits a stochastic process on a term structure of futures prices. In this model, we show the equivalence between the absence of arbitrage and the existence of an equivalent martingale measure. Since we work in a complete market, the results of Harrison and Pliska [1981] imply that this measure is unique. We illustrate the martingale measure methodology for both European and American-style options. In the third section, we review existing discrete-time option models and show they may be considered as special cases of our general framework. The fourth section discusses the implementation of our futures term structure model. The final section concludes.

2. The general framework

This section presents the general framework for valuing derivative securities. Every existing arbitrage-free derivatives pricing model will be shown to be a special case of this approach.

2.1. The model

Consider a frictionless economy with discrete trading dates $t \in [0, 1, 2, \ldots, \tau]$, where for simplicity, the trading horizon is finite ($\tau < \infty$). At each trading date, investors can borrow or lend risklessly and trade in a term structure of futures contracts. At date $t \in [0, \tau]$, the (gross) spot riskless rate is denoted by $r_t \geq 1$ and the futures price is denoted by $F_{t,T}$, where $T \in [t, \tau]$ is the the delivery date. We assume marking-to-market occurs once[1] per period for simplicity. In other words, an investor going long one futures contract with maturity T at time t will receive $F_{t+1,T} - F_{t,T}$ in cash at time $t + 1$.

For simplicity, we use a binomial tree to describe the evolution of the entire futures price curve and spot interest rate over time. The tree starts out at time 0 with the $(\tau + 2)$ vector $[S_0, F_{0,1}, F_{0,2}, \ldots, F_{0,\tau}; r_0]$. It evolves over the first period as given below:

$$\begin{pmatrix} S_0 \\ F_{0,1} \\ F_{0,2} \\ \vdots \\ F_{0,\tau} \\ \cdots\cdots \\ r_0 \end{pmatrix} \begin{array}{l} \overset{p_0}{\nearrow} \begin{pmatrix} S_1^{\mathrm{u}} \equiv F_{0,1} \cdot u_{0,1} \\ F_{1,2}^{\mathrm{u}} \equiv F_{0,2} \cdot u_{0,2} \\ \vdots \\ F_{1,\tau}^{\mathrm{u}} \equiv F_{0,\tau} \cdot u_{0,\tau} \\ \cdots\cdots \\ r_1^{\mathrm{u}} \end{pmatrix} \\ \\ \underset{1-p_0}{\searrow} \begin{pmatrix} S_1^{\mathrm{d}} \equiv F_{0,1} \cdot d_{0,1} \\ F_{1,2}^{\mathrm{d}} \equiv F_{0,2} \cdot d_{0,2} \\ \vdots \\ F_{1,\tau}^{\mathrm{d}} \equiv F_{0,\tau} \cdot d_{0,\tau} \\ \cdots\cdots \\ r_1^{\mathrm{d}} \end{pmatrix} \end{array}$$

[1] Under *deterministic* interest rates, it is well-known that the futures price for any marking-to-market frequency is equal to the forward price. Consequently, the frequency of marking-to-market would have no effect on the futures price.

where $u_{0,T} > d_{0,T} > 0$ for all $T \in \{0, 1, 2, \ldots, \tau\}$. The entire curve moves 'up' with probability $p_0 \in (0, 1)$ or 'down' with probability $1 - p_0$. As the curve evolves, there is one less futures price available as $F_{0,1}$ becomes the new spot price S_1 with value $S_1^{\mathrm{u}} \equiv F_{0,1} \cdot u_{0,1}$ if the process moves up and value $S_1^{\mathrm{d}} \equiv F_{0,1} \cdot d_{0,1}$ if the process moves down. The first element S_0 in the vector disappears. Each futures price is allowed to have its own up and down price relative. For example, $u_{0,1}$ can differ from $u_{0,2}$.

The evolution of the spot interest rate is appended onto each vector. The initial spot rate r_0 changes to r_1^{u} with probability p_0 and to r_1^{d} with probability $1 - p_0$. The implicit assumption here is that the futures price curve and spot interest rate are driven by the same factor. This assumption can be easily relaxed by adding additional branches to the tree. Three branches emanating from each node would imply a two factor model; four branches would imply a three factor model, and so on. Our restriction of two branches is easily relaxed; the generalization is left to the reader.

At an arbitrary step t to $t + 1$, the tree looks like:

$$\begin{pmatrix} S_t \\ F_{t,t+1} \\ F_{t,t+2} \\ \vdots \\ F_{t,\tau} \\ \cdots \\ r_t \end{pmatrix} \begin{array}{l} \xrightarrow{\;p_t\;} \begin{pmatrix} S_{t+1}^{\mathrm{u}} \equiv F_{t,t+1} \cdot u_{t,t+1} \\ F_{t+1,t+2}^{\mathrm{u}} \equiv F_{t,t+2} \cdot u_{t,t+2} \\ \vdots \\ F_{t+1,\tau}^{\mathrm{u}} \equiv F_{t,\tau} \cdot u_{t,\tau} \\ \cdots\cdots \\ r_{t+1}^{\mathrm{u}} \end{pmatrix} \\ \xrightarrow{\;1-p_t\;} \begin{pmatrix} S_{t+1}^{\mathrm{d}} \equiv F_{t,t+1} \cdot d_{t,t+1} \\ F_{t+1,t+2}^{\mathrm{d}} \equiv F_{t,t+2} \cdot d_{t,t+2} \\ \vdots \\ F_{t+1,\tau}^{\mathrm{d}} \equiv F_{t,\tau} \cdot d_{t,\tau} \\ \cdots\cdots \\ r_{t+1}^{\mathrm{d}} \end{pmatrix} \end{array}$$

where $p_t \in (0, 1)$ and $u_{t,T} > d_{t,T} > 0$ for all $T \in [t + 1, \ldots, \tau]$.

At the last step from $\tau - 1$ to τ, the process is:

$$\begin{pmatrix} S_{\tau-1} \\ F_{\tau-1,\tau} \\ \cdots \\ r_{\tau-1} \end{pmatrix} \begin{array}{l} \xrightarrow{\;p_{\tau-1}\;} \begin{pmatrix} S_\tau^{\mathrm{u}} \equiv F_{\tau-1,\tau} \cdot u_{\tau-1,\tau} \\ \cdots\cdots \\ r_\tau^{\mathrm{u}} \end{pmatrix} \\ \xrightarrow{\;1-p_{\tau-1}\;} \begin{pmatrix} S_\tau^{\mathrm{d}} \equiv F_{\tau-1,\tau} \cdot d_{\tau-1,\tau} \\ \cdots\cdots \\ r_\tau^{\mathrm{d}} \end{pmatrix} \end{array}$$

where $p_\tau \in (0, 1)$ and $u_{\tau-1,\tau} > d_{\tau-1,\tau} > 0$. The process ends here. By definition, $S_\tau^{\mathrm{u}} \equiv F_{\tau-1,\tau} \cdot u_{\tau-1,\tau}$ is the spot price at τ if the process moves up over the last period and $S_\tau^{\mathrm{d}} \equiv F_{\tau-1,\tau} \cdot d_{\tau-1,\tau}$ is the spot price at τ if the process moves down.

We have assumed that the probabilities p_t and $1 - p_t$ and the price relatives $u_{t,T}$ and $d_{t,T}$ are strictly positive. If either probability is ever zero, then the process is locally riskless, which is economically uninteresting. If the down price relative is ever zero, then the process absorbs at the origin the first time that such a down jump occurs. For simplicity of the notation and presentation, we have assumed that these probabilities and price relatives do not depend on the state (i.e. node in the tree) or path. The generalization to state or path-dependent probabilities or price relatives is straightforward.

The futures contracts of different maturities are close substitutes, having the same underlying asset with only differing delivery dates. Consequently, when exogenously specifying the stochastic process for the futures price curve, we must be concerned that the process specified admits no arbitrage opportunities. This is the topic of the next subsection.

2.2. *Arbitrage opportunities, market completeness, and martingale probabilities*

Given the stochastic process for the evolution of the futures price curve, we next determine the restrictions required on the up and down price relatives $u_{t,T}$ and $d_{t,T}$ across maturities $T \in [t, \tau]$, $t \in [0, \tau]$ such that there are no arbitrage opportunities.

First, consider the futures price of a fixed maturity T. Over the interval $[t, t+1]$, the evolution of this futures price and the spot interest rate is:

$$\begin{pmatrix} F_{t,T} \\ \cdots \\ r_t \end{pmatrix} \begin{array}{l} \xrightarrow{\;p_t\;} \begin{pmatrix} F^{\mathrm{u}}_{t+1,T} \equiv F_{t,T} \cdot u_{t,T} \\ \cdots\cdots \\ r^{\mathrm{u}}_{t+1} \end{pmatrix}, \quad \text{if 'up'} \\[2ex] \xrightarrow{\;1-p_t\;} \begin{pmatrix} F^{\mathrm{d}}_{t+1,T} \equiv F_{t,T} \cdot d_{t,T} \\ \cdots\cdots \\ r^{\mathrm{d}}_{t+1} \end{pmatrix}, \quad \text{if 'down'.} \end{array}$$

We claim that there are no arbitrage opportunities between these two securities only if[2]

$$u_{t,T} > 1 > d_{t,T} \text{ for all } t \in [0, \tau] \text{ and for all } T \in [t, \tau]. \tag{1}$$

Otherwise, for example, if $1 \leq d_{t,T} < u_{t,T}$, then an arbitrage opportunity is generated by going long the futures at t and receiving at least $F_{t,T}(d_{t,T} - 1) \geq 0$ at the next marking-to-market at $t + 1$. The arbitrageur then reverses the long position costlessly. Conversely, if $1 \geq u_{t,T} > d_{t,T}$, then an arbitrage opportunity is generated by going short the futures at t and receiving at least $F_{t,T}(1 - u_{t,T}) > 0$ at $t + 1$. These contradictions yield the result.

[2] Condition (1) is also sufficient for no arbitrage. A sketch of the proof is that (4) is equivalent to (1), and (4) implies V_t/B_t in (8) is a martingale. An arbitrage opportunity would contradict that V_t/B_t is a martingale (for the arbitrage opportunity). This completes the argument.

Expression (1) holds if and only if there exists a *unique* number $\pi_{t,T}$ satisfying $0 < \pi_{t,T} < 1$ such that:

$$\pi_{t,T} \cdot u_{t,T} + (1 - \pi_{t,T}) \cdot d_{t,T} = 1. \tag{2}$$

The unique number $\pi_{t,T}$ is called a *pseudo-probability* or *a martingale probability*. To see this latter interpretation, multiply expression (2) by $F_{t,T}$:

$$\pi_{t,T} F_{t,T} \cdot u_{t,T} + (1 - \pi_{t,T}) F_{t,T} \cdot d_{t,T} = F_{t,T}. \tag{3}$$

or

$$E_{t,T} F_{t+1,T} = F_{t,T}, \tag{4}$$

for all $T \in [t+1, \tau]$. To prove $E_{t,T} F_{t+i,T} = F_{t,T}$ for all $i = 1, \ldots \tau - t$ and $T \in [t+i, \tau]$, use induction and the law of iterated expectations. Thus, $F_{t,T}$ is a martingale using the pseudo-probability $\pi_{t,T}$. We can solve for $\pi_{t,T}$ explicitly using (2):

$$\pi_{t,T} \equiv \frac{1 - d_{t,T}}{u_{t,T} - d_{t,T}}, \tag{5}$$

for all $T \in [t, \tau]$.

In summary, for each delivery date T, no arbitrage in a futures contract of that maturity is equivalent to:

$$u_{t,T} > 1 > d_{t,T}. \tag{6}$$

or equivalently there exists a unique $\pi_{t,T}$ for all $t \in [0, \tau]$ and for all $T \in [t, \tau]$ such that:

$$0 < \pi_{t,T} < 1 \text{ and } E_{t,T} F_{t+1,T} = F_{t,T}, \tag{7}$$

where $E_{t,T}$ represents expectations with respect to $\pi_{t,T}$ at time t.

But what about arbitrage opportunities across the futures contracts and riskless lending or borrowing opportunities? To guarantee that these don't exist, we need to consider the construction of synthetic futures contracts. This involves the concept of *market completeness*, to which we now turn.

First, for $t \in [0, \tau)$, consider forming a portfolio consisting of n_t futures contracts with maturity $T_1 \in (t, \tau]$ and lending[3] β_t risklessly. Its time t value is:

$$V_t \equiv n_t \Phi_{t,T_1} + \beta_t, \tag{8}$$

where $\Phi_{t,T_1} = 0$ is a placeholder to remind us of our costless investment in futures. The portfolio's time $t+1$ value, including cash flows, is:

$$\begin{aligned} V^{\mathrm{u}}_{t+1} &\equiv n_t F_{t,T_1}(u_{t,T_1} - 1) + \beta_t r_t, \text{ if 'up', or} \\ V^{\mathrm{d}}_{t+1} &\equiv n_t F_{t,T_1}(d_{t,T_1} - 1) + \beta_t r_t, \text{ if 'down'.} \end{aligned} \tag{9}$$

[3] If $\beta_t < 0$, then the investor is borrowing $|\beta_t|$ risklessly.

Since the matrix $\begin{pmatrix} u_{t,T_1}-1 & 1 \\ d_{t,T_1}-1 & 1 \end{pmatrix}$ is invertible for all $t \in [0, \tau)$ and for all $T_1 \in (t, \tau]$, by selecting (n_t, β_t) appropriately, the above portfolio can generate any desired payoff vector at time $t+1$. For example, suppose we wish to obtain the time $t+1$ payoff $[X^{\mathrm{u}}, X^{\mathrm{d}}]$. This can be done by choosing:

$$\begin{aligned} n_t^* &= \frac{X^{\mathrm{u}} - X^{\mathrm{d}}}{F_{t,T_1}(u_{t,T_1} - d_{t,T_1})} \qquad \text{and} \\ \beta_t^* &= \frac{X^{\mathrm{d}} - n_t^* F_{t,T_1}(d_{t,T_1}) - 1}{r_t} \\ &= \frac{X^{\mathrm{d}} + (X^{\mathrm{u}} - X^{\mathrm{d}})\pi_{t,T_1}}{r_t} \\ &= r_t^{-1} E_{t,T_1} X_{t+1}. \end{aligned} \tag{10}$$

Note that the value of the portfolio at time t is then:

$$V_t^* \equiv n_t^* \Phi_{t,T_1} + \beta_t^* = r_t^{-1} E_{t,T_1} X_{t+1}.$$

Because this is true for all times $t \in [0, \tau)$, the market is said to be *dynamically complete*.

To understand these results, consider a graph of the desired payoff X_{t+1} against the futures price change $F_{t+1,T_1} - F_{t,T_1}$. In a binomial framework, the desired payoff, X_{t+1}, may be represented by a straight line with slope $m_x \equiv (X^{\mathrm{u}}_{t+1} - X^{\mathrm{d}}_{t+1})/(F^{\mathrm{u}}_{t+1,T} - F^{\mathrm{d}}_{t+1,T})$ and vertical intercept $X^{\mathrm{u}}_{t+1} - m_x(F^{\mathrm{u}}_{t+1,T_1} - F_{t,T_1})$. The time $t+1$ marking-to-market proceeds from going long n_t futures contracts, $F_{t+1,T_1} - F_{t,T_1}$, is represented by a straight line going through the origin with slope n_t. The time $t+1$ future value of lending β_t at t, $\beta_t r_t$, is given by a horizontal line with vertical intercept $\beta_t r_t$. The desired number of futures contracts, n_t^*, rotates the slope of the time $t+1$ portfolio value, V_{t+1}, to match that of the desired payoff, X_{t+1}. The desired amount of lending, β_t^*, then moves the vertical intercept of this portfolio to match that of the desired payoff. This vertical intercept simultaneously represents the expected payoff, $E_{t,T_1} X_{t+1}$, the expected replicating portfolio value, $E_{t,T+1} V_{t+1}$, and the future market value of the riskless component of this replicating portfolio, $\beta_t^* r_t$.

Given these insights, we can now determine the additional restrictions on the price relatives $u_{t,T}$ and $d_{t,T}$ needed to guarantee that there is no arbitrage among all futures contracts and riskless lending and borrowing opportunities. To obtain this restriction, consider forming a portfolio of the futures contract with maturity T_1 and riskless lending, as above, to duplicate the marking-to-market proceeds of a different futures contract with maturity $T_2 \geq t+1$. That is, choose:

$$\begin{aligned} X^{\mathrm{u}} &= F_{t,T_2}(u_{t,T_2} - 1) \qquad \text{and} \\ X^{\mathrm{d}} &= F_{t,T_2}(d_{t,T_2} - 1) \end{aligned}$$

in expression (10). Consequently, the number of futures contracts held and the amount lent are:

$$n_t^* = \frac{F_{t,T_2}(u_{t,T_2} - d_{t,T_2})}{F_{t,T_1}(u_{t,T_1} - d_{t,T_1})} \quad \text{and}$$
$$\beta_t^* = r_t^{-1} E_{t,T_1}(F_{t+1,T_2} - F_{t,T_2}), \tag{11}$$

while the time t value of this replicating portfolio is:

$$V_t^* = r_t^{-1} E_{t,T_1}(F_{t+1,T_2} - F_{t,T_2}).$$

There is no arbitrage among these securities if and only if the time t value of this portfolio equals the time t value of the futures contract with maturity T_2, i.e.,

$$r_t^{-1} E_{t,T_1}(F_{t+1,T_2} - F_{t,T_2}) = \Phi_{t,T_2} = 0. \tag{12}$$

Equivalently, tomorrow's expected futures price is just today's under an equivalent martingale measure, i.e. if and only if:

$$E_{t,T_1} F_{t+1,T_2} = F_{t,T_2}. \tag{13}$$

However, by (4):

$$E_{t,T_2} F_{t+1,T_2} = F_{t,T_2}, \tag{14}$$

and thus, by the uniqueness of π_{t,T_2}:

$$\pi_{t,T_1} = \pi_{t,T_2}. \tag{15}$$

Condition (15) states that the martingale probabilities are independent of the maturity of the particular futures contract selected. In summary, therefore, we have the following proposition:

Proposition 1 (No arbitrage opportunities). *There are no arbitrage opportunities in the above economy if and only if:*

(1) there exists a unique π_t for $t \in [0, \ldots, \tau)$ such that:

$$E_t F_{t+1,T} = F_{t,T} \text{ for all } T \in (t, \ldots, \tau] \tag{16}$$

where $E_t(\cdot)$ represents expectations with respect to $(\pi_t, \pi_{t+1}, \ldots \pi_{\tau-1})$ at time t, and

(2) the unique π_t is given by:

$$\pi_t = \frac{1 - d_{t,T_1}}{u_{t,T_1} - d_{t,T_1}} = \frac{1 - d_{t,T_2}}{u_{t,T_2} - d_{t,T_2}} \quad \text{for all } t \in [0, \tau) \text{ and for all } T_1, T_2 \in (t, \tau]. \tag{17}$$

Condition (17) provides the necessary and sufficient restrictions required on the up and down price relatives $u_{t,T}$ and $d_{t,T}$ across maturities T, such that there are no arbitrage opportunities in the economy. We assume for the remainder of this paper that these restrictions are satisfied.

2.3. Contingent claim valuation and delta hedging

Given the traded term structure of futures prices, riskless lending and borrowing opportunities, and the arbitrage-free restrictions, we can now discuss the pricing of options and contingent claims. Contingent claims are divided into two styles: European or American. A *European-style* contingent claim is defined to be any time sequence of cash flows which are dependent on the history of the evolution of the term structure of futures prices. An *American-style* contingent claim is defined to be a *set of* sequences of cash flows dependent upon the history of the evolution of the term structure of futures prices *and* an optimal stopping time[4] which determines which sequence in the set of cash flow sequences is received.

For example, a European-style call option on the spot price of an asset with maturity date $\bar{t} \leq \tau$ and strike price $K \geq 0$ has a cash flow at time $\bar{t}$ equal to $\max[S_{\bar{t}} - K, 0]$. In contrast, the corresponding American-style call option has the set of cash flows, $\max[S_t - K, 0]$ for $t \in [0, \bar{t}]$ possible, where the stopping time $\tilde{t} \in [0, \bar{t}]$ determines which of these is received. The stopping time $\tilde{t}$ depends on (at most) the history of the evolution of the term structure of futures prices up to the time it is stopped. Given a stopping time $\tilde{t}$, the cash flow received is $\max[S_{\tilde{t}} - K, 0]$.

2.4. European-style contingent claims

To value contingent claims, we first start with the simplest case, and then complicate the analysis as our knowledge increases. First, consider a European-style contingent claim, i.e. a security which pays off a a cash flow at a fixed date, or possibly at multiple fixed dates. Given are a time sequence of the possibly *path-dependent* cash flows. By path-dependent, we mean that the cash flows received can depend upon the particular history of the evolution of the term structure of futures prices prior to the node of the tree at which the cash flow is received. In general, there may be multiple payout dates associated with the European-style contingent claim. However, the simplest case is where a cash flow is received at only one date, say time $\bar{t} \in (t, \tau)$.

To value this claim by the arbitrage-pricing methodology, start at time $\bar{t} - 1$. At this date, the term structure of futures prices is:

[4] A *stopping time* $\tilde{t} : \Omega \to [0, \infty]$ is defined as a function such that $\{\omega \in \Omega : \tilde{t}(\omega) \leq t\}$ is measurable with respect to the σ-algebra generated by the futures price curve as it evolves through time. The set Ω represents the 2^{τ} possible paths through the binomial tree.

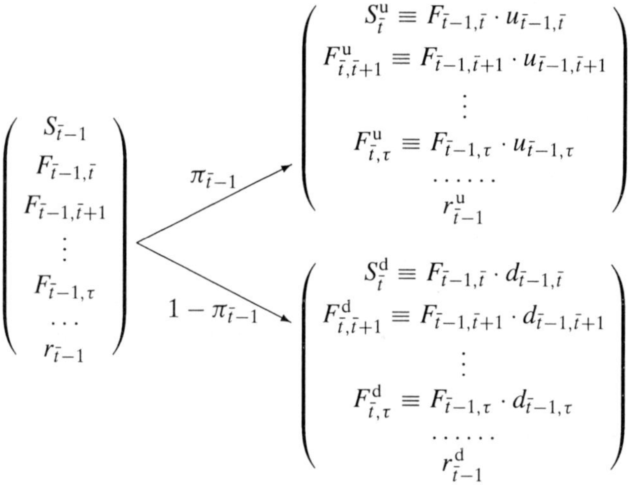

$$\begin{pmatrix} S_{\bar{t}-1} \\ F_{\bar{t}-1,\bar{t}} \\ F_{\bar{t}-1,\bar{t}+1} \\ \vdots \\ F_{\bar{t}-1,\tau} \\ \cdots \\ r_{\bar{t}-1} \end{pmatrix} \begin{matrix} \xrightarrow{\pi_{\bar{t}-1}} \begin{pmatrix} S^{\mathrm{u}}_{\bar{t}} \equiv F_{\bar{t}-1,\bar{t}} \cdot u_{\bar{t}-1,\bar{t}} \\ F^{\mathrm{u}}_{\bar{t},\bar{t}+1} \equiv F_{\bar{t}-1,\bar{t}+1} \cdot u_{\bar{t}-1,\bar{t}+1} \\ \vdots \\ F^{\mathrm{u}}_{\bar{t},\tau} \equiv F_{\bar{t}-1,\tau} \cdot u_{\bar{t}-1,\tau} \\ \cdots\cdots \\ r^{\mathrm{u}}_{\bar{t}-1} \end{pmatrix} \\ \xrightarrow{1-\pi_{\bar{t}-1}} \begin{pmatrix} S^{\mathrm{d}}_{\bar{t}} \equiv F_{\bar{t}-1,\bar{t}} \cdot d_{\bar{t}-1,\bar{t}} \\ F^{\mathrm{d}}_{\bar{t},\bar{t}+1} \equiv F_{\bar{t}-1,\bar{t}+1} \cdot d_{\bar{t}-1,\bar{t}+1} \\ \vdots \\ F^{\mathrm{d}}_{\bar{t},\tau} \equiv F_{\bar{t}-1,\tau} \cdot d_{\bar{t}-1,\tau} \\ \cdots\cdots \\ r^{\mathrm{d}}_{\bar{t}-1} \end{pmatrix} \end{matrix}$$

Let the cash flow to the contingent claim at time $\bar{t}$ be $[X^{\mathrm{u}}, X^{\mathrm{d}}]$ at the two possible states.

Because the market is complete, we know that by mixing a futures contract maturing at $T_1 > \bar{t}$ with riskless lending or borrowing, we can form a portfolio at time $\bar{t}-1$ as in expressions (8)–(10) which will duplicate this cash flow at time $\bar{t}$. To avoid arbitrage, the price of this contingent claim at time $\bar{t}-1$, denoted $C_{\bar{t}-1}$, should equal the value of the portfolio, i.e.,

$$\begin{aligned} C_{\bar{t}-1} &= n_{\bar{t}-1}\Phi_{\bar{t}-1,T_1} + \beta_{\bar{t}-1} = \\ &= r^{-1}_{\bar{t}-1} E_{\bar{t}-1}(X_{\bar{t}}) = r^{-1}_{\bar{t}-1}[\pi_{\bar{t}-1} X^{\mathrm{u}}_{\bar{t}} + (1-\pi_{\bar{t}-1}) X^{\mathrm{d}}_{\bar{t}}] \end{aligned} \tag{18}$$

where

$$X_{\bar{t}} \equiv \begin{cases} X^{\mathrm{u}}_{\bar{t}}, & \text{if 'up'} \\ X^{\mathrm{d}}_{\bar{t}}, & \text{if 'down'.} \end{cases}$$

The value of the contingent claim at time $\bar{t}-1$ is seen to be the discounted expected value of the time $\bar{t}$ cash flows to the contingent claim using the martingale probabilities. This is the same price that would be obtained in a risk-neutral economy with probability beliefs π. Hence, this is called *risk-neutral valuation* and the approach called the *risk-neutrality argument*.

The hedge ratio (or delta) of the contingent claim at time $\bar{t}-1$ is the quantity $n^*_{\bar{t}-1}$ for the futures contract with maturity T_1. By going long $n^*_{\bar{t}-1}$ futures and lending the current model value $C_{\bar{t}-1}$ risklessly, the contingent claim is *synthesized*.

Next, to value this contingent claim at time $\bar{t}-2$, we follow a recursive procedure. At this step, the 'cash flows' received at time $\bar{t}-1$ are given by $[C^{\mathrm{u}}_{\bar{t}-1}, C^{\mathrm{d}}_{\bar{t}-1}]$ where the superscripts u and d correspond to the up and down branches. Consequently, the value of the contingent claim at time $\bar{t}-2$ is given by expression (18) with $X^{\mathrm{u}}_{\bar{t}}$ replaced with $C^{\mathrm{u}}_{\bar{t}-1}$ and $X^{\mathrm{d}}_{\bar{t}}$ replaced with $C^{\mathrm{d}}_{\bar{t}-1}$:

$$C_{\bar{t}-2} = r_{\bar{t}-2}^{-1}\left[\pi_{\bar{t}-2}^{*}C_{\bar{t}-1}^{\mathrm{u}} + (1-\pi_{\bar{t}-2}^{*})C_{\bar{t}-1}^{\mathrm{d}}\right]$$
$$= r_{\bar{t}-2}^{-1}E_{\bar{t}-2}\left(C_{\bar{t}-1}\right). \tag{19}$$

The hedge ratio over $[\bar{t}-2, \bar{t}-1]$ is again obtained from expression (10) with the stated replacements for X^{u} and X^{d}.

Substitution of (18) into (19), and the law of iterated expectations yields:

$$C_{\bar{t}-2} = E_{\bar{t}-2}\left(\frac{x}{r_{\bar{t}-2}\cdot r_{\bar{t}-1}}\right). \tag{20}$$

Again, the contingent claim's value is seen to be the expected value of its cash flows, appropriately discounted, and using the martingale probabilities.

It is now easy to see that by induction:

$$C_0 = E_0\left(\frac{x}{r_0\cdot r_1\cdot\ldots\cdot r_{\bar{t}-1}}\right). \tag{21}$$

Recall that the martingale probabilities are given by $\pi_t = (1-d_{t,T})/(u_{t,T}-d_{t,T})$ for any $T > t$. Expression (21) yields a very general procedure for calculating present values in the above economy. Notice that in the valuation formula, the original probabilities $(p_0, p_1, \ldots, p_{\tau-1})$ do not appear. Instead, they are replaced by the pseudo-probabilities $(\pi_0, \pi_1, \ldots, \pi_{\tau-1})$. The pseudo-probabilities can be thought of as the original probabilities, adjusted for risk aversion, so that the risk-neutral valuation procedure is valid.

An example will help to illustrate the above procedure. Consider a European-style call option on the spot price of the asset with maturity date $\bar{t} \leq \tau$ and strike price $K \geq 0$. By expression (21), the call's value at time 0 is given by:

$$C_0 = E_0\left(\frac{\max\left[S_{\bar{t}} - K, 0\right]}{r_0\cdot r_1\cdot\ldots\cdot r_{\bar{t}-1}}\right). \tag{22}$$

An explicit calculation is possible given particular values for $(u_{t,T}, d_{t,T})$ and $\left(S_0, F_{0,1}, \ldots, F_{0,\tau}; r_0\right)$.

Example (Black's formula). For example, if $u_{t,\bar{t}}$, $d_{t,\bar{t}}$, and r_t are constant at u, d, and r respectively, then the binomial version of Black's model emerges. To see this, let $F_{0,\bar{t}}$ be the futures/forward price for delivery at the option's expiration. Then convergence assures that the terminal futures price is the spot price, i.e. $F_{\bar{t},\bar{t}} = S_{\bar{t}}$. Let $1_{F_{\bar{t},\bar{t}}>K}$ denote the indicator function of the event that the call finishes in-the-money. Since $\max[S_{\bar{t}} - K, 0] = \max[F_{\bar{t},\bar{t}} - K, 0] = 1_{F_{\bar{t},\bar{t}}>K}F_{\bar{t},\bar{t}} - 1_{F_{\bar{t},\bar{t}}>K}K$, the European call's value at time 0 in the binomial model is:

$$C_0 = r^{-\bar{t}}\left\{E_0\left[1_{F_{\bar{t},\bar{t}}>K}F_{\bar{t},\bar{t}}\right] - K E_0\left[1_{F_{\bar{t},\bar{t}}>K}\right]\right\}. \tag{23}$$

The latter expectation is the probability that the call finishes in-the-money:

$$E_0\left[1_{F_{\bar{t},\bar{t}}>K}\right] = P_0(F_{\bar{t},\bar{t}} > K) = \sum_j 1_{F_{\bar{t},\bar{t}}>K}\binom{\bar{t}}{j}\pi^j(1-\pi)^{\bar{t}-j}, \tag{24}$$

where $\pi \equiv (1-d)/(u-d)$ and where j is the realized number of up jumps that occur over the $\bar{t}$ periods. Since $F_{\bar{t},\bar{t}} = F_{0,\bar{t}} u^j d^{\bar{t}-j}$, the first expectation evaluates to:

$$E_0\left[1_{F_{\bar{t},\bar{t}}>K} F_{\bar{t},\bar{t}}\right] = F_{0,\bar{t}} \sum_j 1_{F_{\bar{t},\bar{t}}>K} \binom{\bar{t}}{j} [\pi u]^j [(1-\pi)d]^{\bar{t}-j}$$
$$= F_{0,\bar{t}} \sum_j 1_{F_{\bar{t},\bar{t}}>K} \binom{\bar{t}}{j} \hat{\pi}^j (1-\hat{\pi})^{\bar{t}-j}$$

where $\hat{\pi} \equiv \pi u$, and consequently $1-\hat{\pi} = (1-\pi)d$, since $\pi u + (1-\pi)d = 1$. Substituting $\hat{P}_0(F_{\bar{t},\bar{t}} > K) = \sum_j 1_{F_{\bar{t},\bar{t}}>K} \binom{\bar{t}}{j} \hat{\pi}^j (1-\hat{\pi})^{\bar{t}-j}$ and (24) into (23) gives the European call value as:

$$C_0 = r^{-\bar{t}} \left\{ F_{0,\bar{t}} \hat{P}_0(F_{\bar{t},\bar{t}} > K) - K P_0(F_{\bar{t},\bar{t}} > K) \right\}. \tag{25}$$

In words, the forward/futures price and strike price are each multiplied by a probability of finishing in-the-money, and then their difference is discounted for time. These probabilities can be expressed in terms of binomial distribution functions, which have the advantage of being tabulated and furthermore, are well-approximated by normal distribution functions. Let a be the minimum number of up jumps required to finish in-the-money, i.e. a is the smallest nonnegative integer such that $F_{0,\bar{t}} u^a d^{\bar{t}-a} > K$, or equivalently, $a > [\ln(K/F_{0,\bar{t}} d^{\bar{t}})]/[\ln(u/d)]$. Then:

$$P_0(F_{\bar{t},\bar{t}} > K) = \sum_{j=a}^{\bar{t}} \binom{\bar{t}}{j} \pi^j (1-\pi)^{\bar{t}-j} = \sum_{i=0}^{\bar{t}-a} \binom{\bar{t}}{i} (1-\pi)^i \pi^{\bar{t}-i},$$

where $i = \bar{t} - j$. Letting $B(k; n, p) \equiv \sum_{i=0}^{k} \binom{n}{k} p^i (1-p)^{n-i}$ be the binomial distribution function, we have: $P_0(F_{\bar{t},\bar{t}} > K) = B(\bar{t}-a; \bar{t}, 1-\pi)$, and similarly, $\hat{P}_0(F_{\bar{t},\bar{t}} > K) = B(\bar{t}-a; \bar{t}, 1-\hat{\pi})$. Substituting into (25) gives the binomial version of Black's formula:

$$C_0 = r^{-\bar{t}} \left\{ F_{0,\bar{t}} B(\bar{t}-a; \bar{t}, 1-\hat{\pi}) - K B(\bar{t}-a; \bar{t}, 1-\pi) \right\}. \tag{26}$$

This completes the example.

Now consider an alternative European-style claim, where there is a sequence of time and path-contingent cash flows given by $X_1, X_2, \ldots, X_{\bar{t}}$. Using expression (21), we can value each time's cash flow separately. The generalized contingent claim's arbitrage-free value, denoted C_t, will be the sum of these, i.e.,

$$C_0 = \sum_{t=1}^{\bar{t}} E_0 \left(\frac{X_t}{r_0 \cdot r_1 \cdot \ldots \cdot r_{t-1}} \right). \tag{27}$$

2.5. American-style claims

Finally, we value American-style claims, i.e. claims where the time at which the cash flow is paid out is selected by the owner, rather than being fixed in advanced. Consider a random payout X_t, where the time the payout is received is determined by selection of a stopping time $\tilde{t}$. The arbitrage-free value of the claim is given by:

$$C_0 = E_0\left(\frac{X_{\tilde{t}}}{r_0 \cdot r_1 \cdot \ldots \cdot r_{\tilde{t}-1}}\right), \tag{28}$$

where $\tilde{t} \in$ {stopping times on $[0, \tau]$}. The stopping time $\tilde{t}$ is called the *exercise date*. To see why expression (28) holds, consider the situation where the contingent claim has not been exercised by date $\bar{t} - 1$. The cash flow from the claim at time $\bar{t}$ is $[X^{\text{u}}_{\bar{t}}, X^{\text{d}}_{\bar{t}}]$ depending upon whether 'up' or 'down' is achieved. There is no early exercise decision to be made at this date.

At time $\bar{t} - 1$, if no exercise is chosen, the contingent claim's value is given by expression (21), denoted $C^{\text{n}}_{\bar{t}-1}$ where the superscript 'n' stands for not exercised, i.e.,

$$C^{\text{n}}_{\bar{t}-1} = r^{-1}_{\bar{t}-1} E_{\bar{t}-1}\left(X_{\bar{t}}\right). \tag{29}$$

Now, if exercise is chosen at time $\bar{t} - 1$, the contingent claim's value is denoted by $C^{\text{e}}_{\bar{t}-1}$, where the superscript 'e' stands for exercised, and it is given by:

$$C^{\text{e}}_{\bar{t}-1} = X_{\bar{t}-1}. \tag{30}$$

The value of the contingent claim at time $\bar{t} - 1$ is the larger of these two, i.e.,

$$\begin{aligned} C_{\bar{t}-1} &= \max\left[C^{\text{e}}_{\bar{t}-1}, C^{\text{n}}_{\bar{t}-1}\right] \\ &= \max\left[X_{\bar{t}-1}, r^{-1}_{\bar{t}-1} E_{\bar{t}-1}\left(X_{\bar{t}}\right)\right]. \end{aligned} \tag{31}$$

Thus, the optimal stopping time is:

$$\tilde{t} = \begin{cases} \bar{t} - 1, & \text{if } X_{\bar{t}-1} > r^{-1}_{\bar{t}-1} E_{\bar{t}-1}\left(X_{\bar{t}}\right) \\ \bar{t}, & \text{otherwise.} \end{cases}$$

Next, consider moving back to time $\bar{t} - 2$. The contingent claim's value at time $\bar{t} - 1$, if not exercised at time $\bar{t} - 2$, will be given by expression (28) in an 'up' and 'down' state, i.e., $\left[C^{\text{u}}_{\bar{t}-1}, C^{\text{d}}_{\bar{t}-1}\right]$. Consequently, we have by expression (21) that the contingent claim's value at time $\bar{t} - 2$, if not exercised, is:

$$C^{\text{n}}_{\bar{t}-2} = r^{-1}_{\bar{t}-2} E_{\bar{t}-2}\left(C_{\bar{t}-1}\right). \tag{32}$$

If exercised, it equals:

$$C^{\text{e}}_{\bar{t}-2} = X_{\bar{t}-2}. \tag{33}$$

The claim's value at time $\bar{t}-2$ is the larger of these two, i.e.,

$$\begin{aligned} C_{\bar{t}-2} &= \max\left[C^{\mathrm{e}}_{\bar{t}-2}, C^{\mathrm{n}}_{\bar{t}-2}\right] \\ &= \max\left[X_{\bar{t}-2}, r^{-1}_{\bar{t}-2} E_{\bar{t}-2}\left(C_{\bar{t}-1}\right)\right], \end{aligned} \tag{34}$$

where the optimal stopping time is expanded to:

$$\tilde{t} = \begin{cases} \bar{t}-2, & \text{if } X_{\bar{t}-2} > r^{-1}_{\bar{t}-2} E_{\bar{t}-2}\left(C_{\bar{t}-1}\right); \\ \bar{t}-1, & \text{if } X_{\bar{t}-1} > r^{-1}_{\bar{t}-2} E_{\bar{t}-1}\left(X_{\bar{t}}\right) \text{ and not exercised earlier}; \\ \bar{t}, & \text{otherwise.} \end{cases}$$

This recursive procedure is easily continued until time 0, at which date the optimal stopping time $\tilde{t}$ will be completely specified, and the value C_0 determined. The resulting value will satisfy expression (28). This is known as Bellman's principle of optimality.

Delta hedges for these American contingent claims can be determined according to expression (10) for any time step $(t, t+1)$ where the claim is unexercised. When the claim is exercised, delta hedging is no longer required. This then completes the general framework for contingent claims valuation and hedging. Since many contingent claims are written on the spot price of the underlying asset, the next section discusses the relationship between spot and futures prices in our model.

2.6. *Spot price process*

At an arbitrary date t, the spot price process under the equivalent martingale measure is given by:

$$S_t \begin{cases} \xrightarrow{\pi_t} S^{\mathrm{u}}_{t+1} \equiv F_{t,t+1} \cdot u_{t,t+1} \\ \xrightarrow{1-\pi_t} S^{\mathrm{d}}_{t+1} \equiv F_{t,t+1} \cdot d_{t,t+1} \end{cases}$$

where $u_{t,t+1} > d_{t,t+1} > 0$. Our model has assumed that investors can trade futures contracts of any maturity $T \in [t, \tau]$. However, we have not yet required that investors be able to store the underlying asset from date t to $t+1$. At date t, if an investor desires possession of the underlying asset at date $t+1$, he can go long one futures maturing in one period. Similarly, if an investor desires a short position in the underlying asset at date $t+1$, he can go short one futures at date t. This level of generality is useful when dealing with underlying assets which are not easily held (eg. catastrophe insurance) or stored (eg. eggs) or easily shorted (eg. illiquid stocks). The analysis is also particularly applicable to real options, when futures contracts trade on the underlying, eg. for agricultural or mineral concerns.

In contrast, traditional option valuation models explicitly assume that the underlying asset can be held over time, where the net benefit from borrowing to buy the asset can be positive eg. for high interest rate currencies, or negative, eg. for low interest rate currencies. For the moment, we continue to assume that the underlying asset need not be storable. Define the *relative basis*, y_t, at date t by:

$$y_t \equiv \frac{r_t S_t - F_{t,t+1}}{S_t} = r_t - \frac{E_t S_{t+1}}{S_t}. \tag{35}$$

Thus, the relative basis at t is the difference between the future value, $r_t S_t$, of the spot price at $t+1$, and the time t futures price, where this difference is expressed as a proportion of the current spot price. The relative basis can be positive, zero, or negative. Re-arranging the first equality in the above equation implies:

$$F_{t,t+1} = S_t(r_t - y_t). \tag{36}$$

Expression (36) is often referred to as the 'cost of carry relation'. This name is justified below. Substituting (36) into the above spot price process implies that it can be reformulated as:

$$S_t \begin{cases} \xrightarrow{\pi_t} S^{\mathrm{u}}_{t+1} = S_t \cdot U_t \\ \xrightarrow{1-\pi_t} S^{\mathrm{d}}_{t+1} = S_t \cdot D_t \end{cases}$$

where $U_t \equiv S^{\mathrm{u}}_{t+1}/S_t = (r_t - y_t)u_{t,t+1}$ and $D_t \equiv S^{\mathrm{d}}_{t+1}/S_t = (r_t - y_t)d_{t,t+1}$. At date t, the expected spot price appreciation under the martingale measure is the riskless rate less relative basis:

$$\pi_t U_t + (1-\pi_t)D_t \equiv \frac{E_t S^{\mathrm{u}}_{t+1}}{S_t} = r_t - y_t,$$

by (35). Consequently, the risk-neutral probabilities are determined by r_t, y_t, and the spot price process parameters:

$$\pi_t = \frac{r_t - y_t - D_t}{U_t - D_t}.$$

A computational issue which arises for derivative securities whose payoff depends directly on the spot price is that in general the spot price tree does not recombine. The tree below illustrates the point by setting $\tau = 2$ for simplicity:

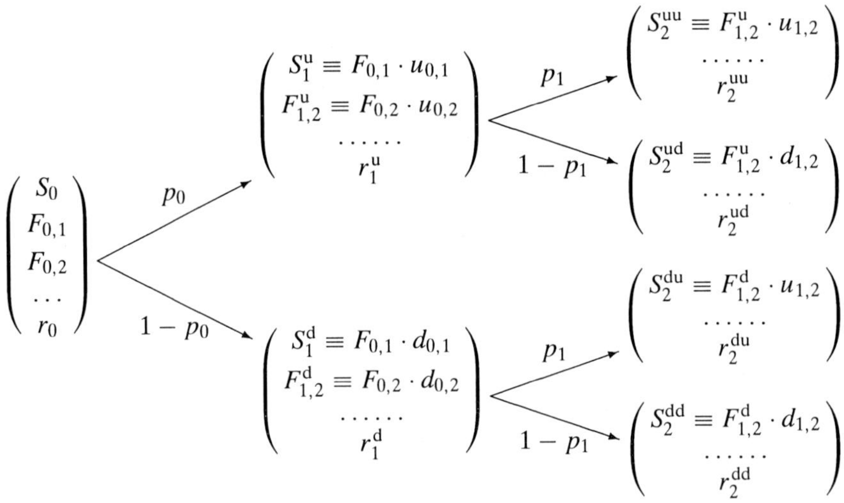

The tree will recombine if

$$F^{\mathrm{u}}_{1,2}d_{1,2} = F^{\mathrm{d}}_{1,2}u_{1,2}, \qquad r_2^{\mathrm{ud}} = r_2^{\mathrm{du}},$$

or equivalently:

$$u_{0,2}d_{1,2} = d_{0,2}u_{1,2}, \qquad r_2^{\mathrm{ud}} = r_2^{\mathrm{du}}.$$

If this equation does not hold for equal length periods, the period lengths can sometimes be chosen so that the tree recombines.

We now assume as in traditional models that *the underlying asset can be stored or short sold without restriction*. Let δ_t denote the 'dividend yield' of the underlying asset at date t, achieved by purchasing the asset at date t and storing it to date $t+1$. This dividend yield is the amount of dollars received at date $t+1$, expressed as a fraction of the time t spot price. If the underlying asset is a currency, $\delta_t > 0$ is the foreign riskfree rate. If the underlying asset is a non-dividend paying stock, then $\delta_t = 0$. If the underlying asset is a commodity, $\delta_t < 0$ may represent proportional storage costs. Using the standard cost-of-carry argument[5], we have:

$$F_{t,t+1} = S_t(r_t - \delta_t). \tag{37}$$

Comparing with (36) implies that the relative basis is this dividend yield:

$$y_t = \delta_t. \tag{38}$$

The analysis easily generalizes to random dividend yields of δ_t^{u} if the underlying asset jumps up, and of δ_t^{d} if the underlying jumps down. The generalized expression is $F_{t,t+1} = S_t(r_t - E_t\delta_t)$.

[5] The standard cost of carry argument is that buying the asset on the spot market, borrowing to finance the purchase, and storing the asset is equivalent to purchasing the asset forward.

We have shown how a binomial process on a term structure of futures leads to a binomial process on the spot price of the underlying asset. The traditional model reverses this analysis. It starts with a binomial process on spot prices and derives the resultant binomial process for futures prices of every maturity. Both models imply the existence of unique pseudo-probabilities, as proved next. No arbitrage between trading in the spot market for the underlying asset and riskless borrowing and lending opportunities implies:

$$U_t > r_t - \delta_t > D_t.$$

Consequently, there exists a unique number $\tilde{\pi}_t \in (0, 1)$ such that:

$$\tilde{\pi}_t U_t + (1 - \tilde{\pi}_t) D_t = r_t - \delta_t.$$

Solving for this pseudo-probability gives:

$$\tilde{\pi}_t = \frac{r_t - \delta_t - D_t}{U_t - D_t}. \tag{39}$$

Considering the futures price, $F_{t,T}$, as a 'derivative' on S_t, the standard dynamic replication argument gives that at time $T - 1$:

$$0 = \frac{\tilde{\pi}_{T-1}(S_T^{\mathrm{u}} - F_{T-1,T}) + (1 - \tilde{\pi}_{T-1})(S_T^{\mathrm{d}} - F_{T-1,T})}{r_{T-1}},$$

or:

$$F_{T-1,T} = \tilde{E}_{T-1}(S_T).$$

At time $T - 2$,

$$0 = \frac{\tilde{\pi}_{T-2}(F_{T-1,T}^{\mathrm{u}} - F_{T-2,T}) + (1 - \tilde{\pi}_{T-2})(F_{T-1,T}^{\mathrm{d}} - F_{T-2,T})}{r_{T-2}},$$

or

$$F_{T-2,T} = \tilde{E}_{T-2}(F_{T-1,T}).$$

Continuing, at time t:

$$F_{t,T} = \tilde{\pi}_t F_{t+1,T}^{\mathrm{u}} + (1 - \tilde{\pi}_t) F_{t+1,T}^{\mathrm{d}}.$$

Substituting $F_{t+1,T}^{\mathrm{u}} = F_{t,T} u_{t,T}$ and $F_{t+1,T}^{\mathrm{d}} = F_{t,T} d_{t,T}$ and algebra gives:

$$\tilde{\pi}_t = \pi_t \text{ for all times } t.$$

Thus, the models can be specified to imply the same prices and hedge ratios of derivative securities. The differences arise in the assumptions. The traditional approach requires that the underlying asset be storable and shortable, whereas our model alternatively assumes that futures contracts of every maturity can be traded. The traditional model characterizes the pseudo-probabilities in terms of the spot price process, whereas our model characterizes these probabilities using the futures price process of any maturity. The next section compares the two models for various categories of underlying assets.

3. Existing models

This section reviews the existing models for pricing options on various commodities and shows how they fit into the above analysis.

3.1. Stock options

All listed stock options are American-style. As a result, the standard model for valuing stock options is the binomial model of Cox, Ross & Rubinstein [1979] (henceforth CRR). In the CRR model, the underlying stock is assumed to be storable and shortable without restriction. If short sales restrictions such as the uptick rule are binding, then the CRR model value becomes an upper bound on call prices and a lower bound on put prices. The spot price relatives U and D, the spot rate r, and the dividend yield δ are usually assumed constant, in order that the tree recombine. The CRR binomial model formula can be obtained from the binomial version of Black's formula (26) using the fact that $F_{0\bar{t}} = S_0\,(r-\delta)^{\bar{t}}$. Substitution gives:

$$\begin{aligned} C_0 &= r^{-\bar{t}}\left\{S_0(r-\delta)^{\bar{t}}B(\bar{t}-a;\bar{t},1-\hat{\pi}) - KB(\bar{t}-a;\bar{t},1-\pi)\right\} \\ &\approx S_0(1-\delta)^{\bar{t}}B(\bar{t}-a;\bar{t},1-\hat{\pi}) - Kr^{-\bar{t}}B(\bar{t}-a;\bar{t},1-\pi), \end{aligned}$$

where $\pi = (1-d)/(u-d) = (r-\delta-D)/(U-D)$ and where $\hat{\pi} \equiv \pi u = [(r-\delta-D)/(U-D)][U/(r-\delta)]$. When the parameters U, D, r, and δ are time-dependent, unequal time steps can often be used to achieve path-independence. When constant dollar dividends are paid aperiodically (eg. quarterly), path-independence is achieved by escrowing out the dividends and imposing a binomial process on the escrowed stock price. At any exercise date, the exercise value is computed by adding back the present value of the dividends to this escrowed price [6].

There are no futures contracts trading on individual stocks. Consequently, to implement our model for stock options, forward prices can be used instead of of futures prices, where these forward prices are implied out of (preferably European) put and call stock options. If forward prices are used in our framework, one should also assume that interest rates are deterministic. Since forward prices equal futures prices under deterministic interest rates, our analysis goes through with F interpreted as the forward price. When interest rates are stochastic, any correlation [7] between spot interest rates and futures prices of stocks leads to theoretical differences between forward and futures prices.

One important difference in the two approaches is that our model does not impose any assumptions on dividends whatsoever. Furthermore, European

[6] For calls, the cum-dividend stock price is used to compute exercise value, while for puts, the ex-dividend price is used.

[7] In the one factor model presented, there is perfect correlation between spot interest rates and futures prices.

options can be valued knowing only the process for the forward maturing with the option, while American options require a maturity corresponding to each potential exercise date. Finally, there is no counterpart to the uptick rule for options, forwards, or futures, so this aspect of the frictionless market assumption is more reasonable.

3.2. Stock index options

The traditional model for valuing index options is also CRR. When compared to valuing options on individual stocks, the implicit assumption in index option models that all of the stocks in the index can be immediately bought or short-sold without restriction is less reasonable. In contrast to stock options, there is a very liquid market in futures on stock indices. Furthermore, American options on stock index futures trade. For options on the spot price of the index, we suggest using our model to characterize the risk-neutral probabilities, π_t, in terms of the implied spot price parameters, U_t and D_t. For options on stock index futures, these probabilities can be characterized in terms of the assumed futures price parameters $u_{t,T}$ and $d_{t,T}$, where T is any sufficiently long maturity. When the maturity used is the same as that of the underlying futures, our model reduces to a binomial version of Black's model.

3.3. Currencies

As in the case of indices, options exist on both the spot and futures exchange rates of currencies. The standard models are Garman & Kohlhagen [1983] for European spot options, Black's model for European futures options, and CRR for American options. With the exception of Black's model, these models assume that domestic and foreign interest rates are constant. However, interest rates are about as volatile as the exchange rates themselves. Since our term structure model assumes stochastic domestic interest rates and makes no assumptions on foreign interest rate behavior, it captures this important element of currency option pricing.

3.4. Commodities

As in the case of currencies, options exist on both the spot and futures prices of commodities. For commodities such as oil however, the spot market is not well-developed, which makes shorting the physical commodity difficult. Furthermore, convenience yields, which are of significant economic magnitude, are difficult to observe directly, and are even harder to forecast. Nevertheless, commodity option models such as Gibson & Schwartz [1990] specify the spot price process directly, requiring the user to input current spot prices and convenience yields.

Commodities such as oil enjoy a rich term structure of futures prices. This term structure can be used in our model to value and hedge derivatives without the need to observe or forecast convenience yields. Since futures are easily shorted, this aspect of the frictionless market ideal is less troubling than for the conventional models described above. Options on futures are easily handled in the specialization of our model to the binomial version of Black [1976]. Furthermore, exotic options, such as options on maturity spreads, are also easily handled in our term structure model.

3.5. Interest rate options

There exist various types of interest rate options such as caps, floors, collars, etc. Standard models are obtainable as special cases of Heath, Jarrow & Morton [1992]. To get the HJM model, one can use the traditional spot price process approach by letting $P(t)$ be the *vector* of zero coupon bond prices of every maturity. Since the spot rate at each date is determined by the price of the shortest maturity zero coupon bond, this additional restriction is also added to the tree:

$$\begin{pmatrix} P(t,\tau) \\ P(t,\tau-1) \\ \vdots \\ P(t,t+1) \\ \cdots \\ r_t = \dfrac{1}{P(t,t+1)} \end{pmatrix} \begin{array}{l} \nearrow^{p_t} \begin{pmatrix} P^{\mathrm{u}}(t+1,\tau) \\ P^{\mathrm{u}}(t+1,\tau-1) \\ \vdots \\ P^{\mathrm{u}}(t+1,t+2) \\ 1 \\ \cdots\cdots \\ r^{\mathrm{u}}_{t+1} = \dfrac{1}{P^{\mathrm{u}}(t+1,t+2)} \end{pmatrix} \\ \searrow_{1-p_t} \begin{pmatrix} P^{\mathrm{d}}(t+1,\tau) \\ P^{\mathrm{d}}(t+1,\tau-1) \\ \vdots \\ P^{\mathrm{d}}(t+1,t+2) \\ 1 \\ \cdots\cdots \\ r^{\mathrm{d}}_{t+1} = \dfrac{1}{P^{\mathrm{d}}(t+1,t+2)} \end{pmatrix} \end{array}$$

The no arbitrage condition (39) is satisfied for each bond maturity. This pseudo-probability must be the same across all bond maturities for the zero-coupon bond price curve to be arbitrage-free. This is the same argument used to get Proposition 1 [see Jarrow, 1995, this volume].

It is possible to use the futures price curve approach here as well. It entails specifying a term structure of futures prices for *each maturity* of the underlying zero coupon bond. The generalization of the no arbitrage condition in Proposition 1 would be that the pseudo-probabilities implied from the evolution of the futures price curve must be the same across all delivery dates for a particular bond maturity *and* across all possible bond maturities. This approach may be most reasonable for Eurodollar or Treasury bond and note futures, where a variety of maturities trade actively.

4. Implementation

This section discusses the implementation of our futures term structure model. We assume that there exists a term structure of contracts with current futures prices given by the vector $[S_0, F_{0,1}, F_{0,2}, \ldots, F_{0,\tau}]$. Another set of inputs to the model are the current spot rate, r_0, and all future state contingent spot rates. We refer the reader to Jarrow [1995, this volume] for guidance on estimating the spot rate process. The final set of inputs to the model are a lower diagonal matrix of up price relatives, $u_{t,T}$:

$$u_{t,T} = \begin{pmatrix} u_{0,1} & 0 & 0 & \ldots & 0 \\ u_{0,2} & u_{1,2} & 0 & \ldots & 0 \\ \vdots & \vdots & \vdots & \ddots & \vdots \\ u_{0,\tau} & u_{1,\tau} & u_{2,\tau} & \ldots & u_{\tau,\tau} \end{pmatrix}$$

and a lower diagonal matrix of down price relatives, $d_{t,T}$:

$$d_{t,T} = \begin{pmatrix} d_{0,1} & 0 & 0 & \ldots & 0 \\ d_{0,2} & d_{1,2} & 0 & \ldots & 0 \\ \vdots & \vdots & \vdots & \ddots & \vdots \\ d_{0,\tau} & d_{1,\tau} & d_{2,\tau} & \ldots & d_{\tau,\tau} \end{pmatrix}.$$

Letting Δ be the length of each time step, we reparametrize the price relatives $u_{t,T}$ and $d_{t,T}$ by:

$$u_{t,T} = \exp\left(\mu_{t,T}\Delta + \sigma_{t,T}\sqrt{\Delta}\right).$$

and

$$d_{t,T} = \exp\left(\mu_{t,T}\Delta - \sigma_{t,T}\sqrt{\Delta}\right),$$

where $p_t = 1/2 + \eta_t\Delta$ for some $\eta_t \in \Re$. p_t are the empirical probabilities. At time $t+1$, the log price relatives are:

$$\ln(F_{t+1,T}/F_{t,T}) = \begin{cases} \mu_{t,T}\Delta t + \sigma_{t,T}\sqrt{\Delta} & \text{if 'up'} \\ \mu_{t,T}\Delta t - \sigma_{t,T}\sqrt{\Delta} & \text{if 'down'}. \end{cases}$$

Simple algebra gives:

$$E^p\left(\ln\left(\frac{F_{t+1,T}}{F_{t,T}}\right)\right) = \mu_{t,T}\Delta + O\left(\Delta^{\frac{3}{2}}\right),$$

$$\sqrt{\mathrm{Var}^p}\left(\ln\left(\frac{F_{t+1,T}}{F_{t,T}}\right)\right) = \sigma_{t,T}\sqrt{\Delta} + O\left(\Delta^{3/2}\right),$$

where $\lim_{\Delta \downarrow 0} O(\Delta^{3/2})/\Delta = 0$. Thus, $\mu_{t,T}$ has the interpretation as the instantaneous expected growth rate in $F_{t,T}$ and $\sigma_{t,T}$ has the interpretation as the instantaneous expected volatility of relative changes in $F_{t,T}$ [8].

For valuation, we need to understand the process under the risk-neutral probability $\pi_t \equiv (1 - d_{t,T})/(u_{t,T} - d_{t,T})$. We have:

$$\pi_t = \frac{1 - \exp(\mu_{t,T}\Delta - \sigma_{t,T}\sqrt{\Delta})}{\exp(\mu_{t,T}\Delta + \sigma_{t,T}\sqrt{\Delta}) - \exp(\mu_{t,T}\Delta - \sigma_{t,T}\sqrt{\Delta})}.$$

Since we have a free parameter, without loss of generality, we can set $\pi_t = 1/2$ for all t. Then:

$$\exp(-\mu_{t,T}\Delta) = \frac{1}{2}\left[\exp(\sigma_{t,T}\sqrt{\Delta}) + \exp(-\sigma_{t,T}\sqrt{\Delta})\right].$$

Thus:

$$1 - \mu_{t,T}\Delta + O\left(\Delta^{\frac{3}{2}}\right) = \frac{1}{2}\left[1 + \sigma_{t,T}\sqrt{\Delta} + \frac{\sigma_{t,T}^2}{2}\Delta + \right.$$
$$\left. + 1 - \sigma_{t,T}\sqrt{\Delta} + \frac{\sigma_{t,T}^2}{2}\Delta + O\left(\Delta^{\frac{3}{2}}\right)\right].$$

This gives $\mu_{t,T}\Delta = -(\sigma_{t,T}^2/2)\Delta + O\left(\Delta^{3/2}\right)$. In summary, the valuation process is approximated by:

$$u_{t,T} = \exp\left(-\frac{\sigma_{t,T}^2}{2}\Delta + \sigma_{t,T}\sqrt{\Delta}\right).$$

and

$$d_{t,T} = \exp\left(-\frac{\sigma_{t,T}^2}{2}\Delta - \sigma_{t,T}\sqrt{\Delta}\right),$$

with $\pi_t = 1/2$. This process depends only on the instantaneous volatility of relative changes in futures prices, and is arbitrage-free.

When there is a term structure of futures options trading, these instantaneous volatilities can be obtained from a term structure of implied volatilities. If no futures options trade, one can use a term structure of options on the spot. The implied volatility can be obtained via any of the previously discussed models. If no options are available, historical volatility can be used, if one assumes that $u_{t,T}$ and $d_{t,T}$ depend on their arguments only through their difference $T - t$. In any case, given a vector of volatilities $[\sigma_{01}, \sigma_{02}, \ldots \sigma_{0\tau}]$, then by definition, the *forward*

[8] Given certain technical restrictions on $(\mu_{t,T}, \sigma_{t,T})$, this process will converge weakly, as $\Delta \downarrow 0$, to:

$$\frac{dF_{t,T}}{F_{t,T}} = \left(\mu_{t,T} + \frac{\sigma_{t,T}^2}{2}\right) dt + \sigma_{t,T} dW_t,$$

where $\{W_t, t \in [0, \tau]\}$ is a standard Brownian motion [see He, 1990].

volatilities of futures $\sigma_{t,T}$ satisfy the following relationship:

$$\sigma_{0,t}^2 t + \sigma_{t,T}^2 (T - t) = \sigma_{0,T}^2 T,$$

i.e.

$$\sigma_{t,T} \equiv \sqrt{\frac{\sigma_{0,T}^2 T - \sigma_{0,t}^2 t}{T - t}}.$$

5. Summary

This paper provided an analytic synthesis of the option pricing literature, using a term structure of futures prices approach. Postulating a process for the evolution of the term structure of futures prices, it is shown how to price derivative securities in an arbitrage-free manner. Complete markets are assumed.

This approach generalizes the traditional methodology by relaxing the assumption of a frictionless spot market (or even the existence of a spot market) and that the underlying commodity is storable. Thus, this method is consistent with short sale constraints in the spot market for the underlying commodity. When short sale restrictions are removed, the traditional option pricing models are shown to be obtainable as special cases. This includes the binomial model of CRR, as well as its applications to index options, currency options and commodity options. The new interest rate options models of HJM are also shown to be a subset of this framework. A brief discussion of how to empirically implement the model is also provided. References are given to reviews of the empirical literature and historic surveys of the model development.

References

Babbs, S., and M. Selby (1992). Contingent claims analysis, in: J. Eatwell, M. Milgate and P. Newman (eds.), *The New Palgrave Dictionary of Money and Finance*, MacMillan, 437–440.

Bhattacharya S., and G. Constantinides, eds. (1989). *Theory of Valuation: Frontiers of Modern Financial Theory*, Vol. 1, Rowman and Littlefield, Totowa, NJ.

Black, F. (1976). The pricing of commodity contracts. *J. Financ. Econ.* 3, 167–179.

Black, F., and M. Scholes (1973). The pricing of options and corporate liabilities. *J. Polit. Econ.* 81, 637–659.

Bookstaber, R. (1987). *Option Pricing and Investment Strategies*, Probus Publishing, Chicago IL.

Brenner, M., ed. (1983). *Option Pricing*, Lexington books, Lexington MA.

Chance D. (1989). *An Introduction to Options and Futures*, Dryden Press, Orlando, FL.

Chance D. and R. Trippi, eds. (1993). *Advances in Futures and Options Research*, Vol. 6, JAI Press, Greenwich, CT.

Clewlow L., S. Hodges, M. Selby, C. Strickland and X. Xu (1992). Recent developments in derivative securities, working paper, University of Warwick.

Cox, J., and C. Huang (1989). Option pricing theory and its applications, in: S. Bhattacharya and G. Constantinides, (eds.), *Theory of Valuation*, Rowman and Littlefield, Totowa, NJ.

Cox, J., and M. Rubinstein (1983). A survey of alternative option-pricing models, in: M. Brenner (ed.), *Option Pricing*, Lexington books, Lexington, MA.

Cox, J., and M. Rubinstein (1985). *Options Markets*, Prentice-Hall, Englewood Cliffs, NJ.

Cox, J., S. Ross and M. Rubinstein (1979). Option pricing: A simplified approach. *J. Financ. Econ.* 7, 229-63.

Dothan, M. (1990). *Prices in Financial Markets*, Oxford University Press, NY.

Duffie, D. (1989). *Futures Markets*, Prentice Hall, NY.

Duffie, D. (1992). *Dynamic Asset Pricing Theory*, Prentice Hall, NY.

Fabozzi, F., ed. (1991). *Advances in Futures and Options Research*, Volumes 1–5, 1986–1991, JAI Press, Greenwich, CT.

Field, P., Jaycolbs, R. and R. Tompkins (1992). *From Black Scholes to Black Holes*, Risk/FINEX, London.

Figlewski, S., W. Silber and M. Subrahmanyam (1990). *Financial Options*, Business One Irwin, Homewood, IL.

Finnerty, J. (1992). Financial engineering, in: J. Eatwell, M. Milgate and P. Newman (eds.), *The New Palgrave Dictionary of Money and Finance*, MacMillan, pp. 56–63.

Galai, D. (1983). A survey of empirical tests of option-pricing models, in: M. Brenner (ed.), *Option Pricing*, Lexington books, Lexington, MA.

Garman, M., and S. Kohlhagen (1983). Foreign currency option values. *J. Int. Money Finance* 2, 231–37.

Gastineau G. (1988). *The Options Manual*, 3rd edition, McGraw Hill, New York, NY.

Geske, R. and S. Trautmann (1986). Option valuation: Theory and empirical evidence, in: G. Bamberg and K. Spremann (eds.), *Capital Market Equilibria*, Springer Verlag.

Gibson. R., and E. Schwartz (1990). Stochastic convenience yield and the pricing of contingent claims. *J. Finance* 45, 959–976.

Harrison, J. M. and S. Pliska (1981). Martingales and stochastic integrals in the theory of continuous trading. *Stoch. Processes Appl.* 11, 215–260.

He, H. (1990). Convergence from discrete- to continuous-time contingent claims prices. *Rev. Financ. Studies* 3(4), 523–546.

Heath, D., R. Jarrow and A. Morton (1992). Bond pricing and the term structure of interest rates: A new methodology for contingent claims valuation, *Econometrica* 60(1), 77–105.

Hodges, S., ed. (1990). *Options: Recent Advances in Theory and Practice*, Vols. 1 and 2, Manchester University Press, Manchester.

Huang C. F. and R. Litzenberger (1988). *Foundations for Financial Economics*, North-Holland, New York, NY.

Hull, J. (1991). *Introduction to Futures and Options Markets*, Prentice Hall, Englewood Cliffs, NJ.

Hull, J. (1992). *Options, Futures, and Other Derivative Securities*, 2nd edition, Prentice Hall, Englewood Cliffs, NJ.

Ingersoll, J. (1987). *Theory of Financial Decision-Making*, Rowman & Littlefield, Totowa, NJ.

Ingersoll, J. (1992). Option pricing theory, in: J. Eatwell, M. Milgate and P. Newman (eds.), *The New Palgrave Dictionary of Money and Finance*, MacMillan, 83–93.

Ingersoll, J. (1992). Derivative products, in: J. Eatwell, M. Milgate and P. Newman (eds.), *The New Palgrave Dictionary of Money and Finance*, MacMillan, 645–47.

Jarrow, R. (1992). Diffusion processes in finance, in: J. Eatwell, M. Milgate and P. Newman, (eds.), *The New Palgrave Dictionary of Money and Finance*, MacMillan, 670–671.

Jarrow, R. (1995). Pricing interest rate options, in: R. Jarrow, V. Maksimovic and W.T. Ziemba (eds.), *Finance*, Handbooks in Operations Research and Management Science, Vol. 9., North Holland, Amsterdam, 251–272 (this volume).

Jarrow, R., and A. Rudd (1983). *Option Pricing*, Richard D. Irwin Inc., Homewood, IL.

Jarrow, R., and S. Turnbull (1992). A unified approach for pricing options on contingent claims on multiple term structures, working paper, Cornell University.

Jarrow, R. and J. Wiggins (1989). Option pricing and implicit volatilities: A review and a new perspective. *J. Econ. Surv.* 3(1), 59–82.

Kolb, R. (1991). *Understanding Futures Markets*, Kolb Publishing, Boulder, CO.

Kolb, R. (1992). *The Financial Derivatives Reader*, Kolb Publishing, Boulder, CO.

Mason, S., and R. C. Merton (1985). The role of contingent claims analysis in corporate finance, in: E. Altman and M. Subrahmanyam (eds.), *Recent Advances in Corporate Finance*.

McMillan L. (1993). *Options as a Strategic Investment*, 3rd edition, New York Institute of Finance, New York, NY.

Merton, R. (1973). Theory of rational option pricing. *Bell J. Econ. Manage. Sci.* 4, 141–183.

Merton, R. C. (1990a). Further developments in option pricing theory, in: *Continuous-Time Finance*, Basil Blackwell and Company, chapter 10.

Merton, R. C. (1992). Options, in: J. Eatwell, M. Milgate and P. Newman (eds.), *The New Palgrave Dictionary of Money and Finance*, MacMillan, pp. 90–93.

Ritchken, P. (1987). *Options: Theory, Strategy, and Applications*, Scott, Foresman, and Co., Glenview, IL.

Ross, S. (1992). Finance, in: J. Eatwell, M. Milgate and P. Newman (eds.), *The New Palgrave Dictionary of Money and Finance*, MacMillan, pp. 26–41.

Rubinstein, M. (1987). Derivative assets analysis. *J. Econ. Perspect.* 1(2), 73–94.

Rubinstein, M., and E. Reiner (1992). Exotic options, working paper, Berkeley University.

Schachter, B. (1992). Options markets, in: J. Eatwell, M. Milgate and P. Newman (eds.), *The New Palgrave Dictionary of Money and Finance*, MacMillan, pp. 93–95.

Shimko, D. (1991). *Finance in Continuous Time: A Primer*, Kolb Publishing, Boulder, CO.

Smith, C. (1976). Option pricing: A review. *J. Financ. Econ.* 3: 3-51.

Smith, C. (1979). Applications of option pricing analysis, in: J. Bicksler (ed.), *Handbook of Financial Economics*, North-Holland, New York, NY.

Smith C., and C. Smithson (1990). *The Handbook of Financial Engineering*, Harper and Row, New York, NY.

Stoll H., and R. Whaley (1993). *Futures and Options: Theory and Applications*, South-Western Publishing Co., Cincinnati, OH.

Van Hulle, C. (1988). Option pricing methods: An overview. *Insurance: Math. Econ.* 7, 139–152.

Whaley, R., ed. (1992). *Inter-Relationships Among Futures, Options, and Futures Options Markets*, Book VI in Selected Writings on Futures Contracts, CBOT, Chicago IL.

Wilmott, P., J. DeWynne, and S. Howison (1993). *Option Pricing: Mathematical Models and Computation*, Oxford Financial Press, Oxford.

R. Jarrow et al., Eds., *Handbooks in OR & MS, Vol. 9*

Chapter 8

Pricing Interest Rate Options

Robert Jarrow
Johnson Graduate School of Management, Cornell University, Ithaca, NY 14853, U.S.A.

1. Introduction

After lying dormant for many years, the theory for pricing interest rate options has recently experienced an explosive expansion.[1] This expansion has been fueled, at least in part, by an increased understanding of the martingale pricing technology.[2] The purpose of this paper is to review and to synthesize this expanding literature. A secondary purpose is to clarify the use of the martingale pricing methodology in the context of interest rate options.

For pedagogical reasons, this theory is presented in the context of a discrete trading, discrete state space economy. The continuous trading economies studied in the literature can be obtained (formally and intuitively) by taking limits. However, all the relevant concepts and insights are illustrated in this simpler setting, for use in the continuous time analogue. Furthermore, most continuous trading models must be implemented, in practice, through a discrete trading, discrete state space approximation. Consequently, little is lost by taking the discrete time perspective.

This paper is divided into two parts. Each part studies a different problem to which the interest rate option pricing theory is applied. The first problem is to value the entire zero coupon bond price curve, given the prices of only a few bonds (one, two or three) which lie upon it. This is the academic's version of 'arbitraging the yield curve'. This problem was analyzed first historically as well [see Vasicek, 1977; Dothan, 1978; Richard, 1978; Brennan & Schwartz, 1979; Langetieg, 1980; Rendleman & Bartter, 1980; Courtadon, 1982; Ball & Torous, 1983; Cox, Ingersoll & Ross, 1985; Artzner & Delbaen, 1989; Longstaff, 1989].

The second problem is to price contingent claims (options) on the zero coupon bond price curve. Here, however, we are given the prices of *all* the zero coupon bonds. This literature is more current and has recently exploded [see Ho & Lee, 1986; Bliss & Ronn, 1989; Heath, Jarrow & Morton, 1990, 1991, 1992; Hull & White, 1990; Babbs, 1990; Turnbull & Milne, 1991; Shirakawa, 1991]. Of course,

[1] See the references to this paper.

[2] See Harrison & Kreps [1979], Harrison & Pliska [1981], Heath & Jarrow [1987].

the two problems are related, and this relationship is analyzed below. To simplify the subsequent discussion, let us refer to the first problem as 'zero-curve arbitrage' and the second problem as 'option pricing'.

One contribution of this review is the identification of a theoretical difference between the model structures used to solve these two different problems. The distinction relates to the manner in which the spot rate process' parameters are specified within the model. Zero curve arbitrage models require an exogenous specification of the spot rate process. In option pricing models, however, the spot rate process is endogenously determined by an exogenous specification of the evolution of the entire zero coupon bond price curve. This distinction will be important in the subsequent analysis.

This paper is subdivided into six sections. Section 2 introduces the notation and terminology. This is the most difficult section to master. Section 3 studies the zero-curve arbitrage models. It is subdivided into the two standard approaches utilized (spot rate process models and bond price process models). The equivalence between these two approaches is studied using the martingale pricing technology. Section 4 studies the option pricing models. It is also subdivided into the two different approaches utilized (spot rate process models and bond price process models). A comparative analysis of these two approaches is provided. Section 5 explores the continuous time empirical specifications of the various models, and a summary section completes the paper.

2. The model: terminology and notation

The most difficult part of the interest rate options literature is the terminology and notation. This section presents the general framework, from which all the subsequent models will be derived. For simplicity, and simplicity alone, a one factor economy (a binomial branching process) is provided. Extension to multiple factors (multinomial branching processes) is straightforward and briefly discussed where appropriate.

We consider a discrete time, discrete state space economy. The trading intervals are $\{0, 1, 2, \ldots, T\}$ where $T < +\infty$. The state space for the economy is best described by examining the tree diagram given in Figure 1. The model starts at time 0. At time 1, one of two states occur: *up* denoted by 'u' and *down* denoted by 'd'. Up occurs with probability $q_0 > 0$ and down occurs with probability $1 - q_0 > 0$. To avoid an overly complicated diagram, only the up probabilities are displayed. We let s_1 denote the state at time 1, i.e., $s_1 \in \{\text{u}, \text{d}\}$.

Next, depending upon the state at time 1, the process can go up again or down. There are four possible states at time 2: {uu, ud, du, dd}. These are *distinct* states as the ordering is important. We let s_2 denote an arbitrary state at time 2. We allow the probability of jumping up at time 1, $q_1(s_1)$, to depend upon the state at time 1.

The state process continues in this fashion until time T. At time T there are 2^T possible states, represented by all sequences of 'u's and 'd's where the ordering is

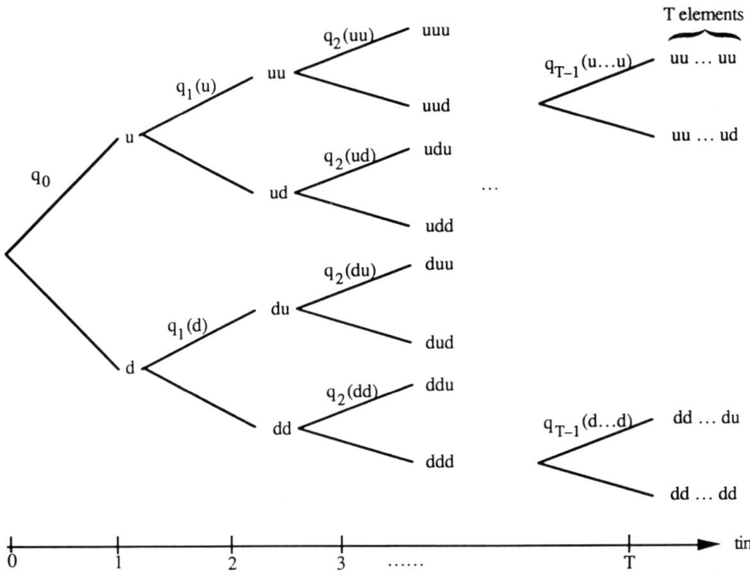

Fig. 1. Tree diagram representation of the state space. $s_1 \in \{u, d\}$; $s_2 \in \{uu, ud, du, dd\}$; $s_3 \in \{uuu, uud, udu, duu, dud, ddu, ddd\}$; $\ldots$; $s_T \in$ {all T sequences of 'u' and 'd' where order is important}.

important. A generic element is denoted s_T. The probability of an upward jump at time $T-1$, $q_{T-1}(s_{T-1})$, depends upon the state (or history of the process) at time $T-1$.

In summary, at time t, the state of the process is denoted by s_t with $s_t \in$ {all t sequences of u's and d's (where the ordering is important)}. The probability of jumping up at time t is $q_t(s_t) > 0$. If the process jumps up, the new state is s_tu. Otherwise, it is s_td. The generalization of this process from two branches to three or more branches is straightforward and omitted.

Traded are all maturity zero coupon bonds and a money market account. We let $P(t, \tau; s_t)$ denote the time t price at state s_t of a default free zero-coupon bond paying 1 dollar at time τ for sure where $0 \le t \le \tau \le T$. We require that bond prices are strictly positive, i.e., $P(t, \tau; s_t) > 0$ for all t, τ and s_t; and that the bonds are default free, i.e., $P(\tau, \tau; s_\tau) = 1$ for all τ and s_τ.

The time t *forward rate* at state s_t for the period $[\tau, \tau+1]$, denoted $f(t, \tau; s_t)$, is defined by

$$f(t, \tau; s_t) \equiv \frac{P(t, \tau; s_t)}{P(t, \tau+1; s_t)} \quad \text{where } 0 \le t \le \tau < T. \tag{1}$$

This corresponds to the rate contractible at time t for a riskless loan over the time period $[\tau, \tau+1]$. Note that this is a modification of the usual definition because the magnitude of $f(t, \tau; s_t)$ is one plus a percent. Expression (1) can be re-written as:

$$P(t,\tau;s_t) = \prod_{j=t}^{\tau-1}\left(\frac{1}{f(t,j;s_t)}\right) \quad \text{for } t \le \tau - 1. \tag{2}$$

The *spot rate* at time t under state s_t, denoted $r(t;s_t)$, is defined by

$$r(t;s_t) \equiv f(t,t;s_t). \tag{3}$$

Lastly, the money market account's time t value under state s_t denoted $B(t;s_{t-1})$ given an initial dollar investment at time 0 is defined by

$$B(t;s_{t-1}) = \prod_{j=0}^{t-1} r(j;s_j) \quad \text{for } t \ge 1 \text{ where } B(0) \equiv 1 \tag{4}$$

and where the s_j's on the right side of expression (4) are the first j coordinates of s_{t-1} on the left side of expression (4). The time t value of this account is known at time $t-1$ because it earns the spot rate over $[t-1,t]$, and this is known at time $t-1$. This observation accounts for the fact that the state s_{t-1} and not s_t is within expression (4). We can rewrite expression (4) recursively as:

$$B(t;s_{t-1}) = B(t-1;s_{t-2})r(t-1;s_{t-1}) \quad \text{for } t \ge 1. \tag{5}$$

Next, we turn to the description of the stochastic processes followed by the above quantities. For the moment, we concentrate on the evolution of the zero-coupon bond price curve and the spot rate of interest.

It is easiest to describe the evolution of the zero-coupon bond price curve as given in Figure 2. At time 0 we have an initial zero-coupon bond price curve which is represented as the $T+1$ vector of prices: $(P(0,T), P(0,T-1), \ldots, P(0,1), 1)$. At time 1 it either moves 'up' to a different T-vector of prices or 'down' to a T-vector of prices. The shortest maturity bond paying off a dollar at time 0 is removed from this new vector at time 1. The last entry in this new vector is the

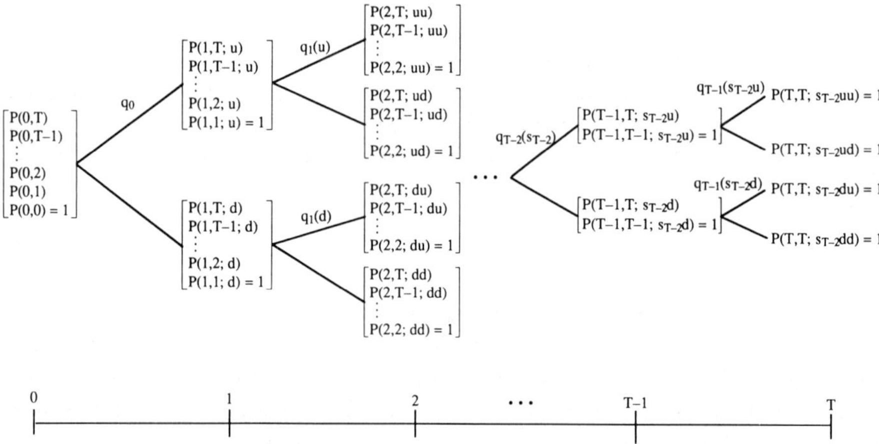

Fig. 2. Tree diagram representation of the zero-coupon bond price curve evolution.

bond which had one period until maturity at time 0 ($P(0, 1)$), and it pays one dollar for sure (independent of the state which occurs) at time 1. Note that each new T-vector of bond prices depends upon the state which occurs (u or d). The probability of going up at time 1 is the probability that $s_1 = \mathrm{u}$, and it is given as q_0. The probability of going down is the complement, $1 - q_0$.

Next, at time 2, the T-vector of prices moves up or down to a new and reduced $(T - 1)$-vector of prices. At each time step, the shortest maturity zero-coupon bond is removed from the price curve after it matures. This reduces the remaining price curve vector by one. Each price vector depends upon the state of the process. The probabilities of moving up or down at time 2 are also state dependent and are given by $q_1(s_1)$ and $1 - q_1(s_1)$, respectively.

Continuing to the second to last date in the tree, time $T - 1$, only one zero-coupon bond remains and it matures at time T. The probabilities for each state possible at time T, s_T, are given by $q_{T-1}(s_{T-1})$ for up and $1 - q_{T-1}(s_{T-1})$ for down. Finally, at time T the bond matures and pays one dollar independent of the state which occurs.

For analysis and without loss of generality, we decompose the bond price process in Figure 2 as follows:

$$P(t, \tau; s_t) = \begin{cases} P(t-1, \tau; s_t)\mathrm{u}(t-1, \tau; s_{t-1}) & \text{if } s_t = s_{t-1}\mathrm{u} \\ P(t-1, \tau; s_t)\mathrm{d}(t-1, \tau; s_{t-1}) & \text{if } s_t = s_{t-1}\mathrm{d} \end{cases}$$
$$\text{for all } \tau > t, s_{t-1} \tag{6}$$

where

$$\mathrm{u}(t, t+1; s_t) = \mathrm{d}(t, t+1; s_t) \equiv \frac{1}{P(t, t+1; s_t)} \quad \text{for all } t, s_t$$

and

$$\mathrm{u}(t-1, \tau; s_{t-1}) > \mathrm{d}(t-1, \tau; s_{t-1}) \quad \text{for all } t-1, \tau, s_{t-1}.$$

The zero-coupon bond price moves up at time t by the proportion $\mathrm{u}(t-1, \tau; s_{t-1})$ or down at time t by the proportion $\mathrm{d}(t-1, \tau; s_{t-1})$. Note that the first restriction following expression (6) guarantees that each bond pays one dollar for sure at maturity, i.e., $P(t+1, t+1; s_{t+1}) = 1$ for all s_{t+1}. By definition, the time t spot rate is:

$$\mathrm{r}(t; s_t) \equiv \mathrm{u}(t, t+1; s_t) = \mathrm{d}(t, t+1; s_t) = \frac{1}{P(t, t+1; s_t)} \tag{7}$$

The stochastic process for the spot rate is depicted in Figure 3. At time 0, the spot rate is $r(0)$. At time 1, the spot rate is either $r(1; \mathrm{u})$ or $r(1; \mathrm{d})$ depending upon whether the state is u or d. The probability of moving up is given by q_0 and the probability of moving down by $1 - q_0$. As before, this process continues until time T. For analysis and without loss of generality, we decompose the spot rate process as in expression (8):

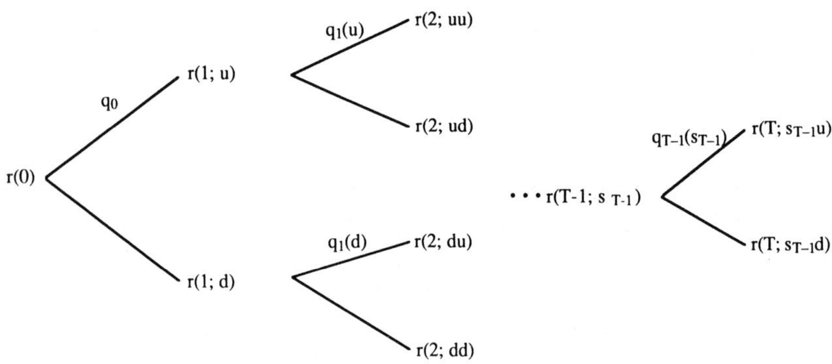

Fig. 3. Tree diagram description of the spot rate process.

$$r(t; s_t) = \begin{cases} r(t-1; s_{t-1})\alpha(t-1; s_{t-1}) & \text{if } s_t = s_{t-1}\text{u} \\ r(t-1; s_{t-1})\beta(t-1; s_{t-1}) & \text{if } s_t = s_{t-1}\text{d} \end{cases} \tag{8}$$

where $\alpha(t; s_t) \neq \beta(t; s_t)$ for all t, s_t.

The spot rate jumps at time t by the proportionality factor $\alpha(t-1; s_{t-1})$ if u occurs, or by the proportionality factor $\beta(t-1; s_{t-1})$ if d occurs. By expression (7), if the bond price $P(t, t+1; s_t)$ moves up at time t, then $r(t; s_t)$ moves down (and vice-versa). The probability of u occurring is $q_{T-1}(s_{T-1})$.

From expressions (6) and (8) we can derive the stochastic process followed by forward rates and the money market account, respectively. These processes are obtained by direct substitution of expression (6) into expression (1) for forward rates; and expression (8) into (4) for the money market account. This analysis is left for the reader. Given the above, it is now easy to see how to extend the processes to incorporate multiple branches. Simply, at each node, the tree expands into multiple directions and the notation must be expanded accordingly. This expansion can incorporate three branches, four branches, five branches, etc.

3. Zero curve arbitrage

This section studies the valuation models designed to price all bonds on the zero-coupon bond price curve using only the price of a few bonds and an exogenous specification of the spot rate process (or equivalently, a money market account). There are two forms taken by these models. The first model type focuses solely upon the spot rate process, using it as the focal point of the analysis. The second model type focuses upon the specification of a few bond price processes and the money market account. These two types of zero-curve arbitrage models, under various reparameterizations, are the discrete time analogues of Vasicek [1977], Dothan [1978], Richard [1978], Brennan & Schwartz [1979], Langetieg [1980], Rendleman & Bartter [1980], Courtadon [1982], Ball

& Torous [1983], Cox, Ingersoll & Ross [1985], Schaefer & Schwartz [1987], Longstaff [1989].

3.1. Spot rate process models

This class of models takes as its initial specification the spot rate process given in Figure 3 and the decomposition provided by expression (8), i.e., given are: $\{r(0), (\alpha(t), \beta(t){:}\ 0 \leq t \leq T-1)\}$. This initial value $r(0)$ and the stochastic processes $(\alpha(t), \beta(t){:}\ 0 \leq t \leq T-1)$ completely specify the spot rate process given in Figure 3. The purpose of this model is to endogenously determine $(P(0,\tau)$ for $\tau = 1, 2, \ldots, T)$ and $(\mathrm{u}(t,\tau), \mathrm{d}(t,\tau){:}\ 0 \leq t < \tau \leq T)$.

The model is completed with the following assumption.

Assumption R (Existence and uniqueness of equivalent martingale probabilities). There exist unique strictly positive (time and state) conditional probabilities[3] $(\pi_0, \pi_1(s_1), \pi_2(s_2), \ldots, \pi_{T-1}(s_{T-1})) \equiv \Pi$ such that $P(t,\tau;s_t)/B(t;s_{t-1})$ are martingales with respect to Π for all $\tau \in \{1, \ldots, T\}$.

This assumption states that the time t conditional expected value under the probabilities Π of a bond's payout at maturity is its time t value, after normalization by the money market account:

$$E_t^{\Pi}\left(\frac{1}{B(\tau;s_{\tau-1})}\right) = \frac{P(t,\tau;s_t)}{B(t;s_{t-1})} \quad \text{for all } 0 \leq t \leq \tau \leq T \tag{9}$$

where $E_t^{\Pi}(\cdot)$ is the conditional expectation at time t with respect to the probabilities Π.

Using expression (4), we can rewrite expression (9) as:

$$E_t^{\Pi}\left(\frac{1}{\prod_{j=t}^{\tau-1} r(j;s_j)}\right) = P(t,\tau;s_t). \tag{10}$$

This shows that all the bond prices $(P(0,\tau){:}\ 0 \leq \tau \leq T)$ and the stochastic processes determining their evolution through time $(\mathrm{u}(t,\tau), \mathrm{d}(t,\tau){:}\ 0 \leq t < \tau \leq T)$ are specified by knowing: $\{\Pi, r(0), (\alpha(t), \beta(t){:}\ 0 \leq t \leq T)\}$. Note that knowing the spot rate $r(0)$ is equivalent [by expression (7)] to knowing the first bond price $P(0,1)$. Hence, one bond price on the curve and knowledge of the quantities $(\Pi, (\alpha(t), \beta(t){:}\ 0 \leq t \leq T))$ is sufficient to determine all the remaining zero-coupon bond prices $(P(0,2), \ldots, P(0,T))$. If these calculated prices differ from the observed market prices, then the price discrepancy indicates the existence of 'profitable' trading opportunities. These 'profitable trading' opportunities will be discussed in a subsequent section.

[3] Formally, the product of these conditional probabilities $\pi_0\pi_1(s_2)\pi_2(s_2)\ldots\pi_{T-1}(s_{T-1})$ forms a probability measure Π on the discrete state space consisting of all possible s_T.

Note that the bond valuation formula given in expression (10) is *independent* of the actual probabilities $q_t(s_t)$ driving the spot rate process. This implies that two different traders who disagree about $q_t(s_t)$ but agree on $\{\Pi, r(0), (\alpha(t), \beta(t): 0 \le t \le T-1)\}$, will agree on the bond prices. This is a trivial, but important observation.

The procedure for constructing a synthetic zero-coupon bond from another zero-coupon bond and the money market account, in the above model, will be discussed in Section 3.3 below. The papers for which the above spot rate process model can be interpreted as the discrete time analogue include Vasicek [1977], Dothan [1978], Richard [1978], Brennan & Schwartz [1979], Rendleman & Bartter [1980], Courtadon [1982], Cox, Ingersoll & Ross [1985] and Longstaff [1989].

3.2. Bond price process models

This class of models takes as its initial specification *one* maturity bond process $(P(t,T))$ from the vector stochastic process given in Figure 2 with the decomposition as in expression (6), *plus* the specification of the spot rate process given in Figure 3 with the decomposition as in expression (8). That is, given are:

$$\begin{aligned} &\{P(0,T), (\mathrm{u}(t,T), \mathrm{d}(t,T): 0 \le t \le T-1)\} \quad \text{and} \\ &\{r(0), (\alpha(t), \beta(t): 0 \le t \le T-1)\} \end{aligned} \tag{11}$$

The purpose of this model is to endogenously determine $(P(0,\tau)$ for $\tau = 1, 2, \ldots, T-1)$ and $(\mathrm{u}(t,\tau), \mathrm{d}(t,\tau)\colon\ 0 \le t < \tau \le T-1)$.

Given these exogenous processes, we can prove the following lemma.

Lemma 1 (Complete markets). Given $\{P(0,T), (\mathrm{u}(t,T), \mathrm{d}(t,T)\colon\ 0 \le t \le T-1)\}$ and $\{r(0), (\alpha(t), \beta(t)\colon\ 0 \le t \le T-1)\}$ as in expressions (6) and (8), respectively; the market is complete.

By *complete*, we mean that given any time $T-1$ state contingent payout $X(s_{T-1}) \in (X^{\mathrm{u}}(s_{T-2}), X^{\mathrm{d}}(s_{T-2}))$, there exists a dynamic *self-financing* trading strategy initiated at time 0 in the bond $P(t,T)$ and the money market account $B(t)$ with share holdings $(n_P(t;s_t), n_B(t;s_t))$ at time t under state s_t for all $t \in \{0, 1, \ldots, T-2\}$ such that the payoff to the portfolio at time $T-1$ matches $X(s_{T-1})$, i.e.,

$$\begin{aligned} &n_P(T-2; s_{T-2})P(T-1, T; s_{T-1}) + \\ &\quad + n_B(T-2; s_{T-2})B(T-1, T; s_{T-1}) = X(s_{T-1}) \quad \text{for all } s_{T-1} \end{aligned} \tag{12}$$

By *self-financing* we mean that there are no cash inflows or outflows from the portfolio after its initiation, i.e.,

$$n_P(t;s_t)P(t+1,T;s_{t+1}) + n_B(t;s_t)B(t+1;s_{t+1}) = \\ = n_P(t+1;s_{t+1})P(t+1,T;s_{t+1}) + n_B(t+1;s_{t+1})B(t+1;s_t) \\ \text{for all } t, s_{t+1}. \quad (13)$$

Two observations about this definition are important. First, the contingent claim's payoff must terminate at time $T-1$ as there is no security trading whose payouts differ across the states at time T (see Figure 2). Second, any contingent claim whose payoffs occur prior to time $T-1$ can also be duplicated using this type of dynamic self-financing trading strategy. The trick is to deposit the contingent claim's payoff at the earlier date into a money market account which transfers it to time $T-1$. The above self-financing trading strategy then applies.

The proof of the lemma contains some important expressions useful for hedging options (or equivalently, constructing synthetic options).

Proof. The proof is by backward induction. Consider forming a portfolio at time $T-2$ given state s_{T-2} to duplicate $X(s_{T-1})$. The desire is to find $n_P(T-2;s_{T-2}), n_B(T-2;s_{T-2})$ such that at time $T-1$:

$$n_P(T-2;s_{T-2})P(T-1,T;s_{T-2}\mathrm{u}) + \\ + n_B(T-2;s_{T-2})B(T-1;s_{T-2}) = X^{\mathrm{u}}(s_{T-2}) \quad (14a)$$

and

$$n_P(T-2;s_{T-2})P(T-1,T;s_{T-2}\mathrm{d}) + \\ n_B(T-2;s_{T-2})B(T-1;s_{T-2}) = X^{\mathrm{d}}(s_{T-2}). \quad (14b)$$

Substitution of expression (6) into (14), algebra, and noting that $\mathrm{u}(T-2,T;s_{T-2}) > \mathrm{d}(T-2,T;s_{T-2})$ implies that equation (14) has a solution, and it is uniquely given by

$$n_P(T-2;s_{T-2}) = \\ = \frac{X^{\mathrm{u}}(s_{T-2}) - X^{\mathrm{d}}(s_{T-2})}{P(T-2,T;s_{T-2})[\mathrm{u}(T-2,T;s_{T-2}) - \mathrm{d}(T-2,T;s_{T-2})]} \quad (15a)$$

and

$$n_B(T-2;s_{T-2}) = \quad (15b) \\ = \frac{X^{\mathrm{d}}(s_{T-2})\mathrm{u}(T-2,T;s_{T-2}) - X^{\mathrm{u}}(s_{T-2})\mathrm{d}(T-2,T;s_{T-2})}{B(T-2,T;s_{T-2})r(T-2;s_{T-2})[\mathrm{u}(T-2,T;s_{T-2}) - \mathrm{d}(T-2,T;s_{T-2})]}$$

The time $T-2$ value of this position, denoted $X(s_{T-2})$, is

$$X(s_{T-2}) \equiv n_P(T-2;s_{T-2})P(T-2,T;s_{T-2}) + \\ + n_B(T-2;s_{T-2})B(T-2;s_{T-2}). \quad (16)$$

This can be written as:

$$X^{\mathrm{u}}(s_{T-3}) \equiv n_P(T-2; s_{T-3}\mathrm{u})P(T-2, T; s_{T-3}\mathrm{u}) + \\ + n_B(T-2; s_{T-3}\mathrm{u})B(T-2; s_{T-3}\mathrm{u}) \tag{17a}$$

$$X^{\mathrm{d}}(s_{T-3}) \equiv n_P(T-2; s_{T-3}\mathrm{d})P(T-2, T; s_{T-3}\mathrm{d}) + \\ + n_B(T-2; s_{T-3}\mathrm{d})B(T-2; s_{T-3}\mathrm{d}). \tag{17b}$$

The next goal is to find $n_P(T-3; s_{T-3}), n_B(T-3; s_{T-3})$ such that at time $T-2$:

$$n_P(T-3; s_{T-3})P(T-2, T; s_{T-3}\mathrm{u}) + \\ + n_B(T-3; s_{T-3})B(T-2; s_{T-3}) = X^{\mathrm{u}}(s_{T-3}), \tag{18a}$$

and

$$n_P(T-3; s_{T-3})P(T-2, T; s_{T-3}\mathrm{d}) + \\ + n_B(T-3; s_{T-3})B(T-2; s_{T-3}) = X^{\mathrm{d}}(s_{T-3}). \tag{18b}$$

But, the system in (18) is identical to the problem given in expression (14), except for a time change. As we have already solved that problem, the solution is again given by (15) but with the appropriate time change ('$T-2$' replaced with '$T-3$').

By backward induction, we can finally get the shares at time 0, $(n_P(0), n_B(0))$ which yield a position at time 1, which in turn yield a position at time 2, ..., so forth, which in turn yields $X(s_{T-1})$ at time $T-1$. By construction [expressions (17) and (18)] this portfolio is self-financing. This completes the proof. □

We point out, in passing, that if Figure 1 was a trinomial process, then the completeness condition [expression (14)] would involve the nonsingularity of a system of three equations involving the 'u's and d's of two distinct maturity zero-coupon bonds (e.g., the bonds with maturities $T-1$ and T) plus the money market account. The analysis and proof is a straightforward extension of the above. This can be further generalized to four branches, five branches, and so forth.

An *arbitrage opportunity* is defined to be any dynamic, self-financing trading strategy initiated at time 0 $(n_P(t; s_t), n_B(t; s_t)\text{: } 0 \le t \le T-1)$ such that its time $T-1$ value, $X(s_{T-1})$, satisfies

$$\begin{aligned} &X(s_{T-1}) \ge 0 \quad \text{for all } s_{T-1}, \\ &X(s_{T-1}) > 0 \quad \text{for some } s_{T-1}; \end{aligned} \tag{19a}$$

and its time 0 value is nonpositive, i.e.,

$$n_P(0)P(0, T) + n_B(0)B(0) \le 0. \tag{19b}$$

Such a portfolio has positive or zero initial cash flow at time 0, and positive or zero cash flow at time $T-1$. It is a 'money pump'.

To finish the description of the model, we add:

Assumption P (No-arbitrage opportunities). There exist no-arbitrage opportunities in this economy.

We have as a direct consequence of Assumption P:

Lemma 2 (The money market account return versus the T-maturity bond return). Given Assumption P,

$$\mathrm{u}(t, T; s_t) > r(t; s_t) > \mathrm{d}(t, T; s_t) \quad \text{for all } s_t \text{ and } t < T + 1 \tag{20}$$

Proof. Suppose not, say that $r(t; s_t) \geq u(t, T; s_t)$ for some t, s_t. Then, an arbitrage opportunity can be constructed. To see this, note that over $[t, t+1]$, the money market account pays off more than the T-maturity bond given the state s_t occurs at time t. So at time t, if state s_t occurs, buy one unit of the money market account and finance it (zero investment) by selling the T-maturity bond. The resulting portfolio at time t satisfies expression (19b) and at time $t+1$, expression (19a). It is straightforward to transform this zero initial wealth position to time 0 (do nothing until time t). This arbitrage opportunity yields a contradiction of Assumption P, and completes the proof. □

Lemma 2 relates the returns on the T-maturity zero-coupon bond with those of the money market account. But, Assumption P is even stronger. It also relates the returns on the T-maturity bond and the money market account to *all* the other zero-coupon bonds. To see this, we need to expand the above definitions of a trading strategy and arbitrage opportunity. The previous definitions only involve the T-maturity bond and the money market account. The corresponding generalization of the definition of a trading strategy and the definition of an arbitrage opportunity to include the remaining zero-coupon bonds is straightforward.

Lemma 3 (Zero-curve valuation). Given Assumption P, let $(n_P(t; s_t), n_B(t; s_t)$: $0 \leq t \leq \tau - 1)$ be the dynamic self-financing trading strategy in the bond with maturity T and the money market account which pays one dollar at time τ across all states s_τ (this exists by Lemma 1), then

$$n_P(0) P(0, T) + n_B(0) B(0) = P(0, \tau). \tag{21}$$

Proof. The proof is simple. If expression (21) is violated, say the left side is strictly less than the right side, then form the portfolio $(n_P(t; s_t), n_B(t; s_t)$: $0 \leq t \leq \tau - 1)$ and short one bond maturing at time τ. By construction, this is an arbitrage opportunity. This contradicts Assumption P. Thus, the left side of expression (21) must be greater than or equal to the right side. If the inequality is strict, repeat the above argument, but reverse the signs of the positions. This also yields a contradiction, and the result. □

Expression (21) shows that all the bond prices $(P(0, \tau)$: $0 \leq \tau \leq T)$ and the stochastic processes for its evolution through time $(\mathrm{u}(t, \tau), \mathrm{d}(t, \tau)$: $0 \leq t < \tau \leq T-1)$ can be determined by knowing $\{P(0, T), (\mathrm{u}(t, T), \mathrm{d}(t, T)$: $0 \leq t \leq T-1)\}$ and $\{r(0), (\alpha(t), \beta(t)$: $0 \leq t \leq T-1)\}$. If the prices given by expression (21) differ from the observed market prices, then the price discrepancy indicates the existence of an arbitrage opportunity. We label such an arbitrage opportunity, 'zero-curve arbitrage'.

The above procedure, in expression (21) and by implication [expression (15)], gives the procedure for constructing a synthetic zero-coupon bond from another zero-coupon bond (maturity T) and the money market account. This synthetic construction of a zero-coupon bond is an important attribute of the bond price process models.

3.3. Equivalence between the spot rate process and bond price process models

This section shows the equivalence between the spot rate process and bond price process models using the martingale pricing technology. This equivalence follows through a sequence of two propositions.

Proposition 1 (The spot rate model implies the bond price model)**.** Given the spot rate process model, assumption R, implies that

(i) the market is complete, and

(ii) expressions (20) and (21) hold for the bond price process (6) constructable from expression (10).

Proof. *Step (i)*. Expression (10) together with $\alpha(t; s_t) \neq \beta(t; s_t)$ implies $\mathrm{u}(t, T; s_t) > \mathrm{d}(t, T; s_t)$. This is the crucial condition in Lemma 1, so the proof of Lemma 1 applies as written.

Step (ii). Expression (6), (9) and algebra yield

$$\frac{\mathrm{u}(t, T; s_t)}{r(t; s_t)} \pi(t; s_t) + \frac{\mathrm{d}(t, T; s_t)}{r(t; s_t)} (1 - \pi(t; s_t)) = 1.$$

Together with $\mathrm{u}(t, T; s_t) > \mathrm{d}(t, T; s_t)$, this implies (20).

From step (i), let $(n_P(t; s_t), n_B(t; s_t)$: $0 \leq t \leq \tau - 1)$ be the self-financing trading strategy generating $P(t, \tau)$. From the proof of Lemma 1 we have at time τ:

$$n_P(\tau-1; s_{\tau-1}) P(\tau, T; s_\tau) + n_B(\tau-1; s_{\tau-1}) B(\tau; s_{\tau-1}) = 1 \quad \text{for all } s_\tau.$$

Taking expected values of both sides under Π [using (6)] gives

$$n_P(\tau-1; s_{\tau-1}) P(\tau-1, T; s_{\tau-1}) + \\ + n_B(\tau-1; s_{\tau-1}) B(\tau-1; s_{\tau-2}) = P(\tau-1, \tau; s_{\tau-1}).$$

This is expression (21) at time $(\tau - 1)$.

Next, using the self-financing conditions [(17) and (18)], we get

$$n_P(\tau-2;s_{\tau-2})P(\tau-1,T;s_{\tau-1})+ \\ +n_B(\tau-2;s_{\tau-2})B(\tau-1;s_{\tau-2})=P(\tau-1,\tau;s_{\tau-1}).$$

Taking expectations under Π [using (6)] gives (21) at time $(\tau-2)$. Continuing by backward induction yields (21). □

Proposition 1 shows that the spot rate process model in conjunction with Assumption R, implies the bond price process model. The bond price model is defined to be expression (11) and the results given in expressions (20) and (21). These results are the implications of assumption P. In fact, expressions (20) and (21) are equivalent to assumption P, but this fact requires a more sophisticated argument and is therefore omitted. For practical applications, expressions (20) and (21) are the relevant conditions.

The order of argument in Proposition 1 is important, however. Given are $\{r(0),(\alpha(t),\beta(t)\colon\ t\in[0,T])\}$ *and* Π. These, in turn, via expression (10) determine $\{P(0,\tau),(\mathrm{u}(t,\tau),\mathrm{d}(t,\tau))$ for all $\tau\}$. These derived quantities enable us to calculate the hedge ratios (or deltas) needed to construct a synthetic zero-coupon bond from another distinct zero-coupon bond and the money market account. The deltas are given in expression (15). These deltas are essential in order to execute any zero-curve arbitrage discovered via expression (10). Next, we state and prove the converse to Proposition 1.

Proposition 2 (The bond price model implies the spot rate model)**.** Expressions (20) and (21) imply Assumption R; in particular, Π is given by

$$\pi^T(t;s_t)=\frac{r(t;s_t)-\mathrm{d}(t,T;s_t)}{\mathrm{u}(t,T;s_t)-\mathrm{d}(t,T;s_t)}\quad\text{for all } 0\le t\le T-1 \text{ and } s_t. \tag{22}$$

Proof. First, by expression (20), there exists a unique $\pi^T(t;s_t)\in(0,1)$ such that

$$\pi^T(t;s_t)\mathrm{u}(t,T;s_t)+(1-\pi^T(t;s_t))\mathrm{d}(t,T;s_t)=r(t;s_t).$$

In fact, the unique $\pi^T(t;s_t)$ is given in expression (22). To show that $P(t,\tau;s_t)/B(t;s_{t-1})$ is a martingale under the π^T given in expression (22) we use expression (21) [and (15)]. The cash flow at time τ to be duplicated is $X(s_\tau)=1$ if $s_\tau=s_{\tau-1}\mathrm{u}$ and 1 if $s_\tau=s_{\tau-1}\mathrm{d}$. Substitution of (15) in (21) evaluated at time $\tau-1$ and algebra yields

$$\frac{P(\tau-1,\tau;s_{\tau-1})}{B(\tau-1;s_{\tau-2})}= \\ =\frac{\pi^T(\tau-1;s_{\tau-1})P(\tau,\tau;s_{\tau-1}\mathrm{u})+\big(1-\pi^T(\tau-1;s_{\tau-1})\big)P(\tau,\tau;s_{\tau-1}\mathrm{d})}{B(\tau;s_{\tau-1})}.$$

This is the result for time $\tau-1$. Continuing this procedure in a backward inductive fashion completes the proof. □

Proposition 2 shows that the bond price process model, i.e., expressions (11), (20) and (21), imply the spot rate process model. The order of the argument is, again, important. Given are $\{r(0), (\alpha(t), \beta(t)\colon\ t \in [0, T]\}$ *and* $\{P(0, T), (\mathrm{u}(t, T), \mathrm{d}(t, T)\colon\ t \in [0, T-1])\}$. These, in turn, via expression (22) determine Π. These Π enable us to use expression (10) to calculate the values of the remaining zero-coupon bonds as discounted expected values. This present value procedure facilitates numerical computations within the bond price process model.

3.4. Summary

The two models just analyzed provide a method for arbitraging price discrepancies across the zero-coupon bond price curve. In fact, this procedure can also be extended to price contingent claims (or options) written on the zero-coupon bond price curve evolution. A *contingent claim* is defined as a state contingent cash flow received at a particular date, say $X(s_{T-1})$ received at time $T-1$. The identical argument used as in the proof of Proposition 2 implies (under either model) that the arbitrage free value of this contingent claim at time 0, denoted $X(0)$, is given by:

$$X(0) = E_0^{\Pi}\left(\frac{X(s_{T-1})}{B(T-1; s_{T-2})}\right) B(0). \tag{23}$$

This argument can be extended to incorporate multiple cash flows and random stopping times, see Carr & Jarrow [1995].

Although this approach has been utilized in the literature [see Vasicek, 1977; Brennan & Schwartz, 1979; Courtadon, 1982; Cox, Ingersoll & Ross, 1985; Longstaff, 1989], it has some problems. The problems are related to the observation that the theoretical zero-coupon bond price curve generated by these models will (almost certainly) differ from the observed zero-coupon bond price curve. This is true because all models, including this one, are approximations to reality and contain errors. These are isolated as arbitrage opportunities in the above models. As such, for any nontrivial contingent claim dependent on the zero bond price curve (with multiple cash flows across multiple dates), the theoretical price in expression (23) will also differ from the observed price due to these zero coupon bond price differences. Again, this indicates an arbitrage opportunity.

With respect to the *observed* zero-coupon bond price curve, however, there may in fact be no-arbitrage opportunities using these contingent claims. The relative prices of the contingent claims (relative to the *observed* zero coupon bond price curve) may be arbitrage free. The above models do not incorporate this distinction. This distinction is best handled by using the class of models directly developed for pricing interest rate contingent claims. This is the topic of the next section.

4. Option pricing

This section shows how to extend the previous zero-curve arbitrage models to contingent claim valuation models where the *entire* initial zero-coupon bond price curve is given. The major difference between this approach and the previous one is that we now deduce the spot rate process endogenously from the bond price process given in Figure 2. Indeed, as each bond matures, it determines the spot rate for that period. The ability to construct the spot rate process from the bond price process in Figure 2 is the key insight to what follows.

4.1 Spot rate process models

This section shows how to extend the spot rate process model of the previous section to price contingent claims taking the entire initial zero-coupon bond price curve as a given. This class of models, under various reparameterizations, include Black, Derman & Toy [1990] and the discrete time analogue of Hull & White [1990]. The purpose of this approach is to endogenously determine Π and $(\alpha(t), \beta(t)\colon\ 0 \le t \le T-1)$ to match the initial bond price curve.

This extension reduces to one of solving a system of simultaneous equations in multiple unknowns. The equations are given by expression (10) for $\tau = 0, 1, \ldots, T$ ($T+1$ equations). Given now are $(P(0,1), \ldots, P(0,T))$, the right side of expression (10). The unknowns are Π and $\{(\alpha(t), \beta(t))\colon\ 0 \le t \le T-1\}$ from Figure 3 and expression (8). There are 2^T unknowns within $(\alpha(t), \beta(t)\colon\ 0 \le t \le T-1)$ and $[T-1][T-2]/2$ unknowns within Π. The goal is to find solutions for the unknowns $(\Pi,\ (\alpha(t), \beta(t)\colon\ 0 \le t \le T-1))$ such that the $(T+1)$ equations implied by expression (10) with the observed bond prices are satisfied. This overabundance of unknowns implies that we can usually find a solution to this system.

It is usual practice [see Black, Derman & Toy, 1990] to arbitrarily set each element in Π equal to (1/2). This reduces the number of unknowns considerably. The determination of $(\alpha(t), \beta(t)\colon\ 0 \le t \le T-1)$ from the system of equations described above must be done numerically (in general). Fortunately, a forward inductive procedure can be utilized. At step 1, $\alpha(0;\mathrm{u})$ and $\beta(0;\mathrm{d})$ are determined by expression (10) and $P(0,2)$. Given these, step 2 solves for $\alpha(1;\mathrm{uu}), \alpha(1;\mathrm{du}), \beta(1;\mathrm{dd}), \beta(1;\mathrm{ud})$ given expression (10) and $P(0,3)$. The process continues in this fashion until all bond prices $(P(0,1), \ldots, P(0,T))$ are used. Counting equations and unknowns reveals (even given Π's elements equal 1/2) that additional constraints can be imposed (for example, the binomial tree for $r(t)$ could be required to recombine). The above procedure guarantees that the spot rate process evolution yields bond prices [under expression (10)] that match the observed initial bond price curve.

To value contingent claims written on the zero-coupon bond price curve evolution, we use expression (23) with the spot rate process and Π as determined above. The quality of this class of models for pricing options is determined by the goodness of fit of the spot rate process (just determined) to the empirically observed spot rate process. Empirical research is needed along these lines.

4.2. Bond price process models

This section shows how to extend the bond price process model of the previous section to price contingent claims taking the entire initial zero-coupon bond price curve as a given. This class of models includes under various reparameterizations those of Ho & Lee [1986], Bliss & Ronn [1989], Heath, Jarrow & Morton [1990, 1991, 1992], Babbs [1990], and Shirakawa [1991].

The first step in this extension is to expand the initial specification of the model to include the stochastic process for *all* the zero-coupon bonds (and not just the T-maturity bond). This implies that given exogenously is now the *entire* process in Figure 2 and its decomposition as in expression (6), i.e., $\{(P(0,1),\ldots,P(0,T)), (\mathrm{u}(t,\tau), \mathrm{d}(t,\tau)\text{: for all } t,\tau)\}$. From this specification, the spot rate process is determined as given in expression (7). The next step in the procedure is to determine the additional restrictions that the implication of Assumption P, the absence of arbitrage, has on the remaining parameters $(\mathrm{u}(t,\tau), \mathrm{d}(t,\tau)\text{: for } 0 \le \tau \le T-1)$ in the bond price processes. This additional restriction is given in the next proposition.

Proposition 3 (Arbitrage restrictions on the zero-coupon bond price processes). Given the specification of $\{(P(0,1),\ldots,P(0,T))$ and $(\mathrm{u}(t,\tau), \mathrm{d}(t,\tau)\text{: for all } t,\tau)\}$, expressions (20) and (21) hold if and only if

$$1 > \frac{r(t;s_t) - \mathrm{d}(t,T;s_t)}{\mathrm{u}(t,T;s_t) - \mathrm{d}(t,T;s_t)} = \frac{r(t;s_t) - \mathrm{d}(t,\tau;s_t)}{\mathrm{u}(t,\tau;s_t) - \mathrm{d}(t,\tau;s_t)} > 0 \qquad \text{for all } 0 \le t \le t \le T-1 \text{ and } s_t. \tag{24}$$

Proof. *Step 1.* From Lemma 3 and Proposition 2 we have

$$\frac{P(t,\tau;s_t)}{B(t;s_{t-1})} = \pi^T(t;s_t)\frac{P(t,\tau;s_t)\mathrm{u}(t,\tau;s_t)}{B(t;s_{t-1})r(t;s_t)} + \\ + \left(1 - \pi^T(t;s_t)\right)\frac{P(t,\tau;s_t)\mathrm{d}(t,\tau;s_t)}{B(t;s_{t-1})r(t;s_t)}.$$

Algebra gives (24).

Step 2. First, note that the strict inequalities in (24) imply (20). Second, reversing the algebra in step 1 gives that expression (9) holds. But this was all that was required for the proof of Proposition 1 [step (ii)] to obtain expression (21). □

Proposition 3 provides necessary and sufficient conditions upon the specification of the bond price process parameters $(\mathrm{u}(t,\tau), \mathrm{d}(t,\tau)\text{: } 0 \le t \le \tau \le T)$ such that expression (23) can be used to price contingent claims on the evolution of the zero-coupon bond price curve, taking the initial curve $(P(0,1),\ldots,P(0,T))$ as given. The probabilities Π are given by expression (22). Expression (24) implies that these probabilities are independent of the particular maturity zero-coupon bond selected. These restrictions allow a great degree of flexibility in the selection of the bond price process.

4.3. A comparison of the spot rate process and bond price process models

By the equivalence propositions of section 3, both models will give the identical contingent claim values *if* each process generates the other. The models only differ in the initial parameterization and the manner in which the initial zero-coupon bond price curve is introduced into the model specification. The spot rate process approach takes the spot rate process and the martingale probabilities as the given, and then inverts the valuation procedure [expression (10)] to find those spot rate processes such that the theoretical bond prices match the observed initial zero-coupon bond price curve. In contrast, the bond price approach takes the entire bond price *curve* process as a given, but restricts the parameters of its stochastic process to guarantee that the evolution of the initial curve through time is consistent with the absence of arbitrage. The different models are just 'opposite sides of the same coin'.

Of the two approaches, for the exponentially expanding trees in Figures 2 and 3, the bond price process approach appears to be the simplest from a computational perspective. Indeed, it requires no inversion to determine the spot rate processes parameters. This inversion process usually entails numerical approximation procedures. However, this preference for the bond price process approach may no longer hold for special cases of the general model. In special cases, the spot rate process may have a recombining tree whereas the bond prices process may not. This could lead to computational efficiencies in constructing the tree which dominate the inversion difficulties. Additional research is needed to resolve these issues.

5. Empirical specifications

To implement these models, it is convenient to specify either the spot rate process's parameters (for the spot rate process models) or the bond price process's parameters (for the bond price process models) in terms of the continuous time limits. The motivation for this specification is that the discrete time, discrete state space model is, in fact, only a reasonable approximation to reality for small time steps between trading intervals. As such, the continuous time limit is the relevant process being approximated.

To illustrate this procedure, two examples are provided. One, for the spot rate process models, and two, for the bond price process models. We only consider the specifications for the option pricing application, although the same techniques can be applied for zero-curve arbitrage. For notational convenience, denote the unit of time between each trading interval $[t, t+1]$ by Δ. The exact size of Δ is usually determined by the particulars of the application itself. We will be interested in the limits of the various processes as $\Delta \to 0$.

5.1. *Spot rate process models*

To illustrate this procedure, we give the specification contained in Black, Derman & Toy [1990]. Recall that in the spot rate process model, given are $\{r(0), \Pi, (\alpha(t), \beta(t)\colon\ 0 \le t \le T-1)\}$. To simplify the parameterization, first set all the probabilities in Π equal to 1/2. Second, let $\alpha(t), \beta(t)$ be dependent only on time, and *independent of the state* of the process. To facilitate estimation, let us reparameterize the model by defining $\mu(t), \sigma(t)$ as:

$$\sigma(t) \equiv \frac{\log(\alpha(t)/\beta(t))}{2\sqrt{\Delta}} \tag{25a}$$

and

$$\mu(t) \equiv \frac{\log\big(\alpha(t)\beta(t)\big)}{2\Delta} \tag{25b}$$

This implies

$$\alpha(t) = \mathrm{e}^{\mu(t)\Delta+\sigma(t)\sqrt{\Delta}} \tag{26a}$$

and

$$\beta(t) = \mathrm{e}^{\mu(t)\Delta-\sigma(t)\sqrt{\Delta}} \tag{26b}$$

Expressed in terms of the spot rate process given in expression (8), we get:

$$r(t+\Delta; s_{t+\Delta}) = \begin{cases} r(t;s_t)\mathrm{e}^{\mu(t)\Delta+\sigma(t)\sqrt{\Delta}} & \text{if } s_{t+\Delta} = s_t\mathrm{u} \\ r(t;s_t)\mathrm{e}^{\mu(t)\Delta-\sigma(t)\sqrt{\Delta}} & \text{if } s_{t+\Delta} = s_t\mathrm{d} \end{cases} \tag{27}$$

From (27) we see that $\mu(t) = E_t^{\Pi}\big(\log r(t+\Delta; s_t+\Delta) - \log r(t;s_t)\big)/\Delta$ and $\sigma(t)^2 = \mathrm{var}_t^{\Pi}\big(\log r(t+\Delta; s_t+\Delta)\big)/\Delta$ where $\mathrm{var}_t^{\Pi}(\cdot)$ is the Π-conditional variance given t. Thus, these parameters can be interpreted as the instantaneous mean and volatilities of changes in the spot rate.

Using standard techniques, it can be shown that the limiting distribution of the spot rates as $\Delta \to 0$ is a lognormal. Black, Derman & Toy [1990] select $(\sigma(t)\colon\ 0 \le t \le T-1)$ to match the term structure of volatilities, and determine $(\mu(t)\colon\ 0 \le t \le T-1)$ such that expression (10) matches the initial bond price curve $(P(0,1), \ldots, P(0,T))$. This completes the specification. Other specifications can be found in Hull & White [1990].

5.2. *Bond price process models*

The empirical specification for the bond price process models is much more subtle than for the spot rate process models. This is due to the facts that (i) each zero-coupon bond must equal a dollar for sure at maturity, and (ii) the no-arbitrage restriction (24) needs to be satisfied. Recall that in the bond price process model, given are $\{(P(0,1), \ldots, P(0,T)), (\mathrm{u}(t,\tau), \mathrm{d}(t,\tau)\colon \text{for all } t, \tau)\}$.

To illustrate this procedure, we give the continuous time specification of Ho & Lee [1986] contained in Heath, Jarrow & Morton [1990, 1991, 1992]. The easiest method for guaranteeing that each bond equals a dollar for sure at maturity is not to specify $(\mathrm{u}(t, \tau), \mathrm{d}(t, \tau)$: for all $t, \tau)$ directly; but, to specify a stochastic process for forward rates instead. Expression (2) can be then used to guarantee that each bond's value at maturity is a dollar, and the $(\mathrm{u}(t, \tau), \mathrm{d}(t, \tau)$: for all $t, \tau)$ deduced from it.

Following this approach, let the state *independent* parameters $\mu(t, \tau)$, σ be given and let the forward rate process satisfy the following expression:

$$f(t+\Delta, \tau; s_{t+\Delta}) = \begin{cases} f(t, \tau; s_t)\mathrm{e}^{\mu(t,\tau)\Delta - \sigma\sqrt{\Delta}} & \text{if } s_{t+\Delta} = s_t\mathrm{u} \\ f(t, \tau; s_t)\mathrm{e}^{\mu(t,\tau)\Delta + \sigma\sqrt{\Delta}} & \text{if } s_{t+\Delta} = s_t\mathrm{d} \end{cases} \quad \text{for } t + \Delta \leq \tau. \tag{28}$$

This implies, in the limit, that these discrete forward rates are lognormally distributed. Expression (2), rewritten in terms of Δ's is:

$$P(t+\Delta, \tau; s_{t+\Delta}) = \prod_{j=t+\Delta}^{\tau-\Delta} \frac{1}{f(t+\Delta, j; s_{t+\Delta})} \quad \text{for } t+\Delta \leq \tau - \Delta \tag{29}$$

Substitution of (28) into (29) yields:

$$P(t+\Delta, \tau; s_{t+\Delta}) = \begin{cases} \displaystyle\prod_{j=t+\Delta}^{\tau-\Delta} \frac{1}{f(t, j; s_t)} \mathrm{e}^{-\sum_{j=t+\Delta}^{\tau-\Delta} \mu(t,j)\Delta + \sigma(\tau - t - \Delta)\sqrt{\Delta}} & \text{if } s_{t+\Delta} = s_t\mathrm{u} \\ \displaystyle\prod_{j=t+\Delta}^{\tau-\Delta} \frac{1}{f(t, j; s_t)} \mathrm{e}^{-\sum_{j=t+\Delta}^{\tau-\Delta} \mu(t,j)\Delta - \sigma(\tau - t - \Delta)\sqrt{\Delta}} & \text{if } s_{t+\Delta} = s_t\mathrm{d} \end{cases} \tag{30}$$

$$= \begin{cases} P(t, \tau; s_t) r(t; s_t) \mathrm{e}^{-\sum_{j=t+\Delta}^{\tau-\Delta} \mu(t,j)\Delta + \sigma(\tau - t - \Delta)\sqrt{\Delta}} & \text{if } s_{t+\Delta} = s_t\mathrm{u} \\ P(t, \tau; s_t) r(t; s_t) \mathrm{e}^{-\sum_{j=t+\Delta}^{\tau-\Delta} \mu(t,j)\Delta - \sigma(\tau - t - \Delta)\sqrt{\Delta}} & \text{if } s_{t+\Delta} = s_t\mathrm{d} \end{cases}$$

Thus, we can identify:

$$\mathrm{u}(t, \tau; s_t) \equiv r(t; s_t)\mathrm{e}^{-\sum_{j=t+\Delta}^{\tau-\Delta} \mu(t,j)\Delta + \sigma(\tau - t - \Delta)\sqrt{\Delta}} \quad \text{for } t \leq \tau - 2\Delta, \tag{31a}$$

$$\mathrm{d}(t, \tau; s_t) \equiv r(t; s_t)\mathrm{e}^{-\sum_{j=t+\Delta}^{\tau-\Delta} \mu(t,j)\Delta - \sigma(\tau - t - \Delta)\sqrt{\Delta}} \quad \text{for } t \leq \tau - 2\Delta, \tag{31b}$$

and

$$\mathrm{u}(t, t+1; s_t) = (t; s_t) = \mathrm{d}(t, t+1; s_t). \tag{31c}$$

Next, we impose the no-arbitrage restriction (24). This implies that:

$$\frac{r(t;s_t) - r(t;s_t)\mathrm{e}^{-\sum_{j=t+\Delta}^{\tau-\Delta} \mu(t,j)\Delta - \sigma(\tau-t-\Delta)\sqrt{\Delta}}}{r(t;s_t)\mathrm{e}^{-\sum_{j=t+\Delta}^{\tau-\Delta} \mu(t,j)\Delta + \sigma(\tau-t-\Delta)\sqrt{\Delta}} - r(t;s_t)\mathrm{e}^{-\sum_{j=t+\Delta}^{\tau-\Delta} \mu(t,j)\Delta - \sigma(\tau-t-\Delta)\sqrt{\Delta}}} =$$

$$= \pi(t;s_t) \qquad \text{for all } t \leq \tau - 2\Delta \text{ and } \tau \leq T. \tag{32}$$

Simplification generates:

$$\frac{1 - \mathrm{e}^{-\sum_{j=t+\Delta}^{\tau-\Delta} \mu(t,j)\Delta - \sigma(\tau-t-\Delta)\sqrt{\Delta}}}{\mathrm{e}^{-\sum_{j=t+\Delta}^{\tau-\Delta} \mu(t,j)\Delta + \sigma(\tau-t-\Delta)\sqrt{\Delta}} - \mathrm{e}^{-\sum_{j=t+\Delta}^{\tau-\Delta} \mu(t,j)\Delta - \sigma(\tau-t-\Delta)\sqrt{\Delta}}} = \pi(t;s_t)$$

$$\text{for all } t \leq \tau - 2\Delta \text{ and } \tau \leq T. \tag{33}$$

First, note that as $\Delta \to 0$, by a Taylor series expansion, the left side of expression (33) is approximately $(\sum_{j=t+\Delta}^{\tau-\Delta} \mu(t, j)\Delta + \sigma(\tau - t)\sqrt{\Delta})/(2\sigma(\tau - t)\sqrt{\Delta})$. Thus, we see that:

$$\pi(t;s_t) = \tfrac{1}{2} + 0(\sqrt{\Delta}) \text{ where } \lim_{\Delta\to 0} 0(\sqrt{\Delta}) = 0 \text{ and } \lim_{\Delta\to 0} \frac{0(\sqrt{\Delta})}{\sqrt{\Delta}} < +\infty \tag{34}$$

For computational convenience, set $\pi(t;s_t) = 1/2$. Under this restriction, expression (33) uniquely determines $\mu(t, \tau)$. It implies that

$$\mathrm{e}^{+\sum_{j=t+\Delta}^{\tau-\Delta}} = \left(\tfrac{1}{2}\mathrm{e}^{\sigma(\tau-t-\Delta)\sqrt{\Delta}} + \tfrac{1}{2}\mathrm{e}^{-\sigma(\tau-t-\Delta)\sqrt{\Delta}}\right) \qquad \text{for all } t \leq \tau - 2\Delta \text{ and } \tau \leq T$$

$$\equiv \cosh\left(\sigma(\tau - t - \Delta)\sqrt{\Delta}\right). \tag{35}$$

Expression (35) is the necessary and sufficient condition for no arbitrage.

In summary, an arbitrage-free empirical specification of the bond price process model is given by $\{(P(0, 1), \ldots, P(0, T)), (\mathrm{u}(t, \tau), \mathrm{d}(t, \tau)\text{: all } t, \tau)\}$ where

$$\mathrm{u}(t, \tau; s_t) \equiv \left(\frac{1}{P(t, t+\Delta; s_t)}\right) \frac{\mathrm{e}^{\sigma(\tau-t-\Delta)\sqrt{\Delta}}}{\cosh\left(\sigma(\tau - t - \Delta)\sqrt{\Delta}\right)} \tag{36a}$$

$$\mathrm{d}(t, \tau; s_t) \equiv \left(\frac{1}{P(t, t+\Delta; s_t)}\right) \frac{\mathrm{e}^{-\sigma(\tau-t-\Delta)\sqrt{\Delta}}}{\cosh\left(\sigma(\tau - t - \Delta)\sqrt{\Delta}\right)} \qquad \text{for } t \leq \tau - 2\Delta, \tag{36b}$$

and

$$\mathrm{u}(t, t+\Delta; s_t) = \mathrm{d}(t, t+\Delta; s_t) = \frac{1}{P(t, t+\Delta; s_t)} \tag{36c}$$

or equivalently,

$$P(t+\Delta, \tau; s_{t+\Delta}) = \begin{cases} \left(\dfrac{P(t, \tau; s_t)}{P(t, t+\Delta; s_t)}\right) \dfrac{\mathrm{e}^{\sigma(\tau - t - \Delta)\sqrt{\Delta}}}{\cosh\left(\sigma(\tau - t - \Delta)\sqrt{\Delta}\right)} \\ \qquad\qquad \text{if } s_{t+\Delta} = s_t \mathrm{u} \\ \left(\dfrac{P(t, \tau; s_t)}{P(t, t+\Delta; s_t)}\right) \dfrac{\mathrm{e}^{-\sigma(\tau - t - \Delta)\sqrt{\Delta}}}{\cosh\left(\sigma(\tau - t - \Delta)\sqrt{\Delta}\right)} \\ \qquad\qquad \text{if } s_{t+\Delta} = s_t \mathrm{d} \end{cases}$$

$$\text{and all } 0 \le t \le \tau - 2\Delta \text{ and } \tau \le T. \tag{37}$$

For calculating interest rate option prices with expression (23), this implies (through expression (24)) that Π is identically equal to (1/2). Furthermore, by expression (36), the entire evolution of the zero-coupon bond price curve is determined by $(P(0, 1), \ldots, P(0, T))$ and the *single parameter* σ, which corresponds to the volatility of the forward rate process given in (28). This completes the empirical specification. Other empirical specifications can be found in Heath, Jarrow & Morton [1992].

6. Conclusion

This paper has reviewed and synthesized the various approaches to pricing interest rate options. The review has concentrated on a discrete time, discrete state space model. Because of space limitations, the continuous time analogues were not discussed in great detail. This is an important area of research for which the reader must necessarily consult the literature. Before concluding, however, a comment is appropriate. As true in the field of option pricing in general, the empirical literature on interest rate options lags behind the available theory. Little is currently known about which subcase of the above models provides the 'best' pricing method for interest rate options. This determination still awaits further research.

References

Artzner, P., and F. Delbaen (1989). Term structure of interest rates: The martingale approach. *Adv. Appl. Math.* 10, 95–129.

Babbs, S. (1990). The term structure of interest rates: Stochastic processes and contingent claims, Ph.D. thesis, Imperial College.

Ball, C., and W. Torous (1983). Bond pricing dynamics and options, *J. Financ. Quant. Anal.* 18, 517–531.

Black, F., E. Derman and W. Toy (1990). A one-factor model of interest rates and its application to treasury bond options. *Financ. Anal. J.* January-February, 33–39.

Bliss, Jr., R., and E. Ronn (1989). Arbitrage-based estimation of non-stationary shifts in the term structure of interest rates, *J. Finance* 44, 591–610.

Brennan, M.J., and E.S. Schwartz (1979). A continous-time approach to the pricing of bonds, *J. Banking Finance* 3, 135–155.

Brenner, R., and R. Jarrow (1993). A simple Formula for options on Discount Bonds, *Adv. Futures Options Res.* 6, 45–51.

Carr, P., and R. Jarrow (1995). A Discrete Time Synthesis of Derivative Security Valuation using a Term structive of Futures Prices, in: R. Jarrow, V. Maksimovic and W.T. Ziemba (eds.), *Finance*, Handbooks in Operations Research and Management Science, Vol 9, Elsevier, Amsterdam, pp. 225–250 (this volume).

Cheng, S. T. (1987). On the feasibility of arbitrage-based option pricing when stochastic bond price processes are involved, unpublished manuscript, Columbia University.

Courtadon, G. (1982). The pricing of options on default-free bonds, *J. Financ. Quant. Anal.* 17, 75–100.

Cox, J.C., J.E. Ingersoll and S.A. Ross (1985). A theory of the term structures of interest rates, *Econometrica* 53, 385–407.

Dothan, L. (1978). On the term structure of interest rates, *J. Financ. Econ.* 6, 59–69.

Harrison, J.M., and D. Kreps (1979). Martingales and arbitrage in multiperiod securities markets, *J. Econ. Theory* 20, 381–408.

Harrison, J.M., and S. Pliska (1981). Martingales and stochastic integrals in the theory of continuous trading, *Stoch. Processes Appl.* 11, 215–260.

Heath, D., and R. Jarrow (1987). Arbitrage, continuous trading, and margin requirements, *J. Finance* 42, 1129–1142.

Heath, D., R. Jarrow and A. Morton (1990). Bond pricing and the term structure of interest rates: A discrete time approximation, *J. Financ. Quant. Anal.* 25(4), 419–440.

Heath, D., R. Jarrow and A. Morton (1991). Contingent claim valuation with a random evolution of interest rates, *Rev. Futures Markets*, 54–76.

Heath, D., R. Jarrow and A. Morton (1992). Bond pricing and the term structure of interest rates: A new methodology for contingent claims valuation, *Econometrica* 60(1), 77–105.

Ho, T.S., and S. Lee (1986). Term structure movements and pricing interest rate contingent claims, *J. Finance* 41(5), 1011–1028.

Hull, J., and A. White (1990). Pricing interest rate derivative securities, *Rev. Financ. Studies* 3(4), 573–592.

Jamshidian, F. (1989). An exact bond option formula, *J. Finance* 44(1), 205–209.

Langetieg, T.C. (1980). A multivariate model of the term structure, *J. Finance* 35(1), 71–97.

Longstaff, F. (1989). A nonlinear general equilibrium model of the term structure of interest rates, *J. Financ. Econ.* 23 195–224.

Rendleman, R., and B. Bartter (1980). The pricing of options on debt securities, *J. Financ. Quant. Anal.* 15, 11–24.

Richard, S. (1978). An arbitrage model of the term structure of interest rates, *J. Financ. Econ.* 7, 38–58.

Schaefer, S., and E. Schwartz (1987). Time-dependent variance and the pricing of bond options, *J. Finance* 42(5), 1113–1128.

Shirakawa, H. (1991). Interest rate option pricing with Poisson-Gaussian forward rate curve processes, *Math. Finance* 1(4), 77–94.

Turnbull, S., and F. Milne (1991). A simple approach to interest-rate option pricing, *Rev. Financ. Studies* 4(1), 87–120.

Vasicek, O. (1977). An equilibrium characterization of the term structure, *J. Financ. Econ.* 5, 177–188.

R. Jarrow et al., Eds., *Handbooks in OR & MS, Vol. 9*

Chapter 9

Term Structure of Interest Rates and the Pricing of Fixed Income Claims and Bonds

Terry A. Marsh

U.C. Berkeley, Walter A. Haas School of Business, 350 Barrows Hall, Berkeley, CA 94720, U.S.A.

1. Introduction

The *term structure of interest rates* is an array ('structure') of prices or yields on bonds with different terms to maturity. The term structure is computed from the observed prices of Government bonds which are typically regarded as default-free in developed countries, or from the prices of liquid claims which replicate bonds, such as interest-rate swaps. The relation among the bonds' yields — the term structure — varies over time. For example, if the yields on long-term bonds are above those on short term bonds, as they were in the U.S. in mid-1993, the term structure is said to be *upward* sloping. By contrast, the term structure was *downward sloping* in the U.S. in 1973 and the early 1980s — short-term yields were above long-term yields.

Until the mid- to late-1970s, term structure analysis and related research on fixed income management more or less existed as a stand-alone field in finance. Basic default-free bond concepts and terminology such as *yields*, *spot* and *forward* rates, *immunization*, *duration*, and the *liquidity preference* and *expectations* hypotheses concerning *term premiums* were neither influenced, nor had much influence on, asset pricing model development. The latter dealt with the *price of risk* whereas term structure models dealt with *the price of time* alone [1] — in the one-period and partial equilibrium portfolio allocation and asset

[1] This is not to say that portfolio theory and asset pricing concepts were *never* used to study the term structure of interest rates. For example, Stiglitz [1970] derived the relative demands for one-period ('short' term) and two-period ('long' term) bonds from a model in which investors make investment and consumption decisions to maximize expected lifetime utility. Long [1974] derived investor demand functions and prices for stocks, bonds, and commodity 'futures' contracts in the presence of multiperiod uncertainty about consumption good prices, changes in the investment opportunity set, and (nominal) wealth. Long's paper, along with various sections of Merton's [1971, 1975a] papers, foreshadowed much of the subsequent general equilibrium term structure analysis. On the empirical side, Roll [1970, 1971] applied a recursive version of the Sharpe–Lintner capital asset pricing model to monthly returns on longer-term bonds. Marsh [1985] tested whether consumption-based and one-period asset pricing model constraints across the monthly returns on bonds with different maturities were satisfied.

pricing models prior to the mid-1970s, one-period bonds were no more than numeraire.

In the last ten years, however, fixed income models have become increasingly integrated with mainstream models of asset allocation and asset pricing. The 'enabling' technology for this integration has been the intertemporal equilibrium asset pricing theory and risk-neutral valuation techniques developed in the mid- to late-1970s. The extension of this new technology to bonds has undoubtedly been stimulated by the increased volatility of interest rates, along with the rapid expansion of the cash market (e.g. the issuance of Government bonds in the U.S. and Japan),[2] and derivative markets (e.g. mortgage-backed securities, bond futures, interest-rate swaps, and the like) in fixed income securities. Continual improvement in the technology has, in turn, stimulated further growth of the derivatives market.

The primary objective of this chapter is to explain how the intertemporal and risk neutral pricing techniques have been applied in the fixed income area. The exposition follows essentially the reverse of the chronological order in which the applications took place. It begins with an explanation of how the risk-neutral approach has been adapted from the options pricing literature. It then turns to the equilibrium bond pricing models which were the focus of research in the late 1970s and early 1980s. Both the risk-neutral and equilibrium approaches are initially presented under the assumption that term structure movements depend upon only a single factor — the short rate of interest. This factor, and thus movements in bond prices, can then be represented in the 'tree' diagram which is now routinely used in explaining contingent claim pricing methods. Once the arbitrage-free and equilibrium approaches to modelling the term structure have been introduced, questions such as how many factors are needed in practice to adequately describe term structure movements, and the extent to which the equilibrium and risk neutral approaches 'incorporate' the information in the current term structure, are discussed. Finally, some of the issues which arise in fitting the fixed income models and applying them in the valuation of interest rate derivatives are addressed.

For the most part, the paper deals with the term structure of default-free *zero coupon* or *discount* bond prices, or equivalently, the *spot* and *forward* rates of interest implied by those prices. In principle, a coupon bond can be decomposed into a portfolio of zero-coupon bonds, each with a face value equal to the coupon, as if it were stripped from the coupon bond and priced separately. For example, a two-year 8% coupon bond with face value $1,000 makes a $40 coupon payment at the end of 6, 12, and 18 months, and a $1,040 payment at the end of two years — this final payment is the face value of principal plus the final coupon payment. As such, the 8% coupon bond notionally consists of a portfolio of three zero-coupon bonds paying $40 at the end of 6 months, 12 months, and

[2] In 1990 fixed income securities account for about half of the estimated $22 trillion worth of outstanding world stocks, bonds, and cash, though not all of these securities are freely traded; some 30%–40% of Government bonds are held by central banks, for example.

eighteen months respectively, together with a $1,040 zero with a maturity of 2 years.[3]

In practice, it is well-known that 'coupon' effects, tax effects, 'on-the-run' effects, and various other idiosyncrasies are important in pricing Treasury securities. Data errors, stale quotes, and the like must also be taken into account when fitting a term structure to bond prices, i.e. in deriving *implied zero coupon* yields. These important practical issues cannot be addressed here. Typically, spline fitting techniques are used to (cross-sectionally) 'smooth out' the idiosyncrasies in bond prices when fitting the term structure at each point in time[4] (cf. Nelson & Siegel [1987], Beim [1992] and Diament [1993] for discussion and references). Unfortunately, the design and pricing of various coupon and payout provisions on debt cannot be covered here either. Cox, Ingersoll & Ross [1980] and Ramaswamy & Sundaresan [1986] are examples of this work. Finally, by ignoring coupons, duration and immunization measures are not per se discussed here, though the models of interest rate movements on which their validity depends are; Ingersoll, Skelton & Weil [1978] contains a good overview of the duration literature; see also Boyle [1978].

The focus of the paper is on dynamic models for the time series of term structures of implied zero-coupon bond yields. Maturity-specific idiosyncrasies in bond prices and yields are smoothed out. The smoothing is assumed to have been done in a first step; the dynamic modelling is then a second step. In a *state-space* framework, these two steps could be *integrated*. In such a framework, the discount function would be defined as a state variable whose dynamics are modelled in a *state equation*. Differences between the observed term structure and the discount function — the differences which are 'smoothed' away in a separate step before fitting dynamic models, would then be simultaneously handled in a measurement equation.[5]

Whether obtained in a state-space framework or by the two step procedure of smoothing and then fitting a dynamic model to the smoothed term structure, the fitted discount function ends up being 'smoothed' in *two* ways relative to the term structures of actual discount bond prices at successive points in time. First, as just discussed, estimated idiosyncrasies such as coupon effects, on-the-run effects, data errors, stale bond quotes, etc., are eliminated as residuals or 'model measurement errors' in the measurement equation. Second, if the dynamic model is to have

[3] In 1984, the U.S. Treasury allowed coupons which are stripped like this from its outstanding obligations to be held as Strips, an acronym for Separate Trading of Registered Interest and Principal of Securities, whereby stripped securities can be held in separate book-entry form at the Federal Reserve. After 1987, bonds could also be reconstructed from Strips.

[4] 'Smoothing out' the effects doesn't necessarily mean 'smoothing away', e.g. if there are no zero-coupon bonds traded, it is not possible to isolate all coupon effects, and they will be smoothed into the fitted yield curve.

[5] As an example of why it is useful to integrate the measurement and state equations, consider liquidity effects on bond prices. One could possibly choose to model liquidity, or systematic factors responsible for it, as something priced in the state equation, or alternatively relegate it to the measurement equation. Integration should also force the user to think about the consequences of estimation error — presumably the loss function for errors in measuring the term structure at the long end is not the same as at the short end.

'teeth', it must have a small number of factors (potentially the prices of a subset of bonds themselves) to explain movements in the smoothed discount function — the state equation.

In Section 2 a brief explanation of equilibrium and risk-neutral valuation of assets, and their application to bonds, is given. In Section 3, a detailed exposition is presented of the risk-neutral method in a simple 'tree-diagram' context. In Section 4, the calibration of the risk-neutral model with the observed term structure is discussed. Equilibrium models of the term structure are introduced in more detail in Section 5, where the relative degree to which equilibrium and risk-neutral models fit the observed term structure is also discussed. The issue of the number of factors underlying shifts in the term structure is discussed in Section 6. Finally, Section 7 contains a brief summary and discussion of issues for future research.

2. Brief overview of asset valuation methods applied to bonds

2.1. Introduction

The analysis here will deal with the pricing of zero-coupon bonds which pay, with certainty, a standardized face value of 100 at maturity date T, $T = 1, \ldots \overline{T}$, where $\overline{T}$ is the longest maturity bond.[6] The payoff 100 is in units of a given country's currency, e.g. \$100 in the U.S. or Y100 in Japan. Given *covered interest rate parity*, a U.S. investor will be indifferent between a U.S. Government bond or a fully hedged investment in Japanese Government bonds.[7]

Current time will be denoted by t. 'States' $i = 1, \ldots S$ are used to represent uncertainty: today's state $\bar{i}$ is known, but future states are unknown. The abstract-sounding states will become nodes in 'tree diagrams' used to illustrate the uncertainty in bond prices. To fix ideas, a state could refer to a level of production

[6] Interestingly, the maturity range $\overline{T}$ seems to differ substantially across countries — 30 year Government bonds and now 50 year corporates in the U.S., but rarely more than 10 year maturities with any liquidity outside the U.S. Further, the maturity structure of debt (especially corporate debt) seems to shift substantially over time within countries. There does not seem to be much analysis of the economic and institutional factors responsible for these differences.

[7] Let $S(t)$ be the spot exchange rate at time t in dollars per yen. Let $F(t, t+1)$ be the one-period forward exchange price, at time t, of dollars per yen. A U.S. investor who invests one dollar to buy a (t+1) maturity U.S. Government bond for $P(t, t+1, \bar{i})$ earns a known return of $R(t, t+1, \bar{i})$. Alternatively, the investor can convert the dollar to $1/S(t)$ yen, which when invested in Japanese Government bonds, will earn the yen-denominated riskless return $R^*(t, t+1, \bar{i})$. This payoff can be sold forward for $[(1+R^*)F(t, t+1)]/S(t)$ dollars at time t (assuming no default risk on the forward market). If *covered interest rate parity* $(1+R) = (F/S)(1+R^*)$ obtains, as it must to rule out the possibility of arbitrage profits, then the U.S. investor will be indifferent between the two alternatives. (Actually, the location of the investor becomes unimportant — the 'U.S. investor' is one who purchases consumption goods in the U.S.). Interestingly, *uncovered interest rate parity*, in which the U.S. investor does *not* hedge the yen investment and thus expects to receive $[1/S(t)](1+R^*)E_t\left[S(t+1)\right]$, where $E_t\left[S(t+1)\right]$ is the time t expectation of the time $t+1$ price of dollars in yen, does not seem to hold very well historically.

technology on which payoffs on some of the investments in individuals' portfolios depend, or to something that influences enjoyment from consumption — a 'consumption technology'.

The price of a *discount bond* will in general be a function of the current time t, the bond's maturity T, and the current state $\bar{i}$. The following time line illustrates the time sequence:

0	t	$t+1$		T	$\bar{T}$
	$P(t, T, \bar{i})$			100	

The *term structure* of bond prices at time t and state $\bar{i}$ is the shape of $P(t, T, \bar{i})$ for increasing T.

If a bond matures at time $T = t + 1$, then its price at time $t + 1$ must, with certainty, equal 100. At time t, its price in state $i = \bar{i}$ can be set equal to:

$$P(t, t+1, \bar{i}) = \frac{100}{R(t, t+1, \bar{i})} \tag{1}$$

which defines the one-period *riskless return* $R(t, t + 1, \bar{i})$ as the return that an investor would receive *with certainty* by buying the bond at time t for $P(t, t + 1, \bar{i})$ and redeeming it at time $t + 1$ for 100. Next, consider bonds which mature at time $t + 2$ and beyond. Even though these bonds have a sure payoff at maturity, their time $t+1$ prices are *uncertain* at time t — time $t+1$ states are uncertain, and thus so are future bond prices and interest rates. Figure 1, reproduced from Ho & Lee [1986], shows *bond* term structures (*discount functions*) at time 0, 1, and 2. In the diagram, as time changes from 0 to 1, the bond which is specifically highlighted as a 3 year bond at time 0 becomes a two year bond at time 2, and its time 1 price depends upon whether state 1 or state 0 is realized. At time 2, it will be a one-year bond, and its price will depend upon which of the three time 2 states is realized. In general, as time passes, the bond's price approaches its par value of 100 and price volatility decreases.

2.2. Equilibrium pricing models

How are the time t prices of bonds determined, given the uncertainty in $t + 1$ prices? In an *equilibrium* approach to asset pricing, bonds are treated as just one asset in an investor's portfolio.[8] In the standard analysis, representative investors are assumed to make their consumption and portfolio decisions so as to maximize the sum of their (additively separable) expected utilities of consumption at each time t in state $\bar{i}$, $u[C(t, \bar{i})]$. A necessary condition for an interior maximum is that, at any time t, the decrease in an investor's satisfaction from selling a marginal dollar's worth of assets at t and thereby giving up expected future consumption, must just balance the increase in marginal utility from consuming

[8] If the bonds are in zero gross supply, the bond prices will be shadow prices.

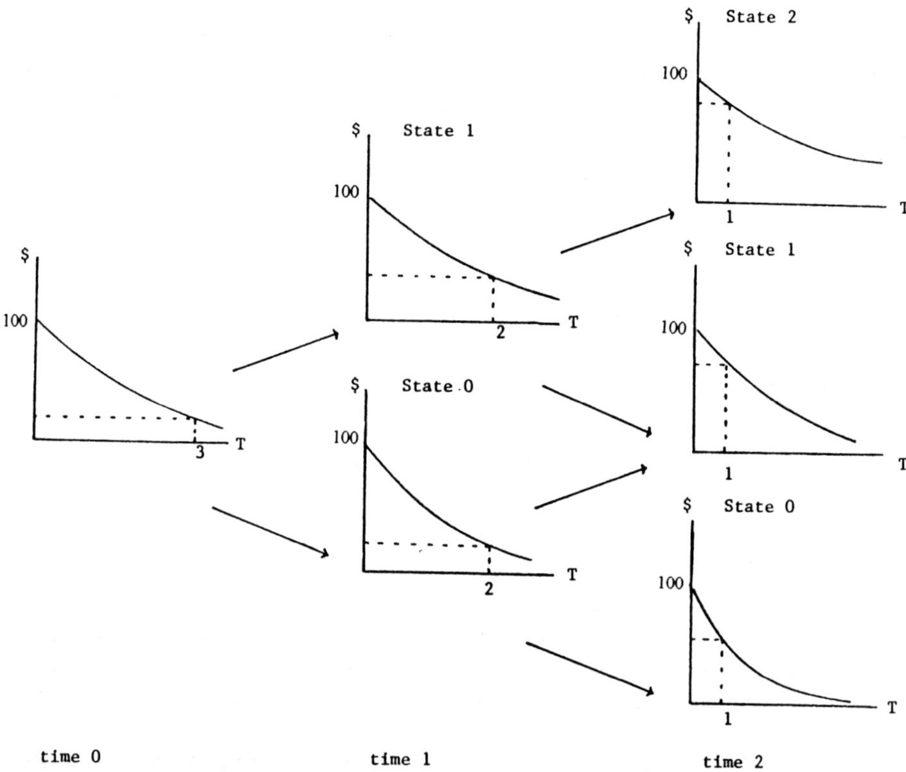

Fig. 1. Example of dynamics in the discount function (reproduced from Ho & Lee [1986]).

the proceeds at t. Suppose that the asset which is sold is the T-maturity bond at price $P(t, T, \bar{i})$. Consuming the proceeds from the sale would give a *marginal* increase in satisfaction of $P(t, T, \bar{i})u_C[C(t, \bar{i})]$, where $u_C[.]$ is the first derivative of the investor's utility function with respect to consumption. The expected loss in utility from selling the bond is the expectation of its uncertain liquidation value at $t+1$, $P(t+1, T, i)$, times the marginal utility from consuming these (uncertain) proceeds at $t+1$, $u_C[C(t+1, i)]$. If $P(t+1, T, i)$ is the equilibrium price, then the expected loss just balances the expected gain for the representative investor. That is:

$$P(t, T, \bar{i})u_C[C(t, \bar{i})] = \sum_{i=1}^{S} Q_i P(t+1, T, i)u_C[C(t+1, i)] \tag{2}$$

where Q_i is the probability of state i at time $t+1$.[9] It is convenient to define $m_i(t, t+1, \bar{i}) \equiv u_C[C(t+1, i)]/u_C[C(t, \bar{i})]$; in words, $m_i(t, t+1, \bar{i})$ is the price at

[9] This transition probability could depend upon the state at time t, and it will definitely depend upon the time-to-maturity of the bond, but the dependence is suppressed for the time being to simplify notation.

which, at the margin, time-t consumption in state $\bar{i}$ is traded off against (uncertain) time-$(t+1)$ consumption in state $i = 1, \ldots, S$. The restriction implied by the equilibrium in (2) is that m_i does not depend upon the specific asset which is used as the investment vehicle to transfer a dollar to time $t+1$: all assets are equally desirable at the margin. Using the definition of m_i and rearranging (2) gives:

$$P(t, T, i = \bar{i}) = \sum_{i=1}^{S} Q_i \left[m_i(t, t+1, \bar{i}) P(t+1, T, i) \right] \tag{3}$$

The Euler equation (2) has to hold between time t and any future point in time, not just between t and $t+1$. In particular, it must hold between t and the maturity time T of each bond. Thus, (3) can be rewritten as:

$$P(t, T, \bar{i}) = 100 \sum_{i=1}^{S} Q_i m_i \equiv \frac{100}{\left[R(t, T, \bar{i})\right]^{T-t}} \tag{4}$$

where $R(t, T, \bar{i})$ is defined as the $(T-t)$-period *spot rate of interest* or *zero-coupon yield-to-maturity*. Plotting $(T-t)$-period yields against time-to-maturity $(T-t)$ for increasing T produces a *yield curve*. Yield curves at a point in time t are typically described as *upward sloping*, *downward sloping*, *flat*, or *humped*, as illustrated in Figure 2. The challenge is to build term structure models which can produce these different yield curve shapes, and enable changes in the shapes to be hedged if so desired.

The Euler equation (2) is a necessary condition on consumption and investment for individuals to maximize their expected utility of lifetime consumption, e.g. Samuelson & Merton [1969], Merton [1971], Rubinstein [1976], and Lucas [1978]. LeRoy [1982] and Breeden [1986] specifically discuss the implications of the Euler equation for bond pricing. As stated in (2), the Euler condition ignores potentially important factors influencing investor decisions such as transactions costs, bankruptcy and borrowing constraints, and lack of time-additivity in their utility functions. The one-period capital asset pricing model, the intertemporal

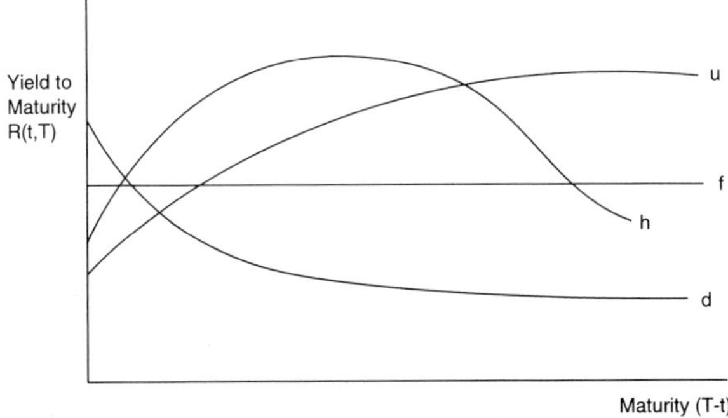

Fig. 2. Alternative potential shapes of the yield curve at time t; u = upward sloping yield curve; D = downward sloping yield curve; f = flat yield curve; and h = humped yield curve.

capital asset pricing model, and the arbitrage pricing theory can all be derived from (2), so bond pricing [10] in this framework makes it consistent with these models.

The concept of states is not fully exploited in the development of (3). The most primitive securities in the state pricing framework are those that pay a dollar in a given state and zero otherwise. Any asset can be 'assembled' from these primitive securities and priced *relative to* them by arbitrage-free techniques. For example, since the $(T-t)$ maturity bond pays off in all states at time T, its price $P(t, T, \bar{i})$ in (4) must be *equal* to the sum of the prices of the primitive securities, each paying off in a different state at time T. If it isn't, arbitrage profits could be earned by making a portfolio of all the primitive securities which, like the bond, would be guaranteed to pay off in every state at time T, but would have a time t price which is different from the bond. Breeden & Litzenberger [1978] and Banz & Miller [1978] show that the prices of the primitive securities — state prices — can be obtained as the prices of options on aggregate consumption and the market index, respectively. The prices of bonds can then be calculated in terms of the state prices. Alternatively, options on bonds could be used to 'back out' the state prices of aggregate consumption. These state prices, and thus bond prices, will still reflect the same probabilities of consumption payoffs and their marginal utility in the payoff states, just as in (2) above.

Many empirical tests find that the Euler condition fails to hold as a restriction across the period-by-period returns on assets, including default-free Treasury securities [e.g. Hansen & Singleton, 1982]. However, it is difficult to know how to interpret these test results. The generality of the Euler condition as a null hypothesis regarding asset returns is, ipso facto, a weakness insofar as its rejection for any particular specification of the utility function doesn't tell us much — the generality admits a plethora of alternatives, one of which will eventually fit the data. In Stigler's words, 'it takes a model to beat a model', which can only be done by putting more flesh around the Euler equation by developing more detailed models of the pricing operator $m_i(t, t+1, \bar{i})$. This is the subject of Section 5. An alternative approach, which *does* accomplish the objective which seems to underlie the Euler equation tests, is to formulate the conditions on prices which are necessary to rule out arbitrage opportunities. Such opportunities must, of course, be absent in any equilibrium.[11] Assuming that arbitrage opportunities can't exist,

[10] The pricing formula can be derived in terms of either real consumption or nominal consumption expenditures, so it can be considered an equilibrium model for either the *real* or *nominal* term structure and bond prices. If the investor's known consumption bundle consists of, say, a home in the U.S., a Japanese car, and vacations in Paris, the known payoffs would be converted using *forward* currency rates which are known at time t. Uncertainty about the relative prices of consumption goods can affect real spot rates of interest, however.

[11] Partial equilibrium models, in which the $m_i(t, t+1, \bar{i})$ is partly given exogenously (e.g. exogenous risk premiums) could be considered another 'less ambitious' way to go. However, as Cox, Ingersoll & Ross [1985] emphasized, arbitrarily specifying some components of the equilibrium is a dangerous business, since there is no longer any guarantee that the equilibrium so constructed does indeed imply the absence of arbitrage opportunities. Constantinides [1992] points out that it is possible to specify the time series properties of the bond pricing kernel either directly, or indirectly by deriving them from a fully-fledged structural model of equilibrium. If one has a direct time

then these will be minimal conditions which must hold on prices. From a practical point of view, if the conditions are not satisfied, 'yield curve arbitrage' profits are possible.[12] In addition, following Black & Scholes [1973], Merton [1973], and Cox & Ross [1976], the no-arbitrage conditions are all that will be needed for pricing contingent claims. The no-arbitrage conditions on bond prices are now derived.

3. Arbitrage-free restrictions on default-free bond prices [13]

3.1. Introduction

Since the one-period riskless return $R(t, \bar{i})$ is a known constant conditional on the state at time t, the equilibrium pricing equation (3) can be rewritten:

$$P(t, T, i = \bar{i}) = \frac{1}{R(t, \bar{i})} \sum_{i=1}^{S} Q_i \big[m_i R(t, \bar{i}) P(t+1, T, i) \big] \tag{5}$$

Cox & Ross [1976], Ross [1978], Garman [1978], and Harrison & Kreps [1979] pointed out that, *if* arbitrage opportunities do not exist, then (5) can be formulated as:

$$P(t, T, i = \bar{i}) = \frac{\sum_{i=1}^{S} \theta_i P(t+1, T, i)}{R(t, \bar{i})} \tag{6}$$

where the nonnegative numbers θ_i are valid probabilities:

$$\sum_{i=1}^{S} \theta_i = 1 \tag{7}$$

series representation for the pricing kernel, the equilibrium specification becomes unnecessary.

[12] Checking the nonarbitrage conditions is not completely mechanical in practice due to the potential effects on bond prices of illiquidity, high or low coupon rates, and other idiosyncrasies like those discussed in Section 1. It is also not mechanical in the sense that there are only potential arbitrage opportunities among N points on the yield curve if they are spanned by $k \ll N$ risk factors. This is a matter of risk model specification, e.g. early writers such as Culbertson [1957] believed that the market for bonds of different maturities was partly segmented, i.e. there were in principle as many factors as maturities.

[13] The exposition in this section and the next most closely resembles that in Cox [1986] and Black, Derman & Toy [1990]. The basics are due to Black & Scholes' [1973] and Merton's [1973] ideas on the basic role of replication, and to Cox, Ross & Rubinstein's [1979] paper in which these ideas were cast in the 'tree diagram' context used here. (Mark Rubinstein credits William Sharpe with suggesting the binomial approach during a break at a 1975 conference in Din Bokek, Israel.) In addition, Vasicek [1977], Richard [1978] and Dothan [1978] derived closed-form expressions for the term structure in continuous-time under the assumption that bond prices are a function of the (instantaneous) short nominal or real rate of interest, as is the case in discrete-time-space in this section. If their models are solved 'as if' investors are risk-neutral, their approach is the continuous-time analog of that used here; Indeed, this interpretation of their models is perhaps most appropriate since the partial-equilibrium dynamics they used were not intended to be endogenous to some full-fledged representation of the actual economy.

The θ_i are called *pseudo* probabilities or *risk neutral* probabilities. The reason for this terminology is readily seen if equation (6) is rearranged as:

$$E_\theta\big[P(t+1, T, .)\big] = P(t, T, \bar{i}).R(t, \bar{i}) \tag{8}$$

where E_θ is the expectation of the one-period-ahead bond price $P(t+1, T, .)$ using the risk-neutral probabilities $\{\theta_i\}$. That is, the bond's expected return computed using the risk neutral probabilities $\{\theta_i\}$, $E_{\theta_i}\big[P(t+1, T, .)\big]/P(t, T, \bar{i})$ equals the riskless return, just as it would if investors were risk-neutral.[14] Since the $\{\theta_i\}$ are nonnegative and sum to unity, (7) says that nonarbitrage implies the existence of a linear pricing operator which can be used to value assets [e.g. Ross, 1978].

Garman derived (6) and (7) by using Farkas' lemma. Harrison & Kreps [1979] provided a recipe for calculating the risk neutral probabilities $\{\theta_i\}_i$ in (5) from the probabilities $\{Q_i\}_i$ in (6). They showed that the probability measure for the risk-neutral probability distribution, which here makes the discounted bond prices[15] a martingale, is a transformation of the original probability distribution $\{Q\}$. If investors have Von Neumann–Morgenstern utilities, then this transformation impounds any aversion to risk in the probability distribution $\{Q\}$ by weighting the probability of each outcome by the marginal utility of wealth of that outcome — the $m_i(t, t+1, \bar{i})$ in (5). Samuelson & Merton [1969] referred to these transformed probabilities as 'effective probabilities' and 'util probs'. Sharpe [1993] points out that the transformed probabilities can also be interpreted as state-dependent *forward prices*, and suggests that it is confusing to refer to them as 'probabilities'. Cheng [1991] gives some examples of the transformation in the fixed income context, where $\{Q\}$ describes bond price movements. If markets are complete, the transformation is unique, i.e. the risk neutral probabilities $\{\theta_i\}$ are unique [Harrison & Pliska, 1981; Huang & Litzenberger, 1988].

The remainder of this section is devoted to a further explanation of this risk-neutral valuation formula (6). It is important to realize that the formula is not necessarily a model of changes in bond prices per se; rather it is the valuation formula that applies when we treat the economy *as if* investors are risk neutral and arbitrage opportunities are ruled out in the pricing of fixed income claims.

3.2. Bond pricing with binomial interest rate movements

Suppose that there is only a single 'state variable', the one-period rate of interest, forcing movements in bond prices [e.g. Cox, Ingersoll & Ross, 1985]. In this case, the uncertainty in (say) two-period discount bond prices can be spanned by a portfolio consisting of the three period bond and riskless borrowing and

[14] The hypothesis that investors are risk-neutral is typically referred to as the *expectations* or *local expectations* hypothesis in the term structure literature. The actual probabilities of bond price movements will not equal the risk-neutral probabilities unless this local expectations hypothesis holds.

[15] More precisely, the discounted pricing functional. The discounting operation is the same as making one-period bonds the numeraire in pricing.

lending. As illustrated below, the proportion of three-period bonds which must be held in the spanning portfolio will depend upon the sensitivity or *delta* of the three-period bond's price, relative to the two-period bond's price, with respect to movements in the interest rate, which is the single source of uncertainty in bond prices. Spanning the two period bond with a portfolio of the three period and one period bonds is analogous to replicating a stock option's payoff with a portfolio of the underlying stock and riskless borrowing and lending.[16]

This parallel between arbitrage-free or risk-neutral bond pricing and arbitrage-free option pricing is now explained more fully and numerically illustrated. It will simplify notation to refer to the price now (time $t = 0$) of the two period bond, $P(0, T = 2, i = \bar{i})$ as G, the present price of the three period bond, $P(0, T = 3, i = \bar{i})$, as H, and the riskless return (one plus the rate of interest) $R(t, \bar{i})$ simply as R. Next, assume that at time $t = 1$, interest rates, and thus bond prices G and H, can move to one of only two possible states — that is, prices can only move either up or down, to H_U or H_D and G_U or G_D respectively, when one plus the interest rate moves down to R_D or up to R_U. The range of movement in the three-period bond ($[H_U - H_D]/H$) will be larger than that of the two-period bond ($[G_U - G_D]/G$) because bond G's time-to-maturity is shorter, and all default-free bond prices must approach their face values as maturity approaches[17]

These binomial movements in R, G, and H are plotted on a 'tree diagram' in Figure 3a. At the end of period 1, bond G will become a one-period bond whose default-free time 2 payoff is known with certainty because the period 2 interest rate will then be known with certainty. In the case of bond H, its price moves up or down again in the second period in response to the change in one-period interest rates from time 1 to time 2. At time 2, it also becomes a one-period bond. In Figure 3, the movements in interest rates and the price of bond H are assumed to be *path independent*. That is, the bond price at time 2 is the same irrespective of whether it went up in the first period and down in the second period, or down in the first period and up in the second period. Here, path independence requires that the *volatility* of percentage changes in the bond price do not depend upon the level of the bond price.

In Figure 3b, numerical values have been attached to the branches of the tree, and these will be used to illustrate results as they are developed. The first period

[16] Note that, so long as stock prices follow a geometric Brownian motion, it can be shown that the no-arbitrage price of the stock option *must* depend upon the price of the stock, and *only the* price of the stock [Merton, 1977]. In the bond example here, it was necessary to make a *structural assumption* that a single state variable underlies bond price movements. However, it can also only be a *structural* assumption that stock prices are a geometric Brownian motion; if stock price volatilities are not constant, for example, option prices can depend upon those volatilities as a second state variable. Generally, there are several important assumptions that are built into stock price trees, particularly path independence (or the process which is transformed to path independent).

[17] This could be regarded as a minimum condition on the behavior of a bond's volatility over time.

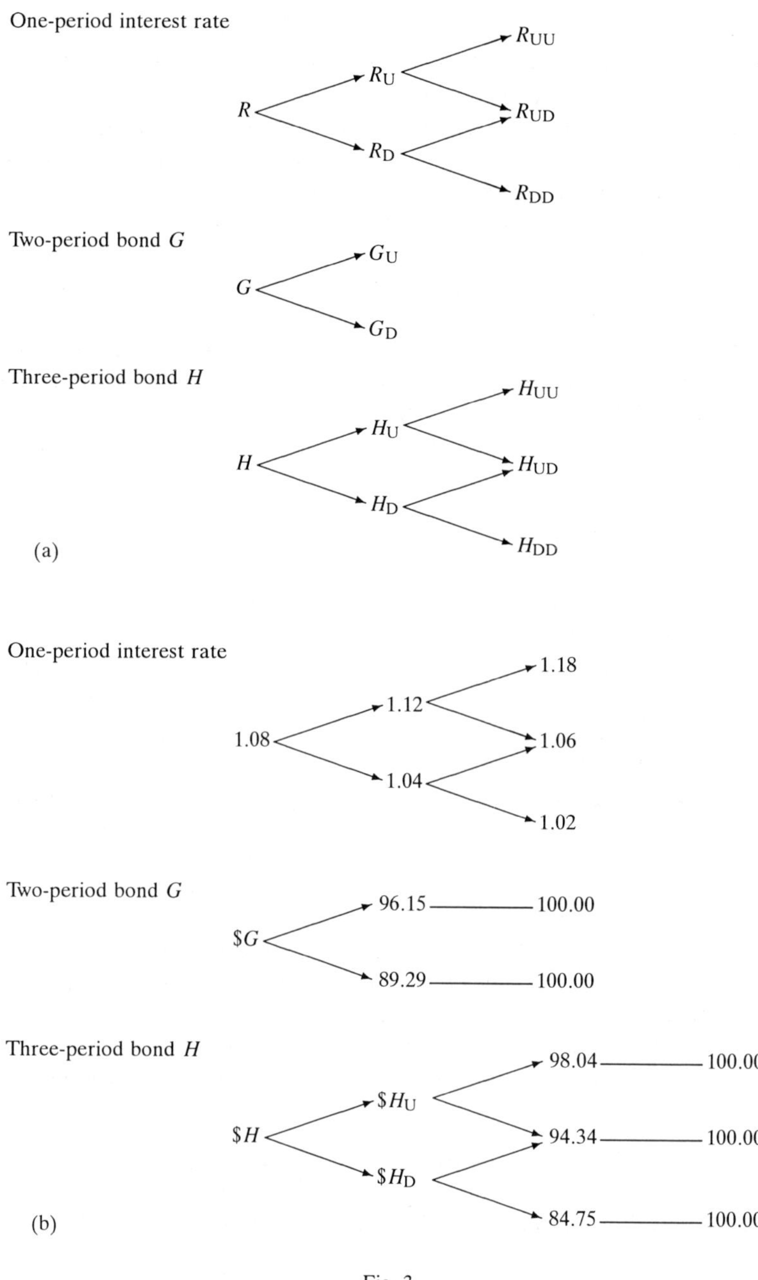

Fig. 3.

interest rate is assumed to be 8% (remember, one plus the interest rate is plotted in Figure 3b). It is assumed that the interest rate will go up or down by 50% in the second period. That is, it will go up to $8\% \times (1 + 0.5) = 12\%$ or down to

$8\% \times (1 - 0.5) = 4\%$.[18] Bond G will then be worth either \$96.15 (if $R_2 = 1.04$) or \$89.29 (if $R_2 = 1.12$). Bond H's price is known at time 2, when it becomes a one-period bond.

Equation (5) tells us that, if arbitrage opportunities are ruled out, the time 0 value of bond G in Figure 1b is some weighted average of $G_U = \$96.15$ and $G_D = \$89.29$, discounted at the period 1 riskless rate of interest of 8%. The weights, which are the risk neutral probability weights in equation (7), are now derived.

So long as there is a single interest rate factor which causes (perfectly correlated) shifts in bond prices of all maturities, the end-of-period 1 value of bond G can be replicated by creating a portfolio of bond H and riskless borrowing at time 0. In particular, the portfolio must contain Δ units of bond H and a one-period default-free loan of B, where Δ and B are chosen such that:

$$\Delta H_U + RB = G_U \tag{9}$$

$$\Delta H_D + RB = G_D \tag{10}$$

Solving these equations gives:

$$\Delta = \frac{G_U - G_D}{H_U - H_D} \tag{11}$$

$$B = \frac{H_U G_D - G_U H_D}{(H_U - H_D)R} \tag{12}$$

Since the portfolio has the same payoff as bond G, the time 0 value of bond G must be:

$$G = \Delta H + B \tag{13}$$

To see the restriction which this no-arbitrage constraint implies across the term structure of bond prices at a point in time, it is necessary to introduce probabilities for interest rate, and thus bond price, changes. Let Q be the probability of a downward movement in interest rates, and thus the probability of an upward movement in bond prices. Then, multiplying (9) by Q and (10) by $(1 - Q)$ and adding them together:

$$QG_U + (1 - Q)G_D = \Delta\left[QH_U + (1 - Q)H_D\right] + RB \tag{14}$$

Imposing the no-arbitrage condition $G = \Delta H + B$, equation (14) becomes:

$$QG_U + (1 - Q)G_D - RG = \Delta\left[QH_U + (1 - Q)H_D - RH\right] \tag{15}$$

[18] Although this specification is for illustration only, the empirical results in Marsh & Rosenfeld [1983] and Chan, Karolyi, Longstaff & Sanders [1992] suggest that such a model of proportional interest rate changes is not wildly unreasonable for nominal short interest rates measured over short intervals.

Further, the *delta* of the no-arbitrage portfolio is $\Delta = (G_U - G_D) \div (H_U - H_D)$, so equation (15) becomes:

$$\frac{QG_U + (1-Q)G_D - RG}{G_U - G_D} = \frac{QH_U + (1-Q)H_D - RH}{H_U - H_D} \equiv \lambda \tag{16}$$

Equation (16) has an easy economic interpretation which is the same as that of its counterpart in option pricing. It says that the *return premium* on all bonds, per unit of risk measured by the *range of movement* in the bond prices, must be identical across bonds. That is, a bond's premium per unit of risk cannot depend upon its maturity, though it could change as a function of the level of interest rates or calendar time. In general, it will also be a function of the length of the time interval in the tree diagram.

Rewriting equation (16) for bond G, the no-arbitrage equation (6) becomes, in this binomial context:

$$G = \frac{[\theta G_U + (1-\theta)G_D]}{R} \tag{17}$$

where $\theta \equiv (Q - \lambda)$ is the *risk aversion adjusted, risk neutral*, or *pseudo* probability θ in equation (7). Equation (17) can be termed a *risk neutral valuation* formula, though as Sharpe [1993] emphasizes, it is really just a forward valuation equation in which the risk-neutral 'probabilities' are Arrow–Debreu forward prices of the payouts G_U and G_D.

The derivation of the nonarbitrage constraint on bond prices resembles the now-standard derivation of the binomial stock option pricing formula. The difference here is that the changes in bond prices were assumed to have been induced by movements in interest rates (or equivalently one-period bond prices). The constant proportional changes in interest rates don't translate into constant proportional movements in bond prices [19], whereas constant proportional stock price movements are assumed directly in the standard options analysis. Since bond prices must converge to their default-free par values at maturity, they cannot have constant proportional price movements over time.[20]

[19] For example, if the pseudo probability of a down-move in interest rates goes to unity, the up-step in the bond price goes toward one plus the current rate of interest, which clearly is not constant.

[20] Some insight may perhaps be gained by seeing how the pricing formula for bond G would resemble the option pricing formula if it were pretended that $H_U/H \equiv u$ and $H_D/H \equiv d$ were constant, in parallel with the geometric Brownian motion assumption for stock price movements which underlies the Black–Scholes option valuation formula. In the stock option pricing model, if λ is interpreted as an expected stock price change in excess of the return on a riskless bond position, and Q the probability that the underlying stock's price moves up, then it may be verified that the binomial call option pricing formula can be written (using the terminology of Cox & Rubinstein, pp. 172–173), as:

$$C = \frac{(Q-\lambda)C_U + [1-(Q-\lambda)]C_D}{R}$$

When written this way, the call option price C depends upon the risk premium on the stock, as well as on the probability of stock price movements. However, C can be rewritten [Cox & Rubinstein,

3.3. Risk (liquidity) premiums on bonds

If the *local expectations* hypothesis holds, then $\lambda \equiv 0$ and the *risk neutral* probabilities are the *actual probabilities* of bond price movements. If $\lambda(R_{\mathrm{U}} - R_{\mathrm{D}}) > 0$, the holding period returns on a long-term bond exceed the riskless return on a one-period bond. So long as the uncertainty in interest rates, $R_{\mathrm{U}} - R_{\mathrm{D}}$, reflects the variation in the representative investor's marginal utility of wealth, then the risk premium on bonds is compensation for the *systematic risk* of bond price movements. It is unclear whether this explanation for the risk premium is consistent with Keynes' argument that long-term bonds are priced to yield a premium because investors have a *liquidity preference* — Keynes [1935, p. 169] proposed that one source of liquidity preference is the '...risk of a loss being incurred in purchasing a long-term debt and subsequently turning it into cash' because 'the future rate of interest is uncertain'; if the uncertainty in interest rates is due to the same factors that cause uncertainty in investors' marginal utilities of wealth, Keynes' liquidity premium is essentially the same as the risk premium here.

3.4. Numerical example (contd.)

To illustrate the risk-neutral valuation result (17), the numerical example in Figure 1b will now be completed. The risk-neutral probability θ is set to $\theta = 0.3$; its determination will be discussed later. Given this value of θ, the risk-neutral prices of bond H at times 0 and 1 are given in Figure 4.

For example, in Figure 4, the value of bond H at time 1 if interest rates had gone up in the first period is:

$$\begin{aligned} H_{\mathrm{D}} &= \left[\theta H_{\mathrm{UD}} + (1-\theta) H_{\mathrm{DD}}\right] \div R_{2,U} \\ &= \left[0.3(94.34) + 0.7(84.75)\right] \div 1.12 \\ &= 78.24 \end{aligned} \tag{18}$$

p. 173–173] in terms of risk-neutral probabilities which depend only upon parameters defining movements in the stock's price, u and d (as well as the interest rate):

$$C = \frac{pC_{\mathrm{U}} + (1-p)C_{\mathrm{D}}}{R}$$

where:

$$p \equiv \frac{(R-d)}{(u-d)} \quad \text{and} \quad (1-p) \equiv \frac{(u-R)}{(u-d)}$$

In like fashion, the formula for the price of bond G in (12) could then be rewritten as:

$$G = [pG_{\mathrm{U}} + (1-p)G_{\mathrm{D}}] \div R$$

where:

$$p = \left[\frac{(RH - H_{\mathrm{D}})}{(H_{\mathrm{U}} - H_{\mathrm{D}})}\right] = \left[\frac{(R - H_{\mathrm{D}}/H)}{(H_{\mathrm{U}}/H - H_{\mathrm{D}}/H)}\right] = \left[\frac{(R-d)}{(u-d)}\right]$$

Now the parameters for the interest rate probability and bond risk premium would be impounded in the price of bond H, and movements in this price could be used in pricing bond G but for the deficient assumption that u and d are constant.

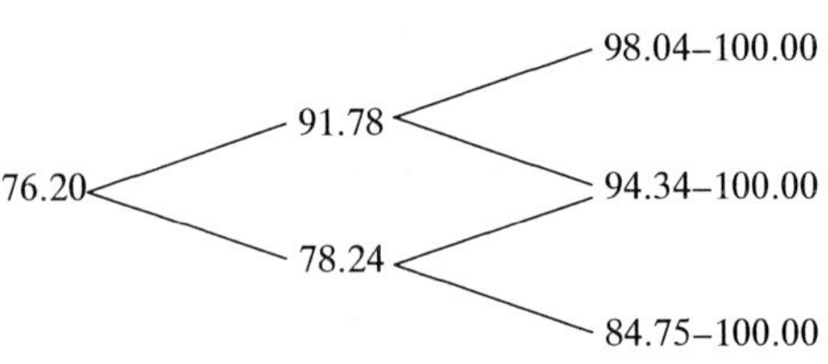

Fig. 4. Bond H.

Similarly, $H_U = 91.78$. H is then:

$$\begin{aligned} H &= \left[\theta H_U + (1-\theta) H_D\right] \div R \\ &= \left[0.3(91.78) + 0.7(78.24)\right] \div 1.08 \\ &= 76.20 \end{aligned} \tag{19}$$

The *dispersion* of possible percentage price changes over the first period is greater for the three-year bond H than for the two-year bond G. Bond H's price increases from 76.20 at the beginning of the period to 91.78 if interest rates go down, but increases to only 78.24 if interest rates go up. These are percentage changes of 20.4% or 2.68% respectively; the volatility of the change is 11.54%. Bond G's price increases by 13.67% or 5.56% in these same two interest rate scenarios; the volatility is 9.61%. The greater range of uncertainty in the returns on the longer-term bond is not specific to the illustration. Long-term bond prices fluctuate more, over short holding periods, than short-term bond prices. The illustration makes clear that the reason for this is roughly the one usually given in practice — if interest rates go up or down, the long-term bond's payoff must be discounted for more periods at the higher or lower interest rates along higher or lower branches of the tree. The qualification is that, if interest rates tend to revert to a long-run steady-state, the changes in interest rates along the higher branches are not independent from one node to the next, so there are less 'effective' than actual periods.

To summarize, the risk-neutral pricing of bonds is, by construction, straightforward once the risk neutral probabilities and up–down movements in interest rates and thus bond prices are specified. The latter can be inferred once interest rate movements are given because the terminal condition is that maturing bonds repay their face value with certainty. The obvious question is: where do these interest rate (or bond price) movements, and risk-neutral probabilities, come from? Or, yield curve arbitrage opportunities aside, why would we be interested in risk-neutral bond prices anyway if they are only relevant to a fictional risk-neutral world? The answer is that risk-neutral bond price movements are sufficient for pricing contingent claims on the bonds as long as the price movements can be hedged. As a result, the emphasis is not on the derivation of today's risk-neutral price. Rather, spot prices for bonds are 'plugged into' an equation such as (21) and the up and down movements in

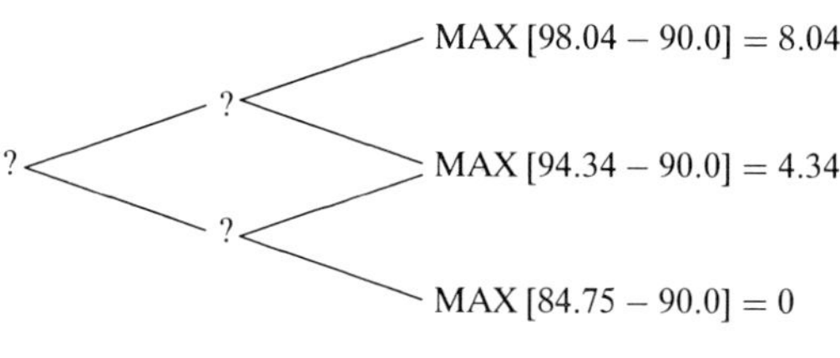

Fig. 5.

bond prices which are consistent with these spot prices are 'backed out', i.e. the tree is calibrated with observed bond prices. Contingent claims, whose values depend upon these future movements, can then be priced consistently with today's observed prices by using the tree, provided that the tree is properly specified.

3.5. *Pricing fixed income contingent claims*

Contingent claims on fixed income securities can all be priced, and hedges computed, from the same lattice, like that plotted in Figure 3, on which interest rate and arbitrage-free bond price movements are drawn.[21]

To illustrate the pricing of claims, suppose that we want to find the time 0 value of a European call option on the three-year bond H, with a strike price of \$90.00 and a maturity of two years. The terminal payoffs on the bond, which are given in Figure 5, can be used to calculate the option payoffs.

For example, if the period-3 interest rate turns out to be 2%, then the value of bond H at the beginning of the third period — the time at which the call option matures — is \$98.04, and the option payoff is \$8.04. Once the terminal payoffs on the call option are determined, we can follow a backward recursion along the branches of the tree, using the risk-neutral valuation formula, to find the time 0 value of the option. Letting C_{U} and C_{D} refer to the time 1 value of the option if bond prices go up or down respectively in period 1:

$$C_{\mathrm{U}} = \{0.3(8.04) + 0.7(4.34)\} \div 1.04 = 5.24 \tag{20}$$

$$C_{\mathrm{D}} = \{0.3(4.34) + 0.7(0)\} \div 1.12 = 1.16 \tag{21}$$

Finally, at time 0, the value of the call option C is:

$$C = [0.3(5.24) + 0.7(1.16)] \div 1.08 = 2.21 \tag{22}$$

[21] Using the same lattice for *all* contingent claims will ensure that they are priced consistently, that hedged positions can be aggregated for risk management, etc.. On the other hand, the one lattice won't generally be the most precise possible for any one security.

The tree diagram for the call option values is:

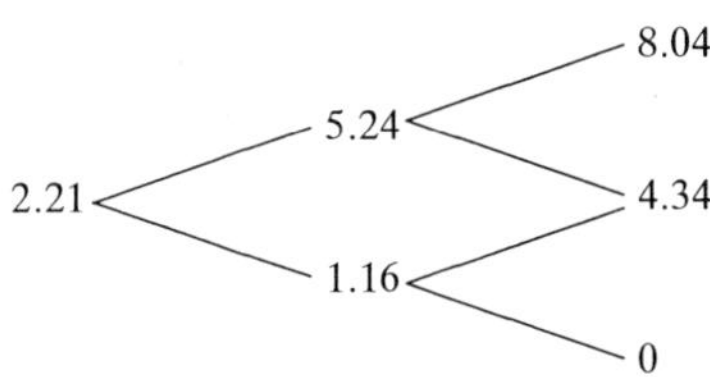

The delta for the call option can be calculated in the standard way. For example, if the interest rate moves to 12% at the end of period 1, $\Delta = (4.34 - 0)/(94.34 - 84.75) = 0.4526$, while if the interest rate moves to 4%, $\Delta = (8.04 - 4.34)/(98.04 - 94.34) = 1.0$. (Note that, in this example, if the period-2 interest rate is 4%, the option will finish in-the-money whatever the outcome for the period-3 interest rate). The delta at time 0 is: $\Delta = (5.24 - 1.16)/(91.78 - 78.24) = 0.3013$.

In calculating the risk-neutral value of the call option to be 2.21, the risk-neutral probabilities θ and $(1 - \theta)$ were required. The value of θ must be specified jointly with the dynamics for interest rates and bond prices. Given $\theta = 0.3$ and the assumed interest rate dynamics, $H = 76.20$, $H_{\mathrm{U}} = 91.78$, and $H_{\mathrm{D}} = 78.24$. Alternatively, given H, H_{U}, H_{D}, (21) can be rearranged to give $\theta = (RH - H_{\mathrm{D}})/(H_{\mathrm{U}} - H_{\mathrm{D}}) = (1.08(76.20) - 78.24)/(91.78 - 78.24) = 0.3$. If the period-length in the tree is decreased, thus decreasing H_{U} and H_{D}, then θ will change, i.e. it depends upon the length of the period.

3.6. Tree diagrams in spot rates, forward rates, or bond discount functions?

For the purposes of pricing contingent claims on bonds, Heath, Jarrow & Morton [1989, 1990, 1992] have suggested transforming the no-arbitrage restrictions on bond prices into equivalent restrictions on the forward rates implied by those bond prices. To explain this forward rate approach, it is simplest to express bond prices in terms of their continuously compounded forward rates of return:

$$P(t, T) \equiv \mathrm{e}^{-\int_t^T f(t,\tau)\,\mathrm{d}\tau} \tag{23}$$

where the *forward rate* $f(t, \tau)$ is the rate of return, established at time t, on a default-free loan to be made at time τ in the future for an instant's duration. By construction, $f(t, t)$ is equal to the instantaneous riskless rate of interest at time t.

Given the relation (23) between bond prices and forward rates, probability models for bond prices can be transformed into probability models for the forward rate, and vice versa. In particular, given an assumed volatility of forward rates, the constraint that expected bond prices equal the riskless rate [equation (18)] can be transformed into an adjustment to the drift of the stochastic process for forward rates.[22]

[22] Note that the forward rate drift adjustment will incorporate both the risk premium in actual probabilities of bond price movements and the fact that the bond price is nonlinear in the

To illustrate the calculation of forward rate probabilities which are consistent with risk-neutral bond values, consider first the two-period bond G in our example. It has a current risk-neutral value of \$84.58, which will rise to \$96.15 if interest rates drop to 4% at the end of the year, or will rise to \$89.29 if interest rates rise to 12%.[23] Then, using the terminology $f(0, 1)$ to refer to the (implied) forward rate *under risk-neutral valuation* at time 0, for a dollar loan from the end of year 1 to the end of year 2, we can solve:

$$84.58 = \frac{100}{(1.08)(f(0, 1))} \tag{24}$$

to find $f(0, 1) \approx 9.47\%$ *under the risk-neutral valuation*. Similarly, using the relative prices of bonds G and H, we can calculate that $f(0, 2) \approx 11.00\%$ under risk-neutral valuation. Thus, under risk-neutral valuation, the forward rate curve at time 0 is: $\left[f(0,0),\, f(0,1),\, f(0,2)\right] = \left[0.08, 0.0947, 0.11\right]$.

Now, what is the change in forward rates from time 0 to time 1, subject to the no-arbitrage restriction on bond prices (i.e. under risk-neutral valuation)? If the one-period spot interest rate decreases to 4%, it can be verified that: $\left[f(1,1),\, f(1,2)\right] = \left[0.04, 0.0476\right]$; if the rate goes up to 12%, $\left[f(1,1),\, f(1,2)\right] = \left[0.12, 0.229\right]$.[24] We cannot decompose this variation between time 0 and time 1 in forward rates into a 'drift' component and a 'volatility' component until we have some specification for the volatility, i.e. the adjustment to the drift of the forward rate process which is consistent with risk-neutral pricing depends upon the forward rate volatility.[25]

An interesting question, especially from a practical standpoint, is whether there is any reason to prefer that term structure uncertainty be specified in terms of the bond *discount function*, *forward rates*, or *spot rates of interest.* Equation (23) gives bond prices as a function of forward rates. The 'zero maturity' forward rate is, in turn, just the instantaneous spot rate. The spot rate is, by definition, the rate of discount which makes a bond's present value equal to its price. So analysis in which it is assumed that forward rates are generated by, say, a one-factor diffusion process, could be transformed into an equivalent analysis in terms of bond prices by using (23) and Ito's lemma. When bond prices which are derived for, say, a particular specification of forward rate movements, are expressed instead as a function of spot interest rates, the corresponding spot interest rate dynamics can be expected to contain restrictions. But at least in the 'easiest' cases, it does seem possible to characterize the mappings and restrictions, and in principle it seems possible to make a computer program with a 'front-end' which

forward rate, e.g. if investors were risk-neutral, and thus risk-neutral probabilities and actual probabilities were equal, there would still be a drift adjustment in the forward rate to make it risk-neutral-consistent.

[23] Note that the beginning-of-year 2 values are trivially risk-neutral values, since at that time bond G will be a one-year bond whose payoff is known with certainty.

[24] If we added a new three year bond at time 1, there would, of course, still be a 3-dimensional vector of forward rates.

[25] See the discussion in Heath, Jarrow & Morton [1989, (11) and section 6].

transforms derivative payoffs expressed in the most natural terms (e.g. interest rate cap payoffs in terms of forward or spot rates) to a desired common stochastic environment.[26] As long as things are done correctly, identical contingent claim values should be obtained in any of the three environments. Unfortunately, the transformations must usually be done numerically from, say, the 'extended' or multi-factor models for spot rates. In these instances, it is difficult to obtain general expressions for the restrictions on a parameterization in forward rates implied by a parameterization in bond prices or interest rates, e.g. to express the restrictions on a forward rate process in Heath, Jarrow & Morton implied by, say, the extended Cox, Ingersoll & Ross model advocated by Hull & White [1990].

4. Calibrating bond pricing dynamics with the observed term structure

4.1. Introduction

The procedure in the previous section was to specify a lattice for interest rate or bond price movements, and then derive arbitrage-free constraints on bond prices. As Ho & Lee [1986] pointed out, this procedure can be reversed: bond prices can be used to calibrate or specify the lattice, which would then be used for pricing other bonds or interest rate derivatives. The logic parallels that in stock option pricing. There, the pricing function, e.g. the Black–Scholes formula, can be inverted to obtain the *implied volatility* of stock prices which is consistent with observed option and stock prices at a point in time.[27]

4.2. Calibration in the binomial example

To illustrate the calibration procedure using the numerical example of the previous section, recall that at time 0, the no-arbitrage prices of bonds G and H were calculated as \$84.58 and \$76.20 respectively. These prices were derived using risk-neutral probabilities and an assumed process for interest rate dynamics. Now, assume that we *don't* know the stochastic process for interest rates, but that current bond prices are *observed*; we then want to back out the parameters of the

[26] In the risk neutral versions of models based on any of the three variables, risk premiums are not required; if forward rates are covariance stationary, then percentage changes in discount bond prices, which are just linear aggregations of forward rate changes, will also be stationary; the nonnegativity restriction on forward rates can be applied directly to the discount function (shorter maturity pure discount bond values cannot be less than longer-maturity values); in the bond price formulation, the volatility parameter for a given bond must change over time as its maturity decreases, but the cross-section of volatilities for the discount function need not change as long as the function spans the same range of maturities.

[27] In practice, it is not often possible to find an observed term structure of bonds which are free of imbedded options. In principle, this means that if the risk-neutral model is being calibrated for the purpose of valuing such options, we are implicitly searching for a fixed point in the fit of the term structure which is both adjusted for imbedded options using the model and which serves as a basis for valuing nonnested options.

interest rate or bond price process that are consistent with these prices. The local expectations hypothesis *does not* have to be correct in order for us to use observed prices to calibrate the risk-neutral model.

Suppose that the following term structure is *observed* at the beginning of period 1: a one-period spot interest rate of 8%, i.e. the price of a zero-coupon bond which matures at the end of period one is \$92.59; the price of the two-period bond is $G = \$84.58$, which implies a two-period spot rate (or yield) of 8.734%; and the price of a three-year bond $H = \$76.20$, implying a three-period yield of 9.483%. Suppose for the moment that the risk-neutral probability of a down-move in interest rates, θ, is set at 0.3. Suppose that we also know that the interest rate changes geometrically, i.e. if i is the *rate* of interest $R - 1$, then $i_U = i(1+k)$, $i_D = i(1-k)$. Then:

$$84.58 = \left[\theta \frac{100}{R_D} + (1-\theta)\frac{100}{R_U}\right] \div 1.08 \tag{25}$$

$$= \left[\theta \frac{100}{(1+i(1-k))} + (1-\theta)\frac{100}{(1+i(1+k))}\right] \div (1+i) \tag{26}$$

With $\theta = 0.3$, this one equation can be solved for k; of course, $k = 0.50$.

In general, this implied volatility will be approximately that of the actual probability distribution of bond price changes so long as the interval of time in each step is short.

What can we learn by bringing in the observed price of the three-year bond, bond H? If we continue to assume that $\theta = 0.3$, then:

$$76.20 = \left[0.3H_U + 0.7H_D\right] \div 1.08 \tag{27}$$

$$\begin{aligned} H_U &= \left[0.3H_{UU} + 0.7H_{UD}\right] \div [1 + 0.08(1-k)] \\ &= \left[0.3\frac{100}{1+0.08(1-k)(1-k)} + 0.7\frac{100}{1+0.08(1-k)(1+k)}\right] \div \\ &\quad \div 1 + 0.08(1-k) \end{aligned} \tag{28}$$

$$\begin{aligned} H_D &= \left[0.3H_{UD} + 0.7H_{DD}\right] \div 1 + 0.08(1+k) \\ &= \left[0.3\frac{100}{1+0.08(1-k)(1+k)} + 0.7\frac{100}{1+0.08(1+k)(1+k)}\right] \div \\ &\quad \div 1 + 0.08(1+k) \end{aligned} \tag{29}$$

If H_U and H_D are substituted into the equation for H, it may be verified that the positive root is $k = 0.50$.

Of course, under the assumption of *constant* proportional interest rate movements, the solution for k obtained from the three-year bond is redundant. However, still under the assumption that θ is known, the value of k could be allowed to be different in periods two and three: i.e. we could calibrate a model with a term structure of volatilities from the bond prices. In fact, it is very common for practitioners to calibrate bond pricing models using the volatility of estimated zero-coupon yields on bonds with different maturities. Empirically, the typical term structure of *yield volatility* is downward sloping — i.e. period-to-period variation in zero-coupon yields are a decreasing function of maturity [e.g. Murphy, 1987, chapter 5]. [Since the yields are just geometric averages of spot and forward rates (up to a Jensen's inequality difference), this reflects the regressivity of those rates.] A more detailed discussion of what features of the data can be matched with what models is given below.

It might also appear that we could use the information in a cross-section of two-period and three-period bond prices to solve jointly for θ and the constant interest rate volatility k under the assumption that the former is not known. However, the risk-neutral probability θ is *not* a free parameter. It is easy to see the reason by recalling that bond G's price was derived as:

$$84.58 = \left[\theta \frac{100}{R_{\mathrm{D}}} + (1-\theta)\frac{100}{R_{\mathrm{U}}}\right] \div R \tag{30}$$

Since the return on one-period bonds R is known, once a specification is made for the up and down interest rate movements, θ must be set so as to make the risk-neutral return on bond G equal to R if arbitrage opportunities are to be precluded. In the calibration step, picking a different value for θ will simply change the value of k. If the length of a period in the tree diagram converges to zero, the limiting value of θ will depend upon how the parameters of the limiting continuous-time distribution for interest rates are mapped to the step sizes in the discrete-time tree (because the constraint on θ must hold in the continuous time limit if arbitrage is to be ruled out).

Perhaps the easiest way to see that the risk-neutral probability is not a 'free parameter' is to remember that it is really just a forward price of the payouts on bond G in the up-state (see Sharpe [1993] for discussion). To prevent arbitrage, the value G of the bond must equal the discounted value of these forward prices multiplied by the payouts G_{U} and G_{D}; conversely, when we know G, G_{U}, G_{D}, and the one-period spot interest rate, we know the state-dependent forward prices.

In practice, bond values are typically stated in terms of yield-to-maturity. The *yield-to-maturity* on a zero-coupon bond which has $T - t$ periods to maturity and a current price $P(t, T)$ per dollar of face value is defined as $y(t, T)$ where $P(t, T) = [1 + y(t, T)]^{-(T-t)}$. In the case of zero-coupon bonds, the $(T - t)$ yield-to-maturity is also the $(T - t)$ *spot rate* of interest. Turning to the example, the *actual* prices of bonds G and H are 84.58 and 76.20 respectively, implying yields of 8.734% and 9.483%, respectively. In a risk-neutral economy, the *term structure* of yields is then (8.0%, 8.734%, 9.483%) for one, two, and three period maturities, i.e. it is upward-sloping.

The term structure of yields is, of course, related to assumed interest rate behavior. If investors are risk-neutral, then $\lambda = 0$, and the actual probability of the interest rate increasing from 8% to 12% in the next period is 0.7, while the probability of a decrease in the rate to 4% is 0.3. That is, the interest rate is expected to increase from 8% to 9.6% in period two and 9.82% in period three. However, the yields-to-maturity on the bonds are *lower* than their expected returns to maturity as implied by these interest rates (and risk-neutral or local expectations pricing). For example, the expected return on the two-period bond G is $(1.08)(1.096) = 1.184$, or 8.80% per period, while the two-period yield is $(1.08734)^2 = 1.182$, or 8.73% per period.

This result that the yield-to-maturity is below the expected bond return under risk-neutrality (the expectations hypothesis) is well-known to be due to the convexity of bond prices as a function of interest rates. The price and yield of bond G, for example, was computed as:

$$G = \frac{1}{R_1} E\left[\frac{100}{\tilde{R}_2}\right] \equiv \frac{100}{(1 + y(0,2))^2} \tag{31}$$

where $\tilde{R}_2 = \{1.04, 1.12\}$. Since $E\,(1/X) > (1/E(X))$, $y(0,2) < R_1 E(\tilde{R}_2)$.[28]

The above procedure involves calibrating the proportional interest rate model with cross-sections of bond prices. However, if additional information about the distribution of bond prices is available, it can be used to obtain the values of the future possible interest rates, not just their spread. For example, Black, Derman & Toy [1990] use the information in yield volatilities to infer interest rates at nodes in the tree. To see how this can be done, let's consider the observed price of the two-period bond in the example:

$$84.58 = \left[\theta \frac{100}{R_\text{D}} + (1-\theta)\right]\frac{100}{R_\text{U}}\Bigg] \div 1.08 \tag{32}$$

With $\theta = 0.3$, notice that this one equation cannot be solved uniquely for the two unknown period-2 interest rates R_U and R_D. But, *if* the *actual* probability Q of an up-move or a down-move in interest rates is the same, the expected interest rate in period 2, $[0.5(R_\text{U}) + 0.5(R_\text{D})]$, is 0.08. The volatility of interest rates in period 2 is then $\left[0.5(R_\text{U} - 1.08)^2 + 0.5(R_\text{D} - 1.08)^2\right]^{0.5}$. Setting this expression for the volatility of period-2 rates equal to the observed volatility constitutes a second equation which can be used in solving for R_U and R_D. If, for example, we know that the volatility of the two-period spot rate equals 0.0432, then the volatility of the period-2 rate, $\tilde{R}_2$ is 0.04. In the special case of the proportional interest rate model used in the example, it may be verified that the only period 2 interest rates which are consistent with a time 0 price of \$84.58 for the two-period bond and a two-period zero-coupon yield volatility of 0.0432 are $R_\text{U} = 1.12$ and $R_\text{D} = 1.04$. Alternatively, we could infer that the volatility of the percentage *change* in interest rates between time 0 and time 1 is 50%.

[28] The difference between yields and expected interest rates is perhaps easiest to see when the risk-neutral probabilities of up moves and down moves in the interest rate, θ, and $(1-\theta)$, are equal to 0.5, so that the expected interest rate in the example is 8% in all periods. Under risk neutrality (the expectations hypothesis), 8% is then also the expected rate of return on bonds G and H in each period. However, it may be verified that bond G's yield is 7.93% (its price is \$85.85 under these probabilities), and bond H's is 7.80% (with a price of \$79.83). That is, the yields-to-maturity become increasingly lower with maturity relative to the expected spot rate of 8.0%.

The three-period bond H provides two more pieces of information — the price of the three-period bond and the volatility of the three-period yield. Repeating the procedure above to back out $R_{\rm UU}$, $R_{\rm UD}$, and $R_{\rm DD}$, it is necessary to ensure that *both* the volatility of the period-3 rate conditional on $R_{\rm U}$, **and** the volatility of the period-3 rate conditional on $R_{\rm D}$, are consistent with these two additional pieces of information. In the special case of proportional interest rate changes in the example here, the previously calculated $R_{\rm U}$ and $R_{\rm D}$ can be used together with the observed three-period spot rate volatility to solve for $R_{\rm UU} = 18\%$, $R_{\rm UD} = 6\%$, and $R_{\rm DD} = 2\%$. Alternatively, under the proportionality assumption, it could be inferred that the volatility of the percentage change in interest rates from period 2 to period 3 is 50%, *irrespective* of whether the second period riskless return is $R_{\rm U}$ or $R_{\rm D}$.

4.3. Calibration techniques generally

At this point, one might reasonably wonder whether there are any general principles to guide the calibration procedure. At one level, the answer is obvious — observable bond prices or yields plus moments of their distribution are 'inputs', and the parameters or nodes of the lattice are the 'outputs' (the pseudo-probabilities are not free parameters, and they should satisfy the constraint that they lie between zero and one as soon as the bond price (interest rate) dynamics are specified). Loosely, there need to be enough inputs to derive the outputs. Though the discussion here has always assumed that prices and volatilities of cash market prices (or swaps) are used as 'inputs', contingent claim prices (e.g. caps, swaptions) could also be used as a source of 'inputs'.

In recent work, the tendency has been to generalize the models of bond price (interest rate) dynamics so that they have enough parameters to fit the observed term structure of bond prices and bond price volatilities. For example, Hull & White [1990] allow time dependence in the drift and diffusion parameters in the Vasicek [1977] and Cox, Ingersoll & Ross [1985] interest rate models in such a way that they are exactly identified from the current term structure of interest rates, the current and future volatilities of the short-term interest rate, and the current term structure of spot or forward rate volatilities. Heath, Jarrow & Morton [1992] introduced a multi-factor model for forward rates with a parameterization that will fit any existing term structure and any specified volatility structure. Finally, Rubinstein [1994] has recently proposed a set of identification conditions on a binomial tree (for stock prices) for which parameters can be calibrated with option prices, i.e. a recipe for what might be called the ultimate 'extended' model.[29]

If we interpret the 'tree' models of the term structure, or their continuous time counterparts, as essentially 'trees' of Arrow–Debreu time–state-contingent prices, then perhaps it is natural to extend their parameterization so as to have the finest grid of states and state prices consistent with observed bond and claim prices. Yet the models and their associated state prices are only as good as the exogenous

[29] His discussion is in terms of stock options.

specification of the tree. Since the extended models are of a reduced-form nature and are parameterized so as to fit exactly the desired characteristics of the bond price and/or interest rate-contingent claim data, the exogenous specification can be evaluated only[30] by: (1) analyzing the properties of, and restrictions on, the future behavior of the term structure that are implied when the model parameters are calibrated with the desired features of the current term structure [e.g. Carverhill, 1992b; Webber, 1992]. For a *given* set of selected features of the data (moment conditions), the looser the parameterization, the less chance that fitted functions, such as the volatility of the short rate, will have to be 'strange-looking' to make them consistent with the data.[31]; or (2) simulating their performance in pricing interest rate dependent contingent claims, which is essentially doing (1), but using the contingent claim prices as the loss function in terms of which to evaluate the models. For example, Hull & White [1990] assess the performance of their extended models in pricing bond options and interest rate caps. The extended models are compared with each other, and also with a special two-factor model. Flesaker [1990] and Amin & Morton [1993] fit various versions of the Heath, Jarrow & Morton [1992] model to Eurodollar futures option prices. They find that put options tend to be overpriced relative to call options, and that there are significant biases in prices as a function of strike price and maturity for all versions of the Heath, Jarrow and Morton model that they study. Amin and Morton also find enough instability in their two parameter specifications for volatility in the Heath, Jarrow and Morton model to suggest that a one parameter specification is preferable for valuing options (or at least options like Eurodollar futures options) with maturities less than one year — intuitively, a single short-term interest rate volatility explains most of the variation in the prices of short maturity bonds.

The above procedures involve the calibration of *prespecified* models for interest rate or bond price dynamics with the observed term structure (under the local expectations hypothesis). For example, in the numerical illustration, the assumption that percentage changes in a single state variable — the one-period interest rate — have a constant volatility formed the basis for the arbitrage restrictions, not vice versa. In general, the interest rate tree must encompass *all* possible future paths for interest rates (or the bond price tree must incorporate all future bond price paths, etc.). Next period, the realized interest rate must be one of the nodes contemplated on this period's tree; otherwise the tree has to be 'redrawn'. But redrawing the tree involves irrational model expectations, in the sense of Muth [1961] — changes in future spot rates as a function of the time 1 realization of the term structure are not incorporated in the typical tree-diagram dynamics when

[30] Perhaps a third criterion should be computational tractability, since extended models will typically not have closed form solutions (the lattice becomes path-dependent, rather than path-independent, as in the illustration in Section 3). But computer power keeps increasing.

[31] For example, in the Section 4 example (and Black, Derman & Toy [1990]), a time dependent volatility parameterization was calibrated with an observed term structure of bond prices and term structure of volatilities. To 'shoehorn' the observed data into this parameterization with a constant interest rate drift can produce an implausible fitted time dependence in volatility. Broadening the parameterization to include a mean-reverting drift in interest rates can alleviate this problem.

they are calibrated with the term structure at time 0. The inconsistency is similar to that which occurs in the case of stock options when (say) the Black–Scholes formula, which assumes a constant stock price volatility, is used to compute a new implied volatility each period.

There is no direct distinction between permanent and transitory components of interest rate changes in the tree; if a transitory interest rate realization occurs, then in principle the *up* and *down* steps following that realization will have to reflect its transitory nature, e.g. a positive 'transitory' will be followed by a down-step. Embedding transitories in the tree is consistent with the use of the tree for pricing interest-rate contingent claims, where it is the *dispersion* of interest rates that matters. However, it is not clear that today's typical tree specification is so flexible, e.g. the proportional interest rate dynamics in the example earlier automatically assumes that all unexpected changes in interest rates are permanent.

When the tree specification is calibrated using all available data, errors in data are of special concern — there is no 'residual' in such a 'fit' which can incorporate measurement error in, say, bond prices or volatility estimates. Further, since there are no 'residuals' in the model fit, there are none of the other typical diagnostics for specification that econometricians use.

Finally, it is sometimes believed that by calibrating the arbitrage-free values of bonds with the observed term structure, information can be extracted from that term structure which will be useful in trading default-free bonds. However, assuming that the arbitrage-free restriction is satisfied, all the information is endogenous to the existing term structure; it is not possible to make superior 'bets' on shifts in the yield curve per se using only the information in the yield curve itself. The information is useful *only* for pricing contingent claims on the term structure at a point in time, or of course for identifying direct yield-curve arbitrage opportunities if they are not assumed away.

5. Equilibrium models

5.1. Introduction

When the pricing of bonds is integrated with that of other assets,[32] the pricing formula can be expressed as follows:

$$P(t, T, \bar{i}) = E_Q\big[m_i P(t+1, T, i)\big] \tag{33}$$

[32] This integration should help in understanding equity pricing: Since default-free bonds have known payoffs, it follows that, commodity price level aside, the *only* reason that they have uncertain returns over their terms to maturity is because of technological uncertainty concerning the opportunities for investment of their payoffs and uncertainty about the marginal utility of investors' consumption at time of payoff. By contrast, the payoffs on, say, corporate stocks, are affected by substantial company-specific uncertainty. As a result, default-free bonds may be very good hedges for economy-wide technological uncertainty in production, and if so, bond returns will be good instruments in tests of the effect of this technological uncertainty on the pricing of equities.

where $E_Q[.]$ is the (conditional) expectation at time t taken with respect to the probability distribution of states at time $t+1$, and m_i is the (Arrow–Debreu) price at which investors trade off consumption at times t and $t+1$, and which must therefore be the same across all assets at time t. Dividing both sides of (33) by the time t price $P(t, T, \bar{i})$ gives:

$$1 = E_Q[m_i Z_i] \tag{34}$$

where $Z_i \equiv P(t+1, T, i)/P(t, T, i = \bar{i})$, is the return earned by buying the time-T maturity bond at time t and reselling it at time $t+1$.

If the risk neutral pricing equation (6) is rearranged as:

$$1 = \sum_{i=1}^{S} \left[\frac{\theta_i}{R_i}\right] \frac{P(t+1, T, i)}{P(t, T, \bar{i})} \tag{35}$$

i.e.

$$1 = E_\Theta[\Theta_i Z_i] \tag{36}$$

then equation (34) can be considered a special case of equation (6), or perhaps vice-versa. In words, an equilibrium model (34) can be transformed into a risk neutral world in which arbitrage opportunities are absent.

Many authors, among them Beja [1979], Ferson [1981], Sundaresan [1984], Cox, Ingersoll & Ross [1985], Breeden [1986], and Benninga & Protopapadakis [1986] have derived endogenous bond returns Z_i along with optimal paths of consumption and m_i in models where a more detailed specification concerning exchange and production uncertainty is superimposed on (34).[33] In these models, real bond yields are typically positively related to production and consumption growth rates and negatively related to uncertainty about future real production opportunities. The model parameters can be identified by fitting bond return (and other asset return) data. Constantinides [1992] proposes that the m_i (or Θ_i) pricing kernel be modelled directly as a reduced form statistical process.

The expectation in (33) is taken with respect to a discrete grid of states i=1,...,S. The probabilities $\{Q_i\}$ will depend upon the length of the interval of time $[t, t+1]$ over which the states change. Frequently, equilibrium models are developed where the interval of time $[t, t+1]$ is taken to a limit of zero, i.e. in continuous time. The continuous time environment is particularly useful if it produces analytically tractable results.[34] In the following, the widely-studied Cox, Ingersoll & Ross [1985] continuous time equilibrium bond pricing model is briefly

[33] Merton's [1975a] analysis, which 'rolls back' the level of exogeneity to the growth model, rightly belongs in this list also, although that paper's purpose was not to draw out the term structure 'throwoffs' (to use Merton's own word).

[34] For a discussion of the merits of focusing on the continuous-time limit, see Merton [1975b]. In general, any difference between the length of the interval over which price changes are observed and the length of the investor's decision interval in the model will have to be taken into account in the econometrics to avoid biased estimates of model parameters.

described. The continuous time model is then related to the discrete time example presented in earlier sections.

5.2. *The Cox, Ingersoll & Ross one-factor model*

On the demand side, Cox, Ingersoll & Ross's nonmonetary economy has identical log-utility investors, while on the supply side, changes in the economy's productive opportunities over time are described by a single state variable following a 'square root' diffusion process with mean reversion. Under these assumptions, the riskless *real* return, defined as r, also follows a square-root process and reverts to a long-run rate of interest r_∞:[35]

$$\mathrm{d}r = \kappa(r_\infty - r)\mathrm{d}t + \sigma\sqrt{r}\,\mathrm{d}Z \tag{37}$$

At time t when the interest rate is r, the price of a discount bond which matures at time T, $P(r, t, T)$, is the solution to:

$$\tfrac{1}{2}\sigma^2 r P_{rr} + \kappa(r_\infty - r)P_r + P_t - \lambda r P_r = 0 \tag{38}$$

where the boundary condition is $P(r, T, T) = 1$, and where λ is a risk aversion coefficient which is *endogenous* to the model.

The solution is:

$$P(r, t, T) = A(t, T)\mathrm{e}^{-B(t,T)r} \tag{39}$$

where:

$$A(t, T) \equiv \left[\frac{2\gamma \mathrm{e}^{\left[(\kappa+\lambda+\gamma)(T-t)\right]/2}}{(\gamma+\kappa+\lambda)(\mathrm{e}^{\gamma(T-t)} - 1) + 2\gamma}\right]^{2\kappa\theta/\sigma^2}$$

$$B(t, T) \equiv \frac{2(\mathrm{e}^{\gamma(T-t)} - 1)}{(\gamma+\kappa+\lambda)(\mathrm{e}^{\lambda(T-t)} - 1) + 2\gamma}$$

$$\gamma \equiv \left[(\kappa+\lambda)^2 + 2\sigma^2\right]^{1/2}$$

The expected instantaneous real return on bond H is $\mathrm{r}+\lambda \mathrm{r} P_r/P$. In Cox, Ingersoll & Ross's model, λr is the covariance between the instantaneous ('short') rate of interest r and investors' returns on their optimally invested portfolios of assets — the virtue of the equilibrium model is that, within the Cox, Ingersoll & Ross economy, this risk measure is consistent across all assets. With $P_r/P < 0$, a *negative* covariance between interest rates and portfolio returns ($\lambda < 0$) results in a positive risk premium.

[35] Longstaff [1989] examines the term structure implications of specifying that the regressivity in the short-term (instantaneous) rate is proportional to $(r_\infty - \sqrt{r})$ rather than $(r_\infty - r)$, as in (37). Beaglehole & Tenney [1992] point out that it is really an Ornstein–Uhlenbeck process for interest rates that gives the Longstaff term structure solution.

5.3. Estimation

If we assume that the Cox, Ingersoll & Ross model (39) can be applied directly to nominal bonds and that the 'short' rate is observable, or to real returns on bonds where the real short rate r is observable, there are four parameters — κ, θ, σ, and λ — to estimate. However, κ and λ always appear as a sum in (39) [because $\kappa + \lambda$ is the coefficient of $r P_r$ in (38)]. Thus it is not possible to identify κ and λ separately without data on the time series of interest rates r_t, though even with this data, the estimates are typically very 'noisy' in practice. Various parametric estimation procedures for the model in (39) are discussed in Brennan & Schwartz [1982], Marsh [1980], Brown & Dybvig [1986], Gibbons & Ramaswamy [1993], Pearson & Sun [1989], and Brown & Schaefer [1994].

Regarding the adequacy of the square root specification per se for short term interest rates in (37), results in Marsh & Rosenfeld [1983] and Chan, Karolyi, Longstaff & Sanders [1992] suggest that nominal short-term interest rates tend to display more heteroscedasticity than allowed for in the square root model, though perhaps more strongly in some periods than in others. The same heteroscedasticity is picked up in the ARCH/GARCH models (see Bollerslev, Chou & Kroner [1992] for a review of this evidence).[36] More recently, Ait-Sahalia [1992] has applied a nonparametric kernel estimator of both the marginal density of the spot interest rate and the transition density between successive interest rates in order to *identify* the diffusion function for interest rates (he parameterizes the drift, and the effects of this parameterization show up in the estimated diffusion function). Looking at Treasury Bill and Federal funds rates, he finds that interest rate diffusion is globally increasing as a function of the level of the interest rate up to 18%, but that after the rate gets this high, there is so much mean regressivity coming from the drift that the diffusion function decreases sharply. Also recently, Hamilton [1988], Cai [1992], and Gray [1993] have proposed modelling interest rate movements as regime switches. Although it is not yet clear whether a regime switching model constitutes a good and parsimonious representation for continuous variables like interest rates, the potential isomorphism between regime switching and lattice movements seems interesting. Finally, it is worth noting that the moments used in both the parametric and nonparametric estimation procedures include the volatility structure of bond prices (or interest rates); in this sense, equilibrium models are 'calibrated' with the volatility structure of yields, just as is the risk-neutral model in Section 4.

There is also a large, more 'traditional', literature concerned with hypotheses about expected returns and term- or risk-premiums on bonds with different maturities. The hypotheses are often framed in terms of the *expectations hypothesis* that: (i) the expected returns from holding a bond of any maturity for a specific period are equal; (ii) the (guaranteed) return from holding any discount bond to

[36] The GARCH models seem more appropriate than the typical diffusion models like (37) because they allow (serially dependent) variation over time in the 'amplitude' parameter σ and thus don't force all the variation in the volatility to be a function of the level of interest rates.

maturity is equal to the return expected from rolling over a series of single-period bonds over the same period; or (iii) forward rates are unbiased predictors of future interest rates. Cox, Ingersoll & Ross [1981] show that these three expressions of the *expectations hypothesis* are strictly (pairwise) inconsistent. Good surveys of the literature, which generally finds that the expectations hypothesis fails, can be found in Malkiel [1966] and Melino [1988]. The most recent tests in this literature, which remain primarily reduced form tests, focus on shifts in the predictability in interest rates (when testing whether forward rates equal *expected* spot rates), and/or variation in the term premiums if they exist.

5.4. Binomial trees and continuous time models

We now return to the linkage between discrete-time equilibrium bond pricing models like (33) and continuous time models like Cox, Ingersoll & Ross's.[37] Ignoring estimation for a moment, the linkage can be addressed by asking under what conditions can a time–state grid be constructed for the discrete-time model that will converge to a given continuous time model as a limit when the time interval shrinks to zero. He [1990] shows that, when a continuous-time equilibrium or no-arbitrage bond price depends upon an N-dimensional state variable vector that follows a diffusion process, it can be approximated by an $N+1$ dimensional multinomial process (thus the one-state variable model used in the example in Section 2 can be approximated by a binomial process). The multinomial 'util probs' are Arrow–Debreu state prices. Willinger & Taqqu [1991] and Duffie & Protter [1992] also discuss the conditions under which finite state space, discrete-time models converge to continuous time limits.

In the one-state variable case, Nelson & Ramaswamy [1990] explore the conditions under which it is possible to construct computationally feasible 'binomial' approximations for limiting diffusion processes. When the limiting process for the state variable does not have a constant volatility, such as the interest rate process in (37), they transform the state variable to make the volatility constant. Then movements over time in the transformed variable can be approximated with a binomial tree in which the nodes are path-independent (like the tree in Figure 1). In path-independent trees, the number of nodes increases linearly in the number of time steps. To extend the Nelson and Ramaswamy results to the N-dimensional case using He's multinomial approach would require that each state variable's volatility depend only upon that variable.

5.5. Estimating equilibrium models versus calibrating lattice models

It is sometimes argued that a major disadvantage of equilibrium term structure models is that they involve several unobservable parameters and do not provide a perfect fit to the term structure of interest rates at a point in time. By contrast, it

[37] See Vetzal [1994] for a good survey of continuous time models of the term structure in the literature.

is argued, the valuation of contingent claims in an *as if* risk-neutral economy does not involve unobservable parameters and can be calibrated with the observed term structure at a point in time.

However, the fact that risk premium and interest rate regressivity parameters are not identified in the risk-neutral distribution is an advantage or disadvantage, depending upon one's level of confidence in the volatility specification. Certainly the risk neutral approach is attractive, in that it has 'fewer moving parts' as a tool for valuing derivatives. At the same time, fewer moving parts is not necessarily better at the *design* stage, where the jettisoned parts may help in understanding the remaining components. As an illustration of the point, when Ait-Sahalia [1992] *identifies* the interest rate diffusion function using nonparametric techniques and a parameterization for the drift, he finds substantial interaction between the estimated diffusion function and the drift specification — as would be expected, the interaction is strong when the interest rate is high and thus mean regressivity is strong. He & Leland [1992] also derive equilibrium asset price processes in which the expected return-risk premium and volatility specifications are internally consistent, and the former provides information about the latter. The tradeoff is really whether the risk premium and drift parameters in bond returns[38] are small and unstable enough relative to the conditional volatility of interest rates (this will depend in part on the periodicity of the returns)[39] to make it better to treat them as nuisance parameters, which they certainly become for pricing derivative assets once the stochastic process assumption for underlying bond prices or interest rates is given.

Whether the risk-neutral model or equilibrium model 'perfectly' fits the observed term structure is not a point of difference between the models; rather it is simply an issue of how many bond price observations there are relative to parameters. If we have N parameters or jointly-identified parameters and N observations, then the equilibrium model will fit the observations just as 'perfectly' (or imperfectly) as the risk-neutral model.

What happens when there are more bonds than parameters? One solution is to simply expand the parameterization of the equilibrium models by, say, replacing constants by deterministic functions of time [e.g. Jamshidian, 1989; Hull & White, 1990]. This creates more parameters so that the enhanced model can be fit exactly to the existing term structure. Alternatively, one can recognize that the existing parameters are overidentified. Unfortunately, *neither the risk-neutral model nor the equilibrium model* themselves contain information to help deal with this overidentification problem. As Professor A. Zellner often reminds his students,

[38] As we just saw for the Cox, Ingersoll & Ross model, these parameters won't always be independently required.

[39] Marsh [1985] reported that, for monthly data over the period 1958–1978, there was a peak in term premiums on bonds between one and two years in maturity, i.e. unconditional term premiums are 'humped' as a function of maturity. McCulloch [1985] also reports low (negative) term premiums on bonds with maturities beyond two years over the period 1951–1982. Unfortunately, because of the variability of longer-term bond returns, it is difficult to be confident that the premiums on long-term bonds are significantly below those on one to two-year bonds.

it is perilous to take care of the overidentification by, say, simply tacking on an additive error term which is outside the model.[40]

6. Sources of interest rate uncertainty: how many factors?

6.1. Introduction

In the foregoing, it has been assumed that there is only one factor or state variable that causes movements in bond prices — the short-term rate of interest. Even fairly simple economic models and casual observation suggest that this is, in principle, a narrow assumption. In a real economy in which investor heterogeneity is not important, the assumption that real interest rates are the only determinant of real bond prices requires that investors are not uncertain about future investment opportunities, or don't care about these uncertainties. For example, in the Cox, Ingersoll & Ross model, investors are assumed to have log utility, so they don't want to hedge against changes in investment opportunities — the interest rate is then proportional to a single state-variable in their model.

The 'real' world is not a real economy. Default-free bonds are usually redeemed in units of currency[41]. Thus, it is reasonable to think that inflation and inflation uncertainty will be important factors in nominal bond prices. On the empirical side, it is easy to find time-periods with approximately the same short rate of interest but very different shapes of the term structure. In general, long-term bond yields tend to be more variable than predicted by the single factor model, where those yields converge to a constant at extreme (infinite) maturities.

It is not difficult to come up with a 'laundry list' of factors which could affect nominal bond prices. The list might include uncertainty about consumption good prices, differences among investors in investment horizons and wealth, uncertainty about future production opportunities, illiquidity, and changes in regulation and taxes. The task is, of course, to come up with a parsimonious model which accounts for the 'important' stochastic factors and either approximates the rest by time-varying deterministic functions or relegates them to a measurement equation.

6.2. Two-factor term structure models

The next most parsimonious stochastic model to the one-factor model is a two-factor model. The evidence, which is discussed below, suggests that two (linear) factors can account for much of the variation in bond prices, so the two-factor class of models (and sometimes a one-factor specialization) seems likely

[40] The situation is exactly the same as that encountered when there are multiple options trading on a stock and Black–Scholes *implied volatilities* calculated from each option are not equal.

[41] Exceptions include Israeli index-linked bonds, the British Government index-linked bonds studied by Wilcox [1985] and Brown & Schaefer [1994], and the 1988 REALS (Real Yield Securities) underwritten by Morgan Stanley & Co. and issued by Franklin Savings (see Rogalski & Werlin [1988] for a description), all of which are indexed for *general* price level changes.

to be sufficient in many practical applications — especially when specification and estimation error are taken into account. Two-factor models that have been developed include: (i) the long rate–short rate model of Brennan & Schwartz [1982]; (ii) models with one real factor and one nominal factor; and (iii) models in which the second factor is a measure of the stochastic volatility of interest rates.

If it is assumed that variation in bond prices can be attributed to two factors, bond prices could simply be factor analyzed and factor scores estimated. Brennan & Schwartz [1982] suggest that if bond prices are a function of two unobervable state variables, then two combinations of observable but endogenous bond prices can be used as 'instruments' to mimic the behavior of the factors, so long as the bond pricing function is invertible. Brennan and Schwartz choose a short rate of interest and a long rate of interest as the two instruments. In a similar vein, Schaefer & Schwartz [1984] use the long rate and the *spread* between the long rate and the short rate as the two instruments. Effectively, the Brennan and Schwartz approach uses short rates and long rates to span the movements in intermediate maturity interest rates. If the mapping from underlying state variables to short and long rates is nonlinear, the length of the time interval over which bond prices are observed will be an important determinant of the adequacy of this spanning.

Canabarro [1993] compares the errors produced by various one- and two-factor models when they are used to compute deltas for constructing portfolios of bonds to replicate a given maturity bond. While the one- and two-factor models have roughly the same replication error when term structures are simulated from a one-factor Cox, Ingersoll & Ross model, the two-factor models have a much lower replication error for long term bonds when actual term structure data is used. This is because the variability of long rates is higher than that which can be captured by the one-factor models, even the 'extended' versions which are 'recalibrated' each period.[42]

The second two-factor formulation involves the nontrivial introduction of a monetary sector into the real equilibrium models, so that nominal bond prices can then be expressed as a function of a real factor and an inflation factor. To relate this to the first formulation, inflationary expectations might be identified with the short rate while the real factor is identified with the long rate or some transformation of the long-run and short-run rates, e.g. the difference between them. The real factor–nominal factor route seems to be a promising direction to go if nominal bonds are the object of study: even if one subscribes to the 'judge a model by its results' school, it does seem a bit incongruous to take detailed derivations of bond prices in general equilibrium real economies and then superimpose highly stylized inflation effects (e.g. price level homogeneity) in order to apply them to nominal bonds.

Casual empiricism suggests that commodity price level uncertainty could be at least as important as real interest rates or consumption growth rates in explaining

[42] As noted earlier, the period-by-period recalibration of the deterministic time-dependent parameters in the extended models can't pick the dynamics of a higher dimensional stochastic process.

movements in nominal bond prices, and the financial periodicals use a lot of ink in explaining how money supply changes affect interest rates. The difficulty, of course, is to account for interaction between inflation and real economic variables. Cox, Ingersoll & Ross briefly consider general price level (single good price) uncertainty as a second factor with no real effects in their model. Richard [1978] derives closed form bond prices in a two-factor model where real interest rates and inflation are assumed to move independently of each other and have constant prices of risk. Breeden [1986] introduces multiple good prices which can covary with instantaneous real consumption expenditures and thereby affect interest rates. Pennacchi [1991] develops a two-factor nominal bond pricing model in which the two factors — real interest rates and expected inflation, are allowed to be interdependent. Given his identification assumptions, he reports that the two factors are significantly negatively correlated, and that the real interest rate is more volatile than the expected inflation rate.

Structural models to account for the covariation between a real factor and expected inflation could arise in at least the following ways: (i) the 'Mundell effect' where an increase in expected inflation and nominal rates causes substitution from money to capital which lowers the expected real rate of return on capital; (ii) the endogenity of commodity price levels to the same state variables (including economic uncertainty) that cause changes in real rates of interest [e.g. Black, 1972; Shi, 1994a, b]; (iii) imperfect indexation of private contracts; (iv) taxation of nominal interest income [e.g. Fischer & Modigliani, 1978].

There is also a substantial literature on co-movements in the term structure and business cycle variables like growth of consumption, GNP, and stock prices, and seasonality. In the absence of compelling structural macro-models of these co-movements, the results are usually reduced form. References include Friedman & Schwartz [1963], Kessel [1965], Keim & Stambaugh [1986], Harvey [1988], and Friedman & Kuttner [1992].[43]

A third two-factor formulation is to model the two factors affecting the nominal bond price as (say) the short term interest rate and a stochastic volatility of that rate. More generally, the first factor could be interpreted as 'the level' of the term structure, while the second is the stochastic variation in 'term structure uncertainty'. Various formulations where stochastic volatility is introduced as a second factor are considered in Longstaff & Schwartz [1992], Fong & Vasicek [1991a,b], He & Marsh [1991], and Vetzal [1992].[44] The models have the advantage that they can usually be expressed so as to nest GARCH-like variation in interest rates, such as that reported by Engle & Ng [1991] for Treasury Bills. They are also consistent with various threads of evidence that the covariation between T-Bill returns and other asset returns is not very stable. Finally, they also accord roughly

[43] Romer & Romer [1990] present interesting evidence which they interpret as suggesting that the power of the term structure slope to predict subsequent economic activity is much stronger in episodes in which the Federal Reserve deliberately shifts its monetary policy.

[44] Gennotte & Marsh [1993] present a different model in which the volatility that affects interest rates is not that of interest rates directly, but rather that of aggregate cash flows; the latter then becomes a state variable underlying term structure movements.

with the practice of many practitioners who fit, by one means or another, volatility structures to the data as a first step their analysis.

6.3. Empirical evidence on the dimensionality of term structure movements

On the empirical side, Garbade [1986] and Litterman & Scheinkman [1991] estimate an implicit linear factor model for implied zero coupon bond returns.[45] Both papers report that *three* implicit factors explain some 98% of the variation in returns. The first factor, called a *level* factor because changes in the yields on bonds of all maturities have roughly the same loading on this factor, explains about 90% of the variation in returns. The second factor, called a *steepness* factor because it causes opposite changes in the yields of short-term and long-term bond yields, explains about 81% of the remaining variation. Garbade and Litterman & Scheinkman call their third factor a *curvature* factor because the estimated loadings for different bonds give it the effect of changing the curvature of the yield curve. This third factor never accounts for more than about 5% of the total explained variance of returns for bonds at any maturity.

An interesting issue raised by the factor analysis concerns the importance and operation of the third implicit factor. Clearly it is not, *on average*, of great importance. It could reflect the presence of nonlinearity in the bond return dynamics when the linear factor model is applied. Alternatively, it could reflect an asymmetry in returns or instability in the parameters of the distribution of bond returns, which would also masquerade as an extra 'factor'.[46]In either case, the importance of the third factor in price changes on occasional days (or weeks) is potentially much greater than 'just' an extra 5%. As a result, it might be very important in practice where it can cause an apparently perfect hedge to incur losses (or gains).

7. Summary and discussion

The purpose of this chapter has been to outline how risk-neutral and equilibrium asset pricing techniques have come to be applied in the fixed income area over the last five to ten years. These techniques, together with the assumption that term structure movements can be attributed to a small number of factors, lead to pricing and risk hedging formulae for fixed income, and fixed income derivative, securities. The pricing formulae can be interpreted as restrictions across the prices of the fixed income securities. The arbitrage-free pricing restrictions provide a

[45] In a series of papers, K. Garbade extended the analysis to: Treasury Strip and Federal Agency bonds, in Garbade [1987]; to an international comparison of yield curve movements, in Garbade & Urich [1988]; applied it in measuring the risk of portfolios or cross-sections of bonds, in Garbade [1989a, b]; and allowed for shifts over time in the parameters of the factor model [Garbade, 1990, and Baron, 1989].

[46] Litterman, Scheinkman & Weiss [1991] consider one way in which volatility in the volatility of returns could cause the curvature effect.

basis for 'yield curve arbitrage' and for the pricing of fixed income derivatives. The equilibrium pricing restrictions are those which integrate the pricing of fixed income securities with the pricing of all other assets, and a fortiori they imply the absence of arbitrage opportunities.

Leaving aside the general but obvious questions surrounding the dimensionality and specification of the factor structure of term structure movements, there are at least two broad areas which still seem to be unsettled, and thus to leave room for future research and industry development. First, many alternative parameterizations of term structure uncertainty have been proposed: in terms of *bond price* movements, as in Ho & Lee [1986]; in *forward rate* formulations, as in Heath, Jarrow & Morton [1992]; and in terms of *interest rate* movements, as in the original (equilibrium model) formulation by Cox, Ingersoll & Ross [1985] and the 'extended' Cox, Ingersoll & Ross [1985] and Vasicek [1977] models suggested by Hull & White [1990]. When the parameterization of the term structure uncertainty in terms of the stochastic process for the selected one of these three variables becomes complicated, it can be difficult/impossible to transform among the three alternatives. In practice, this often means that instead of using a common stochastic model for all interest rate-sensitive securities, different models are used for different securities. Even ignoring scientific niceties, this makes it hard to aggregate risk positions, etc. in practice.

Moreover, the tendency has been to increase the parameterization of the models, expressed in whichever of the three variables is chosen, so that they can be calibrated exactly to at least the observed term structure and term structure of volatilities for the purpose of pricing derivatives. The logic of calibrating a model with the observed moments of the term structure to price derivatives is appealing — when the model is represented as a binomial tree, it can easily be seen that the calibration procedure is just like inverting observed prices to obtain Arrow–Debreu state prices. In addition, the approach in which the stochastic process for term structure movements is represented in a lattice which is then calibrated with observed bond prices and moments follows the recent trend in the statistics and econometrics literature toward use of nonparametric and empirically fitted models, and away from analytical parametric models (this trend undoubtedly follows the trend in computer power). But the calibrated model is only as good as its original specification; if the tree is wrong in the sense that over time it is found that future interest rate or bond price realizations are not on one of the paths in the tree, it will have to be 'redrawn'; since the reconstruction of the tree in response to the realizations is not itself represented in tree, this is a form of Muthian irrationality. Use of 'all the data' in calibrating tree models is, ipso facto, an advantage; but it leaves no 'residuals' to absorb data errors and the like.

Second, it seems unlikely that there is a single term structure specification that is best for pricing all fixed income derivatives.[47] For example, a one-factor model in which yields on bonds with different maturities are (instantaneously) perfectly

[47] This doesn't mean that the derivatives can't all be priced and hedged in terms of a common model which nests the specialized (restricted) versions best for various derivatives.

correlated does not, a priori, seem a good candidate for valuing options to exchange one segment of the yield curve for a different segment (e.g. the SYCURVE options offered by Goldman Sachs),[48] though it might produce reasonable results in valuing some short-term options on bond prices. More generally, several of the most recent exotic interest rate options 'lever' volatility assumptions in the underlying tree, thus making their pricing and hedging much more sensitive to gyrations in the market which weren't contemplated in the tree. Unfortunately, there are currently few guidelines available to guide the selection of which model features are important for pricing and hedging which interest rate contingent claims. It would be interesting to investigate whether bounds can be placed on the underlying interest rate uncertainty, and thus on which features of uncertainty are important, given some categorization of the various derivatives contracts.[49]

Acknowledgements

I am grateful to the Yamaichi Securities Co. Ltd. for financial support through the Yamaichi Chair in Finance at the University of Tokyo while part of this work was completed, and to Raoul Davie, Paul Pfleiderer, Kenneth Vetzal, and especially David Pyle for helpful comments on earlier drafts.

References

Ait-Sahalia, Y. (1992). Nonparametric pricing of interest rate derivative securities, Paper based on Ph.D. Dissertation, Department of Economics, MIT, 50 Memorial Drive, Cambridge, MA 02139.

Amin, K.I., and Morton, A.J. (1993). Implied volatility functions in arbitrage-free term structure models, unpublished paper, School of Business Administration, The University of Michigan.

Banz, R.W., and Miller, M.H. (1978). Prices for state-contingent claims: Some estimates, and applications. *J. Bus.* 51(4), 653–672.

Baron, K.C., (1989). Time variation in the modes of fluctuation of the Treasury yield curve. *Bankers Trust Company*, Topics in Money, and Securities Markets, No. 57, October.

Beaglehole, D. R., and M.S. Tenney (1991). Corrections, and additions to 'A nonlinear equilibrium model of the term structure of interest rates,' *J. Financ. Econ.* 32, 345–353.

Beim, David, (1992). Term structure, and the non-cash values in bonds, paper presented at the Berkeley Program in Finance meeting, Carmel Valley, August 1993.

Beja, A., (1979). State preference, and the riskless interest rate: A markov model of capital markets. *Rev. Econ. Studies* XLVI(3), 144, 435–446.

Benninga, S., and A. Protopapadakis (1986). General equilibrium properties of the term structure of interest rates. *J. Financ. Econ.* 16(3), 389–410.

Black, F. (1972). Active, and passive monetary policy in a neoclassical model. *J. Finance* 27(4), 801–814.

Black, F. (1988). A simple discounting rule. *Financ. Manage.* 17(2), 7–11.

[48] Perhaps a one-factor model for the yield curve *spread* could work, but it would be specific to the points on the yield curve defining the spread, and could probably be dominated by a model using a second 'curvature' type factor.

[49] The intuition is similar to that behind Grundy's [1991] derivation of bounds on asset price distributions implied by option prices.

Black, F., E. Derman, and W. Toy (1990). A one-factor model of interest rates, and its application to Treasury bond options, *Financ. Anal. J.* January–February, 33–39.

Black, F., and M. Scholes (1973). The pricing of options, and corporate liabilities. *J. Polit. Econ.* 81, 637–659.

Bollerslev, T., R. Chou, and K. Kroner (1992). ARCH modelling in finance. *J. Econometr.* 52, 5–59.

Boyle, P.P., (1978). Immunization under stochastic models of the term structure. *J. Inst. Actuaries* 105, 177–187.

Breeden, D.T. (1986). Consumption, production, inflation, and interest rates: A synthesis. *J. Financ. Econ.* 16, 3–39.

Breeden, D.T., and R.H. Litzenberger (1978). Prices of state-contingent claims implicit in option prices. *J. Bus.* 51, 621–651.

Brennan, M.J., and E.S. Schwartz (1982). An equilibrium model of bond pricing, and a test of market efficiency. *J. Financ. Quant. Anal.* 62(3), 301–329.

Brown, S.J., and P.H. Dybvig, (1986). The empirical implications of the Cox, Ingersoll, Ross theory of the term structure of interest rates, *J. Finance* 61(3), 616–630.

Brown, R.H., and S.M. Schaefer (1994). The term structure of interest rates, and the Cox, Ingersoll & Ross model. *J. Financ. Econ.* 35, 3–42.

Cai, J. (1992). A Markov model of unconditional variance in ARCH, unpublished paper, Northwestern University.

Canabarro, E. (1993). Comparing the dynamic accuracy of yield-curve-based interest rate contingent claim pricing models. *J. Financ. Eng.* 2(4), 365–401.

Carverhill, A. (1992a). Term structure dynamics, and associated option valuations: An evolutionary approach, unpublished paper, Hong Kong University of Science, and Technology, Clear Water Bay, Kowloon, Hong Kong.

Carverhill, A. (1992b). Interest rate option valuation models: A note about the behavior of the volatility structure, Unpublished paper, Hong Kong University of Science, and Technology, Clear Water Bay, Kowloon, Hong Kong.

Chan, K.C., Karolyi, G.A., F.A. Longstaff, and A.B. Sanders (1992). An empirical comparison of alternative models of the short term interest rate. *J. Finance* 67(3), 1209–1227.

Cheng, S.T. (1991). On the feasibility of arbitrage-based option pricing when stochastic bond price processes are involved. *J. Econ. Theory* 53, 185–198.

Constantinides, G. M. (1992). A theory of the nominal term structure of interest rates. *Rev. Financ. Studies* 5(4), 531–552.

Courtadon, G. (1982). The pricing of options on default-free bonds. *J. Financ. Quant. Anal.* 62(1), 75–100.

Cox, J.C. (1986). Term structure models, lecture presented at the Berkeley Program in Finance Seminar, Lake Tahoe, March 16–19.

Cox, J.C., J.E. Ingersoll, Jr., and S.A. Ross (1980). An analysis of variable rate loan contracts, *J. Finance* 35, 389–403.

Cox, J.C., J.E. Ingersoll, Jr., and S.A. Ross (1981). A re-examinations of traditional hypothesis about the term structure of interest rates. *J. Finance* 36(4), 769–799.

Cox, J.C., J.E. Ingersoll, Jr., and S.A. Ross (1985). A theory of the term structure of interest rates, *Econometrica* 53(2), 385–407.

Cox, J.C., and S.A. Ross (1976). A survey of some new results in financial option pricing theory. *J. Finance* 31(2), 383–402.

Cox, J.C., S.A., Ross, and M.R. Rubinstein (1979). Option pricing: A simplified approach. *J. Financ. Econ.* 7, 229–263.

Cox, J.C., and M. Rubinstein (1985). *Options Markets*, Prentice-Hall, Englewood Cliffs, NJ.

Culbertson, J. (1957). The term structure of interest rates. *Q. J. Econ.* 71(4), 485–517.

Dietrich-Campbell, D., and E. Schwartz (1986). Valuing debt options. *J. Financ. Econ.* 16, 321–343.

Diament, P., (1993) Semi-empirical smooth fit to the Treasury yield curve. *J. Fixed Income* 3(1), 55–70.

Dothan, L.U. (1978). On the term structure of interest rates. *J. Financ. Econ.* 6(1), 59–69.

Duffie, D., and P. Protter (1992). From discrete- to continuous-time finance: Weak convergence of the financial gain process. *Math. Finance* 2(1), 1–15.

Engle, R.F., D.M. Lilien, and R.P. Robins (1987). Estimating time varying risk premia in the term structure: The ARCH-M model, *Econometrica* 55(2), 391–407.

Engle, R.F., and V.K. Ng (1991). Time-varying volatility, and the dynamic behavior of the term structure, unpublished paper, Department of Economics, U.C.S.D., La Jolla, CA.

Estrella, A., and G. Hardouvelis (1991). The term structure as a predictor of real economic activity. *J. Finance* 46(2), 555–576.

Ferson, W. (1981). Expectations of real interest rates, and aggregate consumption: Empirical tests. *J. Financ. Quant. Anal.* 18(4), 477–497.

Fischer, S., and F. Modigliani (1978). Towards an understanding of the real effects, and costs of inflation. *Weltwirtsch. Archiv* 114, 810–832.

Flesaker, B. (1990). Estimation, and testing of the constant volatility Heath, Jarrow, Morton model of interest rate contingent claims pricing, unpublished paper, University of Illinois at Urbana-Champaign.

Fong, H.G., and Vasicek, O.A. (1991a). Interest rate volatility as a stochastic factor, unpublished paper, Gifford Fong Associates, 160 Pringle Drive, Walnut Creek, CA.

Fong, H.G., and Vasicek, O.A. (1991b). Fixed-income volatility management. *J. Portfolio Manage.* Summer, 41–46.

Friedman, M., and A. Jacobson Schwartz, (1963). *A Monetary History of the United States*, Princeton University Press, Princeton.

Friedman, B., and K. Kuttner, (1992). Money, income, prices, and interest rates. *Am. Econ. Rev. 82(3)*, 472–492.

Garbade, K.D., (1986). Modes of fluctuation in bond yields — An analysis of principal components. *Bankers Trust Company*, Topics in Money, and Securities Markets, No. 20, June.

Garbade, K.D., (1987). Modes of fluctuation in Treasury Strip, and Federal Agency bond yield curves. *Bankers Trust Company*, Topics in Money, and Securities Markets, No. 25, March.

Garbade, K.D., (1989a). Risk constrained portfolio reallocations, and the prices of interest rate risk. *Bankers Trust Company*, Topics in Money, and Securities Markets, No. 51, June.

Garbade, K.D., (1989b). Consistency between the shape of the yield curve, and its modes of fluctuation in a multi-factor framework. *Bankers Trust Company*, Topics in Money, and Securities Markets, No. 59, December.

Garbade, K.D., (1990). Recent time variation in the modes of fluctuation of the spot Treasury yield curve. *Bankers Trust Company*, Topics in Money, and Securities Markets, No. 70, December.

Garbade, K.D., and Urich, T.J., (1988). Modes of fluctuation in Sovereign bond yield curves: An international comparison. *Bankers Trust Company*, Topics in Money, and Securities Markets, No. 42, October.

Garman, M.B. (1978). A synthesis of the equilibrium theory of arbitrage, Unpublished paper, U.C. Berkeley, June, 1978.

Gibbons, M.R., and K. Ramaswamy (1993). The term structure of interest rates: Empirical evidence. *Rev. Financ. Studies* 6(3), 619–658.

Gennotte, G., and T.A. Marsh (1993a). Variations in economic uncertainty, and risk premiums on capital assets. *Eur. Econ. Rev.* 37(5), 1021–1041.

Gennotte, G., and T.A. Marsh (1993b). The term structure, equity returns, and yield premiums on risky bonds, unpublished paper, U.C. Berkeley, and University of Tokyo.

Gray, S. (1993). Regime-switching models: A new approach, unpublished paper, Graduate School of Business, Stanford University, Stanford, CA 94305, November.

Grundy, B.D. (1991). Option prices, and the underlying asset's return distribution. *J. Finance* 56(3), 1045–1069.

Hamilton, J., (1988). Rational expectations econometric analysis of changes in regime: An investigation of the term structure of interest rates. *J. Econ. Dyn. Control* 12, 385–423.

Hansen, L.P., and K.J. Singleton (1983). Stochastic consumption, risk aversion, and the temporal behavior of asset returns. *J. Polit. Econ.* 91(2), 249–265.

Harrison, J.M., and D.M. Kreps (1979). Martingales, and arbitrage in multiperiod security markets. *J. Econ. Theory* 20, 381–408.

Harrison, J.M., and S. Pliska (1981). Martingales, and stochastic integrals in the theory of continuous trading. *Stoch. Processes Appl.* 11, 215–260.

Harvey, C., (1988). The real term structure, and consumption growth, *J. Financ. Econ.* 22, 305–333.

He, H. (1990). Convergence from discrete- to continuous-time contingent claims prices. *Revi. Financ. Studies* 3(4), 523–546.

He, H., and H., Leland (1992). Equilibrium asset price processes, unpublished paper, Walter A. Haas School of Business, U.C. Berkeley, 350 Barrrows Hall, Berkeley, CA.

He, H., and T.A., Marsh (1991). Modelling term structure uncertainty, unpublished paper: Walter A. Haas School of Business, U.C. Berkeley, 350 Barrrows Hall, Berkeley, CA.

Heath, D., R. Jarrow, and A. Morton (1989). Contingent claim valuation with a random evolution of interest rates, unpublished paper: Cornell University, Ithaca, NY.

Heath, D., R. Jarrow, and A. Morton (1990). Bond pricing, and the term structure of interest rates: A discrete time approximation. *J. Financ. Quant. Anal.* 25(4), 419–440.

Heath, D., R. Jarrow, and A. Morton (1992). Bond pricing, and the term structure of interest rates: A new methodology for contingent claims valuation. *Econometrica* 60, 77–105.

Hicks, J.R. (1939). *Value, and Capital.*

Ho, T.S.Y., and S. Lee (1986). Term structure movements, and pricing interest rate contingent claims. *J. Finance* 51(5), 1011–1029.

Huang, C., and R. Litzenberger (1988). *Foundations for Financial Economics*, North Holland–Elsevier Science Publishing Company, New York, NY.

Hull, J., and White, A. (1990). Pricing interest-rate-derivative securities. *Rev. Financ. Studies*, 3(4), 573–592.

Ingersoll, J., Jr., J. Skelton, and R. Weil. (1978). Duration forty years later. *J. Financ. Quant. Anal.* November, 627–650.

Jamshidian, F. (1989). An exact bond option formula. *J. Finance* 44(1), 205–210.

Jarrow, R.A. (1994). Pricing interest rate options, in: R. Jarrow, V. Maksimovic, and W.T. Ziemba (eds.), Finance, Handbooks in Operations Research, and Management Science, Vol. 9., North Holland, Amsterdam, pp. 251–272 (this volume).

Keim, D., and R. Stambaugh, (1986). Prediting returns in the stock, and bond markets. *J. Financ. Econ.* 17(2), 357–390.

Kessel, R. (1965). The cyclical behavior of the term structure of interest rates, occasional paper 91, National Bureau of Economic Research.

Keynes, J.M. (1935) *The General Theory of Employment, Interest, and Money*, Harcourt, Brace & World, Inc., New York, NY.

Kuwahara, H., and T.A. Marsh (1994). Exploration of a methodology for choosing interest rate models appropriate for pricing, and hedging interest rate derivatives, unpublished paper, Department of Economics, University of Tokyo.

LeRoy, S.F. (1982). Risk-aversion, and the term structure of real interest rates. *Econ. Lett.* 10, 355–361.

LeRoy, S.F. (1984). Nominal prices, and interest rates in general equilibrium: Endowment shocks. *J. Bus.* 57(2), 197–213.

Litterman, R., J. Scheinkman, and L. Weiss (1991). Volatility, and the yield curve. *J. Fixed Income* 1(1), 49–53.

Litterman, R., and J. Scheinkman (1991). Common factors affecting bond returns. *J. Fixed Income* 1(1), 54–61.

Long, J.B., Jr. (1974). Stock prices, inflation, and the term structure of interest rates. *J. Financ. Econ.* 1(2), 131–170.

Longstaff, F. (1989). A nonlinear general equilibrium model of the term structure of interest rates. *J. Financ. Econ.* 23, 195–224.

Longstaff, F.A. (1990). The valuation of options on yields. *J. Financ. Econ.* 26, 97–121.

Longstaff, F., and E.S. Schwartz (1992). Interest rate volatility, and the term structure: A two-factor general equilibrium model. *J. Finance* 47(4), 1259–1282.

Lucas, R.E., Jr. (1978). Asset prices in an exchange economy. *Econometrica* 46, 1429–1445.

McCulloch, J.H. (1985). Interest-risk sensitive deposit insurance premia. *J. Banking Finance* 9, 137–156.

Malkiel, B. (1966). *The Term Structure of Interest Rates: Expectations, and Behavior Patterns*, Princeton University Press, Princeton, NJ. .

Marsh, T.A. (1980). Equilibrium term structure models: Test methodology. *J. Finance* 35(5), 421–438.

Marsh, T.A. (1985). Asset pricing model specification, and the term structure of interest rates, NBER working paper No. 1612, November.

Marsh, T.A., and E.R. Rosenfeld (1983). Stochastic processes for interest rates, and equilibrium bond prices. *J. Finance* 38, 635–646.

Melino, A. (1988). The term structure of interest rates: Evidence, and theory. *J. Econ. Surv.* 4, 335–366.

Merton, R.C., (1971). Optimum consumption, and portfolio rules in a continuous-time model. *J. Econ. Theory* 3, 373–413.

Merton, R.C., (1973). Theory of rational option pricing. *Bell J. Econ. Manage. Sci.* 4, 141–183.

Merton, R.C., (1975a). An asymptotic theory of growth under uncertainty. *Rev. Econ. Studies* 42(3), 375–393.

Merton, R.C., (1975b). Theory of finance from the perspective of continuous time. *J. Financ. Quant. Anal.* 10(4), 659–674.

Merton, R.C., (1977). On the pricing of contingent claims, and the Modigliani–Miller theorem. *J. Financ. Econ.* 5(2), 241–249.

Merton, R.C., (1982). On the microeconomic theory of investment under uncertainty, in: K.J. Arrow, and M.D. Intrilligator (eds.). *Handbook of Mathematical Economics, Vol. II*, North-Holland, Amsterdam.

Merton, R.C., (1990). The financial system, and economic performance. *J. Financ. Serv. Res.* , 4(4) December, 263–300.

Miller, M.H., (1986). Financial innovation: The last twenty years, and the next. *J. Financ. Quant. Anal.* 21, 459–471.

Murphy, J.E., Jr., (1987). *With Interest: How to Profit from Interest Rate Fluctuations*, Dow Jones Irwin, Homewood, IL.

Muth, J., (1961). Rational expectations, and the theory of price movements. *Econometrica* 29, 315–335.

Nelson, C.R., and A.F. Siegel (1987). Parsimonious modeling of yield curves. *J. Bus.* 60(4), 473–489.

Nelson, D.B., and K. Ramaswamy (1990). Simple binomial processes as diffusion approximations in financial models. *Rev. Financ. Studies* 3(3), 393–430.

Pearson, N.D., and T. Sun (1989). A test of the Cox, Ingersoll, Ross model of the term structure of interest rates using the method of maximum likelihood, unpublished paper, Sloan School of Management, MIT, Cambridge, MA.

Pennacchi, G. (1991). Identifying the dynamics of real interest rates, and inflation: Evidence using survey data. *Rev. Financ. Studies* 4, 53–86.

Ramaswamy, K., and S. Sundaresan (1986). The valuation of floating-rate notes. *J. Financ. Econ.* 17, 251–272.

Richard, S.F. (1978). An arbitrage model of the term structure of interest rates. *J. Financ. Econ.* 6(1), 33–57.

Rogalski, R., and E. Werlin (1988). What's new: A real interest rate bond. *Invest. Manage. Rev.* 2(2), 20–27.

Roll, R. (1970). *The Behavior of Interest Rates: An Application of the Efficient Market Model to U.S. Treasury Bills*, Basic Books, New York, NY.

Roll, R. (1971). Investment diversification, and bond maturity. *J. Finance* 26, 51–66.

Romer, C., and D. Romer, 1990, New evidence on the monetary transmission mechanism. *Brookings Pap. Econ. Activity*, 1, 149–198.
Ross, S.A. (1978). A simple approach to the valuation of risky streams. *J. Bus.* 51(3), 453–475.
Rubinstein, M. (1976). The valuation of uncertain income streams, and the pricing of options. *Bell J. Econ.* 7, 407–425.
Rubinstein, M. (1994). Implied binomial trees, (American Finance Association Presidential Address) Finance working paper No. 232, U.C. Berkeley, Research Program in Finance Working Paper Series, January.
Samuelson, P.A., and R.C. Merton (1969). A complete model of warrant pricing that maximizes utility. *Indust. Manage. Rev.* 10(2), 17–46.
Schaefer, S.M., and E.S. Schwartz (1984). A two-factor model of the term structure: An approximate analytical solution. *J. Financ. Quant. Anal.* 19, 413–424.
Sharpe, W. (1993). Nuclear financial economics, forthcoming.
Shi, W. (1994a). The term structure of nominal interest rates: An equilibrium model, unpublished Paper, Haas School of Business, U.C. Berkeley, Berkeley, CA.
Shi, W. (1994b). The term structure of nominal interest rates: An econometric test, unpublished paper, Haas School of Business, U.C. Berkeley, Berkeley, CA.
Stiglitz, J.E. (1970). A consumption-oriented theory of demand for financial assets, and the term structure of interest rates. *Rev. Econ. Studies* 37, 321–351.
Sundaresan, M. (1984). Consumption, and equilibrium interest rates in stochastic production economies. *J. Finance* 39, 77–92.
Tobin, J. (1958). Liquidity preference as behavior towards risk. *Rev. Econ. Studies* 25, 65–86.
Van Horne, J.C. (1985). Of financial innovations, and excesses. *J. Finance* 40, 621–631.
Vasicek, O. (1977). An equilibrium characterization of the term structure. *J. Financ. Econ.* 5, 177–188.
Vetzal, K. (1992). The impact of stochastic volatility on bond option prices, research report 92-08, Institute of Insurance, and Pension Research, University of Waterloo, Waterloo, Ont.
Vetzal, K. (1994). A survey of stochastic continuous time models of the term structure of interest rates, forthcoming.
Webber, N.J. (1992). The consistency of term structure models: The short rate, the long rate, and volatility, Financial Options Research Center, Warwick Business School, University of Warwick, Coventry, FORC Reprint 92/20.
Wilcox, J.A. (1985). Short-term movements of long-term real interest rates: Evidence from the U.K. indexed bond market, Working Paper No. 145, Institute for Business, and Economic Research, U.C. Berkeley, Berkeley, CA.
Willinger, W., and M.S. Taqqu (1991). Toward a convergence theory for continuous stochastic securities models. *Math. Finance* 1(1), 55–99.

R. Jarrow et al., Eds., *Handbooks in OR & MS, Vol. 9*
1995 Elsevier Science B.V.

Chapter 10

Program Trading and Stock Index Arbitrage

Linda Canina
School of Hotel Administration, Cornell University, Ithaca, NY 14853, U.S.A.

Stephen Figlewski
Stern School of Business, New York University, New York City, NY 10012, U.S.A.

1. Introduction

The creation of futures contracts based on stock market indexes and the development of program trading are among the most important, and also the most controversial, financial market innovations of the 1980s. On the one hand, index futures are an extremely useful and inexpensive risk management tool that allows an institutional investor to adjust the market risk exposure of an investment portfolio quickly, easily, and cheaply without disturbing the equity holdings in the portfolio. Futures greatly facilitate the management of equity portfolio risk by large scale institutional investors such as pension plan sponsors, first because transactions costs are significantly reduced, but also because they permit decentralized investment decision-making. In which individual portfolio managers are free to invest the funds allocated to them as they choose while overall market exposure is set by a futures overlay strategy that is implemented at the plan sponsor level.

On the other hand, with the ease of trading and the high leverage that these instruments permit, transitory fluctuations in market sentiment can produce powerful effects in the futures market which are then transmitted by arbitrage to the underlying stock market. On numerous occasions during the 1980s, trading in stock index futures was widely blamed as a cause of, or at least a contributor to, turmoil in the stock market, and various constraints were placed on the futures market and on the arbitrage process. The most extreme example, of course, was in the crash of October 19, 1987 and its aftermath, when the New York Stock Exchange (NYSE) imposed a ban on program trading for several weeks, and a variety of measures to curb index futures trading were introduced thereafter.

In this chapter, we will discuss the instruments, the trading strategies, and to some extent, the controversies surrounding index futures and program trading in stocks.

2. Stock index futures contracts and program trading

2.1. Index futures

A futures contract based on a stock index was first proposed by the Kansas City Board of Trade (KCBOT) in 1978. Although the most widely followed stock index in the U.S. is the Dow Jones Industrial Average, the Dow Jones Company opposed the use of their index for futures trading at the time, and continues to do so to this day. The KCBOT therefore proposed a contract based on the Value Line Composite Index, a very broad market index covering about 1700 major stocks. Financial futures were quite new at that time, and to the Commodity Futures Trading Commission (CFTC) which has the responsibility of approving all new futures contracts, the unique design of the proposed contract seemed to pose serious problems. One of the most important was that there was to be no provision for delivery of the underlying stocks.

While few of the contracts outstanding at any one time in a futures market actually result in delivery of the underlying commodity or financial instrument, it is the *possibility* of delivery that ties the futures price to the cash price at maturity, which is a requirement for effective hedging. However, the stock market is much more active and liquid than the cash market for other futures. There is no difficulty or ambiguity in *pricing* a broad portfolio of stocks, such as the Standard and Poor's 500 index portfolio, or in calculating the value of an index like the Value Line.[1] But it would be highly impractical, and in some cases impossible, to deliver the 'stock index' itself.[2] In other words, the expiration value of an index futures contract is easily determined by looking at the closing value of the index in the stock market, but the only settlement procedure that makes sense is cash settlement based on price differences. The CFTC was not prepared in 1978 to approve the KCBOT's proposed cash-settled stock index futures contract.

Only in 1982, after the regulatory climate changed under the Reagan Administration, did the CFTC finally allow stock index futures to trade. In that year, the KCBOT won approval for its Value Line contract, the Chicago Mercantile Exchange (CME) introduced the Standard and Poor's 500 (S&P 500) contract, and the New York Stock Exchange opened an affiliated futures exchange. The New York Futures Exchange's (NYFE) primary contract was an index future based on the NYSE composite index.

[1] The original Value Line Index is computed as a geometric average from the returns on the individual component stocks, meaning that there was no actual stock portfolio whose value was represented by the Value Line Index. In 1988, Value Line introduced an arithmetic average index, which was adopted as the underlying index for Value Line futures. The new index measures the value of an equally weighted portfolio of all of the component stocks.

[2] Unlike most stock index futures contracts, the Osaka Stock Futures 50 (OSF50) was settled by physical delivery of the underlying securities. This contract was delisted in 1993 because of the lack of volume since 1988, when the Osaka Securities Exchange introduced the Nikkei Stock Average and the Tokyo Stock Exchange introduced the TOPIX futures contracts.

All three contracts were similar in design. The underlying asset was $500 times the index, with settlement exclusively in cash. Contract months were March, June, September, and December. Like all futures, contracts were guaranteed by the exchange Clearing House, both parties to a trade had to post initial margin, and the margin accounts were marked to market every day. These procedures essentially eliminated default risk. Also, because the margin procedure prevented a trader from building up large losses on any position that could lead to a default, as in other futures the margin level could be safely set quite low, 5% of the value of the stocks underlying the contract or less.

For example, consider a trader who buys December S&P 500 futures on November 1 at a price of 450, and on expiration day in December the S&P index ends at 455. The total return on the long position will be received in the form of a stream of daily margin flows over the holding period, as the contracts are marked to market at each day's futures settlement price. The daily cash payment is $500 per contract times the price change from the previous day. The cumulative value the trader receives over the entire period will be $\$500 \times (455 - 450) = \$2500$. On expiration day, there is one final payment as all outstanding contracts are marked to the level of the actual S&P index, and then they expire.

Stock index futures were an extraordinary success, with trading volume growing rapidly to many thousands of contracts per day. However, as is frequently found with duplicative futures contracts, one market quickly became dominant and attracted the lion's share of the trading volume, and the others soon became satellites of the primary market. In this case, it was the CME's S&P 500 contract that became dominant.[3]

In time, other index futures were proposed, some of which were introduced, but there were few successes in the U.S. For a time, in the middle 1980s, futures on the Major Market Index became active. This index was designed to be very much like the Dow Jones: It is comprised of 20 large stocks, of which nearly all are components of the Dow, and the weighting procedure is the same.[4] Additional support for this contract came from the fact that there was active trading in stock index options based on the same index. Other futures contracts tied to small stocks, such as the Russell 2000, or to different types of indexes were attempted, but so far the S&P 500 is by far the most important index future in the U.S.

In the last few years, stock index futures have been introduced in many

[3] As of December 27, 1983 the open interest on the S&P 500, NYSE composite and the Value Line futures contracts was 24,576, 11,237 and 3,755, respectively. While, the open interest on the S&P 500, the NYSE composite and the Value Line futures contracts was 117,944, 5,264 and 1,444, respectively, as of December 27, 1988.

[4] Unlike the S&P and most other broad market indexes that weight each component stock in proportion to the total capitalization of the firm ('cap' weighting), a few indexes, including the Dow and the Japanese Nikkei 225 are essentially based on the value of a portfolio containing one share of each stock. This causes the return on a given stock to affect the index in proportion to its price ('price' weighting). The third common weighting procedure for a stock index is equal weighting, in which the percent change in the index is computed as a simple average of the returns on the component stocks. In 1994 the cap weighted Nikkei 300 was introduced in Japan.

Table 1

Major stock index futures around the world

Country	Index	# Stocks	Weight [a]	Volume (7/27/94)	Open interest (7/27/94)
North America					
U.S.	S&P 500	500	cap	47,481	218,769
	NYSE composite	2089	cap	1,299	3,820
	Major market	20	price	46	3,237
	Value line	1665	equal	50	811
	Russel 2000	2000	cap	1,035	3,227
	Nikkei 225 (Japan)	225	equal	2,449	21,745
Canada	TSF 35	35	cap	377	NA
Europe					
U.K.	FT-SE 100	102	cap	17,373	53,474
France	CAC-40	40	cap	45,893	70,336
Germany	DAX	30	cap	16,379	98,263
Switzerland	SMI	23	cap	5,687	NA
Netherlands	EOE	25	cap	1,819	NA
Spain	IBEX 35	35	cap	43,184	257,480
Sweden	OMX	30	cap	3,408	160,064
Far East, Australia					
Japan	Nikkei 225	225	equal	26,696	118,258
	Nikkei 300	300	cap	9,997	145,613
	Topix	1229	cap	8,804	73,238
Singapore	Nikkei 225 (Japan)	225	equal	32,263	92,366
Hong Kong	Hang Seng	33	cap	30,066	42,994
Australia	All ordinaries	274	cap	4,442	71,212

Source: Bloomberg data.
[a] See footnote 4 for an explanation of index weighting methods.

countries. Table 1 shows a selection of index futures from around the world. Clearly, index futures are a financial innovation that has widespread appeal.

2.2. *Index arbitrage and program trading*

Unlike stock values, that are determined by expectations of future supply and demand based on earnings and other fundamental economic factors, the equilibrium stock index futures prices are unambiguous and easily calculated. As a derivative instrument, the fair price for an index futures contract is determined completely by the current level of the index in the stock market and the 'cost of carry', which depends on the risk free interest rate and the dividend yield. This relation is discussed in the next section.

This theoretical price relationship is enforced by arbitrage between the cash and futures markets. For example, if the futures price in the market is higher than its theoretical value, an arbitrage opportunity arises in which the overpriced future is sold and the underlying stock index portfolio is bought, to create a riskless position with a high return. Executing that trade involves simultaneously purchasing all of the component stocks in the correct proportions to duplicate the index. Such a trade of an entire portfolio of stocks at once is known as a 'program trade'. Arbitrage between a stock index future and the underlying index portfolio clearly requires a program trade, but not all program trades are related to index futures. The NYSE defines any simultaneous trade involving 15 or more stocks and a market value of $1 million or more to be a program trade. With this broad definition, by 1992 the NYSE reported that 11.5% of total trading volume was program trading. However, in a study of all program trades done on the NYSE during 4 months in 1989, Neal [1993] finds that only 47.5% were related to stock index arbitrage. Other reasons for program trading included liquidation of portfolios (19.8%), portfolio realignment (12.4%), and a variety of other trading strategies.

Effective index arbitrage trading requires the ability to trade the index futures (or options)[5] contracts and quickly execute a program trade of the underlying stocks. For a broad stock market index portfolio like the S&P 500, simultaneously trading all of the component stocks presents a considerable challenge. In the first few years of index futures trading, there were no formal procedures for program trading and arbitrageurs were forced to enter orders exactly as if each of the stock trades was a separate transaction, a cumbersome process when a large number of stocks were involved. To accelerate execution, they frequently traded surrogate portfolios consisting of a much smaller number of the most liquid stocks in place of the entire index portfolio.

By the middle 1980s, however, trading technology in the U.S. had advanced to the point that it was possible to generate the individual buy or sell orders for exchange-traded stocks by computer and to transmit them electronically through the New York Stock Exchange's Designated Order Turnaround (DOT) system directly to the various exchange trading posts. While trading a surrogate portfolio is still common, it is now possible to buy or sell nearly the entire S&P 500 index portfolio within about 2 minutes and frequently much faster than that. Neal [1993] reports that in 1989, the average number of stocks in the cash leg of an S&P futures arbitrage was 375 (with a standard deviation of 155); the average for an NYSE futures arbitrage was only 292, even though the index contains over 1600 stocks.

The heavy use of computers in the strategy gave rise to a common misconception that the trading decisions in an index arbitrage are made automatically by computer. This is false: the computer's role is essentially the clerical task of generating a large number of orders efficiently and transmitting them electronically into the market. The trading decisions are made by human traders.

[5] Options based on broad stock indexes are also actively traded, but an options arbitrage is much more complicated than a futures arbitrage because the position must be adjusted dynamically as the market moves. The result is that, as Neal [1993] shows, there is actually little program trading associated with index options arbitrage. We confine our attention in this chapter to arbitrage with stock index futures.

Internationally, the nature of program trading and index arbitrage varies considerably from country to country. In Japan and France, like the U.S., portfolio trades may be executed stock by stock electronically throughout the day, while in most other markets (e.g., Germany, Switzerland, the Netherlands) orders have to be carried by hand to the specialists on the trading floor, as they were in the U.S. when index futures trading first began. In the U.K., trading is done by dealers through a screen-based quotation system, like the OTC market in the U.S. The lack of simultaneous execution of the program orders increases execution risk.

3. Stock index arbitrage in theory

3.1. Index futures pricing in a frictionless market

In futures and stock markets, absent transactions costs and other market frictions, the Law of One Price should hold: securities (and portfolios of securities) with identical cash flows must sell for the same price and opportunities for riskless arbitrage profits should not exist. This principle is the basis of the 'cost of carry' pricing relationship for futures contracts.

Consider the strategy of buying the portfolio of stocks that comprise the index at date t and simultaneously selling stock index futures contracts that mature on some later date T. Although there is no way to deliver the stocks to satisfy the short position in the futures market, the futures price at expiration on date T will be set equal to the index level in the stock market at that time, so the futures trade effectively locks in today's futures price as the total amount that will be realized on the stock portfolio when the position is unwound at T. We are treating futures as if they were forward contracts, leaving out the second order pricing effects of initial margin and marking to market. More importantly, for the moment, we are ignoring transactions costs.

In other words, if the initial index value and futures price are $P(t)$ and $F(t, T)$, respectively, and their final values on date T (the same for both the index and the expiring future) are $P(T)$, then the stock trade will earn $P(T) - P(t)$ and the short futures position will yield $F(t, T) - P(T)$, so the total return on the combined position (excluding dividends) is $F(t, T) - P(t)$, which is fixed at the outset. Any difference between the index level at which the stock position is liquidated on date T and the initial date t futures price is offset by a matching profit or loss on the futures.

Thus the arbitrage trade creates a fully hedged riskless position for the period from t to T. The total return is equal to the dividends paid by the stocks over the holding period, plus price appreciation equal to the difference between the date t futures price and spot index level. But since this return is riskless, by the Law of One Price it must be the same as the return on other risk free investments, i.e., the riskless rate of interest. This relationship then yields the equilibrium futures price as a function of the level of the spot index, its future dividend payout and the riskless interest rate:

$$F^{e}(t,T) = P(t)e^{r(T-t)} - \sum_{s=t+1}^{T} D(s)e^{r(T-s)} \tag{1}$$

where $F^{e}(t, T)$ is the theoretical date t price of the futures contract maturing at date T, $P(t)$ is the date t value of the cash index underlying the futures contract, r is the riskless interest rate applicable to the period from t to T (expressed as a continuously compounded percent per day), and $D(s)$ is the date s dividend inflow on the stock portfolio, measured in index units and assumed to be known as of t.

This is commonly called the 'cost of carry' value, because the futures price is equal to the index at date t plus the net cost of carrying the position until futures expiration (i.e., the riskless interest rate less the dividend payout). Equation (1) takes into account the actual dividends paid by the component stocks and the dates on which they are expected to be paid. This is the correct way to handle dividends, but it can be quite burdensome to try to forecast future dividends and payout dates for a large number of stocks. A broad stock portfolio produces a fairly continuous stream of dividend payments.[6] These can vary considerably from day to day, but no single day's payment is a very large percent of the index. For many purposes, equation (1) can be approximated quite closely by the simpler expression in equation (2):

$$F^{e}(t,T) \approx P(t)e^{(r-d)(T-t)} \tag{2}$$

where d is the expected dividend *yield* on the index portfolio over the holding period, expressed at a continuously compounded daily rate.

If the cost of carry relation is not satisfied at every instant t during the futures contract life, then an opportunity exists to make a riskless arbitrage profit equal to the mispricing, that is, the difference between the actual and theoretical futures prices. For example, when the futures price is above the level given in equation (1), a long index arbitrage position should be taken: The stock index portfolio should be purchased and the futures contract should be sold. Exploitation of the mispricing in this way should cause stock prices to be bid up and futures prices down, driving them toward the theoretical alignment.

At expiration, the futures contracts will mature and will be settled in cash. The stock portfolio should be sold simultaneously, so that the futures and cash legs of the trade are unwound at the same price. The end result will be that the total return on the hedged position, from the price appreciation locked in by the futures plus the dividend flow from the stocks during the holding period, will be greater than the interest rate that could have been earned on the same capital by investing in riskless securities. If the arbitrage position can be financed by borrowing the necessary funds at the riskless interest rate, the trade will produce a 'free lunch', i.e., positive profits on no net investment.

[6] In Japan, dividend payments are concentrated in the months of March, the end of the fiscal year, and in September.

Underpriced futures give rise to arbitrage profits from selling (short) the index stocks, investing the proceeds in riskless securities, and going long futures to lock in the effective index level at which the stocks will be repurchased. The interest earned plus the difference between the initial index level (at which the stocks are sold) and the futures price (that fixes where they will be bought back) will exceed the value of the foregone dividends. However, in practice this trade is distinctly harder to execute than the 'cash and carry' long arbitrage, as we will discuss in more detail below.

3.2. Transactions costs

In the real world, traders face market 'imperfections', particularly transactions costs. In the presence of these costs, a small mispricing in the futures contract will not produce an arbitrage opportunity large enough to offset the cost of putting on a trade to exploit it. There will be a band around the theoretical futures price within which the actual price may float freely without inducing arbitrage.

Transactions costs in this case are of two types.[7] First there are brokerage fees, commissions, and possibly other cash outlays associated with trading, such as stock transfer taxes. These can vary considerably from market to market, and from trader to trader. For example, in the U.S., brokerage commission rates are negotiable. They can depend on the brokerage firm, the identity of the customer and the nature of its business relationship with the broker, the specific trading strategy employed (for example, whether the broker guarantees execution of the program trade at a particular index level, or simply gives its 'best efforts' with no guarantee of the outcome), and numerous other aspects of the transaction.

The second element of transactions costs is 'market impact', due to the fact that simply executing a trade will tend to push a security's market price away from its previous level. The bid–ask spread is the major source of this market impact, but it also can happen that a large sized trade will push the market price through the previously reported quote.

The reported index value for U.S. indexes is constructed from the prices at which each of the component stocks *last* traded (not current quotes). Normally there is about the same probability that the most recent trade for a stock will have been at the bid price as at the ask, so the prices in an index like the S&P 500 are *on average* at about the midpoint between bid and ask (leaving aside the issue of 'staleness' of prices for inactively traded stocks).[8] But if an arbitrageur buys the entire index portfolio, all of the stocks will be traded at their current ask prices, causing an immediate, and spurious, jump in the reported index. Similarly, selling the index portfolio will produce an apparent sharp drop in the index. This effect is known as 'bid–ask bounce'. In essence, the index itself has a bid–ask spread.

[7] The description of the trading environment in this section, including the structure of transactions costs and the institutional features of trade execution, are specific to the U.S. markets.

[8] For less actively traded stocks, on occasion the last trade will have taken place sufficiently long ago that the price is not even within the current bid–ask spread. In that case, an index program trade may produce a transaction at a price that is quite far from the reported price for that stock.

The bounce from the center of the market to either the bid or the ask amounts to about 0.5% for the S&P 500, according to Sofianos [1993].

If we denote the bid–ask bounce (i.e., the combined effect for both the stocks and the futures) as B and the commissions and other expenses (for a round trip trade) as C, the arbitrage bounds on the actual futures price in the market become [9]

$$F^{e}(t, T) - B - C \leq F(t, T) \leq F^{e}(t, T) + B + C \tag{3}$$

Equation (3) incorporates the fact that when the arbitrage position is held until expiration it will be unwound at the same settlement level for the future and the index, which eliminates the bid–ask bounce.[10] Thus the total transactions cost will involve paying commissions for both entering and unwinding the trade, but only one market impact.

3.3. Constraints on capital and early unwinding of positions

Equation (3) specifies a price range around the theoretical futures price, and as long as the market price falls within this band, the mispricing can not be risklessly arbitraged away. The width of the no-arbitrage region depends on commissions plus market impact costs of initiating the trade. However, assuming perfect markets except for transactions costs, as soon as the price bound is breached, arbitrageurs should be willing to take essentially unlimited positions. This would effectively turn the Equation (3) bounds into reflecting barriers for the futures price.

In practice, unlimited arbitrage does not happen, for several reasons. One is that as prices move over time, the opportunity to unwind a trade profitably before expiration may arise. This possibility affects the decision on where to get into an arbitrage position: An aggressive arbitrageur may put on a trade inside the equation (3) bounds in the hopes of being able to realize a profit by unwinding early. On the other hand, real world constraints on capital and other limitations,

[9] For exactitude, B and C should be expressed in terms of date T future values. That is, B is the date t bid–ask bounce multiplied by $e^{r(T-t)}$, and all cash payouts for commissions and other trading expenses should be increased at rate r from the date of payout to T.

[10] Unwinding the cash leg of the arbitrage at the precise index level that determines the final settlement of the futures is not necessarily easy. In the U.S., however, this can be done by trading the stocks using 'market on close' or 'market on open' orders for contracts expiring at the close or open, respectively, of the stock market on expiration day. In the case of the S&P 500 contract, the arbitrageur liquidates the cash position at opening prices, which are also the prices that determine the futures settlement value. Prior to June 1987, the S&P futures contract settled at the close. As we will discuss in more detail below, program trading on the quarterly expirations of stock index futures, stock index options, and stock options, referred to as the triple witching hour, can produce price movements in the stock market. The expiration procedures were changed from the close to the opening to reduce the expiration effects on prices. See Stoll & Whaley [1986, 1987, 1990] and Stoll [1988] for a discussion of the expiration-day effects of stock index arbitrage. Market on close or open orders are not possible in every stock market (e.g., the U.K.), which means that market impact must be considered both at the beginning and at the end of an arbitrage.

like exchange-imposed position limits, prevent arbitrageurs from taking infinitely large positions regardless of profit possibilities. In the face of strong market pressures, limited arbitrage trading may not be sufficient to keep the futures price within the no-arbitrage range. Finally, execution risk and other uncertainties (about the amounts and timing of future dividends, for example), along with the existence of a wide range of effective transactions cost structures within the population of potential arbitrageurs can blur the exact location of the price bounds considerably.

The effects of early unwinding and capital constraints on the equilibrium range for index futures prices have been analyzed theoretically by several authors, including Merrick [1989] and Brennan & Schwartz [1990]. If an index arbitrage position is not held until expiration of the futures contract, a second market impact cost will be incurred in closing it. However, if the initial futures mispricing that generated the trade is reversed and futures become mispriced in the other direction by an amount large enough to cover the additional market impact cost, it is rational to unwind the position early, before expiration. In practice, index arbitrageurs may enter and exit arbitrage positions on both sides of the market in the same contract many times within a contract cycle. It is also possible, as Merrick [1989] points out, to extend the holding period past the expiration of one futures contract by rolling the futures component of the trade forward into the next expiration month without liquidating the cash position. Rolling forward at a favorable spread in the futures prices can enhance the arbitrage profit.

Since real world arbitrageurs are constrained by limited capital from taking infinitely large positions, more flexible unwinding of their trades can substantially raise the realized annual arbitrage returns above those guaranteed by the hold-to-expiration investment strategy. These trades are not riskless, however, because the arbitrageurs' profits are now dependent on the path taken by futures prices. In general, traders must wait and hope that the initial mispricing is eliminated, and then reversed by a large enough amount that they can recover all transactions costs. Still, as Merrick [1989] recognized, this possibility can lead arbitrageurs to take positions even when prices are within the transactions cost bounds.

The aggressive risky arbitrage strategy just described is more than a hypothetical possibility: Sofianos [1993] reports that by 1989, nearly 70% of S&P 500 index arbitrage trades were unwound prior to expiration, with the average turnaround time being about 24 hours. The *average* arbitrage trade in his sample was put on when prices were inside the arbitrage bounds, i.e., when the mispricing was not large enough to produce a net profit on a trade that had to be carried to expiration and unwound at fair value.

Brennan & Schwartz [1990] modeled stock index arbitrage activity taking into account the fact that limited capital imposes a constraint on the maximum position an arbitrageur can assume. They assumed a strict limit on the position that could be taken and modeled mispricing as following a Brownian Bridge process. Under these assumptions, they then used option theory to analyze the arbitrage decision. By putting on a position, the trader acquires the option of unwinding it early, while by unwinding, she releases her capital and obtains the option to enter into another trade.

Relaxing the strict position limit assumption made by Brennan and Schwartz [1990], Tuckman & Vila [1992] model the effect of holding costs on arbitrage strategies. Holding costs whose magnitudes depend on the (uncertain) duration of the trade, such as the loss of interest when the investor does not obtain the use of short sale proceeds, can transform riskless arbitrage opportunities into risky investments. Tuckman and Vila derive the partial differential equation governing a risk-averse arbitrageur's optimal dynamic strategy given holding costs and an exogenous mispricing process. It is shown that 1) arbitrageurs will not hold a position unless the potential gains are large enough, 2) they do not trade unlimited amounts, and 3) they may take a position even with an instantaneously negative expected return since any such losses will be accompanied by greater arbitrage opportunities.

Like Brennan and Schwartz [1990], Tuckman & Vila [1992] make the assumption that the mispricing process is exogenous, and not affected by trading. However, this is inconsistent with the empirical evidence reported by MacKinlay & Ramaswamy [1988]. They found that the opportunity to put on arbitrage positions on one side of the market affected subsequent price movements. For example, if overpricing in the futures market leads arbitrageurs to put on long stock-short futures positions, they will unwind them if futures become underpriced in a following period, which will tend to support the futures market, relative to the situation with no preexisting arbitrage positions. Thus the mispricing process is path dependent.

More recently, in Tuckman & Vila [1993] the independence assumption was relaxed by allowing the activity of arbitrageurs to feed back into the mispricing process. In that case, 1) arbitrageurs reduce but do not eliminate mispricings; 2) equilibrium prices are kept inside the riskless arbitrage bounds because arbitrageurs take risky positions even when no riskless profit opportunities are available; 3) arbitrageurs are most effective in eliminating mispricings that are transient and conditionally volatile; 4) it is more difficult to eliminate mispricings of long-term contracts because costs increase with the holding period; and 5) arbitrage activity lowers the conditional volatility of the mispricing process. These results are consistent with the empirical evidence that violations of the cost of carry relation still exist and the level of mispricing is positively related to time until maturity.

3.4. Constraints on short sales

We have alluded to constraints on short selling as impediments to index arbitrage. In the U.S., the stock exchanges do not permit a short sale on a downtick. That is, a stock can not be sold short if it has just dropped in price. The trader must wait until the price ticks up. This introduces a considerable asymmetry between the ease, speed, and risk of executing the arbitrage trade when futures are underpriced versus being overpriced. As we will discuss in the next section, in the early years of index futures trading in the U.S., it was common to observe futures prices falling well below fair value, without much arbitrage trading to offset the mispricing. The difficulty of executing the necessary short sale of the stock index portfolio was a prime explanation. This underpricing of futures contracts still exists frequently for indices heavily weighted by small stocks, such as Value Line.

As one expects in a largely efficient financial market, however, the unexploited arbitrage opportunities such underpricing created were not allowed to persist for very long. Since there is no prohibition on selling stocks on a downtick if the investor already owns them, the many large institutions ('indexers') that follow a basically passive investment strategy of holding the index portfolio were in an excellent position to exploit their natural advantage in doing index arbitrage from the short side.

Within a few years, the indexers had become so adept at the arbitrage trade of buying futures when they were underpriced, selling the index stocks out of their portfolios, and investing the proceeds in Treasury bills (thus risklessly enhancing returns on a passive index strategy) that opportunities on either side of the market had become sparse, small, and risky. It was said that index arbitrage had become a 'commodity business', meaning that it did not require any special expertise, the brokerage firms priced their services very aggressively, and profit rates were fairly limited all around.

4. Empirical evidence on index futures pricing

Many studies since the introduction of index futures contracts in the early 1980s have reported significant and persistent deviations of futures prices from fair values. The market frictions mentioned in the previous section which make risk free arbitrage difficult, including transactions costs, the uptick rule for short sales in the stock market, the limited supply of arbitrage capital and position limits in the futures market may provide most of the explanation for these results. Table 2 provides a capsule summary of a number of empirical studies of index futures pricing.

The cost of carry model for the pricing of index futures contracts has been the basis of many empirical studies. A common finding is that cost of carry pricing does not always hold exactly in actual markets. Stoll & Whaley [1986] report many violations of the arbitrage bounds in excess of transactions costs during the period April 1982 through December 1985. In fact, for the June 1982 contract, the bounds were violated nearly 80% of the time, but for later contracts the rate of violation fell to less than 15%. MacKinlay & Ramaswamy [1988] found that the S&P 500 futures contracts expiring in September 1983 through June 1987 violated the cost of carry relation on average 14.4% of the time.

In the earliest period of index futures trading, from June 1982 to December 1982, index contracts systematically sold at large discounts to their theoretical values. Modest & Sundaresan [1983], Cornell & French [1983a, b] and Figlewski [1984a, b], among others, considered possible explanations for this discount.

A primary issue was whether the discounts indicated large foregone arbitrage opportunities (in which case the market would have been highly inefficient), or were simply a result of market frictions that were not in the basic cost of carry formula. Or perhaps they reflected additional factors that needed to be taken into account in determining the equilibrium futures price. No academic seriously asserted gross market inefficiency. But no single explanation for the discounts became widely accepted at the time.

Modest & Sundaresan [1983] examined the June and December 1982 futures contracts on the S&P500 index to determine whether the discount could be explained by the fact that investors do not normally get full use of the proceeds from short sales of stock, so the true cost of shorting the index should include foregone interest on at least a portion of the proceeds. They found that if the proceeds of selling short the stock index portfolio could be fully invested, future prices regularly violated the transactions cost bounds, creating sizable arbitrage opportunities. But when investors could use no more than half of the short sale proceeds, actual futures prices almost always fell within the (expanded) no-arbitrage bounds.

The difference between the tax treatment of futures and the underlying stocks is another factor that could affect equilibrium futures pricing. For tax purposes, all profits and losses on futures are treated as if they were realized by the end of the year, whereas in stocks, capital gains taxes are not levied until the shares are sold. As a result, stockholders have a 'tax timing option' [11] that is unavailable to futures traders. Cornell & French [1983a, b] examined whether this tax difference could explain the discount in futures prices. They showed that the tax timing option does reduce the theoretical futures prices, but did not relate the possible magnitude of the effect to the size of futures mispricing in the market.

These studies tried to explain the mispricing in terms of institutional factors that were excluded in the formula for the fair futures price in equilibrium. By contrast, Figlewski [1984a, b] hypothesized that the discount represented a situation of informational and institutional *disequilibrium*. As a result, he suggested that the discount was largely the result of unfamiliarity with the new markets and a scarcity of sophisticated arbitrageurs ready to implement the arbitrage trade efficiently. In that case, the mispricing would prove to be a transitory phenomenon. Figlewski [1984a] showed empirically that the futures discount had been decreasing over time for the period June 1, 1982–September 30, 1983.

More recently, MacKinlay & Ramaswamy [1988] used transactions data on S&P 500 index futures prices and the underlying index from September 1983 to June 1987 to examine the intraday behavior of the deviations of futures prices from fair values. Over this period, the mispricing was positive on average, although it was negative for some contracts. They also analyzed the level and the change in mispricing across time and found that the absolute value of the mispricing was positively related to the time until futures maturity. This is consistent with their hypothesis that, in addition to transactions costs, the no-arbitrage boundaries

[11] See Constantinides [1983] for a discussion of the concept of a tax timing option.

Table 2

Summary of empirical studies on stock index futures pricing

<table>
<tr><th>Author</th><th>Contract</th><th>Period</th><th>Frequency of data</th><th>Market frictions [1]</th><th>Results</th></tr>
<tr><td>Modest & Sundaresan [1983]</td><td>SP500</td><td>Apr. 21, 1982–
Sept. 15, 1982</td><td>Daily
SSP</td><td>TC</td><td>Futures prices lie within bounds with use of at most half of short sale proceeds.</td></tr>
<tr><td>Cornell & French [1983]</td><td>SP500
NYSE</td><td>June 1, 1982,
July 1, 1982,
Aug. 2, 1982,
Sept. 1, 1982</td><td>Daily</td><td></td><td>Tax timing option reduces price, but not enough to eliminate the discount found during early period.</td></tr>
<tr><td>Figlewski [1984]</td><td>SP500</td><td>June 1, 1982–
Sept. 30, 1983</td><td>Daily</td><td></td><td><table>
<tr><th>Mean contract SP500</th><th>Full sample</th><th>First 3rd</th><th>Middle 3rd</th><th>Last 3rd</th></tr>
<tr><td>Mean arbitrage return</td><td>0.03</td><td>−2.88</td><td>2.12</td><td>2.54</td></tr>
<tr><td>Standard deviation</td><td>11.25</td><td>13.07</td><td>9.19</td><td>6.23</td></tr>
</table>
Mispricing is negative for the first period and positive thereafter. Mispricing decreases over time.</td></tr>
<tr><td>Stoll & Whaley [1986]</td><td>SP500</td><td>April 1982–
Dec. 1985</td><td>Hourly</td><td></td><td>The percentage of observations in which the mispricing violated the arbitrage bounds ranged from under 6% to 79% by contract. The average percentage across all contracts was 36%.</td></tr>
<tr><td>MacKinlay & Ramaswamy [1988]</td><td>SP500</td><td>June 17, 1983–
June 18, 1987</td><td>15-minute
tick data</td><td></td><td>Average mispricing was 0.12%. Mispricing is positively related to time until maturity. Mispricing is path dependent.</td></tr>
<tr><td>Merrick [1989]</td><td>SP500
NYSE</td><td>May 17, 1982–
May 30, 1986</td><td>Daily</td><td>EU</td><td>Total arbitrage profits of 178.48 index points. Unwinding profits represent 34% of total profits.</td></tr>
<tr><td>Brenner, Subrahmanyam & Uno [1989]</td><td>OSF50
NSA</td><td>June 1987–
May 1988</td><td>Daily</td><td></td><td><table>
<tr><th></th><th colspan="6">Mean percentage</th></tr>
<tr><th></th><th colspan="2">Absolute deviation</th><th colspan="2">Positive</th><th colspan="2">Negative</th></tr>
<tr><th></th><th>Sept. 87</th><th>June 88</th><th>Sept. 87</th><th>June 88</th><th>Sept. 87</th><th>June 88</th></tr>
<tr><td>NSA</td><td>1.48</td><td>0.47</td><td>0.76</td><td>0.17</td><td>−1.73</td><td>−0.61</td></tr>
<tr><td>OSF50</td><td>1.26</td><td>0.57</td><td>1.74</td><td>0.66</td><td>−0.65</td><td>−0.26</td></tr>
</table></td></tr>
</table>

Table 2 (cont'd.)

Yadav & Pope [1990]	FTSE-100	July 1, 1984– June 30, 1988	Daily	EU	The mean percentage mispricing was −0.40% for the overall sample. The option to unwind early or rollover an arbitrage position are valuable. The arbitrage bounds tend to be wider for longer times to expiration.
Brennan & Schwartz [1990]	SP500	June 17, 1983– June 18, 1987	15-minute tick data	EU	Early close out option has value. Profitable to open position even if mispricing does not cover trading costs. Average profit was 0.54 index points.
Habeeb, Hill & Rzad [1991]	SP500	Dec. 21, 1987– June 15, 1990	5-minute tick data	EU EL	Excess return of 5% from both long and short. Excess return of 3% from long or short. Execution lags decrease excess returns.
Sofianos [1993]	SP500	Jan. 15, 1990– July 13, 1990	Tick data Actual arbitrage trades	EU	Mispricings were narrow and short-lived. Most trades were unwound early. Early close out excess return of 0.1 to 4.9% points.
Chung, Kang & Rhee [1994]	NSA	Sept. 9, 1988– Sept.12, 1991	1-minute tick data	EL	The mean percentage mispricing was 0.41% and predominantly positive for the overall sample.

[1] All of the studies assumed the following market imperfections, except when noted: transaction costs (TC); full use of short sale proceeds (SSP); no uptick rule for short sales (UR); no execution lag (EL); and no early unwinding (EU). For example, if transaction costs were not included a TC appears in the column and if an execution lag was imposed, EL appears in the column.

are affected by other factors that depend on the length of the holding period, such as uncertainty about dividends and future mark to market cash flows, and also risk in tracking the stock index with a partial basket of stocks. As a result, larger mispricing may be permitted to develop at longer times to maturity before arbitrageurs will take a position.

As mentioned above, MacKinlay and Ramaswamy [1988] also found the mispricing series to be path-dependent. In particular, conditional on the mispricing having crossed one arbitrage bound, it was less likely to cross the opposite bound. This is because arbitrageurs will close out positions established when the mispricing was outside one bound before it reaches the other bound, thus tending to keep the futures price within the no-arbitrage range.

The discount found during the early period of index futures trading is not unique to U.S. futures markets. Persistent underpricing relative to the cost of carry theoretical value in the early years of trading has been documented in other markets, including Japan and the U.K.

Brenner, Subrahmanyam & Uno [1989a–c] examined the mispricing of the Nikkei 225 Stock Average (NSA) futures contract, traded on the Singapore International Monetary Exchange (SIMEX), and the Osaka Stock Futures 50 (OSF50) futures contract, traded on the Osaka Securities Exchange (OSE),[12] from September 1987 through June 1988. The NSA contract started trading on September 3, 1986 and the OSF50 was introduced on June 9, 1987. The NSA contract is based on an arithmetic average of the prices of 225 stocks traded on the First Section of the Tokyo Stock Exchange (TSE). The spot index for the OSF50 was also an arithmetic price average, but of 50 stocks traded both on the OSE and the TSE. Unlike most stock index futures contracts, the OSF50 contract was settled by physical delivery of the underlying securities during the sample period. This contract was delisted in 1993 because of the lack of trading since 1988 (see footnote 2).

For the NSA contract, the mispricing was predominately negative over the early trading period and the mispricing tended to persist. However, for the OSF50 contract, positive deviations were more frequent. The deviations for the NSA contract were significantly larger than for the OSF50 contract. Over the entire sample period, the mean absolute deviation was 1.22% for the NSA contract versus 0.92% for the OSF50 contract.

More recently, Chung, Kang & Rhee [1994], examined the impact of the Japanese stock market microstructure on the pricing of NSA futures contracts in Osaka using intraday transactions data for the period from September 9, 1988 to September 12, 1991.[13] They found that the NSA futures prices on the OSE have tended to deviate on average 0.41% from theoretical no-arbitrage prices

[12] Bacha and Fremault Vila [1993] examined the mispricing and volume of the NSA futures contract in three different markets (SIMEX, OSE and CME).

[13] In Japan, some of the impediments to arbitrage trading include: high transaction costs, cash margin requirements, relatively long execution lags in the spot market and difficulties in taking short sale positions.

with transaction costs; the contract is predominantly overpriced which is opposite to the results reported by Brenner, Subrahmanyam & Uno [1989a–c] for the SIMEX NSA futures contract during an earlier period; mispricing signals tend to be clustered and persistent; and, the size and frequency of mispricings is positively correlated with the remaining life of the contract.

Yadav & Pope [1990] examined the mispricing of the LIFFE FTSE-100 futures prices over the period July 1, 1984 to June 30, 1988. Their results are very similar to those found for the U.S. futures contracts and the Japanese NSA contract. In addition, like MacKinlay and Ramaswamy [1988] they found that the amount of mispricing was positively related to time until expiration.

The previous research utilized the cost of carry model in a static setting, but Brennan & Schwartz [1990] modeled the mispricing as a Brownian bridge process. We discussed above how they showed that trading costs and position limits in the stock index futures market can make it valuable to close a position before maturity, and therefore it may be worthwhile to open a position even when the costs of opening it plus the costs of closing it at maturity exceed the level of mispricing. The study also included empirical results to support their arguments: the average arbitrage profit including the option value was 0.54 index points.

Merrick [1989] also recognized opportunities to reverse arbitrage positions and/or roll positions into the next contract prior to the expiring contract's expiration. He found that early unwindings and rollovers were valuable. Early unwinding profits represented 34% of total profits.

In practice, investors are unable to execute their trades at the instant at which the mispricing occurs, as was assumed by all of the above studies. Habeeb, Hill & Rzad [1991] relaxed this assumption and assumed a five minute execution lag in their analysis of S&P 500 index arbitrage. They also incorporated various trading costs and allowed for unwinding the trade prior to expiration. The study covers the period December 21, 1987 through June 15, 1990. They found that the periods with the greatest range of mispricing were in 1988 and the first half of 1990. The excess return from one-sided long or short arbitrage was about three percent per year while it was as much as 5% per year when both long and short positions could be taken.

To this point, all of the studies examined only cash and futures prices and simulated the arbitrage trades. Sofianos [1993] was the first to examine actual S&P 500 index arbitrage transactions obtained from the daily program trading reports of NYSE member firms. He estimated the expected return to expiration and the early-closing return for actual S&P 500 index arbitrage transactions over the period January 15 to July 13, 1990. He found that the average annualized expected return to expiration at the initiation of actual S&P 500 index arbitrage positions over this period was 0.5 percentage points *below* the opportunity cost of funds. Most index arbitrage positions were established when the mispricing would not cover transactions costs if the position had to be held to expiration.[14] But in practice, the majority of the trades were unwound early, following profitable

[14] In fact, these were risky positions, not arbitrage positions.

mispricing reversals. These results suggest that the early close-out option described by Brennan and Schwartz [1990] is valuable in practice. In fact, the estimate of the average annualized early close-out return ranged from 0.1 to 4.9 percentage points above the opportunity cost of funds.

5. Program trading and volatility

The largest objection to trading in stock index futures has been due to the perception, and fear, that index futures trading and index arbitrage creates excessive volatility in the stock market. The behavior of the index futures market during the 1987 stock market crash and the well-known and extensive use of stock index futures in 'portfolio insurance' strategies at the time produced some of the most extreme concerns and criticisms along these lines, but similar concerns had been voiced earlier, and continue to be heard today.

5.1. The Triple Witching Hour

An early indication that index futures trading could have a disruptive effect on the underlying stock market was that stock prices were sometimes observed to behave very peculiarly at the time of the quarterly expirations of index futures and other equity derivatives. Specifically, on expiration day the stock market would occasionally experience an unexplained wave of buy or sell orders in the last few minutes of trading, that would take traders by surprise and drive prices sharply up or down. Large swings in traders' profits and losses could occur in seconds; options that appeared to be well out-of-the-money with only minutes to go before they expired could suddenly turn into major losses for unwary writers; and generally strange and frightening occurrences seemed possible.

Because these events were unusual and unexplained, and they seemed to be associated with the simultaneous expiration of four kinds of equity derivatives, stock index futures, stock index options, stock index futures options, and some options on individual stocks, the period just before the close of trading on the quarterly expiration date came to be known as the 'Triple Witching Hour'.[15]

The explanation for the Triple Witching Hour events is actually not hard to understand. They *are* a result of the expiration of stock index contracts, primarily the index futures, and are produced by the unwinding of index arbitrage trades, as we have described above. Consider an arbitrageur who arrives at the futures expiration date holding a long position in the S&P 500 stocks and a short position in S&P futures contracts. The futures will mature at the close of trading, at which point they will be marked to market at the closing level of the S&P index. In order to unwind the arbitrage position without paying a second market impact and also bearing execution risk, the trader will try to liquidate the position by selling

[15] See Stoll & Whaley [1986, 1987, 1990] and Stoll [1988] for an excellent analysis of the expiration day effects of stock index arbitrage.

the stocks simultaneously with expiration of the futures contracts, at the market's close. This can even be done with 'market on close' orders that lie dormant until the last minute of trading, at which point they become market orders and are executed at whatever the prevailing market price is. Even if this style of trading at the last second were to push the prices received on the stocks down sharply, there would be additional profits on the not-yet-expired short futures position that would offset the losses.

A priori, one might expect that the arbitrage positions that remain to be unwound at futures expiration would be fairly balanced between the long and the short side, so that unwinding them simultaneously at the close would produce largely offsetting trades in the underlying stocks. This often was not the case. In some periods, the arbitrage opportunities tended to lie all on one side of the market, with little or no chance of unwinding the positions profitably before expiration. It was on those occasions that the Triple Witching Hour trades, nearly all in the same direction, could produce sharp market moves.

For example, in early September 1986 the stock market experienced a sharp two-day sell-off. Although it's magnitude, about 120 points on the Dow Jones average, is small in comparison to the October 1987 crash, at the time, it was the largest market drop since 1929 and it made a large impression on the market. For many weeks afterwards, stock index futures traded well below fair value, which allowed large short stocks–long futures arbitrage positions to be established with the December futures contract.

Since futures remained underpriced throughout the quarter, the arbitrageurs were unable to unwind these positions profitably before expiration. Thus, when they were unwound at the Triple Witching Hour on December 19, 1986, over 85 million shares (more than one third of the entire day's volume) were purchased in the last minute of trading, with the result that stock prices surged upwards.

In 1987, to ease the pressure the Witching Hour caused for stock exchange specialists and others, the expiration procedure was changed for S&P 500 futures. Starting with the June 1987 expiration, final settlement is based on stock prices at the *opening* on the expiration Friday. The opening procedure on the NYSE is better suited to managing order imbalances, so there is less price disruption when large arbitrage positions are unwound. Other index related contracts did not change their expiration procedures, with the result that the Triple Witching Hour price effects are now effectively spread out over the day.

5.2. The debate on program trading after October 1987

Following October 1987, futures trading and index arbitrage were thoroughly examined in a variety of studies sponsored by government authorities, the exchanges, and others. Although they produced a large amount of discussion and statistical evidence, these studies did not produce widespread agreement on the principle issues. Nevertheless, several formal changes to the way index futures are traded were imposed in the aftermath of the crash. As mentioned above, immediately after the crash the NYSE banned the use of the DOT system for arbitrage trades for several weeks. This had the effect of disconnecting the index futures market from the underlying cash market and permitted large deviations from theoretical pricing to develop and persist.[16]

Margin requirements on index futures were also raised significantly. Prior to October 1987, margins were comparable in size to those for other futures, typically less than 5% of the nominal value of the futures contract. For example, if the S&P 500 index were at a level of 400, the value of the stock underlying an S&P futures contract would be $\$500 \times 400 = \$200,000$. Before 1987, the initial margin requirement on the contract might have been less than \$5000. It must be emphasized that 'margin' in a futures market is qualitatively different from margin on a stock purchase, which represents a partial payment for securities that are transferred immediately. The futures margin is essentially a performance bond on a contract that only binds the parties to make a transaction at a later date. The purpose of the futures margin deposit is to guarantee that both counterparties will be able to cover any (paper) losses on their commitments prior to maturity.

Given the daily mark to market that keeps the actual margin deposits current as the market prices move, these low margin levels were adequate for the purpose of assuring the financial integrity of the futures contracts. But in comparison to the 50% margin required for a stock transaction, futures margins permitted a much greater degree of leverage. Many cash market participants worried that low margins led to speculative excesses in index futures, which then spilled over into the stock through stock index arbitrage trading and produced high volatility there. While calls for government regulation of index futures margins after the crash were not satisfied, the futures exchanges themselves elected to raise stock margin requirements sharply — not to 50%, but to the 10 to 15% range. In March 1994, following several years of unusually low volatility, the S&P 500 index was at about 450, which translates to a futures contract representing about \$225,000 worth of stock, and the initial margin requirement was \$9000, about 4%.

In addition to higher margins following the crash, the exchanges established a system of 'circuit breakers', designed to stop or slow trading, and specifically index arbitrage, in periods of high market volatility. Several different forms of circuit breakers were tried. The current system, which has been in place for a number of years, calls for suspension of futures trading for one half hour if the Dow Jones index falls by 50 points or more in a day; longer trading halts after further market drops; and the 'sidecar' which shunts aside program trades in the DOT system and delays their execution for 5 minutes once the SP500 futures contract declines 12 points from the previous day's close.

Academic economists tend to differ sharply with other public commentators on the merits of the basic arguments about index arbitrage and market volatility, as

[16] One result was that arbitrageurs who did succeed in putting on short stocks–long futures positions after the crash ended up unwinding them on expiration day. As in 1986, the Triple Witching Hour (or Day) in December 1987 produced a sharp rise in stock prices, 50.90 index points in the Dow index for the day

well as about proposed procedures to deal with the problem.[17] A full analysis of the issues is beyond the scope of this chapter, so we will only mention some of the points of debate.

Opponents of futures argue that they facilitate destabilizing speculation that pushes the futures price out of line with the true value of the underlying stocks. Index arbitrage then transmits the price disruption into the stock market. In this way, it is claimed, index futures and arbitrage activity significantly increase volatility and are detrimental to the stock market. The appropriate policy is therefore to restrain index futures arbitrage, especially during volatile market conditions.

Academic research has produced counterarguments to nearly all of these assertions. First, there is disagreement about whether speculation by futures traders is, or can be, destabilizing to the underlying cash market, a question that has been studied at great length by economists without reaching a consensus. However, it is a mistake to draw a large distinction between stock index futures traders and investors in stocks. As pointed out in the Brady Commission report [1988] that analyzed the 1987 crash, it is more appropriate to consider the markets for stocks and all of the derivative instruments based on stocks as being different components of a single integrated equity market. Futures trading is done by essentially the same large investors whose activities cause price changes in the cash market. Moreover, the nature of arbitrage trading is that it pushes prices down in one part of the unified stock market, but simultaneously raises prices in another. The resulting change in *relative* values should not cause any net change in the overall level of stock prices, properly defined.

Second, it is not clear that stock price volatility is actually greater now than before index futures existed, or even that higher volatility would necessarily be undesirable. Mathematically, volatility is the annualized standard deviation of stock returns. This has been found to vary considerably from year to year. It also depends on the time interval between prices in the data sample (i.e., daily, monthly, etc.), because of the effect of the complex pattern of serial correlation in stock returns.[18] Except for October 1987, there is little evidence that volatility measured at intervals longer than a day has increased. Indeed, realized volatility of the S&P index during 1993 was only 8.4%. This is exceedingly low by comparison with the historical average over the last 40 years of close to 14%.[19]

Intraday price movements over very short intervals are larger than previously, but economists argue that higher measured volatility may actually correspond to an *improvement* in the quality of prices, if it means that they are adjusting more rapidly than before to new information. A reduction in the serial correlation of daily returns in recent years suggests that this may have happened.

[17] See Miller [1993] for a discussion of the politics of index arbitrage in the U.S. and in Japan.

[18] See Figlewski [1994] for empirical evidence of time-variation in stock market volatility as well as a discussion of the statistical problems in measuring volatility. Brown [1990] gives an illustration of the effect of the differencing interval on measured volatility.

[19] See Bach and Fremault Vila [1994] for evidence on the affect of the introduction of the Nikkei 225 stock index futures contract on volatility in the stock market.

Third, the fact that large futures price changes tend to precede similar movements in the underlying stocks is not proof that volatility originates in the futures market and is transmitted by index arbitrage into the cash market. Stock index futures are much more liquid than individual stocks and permit investors to change their exposure to the entire stock market quickly and with low transactions costs. Events with a market-wide impact can therefore be expected to be reflected initially in the futures market and then later in the stock market. Futures price movements will tend to lead those in the stock market even if the futures market is only serving as a kind of barometer for fluctuations in general investor sentiment.

Next, academics disagree that index futures trading and arbitrage are responsible for the 1987 stock market crash. The Brady Report [1988] pointed to portfolio insurance, as being closely linked to the severity of the price decline on October 19. On the other hand, Roll [1988] analyzed the behavior of stock markets around the world during the crash, and found little difference between the experience of those that had no index futures market or portfolio insurance trading and those that did. However, one can safely say that stock index arbitrage per se was not a factor in the crash. On October 19, huge backlogs of orders built up in the stock market and essentially precluded execution of arbitrage trades, and the subsequent ban on using the DOT system for arbitrage severely restricted the practice thereafter. This cut off the futures market from the cash market, and kept arbitrage from eliminating futures mispricing that was frequently extreme.

Lastly, academics mostly argue against trading halts as a way to reduce market volatility. Impeding arbitrage weakens the tie between futures prices and the underlying stock market, which reduces the value of index futures as a dependable hedging vehicle. Moreover, there is a concern that as prices approach the point at which trading will be cut off, there is a kind of 'gravitational pull' toward that market level, as traders rush to complete trades before the circuit breaker is tripped. McMillan [1991] presents evidence that the circuit breakers in practice may not produce the calming effect that was hoped for.

Grossman [1988b] examined the relationship between both program trading and nonprogram trading and stock market volatility, using daily data over the January 2, 1987–October 30, 1987 period. The correlation between program trading intensity and volatility was statistically and economically insignificant. However, the results showed a statistically significant and positive relationship between volatility and nonprogram trading intensity.

Harris, Sofianos & Shapiro [1992], using 2,346 reported program trades executed at the NYSE in June 1989, analyzed the relationship among program trading, intraday stock index returns and stock index futures returns in the fifty minutes on either side of a program trade. They found many interesting results: 1) average trading frequency begins to increase before the program trade and remains high for about 10 minutes after it; 2) the value of the cash index and the futures price begin to change before the program trade is initiated — in fact about half of the total change occurs before the trade; 3) the absolute value of the difference between the index and the futures price is greatest before the program trade; 4) on average, there is no price reversal within the 50 minutes following the trade; and 5) program trading is positively related to intraday volatility.

The first three of these findings imply that causality does not run exclusively from the futures to the stock market. The fourth, an important result, shows that program trading does not appear to cause overshooting and subsequent price corrections that would be associated with destabilization of the market. Points 4) and 5) together support the argument that price changes around program trades may show increased volatility, this is due to new information entering the market. If so, the volatility is not 'excess' volatility but rather fundamental volatility.

6. Conclusion

In this chapter, we have described a little of the development of the market in stock index futures. We showed the theoretical relationship between the futures price on a stock index contract and the current level of its underlying index, and explained how prices are kept in line by arbitrage. In describing how the arbitrage is actually done, we discussed program trading and generalized the cost of carry model to include the effects of transactions costs and the possibility of unwinding an arbitrage trade early. Reviewing the literature on empirical tests of the pricing model, we found that most analysts found apparent futures mispricing, both in the U.S. and in foreign markets. Mispricing tended to be larger at the outset and to diminish over time as arbitrageurs developed more efficient information and execution procedures, such as electronic transmission of computer-generated orders into the market.

Lastly, we discussed the arguments that trading in stock index futures, and especially arbitrage against the underlying stocks, led to increased volatility in the stock market. We argued that, except for the Triple Witching Hour where the link between futures and the potential for sharp price changes in the underlying stock is clear, the claim that index futures destabilize the stock market is not supported. Nor would an increase in volatility indicate that trading in index futures should be curbed — higher volatility in many cases is a result of greater informational efficiency.

One sign of the importance of futures contracts based on broad stock indexes is the fact that so many have been introduced worldwide. As Table 1 shows, despite any controversy these instruments may have generated in the U.S. over the years, countries with well developed capital markets (including the U.S., we argue) have found that the advantages of index futures trading greatly outweigh the concerns.

Acknowledgements

The authors would like to thank Joanne Hill of Goldman Sachs and William T. Ziemba, the editor, for helpful discussions.

References

Bacha, O., and A. Fremault Vila (1993). Multi-market trading and patterns in volume and mispricing: The case of the Nikkei Stock Index futures market, working paper 92-33, Boston University School of Management.

Bacha, O., and A. Fremault Vila (1994). Futures markets, regulation and volatility: The case of the Nikkei Stock Index futures market, forthcoming.

Brady, N., J. Cotting, R. Kirby, J. Opel and H. Stein (1988). Report of the Presidential Task Force on market mechanisms, U.S. Government Printing Office, Washington D.C.

Brennan, M., and E. Schwartz (1990). Arbitrage in stock index futures. *J. Bus.* 63(1), S7–S31.

Brenner, M., M. Subrahmanyam, M., and J. Uno (1989a). Arbitrage opportunities in the Japanese stock and futures markets. *Financ. Anal. J.* 46, pp. 14–24.

Brenner, M., M. Subrahmanyam, M., and J. Uno (1989b). The behavior of prices in the Nikkei spot and futures markets. *J. Financ. Econ.* 23, pp. 363–383.

Brenner, M., M. Subrahmanyam, M., and J. Uno (1989c). Stock index-futures arbitrage in the Japanese markets, in: R. Sato, ed. *Japan and the World Economy 1*, Elsevier Science Publishers B.V. North Holland, pp. 303–330.

Brown, S. (1990). Estimating volatility, in: S. Figlewski et al. (eds.), *Financial Options: From Theory to Practice*, Business One Irwin, Homewood, IL, pp. 516–37.

Chung, Y.P. (1991). A transactions data test of stock index futures market efficiency and index arbitrage profitability. *J. Finance* pp. 1791–1809.

Chung, Y.P., J.-K. Kang and S.G. Rhee (1994). Index-futures arbitrage in Japan,University of California, Riverside, working paper.

Constantinides, G.M. (1983). Capital market equilibrium with personal tax. *Econometrica*, 51, 611–636.

Cornell, B. (1985). Taxes and the pricing of stock index futures: Empirical results. *J. Futures Markets* 3, 1–14.

Cornell, B., and K. French (1983a). The pricing of stock index futures. *J. Futures Markets* 3, 1–14.

Cornell, B., and K. French (1983b). Taxes and the pricing of stock index futures. *J. Finance* 38, 675–694.

Figlewski, S. (1984a). Hedging performance and basis risk in stock index futures. *J. Finance* 39, 657–699.

Figlewski, S. (1984b). Explaining the early discounts on stock index futures: The case of disequilibrium. *Financ. Anal. J.* July/August, 43–47.

Figlewski, S. (1994). Forecasting volatility with historical data, New York University Salomon Center, working paper.

Finnerty, J.E., and H.Y. Park (1988). How to profit from program trading. *J. Portfolio Manage.* 14, 41–46.

Grossman, S. (1988a). An analysis of the implications for stock and futures price volatility of program trading and dynamic hedging strategies. *J. Bus* 61, 275–298.

Grossman, S. (1988b). Program trading and market volatility: A report on interday relationships. *Financ. Anal. J.* July/August, 413–419.

Grünbichler, A., and T.W. Callahan (1993). Stock index futures arbitrage in Germany: The behavior of the DAX index futures prices, University of Graz, Austria, working paper.

Habeeb, G., J.M. Hill and A.J. Rzad (1991). Potential rewards from path-dependent index arbitrage with S&P 500 futures. *Rev. Futures Markets* 10(1), 180–203.

Harris, L., G. Sofianos and J. Shapiro (1992). Program trading and intraday volatility, working paper, #90-03, New York Stock Exchange.

MacKinlay, A.C., and K. Ramaswamy (1988). Index-futures arbitrage and the behavior of stock index futures prices. *Rev. Financ. Studies* 1, 137–158.

McMillan, H. (1991). Circuit breakers in the S&P 500 futures market: Their effect on volatility and price discovery in October 1989. *Rev. Futures Markets* 10, 248–274.

Merrick, J. (1989). Early unwindings and rollovers of stock index arbitrage programs: Analysis and implications for predicting expiration day effects. *J. Futures Markets* 9, 101–111.

Miller, M.H. (1993). The economics and politics of index arbitrage in the U.S., and Japan. *Pac.-Basin Finance J.* 1, 3–11.

Modest, D.M., and M. Sundaresan (1983). The relationship between spot and futures prices in stock index futures markets: Some preliminary evidence. *J. Futures Markets* 3, 15–42.

Neal, Robert (1993). Is program trading destabilizing?. *J. Derivatives* 1, Winter, 64–77.

Pope, P.F., and P.K. Yadav (1994). The impact of short sales constraints on stock index futures prices: Direct empirical evidence from FTSE 100 futures. *J. Derivatives* 1, 15–26.

Roll, R. (1988). The international crash of October 1987. *Financ. Anal. J.* 46, 15–42.

Sofianos, G. (1993). Index arbitrage profitability. *J. Derivatives* 1, 6–20.

Stoll, H.R. (1988). Index futures, program trading and stock market procedures. *J. Futures Markets* 8(4), 391–412.

Stoll, H.R., and R.E. Whaley (1986). Expiration day effects of index options and futures, in: *New York University Monograph Series in Finance and Economics*, Monograph 1986-3, Salomon Center for the Study of Financial Institutions, New York University, NY.

Stoll, H.R., and R.E. Whaley (1987). Program trading and expiration-day effects. *Financ. Anal. J.* March–April, 16–28.

Stoll, H.R., and R.E. Whaley (1990). Program trading and individual stock returns: Ingredients of the triple-witching brew. *J. Bus* 63(1), S165–S192.

Tuckman, B., and J.-L. Vila (1992). Arbitrage with holding costs: A utility-based approach. *J. Finance* 4, 1283–1302.

Tuckman, B., and J.-L. Vila (1993). Holding costs and equilibrium arbitrage, New York University Salomon Center, working paper.

Yadav P.K., and P.F. Pope (1990). Stock index futures pricing: International evidence. *J. Futures Markets* 10, 573–603.

R. Jarrow et al., Eds., *Handbooks in OR & MS, Vol. 9*

Chapter 11

Mortgage Backed Securities

Walter N. Torous
Anderson School of Management, University of California, Los Angeles, CA 90095, U.S.A.

1. Introduction

A mortgage is a loan originated by a bank or thrift institution and secured by underlying property. A mortgage backed security is a financial instrument whose cash flows depend upon the cash flows of an underlying pool of mortgages. The mortgage backed securities market, a recent innovation, has grown dramatically in both size and importance: only $500 million of mortgage pass-through securities were issued in 1977, while over $1 trillion were issued by 1990.

Most mortgage backed securities are backed by a pool of fixed rate mortgages which differ little, if at all, in their coupon rates, terms to maturity, and other contractual features. The homogeneous nature of this underlying collateral facilitates its securitization. In contrast, adjustable rate mortgages (ARMs) are more heterogeneous, for example, differing in the underlying index which the coupon rate varies with, and various cap provisions which limit movements in the coupon rate. Nevertheless, given the popularity of ARMs, their securitization will become increasingly important, especially as ARMs become more homogeneous in their contractual features.

Mortgage backed securities or their underlying collateral are typically guaranteed against default by the federal government or government-sponsored enterprises (GSEs). However, mortgage backed securities are *not* risk free. Since residential mortgages are typically prepayable, mortgage backed securities are subject to prepayment risk. For example, if high coupon mortgages are prepaid in a low refinancing rate environment, the investor must reinvest the resultant principal at unfavorable rates. This prepayment risk is further complicated by the fact that some borrowers prepay low coupon mortgages in a relatively high refinancing rate environment, while others do not prepay high coupon mortgages in a relatively low refinancing rate environment. The modeling of prepayment behavior, therefore, is critical to the valuation of mortgage backed securities.

The growth of the mortgage backed securities market has been characterized by innovation. While the earliest securities simply passed through underlying mortgage cash flows to the investor on a pro rata basis, more recent innovations, such as interest only strips (IOs), principal only strips (POs), and collateralized mortgage obligations (CMOs), rearrange mortgage cash flows to provide investment opportunities heretofore unavailable. As such, mortgage backed securities play an important role in completing securities markets.

The plan of this chapter is as follows. Section 2 reviews mortgage markets and describes mortgage cash flows. A thorough understanding of underlying mortgage cash flows is necessary in order to understand mortgage backed securities. Given their importance, we consider not only fixed rate mortgages, but also ARMs. Mortgage backed securities are detailed in Section 3, where we describe the major pass-through programs and introduce CMOs. In Section 4, we investigate the statistical modeling of borrower prepayment behavior. The more accurately prepayments are estimated, the more accurately mortgage backed securities can be valued. Given a sample of residential mortgage prepayments, we use Poisson regression techniques to illustrate the estimation of prepayment models. The valuation of mortgage backed securities is reviewed in Section 5, while Section 6 concludes with a chapter summary.

2. Mortgages

The growth of the mortgage backed securities market derives from the importance of the underlying mortgage market and the consequent availability of relatively homogeneous collateral.

Mortgages are loans secured by underlying property. The mortgage agreement stipulates that if the borrower defaults, the lender may foreclose the loan and force the sale of the property. Typically mortgages are fully amortizing so that the principal amount is repaid over the life of the loan. The mortgage agreement specifies the future payments and defines the interest rate, term to maturity, as well as the payment frequency used to calculate these payments.

The mortgage market is an important component of the U.S. capital market. As of the beginning of 1990, \$3.5 trillion of mortgage debt was outstanding, dominating both the corporate debt market, \$1.4 trillion outstanding, and the government debt market, \$1.9 trillion outstanding.

Residential mortgages are the most important component of the U.S. mortgage market. The majority of mortgage backed securities are based on residential mortgages. These residential mortgages can be insured against default under a variety of government mortgage programs. For example, if the borrower and property qualify, Federal Housing Administration (FHA) mortgage insurance insures the lender against any default losses. The Veterans Administrations (VA) partially guarantees mortgage loans of qualified veterans. Of course, conventional residential mortgages, that is non-FHA insured or non-VA guaranteed loans, can be privately insured against default losses.

2.1. Fixed rate mortgages

The interest rate on a fixed rate mortgage does not change over the life of the loan. Fixed rate mortgages also require constant or level monthly payments. The monthly payment is computed to fully amortize the principal by the mortgage's maturity. Most fixed rate mortgages have thirty-year terms to maturity at origination, although fifteen year maturities are becoming increasingly common.

Consider a fully amortizing fixed rate mortgage having an original principal of $F(0)$ and an original term to maturity of T years. For expositional purposes, assume the mortgage has a fixed, continuously compounded interest rate of c. Then the payout rate, C, which fully amortizes the loan by the end of T years, is given by the following annuity factor

$$C = \frac{cF(0)}{1 - \exp(-cT)}.$$

The principal on a continuously compounded fixed rate mortgage declines over time as follows

$$\mathrm{d}F(t) = cF(t) - C.$$

The solution to this first-order ordinary differential equation subject to the terminal condition $F(t) = 0$ (that is, the loan being fully amortized in T years) gives the mortgage's principal outstanding at time t $(0 < t < T)$

$$F(t) = F(0)\frac{1 - \exp\big(-c(T - t)\big)}{1 - \exp(-cT)}.$$

Each level mortgage payment has an interest component as well as a component reflecting the repayment of the loan's principal. Early in the mortgage's life the interest component is relatively large, but as the mortgage ages or seasons and the principal is reduced via amortization, the interest component becomes relatively less important.

The analysis to this point has not considered the fact that residential mortgages are typically prepayable. For example, if interest rates have fallen, a borrower can prepay the principal outstanding on a loan by taking out a new mortgage at the lower prevailing rate of interest. While conventional mortgages are typically prepayable subject to a prepayment penalty, FHA-insured and VA-guaranteed loans are prepayable without penalty. Once a mortgage is prepaid, it ceases to exist and, as such, its cash flows also terminate. Consequently, prepayment affects the timing of a mortgage's cash flows and therefore influences the valuation of mortgages and mortgage backed securities. While a majority of prepayments are motivated by borrowers attempting to minimize their interest costs, as we shall see later, other factors also influence prepayment decisions.

2.2. ARMs

The interest rate on an ARM varies with prevailing market interest rate conditions. Federally-chartered thrift institutions were permitted to originate ARMs in April of 1981. Previously, thrifts originated long-term, fixed rate mortgages financed primarily by short term deposits, thereby exposing them to considerable interest rate risk. ARMs reduce the gap between a thrift's asset and liability maturities and hence reduce interest rate risk.

However, ARMs do not eliminate a thrift's interest rate risk exposure, since the many contractual features of an ARM result in an imperfect adjustment of its coupon rate to changes in the thrift's cost of funds. For example, Section 3806 of the Alternative Mortgage Transaction Parity Act of 1982 states that 'adjustable rate mortgage loans originated by a creditor shall include a limitation on the maximum interest rate that may apply during the term of the loan'. The presence of a lifetime cap and other contractual features prevents a timely and full adjustment in the ARM's coupon rate.

The essential contractual features of ARMs may be summarized as follows.

Index. An ARM's coupon rate varies with its contractually specified index. The two most widely used indices are a cost of funds index (COFI) and a constant maturity (one year or five year) Treasury index. The former represents a weighted average of the actual book cost of funds of thrifts located in the Federal Home Loan Bank's 11th district (Arizona, California, and Nevada), while the latter is constructed from the current yields of Treasury securities.

Margin. The ARM's coupon rate is given by the sum of the prevailing level of the index and the contractually specified margin, subject to initial discounts and restrictions to be discussed below. The size of the margin reflects the value of the various options embedded in the ARM, including the option to prepay, as well as the costs of servicing the loan.

Adjustment period. An ARM's coupon rate is adjusted periodically at a contractually stipulated frequency. The adjustment period is the minimum period of time over which its coupon cannot be changed. Typical adjustment periods are six months or one year.

Teaser rate. At origination, the ARM's coupon rate is frequently set below its fully indexed level, index plus margin, so as to provide an inducement to the borrower. This initial coupon rate is referred to as the ARM's teaser rate. Typically, the teaser rate is in effect for the initial adjustment period.

Lifetime cap. An ARM's lifetime cap contractually stipulates an upper bound which its coupon rate cannot exceed. If at adjustment the ARM's coupon rate exceeds the lifetime cap, then the coupon rate remains fixed at the lifetime cap. The coupon rate is fixed at the lifetime cap until the fully indexed rate falls below the lifetime cap at a subsequent adjustment.

Lifetime floor. An ARM's lifetime floor contractually stipulates a lower bound below which its coupon rate cannot drop. If at adjustment the ARM's coupon rate falls below the lifetime floor, then the coupon rate remains fixed at the lifetime floor. The coupon rate is fixed at the lifetime floor until at a subsequent adjustment the fully indexed rate exceeds the lifetime floor. As opposed to the lifetime cap, which is beneficial to the borrower, the lifetime floor is generally viewed as being advantageous to the originator. However, it should be noted that the lifetime floor will typically not be binding, since most interest sensitive borrowers will prepay at sufficiently low interest rates to lock in low fixed refinancing costs.

Periodic cap. The periodic cap limits the amount by which the ARM's coupon rate can increase or decrease over any adjustment period. In other words, if the underlying index increases or decreases by more than the periodic cap, the ARM's coupon rate changes only by the magnitude of the periodic cap. Periodic caps effect lags in ARM coupon rate changes to changes in a thrift's cost of funds, though in the case of falling interest rates the consequences are beneficial to the originator.

2.3. *ARM cash flows*

We consider a fully amortizing mortgage having an original principal of $P(0)$ and an original term to maturity of T years, with a continuously compounded teaser rate of $c(0)$. As a result, the ARM's payout rate over the initial adjustment period is $C(0)$, where

$$C(0) = \frac{c(0)F(0)}{1 - \exp(-c(0)T)}.$$

The loan's principal outstanding, $F(t)$, during the initial adjustment period is given by

$$F(t) = F(0)\frac{1 - \exp\big(-c(0)(T-t)\big)}{1 - \exp(-c(0)T)}.$$

At the ARM's ith adjustment, at time t_i, with a coupon rate of $c(t_i)$, the ARM's payout rate, $C(t_i)$, is now given by

$$C(t_i) = c(t_i)F(t_i)\big[1 - \exp\big(-c(t_i)\big)\big(T - t_i\big)\big)\big],$$

while during the ith adjustment period the loan's principal outstanding is given by

$$F(t) = F(t_i)\frac{1 - \exp\big(-c(t_i)(T-t)\big)}{1 - \exp\big(-c(t_i)(T-t_i)\big)}.$$

The ARM's coupon rate at adjustment is determined by adding the contractually specified margin, m, to the prevailing level of the underlying index, $x(t)$, subject to the ARM's lifetime and periodic cap constraints. Let $c^*(t)$ represent the fully indexed loan rate in the absence of any cap constraints

$$c^*(t_i) = x(t_i) + m.$$

If $c^*(t_i) > c(t_{i-1})$, then the ARM coupon rate is given by

$$c(t_i) = \min\left[c^*(t_i), c_{\mathrm{L}}, c(t_{i-1}) + c_{\mathrm{P}}\right],$$

where c_L denotes the ARM's lifetime cap and c_p the ARM's periodic cap. Conversely, if $c^*(t_i) < c(t_{i-1})$, then the ARM's coupon rate is given by

$$c(t_i) = \min\left[c^*(t_i), c_F, c(t_{i-1}) - c_P\right],$$

where c_F denotes the ARM's lifetime floor.

3. Mortgage backed securities

Mortgage backed securities range from relatively simple mortgage pass-through securities to more complicated CMOs. In this section, we detail the various agency pass-through programs and introduce CMOs.

3.1. Mortgage pass-through securities

The investor in a mortgage pass-through security owns an interest in an underlying pool of mortgages. The corresponding mortgage cash flows, including both principal and interest, are passed to the investor through an intermediary who retains a portion of the cash flows as compensation for services rendered. Services rendered include guaranteeing the pass-through payments and collecting mortgage payments, as well as making pass-through payments to the investor in a timely fashion. The pass-through security is also typically reinsured by a federal agency which guarantees the timely payment of interest and principal in the event of default by the borrower and the intermediary's inability to pass through principal and interest to the investor.

The first mortgage pass-through security was issued in 1970 under the auspices of the Government National Mortgage Association (GNMA). Only \$.3 billion of GNMA securities were issued in 1970. However, this market has grown dramatically so that by the end of 1991, over \$400 billion of GNMA securities were outstanding. This spectacular growth was fueled by the large volume of fixed rate mortgage originations since 1970, together with the fact that the guarantee of GNMA pass-through payments is backed by the full faith and credit of the U.S. government. As a result, significant amounts of investment funds have been attracted away from corporate and other government securities markets and into the pass-through securities market.

Mortgage pass-through security cash flows

To illustrate mortgage pass-through security cash flows, consider a hypothetical pass-through security backed by a fully amortizing fixed rate mortgage having a continuously compounded interest rate of c, an original principal of $F(0)$, and an original term to maturity of T years.

Given the characteristics of the underlying mortgage, the pass-through security also has an original principal of $F(0)$, as well as an original term to maturity of T years. We assume a continuously compounded fixed pass-through rate of $p < c$, the difference representing the servicing and insurance rate received by the intermediary and federal agencies, respectively. Therefore, the payout rate to the pass-through security, $P(t)$, is given by

$$P(t) = C - (c - p)F(t).$$

Notice that while the mortgage's payout rate C is constant, the pass-through security's payout rate $P(t)$ is not. It increases with time as the underlying mortgage principal outstanding, $F(t)$, decreases as a result of amortization.

However, it should be emphasized that mortgage pass-through securities are subject to potentially significant prepayment risk. In particular, if underlying mortgages prepay, then the principal is passed through to the investor via the intermediary. To the extent that prepayment affects the timing of a mortgage's cash flows, it also affects the timing of a mortgage pass-through security's cash flows.

Federal agency-sponsored pass-through programs

Different federal agency-sponsored mortgage pass-through programs differ in the magnitude of their servicing spread, $c - p$, as well as in the nature of the underlying guarantee. We now briefly summarize the features of the major federal agency-sponsored pass-through programs.

Government National Mortgage Association (GNMA or Ginnie Mae). GNMA is a wholly owned U.S. government corporation within the Department of Housing and Urban Development (HUD). GNMA is authorized to guarantee the timely payment of principal and interest of pass-through securities that are collateralized by FHA-insured or VA-guaranteed mortgages. GNMA's guarantee is backed by the full faith and credit of the U.S. government.

The GNMA-I program, begun in 1970, pools current mortgages and is the most important of GNMA's securitization programs. In particular, mortgages are pooled within a year of their origination and are gathered into pools with matching coupons and matching maturities. All GNMA-I pools have a 50 basis points servicing fee (44 basis points retained by the intermediary and 6 basis points retained by GNMA). GNMA-I pools are originated and serviced by mortgage bankers, thrift institutions, savings banks, and, to a lesser extent, commercial banks.

Federal Home Loan Mortgage Corporation (FHLMC or Freddie Mac). FHLMC is a GSE with its common stock being publicly traded since the passage of Financial Institutions Recovery, Reform Emergency Act (FIRREA) in 1989. While GNMA is mandated to increase the liquidity of FHA-insured and VA-guaranteed mortgages, FHLMC was established in 1970 with a directive to increase liquidity and available credit in the conventional mortgage market by maintaining a secondary market for nongovernment insured mortgages. To that end, FHLMC purchases mortgages, manages several pass-through programs, and issues debt, including CMOs, to finance its activities.

FHLMC pass-throughs differ from GNMA pass-throughs in several important respects. First, for participation certificates issued prior to October 1990, FHLMC guarantees timely payment of interest and only eventual repayment of principal.

Furthermore, these securities are not backed by the full faith and credit of the U.S. government but rather by FHLMC itself. However, in the event that FHLMC is unable to meet its obligations, it is implicitly assumed that the U.S. government would do so, thereby giving FHLMC securities U.S. agency status in credit markets. Finally, many FHLMC pools contain seasoned mortgages and, as such, the underlying mortgage maturities may vary over a wide range. Furthermore, the rates on mortgages included in FHLMC pools can vary from 50 to 250 basis points above corresponding pass-through rates.

Federal National Mortgage Association (FNMA or Fannie Mae). FNMA is also a GSE authorized to purchase and sell conventional, FHA-insured, and VA-guaranteed mortgage loans. To that end, FNMA introduced its mortgage pass-through program in 1981.

As with FHLMC, the majority of FNMA mortgage backed securities are issued against pools of conventional mortgages. FNMA mortgage backed securities may be backed by mortgages from FNMA's own portfolio, or mortgages aggregated by a single issuer which are then swapped for mortgage backed securities. The original term to maturity of mortgages included in FNMA pools ranges between 10 and 30 years and like FHLMC participation certificates, the underlying mortgage coupon rates can vary widely.

FNMA guarantees the timely payment of both principal and interest on its mortgage backed securities. FNMA mortgage backed securities are backed by FNMA itself. In the event that FNMA is unable to meet its obligations, it is also implicitly assumed that the federal government would do so.

3.2. Collateralized mortgage obligations

CMOs represent one of the most important recent innovations in capital markets. Agency-backed CMOs have increased from some \$3 billion outstanding in 1983 to over \$1 trillion outstanding in 1993.

CMOs are multiple-class financial instruments based on either mortgages or mortgage pass-through securities. In particular, CMOs take mortgage cash flows and redirect them into a series of bond-like classes or tranches. By redirecting mortgage cash flows, the inherent prepayment risk is also redistributed, both to more certain tranches as well as less certain tranches. Instead of investors taking on all the risks of a particular mortgage pass-through security, CMOs in essence reallocate this risk to appropriate investors.

Today's CMOs consist of what can best be referred to as scheduled and unscheduled classes. Scheduled classes provide a more well-defined average life of principal payments which are, by construction, robust to a variety of prepayment speeds. Therefore, scheduled classes have reduced prepayment risk. The unscheduled classes, loosely speaking, receive everything else that is left over. Their role is to support the scheduled classes by taking on prepayment risk. Accordingly, they have high initial yields, as well as a variety of unique features to attract investors, such as floating and inverse floating rates of interest.

PACs (planned amortization classes)

PACs are the most popular of scheduled classes. A PAC is designed to meet its principal payment schedule over a *range* of prepayment speeds.

PACs have first priority in receiving collateral principal payments. Excess principal is then allocated to other classes. If prepayments are fast and there is excess principal after all scheduled classes have been paid, then this principal is paid as follows:

- support classes receive principal until they are retired;
- then junior scheduled classes receive principal until they are retired;
- if excess principal still remains, it is paid to the PACs without regard to their planned balances.

If prepayments are slow and there is insufficient principal to pay the PACs, then

- each PAC is paid up to its planned balance in the order set by the payment rules until available funds are exhausted;
- other classes receive no principal payments in these circumstances;
- PACs that are behind their planned balances must be caught up before other classes receive principal payments.

TACs (targeted amortization classes)

A TAC is designed to meet its principal payment schedule for a single prepayment scenario. A TAC receives enough principal each month to reduce the amount outstanding to its targeted balance for that payment date. Excess principal then goes to support tranches until they are retired. Once support tranches are retired, excess principal is distributed to remaining TACs. If there are PACs in a deal, TACs, in effect, become support classes.

Interest rate types

For CMOs practically any interest rate type can be associated with any principal payment type:

Fixed rate — the most popular of coupons and predominant among PAC classes;

Floating rate — coupons vary with an underlying index and are reset periodically. For example,

$$\text{LIBOR} + 0.7\% \text{ s/t minimum} = 0.7\%, \text{ maximum} = 10.5\%.$$

Notice that there is a cap as well as a floor associated with the floating coupon rate. To create a floating rate tranche from fixed rate collateral it is customary to include an inverse floating rate tranche.

Inverse floating rate — the coupon rate varies inversely with the index. For example,

$$103.75\% - (\text{LIBOR} \times 10) \text{ s/t min} = 0\%, \text{ max} = 10.0\%.$$

Super floating rate — the coupon rate varies multiplicatively, rather than additively, with the underlying index. For example,

$$(\text{LIBOR} \times 1,080) - 10,125\% \text{ s/t min} = 0\%, \text{ max} = 1080\%.$$

4. Mortgage prepayments

Most residential mortgages are prepayable. If refinancing rates are sufficiently low, a borrower may find it financially advantageous to replace the existing mortgage by taking out a new loan at prevailing rates. However, individuals often prepay residential mortgages for reasons other than to minimize their interest costs. A job relocation or a change in marital status may prompt a prepayment. Alternatively, individuals often do not prepay when it would appear to be financially advantageous to do so. Many 10% coupon mortgages continue to survive in an 8% refinancing environment.

Since prepayment is critical to the valuation of mortgage backed securities, there have been many efforts to explicitly characterize borrower prepayment behavior. When mortgage backed securities were first introduced in the 1970s, a twelve-year prepaid life assumption was commonly made. In other words, mortgage backed cash flows were assumed to consist of contractually specified principal and interest cash flows for the first twelve years of a pool's life, with the remaining principal being prepaid in full at the end of the twelfth year. Alternatively, mortgages were assumed to prepay according to FHA experience. That is, historical mortality rates tabulated by HUD for FHA loans were used as prepayment rates for mortgages. More recently, according to the Public Securities Association's (PSA) prepayment standard, annual prepayment rates are assumed to increase linearly at 0.2% per month for 30 months, thereafter remaining constant at an annual prepayment rate of 6%.

Today, in contrast, much effort is been expended on estimating prepayment models which more accurately recognize the effects of a changing economic environment on borrower prepayment behavior.

4.1. Prepayment models

A prepayment model relates the incidence of prepayments in a sample of mortgages to a variety of explanatory variables or covariates. The statistical analysis of a prepayment model allows us to calibrate and assess the statistical influence of posited covariates on a borrower's prepayment decision.

A borrower's prepayment decision is clearly influenced by the level of prevailing refinancing rates: the lower refinancing rates are relative to the mortgage's coupon rate then, all else equal, the more likely prepayment. Seasoning or the age of the mortgage may also influence prepayments. For example, newly originated mortgages may be expected to be less likely to prepay than seasoned mortgages. In addition, the region of the country in which a mortgage is originated affects a borrower's propensity to prepay, since borrowers tend to be more mobile in economically robust regions. Other covariates, such as seasonality, also influence prepayment decisions.

Poisson regression provides a comprehensive framework in which to estimate prepayment models. In particular, the number of mortgages prepaid per unit time are treated as independent Poisson random variables with the incidence rate per unit time hypothesized to depend on various covariates. The effectiveness of Poisson regression techniques stems from the fact that the censored nature of prepayment data can be easily accommodated and, more importantly, the ease with which the statistical effects of time-varying covariates can be analyzed.

Let λ represent the rate per unit time that mortgages in a pool prepay. Alternatively, λ can be thought of as the probability that a particular mortgage will be prepaid, conditional on not having been previously prepaid. If η_t is the number of mortgages in the pool outstanding at the beginning of period t, then the expected number of prepayments during period t, μ_t, is given by

$$\mu_t = \eta_t \lambda(\underline{X}_t, \underline{\beta})$$

where $\underline{X}_t$ represents a vector of covariates and $\underline{\beta}$ represents the corresponding vector of parameters to be estimated. It is convenient to assume that the prepayment function has a log-linear form

$$\lambda(\underline{X}_t, \underline{\beta}) = \exp(\underline{X}_t \underline{\beta}).$$

Let c_t denote the number of prepayments in period t, $t = 1, \ldots, T$. We assume that the $\{c_t\}$ are independent and follow a Poisson distribution with parameter $\lambda(\underline{X}t, \underline{\beta})$. It follows that

$$E(c_t) = \eta_t \lambda(\underline{X}_t, \underline{\beta}).$$

We use maximum likelihood techniques to estimate $\underline{\beta}$. That is, we determine that value of $\underline{\beta}$ which is most likely under the Poisson assumption given observed prepayment data $\{c_t\}$. The contribution of time period t to the log-likelihood function is proportional to

$$L_t = c_t \ln(\eta_t \lambda(\underline{X}_t, \underline{\beta}) - \eta_t \lambda(\underline{X}_t, \underline{\beta}).$$

The log-likelihood function is the sum of the L_t over all the time periods

$$L = \sum_t L_t.$$

For illustrative purposes, we estimate a prepayment model based on the refinancing experience of 11 distinct FNMA single family pools with pass-through rates ranging from 4% to 15% over the January to June 1990 sample period. The following covariates are included:

Refinancing opportunities: To capture the effects of refinancing opportunities, we include a covariate, *rf7*, which measures the ratio of the contemporaneous 7 year Treasury bond rate to a pool's weighted-average-coupon (WAC).

Age or seasoning: The age of a mortgage affects prepayment decisions. Newly originated mortgages are unlikely to be prepaid, while aged mortgages, for example, held by retirees, are more likely to be prepaid. We include a covariate, $\pi_0(t)$, for each age t included in our sample.

Seasonality: The time of year affects prepayments. Spring and summer months tend to experience greater prepayment activity. To capture these seasonal effects in prepayments, we include a dummy variable, *season*, which takes on the value of one for the months of April through September, and is zero elsewhere.

Burnout: Borrowers are heterogeneous in their response to refinancing opportunities. Once eager to prepay borrowers have refinanced, the remaining borrowers may be expected to be laggard in their prepayment decisions. In other words, pools which have experienced significant prepayment activity are burned out with a subsequent slow down expected in their future prepayments. Burnout is modeled as the ratio of a pool's current principal to what its principal would have been if borrowers prepaid according to an assumed prepayment schedule (the PSA standard). The smaller the value of this covariate, *burnout*, the more burned out the pool.

The following model was estimated using Poisson regression techniques

$$\pi(t) = \pi_0(t) \exp\left(\beta_1 rf7 + \beta_2 \ln(burnout) + \beta_3 season\right)$$

with the following results

Parameter	Estimate	Standard error
β_1	−10.93	0.19
β_2	0.97	0.07
β_3	0.86	0.07
$\pi_0(2)$	0.80	0.03
$\pi_0(5)$	2.24	0.08
$\pi_0(6)$	2.80	0.11
$\pi_0(8)$	2.43	0.19
$\pi_0(9)$	2.46	0.29
$\pi_0(10)$	1.40	0.20
$\pi_0(11)$	4.73	0.55
$\pi_0(12)$	6.03	0.84
$\pi_0(15)$	6.42	1.04
$\pi_0(16)$	4.74	0.36
$\pi_0(19)$	17.19	2.00

As evidenced by the significantly negative coefficient on *rf7*, these empirical results are consistent with prepayments increasing with decreasing refinancing rates. Also, the less burned out a pool [and so the larger ln(*burnout*)], the faster prepayments. Prepayments are also significantly faster in the spring and summer months. Finally, prepayments initially increase with increasing age, peak at approximately 6 years, thereafter decrease with increasing age, then again increase with increasing age.

5. Valuation

Mortgage backed securities are interest rate contingent securities and, as such, can be valued using fixed income valuation techniques. Rather than review these techniques, we concentrate only on issues unique to mortgage backed securities, in particular, the valuation effects of prepayment behavior.

To that end, we couch our analysis in Cox, Ingersoll and Ross's single factor framework and, without loss of generality, consider our previous example of a mortgage pass-through security with continuous payout rate, in the absence of prepayments, given by

$$P(t) = C - (c - p)F(t).$$

The single state variable is assumed to be the instantaneous riskless rate, $r(t)$, whose dynamics are given by

$$\mathrm{d}r = \kappa(\theta - r)\mathrm{d}t + \sigma\sqrt{r}\,\mathrm{d}Z$$

where

κ ≡ the speed of adjustment coefficient;
θ ≡ the long-term mean instantaneous riskless rate;
$\sigma^2 r$ ≡ the instantaneous variance of increments in r
Z ≡ a standardized Wiener process.

In this single factor framework, the value of the mortgage pass-through security, V, depends only on the state variable $r(t)$:

$$V = V(r;t).$$

Prepayment behavior is critical to the valuation of the mortgage pass-through security. We assume that prepayments follow a Poisson process. In particular, the Poisson random variable equals zero if the underlying mortgage is not prepaid, but jumps to one if and when the mortgage is prepaid and the pass-through security ceases to exist. The intensity of this Poisson process, λ, is given by

$$\lambda = \lambda(r;t)$$

and can be interpreted as the probability per unit time that the borrower will prepay, or equivalently, the rate per unit time that outstanding mortgages are prepaid. Recall our previous discussion of estimating λ using Poisson regression techniques.

In the absence of arbitrage opportunities, the preceding assumptions together with the assumption that prepayment decisions are purely nonsystematic imply that the value of the mortgage pass-through security must satisfy the following second-order partial differential equation

$$\frac{1}{2}\sigma^2 r\frac{\partial^2 V}{\partial r^2} + (\kappa(\theta - r) - \xi r)\frac{\partial V}{\partial r} - rV + P(t) + \lambda(F(t) - V) = -\frac{\partial V}{\partial t},$$

where ξ equals the market price of interest rate risk. Since the underlying mortgage is fully amortizing, the value of the mortgage pass-through security must satisfy the terminal condition

$$V(r;T) = 0,$$

where T denotes the maturity date of the mortgage.

Notice that what differentiates the mortgage pass-through security from other default-free securities is its payout rate

$$P(t) + \lambda(F(t) - V).$$

In the absence of prepayment ($\lambda \equiv 0$), the mortgage pass-through security can be viewed as a default-free security with payout rate $P(t)$. However, with probability λ the underlying mortgage is prepaid and the pass-through investor receives the principal outstanding $F(t)$ in lieu of V. Clearly as λ changes, the mortgage pass-through security's payout rate changes, thereby altering the security's value.

Schwartz & Torous [1989], among others, provide numerical results demonstrating the effects of these varying prepayment assumptions on mortgage values. In particular, they consider a hypothetical 11%, 25-year, default-free fully amortizing mortgage originally issued five years ago. Fixing the short rate of interest at $r = 7\%$, if the mortgage is assumed to be nonprepayable, its price per \$100 principal is \$144.95 for a relatively low long rate of interest of $\ell = 7\%$, but falls to \$86.89 for a relatively high long rate of $\ell = 13\%$. If the mortgage is prepayable and mortgagors are assumed to follow an optimal, value-minimizing call policy, its price is \$100 for $\ell = 7\%$; that is, the mortgage is called, and decreases to \$85.19 for $\ell = 13\%$. However, if borrowers are assumed to prepay according to an empirically estimated prepayment function, the mortgage's price is \$117.97 for $\ell = 7\%$, reflecting the fact that most but not all borrowers now prepay. If $\ell = 13\%$, the mortgage's price is \$88.88, since most borrowers do not prepay in this relatively high refinancing rate environment.

Prepayment behavior is also critical to the choice of numerical techniques used to solve the partial differential equation and therefore value the mortgage pass-through security. If prepayment behavior is assumed to be path independent — prepayments today do not depend on the past history of the assumed state variables — then standard solution techniques, such as finite difference or binomial methods, can be used. These numerical techniques solve the partial differential equation starting at the security's terminal date and then proceed backwards from this date to arrive at the security's current value. Unfortunately, as previously argued, prepayment behavior is more accurately modeled as being path dependent — prepayments today do depend on the past history of the assumed state variables — rendering these standard solution techniques inapplicable since prior information is not reflected in the security's current value.

Fortunately, Monte Carlo simulation methods can be used to solve the partial differential equation while accommodating a path dependent prepayment function. Returning to our previous example, the Monte Carlo method requires that the single state variable r be generated by the following risk-adjusted process:

$$\mathrm{d}r = (\kappa(\theta - r) - \xi r)\mathrm{d}t + \sigma\sqrt{r}\,\mathrm{d}Z.$$

To value the pass-through security, we generate corresponding realizations of r at every month during the life of the security. Given the probability that the mortgage will be prepaid during that month, we determine the cash flows — contractually obligated and prepayments — to the security holder. The present value of these cash flows gives a particular realization of the mortgage pass-through security's value. By repeating this procedure, the average of the corresponding realizations gives the solution of the partial differential equation.

6. Summary

Securitization has transformed the mortgage market into one of the most innovative financial markets in the world. This innovation has been characterized by reallocating underlying mortgage cash flows to satisfy the continually evolving financial needs of investor clienteles.

In the years to come, mortgage collateral will be reallocated in still different ways to satisfy investor clienteles. For example, nonagency or 'private label' mortgages, where both prepayment and default risk must be modeled, will become increasingly important. And as witnessed by the recent growth in the market for asset backed securities (ABSs), the underlying collateral need not be mortgages. However, the principles underlying the continuing success of the mortgage backed securities market are equally applicable to this and other markets.

Acknowledgement

Thanks to Bob Jarrow for his comments and suggestions.

Bibliography

Brennan, M., and E.S. Schwartz (1985). Determinants of GNMA mortgage prices. *AREUEA J.* 13(1), 209–228.

Buser, S.A., and P.H. Hendershott (1984). Pricing default-free fixed rate mortgages. *Housing Finance Rev.* 3(4), 248–260.

Cox, J.C., J.E. Ingersoll, Jr. and S.A. Ross (1985). A theory of the term structure of interest rates. *Econometrica* 53, 385–407.

Cunningham, D., and P.H. Hendershott (1984). Pricing FHA default insurance. *Housing Finance Rev.* 3(4), 383–392.

Dunn, K., and J.J. McConnell (1981). Valuation of GNMA mortgage-backed securities. *J. Finance* 36, 599–617.

Foster, C., and R. Van Order (1984). An option-based model of mortgage default. *Housing Finance Rev.* 3(4), 351–372.

Foster, C., and R. Van Order (1985). FHA terminations: A prelude to rational mortgage pricing. *AREUEA J.* 13(3), 273–291.

Green, J., and J. Shoven (1986). The effects of interest rates on mortgage prepayments. *J. Money, Credit, Banking* 18, 41–59.

Hall, A. (1985). Valuing mortgage borrowers prepayment option. *AREUEA J.* 13(3), 229–247.

Hendershott, P.H., and R. Van Order (1987). Pricing mortgages: An interpretation of the models and results. *J. Financ. Serv. Res.* 1, 77–111.

Kau, J.B., D.C. Keenan, W.J. Muller, III, and J. Epperson (1990). The valuation and analysis of adjustable rate mortgages. *Manage. Sci.* 36, 1417–1431.

Kau, J.B., D.C. Keenan, W.J. Muller, III, and J. Epperson (1992). A generalized valuation model for fixed-rate residential mortgages. *J. Money, Credit, Banking* 24(3), 279–299.

Quigley, J.M. (1987). Interest rate variations, mortgage prepayment, and household mobility. *Rev. Econ. Stat.* 69(4), 636–644.

Schwartz, E.S., and W.N. Torous (1989). Prepayment and the valuation of mortgage backed securities. *J. Finance* 44, 375–392.

Schwartz, E.S., and W.N. Torous (1991). Caps on adjustable rate mortgages: Valuation, insurance, and hedging, in: R.G. Hubbard (ed.), *Financial Markets and Financial Crises*, University of Chicago Press, Chicago, IL.

Schwartz, E.S., and W.N. Torous (1992). Prepayment, default, and the valuation of mortgage pass-through securities. *J. Bus.* 65(2), 221–239.

Titman, S. and W.N. Torous (1989). Valuing commercial mortgages: An empirical investigation of the contingent claims approach to valuing risky debt. *J. Finance* 44, 345–373.

R. Jarrow et al., Eds., *Handbooks in OR & MS, Vol. 9*

Chapter 12

Market Microstructure

David Easley
Department of Economics, Cornell University, Ithaca, NY 14853-4201, U.S.A.

Maureen O'Hara
Johnson Graduate School of Management, Malott Hall, Cornell University, Ithaca, NY 14853-4201, U.S.A.

1. Introduction

Market microstructure is the study of the process and outcomes of exchanging assets under explicit trading rules. While much of economics is concerned with the trading of assets, market microstructure research focuses on the interaction between the mechanics of the trading process and its outcomes, with the specific goal of understanding how actual markets and market intermediaries behave. This focus allows researchers to pose applied questions regarding the performance of specific market structures, as well as more theoretical queries into the nature of price adjustment.

That the structure of specific trading mechanisms and intermediaries affects the behavior of prices is at once an old and a new idea. For several generations of scholars, the fiction of a Walrasian auctioneer automatically clearing markets was a powerful, and convincing, format for characterizing price formation. But there were always some (Demsetz [1968]; Working [1953] to name but two) who questioned whether such a level of abstraction from actual market mechanisms might not beg important and fundamental issues. In particular, the intertemporal aggregation of supply and demand in markets was not well captured in models assuming that equilibrium would naturally arise. These aggregation issues, termed the market microstructure by Garman [1976] in an important paper on dealer behavior, have grown to be one of the foremost areas of financial research.

In this article, we survey important aspects of the market microstructure literature. The recent interest in markets in general and market making in particular suggests that a critical review of the literature would be a valuable contribution. But because the research area per se is vast, and involves both theoretical and empirical investigations, any attempt to survey market microstructure in its totality would be doomed to failure. Our goal in this survey is more modest. We attempt to analyze the theoretical approaches to the behavior of security prices and markets in the presence of differential information. This focus reflects both our own research interests and the fact that much current research involves applications of several existing models to specific market problems. Moreover, the large and growing empirical literature in this area also builds from these underlying theoretical constructs. It is our hope to establish how such models work, what they imply for market behavior, and where (and how) they can be applied to study problems in securities markets.

This theoretical focus comes at some cost, however. Many important and provocative articles in this area have been empirical, establishing properties of price and market behavior often not predicted by existing theoretical models. Moreover, the information focus we adopt here is also restrictive. Most of the early papers in market microstructure are inventory models, viewing the behavior of the dealer in a context devoid of any private information. These inventory analyses [see for example Amihud & Mendelson, 1980; Stoll, 1978; Ho & Stoll, 1981; Cohen, Maier, Schwart & Whitcomb, 1981; O'Hara & Oldfield, 1986] capture a large and important component of market behavior. And it is clearly not the case that the 'important' work in market microstructure began with the information-based models. But it is in this direction that most recent research efforts have gone, and hence, our focus reflects to a large extent the movement of the literature.

In the next section we begin our survey by reviewing the Walrasian (batch) market approach to modeling security market behavior in the presence of differential information. From this point of view there is a single market-clearing price set by some specified market intermediary. Because trades are aggregated and markets operate at specific points in time, this framework is closely related to rational expectations models. In Section 3 we review an alternative modeling approach, that of the sequential trade model. Here trades occur one at a time, different prices to buy and sell are quoted by a market specialist, and the sequence of orders may affect market behavior. From this point of view there is no market price; the price in any transaction will differ depending upon myriad factors such as whether the trade is large or small, the order arose from a buyer or seller, the order is a limit or a market, etc.

These two general approaches have been used to analyze a wide range of market problems and issues, and in Section 4 we briefly review a few of these applications. Because the underlying modeling approaches are not always generalizable, our discussion here considers what we have learned of a general nature from research on these issues. What is of perhaps more interest are the issues not yet resolved. We conclude our survey with a discussion of some of the open questions for future market microstructure research.

2. Walrasian (batch) models

We begin our exposition of the batch model approach to market microstructure with a review of the (micro) Rational Expectations Equilibrium (REE) concept. This is useful not because the batch models build explicitly from the REE literature (although some, such as Kyle [1989], do), but because they all use the rational expectations concept. Further, from a theoretical perspective the difficulties with the REE approach demonstrate the need to take market institutions into account.

2.1. Rational expectations

In a security market, price will typically reflect traders' information. If traders begin with differential information they may attempt to infer others' information from prices and thus revise their beliefs about the value of securities. This information bearing role for prices creates difficulties that the REE concept was designed to solve. We will not survey the REE literature here (see Jordan & Radner [1982] for a survey). Instead we consider a simple example to illustrate the rational expectations idea and some problems with REEs.

Consider an asset market with two (price taking) traders, $i = 1, 2$, who receive payoff relevant signals, $s^i \in S^i$. These traders begin with endowments, w^i, of the securities and purchase portfolios x^i. The traders have payoff functions (which can be viewed as conditional expected utility), $U^i(x^i, s)$ for $s \in S^1 \times S^2$ the joint signal. In this economy, prices will depend on the joint signal through a price relation $P(s)$. We let p denote a realization of this relationship.

A rational trader who knows the price function and the actual price p will select a portfolio to solve.[1]

$$\begin{aligned} &\text{Max } E^i[U^i(x^i, s) \mid s^i, s \in P^{-1}(p)] \\ &\text{s.t.} \quad p \cdot (x^i - w^i) = 0. \end{aligned} \tag{1}$$

this generates a demand relation for trader i denoted by $D^i(p, s^i, P(\cdot))$. A REE is a price relation $P(\cdot)$ such that

$$D^1(P(s), s^1, P(\cdot)) + D^2(P(s), s^2, P(\cdot)) = w^1 + w^2. \tag{2}$$

for all s.

Even if we assume that preferences and endowments satisfy classical assumptions, REE do not exist for some economies.[2] Of perhaps more importance is that these equilibria exhibit several fundamental problems. First, the equilibrium concept is too coarse. Examples can be constructed in which prices reveal trader 1's information to trader 2 even if trader 1's payoffs do not depend on his information. But it should not be possible for 1's information to get into prices if he does not use it. Second, unless noise is added, prices are typically fully revealing or approximately fully revealing [Grossman & Stiglitz, 1980]. Moreover, if traders

[1] The assumption that rational traders know the price function is far from trivial. The usual argument that Bayesian learning is consistent does not directly apply here as the price function is an endogenous relationship. For surveys of the literature on learning and REEs see Blume, Bray & Easley [1982] and Blume & Easley [1992].

[2] However, except in the case where the dimension of S equals the number of securities minus one, REEs exist for a generic set of economies. See Jordan & Radner [1982].

are allowed to condition on trades as well as prices, then generically these market statistics provide a sufficient statistic for all information to each trader [Jordan, 1982]. But then there is no advantage to being informed. So why would any trader acquire information? Third, unless a restrictive condition on the distribution of information is met, there is no trading mechanism that could implement REEs.[3] That is, there is no trading game whose Bayes–Nash equilibrium are REE even in large economies.

Taken together these difficulties suggest that although the rational expectations concept may be useful, the (competitive) REE definition may not provide a good approximation to the working of actual security markets. Radner [1979] noted this, 'A thorough theoretical analysis of this situation probably requires a more detailed specification of the trading mechanism than is usual in general equilibrium analysis'. One difficulty in providing this detailed specification, however, is the complexity of actual security markets. Unlike the simplicity of the Walrasian auctioneer, actual trading mechanisms possess myriad features: Order form, timing conventions, order size and regulatory constraints all can differ between markets. This complexity dictates that any modeling approach must abstract from a least some features of the trading mechanism. The simplest framework to do so involves analyzing the performance of a batch market with market orders.

2.2. Market orders

In the batch model approach to the study of security price formation a market maker observes the net order flow from traders and sets a single price at which all orders are cleared. These orders are simply requests to buy or sell at the prevailing market price, and hence, are not price-contingent. Thus, these models do not permit a characterization of the bid–ask spread or of transaction prices on a trade-by-trade basis. What they do allow is a characterization of informed traders' strategies and their effect on prices.

The first models to address these strategic aspects of trading in a market microstructure model were Kyle [1984, 1985]. We will focus on Kyle's [1985] analysis of a single risk neutral informed trader, a group of noise traders and a single risk neutral market maker. These individuals trade an asset with liquidation value given by the random variable v. The informed trader observes v. The market maker does not know v, but instead has a prior on v which is normal with mean p_0 and variance σ_μ^2. What the market maker does know is the aggregate net order flow from the informed and uninformed traders. The role of the uninformed traders is to provide noise in this aggregate order flow. They do not act strategically, but rather submit an aggregate order, μ, which is normally

[3] This condition requires that no trader have private information which would affect the prediction of the payoff relevant state given all other traders' information. See Blume & Easley [1990]. In a large economy, this condition is satisfied in the standard example where traders' signals are all $N(s, \sigma^2)$, are independent (given s) and only s is payoff relevant.

distributed with mean 0 and variance σ_μ^2. The market maker is assumed to select efficient prices. This means that given an order flow of x from the informed trader and μ from noise traders the price p is set equal to the expected value of the asset conditional on observing $x + \mu$. Let the induced pricing function be $P(x + \mu)$. Then

$$P(x + u) = E[v \mid x + \mu]. \tag{3}$$

The informed trader has rational expectations, in particular, he knows the pricing function and the distribution of noise trades. He does not know the realization of the noise trade, nor does he know the price. The informed trader simply selects a market order, a quantity, to maximize his expected profits. Let $X(v)$ be his order strategy and $\Pi(X(\cdot), P(\cdot))$ his profit function. Then optimality requires that $X(v)$ maximizes $E[\Pi(X(\cdot), P(\cdot)) \mid v]$ for each v. An equilibrium is then an efficient price function $P(\cdot)$ and an expected profit maximizing $X(\cdot)$.

There are several features to note about this framework. First, this is not a game theoretic model, but it can be made into one either by including additional market makers who have common information and compete through prices or by assigning the market maker an objective function leading to the optimality of efficient prices. With either modification the equilibrium becomes a subgame perfect equilibrium in the sense that each players' strategy is a best response given his information at each stage in the game. Second, because the informed player does not know μ or p when he submits an order, and orders are not functions of p, this game could not implement a REE even if multiple informed traders existed. This is not a serious shortcoming, however, as the objective here is to represent important aspects of the working of real securities markets. Finally, as in most market microstructure models the noise trader plays an important role. In effect, the informed trader (partially) hides in the noise such traders induce in the order flow. Because the market maker has zero expected profit, and the informed trader maximizes expected profit, the noise traders have expected losses. This does not mean that they are necessarily irrational; they may have other objectives and may be trading for liquidity purposes.

Kyle demonstrates that there is an equilibrium in which

$$\begin{aligned} X(v) &= \beta(v - p_0), \\ P(x + u) &= p_0 + \lambda(x + u), \end{aligned} \tag{4}$$

where

$$\beta = \left(\frac{\sigma_u}{\sigma_0}\right) \quad \text{and} \quad \lambda = \frac{1}{2}\left(\frac{\sigma_0}{\sigma_u}\right).$$

Given the market makers' pricing function, optimality of the linear strategy for the informed trader is immediate. The derivation of the pricing rule is more interesting. Using his hypothesized knowledge of $X(\cdot)$, the order flow allows the market maker to construct an observable random variable which is normally distributed with mean v and variance σ_u^2/β^2. An application of Bayes rule shows that the market maker's posterior on v is normal with mean $p_0 + \lambda(x + u)$ and variance $(1/2)\sigma_0^2$. So regardless of the trade realized, the posterior variance of v is one-half its prior variance.

Kyle also constructs a multiperiod version of his model in which the informed trader takes into account the affect of current trades on both current and future profits. This result is an equilibrium of the form (for a period length of one):

$$\begin{aligned} X_t(v) &= \beta_t(x - p_{t-1}) \\ P_t(x_t + u_t) &= p_{t-1} + \lambda_t(x_t + u_t), \end{aligned} \tag{5}$$

where

$$\beta_t = \frac{\sigma_u^2}{\sigma_{t-1}^2}, \quad \sigma_t^2 = \frac{1}{2}\sigma_{t-1}^2 \quad \text{and} \quad \lambda_t = \frac{1}{2}\frac{\sigma_{t-1}^2}{\sigma_u^2}.$$

Here σ_t^2 is the market maker's posterior variance of v at period t.

While we present this multi-period behavior in a discrete fashion, Kyle also considers the problem in a continuous framework. In particular, Kyle assumes that the uninformed trades $\tilde{\mu}(t)$ follow a Brownian motion. One implication of this assumption is that the uninformed quantity traded at one auction is independent of the uninformed quantity traded at other auctions. Since this will not be true of the quantity traded by the informed trader, it is this linkage of information and quantity that will ultimately cause prices to reflect all underlying information.

Of particular interest is how the informed trader chooses to strategically exploit his information across time. A key result of the Kyle model is that smoothing behavior by the informed trader results in prices that have constant volatility as the time periods of the model are shortened to approach a continuous auction.[4] As expected, the price path also has the property that prices follow a martingale, so prices are 'efficient' in the sense that an uninformed observer's expectation of any future price is today's price. Kyle further demonstrates that prices will eventually reflect the informed trader's new information.

One consequence of this equilibrium is that the informed trader profits more by continuously trading rather than by attempting to manipulate prices through some mixed strategy. Unlike in sequential trade models, however, it is not the case that the informed trader trades the same amount every period. Indeed, it is this ability to vary the trade size that allows the trader to 'hide' from the market maker. Because the informed trader is eventually 'found' by the market maker, Kyle is able to show that his profits are bounded and hence, the return to information can be calculated.

The Kyle model thus provides an elegant way to characterize how a single informed trader optimally exploits his informational advantage and what this,

[4] This constant volatility property is also a characteristic of a random walk. Hence, in the Kyle model security prices will follow a random walk. While this behavior is theoretically consistent with 'efficient' markets, it does not appear to be consistent with the empirical behavior of prices, see Lo & McKinley [1988]. See also Back [1992] for a continuous time refinement of Kyle's model.

in turn, implies for the price process. While the model does not capture the evolution of prices (or quotes) in response to individual trades as the sequential trade models do, it does allow the return to information to be explicitly calculated.

There are, of course, a number of abstractions in the model that may affect the equilibrium outcome. For example, the timing conventions of the model dictate that the market maker observe only the aggregated order flow, and not any of its component parts. From a purely technical perspective, this prevents the market maker from observing the informed's orders, and hence, preserves the 'nonrevealing' nature of the equilibrium. But what if the market maker knew at least something about the uninformed order flow? Given the market maker's central position in most trading mechanisms, it seems likely that she could know more about the distribution of orders than the market as a whole. In this case, the game changes to one in which the informed trader knows more about the asset's value, but the market maker knows more about the order flow. This framework is the setting for research by Lindsay [1990], Forster & George [1992], and Holden & Bagnoli [1992].[5] Their models suggest that the ability of the informed to extract profits in such a setting can be drastically reduced, with prices reflecting information much more quickly.

Another extension of the model that greatly affects its results is the inclusion of multiple informed traders. The elegance and simplicity of the Kyle model derives, in part, from the single informed trader's ability to control the flow of information. But since the informed trader makes positive profits, it follows that other traders might also seek information on the asset, breaking down the 'information monopolist' setting. While this issue was considered by Kyle in a two-period setting [see Kyle, 1984], Holden & Subrahmanyam [1992], and Foster & Vishwanathan [1993] extend the Kyle [1985] framework to include multiple informed traders.

Holden and Subramanyan show that the competition between informed traders forces prices to full information levels almost immediately. Thus, the smoothing behavior which allowed prices to gradually adjust to new information, and thereby provide a return to the informed trader, disappears. Instead, the equilibrium now becomes that of the standard rational expectations models in which the trading behavior of the informed results in a revealing equilibrium in which prices instantly reflect all private information. Foster & Vishwinathan [1993] demonstrate that a similar result can occur if the normality assumption is relaxed. They derive a model with a public signal in which the randomness is characterized by an elliptically contoured distribution as opposed to the more restrictive normal class. Their analysis suggests that the Kyle model may not easily generalize beyond the normal class. These results are particularly important because they suggest a frailty to the ability of at least this simple trading process to avoid the information revelation conundrum so bedeviling to economic analyses.

[5] Models in which the market makers knows some information about the uninformed order flow are also found in Admati & Pfleiderer [1991], Gennotte & Leland [1990], Roell [1990], and Madhavan [1992].

One possible direction to remedy this problem is to consider a more complex trading mechanism. In actual markets, a wide variety of order formats exist, allowing traders greater control over at least some aspects of their trade behavior. Given the batch nature of trading modelled here a more natural characterization might be to trade via limit orders which allow the trader to vary the size of his trade with the market price. This issue of strategic behavior and the trading mechanism is considered in Kyle [1989].

2.3. *Price-contingent orders*

The Kyle [1989] paper returns to a more standard rational expectations framework in which traders submit demand functions to a centralized market. This market is run by a Walrasian auctioneer who clears all trades at a single price. In addition to the fictional auctioneer there are three types of participants in this market: noise traders, uninformed traders and speculators. The noise traders play the same role as in the previous analysis. The other traders submit optimally chosen demand functions. Since such price contingent (or limit) orders are available in actual markets, this mechanism incorporates some additional realism, but at the expense of dropping an active market maker.

The speculators receive signals which are correlated with the value of the asset, but which are independently distributed given this value. As is usual in this literature all variables are normally distributed. But here, unlike in previous market microstructure models, uninformed traders and speculators have negative exponential utility of final profit. Each speculator chooses a strategy or demand function, $X_n(p; i_n)$, where p is the price and i_n is n's signal, to maximize expected utility. Similarly, each uninformed trader selects a strategy or demand schedule $Y_m(p)$.

The optimal demand schedules $X = (X_n(p; i_n))_n$ and $Y = (Y_m((p))_m$ and the quantity demanded by noise traders are communicated to the auctioneer. His role is to choose a price p and allocations $(X_n)_n$ and $(Y_m)_m$ to clear the market. The outcome of this process will be price and allocation functionals $P(X, Y)$, $(X_n^*(X, Y))_n$ and $Y_m^*(X, Y))_m$. In these functionals we have suppressed the dependence on the noise traders' demand. Note that the auctioneer's only role is to clear markets; he does attempt to set efficient prices or even to infer information from the schedules submitted to him.

An imperfectly competitive rational expectations equilibrium is a Bayes–Nash equilibrium in demand schedules. That is, (X, Y) is an equilibrium if, markets clear at $p(\cdot)$, $(X_n^*(\cdot))_n$ and $(Y_m^*(\cdot))_m$, and:

$$
\begin{aligned}
&E\big[U_n\big\{(v - p(X, Y))X_n^*(X, Y)\big\} \mid i_n\big] \geq \\
&\quad \geq E\big[U_n\big\{(v - p(X', Y))X_n^*(X', Y)\big\} \mid i_n\big], \\
&\quad \text{for any } X' = X \text{ except in the } n\text{th coordinate and for any } i_n, \qquad (6a)
\end{aligned}
$$

$$
\begin{aligned}
&E\big[U_m\big\{(v - p(X, Y))Y_m^*(X, Y)\big\}\big] \geq E\big[U_m\big\{(v - p(X, Y'))Y_m^*(X, Y')\big\}\big], \\
&\quad \text{for any } Y' = Y \text{ except in the } m\text{th coordinate.} \qquad (6b)
\end{aligned}
$$

Notice that this equilibrium differs from the competitive outcome in that informed traders take account of the effect of their actions on the market price. While this may seem to be a subtle change, it has a number of important implications for the amount of information traders need to know. In particular, in the competitive rational expectations equilibrium, to determine their optimal strategies, traders are assumed to know their own preferences, the structure of the market, and the function that translates information into prices. In the imperfect competitive equilibrium traders must again know all of this information, but in addition they must also know the function translating demands into prices and allocations as well as everybody's demand schedule (or everybody's preferences so that they can calculate the demand schedules). Moreover, it will be the case that each trader needs to know the exact number of traders N and M; changes in the number of either type will affect the equilibrium. Such extensive information requirements are somewhat difficult to reconcile with actual market characteristics.

As in any rational expectations equilibrium it must be the case that the strategies traders expect to prevail are, in fact, the strategies that do prevail. Kyle demonstrates that under certain conditions there will exist a symmetric linear equilibrium. For this equilibrium to occur, a sufficient number of speculators is needed to ensure a reasonably 'competitive' outcome. In the absence of this, the assumption that noise traders' demands are price inelastic means that a single informed trader (or even a single uninformed speculator if he is the only nonpassive agent) will make infinite expected profits. If there are 'enough' speculators, however, they essentially compete among themselves so that this monopolistic outcome cannot occur. In this sense, this result is similar to that demonstrated in Kyle [1984].

An important property of this imperfectly competitive equilibrium is that prices are less informative than they are in a competitive rational expectations equilibrium. Because traders recognize the impact of their trades on the market price they will not completely 'trade away' their informational advantage. In this example, therefore, it will be the case that with strategic behavior, the rational expectations equilibrium will both exist and have the reasonable property that informed traders earn a positive return to information.

2.4. *Strategic uninformed traders*

An important restriction of the analyses surveyed in Sections 2.2 and 2.3 is that uninformed traders are not permitted to act strategically. Instead, noise traders are assumed to transact every period for reasons exogenous to the model, an assumption also made in the sequential trade models. Yet, if it is profitable for an informed trader to time his trades, it may be profitable for the uninformed to do so as well. Moreover, if the uninformed trade differently, it will be the case that the optimal informed strategy will also change. The issue of uninformed strategic behavior, therefore, introduces a number of interesting dimensions into the analysis of market behavior.

One reason for considering this aspect of the trading process is that it may allow the uninformed to reduce the losses they incur in trading. The uninformed, and their losses, are necessary in information-based microstructure models, as they generate the gains made by the informed. Nevertheless, it is troubling that the only role played by the uninformed is that of being 'taken' by the informed traders.[6]

Allowing the uninformed to time their trades also introduces the possibility that uninformed trades could themselves have interesting price effects. In particular, if the uninformed attempt to 'hide' from the informed traders, then patterns of trade may arise. Such trade patterns are characteristic of actual security trading, with several researchers [see Jain & Joh, 1988; French & Roll, 1986] empirically documenting both within and across day patterns. Given a passive role for the uninformed, it does not appear that strategic decisions by informed traders will result in such variations in the timing and volume of trade. Moreover, in the microstructure models considered thus far, market makers play only a passive role by accommodating, rather than initiating, trades so their role in introducing price patterns is unclear. This suggests that, to understand trade patterns, the role of the uninformed must be specified in greater detail.

Numerous authors have addressed this issue of uninformed strategic behavior in a variety of contexts. Admati & Pfleiderer [1988, 1989] focus on the timing decisions of uninformed traders transacting within a single day. Foster & Vishwanathan [1990] are concerned with interday strategic effects induced by varying levels of public and private information across trading days. Seppi [1990] analyzes the factors that influence a large uninformed trader's decision to trade blocks versus round lots. In all of these applications, the focus is on the ability of the uninformed to choose strategically either the composition or the timing of their orders.

Admati & Pfleiderer [1988] consider a world in which informed traders repeatedly receive information one period before it will become public. So unlike in Kyle [1985] the informed have no real timing decision to make; they need only chose their optimal order size in each period. Alternatively, uninformed discretionary traders have exogenous liquidity needs and cannot split trades. Their only decision is when to trade. There are also nondiscretionary liquidity traders who provide the familiar noise in the market. Finally, the market structure is the same as the discrete time version of Kyle [1985].

The interesting question here is the optimal behavior of discretionary traders and their effect on patterns of trade. If these traders behave strategically they should each recognize that their order strategy affects the pricing functions as well as realized prices. This would lead to a complex problem and Admati and Pfleiderer do not focus on it. Instead, uninformed traders are assumed to act competitively and thus take prices as given. This reduces their decision problem to choosing the period in which trade is least costly. In equilibrium the uninformed

[6] Glosten [1989] and Hindy [1991] present market microstructure models in which noise traders are not present. Bhattacharya & Spiegel [1991] analyze the effect of noise trader behavior on market prices.

'clump' together in an attempt to separate their trades from the adverse effects of the informed traders. It seems likely that if the uninformed were to take account of the price effects of their trades then this would simply reinforce the clumping behavior. Of course, the uninformed cannot completely separate themselves from the informed because by assumption the informed traders cannot time their trades and so are always present in the market. Moreover, it must also be the case that in every period there are some nondiscretionary uninformed traders active in the market or else the trades of the informed would instantly reveal their information to the market. Nonetheless, by clumping together, the discretionary uninformed traders can increase the liquidity (in the period in which they trade) of the market and thereby reduce their losses to the informed.

The decisions of the uninformed traders, in turn, affect the choices of the informed traders. Since the optimal informed order quantity depends on the variance of the uninformed trade, it follows that the informed trade quantity will also follow the pattern set by the uninformed traders. In particular, in periods where the uninformed volume is large, the informed volume will also increase and conversely in periods where the uninformed volume is small. The strategic decisions of the informed traders will thus serve to exacerbate the patterns introduced by the uninformed traders.

A crucial assumption underlying this analysis, however, is the independence of trade between periods. Unlike in either the sequential trade models or Kyle [1985], trade in one period is not informative about trade in any subsequent period. This reflects the dual assumptions that informed traders' information lives only one period and that uninformed traders are not permitted to split their trade between periods. In this setting, therefore, there is no endogenous learning problem for either the uninformed or the market makers because there is nothing to be learned from market statistics; subsequent prices will not reflect the effects of previous order flows.

One reason why this is important is that it greatly affects the nature of the equilibrium, and hence, the qualitative predictions, that emerge from these models. For example, Admati & Pfleiderer consider a simple extension in which the uninformed are permitted to split their trades across two periods. Two problems immediately arise in characterizing this solution. First, it is not clear that a pure-strategy equilibrium will always exist, and even if it does exist, it is not generally possible to find a closed form solution. A second problem is that there is no way to guarantee that if we find an equilibrium that it is in fact the only equilibrium. Once we allow traders to act strategically across periods, the potential for multiple equilibrium becomes a major concern.

The fragility of equilibrium with strategic trade is also a problem if the assumptions regarding trader behavior are relaxed. Subrahmanyam [1991b] demonstrates that if informed traders are risk averse then it need not be the case that periods with more informed traders result in better prices for the uninformed. He shows that with a small number of informed, an increase in informed trading can actually worsen the 'terms of trade', suggesting that the aggregation or clumping tendency of the market need not hold if traders are risk averse.

If uninformed trade flows do become informative over time, then Admati & Pfleiderer argue that uninformed traders will be more likely to trade early in the day than later. A similar earlier versus later in the trading period story is also considered in an analysis of interday trading patterns by Foster & Vishwanathan [1990].[7] Their analysis involves a variant of Kyle's [1985] model in which trade occurs only once a day and information is 'lumpy'. An interesting aspect of this paper is that the informed trader's information can persist across more than one trading interval, allowing both informed and uninformed traders to time their trades.

The basic issue considered in Foster & Vishwinathan is the trade pattern that arises when the informational advantage of the informed trader can deteriorate across time. Their model uses the basic structure of the discrete time version of the Kyle [1985] model. There is a single, risk neutral informed trader who receives a private signal every day. There is also a noisy public signal available to all traders at the close of trading each day.

As was also true in Admati & Pfleiderer, the uninformed discretionary traders do not take account of their effect on the terms of trade and so act competitively rather than strategically in choosing when to trade. The discretionary traders are limited in their ability to time their trades in that they may only delay trading by one period (a day in this model) and are not permitted to push trading off over the weekend. One difference between this model and that of Admati & Pfleiderer is that since Foster & Viswanathan have only a single informed trader the dissipative effect on information that arises with multiple informed traders does not arise in this model. Hence, even if discretionary traders are able to delay trading, if there is no public signal then the single informed trader simply adjusts her trading volume to offset the discretionary effects. In this case, the behavior of the uninformed only affects the profit of the informed trader and, with entry precluded, there is no pattern in security prices and variances.

When there is a public signal however, the informed trader cannot offset the uninformed's order flow behavior and patterns may emerge. Indeed, Foster & Viswanathan show that multiple equilibria are possible with single or dual periods of trade concentration possible. In these equilibria it is always the case that Monday volume is lowest because the uninformed always delay trading to avoid the informed trader's large informational edge.[8] Similarly, the variance of returns on Mondays will differ from other days because of this differential trading behavior. Foster & Viswanathan argue that this trading behavior may explain the daily variance differences empirically found by French & Roll [1986].

In both the Admati & Pfleiderer and Foster & Viswanathan models, therefore, the ability of uniformed traders to delay trades can introduce patterns in trade behavior. Since empirical work suggests that such patterns exist, these models serve to highlight assumptions sufficient to establish such patterns theoretically.

[7] Pagano & Roell [1992] provide a different result showing conditions under which uninformed traders would prefer to trade at the end of an 'information' period.

[8] In this model, informed traders continue to receive private information over the weekend and hence start the week with an informational advantage.

What appears to be important is some impediment on the behavior of the informed which restricts them from offsetting the effects of the uninformed. As we have discussed, it is possible to obtain such results but their generality is constrained by the need to retain the tractable, linear structure needed to characterize equilibrium.

3. Sequential trade models

The batch model approach surveyed in the previous section provided a number of important insights into the behavior of market prices. By its very nature however, this approach cannot provide information about the fine details of the security price process. Transactions cannot be examined on a trade-by-trade basis so that the precise evolution of prices across time cannot be addressed. Equally important, the determinants of the bid–ask spread cannot be identified.

A parallel literature has developed to analyze these issues in the context of a sequential trading process. The origin of this literature is usually credited to a simple paper by Bagehot [1971]. He argued that the presence of traders with superior information could explain much of the market maker's behavior. If informed traders buy when the stock is priced too low (given their information) and sell when it is too high, then the market maker loses to them. To offset these losses by gains from trading with uninformed traders, a bid–ask spread develops.

This idea was first formalized in a one period model by Copeland & Galai [1983]. They view the market maker as setting bid and ask prices to maximize expected profit. The bid–ask spread arises from the assumption that some traders are informed of the true value of the stock and buy price elastic amounts when the value is above the ask and conversely sell when it is below the bid. The remaining traders are uninformed and have trades determined by their demand function. They show that a spread does arise and they characterize how it depends on the traders' demands.

This approach provides a cogent explanation of why a bid–ask spread may exist, but the assumption that the value of the stock is known at the end of the period makes it inappropriate for a study of the evolution of asset prices. In a sequential framework the market maker, and traders, should learn from previous trades and adjust their behavior over time.

It was this insight that Glosten & Milgrom developed in their 1985 model of the market maker's pricing decisions. Their model is driven by the fact that in a competitive market, informed agents' trades will reflect their information. If an order to sell is delivered anonymously to the market maker it could be that the agent who placed the order knew bad news. But it could also be that the trader was uninformed and simply needed liquidity. As the market maker does not know which is true, the arrival of a sell order will lower his expectation of the assets' value. Similarly, the arrival of a buy order will raise his expectation of the value. Thus, a market maker who sets efficient prices will quote an ask price greater than his bid price, and a spread will arise. The interesting questions here are the determinants of the spread and the evolution of prices over time.

We consider a simplified version of the Glosten & Milgrom [1985] model to illustrate the pricing problem. All traders are risk neutral and act competitively. They trade an asset, with random eventual value v, and money. Each trade involves one unit of the asset, trades take place sequentially, and all trades take place at either the market maker's bid or ask price. Some fraction of these trades come from uninformed traders who, as in the batch models, have exogenously specified behavior. The remainder of the trades come from informed traders. To make the analysis simple suppose these informed traders all either observe good news (G) or bad news (B) with $E[v \mid G] > E[v \mid B]$.

The market maker sets bid and ask prices such that his expected profit on any trade is zero. The rationale for this assumption is price competition among risk neutral market makers. The result of this structure is that the bid (ask) price must be the expected value of the asset conditional on the arrival of a sell (buy) order. The market maker's inventory is irrelevant here; his pricing problem reduces to calculating conditional expected values.

The ask price that the market maker quotes for the first trade of the trading day is

$$a_1 = E[v \mid G]\Pr[G \mid S_1] + E[v \mid B]\Pr[B \mid S_1] \tag{7}$$

where S_1 denotes the event that the first order to arrive is a sell order. Rationality on the market maker's part dictates that these probabilities are determined by Bayes rule, so $\Pr[B|S_1] = \Pr[B]\Pr[S_1|B]/\Pr[S_1]$ where $\Pr[B]$ is the initial probability of bad news and $\Pr[S_1]$ is the unconditional probability of a sell order at time one. Since the informed sell upon receipt of bad news and buy upon receipt of goods news we have $\Pr[S_1 \mid B] > Pr[S_1 \mid G]$. Thus, $\Pr[B \mid S_1] > Pr[B]$. That is, a sale raises the conditional probability of bad news and so lowers the expected value of the asset. Similarly, a buy raises the expected value of the asset.

Given these initial quotes some first trade will occur. Suppose that the actual trade is a sale. To determine his quotes for the next trade the market maker goes through the same process except that the new prior probabilities of bad or good news are the posterior probabilities $\Pr[B \mid S_1]$ and $\Pr[G \mid S_1]$. So to understand the evolution of prices we need only track the evolution of the market maker's beliefs. That is, the ask price at time two will be

$$a_2(S_1) = E[v \mid G]\Pr[G \mid S_1, S_2] + E[v \mid B]\Pr[B \mid S_1, S_2] \tag{8}$$

given that a sale, S_1, occurred at time one.

The determination of beliefs and quotes for subsequent periods proceeds in the same way. Because the distribution of trades differs if good or bad news has occurred and the market maker observes trades, he will eventually learn the informed's information. Prices will thus converge to their full-information values and the spread will disappear. Along the way of course, prices are not full-information efficient. But they are weak-form efficient in the sense that prices follow a martingale. The price at any date is the (market maker's) expectation of the value of the asset, $p_t = E[v \mid I_t]$ where I_t is the market maker's information at date t. So $E[p_{t+1} \mid I_t] = E[E[v \mid I_{t+1}] \mid I_t] = E[v \mid I_t] = p_t$.

What preserves the gradual adjustment of prices to information in the sequential trade model is the probabilistic structure of the order process. In this model, traders are constrained to buy or sell one unit at any point in time. An informed trader, knowing the asset's true value, would clearly prefer to continue trading until prices reach their full information level. But this is precluded by assumption. Instead, each trader has some probability of being able to trade, and it is this limitation that keeps informed traders from immediately forcing prices to their true level.

With prices gradually adjusting to information it follows that the bid–ask spread plays an important role in reflecting the risk of informed trading. Glosten and Milgrom characterize the spread, $a_t - b_t$, showing how it depends on the number of informed, trading elasticities and other parameters of the model. They also show that if the adverse selection problem is too severe the market maker may set the spread so wide that the market collapses. This is the analog for securities markets of the 'lemons problem' discussed by Akerlof [1970].

The sequential trade approach has been used by several authors to address market microstructure questions other than the existence of a bid–ask spread. One obvious question is the effect of trade size on the bid–ask spread. Market makers do not quote single bid and ask prices, rather the quote depends on the number of shares to be traded. Large sales depress prices and large buys raise price. In addition, when small trades follow large trades, prices tend to recover.

Easley & O'Hara [1987] consider a sequential trade model in which individuals submit orders for either large or small trades. The uniformed are assumed to use both order sizes. The informed choose an order size to maximize their expected profits. If the spread was constant across trade sizes the informed would make more money from large trades than from small trades. This would lead them to submit only large orders. But then the spread could not be constant as large trades would have a greater information content than small trades. In any equilibrium, therefore, the spread must increase with trade size.

Depending on market characteristics two types of equilibria are possible. In a (semi-)separating equilibrium the informed use only large trades. In this equilibrium there is no spread for small trades but there is a spread for large trades. In a pooling equilibrium the informed are indifferent between large and small trades. Here there is a spread at all trade sizes, but the spread widens as trade size increases.

The price recovery following large trades suggests that no matter what the equilibrium, the arrival of a small order must carry information. This is incorporated in the Easley & O'Hara [1987] analysis by having the market maker be uncertain about whether an information event has occurred as well as about whether any news was good or bad. Now as small trades are more likely to come from the uninformed than from the informed, a small trade raises the conditional probability that an information event has not occurred. This causes the spread to shrink. So when a small trade follows a large sale prices partially recover.

The multiple trade size issue introduces a single strategic element into the sequential trade approach. Much subsequent research considers other, often more complex, strategic issues. But on this topic the sequential trade approach is limited. The inability to specify the trading protocol in more, but still tractable, detail makes it difficult to pose questions of market manipulation by informed trades. For this purpose the batch models seem more promising. However, the strategic analysis of equilibrium with alternative trade size is, in fact, applicable to other related topics. For example, for multiple-listed securities, the choice of trading venue is isomorphic to the equilibrium analyzed above, as are questions regarding trade between related markets, such as the option and the stock. In these settings, the equilibrium involves the same characteristics as that derived in the trade size model.

The sequential trade approach has also been used to analyze the role of time in the trading process. In the models discussed so far, time was order arrival time rather than clock time. With this approach any information contained in the amount of time between trades or in the number of trades per day (a proxy for volume) is lost. The notion of time as a factor in pricing was developed in papers by Diamond & Verrecchia [1987] and Easley & O'Hara [1992a]. Diamond & Verrecchia show how short sale constraints can affect the security price process. If some informed traders face binding short sale constraints then trading intensity will be lower when bad news arrives than when good new arrives. Market makers thus interpret no-trade intervals as signals of bad news and lower their quotes. Diamond and Verrecchia also show that prohibiting short sales shows the adjustment of the market to bad news.

An alternative explanation of the role of time is offered by Easley & O'Hara [1992a]. The focus here is on whether an information event has occurred and on how trading intensity provides a signal about the existence of new information. Here a no-trade interval lowers the market maker's probability on an information event having occurred. Since only actual trades carry information about the type of news, the market maker keeps the relative probabilities on good and bad news unchanged, but lowers their absolute amounts. So following a no-trade interval the spread shrinks as the ask falls and the bid rises. This approach makes the number of trades, or volume, endogenous and permits a characterization of the affect of volume on the speed of adjustment of prices to strong form efficient prices. This focus on time also reveals important differences between the process of quotes and the transactions price process, with the latter being biased by potentially severe sampling problems.

4. Applications

The models surveyed in the previous two sections provide cogent and tractable frameworks for analyzing the behavior of securities markets. While the general theoretical properties of security prices are clearly important, there are also many specific issues in security market structure, regulation, and design that merit analysis. Most recent work in market microstructure has focused on such issues. In this section, we provide a partial and very brief discussion of some of these applications. As will be apparent, these applications demonstrate the variety of issues and problems addressed in the microstructure area.

4.1. Market structure

A fundamental question in security market organization is how should the trading mechanism be structured. In actual markets, a plethora of structures exist, ranging from simple call markets to more complex continuous markets, from highly centralized exchanges with a single specialist to fragmented markets with multiple dealers, and even extending to automated screen-driven mechanisms with no explicit price-setting agent. This diversity of trading mechanisms may be due to historical factors, or it may be the result of more effective trading mechanisms prevailing over time. Why some institutional arrangements dominate in some market settings and not others, however, is not obvious.[9]

There has been extensive research investigating the role played by specific mechanisms, as well as more general questions regarding the link between the trading mechanism and the stability and performance of the market. Fundamental to these analyses is the question of market viability. In particular, as we noted earlier, Glosten & Milgrom [1985] raise the spector that if information problems were severe enough, then in the competitive specialist framework there may be no market clearing price at which trades can take place. The difficulty is that a high enough threat of information based trading may induce uninformed traders to leave the market, resulting in a sure loss to any trader on the other side.[10]

Several researchers have argued that there may be features of the trading mechanism that can overcome this information-induced failure. Glosten [1989] considers whether the monopoly position of the specialist, as found for example, on the NYSE, might provide this needed stability. The intuition underlying this argument is that a monopoly specialist is not concerned with the profit arising from any individual trade, but rather may chose a price schedule to maximize profits. Glosten shows that a monopolistic specialist who chooses a schedule of prices resulting in expected losses on some trades and expected gains on others will continue to operate after a competitive market has ceased to exist. In Glosten's model, this averaging takes place across trade sizes. Gammill [1989] pursues a similar averaging idea with respect to intertemporal price behavior in his analysis of competitive versus monopolist market structure.

Madhavan [1992] demonstrates that another solution to the stability problem may be to organize trading as a call market. In a call market, orders are aggregated and cleared at a single price. With orders lumped together, the market maker can

[9] For an excellent discussion of market structure issues see Stoll [1990]. The effect of market structure parameters on market efficiency is discussed in Easley & O'Hara [1992b].

[10] This problem is related to the no-trade equilibrium demonstrated by Milgrom & Stokey [1982]. Bhattacharya & Spiegel [1991] analyze the market failure problem in a rational expectations framework.

essentially price on average in much the way the monopolistic specialist behaves in the Glosten analysis. The NYSE operates just such a call market to begin trading every day, with the mechanism shifting to a continuous auction framework for subsequent trades. Since information problems may be more severe at the open, Madhaven's analysis suggests one reason why this market mechanism has remained viable.

One limitation to this line of research, however, is that while these analyses have demonstrated the stability properties of particular market mechanisms, there has been no analysis determining the *optimal* mechanism for achieving stability in market clearing.[11] Moreover, while Glosten considered some general welfare issues, the explicit welfare properties of alternative market structures has not been addressed. Consequently, the important question of what markets *should* look like remains unanswered. This is undoubtedly an important, and necessary direction for future research on the design of market trading mechanisms.

While these analyses have addressed the viability of market mechanisms, there are numerous other issues relating to the performance of alternative market structures. For example, whether trading is constrained to a single entity (as is the case in a monopolistic framework or a call market) or can be divided amongst several venues is an issue of obvious importance. The recent development of purchased order flow by third market providers as well as the general expansion of regional exchanges [see McInish & Wood, 1992] are evidence of greater fragmentation in security markets. Glosten [1991a] examines theoretically how the ability to skim orders from exchanges affects market liquidity, while Lee [1993] presents empirical evidence of differential trading prices across trading venues. While these analyses are provocative, more extensive research will be needed to establish how the increasing tendency to fragment order flow will affect market stability or performance.

A related issue involves the role of the dealer or broker in the trading mechanism. Although the NYSE specialist cannot trade on his own account before customer orders, this is not the case for all markets (or market participants). In the London stock market and in most futures markets, for example, brokers can dual trade, meaning that they can act both to place orders for customers and enter orders for their own account. Roell [1990] analyzes the effect of dual trading on the quality of the market, and finds that transactions costs fall for liquidity motivated traders, and rise for traders who may be information traders. Overall, however, the liquidity of the market is shown to worsen when dual trading is permitted. Fishman & Longstaff [1992] investigate this issue empirically using futures market data and find that dual traders do better than brokers who do not dual trade. Chang & Locke [1992] also address this issue extensively using evidence from the eurodollar futures markets.

The role of the block trader is also of obvious importance in understanding the behavior of security markets and prices. Block trades (or orders for more

[11] This issue of stability is addressed further in other chapers of this handbook, see Kleidon [1995].

than 10,000 shares) accounted for more than 50% of NYSE volume in 1990 (see Keim & Madhavan [1993] for discussion). Most of these trades involve an entirely different trading mechanism involving the services of a block trader, or 'upstairs' market maker, who forms a syndicate to buy or sell the desired quantity. Once the syndicate is assembled, the trade is then crossed on the floor of the exchange.

This block syndication process raises a number of interesting questions relating to the optimality of this trading mechanism vis a vis the more standard 'downstairs' specialist market. Burdett & O'Hara [1987] analyze the block trader's optimal strategy and show how information on the very existence of a block trade can have price effects on the stock. They determine the factors affecting the decision of the block trader to continue searching for additional syndicate participants or to end the process by buying the remaining shares. Seppi [1990] examines the question of why traders might prefer to trade blocks rather than break orders into smaller trades. He concentrates on analyzing the ability of block traders to contract on trader behavior subsequent to the block trade. Grossman [1991] considers informational differences between the 'upstairs' and 'downstairs' markets. This research suggests that the block trading mechanism may allow uninformed traders to minimize the adverse selection costs faced in trading large orders.

One market structure issue that will undoubtedly be the focus of much future research is the trend toward greater automation in the trading mechanism [see Domowitz, 1990]. If trading shifts from the traditional specialist mechanism to an electronic clearing framework, then the exact clearing rules of the mechanism will affect the resulting stochastic process of prices. These trading rules typically involve the ability to use alternative order structures, and hence, we consider this order form issue in more detail.

4.2. Order form

A feature of most microstructure models considered thus far is that orders are assumed to be for immediate execution.[12] While such 'market orders' are indeed found in actual markets, this focus is far too restrictive; many other order forms exist and are widely used in trading venues. These orders can range from simple 'limit orders' specifying a price (better than the current quote) at which the trade should execute and 'stop loss orders' dictating a price (below the current price) at which the stock is to be sold, to more esoteric 'market at close' or 'fill or kill' orders. What is significant about each of these alternative trade forms is that they are all contingent orders, providing for execution only if a prespecified event occurs.

This contingent feature introduces a number of important complexities into the trading process. By allowing traders to link execution with future events, such orders allow traders greater control over their trading behavior. But this also greatly complicates the link between traders' demands and market behavior.

[12] An exception is the Kyle [1989] model which considers only limit orders, but in that one-period model there is no specialist, or bid–ask spread.

For example, limit orders allow traders to provide liquidity to the market and thus compete with the market maker, while stop orders permit traders to take liquidity from the market and hence, force the market maker to accommodate their trades. Consequently, such order strategies affect the price-setting problem faced by the market maker, dictating that the behavior of security prices may be greatly affected by the types of orders permitted in a market.

Because of the complexity of these orders, early work on the role of order form focused on the symmetric information case. For example, Cohen, Maier, Schwartz & Whitcomb [1981] developed a 'gravitational pull' model of trader order strategy in which the certain execution of the market order dominated the uncertain execution of a limit order over some price ranges. Similarly, O'Hara & Oldfield [1986] considered the supply and demand information that the book of limit orders provides to the market maker. But neither analysis considered how the book and hence, market prices are affected if there can be private information, nor did they examine the price adjustment or efficiency effects associated with alternative order arrangements.

This interaction of the book and prices was examined by Rock [1991]. In his model, the book is formed of limit orders submitted by risk neutral uninformed traders. The market maker, who is risk averse, posts bid and ask prices and thus essentially competes with the orders in the book. But in this competition the market maker has a distinct advantage: he knows the size of the trade. Since a large order is more likely to be information-related, the market maker can forego such trades and leave them to the book. This adverse selection problem results in orders on the book losing money since the market maker preempts profitable trades. What allows the book to survive in the Rock framework is the inventory exposure of the market maker. Since the specialist is risk averse, he may forego profitable but inconvenient trades because of his risk exposure, thus allowing the limit order traders to profit.

This adverse selection problem between the market maker and the book highlights an important facet of the role of order form in the trading mechanism. With the advent of electronic trading systems and clearing networks, the issue of trade priority and who has access to trade information has become (and will continue to be) an important issue.[13] A related issue is the effect that alternative order forms have on market performance. The rise of mechanistic trading strategies (such as portfolio insurance) coupled with the ability to electronically transmit orders has magnified the importance of price-contingent orders.

These market performance effects of price-contingent orders are examined by Easley & O'Hara [1991]. Their model analyzes the market maker's price-setting problem in a world of private information when traders can use either market orders or stop orders. Because a stop order specifies a price at which a security is to be sold, these orders are typically used by uninformed traders seeking to limit losses on their portfolio. Easley & O'Hara demonstrate that the diversion of uninformed orders to this alternative order form increases the informativeness of

[13] See Glosten [1991b] for an analysis of an electronic trading mechanism.

the market order stream. Consequently, if the market maker knows which orders are stops and which are markets, he sets a larger spread and adjusts prices faster than if price-contingent orders were not allowed. Perhaps more intriguing, if the composition of orders is not known, then uncertainty over order type reduces the variance of prices but with a corresponding loss in price informativeness.

This ability of alternative order forms to change the stochastic process of prices raises a number of important issues for researchers. One such issue concerns the effects of the more commonly used limit orders on price behavior. While Rock's model is suggestive, there has not yet been an analysis of limit orders in a dynamic context. Hence, how limit orders affect the adjustment of prices to information is not apparent. A second issue concerns the relation of order form and market stability. In the Easley & O'Hara model, the sequence property of price-contingent orders increases the probability of episodic large price movements, even though the price variance of the overall price process is decreased. They note that such behavior is consistent with empirical properties of the market surrounding the crash in 1987. Several researchers [Grossman, 1988; Gennotte & Leland, 1990; Jacklin, Kleidon & Pfleiderer, 1992] have also argued that order strategies were at least partially to blame for market performance at this time. The appropriate regulatory response in light of this finding has been an issue addressed by several researchers.

These observations suggests that policy issues may be the focus of much future research in microstructure. While there is a large body of theoretical research in the literature, much of it is directed toward investigating general properties of security market equilibrium. What is not yet well developed are analyses of how markets should be structured given the important effects on welfare that can arise from market behavior. This issue will doubtless benefit from increased scrutiny by market microstructure researchers.[14]

4.3. Multi-market behavior

A third, but by no means final, area in which research is currently being conducted is on the linkages between markets. Most analyses of microstructure issues have focused on the behavior of a market maker acting in a single market setting. But this characterization is clearly limited. Both equities and futures routinely trade in multiple locations, and the behavior of derivatives (such as baskets and options) surely cannot be viewed in isolation from their underlying securities.

Viewing the trading process in multiple venues introduces a number of important dimensions to microstructure research. The role of liquidity, for example, becomes fundamental to both the behavior or prices and the viability of the market.[15] Pagano [1989] considers the questions of whether multiple markets can exist given that liquidity is an increasing function of scale. His model abstracts

[14] For example, Admati & Pfleiderer [1991] discuss sunshine trading, and Lee, Ready & Seguin [1992] examine trading halts.

[15] See Grossman & Miller [1988] for a model of liquidity when information is symmetric.

from information and instead focuses on the role of traders' expectations of other traders' actions in affecting market behavior. He shows that in the absence of some impediment to trade a two-market equilibrium will not generally exist. If there are transaction costs, however, then for some traders the ability to transact in a deeper but more expensive market may dominate a cheaper but illiquid setting. Chowdry & Nanda [1991] examine similar issues in a model with asymmetric information.

Subrahmanyan [1991a] examines the related question of whether traders will concentrate in a basket of securities or trade the underlying securities. His analysis demonstrates that liquidity traders may benefit from trading in the basket if it allows them to avoid the detrimental effects of private information on individual security values. But the basket security does allow traders to transact based on systematic information, and hence, it is not immediately obvious what equilibrium will arise, making policy comparison between markets difficult.

If multiple markets do exist, then the linkages between them are clearly important. Kumar & Seppi [1990] analyze a model of a security market and a futures market trading index futures on the securities. Their analysis focuses on the differences in information flows between markets when there may be lags in observing prices in the other markets. Their analysis provides the interesting result that the existence of index arbitrageurs can actually reduce market liquidity because the market makers increase the spread to offset their losses to these agents who know more than they do. Clearly more research is need to fully document the effects of market linkages on price and trader behavior.

An interesting issue to consider in future research is the differential learning that alternative market settings permit market participants. An emerging, and potentially important, literature has considered the role of 'price discovery' in securities markets [see Leach & Madhaven, 1993]. In the context considered here, such price discovery could arise if price patterns in one market are informative about future price behavior in another market. Subrahmanyan's paper suggests that if agents have symmetric access to both systematic and idiosyncratic information then in his two market model neither market can act as a dominant price discovery venue. Whether this holds more generally is of obvious importance.

5. Conclusions and future research

What then remains for future research in market microstructure? The research conducted in the last decade has provided a wealth of knowledge and insight both into the behavior of markets and into the more fundamental issues of price formation and behavior. But while much has been gleaned, much remains to be learned. In this concluding section, we discuss our view of at least some of the issues likely to be important over the next decade of microstructure research. As will be apparent, despite the recent plethora of research in market microstructure, much of the important work in this research area remains to be done, suggesting that market microstructure issues will remain the dominant research agenda in finance over the next decade.

One area of unquestioned importance is the development of more general microstructure models. The seeming abundance of theoretical work aside, the extant models suffer from a lack of generality. The Kyle model, despite supporting almost a cottage industry of microstructure researchers, is still essentially an example. And, as greater generality is added to that model, the work of Holden & Subrahmanyan, Spiegel & Subrahmanyan and others suggests that the robustness of its results is questionable. A similar criticism can be directed at the sequential trade framework, where deviations from its basic probabilistic structure are not easily incorporated.

In both models, one obvious difficulty is the exclusion of any role for inventory effects. In earlier microstructure research, a wide variety of price phenomena could be related to the risk exposure inventory imposed on the market maker. But the focus on information issues dictated a parsimony to models achievable only by restricting their domain. The result is a schizophrenia in the literature where inventory models generally assume risk averse specialists while information models assume risk neutral ones. Certainly, this dichotomy is neither accurate nor acceptable. What is needed are models capable of incorporating not only both information and inventory, but their interaction as well.

Yet, while this is an obvious direction for future work, it is not an easy one. The multi-period analyses of market behavior with inventory such as Amihud & Mendelson [1980] and Ho & Stoll [1981] proved remarkably complex even in the absence of information considerations. A definitive multi-period model incorporating all dimensions of the dealer's problem is not likely to be feasible in the near future.

A second, and related, area where researchers have much to contribute is in defining the important link between the theoretical models of market behavior and the empirical or statistical properties of security prices. While models of price formation abound, there has as yet been little testing of these models, or even development of formal hypotheses for price behavior. Yet it is precisely here that microstructure research should have much to offer. The statistical properties of asset prices form the basis of most finance and accounting research. The power of microstructure models is that they should provide predictions for the resulting stochastic process of prices. Such predictions could indicate, for example, the variance process characterizing security prices or the serial correlation properties of prices, topics clearly of interest to empirical researchers.

Perhaps equally important, investigating the statistical predictions of models provides a way to determine the validity or at least usefulness of theoretical models. To date, the development of theoretical models has not yet progressed to the point where we can reject models or even evaluate their significance. If our theoretical models are to be more than arcane exercises, it must be because they provide predictive ability for the behavior of security prices or markets. In the absence of this, microstructure models may be useful descriptors, but will never attain the power of explaining market behavior.

It is in this direction that our own research is directed. We are investigating the statistical properties of security prices, quotes, and volume with the hope of providing testable hypotheses for their behavior.[16] Because our models of dealer behavior dictate the resulting stochastic process of prices, it is possible to recover the theoretical factors determining price behavior. And this, in turn, allows for testing of the model. It is likely that our current models will 'fail' in the sense of having little predictive power or marginal statistical significance. But it is only through the process of establishing this that the value of microstructure models of price formation can be determined.

A third, and perhaps the most important, direction for future microstructure research lies in greater empirical investigations of price and market behavior. It may seem surprising that we conclude a review of theoretical work with a discussion of the importance of empirical work. But the recent availability of intraday data on dealers' prices, quotes, inventories and order flows provides enormous potential for important discoveries. A promising start illustrating this can be found in recent work by Madhaven & Smidt [1991, 1992] and Hasbrouck & Sofianos [1992]. Their research looking at the empirical behavior of dealer's prices, quotes, and inventories suggests a complexity to market behavior not yet captured by existing theoretical models.

The ability to track the effects of different types of orders, to measure the incorporation of information into prices on a trade-by-trade or even minute-by-minute basis, to investigate how different order strategies affect the process of prices, and to control for factors such as bid–ask bounce means that researchers can devise better methods to test economic phenomena. And this suggests that future empirical research in virtually every area of finance will be affected by microstructure factors. Moreover, the increasing availability of international data of similar quality provides unprecedented ability to investigate empirical phenomena in alternative settings. These developments dictate that market microstructure research will have an applicability and importance far beyond its current state.

Acknowledgements

We would like to thank Craig Holden, Ananth Madhavan, Ailsa Roell, Matthew Spiegel, and S. Viswanathan for helpful comments.

References

Admati, A., and P. Pfleiderer (1988). A Theory of intraday patterns: Volume and price variability. *Rev. Financ. Studies* 1, Spring, 3–40.

Admati, A., and P. Pfleiderer (1989). Divide and conquer: A theory of intraday and day-of-the-week mean effects. *Rev. Financ. Studies* 2, 189–224.

[16] The role of volume is a subject of much recent work. Gallant, Rossi & Tauchen [1992] provide an excellent statistical analysis of volume, while Kim & Verrechia [1990] and Blume, Easley & O'Hara [1993] provide theoretical analysis of this variable.

Admati, A., and P. Pfleiderer (1991). Sunshine trading and financial market equilibrium. *Rev. Financ. Studies*, 4(3), 443–482.

Akerlof, G. (1970). The market for lemons: Qualitative uncertainty and the market mechanism. *Q. J. Econ.* 89, 488–500.

Amihud, Y., and H. Mendelson (1980). Dealership market: Market making with inventory. *J. Financ. Econ.* 8, 31–53

Bagehot, W. (pseud) (1971). The only game in town. *Financ. Anal. J.* 27, 12–14, 22.

Back, K. (1992). Insider trading in continuous time. *Rev. Financ. Studies*, 5(3), 387–410.

Bhattacharya, U., and M. Spiegel (1991). Insiders, outsiders, and market breakdowns. *Rev. Financ. Studies* 4, 255–282.

Blume, L., M.M. Bray and D. Easley (1982). Introduction to the stability of rational expectations equilibria. *J. Econ. Theory* 26, 313–317.

Blume, L., and D. Easley (1990). Implementation of Walrasian expectations equilibria. *J. Econ. Theory* 51, 207–227.

Blume, L., and D. Easley (1992). What has the rational learning literature taught us?, in: A. Kirman and M. Salmon (eds.), *Essays in Learning and Rationality in Economics*, Basil Blackwell Press.

Blume, L., Easley, D. and M. O'Hara (1993). Market statistics and technical analysis: The role of volume, forthcoming.

Burdett, K., and M. O'Hara (1987). Building blocks: An introduction to block trading. *J. Banking Finance* 11, 193–212.

Chang, E.C., and P.R. Locke (1992). The performance and market impact of dual trading: Re CME Rule 552, working paper, CFTC.

Chowdry, B., and V. Navda (1991). Multi-market trading and market liquidity. *Rev. Financ. Studies*, 4(3), 483–512.

Cohen, K., S. Maier, R. Schwartz, and D. Whitcomb (1981). Transaction costs, order placement strategy, and existence of the bid–ask spread. *J. Polit. Econ.* 89, 287–305.

Copeland, T., and D. Galai (1983). Information effects and the bid–ask spread. *J. Finance* 38, 1457–1469.

Demsetz, H. (1968). The cost of transacting. *Q. J. Econ.* 82, 33–53.

Diamond, D.W., and R.E. Verrechia (1987). Constraints on short-selling and asset price adjustments to private information. *J. Financ. Econ.* 18, 277–311.

Domowitz, I. (1990). The mechanics of automated trade execution. *J. Financ. Intermed.* 1, 167–194.

Easley, D., and M. O'Hara (1987). Price, trade size, and information in securities markets. *J. Financ. Econ.* 19, 69–90.

Easley, D., and M. O'Hara (1991). Order form and information in securities markets. *J. Finance* 46, 905–927.

Easley, D., and M. O'Hara (1992a). Time and the process of security price adjustment. *J. Finance*, 47(2), 577–607.

Easley, D., and M. O'Hara (1992b). Adverse selection and large trade volume: The implications for market efficiency. *J. Financ. Quant. Anal.* 27, 185–208.

Fishman, M., and F. Longstaff (1992). Dual trading in futures markets. *J. Finance*, 47(2), 643–672.

Forster, M., and T. George (1992). Anonymity in securities markets. *J. Financ. Intermed.* 2(2), 168–206.

Foster, F.D., and S. Viswanathan (1990). A theory of the intraday variations in volume, variance and trading costs in securities markets. *Rev. Financ. Studies* 3.

Foster, F.D., and S. Viswanathan (1993). The effect of public information and competition on trading volume and volatility. *Rev. Financ. Studies*, 6(1), 23–56.

French, K.R., and R. Roll (1986). Stock return variances: The arrival of information and the reaction of traders. *J. Financ. Econ.* 17, 5–26.

Gallant, A.R., P.E. Rossi and G. Tauchen (1992). Stock prices and volume. *Rev. Financ. Studies*, 5(2) 199–242.

Gammill, J.F. (1989). The organization of financial markets: Competitive versus cooperative market mechanisms, working paper 90–010, Harvard University.

Garman, M. (1976). Market microstructure. *J. Financ. Econ.* 3, 257–275.

Gennotte, G., and H. Leland (1990). Market liquidity, hedges and crashes. *Am. Econ. Rev.* 80, 999–1021.

Glosten, L. (1989). Insider trading, liquidity, and the role of the monopolist specialist. *J. Bus.* 62, 211–236.

Glosten, L. (1991a). Asymmetric information, the third market and investor welfare, working paper, Graduate School of Business, Columbia University.

Glosten, L. (1991b). The inevitability and resilience of an electronic open limit order book, working paper, Graduate School of Business, Columbia University.

Glosten, L., and P. Milgrom (1985). Bid, ask, and transaction prices in a specialist market with heterogeneously informed traders. *J. Financ. Econ.* 13, 71–100.

Grossman, S.J. (1988). An analysis of the implications for stock and futures: Price volatility of program trading and dynamic hedging strategies. *J. Bus.* 61, 275–298.

Grossman, S. J. (1991). The informational content of upstairs and downstairs trading, working paper, Wharton School.

Grossman, S.J., and M.H. Miller (1988). Liquidity and market structure. *J. Finance* 43, 617–633.

Grossman, S.J., and J.E. Stiglitz (1980). On the impossibility of informationally efficient markets. *Am. Econ. Rev.* 70, 393–408.

Hasbrouck, J., and G. Sofianos (1992). The trades of market-makers: An analysis of NYSE specialists, working paper, The New York Stock Exchange.

Hindy, A. (1991). An equilibrium model of futures markets dynamics, working paper, Sloan School of Management, Massachusetts Institute of Technology.

Ho, T, and H. Stoll (1981). Optimal dealer pricing under transactions and return uncertainty. *J. Financ. Econ.* 9, 47–73.

Holden, C., and M. Bagnoli (1992). Toward a general theory of market making, working paper, Indiana University.

Holden, C.W., and A. Subrahmanyam (1992). Long-lived private information and imperfect competition. *J. Finance* 47, 247–270.

Jacklin, C.J., A.W. Kleidon and P. Pfleiderer (1992). Underestimation of portfolio insurance and the crash of October 1987. *Rev. Financ. Studies* 5, 35–63.

Jain, P.C., and G.-H. Joh (1988). The dependence between hourly prices and trading volume. *J. Financ. Quant. Anal.* 23, 269–284.

Jordan, J. (1982). The generic existence of rational expectations equilibria in the higher dimensional case. *J. Econ. Theory* 26, 224–243.

Jordan, J., and R. Radner (1982). Rational expectations in microeconomic models: An overview. *J. Econ. Theory* 26, 201–223.

Keim, D. B., and A. Madhavan (1993). The upstairs market for large block transactions: Analysis and measurement of price effects, working paper, Wharton School.

Kim, O., and R.E. Verrecchia (1990). Trading volume and price reactions to public announcements, working paper, Wharton School.

Kleidon, A.W. (1995). Stock market crashes, in: R. Jarrow, V. Maksimovic and W.T. Ziemba (eds.), *Finance*, Handbooks in Operations Research and Management Science, Vol 9, Elsevier, Amsterdam, pp. 465–496 (this volume).

Kumar, P., and D. Seppi (1990). Information and index arbitrage, working paper, University of Pennsylvania.

Kyle, A.S. (1984). Market structure, information, futures markets, and price formation, in: G. Story, A. Schmitz and A. Sarris (eds.), *International Agricultural Trade: Advanced Readings in Price Formation, Market Structure, and Price Instability*, Westview Press, Boulder and London.

Kyle, A.S. (1985). Continuous auctions and insider trading. *Econometrica* 53, 1315–1336.

Kyle, A.S. (1989). Informed speculation with imperfect competition. *Rev. Econ. Studies* 56, 317–355.

Leach, J.C., and A.N. Madhavan (1993). Price experimentation and security market structure. *Rev. Financ. Studies*, 6(2) 375–405.
Lee, C.M.C. (1993). Market integration and price execution for NYSE-listed securities. *J. Finance*, 48(3) 1009–1038.
Lee, C.M.C., M.J. Ready and P.J. Sequin (1992). Volume, volatility and NYSE trading halts, working paper, University of Michigan.
Lindsay, R. (1990). Market makers, asymmetric information and price formation, working paper, Hass School of Management, University of California at Berkeley.
Lo, A.W., and A.C. MacKinlay (1988). Stock market prices do not follow random walks: Evidence from a simple specification test. *Rev. Financ. Studies* 1, 3–40.
Madhavan, A. (1992). Trading mechanisms in security markets. *J. Finance*, 47(2), 607–642.
Madhaven, A., and S. Smidt (1991). A Bayesian model of intraday specialist pricing. *J. Financ. Econ.*, 30, 99–134.
Madhaven, A., and S. Smidt (1992). An analysis of daily changes in specialists inventories and quotations, working paper, Wharton School.
McInish, T.H., and R.A. Wood (1992). Price discovery, volume, and regional/third market trading, working paper, Memphis State University.
Milgrom, P., and N. Stokey (1982). Information, trade, and common knowledge. *J. Econ. Theory* 26, 17–27.
O'Hara, M., and G. Oldfield (1986). The microeconomics of market making. *J. Financ. Quant. Anal.* December, 361–376.
Pagano, M. (1989). Trading volume and asset liquidity. *Q. J. Econ.* May, 255–274.
Pagano, M., and A. Roell (1992). Transparency and liquidity: A comparison of auction and dealer markets with informed trading, LSE Financial Markets Group Discussion paper No. 150.
Radner, R. (1979). Rational expectations equilibrium: Generic existence and the information revealed by price. *Econometrica* 47, 655–678.
Roell, A. (1990). Dual-capacity trading and the quality of the market. *J. Financ. Intermed.* 1, 105–124.
Rock, K. (1991). The specialist's order book. *Rev. Financ. Studies*.
Seppi, D. (1990). Equilibrium block trading and asymmetric information. *J. Finance* 45, 73–94.
Spiegel, M., and A. Subrahmanyan (1992). Informed speculation and hedging in a non competitive securities market. *Rev. Financ. Studies*, 5(2), 307–329.
Stoll, H. (1978). The supply of dealer services in securities markets. *J. Finance* 33, 1133–1151.
Stoll, H. (1990). Principles of trading market structure, working paper 90-31, Owen Graduate School, Vanderbilt University.
Subrahmanyam, A. (1991a). A theory of trading in stock index futures. *Rev. Financ. Studies* 4, 17–52.
Subrahmanyam, A. (1991b). Risk aversion, market liquidity, and price efficiency. *Rev. Financ. Studies* 4(3), 417–442.
Working, H. (1953). Futures trading and hedging. *Am. Econ. Rev.* 43, 314–343.

R. Jarrow et al., Eds., *Handbooks in OR & MS, Vol. 9*

Chapter 13

Financial Decision-Making in Markets and Firms: A Behavioral Perspective

Werner F.M. De Bondt
School of Business, University of Wisconsin, Madison, WI 53705, U.S.A.

Richard H. Thaler
Graduate School of Business, University of Chicago, Chicago, IL 60637, U.S.A.

The economist may attempt to ignore psychology, but it is sheer impossibility for him to ignore human nature. . . . If the economist borrows his conception of man from the psychologist, his constructive work may have some chance of remaining purely economic in character. But if he does not, he will not thereby avoid psychology. Rather, he will force himself to make his own, and it will be bad psychology.

— John Maurice Clark, *Economics and Modern Psychology*, Journal of Political Economy, 1918, Vol. 26, p. 4.

1. Introduction

Financial economics is, perhaps, the least behavioral of the various subdisciplines of economics. In other areas, what people actually do is, if not in the foreground, at least part of the picture. Labor economists investigate how people choose where to work and how much education to obtain. In public finance there is concern about how taxpayers respond to changes in the law. Even in macroeconomics, analyses of consumption and saving start with people making choices. In contrast, in finance, we simply insist that, whatever people do, they do it right. People optimize but otherwise their behavior is like a black box. The finance literature reveals little interest in investor decision processes or in the quality of judgment. As a result, it is nearly devoid of 'people'.[1]

It has not always been this way. Earlier generations of economists such as Irving Fisher, John Maynard Keynes, and Benjamin Graham (as well as many others, see Loewenstein & Elster [1992, chapter 1]) put great emphasis on the fallible nature of human decision-making. Modern finance replaces these realistic characterizations of human conduct with representative agent models in which

[1] Indeed, successful finance texts such as Brealey & Myers [1988] or, at the doctoral level, Ingersoll [1987] do not even list an index entry for 'investor psychology'. However, Brealey and Myers consider the question of 'How are major financial decisions made?' as one of ten major 'unsolved problems that seem ripe for productive research' [p. 883].

everyone in the economy is assumed to be as smart as Sandy Grossman and everyone looks toward the future in a way that would make econometricians proud.[2] Most economists readily agree that the behavior of the people they observe most often (e.g., their spouses, colleagues, and Deans) does not fit this model. Yet, the rational agent paradigm endures. Why?

There are two standard justifications for retaining the assumption of universal rationality. The first, often attributed to Milton Friedman [1953], is the 'as if' defense. Although a baseball outfielder cannot solve the set of differential equations necessary to compute where a fly ball will land, he nonetheless can run to exactly the right place to catch it. He acts 'as if' he could solve the problem. Friedman argues that theories should be judged not on the basis of their assumptions but rather on the validity of their predictions. Theory unavoidably involves simplification! Although we are happy to accept this criterion for evaluating theories, we do not find the evidence of great comfort.[3] Firms pay dividends. Closed-end funds sell at prices that diverge from net asset value. Most stock portfolios are actively managed even though portfolio managers typically underperform index funds. Stock returns run in seasonal patterns and are more predictable than anyone ever suspected, even five years ago. And, of course, on October 19, 1987 prices fell over 20% on a day in which the only financial news was the crash itself.[4]

With facts such as these, it may be time to have another look at the assumptions. A close look does suggest problems. Over the past twenty years, psychologists (most notably Daniel Kahneman and Amos Tversky) have found again and again that the usual axioms of finance theory (expected utility theory; risk aversion; Bayesian updating; rational expectations) are descriptively false. For example, people display overconfidence in their own judgment, and they make decisions that depend as much on how a problem is 'framed' as on its objective payoffs. Importantly, deviations from the normative model are systematic. Therefore, they do not disappear with simple aggregation.

The second line of defense relies on market forces. In competitive markets, the argument goes, irrational agents lose their wealth and go out of business, or somehow are rendered irrelevant by smart arbitrageurs who jump in to exploit the opportunities created by irrationality. In financial markets, where

[2] Emphasizing its normative appeal, Herbert Simon [1983] calls this vision of rationality the 'Olympian model'. It 'serves, perhaps, as a model of the mind of God, but certainly not as a model of the mind of man' [p. 34]. Hayek [1948] traces the Olympian model back to Descartes' *Discourse on Method*. He contrasts the 'false' Cartesian view with the antirationalistic approach of 18th century English individualism (e.g., Adam Smith, Edmund Burke, or Bernard Mandeville) which regards man as a '...fallible being, whose individual errors are corrected only in the course of a social process' [pp. 8–9]. (These and other concepts of rationality are discussed in Elster [1979, 1983, 1989].)

[3] Indeed, we have heard the following joke: finance consists of theories for which there is no evidence and empirical facts for which there is no theory.

[4] French & Roll [1986] and Roll [1988] provide more systematic evidence suggesting that the stock market 'has a life of its own'. Romer [1993] offers two rational interpretations of price movements without news.

stakes are large and transactions costs small, this argument is thought to have special force.[5]

One way to investigate this issue carefully is to construct models with two kinds of agents, some fully rational and some less so (i.e., quasi-rational or noise traders) [see, e.g., De Long, Shleifer, Summers & Waldmann, 1990a, and Russell & Thaler, 1985]. What are the conditions for market prices to be identical to what they would be if all agents were rational? One needs: (1) a date T at which the true value becomes known; (2) costless short-selling over a period long enough to include T; (3) investors with time horizons that include T; (4) not 'too many' quasi-rational traders; (5) short selling by rational traders only.[6] These conditions are not likely to be met. Thus, the simple point is that, even if price diverges from intrinsic value, that fact does not always per se create an arbitrage opportunity [see also Black, 1986; and Shleifer & Summers, 1990].

It is similarly dangerous to argue that irrational investors necessarily lose wealth over time when interacting with rational traders.[7] De Long, Shleifer, Summers & Waldmann [1990b, 1991] show that, in some circumstances, noise traders may actually earn higher returns than rational traders. Since they do so by unintentionally bearing more risk, the noise traders have lower expected utility but higher wealth. Also, rational people may have an incentive to join the crowd rather than to go against it. In general, evolutionary forces tend to be slow in their effects, so even if noise traders do earn lower expected returns, they will still affect asset prices.

As is true in other branches of economics, the problems with modern finance theory are created by its presumed dual purpose, characterizing optimal choice and describing actual choice. The validity of the theory for the first purpose is not in question. However, since it is assumed that actual people do optimize (or behave as if they did), the theories are also thought to be good descriptive models. Of course, if people fail to optimize, this is not the case.[8] The solution is to retain the normative status of optimization (e.g., teach students to maximize expected utility and to use Bayes' rule) but develop explicitly descriptive models of behavior in markets and organizations. We call this effort behavioral finance.

[5] Graham & Dodd [1934] give color to this question by asking whether the stock market is 'a *weighing machine*, on which the value of each issue is recorded by an exact and impersonal mechanism' or a '*voting machine*, whereon countless individuals register choices which are the product partly of reason and partly of emotion' [p. 27].

[6] This last condition is necessary because, if quasi-rational traders are allowed to sell short, no equilibrium exists.

[7] In other words, here rationality is seen as evolutionary adaptation and 'it isn't important *how* people go about making decisions' (Simon, 1983, p. 38). The fact itself that people survive is sufficient proof that they make rational decisions. See Lucas [1986].

[8] In some cases, the axioms of rationality are 'too strong'. While they describe what a well-informed investor may want to do, bounded rationality prevents maximizing agents from taking truly optimal decisions. In other circumstances, the reverse problem occurs. That is, the standard axioms are 'too weak'. For instance, Kreps [1990] makes the case for bounded rationality and retrospection based on the observation that important problems in game theory have many Nash equilibria and the theory 'isn't any help' (p. 97) in choosing between them.

This paper provides a selective review of recent work in behavioral finance.[9] Our goal is a modest one. We wish to establish that the optimal quantity of research on this topic is strictly positive. Consistent with this limited goal, we believe that the assumptions and results of modern finance are often adequate and that many aspects of the perfect markets–perfect people approach should be retained. For example, the assumptions that the typical investor in the stock market is motivated by self-interest and prefers more wealth to less even when wealth is very large (nonsatiation) are good first approximations, even if some investors have a preference for politically correct portfolios and if some wealthy people give away large sums of money. Similarly, the Black–Scholes formula serves admirably well both as a characterization of option prices in a rational world and as a description of actual prices. (Notice that the conditions for a rational equilibrium described above are met in this case.) Nevertheless, exploring the implications of psychology for financial markets does offer the promise of helping us understand aspects of finance that appear puzzling within the standard paradigm.

To some, it will seem that the introduction of psychological factors conflicts with 'good' economic theory and that it is merely a clever way to introduce free parameters. Cochrane [1991], for instance, states that 'the central problem for fad models' is overcoming the charge that 'they are just a catchy name for a residual' [p. 480].[10] Not surprisingly, we disagree. Following Akerlof [1984], our view of good theory is that 'it poses interesting "if . . . then" propositions relevant to some economic issue' [p. 3]. This maxim does not rule out unconventional assumptions and, certainly, the research in behavioral finance has not been criticized for boredom! Miller [1986a] argues instead that behavioral finance is 'too interesting and thereby distracts us from the pervasive market forces that should be our principal concern' [p. 283].

The problem with the 'lack-of-discipline' criticism is that it is applied asymmetrically. Of course, free parameters can be used to shore up any theory. But rational models are not immune to this disease. Rationality itself is often ill-defined and does not impose enough discipline.[11] Furthermore, skillful theorists can rationalize almost any empirical fact, a practice Fama [1991, p. 1593] refers to as 'model dredging'. In an important sense, therefore, behavioral research is more disciplined than the rational paradigm. At least, it wants to start the analysis with assumptions that are approximately true! That is, the basic building blocks of new theory must derive empirical and experimental support from our sister social sciences. As stated eloquently by John Maurice Clark, our constructive theoretical work thereby retains a chance 'of remaining purely economic in character'. In this chapter, we hope to show that a concern with the quality of financial decision-making can produce many interesting, relevant, and refutable theories.

[9] For a collection of relevant papers, see Thaler [1993].

[10] Presumably, the same perspective leads Schwert to ask, in his discussion of the small firm effect, that new theory 'be developed that is consistent with rational maximizing behavior on the part of *all* actors in the model' [1983, p. 10, our emphasis].

[11] As Arrow [1986] points out, rationality per se does not yield much predictive power. The rational paradigm often derives its predictions from subsidiary assumptions such as homogeneity.

2. Micro-foundations of behavioral finance: a sampler

Although modern finance typically makes predictions about market outcomes and the behavior of firms, there is an underlying set of assumptions about individual behavior that are used to derive these predictions. Specifically, people are said to be risk averse expected utility maximizers and unbiased Bayesian forecasters. In other words, agents make rational choices based on rational expectations. This set of assumptions can be criticized on two counts: 1. some assumptions are false, e.g., people violate the substitution axiom of expected utility theory; 2. the set is incomplete. That is, the theory has little to say about important aspects of economic behavior such as the role of social norms. Thus, to make progress, one needs to better characterize behavior in the usual domains of finance theory (e.g., portfolio selection) and to enrich the theory to incorporate new domains upon which finance has been silent. Efforts along these lines are made both by behavioral economists and by other social scientists, especially psychologists and sociologists. Of course, we cannot adequately summarize this work in this chapter. Instead, we offer a selection of behavioral concepts that we find most useful to finance.[12]

2.1. Overconfidence

Perhaps the most robust finding in the psychology of judgment is that people are overconfident [e.g., Lichtenstein, Fischhoff & Phillips, 1982]. One manifestation of this phenomenon is that people overestimate the reliability of their knowledge. When people say that they are 90% sure that an event will happen or that a statement is true, they may only be correct 70% of the time. Similarly, elicited confidence limits are too narrow. People also overestimate their abilities. One famous finding is that 90% of the automobile drivers in Sweden consider themselves 'above average' [Svenson, 1981]. Comparable results occur for other traits: nearly all people consider themselves above average in their ability to get along with others. A specific finding of relevance to finance is that the degree of overconfidence varies across domains. People are more confident of their predictions in fields where they have self-declared expertise, holding their actual predictive ability constant [Heath & Tversky, 1991].

2.2. Non-Bayesian forecasting

Are predictions and forecasts made as if people have a working knowledge of Bayes' rule? Numerous studies conclude that the answer to this question is no. Kahneman & Tversky show that, instead of using Bayes' rule, people appear to make probability judgments using similarity or what they call the

[12] More discussion of specific psychological concepts relevant to economics is found in Mitchell [1914], Clark [1918], Hayes [1950], Katona [1951], Slovic [1972], Thaler [1987], and Loewenstein & Elster [1992]. Kahneman, Slovic & Tversky [1982] and Nisbett & Ross [1980] provide a systematic overview of the literature on judgment and decision-making.

'representativeness heuristic'. People evaluate the probability of an uncertain event, or a sample, 'by the degree to which it is: (i) similar in essential properties to its parent population; and (ii) reflects the salient features of the process by which it is generated' [1972, p. 431]. Although the heuristic is generally useful, it can lead to systematic errors. In the context of Bayes' rule, representativeness induces people to give too much weight to recent evidence and too little weight to the base rate or prior odds. For example, subjects were asked to judge from the description of a man whether he was a lawyer or an engineer. Their answers were insensitive to whether they had been told that the description came from a sample with 70% lawyers or 30% lawyers. Grether [1980] obtained similar findings in a design in which subjects had a financial incentive to give correct answers.

Representativeness also leads people to make forecasts that are too extreme, given the predictive value of the available information. Another Kahneman & Tversky [1973] experiment illustrates this finding. Subjects were asked to predict a student's raw grade point average (GPA) using the percentile scores of one of three variables: the student's GPA, the results of a test of mental concentration, and of a test of sense of humor. Since the percentile score for sense of humor is a much worse predictor of raw GPA than the percentile GPA score, subjects should have provided less extreme forecasts when given the former predictor. Instead, the variability of the forecasts was similar in the three cases. The subjects can be said to be 'overreacting' to the data about sense-of-humor.

2.3. Loss aversion, framing, and mental accounting

A strong intuition about preferences is that people treat gains and losses differently and, in particular, that losses loom larger than gains. This intuition was expressed by Markowitz [1952] — who suggested semi-variance might be a better measure of risk than variance — and was formally incorporated into Kahneman and Tversky's prospect theory, a descriptive theory of decision making under uncertainty. In prospect theory the carriers of value are changes in wealth, rather than levels, and negative changes are weighted more heavily than gains. (Empirical tests indicate that losses are weighted about twice as heavily as gains. See Kahneman, Knetsch & Thaler [1990].)

Loss aversion implies that decision-making is sensitive to the description of the action choices, that is, to the way the alternatives are 'framed' [Tversky & Kahneman, 1981]. For example, a store that offers cash customers a discount is less likely to upset its credit card clientele than another store — with the same prices — that imposes a credit card surcharge [Thaler, 1980]. Individuals also have opportunities to create their own frames, a process called mental accounting [Thaler, 1985]. Consider, e.g., an investor holding 1000 shares each of two stocks, both with a current price of $10 per share. One stock was purchased at $5, the other at $13. If the investor contemplates selling the stocks separately he may resist selling the loser because of loss aversion, but if the two transactions are combined, producing a net gain, no loss need be felt. Mental accounting may also be used to mitigate self-control problems, for example by setting up special accounts (e.g., the children's education account) that are considered off-limits to spending urges [Thaler & Shefrin, 1981].

2.4. Fashions and fads

An obvious fact of life is that people are influenced by each other. Twenty years ago, joggers were considered health nuts, mineral water was difficult to find in America, and many people wore bell-bottomed trousers and leisure suits. Fashions change. What we once considered odd or distasteful somehow becomes normal and even desirable. Far from controversial, these remarks would be judged banal in any other field of social science. In economics, however, it is not yet fashionable to discuss fashions.

We will not attempt here to summarize all of sociology and social psychology. It is enough to stress that people are influenced by their social environment and that they often feel pressure to conform [Aronson, 1991]. It is certainly possible to construct models in which such behavior is 'rational' [see, e.g., Bikhchandani, Hirshleifer & Welch, 1992]. Safety-in-numbers is, after all, one reason why animals herd. However, as with other heuristics, herding may also lead people astray, e.g., when they follow a market guru. Regardless, for our purposes, the normative status of this behavior is less important than its pervasiveness. Fashions and fads are as likely to emerge in financial markets as anywhere else.

2.5. Regret, responsibility, and prudence

Regret is the feeling of ex-post remorse about a decision that led to a bad outcome. Even for those trained to differentiate between bad decisions and bad outcomes, it is often difficult not to feel regret after a bad outcome. Regret becomes of interest to theorists if decision-makers take steps to avoid regret [Bell, 1982]. One tactic is to shift the responsibility for a decision onto someone else, i.e., hiring an agent. This introduces what amounts to a negative agency cost. Holding the quality of decisions constant, if the agency relationship reduces the regret felt, the expected utility of the principal rises.

Another way to reduce anticipated regret is to follow standard social and legal norms of 'prudent' decision-making. Regret is larger for an unconventional decision than for a routine one. For example, a portfolio of three large blue chip stocks may be considered more prudent than a portfolio of 30 AMEX companies, regardless of the objective risk characteristics of the two portfolios. Thus, prudence may be relevant for asset pricing. It raises the required return for small firms, especially if they are unsuccessful, but it lowers the return for large well-established corporation and 'glamour stocks' that get favorable news coverage [Shefrin & Statman, 1993b].

3. Investor psychology and market prices

The previous sections have established two necessary conditions for the study of behavioral finance to be interesting and valuable. First, in direct tests, the axioms of rationality upon which modern finance is based are often violated, and the departures are systematic. Second, markets cannot, in general, be relied upon to eliminate traces of irrationality. With this established, where should we expect the new tools to be applied most productively? As suggested by Thomas Kuhn [1970], a reasonable place to start is with the study of anomalies, i.e., empirical facts for which there is wide agreement that the standard paradigm lacks explanatory power.[13] Notice that this strategy is completely in keeping with Friedman's positive approach. If the theory predicts well, we care less about the realism of the assumptions. Therefore, this review emphasizes the anomalous domains where psychology is likely to be useful. In so doing we do not intend to suggest that these domains are the most important, merely that they highlight the potential of a new approach. Conversely, by discussing these limited domains, we do not wish to imply that psychological factors are only present in the periphery but rather that these are situations where the role of psychology is most apparent.

3.1. Trading and active portfolio management

By-and-large, the past literature on capital markets has paid only peripheral attention to trading volume. In rational expectations models, differences in private information may cause disagreement among investors. However, without noise traders (dropped into the model as a deus ex machina), the lack of consensus will not generate trading if rationality is common knowledge [Aumann, 1976; Milgrom & Stokey, 1982]. This is sometimes called the Groucho Marx Theorem. Just as Groucho did not want to join any club that would have him as a member, no rational trader would want to trade with another rational trader (if she is selling, why should I buy?). In reality, many investors 'agree to disagree' and they actively bet on their information. This seems to reflect the belief of investors that they can outwit other market participants. In other words, investors with access to the same information disagree about its proper interpretation [Harris & Raviv, 1992]. While some trading may occur for the purposes of consumption or portfolio rebalancing, it is hard to see how these motives by themselves can produce 200 million shares of daily volume on the NYSE.

The high trading volume on organized exchanges is perhaps the single most embarrassing fact to the standard finance paradigm. Lowenstein [1988] reports

[13] Of course, some 'anomalies' may be statistical illusions, the products of relentless data mining. (Lakonishok & Smidt [1988] and Lo & MacKinlay [1990b] discuss data-snooping.) However, many financial market regularities are observed world-wide. See, e.g., Ziemba [1993] and Hawawini & Keim [1995, chapter 17 of this volume]. Also, some anomalies are confirmed for later time periods. The concept that 'good ideas made public carry the seeds of their own destruction' does not always hold. For instance, Hensel, Sick & Ziemba [1994] find a turn-of-the-month anomaly for stock index futures between 1982 and 1992. Ariel's well-known [1987] study of this effect was based on data for the 1963–1981 period.

that, in 1987, annual market-wide trading costs for S&P companies equalled 17.8% of the annual earnings reported by these firms. It must be stressed that the high volume is not produced by amateur investors. The average turnover rate for institutional investors is much higher than the rate for individuals. Of course, high volume is only one aspect of a more general puzzle. Why are most funds actively managed? It has been known for years [see, e.g., Jensen, 1968, or Ippolito & Turner, 1987] that few active portfolio managers earn returns above the S&P 500, and yet index funds (with lower fees) still garner a modest share of the market.

The key behavioral factor needed to understand the trading puzzle is overconfidence. Overconfidence explains why portfolio managers trade so much, why pension funds hire active equity managers, and why even financial economists often hold actively managed portfolios — they all think they can pick winners. High trading volume and the pursuit of active investment strategies thus seem inconsistent with common knowledge of rationality.[14]

3.2. Contrarian investment strategies

An important tenet of the efficient market hypothesis (EMH) is that one cannot earn abnormal profits by trading on publicly available information. Over the last decade, numerous apparent 'exceptions' to this rule have been documented. Because Hawawini & Keim [1995, chapter 17 of this volume] review the asset pricing anomalies, we focus here on results that fall under the general category of contrarian investment strategies.

At least since the publication of Graham & Dodd's *Security Analysis* [1934], there has been a school of investors who follow value-based investment strategies.[15]

[14] The agency relationship between clients and money managers also plays a role (De Bondt, 1992a). It is difficult to distinguish luck from skill in investment. Merely by chance, there will always be *some* investment advisors who look like true gurus. But representativeness makes it hard to recognize this. Also, clients may *want* to believe that investment advice can be valuable (cognitive dissonance). Either way, money managers are forced to signal competence, e.g., through hard work, elegant presentations, and the employment of celebrated analysts. Most importantly, among themselves, the advisors play a performance ranking game. It is critical that, besides dollar profits, *rank* matters. This rule rewards prudent investing in conventional/fashionable stocks. Also, with frequent evaluation, portfolio insurance and other stop-loss strategies that limit downward risk are seen to fulfill useful roles.

[15] As far as we can determine, the terms 'contrary thinking' or 'contrarian investing' were first popularized by Humphrey Neill [1954]. Neill, in turn, credits William Stanley Jevons with the concept. Jevons stated in his *Primer of Political Economy* that 'in making investments it is foolish to do just what other people are doing, because there almost sure to be too many people doing the same thing' [quoted in Neill, 1985, pp. 64–65].
Traditionally, contrarian investment strategies require much 'patience' and they look for prices to gravitate towards value over a period of several months or years. Below, we narrow our discussion to these longer-term strategies. However, there is also a growing literature on short-term overreaction in stock prices [see, e.g., De Bondt & Thaler, 1989; Jegadeesh, 1990; Lehmann, 1990; Lo & MacKinlay, 1990a] and the overreaction of long-maturity option prices to the implied volatility of short-maturity options [Stein, 1989]. The speculative dynamics of asset price behavior are further discussed in Cutler, Poterba & Summers [1991] and Jegadeesh & Titman [1993].

Presumably, unusual returns could be earned by buying out-of-favor stocks and holding them for the long term. We include in this category companies with low price-earnings (P/E) ratios [Basu, 1977; Jaffe, Keim & Westerfield, 1989], low ratios of market value to book value, and low past returns [De Bondt & Thaler, 1985, 1987].

Graham's original logic for adopting a contrarian strategy was certainly based on psychology. In his view, the prices of out-of-favor firms are irrationally depressed by investors focusing on the here-and-now: 'The market is always making mountains out of molehills and exaggerating ordinary vicissitudes into major setbacks' [1959, p. 110]. Dreman [1982] went further and made explicit use of modern psychology. He argued that P/E ratios can be interpreted as market forecasts of future profit growth. In practice, the forecasts of many investors are naive extrapolations of recent experience. But predicting future profits is difficult. This means that rational earnings forecasts should lie in a narrow range, especially if they are long-term. In fact, the extreme variability of P/E ratios suggests that consistent with representativeness earnings forecasts are systematically too extreme. Interestingly, the data confirm this theory for security analysts [De Bondt & Thaler, 1990]. But, if the bias applies to experts, it seems likely that it also applies to common investors.[16] Thus, too extreme earnings expectations may explain the anomaly that low P/E stocks outperform high P/E companies.

De Bondt & Thaler [1985] extended Dreman's reasoning to predict a new anomaly. We reasoned that, if the excessive optimism or pessimism about future prospects was real, it should be possible to earn excess returns simply by investing in the stocks of companies that had done extremely poorly in past years. In other words, past performance would serve a proxy for investor sentiment. Consistent with this hypothesis, a strategy of buying extreme losers over the past two to five years (the rank period) earns significant excess returns over later years (the test period). Prior losers outperform prior winners by about 8% per year [see also Chopra, Lakonishok & Ritter, 1992].

A common critique of contrarian strategies is that the firms selected are risky rather than undervalued [e.g., Chan, 1988; Ball & Kothari, 1989].[17] Of course, in

[16] Perhaps as a consequence, it is possible to earn abnormal profits by systematically betting against financial analysts' earnings forecasts. See De Bondt [1992b].

[17] A recent paper by Conrad & Kaul [1993] raises two more issues. First, they correctly question De Bondt & Thaler's use of cumulative average returns because these returns assume costless monthly portfolio rebalancing and are not truly obtainable by investors. Buy-and-hold returns are a better performance measure. Second, they claim that much of the return to losers is a low price effect.

The arguments are rebutted by Loughran & Ritter [1994]. As it turns out, the use of buy-and-hold returns increases the performance differential between winners and losers. Second, the relationship between price levels and returns in Conrad & Kaul is largely (although not entirely) due to the confounding of time-series and cross-sectional return patterns. That is, high returns to low-priced stocks occur mostly during the 1930s and 1940s when most stocks had low prices, and the negative returns to high-priced stocks occur during the late 1960s when most stocks had high prices. Thus the low price effect partly reflects mean reversion at the market level. Also, almost all low-priced stocks on the NYSE have been big losers over some prior interval.

principle, one can attribute any apparent abnormal returns to some unmeasured risk factor but this tautological approach does not help. If a strategy is said to be risky, the investors that use it should be exposed to the chance of being worse off. Different methods have been tried to test this explanation. Using capital asset pricing model betas as measures of risk, De Bondt & Thaler [1987] found that during the test period past losers are more risky than winners, though not nearly enough to explain the difference in returns. Furthermore, we found that loser firms only had higher betas in years when the market was rising. Betas in 'up markets' were on average 1.39 while betas in down markets were only 0.88, not an unattractive combination.

In our [1987] paper, we also observed that other contrarian strategies earn excess returns, for instance, buying stocks with low market- to book-value ratios (MVBV) — a result later replicated by Fama & French [1992]. Lakonishok, Shleifer & Vishny [1993] ask whether the apparent predictive power of MVBV-ratios may yet be interpreted as proper compensation for risk. If value-based strategies outperform 'glamour stocks', an interesting question is whether the strategy does poorly at times when the marginal utility of consumption may be expected to be high, i.e., in recessions. As it turns out, value strategies do well even in these 'bad states of the world'.

While traditional risk measures seem unable to explain the success of contrarian investing, risk may yet be an important part of the story. For example, there is no denying that equity risk premia are time-varying. However, we think it essential to distinguish perceived risk from true objective risk [see also Arrow, 1982]. People often misjudge probabilities, e.g., counter to fact, homicides are generally judged more frequent than suicides. Because companies selected by value money managers definitely have the appearance of extreme riskiness (e.g., because of declining earnings or big losses), investing in such companies requires courage and it goes against the consensus summarized in the market price. Unconventional choices repel since investors are aware that they may cause regret. Also, to outsiders, these decisions are likely to look imprudent.[18]

Notice that the mere appearance of imprudence or risk can raise the required rate of return. If, for any reason, investors are reluctant to hold certain assets and if not enough rational traders are willing to step in, then perceived risk and true risk have a similar effect on asset prices. This argument is precisely the same as the ritual disclaimer in finance that all efficient market tests are joint tests with an asset pricing model. While Fama & French [1988] conclude that it may be hopeless to distinguish behavioral from rational explanations of return predictability, we are considerably less pessimistic. A future horse race between models is possible

[18] And 'worldly wisdom teaches that it is better for reputation to fail conventionally than to succeed unconventionally' [Keynes, 1936, p. 158]. Lynch [1990] argues similarly that 'between the chance of making an unusually large profit on an unknown company and the assurance of losing only a small amount on an established company, the normal ... portfolio manager would jump at the latter. ... If IBM goes bad and you bought it, the clients ... will ask "What's wrong with that damn IBM lately?" But if La Quinta Inns goes bad, they'll ask: "What's wrong with you?"' [p. 44]. See also Shefrin & Statman [1993b].

as soon as a behavioral theory of the equilibrium trade-off between return and perceived risk is formulated.

The behavioral explanation for the success of contrarian strategies relies on the combination of biased forecasts of future profit and misperceptions of risk. It is not, however, the case that on a minute-by-minute basis stock prices always overreact. At this time, we do not have a complete psychological theory of the impact of new information on security prices. Underreaction, rather than overreaction, to specific news items is suggested by the literature on the post-earnings announcement drift. Bernard & Thomas [1989, 1990] examine the stock price reaction to quarterly earnings announcements made by publicly-traded companies for the years between 1971 and 1986, in total nearly 90,000 earnings reports. Earnings reports deserve our attention because we want to know whether the market reacts properly to what is likely the most visible piece of company information. Generally, good quarterly earnings news follows good news and bad follows bad. However, after the initial announcement of unusually high earnings, the market is apparently 'surprised' to receive more good news during the next three quarters. Further, while extremely good earnings are rarely matched in the corresponding quarter of the following year, the market appears 'surprised' at that. Thus, on average, the post-earnings announcement return drift lasts for three quarters and then is partially reversed. The abnormal profit that can be obtained by selling 'bad earnings' stocks and buying 'good earnings' stocks is about eight percent per year. It is even more impressive for small companies.

3.3. Asset pricing and investor sentiment

Another tenet of efficient markets is that asset prices are equal to intrinsic value. But this hypothesis is not easy to test because intrinsic value is typically unobservable. The variance bounds tests proposed by Shiller [1981, 1989] — which rely on the contrast between observed market volatility and the variability in the ex-post present value of dividends paid to shareholders — offer an illustration of how difficult such tests can be.

In contrast, closed-end mutual funds offer a much easier test of market efficiency. Since, by law, these funds are required to report the net value of the assets held in the portfolio (NAV), the figures can be compared with share prices (P) directly. Indeed, the *Wall Street Journal* publishes both sets of numbers every week.

Closed-end funds usually sell at a discount from net asset value, i.e., $P < NAV$. Graham [1959] observed that this discount 'may be viewed as an expensive monument erected to the inertia and stupidity of stockholders' [p. 242]. On occasion, some funds sell at a premium ($P > NAV$). For example, at the end of the 1980s, we observed a remarkable bubble in closed-end 'country' funds. For several months, the prices of the Spain and Germany funds exceeded the NAV by as much as 100%! Although high management fees, other agency costs, or unrealized capital gains liabilities may partially explain why price might be less than net asset value, it is somewhat of a mystery why anyone would pay \$2 to acquire $1 worth of assets in countries with few restrictions on foreign investment.

A behavioral interpretation of closed-end fund pricing is offered by De Long, Shleifer, Summers & Waldmann [1990a] in the context of a noise trader model. Briefly, they propose that investor sentiment varies through time. For example, when noise traders are optimistic, the prices of closed-end funds rise, causing the discounts to narrow (or premia to increase). Rational traders are subject to two types of risk: (1) fundamental risk that *NAV* may decline; and (2) noise trader risk that the discount may widen. To compensate for this risk, rational traders only buy closed-end funds at a discount.

This theory is tested by Lee, Shleifer & Thaler [1991] who find many aspects of the data consistent with the noise trader model. First, closed-end fund discounts move together through time, so that the average discount can indeed be seen as a sentiment index. Secondly, new funds often get started when discounts on existing funds are low. Third, the stock returns of small firms vary inversely with the discount. That is, when the discounts shrink, small stocks do well (even controlling for the macro-factors that vary with security returns in general). Finally, in later work, Bodurtha, Kim & Lee [1993] find that the discounts of closed-end country funds traded in the U.S. also move together. The fund returns reflect the performance of U.S. stocks rather than the performance of the stock indices of the countries in which they invest [see also Bailey & Lim, 1992].

The relevance of small individual investors to the pricing of closed-end funds suggests that in other circumstances where these investors are disproportionately represented — e.g., the case of initial public offerings of stock (IPOs)–behavioral factors may also play a role. IPO volume moves to some extent with the major market indices and it comes in industry 'waves'. The prices of firms issued in high-volume ('hot') markets not only rise sharply right after issuance [Ritter, 1984] but also exhibit the poorest subsequent performance. Initially, IPOs appear to be (on average) 'underpriced'.[19] But, from a long run perspective, the issues seem 'overpriced'. For example, considering all major IPOs during the 1975–1984 period, Ritter [1991] finds that an investor who purchased these companies at the end of the first day of public trading would have been left, three years later, with 83 cents relative to each dollar from a group of comparable firms. Nevertheless, the average IPO outperformed the market by 14.1% on its first trading day. Both the under- and overpricing are even stronger for small-size start-up firms

[19] The theoretical literature on this topic is large. It almost always assumes that the offering price is too low rather than the first aftermarket price too high. Possible underpricing rationales include: (1) Underwriters collude and, as monopsonists, underpay entrepreneurs. The IPOs are offered to favorite customers as a way of rebating commissions. (2) Underwriters know more than entrepreneurs about the market value of the IPO. The low offering price reduces the investment bankers' risk that the IPO 'doesn't sell'. (3) The underpricing is necessary to attract uninformed investors bedeviled by the winner's curse. (4) The low offering price is seen as 'insurance' against liability suits. (5) Underwriters want 'to leave a good taste' with investors so that future underwritings (of the same or a different company) are sold more easily. They may also want to create a shortage illusion. For detailed references, see Ibbotson, Sindelar & Ritter [1988] and Ibbotson & Ritter [1995].

with little or no prior sales. From an aggregate time-series perspective, the initial underpricing — i.e., the average return on the first day of trading for all firms that go public during the month — typically leads total IPO volume by 6 to 12 months.

The data clearly suggest a scenario where, at times, investors are overoptimistic about the profit potential of growth companies and where entrepreneurs (with the help of investment bankers) take advantage of these opportunities. In the majority of cases, the excitement turns to disappointment. It is important to ask: What is the source of the initial 'optimism'? It often seems as if a 'concept' is sold (rather than a proven record). For example, in the early 1990s, new software firms have often been marketed as 'the next Microsoft'. This is consistent with representativeness. An altogether different interpretation is that investors buy IPOs as lottery tickets and are willing to lose on average in order to obtain some chance for a large gain. Finally, it may be that investment bankers act as impresarios and purposely underprice some IPOs to create excess demand and to enhance their reputation [Shiller, 1990]. When later IPOs are launched, people who missed out are eager to buy, so as to escape more future regret.

3.4. *The equity premium puzzle*

A topic that has received much attention in recent years is the return differential between stocks and the risk free rate, the equity premium. In the U.S., the real return on equities from 1926 to the early 1990s is roughly 7%, while the return on long-term bonds is about 1%. This is an impressive gap, especially when the rates are compounded over sixty or more years! Many observers wonder: Is the equity premium too large to be consistent with standard rational models? Mehra & Prescott [1985] first posed this question formally. They investigate how risk averse the representative investor (with an additively separable expected utility function) has to be in order to explain the historical return data. They conclude that the equity premium would only be this large if people were extraordinarily risk averse. As a result, Mehra and Prescott declare the magnitude of the equity premium a puzzle.[20]

There have been several attempts to explain the puzzle, some with a behavioral character. For example, Constantinides [1990] proposes a theory based on habit formation, in which investors are reluctant to reduce their consumption from one period to the next. Also, Epstein & Zin [1990] question the assumption of expected utility maximization and replace it with an alternative model. Neither approach is completely successful. Benartzi & Thaler [1993] offer a more explicitly behavioral explanation that builds on the concepts of loss aversion and mental

[20] The estimated coefficient of relative risk aversion is about 40. This number is not only much higher than other estimates (usually close to 1.0) but, in the Mehra–Prescott model, high risk aversion implies a low intertemporal elasticity of substitution which is inconsistent with the low risk free rate.

accounting. Loss aversion agrees with Kahneman & Tversky's prospect theory, in which the disutility of a marginal loss is roughly twice as large as the utility of a marginal gain. Mental accounting plays a role because, in this model, the attractiveness of a risky investment depends on the frequency with which it is evaluated. The intuition is straightforward. Suppose an investor checks the value of her portfolio every day, and values the change according to prospect theory. This investor will find equities very unattractive since, on a daily basis, stocks fall about as often as they rise, and losses are felt twice as keenly as gains. Compare this case with an investor who buys an equity portfolio and then forgets about it for twenty years. The second investor faces a very small chance of a loss, and so would find equities attractive. Within this framework, Benartzi and Thaler ask how often investors would have to reevaluate their portfolios in order to make stocks and bonds equally attractive. The answer is about one year. The authors dub this combination of short horizons and sensitivity to losses 'myopic loss aversion'. They estimate that, if the horizon of the typical investor were 20 years, the equity premium would fall to 1.5%.

4. Financial decision-making in corporations

Like proprietorships, partnerships, or nonprofits, corporations are a type of organization, i.e., a 'system of coordinated action among individuals and groups whose preferences, information, interests, or knowledge differ' [March & Simon, 1993, p. 2]. Of course, much economic action is coordinated by market processes. As Ronald Coase [1937] initially observed, economic theory should explain why organizations exist and it should rationalize their structure. The Modigliani–Miller irrelevance propositions for financing and dividend policy — the traditional starting points in the study of corporate finance — may be interpreted as special cases of Coase's later [1960] theorem. That is, in the absence of contracting costs, taxes, and other frictions, the assignment of property rights should not affect either the firm's operations or its market value. Starting from this polar case, modern corporate finance studies (1) the various ways in which taxes, information asymmetries, and self-interest in contracting relationships change optimal financing and investment decisions, and (2) the economic forces that push the organization toward its optimal (equilibrium) ownership structure.

Thus, modern finance emphasizes the essential contractual nature of organizations [Jensen & Meckling, 1976; Fama & Jensen, 1983]. Accordingly, the decision-making behavior of the various constituencies (shareholders, bondholders, management, suppliers, customers, etc.) that make up the firm becomes very relevant. In particular, insofar as actual decisions differ from their normative ideal, corporate finance takes on a new dimension. Our examples below are meant to illustrate this general proposition. First, we ask how shareholders' preference for dividends affects dividend policy. Next, we describe executives' efforts to manage investors' perceptions of firm value. Finally, we discuss two aspects of managerial behavior that mattered a great deal in the corporate restructuring of the 1980s: (1) hubris, and (2) the reluctance to walk away form money-losing projects.

4.1. Dividend policy

Why do firms pay dividends? To repeat, in perfect markets, dividend policy does not matter to the value of the firm [Miller & Modigliani, 1961]. But, when dividends are taxed at a higher rate than capital gains, stockholders should complain if a firm pays cash dividends. Instead, stockholders often do the opposite — they complain when dividends are cut. A different way to think about this puzzle is from the perspective of management. Over long periods, corporate executives seem to fail to respond to large tax incentives. Firms could hoard cash and purchase their own securities or the securities of other firms. But, in fact, managers systematically fail to benefit their shareholders by converting high-taxed dividends to low-taxed capital gains.[21]

Shefrin & Statman [1984] offer a behavioral explanation based on mental accounting and self-control. Essentially, dividends are paid because investors want them. People psychologically resist dipping into capital. (Until recently, colleges and universities usually did not spend the capital gains earned by their endowments.) This rule is a self-control device. Also, dividends can be savored as a separate gain when the stock price rises and used as a silver lining if the price drops. This is a mental accounting explanation. Financing consumption out of dividends further avoids the anticipated regret of selling a stock that rises in value. Shefrin & Statman's theory suggests clientele effects that are in fact observed. For example, retired investors typically hold a larger portion of their stock portfolio in income securities than do young investors. In surveys, retirees also rate 'dividend income' as a much more important investment goal than 'short-term capital gains' [Lease, Lewellen & Schlarbaum, 1976].

We speculate that other aspects of dividend policy are similarly influenced by public relations and the need to manage shareholder perceptions. Among other things, modern finance fails to explain dividend smoothing, stock dividends, and why dividends have labels. For instance, some dividends are designated as 'special'. A psychological perspective suggests that, in this way, subsequent elimination is not experienced as a loss. Stock dividends create a different illusion: the mirage of an actual dividend without a dollar payout. Perhaps this technique softens the blow on investors as they sell off shares. Finally, in his classic study of dividend smoothing, John Lintner suggested that the practice 'helps to minimize adverse stockholder reactions' [1956, p. 100]. This makes sense if, as predicted by the self-control theory, consumption closely tracks (dividend) income.

[21] Easterbrook [1984] offers two rationales for dividends based upon agency theory. The first is the need to monitor corporate management. The other is to ensure that managers do not reduce risk. However, stock repurchases that force managers to frequent the capital markets accomplish the same objective and they are cheaper than dividends. Notice that, from a (third) signalling perspective, stock repurchases may also dominate dividends.

4.2. Earnings management

Executives also pay careful attention to reported earnings-per-share. For example, many managers and investors seem to like a steady upward trend in earnings with clear future targets [Barth, Elliott & Finn, 1992]. Other firms maximize short-term earnings.[22] Managers often behave as if there were a mechanical relation between reported accounting earnings and stock prices. For example, Hand [1989] finds that many firms report paper gains on debt-equity swaps in ways that smooth a transitory fall in earnings.[23] More generally, Brealey & Myers admit that managers 'seem to assume that investors suffer from financial illusion'. 'Some firms devote enormous ingenuity to the task of manipulating earnings to stockholders ... choosing accounting methods which stabilize and increase reported earnings' [1984, p. 276].

The intellectual challenge posed by earnings management is why it happens if (1) an efficient market looks through the manipulation and (2) it wastes time and resources. Schipper offers the possibility that (2) is false because earnings management provides 'a means for managers to reveal their private information' [1989, p. 91]. Earnings management may also be self-serving, e.g., if reported earnings are tied to executive compensation. But managers often feel ambushed by a short-sighted stock market. With bad earnings news, they say, their companies easily turn into takeover targets.

4.3. Corporate growth, decline, and reorganization

Corporate expansion can take two forms: internal growth or external acquisition of assets. Similarly, corporate retrenchment either occurs through plant closings, or through divestitures and a company break-up. Clearly, all the evidence suggests that expansion occurs more readily than the redeployment or destruction of existing assets. For example, event studies show that the market often reacts positively to sell-offs and project cancellations [see, e.g., Hite, Owers & Rogers, 1987] and that it believes that some CEOs enhance their effectiveness with death.

Jensen blames information problems, agency costs, as well as the 'mindset of managers' [1993, p. 847] for the myopic focus on sunk costs and the difficulty of exit. 'Even when managers do acknowledge the requirement for exit, it is often difficult for them to accept and to initiate the shutdown decision. ... firms with large positive cash flow will often invest in even more money-losing capacity...' [1993, p. 848]. Jensen's psychological insights agree with the literature on status quo bias [Samuelson & Zeckhauser, 1988] and the nonrational 'escalation of

[22] Further examples of earnings management include (1) the tendency to delay bad earnings reports, and (2) the so-called big bath. In years of unusually low profits or losses, earnings are reduced further 'to clear the deck'. Accounting write-offs that are taken now improve the chances for improved earnings later.

[23] Does it work, or do stock prices behave instead as if investors unscramble the true cash flow implications of the accounting data? Hand [1990] concludes that prices are set in part by unsophisticated investors, 'functionally fixated' on reported earnings.

commitment' [Staw, 1976]. Decision makers who have chosen a particular course of action tend to 'throw good money after bad', perhaps to reaffirm the wisdom of the initial decision (and to protect their professional reputation). There appear to be multiple reasons why escalation comes about [see Bazerman, 1986, chapter 4]. One explanation relies on framing and the role of reference points. Entrapment occurs as people become effectively risk-seeking in their attempts to recoup past losses and to 'break-even'.

Of course, in addition, we should not forget that executives gain from running large companies and managing more assets. Perhaps the most robust finding in the literature on executive pay is that dollar compensation is strongly and positively related to firm size [see, e.g., Baker, Jensen & Murphy, 1988]. The consumption value of perquisites and status are also likely to increase with firm size.

Corporate expansion brings us to the literature on mergers and takeovers, reviewed by Jensen & Ruback [1983] and Jarrell, Brickley & Netter, 1988]. Many takeovers can be explained by synergy, inefficient target management, or taxes. However, while target firm shareholders typically do very well when their firm is purchased, stockholders in the acquiring firm do not appear to make any money. In fact, in most cases, they lose wealth. For the 1980s, Servaes [1991] finds statistically significantly negative returns of −3.4% on the announcement date [see also Bradley, Desai & Kim, 1988; Jarrell & Poulsen, 1989; or Loderer & Martin, 1990]. Based on an exhaustive sample of mergers and tender offers with returns on CRSP between 1955 and 1987, Agrawal, Jaffe & Mandelker, 1992] report a significant loss of about 10% over the five-year post-merger period.[24]

What causes mergers and acquisitions if the profits are one-sided? Roll [1986] offers the hubris hypothesis as an answer. Put simply, managers of bidder firms, flush with cash from recent successes (perhaps due to luck), are convinced that they can run the target firm better than current management. As a result, they systematically overestimate the benefits of corporate combination. In Roll's words, '... If there really are no gains in takeovers, ... the phenomenon depends on the overbearing presumption of bidders that their valuations are correct'. Hubris is consistent with a large body of evidence in psychology and increasing evidence in finance [e.g., Giliberto & Varaiya, 1989] that individuals tend to be overconfident.[25]

[24] The returns tend to be more negative if (1) the Tobin's q of the bidder is 'low' [Lang, Stulz & Walkling, 1989], (2) top executives own a smaller percentage of the bidding firm [Lewellen, Loderer & Rosenfeld, 1985], (3) the takeover is financed with equity issues rather than cash [Travlos, 1987], (4) the acquisition turns out to be 'a failure' ex post [Kaplan & Weisbach, 1992].
The post-outcome negative bidder returns are 'unsettling' to Jensen & Ruback [1983] 'because they are inconsistent with market efficiency and suggest that changes in stock prices during takeovers overestimate the future efficiency gains from mergers' [p. 20].

[25] Referring to Adam Smith and others, Knight [1921] argues similarly that, on average, entrepreneurs may not be properly compensated for their risk-taking. According to Knight, '... these 'risks' do not relate to objective external probabilities, but to the value of the judgment and executive powers of the person taking the chance. It is certainly true that ... most men have an irrationally high confidence in their own good fortune, and that is doubly true when their personal prowess comes into the reckoning, when they are betting on themselves. ... To these considerations must be added the stimulus of the competitive situation, ..., as in an auction sale,

Roll's view of the takeover research is that managers are boundedly rational but that markets are not. His reliance on event-study results assumes market efficiency.

A competing view says that opportunistic executives *knowingly* overpay for target firms because they gain personally through job security, diversification of human capital, and further nonpecuniary benefits [Morck, Shleifer & Vishny, 1990]. Seyhun [1990] studies the trading behavior of insiders to make inferences about their motivation. He finds that, prior to takeover announcements, top executives of bidder firms increase their net purchases. This suggests that, even if managers understand the winner's curse, they nevertheless persist in their beliefs because of overweening pride.

5. Conclusion

Modern finance assumes that the study of substantively rational solutions to normative problems forms an adequate basis for understanding actual behavior. Of course, substituting mathematical logic for empirical observation is convenient. Financial economists can cut down on their reading and they can (sometimes proudly) admit to being ignorant about advances in other social sciences. In addition, the optimality principle is less 'messy' than the complexity of the real world. Many ideas do not easily lend themselves to mathematical representation. This puts a premium on simple notions and tractable models, so long as they offer testable predictions.[26]

However, an uncritical reliance on the optimality principle also has substantial costs. First, it diverts our attention from actual decision processes, perhaps based on the view that process does not affect outcome. As a result, numerous engaging questions do not even get posed. But people trade in financial markets. Are the vital statistics that describe these markets (prices, transaction volumes, etc.) any different because of their presence? For the most part, we do not know. Second, the optimality principle sometimes results in tortuous and absurd rationalization — where auxiliary assumptions play a big role (e.g., who knows what?) and where, ultimately, the premises are derived from the conclusions. Finally, there is the danger of a stubborn confirmation bias that repeats 'if it could still be rational, it must be'.[27]

where things often bring more than any one thinks they are worth. Another large factor is ... tenacity [where], once committed, ... the general rule is to hold on to the last ditch ... The prestige of entrepreneurship ... must also be considered' [pp. 365– 366].

[26] Yet, we should not confuse what is tractable with what is right. Neither should we confuse what is internally consistent (starting from so-called first principles) with what is right. To repeat our discussion above, models that build on the optimality principle may yet be useful as normative tools or as benchmarks to evaluate the quality of actual investor decision-making. Also, they may describe the synchronous behavior of two financial markets if arbitrage between these markets is nearly costless and risk-free. Finally, these models may capture long-run equilibrium outcomes when behavior is fully adapted to changing conditions.

[27] For a broader discussion of the optimality principle as a heuristic of science, see Schoemaker [1991].

The purpose of this paper has not been to diminish the achievements of modern finance. Rather, we have argued that, in order to make scientific progress, some diversity in methods is probably a good thing. In particular, much is gained — and, possibly, some anomalies could be resolved — by careful observation of what people actually do. We look for general behavioral principles that apply in multiple economic contexts, e.g., excessive self-confidence. Some principles are suggested and confirmed by psychological experiments. Others are age-old.

Admittedly, past work on the psychology of financial markets was often sketchy and anecdotal. It relied on dramatic evidence relating to stock market crashes, banking panics, and other memorable events, e.g., the Florida land price bubble of the 1920s or the 17th century Dutch tulipmania (Kindleberger [1989]; for a critique, see Garber [1990]). Maybe because the facts were so unusual, there was a tendency to explain each instance by unique historical circumstances.[28]

In contrast, we have provided a systematic review of evidence that behavioral factors matter outside the laboratory, i.e., even when a lot of money is at stake. The papers that were discussed are best described as pragmatic empirical work. Their purpose is to collect a set of robust empirical facts that stand out, no matter which way one cuts the data. (Thus, the results rely less on statistical acrobatics than on judiciously chosen natural experiments.) Following Friedman [1946] and Summers [1990], our view of theory is that 'it should generalize interesting facts'.

The study of financial decision-making (at the level of the individual, the market, the organization) is a wide-open field. Commenting on the extensive downsizing and exit that will be required from mature industries in the 1990s, Jensen laments that finance 'has concentrated on how capital investment decisions should be made, with little systematic study of how they actually are made in practice' [1993, p. 870]. He calls for positive (descriptive) theories of organizations. The possible 'fragmentation' of the finance profession he calls 'progress, not failure' [p. 872]. Obviously, we concur.

One topic that especially draws our attention is the unprecedented financial innovation during the last few decades. Merton [1990] sees three driving forces: (1) the demand for 'completing the market'; (2) the lowering of transactions costs; and (3) reductions in agency and monitoring costs. Miller [1986b] interprets the innovation as a response to regulatory changes. Our own view is that these forces, while relevant, leave out the central question of the design and the marketing of financial products [Shefrin & Statman, 1993a]. Consider, for example, portfolio insurance. This product became more popular on Wall Street once it was framed as 'insurance'. Neither the success nor the faltering of portfolio insurance are easily explained by the traditional arguments, but 'to know thy customers' may well be key.

[28] Witness, similarly, all the attempts to explain the world- wide 1987 stock market crash with institutional factors that are specific to the United States, e.g., portfolio insurance. Whatever their merits, such exercises evidently do not lead us towards a general theory of financial panics. For more discussion, see Kleidon [1995, chapter 16 of this volume].

Acknowledgements

Earlier versions of this paper were presented at CentER and TIAS (Tilburg, The Netherlands), the 7. Kolloquium 'Empirische Kapitalmarktforschung' in Osnabruck (Germany), the University of Manchester, the Norwegian School of Management and the University of Wisconsin–Madison. We thank the participants for helpful comments. We also thank Bill Ziemba (the editor), Warren Bailey, Peter Bossaerts, Ken French, Narasimhan Jegadeesh, Jay Ritter, and Alex Triantis.

References

Aronson, E. (1991). *The Social Animal*, 6th edition, W.H. Freeman, New York, NY.

Agrawal, A., J.F. Jaffe, and G.N. Mandelker (1992). The post-merger performance of acquiring firms: A re-examination of an anomaly. *J. Finance* 47(4), 1605–1621.

Akerlof, G.A. (1984). *An Economic Theorist's Book of Tales*, Cambridge University Press, Cambridge.

Ariel, R.A. (1987). A monthly effect in stock returns. *J. Finance Econ.* 12, 387–404.

Arrow, K.J. (1982). Risk perception in psychology and economics. *Econ. Inq.* 20, 1–9.

Arrow, K.J. (1986). Rationality of self and others in an economic system, in: R.M. Hogarth and M.W. Reder (eds.), *Rational Choice: The Contrast Between Economics and Psychology*, University of Chicago Press, Chicago, IL.

Aumann, R.J. (1976). Agreeing to disagree. *Ann. Stat.* 4(6), 1236–1239.

Bailey, W., and J. Lim (1992). Evaluating the diversification benefits of the New Country Funds. *J. Portfolio Manage.* Spring, 74–80.

Baker, G.P., M.C. Jensen and K.J. Murphy (1988). Compensation and incentives: Practice vs. theory. *J. Finance* 43, 593–616.

Ball, R., and S.P. Kothari (1989). Nonstationary expected returns: Implications for tests of market efficiency and serial correlation in returns. *J. Financ. Econ.* 25, 51–74.

Barth, M.E., J.A. Elliott, and M.W. Finn (1992). Market rewards for increasing earnings patterns, working paper #93-041, Harvard Business School.

Basu, S. (1977). Investment performance of common stocks in relation to their price-earnings ratios. *J. Finance* 32(3), 663–682.

Bazerman, M.H. (1986). *Judgment in Managerial Decision Making* Wiley, New York, NY.

Bell, D.E. (1982). Regret in decision-making under uncertainty. *Oper. Res.* 10, 961–981.

Benartzi, S., and R.H. Thaler (1993). Myopic loss aversion and the equity premium puzzle, working paper, Johnson Graduate School of Management, Cornell University.

Bernard, V.L., and J.K. Thomas (1989). Post-earnings-announcement drift: Delayed price response or risk premium?. *J. Account. Res.* 27, Supplement 1–48.

Bernard, V.L., and J.K. Thomas (1990). Evidence that stock prices do not fully reflect the implications of current earnings for future earnings. *J. Account. Econ.* 13, 305–340.

Bikhchandani, S., D. Hirshleifer, and I. Welch (1992). A theory of fads, fashion, custom, and cultural change as informational cascades. *J. Polit. Econ.* 100, 992–1026.

Black, F. (1986). Noise. *J. Finance* 41, 529–543.

Bodurtha, J.N., Jr., D.-S. Kim, and C.M.C. Lee (1993). Closed-end country funds and U.S. market sentiment, working paper, University of Michigan.

Bradley, M., A. Desai, and E.H. Kim (1988). Synergistic gains from corporate acquisitions and their division between the stockholders of target and acquiring firms. *J. Financ. Econ.* 21, 3–40.

Brealey, R.A., and S.C. Myers (1984/1988). *Principles of Corporate Finance*, McGraw-Hill, New York, NY.

Camerer, C.F. (1987). Do biases in probability judgment matter in markets? Experimental evidence. *Am. Econ. Rev.* 77(5), 981–997.

Chan, K.C. (1988). On the contrarian investment strategy. *J. Bus.* 61(2), 147–163.

Chopra, N., J. Lakonishok, and J.R. Ritter (1992). Measuring abnormal performance: Do stocks overreact?. *J. Financ. Econ.* 31, 235–268.

Clark, J.M. (1918). Economics and modern psychology. *J. Polit. Econ.* 26(1), 1–30.

Coase, R.H. (1937). The nature of the firm. *Economica* 4, 386–405.

Coase, R.H. (1960). The problem of social cost. *J. Law Econ.* 3, 1–44.

Cochrane, J.H. (1991). Volatility tests and efficient markets. *J. Monetary Econ.* 27, 463–485.

Conrad, J., and G. Kaul (1993). Long-term market overreaction or biases in computed returns?. *J. Finance* 48(1), 39–64.

Constantinides, G.M. (1990). Habit Formation: A resolution of the equity premium puzzle. *J. Polit. Econ.* 98(3), 519–543.

Cutler, D.M., J.M. Poterba, and L.H. Summers (1991). Speculative dynamics. *Rev. Econ. Studies* 58, 529–546.

De Bondt, W.F.M. (1992a). What are investment advisors paid for? The Shefrin–Statman and competing views, in: J.B. Guerard, Jr. and M.N. Gultekin (eds.), *Handbook of Security Analyst Forecasting and Asset Allocation*, JAI Press, Greenwich, CT.

De Bondt, W.F.M. (1992b). *Earnings Forecasts and Share Price Reversals*, Institute of Chartered Financial Analysts, Charlottesville.

De Bondt, W.F.M. and R.H. Thaler (1985). Does the stock market overreact?. *J. Finance* 40(3), 793–805.

De Bondt, W.F.M., and R.H. Thaler (1987). Further evidence on investor overreaction and stock market seasonality. *J. Finance* 42(3), 557–581.

De Bondt, W.F.M., and R.H. Thaler (1989). A mean-reverting walk down Wall Street. *J. Econ. Perspect.* 3(1), 189–202.

De Bondt, W.F.M., and R.H. Thaler (1990). Do security analysts overreact?. *Am. Econ. Rev.* 80(2), 52–57.

De Long, J.B., A. Shleifer, L.H. Summers, and R.J. Waldmann (1990a). Noise trader risk in financial markets. *J. Polit. Econ.* 98(4), 703–738.

De Long, B.J., A. Shleifer, L.H. Summers, and R.J. Waldmann (1990b). Positive feedback investment strategies and destabilizing rational speculation. *J. Finance* 45(2), 379–395.

De Long, B.J., A. Shleifer, L.H. Summers, and R.J. Waldmann (1991). The survival of noise traders in financial markets. *J. Bus.* 64(1), 1–20.

Dreman, D.N. (1982). *The New Contrarian Investment Strategy*, Random House, New York, NY.

Easterbrook, F.H. (1984). Two agency-cost explanations of dividends. *Am. Econ. Rev.* 74, 650–659.

Elster, J. (1979). *Ulysses and the Sirens*, Cambridge University Press, Cambridge.

Elster, J. (1983). *Sour Grapes*, Cambridge University Press, Cambridge.

Elster, J. (1989). *Solomonic Judgements*, Cambridge University Press, Cambridge.

Epstein, L.G., and S.E. Zin (1990). First-order risk aversion and the equity premium puzzle. *J. Monetary Econ.* 26, 387–407.

Fama, E.F. (1991). Efficient capital markets: II. *J. Finance* 46(5), 1575–1617.

Fama, E.F., and K.R. French (1988). Permanent and temporary components of stock market prices. *J. Polit. Econ.* 96, 246–273.

Fama, E.F., and K.R. French (1992). The cross-section of expected stock returns. *J. Finance* 47, 427–465.

Fama, E.F., and M.C. Jensen (1983). Separation of ownership and control. *J. Law Econ.* 26, 301–325.

French, K.R., and R. Roll (1986). Stock return variances: The arrival of information and the reaction of traders. *J. Financ. Econ.* 17, 5–26.

Friedman, M. (1946). Lange on price flexibility and employment. A methodological criticism. *Am. Econ. Rev.* 36, 613–631.

Friedman, M. (1953). *Essays in Positive Economics*, University of Chicago Press, Chicago, IL.

Garber, P.M. (1990). Famous first bubbles. *J. Econ. Perspect.* 4(2), 35–54.

Giliberto, S.M., and N.P. Varaiya (1989). The winner's curse and bidder competition in acquisitions: Evidence from failed bank auctions. *J. Finance* 44(1), 59–75.

Graham, B. (1959). *The Intelligent Investor. A Book of Practical Counsel*, 3rd edition, Harper & Brothers, New York, NY.

Graham, B., and D. Dodd (1934). *Security Analysis*, McGraw-Hill, New York, NY.

Grether, D.M. (1980). Bayes' rule as a descriptive model: The representativeness heuristic. *Q. J. Econ.* 95, 537–557.

Hand, J.R.M. (1989). Did firms undertake debt-equity swaps for an accounting paper profit or true financial gain?. *Account. Rev.* 64(4), 587–623.

Hand, J.R.M. (1990). A test of the extended functional fixation hypothesis. *Account. Rev.* 65(4), 739–763.

Harris, M., and A. Raviv (1992). Differences of opinion make a horse race, working paper, University of Chicago.

Hawawini, G., and D.B. Keim (1995). On the predictability of common stock returns: World-wide evidence, in: R. Jarrow, V. Maksimovic and W.T. Ziemba (eds.), *Finance*, Handbooks in Operations Research and Management Science, Vol. 9, North-Holland, Amsterdam, pp. 497–544 (this volume).

Hayek, F.A. (1948). *Individualism and Economic Order*, University of Chicago Press, Chicago, IL.

Hayes, S.P., Jr. (1950). Some psychological problems of economics. *Psychol. Bull.* 47(4), 289–330.

Heath, C., and A. Tversky (1991). Preference and belief: Ambiguity and competence in choice under uncertainty. *J. Risk Uncertainty* 4, 5–28.

Hensel, C.R., G.A. Sick, and W.T. Ziemba (1994). The turn-of-the-month effect in the U.S. stock index futures markets, 1982–1992, forthcoming.

Hite, G.L., J.E. Owers and R.C. Rogers (1987). The market for interfirm asset sales: Partial sell-offs and total liquidations. *J. Financ. Econ.* 18, 229–252.

Ibbotson, R.G., and J.R. Ritter (1995). Initial public offerings, in: R. Jarrow, V. Maksimovic and W.T. Ziemba (eds.), *Finance*, Handbooks in Operations Research and Management Science, Vol. 9, North Holland, Amsterdam, pp. 993–1016 (this volume).

Ibbotson, R.G., J,.L. Sindelar, and J.R. Ritter (1988). Initial public offerings. *J. Appl. Corp. Finance* 1, 37–45.

Ingersoll, J.E., Jr. (1987). *Theory of Financial Decision Making*, Rowman & Littlefield, Totowa, NJ.

Ippolito, R.A., and J.A. Turner (1987). Turnover, fees, and pension plan performance. *Financ. Anal. J.* November/December, 16–26.

Jaffe, J., D.B. Keim, and R. Westerfield (1989). Earnings yields, market values and stock returns. *J. Finance* 54, 135–148.

Jarrell, G.A., J.A. Brickley, and J.M. Netter (1988). The market for corporate control: The evidence since 1988. *J. Econ. Perspect.* 2, 49–68.

Jarrell, G.A., and A.B. Poulsen (1989). The returns to acquiring firms in tender offers: Evidence from three decades. *Financ. Manage.* 18, 12–19.

Jegadeesh, N. (1990). Evidence of predictable behavior of security returns. *J. Finance* 45, 3, 881–898.

Jegadeesh, N., and S. Titman (1993). Returns to buying winners and selling losers: Implications for stock market efficiency. *J. Finance*. 48(1), 65–92.

Jensen, M.C. (1968). The performance of mutual funds in the period 1945–1964. *J. Finance* 23, 389–416.

Jensen, M.C. (1993). The modern industrial revolution, exit, and the failure of internal control systems. *J. Finance* 48(3), 831–880.

Jensen, M.C., and W. Meckling (1976). Theory of the firm: Managerial behavior, agency costs and ownership structure. *J. Financ. Econ.* 3, 305–360.

Jensen, M.C., and R.S. Ruback (1983). The market for corporate control: The scientific evidence. *J. Financ. Econ.* 11, 5–50.

Kahneman, D., J.K. Knetsch, and R. Thaler (1990). Experimental tests of the endowment effect and the Coase theorem. *J. Polit. Econ.* 98, 1325–1348.

Kahneman, D., P. Slovic, and A. Tversky, eds. (1982). *Judgment under Uncertainty: Heuristics and Biases*, Cambridge University Press, Cambridge.

Kahneman, D., and A. Tversky (1972). Subjective probability: A judgment of representativeness. *Cogn. Psychol.* 3, 430–454.

Kahneman, D., and A. Tversky (1973). On the psychology of prediction. *Psychol. Rev.* 80, 237–251.

Kaplan, S.N., and M.S. Weisbach (1992). The success of acquisitions: Evidence from divestitures. *J. Financ. Econ.* 24, 137–154.

Katona, G. (1951). *Psychological Analysis of Economic Behavior*, McGraw-Hill, New York, NY.

Kindleberger, C. (1989). *Manias, Panics, and Crashes: A History of Financial Crisis*, revised edition, Basic Books, New York, NY.

Keynes, J.M. (1936). *The General Theory of Employment, Interest and Money*, Harcourt Brace Jovanovich, London.

Kleidon, A.W. (1995). Stock market crashes, in: R. Jarrow, V. Maksimovic and W.T. Ziemba (eds.), *Finance*, Handbooks in Operations Research and Management Science, Vol. 9, North-Holland, Amsterdam, pp. 465–495 (this volume).

Knight, F.H. (1971). *Risk, Uncertainty, and Profit*, University of Chicago Press, Chicago (Originally published by Houghton Mifflin Company, 1921).

Kreps, D.M. (1990). *Game Theory and Economic Modelling*, Oxford University Press, Oxford.

Kuhn, T.S. (1970). *The Structure of Scientific Revolutions*, 2nd edition, University of Chicago Press, Chicago.

Lakonishok, J., A. Shleifer, and R.W. Vishny (1993). Contrarian investment, extrapolation, and risk, working paper, University of Illinois at Urbana, Champaign

Lakonishok, J., and S. Smidt (1988). Are seasonal anomalies real? A ninety-year perspective. *Rev. Financ. Studies* 1(4), 403–425.

Lang, L.H.P., R. Stulz, and R.A. Walkling (1989). Managerial performance, Tobin's q, and the gains from successful tender offers. *J. Financ. Econ.* 24, 137–154.

Lease, R.C., W.G. Lewellen, and G.G. Schlarbaum (1976). Market segmentation: Evidence on the individual investor. *Financ. Anal. J.* 32, 32–40.

Lee, C.M.C., A. Shleifer, and R.H. Thaler (1991). Investor sentiment and the closed-end fund puzzle. *J. Finance* 46, 75–109.

Lehmann, B.N. (1990). Fads, martingales, and market efficiency. *Q. J. Econ.* 105(1), 1–28.

Lewellen, W., C. Loderer, and A. Rosenfeld (1985). Merger decisions and executive ownership in acquiring firms. *J. Account. Econ.* 7, 209–231.

Lichtenstein, S., B. Fischhoff, and L.D. Phillips (1982). Calibration of probabilities: The state of the art to 1980, in D. Kahneman et al. (eds.), *Judgment Under Uncertainty: Heuristics and Biases*, Cambridge University Press, Cambridge.

Lintner, J. (1956). Distribution of incomes of corporations among dividends, retained earnings and taxes. *Am. Econ. Rev.* 46, 97–113.

Lo, A.W., and A.C. MacKinlay (1990a). When are contrarian profits due to stock market overreaction?. *Rev. Financ. Studies* 3(2), 175–205.

Lo, A.W., and A.C. MacKinlay (1990b). Data-snooping biases in tests of financial asset pricing models. *Rev. Financ. Studies* 3(3), 431–468.

Loderer, C., and K. Martin (1990). Corporate acquisitions by listed firms: The experience of a comprehensive sample. *Financ. Manage.* 19, 17–33.

Loewenstein, G., and J. Elster (1992). *Choice Over Time*, Russell Sage Foundation, New York, NY.

Loughran, T., and J.R. Ritter (1994). Long-term market overreaction: The effect of low-priced stocks, working paper, University of Iowa.

Lowenstein, L. (1988). *What's Wrong with Wall Street*, Addison-Wesley, New York, NY.

Lucas, R.E., Jr. (1986). Adaptive behavior and economic theory, in: R.M. Hogarth and M.W. Reder (eds.), *Rational Choice: The Contrast Between Economics and Psychology*, University of Chicago Press, Chicago, IL.

Lynch, P. (1990). *One Up on Wall Street*, Penguin Books, New York, NY.
March, J., and H. Simon (1993). *Organizations* (first edition: 1958), Blackwell Publishers, Cambridge, MA.
Markowitz, H. (1952). The utility of wealth. *J. Polit. Econ.* 60, 151–158.
Mehra, R., and E. Prescott (1985). The equity premium: A puzzle. *J. Monetary Econ.* 15, 145–161.
Merton, R.C. (1990). The financial system and economic performance. *J. Financ. Serv. Res.* 263–300.
Miller, M.H. (1986a). Behavioral rationality in finance: The case of dividends, in: R.M. Hogarth and M.W. Reder (eds.), *Rational Choice: The Contrast Between Economics and Psychology*, University of Chicago Press, Chicago, IL.
Miller, M.H. (1986b). Financial innovation: The last twenty years and the next. *J. Financ. Quant. Anal.* 21, 459–471.
Miller, M.H., and F. Modigliani (1961). Dividend policy, growth, and the valuation of shares. *J. Bus.* 34(4), 411–433.
Milgrom, P., and N. Stokey (1982). Information, trade, and common knowledge. *J. Econ. Theory* 26, 17–27.
Mitchell, W.C. (1914). Human behavior and economics: A survey of recent literature. *Q. J. Econ.* November, 1–47.
Morck, R.A., A. Shleifer, and R.W. Vishny (1990). Do managerial objectives drive bad acquisitions?. *J. Finance* 45, 31–48.
Neill, H.B., (1985). *The Art of Contrary Thinking*, 5th edition (first published in 1954), Caxton Printers, Ltd., Caldwell, ID.
Nisbett, R., and L. Ross (1980). *Human Inference: Strategies and Shortcomings of Social Judgment*, Prentice-Hall, Englewood Cliffs, NJ.
Ritter, J.R. (1984). The hot issue market of 1980. *J. Bus.* 57(2), 215–240.
Ritter, J.R. (1991). The long-term performance of initial public offerings. *J. Finance* March, 3–27.
Roll, R. (1986). The hubris hypothesis of corporate takeovers. *J. Bus.* 59(2), 197–216.
Roll, R. (1988). R^2. *J. Finance* 43(2), 541–566.
Romer, D. (1993). Rational asset-price movements without news. *Am. Econ. Rev.* 83(5), 1112–1130.
Russell, T., and R.H. Thaler (1985). The relevance of quasi rationality in competitive markets. *Am. Econ. Rev.* 75, 1071–1082.
Samuelson, W., and R. Zeckhauser (1988). Status quo bias in decision-making. *J. Risk Uncertainty* 1, 7–59.
Schipper, K. (1989). Earnings management. *Account. Horizons* 3(4), 91–102.
Schoemaker, P.J.H. (1991). The quest for optimality: A positive heuristic of science?. *Behav. Brain Sci.* 14(2), 205–245.
Schwert, G.W. (1983). Size and stock returns, and other empirical regularities. *J. Financ. Econ.* 12, 3–12.
Servaes, H. (1991). Tobin's *q*, agency costs, and corporate control. *J. Finance* 46, 409–419.
Seyhun, H.N. (1990). Do bidder managers knowingly pay too much for target firms?. *J. Bus.* 63(4), 439–464.
Shefrin, H., and M. Statman (1984). Explaining investor preference for cash dividends. *J. Financ. Econ.* 13, 253–282.
Shefrin, H., and M. Statman (1993a). Behavioral aspects of the design and marketing of financial products. *Financ. Manage.* 22(2), 123–234.
Shefrin, H., and M. Statman (1993b). A behavioral framework for expectations about stock returns, working paper, Leavey School of Business, Santa Clara University.
Shiller, R.J. (1981). Do stock prices move too much to be justified by subsequent changes in dividends?. *Am. Econ. Rev.* 71(3), 421–436.
Shiller, R.J. (1989). *Market Volatility*, MIT Press, Cambridge, MA.
Shiller, R.J. (1990). Speculative prices and popular models. *J. Econ. Perspect.* 4(2), 55–65.
Shleifer, A., and L.H. Summers (1990). The noise trader approach to finance. *J. Econ. Perspect.* 4(2), 19–33.

Simon, H.A. (1983). *Reason in Human Affairs*, Stanford University Press, Stanford, CA.

Slovic, P. (1972). Psychological study of human judgment: Implications for investment decision making. *J. Finance* 27, 779–799.

Slovic, P. Information processing, situation specificity, and the generality of risk-taking behavior. *J. Pers. Social Psychol.* 22(1), 128–134.

Staw, B.M. (1976). Knee-deep in the big muddy: A study of escalating commitment to a chosen course of action. *Organ. Behav. Human Perform.* 16, 27–44.

Stein, J. (1989). Overreactions in the options market. *J. Finance* 44(4), 1011–1023.

Summers, L.H. (1990). The scientific illusion in empirical macroeconomics, in: S. Hylleberg and M. Paldam (eds.), *New Approaches to Empirical Macroeconomics*, Ebertoft, Denmark,

Svenson, O. (1981). Are we all less risky and more skillful than our fellow drivers?. *Acta Psychol.* 47, 143–148.

Thaler, R.H. (1980). Toward a positive theory of consumer choice. *J. Econ. Behav. Organ.* 1, 39–60.

Thaler, R.H. (1985). Mental accounting and consumer choice. *Marketing Sci.* 4, 199–214.

Thaler, R.H. (1987). The psychology of choice and the assumptions of economics, in: Alvin E. Roth (ed.), *Laboratory Experimentation in Economics: Six Points of View*, Cambridge University Press, Cambridge.

Thaler, R.H., ed. (1993). *Advances in Behavioral Finance*, Russell Sage Foundation, New York, NY.

Thaler, R.H., and H. Shefrin (1981). An economic theory of self-control. *J. Polit. Econ.* 89, 392–410.

Travlos, N.G. (1987). Corporate takeover bids, methods of payment, and bidding firms' stock returns. *J. Finance* 42, 943–964.

Tversky, A., and D. Kahneman (1974). Judgment under uncertainty: heuristics and biases. *Science* 185, 1124–1131.

Tversky, A., and D. Kahneman (1981). The framing of decisions and the psychology of choice. *Science* 211, 453–458.

Ziemba, W.T. (1993). World wide security market regularities, forthcoming.

R. Jarrow et al., Eds., *Handbooks in OR & MS, Vol. 9*

Chapter 14

Volatility

Stephen F. LeRoy
Curtis L. Carlson School of Management, University of Minnesota, Minneapolis, MN 55455, U.S.A.

Douglas G. Steigerwald
Department of Economics, University of California, Santa Barbara, CA 93106, U.S.A.

1. Introduction

Until the mid-1970s, capital market efficiency was tested using what are now known as returns tests. In these tests the analyst sought to determine whether information currently available to investors is correlated with future asset returns. For example, past returns, detailed firm data and such macroeconomic variables as GNP were all considered as possible explanatory variables in a linear model of equity returns. If nonzero correlations were found, one inferred that the current price could be improved upon as a predictor of future prices, suggesting that capital markets are not informationally efficient.

If capital markets are not informationally efficient in this sense then (under additional assumptions) investors who trade actively to exploit these correlations can hope to do better on average than investors who buy and hold. If, however, markets are informationally efficient, then prices 'fully reflect' available information and there are no exploitable correlations between future returns and current information. In the absence of exploitable correlations, active trading rules cannot succeed on average.

Most of the evidence accumulated prior to the 1980s implied that asset markets are informationally efficient, at least as a first approximation. Fama's influential [1970] paper surveyed the empirical evidence available up to that date and established the conclusion in favor of market efficiency to most academic readers' satisfaction (see Fama 1991 for an update).

LeRoy & Porter [1981] and Shiller [1981], working independently, proposed an alternative test of market efficiency. This test exploited Samuelson's [1965] demonstration that, in the context of the stock market, the present-value relation is equivalent (subject to a convergence assumption) to the null hypothesis tested in the returns tests. The present-value relation states that the current actual stock price is the best predictor of the discounted value of future actual dividends, referred to as the ex-post rational price. More precisely, the present-value relation states that actual current price equals the mathematical expectation of ex-post rational price conditional on whatever information investors have available:

$$p_t = E(p_t^* \mid I_t), \tag{1.1}$$

where

$$p_t^* \equiv \sum_{i=1}^{\infty} \beta^i d_{t+i}. \tag{1.2}$$

This version of the market efficiency hypothesis suggested to LeRoy & Porter and Shiller a strategy for empirical testing which was different from the returns tests surveyed by Fama. If price equals discounted expected dividends, then price changes occur only when expected dividends change. Expected dividends, unfortunately, are not easily measured. However, under rational expectations the volatility of changes in expected dividends is related systematically to the volatility of changes in actual dividends, which can be estimated. LeRoy & Porter and Shiller exploited this line of reasoning to derive the bounds on stock price volatility implied by measured dividend volatility. The simplest variance bounds relation is

$$V(p_t) \leq V(p_t^*), \tag{1.3}$$

which follows from (1.1) plus the result from probability theory that the variance of the conditional expectation of a random variable is less than or equal to the variance of the random variable itself. LeRoy & Porter and Shiller found that these bounds were violated, suggesting that the common journalistic observation that stock price changes are in some sense excessive relative to fundamentals may have substance.

Returns tests appeared to accept market efficiency, volatility tests to reject it. Both LeRoy & Porter and Shiller suggested a possible explanation for this discrepancy: volatility tests have greater power than returns tests. To be sure, Shiller provided little, and LeRoy & Porter nothing, by way of specific support for this claim. The subsequent variance-bounds literature has returned periodically to the question of power, particularly in comparing volatility tests with conventional returns tests of market efficiency. The results achieved so far have not been conclusive. We believe that this concern with statistical power is not misplaced: power is the central concept in analyzing econometric aspects of the variance-bounds tests. The related topic of bias in parameter estimation, which has been the main focus in much discussion of econometric aspects of the variance-bounds literature, is in fact subsidiary: bias causes problems only insofar as it reduces the power of a test (for given size), and there is generally no presumption that this occurs.

In Sections 2–4 of this paper we survey the variance-bounds literature and the parallel evolution of the literature on returns tests of market efficiency, taking power as the organizing principle. In Section 5 we present some new results on the comparative power of volatility and returns tests. Section 6 is the conclusion.

We recognize that some readers — particularly those who want to get the flavor of the variance-bounds literature without delving deeply into its econometric side — may prefer a more general treatment. Such readers should consult LeRoy [1984] and West [1988]. LeRoy [1989] discussed the variance-bounds literature in its relation to the general question of asset market efficiency. Shiller's [1989] book gave introductory treatment, as did Cochrane's [1991] review. Finally, Gilles & LeRoy's [1991] survey provided an elementary econometric survey of the variance-bounds literature, as here, but focused on bias in parameter estimators rather than power.

2. Variance-bounds tests of capital market efficiency

2.1. Statistical hypothesis testing

It became clear at an early stage of the development of the variance-bounds literature that there is a trivial sense in which variance-bounds tests — some, at least — are in fact more powerful than returns tests. To explain this, it is necessary first to review the basics of statistical hypothesis testing.

Whenever a statistical test is constructed, inferences made about the null or alternative models are probabilistic rather than deterministic. There is virtually always some probability that even if the true data-generating process is the null model, the particular data realization sampled by the researcher leads to rejection of the null model. Correspondingly, there is generally some chance that even though the null model is incorrect, the data under observation conform to it so closely that the model cannot be rejected. These ideas lead directly to the concepts of size and power.

A test of the null hypothesis is based upon the estimated values of certain parameters in the model. The *critical region* denotes the range of estimated parameter values for which the null model is rejected. The *size* of the test is the probability that the parameter estimate lies in the critical region when the null hypothesis is true, so that the null model is incorrectly rejected. The *power* of the test is the probability of the same event when the alternative model is true, so that the null model is correctly rejected.

One wants a test that is powerful against all relevant alternative models. This can be achieved simply by specifying a large critical region. Unfortunately, specifying a large critical region also increases the size of the test. Because of this relation between size and power, there is a trivial sense in which any test can be made to have high power: enlarge the critical region. Such a test will produce the correct answer with high probability when the null hypothesis is false, but only because the test has a high probability of rejecting the null whether it is true or false.

It follows that in comparing the power of two econometric tests, size must be held constant. Otherwise the comparison is pointless.

2.2. Size and power in variance-bounds tests

Let us see how these considerations bear on the variance-bounds tests. The simplest and best-known of the variance-bounds theorems, introduced as (1.3) above, says that the variance of actual stock prices p_t is bounded above by the variance of the ex-post rational price p_t^*. One natural way to test (1.3) is to examine the volatility statistic, defined to be the difference between the estimated variance of p_t^* and that of p_t. There are several problems involved in constructing the statistic, of which the most serious involves trend correction. If p_t and p_t^* have not been corrected for trend the population means and variances are time-dependent, implying that population variances cannot be consistently estimated by sample variances. The first-generation variance-bounds papers of LeRoy & Porter and Shiller ran into difficulty with trend-correction. Subsequent papers, however, have remedied this problem [Campbell & Shiller, 1988; LeRoy & Parke, 1992]. This material is reviewed in Gilles & LeRoy [1991]; repetition here would divert attention from the topic of power, so we simply assume that a satisfactory trend-correction algorithm has been implemented, implying that p_t and p_t^* are stationary.

It is known that $V(p_t)$ is accurately estimated by its sample variance for reasonable sample sizes and specifications of investors' information sets, but $V(p_t^*)$ is more problematic. The fact that p_t^* depends on dividends beyond any finite horizon implies that p_t^* is unobservable in any finite sample. Grossman & Shiller [1981] resolved this problem by defining an observable proxy $p_{t|T}^*$ for the unobservable p_t^* by setting the terminal value $p_{T|T}^*$ equal to p_T and deriving earlier values from the recursion

$$p_{t|T}^* = \beta(p_{t+1|T}^* + d_{t+1}), \tag{2.1}$$

an implication of (1.2). They estimated $V(p_t^*)$ by taking the sample variance of $p_{t|T}^*$.

It happens that the estimator of $V(p_t^*)$ just described is severely downward-biased in small samples [Flavin, 1983; Kleidon, 1986; see Gilles & LeRoy, 1991, for an exposition]. This implies that the mathematical expectation of the volatility statistic is smaller than the corresponding population value, and in fact may be negative even if the present-value model is true. If the critical region associated with a test of the null hypothesis that the present-value model is correct consists of all negative values of the volatility statistic, then the downward bias just described ensures that the size of the test will be large. Hence even if (1.3) holds in the population our sample estimators will typically indicate excess volatility (the inequality in the sample counterpart of (1.3) is reversed).

It has become common to conclude from such reasoning that variance-bounds tests are biased toward rejection, and therefore are not credible. This reasoning is incorrect, as the choice of zero as a critical value for the volatility statistic is entirely arbitrary. To the extent that $V(p_t^*)$ is estimated with downward bias, the probability of incorrectly rejecting the present-value model is increased, but since the size of the test was unspecified in the first place, it is difficult to understand in what sense we have a biased test. It would be more accurate to conclude that in the absence of some means of controlling the size, we have no real test at all. This is true whether or not point estimates of parameters are biased.

It is now easy to see the trivial sense in which variance-bounds tests may have higher power than conventional returns tests. The downward bias in the estimate of $V(p_t^*)$ just described means that if the rejection region is specified to be the negative values of the volatility statistic, the variance-bounds tests may be prone to reject the null of market efficiency whether it is false or not. This is a point against variance-bounds tests if market efficiency is in fact true, but is a point in their favor if it is false. Thus by adopting a biased estimator of $V(p_t^*)$, we have increased the power of the test at the cost of increasing its size. This does not provide a useful benchmark for comparing variance-bounds tests with returns tests since we could increase both the size and power of a returns test by enlarging its critical region. A claim for the superiority of variance-bounds tests can be based only on a showing that they are more powerful than returns tests for given size, and a claim for their inferiority must demonstrate the opposite. Nothing in the discussion so far shows either point.

To construct a true econometric test based on the volatility statistic and to compare this test with conventional market efficiency tests, it is necessary to determine how to choose the critical value of the test statistic so that the size is held to some preassigned level. That the estimator of $V(p_t^*)$ constructed as described above is biased is not necessarily a problem, even if the bias is difficult to evaluate analytically. Assuming that Monte Carlo methods are used to construct critical values, then as long as the estimate of $V(p_t^*)$ is constructed in the same way on the artificially generated data as on real-world data, the bias is automatically allowed for in the choice of the critical value.[1]

2.3. *The nuisance parameter problem in testing variance bounds*

The fact that variance-bounds tests are tests of an inequality causes a major problem. The efficient markets model makes no restriction on investors' information sets; equivalently, inequality (1.3) holds no matter how much or little information investors have. Thus there are many versions of the null hypothesis, indexed by a measure of investors' information. This causes a problem in setting the critical value of the volatility statistic: different specifications of investors' information lead to different critical values. The better the information investors have about future dividends, the greater will be the volatility of stock prices under the efficient markets model, and therefore the lower will be the value of $V(p_t^*) - V(p_t)$ that is implied by market efficiency. The fact that the population value of $V(p_t^*) - V(p_t)$ associated with the present-value model depends on the

[1] This point lay behind Shiller's [1988] reply to Kleidon's [1986] criticism: Shiller granted that his estimator of $V(p_t^*)$ is biased under the conditions assumed by Kleidon, but used simulation results to argue that even so the real-world value of the volatility statistic was too far below zero to be consistent with market efficiency.

extent of investors' information suggests that the same will be true of the critical value of the associated sample statistic. (This is not necessarily the case, however, because the sample variability of the volatility statistic also depends on the extent of investors' information, which complicates the picture). The Monte Carlo simulations reported in LeRoy & Parke [1992] imply that for reasonable parameter values the critical level of the volatility statistic does indeed depend strongly on the extent of investors' information.

The question becomes how one sets the critical value of the volatility statistic, given the dependence of its distribution on a nuisance parameter. One potential solution is to vary the amount of information agents are assumed to have, and then choose the critical value so that the maximum size of the test is held to some preassigned level like 5%. The problem is that in the present setting the nuisance parameter problem is so severe that for most versions of the null hypothesis rejection will occur with probability much lower than 1% when the nominal probability of Type I error is set at 5%. With the acceptance region set so large, the test will have very low power. There is no way to avoid the fact that when a severe nuisance parameter problem occurs, the size and power of any statistical test are essentially impossible to evaluate no matter how one chooses the rejection region.

This argument, presented in LeRoy & Parke [1992], implies that hypothesis testing of the variance-bounds inequality is essentially impossible. The point was not noticed earlier, and is still not widely appreciated, because of the practice prevailing in the variance-bounds literature (discussed above) of implicitly identifying the critical value of the volatility statistic with zero — so that the present-value model is accepted if $\hat{V}(p_t) \leq \hat{V}(p_t^*)$ and rejected in the opposite case — despite the absence of any justification for this identification. We already saw that if the critical value of the volatility statistic is set equal to zero and if a downward-biased estimate of $V(p_t^*)$ is used, rejection of market efficiency is to be expected, but these tests have a large size. More recent papers, such as Cochrane [1992], use better estimates of $V(p_t^*)$ and fail to reject the efficient market model based on the sample counterpart of the variance-bounds inequality. However, these papers do not take cognizance of the nuisance parameter problem.

2.4. Summary

Thinking about statistical power in the context of variance-bounds tests leads to serious questions about their interpretation: it is pointless to compare the power of variance-bounds and returns tests without holding size constant. But because the probability distribution of the volatility statistic depends on the extent of investors' information, which is unrestricted under market efficiency, there is no way to hold constant the size of a variance-bounds test.

The practice in the variance-bounds literature has been to reject market efficiency when the sample counterpart of the variance inequality is not satisfied. This arbitrary choice of rejection region has the obvious implication that if a downward-biased estimator of $V(p_t^*)$ is used, and if investors have considerable information about future dividends (so that $V(p_t)$ is high under the null hypothesis) then the test is likely to have a large size and, correspondingly, high power. If an unbiased estimator of $V(p_t^*)$ is used, the size is smaller, but the power is lower as well. It appears that little is learned by actually conducting such tests: there is no point in verifying that some particular variance-bounds test rejects or fails to reject market efficiency if one has no way to evaluate the probabilities of these outcomes under the null hypothesis of market efficiency or under some alternative.

3. Returns tests

Defenders of efficient capital markets rejected the contention that the variance-bounds tests demonstrated the excess volatility of asset prices, and the discussion of the preceding section suggests that they had some justification for doing so. The main problem, as we saw, was that nothing can be concluded from the fact that point estimates of $V(p_t)$ and $V(p_t^*)$ reverse the variance-bounds inequality in the absence of a showing that such an outcome would be unlikely if the present-value model were correct.[2] Further, the critical value of the volatility statistic depends upon a nuisance parameter that reflects how much information agents have. Because the present value model does not specify the amount of information agents have, it appears that there is no way to remedy this problem and draw valid inferences from variance-bounds tests.

However, just as researchers were dismissing the conclusion of variance bounds tests in favor of those of returns tests, and thereby reaffirming the earlier conclusion in favor of the present-value model, the latter tests were undergoing a major reappraisal. Fama & French [1988] and Poterba & Summers [1988] reexamined the autocorrelation of rates of return on stock. Unlike the earlier papers discussed in Fama [1970], in which daily and weekly returns were used, Fama & French and Poterba & Summers looked at autocorrelation of returns averaged over months and years. They found that over these long horizons returns are significantly autocorrelated. The average return from $t-T$ to T predicts about 35% of the variation of the average return from t to $t+T$, for T on the order of three to five years. The correlation is negative, so that low returns in the past predict high returns in the future.

The finding that stock returns are autocorrelated at long horizons parallels the excess volatility findings: many of the alternatives to the present-value model that would produce negatively autocorrelated returns would also generate excess volatility. For example, investor overreaction to relevant information would produce both negative return autocorrelation and excess price volatility. Alternatively,

[2] LeRoy & Porter [1981] presented evidence that the rejections implied by the point estimates of volatility parameters were of borderline statistical significance at conventional levels, based on asymptotic distributions. However, because of bias induced by faulty trend correction this evidence was of questionable validity. Also, a showing of small-sample bias raised questions about the applicability of asymptotic distribution theory.

suppose that stock prices are modeled as the sum of the value implied by the present-value relation and a noise term which is independent of fundamentals. Again, both negatively autocorrelated returns and excess volatility would result.

The finding that stock prices contain a mean-reverting component, like the finding of excess volatility, has been subjected to criticism. Kim, Nelson & Startz [1991] contended that much or all of the evidence of mean-reversion disappears if data from the 1930s are dropped from the sample (however, this finding has been questioned by Cogley [1991]). Similarly, Richardson [1993] took issue with Fama & French's analysis on econometric grounds.

The contrasting outcomes of variance-bounds and returns tests reported in the introduction appears now to be reversed. The original variance-bounds tests rejected the present-value model, whereas the earlier returns tests accepted it; the upshot of the discussion so far, however, is that the best evidence rejecting the present-value model comes from returns tests, not variance-bounds tests.

4. Orthogonality tests

4.1. Introduction

In criticizing volatility tests, we followed precedent in identifying these with the bounds test

$$V(p_t) \leq V(p_t^*), \tag{4.1}$$

the simplest and best-known volatility implication of the present-value relation. We saw that inequality (4.1) is essentially untestable because the present-value relation leaves investors' information unrestricted, rendering it impossible to set critical values for the rejection region. However, bounds tests are not the only kind of volatility test; we also have orthogonality tests. These, although less familiar, are better-behaved econometrically than bounds tests: as we will see, they are less subject than bounds tests to the nuisance parameter problem discussed in Section 2.

The simplest orthogonality test is derived by iterating the definition of returns (as the sum of dividends plus capital gain) to obtain

$$p_t^* = p_t + \sum_{i=1}^{\infty} \beta^i (p_{t+i} + d_{t+i} - \beta^{-1} p_{t+i-1}). \tag{4.2}$$

Taking variances in (4.2) and invoking the orthogonality of the two terms on the right-hand side of (4.2) yields

$$V(p_t^*) = V(p_t) + \frac{\beta^2 V(p_{t+1} + d_{t+1} - \beta^{-1} p_t)}{1 - \beta^2}, \tag{4.3}$$

assuming that these variances are constant over time [see LeRoy, 1989, and Gilles & LeRoy, 1991, for more discussion].

The orthogonality test (4.3) has a somewhat different interpretation from the bounds test (4.1). The present-value model is seen in (4.3) to provide a joint restriction on the volatility of price and that of excess payoffs, not just on the volatility of price as with the bounds test. Because (4.3) holds as an equality for any specification of investors' information, the orthogonality test provides a way of partly circumventing the nuisance parameter problem that plagues the bounds test (4.1): variations in m affect $V(p_t)$, but the effect is precisely offset by an equal and opposite effect on the right-most term of (4.3).[3] Both effects are allowed for in the test. It was for this reason that LeRoy & Porter placed primary reliance on their version of the orthogonality test rather than the bounds test in concluding that volatility is excessive (although the reader will not find a clear discussion of the distinction between bounds and orthogonality tests in that paper).

Orthogonality tests provide statistically significant evidence of excess volatility [LeRoy & Parke, 1992]: no matter how one specifies investors' information, the volatility statistic based on (4.3) (i.e., its left-hand side less its right-hand side, with population parameters replaced by their sample counterparts) is significantly negative.

4.2. Relative power of volatility and returns tests

The empirical evidence to date indicates that both returns tests and volatility tests reject the present-value model. Rejection appears to be of borderline significance in the case of returns tests (and is subject to question on econometric grounds), but is clearly significant in the case of volatility tests. Since both types of test give essentially the same answer, determining which of these tests is more powerful — the focus of this paper — is a less urgent topic than it would be if their outcomes differed. Nonetheless, it is well worth investigating, and we now do so.

It seems unlikely that any conclusion about the general superiority of one test over the other will be forthcoming. Instead, volatility tests are likely to be more powerful than returns tests under some alternatives and less powerful under others. To see that the relative power of two tests of some null hypothesis generally depends on the alternative hypothesis, we turn to a more familiar example. Consider testing the irrelevance of x_1 and x_2 in the linear regression model

$$y_t = \beta_0 + \beta_1 x_{1t} + \beta_2 x_{2t} + \epsilon_t. \tag{4.4}$$

One straightforward approach is based upon testing

$$H_0: \qquad \beta_1 = \beta_2 = 0 \tag{4.5}$$

against the alternative

$$H_1: \qquad \beta_1 \text{ or } \beta_2 \neq 0. \tag{4.6}$$

[3] However, even for the orthogonality test the sample characteristics of the statistic corresponding to this parameter depend on investors' information, as will be seen below. Therefore even under the orthogonality test the nuisance parameter problem, although much mitigated, is still with us.

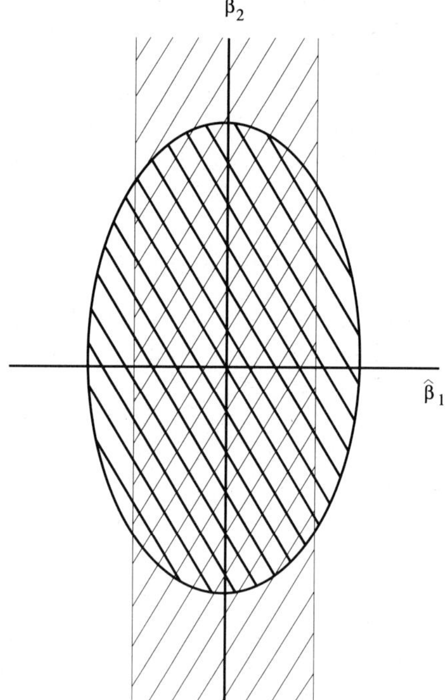

Fig. 1. Critical regions for testing $\beta_1 = \hat{\beta}_2 = 0$.

Since the test statistics are the sample regression coefficients $\hat{\beta}_1$ and $\hat{\beta}_2$, the critical region is given by the ellipsoid in Figure 1.

One could also form a test of $\beta_1 = \beta_2 = 0$ based only upon β_1, leading to $H_0' : \beta_1 = 0$ and $H_1' : \beta_1 \neq 0$. The critical region for this test is given by the area between the two vertical lines in the figure. If the size of each test is 5%, for example, then the probability of obtaining values in the ellipsoid given H_0 is equal to the probability of obtaining values between the two vertical lines given H_0'. Thus by construction the two tests work equally well when H_0 is true.

There is no presumption that under an alternative hypothesis the probabilities of the regions in which the tests give different outcomes is the same. For example, under an alternative hypothesis with $\beta_1 = 0$ and $\beta_2 \neq 0$ the test that ignores the implication of the model for β_2 is likely incorrectly to fail to reject the null. However, if the alternative hypothesis has $\beta_1 \neq 0$ and $\beta_2 = 0$, ignoring the implications of the model for β_2 is a virtue since the test involving only the statistic for β_1 is more likely to reject the null hypothesis when it is false.[4]

[4] Cochrane [1991] argued that because volatility tests and return tests use the same instruments, they are likely to have the same power. This argument ignores the fact, just discussed, that the power of different tests generally depends on the alternative hypothesis, even if the tests use the same instruments. It follows that return and volatility tests do not necessarily have equal power

LeRoy & Porter and Shiller supposed that something similar was occurring with the volatility tests: by ignoring some implications of the present-value relation in order to focus on its implications for price and return variance, the volatility tests were in effect searching for violations in the right direction, whereas a test that searches in all directions for violations necessarily searches less thoroughly. Although LeRoy & Porter and Shiller suggested this possibility, they provided no concrete evidence supporting the suggestion.

4.3. Two orthogonality tests for the geometric random walk

The orthogonality test discussed above says that the variance of actual price plus that of returns (multiplied by a constant) equals the variance of the ex-post rational price (4.3). This version of the orthogonality test has the virtue of simplicity, but also has the major drawback that it requires the assumption that dividends are stationary, necessitating a trend correction. To avoid trend-correction questions, we replaced (4.3) with

$$V(p_t^*/d_t) = V(p_t/d_t) + \frac{\beta^2\left\{V(p_t/d_t) + [E(p_t/d_t)]^2\right\}}{1-\beta^2(\sigma^2+\mu^2)}V(r_t) \tag{4.7}$$

[see LeRoy & Parke, 1992, for a derivation]. Here μ and σ are the mean and standard deviation, respectively, of the dividend growth rate. Equation (4.7) is analogous to (4.3) except that in (4.7) the extensive variables p_t^*, p_t and $p_{t+1} + d_{t+1} - \beta^{-1}p_t$ are replaced by the intensive variables p_t^*/d_t, p_t/d_t and r_t, (the rate of return: $r_{t+1} \equiv [p_{t+1} + d_{t+1} - p_t]/p_t$). Qualitatively, the interpretation of (4.7) is the same as that of (4.3): in (4.7) the variance of the price–dividend ratio plus (a function of) the variance of the rate of return equals the variance of the ex-post rational price–dividend ratio. The more information investors have, the higher is $V(p_t/d_t)$ and the lower is $V(r_t)$.

Just as (4.3) required that the extensive variables p_t^*, p_t and $(p_{t+1} + d_{t+1} - \beta^{-1}p_t)$ have constant variances, (4.7) requires that the intensive variables p_t^*/d_t, p_t/d_t and r_t have constant variances. If dividends are generated by a log-linear process (and assuming that information revelation is regular), this property will be satisfied for the intensive variables even though dividends, and therefore stock prices, have upward trends. Thus no further trend-correction is necessary.

The volatility statistic associated with (4.7) is computed by calculating the sample moments $\hat{V}(p_t/d_t)$, $\hat{V}(r_t)$, $\hat{E}(d_{t+1}/d_t)$ and $\hat{V}(d_{t+1}/d_t)$, where the sample variances are the average squared deviations around sample means, and substituting these for $V(p_t/d_t)$, $V(r_t)$, μ and σ^2 in (4.7). We estimated β from

$$\hat{E}(p_t/d_t) = \frac{\hat{\beta}\hat{\mu}}{1-\hat{\beta}\hat{\mu}}. \tag{4.8}$$

against any particular alternative. Also, Cochrane's argument makes no allowance for the fact that because return tests and volatility tests use different auxiliary hypotheses, they are in effect tests of different versions of market efficiency.

It remains to select an estimator of $V(p_t^*/d_t)$. There are two types of estimators of $V(p_t^*/d_t)$: model-free and model-based [Gilles & LeRoy, 1991]. A model-free estimator directly constructs an observable counterpart to the unobservable p_t^* series and takes the sample variance of the implied p_t^*/d_t series. A model-based estimator is derived by postulating a dividends model and deriving an expression for $V(p_t^*/d_t)$ in terms of β and the parameters of the dividends model. Then $V(p_t^*/d_t)$ is estimated by substituting parameter estimates in the derived expression. Model-free estimators have the advantage that they do not add a dividends model to the null model being tested, but model-based tests have the advantage that they are much less subject to sample variation [LeRoy & Parke, 1992]. Our model-free estimator of $V(p_t^*/d_t)$ was the sample variance of $p_{t|T}^*/d_t$, where $p_{t|T}^*$ is defined in (2.1).

Our model-based estimator of $V(p_t^*/d_t)$ was constructed from the geometric random walk:

$$d_{t+1} = d_t \epsilon_{t+1}, \tag{4.9}$$

where $E(\epsilon_t) = \mu$, $V(\epsilon_{t+1}) = \sigma^2$, and the ϵ_t are independently and identically distributed. Under the geometric random walk

$$V(p_t^*/d_t) = \frac{\beta^2\sigma^2}{[1-\beta^2(\sigma^2+\mu^2)](1-\beta\mu)^2}, \tag{4.10}$$

implying that the model-based estimate of $V(p_t^*/d_t)$ is:

$$\hat{V}(p_t^*/d_t) = \frac{\hat{\beta}^2\hat{\sigma}^2}{[1-\hat{\beta}^2(\hat{\sigma}^2+\hat{\mu}^2)](1-\hat{\beta}^2\hat{\mu}^2)}. \tag{4.11}$$

In each case the sample statistic $\hat{S}$ is just the left-hand side of (4.7) less its right-hand side, with sample statistics replacing population parameters as just indicated. If the model being tested is that which actually generated the data, $\hat{S}$ should be near zero; if $\hat{S}$ is significantly different from zero, the model is rejected. Specifically, excess volatility would cause $\hat{V}(p_t/d_t)$ and $\hat{V}(r_t)$ to be high, leading to a significantly negative value of $\hat{S}$.

5. Monte Carlo tests

5.1. Monte Carlo evaluations of volatility tests

We constructed Monte Carlo evaluations of the size and power of the model-based bounds test, and both the model-free and model-based orthogonality tests, by assuming that dividends were generated by a geometric random walk with normal innovations.[5] We set the mean and standard deviation of the dividend

[5] We conducted tests of the model-free bounds test, but do not report them because they are subject to the same critical shortcomings as the model-based bounds test, reported below.

growth rate equal to those reported by LeRoy & Parke [1992] for annual US aggregate dividends ($\mu = 1.0216$, $\sigma^2 = 0.0153$). Simulated stock prices were calculated using an annual discount factor of 0.9350, the value estimated by LeRoy & Parke. For each iteration, we simulated a time-series for both prices and dividends of length 117 to accord with our annual data set. We performed 10,000 iterations, each time saving the values of the test statistics, which we used to construct a simulated distribution. The critical values for our test statistics were then based on the 5%-tail of the simulated distribution in the direction associated with excess volatility.

As noted in Section 2 the present-value model being tested is a compound null hypothesis, with different versions implied by different specifications of investors' information. The stock price series associated with a given dividend sample path depends on how much information investors are assumed to have, implying that for bounds tests the population parameter corresponding to the test statistic, $V(p_t^*/d_t) - V(p_t/d_t)$, takes on different values under different versions of the null hypothesis. A major advantage of the orthogonality test is that this problem does not occur: the parameter being tested equals zero under all versions of the null hypothesis.

To parametrize the dependence of stock price on investors' information, we assumed that investors have information variables which enable them to see ahead exactly m periods, for various values of m. This device was used by Gilles & LeRoy [1991] and LeRoy & Parke [1992]. For $m = 0$ investors extrapolate future dividends from current dividends using the constant growth rate implied by the geometric random walk, implying that the price–dividend ratio is constant over time. Investors at t know actual dividends up to $t + m$ and extrapolate dividends beyond $t + m$ by applying a constant growth rate to d_{t+m}. The higher the value of m, the higher is $V(p_t/d_t)$ and the lower is $V(r_t)$; as m approaches infinity, $V(p_t^m/d_t)$ approaches $V(p_t^*/d_t)$ and $V(r_t)$ approaches zero.

We limited the Monte Carlo runs to $m \leq 5$. The reason is that with $m = 5$ the predicted volatility of the price–dividend ratio under the null hypothesis approximately equals the volatility of the real-world price–dividend ratio [LeRoy & Parke, 1992]. Thus for $m > 5$ the volatility of the price–dividend ratio predicted by the model is greater than that observed in the real-world data under both the null hypothesis and the alternative, so these cases can be discarded at the outset as empirically irrelevant.

To evaluate the power of the test just described, we repeated the calculations of the mean and standard deviation of the test statistic assuming that stock prices equal those implied under various values of m by the null hypothesis plus a white noise term:

$$p_t/d_t = E(p_t^*/d_t \mid I_t) + \eta_t, \tag{5.1}$$

where η_t has unit variance, as compared to a variance of p_t^*/d_t of 89.3. We then calculated power by estimating the mean and standard deviation of the test statistic over 10,000 simulated time series generated under this alternative hypothesis. Again using the simulated finite-sample distribution, we calculated the power of each test as the probability that the test statistic generated under the alternative lies in the rejection region as computed under the null.

5.2. Regression tests as a benchmark

As a benchmark to evaluate the power of the bounds and volatility tests, we performed similar power calculations for two regression tests:

$$r_{t+1} = \alpha + \beta r_t + \xi_{1t} \tag{5.2}$$

and

$$r_{t+1} = \gamma + \delta \left(\frac{p_t}{d_t} \right) + \xi_{2t}. \tag{5.3}$$

The null hypothesis implies that $\beta = 0$ and $\delta = 0$. Under the alternative hypothesis, β and δ are negative. This is so because a positive realization of the noise term at t is correlated with high values of r_t and p_t/d_t, and also with low values of r_{t+1}. Therefore a one-tail test of the present-value model can be constructed by setting the rejection region as the lower 5% tail of $\hat{\beta}$ and $\hat{\delta}$.

The reason we concentrated on a white noise alternative — despite the fact that fads are usually modeled as highly autocorrelated noise processes — is that under a white noise alternative it is easy to determine the most powerful regression test of the present-value model: regress r_{t+1} on r_t. Including lagged returns as regressors will only dissipate degrees of freedom since lagged returns have population coefficients of zero under both the null and the alternative. However, we present evidence below that our results on power carry over when noise is autocorrelated.

The regression tests just outlined have the major advantage that, under the null hypothesis, they are free of nuisance parameter problems. For the regression tests, like the orthogonality test but unlike the bounds test, the value of the population parameter is zero under all versions of the null hypothesis (i.e., under any specification of investors' information). However, it is also true of regression tests, unlike both the volatility tests, that the probability distribution of the corresponding test statistic does not depend on investors' information. Put differently, in the regressions the t-test for $\beta = 0$ and $\delta = 0$ allows construction of a 5% rejection region under any specification of investors' information. Under the orthogonality tests, in contrast, it is necessary to make allowance for the fact that for any critical value of the test statistic the size of the test may depend on investors' information. This dependence complicates the interpretation of the results.

5.3. Monte Carlo results

Tables 1 and 2 report the mean and standard deviation of the test statistic for each of the five tests outlined above — three volatility tests and two regression tests — under the null hypothesis and the alternative hypothesis, respectively.

Table 1

Mean / standard deviation of test statistics; null hypothesis: present-value model

m	Volatility tests			Regression tests	
	(1) Bounds	(2) Model-free orthogonality	(3) Model-based orthogonality	(4) r_{t+1} on r_t	(5) r_{t+1} on p_t/d_t
1	83.2 / 13.1	−43.2 / 37.5	−0.0 / 1.0	0.0 / 0.09	0.0 / 0.004
2	77.2 / 12.7	−42.4 / 38.4	0.3 / 2.2	0.0 / 0.09	0.0 / 0.004
3	71.7 / 12.9	−41.3 / 39.8	0.9 / 3.6	0.0 / 0.09	0.0 / 0.002
4	66.8 / 13.6	−40.3 / 39.5	1.6 / 5.3	0.0 / 0.09	0.0 / 0.002
5	62.5 / 14.6	−39.2 / 38.2	2.5 / 7.2	0.0 / 0.09	0.0 / 0.002

Table 2

Mean / standard deviation of test statistics; alternative hypothesis: present-value model plus noise

m	Volatility tests			Regression tests	
	(1) Bounds	(2) Model-free orthogonality	(3) Model-based orthogonality	(4) r_{t+1} on r_t	(5) r_{t+1} on p_t/d_t
1	82.2 / 13.1	−86.7 / 42.8	−29.1 / 11.1	−0.13 / 0.09	−0.0004 / 0.005
2	76.2 / 12.7	−88.7 / 41.4	−30.4 / 11.2	−0.14 / 0.09	−0.0004 / 0.003
3	70.7 / 13.0	−90.0 / 43.0	−31.4 / 11.9	−0.16 / 0.09	−0.0005 / 0.003
4	65.8 / 13.7	−89.9 / 43.2	−31.8 / 12.6	−0.17 / 0.09	−0.0005 / 0.002
5	61.5 / 14.7	−91.2 / 41.9	−32.3 / 14.1	−0.18 / 0.09	−0.0006 / 0.002

Column 1 of Table 2 shows that, as expected, the mean value of the test statistic under the bounds tests decreases with m. Comparison of column 1 of Tables 1 and 2 shows that, again as expected, the noise term lowers the mean of the test statistic. However, the effect is minor relative to both the standard deviation of the test statistic and the effect of m on the test statistic. We see already that the bounds test is likely not to be very good at detecting the presence of noise.

Column 2 of Table 1 shows that under the null hypothesis the test statistics for the model-free orthogonality test average about one standard deviation below zero, reflecting the well-documented downward bias in the model-free estimate of $V(p_t^*/d_t)$. The corresponding column of Table 2 shows that the test statistic averages about two standard deviations below zero when white noise is present. In sharp contrast to the bounds test, the behavior of the test statistic under either the null or the alternative does not depend significantly on investors' information. The reason that the noise has a greater effect on the test statistic under the model-free orthogonality test is that in the rightmost term in (4.7), $V(r_t)$ is multiplied by a large number; the effect of the noise term on $V(p_t/d_t)$ is minor by comparison. In the model-based orthogonality test the effect of noise on the test statistic (column 3) is comparable in magnitude to its effect in the model-free test. However, sampling variation is much lower with the model-based orthogonality test, especially under the null hypothesis. In the regression tests, the white noise term induces negative autocorrelation of borderline statistical significance in successive rates of return (Table 2, column 4). In contrast, the coefficient in the regression of r_{t+1} on p_t/d_t is essentially zero under the alternative.

Tables 3 and 4 show the size and power of the five tests under consideration. We computed size and power under a representative value of m: $m = 2$ (Table 3), and under the maximum reasonable value of m: $m = 5$ (Table 4). Column 1 of either Table 3 or Table 4 shows that the size and power of the bounds test depend

Table 3 *

Size / power of tests; critical region based on $m = 2$

m	Volatility tests			Regression tests	
	(1) Bounds	(2) Model-free orthogonality	(3) Model-based orthogonality	(4) r_{t+1} on r_t	(5) r_{t+1} on p_t/d_t
1	0.01 / 0.01	0.04 / 0.63	0.00 / 0.99	0.06 / 0.40	0.06 / 0.06
2	0.03 / 0.04	0.05 / 0.66	0.04 / 0.99	0.06 / 0.47	0.06 / 0.06
3	0.11 / 0.13	0.04 / 0.65	0.11 / 0.99	0.06 / 0.52	0.07 / 0.05
4	0.23 / 0.26	0.04 / 0.67	0.16 / 0.99	0.06 / 0.58	0.07 / 0.05
5	0.37 / 0.39	0.04 / 0.65	0.19 / 0.99	0.06 / 0.65	0.08 / 0.06

Size = probability of rejecting the present-value model when it is true; power = probability of rejecting the present-value model when it is false.

Table 4 *

Size / power of tests; critical region based on $m = 5$

m	Volatility tests			Regression tests	
	(1) Bounds	(2) Model-free orthogonality	(3) Model-based orthogonality	(4) r_{t+1} on r_t	(5) r_{t+1} on p_t/d_t
1	0.00 / 0.00	0.06 / 0.66	0.00 / 0.97	0.06 / 0.40	0.06 / 0.06
2	0.00 / 0.00	0.05 / 0.68	0.00 / 0.98	0.06 / 0.47	0.06 / 0.06
3	0.00 / 0.00	0.04 / 0.67	0.01 / 0.98	0.06 / 0.52	0.07 / 0.06
4	0.01 / 0.01	0.05 / 0.69	0.03 / 0.98	0.06 / 0.58	0.07 / 0.05
5	0.03 / 0.04	0.05 / 0.67	0.06 / 0.99	0.06 / 0.65	0.08 / 0.06

Size = probability of rejecting the present-value model when it is true; power = probability of rejecting the present-value model when it is false.

* Note that some of the values which should equal 0.05 from the construction of the tables actually equal 0.03, 0.04 or 0.06. This discrepancy primarily reflects the normal approximation used to set rejection regions. Also, sample variation is important in estimating tail probabilities, even with 10,000 draws. Finally, the reported values reflect roundoff error.

strongly on m, and also that size is virtually equal to power. Thus, as expected from the discussion of Tables 1 and 2, the bounds test is virtually useless in detecting the presence of the noise term.

Column 2 of Tables 3 and 4 shows that, when the rejection region for the model-free orthogonality test is chosen so that the null is rejected with 5% probability when it is true, it is rejected about two-thirds of the time when it is false. These figures are essentially unaffected by m. In contrast, the fact that the mean and standard deviation of the model-based orthogonality test statistic depend on m means that for fixed rejection region the size and power of the test do so as well (column 3). However, the very low sampling variation of the model-based orthogonality test statistic means that the nuisance parameter problem can be easily handled: setting a large acceptance region, as in Table 4, implies that the null hypothesis is almost sure not to be rejected if it is true and is almost sure to be rejected if it is false.

The regression of r_{t+1} on r_t has power that ranges from 0.40 to 0.65, depending on m, when size is set at 0.05 (column 4). Thus a regression of r_{t+1} on r_t has some ability to detect noise, but much less than the model-based orthogonality test. It is interesting to observe that the nuisance parameter problem reappears with the test based on regressing r_{t+1} on r_t: even though size does not depend on m, the power of the test does. (Note that, while regression theory guarantees that regression tests are free of nuisance parameter problems under the null, it provides no such assurance under the alternative). Finally, the regression of r_{t+1} on p_t/d_t (column 5), like the bounds test, is completely unable to detect the presence of noise. In fact, for some values of m ($m = 3, 4, 5$), the presence of noise actually increases the probability that we fail to reject the null hypothesis. This occurs because the correlation between the noise and p_t/d_t is so low that the noise acts essentially only to increase the variance of p_t/d_t, leading the coefficient in the regression of r_{t+1} to be biased toward zero. This effect is familiar from the errors-in-variables problem of econometrics.

It is important to understand why the model-based orthogonality test performs so much better than the other tests. Observe that if a researcher knew m, then both $V(p_t/d_t)$ and $V(r_t)$ could be expressed as functions of β, m, μ and σ^2, just as $V(p_t^*/d_t)$ is given by (4.10) as a function of β, μ and σ^2. Observe further that if these functions, along with expression (4.11) for $V(p_t^*/d_t)$, are inserted in (4.7), the result is an identity in β, m, μ and σ. Consequently, $\hat{S}$ equals zero for any m even though the estimated values of β, μ and σ are substituted for their population counterparts in (4.7).

Of course, the researcher who does not know m must use the model-free estimates of $V(p_t/d_t)$ and $V(r_t)$ — i.e., their sample variances. It follows that if the null hypothesis is true, variations in $\hat{S}$ are entirely attributable to the differences between the model-free estimates of $V(p_t/d_t)$ and $V(r_t)$ and their model-based counterparts. These differences are small, and are correlated in such a way that the orthogonality test statistic has low variance under the null hypothesis (Table 1). Therefore the orthogonality test is very likely to detect noise if it is present. This argument is similar to that of Durlauf & Hall [1989] to the effect that orthogonality tests are more powerful than bounds tests.

5.4. Robustness to respecified dividend processes

These results show that the model-free orthogonality test has somewhat better ability to detect noise than the most powerful regression test, particularly for low m. For the model-based orthogonality test, power is far greater. However, it will be objected that the playing field is not level. Both versions of the orthogonality test required, in addition to the present-value model, the specification that $V(p_t^*/d_t)$, $V(p_t/d_t)$ and $V(r_t)$ are constant over time. The model-based orthogonality test required further that dividends be generated by a geometric random walk. The regression tests, in contrast, do not require either assumption. The simulations used to evaluate the tests were based on the geometric random walk model, so that the additional specifications adopted for the orthogonality tests were satisfied by construction in the population used to evaluate the two classes of test. It is not surprising that the tests requiring a more restrictive specification perform better than the tests not requiring the more restrictive specification, given a setting in which the added restrictions are valid by assumption.

The suggestion is that the superiority of the orthogonality tests may disappear in settings where the moment variances are nonconstant or where the geometric random walk is a misspecification. That the orthogonality test lacks robustness to alternative dividend specifications is a very real possibility, and this question deserves more thorough study than we have given it. However, we have two preliminary results to report.

We considered an environment in which the geometric random walk is a gross misspecification: if dividends are generated by a stationary model rather than an integrated model the orthogonality relation (4.7) is invalid. We verified by Monte Carlo methods that application of (4.7) resulted in virtually 100% rejection frequencies if dividends are stationary whether the null hypothesis was true or false. Analysts who are not willing to stipulate that dividends have a unit root will regard as a major limitation of the orthogonality test the fact that it breaks down if the form (stationary or unit root) of the dividend process is misspecified.

What happens if dividends are log-linear and have a unit root, but are generated by a model less parsimonious than the geometric random walk? In that setting the model-free orthogonality test remains valid, but the model-based test does not since then expression (4.10) for $V(p_t^*/d_t)$ in terms of μ, σ and β is a misspecification. To investigate the extent to which our characterization of the size and power of the orthogonality test carry over in this more general setting, we based Monte Carlo simulations on the AR(2) model

$$\frac{d_{t+1}}{d_t} = 1.03 + 0.18\frac{d_t}{d_{t-1}} - 0.19\frac{d_{t-1}}{d_{t-2}} + \eta_t, \tag{5.4}$$

($V(\eta_t) = 0.0149$), which gives a more accurate characterization of US dividends than the more parsimonious geometric random walk [LeRoy & Parke, 1992, supplement]. Table 5 compares the size and power of the geometric random walk model on the left (this column coincides with Table 4, column 3) with the AR(2)

Table 5
Size / power of tests; critical region based on $m = 5$

m	Geometric random walk	AR(2)
1	0.00 / 0.97	0.00 / 0.96
2	0.00 / 0.98	0.00 / 0.98
3	0.01 / 0.98	0.01 / 0.98
4	0.03 / 0.98	0.03 / 0.96
5	0.06 / 0.99	0.05 / 0.94

model on the right. As is evident, the size and power are not much affected by the geometric random walk misspecification if dividends are generated by the AR(2) model (5.4).

One interpretation of these results is that the orthogonality test is robust, at least within the class of log-linear unit-root models. Another interpretation, however, is that the geometric random walk is a good approximation to less parsimonious dividend models; given that the AR(2) is close to the geometric random walk it is not surprising that size and power are nearly the same in the two cases. From this vantage, it would be observed that little can be concluded about robustness without considering dividend models less similar than our estimated AR(2) to the geometric random walk.

In conclusion, the second of these results suggests that the orthogonality test is not critically sensitive to the geometric random walk assumption, contrary to what might have been expected. However, we again emphasize that we have not provided definitive evidence on this point.

5.5. *Robustness to autocorrelated noise process*

As noted above, we concentrated our attention on a white noise alternative in order to identify easily the regression test which is optimal against the alternative. However, the alternative hypothesis that is relevant empirically (at least on some accounts) incorporates highly autocorrelated noise rather than white noise. To evaluate the effect of noise autocorrelation on power, we recalculated power assuming that the noise is given by

$$\eta_t = \rho\eta_{t_1} + \epsilon_t, \tag{5.5}$$

with σ_ϵ^2 adjusted so that $\sigma_\eta^2 = 1$ for each value of ρ. Table 6 shows that the effect of noise autocorrelation on the power of both the bounds test and the model-based orthogonality test is negligible for low and moderate levels of noise: for ρ less than 0.9 the bounds test seldom rejects and the orthogonality test almost always rejects, as with white noise. However, when the noise process is almost a random walk, the noise increases the sample volatility of the test statistic: for ρ = 0.99 the test statistic lies in the rejection region with 39% probability (71%) for the bounds (orthogonality) test. Thus highly autocorrelated noise somewhat

Table 6

Power under autocorrelated alternative; critical region based on $m = 5$

ρ	Volatility tests		Regression tests	
	(1) Model-based bounds	(2) Model-based orthogonality	(3) r_{t+1} on r_t	(4) r_{t+1} on p_t/d_t
0.0	0.04	0.99	0.40	0.06
0.1	0.04	0.99	0.32	0.08
0.2	0.04	0.99	0.25	0.10
0.3	0.04	0.98	0.20	0.11
0.4	0.04	0.96	0.15	0.12
0.5	0.04	0.95	0.12	0.13
0.6	0.05	0.93	0.10	0.13
0.7	0.05	0.90	0.09	0.12
0.8	0.08	0.87	0.08	0.11
0.9	0.14	0.84	0.07	0.09
0.95	0.24	0.80	0.07	0.08
0.99	0.39	0.71	0.07	0.07

improves the poor performance of the bounds test, but somewhat degrades the excellent performance of the model-based orthogonality test.

As expected, the power of the regression of r_{t+1} on r_t falls as ρ rises. For very high values of ρ the noise component of r_{t+1} is virtually equal to that of r_t, so the negative autocorrelation of rates of return associated with low values of ρ disappears. Also as expected, the regression of r_{t+1} on p_t/d_t gains power as ρ rises from low to moderate values.[6] However, for all values of ρ the regression tests of the present value model remain greatly inferior to the model-based orthogonality test.

6. Conclusion

Both the model-free and model-based orthogonality tests are better-behaved econometrically than the returns test that is optimal (among returns tests) against the alternative we assumed. The model-free orthogonality test has somewhat higher power than the benchmark returns test when size is held constant. Further, unlike the regression test the model-free orthogonality test is not subject to the nuisance parameter problem under either the null or the alternative. The model-based orthogonality test, in contrast, is subject to the nuisance parameter problem under both the null and the alternative. However, sampling variation is so low under both the null and the alternative — but particularly so under the

[6] Campbell [1993] verified analytically that long-horizon return autoregressions are more powerful than short-horizon return autoregressions when the alternative is highly autocorrelated. Regressing r_{t+1} on p_t/d_t is similar to a long-horizon return autoregression.

null — that the nuisance parameter problem does not distort the outcome: in assessing the presence or absence of noise, the critical region for the model-based orthogonality test can be set so that the test almost always returns the correct diagnosis. However, the model-based test requires the assumption that dividends follow a geometric random walk, so this verdict in favor of the model-based orthogonality test might require revision to the extent that that specification is incorrect.

If the real-world data were generated by the alternative hypothesis assumed in our Monte Carlo runs — stock price equals the present value of expected dividends plus white noise, where dividends follow a geometric random walk — with approximately the same parameter values, we would expect to find exactly the pattern observed with real-world data: failure to reject or marginal rejection with returns tests: stronger rejection with variance-bounds tests. These results support LeRoy & Porter and Shiller's original conjecture that the differing outcomes of returns and variance-bounds tests reflect the greater power of the latter tests. There is nothing paradoxical about this: we argued above that different tests of the same null hypothesis will generally have different power against any particular alternative hypothesis, even if they use the same instruments.

The difference in power may also be due to a difference in the auxiliary hypotheses assumed in constructing the test statistic. The volatility tests which we used made hard use of the assumption that $V(p_t^*/d_t)$, $V(p_t/d_t)$ and $V(r_t)$ are constant over time. This constancy property was assumed satisfied under both the null and alternative hypotheses which we specified. If we had specified either a null or an alternative hypothesis that failed to satisfy this property, it is unlikely that our results would have been as favorable to the volatility test as those reported here.

There are other possible explanations for the fact that volatility tests show stronger rejection of the present-value model than returns tests. Model-based volatility tests can detect the present of rational speculative bubbles, whereas returns tests cannot since the latter do not impose a convergence condition. Therefore if stock prices have bubble components, rejection of the present-value model will be stronger under volatility tests than return tests, consistent with our stylized fact.

We have dealt with the procedural question of the relative ability of different types of statistical tests to detect departures from the present-value model. We have not considered the substantive question of how to interpret rejection of the present-value model. LeRoy [1989] discussed this question but, again, not conclusively: no consensus exists as to whether statistical rejection of the present-value model has implications for the broader question of capital market efficiency. A minimalist interpretation of the statistical rejection of the present-value model would emphasize that what is rejected is the assumption that discount rates are constant over time. However, nothing about capital market efficiency precludes time-varying discount rates. Also, it is known that small but highly autocorrelated departures from constant discount rates may be consistent with price volatility greatly in excess of that implied by the (constant discount rate version of the) present-value model. Therefore even highly excessive price volatility might give rise to only marginally profitable trading rules. Along these lines the interpretation of the variance-bounds rejections might be that the present-value model has only weak implications for the unconditional variance of asset prices (except in the restrictive constant discount rate case), not that market efficiency is violated.

Others, such as Shiller, have drawn more sweeping conclusions from the excess volatility in financial markets. They point out that models with time-varying discount rates perform little better than the constant discount rate version in explaining real-world asset price changes. Also, they would situate excess volatility with the other anomalies of financial markets, which collectively establish a strong case against market efficiency even though individually these anomalies may be subject to question.

Acknowledgements

Without implicating them, we thank F. Black, S. Blough, T. Bollerslev, J. Cochrane, S. Durlauf, J. Geweke, R. Hodrick, R. Jagannathan, W. Parke and W. Ziemba for comments.

References

Campbell, J. (1993). Why long horizons? A study of power against persistent alternatives. Reproduced, Princeton University.

Campbell, J.Y., and R.J. Shiller (1988). The dividend-price ratio and expectations of future dividends and discount factors. *Rev. Financial Stud.* 1, 195–228.

Cochrane, J.H. (1991). Volatility tests and efficient markets: A review essay. *J. Monetary Econ.* 27, 463–485.

Cochrane, J.H. (1992). Explaining the variance of price-dividend ratios. *Rev. Financial Stud.* 5, 243–280.

Cogley, T. (1991). Out-of-sample predictive power of dividend yield regressions. Reproduced, University of Washington.

Durlauf, S.N., and R.E. Hall (1989). Measuring noise in stock prices. Reproduced, Stanford University.

Fama, E.F. (1970). Efficient capital markets: A review of theory and empirical work. *J. Finance* 25, 283–417.

Fama, E.F. (1991). Efficient capital markets, II. *J. Finance* 46, 1575–1617.

Fama, E.F. and K.R. French (1988). Permanent and transitory components of stock prices. *J. Political Econ.* 96, 246–273.

Flavin, M. (1983). Excess volatility in the financial markets: A reassessment of the empirical evidence. *J. Political Econ.* 91, 929–956.

Gilles, C., and S.F. LeRoy (1991). Econometric aspects of the variance-bounds tests: A survey. *Rev. Financial Stud.* 4, 753–791.

Grossman, S.J., and R.J. Shiller (1981). The determinants of the variability of stock prices. *Am. Econ. Rev. Pap. Proc.* 71, 222–227.

Kim, M.J., C.R. Nelson and R. Startz (1991). Mean reversion in stock prices? A reappraisal of the empirical evidence. *Rev. Econ. Stud.* 58, 515–528.

Kleidon, A.W. (1986). Bias in small-sample tests of stock price rationality. *J. Business* 59, 237–261.

LeRoy, S.F. (1984). Efficiency and the variability of asset prices. *Am. Econ. Rev. Pap. Proc.* 74, 183–187.

LeRoy, S.F. (1989). Efficient capital markets and martingales. *J. Econ. Literature* 17, 1583–1621.

LeRoy, S.F., and W.R. Parke (1992). Stock price volatility: Tests based on the geometric random walk. *Am. Econ. Rev.* 82, 981–992.

LeRoy, S.F., and R.D. Porter (1981). Stock price volatility: Tests based on implied variance bounds. *Econometrica* 49, 555–574.

Poterba, J.M., and L.H. Summers (1988). Mean reversion in stock prices: Evidence and implications. *J. Financial Econ.* 22, 27–59.

Richardson, M. (1993). Temporary components of stock prices: A skeptic's view. *J. Business Econ. Statistics* 11, 199–207.

Samuelson, P.A. (1965). Proof that properly anticipated prices fluctuate randomly. *Ind. Manage. Rev.* 6, 41–49.

Shiller, R.J. (1981). Do stock market prices move too much to be justified by subsequent changes in dividends?. *Am. Econ. Rev.* 71, 421–36.

Shiller, R.J. (1988). The probability of gross violations of a present value variance inequality. *J. Political Econ.* 96, 1089–1092.

Shiller, R.J. (1989). *Market Volatility*, Cambridge, MIT Press.

West, K. (1988). Bubbles, fads and stock price volatility: A partial evaluation. *J. Finance* 43, 636–656.

R. Jarrow et al., Eds., *Handbooks in OR & MS, Vol. 9*

Chapter 15

Asset and Liability Allocation in a Global Environment

John M. Mulvey

School of Engineering and Applied Science, Department of Civil Engineering and Operations Research, Princeton University, Princeton, NJ 08544, USA

William T. Ziemba

Faculty of Commerce and Business Administration, University of British Columbia, 2053 Main Mall, Vancouver, B.C. Canada V6T 1Z2

1. Introduction

A fundamental investment decision is the selection of asset categories and the accompanying proportion of wealth placed in each of the categories over time. This problem is called *dynamic asset allocation*. It sets the stage for tactical decisions concerning the purchases/sales of individual securities and the timing therein, for example, for tax or cashflow purposes. For investors who possess substantial financial wealth, such as institutional investors, and especially those who are well diversified, portfolio risk depends to a large degree on asset allocation choices rather than the selection of individual stocks or bonds; see e.g. Brinson, Hood & Beebower [1986] and Hensel, Ezra & Ilkiw [1990]. In addition, asset allocation provides a natural mechanism for evaluating portfolio managers — the performance attribution issue as discussed by Grinblatt & Titman [1995] in this volume.

The allocation decision involves the proportion of major asset categories within a portfolio. A popular benchmark for pension plans is the 60–40 mix. This portfolio places 60% of its assets in a broad stock index (typically the S&P 500) and the remainder in a bond fund (such as the Salomon government/corporate index). The 60–40 mix has been a traditional benchmark for U.S. institutional pension fund portfolios. However, the growing realization that foreign assets and other categories of domestic assets generally improve portfolio performance has led large pension fund consultants to recommend broader mixes; see Table 1. For example, Mr. George Russell the chairman of the world's largest such firm, the Frank Russell Company in Tacoma, Washington, which advises on client assets of more than $ 500 billion, US equities suggested the following typical asset mix in an interview on Wall Street Week in January 1995: 25% in large cap US equities, 10% in small cap US equities; 20% in international equities divided among 15% in known markets and 5% in emerging markets for a 55% equity exposure, plus 40% in a mixture of fixed income assets and 5% in real estate.

Table 1

Typical asset categories for institutional and individual investors. The list of secondary asset can become large depending upon investor requirements.

Major assets	Large capitalized stock index (S&P500) Government/corporate bond index Money market (cash)

Secondary assets	Foreign stocks
	  Pacific Rim stocks
	  European stocks
	  Emerging markets

	Foreign bonds
	  intermediate
	  long

	Small stocks
	Growth stocks
	Value stocks
	Real-estate funds
	  office buildings
	  shopping centers
	  apartments

	Venture capital markets Precious metals (gold, silver, platinum) Commodities (oil, copper) Tax exempt bonds (mostly for individuals) Annuities and insurance policies (mostly for individuals)

To show the performance of this mix, we must make a choice concerning the updating of the portfolio. For example, we might rebalance the portfolio at the beginning of each period to recover the target ratio. Alternatively, we could simply make no transaction except reinvest any dividends and interest — a buy and hold strategy. For convenience, the reinvestment issue is generally resolved by assuming that the cashflows are reinvested in the generating asset category. Figure 1 depicts the historical results of pure strategies and several popular benchmarks. Both buy-and-hold and fixed-proportions are indicated. The geometric returns and the annualized variance of returns are plotted. There are several noteworthy points. First, of course, the performance will vary over subsets of the target period and over other historical periods. Nevertheless, we can make several general observations about the patterns of returns. Risk is reduced by international diversification (as discussed in the next subsection). Investors would have been better served by keeping a proportion of their wealth outside their home country. A well diversified portfolio provides returns that are higher than the geometric averages for the pure equity strategy (S&P500) with much less risk (10.5% versus 15%). These portfolio returns are generated under the assumptions of neither transaction nor market impact costs. This assumption is reasonable for institutional investors who possess the three major asset categories (S&P500, G/C bonds, and Cash), but the results become more tenuous for individuals who must

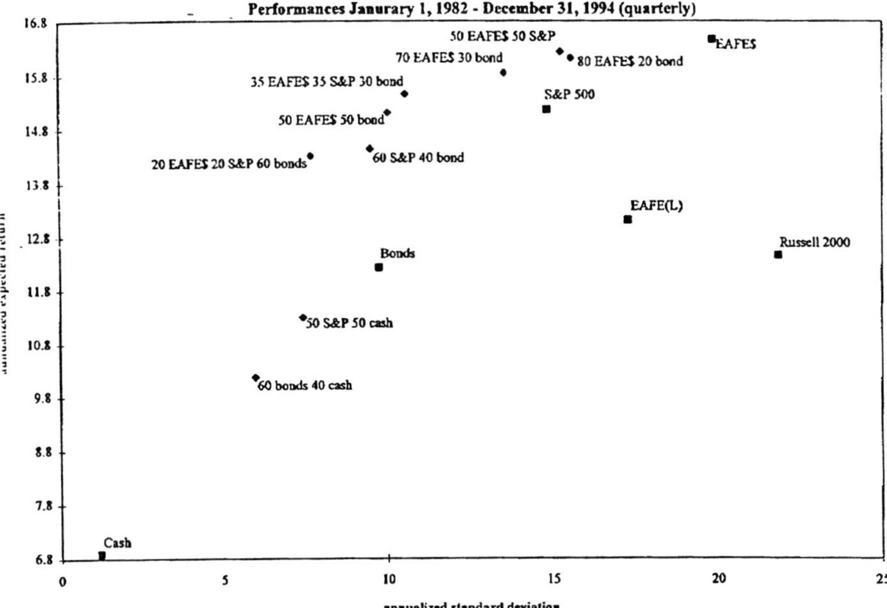

Fig. 1. Historical performance of some asset categories; 1-1-1982 to 12-31-1994.

pay substantial taxes and other transaction costs and for institutions who would like to refine the asset allocation decision by dividing the investment universe into a larger number of asset categories. Additionally, individuals need to take a systematic approach to portfolio management by monitoring both assets and liabilities [Wendt, 1994]. For many investors, there is a large gap between the idealized (model) portfolios and the decisions that they must make to manage their own portfolios. We will show that this gap can be reduced by the use of an integrated multi-period stochastic programming asset-liability investment system.

1.1. Historical performance of global markets

Historically investors have tended to make equity, bond and other investments at home. Some of the reasons for this emphasis are shown below [Ziemba & Schwartz, 1991]:

- The comfort factor: individuals, pension boards and investment companies are more comfortable with what they think they know — their home market.
- Regulations: most tax-exempt plans have limits on asset allocation classes such as 10% in foreign investments.
- Fear: there is fear involved with having one's resources invested abroad because of possible currency, repatriation and nationalization changes.
- Transaction costs: the cost of investing abroad both in terms of costs of currency exchange, taxes, transaction costs, and management fees exceeds that of local investments.

Table 2

Equity proportions for US, Japan and UK investors. Source: French & Poterba [1991].

	U.S.	Japan	U.K.
United States	93.8	1.3	5.9
Japan	3.1	98.1	4.8
United Kingdom	1.1	0.2	82.0
France	0.5	0.1	3.2
Germany	0.5	0.1	3.5
Canada	1.0	0.1	0.6

- Prejudice: some pension trustees perceive investment abroad and particularly in Japan as giving help to a competitor.
- Lack of knowledge: less is known about foreign investment and its advantages and disadvantages.
- Currency risk: foreign investment naturally involves currency risk, so that the total return is the return in local currency plus the currency gain or loss from the naked or hedged position.

The amount of foreign investment is well below what modern portfolio theory suggests would be appropriate. For example, French & Poterba [1991] estimated that at the end of 1989 U.S., Japanese, and U.K. equity investments were 6.2%, 1.9%, and 18.0% abroad, respectively. For these three countries the equity portfolio weights of investors is shown in Table 2.

Data such as that in Table 3, which shows the returns in local currencies and U.S. dollars for the twenty four plus years from January 1, 1970 to March 3, 1994, indicates that more investment abroad seems advisable to both increase return and lower risk through greater diversification.

Solnik & Noetzlin [1982] and Jorion [1989] have presented studies measuring the benefits that would have been obtained by foreign investments for a U.S. investor during the periods 1970–80 and 1978–88, respectively. For example, using a mean-variance approximation to the growth optimal logarithmic utility function, Jorion estimated that an investor would have gained about 6.8% mean return per year from a 60–40 benchmark portfolio with the inclusion of foreign stocks and bonds hedged and unhedged with the same volatility (Figure 2). The volatility reducing benefits of foreign bonds during the period 1978–88 are illustrated in Figure 3.

A variety of simulations with portfolio weight constraints and investment in weak and strong dollar periods showed that the optimal investment in foreign assets was well above what investors typically hold and especially so for hedged foreign bonds. See also Peta [1993] who arrives at the same conclusion with a different analysis and data set. As of 1987 foreign bonds were only 17% of foreign total investment whereas simulations indicate a 40% plus optimal allocation.

Due to their lack of dependence on local economic conditions, international markets can be employed successfully to reduce portfolio risks. Figure 4 depicts

Table 3

Returns in local currency and US dollars, January 1, 1970 to March 3, 1994. Base = 100 on January 1, 1970. Source: Morgan Stanley Capital Index

	Total Return		Annual US$	Total value in US$ Bil	MSCI World Index Weight
	Local currency	US$			
Hong Kong	6693.6	4810.2	18.20%	383.2	3.1
Japan	951.1	3295.3	16.28%	2885.4	23.9
Singapore	1198.4	2330.4	14.56%	94.9	0.7
Sweden	1954.3	1264.3	11.57%	101.5	0.9
Switzerland	356.8	1069.6	10.77%	243.8	3.0
EAFE	595.3	1029.6	10.59%	6850.5	60.7
Austria	470.0	1016.0	10.52%	28.2	0.3
Denmark	877.9	985.6	10.38%	39.6	0.4
Norway	935.5	901.6	9.96%	26.4	0.2
Netherlands	467.4	881.9	9.85%	171.2	2.0
Belgium	503.5	714.8	8.96%	76.1	6.7
Germany	300.6	643.7	8.37%	442.6	4.1
France	660.6	630.3	8.27%	453.4	3.9
UK	1000.1	623.0	8.22%	1189.9	11.0
The World	*472.1*	*616.6*	*8.17%*	*11637.9*	*100.0*
USA	432.6	432.6	6.53%	4467.0	36.7
Canada	454.9	363.0	5.72%	296.6	2.4
Malaysia	302.6	350.0	5.56%	202.3	1.8
Asia	443.0	279.5	4.54%	196.2	1.7
Italy	547.7	203.5	3.11%	135.0	1.3
Ireland	192.3	165.5	2.20%	17.0	0.2
Spain	286.3	143.2	1.56%	114.9	1.2
Finland	141.1	100.5	0.02%	23.5	0.2
New Zealand	100.2	93.6	−0.29%	25.4	0.2

a mean-standard deviation efficient frontier for the period January 1, 1982 to December 31, 1994 with and without the EAFE (Europe, Australia, & Far East) asset category. Table 4 shows the corresponding asset proportions. Adding EAFE to the investor's portfolio would have reduced volatility or increased expected returns during these past thirteen years.

1.2. Managing currency risks

An inevitable issue related to international investing is the decision to hedge currency risks. There are many strategies for handling currency risks — and almost as many controversies regarding the suitability of these strategies. Indeed, many investors do not hedge and even major pension fund consultants often do not recommend hedging. Several critical topics that must be addressed:

(a) The local currency asset return is not accessible — but rather the actual value depends upon the future/forward market and the relative interest rates between the two countries. Hedging cannot be done in a costless fashion [Brinson, Hood & Beebower, 1986; and Brinson, 1993].

Table 4

Asset proportions for points on efficient frontier with EAFE.

Optimal asset allocations using mean-variance analysis January 1, 1982–December 31, 1994 (quarterly)											
Annualized S.D.	1.171802	1.706537	2.645196	3.690806	4.773598	5.873041	6.981274	8.298454	11.6373	16.24679	19.85882
Mean	7	8	9	10	11	12	13	14	15	16	16
EAFE($)	1	3.9	6.6	9.2	11.8	14.4	17.1	24.1	39.3	64.2	100
S&P	0	3.4	6.6	9.8	13.1	16.3	19.5	25.7	37.7	35.8	0
Bonds	0	3.4	17.4	26.5	35.5	44.6	53.7	50.2	23	0	0
Cash	98.7	84.3	69.4	54.5	39.6	24.7	9.7	0	0	0	0
Russell	0.3	0	0	0	0	0	0	0	0	0	0
EAFE(Local)	0	0	0	0	0	0	0	0	0	0	0

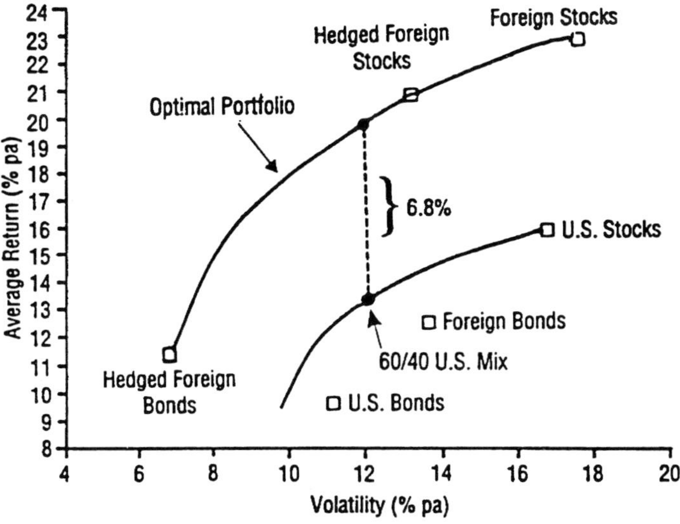

Fig. 2. Efficient frontier with hedged foreign assets, 1978–1988. Source: Jorion [1989].

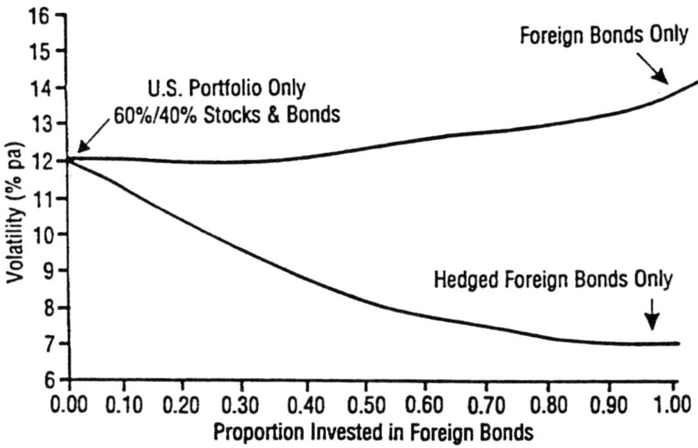

Fig. 3. Portfolio volatility with foreign bonds, 1978–1988. Source: Jorion [1989].

(b) To accurately evaluate the desirability of currency hedging requires an estimate of the investor's future cash needs. For instance, a multi-national corporation who produces and sells in multiple countries will generate both positive and negative cashflows around the globe. The projected cashflows should be estimated for each country and must address the uncertainties in a direct fashion. Liabilities must be included in the analysis.

(c) The 'optimal' hedging decision will be inevitably different for investors in different countries. The expectations and hedging costs will vary. What is a

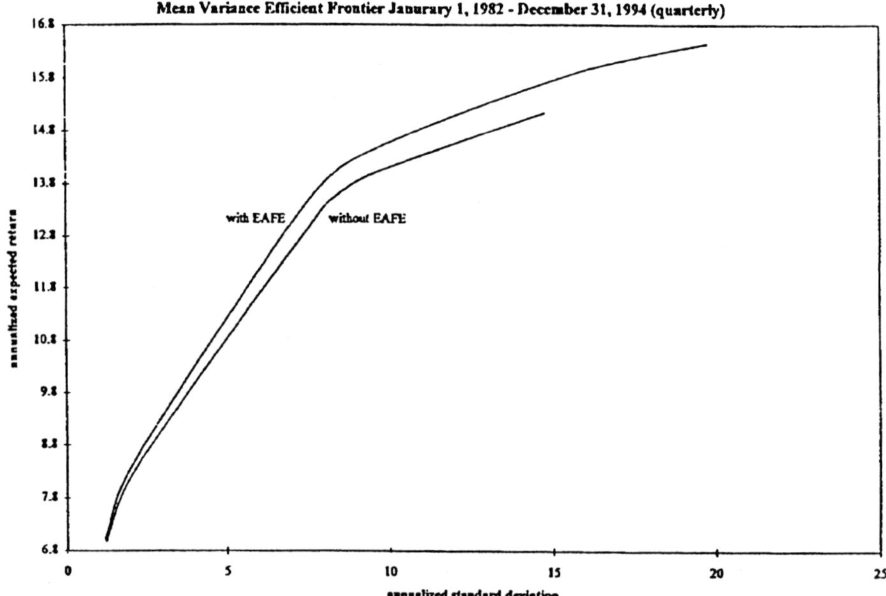

Fig. 4. Ex post efficient frontiers with and without EAFE (1-1-1982 to 12-31-1994).

premium in for one will be a discount for the other. Also, realized currency return is typically positive for currencies trading at discounts in the futures markets because of their higher domestic interest rates [Froot and Thaler, 1990] even though expected return is zero.

(d) Some amount of currency risk can be diversified away, for example, by using the futures market for hedging against the rise of interest rates in the foreign country. This would also hedge the return on fixed income investments as well.

(e) But other currency related risks cannot be eliminated in a reasonable manner, for instance, political risks that cause rapid devaluation of a foreign currency.

Typically, the hedging decision is subordinate to asset allocation. The first decision fixes the amount of foreign stocks and bonds. Next, the investor must choose to hedge actively or passively. As mentioned, hedging cannot be done so that the local returns are generated due to the forward rate bias and due to the uncertainty involving the amount of currency to hedge. These uncertainties must be addressed when designing a currency hedging strategy.

Optimization models can be employed for the task of managing hedging portfolios across a number of countries. For example, Salomon Brothers uses a mean-variance approach for selecting a basket of currencies to hedge [Sorensen, Mezrich & Thadani, 1993]. The composition of the hedging portfolio depends upon the recommendations of running the optimization system. A critical feature according to Salomon is the model's ability to adjust the forecasting projections as conditions change. A GARCH forecasting procedure tracks volatility and the direction of the various currencies. The goal of the Salomon system is to reduce currency risks while increasing expected profit. In backtesting, the system gained 2–3% annual returns over naive strategies. The advantage of the optimization method is to carry out a cross-hedging strategy so that the full forward costs are avoided.

Another approach is to treat currency forward contracts as a separate asset category and to include this asset in the portfolio mix decision [Kritzman, 1993]. Historically since the deregulation of currency markets in 1973, hedgers have performed best when they sold foreign forward contracts when a premium existed. Various strategies can take advantage of this pattern and other trends. See Adler & Jorion [1992], Gillies & Turner [1990], Solnik [1989] and Ziemba [1991] for further discussions of currency hedging. A multi-stage optimization model is ideal for implementing the hedging decision in concert with asset allocation.

2. Asset allocation framework

This section discusses the asset and liability allocation decision as a multi-stage stochastic program as presented in Mulvey [1989, 1993a, 1994a,b]. Many allocation and liability problems can be posed as special cases of this model. The stochastic program is portrayed as a network graph (Figure 5). Some practical issues are difficult to accommodate within a network and must be handled as general linear constraints as discussed below. Nevertheless, the network provides a visual reference for the asset-liability planning system.

The first critical issue is to define the requisite planning period. In Figure 5,

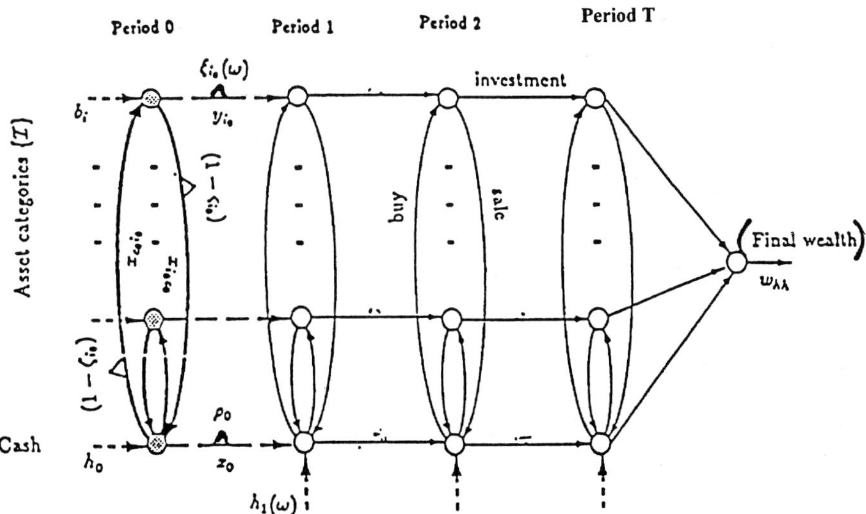

Fig. 5. Basic framework for asset allocation investment model indicating flows of funds between asset. Categories and cash for each time period during planning horizon. Source: Mulvey & Vladimirou [1992].

the planning horizon has time discretized into two intervals: $t = \{0, 1, \ldots, \tau\}$ and $t = \{\tau + 1, \ldots, T\}$. The former corresponds to the period in which investment decisions are to be made. The latter is used to compute the present value of the liabilities at the end of the planning period and to handle distortions that can occur at the horizon. Investment decisions are made at the last instant of each stage. Much flexibility exists in this context. An active trader might view the time interval as short as minutes, whereas a pension plan advisor might be more interested in twelve monthly time steps corresponding to the dates between the annual Board of Directors' meetings. It is possible for the time steps to vary; for instance, short time periods may be used at the beginning of the planning period and longer time steps towards the end. The second interval $t = \{\tau + 1, \ldots, T\}$ is needed in order to properly handle the horizon at time τ. The model will calculate economic and other factors beyond period τ up to period T and these may depend upon the resolution of previous uncertainties. The investor cannot render any active decisions after period τ.

Asset investment categories are defined using the set $i = \{1, 2, \ldots, I\}$.The decision variables represent generic investments as shown in Table 1, such as stocks, bonds, or real estate. It is desirable to have an index available which tracks the market segment — such as the S&P 500 index, or the Russell 3000 index. The level of aggregation depends upon the investor's circumstances. Individuals may need only 5 or 6 categories, whereas institutional investors such as insurance companies may be able to handle 30 to 40 categories.

A critical issue involves the handling of uncertainty. We employ the notion of *scenarios* for modeling random parameters. This corresponds to the robust optimization strategy posed in Mulvey [1993a, 1994a], and Mulvey, Vanderbei & Zenios [1995]. A scenario depicts a single plausible set of outcomes for all of the random coefficients over the entire planning period $t = \{1, \ldots, \tau, \ldots, T\}$. We extend the horizon beyond period τ for some of the economic factors, such as interest rates or currencies, allowing for a concise procedure for modeling the end of the planning period. We assume that a representative set of scenarios has been constructed which 'covers' the set of possibilities to a sufficient degree. Developing this representative set is a topic of current research; see Mulvey [1995]. The issues in forecasting a single scenario, say for placing investments are different than those that involve the development of a spectrum of possibilities. See section 2.4 for more details on the scenario generation process. See Chow [1993, 1994], Dantzig & Infanger [1993], Davis [1993], Dixit & Pindyck [1994] and their references for competing techniques which address the modeling of the stochastic processes and the solution of dynamic optimization problems.

The primary decision variable $x^s_{i,t}$ represents the investment in asset category i at the beginning of time period t under scenario s. These variables define the state of the system after the rebalancing decisions have been made. The investor's total assets are defined as:

$$\sum_i x^s_{i,t} = a^s_t, \quad s \in S,\ t \in T. \tag{1}$$

The single-period returns $r^s_{i,t}$ for the asset categories — for asset i, time t, and scenario s — are projected by the stochastic modeling subsystem for each scenario. Thus, the wealth accumulated at the end of the tth period before rebalancing in asset i is

$$x^s_{i,t}(1 + r^s_{i,t}) = v^s_{i,t}, \quad \forall i \in I,\ t \in T,\ s \in S. \tag{2}$$

Rebalancing decisions are made at the end of each period. Purchases and sales of assets are represented by the variables $y^s_{i,t}$ and $z^s_{i,t}$ with transaction costs defined via the coefficients ζ_i assuming symmetry in the transaction costs.

Using the terminology of robust optimization [Mulvey, Vanderbei & Zenios, 1994], we next define the relationships of the various investment categories at each period as the structural constraints. The flow balance constraint for each asset category and time period is

$$x_{i,t} = v^s_{i,t-1} + y^s_{i,t-1}(1 - \zeta_i) - z^s_{i,t-1}, \quad \forall i \in I,\ t \in T,\ s \in S. \tag{3}$$

This equation restricts the cashflows at each period to be consistent. It is assumed that dividends and interest are forthcoming simultaneously with the rebalancing decisions. Thus, the z variables consist of two parts corresponding to the involuntary cash outflow — dividend or interest — and a voluntary component for the cashflow — the amount actively sold (*sales*), namely

$$z^s_{i,t} = d^s_{i,t} + u^s_{i,t}, \quad \forall i \in I,\ t \in T,\ s \in S, \tag{4}$$

where d represents the dividends and u the amount of assets actually sold. The dividend equation is

$$d^s_{i,t} = x^s_{i,t}(d_Y)^s_i, \tag{5}$$

where $(d_Y)^s_i$ indicates the dividend payout percentage ratio for asset i under scenario s. The cash node at each period t also requires a flow balancing equation

$$\begin{aligned} c^s_t = g^s_{t-1} + \sum_i (u^s_{i,t-1}(1 - \zeta_i) + d^s_{i,t-1}) - \\ \sum_i y^s_{i,t} - b^s_{t-1}(1 - \delta^s_t) + c^s_{t-1} - e^s_{t-1} - l^s_{t-1} + b^s_t, \quad \forall t \in T,\ s \in S, \end{aligned} \tag{6}$$

with three new decision variables: b^s_t corresponding to the amount of borrowing in each period t at the borrowing rate δ^s_t; e^s_{t-1} the cash outflows; g^s_{t-1} the cash inflows; and l^s_{t-1} the paydown of loan principle in period $t - 1$, scenario s. Any of these decisions may be dependent upon the state of the world represented by scenario s. For simplicity, assume that all borrowing is done on a single-period basis. Adding new decision variables for each category of multi-period borrowing avoids the assumption. Define initial wealth in asset $i \in I$ at the end of period 0 as $v_{i,0}$.

The cash inflows variables g^s_{t-1} provide a great deal of flexibility. They can depict the savings for an individual investor. The amount of savings could be a determined proportion of the investor's wealth or income or could be a more complex function of the scenario conditions. Inflow decisions can be fixed or variable. For pension plans, mandatory contributions fall under his domain. Actuarial and other rules such as relating to tax deductibility form the basis for calculating the amount of the cash inflows at each period and under each scenario. Company policy must also factored into the contribution decision.

The cash outflow variables e_{t-1}^s can be employed for a number of external decisions under the control of the investor. An individual investor may wish to use investment funds to pay for consumption expenditures. These expenses could be dependent upon the detailed circumstances of the scenario — such as an investor giving away part of his wealth once a fixed goal is reached. Assume that once the funds are committed in this category they are lost to the investor and do not contribute to the wealth function in that or future time periods.

If one would like to spend funds for certain substantial durable expenditures, say a sailboat or expensive automobile and this expense increase one's wealth, we must create a new asset category in order to account for this investment. The investment decision is then triggered by a set of pre-specified conditions. In the case of a pension plan that wishes to make a voluntary contribution to increase the fund's surplus or to reduce its unfunded deficit, we would extend the cash inflow variable g_{t-1}^s to be a function of the new set of conditions.

In practice, investors restrict their investments in asset categories for a variety of purposes such as company policy, legal and historical rules and other considerations. These policy constraints may take any form, such as the set of linear restrictions

$$A^s x^s = b^s, \quad \forall s \in S. \tag{7}$$

These linear constraints arise for numerous purposes. For example, investors may set a lower limit — say 5% — on cash for liquidity considerations. They may wish to restrict foreign exposure to a specified range such as 10–20% of their portfolio's value. There might be a constraint that limits the stock-to-bond ratio to a value such as 0.7. Another common restriction is to limit small stocks to the percentage of small stocks in the Russell 3000 index. Or the investor might constrain the annual turnover in the portfolio to some percentage, such as 50%. Equations (7) encompass any general linear constraints.

Giving investors the opportunity to control the recommendations is valuable on several counts. First, it improves the chances that recommendations will be implemented. If an institutional investor must observe a legal constraint, there is little purpose in proposing an investment mix that cannot be made. Second, the investor becomes actively engaged in the investment decision. The investor will learn a great deal by setting up alternative constraints. Information can be gained by observing the dual variables on constraints that are binding at the proposed solution. These dual variables can guide the investor who is exploring alternative investment strategies. The use of constraints is the most direct way to approach the what-if analysis that is a critical byproduct of asset allocation studies. Investors who places constraints on the feasible region becomes part of the solution algorithm. The investor must be convinced that the proposed recommendations are sound. Otherwise asset allocation will not result in action. See Cariño, Kent, Myers, Stacy, Sylvanus, Turner, Watanabe & Ziemba [1994], Holmer [1994], Kusy and Ziemba [1986], and Mulvey [1994a] for further details regarding successful implementations of asset-liability investment systems.

The proposed asset-liability model uses the split-variable representation of the multi-stage stochastic program [Mulvey & Ruszczynski, 1994]. Under this structure, we define decision variables for *each* scenario and asset category — despite the fact that decisions cannot be made dependent upon knowing the actual scenario that will occur. To reflect reality, we must add a set of constraints to prevent the optimization model from anticipating the future. The constraints are known as non-anticipativity conditions; they have a particularly simple structure. Although the split-variable model is much larger than the traditional (compact) stochastic optimization model, it has several benefits. It is easy to describe. It readily accommodates a wide variety of dynamic decision policies. Last, the split variable model is easier to solve than the compact model in some situations [Lustig et al., 1991].

There are several alternatives for addressing non-anticipativity. In stochastic programming, for example, the path of uncertainties is typically revealed as a scenario tree; see Mulvey & Ruszczynski [1995]. The non-anticipativity conditions stipulate that decision variables (x, y, z, b, v, etc.) must be equal to each other whenever they inherent a common historical past — until some time t in the planning horizon $\{0, 1, \ldots, \tau\}$.

This restrictions can be written as

$$x_{i,t}^{s} = x_{i,t}^{s'} \tag{8}$$

for scenarios s and s' inheriting a common past up to time t. Similar constraints are needed for each of the decision variables appearing in the scenario tree (Fig. 6). These constraints can be extremely numerous, but their simple form — a pair of $+1$ and -1 for each row — can be taken advantage of by solution algorithms [Mulvey & Ruszczynski, 1995]. The non-anticipativity Equations (8) are commonly used in the stochastic programming field.

An alternative method for handling non-anticipativity is to reduce the decision space to a set of policies that do not depend upon knowing the future. This approach is called 'dynamic stochastic control' (DSC). For a simple example, investment decisions at each stage could be limited to a fixed-proportion rule. Letting $\Lambda_{i,t}^{s}$ be the percentage of asset wealth invested in category i under scenario s, at period t, define a set of constraints which prevent the model from using unavailable information in rendering its decisions. A set of constraints that enforce this policy is

$$\Lambda_{i,t}^{s_1} = \Lambda_{i,t}^{s_2}, \quad \forall s_1, s_2 \in S,\ t \in T,\ i \in I, \tag{8a}$$

where

$$\Lambda_{i,t}^{s} = \frac{x_{i,t}^{s}}{a_t^{s}}$$

for asset i at time t. In each period, the investor rebalances to a target investment mix. The solution to the asset allocation decision provides the recommended proportions. Adding constraint (8a) turns the model into a nonconvex optimization problem. See Maranas, Androulakis, Floudas, Berger & Mulvey [1994] for details on a practical global algorithm for solving this nonconvex problem.

The fixed-mix investment policy may lead to sub-optimal performance since it restricts the decision universe at each step during the planning horizon. For examples of alternatives to the fixed-mix rule, Perold & Sharpe [1988] discuss control policies in the context of portfolio insurance strategies. Fixed-mix can be considered a form of selling portfolio insurance and would perform best when markets are volatile and drifting sideways (see Perold and Sharpe [1988]). There are many other investment policies to consider, but in most cases they lead to non-convex optimization problems due to the inclusion of non-linear dynamics when rebalancing the portfolio at the beginning of each period. The recent results in global optimization [Maranas, Androulakis, Floudas, Berger & Mulvey, 1994] will be significant since these highly efficient algorithms, which provide performance guarantees, can be readily applied to other classes of stochastic control policies.

There are many issues to consider when proposing a control. These include the background and the experience of the investor as well as their computer capabilities. Many investors are unable to formulate and run multi-stage stochastic optimization models at each time period as proposed by the model implied by Equation (8). On the other hand once specified, the dynamic control strategy [e.g. Equation (8a)] is generally very easy to understand and implement. In addition, the control approach can be readily tested with out-of-sample scenarios. In the end, however, the stochastic programming approach should provide superior returns all else being equal since it generates a larger feasible region. Further testing is needed in order to fully understand the pros and cons of alternative modeling frameworks.

2.1. Objective functions

A critical issue in a financial modeling effort is to determine the choice of an objective function and an underlying preference structure. There are numerous possibilities. In our basic model, the first proposed objective is to maximize the investor's wealth at the end of period τ — subject to the payout of intermediate cash outflows (liabilities) under each of the scenarios. Wealth at the end of the planning horizon period τ is:

$$w_\tau^s = \sum_i v_{i,\tau}^s - PV(l_{\tau,T}^s) - (b)_\tau^s, \tag{9}$$

where $l_{\tau,T}^s$ is the liability stream from period τ to period T, and $(b)_\tau^s$ is the amount of loans outstanding at time period τ. This calculation may cause no particular difficulty for investors. At times, however, the investor's liabilities are not readily marketable and must be projected along with the accompanying discount factors. Take the case of a pension plan. Actuaries project cashflows to pay pension

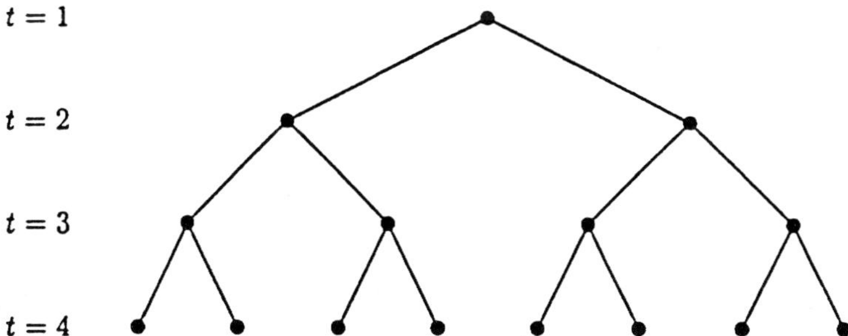

Fig. 6. A scenario tree for generating the path of uncertainties and associated conditional decisions.

beneficiaries as they are demanded. Discounting the cashflows depends upon the current long term government interest rates — 30-Year Treasury Bonds. In this situation, we must estimate market value by calculating the present value of the liabilities under a variety of possible forecasts — scenarios. Part of the right hand side of Equation (9) must therefore be estimated through actuarial simulation models. In fact, the actual cash liabilities will depend upon the scenario that occurs. Pension plans generally payout greater amounts during times of high inflation. Hence, the liabilities must be conditioned on the scenario and may be partially under the control of the decision maker, e.g. for insurance companies when they price their life insurance products.

There are numerous alternative objective functions. The first possibility is to employ mean-variance for a special time point τ as follows:

$$\text{Maximize} \quad \exp(w_\tau) - \beta \mathrm{Var}(w_t), \tag{10a}$$

where β indicates the relative significance of risk (a.k.a. standard deviation) as compared with expected value. This objective lead to an efficient frontier of wealth (or surplus) at period τ. There are many practical techniques for selecting a point on the efficient frontier, depending upon the risk tolerance of the investor and other factors. See Markowitz [1959], Kallberg & Ziemba [1983] and Ankrim [1992] for discussions. The basic idea is to find the investor's preferred marginal rate of substitution. Kallberg and Ziemba show that the form of the utility function is not crucial, it is the average risk aversion that determines portfolio choice.

An alternative to mean-variance is the von Neumann–Morganstern expected utility (EU) of wealth at period τ. The objective is

$$\text{Maximize} \quad \sum_s p_s \mathit{Utility}\,(w_\tau^s), \tag{10b}$$

where p_s is the probability of scenario s, and *Utility* (w) is the von Neumann–Morganstern utility function which may be estimated using derived certainty equivalence and risk premium questions; see Keeney & Raiffa [1976, 1993].

Temporal issues play a role in the determination of an objective function when the time horizon is long. Investors who approach their goal (e.g. as they near retirement age) should become more risk averse. Conversely, young investors should be relatively more aggressive with their retirement funds than someone who is closer to retirement. The standard approach for addressing these temporal choice issues is to maximize a discounted consumption function such as:

$$\text{Maximize} \quad \sum_s \sum_t p_s^* \left(\frac{1}{(1+\rho)^t} \right) \mathit{Utility}\,(e_t^s), \tag{10c}$$

where the discount parameter is equal to ρ. This discounted consumption function has been the focus of theoretical analysis since the early work of Samuelson [1969], Merton [1969] and others. Koopmans [1972] presents a study of discounted utility, including assumptions that lead to the use of this function. A survey of the literature appears in Ziemba & Vickson [1975].

Another approach for addressing temporal preferences is a direct extension of the expected utility model. Most investors are interested not only in their wealth at the end of a planning horizon but also in the form of the wealth trajectories during the planning horizon. An example is the rapid attainment of a certain level of wealth and then flattening of the wealth curve, as compared with a trajectory in which the growth in wealth comes at the end of the planning horizon. Given these two paths, most investors would prefer the former. To accommodate these preferences, we model intermediate preferences and the path to achieve a target wealth. A multi-objective formulation is an ideal mechanism for conducting this rather than the previous single EU attribute in which the goal focuses on wealth at beginning of period τ. Several dimensions are added to the certainty equivalence EU questions: corresponding to the investor's wealth at several key junctures during the planning period. This extension is clearly a multi-objective problem that can be addressed using the efficient algorithms discussed in the literature. See Keeney & Raiffa [1976, 1993], Spronk [1981], Zionts [1978] among others. A general formulation for this problem is:

$$\text{Maximize} \quad \sum_s p_s \mathit{Utility}\,(w_1^s, w_2^s, \ldots, w_\tau^s). \tag{10d}$$

The recommended course for implementing this temporal multicriteria problem is an issue for future research. Mulvey & Atkins [1994] describe an approach which combines the discounted utility function and the multi-attribute utility function. This results in their Financial Goal Index — a parameter which takes into account the time path and the expectations of meeting future goals and liabilities.

The complete asset-liability optimization system is to maximize one of the alternative objective functions (10a,10d) subject to the restrictions implied by Equations (1)–(9). In most cases, the proposed model is a nonlinear stochastic program with linear constraints.

2.2. Special cases

A special case of the asset-liability system is the mean-variance model [Markowitz, 1959]. This single-period quadratic program is popular among investment advisors [e.g. Black & Litterman, 1992]. The usual objective function possess two conflicting terms: the expected value and the variance of assets at the end of the single planning period $\tau = 1$. Variance of assets provides a surrogate for risk in this framework. The mean-variance model has been extended in several directions. Konno, Shirakawa & Yamazaki [1993] and Markowitz, Todd, Xu & Yamaneet [1993] and others [King, 1993] have proposed a modified objective in which risk is defined differentially between upside (profit) and downside (loss). Another idea is to penalize the absolute value deviations from a target wealth [Konno and Yamazaki, 1991].

Another special case of the asset-liability model is maximizing the single-period expected utility (EU) of assets. This myopic strategy presents an obvious special case of the proposed investment model in which $\tau = 1$ and there are no liabilities. Grauer & Hakansson [1985] and Mulvey [1989, 1994a] showed that the expected utility approach can generate superior returns when evaluated by means of historical evidence. This type of ex post backtesting is a common approach for performance attribution.

2.3. Why a multi-period framework?

The single period models possess several inherent drawbacks that can be avoided by modeling the dynamic aspects of the investment problem within a multi-period context. These difficulties include: (1) handling of transaction and market impact costs; (2) the lack of temporal independence for many of the economic factors, e.g. interest rates; (3) a consistent specification of risk over time; and (4) the ability to make tradeoffs between short-term risk and long-term gains.

The first factor — market impact costs — is generally ignored in investment studies, partially because of the difficulty in measuring the degree of this factor and the consequential increase in modeling complexity [Mulvey & Vladimorou, 1992]. In many real world cases and especially in severe market downturns, however, the market impact costs can be substantial. For example, an investor in real estate might wish to sell his building once the market begins dropping, before the price drops even further. Selling in these situations can be quite expensive in terms of causing continued erosion in prices and high transaction costs and in terms of market psychology. A symmetric situation occurs when buying during an inflationary spiral. Many institutional investors are faced with similar phenomena when they invest in thinly traded markets or when they are dealing with substantial positions that must be unwound.

The second issue — intertemporal dependencies — has gained in importance because evidence is that certain economic factors display mean reversion over time. For instance, most interest rate models are stochastic processes that mean revert, such as the Ornstein–Ulenbeck process that forms the basis for the Cox, Ingersoll and Ross single factor model [Ingersoll, 1987]. See DeBondt & Thaler [1989]. Research on equities has shown that the variance of long term returns is inconsistent with short term variance, if temporal independence exists. The historical variance ratio is too small to support the case of independence.

The third and fourth issues involves definition of a preference function that can be employed successfully over a number of years. One of the advantages of a systematic approach to investing is consistency — year after year maintaining a unified plan of action. It does the investor no good to become conservative after a dramatic drop in price — selling all of his stocks! This behavior is easy to understand from a psychological standpoint, but makes poor sense for investors and especially for long term investors. A multi-year asset-liability optimization system provides an opportunity for the investor to look both at the long and the short term consequences of today's investment decisions. For example, investing in stocks over the long run has dominated most other forms of asset investments. Yet many individuals are hesitant to place a majority of their assets in stocks, even for long term investments such as pension plans (401s or IRAs). A multi-period planning system shows the consequences of this form of severe risk aversion.

2.4. *Modeling stochastic parameters*

The stochastic parameters that are needed for the asset-liability system can be placed in three groupings: (1) a small set of economic factors; (2) projected returns for the asset categories implied by the values of the economic factors in the prior group; and (3) projected liabilities based on the implied values of the same economic factors. Scenarios are critical to the scenario generation process. A scenario consists of a complete and consistent set of parameters across the extended planning horizon — $t = \{1, \ldots, \tau, \ldots, T\}$.

There are several goals when building a stochastic model. First, of course, the procedures must be based on sound economic principles. Interest rates must be consistent with the returns for the fixed-income asset categories. International investments must separate currency returns from foreign market returns. Basic trends should be preserved whenever possible — such as mean reversion in interest rates over extended horizons. The projections should be compared with regard to their fit with historical trends.

A second goal is to design a stochastic process that is flexible enough so that the system can be tailored to the individual investor's circumstances. It is unlikely that an investor will trust the recommendations of a planning system unless he or she is confident that the investor's general beliefs are properly portrayed in the stochastic models. The model should be simple enough so that the investor can understand the basic philosophy and the key linkages among the modeling components. An understandable model will go a long way to gaining the confidence of the investor — thus increasing the chances that an asset liability system will be employed in an active manner.

The scenario generation process constructs scenarios that represent the universe of possible outcomes. This objective is different than the generation of a single scenario, say for forecasting and trading strategies. We are interested in constructing a *representative* set of scenarios that are both optimistic and pessimistic within

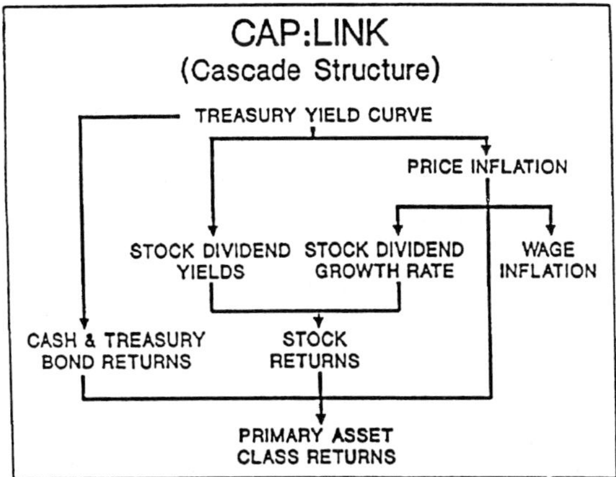

Fig. 7. Overview of Towers Perrin's scenario generation process using a cascade structure.

a general modeling framework. Such an effort was undertaken by Towers Perrin (one of the largest actuarial firms in the world). Their scenario generation process is called CAP:Link for capital market projections and the overall design is shown in Figure 7 [Mulvey, 1995]. The process entails a cascading set of submodels, starting with the interest rate component. Towers Perrin employs a version of the Brennan–Schwartz [1982] two factor interest rate model as modified in order to avoid the problem cited by Hogan [1993]. The other submodels are driven by the interest rates and other economic factors. This market projection system has been implemented in over 12 countries in Europe and North America.

The Towers Perrin scenario projections are long term — over 10 years. For this horizon, the covariances between asset returns are unreliable; hence Towers Perrin could not use a simple multinormal covariance structure for their generation. This would be inconsistent with historical evidence. However, an investor who has a short horizon and who is actively trading and rerunning her model might be able to use a covariance matrix to generate the requisite scenarios. It all depends upon the characteristics of the investor and his or her aims for using a financial planning system.

3. Integrating assets and liabilities

In most cases, investors apply the mean-variance model without reference to the liabilities or the uses of the funds. Focusing on assets alone misrepresents the risks and relative rewards, especially for investors who are risk averse. The key equation is

$$\text{Investor Wealth} = \sum_i x_i - PV(\mathit{liabilities}).$$

The vast majority of asset allocation work ignores the second term in this equation. Risk is defined with respect to the assets. However, in many realistic situations, the present value of the liabilities can change — by movements in the discount rate, by changes in the cashflows, or by both conditions. Thus, in order to assess the risks relative to wealth, the investment models must consider both terms in an integrative fashion — assets and liabilities. This concept is well understood in the fixed-income field where immunization and other asset-liability techniques are common, but it has received little attention in the general asset allocation area.

To accommodate the integration of asset allocation and liability projections requires a set of scenarios that bring together the two sides of the investment equation. Generally, historical data is used for calibrating the assets. However, forward looking simulations must be designed for the projection of the liabilities. These simulations must also consider the decisions of the organization with regard to the liabilities. For instance, an insurance company can adjust their payouts for some of their products such as annuities. These decisions must be considered in light of the investment choices to determine what overall risks are acceptable for the organization.

Both the stochastic programming and the dynamic stochastic control approaches discussed above provide an ideal framework to conduct this form of strategic planning for a large financial organization. There is no excuse for a financial entity to misunderstand the risks that it encounters, such as occurred in the 1980s for the U.S. savings and loan crisis; (see Pyle [1995]). Once it becomes clear that a risk is present, say for one or more scenarios, the financial organization can hedge this risk in the market, for example, through the use of derivatives, or by contracting with a Wall Street firm for a custom tailored product that exactly matches the firm's needs. To this end, an integrative asset-liability system provides an ideal vehicle for assessing risks for a financial organization.

There are several noteworthy examples of asset-liability investment systems. One of these is the Russell–Yasuda–Kasai effort. This project received second prize in the 1993 Franz Edelman competition for the best application in Management Science; see Cariño, Kent, Myers, Stacy, Sylvanus, Turner, Watanabe & Ziemba [1994], Cariño & Ziemba [1995], and Cariño, Myers & Ziemba [1995]. The model coordinates the major strategic decisions for a large Japanese insurance company. Figure 8 shows how the model fits into the overall planning process of this $26 billion dollar company. The model was implemented in April 1991 and has been used in an integral way by Yasuda–Kasai in the following years. For fiscal 1991 and 1992, April 1991–March 1993, estimated additional return over the previous technology (static mean-variance analysis) were estimated to be $79 million.

The second example involves the world-wide benefit consulting company — Towers Perrin. The objectives of the Towers Perrin asset-liability investment system are to provide actuarial advice regarding the soundness of pension plans and to render recommendations as asset consultants. The Towers Perrin system depends upon dynamic stochastic control, rather than the multi period stochastic program employed in the Russell system. The Towers Perrin staff devoted considerable

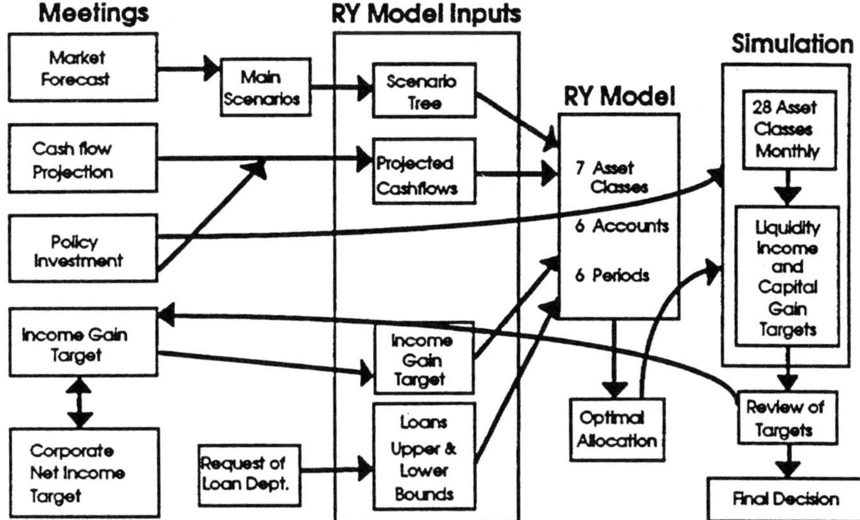

Fig. 8. The RY model is central to Yasuda Kasai's asset/liability decision process. The process begins with a series of meetings to prepare the market forecasts, scenarios, cash-flow projections, targets, loan bounds, and other inputs. Planners then run the model, simulate the allocations, review the targets, and report a final decision.

effort in the definition of the scenario generation routines as discussed in Mulvey [1995]. The scenario generation program assists both actuaries for setting return and other assumptions as well as providing support for the asset consultants who make recommendations concerning the risk/rewards for investment strategies.

Other examples of asset liability systems are: Holmer for Fannie Mae [1994], Nielsen & Zenios for funding insurance products [1992], and King & Warden for an insurance company [1994]. Also see the recent Ph.D. thesis by Dert [1995]. An early model in this arena is Kusy & Ziemba [1986].

4. Solution strategies

Large realistic-size multistage stochastic optimization problems can now be solved in a practical fashion. Part of the reason for the technological advance is due to the exponential increases in computer hardware capabilities and the resulting decreases in cost pursuant of computation. Also related are the commensurate improvements in the efficiency of optimization algorithms. The use of parallel and distributed computing is essential to the effort. This section reviews solution algorithms that apply to multi-stage asset-liability systems as described in Section 2. We are concerned with the solution of problems possessing discrete-time with 10 to 20 periods, a modest number of scenarios — typically between 500 and 5000, and nonlinear risk-oriented objective functions.

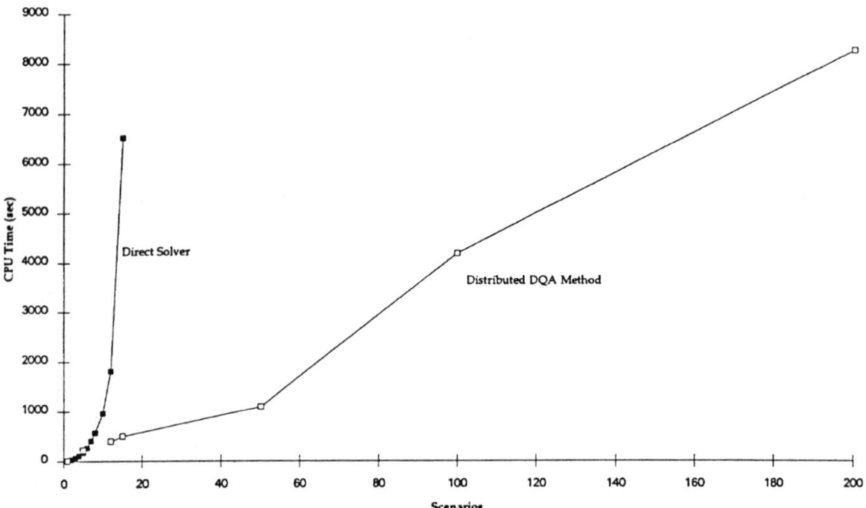

Fig. 9. Solution times for solving nonlinear asset-liability investment system. Source: Berger, Mulvey & Ruszczynski [1994].

The size of the asset-liability model depends upon the form of the non-anticipativity rules that are chosen. If the classical stochastic or robust program is selected, the asset-liability model becomes a linear or convex nonlinear program whose size hinges on the number of scenarios that are placed in $\{S\}$. On the other hand, if a dynamic stochastic control approach is selected, problem size is much smaller. Solution strategies for both formulations are discussed in the next sections.

4.1. Stochastic programs

The most direct way to solve linear stochastic programs is to employ one of the modern efficient linear programming solvers. CPLEX and IBM's OSL are the two leading systems. In some cases, the nonlinear terms in the objective function can be piecewise linearized. The Russell Yasuda Kasai team, for example, linearized the penalty terms for missing target contributions so that OSL could be employed; see Cariño & Ziemba [1995]. Of course, this transformation requires separable terms. The interior-point algorithms are well suited to the scenario structure of multi-stage stochastic programs.

Over the past few years, substantial progress has been made on the design of efficient algorithms for stochastic programs. Dantzig & Infanger [1993], Rockafellar & Wets [1991], Mulvey & Vladimirou [1992], and Nielsen & Zenios [1993] have developed solution strategies for solving multi-stage stochastic programs. Also, see the recent books by Kall & Wallace [1994] and by Infanger [1994] and the references contained therein. The proposed algorithms take advantage of the problem's structure during the calculations and in several cases are implemented in a parallel or distributed computing environment. The use of parallel computers will greatly accelerate over the next decade. This avenue of research — parallel implementations — is very promising. In the original stochastic programs, the model maximizes the expected value of the investments. However, the inclusion of risk aversion means that nonlinear objectives must be an essential part of the multi-period asset liability model. Recently, nonlinear algorithms have been developed that appear to be well suited to solving the stochastic program. For example, Carpenter et al. [1993] extended the OB1 code to handle nonlinear objectives within an efficient interior-point algorithm. This work has been extended by Vanderbei and his colleagues [Berger, Mulvey, Rothberg & Vanderbei, 1995] at Princeton University. Also, Berger, Mulvey and Ruszczynski [1994] have extended their DQA method to handle convex objectives as specified by the risk averse EU functions. To illustrate the efficiency of the convex-DQA algorithm, Figure 9 plots the solution time as a function of the number of scenarios for a large planning model. A single scenario for this problem has about 1400 variables and 600 constraints. The largest problem in this domain that has been solved to date had over 3000 scenarios with 450,000 total variables and almost 300,000 constraints.

Although these problems have been exceedingly difficult to solve, the integrative models are generally employed for long term planning — hence the execution time is not a concern as long as a number of examples can be solved so that the investor gains an understanding of the range of possible recommendations under differing sets of assumptions. When the investor is interested in almost real time planning, the use of massively parallel computing can be used to advantage as discussed in Zenios [1991] and Nielsen & Zenios [1993]. Cariño, Myers & Ziemba [1995] present a comparison of the performance of alternative stochastic programming and large-scale solution methods. They concluded that for the Russell–Yasuda type models that the larger and more difficult the problem becomes the more advantageous are solution methods based on Bender's decomposition through parallel processing.

A useful problem transformation in the case of the mean-variance model is to convert the covariance matrix Q into two component parts:

$$Q = F^t F, \tag{11}$$

where F is a $(k \times n)$ matrix of factors and $k \ll n$. Then we can convert the mean-variance objective function into a separable function by introducing new *y-variables* such that

$$y = Fx. \tag{12}$$

The variance term $x'Q'x$ is set equal to the separable product $y'y$. Adding constraints (12) to the model completes the problem transformation.

As long as the number of constraints k is relatively small, such as when the number of scenarios is modest, the new problem can be solved much more efficiently than the original dense nonseparable model. Konno & Suzuki [1992] showed that the new problem can be addressed via piecewise linearization, whereas Vanderbei & Carpenter [1993] proved that nonlinear interior methods can take great advantage of the separable structure. Indeed, interior methods are not dependent on the number of constraints, but rather on the buildup density of the Cholesky factors. A similar transformation is possible with the expected utility objectives as discussed in Berger, Mulvey & Ruszczynski (1994). In fact with this transformation, the solution of nonlinear objectives is not much harder than solving linear programs of the same structure. These developments will greatly improve the chances that nonlinear risk aversion is handled directly in the financial planning model.

Recently, Berger, Glover & Mulvey [1995] designed a new technique for pre-ordering the problem before employing a nonlinear interior-point algorithm. This tree dissection method improves computational performance by over 200 times as compared with the standard interior-point methods for solving problems (e.g. CPLEX and LOQO). For example, they solved a 512 scenario 6-stage investment problem in 448 seconds using a single-processor SGI workstation [Berger, Glover & Mulvey, 1995]. This time is less than the time it took CPLEX to order the matrix. The group was able to extend the methodology to a 4096 scenario 6-stage problem. In all cases, the algorithm took less than 70 iterations to find the optimal solution. This performance level promises to eliminate the need for decomposition methods for classes of applications.

4.2. Dynamic stochastic control

Much of the early research on dynamic investment strategies centered on the area of dynamic programming and control theory. Merton [1969], for example, showed that the investment/consumption decision strategy can be solved for certain assumed cases. Others have continued the research to find closed form solutions [Karatzas, Lehoczky, Sethi & Shreve 1986; Davis & Norman, 1990; Sethi, Taksar & Presman, 1992]. Karatzas et al. [1986] allows for bankruptcy, Davis & Norman [1990] include transaction costs, and Sethi et al. [1992] incorporate a positive minimum level of consumption. In most of this work, the stochastic model has a random walk structure, and the objective a special case of the discounted consumption function (e.g. Merton) or a special case of the iso-elastic class (e.g. log utility or expected value). The general asset-liability model has not been solved in a practical way using dynamic programming, primarily due to the explosion in the size of the state space.

Another approach is to assume the discretizations implied by the asset-liability model discussed in Section 2 — discrete time and discrete scenarios — and to couple that with a specific form of the investment decisions at each stage. We call this strategy: Dynamic Stochastic Control. The fixed-mix strategy described in Section 2 fits this framework. While extraordinarily simple, the fixed-mix strategy has a theoretical underpinning from the results of Merton, Karatzas et al. and others who have shown that variants of fixed-mix are optimal for a variety of dynamic investment models. Of course, there are many variants of DSC strategies. See Perold & Sharpe [1988] for a discussion of the portfolio insurance (momentum) strategies. Fixed-mix can be placed in this context by perceiving it as a sale of portfolio insurance. Berger, Glover & Mulvey [1995] showed that the lifecyle investment strategies can be posed as variants of stochastic control strategies.

There are several distinct advantages to the dynamic stochastic control framework. It is not susceptible to the curse of dimensionality; the number of decision variable is greatly restricted to some small multiple of the number of asset categories. The investment rules are well understood by the investing public. And the precision of the recommendations can be evaluated by means of out-of-sample experiments. Unfortunately, the fixed-mix model results in a nonconvex program. Thus, an optimization model may local a local optimal solution which may not be the global solution. This situation greatly complicates the search for the best recommendation. See Maranas, Androulakis, Floudas, Berger & Mulvey [1994] for an instance of a practical algorithm for solving this difficult optimization model.

Brennan, Schwartz and Lagnado [1993] consider the problem of strategic asset allocation with time varying asset returns dependent upon state variables. They provide an analysis and computations in the dynamic tradeoff of cash, stock and bond returns. They study the impacts on asset weights of varying investor time horizons. The asset weights are extremely sensitive to small changes in asset return predictions.

5. Conclusions

Asset allocation choices are critical issues for investors who possess substantial wealth and who are attempting to assess the risks for various investment and related decisions over time. The proposed asset liability model provides a general framework for integrating asset, liability and expensing decisions for a large financial entity — such as an insurance company, bank or pension plan. This comprehensive approach is needed in order to properly measure the risk and returns of alternative investment strategies. Without a comprehensive and integrative model, investors will be unable to properly measure risks to their *wealth*. The usual asset-only models inadequately evaluate the impact of the investment decisions on the investor's wealth, especially for risk averse decision makers or organizations, and provide only limited assistance with the important temporal tradeoffs. Investment models must be tailored to individual circumstances. The multi-stage stochastic program provides an ideal vehicle for developing a financial planning system for the user's needs.

Although an integrative asset-liability investment system may result in a large stochastic program or a nonconvex optimization model, efficient algorithms are now available for solving these models. The continued sharp decrease in computer costs along with improvements in software algorithms and the commensurate increase in usability will improve the prospects that asset-liability investing will become a common place in large financial organizations and for individual investors.

Acknowledgements

This research was supported in part by Towers Perrin, the US NSF (CCR-9102660), the Frank Russell Company, and NSERC grant 5-87147.

References

Adler, M. and P. Jorion (1992). Universal currency hedges for global portfolios, *J. Portfolio Management* Summer, 28–35.

Ankrim, E.M. (1992). Risk tolerance, sharpe ratios, and implied investor preferences for risk, *Frank Russell Company*, July.

Ankrim, E.M. and C.R. Hensel (1993). Commodities in asset allocation: a real asset alternative to real estate, *Financial Analysts J.* May–June, 20–29.

Berger, A.J., F. Glover and J.M. Mulvey (1995). Solving global optimization problems in long-term financial planning, *Statistics and Operations Research Technical Report*, Princeton University, January.

Berger, A., J. Mulvey, E. Rothberg and R. Vanderbei (1995). Solving multi-stage stochastic programs via a nonlinear interior-point algorithm and tree dissection, *Statistics and Operations Research Technical Report*, Princeton University,

Berger, A.J., J. Mulvey and A. Ruszczynski (1994). An extension of the DQA algorithm to convex stochastic programs, *SIAM J. on Optimization* 4, 735–753.

Black, F. and R. Litterman (1992). Global portfolio optimization, *Financial Analysts J.* September–October, 28–43.

Brennan, M.J. and E.S. Schwartz (1982). An equilibrium model of bond pricing and a test of market efficiency, *J. Financial and Quantitative Analysis*, 17, 75–100.

Brennan, M.J., E.S. Schwartz and R. Lagnado (1993). Strategic asset allocation, *mimeo UCLA*, October.

Brinson, G. (1993). You can't access local-currency returns, *Financial Analysts J.* May–June, 10.

Brinson, G., R. Hood and G.L. Beebower (1986). Determinants of portfolio performance, *Financial Analysts J.* July–August, 39–44.

Cariño, D.R., T. Kent, D.H. Myers, C. Stacy, M. Sylvanus, A. Turner, K. Watanabe and W. T. Ziemba (1994). The Russell–Yasuda Kasai model: an asset liability model for a Japanese insurance company using multi-stage stochastic programming, *Interfaces* 24, January–February, 29–49.

Cariño, D.R., D.H. Myers and W.T. Ziemba (1995). Concepts, technical issues and uses of the Russell–Yasuda Kasai financial planning model, *Frank Russell Company*, Tacoma, WA, June.

Cariño, D.R. and W.T. Ziemba (1995). Formulation of the Russell–Yasuda Kasai financial planning model, *Frank Russell Company*, Tacoma, WA, June.

Carpenter, T.J., I.J. Lustig, J.M. Mulvey and D.F. Shanno (1993). Separable quadratic programming via a primal-duel interior point method and its use in a sequential procedure, *ORSA Journal on Computing* 5(2), 182–191.

Chopra, V.K. and W.T. Ziemba (1993). The effect of errors in means, variances, and covariances on optimal portfolio choice, *J. Portfolio Management*, Winter, 6–11.

Chow, G.C. (1993). Optimal control without solving the Bellman equation, *J. Economic Dynamics and Control*, 17, 621–630.

Chow, G.C. (1994). The Lagrange method of optimization in finance, *Econometric Research Program Memorandum 369*, Princeton University.

Dantzig, G. and G. Infanger (1993). Multi-stage stochastic linear programs for portfolio optimization, *Ann. Oper. Res.* 45, 59–76.

Davis, M.H.A. (1993). Markov models and optimization, *Monographs on Statistics and Applied Probability*, Chapman and Hall, 49.

Davis, M.H.A. and A.R. Norman (1990). Portfolio selection with transaction costs, *Math. Oper. Res.* 15, 676–713.

DeBondt, W.F.M. and R. Thaler (1989). A mean-reverting walk down Wall Street, *J. Economic Perspectives* 3 (1), 189–202.

Dert, C. (1995). *A Multi-Stage Chance Constrained Programming Approach to Asset-Liability Management for Pension Funds*, Ph.D. Thesis, Erasmus University, Rotterdam, The Netherlands.

Dixit, A.K. and R.S. Pindyck (1994). *Investment Under Uncertainty*, Princeton University, Princeton, NJ.

Fama, E.F. (1991). Efficient capital markets: II, *J. Finance* 46, 1575–1617.

Floudas, C.A. and V. Visweswaran (1993). Primal-relaxed dual global optimization approach, *J. Optimization Theory and its Application*, 78 (2).

French, K.R. and J.M. Poterba (1991). Investor diversification and international equity markets, *Am. Economic Rev.* 81, 222–226.

Froot, K.A. and R.H. Thaler (1990). Foreign exchange, *J. Economic Perspectives*, 4, 179–192.

Gillies, J.M. and A.L. Turner (1990). On the relationship between currency hedging and local rates of return, *Frank Russell Company*, Tacoma, Washington, March.

Grauer, R.R. and N.H. Hakansson (1985). Returns on levered actively managed long-run portfolios of stocks, bonds and bills, *Financial Analysts J.* September, 24–43.

Grinblatt, M. and S. Titman (1995). Performance evaluation, in: R. Jarrow, V. Maksimovic and W.T. Ziemba (eds.), *Finance*, Handbooks in Operations Research and Management Science, Vol 9, Elsevier, Amsterdam, pp. 581–610 (this volume).

Hensel, C.R., D.D. Ezra and J.H. Ilkiw (1990). The value of asset allocation decisions, *Res. Commentary,* Frank Russell Company, Tacoma, WA, March.

Hensel, C.R. and W.T. Ziemba (1995). US investment returns during democratic and republican administrations, 1928–1993, *Financial Analysts J.* March/April, 61–69.

Hogan, M. (1993). Problems in certain two-factor term structure models, *The Annals of Applied Probability*, 3 (2), 576–581.

Holmer, M. (1994). The asset/liability management strategy at Fannie Mae, *Interfaces* 24 (3), 3–21.

Holmer, M. and S. Zenios (1993). *The Productivity of Financial Intermediation and the Technology of Financial Product Management*, Wharton Report 93-02-01, University of Pennsylvania.

Infanger, G. (1994). *Planning Under Uncertainty: Solving Large-Scale Stochastic Linear Programs*, Boyd and Fraser.

Ingersoll, J.E. Jr. (1987). *Theory of Financial Decision Making*, Rowman & Littlefield.

Jorion, P. (1989). Asset allocation with hedged and unhedged foreign stocks and bonds, *J. Portfolio Management*, 15, 49–54.

Kall, P. and S.W. Wallace (1994). *Stochastic Programming*, John Wiley.

Kallberg, J.G. and W.T. Ziemba, 1983. Comparison of alternative utility functions in portfolio selection problems, *Management Science*, 29, 1257–1276.

Karatzas, I. and S. Shreve (1988). *Browian Motion and Stochastic Calculus*, Springer-Verlag.

Karatzas, I., J. Lehoczky, S.P. Sethi and S.F. Shreve (1986). Explicit solution of a general consumption/investment problem, *Math. Oper. Res.* 11, 261–294.

Keeney, R. and H. Raiffa (1993). *Decisions with Multiple Objectives: Preferences and Value Tradeoffs*, John Wiley, 1976, reprinted by Cambridge University Press.

King, A.J. (1993). Asymmetric risk measures and tracking models for portfolio optimization under uncertainty, *Ann. Oper. Res.* 45, 165–178.

King, A.J. and T. Warden (1994). Stochastic programming for strategic portfolio management, *15th International Programming Symposium*, Ann Arbor, August.

Konno, H., S. Pliska and K. Suzuki (1993). Optimal portfolio with asymptotic criteria, *Ann. Oper. Res.* 45, 187–204.

Konno, H., H. Shirakawa and H. Yamazaki (1993). A mean-absolute deviation-skewness portfolio optimization model, *Ann. Oper. Res.* 45, 205–220.

Konno, H. and K. Suzuki (1992). A fast algorithm for solving large scale mean-variance models by compact factorization of covariance matrices, *J. Oper. Res. Society of Japan* 35, 93–104.

Konno, H. and H. Yamazaki (1991). Mean-absolute deviation portfolio optimization model and its applications to Tokyo stock market, *Management Science*, 37 (5), 519–531.

Koopmans, T.C. (1972). *Representation of Preference Orderings over Time, in Decision and Organization*, C. McGuire and R. Radner (eds.), North-Holland.

Kritzman, M. (1993). The optimal currency hedging policy with biased forward rates, *J. Portfolio Management* Summer, 94–100.

Kroll, Y., H. Levy and H. Markowitz (1984). Mean variance versus direct utility maximization, *J. Finance* 39, 47–62.

Kusy, M.I. and W.T. Ziemba (1986). A bank asset and liability management model, *Oper. Res.* 34, 356–376.

Lustig, I.J., J.M. Mulvey and T.J. Carpenter (1991). Formulating two-stage stochastic programs for interior point methods, *Oper. Res.* 39(5), 757–770.

Maranas, C.D., I.P. Androulakis, C.A. Floudas, A.J. Berger and J.M. Mulvey (1994). Solving stochastic control problems in finance via global optimization, *Statistics and Operations Research Technical Report* 94-01, Princeton University.

Markowitz, H.M. (1959). *Portfolio Selection: Efficient Diversification of Investments*, John Wiley, New York.

Markowitz, H.M., P. Todd, G. Xu and Y. Yamane (1993). Computation of mean-semivariance efficient sets by the critical line algorithm, *Ann. Oper. Res.* 45, 307–318.

Merton, R.C. (1969). Lifetime portfolio selection under uncertainty: the continuous time case, *Rev. Economics and Statistics* 3, 373–413.

Merton, R.C. (1990). The financial system and economic performance, *J. Financial Services Research*, December, 263–300.

Michaud, R.O. (1989). The Markowitz optimization enigma: is 'optimized' optional?, *Financial Analysts J.* January–February, 31–42.

Mulvey, J.M. (1989). A surplus optimization perspective, *Investment Management Rev.* 3, 31–39.

Mulvey, J.M. (1993a). Incorporating transaction costs in models for asset allocation, in: S. Zenios (ed.), *Financial Optimization*, Cambridge University Press, 243–259.

Mulvey, J.M. (1993b). Fixed-mix investment strategies, *Statistics and Operations Research Technical Report*, 93-14, Princeton University.

Mulvey, J.M. (1994a). An asset-liability investment system, *Interfaces* 24 (3), 22–33.

Mulvey, J.M. (1994b). Integrating assets and liabilities for large financial organizations, Chapter in: *New Directions in Computational Economics*, W.W. Cooper and A.B. Whinston (eds.), Kluwer Academic Publishers, 135–150.

Mulvey, J.M. (1995). Generating scenarios for the Towers Perrin investment systems, *Statistics and Operations Research Technical Report*, Princeton University; *Interfaces*, to appear.

Mulvey, J.M. and C.A. Atkins (1994). The HOME account: financial analysis, planning, and management system for individuals, *Technical Report, Proprietary Financial Products*, Charleston, SC.

Mulvey, J.M. and A. Ruszczynski (1992). A diagonal quadratic approximation method for large scale linear programs, *Oper. Res. Lett.* 12, 205–215.

Mulvey, J.M. and A. Ruszczynski (1995). A new scenario decomposition method for large-scale stochastic optimization, *Oper. Res.* 43(3), 477–490.

Mulvey, J.M., R. Vanderbei and S. Zenios (1995). Robust optimization of large-scale systems, *Oper. Res.* 43(2), 264–281.

Mulvey, J.M. and H. Vladimirou (1992). Stochastic network programming for financial planning problems, *Management Science*, 38 (11), 1642–1664.

Mulvey, J.M. and S.A. Zenios (1994). Diversifying a portfolio of fixed-income securities: modeling dynamic effects, *Financial Analysts J.* January–February, 30–38.

Nielsen, S. and S. Zenios (1992). A stochastic programming model for funding single premium deferred annuities, *Technical Report, The Wharton School*, The University of Pennsylvania, August.

Nielsen, S. and S. Zenios (1993). A massively parallel algorithm for nonlinear stochastic network problems, *Oper. Res.* 41 (2), 319–337.

Onorato, M. (1993). Multifactor asset and liability risk management approach: a procedure to evaluate bank strategic performance, *Report R9323/F, Rotterdam Institute for Business Economic Studies*, Erasmus University, Rotterdam, The Netherlands, December.

Perold, A.F. (1984). Large-scale portfolio optimization, *Management Science* 30, 1143–1160.

Perold, A.F. and W.F. Sharpe (1988). Dynamic strategies for asset allocation, *Financial Analysts J.* January, 16–27.

Peta, J.L. (1993). International bond diversification from a U.S. perspective, *Research Commentary, Frank Russell Company*, Tacoma, Washington, February.

Pyle, D.H. (1995). The U.S. Savings and Loan Crisis, in: R. Jarrow, V. Maksimovic and W.T. Ziemba (eds.), *Finance*, Handbooks in Operations Research and Management Science, Vol 9, Elsevier, Amsterdam, pp. 1105–1126 (this volume).

Rockafellar, R.T. and R.J.-B Wets (1991). Scenarios and policy aggregation in optimization under uncertainty, *Math. Oper. Res.* 16, 119–147.

Samuelson, P. (1969). Lifetime portfolio selection by dynamic stochastic programming, *Rev. Economics and Statistics* 57, 239–246.

Sethi, S.P., M.I. Taksar and E. Presman (1992). Explicit solution of a general consumption/portfolio problem with subsistence consumption and bankruptcy, *J. of Economic Dynamics and Control* 16, 747–768.

Solnik, B. (1989). Optimal currency hedge ratios: the influences of the interest rate differential, in: S.G. Rhee and R.P. Chang (eds.), *Pacific-Basin Capital Market Research*, Amsterdam, North-Holland, 441–465.

Solnik, B. and B. Noetzlin (1982). Optimal international asset allocation, *J. Portfolio Management* 9, 11–21.

Sorensen, E., J. Mezrich and D. Thadani (1993). Currency hedging through portfolio optimization, *J. Portfolio Management*, Spring, 78–85.

Spronk, J. (1981). *Interactive Multiple Goal Programming: Applications to Financial Planning*, Martinus Nijhoff Publishing, Boston.

Vanderbei, R.J. and T.J. Carpenter (1993). Symmetric indefinite systems for interior-point methods, *Mathematical Programming* 58, 1–32.

Wendt, R.Q. (1994). Strategic asset allocation: asset/liability forecasting, in: J. Lederman and R. Klein (eds.), *Global Asset Allocation*, John Wiley, New York.

Worzel, K., C. Vassiadou-Zeniou and S.A. Zenios (1995). Integrated simulation and optimization models for tracking fixed-income indices, *Oper. Res.*, to appear.

Zenios, S.A. (1991). Massively parallel computations for financial planning under uncertainty, in: J. Mesirov (ed.) *Very Large Scale Computing in the 21-st Century*, SIAM, Philadelphia, PA.

Zenios, S.A. (ed.) (1993). *Financial Optimization*, Cambridge University Press.

Ziemba, W.T. (1991). Currency hedging strategies for U.S. investments in Japan and Japanese investment in the U.S., in: W.T. Ziemba, W. Bailey and Y. Hamao (eds.), *Japanese Financial Market Research*, North-Holland, Amsterdam, pp. 313–336.

Ziemba, W.T. (1994). Worldwide security market regularities, *Eur. J. Oper. Res.* 74, 198–229.

Ziemba, W.T., W. Bailey, and Y. Hamao (eds.), (1991). *Japanese Financial Market Research*, North-Holland, Amsterdam.

Ziemba, W.T. and S.L. Schwartz (1991). *Invest Japan: The Structure, Performance and Opportunities of the Stock, Bond and Fund Markets*, Probus Publishing, Chicago, Il.

Ziemba, W.T. and R.G. Vickson (eds.), (1975). *Stochastic Optimization Models in Finance*, Academic Press, New York.

Zionts, S. (ed.), (1978). *Multiple Criteria Problem Solving*, Springer, Berlin.

R. Jarrow et al., Eds., *Handbooks in OR & MS, Vol. 9*

Chapter 16

Stock Market Crashes

Allan W. Kleidon
Cornerstone Research, 1000 El Camino Real, Menlo Park, CA 94025-4327, U.S.A. School of Law, Stanford University, Stanford, CA 94305-8610, U.S.A.

1. Introduction

Stock market crashes, defined as precipitous declines in value for securities that represent a large proportion of wealth [Garber, 1992], are rare, difficult to explain, and potentially catastrophic. During four trading days in the crash of October 1987, the U.S. stock market fell by about thirty percent, wiping out roughly one trillion dollars of equity. On October 19 alone, Black Monday, the market fell by over twenty percent. Roll [1989] documents simultaneous declines in markets around the world, irrespective of the level of technical sophistication, with concurrent panics that evoked memories of 1929 and the Great Depression.

What causes such events? Do they signal important failures in the financial system? Are they the forerunners of macroeconomic difficulties such as the Great Depression? What are appropriate responses? Adding to the importance of these questions is the potential for interaction. For example, although there may be incentives for a quick response such as the Presidential Task Force or Brady Report [1988], the adequacy of the response is clearly tied to how well the causes are understood.

The twenty-five largest daily percentage stock market crashes from 1885–1991 are listed in Schwert [1992], and some are relatively straightforward to understand. Declines on May 14 and May 21, 1944 corresponded to news about the German invasion of France, for example. More recently, the decline on October 26, 1989 can be traced to information about the failure of a well publicized takeover attempt and was concentrated in potential takeover targets. However, the largest single day decline on October 19, 1987 has proven much more difficult to explain in terms of standard valuation models, leading some to ask whether irrationality must inevitably have been the cause. One theme of this paper is that such complex events can extend our appreciation of the wide range of phenomena that are, in fact, consistent with rational individual behavior.

In some ways the deepest questions raised by crashes concern the aggregation of individuals' beliefs and actions into market data such as prices and volumes. Adam Smith's 'invisible hand' is but one expression of the difficulty in explaining how the actions of imperfect individuals, who share (at least on average) predictable biases in judgement, are meshed in some fashion to produce aggregate market phenomena. This topic is so basic yet so poorly understood that its periodic recurrence as the focus of economists' attention is no surprise. Nor is it surprising that other disciplines such as the behavioral sciences, and the public in general, sometimes regard the economists' paradigms as simplistic at best or even highly suspect.

The traditional response exemplified by Friedman [1956] is that models are by construction simplifications, and the proof of the pudding is in the eating: Does the model explain the facts or predict the phenomena under consideration with sufficient accuracy to warrant its continued acceptance? While the justification for this response is persuasive at one level, at another level it is unsatisfying. Even if economic models of aggregate behavior were to work perfectly, it would be pleasing to know *how* the actions of individuals are aggregated to conform to the predictions of models based on the 'economic human', who is often characterized as performing complicated mathematical operations instantaneously and bias free. Work such as Alchian [1950] goes some way to fill the void. His approach is to assume that evolutionary forces will leave as survivors those who, for whatever reason (rational or irrational), behave as predicted by the economic models. But there is currently a large gap between what we know of individual behavior, with all its warts and biases, and what we know of aggregate market behavior.[1]

Complete articulation of aggregation theorems that take us from individuals to markets may prove something of a holy grail, and we are certainly not there yet. Individual minutia can distract from understanding the workings of a marketplace, yet investigation of actual markets is typically plagued by the complexities of environments with great uncertainty on most dimensions of interest. How does one sort out the effects of assumptions of individual behavior versus other potential uncertainties in the marketplace?

There is a middle ground between the description of individual action and the analysis of data from real markets that is, in my view, under-exploited. Laboratory experiments with live subjects in controlled settings of asset markets offer the possibility of systematic examination of the effects of different market and information structures on aggregate market prices and quantities. Such results do not explicitly link back to the aggregation theorems we may like to assume exist, since their goals are much more limited: How do information and market structures map into price and volume behavior? Yet they clearly have the potential to give much more information on the kinds of market conditions that are likely to lead to aggregate behavior predicted by economic models.

Moreover, such behavioral experiments with laboratory asset markets have the potential to guide the construction of actual markets. For example, if it appears that certain conditions are necessary for market prices to converge to those predicted by rational expectations models, and if it were held as a matter of policy

[1] See, e.g, Khaneman, Slovic & Tversky [1982] and references therein for examples of individual behavior that differs from the typical assumptions of economic models. See also Ziemba & Hausch [1987].

that society benefits from prices behaving in this fashion, then a focus of attention on whether actual markets provide those characteristics may be in order.

Conversely, if we can learn about the path that prices typically take on their way to convergence to the predictions of rational expectations models — that is, if we can learn about the dynamics of prices under general conditions that will, eventually, lead to what may be desirable behavior — then we may know more of what to expect from real prices. A conclusion of this paper is that we gain considerable insight from the results in experimental markets into the nature and causes of stock market crashes and consequently how we should respond to them.

The paper first outlines evidence from experimental securities markets (Section 2). A standard economics literature examines theoretical conditions for a fully revealing rational expectations equilibrium in which prices completely and accurately aggregate the information of all individuals. The experimental literature examines a variety of market settings. Based on the economic analysis, not all of the laboratory markets would be expected to result in fully revealing prices, and indeed some experimental settings result in prices that do not completely aggregate individuals' private information. The laboratory results provide insight into when imperfect aggregation is more likely to occur, namely an absence of common information about preferences or beliefs of other traders and a lack of traders' experience in the market setting. These findings are consistent with the extant economics literature concerning information aggregation.

Section 3 examines various proposed explanations of the crash, based on a taxonomy suggested by the results in Section 2. Section 3.1 examines models of new 'external' information about fundamentals, that is, information about expected future cash flows or discount rates that reaches *any* trader or investor for the first time. These models explicitly or implicitly assume a fully revealing rational expectations equilibrium. Under this assumption, price changes can only occur if some new 'external' information reaches the market as a whole.

Section 3.2 examines models of new 'internal' information about fundamentals. Not all market conditions result in fully revealing prices, either theoretically or in laboratories. Several recent economic models demonstrate that if prices do not fully reveal all individuals' private information, then they can deviate from the levels that would prevail based on the aggregate or external information about fundamentals; that some trigger event can serve to provide the common beliefs that facilitate aggregation of private information; and that stock market crashes can result from the consequential change in 'internal' information about fundamentals. This language serves to underscore that rational price movements can occur even in the absence of any identifiable external news, since the issue is not one of new information coming to the market in aggregate, but rather one of aggregation of diverse information already known to separate individuals.[2]

[2] Kleidon [1992b] distinguishes between fundamentals that are narrowly defined versus broadly defined to convey exactly the same sense as external versus internal information about fundamentals. The terms 'external news' and 'internal news' are used in D. Romer [1993].

The models of Sections 3.1 and 3.2 share the characteristic that price changes, including crashes, are caused by new information about fundamentals within a framework of rational expectations. The distinguishing feature is whether or not the models assume fully revealing, complete aggregation of private information. Section 3.3 examines a very different class of model in which stock market crashes are not due to rational updating of information about fundamentals. These models have gained some recent currency, in large part because of the perception that rational models can explain stock price changes only in terms of changes in *external* information about fundamentals. Such a perception is incorrect. Although it is generally accepted that changes in external fundamentals are implausible as explanations of the crashes of 1929 and 1987, rational changes in internal information about fundamentals are an entirely different matter.

In light of the results of Section 3, Section 4 examines various proposed responses to crashes. Such responses include the Brady Commission's proposals for a single regulatory authority to oversee the stock, futures and options markets, unified margin requirements, and circuit breakers. The section also examines sunshine trading, securities transactions taxes, and the responses of monetary authorities to crashes. Section 5 concludes the paper.

2. Evidence from experimental markets

2.1. Current laboratory evidence

A useful summary of results from laboratory experiments on information aggregation is given in Camerer [1989, section 6.2.3, p. 28]; see also Forsythe & Lundholm [1990] and Smith, Suchanek & Williams [1988]. These experiments typically examine a controlled environment in which single or multiple securities are traded, the value of which depend on dividends and a terminal payout. Sometimes preferences differ across agents, and sometimes trading takes place in a multi-period setting. Within each period, it is possible to have multiple rounds of trade prior to resolution of uncertainty.

The central question in these experiments is how well prices match the predictions of the fully revealing rational expectations hypothesis, as articulated in Plott & Sunder [1988, p. 1090]: 'All traders choose in equilibrium as if they are aware of the pooled information of all traders in the system regarding the underlying state.' Camerer [1989, p. 25] defines deviations of prices from their value based on pooled information as 'information bubbles', and notes that such 'bubbles' may or may not be rational. This definition of information bubbles includes the strong form of market efficiency [Fama, 1970]; that is, if prices do not fully reflect all public and private information, Camerer's classification would label prices as containing an information bubble.

This is a strong benchmark against which to compare prices. A standard economics literature, following early work such as Grossman & Stiglitz [1976], examines conditions under which prices will fully reveal individuals' information. For example, Hellwig [1980] highlights the importance of the number of sources of uncertainty relative to prices and concludes that under typical conditions prices will be inefficient in aggregating individuals' information. Not all experimental markets satisfy the theoretical conditions for full revelation of information. One justification given for using this stringent benchmark, even when the experimental market does not meet theoretical requirements, is that a finding of fully revealing prices under such settings provides 'much more convincing evidence for the 'real world' relevance of common knowlede [sic] theories' than if there were literally common knowledge in the experiments [Copeland & Friedman, 1991, footnote 5, p. 270].

Four major conclusions emerge from the experimental studies of securities markets. First, the fully revealing rational expectations equilibrium [REE] performs well when some traders are fully informed and some are uninformed [Forsythe & Lundholm, 1990, p. 310]. This model corresponds to the assumed framework underlying many of the current financial information models such as Grossman & Stiglitz [1980] and Kyle [1985].

This first result does not tackle the more difficult problem of the aggregation of information in a market where many individuals have information, but no one observes the *collective* information. However, a second finding is that the fully revealing REE also performs well in many settings which require such information aggregation. Camerer reports [1989, p. 28], 'In most experiments prices aggregate information well: after several trading periods of experience, there are usually no information bubbles (or they vanish quickly, in a minute or less after information is released).' This demonstrates the classic point made by Friedman and repeated in standard economics: The aggregate behavior of individuals may be modelled very effectively without explicit recognition of the differences between actual individual behavior and the model's assumptions.

Given the reliance placed by society on market prices, these two findings are important and reassuring, but they do not directly help in explaining stock market crashes. A hint is provided by the result that several trading periods' worth of experience may be necessary before prices behave as dictated by a fully revealing REE. There is not an automatic black-box of information aggregation, but real people can typically learn how to trade, at least in simple situations.

Third, however, certain more complicated market settings can readily generate deviations of prices from the fully revealing REE, with accompanying 'bubbles' and 'crashes' [Plott & Sunder, 1988; Smith, Suchanek & Williams, 1988; Forsythe & Lundholm, 1990]. Again, learning plays a key role in price formation since in these more complex settings, as in simpler markets, deviations from the REE frequently occur until subjects are experienced. Even with experienced subjects, however, some market and information structures generate such bubbles and crashes. There appear to be limitations on the ability of individuals to sort through the demands of particular information or market structures to reach the fully revealing REE solutions that are typically the outcome of simpler settings.

The fourth and most insightful outcome of this research, for our current purposes at least, concerns the apparent regularities that define situations in which the REE is not achieved. One market setting that can generate violations of the fully revealing REE, even if information aggregation is not required, is where there is only one potentially informed trader (a fact that everyone knows). In this setting, Friedman and Von Borries [1988] find 'information mirages;' that is, uninformed traders may incorrectly (but possibly rationally) draw inferences from purely noninformational liquidity trades when, unknown to them, the potentially informed trader in fact has no information. Camerer [1989, p. 28] reports other studies in which few or no mirages were found, especially with experienced traders; the Friedman and von Borries result is attributed to lack of competition among informed traders.

Plott & Sunder [1988] study markets in which individuals have differing information and no individual has complete information, but in which collectively the market is informationally complete. Such a setting more directly addresses the issue of individual versus aggregate behavior. Plott and Sunder find support for the REE when a complete set of contingent securities is traded, or when traders have identical preferences. However, if there is a single security and diverse preferences, then the REE is frequently not achieved.

Forsythe & Lundholm [1990] further analyze the market structure in Plott & Sunder [1988] and seek sufficient conditions for REE convergence. In particular, they find [p. 310] 'that trading experience and common knowledge of payoffs are jointly sufficient to achieve an RE equilibrium, but that neither is a sufficient condition by itself'. Operationally, they find that markets without common knowledge of dividend payoff schedules do not support the REE even with experienced traders. Moreover, although some experience was necessary even with common knowledge of dividends, the experience did not have to be with the same dividend parameter set or market design, since experienced traders were able to rapidly adjust to new market settings.

Forsythe and Lundholm note that they cannot regard any particular treatment as necessary to achieve the fully revealing REE since they have not investigated all possible market structures in the absence of that treatment. Copeland & Friedman [1991] illustrate the point since they examine a market in which information is asymmetrically distributed across traders, with traders purchasing (complete) information sequentially, but in which there is no common knowledge of traders' payoffs or information acquisition. They find that the fully revealing REE best explains prices but that a partially revealing model better explains the market value and allocation of purchased information, and the allocation of assets.

2.2. *Evaluation of findings*

One caveat to an interpretation of findings from the experimental markets concerns the benchmark typically employed in such studies, namely a fully revealing REE in which all information by any individual is revealed in prices. It should come as no surprise that this standard may be violated under conditions that do not satisfy the theoretical requirements for full relevation. In a similar vein, while Camerer [1989] defines information bubbles to include situations where any private information is not revealed in prices, this definition of bubbles is considerably stronger than the typical use in finance, and in effect implies that all stock prices contain 'bubbles'.

One lesson that can be brought from the experimental markets to an investigation of stock market crashes is that some learning period is typically required before traders aggregate information as predicted by a fully revealing REE. A distinction is drawn in the experimental literature between temporary deviations from a final price which conforms to the REE, and a failure of the price sequence to converge to the REE even in the limit. For example, Plott & Sunder [1988, footnote 6, p. 1104] state: 'Rational expectations can be seen either as a static theory of markets (e.g., in the efficient market literature in finance) or as an end-point of a dynamic path of adjustment' and favor the second interpretation based on their previous work. Smith, Suchanek & Williams [1988, p. 1150] also reach a general conclusion that the rational expectations model of asset prices 'is supported only as an *equilibrium concept* underlying an adaptive capital gains price adjustment process'.

A second lesson seems to be that if information aggregation is required because no individual knows all the relevant information, then agents need to be able to understand the market structure before reliable laboratory convergence to fully revealing REE can be demonstrated. In the information mirages of Camerer & Weigelt [1991], 'people see information which is not there' because the market setting is one where no trader has any information but nobody knows that no trader has any information [Camerer, 1989, p. 26]. Plott & Sunder [1988, p. 1116] conclude, 'Some sort of knowledge of others' preferences appears to be a necessary condition for aggregation of diverse information.' Forsythe & Lundholm [1990, p. 341] conclude that 'common knowledge of dividends and a similar prior experience are jointly, but not separately, sufficient to achieve an RE equilibrium'.

Smith, Suchanek & Williams [1988, p. 1148] comment:

> Real people in any environment usually do not come off the stops with common expectations; they usually do not solve problems of maximization over time by ex-ante reasoning and backward induction, *nor is this irrational when there is insufficient reason to believe that expectations are common*. ... a common dividend, and common knowledge thereof is insufficient to induce initial common expectations. As we interpret it this is due to agent uncertainty about the behavior of others. With experience, and its lessons in trial-and-error learning, expectations tend ultimately to converge and yield an [REE]. [Emphasis added]

The third lesson is that, under a wide variety of conditions, experimental markets demonstrate that real traders in security markets are able to produce aggregate market phenomena that match the predictions of rational economic models. It should not be overlooked that when conditions are suitable for the inference of information from other traders' actions — which can be as subtle as the existence of a complete set of contingent securities [Plott & Sunder, 1988] — the consistent finding is that experienced traders trade to the REE. Stated in the alternative, it is simply not the case that individual biases and limitations imply that aggregate prices must display irrational behavior. To the contrary, the tendency is toward rational aggregate behavior.

One possible explanation of crashes exploited by several models in the next section is that market conditions may evolve over time from an early state in which traders do not share common knowledge to one in which their preferences and beliefs are commonly revealed. This is particularly interesting since the medium for revelation of individual preferences or beliefs can easily be the trading process itself, consistent with the experimental findings that a period of learning often teaches traders how to extract information. These models demonstrate that market evolution may change the possibilities for such information extraction, allowing for rational deviations from and returns to the fully revealing REE.

3. Potential explanations of stock market crashes

The findings from experimental markets lead naturally to two, and possibly three, potential explanations for observed stock market crashes. Each has received attention in popular or academic literature.

At one extreme, it is possible that prices at all times conform to the predictions of fully revealing rational expectations models and that a crash results from a discrete and large change in the external information about fundamentals on which such models operate. The most common articulation of this explanation regards prices as the present value of expected future cash flows, and a crash corresponds to new information about either future cash flows (earnings or dividends) or discount rates. An important issue concerns whether the term 'fundamentals' is to be applied narrowly or broadly. In particular, if there is no change in the *collective* information in the market about cash flows or discount rates, has there been a change in fundamentals? As noted in Kleidon [1992b, p. 653], there may be no changes in fundamentals narrowly defined with respect to collective information (denoted in D. Romer [1993] as external news about fundamentals), yet there may be rational movements in prices because of changes in the knowledge that traders have about the behavior of other traders.

A change that enables information aggregation will potentially change expectations of future cash flows for every trader, yet there need be no change in the collective information. The extreme position of fully revealing prices means that there is no distinction between external and internal information about fundamentals since all individual information is assumed to be perfectly aggregated.

A second, intermediate position is that prices tend to converge to the predictions of rational expectations models, but that natural changes in the trading environment can lead to periods during which the conditions for aggregating diverse information and achieving the fully revealing REE are violated. For example, conditions may change so that investors no longer have common knowledge about other traders' beliefs or preferences. This initially results in (possibly substantial) deviations from the REE that would obtain in the presence of common beliefs. If some 'trigger event' results in substantial revision of beliefs about some aspects of other traders then an abrupt change in stock price may result. For example, if some trigger serves to provide common beliefs then the price may rapidly move to the fully revealing REE.

Third, another extreme view is that stock market crashes can only be explained in terms of capricious and temperamental changes in world view at the individual level and hence cannot be linked in a rational fashion to either changes in external information about fundamentals or to new rational learning by individuals about fundamentals. This view, based on irrational or nonrational assumptions, does not necessarily flow from the experimental evidence, but it has received some attention in the literature and completes the taxonomy.

3.1. Changes in external information about fundamentals

One potential cause of market crashes is a change in external information about fundamentals, and indeed some large price declines can be attributed to such causes.[3] For example, the 'minibreak' of Friday October 13, 1989 can be traced to a particular event with relatively straightforward implications for future cash flows. The decline on October 13 began shortly after 2:40 p.m., when it was announced that financing for a proposed takeover of United Airlines had failed and that trading in United's stock was suspended [McMillan, 1991, pp. 252 ff.; U.S. Securities and Exchange Commission (SEC), 1990]. The decline was substantial. By close of trade, the Dow Jones Industrial Average (DJIA) had dropped by 190 points (6.90%), which was the second largest decline in absolute terms (and the twelfth largest in percentage terms). However, consistent with the link to the woes of United Airlines, the decline was concentrated in leveraged buyouts and other potential takeover targets. Thus, this crash seems relatively easily explained in terms of standard valuation models and changes in external fundamentals.

Much more difficult to reconcile with standard models of external fundamentals are the events of October 19, 1987 when the DJIA dropped 508 points or 22.6 percent. From the close of trading on Tuesday October 13, 1987 to the close on October 19 (four trading days), the DJIA fell 769 points or 31%, representing a decline in the value of outstanding U.S. equity of some $1 trillion. Only the 12.8% drop in the Dow on October 28, 1929 and the fall of 11.7% on the following day, which together constituted the crash of 1929, have approached the October 1987 decline in magnitude.

Traditional measures of value suggest that the market was unusually high immediately before the 1987 crash. In August/September 1987 price-earnings [P/E] ratios were close to historical highs. Figure 1 shows quarterly P/E ratios for Standard and Poor's 500 Index (and its predecessors) from 1936 to 1991, and annual P/E ratios from 1926 to 1935. The range for available monthly data is a high of 23.30 in December 1991 to a low of 5.9 in June 1949. The average P/E ratios in August and September 1987 were 22.33 and 22.10, respectively, while in November 1987 it had fallen to 15.81. Figure 1 also shows real yields on long-term

[3] Some of the following material is based on Kleidon & Mehra [1995].

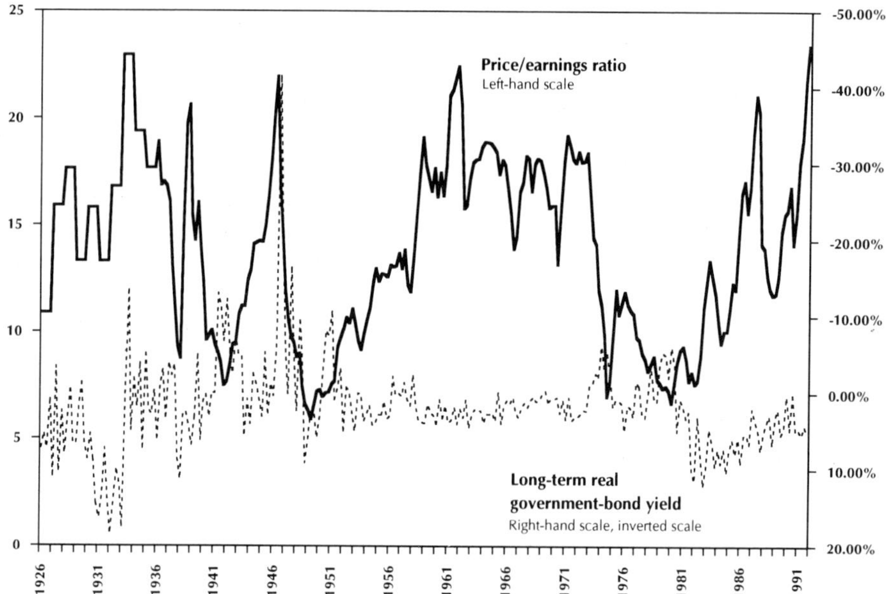

Fig. 1. Price-earnings ratios for the S&P 500 Index and real long-term government bond yields, 1926 to 1991. Data are plotted quarterly, and price-earnings ratios are based on annual data from 1926 to 1935 and quarterly data from 1936:Q1 to 1991:Q4. Real yields are defined as nominal yields less annualized quarterly inflation rates. Sources: S&P Security Price Index Record, 1992; SBBI 1992 Yearbook, Exhibits A-9, B-10, Ibbotson Associates.

government bonds, based on annualized quarterly inflation rates. The high P/E ratios prior to the crash were not accompanied by unusually low real interest rates. Dividend yields were very low just prior to the crash, by historical standards. From 1956 to 1986 the average dividend yield for the DJIA was 3.8%. In September 1987 the yield was only 2.8%, and was back to 3.71% by December 1987. A reasonable inference is that the crash reflected a fundamental shift in equilibrium values, with the market returning from an unusually high price level to a more usual level.

However, the major difficulty for standard valuation models lies in identifying a possible source of the negative information or the increased discount rates that could account for a 31% drop in value from October 13 to October 19, 1987. The SEC Report [1988] notes that some negative news occurred on October 14–16, and Mitchell & Netter [1989] point to antitakeover legislation proposed on October 13 as the fundamental cause of the ten percent price decline by October 16. However, although they regard this initial price decline as consistent with rationality, they provide no explanation of how this 'normal' price movement could trigger the massive decline on October 19.

This stumbling block for standard valuation models has been widely noted. For example, French [1988, p. 279] asks, 'What new information reduced fundamental values by more than 20% on October 19, 1987?' Ziemba & Schwartz [1992,

p. 395] note that an increase in the standard deviation of asset returns can imply sharply higher expected returns and hence lower current prices in standard pricing models but do not identify the source of increased volatility. Schwert [1992] notes that the rise in volatility in 1987 was contemporaneous with the fall in prices, making causal statements difficult; moreover, volatility returned to pre-crash levels by early 1988, but prices did not rebound. Implicitly defining new information about fundamentals in the narrow sense, that is, new information to the collective market, French [1988] agrees with many other commentators that such new external information was absent in October 1987.

However, various authors reach different conclusions about the implications of this finding for models of rational price movements. French [1988, p. 281] concludes that 'prices were above fundamental values before the crash, but that investors did not know they were too high' and believes that it is difficult 'to describe a rational (and plausible) model in which traders can infer that they have made an enormous error from a small amount of bad news'. The alternative, which French favors, 'is to consider the possibility of irrational behavior'.

Gennotte & Leland [1990], Jacklin, Kleidon & Pfleiderer [1992], and D. Romer [1993] all provide models that do not assume irrational behavior but that relax the assumption that prices necessarily fully aggregate individual information. These models are consistent with extant economic theorems that not all market settings will result in full information revelation. They are also in the spirit of results from the experimental markets confirming that certain market conditions prevent information aggregation and allow for deviations from a fully revealing REE, with consequent booms and crashes.

3.2. Models of imperfect information aggregation

3.2.1. Grossman [1988]

An important precursor to explanations of market crashes based on imperfect information aggregation is Grossman [1988], which was in fact developed prior to the crash of October 1987. Grossman examines hedging strategies, called portfolio insurance, that synthesize a put on the market by dynamic replication in the stock (or futures) and bond markets. These dynamic hedging strategies imply mechanical rules that more stock will be purchased following a price rise and that stock will be sold following a fall in stock prices.

Grossman's focus is on the implications for market liquidity of imperfect information by traders about the extent to which other traders are following portfolio insurance strategies. The key element in his model is that the existence of portfolio insurance will affect those traders who want to accommodate demands for trade by those with portfolio insurance. For example, if prices fall, inducing coordinated selling by those following dynamic hedging strategies, then other investors would like to have sufficient liquidity in their portfolios to take the other side of these trades. This is especially so since the mechanistic nature of the dynamic strategies, which are based solely on *past* price movements, implies that there is no adverse information in these sales.

Uncertainty about the extent of portfolio insurance is linked in Grossman's model to imperfect aggregation of information about the preferences of individual traders. If those seeking 'insurance' were to purchase a put directly, then the market price of puts will reveal information about the demand for insurance. However, if a dynamic strategy is followed, it is much more difficult to infer the motives behind current trades since the point of dynamic hedging is to follow a particular price dependent strategy in the *future*.

What happens if there is imperfect information about the extent of portfolio insurance? Grossman argues that there may be higher price volatility caused by nonoptimal portfolio composition for those seeking to provide liquidity for the dynamic hedgers. Following the previous example, if there is more portfolio insurance than anticipated and the price falls then there will be greater subsequent selling than planned for by the providers of liquidity, and the price may fall more than would be the case if the amount of portfolio insurance were known with certainty. In general, this increased 'price pressure' flowing from decreased liquidity implies greater price volatility.

3.2.2. Gennotte & Leland [1990]

The liquidity argument of Grossman [1988] is extended in Gennotte & Leland [1990] and explicitly applied to the stock market crashes of 1929 and 1987. Information about the extent of dynamic hedging strategies, including both formal portfolio insurance (in 1987) and informal stop-loss strategies (in both 1987 and 1929), is assumed to be imperfectly aggregated. This causes price pressure due to lack of liquidity when there is more dynamic hedging than anticipated and the price declines, resulting in more than expected coordinated selling.

Leland and Gennotte extend Grossman's model in order to answer two questions [1990, p. 1000]: '(1) How can relatively small amounts of hedging drive down prices significantly? (2) Why didn't stock prices rebound the moment such selling pressure stopped?' The first question is answered by explicitly modelling the extent to which investors infer information from prices in a rational expectations equilibrium with diverse information across investors. The second question is answered by modelling the effect of imperfect information about the extent of dynamic hedging. If sales by dynamic hedgers are incorrectly interpreted as sales by informed traders, then expectations of future value, and consequently the current price, are permanently revised downward.

3.2.3. Jacklin, Kleidon & Pfleiderer [1992]

The arguments in Grossman [1988] also provide the stimulus for the model in Jacklin, Kleidon and Pfleiderer (JKP) [1992]. However, the emphasis is not on liquidity effects during a crash but rather on imperfect information aggregation during the time leading up to the crash, and on a trigger that serves to provide common information that leads to a crash. Again, the focus is on dynamic hedging strategies that JKP label generically as portfolio insurance (which include informal dynamic hedging such as stop-loss orders). JKP assume, as do Gennotte and Leland, that there is imperfect information about the extent of portfolio insurance, and that there is greater use of dynamic hedging strategies than is commonly believed. They ask [1992, p. 36], 'If the market was surprised at the amount of portfolio insurance selling on October 19 (or more correctly on the previous Friday, October 16), then what are the implications for the price level *before* the amount of portfolio insurance was revealed?'

JKP extend the model of Glosten & Milgrom [1985] to allow uncertainty about individual preferences with respect to portfolio insurance, and conclude that imperfect knowledge of the extent of portfolio insurance can lead to systematic deviations of prices from those that would prevail if the amount of portfolio insurance were common knowledge. In particular, if traders underestimate the extent of dynamic hedging, then stock purchases following a price rise can be incorrectly attributed to purchases based on favorable information rather than to information-free purchases based on a mechanical dynamic strategy. This leads to the price being greater on average than that which would prevail if there were either no portfolio insurance or if the extent of portfolio insurance were common knowledge.

Figure 2 demonstrates the potential effects on expected price paths of uncertainty about the extent of portfolio insurance. Results over 100 periods for four models (examined in detail in JKP) are presented. Models 1 and 2 show situations in which there are unexpectedly high and low amounts of portfolio insurance, respectively. In model 3, there is the same large amount of insurance

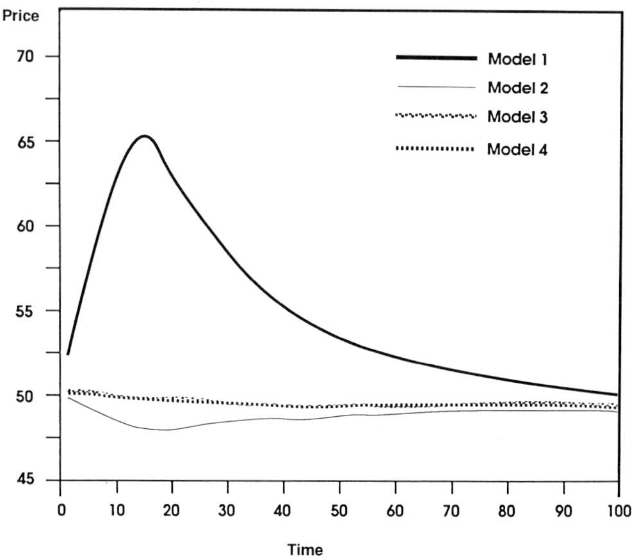

Fig. 2. Averages across 10,000 replications of prices for different models of portfolio insurance: Model 1, high portfolio insurance initially underestimated by the market; Model 2, low portfolio insurance initially overestimated; Model 3, high portfolio insurance known with certainty; and Model 4, no portfolio insurance known with certainty. Source: Jacklin, Kleidon & Pfleiderer [1992].

as in model 1 but the amount is known with certainty by all participants, while in model 4 there is no insurance (which all traders know). The price level defined by external fundamentals is 50, and this price is achieved on average for both models 3 and 4 which are virtually indistinguishable. Thus, large amounts of portfolio insurance do not necessarily cause a deviation of prices from the level implied by external fundamentals, if the amount of such insurance is known by all participants (model 3).

However, uncertainty about the preferences of others can lead to systematic deviations from this level. If the level of portfolio insurance is initially underestimated as in model 1, then rational traders can misinterpret uninformed mechanical purchases as containing favorable information, causing the price to rise above the level based on external fundamentals. The trigger for a crash in this model is a price decline that stimulates coordinated selling by those with portfolio insurance. If there is greater than anticipated selling in response to the price decline, then beliefs concerning the extent of portfolio insurance are revised upward and beliefs about the information content of previous purchases are revised downward — as is the price.[4] The corresponding October 1987 events are the bad news and unexpectedly large portfolio insurance sales prior to October 19, especially on the afternoon of Friday October 16, as discussed in the SEC Report [1988, p. 2–10].

3.2.4. Romer [1993]

D. Romer [1993] also emphasises that imperfect aggregation of individuals' information may result in price movements caused by the revelation of information about future payoffs or discount rates via the trading process itself, that is, internal news rather than outside news.

The particular mechanism he suggests to explain the crash of October 1987 is based on a model of individual trader uncertainty about the quality of other traders' information. Such uncertainty can cause too heavy reliance on the market price as an aggregator of others' information and too little reliance on one's own information (or the converse). Subsequent market behavior, such as the price reaction to liquidity trades, reveals whose information is superior, and rapid price adjustments may result.

3.2.5. Summary and comparison of models

French [1988, p. 284] claims that it is 'hard to imagine a plausible model of fundamental value in which the small amount of information observed on October 19, 1987, could trigger a rational 22% drop in prices'. While the issue of plausibility may lie in the eye of the beholder, it is certainly possible to find rational models

[4] The analysis with respect to model 2, which initially overestimates the amount of insurance, is symmetric. Note that the parameter values underlying Figure 2 assume a ten percent prior probability of high insurance, so that the mispricing that results if insurance is in fact high (model 1) is larger than for model 2. However, assuming the prior probabilities are rational, the outcome in model 1 occurs with only ten percent probability.

in which little or no news about narrowly defined external fundamentals can be reconciled with very large and rapid price changes. The key is not a relaxation of the assumption of individual rationality, but a relaxation of the assumption that prices are perfect aggregators of individual information; that is, the models deal with internal as well as external information about fundamentals.

The important innovation in these models is to allow rational investors to learn, over time, about both the market structure and the information of other traders.[5] Experimental markets confirm that uncertainty about the basic rules of the game — for example, the preferences or beliefs of others — can provide insufficient structure for traders to infer the information possessed by others. Each of the models outlined above is concerned with the same basic issue.[6]

The models of Jacklin, Kleidon & Pfleiderer [1992] and Romer [1993] share many similarities. Both are based on imperfect aggregation of information in the market (albeit from different sources); both produce the result that rational actions by individuals will result in stock prices rising above the level that would prevail if there were perfect aggregation of information, which is consistent with claims that typical market indicators suggested that prices were high prior to the crash [Brady Report, 1988]; both use the trigger of undisputed bad news in the week prior to the crash [Mitchell & Netter 1989] to reveal the extent to which traders' beliefs about the market structure were incorrect; and both explain the crash as the consequent rapid revision of beliefs about the fundamental value of the stock.

These models implicitly assume that the final price after the crash is the rational price based on both external fundamentals and full knowledge of the market structure, including the preferences of other traders as indicated by the proportions of traders following particular strategies (in JKP) and knowledge of the beliefs of other traders (in Romer's model). The models provide a framework within which uncertainty about some parameter of market structure arises naturally and about which there is learning over time. Uncertainty about the proportions of traders following dynamic hedging strategies in JKP is reasonable since the use of

[5] Related work by Brown & Jennings [1989] and Grundy & McNichols [1989] shows that multiple rounds of trade can reveal information about previous amounts of informed versus uninformed trading. Kraus & Smith [1989] consider imperfect information about investor endowments, and Easley & O'Hara [1991] examine the effects of uninformed stop orders on securities prices.

[6] Other papers dealing with the October 1987 crash address related issues. Black [1988, p. 273] attributes the crash to investor awareness that 'the typical investor had more flexible tastes' than previously believed. Leland & Rubinstein [1988, p. 48] assume that in the 'standard model ... all investors are fully aware of the strategies followed by portfolio insurers', and note the possibility that instead 'they may have interpreted the portfolio insurance trades as information-based'. Brennan & Schwartz [1989, p. 471] note the 'possible misinterpretation of the information content of portfolio-insurance-induced transactions' if the amount of such activities is not known, and Miller [1992] also regards portfolio insurance as potentially destabilizing if the absence of information in such trades is not understood. Bulow & Klemperer [1994] observe that traders' 'willingness to pay' will typically be much more elastic than their demand curves based on personal valuations, so that small changes in one individual's valuation can rationally result in a large change in average price. Lee [1992] 'relies on the notion of informational cascades in deriving indistinguishable trade orders after a sequence of good news traders' [p. 2] following Bikhchandani, Hirshleifer & Welch [1992].

formal portfolio hedging was a relatively new phenomenon prior to the 1987 crash. Romer also points to a new economic development as the cause of uncertainty about the beliefs of others, namely the phenomenon of 'unprecedentedly large government budget deficits for the foreseeable future' [1993, p. 15]. Both of these phenomena were cited in surveys as concerns related to the crash.[7]

The one-period model of Gennotte and Leland is somewhat different. In their chronology linking the events of October 1987 to their model [1990, pp. 1011–1012], the market just prior to opening on October 19 is regarded as correctly priced relative to external fundamentals, in contrast to the implications of the other models examined here. Gennotte and Leland's model requires the selling on October 19 by those with portfolio insurance to be misinterpreted as informed selling, which makes it difficult to explain the prior decline in prices in markets that opened before the NYSE [Roll, 1989]. Such a phenomenon is consistent with the other models, since the trigger that caused a revision in prices occurred in the previous week (especially on the afternoon of Friday, October 16). As noted by Romer [1993, p. 17], Gennotte and Leland's model also suggests that the price drop should have been reversed when it became known that the selling on October 19 was not information-based, but such a reversal did not occur.

While each model differs in detail and some implications, all share the basic characteristic that the crash is explained in terms of rational individual action in the context of a trading environment in which it is difficult to aggregate individuals' information. This behavior is closely attuned to the findings of experimental securities markets and is consistent with standard models of non-fully-revealing rational expectations. It differs significantly from the assumptions in the third group of explanations for crashes, namely irrational or extrarational behavior by individuals.

3.3. Models of crashes not based on rational behavior

The explanations for crashes we now examine share the characteristic that they are not based on a model of rational individual behavior and changes in external or internal information about fundamentals. They range from popular explanations that appear in the press or reports such as that of the Brady Commission, through models that bear some relation to rational models but assume that crashes occur for nonrational reasons, such as 'speculative bubbles' and the 'sunspot' literature, to models that explicitly assume irrational behavior by individuals.

3.3.1. Popular explanations for crashes

As in 1929, many popular explanations for the crash of October 1987 quickly appeared, but the analysis was not necessarily based on well structured reasoning. One prominent explanation given in the Brady Report [1988] blamed the programmed trading of index arbitrage and portfolio insurance for a cascade of order flows that precipitated the crash. The suggestion is that prices fell in the cash (stock) market triggering sales in the futures market by those with portfolio

[7] See, for example, the Brady Report [1988] and Shiller [1989].

insurance, which in turn led to index arbitrage sales in the cash market further lowering the cash prices, and so on. This theory was challenged in the reports of the U.S. Commodity Futures Trading Commission [1988] and the Chicago Mercantile Exchange,[8] and empirical evidence against the argument is provided by Santoni [1988].

Other explanations include suggestions that stock prices were too high for some unspecified reason and fell to appropriate levels. For example, prior to the official Report [1988] by the Brady Commission, Nicholas Brady noted in a discussion of possible causes that pre-crash stock prices were 'incredibly high' by usual standards [*Wall Street Journal* 1987, p. 18]. While this view implicitly regards the crash as returning the market to reasonable levels, it does not provide any explanation as to why it was 'incredibly' high before the crash. Moreover, it does not explain in what sense the stock price was unbelievable. For example, although it is true that prices prior to October 1987 were high by historical measures, Bleiberg [1989] demonstrates that these levels were matched in other periods that were followed by booms, not crashes.

However, the general notion of prices being too high followed by an inevitable crash was fairly widespread in popular ex-post accounts of the crash [Santoni, 1988, p. 19], an argument linked to either rational or irrational bubbles.

3.3.2. Rational bubbles and sunspots

Some rational expectations models allow for multiple equilibria. Models have emerged that suggest that price changes may be due to self-fulfilling prophecies of market participants, 'often called 'bubbles' or 'sunspots' to denote their dependence on events that are extraneous to the market' [Flood and Hodrick, 1990, p. 85].[9] Explosive indeterminacies in asset prices within a rational expectations model are usually called rational bubbles, and stochastic versions of rational bubbles allow for crashes with some probability. Nonexplosive indeterminacies or sunspots assume coordinated movement from one equilibrium to another, with the cause of the movement outside the realm of the rational models themselves. The movements could be due to sunspots, for example, as long as all agents agree on the coordinating mechanism to be used [see, e.g., Peck and Shell, 1991]. This approach is something of a hybrid between rational and nonrational models. Prices are rational, within the assumptions of the particular rational expectations model under consideration; however, the choice among potential equilibria is determined from outside the rational framework. One approach to bubbles and sunspots is to add plausible theoretical restrictions to models that rule out many of the potential equilibria. Flood and Hodrick note [1990, p. 87], 'Many researchers argue that empirical tests for bubbles and sunspots are uninteresting because they can be ruled out by certain types of rational economic theories.' Nevertheless, some types of bubbles and sunspots are difficult to rule out with theoretical arguments.

[8] See Miller, Hawke, Malkiel & Scholes [1988]. In gcncral, scc Santoni [1988, p. 20] for detailed references to these reports.

[9] This paper contains an excellent survey and review of the literature. See also Camerer [1989].

Three challenges face this approach. First, sunspot models, in particular, place more demands on the aggregation of individual beliefs and preferences than other models, since all individuals must coordinate their beliefs about which of multiple equilibria will apply at any particular moment based, say, on sunspots. The response by Woodford [1990] presents an overlapping generations model within which particular adaptive learning rules by individuals can lead them to believe in and converge to a stationary sunspot equilibrium.

Second, by their nature, these models do not account for the timing of a crash. A deterministic bubble will never burst — the stock price will rise exponentially without bound above the level determined by fundamentals, a model that seems implausible. A stochastic bubble will rise at a rate greater than the required rate of return while it lasts, although each period there is some chance it will burst; but if the date of collapse were predictable, rationality would preclude the bubble's existence. Moreover, as noted by French [1988, p. 281], there is little evidence that traders generally knew that prices were above fundamentals and a bubble was waiting to burst prior to the crash in October 1987; traders reactions were described as 'stunned disbelief'. Changes from one price level to another in the sunspot literature must also be dictated by stochastic elements such as real sunspots.

Third, tests for rational bubbles are fraught with difficulties, not least being the challenge of specifying a benchmark against which to test for bubbles. In their review, Flood & Hodrick [1990, p. 87] conclude:

> It is our contention that no econometric test has yet demonstrated that bubbles are present in the data. In each case, misspecification of the model or alternative market fundamentals seems the likely explanation of the findings.

West [1988] also concludes in a review of bubbles literature that there is little support for rational bubbles in stock prices. Stone & Ziemba [1993] conclude that there is little evidence of a bubble in Japan's essential land or stock markets despite the dramatic declines in these markets in the early 1990s, although they believe (with caveats based on Flood and Hodrick's analysis) that fat tails in distributions of golf club membership prices is some evidence for a bubble in speculative land prices [see also Ziemba & Schwartz, 1992, chapter 5].

3.3.3. Irrational bubbles and fads

Russell [1988, p. 51] comments that the 'present mania for bubbles in the financial press' started with the crash of October 1987 and the subsequent weakening of journalists' faith in market efficiency, if 'market efficiency' implies that forecasts of future dividends declined by twenty percent in one day. After presenting a cogent critique of bubble theories, Russell concludes that the primary reason for their popularity is the apparent absence of an alternative [1988, p. 52]: 'Until such time as a smoking gun is discovered, market commentators will best be served by jumping on the bubble bandwagon'.

Academic commentators have made similar leaps for the same reason. French [1988, p. 281] believes that rational models cannot account for the apparent change in fundamentals observed in the crash of 1987. Shleifer & Summers [1990, p. 19] believe that 'the stock in the efficient markets hypothesis — at least as it has traditionally been formulated — crashed along with the rest of the market on October 19, 1987', and assume 'as an alternative to the efficient markets hypothesis' that 'some investors are not fully rational'. In contrast with the models of imperfect information aggregation discussed in Section 3.2 above, Shiller [1988, p. 291] believes that 'portfolio insurance is best thought of as an investor fad that, like other fads, has caused an important change in investor behavior'.

Shiller's view is consistent with his general belief [1989, p. 1] that asset prices 'change in substantial measure because the investing public en masse capriciously changes its mind'. Of course, this sentiment goes back at least to the Dutch 'tulip mania' of the seventeenth century, with a recent revival based on apparent excess volatility of stock prices when judged against the benchmark of simple models of fully revealing rational expectations and constant discount rates [LeRoy & Porter, 1981; Shiller, 1981]. The subject has been controversial, with respect to both tulip mania [Garber, 1989, 1992] and excess volatility [Flavin, 1983; Kleidon, 1986; Gilles & LeRoy, 1991; Cochrane, 1992; Ackert & Smith, 1993].

Related work on the bond market demonstrates the hazards of this approach. Early papers by Shiller [1979] and Singleton [1980] concluded that there was excess volatility in bond prices relative to the expectations model. However, based on more data and better statistical methods and interpretation, Shiller [1989] concludes that in fact bond prices do not show excess volatility. This result is very interesting since the pricing of bonds is a much less daunting task than the pricing of equities. It is more likely that the conditions for information aggregation and the adequacy of simple pricing models will exist in the bond market than in the stock market. Moreover, the finding that bond markets apparently conform to simple models of rational pricing raises the question: If investor fads are truly as endemic as this literature believes [Shiller, 1989], then why would they fail to leave a mark in the bond market?

In the context of crashes, much of the current support for irrational models of fads and bubbles stems from a belief that rational models cannot account for rapid revisions of fundamental values in the absence of external news. French [1988, p. 281] notes the traditional reluctance of economists 'to use ad hoc assumptions of irrationality to 'explain' individual anomalies or events', but succumbs 'at the risk of appearing weak-willed'. The more recent work described in Section 3.2 above, which demonstrates the possibility of changes in internal information about fundamentals in the absence of external news, suggests that he may have yielded to temptation prematurely.

4. Responses to crashes

One response to stock market crashes is the stimulation of academic research on causes of such unusual events. The development of our understanding of how the trading process can aggregate information in the absence of new external information, with attendant rapid revisions of value, is no exception.

More immediately related to crashes are specific proposals for changes in the regulatory or structural environment of stock markets, which ostensibly either remove the causes of crashes or ameliorate their effects. The Brady Report [1988] focussed most attention on what it perceived to be the major source of 'the problems of mid-October', namely 'the failure of [stocks, stock index futures, and stock options] to act as one' [1988, Executive Summary, p. vi]. Recommendations included one agency having regulatory authority over all three market segments, coordinated margin requirements, and circuit breakers.

Circuit breakers have also been recommended for reasons that can be linked to the aggregation issues discussed above. To the extent that prices differ from the level of a fully revealing REE, there may be circumstances under which a halt in trading would allow better aggregation of private information. This rationale underlies the traditional trading halts on, say, the NYSE, where either impending announcements or order imbalances signal the possibility of significant asymmetries in information across traders.

Other recommendations also relate to issues of information aggregation. A major source of a failure of complete aggregation of information has been traced in laboratory experiments and in the economic models of Section 3.2 to an absence of common beliefs about traders' preferences or beliefs. One suggestion that may assist in the formation of common beliefs is the provision of greater information about the motives of traders, such as 'sunshine trading' proposals.

Some responses stem from the belief that the cause of crashes is individual irrationality or irresponsibility, typified by such pejorative terms as 'excessive speculation'. If the very existence of stock markets leads to socially unproductive activities, exemplified by booms and crashes, then perhaps the solution is to close them down or at least make it more difficult for individuals to access them. Such proposals have indeed been made, especially in the form of transactions taxes specifically designed to impede the functioning of the stock market.

This section discusses these proposals in turn, and concludes with a brief examination of the response of monetary authorities to the crash of October 1987.

4.1. *A single market of stocks, futures and options*

Most of the official Brady Report [1988] focussed on market disruption during the crash itself. The Brady Commission advocated one regulatory authority across stocks, futures, and options because of the well-documented breakdown between the cash (NYSE) and futures markets, which are regulated by the Securities and Exchange Commission (SEC) and Commodity Futures Trading Commission (CFTC), respectively. However, the argument for unified regulation is significantly weakened by an examination of the behavior of the options market which is also regulated by the SEC. Kleidon & Whaley [1992] demonstrate that during the 1987 crash the cash market was delinked from both the options and futures markets, but the latter markets retained their usual links.

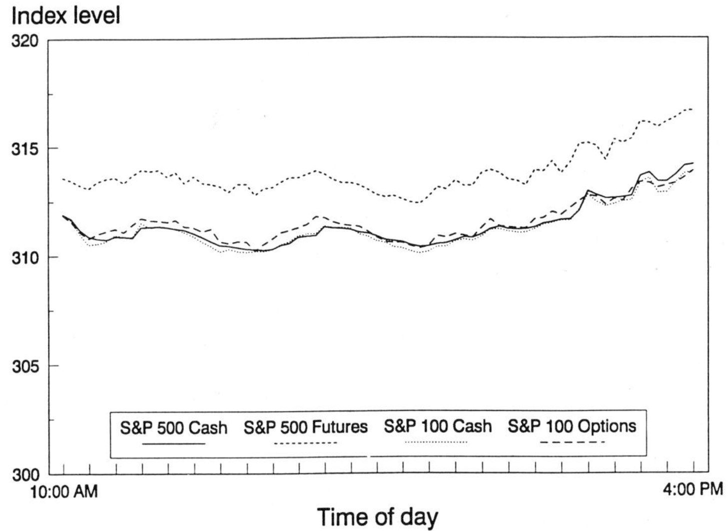

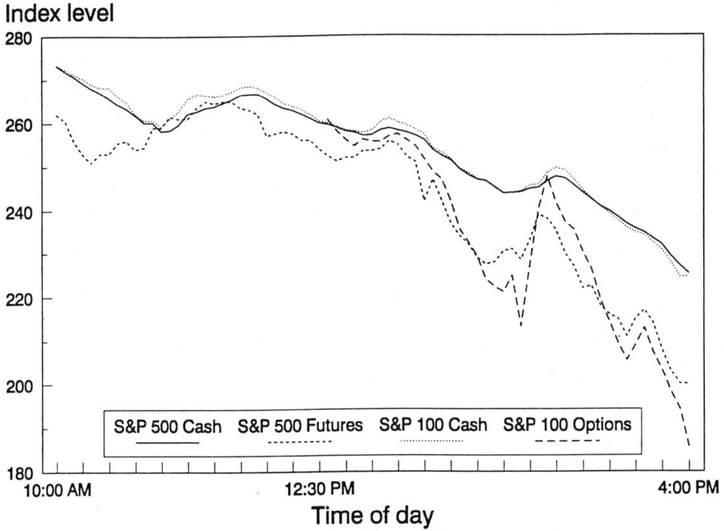

Fig. 3. Levels of the S&P 500 cash index, the December 1987 S&P 500 futures contract, the S&P 100 cash index, and the implied S&P 100 cash index computed from the November 1987 S&P 100 index option price quotes (both S&P 100 indexes normalized to the S&P 500 cash index at 10:00 a.m. EST) for (a) October 13, 1987 and (b) October 19, 1987. Source: Kleidon & Whaley [1992].

Figure 3a illustrates the usual linkage across these three markets, demonstrating the close correspondence between the prices of stocks, futures, and options on October 13, 1987, a typical trading day. Four series are plotted. The cash market (primarily the NYSE) is represented by the S&P 500 and S&P 100 Indexes, which for our purposes can be regarded as identical. The futures contract on the S&P 500 Index is traded on the Chicago Mercantile Exchange, while the options contract on the S&P 100 Index is traded on the Chicago Board Options Exchange. The series plotted in Figure 3 based on the S&P 100 options contract is the price level of the S&P 100 that is implied by the traded options prices.[10] Figure 3a shows that all four series show very similar movements, and that the difference between the futures price and the cash price (called the basis) is positive as is implied by standard cost of carry arbitrage arguments.

Figure 3b shows the strikingly different behavior of these series on October 19, 1987. Again, for our purposes, the cash market series of the S&P 500 and S&P 100 are virtually identical. Both series differ significantly from the S&P 500 futures contract, the fact which attracted so much attention from the Brady Commission. Not only do the cash and futures prices diverge, but for much of the day the basis was *negative*, apparently indicating the violation of arbitrage bounds. However, the Brady Commission did not examine the corresponding behavior in the options market. The S&P 100 options prices are also significantly at odds with the cash market, and in fact are closely related to the futures prices.

These results challenge the claims of the Brady Commission that a single regulatory authority is necessary to ensure the maintenance of close market links during disruptions such as a crash. First, the cash and options markets were delinked on October 19 although both are regulated by the same authority, namely the SEC. Second, the futures and options markets retained much of their usual linkage despite being regulated by the CFTC and the SEC, respectively. A much more accurate description of the events during October 1987 is that the cash market was delinked from the other securities markets.

Kleidon [1992a] traces the major source of market breakdown during the 1987 crash to mechanical order-processing problems on the NYSE that have since been remedied. The NYSE order routing systems then in place meant long delays between the submission and execution of limit orders. There is always the potential for limit orders to be 'picked off' if the equilibrium price based on current information moves through stale limit orders; the limit orders provide a free option to those on the other side of the market. However, the extraordinary volume on October 19, 20 and 21 and the consequent delays in processing of orders greatly exacerbated the problem. For example, by noon on October 19, queues of up to 75 minutes developed at physical printers at NYSE specialists' posts, and software that allowed tracking and cancellation of limit orders did not function properly. Stale limit buy orders were picked off as the equilibrium price, reflected in futures and options prices, fell. This in turn created stale prices in the cash market with a consequent negative basis when the cash prices did not fall as rapidly as the futures prices.[11]

[10] See Kleidon & Whaley [1992] for details of index composition and series construction in Figure 3.

[11] See Kleidon [1992a] for details. Other features of the cash and futures prices during the 1987 crash are also explained by stale prices in the cash market. For example, differential degrees

Some divergences between the cash and futures prices may also have resulted from differences in liquidity across markets, given the problems caused by the huge volume during the crash [Amihud, Mendelson & Wood, 1990; Blume, MacKinlay & Terker, 1989]. However, the primary cause of delinkage was the outdated order processing system on the NYSE which was being replaced at the time of the crash. Kleidon & Whaley [1992, p. 874] conclude, 'The answer to the market integration issue, at least as evidenced by the crash, appears to lie in developing more efficient means of trade order execution in the stock market, rather than in imposing a common regulatory structure.'

4.2. Circuit breakers

If the problems during 1987 on which the Brady Commission focussed can be attributed to mechanical difficulties on the NYSE, it should come as no surprise that remedies such as circuit breakers were not particularly helpful during the next market disruption, namely the mini-crash of October 1989. The first circuit breaker was activated in the S&P 500 futures market at about 3 p.m. on Friday, October 13 when the index fell 12 points. Trading in the contract was suspended for half an hour as required under the regulations, while computerized trades were segregated from the rest of the market and put into a 'side car'. When trading resumed another circuit breaker was triggered at about 3:45 p.m., and trading was suspended for the day. The fact that the market continued to fall was the first hard evidence that market collapses had little to do with computerized trading per se. Moreover, although it is possible that circuit breakers could allow for greater dissemination of information to traders [Greenwald & Stein, 1991; Lauterbach & Ben-Zion, 1991], a careful examination of the workings of circuit breakers in 1989 leads McMillan [1991] to conclude that they have not fulfilled their advertised role of facilitating price discovery.

4.3. Sunshine trading

One suggestion that may assist in information aggregation is for better identification of trading motives, in particular by those trading for liquidity or other noninformation based purposes. Leland & Rubinstein [1988, p. 50] call for greater 'sunshine trading' in which 'an investor attempts to preannounce his trading intentions (his identity, order size and timing) several hours prior to the actual trade hoping to deepen the market during the time his trade takes place'. The ability to identify those traders without information is crucial to the success of this endeavour. Leland and Rubinstein argue [p. 5], 'Presumably, only noninformation based orders would be filled in this way.' Sunshine trading is further analysed in Admati & Pfleiderer [1991]. Gennotte & Leland [1990] and Jacklin, Kleidon &

of staleness across individual stocks resulted in nonsynchronous prices in the cash index (even if stocks traded more or less continuously given the high volume), which accounts for the differences in variances of the cash and futures markets.

Pfleiderer [1992] stress that crashes in their models are caused by a lack of perfect information about the extent of portfolio insurance and not by the insurance itself, with natural policy implications concerning the potential benefits of sunshine trading.

4.4. Securities transactions taxes

To those who believe that smoothly running stock markets are the problem, the solution is Tobin's [1984] suggestion to 'throw sand into the gears'. Summers & Summers [1989, p. 261] agree with Tobin and argue that 'strong economic efficiency arguments' can be made in support of a securities transfer excise tax designed to curb perceived wastage stemming from 'our excessively well-functioning financial markets'. Summers and Summers note [p. 262] that they follow the path of Keynes, who suggested [cited p. 263], 'It is usually agreed that casinos should in the public interest be inaccessible and expensive. And perhaps the same is true of stock exchanges.'

Although related proposals for transactions taxes were made by the Bush administration, they have not been enacted and Summers is cited as having retreated from his earlier position [Teitelman, 1993, p. 43]. One response to the proposal has been to evaluate the example of Sweden which imposed a transactions tax in 1984. Contrary to the beliefs of proponents of transactions taxes, Umlauf [1993] finds that their imposition in Sweden did not reduce volatility in the market, although stock price levels and trading activity did decline. Moreover, when the transactions tax was increased to two percent in 1986, 50% of the turnover in Sweden migrated to London and returned when the tax was abolished [Giarraputo, 1993, p. 102]. As a secondary effect, capital gains tax revenues fell as a result of the lower trading, and revenues from the transaction tax were entirely offset [Umlauf, 1993, p. 229].

Not all commentators have advocated impeding the use of securities markets. One response by the London Stock Exchange to the October 1987 crash was to urge greater use of arbitrage and hedging techniques in the British stock market [*Wall Street Journal*, 1988, p. 26]. A laboratory study designed to examine the impact of programmed trades and futures markets found that their introduction may be crucial in some situations for ensuring the informational efficiency of the spot market [Harrison, 1992]. The addition of more traded securities in this particular market setting appears to play a similar role in completing the market as found in Plott & Sunder [1988].

Perhaps it is not coincidental that Keynes' proposals were made in the aftermath of the crash of 1929 and the subsequent depression, while Summers & Summers make much of both 1929 and 1987. The foundation for their case lies in the inability of observed changes in *external* information about fundamentals to explain stock price movements. Further, Summers & Summmers [1989, p. 269] emphasize results such as French & Roll [1986] that 'suggest the possibility that trading itself may be a source of volatility'. Within the context of models of imperfect information aggregation, of course, that possibility is exactly what drives the distinction between external and internal information about fundamentals.

However, there is no consequent implication that observed volatility is 'excessive' and should be curbed.

4.5. *Monetary authorities*

The 1929 crash was followed by the Great Depression, while the 1987 crash was not accompanied by an equivalent macroeconomic slump. One possibility is that lessons learned in 1929 were applied in 1987, particularly with respect to liquidity and the money supply. At a crucial time between the close of trading on October 19 and the open on October 20, the Federal Reserve staff in Washington released Chairman Alan Greenspan's pledge to supply liquidity during the crisis. The Federal Reserve also persuaded banks to supply liquidity to security firms which were often caught funding the float between clearinghouse demands and payment by individuals. Even with these assurances, the system came perilously close to financial gridlock on October 20 [Stewart & Hertzberg, 1987].

Aside from some immediate purchases of government bonds by the Federal Reserve Bank of New York [C. Romer, 1993], the Federal Reserve in 1929 'had no desire to provide the liquidity that would have been necessary for the banks to [extend broker loans in order to stem the decline]' [Cecchetti, 1992, p. 575], and subsequently acted to lower the money supply [C. Romer, 1993]. Indeed, Cechetti ties the Federal Reserve actions around the 1929 crash to an explicit desire to 'stifle' the stock market by restricting the ability of member banks to make broker loans, while Romer links the Great Depression to the decline in consumer spending following the crash, exacerbated by the subsequent Federal Reserve actions. The absence of a counterpart in 1987 to the Great Depression is a hopeful sign of collective learning about appropriate responses to stock market crashes.

5. Conclusions

Despite the undeniable costs of stock market crashes, one benefit is that standard models of asset pricing are significantly challenged. The major difficulty posed by the crash of October 19, 1987 is finding an explanation for the 23% drop in 'value'. One extreme possibility is that new information about future cash flows or discount rates reached the market as a whole, thus accounting for the drop in terms of external information about fundamentals. This possibility is widely rejected in evaluations of the crash. Another extreme view, often portrayed as the only alternative to the first, is that the drop must have been caused by fads or other irrational behavior.

This paper favors the middle ground of a growing literature: Stock prices can rationally change as information is released through the trading process itself. The central argument applies the well known economic result that not all market conditions allow for the complete aggregation of individuals' information in a fully revealing rational expectations equilibrium. Laboratory evidence confirms that an absence of common knowledge about traders' preferences and beliefs often causes experimental markets to deviate from fully revealing REE, even with experienced traders. Apparently traders are not necessarily able to correctly infer private information if they are simultaneously attempting to learn about the rules of the game, that is, other traders' preferences and beliefs. In contrast, if market conditions do allow for common beliefs on these dimensions — and this can be as subtle as the introduction of derivative assets that span the market — then the consistent finding is that prices in experimental markets with experienced traders converge rapidly to the fully revealing REE.

Changes in external information about fundamentals can explain some crashes, such as October 1989. The crashes of 1929 and 1987, on the other hand, require some form of changes in internal information about fundamentals revealed through the trading process to allow reconciliation with rational models, and such models have emerged since October 1987. This recent literature, discussed in Section 3.2 above, is consistent with the findings from experimental markets.

These models share the feature that large changes in asset prices can occur rapidly as fundamentals are rationally updated based on internal news revealed via the trading process, in the absence of external news about fundamentals. For example, Jacklin, Kleidon & Pfleiderer [1992] show how lack of common knowledge about traders' preferences can cause crashes, while D. Romer [1993] accounts for crashes by lack of common knowledge about traders' beliefs. In both cases the authors link the lack of common knowledge to changes in the trading environment, namely the upsurge in use of portfolio insurance and unprecedented government deficits, respectively. Both models cite the acknowledged external news during the week prior to October 19 as providing the trigger that revealed internal news through the trading process.

There are good reasons to believe that related phenomena frequently occur in securities markets. The economic and trading environments periodically change, potentially providing circumstances under which the aggregation of information may be particularly difficult. Even under relatively stable environments, actual conditions continually change in ways that may make fully revealing prices the exception rather than the rule. If the results from laboratory experiments carry over to real markets, however, prices can be expected to evolve toward the predictions of the fully revealing REE as common knowledge is obtained, and not to some capricious irrationality.

This new approach to asset pricing is attractive on several dimensions. First, it has the potential to explain several empirical findings that have resisted explanation within standard models that assume fully revealing prices. Aside from crashes, such findings include French & Roll's [1986] documentation of stock price volatility that is apparently created by the trading process itself, and other forms of ostensible excess volatility in asset prices.[12] Second, it seems a reasonable con-

[12] Uncertainty about traders' preferences, as examined in Jacklin, Kleidon & Pfleiderer [1992], can be applied to smaller price changes than implied by a 'crash'. D. Romer [1993] notes the applicability of models of uncertainty about investor beliefs to smaller price changes, and also provides an alternative model based on transaction costs.

cession to reality to relax the assumption of common knowledge about all traders' preferences and beliefs. The results from models that relax that extreme assumption are consistent with findings from experimental markets. Third, the models are also consistent with well known results in economics that examine conditions for fully revealing prices. Fourth, if the approach is articulated as an examination of the effects of uncertainty about other traders' preferences and beliefs, then a natural research agenda emerges with potentially broad applications.[13]

While the major challenges concern explanations for crashes, responses are both inevitable and imperfect. Considerable research since 1987 indicates that some proposed responses are based on incomplete information (for example, the Brady Commission theme of the necessity for a single regulator to control an effectively single market in stocks, futures and options). Some proposals assume that the 1987 crash cannot be due to fundamentals and must be caused by irrationality (as in Summers & Summers' [1989] support for a transactions tax). Other proposals, such as circuit breakers and sunshine trading, are potentially consistent with the middle ground taken here that emphasizes the aggregation of individuals' information.

Fortunately, there is evidence of collective learning about stock market crashes. Although the crashes of 1929 and 1987 share many similarities, one important difference is that 1987 was not followed by the counterpart to the Great Depression. This is at least partially attributable to differences in behavior by the Federal Reserve following the two crashes. While one theme of this paper is that knowledge is imperfect, another is that learning over time often leads towards rational outcomes.

Acknowledgements

Support for this research has been provided by Cornerstone Research and the Stanford Program in Finance. Helpful comments from Anat Admati, Stephen Gray, Ming Huang, Charlie Jacklin, Russell Lundholm, David Modest, Paul Pfleiderer, David Romer, Matthew Spiegel and Bill Ziemba, and excellent project administration by Debbie Winford, are gratefully acknowledged.

References

Ackert, L.F., and B.F. Smith (1993). Stock price volatility, ordinary dividends, and other cash flows to shareholders. *J. Finance* 48, 1147–1160.

Admati, A.R., and P. Pfleiderer, (1991). Sunshine trading and financial market equilibrium. *Rev. Financ. Studies* 4, 443–481.

Amihud, Y., H. Mendelson and R.A. Wood (1990). Liquidity and the 1987 stock-market crash. *J. Portfolio Manage.* 16, 65–69.

[13] Related literature, such as Marcet & Sargent [1989] and Vives [1993], examines models of individual learning; Wang [1993] examines learning in an incomplete market with asymmetric information about dividend growth.

Alchian, A.A. (1950). Uncertainty, evolution, and economic theory. *J. Polit. Econ.* 58, 211–221.

Bikhchandani, S., D. Hirshleifer and I. Welch, (1992). A theory of fads, fashions, customs and cultural change as informational cascades. *J. Polit. Econ.* 100, 992–1026.

Black, F. (1988). An equilibrium model of the crash, in: S. Fischer (ed.), *NBER Macroeconomics Annual 1988*, MIT Press, Cambridge, MA, pp. 269–275.

Bleiberg, S. (1989). How little we know. *J. Portfolio Manage.* 15, 26–31.

Blume, M.E., A.C. MacKinlay and B. Terker (1989). Order imbalances and stock-price movements on October 19 and 20, 1987. *J. Finance* 44, 827–848.

Brennan, M.J., and E.S. Schwartz (1989). Portfolio insurance and financial market equilibrium. *J. Bus.* 62, 455–472.

Brown, D.P., and R.H. Jennings (1989). On technical analysis. *Rev. Financ. Studies* 2, 527–551.

Bulow, J., and P. Klemperer (1994). Rational frenzies and crashes, *J. Polit. Econ.* 102, 1–23.

Cecchetti, S.G. (1992). Stock market crash of October 1929, in: P. Newman, M. Milgate and J. Eatwell (eds.), *The New Palgrave Dictionary of Money and Finance*, 3, (Macmillan Press Limited, London, pp. 573–577.

Camerer, C. (1989). Bubbles and fads in asset prices. *J. Econ. Surv.* 3, 3–41.

Camerer, C., and K. Weigelt (1991). Information mirages in experimental asset markets. *J. Bus.* 64, 463–493.

Cochrane, J.H. (1992). Explaining the variance of price–dividend ratios. *Rev. Financ. Studies* 5, 243–280.

Copeland, T.E., and D. Friedman (1991). Partial relevation of information in experimental asset markets. *J. Finance* 46, 265–295.

Easley, D., and M. O'Hara (1991). Order form and information in securities markets. *J. Finance* 46, 905–927.

Fama, E.F. (1970). Efficient capital markets: A review of theory and empirical work. *J. Finance* 35, 383–417.

Flavin, M. (1983). Excess volatility in the financial markets: A reassement of the empirical evidence. *J. Polit. Econ.* 91, 929–956.

Flood, R.P., and R.J. Hodrick (1990). On testing for speculative bubbles. *J. Econ. Perspect.* 4, 85–101.

Forsythe, R., and R. Lundholm (1990). Information aggregation in an experimental market. *Econometrica* 58, 309–347.

French, K.R. (1988). Crash-testing the efficient market hypothesis, in: S. Fischer (ed.), *NBER Macroeconomic Annual 1988*, MIT Press, Cambridge, MA, pp. 277–285.

French, K.R., and R. Roll (1986). Stock return variances: The arrival of information and the reaction of traders. *J. Financ. Econ.* 17, 5–26.

Friedman, D., and A. Von Borries (1988). Monopolist insiders in computerized asset markets: A note on some experimental results, Organized Research Activity in Applied Economics, working paper No. 178, University of California, Santa Cruz.

Friedman, M. (1956). *The methodology of positive economics. Essays in Positive Economics*, University of Chicago Press, Chicago, IL.

Garber, P.M. (1989). Tulipmania. *J. Polit. Econ.* 97, 535–560.

Garber, P.M. (1992). Crashes, in: P. Newman, M. Milgate and J. Eatwell (eds.), *The New Palgrave Dictionary of Money and Finance*, 1, Macmillan Press Limited, London, pp. 511–513.

Gennotte, G., and H. Leland (1990). Market liquidity, hedging and crashes. *Am. Econ. Rev.* 80, 999–1021.

Giarraputo, J.D. (1993). Roundtable: New directions on the exchanges. *Global Finance* 7, 99–103.

Gilles, C., and S.F. LeRoy, (1991). Econometric aspects of the variance-bounds tests: A survey. *Rev. Financ. Studies* 4, 753–791.

Glosten, I.R., and P.R. Milgrom (1985). Bid, ask and transaction prices in a specialist market with hetrogeneously informed traders. *J. Financ. Econ.* 14, 71–100.

Greenwald, B.C., and J.C. Stein (1991). Transactional risk, market crashes, and the role of circuit breakers. *J. Bus.* 64, 443–462.

Grossman, S.J. (1988). Analysis of the implications for stock and future price volatility of program trading and dynamic trading strategies. *J. Bus.* 61, 275–298.

Grossman, S.J., and J.E. Stiglitz (1976). Information and competitive price systems. *Am. Econ. Rev.* 66, 246–253.

Grossman, S.J., and J.E. Stiglitz (1980). On the impossibility of informationally efficient markets. *Am. Econ. Rev.* 70, 393–408.

Grundy, B.D., and M. McNichols (1989). Trade and the revelation of information through prices and direct disclosure. *Rev. Financ. Studies* 2, 495–526.

Harrison, G.W. (1992). Market dynamics, programmed traders and futures markets: Beginning the laboratory search for a smoking gun. *Econ. Record*, Supplement, 46–62.

Hellwig, M.F. (1980). On the aggregation of information in competitive markets. *J. Econ. Theory* 22, 477–498.

Ibbotson Associates (1992). *Stocks, Bonds, Bills and Inflation 1992 Yearbook*, Ibbotson Associates, Inc., Chicago.

Jacklin, C.J., A.W. Kleidon and P. Pfleiderer (1992). Underestimation of portfolio insurance and the crash of October 1987. *Rev. Financ. Studies* 5, 35–63.

Khaneman, D., P. Slovic and A. Tversky (1982). *Judgment Under Uncertainty: Heuristics and Biases*, Cambridge University Press, Cambridge, MA.

Kleidon, A.W. (1986). Variance bounds tests and stock price valuation models. *J. Polit. Econ.* 94, 953–1001.

Kleidon, A.W. (1992a). Arbitrage, nontrading, and stale prices: October 1987. *J. Bus.* 65, 483–507.

Kleidon, A.W. (1992b). Market and environmental uncertainty, in: P. Newman, M. Milgate and J. Eatwell (eds.). *The New Palgrave Dictionary of Money and Finance*, 2, Macmillan Press Limited, London, pp. 651–654.

Kleidon, A.W., and R. Mehra (1995). The stock market crashes of 1987 and 1989, in: D. Glassner (ed.). *Encyclopedia of Business Cycles, Panics, and Depressions*, Garland Press, New York.

Kleidon, A.W., and R.E. Whaley, (1992). One market? Stocks, futures and options during October 1987. *J. Finance* 47, 851–877.

Kraus, A., and M. Smith (1989). Market created risk. *J. Finance* 44, 557–569.

Kyle, Albert S. (1985). Continuous auctions and insider trading. *Econometrica* 53, 1315–1335.

Lauterbach, B., and U. Ben-Zion (1991). Panic behavior and the performance of circuit breakers: Empirical evidence, Work ing paper, Department of Business Administration, Bar Ilan University.

Lee, I.H. (1992). Market crashes and informational cascades, working paper, Department of Economics and Anderson Graduate School of Management, University of California, Los Angeles, CA.

Leland, H., and M. Rubinstein (1988). Comments on the market crash: Six months after. *J. Econ. Perspect.* 2, 45–50.

LeRoy, S.F., and R.D. Porter (1981). The present-value relation: Tests based on implied-variance bounds. *Econometrica* 49, 555–574.

Marcet, A., and T.J. Sargent (1989). Convergence of least squares learning mechanisms in self-referential linear stochastic models. *J. Econ. Theory* 48, 337–368.

McMillan, H. (1991). Circuit breakers in the S&P 500 futures market: Their effect on volatility and price discovery in October 1989. *Rev. Futures Markets* 10, 248–274.

Miller, M.H. (1992). Financial innovation: Achievements and prospects. *Cont. Bank J. Appl. Corp. Finance* 4, 4–11.

Miller, M.H., J.D. Hawke, Jr., B. Malkiel and M. Scholes (1988). *Final Report of the Committee of Inquiry Appointed by the Chicago Mercantile Exchange to Examine the Events Surrounding October 19, 1987*, Chicago Mercantile Exchange Committee of Inquiry, Chicago, IL.

Mitchell, M.L., and J.M. Netter (1989). Triggering the 1987 stock market crash: Antitakeover provisions in the proposed House Ways and Means tax bill? *J. Financ. Econ.* 24, 37–68.

Peck, J., and K. Shell (1991). Market uncertainty: Correlated and sunspot equilibria in imperfectly competitive economies. *Rev. Econ. Studies* 58, 1011–1029.

Plott, C.R., and S. Sunder (1988). Rational expectations and the aggregation of diverse information in laboratory security markets. *Econometrica* 56, 1085–1118.

Presidential Task Force on Market Mechanisms (Brady Commission) 1988. *Report*, U.S. Government Printing Office, Washington, D.C.

Roll, R.W. (1989). The international crash of October 1987, in: R.W. Kamphuis Jr., R.C. Kormendi and J.W.H. Watson (eds.), *Black Monday and the Future of Financial Markets*, Mid-America Institute for Public Policy Research Inc., Irwin, Homewood.

Romer, C.D. (1993). The nation in depression. *J. Econ. Perspect.* 7(2), 19–39.

Romer, D. (1993). Rational asset-price movements without news, *Am. Econ. Rev.* 83, 1112–1130.

Russell, F.X. (1988). The bubble bandwagon. *Intermarket* 5(10), 51–52.

Santoni, G.J. (1988). The October crash: Some evidence on the cascade theory. *Fed. Reserve Bank St. Louis* 70, 18–33.

Schwert, G.W. (1992). Stock market crash of October 1987, in: P. Newman, M. Milgate and J. Eatwell (eds.), *The New Palgrave Dictionary of Money and Finance*, 3, Macmillan Press Limited, London, pp. 577–582.

Shiller, R.J. (1979). The volatility of long-term interest rates and expectations models of the term structure. *J. Polit. Econ.* 87, 1190–1219.

Shiller, R.J. (1981). Do stock prices move too much to be justified by subsequent changes in dividends? *Am. Econ. Rev.* 71, 421–436.

Shiller, R.J. (1988). Portfolio insurance and other investor fashions as factors in the 1987 stock market crash, in: S. Fisher (ed.), *NBER Macroeconomic Annual 1988*, MIT Press, Cambridge, MA, pp. 287–295.

Shiller, R.J. (1989). *Market Volatility*, MIT Press, Cambridge, MA, and London.

Shleifer, A., and L.H. Summers, (1990). The noise trader approach to finance. *J. Econ. Perspect.* 4, 19–33.

Singleton, K. (1980). Expectations models of the term structure and implied variance bounds. *J. Polit. Econ.* 88, 1159–1176.

Smith, V.L., G.L. Suchanek and A.W. Williams (1988). Bubbles, crashes, and endogenous expectations in experimental spot asset markets. *Econometrica* 56, 1119–1151.

Standard and Poor's Corporation (1992). *Security Price Index Record*, New York, NY.

Stewart, J.B., and D. Hertzberg (1987). Terrible Tuesday. *Wall Street Journal* November 20, 1.

Stone, D., and W.T. Ziemba (1993). Land and stock prices in Japan. *J. Econ. Perspect.* 7(3), 149–165.

Summers, L.H., and V.P. Summers (1989). When financial markets work too well: A cautious case for a securities transactions tax. *J. Financ. Serv. Res.* 3, 261–268.

Teitelman, R. (1993). Wall Street and the new economic correctness. *Inst. Invest.* 27(2), 36–44.

Tobin, J. (1984). On the efficiency of the financial system. *Loyds Bank Rev.* 153, 1–15.

Umlauf, S.R. (1993). Transaction taxes and the behavior of the Swedish stock market. *J. Financ. Econ.* 33, 227–240.

U.S. Commodity Futures Trading Commission, Division of Economic Analysis and the Division of Trading and Markets (1988). *Final Report on Stock Index Futures and Cash Market Activity During October 1987*, U.S. Government Printing Office, Washington, D.C.

U.S. Securities and Exchange Commission (1988). *The October 1987 Market Break: Report by the Division of Market Regulation*, U.S. Government Printing Office, Washington, D.C.

U.S. Securities and Exchange Commission (1990). *Trading Analysis of October 13 and 16, 1989*, U.S. Government Printing Office, Washington, D.C.

Vives, X. (1993). How fast do rational agents learn? *Rev. Econ. Studies* 60, 329–347.

Wall Street Journal (1987). Before the fall: Speculative fever ran high in the 10 months prior to Black Monday, December 11, 1, 18.

Wall Street Journal (1988). London Stock Exchange urges more use of arbitrage, hedging in crash report, February 11, 26.

Wang, J. (1993). A model of intertemporal asset prices under asymmetric information. *Rev. Econ. Studies* 60, 249–282.

West, K.D. (1988). Bubbles, fads and stock price volatility tests: A partial evaluation. *J. Finance* 43, 639–656.

Woodford, M. (1990). Learning to believe in sunspots. *Econometrica* 58, 277–307.

Ziemba, W.T., and D.B. Hausch (1987). *Dr. Z's Beat the Racetrack*, William Morrow and Co., Inc., New York, NY.

Ziemba, W.T., and S.L. Schwartz (1992). *Invest Japan: The Structure, Performance and Opportunities of Japan's Stock, Bond and Fund Markets*, Probus Publishing Company, Chicago, IL.

R. Jarrow et al., Eds., *Handbooks in OR & MS, Vol. 9*

Chapter 17

On the Predictability of Common Stock Returns: World-Wide Evidence

Gabriel Hawawini
INSEAD–Euro-Asia Centre, Boulevard de Constance, 77309 Fontainebleau, France

Donald B. Keim
Wharton School, 2300 Steinberg Hall, University of Pennsylvania, Philadelphia, PA 19104, U.S.A.

1. Introduction

In this chapter we examine recent empirical findings on the predictability of stock returns. These findings document persistent cross-sectional and time series patterns in returns that are not predicted by extant theory. As a result, such empirical regularities are often classified as anomalies.[1]

We begin by noting that this chapter is not an essay on the efficiency of world-wide security markets[2]. Admittedly, the nature of the evidence that we discuss is interpreted by many market observers as convincing evidence of market inefficiency. But we remind the reader of the joint null hypothesis underlying such analyses — to wit, security markets are efficient *and* returns behave according to a prespecified equilibrium model (e.g., the capital asset pricing model). If the joint hypothesis is rejected, we cannot specifically attribute that rejection to one or the other branch of the hypothesis. That is, a conclusion that securities markets are not efficient is inapproriate since the rejection may be due to a test design based on an incorrect equilibrium model. While we acknowledge that

[1] The term anomaly, in this context, can be traced to Thomas Kuhn [1970] in his classic book *The Structure of Scientific Revolutions*. Kuhn maintains that research activity in any normal science will revolve around a central paradigm and that experiments are conducted to test the predictions of the underlying paradigm and to extend the range of phenomena it explains. Although research most often supports the underlying paradigm, eventually results are found that don't conform. Kuhn [1970, pp. 52–53] terms this stage 'discovery': 'Discovery commences with the awareness of *anomaly*, i.e., with the recognition that nature has somehow violated the paradigm-induced expectations that govern normal science' (emphasis added).

[2] See Fama [1991] for a survey of the recent evidence on market efficiency. Also see Lehman [1991] for a more selective treatise on current scepticism regarding the efficient market hypothesis, and Blume & Siegel [1992] for a review of asset pricing and market structure.

the strict form of market efficiency discussed in most textbooks is an unlikely description of security price determination[3], the simple fact that so many of these regularities have persisted for more than fifty years suggests that perhaps our benchmark models are less than complete descriptions of equilibrium price formation.

The summary of research that we present is not an exhaustive compilation of the findings on predictable returns. Rather, we focus on the subset of the findings whose existence has proved most robust with respect to both time and the number of stock markets in which they have been observed. We broadly classify the findings as being cross-sectional (e.g., size and E/P effects) or time series (e.g., return autocorrelations, seasonal return patterns) in nature. As such, the discussion is divided along these lines.

The chapter proceeds as follows. Section 2 discusses cross-sectional return predictability by focusing on the cross-sectional relation between returns and size, earnings–price ratios, and price–book ratios. Time series return predictability is examined in three separate sections. Section 3 discusses seasonal patterns in returns relating to calendar turning points such as the turn of the year, beginning of the week, and turn of the month. Section 4 covers the autocorrelation of individual security and portfolio returns measured over short and long horizons. Section 5 examines the evidence on predicting returns with ex-ante observable variables. The paper concludes with a brief summary in Section 6.

2. Cross-sectional return predictability

2.1. *The capital asset pricing model: early tests and ad hoc empirical extensions*

The capital asset pricing model (CAPM) has occupied a central position in financial economics for the thirty years since its origins in the papers by Treynor [1961], Sharpe [1964], Lintner [1965] and Mossin [1966]. Given certain simplifying assumptions, the CAPM states that the rate of return on any security is linearly related to that security's systematic risk (or beta) measured relative to the market portfolio of all marketable securities. Hence, according to the CAPM, the cross-sectional relation between return and risk can be expressed as

$$E(R_i) = a_0 + a_1\beta_i \tag{1}$$

If the model is correct and security markets are efficient, security returns will on *average* conform to this linear relation. Persistent departures, however, represent

[3] In stark contrast to conclusions drawn in his earlier essay on efficient markets in 1970, and conditioned on the accumulation of empirical evidence over the past twenty years, Fama [1991] declares 'The market-efficiency hypothesis, that security prices fully reflect all available information, is an extreme null hypothesis, a point on a continuum, and so almost surely false. The interesting task is not to accept or reject market efficiency but to measure the extent to which the behavior of returns departs from its predictions.'

violations of the joint hypothesis that both the CAPM and the efficient market hypothesis (EMH) are correct.

The strict set of assumptions underlying the CAPM has prompted numerous criticisms. However, since any model proposes a simplified view of the world, the merits of the assumptions do not themselves constitute sufficient basis for its rejection. The rejection or acceptance of a theory should rest on the scientific evidence. Sophisticated tests of the propositions of the CAPM became possible with the creation of the computerized data base of stock prices and distributions at the University of Chicago in the mid 1960s, on the heels of the theoretical development of the CAPM. Numerous studies were conducted in the early 1970s, the most prominent being those conducted by Black, Jensen & Scholes [1972], Blume & Friend [1973], and Fama & MacBeth [1973]. These tests found that the estimated intercept was higher than the risk-free rate [the implied value of a_1 in equation (1)], and the estimated coefficient on beta (a_1 in equation (1), representing an estimate of the market risk premium) was lower than predicted by the CAPM of Sharpe [1964], Lintner [1965], Mossin [1966] and Treynor [1961] and only marginally important in explaining cross-sectional differences in average security returns. The results of these studies were interpreted as being consistent with the Black [1972] version of the CAPM.[4]

Although the early tests lend some support for the CAPM, subsequent research was not always as accommodating. For example, in his 1977 critique of existing tests of the CAPM, Roll argued that tests performed with any 'market' portfolio other than the true market portfolio are not tests of the CAPM and, therefore, cannot be interpreted as evidence for the model. In response to Roll's criticism of the earlier tests, Stambaugh [1982] constructed broader market indexes that included bonds, real estate and consumer durables and found that tests of the model with these broader indexes were not very sensitive to the breadth of the definition of the market proxy.

Since the CAPM was not unambiguously supported by the tests, researchers formulated alternative models. Many developed equilibrium models by relaxing the CAPM assumptions. For example, Mayers [1972] allows for nonmarketable assets such as human capital, and Brennan [1970] and Litzenberger & Ramaswamy [1979] relaxed the no-tax assumption. Others examined *ad hoc* alternatives to the CAPM. For example, Basu [1977] and Banz [1981] found that the ratio of price to earnings and the market capitalization of common equity, respectively, provided considerably more explanatory power than beta. Indeed, Banz found little evidence of explanatory power for beta. These two seminal studies served as a springboard for much subsequent research that has confirmed the ability of P/E and size to explain cross-sectional differences in returns. Other studies have extended the list of predictive variables to include industry-relative P/E ratios, the

[4] Many of the tests were done using equal-weighted portfolio (asset) returns and, unknown to the researchers, their evidence was highly sensitive to the correlation of beta and size, and to the relatively high returns of small firms in January. These issues are discussed in the following sections. Also see Ritter & Chopra [1989].

ratio of price to book, price per share, and other similar variables. These studies have produced far more convincing evidence of cross-sectional return predictability than any of the previous tests concerning the explanatory power of beta. Absent in this literature, though, is any supporting theory to justify the choice of variables. Nevertheless, these findings collectively represent a set of stylized facts that stand as a challenge for alternative asset pricing models. In this section we present a sample of the more important contributions to these stylized facts. To maintain a unifying thread through the following discussion of cross-sectional return predictability, we augment much of our reporting of the original results in the literature with some basic summary statistics that document the findings with a common data set for the same time period using the same empirical methods. Hopefully, this will avoid some of the apples-and-oranges comparisons imposed on literature surveys of research studies which employ widely varying samples, time periods and empirical methods.

2.2. *The size effect*

Most of the research on cross-sectional predictability of stock returns has focused on the relation between returns and the market value of common equity, commonly referred to as the size effect. Banz [1981] was the first to document this phenomenon. For the period 1931 to 1975, Banz estimated a model of the form

$$E(R_i) = a_0 + a_1\beta_i + a_2 S_i \tag{2}$$

where S_i is a measure of the relative market capitalization ('size') for firm i. He found that the statistical association between returns and size is negative and of a greater order of magnitude than that between returns and beta documented in the earlier studies of the CAPM. Similar models have been estimated for Belgium [Hawawini, Michel & Corhay, 1989], Canada [Calvet & Lefoll, 1989], France [Hawawini & Viallet, 1987], Japan [Hawawini, 1991; Chan, Hamao & Lakonishok, 1991], Spain [Rubio, 1988], and the United Kingdom [Corhay, Hawawini & Michel, 1987]. In all countries except France and Japan there is no relation, on average, between return and market risk when all months of the year are considered (i.e., a_1 is statistically indistinguishable from zero). There is, however, a negative relationship between returns and size in all countries except Canada and France (i.e., a_2 is significantly less than zero).[5]

Researchers have also demonstrated the existence of the size effect by examining the returns of portfolios formed on the basis of market capitalization. For example, Reinganum [1981], using daily data over the period from 1963 to 1977, showed that portfolios of small firms have significantly higher average returns than large firms. He found that the difference in returns between the smallest

[5] There is an abundance of convincing evidence that the relation between size and returns is concentrated in the month of January. We discuss this aspect of the size effect in more detail in Section 2.5 below.

Table 1

Monthly returns and others characteristics for value-weighted portfolios of NYSE and AMEX stocks formed on the basis of market capitalization (April 1951–December 1989)

Size portfolio	Mean return	Std. dev. return	Beta	Mkt. cap. ($mill.)	E/P (%)	Price ($)
Smallest	1.65	6.76	1.17	9.7	−6.6	11.13
2	1.48	6.20	1.19	23.2	4.6	16.71
3	1.34	5.77	1.15	41.4	4.5	21.15
4	1.28	5.65	1.17	68.0	7.3	25.31
5	1.33	5.17	1.11	109.8	7.6	29.39
6	1.21	4.82	1.05	178.9	7.6	31.95
7	1.20	4.68	1.04	291.4	7.4	36.83
8	1.23	4.58	1.03	502.3	7.5	40.23
9	1.08	4.41	1.01	902.1	8.0	49.72
Largest	0.99	4.09	0.95	3983.0	7.7	66.92

Prior to 1962, the portfolios contained only NYSE stocks. The portfolios are created on March 31 of each year using March 31 shares outstanding and prices. Aside from new listings and delistings, which are added to or dropped from the portfolios as they occur during the year, the portfolio composition remains constant over the following twelve months. Portfolios contain only December 31 fiscal closers.

and the largest deciles of firms drawn from the NYSE and AMEX was about 30% annually. In response to Roll's [1981] conjecture that the size effect may be a statistical artifact of improperly measured risk due to the infrequent trading of small stocks [see also Hawawini, 1983], Reinganum [1982] estimated betas using methods designed to account for nonsynchronous and infrequent trading [see Scholes & Williams, 1977, and Dimson, 1979].[6] He found that the magnitude of the size effect is not very sensitive to the method of estimating betas. Blume & Stambaugh [1983] demonstrate, however, that the portfolio strategy implicit in Reinganum's paper (requiring *daily* rebalancing of the portfolio to equal weights) produces upward-biased estimates of small-firm portfolio returns due to a 'bid–ask' bounce that is inversely related to firm size. Blume and Stambaugh show that the measured size-related premium is halved in portfolio strategies that avoid this bias.

The bias described by Blume & Stambaugh [1983] is of substantially smaller quantitative importance in value-weighted portfolio returns and in portfolio strategies employing monthly (or quarterly, or annual) rebalancing. Thus, characterization of the size effect using monthly value-weighted portfolio returns should be reasonably free of the bid–ask bias. With this in mind, Table 1 reports average monthly returns for ten size portfolios of NYSE and AMEX stocks for the period

[6] Ordinary least squares estimates of beta coefficients of infrequently traded stocks are lower than their 'true' beta coefficients, and since small firms tend to trade relatively infrequently, their beta coefficients are underestimated.

Table 2

International evidence of a size premium [1]

Country:	Australia	Belgium	Canada	Finland	France	Germany	Ireland	Japan	New Zealand	Spain	Switzer-land	Taiwan	United Kingdom
Test period	1958–81	1969–83	1973–80	1970–81	1977–88	1954–90	1977–86	1965–87	1977–84	1963–82	1973–88	1979–86	1958–82
No. of securities [2]	281–937	170	391	50	529–460	All FSE	40	1st section TSE	about 100	98–140	153	53 to 72	All LSE
No. of size portfolios	10	5	5	10	5	9	5	10	5	10	6	5	10
Market value of largest portfolio of firms divided by market value of smallest portfolio of firma [3]	N.A.	188	67	113	N.A.	N.A.	N.A.	N.A.	60	228	99	17	182
Average monthly return (%) on the smallest portfolio of firms [4]	6.75	1.17	1.67	1.65	1.20	1.54	3.10	2.57	0.69 [7]	0.58 [8]	0.94	0.47 [8]	1.33
Average monthly return (%) on the largest portfolio of firms [4]	1.02	0.65	1.23	0.89	0.30	1.05	2.63	1.37	0.18 [7]	0.02 [8]	0.42	−0.10 [8]	0.93
Size premium (%) (small minus large)	5.73	0.52	0.44	0.76	0.90	0.49	0.47	1.20	0.51 [7]	0.56	0.52	0.57 [8]	0.40
Average risk of smallest portfolio													
– standard beta coefficient [5]	1.04	1.01	N.A.	0.36	N.A.	0.80	N.A.	1.12 [9]	N.A.	N.A.	N.A.	0.79	0.31
– adjusted beta coefficient [6]	N.A.	N.A.	N.A.	0.52	N.A.	N.A.	N.A.	1.22 [9]	0.90	N.A.	N.A.	0.55	0.64
Average risk of largest portfolio													
– standard beta coefficient [5]	0.95	0.98	N.A.	1.00	N.A.	1.08	N.A.	0.81 [9]	N.A.	N.A.	N.A.	0.99	1.01
– adjusted beta coefficient [6]	N.A.	N.A.	N.A.	0.95	N.A.	N.A.	N.A.	0.77 [9]	0.99	N.A.	N.A.	0.72	1.02

[1] Sources: *Australia*, Brown et al. [1983]; *Belgium*, Hawawini et al. [1989]; *Canada*, Berges et al. [1984]; *Finland*, Wahlroos & Berglund [1986]; *France*, adapted from Louvet & Taramasco [1991]; *Germany*, Stehle [1992]; *Ireland*, adapted from Coghlan [1988]; *Japan*, Ziemba [1991]; *New Zealand*, Gillan [1990]; *Spain*, Rubio [1986]; *Switzerland*, Cornioley & Pasquier-Dorthe [1991]; *Taiwan*, Ma & Shaw [1990]; *United Kingdom*, Levis [1985].

[2] TSE = Tokyo Stock Exchange; LSE = London Stock Exchange; NYSE = New York Stock Exchange.

[3] The ratio is based on average market value over the sample period, except for the United States where the ratio is calculated in 1975 and Finland where it is calculated in 1970.

[4] All returns are significantly different from zero at the 0.05 level.

[5] Standard beta coefficients are estimated using ordinary least square regression; N.A. = not available.

[6] Adjusted betas are estimated using the Scholes & Williams [1977] method in the case of France and Taiwan and the Dimson [1979] method in all other cases. These two methods adjust the estimated beta coefficient for the thin trading that characterizes smaller firms; N.A. = not available.

[7] These are abnormal returns calculated with respect to a capital asset pricing model.

[8] For Spain the average returns on the small and the large portfolios are returns in excess of those predicted by the capital asset pricing model; that is, they are risk-adjusted returns. For Taiwan average portfolio returns are calculated using excess returns on individual securities which, in turn, are estimated by subtracting from each individual security return, the return of the portfolio to which a security belongs (five control portfolios are constructed according to the level of systematic risk). Note that another study of the size effect on the Taiwan Stock Exchange [Chou & Johnson, 1990] finds no evidence of a significant size effect after controlling for a P/E effect.

[9] These beta coefficients are from a different sample given in Nakamura & Terada [1984].

1951 to 1989. The size portfolios are drawn from data used in Jaffe, Keim & Westerfield [1989] and updated here to 1989.[7] The negative relation between size and expected returns is clearly evident — the annualized difference in returns between the smallest and the largest size deciles is about 7.9%. The betas of the portfolios decline with increasing size, but the differences are small — the difference between the smallest and largest size portfolios is 0.26. Thus, consistent with research that finds significant coefficients on size in equation (2) after adjusting for the explanatory power of beta, the difference in estimated OLS betas between the smallest and the largest size portfolios is insufficient to explain the difference in returns between the two extreme portfolios.

Additional evidence in Reinganum [1990] suggests that the relative price behavior of small and large firms may differ for Over-the-Counter (OTC) stocks. Using data for the 1973–1988 period, Reinganum finds that small OTC shares have significantly lower returns than NYSE and AMEX firms with the same size, and that the small-firm premium for OTC stocks is much lower than for NYSE and AMEX stocks. Reinganum, motivated by earlier work by Amihud & Mendelson [1986], argues that the differences are related to differences in liquidity between the two markets, suggesting differential costs of trading small stocks in these two types of markets. The implication is that market structure may be an important influence on the measured size effect. If so, analysis of international evidence on the size effect, where we observe very different market organizations and structures, may be quite useful in understanding the cause of the size effect.[8] [9]

Following the discovery of a size premium in the U.S. equity markets, numerous studies have documented its existence in most stock markets around the world. The evidence from these studies is summarized in Table 2 for the Australian, New Zealand, Canadian, Japanese, Taiwanese, and seven European stock markets. We define the size premium as the difference between the average monthly return on the portfolio of smallest stocks and the average monthly return on the portfolio of largest stocks. The monthly size premium is positive in all countries.[10] Its magnitude, however, varies across markets: It is most pronounced in Australia (5.73%) and Japan (1.20%), and is insignificant only in the United Kingdom

[7] See Jaffe, Keim & Westerfield [1989] for a detailed description of the data.

[8] Loughran [1993] finds, however, that of the 5.7% difference in returns between NYSE and NASDAQ stocks in the bottom five size deciles (based on NYSE ranking), 60% is due to the poor (long-run) performance of initial public offerings (IPO's) on NASDAQ. A difference of only 2.3% remains after purging NASDAQ returns of an IPO effect (IPO's are much more heavily concentrated on NASDAQ than on the NYSE).

[9] Fama, French, Booth & Sinquefield [1993] show that small NYSE stocks have substantially lower ratios of price to book value than comparably-small NASDAQ stocks. They argue that the higher returns for small NYSE stocks are related to the lower price/book ratios, a relation that appears to persist independently of the size-return relation (see Section 2.7.2 below).

[10] Contrary to the evidence of a size effect on the Taiwan Stock Exchange reported by Ma & Shaw [1990], Chou & Johnson [1990] find no evidence of a size effect for Taiwan. And according to Kim, Chung & Pyun [1992], there is no evidence of a significant size effect on the Korea Stock Exchange during the period 1980 to 1988 for a sample of up to 224 stocks.

(0.40%) and Canada (0.44% per month).[11] Note, however, that there is a wide range across the twelve markets in terms of the size (market capitalization) differential between the largest and the smallest size portfolios. For example, in Spain the average market capitalization of the stocks in the largest size portfolio is 228 times the average market capitalization of the stocks in the smallest size portfolio. But in the case of Taiwan the largest portfolio is only 17 times larger than the smallest one. Because the size and number of portfolios as well as the sample periods differ across countries, it is difficult to gauge whether the magnitude of the size premium is significantly different across countries.

Can differences in beta risk between the smallest and largest portfolios explain the size premium in these markets? The evidence is found in Table 2. As in the U.S., Japanese small firms have, on average, *higher* beta risk than large firms (see Table 1 for the U.S. evidence), but the higher beta risk of small firms in these two countries cannot explain the size premium — the risk-adjusted size premium is still significantly different from zero. In the remaining countries for which data is available, the systematic risk of the smallest firms is about the same or *lower* than that of the largest firms. As mentioned above, the reason may be that the extreme illiquidity in some of these markets, especially for smaller stocks, may result in downward-biased estimates of beta — even when betas are estimated with monthly returns. Many of these studies do not estimate betas with the methods of Scholes & Williams [1977] or Dimson [1979] which are designed to correct for this downward bias. In the countries where adjusted betas are computed, the adjusted betas of small firms are indeed higher than their standard OLS betas. But even with adjusted betas the size premium remains.

2.3. *The earnings/price (E/P) effect*

Earnings-related strategies have a long tradition in the investment community. The most popular of these strategies, buying stocks that sell at low multiples of earnings, can be traced at least to Graham & Dodd [1940, p. 533] who proposed that 'a necessary but not a sufficient condition' for investing in a common stock is 'a reasonable ratio of market price to average earnings'. They advocated that a prudent investor should never pay as much as 20 times earnings and a suitable multiplier should be 12 or less.

[11] Although Levis [1985] finds that the size effect on the London Stock Exchange is not statistically significant, others report a significant size premium. Banz [1985] provides evidence of a significant size effect on the LSE. His analysis is based on 29 years of monthly returns [1955–1983] taken from the London Share Price Data base (LSPD). With ten value-based portfolios, he reports a compounded annual return of 39.9% for the smallest portfolio versus 13.0% for the largest. Dimson & Marsh [1984] also report evidence of a size effect on the portfolios constructed from a sample of stocks taken from the LSPD. Over the period 1977–1983, the portfolio of smallest stocks earned a compound annual return of 41% and the portfolio of largest stocks realized a compound annual return of 18%. In Banz [1985], the compound annual return on the smallest portfolio exceeded that of the largest by 27%. Dimson & Marsh [1984] report that the difference is 23%, both before adjustment for risk.

Ball [1978] argues that earnings-related variables like E/P are proxies for expected returns. In that case, if the CAPM is an incomplete specification of priced risk, then we would expect E/P to explain the portion of expected return that is in fact compensation for risk variables omitted from the tests. A valid question, then, is whether a documented relation between average returns and E/P is due to the influence of E/P, or whether E/P is merely proxying for other explanators of expected returns.[12]

Nicholson [1960] published the first extensive study of the relation between P/E multiples and subsequent total returns, showing that low P/E stocks consistently provided returns greater than the average stock. Basu [1977] introduced the notion that P/E ratios may explain violations of the CAPM and found that, for his sample of NYSE firms, there was a significant negative relation between P/E ratios and average returns in excess of those predicted by the CAPM. If one had followed his strategy of buying the quintile of lowest P/E stocks and selling short the quintile of highest P/E quintile stocks, based on annual rankings, the average annual abnormal return would have been 6.75% (before commissions and other transaction costs) over the 1957 to 1975 period. Reinganum [1981], analyzing both NYSE and AMEX stocks, confirmed and extended Basu's findings to 1979. In Table 3A we update the relation between monthly expected returns and P/E

Table 3A

Monthly returns and other characteristics for value-weighted portfolios of NYSE and AMEX stocks formed on the basis of the ratio of earnings/price (April 1962–December 1989)

E/P portfolio	Mean return	Std. dev. return	Beta	Mkt. cap. ($ mill.)	E/P (%)	Price ($)
Negative	1.55	8.68	1.46	141.8	−37.7	10.57
Lowest	0.79	5.61	1.09	888.4	2.7	37.55
2	0.90	5.06	1.05	938.4	5.0	38.02
3	0.91	4.94	1.03	849.1	6.4	35.38
4	0.87	4.60	0.95	913.9	7.5	31.91
5	0.79	4.81	0.98	913.5	8.5	31.22
6	0.97	4.65	0.94	808.0	9.4	29.68
7	1.05	4.69	0.96	682.3	10.5	28.11
8	1.13	4.64	0.87	777.8	11.7	27.47
9	1.34	4.65	0.89	656.5	13.3	25.07
Highest	1.25	5.48	1.01	569.8	18.9	21.82

Portfolio are created on March 31 of each year using year-end accounting values and March 31 prices. Aside from new listings and delistings, which are added to or dropped from the portfolios as they occur during the year, the portfolio composition remains constant over the following twelve months. Portfolios contain only December 31 fiscal closers.

[12] The question posed is whether E/P is the determinant of expected returns or whether E/P is simply a proxy for the underlying factor(s) that are the true determinants of expected returns. Of course an alternative question would ask whether E/P captures differences in equilibrium expected returns, or does it simple capture misvaluations of individual securities.

to 1989 using the data file of NYSE and AMEX stocks originally constructed by Jaffe, Keim & Westerfield [1989] through 1987, and updated here through 1989.[13] The average portfolio returns reported in Table 3A confirm the E/P effect documented in previous studies. The average difference in returns between the highest and lowest E/P portfolios is on average 0.46% per month (t = 1.77)[14]. For purposes of comparison, we also separately computed size portfolios for the same sample of firms. The average difference in returns between the smallest and largest size deciles for this same 1962–1989 period is 0.80% per month (t = 2.42). Thus, size and E/P display similar abilities to sort firms according to expected returns.[15]

There are only a few studies which examine the P/E effect in markets outside the United States largely due to a lack of computerized accounting databases which can be used for academic research. In one example, Levis [1989] reports evidence documenting the presence of a significant P/E effect on the London Stock Exchange over the period April 1961 to March 1985. He reports an average monthly premium of 0.58%, 7.0% annually. This is similar to the U.S. results reported in Table 3A, and also to results in Basu [1977, 1983] and Reinganum [1981]. Adjusting portfolio returns for differences in systematic risk does not modify this conclusion.[16]

Aggarwal, Hiraki & Rao [1988] provide evidence of a significant P/E effect for a sample of 574 firms listed on the first section of the Tokyo Stock Exchange during the period from 1974 to 1983. Only firms with positive earnings were included in the sample. Portfolios of low P/E stocks outperformed those with relatively higher P/E stocks even after controlling for differences in systematic risk *and* size across portfolios.

For the Taiwan Stock Exchange, Chou & Johnson [1990] report a significant P/E effect during the period 1979–1988 for a comprehensive sample of shares with

[13] Although the sample in Jaffe, Keim & Westerfield [1989] extends back to 1951, we report results here for the shorter 1962–1989 period to facilitate comparison with other results reported below for this same period. We point out that the sample includes only December 31 fiscal closers.

[14] The table reports total returns that are not adjusted for risk. Since the betas are not substantially different across the portfolios, inferences drawn from total returns should not diverge in a meaningful way from inferences drawn from beta-risk-adjusted returns.

[15] Some have argued that because firms in the same industry tend to have similar E/P ratios, a portfolio strategy that concentrates on low E/P stocks may indeed benefit from higher than average returns, but at a cost of reduced diversification. These arguments also suggest that the E/P effect may in fact be an industry effect. For example, during the 1980s financial firms and utilities comprised anywhere from 45 to 86% of the highest E/P quintile constructed from the sample of firms described in Section 2.3. Peavy & Goodman [1983] address this potential bias and examine the P/E ratio of a stock relative to its industry P/E (PER). They find a significant negative relation between PER's and abnormal returns over the 1970–1980 period. A portfolio strategy that bought the quintile of lowest PER stocks and sold short the highest PER quintiles would have yielded an annualized abnormal return of 20.80% over the period, although this number does not account for transactions costs.

[16] Levis also reports a size effect (see the evidence in Table 2 for the case of a slightly different sample characteristics), but it is weaker than the P/E effect. He reports a large degree of interdependency between the two effects with the P/E effect tending to subsume the size effect.

positive earnings. They show that the average monthly return of the lowest quintile P/E portfolio exceeds that of the highest quintile P/E portfolio by 2.27%, 27.2% annually. Chou and Johnson find that after adjusting for differences in systematic risk, the P/E premium is still significant with an average monthly return of 1.88% (22.6% annually). Ma & Shaw [1990] report a weaker but still significant P/E effect for a smaller sample of stocks over the period 1979 to 1986. Dividing their sample into 5 portfolios, they found a significant average risk-adjusted monthly P/E premium of 0.85% (10.2% annually).

Finally, for the New Zealand Stock Exchange, Gillan [1990] finds no evidence of a P/E effect for the same sample as described in Table 2 for which he reports a significant size effect. Portfolios based on low P/E ratios do not earn significantly higher risk-adjusted returns than portfolios based on high P/E ratios during the period 1977 to 1984. A similar conclusion is reached by Kim, Chung & Pyun [1992] for Korea. They find no evidence of either a size effect or a P/E effect on that market during the period 1980–1988 for a sample of up to 224 stocks.

In summary, the evidence from five markets outside the United States indicates that in the United Kingdom, Japan and Taiwan there is a significant P/E effect similar to that found in the U.S. There is no evidence, however, of a significant P/E effect in New Zealand and Korea. Given the small size and relatively short sample period for the Taiwan, New Zealand and Korean markets, however, it is difficult to draw definitive conclusions from the evidence regarding these three markets.

2.4. A variation on the E/P effect: the ratio of cash-flow-to-price

An alternative to the E/P ratio is the ratio of cash flow to price, where cash flow is defined as reported accounting earnings plus depreciation. Its appeal lies in the fact that accounting earnings may be a misleading and biased estimate of the economic earnings with which shareholders are concerned. Cash flow per share is less manipulable and, therefore, possibly a less biased estimate of economically important flows accruing to the firm's shareholders. The distinction between reported earnings and cash flow is important when examining these effects across countries with different accounting practices regarding the reporting of earnings. In some countries, such as Japan, firms are required to use the same depreciation schedule to calculate earnings reported to shareholders and earnings subject to corporate taxes. As a result, virtually all Japanese firms use accelerated depreciation for financial reporting (to reduce their tax liability) which creates large distortions in reported earnings for firms with large capital investments. In other countries, such as the United States, firms can use accelerated depreciation for tax purposes (which reduces taxable profits) and straight-line depreciation for reporting purposes (which produces relatively higher reported earnings to shareholders). Such accounting differences explain why there is a narrower difference between Japanese and American P/CF ratios compared to the much larger difference in the P/E ratios prevailing in these countries. For example, in August 1990, the market P/CF was 7.6 in the United States and 10.6 in Japan, whereas the market

Table 3B

Monthly returns and other characteristics for value-weighted portfolios of NYSE and AMEX stocks formed on the basis of the ratio of cash flow/price (April 1962–December 1989)

CF/P portfolio	Mean return	Std. dev. return	Beta	Mkt. cap. ($ mill.)	CF/P (%)	E/P (%)
Negative	1.32	10.38	1.53	114.4	−53.5	−77.2
Lowest	0.73	5.73	1.06	969.2	5.1	1.0
2	0.92	5.47	1.05	1159.3	8.9	5.2
3	1.12	5.55	1.07	861.6	11.6	7.0
4	1.14	5.27	1.03	897.5	13.8	8.2
5	0.90	5.37	1.02	1042.1	16.1	9.1
6	1.38	5.49	1.05	800.0	18.5	10.7
7	1.05	5.54	1.03	832.3	21.2	11.1
8	1.32	5.11	0.94	899.5	24.5	12.0
9	1.35	5.20	0.92	1182.2	29.6	13.0
Highest	1.62	5.81	1.03	821.7	50.5	12.9

Portfolio are created on March 31 of each year using year-end accounting values and March 31 prices. Aside from new listings and delistings, which are added to or dropped from the portfolios as they occur during the year, the portfolio composition remains constant over the following twelve months. Portfolios contain only December 31 fiscal closers.

P/E was 15.8 in the United States and 35.3 in Japan (Goldman Sachs Research, August 1990).[17] Chan, Hamao & Lakonishok [1991] find evidence of a significant relation between expected returns and cash-flow yield (CF/P) for Japanese stocks.

Consider the evidence on the CF/P effect summarized in Table 3B. The table reports average returns and other portfolio characteristics for ten decile portfolios based on annual rankings (at March 31) of NYSE and AMEX securities on the ratio of cash-flow per share to price per share (CF/P) for the period 1972 to 1989. Cash flow (CF) is defined as reported earnings plus depreciation. The similarity of the average values of E/P and CF/P for the portfolios shows there is much overlap between the composition of the CF/P portfolios in Table 3B and the E/P portfolios reported in Table 3A. There appears to be some marginal explanatory power provided by CF/P relative to E/P in the evidence on average returns reported in the first column, although the results are for two different time periods. To make the comparison for the 1972–1989 period, the average difference in returns between the two extreme E/P decile portfolios is 0.72% per month

[17] French & Poterba [1991] adjust the E/P ratio for the Japanese and U.S. markets for differences in accounting techniques and report adjusted E/P ratios of 22.8 for Japan and 14.5 for the United States. Thus, holding accounting techniques constant does not eliminate the difference between the estimates. The remaining differences may be explained by a lower level of interest rate and a faster economic growth rate in Japan compared to the United States during that period.

(t = 2.05) and the difference in returns between the two extreme CF/P portfolios is 0.89% per month (t = 2.44). This translates to an average *annual* difference between the two effects of about 2.0%.[18]

2.5. *The price/book (P/B) effect*

Although less research has examined the ability of other variables to predict cross-sectional differences in security returns, the ratio of price per share to book value per share (P/B) deserves mention because of its significant predictive ability. As is the case for the other variables discussed above, there is no theoretical model that predicts P/B should have predictive power. However, investment analysts (e.g., Graham and Dodd) have long argued that the magnitude of the deviation of current (market) price from book price per share is an important indicator of expected returns. A succession of papers [Stattman, 1980; Rosenberg, Reid & Lanstein, 1985; De Bondt & Thaler, 1987; Keim, 1988; and Fama & French, 1992] document a significant negative relation between P/B and returns. To provide some perspective on the magnitude of the P/B effect, Table 4 reports average monthly returns and other portfolio characteristics for ten decile portfolios drawn from the same data used above for the E/P and CF/P results. The average monthly returns for the 1962 to 1989 period in Table 4 show a significant negative relation between P/B and returns. Further, the monthly difference in returns between the extreme P/B portfolios (0.78%, t = 2.35) for the 1972 to 1989 period (not reported in Table 4), is comparable to the corresponding differential return for the E/P effect (0.72%, t = 2.05), CF/P effect (0.89%, t = 2.44) and larger than the size premium (0.56%, t = 1.35) measured over the same period.

There is limited evidence of a P/B effect outside the U.S. A P/B effect has been documented for stocks trading on the Tokyo Stock Exchange [Aggarwal, Rao & Hiraki, 1989; Chan, Hamao & Lakonishok, 1991; and Capaul, Rowley & Sharpe, 1993], and also on stock exchanges in France, Germany, Switzerland and the U.K. [Capaul, Rowley & Sharpe, 1993]. The magnitude of the P/B effect in these markets is smaller than that reported above for the U.S., and only marginally significant. Capaul, Rowley and Sharpe report the following average monthly values for the difference in returns between lowest and highest P/B portfolios: France, 0.53%; Germany, 0.13%; Japan, 0.50%; Switzerland, 0.31%; and the U.K., 0.23%.

[18] An alternative to both the E/P and CF/P ratios is the price-to-sales (P/S) ratio. Compared to earnings and cash flow, sales revenues are probably least influenced by accounting rules and conventions. There is indeed evidence of a P/S effect in both the United States [Senchack & Martin, 1987; Jacobs & Levy, 1988] and Japan [Aggarwal, Rao & Hiraki, 1990]. In these markets, low P/S ratio portfolios have, on average, higher returns than portfolios with relatively higher P/S ratios. For example, during the period 1968 to 1983, a portfolio of Japanese stocks with the lowest P/S ratio had an average monthly return of 1.86% compared with 1.13% for the portfolio of stocks with the highest quintile of P/S.

Table 4

Monthly returns and other characteristics for value-weighted portfolios of NYSE and AMEX stocks formed on the basis of the ratio of price/book (April 1962–December 1989)

P/B portfolio	Mean return	Std. dev. return	Beta	Mkt. cap. ($ mill.)	P/B	Price ($)
Negative	1.66	8.37	1.29	118.6	−7.07	13.62
Lowest	1.49	5.63	1.04	260.5	0.57	15.98
2	1.46	4.98	0.95	401.2	0.83	19.99
3	1.08	4.66	0.90	619.5	1.00	23.56
4	1.12	4.32	0.83	667.7	1.15	25.72
5	0.96	4.56	0.90	641.1	1.31	26.94
6	0.82	4.45	0.91	834.6	1.52	29.97
7	0.86	4.79	0.98	752.3	1.80	31.45
8	0.93	4.87	1.02	813.0	2.20	33.93
9	0.85	5.25	1.11	1000.8	2.95	37.48
Highest	0.91	5.19	1.05	1429.8	8.17	46.66

Portfolio are created on March 31 of each year using year-end accounting values and March 31 prices. Aside from new listings and delistings, which are added to or dropped from the portfolios as they occur during the year, the portfolio composition remains constant over the following twelve months. Portfolios contain only December 31 fiscal closers.

2.6. One effect or many?

The research discussed above documents significant cross-sectional relations between abnormal returns and size, E/P (or CF/P) and P/B. Few would argue that these separate findings are entirely independent phenomena. Several characteristics of the portfolios support such a conclusion. First, the ranking variables all share a common variable — price per share of the firm's common stock. Second, the various effects all display similar return patterns through time. We discuss these common features of the documented effects in this section.

2.6.1 Price as a common denominator

Market capitalization, E/P, P/B and CF/P are computed using a common variable — price per share. Blume & Stambaugh [1983] and Stoll & Whaley [1983] explored the relation between size and price, and reported evidence suggesting a high rank correlation between size and price.[19] Keim [1988], Jaffe, Keim & Westerfield [1989] and Fama & French [1992] have all recently raised this possibility regarding the other effects. That E/P and P/B also produce rankings based, to some extent, on price per share, is evident in the rightmost columns in Tables 3A and 4 where the average share price of the stocks in the size, E/P and P/B portfolios decline monotonically with the respective variables.

[19] Results in Blume & Husic [1973], Stoll & Whaley [1983] and Blume & Stambaugh [1983] also reveal a significant cross-sectional relation between price per share and average returns.

Table 5

Average rank correlations (t-statistics) between several predetermined characteristics for NYSE and AMEX stocks, and also between these characteristics and returns during the following year (1962–1989)

	Market capitalization	Earnings/ price	Price/ book	Dividend yield	Price
Earnings/price	0.05 (1.70)				
Price/book	0.30 (15.09)	−0.29 (−10.99)			
Dividend yield	−0.01 (−0.51)	0.36 (14.50)	−0.47 (−31.03)		
Price per share	0.78 (84.94)	0.11 (4.02)	0.33 (17.40)	−0.13 (−7.12)	
Annual return ($t+1$)	0.03 (0.92)	0.12 (6.09)	−0.07 (−3.45)	0.04 (1.46)	0.04 (1.15)

Correlations are computed annually using ranks of individual stocks. All rankings are conducted at the end of March, using prices at that time and accounting numbers for the previous fiscal year.

To demonstrate the association among these variables, Table 5 reports pairwise rank correlations between each of the variables described above and also for dividend yield, a variable that has also been shown to have cross-sectional return predictability [20]. These rank correlations and the associated t-values are computed as follows. Each year at the end of March all NYSE and AMEX stocks are ranked independently on size, E/P, P/B, D/P, and price (i.e., five separate rankings are produced). Each variable is computed using price per share at March 31 and, when applicable, accounting numbers for the previous year [21]. Pairwise Spearman rank correlations are computed. This procedure is conducted in each year for the period 1962 to 1989, and mean rank correlations and standard errors are computed for the entire time series of values. Consistent with the above conjecture, the rank correlations are generally large and significant. With the exception of the rank correlations for size–E/P and size–dividend yield, the correlations are significantly different from zero, indicating some commonalities among the effects [22]. As suggested in previous work [Blume & Stambaugh, 1983, and Stoll & Whaley, 1983], the rank correlation between market capitalization and

[20] The relation between stock returns and dividend yields is most often attributed to the differential taxation of capital gains and ordinary income as described in the after-tax asset pricing models developed by Brennan [1970] and Litzenberger & Ramaswamy [1979]. For additional evidence, both pro and con, regarding the relation between stock returns and dividends, see Black & Scholes [1974], Blume [1980], Hess [1983], Keim [1985], Miller & Scholes [1982] and Rosenberg & Marathe [1979].

[21] Note that only December fiscal closers are included in the rankings.

[22] This lack of correlation between size and E/P is also evident in Table 3A.

price is significant and by far the largest correlation in the table. The correlation between price and P/B is also quite large (0.33).

2.6.2. Common variation through time: within-year seasonality

The fact that all these effects are most pronounced in the month of January suggests that the effects are associated with some common underlying factor. This January seasonal has been demonstrated for the size effect [Keim, 1983b], E/P effect [Cook & Rozeff, 1984, and Jaffe, Keim & Westerfield, 1989], and the P/B effect [Keim, 1988, and Fama & French, 1991].[23] There is a burgeoning literature on the January effect that is discussed in more detail below in Section 3.2. We merely report on the general stylized facts at this juncture.

Figure 1 summarizes the January seasonal for the size, E/P and P/B effects using portfolios of NYSE and AMEX securities. Considering each effect separately, the difference in return between the two extreme decile portfolios (e.g., smallest size portfolio minus largest size portfolio) is measured separately in each month of the

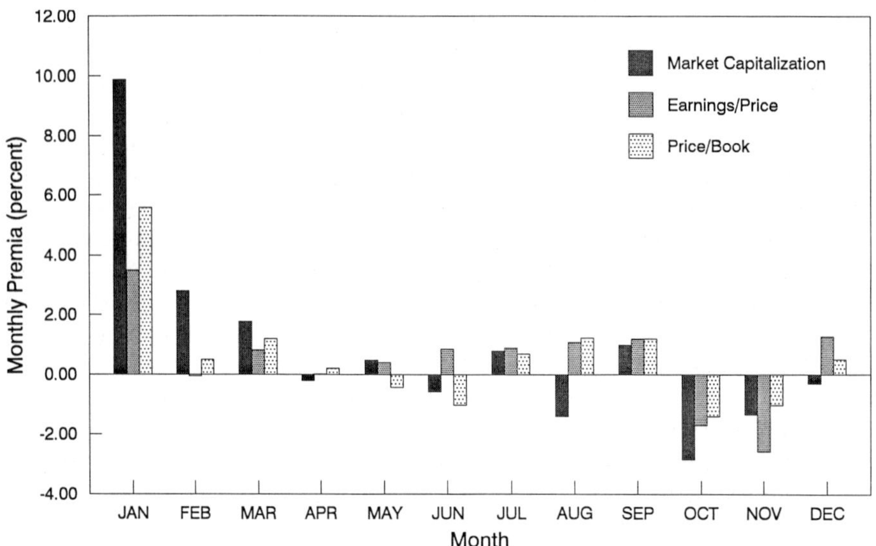

Fig. 1. Monthly difference in returns for extreme deciles (4/62–12/89) (e.g. smallest market cap. – largest market cap.). Based on monthly returns of value-weighed decile portfolios of NYSE and AMEX stocks. Portfolios are (independently) constructed on March 31 of each year using March 31 shares outstanding and prices, and prior-year-end accounting values. Aside from new listings and delistings, which are added to or dropped from the portfolio as they occur during the year, the portfolio composition remains constant over the following twelve months. The portfolios contain only December 31 fiscal closers.

[23] Interestingly, the P/E effect in the Tokyo market manifests itself in all months of the year *except* January. During that month, there is a significant *reverse* P/E effect — that is, high P/E portfolios outperform low P/E portfolios during January.

year and the average for each month is computed. The figure, which reports the month-by-month averages for each of the three effects, clearly shows a January seasonal in the effects.

2.6.3. *Common variation through time: long-term variation*

In addition to the within-year variation, the magnitude of these effects have been shown to vary over longer periods of time. For example, Brown, Kleidon & Marsh [1983] find that the size effect reverses itself for sustained periods: while for most periods there is a small-firm premium, there are a few periods (e.g., 1969–1973) when there is a *large*-firm premium.[24] Stated differently, there are extended periods when small capitalization portfolios underperform large-capitalization portfolios on a risk-adjusted basis. Jaffe, Keim & Westerfield [1989] report similar findings for the E/P effect. Thus, we must distinguish between the unconditional and conditional expected values for the effects. The relatively short period [1972–1989] used in the comparisons reported in Section 2.4 may not be long enough to capture the 'long-run' magnitudes of these effects.

To illustrate the time-varying nature of these effects, Figure 2 plots the annual size, E/P and P/B effects over the 1962 to 1989 period. The magnitude of the effects is measured as the respective differences in returns between the extreme decile portfolios composed of NYSE and AMEX securities. We make several observations. First, and consistent with previous findings, the magnitudes of the effects change substantially over time.[25] Hence, the estimated magnitudes of the effects are quite sensitive to the period in which they are measured. For example, there are extended periods when the effects reverse, especially for the size effect [Brown, Kleidon & Marsh, 1983]. As a case in point, the size effect was inverted for a large portion of the 1980s, which comprises a long segment of the time period used in the 1972–1989 comparison above. As a result, it is not clear that the relative differences in the magnitudes of the effects noted is Section 2.5 are unbiased estimates of the long-run differences in returns arising from portfolio strategies employing these different variables. Second, it also appears that while the annual P/B and E/P effects are significantly related (the simple correlation, r, between the annual P/B and E/P effects is 0.76 and significant), the size effect is less correlated with both the E/P effect ($r = 0.31$) and the P/B effect ($r = 0.36$).

2.7. *Disentangling the effects*

The discussion in Section 2.6 concerns two stylized facts. First, the variables that have been shown to predict cross-sectional variation in returns are all significantly correlated with price per share, which itself has been shown to significantly predict

[24] Note, however, that even in periods when there is, on average, a large-firm premium, there is a significant small-firm premium in January [see Keim, 1983b].

[25] Keim & Stambaugh [1986] examine the *conditional* size effect and show that an ex-ante observable variable (based on the level of small firm prices), chosen to proxy for variation in expected returns, predicts the variation in the size effect. Keim [1990] and Fama & French [1991] note similar capabilities to predict the E/P effect and the P/B effect, respectively.

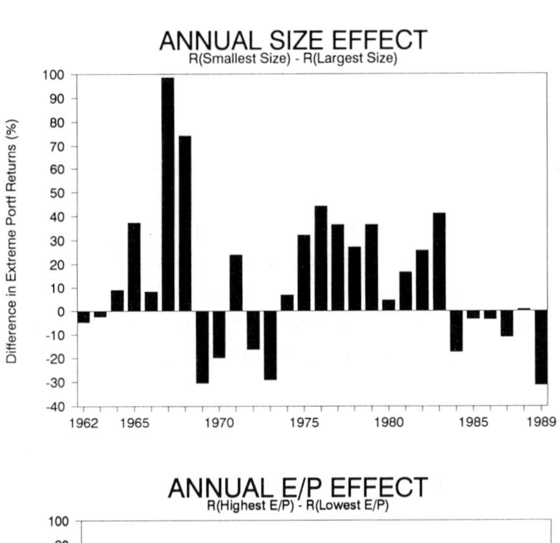

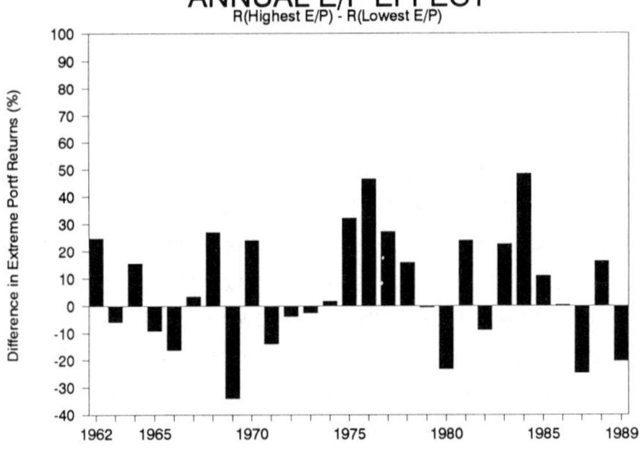

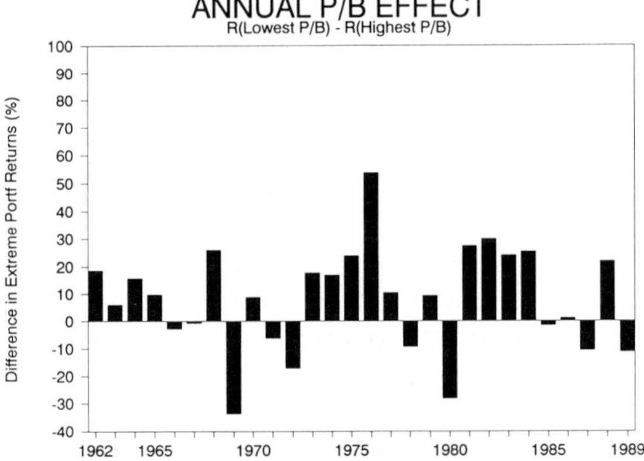

Fig. 2. Annual size, E/P and P/B effects over period 1962–1989. Based on monthly returns of value-weighed decile portfolios of NYSE and AMEX stocks. Portfolios are (independently) constructed on March 31 of each year using March 31 shares outstanding and prices, and prior-year-end accounting values. Aside from new listings and delistings, which are added to or dropped from the portfolio as they occur during the year, the portfolio composition remains constant over the following twelve months. The portfolios contain only December 31 fiscal closers.

cross-sectional differences in returns. Second, the ability of these variables to predict cross-sectional differences in returns is significantly greater in January. Indeed, it is very weak outside of January. The question, then, is whether these separate findings are all a manifestation of the same underlying phenomenon; and if so, which is the cleanest proxy for the underlying effect?

2.7.1. Size and E/P

Much of the research in this area has examined the interrelation between the E/P and size effects. A variety of techniques have been used — ranging from simple analysis of average portfolio returns to sophisticated regression techniques. The disparate methods used often make comparisons difficult. In the end, the results are less than conclusive. For example, Reinganum [1981] argues that the size effect subsumes the E/P effect (i.e., once we control for size, there is no marginal E/P effect). Basu [1983] argues just the opposite. Peavy & Goodman [1983] and Cook & Rozeff [1984], after performing meticulous replications of and extensions to the methods of Basu and Reinganum, reach surprisingly different conclusions. Peavy and Goodman's results are consistent with Basu's, but Cooke and Rozeff conclude that no one effect dominates the other. Banz & Breen [1988] find a size effect but no independent E/P effect, a result similar to Reinganum. Jaffe, Keim & Westerfield [1989] argue that the inability to disentangle the two effects may be attributable to the relatively short time periods used in the above studies (ranging from 8 to 18 years) that do not overlap, and the failure of the studies (with the exception of Cook & Rozeff [1984]) to account for potential differences between January and the other months (see Figure 1). Using data covering a 36-year period, Jaffe, Keim and Westerfield find that after controlling for size there is a significant E/P effect in both January and the other months; controlling for the E/P effect, there is a significant size effect only in January[26]. They also conclude that the results of the earlier studies conflict because the magnitude of the two effects is period specific (see Figure 2). Fama & French [1992] reach similar conclusions regarding the joint significance of size and E/P effects (see the regression results in their table 3).

2.7.2. Size and P/B

Stattman [1980] and Rosenberg, Reid & Lanstein [1985] (RRL) were the first to examine the possible interaction between size and P/B for NYSE and AMEX stocks. Stattman examines average beta-risk-adjusted portfolio returns for the 4/1964 to 4/1979 period and concludes that 'even after taking account for the size effect, there remains a positive relationship between (B/P, the inverse of P/B) and subsequent returns'. RRL examine market model residuals of P/B portfolios that are constructed to be orthogonal to size and other influences. They also find a significant relation between abnormal returns and P/B for the 1973–1984 period. Fama & French [1992] use data for the longer period of 1962–1990. Their sample

[26] This result is consistent with other studies which have found that when examined alone, the size effect is significant only in January [e.g., Blume & Stambaugh, 1983]. See Section 3.2.

includes NYSE and AMEX stocks for the entire period and OTC stocks for the 1973–1990 subperiod. Fama and French estimate an extension of cross-sectional model given in equation (2) with the addition of P/B, using data for individual stocks.[27] Based on their findings, they conclude that size and P/B are sufficient to characterize cross-sectional differences in expected returns.

2.7.3. *E/P and P/B*

The consensus from the research detailed above is that the relation between market capitalization and average returns is quite robust.[28] In addition, variables like E/P and P/B seem to provide explanatory power for average returns beyond the influence of size. Fama & French [1992] (FF) investigate whether these two variables are proxying for the same additional influence by estimating equation (2) with both P/B and E/P as additional independent variables. Based on their results, they conclude that size and P/B together subsume any additional explanatory power of E/P. It may be difficult to compare their results to earlier findings on the E/P effect, though, since FF compute ratios of E/P and P/B using market prices that occur at a point in time before the market knows the value of earnings or book value. In addition, FF's market capitalization values, used in conjunction with these accounting ratios in their tests, are measured with considerably 'fresher' market prices than used in the ratios.[29]

To facilitate comparison of the interaction between the E/P and P/B effects to previous studies of the E/P effect, we use the data described above in Section

[27] Most previous research has demonstrated that estimates of beta do not enter significantly into models like the one represented in equation (2) in the presence of other explanatory variables such as size and E/P (an exception is Chan & Chen [1988]). Thus, Fama and French argue that methodologies that use portfolios for the test assets in equation (2), to avoid estimation error in individual beta estimates, unduly forfeit the valuable information in the cross section of individual security characteristics such as market values or E/P's. This latter point was emphasized earlier in Litzenberger & Ramaswamy [1979] in their analysis of the relation between stock returns and dividend yields.

[28] An exception to the above findings is the recent study by Chan, Hamao & Lakonishok [1991] who find that in the Japanese stock market P/B and CF/P are sufficient to characterize cross-sectional differences in expected returns. That size is unimportant in explaining expected returns appears to be unique to the Japanese and Korean markets.

[29] To see this, consider the treatment of a firm with a December fiscal year-end by FF. They compute E/P or P/B for such a firm using the stock price *at the end of December in year $t-1$* and the earnings or book value as of December (but not known until approximately March of year t), while market capitalization is computed using price *at the end of June in year t*. These values are then jointly compared with returns measured over the period from July in year t to June of year $t+1$. In contrast, other studies typically compute E/P or P/B using stock price *at the end of March in year t*, market cap using price *at the end of March in year t*, and then jointly compare these values with returns measured over the twelve months beginning in April of year t. Thus, as of the test date, the market-determined information in the FF accounting ratios is considerably staler than that in the market cap variable (by 6 months). Hence, the FF values for these characteristics may differ substantially from values used in other studies, especially for stocks that experienced unexpectedly good or bad earnings. For example, FF's E/P ratio (market capitalization) for a stock that announced unexpectedly bad earnings in March would be lower (higher) than the ratio used in other studies.

2.3 to compute returns for portfolios created on the basis of both E/P and P/B, where the market price used in the ratio occurs three months after the end of the firm's fiscal year. Briefly, at the end of March in each year from 1962 to 1989 we sort all NYSE and AMEX stocks by P/B and form five groups of equal numbers of securities based on the P/B ranking. Within each of these groups we again rank the stocks by E/P and create five subgroups within each of the P/B groups.[30] Individual stock returns are adjusted for the influence of the size effect by simply subtracting the return for the size decile (see Table 1) of which that security is a member. The composition of the portfolios remains constant over the next twelve months and value-weighted size-adjusted portfolio returns are computed each month.

The results, reported in Table 6, are consistent with those in Fama & French [1992]. First, there is slight evidence of a relation between E/P and returns, although this relation is largely confined to the lowest P/B category, and extends only through the first four quintiles. Second, there appears to be a relation between P/B and subsequent returns, although this relation is often not monotonic and does not appear in all E/P categories. Curiously, the P/B effect occurs in the E/P categories in which the average price of the securities in the portfolios increases with P/B. (In this regard, recall the significant rank correlations between price and P/B in Table 5.) Although the experiment controls for the influence of market capitalization on expected returns, it does not explicitly control for price, which has also been shown to influence returns. Thus, the high average returns for low P/B stocks may reflect some underlying relation between returns and low price.

An alternative hypothesis involves the prospect that low P/B stocks are simply stocks whose prices have dropped relative to book values that vary little through time. As discussed below in Section 4.1, firms whose stocks have recently declined in price, in the absence of a concomitant decline in the value of the debt, have become more leveraged and, other things equal, more risky. Traditional estimation methods may underestimate 'true' beta risk for such firms and, therefore, overstate 'risk-adjusted' returns.[31] As a result, stocks that have recently declined substantially in price will tend to have underestimated betas and low ratios of P/B. Hence, P/B may be a more accurate proxy for 'true' beta risk than traditional estimates of beta due to the measurement error in the traditional estimates. Given

[30] For purposes of this experiment, we eliminate all stocks with negative values of either P/B or E/P from the sample.

[31] Traditional methods (e.g., OLS) that have been used for estimating betas in most cross-sectional analyses use four or more years of monthly returns data and (implicitly) apply equal weights to all observations in the time series. Clearly, the most relevant observations — the ones that should be given the most weight in the estimation — are those occurring closest to the period of analysis (e.g., portfolio formation date). Thus, the betas used in such studies are 'stale' in that they are estimated using information that, in large measure, is not relevant. This estimation shortfall also applies to studies that use 'future' betas estimated from data occurring after the analysis interval — structural changes that impact firm risk can also affect the post-analysis observations, thereby rendering them less relevant for assessing the firm's risk in the analysis interval.

Table 6

Size-adjusted monthly returns (%) and other characteristics for twenty-five portfolios of NYSE and AMEX stocks ranked first by P/B ratio and then by E/P ratio over the period April 1962–December 1989 [a]

	Earnings/price				
	Lowest	2	3	4	Highest
Returns					
Low P/B	0.23	0.22	0.48	0.50	0.09
	(0.22) [b]	(0.16)	(0.14)	(0.15)	(0.17)
2	0.14	−0.17	0.15	0.12	0.23
	(0.16)	(0.15)	(0.13)	(0.14)	(0.16)
3	−0.06	−0.26	−0.02	0.07	0.06
	(0.14)	(0.13)	(0.12)	(0.13)	(0.14)
4	−0.07	0.02	−0.09	−0.18	0.08
	(0.15)	(0.11)	0.11)	(0.12)	(0.16)
High P/B	−0.04	−0.10	−0.01	−0.03	0.04
	(0.18)	(0.13)	(0.11)	(0.11)	(0.15)
Price/book					
Low P/B	0.69	0.74	0.74	0.74	0.68
2	1.08	1.09	1.08	1.07	1.06
3	1.43	1.44	1.42	1.40	1.40
4	2.05	2.04	2.00	1.97	1.95
High P/B	7.24	5.18	4.52	4.03	5.43
Earnings/price (%)					
Low P/B	4.27	8.85	11.49	13.98	20.61
2	5.56	9.06	10.81	12.38	16.11
3	5.41	8.25	9.68	11.15	14.86
4	4.52	7.02	8.21	9.43	13.24
High P/B	2.80	4.68	5.76	6.98	10.49
Price ($)					
Low P/B	14.25	19.58	21.13	22.05	20.86
2	22.07	27.11	27.22	27.27	23.61
3	29.50	29.73	30.66	29.99	26.40
4	35.27	35.91	35.61	33.23	28.39
High P/B	55.48	49.10	45.08	39.06	31.17
Market capitalization ($ mill.)					
Low P/B	154.97	253.64	445.70	631.84	493.98
2	493.02	727.21	704.08	737.39	764.06
3	651.23	770.02	850.76	859.78	745.37
4	705.64	951.78	921.58	839.79	661.38
High P/B	1519.06	1472.63	1314.98	1282.69	914.91

[a] We define a size-adjusted monthly return for security i as the return for that security minus the monthly portfolio return for the size decile in which security i is a member. P/B and E/P portfolios in the table are value-weighted combinations of these monthly size-adjusted returns. All portfolios are formed on March 31 of each year using year-end accounting values and March 31 market prices. Stocks with negative values of either P/B or E/P are excluded from the sample.

[b] Standard deviations of returns in parentheses ($N = 333$).

their *unobserved* higher levels of risk, the subsequent higher average returns that compensate for this risk appear anomalous.[32] [33]

3. Time series return predictability: seasonal patterns

Consider a model of stock prices in which returns are constant through time. In the next three sections we entertain evidence relating to the validity of such a model. In this section, we examine the evidence regarding 'seasonal' patterns in returns relating to calendar turning points such as the beginning of the week, the month, and the year.

3.1. Patterns in daily returns around weekends

Consider an exchange where trading takes place Monday through Friday. If the process generating stock returns operates continuously, then Monday returns should be three times the returns expected on each of the other days of the week to compensate for a three-day holding period, given that no trading takes place over the two-day weekend. This is known as the calendar-time hypothesis. The alternative is the trading-time hypothesis: returns are generated only during active trading and average returns are the same for each of the five days of the week. The evidence we discuss in this section finds that stock returns, in many Western countries, are on average negative on Monday. This is inconsistent with both the calendar-time and the trading-time hypotheses since the former predicts a *larger* return, and the latter an *equal* return, for Monday relative to the other days of the week.

Cross [1973] and French [1980] document significant negative Monday returns using the S&P composite index beginning in 1953, and Gibbons & Hess [1981] find the same pattern for the Dow Jones Industrial Index of 30 stocks [1962–1978]. Keim & Stambaugh [1984] extend the findings for the S&P composite to include the period 1928–1982, and also find the same pattern in actively-traded OTC stocks. Lakonishok & Smidt [1988] extend the finding for the Dow Jones Industrial Index to include the period 1897–1986.

The weekend effect has also been documented in many other stock markets. The international evidence is summarized in Table 7. The research reported in the table covers periods of various lengths, generally in excess of fifteen years. In each case the study reporting the most extensive data is used, and returns are computed using the closing (end-of-trading) value of the index. In particular, Monday returns are computed from Friday close to Monday close and hence

[32] De Bondt & Thaler [1987] show that such price reversals are most extreme for low P/B stocks.

[33] Recent papers by Kothari, Shanken & Sloan [1993] and Breen & Korajczyk [1993] suggest that the P/B results may be due to survivor biases in samples of stocks drawn from the Compustat files. Compustat tends to include (and add) stocks in their files only after the stock has demonstrated a successful track record. Thus, small firms with low P/B ratios that subsequently perform poorly (or fail) are unlikely to appear on the files.

Table 7

International evidence of daily seasonality in stock market returns [1] (average daily percentage returns)

Country [2]	Period	Index	Monday	Tuesday	Wednesday	Thursday	Friday	Saturday
Australia	1975–84	EWI	0.044	−0.116*	0.045	0.198*	0.157*	–
Belgium	1977–85	VWI	0.098*	−0.032	0.041*	0.111*	0.130*	–
Belgium	1977–85	EWI	0.080*	0.026*	0.046*	0.044*	0.062*	–
Canada	1969–84	TC [3]	−0.157*	−0.003	0.073*	0.075*	0.094*	–
Finland	1977–82	VWI	0.086*	0.066*	0.030	0.070*	0.074*	–
France	1977–89	VWI	−0.050	0.139*	0.126*	0.133*	0.100*	–
France	1977–89	EWI	0.083*	0.117*	0.122*	0.117*	0.013	–
Germany	1970–85	VWI	−0.085*	0.008	0.044	0.060*	0.099*	–
Germany	1970–85	EWI	0.005	−0.026	0.031	0.066	0.107*	–
Greece	1978–86	VWI	0.070*	−0.058	−0.073*	0.041	0.160*	–
Japan	1949–88	VWI [4]	−0.071*	−0.044*	0.115*	0.081*	0.042*	0.133*
Korea	1980–84	VWI	−0.072*	−0.087*	0.087*	0.014*	0.120*	0.230*
Singapore	1969–84	ST [5]	−0.036	−0.107*	0.079*	0.121*	0.100*	–
Spain	1979–83	VWI	–	−0.072*	0.003	0.037	0.071*	–
United Kingdom	1969–84	FT-A [6]	−0.095*	0.106*	0.090*	0.011	0.044	–
United States	1928–52	S&P [7]	−0.223*	0.076*	0.084*	0.066	0.029	0.147*
United States	1952–82	S&P [7]	−0.154*	0.026	0.103*	0.036*	0.092*	–

[1] Starred returns are significantly different from zero at the 0.05 level. Non-starred returns are not significantly different from zero. VWI = value-weighted index; EWI = equally-weighted index.

[2] Sources: *Australia*, Ball & Bowers [1987]; *Belgium*, Corhay [1991]; *Canada, Singapore, United Kingdom*, Condoyanni, O'Hanlon & Ward [1987]; *Finland*, Berglund [1985]; *France*, Hamon & Jacquillat [1991]; *Germany*, Frantzmann [1988]; *Greece*, Condoyanni, McLeay & O'Hanlon [1989]; *Japan*, Ziemba [1991]; *Korea*, Kim [1988]; *Spain*, Santesmases [1986]; *United States*, Keim & Stambaugh [1984].

[3] TC = Toronto composite index.

[4] The Tokyo Stock Exchange is closed on Saturdays since February 1989.

[5] ST = Straits Times index.

[6] FT-A = Financial Times all share index.

[7] S&P = Standard & Poor's composite index. The New York Stock Exchange is closed on Saturdays since June 1952.

include the nontrading weekend period (Friday close to Monday open) as well as Monday's trading hours (Monday open to Monday close). The exchanges in most countries are closed on Saturdays and Sundays. Exceptions are: Japan, where the exchange was open every second, fourth and fifth (if any) Saturday of the month for morning trading (this practice was discontinued in January 1989, see Ziemba [1991]); Korea, where the market is open every Saturday; and the U.S., where the NYSE was open for trading on Saturdays (generally from 10:00 a.m. until noon) during most of the period prior to June 1952. Starred returns are statistically different from zero.

Several observations can be made:

(1) There are significant differences in average daily returns across days of the week in nearly all countries (statistical tests in the corresponding studies confirm

this for all the countries in the sample, except for the equal-weighted index in Germany).

(2) In general, average daily returns during the last three days of the week (Wednesday, Thursday and Friday) are positive. In contrast, average daily returns during the first two days of the week (Monday and Tuesday) are often negative. (However, the Greek index displays significantly negative average returns on Wednesday.)

(3) In most non-Asian markets, average returns on the first day of the trading week — usually Monday — are significantly negative. Note that in Spain, Tuesday returns are negative, corresponding to Tuesday being the beginning of the trading week for the Madrid market during the period examined.

(4) Tuesday returns are significantly negative for the Pacific rim countries of Japan, Korea, Singapore and Australia, sometimes in conjunction with significantly negative Monday returns (Japan and Korea).

(5) In France and Germany, the negative Monday effect manifests itself in the value-weighed index rather than the equally weighted index which means that it is mostly caused by relatively larger firms (large firms are over-represented in the value-weighted index compared to the equal-weighted index). Thus, the Monday effect may be related to firm size.

Related to this last point, Keim & Stambaugh [1984], noting results in Gibbons & Hess that suggest that Friday returns vary cross-sectionally with market value, find that the return differential between small and large firms increases as the week progresses, and is largest on Friday. In addition, Keim [1987] shows that, controlling for the large average returns in January, the 'Friday effect' and the 'Monday effect' are not different in January than in the other months.

All of the studies which document negative Monday returns use Friday-close-to-Monday-close returns, and thus cannot distinguish whether the negative returns are due to the weekend nontrading period or to active trading on Monday. Research that has tried to sort out this issue is not in complete agreement. For example, Harris [1986], for all NYSE stocks for the period 1981–1983, and Smirlock & Starks [1986], for the Dow Jones 30 for the period 1963 to 1973, examine intra-daily returns and show that negative Monday returns accrue both during the nontrading hours over the weekend (Friday close to Monday open) and during trading on Monday. On the other hand, Rogalski [1984] examines intra-daily data for the period 1974–1984 and concludes that negative Monday returns accrue entirely during the weekend nontrading period.

We do not yet have a satisfactory explanation for the weekend effect. The fact that the pattern is robust across so many different markets argues persuasively against many institutionally-motivated explanations. For example, one potential explanation that has been examined in the United States [Gibbons & Hess, 1981, and Lakonishok & Levi, 1982] and the United Kingdom [Theobald & Price, 1984] is based on the delay between trading and settlement (actual transfer of funds) due to check clearing. On the NYSE there is a five-business-day settlement period to which an additional day is added for check clearing. This means that for stocks purchased on a business day other than Friday, the buyer will have eight *calendar* days before transferring funds. For stocks purchased on Friday, he will have ten calendar days and thus two more days of interest. In an efficient securities market the buyer should be willing to pay more for stocks purchased on Friday by an amount not exceeding two days of interest. Consequently, observed returns on Friday should be higher than those on other days of the week and those of Monday should be lower. Gibbons and Hess and Lakonishok and Levi showed that adjusting daily returns for the interest rate reduces the Monday effect, but comes nowhere close to explaining it.

On the London exchange trading takes place over consecutive account periods of two weeks' length beginning every other Monday. Settlement, however, is made on the second Monday after the end of the account. This means that for stocks purchased on the first Monday of the account, the buyer will have 21 calendar days before losing funds; whereas for stocks purchased the preceding Friday, he will have only 10 calendar days. For stocks purchased on the second Monday of the account, the buyer will have 14 calendar days but 17 calendar days for stocks purchased the preceding Friday. According to the settlement-delay hypothesis, the first Monday returns for the account should be higher than the returns on the other days of the week and the second Monday returns should be smaller. However, the fact that stocks generally go ex-dividend on the *first* Monday of the account [Theobald & Price, 1984] will partly offset the rise in price and also the return predicted for that day by the settlement-delay hypothesis. Indeed, returns on non-ex-dividend Mondays are generally negative, whereas returns on ex-dividend Mondays are generally positive.[34] This result is qualitatively consistent with the settlement-delay hypothesis but the magnitude of the Monday effect on the NYSE and the LSE cannot be fully explained by the settlement-delay hypothesis.

The Tuesday effect in Australia, Korea, Japan and Singapore is conjectured as resulting from time zone differences relative to New York [Jaffe & Westerfield, 1985a, b]. These countries are all one day ahead of New York; hence, the Tuesday effect in these countries may reflect the earlier Monday effect in New York.

We also know that the weekend effect is not completely explained by measurement error in recorded prices [Gibbons & Hess, 1981; Keim & Stambaugh, 1984; Smirlock & Starks, 1986], specialist trading activity [Keim & Stambaugh, 1984], and systematic patterns in investor buying and selling behavior [Keim, 1989, and Lakonishok & Maberly, 1990].

What are the implications of the above findings for investment managers? The evidence indicates that the major stock exchanges around the world are

[34] In smaller markets, daily returns, even for frequently traded stocks, are usually correlated. This phenomenon may prevent the detection of a Monday effect in the data. An additional problem may arise from the fact that the returns of market indices containing stocks with low trading frequency are generally serially correlated even if no serial correlation exists in the individual underlying securities returns [Hawawini, 1978, 1980a, b]. Theobald & Price [1984] have shown that in this case seasonal patterns in the daily returns of the individual securities that make up the index will be 'diffused'. Indeed, they report a stronger mean seasonality in more regularly 'traded' indices. Another characteristic of thinly traded stocks which has to be taken into account is the significant deviation of their return distribution from normality.

part of a global market in which the price movements of individual exchanges are interrelated. Lags in the correlation structure of stock returns around the world seem to reflect differences in time zones. The Monday effect reported in North America and the United Kingdom is replaced by a Tuesday effect in many countries outside the New York time zone. There may be some advantages to be gained from that knowledge: investors *planning* to buy stocks should do so preferably on Monday for Canadian, U.S. and U.K. stocks and on Tuesday for most Far Eastern stocks. Similarly, a stock sale should be preferably carried out on a Wednesday, Thursday or Friday.

3.2. Patterns in returns around the turn of the year

Rozeff & Kinney [1976] found that equal-weighted indexes containing all the stocks listed on the NYSE displayed significantly higher returns in January than in the other eleven months over the period 1904–1974. Gultekin & Gultekin [1983] examined the monthly stock returns from 17 countries during the period January 1959 through December 1979 and found that all the countries in their sample exhibited a large and positive January mean return. Average January returns were significantly larger than returns in other months for 13 of the 17 countries analyzed.

Table 8 summarizes the turn-of-the-year effect by reporting average monthly returns of eighteen market indices by month of the year. Several observations can be made. First, there is considerable variation in average returns across months of the year. In particular, average returns during January are always positive and generally significantly higher than during the rest of the year (a notable exception is Korea). Second, the magnitude of the January seasonal depends on the composition of the stock market index. Broader and equally-weighted indices, which emphasize smaller stocks, exhibit a stronger January seasonal than narrower or value-weighted indices. The equal-weighted index of all NYSE shares has an average January return of 5.08% compared to 1.04% for a value-weighted index. The same is true in Japan where the index reported in Table 8 is equally-weighted and exhibits an average January return of 5.58% compared to 4.36% for a value-weighted index containing the same stocks and measured over the same period [see Hawawini, 1991].

Keim [1983b] documented that the magnitude of the size effect varied by month of the year. He found that fifty percent of the annual size premium was concentrated in the month of January. Subsequent research by Blume & Stambaugh [1983] demonstrated that, after correcting for an upward bias in average returns for small stocks that was common to the experimental design in the early studies on the size effect, the size effect is evident only in January. The worldwide evidence of monthly seasonality in the size premium is summarized in Table 9 for the subsample of the countries presented in Table 8 for which evidence is available. The size premium is measured using the same method as the one reported in Table 2 but instead of taking all months of the year into consideration, the size premium is first measured during the month of January and then during the rest of the year (from February through December). In all countries except France and

Table 8

International evidence of monthly seasonality in stock market returns [1] (average monthly percentage returns)

Country	Jan.	Feb.	March	April	May	June	July	Aug.	Sept.	Oct.	Nov.	Dec.	All mths.
1. Australia	2.65	−0.58	0.51	0.84	0.97	0.43	0.66	−0.37	−2.39	2.13	−0.85	3.99	0.67
2. Belgium	3.20	1.09	0.40	1.48	−1.36	−0.84	1.44	−1.17	−1.87	−0.69	0.42	0.09	0.17
3. Canada	2.90	0.07	0.79	0.41	−0.96	−0.30	0.69	0.60	−0.06	−0.82	1.44	2.61	0.61
4. Finland	3.62	2.09	2.63	0.95	−0.02	1.55	2.53	0.97	−0.76	0.77	0.61	2.51	N.A. [2]
5. France	3.72	−0.18	1.98	0.94	−0.66	−1.90	1.53	1.03	−1.21	−0.72	0.43	0.15	0.43
6. Germany	1.62	0.55	2.17	0.80	0.15	1.62	2.11	2.18	−0.50	−0.46	0.93	1.42	1.09
7. Hong Kong	7.98	4.22	−2.34	1.86	2.34	2.40	2.74	−0.86	−1.69	3.21	−2.49	5.45	1.90
8. Japan	5.58	1.00	2.90	0.51	0.18	2.51	0.65	0.92	0.13	0.52	1.81	2.48	1.60
9. Korea	0.42	2.10	3.72	0.73	1.65	2.54	2.91	−0.13	−0.01	−0.67	3.02	3.34	1.64
10. Malaysia	1.70	0.21	−0.07	0.11	0.49	0.04	−0.34	−0.38	−0.10	0.45	−0.25	0.54	0.20
11. Netherlands	3.74	−0.53	0.62	2.49	0.54	−1.43	1.02	−1.69	−3.34	−0.96	−0.80	1.48	0.38
12. Singapore	7.81	0.69	0.28	0.54	3.45	1.76	0.71	−1.12	−0.11	−0.23	−0.07	1.91	1.31
13. Spain	3.04	1.99	0.14	0.14	−0.81	0.59	1.47	1.00	−2.02	0.18	0.36	−0.45	N.A. [2]
14. Taiwan	6.26	3.41	2.40	4.97	3.49	1.24	0.88	3.83	4.01	−3.70	0.47	1.63	2.41
15. United Kingdom	3.40	0.69	1.25	3.13	−1.21	−1.69	−1.11	1.88	−0.24	0.80	−0.61	2.06	0.70
16. U.K. FT-A [3]	3.06	0.79	1.15	3.57	−1.00	−0.85	−0.22	2.62	0.03	1.26	0.16	2.34	1.08
17. United States	1.04	−0.41	1.27	0.96	−1.38	−0.56	0.14	0.34	−0.79	0.78	1.03	1.42	0.32
18. U.S. EW [4]	5.08	0.55	1.55	0.44	−1.42	−1.00	0.73	0.72	−0.42	−0.79	1.79	1.37	N.A. [2]

[1] Sources: *Finland*, Berglund [1985] (the period covered is from January 1970 to December 1983); *United Kingdom*, Levis [1985] (the period covered is from January 1958 to December 1982 for Financial Times all share index); *Spain*, Rubio [1986] (the period covered is from January 1963 to December 1982); *Netherlands*, van der Bergh & Wessels [1985] (the period covered is from January 1966 to December 1982); *Malaysia*, Wong et al. [1990] (the period covered is 1970 to 1985; Index is value-weighted); *Germany*, Stehle [1992] (the period covered is 1954 to 1990; value-weighted index of all stocks listed on the Frankfurt Stock Exchange); *Japan*, Hawawini [1991] (the period covered is from January 1955 to December 1985 for an equally-weighted index of up to 566 stocks); *Hong Kong*, *Korea*, *Taiwan* and *Singapore*, Lee [1992] (the period covered is from January 1970 to December 1989, except *Korea* that begins in 1975; *Hong Kong* index is Hang Seng; *Korea* index is Korea Composite Stock; *Taiwan* index is Taiwan Stock Exchange; *Singapore* index is Straits Times). All other data are from Gultekin & Gultekin [1983] and are based on stock market indexes from Capital International Perspective (value-weighted indexes). The period covered is January 1959 to December 1979.

[2] Not available.

[3] FT-A = Financial Times all share index.

[4] Equally-weighted index of New York Stock Exchanges shares.

Table 9

International evidence of seasonality in the size premium [1]

Country:	Belgium	Finland	France	Germany	Japan	Taiwan	United Kingdom
Test period	1969–1983	1970–1983	1968–1980	1954–1990	1965–1987	1979–1986	1958–1982
Number of securities [2]	170	40	201	All FSE	1st section TSE	53 to 72	All LSE
Number of size portfolios	5	5	5	9	10	5	10
Market value largest portfolio / Market value smallest portfolio	188	113	83	N.A.	N.A.	17	182
January return [3] (%) on:							
– Smallest portfolio	5.4	5.9	3.7	2.8	9.5	N.A.	2.3
– Largest portfolio	3.0	2.5	4.4	1.3	2.3	N.A.	3.6
January size-premium [4] (%)	2.4	3.4	−0.7	1.6	7.2	3.4 [6]	−1.3
Rest-of-the-year monthly return [5] (%) on:							
– Smallest portfolio	0.8	1.8	1.4	1.4	1.9	N.A.	1.2
– Largest portfolio	0.4	1.0	0.7	1.0	1.3	N.A.	0.7
Rest-of-the-year size premium (%)	0.4	0.8	0.7	0.4	0.6	0.3 [6]	0.5

[1] Sources: *Belgium*, Hawawini et al. [1988]; *Finland*, Berglund [1985]; *France*, Hamon [1986]; *Germany*, Stehle [1992]; *Japan*, Ziemba [1991]; *Taiwan*, Ma et al. [1990], and *United Kingdom*, Levis [1985]. Note that except for the cases of Finland and France, the sources used in Table 9 are the same as those used in Table 2.

[2] TSE = Tokyo Stock Exchange; LSE = London Stock Exchange; N.A. = not available.

[3] All monthly mean returns are significantly different from zero.

[4] The January size-premium is significantly different from zero only in Belgium, Finland, Taiwan and Japan.

[5] Monthly mean returns are not significantly different from zero for the largest porfolio.

[6] The size-premium is measured with *excess* return estimated with OLS beta coefficients.

the United Kingdom the size premium is significantly larger during January than during the rest of the year, although it generally remains positive after January.

What explains this phenomenon? The most popular hypothesis attributes the effect to year-end tax-loss selling. The tax-loss selling hypothesis can be summarized as follows:

> The hypothesis maintains that tax laws influence investors' portfolio decisions by encouraging the sale of securities that have experienced recent price declines so that the (short term) capital loss can be offset against taxable income. Small firm stocks are likely candidates for tax-loss selling since these stocks typically have higher variances of price changes and, therefore, larger probabilities of large price declines. Importantly, the tax-loss argument relies on the assumption that investors wait until the tax year-end to sell their common stock 'losers'. For example, in the U.S., a combination of liquidity requirements and eagerness to realize capital losses before the new tax year may dictate sale of such securities at year-end. The heavy selling pressure during this period supposedly depresses the prices of small firm stocks. After the tax year-end, the price pressure disappears and prices rebound to equilibrium levels. Hence small firm stocks display large returns in the beginning of the new tax year. [Brown, Keim, Kleidon & Marsh, 1983, p. 107]

Reinganum [1983] and Roll [1983] both examine the hypothesis and their tests suggest that part, but not all, of the abnormal returns in January is related to tax-related trading. On the other hand, Schultz [1985] finds that prior to 1917 — before the U.S. tax code created incentives for tax-motivated selling — there was no evidence of a January effect for his sample of low-price stocks. This finding is confirmed in a recent paper by Jones, Lee & Apenbrink [1991] who find no evidence of a January effect prior to 1917 for the individual stocks in the Cowles Industrial Index.

Others have tested the hypothesis by examining the month-to-month behavior of returns in countries with tax codes similar to the U.S. code but with different tax year-ends. The tax-loss selling hypothesis predicts that, in the month immediately following the tax year-end, returns of small firms will be large relative to both other months and other firms. The hypothesis makes no predictions regarding the behavior of returns during the other months. The international evidence is far from conclusive. The studies that examine returns in countries with similar tax codes to the U.S. but with different tax year-ends (for example, the U.K. has an April tax year-end and Australia has a June tax year-end) find seasonals after the tax year-end, but often find large returns in January that are not predicted by the hypothesis. There is no January size premium in France, a country that taxes capital gains, while a January size-premium is reported in Japan, a country that did *not* tax capital gains for individual investors until 1989. Of course, the January size-premium in countries that neither tax capital gains nor have a December 31 tax year-end may be induced by foreign investors who pay capital gains taxes in their home country. Some evidence in favor of the tax-induced hypothesis is that no seasonality was detected in the United Kingdom *prior* to the introduction of capital gains taxes in this country in April 1965 [Reinganum & Shapiro, 1987].

After April 1965, seasonality appeared both in January and April.[35] Further, Berges, McConnell & Schlarbaum [1984] find a January seasonal in Canadian stock returns prior to 1972, a period when Canada had no taxes on capital gains.

The inconsistent evidence regarding the tax-loss selling hypothesis has led to other potential explanations. One possibility concerns the impact of institutional 'window dressing' at the end of the year — the practice of selling off 'loser' stocks at year-end so that they don't appear on the year-end statements sent to constituent shareholders [Haugen & Lakonishok, 1987][36]. Although there is some evidence that institutions behave in this fashion, the resulting impact on stock prices is difficult to distinguish from the impact of tax-loss selling. Similar in spirit to the 'price pressure' necessary in the tax-loss-selling and window-dressing stories is the notion that liquidity constraints of market participants may influence security returns, and these effects may have seasonal patterns. For example, periodic infusions of cash into the market as a result of, say, institutional transfers for pension accounts or proceeds from bonuses or profit-sharing plans, may impact the market. For example, Kato & Schallheim [1985] and Hawawini [1991], in an examination of the size effect in Japan, find January *and* June seasonals in small firm returns that coincide with traditional Japanese bonuses paid at the end of December and in June. Further, Rozeff [1986] finds a substantial *upward* shift in the ratio of purchases to sales of common stocks in a sample of individual and institutional investors (who are not members of the NYSE) at the beginning of the year that coincides with the small firm returns in January (although Rozeff interprets this as evidence of tax-loss selling). Ritter [1988] documents a similar pattern in the daily sales to purchases ratio for retail customers of a large brokerage firm, and argues, in conjunction with buying pressure at the beginning of the new year, that the turn-of-the-year price behavior is a result of price pressure. Finally, Ariel [1987] finds a daily pattern in daily stock returns in *every month* but February that parallels precisely the pattern that occurs at the turn of the year (see Section 3.3). Such a consistent pattern at month-ends is likely related to investor buying and selling behavior that is motivated by reasons other than taxes.

The above arguments rely on the notions of price pressure and irrational market participants to translate the buying and selling behavior of market participants into abnormal returns. There is an alternative. Most (all) of the above studies use daily *closing* transaction prices to compute returns for the analyses. These closing prices may be equivalent to dealer (specialist) bid or ask prices depending on whether the trade was seller- or buyer-initiated. Now, as a case in point, if there is a preponderance of seller-initiated transactions at the end of the year (because of tax-loss selling, perhaps) and an abundance of buyer-initiated transactions in the beginning of the new year (as investors rebalance their portfolios with substitute

[35] It is worth noting that in the United Kingdom, the size premium has been shown to be the largest during the month of May when it is equal to 2.45% (1.29% for the smallest portfolio minus −1.16% for the largest portfolio). This represents an annualized return of almost 30%. Interestingly, there is an old British maxim that says 'sell in May and go away'. Obviously the maxim applies to large rather than small firms.

[36] See also the related evidence on market 'overreaction' below in Section 4.1.

securities for the losers they sold in December), and this behavior tended to be particularly pronounced for small stocks (because the losers tend to be heavily populated in that sample), then the large returns we tend to see at the turn of the year could be due to a systematic movement from transactions occurring closer to the bid toward transactions that are closer to the ask. In other words, the turn-of-the-year effect for small stocks may be nothing more than a reflection of the bid–ask spread for these stocks — an artifact of the data. Keim [1989] investigates and confirms this conjecture for OTC National Market System stocks for the 1983–1988 period, and for NYSE and AMEX stocks for the 1988–89 turn-of-the-year period. However, even after adjusting for this 'bias' in returns, Keim still finds evidence of a significant turn-of-the-year effect for the sample period. That is, the prices on small stocks at the end of January are substantially higher than at the end of December.

3.3. *Patterns in returns around the turn of the month*

The monthly effect was found by Ariel [1987] who showed that for the period 1963 to 1981 the average returns for common stocks on the NYSE and AMEX are positive only for the last trading day of the month and for the trading days during the first half of the month. This statement is true even if the large returns around the turn of the year are removed from the sample. During the latter half of the month returns are indistinguishable from zero. Ariel concludes that during his sample period 'all of the market's cumulative advance occurred around the first half of the month, the second half contributing nothing to the cumulative increase'. Results in Lakonishok & Smidt [1988] for the 30 stocks in the Dow Jones Index for the period extending back to 1897 tend to confirm Ariel's finding. Although Ariel is unable to explain the finding, one potential explanation involves portfolio rebalancing of individual and institutional investors related to cash infusions from month-end salaries and contributions (see Ritter [1988] and Ritter & Chopra [1989] for a discussion of these effects at the turn of the year). Results from Japan lend some credence to this story. Ziemba [1991] shows that the index of the 225 stocks listed on the first section of the Tokyo Stock Exchange have significantly higher average returns between day −5 (zero being the beginning of the month) and day +2. The turn-of-the-month effect may begin earlier in Japan because most salaries in Japan are paid on days 20 to 25 of the month with the 25th being the most popular. In the United States most salaries tend to be paid on day −1.

3.4. *Patterns in returns around holidays*

Ariel [1990] finds that over one-third of the return accruing to the index of all stocks on the NYSE and AMEX over the period from 1963 to 1982 was earned on the trading days preceding the eight holidays that result in market closings each year.[37] The finding holds even if New Years day is excluded. Lakonishok

[37] These holidays are New Years, President's Day, Good Friday, Memorial Day, Independence Day, Labor Day, Thanksgiving, and Christmas.

& Smidt [1988] confirm Ariel's findings back to 1897 for the 30 stocks in the Dow Jones Industrial Average. For the Japanese index described in Section 3.3, Ziemba [1991] finds that the average return is +0.31% ($t = 3.10$) before holidays, significantly larger than the average return on the other days. There is a strong holiday effect in Japan on April 28 (with an average daily return of 0.22%); May 2 (0.54%) and May 4 (0.33%). These are the three days preceding the three holidays occurring during the so-called Golden Week on April 29, May 3 and May 5.

4. Time series return predictability: return autocorrelations

Most early work studying the efficiency of the stock market presumed an equilibrium model of stock prices in which expected returns are constant through time (prices follow a 'random walk'). The constant expected returns model implies that if the market is efficient price changes are unpredictable so that the past history of price changes is not informative for the prediction of future price changes. Researchers have examined this notion of market efficiency by testing whether return autocorrelations are equal to zero. We examine the evidence on stock return autocorrelations first for individual securities and then for portfolios.

4.1. Individual security return autocorrelations

In an early examination of return autocorrelations, Fama [1965] examined the autocorrelation of *daily* returns for the individual Dow Jones 30 industrial stocks. He found that 75% of the Dow 30 stocks had significantly positive autocorrelations in the 1957–1962 period. Foerster & Keim [1992] update these results for the 1963 to 1990 period and find that 80% are significantly positive. Although the Dow 30 is a limited sample of relatively homogeneous stocks, they are nevertheless an interesting sample because (1) they represent a sample of stocks widely followed by analysts and other market observers, (2) they are among the most actively traded of all stocks, and, as a result, (3) they have relatively tight bid–ask spreads. Since the Dow 30 stocks also have relatively high prices, they are less subject to potential bid–ask-related biases that might influence estimated returns and, therefore, autocorrelations.[38] Based on the evidence for these very liquid, actively-

[38] In addition to the inferential problems associated with the joint nature of such tests, there are biases and other microstructure-related effects that may induce 'artificial' serial dependencies into returns. For example, Niederhoffer & Osborne [1966] find that successive trades tend to occur alternatively at the bid and then the ask, resulting in negative serial correlation in returns at short frequencies. Indeed, it is this bid–ask bounce that motivated Roll [1984] and others to exploit this negative serial dependency to estimate the (unobservable) effective bid–ask spread. Thus, this negative serial dependency at short frequencies may mask the true underlying process governing price behavior. Such effects will have a larger impact on estimated returns and autocorrelations for smaller stocks which have lower prices and, consequently, for which the bid–ask spread represents a larger percentage of price.

researched stocks, we are left with the impression of an underlying positive serial dependency in stock returns.

French & Roll [1986] computed autocorrelations for all NYSE and AMEX stocks and found that the *daily* autocorrelations are on average negative for exchange-traded stocks. They find, however, that the estimated autocorrelations are inversely related to the market capitalization of the stock: smallest stock autocorrelations are the most negative, and the stocks in the largest decile of market capitalization have positive autocorrelations on average. This latter finding confirms the results above for the Dow 30, while the former result may be a reflection of the influence of a bid–ask bounce discussed in footnote 38.[39]

In most of these studies, the predictable component of returns explains a trivial percentage of total return variability (typically less than 1%). Lo & MacKinlay [1988], who find that *weekly* returns are negatively autocorrelated across all firm sizes, also conclude that the serial correlation is both economically and statistically insignificant.[40] They concur with previous studies that the idiosyncratic variability of individual stocks overwhelms the predictable component. Lehman [1990] directly tests the economic significance of the negative weekly autocorrelations by examining the profitability of a trading rule based on this price pattern. Based on his evidence he concludes that the trading rule is profitable for certain market participants, but his assumption regarding the magnitude of the trading costs necessary to implement the strategy may not fully account for the costs relevant for most market participants. In addition, Conrad, Gultekin & Kaul [1991] replicate Lehman's experiment with closing bid quotes rather than with transaction prices and find that the profits are indistinguishable from zero.

Blume & Friend [1978, p. 170–171], Keim [1983a] and Jegadeesh [1990] find evidence of significant negative autocorrelation using *monthly* returns. In contrast to the above studies that estimate serial correlations, however, these studies estimate cross-sectional regressions like (2) using individual securities, but with the lagged returns as independent variables. Keim & Jegadeesh also control for the size effect when estimating the coefficients. The return 'reversals' they document are, therefore, unlikely to be due to biases related to bid–ask spreads.

The research on return reversals that has had the largest impact on both academics and practitioners is the work of De Bondt & Thaler [1985, 1987]. De Bondt and Thaler examine longer-horizon returns and find that NYSE stocks identified as the biggest losers (winners) over a 3- to 5-year period have the highest (lowest) market-adjusted returns on average over the following period. De Bondt and Thaler attribute the predictability to market 'overreaction' in which

[39] Solnik [1973] finds significant negative autocorrelation of daily returns for the majority of stocks trading on exchanges in Belgium, France, Germany, Italy, Netherlands and the United Kingdom. Lawrence [1986] reports significant negative daily autocorrelations for 31% of the stocks trading on the Kuala Lumpur exchange and 79% of the stocks trading on the Singapore exchange. Butler & Malaikah [1992] report that 36% and all of the stocks trading on the Kuwaiti and Saudi stock markets, respectively, exhibit significant negative daily autocorrelations.

[40] Cootner [1964] earlier found evidence of negative autocorrelation for weekly stock price changes.

stock prices diverge from fundamental value because of (irrational) waves of optimism or pessimism before returning eventually to fundamental values.[41] These findings have generated many contrarian investment strategies whose profitability is predicated on such negatively autocorrelated price changes.[42]

There may be no free lunch, though. Chan [1988] and Ball & Kothari [1989] argue that the abnormal risk-adjusted returns reported for contrarian investment strategies are due to inadequate adjustment for risk. That is, a loser firm whose stock price (and therefore market capitalization) has declined, in the absence of a concomitant decline in the value of the debt, becomes more leveraged and, other things equal, more risky. Traditional methods for computing risk may underestimate the priced risk for these firms and, therefore, overstate the abnormal return. In this vein, Zarowin [1989] shows that loser firms tend to be small firms and winner firms tend to be large firms. After controlling for the size effect, Zarowin finds insignificant evidence of contrarian profits. In contrast to these studies, Chopra, Lakonishok & Ritter [1992] find that after adjusting for size and beta there is an economically important overreaction effect, especially for small stocks. Chopra, Lakonishok & Ritter find, though, that these contrarian profits are 'heavily concentrated in January', suggesting they are related to the January effect. They conclude that their findings are not due to tax-loss selling, but the prominent role played by small stocks in the findings suggests that the buying and selling behavior of individual investors may be important. Clearly, more work is needed to sort out these issues.

4.2. Portfolio return autocorrelations

Because of variance reduction obtained from diversification, portfolio returns provide more powerful tests of the ability of past returns to predict future returns. However, this increased power may be offset by biases and induced autocorrelation caused by the nontrading of securities contained in the portfolios. Fisher [1966] shows that infrequent trading will result in significant portfolio autocorrelation, which will be more serious for portfolios that contain less-frequently traded stocks [see also Hawawini, 1978, 1980b]. Scholes & Williams [1977], Dimson [1979] and Cohen, Hawawini, Maier & Schwartz [1983] develop models of the return process in which OLS estimates of beta computed with returns measured over a short (such as daily) interval will contain a bias related to the degree of nontrading of the stocks in the index.

The extent to which such effects surface in the data became evident in the early 1980s with the accumulation of evidence on the size effect. Reinganum [1981], Roll [1981], Keim [1983b] and others report significant positive autocorrelations (in the vicinity of 0.4) for the daily returns of portfolios composed of small,

[41] See also Poterba & Summers [1988] and De Long, Schleifer, Summers & Waldman [1990].

[42] Jegadeesh & Titman [1993] find, however, that a strategy of buying stocks that have recently performed well and selling stocks that have performed poorly generates significant positive returns over 3- to 12-month holding periods. They argue that such price behavior is consistent with positive-feedback trading.

infrequently-traded stocks. It is plausible that such autocorrelation may merely reflect information being revealed in prices of infrequently-traded shares with a lag due to their infrequent trading, thereby imparting serial correlation in the returns of portfolio that contain small, infrequently-traded shares. However, Lo & MacKinlay [1990a] develop a model of nontrading and conclude that, given plausible levels of nontrading, the model cannot explain the level of autocorrelation found in the data. In addition, recent evidence in Foerster & Keim [1992] on actual levels of nontrading finds that periods when nontrading is highest do not correspond to periods during which daily autocorrelations are largest.

There is also evidence of significant and mostly positive autocorrelations in the daily returns of stock market indexes around the world. For example, in the United Kingdom, the Financial Times All Share Index (a value-weighted index) exhibited significantly positive lag-one autocorrelation in daily returns (0.19) but insignificant positive lag-one monthly autocorrelations (0.13) during the period 1965–1989 [Poon & Taylor, 1992]. Baily, Stulz & Yen [1990] provide evidence of lag-one autocorrelations for indexes of several Pacific-Basin stock markets during the period 1977 to 1985: 0.21 in Australia; 0.06 in Hong Kong; 0,21 in Singapore; 0.30 in Thailand; −0.08 in Taiwan; and −0.09 in Korea (all significantly different from zero). In the case of Japan, Kishimoto [1990] reports a significant daily autocorrelation for the Topix Index (a composite index of all stocks traded on the Tokyo Stock Exchange) for the period 1949–1988.

Recent evidence indicates that daily index autocorrelations have declined during the 1980s. Froot & Perold [1990] and Foerster & Keim [1992] report that daily autocorrelations of returns of portfolios of both large and small stocks are insignificantly different from zero in the last half of the 1980s. In fact, for several short subperiods daily autocorrelations were negative. Froot–Perold and Foerster–Keim suggest that the introduction of index futures contracts and the initiation of new institutional trading practices (program trading, the proliferation of index portfolio management) during this period led to higher correlation of closing prices across stocks (due to increased trading in baskets of stocks) resulting in *portfolio bid–ask bounce*. This induced negative autocorrelation may offset any underlying autoregressive component in returns, resulting in lower (negative) daily autocorrelations. Brenner, Subrahmanyam & Uno [1990] and Kishimoto [1990] find a similar decline in the daily autocorrelations of the Nikkei Stock Average and the Topix Index after September 1988 when futures contracts on these indexes were introduced.

Because of the potential statistical problems associated with measuring autocorrelations of daily portfolio returns, many researchers shifted their focus to longer-interval returns. Since even the smallest firms on the NYSE or AMEX rarely go more than several days without trading, such biases will unlikely contaminate returns measured over intervals of a week or longer. Lo & MacKinlay [1988] examine weekly returns and find evidence of positive autocorrelation that is strongest for the portfolio of smallest stocks (0.42) and weakest for the portfolio of largest stocks (0.14). To determine whether the autocorrelation results for weekly returns are influenced by nontrading biases, Conrad & Kaul [1988] compute portfolio autocorrelations using weekly returns that were computed only with prices that were the result of actual transactions (i.e., stocks that didn't trade were excluded). Their results are very similar to Lo & MacKinlay, suggesting that significant positive weekly autocorrelations are not attributable to nontrading. That the relation between autocorrelations and the size of the firms in the portfolio is not due to nonsynchronous or infrequent trading is reinforced by the results for monthly returns in Keim & Stambaugh [1986]. They find the same relation between market capitalization and autocorrelations for monthly portfolio returns, although it is weaker than the evidence for shorter-interval returns. Over the 1928–1978 period the return autocorrelation for the portfolio comprising the smallest (largest) quintile of market capitalization was 0.17 (0.13).

Cohen, Hawawini, Maier & Schwartz [1983] and Lo & MacKinlay [1990a] develop models of the return-generating process in which positive autocorrelation in portfolio returns is in large part due to significant cross-autocorrelations between securities exhibiting differing degrees of nontrading. Like Roll [1981], Reinganum [1982] and other early research on the size effect that finds lagged values of the return on the market predict subsequent returns on small firm portfolio returns, Lo & MacKinlay find that returns of large-stock (very liquid) portfolios lead the returns of small-stock (less liquid) portfolios. The important contribution of their paper though is the reconciliation of the seemingly paradoxical coexistence of positive portfolio autocorrelations and negative individual stock autocorrelations. They demonstrate that portfolio returns may be significantly autocorrelated even if individual security return autocorrelations are negative (or zero): since the autocorrelation of portfolio returns is the sum of individual security autocovariances and cross-autocovariances, if the cross-autocovariances are sufficiently large relative to the autocovariances, they will overshadow the contribution of the autocovariances [see also Hawawini, 1978, 1980b].

The evidence suggests that, in contrast to individual security autocorrelations, short-horizon portfolio return autocorrelations are statistically significant. However, the estimated autocorrelations are small enough (for example, at the monthly level) that they may not be economically significant. Is the evidence sufficient to reject the joint hypothesis of market efficiency and the model of constant expected returns? If we reject, we are again faced with the standard inferential dilemma: do we interpret the rejection as a rejection of the model in favor of an alternative of time-varying expected returns? or as a violation of the efficient market hypothesis? However, Summers [1986] argues that such tests lack power to reject the null against interesting (controversial) alternative models. For example, Summers [1986] presents a model featuring irrational behavior of market participants where security prices (in aggregate) take long and wide swings from fundamental values, yet this irrationality will not be detectable in tests using short horizon returns (as described above). Stambaugh [1986] concurs with Summers that a uniformly powerful test exists only in the dreams of statisticians. More importantly, though, Stambaugh points out that such security price behavior would manifest itself in significant negative autocorrelations at longer return horizons and he provides some supporting evidence of negative first-order autocorrelations (−0.31) for 5-year S&P 500 returns.

A number of subsequent papers examined the autocorrelation of long-horizon portfolio returns in more detail. For example, Fama & French [1988a] find a U-shaped pattern of autocorrelations as a function of return horizon extending out to 10 years. The largest departures from zero are the estimated autocorrelations of −0.25 to −0.45 for 3- to 5-year returns. However, these strong negative autocorrelations are largely due to the 1926–1936 period which is centered on the stock market crash of 1929. Poterba & Summers [1988] also find evidence of negative autocorrelation in long horizon returns for the longer 1871–1985 period for the annual S&P composite index, backdated to 1871 using the Cowles data as reported in Wilson & Jones [1987]. However, Richardson [1991] shows that data generated by a random walk will naturally induce the type of U-shaped pattern in the autocorrelation observed in the stock price data.

In the end, although the autocorrelation tests for both short- and long-horizon returns are suggestive of time variation in expected returns, the statistical shortcomings of the tests prevent clean inferences. Small sample sizes impair the power of the tests using long horizon returns. In the tests using short-horizon returns, lagged returns have marginal explanatory power. However, there is a more fundamental problem: the variation in expected returns that we try to predict represent only a small component of the total variation in returns. As Fama [1991] points out, past returns do indeed contain information about expected returns, but they are a very noisy signal. A more powerful test should exploit explanatory variables that contain more precise information about expected returns. We turn now to such tests.

5. Time series return predictability: forecasting with ex-ante observable variables

There is a rapidly-growing body of research that has documented the ability of predetermined variables to predict returns. In the earliest work along these lines, researchers [e.g., Bodie, 1976; Jaffe & Mandelker, 1976; Nelson, 1976; and Fama & Schwert, 1977] uncovered a negative relation between short-horizon (monthly) stock returns and expected inflation during the post-1953 period.[43] However, the explanatory power of expected inflation does not generalize to other assets, and even for stocks it is quite low (less than 3%).

More recent research has focused on variables designed to proxy for the expected risk premium in the stock and bond markets using variables related to the current level of asset prices. The idea is that since asset prices are the discounted values of expected future cash flows, where the discount rate is the expected risk premium, changes in asset price levels convey information about the

[43] Fama & Schwert [1977] use the T-Bill yield as a measure of expected inflation and find a particularly strong correlation with stock returns in the post-1953 period. This correlation may be period-specific, however. Keim & Stambaugh [1986] show that this relation between stock returns and T-Bill yields is insignificant in the 1926–1952 period (see their footnote 2).

market's expectations about changing expected risk premiums. Keim & Stambaugh [1986] and Campbell [1987] use such variables to forecast monthly stock and bond returns. For example, Keim & Stambaugh [1986] use a variable that captures the level of small stock prices and a January dummy variable to forecast the returns on long-term government bonds, low- and high-grade corporate bonds and portfolios of NYSE stocks corresponding to quintiles based on market capitalization. They find that the combination of these variables reliably predicts returns across all the asset categories, explaining as much as 14% of the variation in returns in the 1953–1978 period. Keim and Stambaugh also point out that the coefficient on the price level variable is larger for corporate bonds than government bonds, for low-grade bonds than high-grade bonds, for stocks than bonds, and for small stocks than large stocks. This accords with intuition about generally increasing risk across these asset categories. Broadening the set of assets under consideration, Harvey [1991] finds that U.S. dividend yield and term structure variables predict monthly returns on a wide array of foreign common stock portfolios. Campbell & Hamao [1992] find similar evidence for Japanese and U.K. stocks. The common variation in expected returns across the asset categories and the ordering of the coefficients argues more for a time-varying expected returns explanation of the results than an inefficient market explanation.[44]

Other research examines longer-horizon returns. For example, Rozeff [1984] and Shiller [1984] investigate the explanatory power of dividend yields on annual stock returns. Rozeff finds that dividend yields explain 14% of the variation in the S&P composite index over the 1926–1981 period. Shiller also examines the predictability of annual S&P composite returns and finds that dividend yields explain nearly 16% of the variation in the 1946–1983 period. Shiller also finds predictive ability of ratios of earnings to price ($R^2 = 0.106$) in the 1946–1983 period. Shiller reports, however, that both dividend yields and earnings yields have very little predictive power in the 1898–1945 period. Additional research finds that the predictive power of dividend yields and earnings yields increases with the length of the return horizon [Campbell & Shiller, 1988, and Fama & French, 1988b]. For example, Fama & French [1988b] report that dividend yields explain about 25% of the variation in 2- to 4-year returns.

6. Concluding remarks

Research in finance over the past ten to fifteen years has revealed stock price behavior that is inconsistent with the predictions of familiar models. Some of the evidence argues reasonably convincingly for alternatives to existing paradigms — in particular the evidence on cross-sectional predictability based on variables like size, E/P and P/B. Indeed, many authors argue that the findings provide support for multi-factor alternatives to the CAPM like the models of Ross [1976]

[44] Fama & French [1989] find similar results for long-horizon returns across similar asset categories and draw similar inferences.

or Merton [1973]. One of the most significant contributions of this entire line of research is that it has sharpened our focus on potential alternative sources of risk, and future theoretical work should certainly benefit. On the other hand, there are at least two reasons why it is difficult to argue that the evidence constitutes proof that the CAPM is 'wrong'. First, there is Roll's conjecture that such evidence cannot be considered a violation of the CAPM since we can never measure the market portfolio and, hence, cannot test the model. Second, no one has yet conclusively shown that variables like size, E/P and P/B are not simply proxies for measurement error in betas. Are we certain, for example, that variation in ratios of P/B is not picking up variation in leverage which is not reflected in OLS betas that are typically estimated with sixty months of prior (stale) prices? The book is not closed — we think that more research is necessary to resolve these issues.

The research on time series predictability, as a whole, is convincing evidence that expected returns are not constant through time. That most asset pricing models allow for time-varying expected returns renders these results quite appealing; anyway, constant expected returns is a rather confining characterization of stock returns. Some of the temporal patterns in returns — in particular those relating to calendar turning points — are more troubling than others since they defy economic (rational) interpretations. For example, we can sensibly tell a business conditions story about time variation in expected returns, but the institutionally-oriented stories that have been advanced for the calendar-related patterns are harder to swallow since they often (always) require irrational market participants.

Finally, there is the question of believability. That is, is the evidence as robust as the sheer quantity of results would lead us to believe? First, there is the issue of data snooping — many of the papers described above were predicated on previous research that documented the same findings with the same data. Degrees of freedom are lost at each turn, and several authors [Merton, 1985; Lakonishok & Smidt, 1988; and Lo & MacKinlay, 1990b] have warned about adjusting tests of significance for these lost degrees of freedom. Also, the existence of these patterns in our laboratory experiments does not necessarily imply that they exist in the returns of implementable portfolios — that is, returns net of transactions costs. For example, market illiquidity and transactions costs may render a small stock strategy infeasible. Day of the week and other seasonal effects may have practical value only for those investors who were planning to trade (and pay transactions costs) in any event. Finally, that many of these effects have persisted for nearly 100 years in no way guarantees their persistence into the future. How many years of data are necessary to construct powerful tests? Research over the next 100 years will hopefully settle many of these issues.

Acknowledgements

We thank Ted Aronson, Fischer Black, Steve Foerster, Ken French, Bruce Grundy, Ananth Madhavan, Terry Marsh, Matt Richardson, Jay Ritter, Richard

Stehle, Bill Ziemba and participants at the Fall 1992 Berkeley Program in Finance and the Spring 1993 CRSP Seminar for helpful comments and suggestions.

References

Aggarwal, R., T. Hiraki and R. Rao (1988). Earning/price ratios, size, and seasonal anomalies in the Japanese Securities market, working paper, John Carroll University, University Heights, Ohio.

Aggarwal, R., R. Rao and T. Hiraki (1989). Price/book value ratios and equity returns on the Tokyo Stock Exchange: An empirical study, working paper, John Carroll University, University Heights, Ohio.

Aggarwal, R., R. Rao ant T. Hiraki (1990). Equity return regularities based on the price/sales ratio: An empirical study of the Tokyo Stock Exchange, in: S.G. Rhee and R.P. Chang (eds.), *Pacific-Basin Capital Markets Research*, Vol. I, North Holland, Amsterdam.

Amihud, Y., and H. Mendelson (1986). Asset pricing and the bid–ask spread. *J. Financ. Econ.*, 17 (December), 223–250.

Arbel, A., and P. Strebel (1982). The neglected and small firm effects. *Financ. Rev.* 17, 201–218.

Ariel, R.A. (1987). A monthly effect in stock returns *J. Financ. Econ.* 18, 161–74.

Ariel, R.A. (1990). High stock returns before holidays: Existence and evidence on possible causes. *J. Finance*, 45(5), December, 1611–1626.

Baily, W., R.M. Stulz and S. Yen (1990). Properties of daily stock returns from the Pacific Basin stock markets: Evidence and implications, in: S.G. Rhee and R.P. Chang (eds.), *Pacific-Basin Capital Markets Research*, Vol. I, North Holland, Amsterdam.

Ball, R. (1978). Anomalies in relationships between securities' yields and yield-surrogates. *J. Financ. Econ.* 6, 103–26.

Ball, R., and J. Bowers (1987). Daily Seasonals in Equity and Fixed-Interest Returns: Australian Evidence and Tests of Plausible Hypotheses, in: E. Dimson (ed.), *Stock Market Anomalies*, Cambridge University Press, Cambridge.

Ball, R., and S. Kothari (1989). Nonstationary expected returns: Implications for tests of market efficiency and serial correlation in returns. *J. Financ. Econ.* 25, 51–74.

Banz, R. (1981). The relationship between return and market value of common stock. *J. Financ. Econ.*, 9, 3–18.

Banz, R. (1985). Evidence of a size-effect on the London Stock Exchange, unpublished manuscript, INSEAD, Fontainebleau.

Banz, R., and Breen, W. (1986). Sample dependent results using accounting and market data: Some evidence. *J. Finance*, 41, 779–794.

Barnes, P. (1985). Thin trading and stock market efficiency: The case of the Kuala Lumpur Stock Exchange. *J. Bus. Finance Account.*, 12, 609–617.

Barry, C., and Brown, S. (1984). Differential information and the small firm effect. *J. Financ. Econ.*, 13, 283–294.

Basu, S. (1977). Investment performance of common stocks in relation to their price–earnings ratio: A test of the efficient market hypothesis. *J. Finance*, 32, 663–682.

Basu, S. (1983). The relationship between earning's yield, market value and the returns for NYSE common stocks: Further evidence. *J. Financ. Econ.* 12, 129–156.

Berges, A., McConnell, J., and Schlarbaum, G. (1984). The turn of the year in Canada. *J. Finance*, 39, 185–192.

Van den Bergh, W., and R. Wessels (1985). Stock market seasonality and taxes: An examination of the tax-loss selling hypothesis; *J. Bus. Finance Account.*, 12, 515–530.

Berglund, T. (1985). Anomalies in stock returns in a thin security market: The case of the Helsinki Stock Exchange, doctoral thesis, The Swedish School of Economics and Business Administration, Helsinki.

Black, F. (1972). Capital market equilibrium with restricted borrowing. *J. Bus.*, 45, 444–455.

Black, F., M. Jensen and M. Scholes (1972). The capital asset pricing model: Some empirical tests, in: M. Jensen (ed.), *Studies in the Theory of Capital Markets*, Praeger, New York, NY.

Black, F., and M. Scholes (1974). The effects of dividend yield and dividend policy on common stock prices and returns. *J. Financ. Econ.* 1, 1–22.

Blume, M.E. (1980). Stock returns and dividend yields: Some more evidence. *Rev. Econ. Stat.* 62, 567–77.

Blume, M.E., and I. Friend (1973). A new look at the capital asset pricing model. *J. Finance* 28, 19–33.

Blume, M.E., and I. Friend (1978). *The Changing Role of the Individual Investor*, Wiley, New York, NY.

Blume, M.E., and F. Husic (1973). Price, beta and exchange listing. *J. Finance* 28, 283–99.

Blume, M.E., and J.J. Siegel (1992). The theory of security pricing and market structure, *Financial Markets, Institutions and Instruments* 1,1–57.

Blume, M.E., and R.F. Stambaugh (1983). Biases in computed returns: An application to the size effect. *J. Financ. Econ.* 12, 387–404.

Bodie, Z. (1976). Common stocks as a hedge against inflation. *J. Finance* 31, 459–70.

Breen, W.J., and R.A. Korajczyk (1993). On selection biases in book-to-market based tests of asset pricing models, working paper, Northwestern University.

Brennan, M.J. (1970). Taxes, market valuation, and corporate financial policy. *Nat. Tax J.* 23, 417–27.

Brenner, M., M.G. Subrahmanyam and J. Uno (1990). The volatility of the Japanese stock indices: Evidence from the cash and futures market, working paper, NYU.

Brown, P., D. Keim, A. Kleidon and T. Marsh (1983). Stock return seasonalities and the tax-loss selling hypothesis: Analysis of the arguments and Australian evidence. *J. Financ. Econ.* 12, 105–128.

Brown, P., A. Kleidon and T. Marsh (1983). New evidence on the nature of size-related anomalies in stock prices. *J. Financ. Econ.* 12, 33–56.

Butler, K.C., and S.J. Malaikah (1992). Efficiency and inefficiency in thinly traded stock markets: Kuwait and Saudi Arabia. *J. Banking Finance* 16, 197–210.

Calvet, A., and J. Lefoll (1989). Risk and return on Canadian capital markets: Seasonality and size effect. *Finance*, 10, 21–39.

Campbell, J.Y. (1987). Stock returns and the term structure. *J. Financ. Econ.* 18, 373–400.

Campbell, J.Y., and Y. Hamao (1992). Predictable stock returns in the U.S., and Japan: A study of long-term capital market integration. *J. Finance* 47, 43–72.

Campbell, J.Y., and R.J. Shiller (1988). Stock prices, earnings and expected dividends. *J. Finance* 43, 661–76.

Capaul, C., I. Rowley and W.F. Sharpe (1993). International value and growth stock returns. *Financ. Analysts J.* 49(1), 27–36.

Chan, K.C. (1988). On the contrarian investment strategy. *J. Bus.* 61, 147–63.

Chan, K.C., and N.F. Chen (1988). An unconditional asset-pricing test and the role of firm size as an instumental variable for risk. *J. Finance* 43, 309–325.

Chan, L.K.C., Y. Hamao and J. Lakonishok (1991). Fundamentals and stock returns in Japan. *J. Finance* 46, 1739–1764.

Chopra, N., J. Lakonishok and J.R. Ritter (1992). Measuring abnormal returns: Do stocks overreact? *J. Financ. Econ.* 31, 235–268.

Chou, S.-R., and K. Johnson (1990). An empirical analysis of stock market anomalies: Evidence from the Republic of China in Taiwan, in: S.G. Rhee and R.P. Chang (eds.), *Pacific-Basin Capital Markets Research*, Vol. I, North Holland, Amsterdam.

Coghlan, H.A. (1988). Small firms versus large on the Irish Stock Exchange: An analysis of the performances 1977–86. *Irish Bus. Adm. Res.*, 9, 10–20.

Cohen, K.J., G.A. Hawawini, S.F. Maier and R.A. Schwartz (1983). Friction in the trading process and the estimation of systematic risk. *J. Financ. Econ.* 12, 263–78.

Condoyanni, L., J. O'Hanlon and C.W.R. Ward (1987). Day of the week effect on stock returns: International evidence. *J. Bus. Finance Account.*, 14, 159–174.

Condoyanni, L., J. O'Hanlon and S. McLeay (1989). An investigation of daily seasonality in the Greek Equity Market, in: R. Guimaraes, B. Kingsman and S. Taylor (eds.), *A Reappraisal of the Efficiency of Financial Markets,* NATO ASI Series, Springer-Verlag.

Conrad, J., and G. Kaul (1988). Time variation in expected returns. *J. Bus.* 61, 409–25.

Conrad, J., M. Gultekin and G. Kaul (1991). Profitability and riskiness of contrarian portfolio strategies, working paper, University of North Carolina, Chapel Hill.

Cook, T.J., and M.S. Rozeff (1984). Size and earnings/price anomalies: One effect or two?. *J. Financ. Quant. Anal.* 13, 449–66.

Cootner, P.H., ed. (1964). *The Random Character of Stock Market Prices*, MIT Press, Cambridge, MA.

Corhay, A., G. Hawawini and P. Michel (1987). The pricing of equity on the London Stock Exchange: Seasonality and size premium, in: E. Dimson (ed.), *Stock Market Anomalies*, Cambridge University Press, Cambridge.

Corhay, A. (1991). Daily seasonalities on the Brussels Spot Equity Market. *Cah. Econ. Bruxelles*, 132, 415–430.

Corniolay C., and J. Pasquier (1991). CAPM, risk premium seasonality and the size anomaly: The Swiss case (in French). *Finance* (J. French Finance Assoc.) 12(1), 23–44.

Cross, F. (1973). The behavior of stock prices on Fridays and Mondays. *Financ. Anal. J.* 29, 67–9.

De Bondt, W.F.M., and R.H. Thaler (1985). Does the stock market overreact?; *J. Finance* 40, 793–805.

De Bondt, W.F.M., and R.H. Thaler (1987). Further evidence on investor overreactions and stock market seasonality. *J. Finance* 42, 557–81.

De Long, J.B., A. Shleifer, L.H. Summers and R.J. Waldmann (1990). Positive feedback investment strategies and destabilizing rational speculation. *J. Finance* 45, 379–95.

Dimson, E. (1979). Risk measurement when shares are subject to infrequent trading. *J. Financ. Econ.*, 7(2), 197–226.

Dimson, E. (1988). *Stock Market Anomalies*, Cambridge University Press, Cambridge.

Dimson, E. and P. Marsh (1986). Event study methodologies and the size effect: The case of U.K. Press recommendations. J. Financ. Econ 17(1), 113–142.

Fama, E.F. (1965). The behavior of stock-market prices. *J. Bus.* 38, 34–105.

Fama, E. (1970). Efficient capital market: A review of theory and empirical work. *J. Finance*, 25, 382–417

Fama, E.F. (1991). Efficient capital market, II. *J. Finance* 46, 1575–1617.

Fama, E.F., and M.E. Blume (1966). Filter rules and stock-market trading, *J. Bus.* 39, 226–41.

Fama, E.F., and K. French (1988a). Permanent and temporary components of stock prices. *J. Polit. Econ.* 96, 246–73.

Fama, E.F., and K. French (1988b). Dividend yields and expected stock returns. *J. Financ. Econ.* 22, 3–25.

Fama, E.F., and K. French (1989). Business conditions and expected returns on stocks and bonds. *J. Financ. Econ.* 25, 23–49.

Fama, E.F., and K. French (1992). The cross section of expected stock returns. *J. Finance* 47, 427–466.

Fama, E.F., K.R. French, D.G. Booth and R. Sinquefield (1993). Differences in the risks and returns of NYSE and NASD Stocks. *Financ. Analysts J.* 49(1), 37–41.

Fama, E., and J. MacBeth (1973). Risk, return and equilibrium: Empirical tests. *J. Polit. Econ.*, 71, 607–636.

Fama, E.F., and W. Schwert (1977). Asset returns and inflation. *J. Financ. Econ.*, 5, 115–146.

Foerster, S., and D.B. Keim (1992). Direct evidence of non-trading and implications for daily return autocorrelations, unpublished manuscript, University of Pennsylvania.

Fisher, L. (1966). Some new stock-market indices. *J. Bus.* 39, 191–225.

Frantzmann, H.-J. (1988). Return and pricing seasonalities in the German stock market, working paper, Institut für Entscheidungstheorie, University of Karlsruhe.

French, K. (1980). Stock returns and the weekend effect. *J. Financ. Econ.*, 8, 55–69.

French, K.R., and J.M. Poterba (1991). Were Japanese stock prices too high? *J. Financ. Econ.* 29, 337–364.

French, K., and R. Roll (1986). Stock return variances: The arrival of information and the reaction of traders. *J. Financ. Econ.* 17, 5–26.

Froot, K., and A. Perold (1990). New trading practices and short-run market efficiency, working paper no. 3498, NBER.

Gibbons, M., and P. Hess (1981). Day of the week effects and asset returns. *J. Bus.* 54, 579–596.

Gillan, S. (1990). An investigation into CAPM anomalies in New Zealand. The small firm and price earnings ratio effects. *Asia Pac. J. Manage.* 7, 63–78.

Graham, B., and D.L. Dodd (1940). *Security Analysis: Principles and Technique*, McGraw-Hill Book Company, Inc., New York, NY.

Gultekin, M., and B. Gultekin (1983). Stock market seasonality: International evidence. *J. Financ. Econ.*, 12, 469–482.

Hamon, J. (1986). The seasonal character of monthly returns on the Paris Bourse (in French). *Finance*, 7, 57–74.

Hamon, J., and B. Jacquillat (1991). Weekly and daily return seasonalities on the Paris Stock Exchange (in French). *Finance*, 12, 103–126.

Harris, L. (1986). A transaction data study of weekly and intradaily patterns in stock returns. *J. Financ. Econ.*, 16, 99–117.

Harvey, C. (1991). The world price of covariance risk. *J. Finance* 46, 111–157.

Haugen, R., and J. Lakonishok (1987). *The Incredible January Effect*, Dow Jones-Irwin, Homewood, IL.

Hawawini, G. (1978). Temporal aggregation and serial correlation. *Econ. Lett.*, 1, 237–242.

Hawawini, G. (1980a). Intertemporal cross dependence in securities daily returns and the short term intervalling effect on systematic risk. *J. Financ. Quant. Anal.*, 15, 139–149.

Hawawini, G. (1980b). The intertemporal cross price behavior of common stocks: Evidence and implications. *J. Financ. Res.* 3, 153–167.

Hawawini, G. (1983). Why beta shifts as the return interval changes. *Financ. Anal. J.*, 39, 73–77.

Hawawini, G. (1984). *European Equity Markets: Price Behavior and Efficiency*, Monograph Series in Finance and Economics, Salomon Brothers Center for the Study of Financial Institutions, New York University. NY.

Hawawini, G. (1991). Stock market anomalies and the pricing of equity on the Tokyo Stock Exchange, in: W.T. Ziemba, W. Bailey and Y. Hamao (eds.), *Japanese Financial Market Research*, North-Holland, Amsterdam.

Hawawini, G., P. Michel and A. Corhay (1989). A look at the validity of the capital asset pricing model in light of equity market anomalies: The case of Belgian common stocks, in: S. Taylor (ed.), *A Reappraisal of the Efficiency of Financial Markets*, NATO ASI Series, Springer-Verlag.

Hawawini, G., and C. Viallet (1987). Seasonality, size premium and the relationship between the risk and return of French common stocks, working paper, INSEAD and the Wharton School of the University of Pennsylvania.

Hess, P.J. (1983). Tests for tax effects in the pricing of financial assets. *J. Bus.* 56, 537–554.

Jacobs, B., and K. Levy (1988). Disentangling equity return regularities: New insights and investment opportunities. *Financ. Anal. J.* May–June, 18–43.

Jaffe, J., and G. Mandelker (1976). The Fisher effect for risky assets: An empirical investigation. *J. Finance*, 31, 447–458.

Jaffe, J., and R. Westerfield (1985a). The weekend effect in common stock returns: The international evidence. *J. Finance* 40, 433–454.

Jaffe, J., and R. Westerfield (1985b). Patterns in Japanese common stock returns: Day of the week and turn of the year effects. *J. Financ. Quant. Anal.*, 20, 261–272.

Jaffe, J., and R. Westerfield (1989). A twist effect on the monday effect in stock prices: Evidence from the US and foreign stock markets. *J. Banking Finance* 13, 641–650.

Jaffe, J., D.B. Keim and R. Westerfield (1989). Earnings yields, market values and stock returns. *J. Finance* 45, 135–148.

Jegadeesh, N. (1990). Evidence of predictable behavior of security returns. *J. Finance*, 45, 881–898.

Jegadeesh, N., and S. Titman (1993). Returns to buying winners and selling losers: Implications for stock market efficiency. *J. Finance* 48, 65–92.

Jones, S.L., W. Lee and R. Apenbrink (1991). New evidence on the January effect before personal income taxes. *J. Finance* 46, 1909–1924.

Kato, K., and J. Schallheim (1985). Seasonal and size anomalies in the Japanese stock market. *J. Financ. Quant. Anal.*, 20(2), 243–272.

Keim, D.B. (1983a). The interrelation between dividend yields, equity values and stock returns: Implications of abnormal January returns, unpublished dissertation, University of Chicago.

Keim, D.B. (1983b). Size-related anomalies and stock return seasonality: Further empirical evidence. *J. Financ. Econ.*, 12, 13–32.

Keim, D.B. (1985). Dividend yields and stock returns seasonality: Further empirical evidence. *J. Financ. Econ.*, 14, 473–490.

Keim, D.B. (1986). The capital asset pricing model and market anomalies. *Financ. Anal. J.*, 42, 19–34.

Keim, D.B. (1987). The daily returns-size connection. *J. Portfolio Manage.* 13(2), 41–47.

Keim, D.B. (1988). Stock market regularities: A synthesis of the evidence and explanations, in: E. Dimson (ed.), *Stock Market Anomalies*, Cambridge University Press, Cambridge, pp. 16–39.

Keim, D.B. (1989). Trading patterns, bid–ask spreads, and estimated security returns: The case of common stocks at calendar turning points. *J. Financ. Econ.* 25, 75–98.

Keim, D.B. (1990). A new look at the effects of firm size and E/P ratio on stock returns. *Financ. Analysts J.* 46(2), 56–67.

Keim, D.B., and R.F. Stambaugh (1984). A further investigation of the weekend effect in stock returns. *J. Finance* 39, 819–35.

Keim, D.B., and R.F. Stambaugh (1986). Predicting returns in the stock and bond markets. *J. Financ. Econ.* 17, 357–90.

Kim, S.W. (1988). Capitalizing on the weekend effect. *J. Portfolio Manage.* 14(3), 59–63.

Kim, Y.G., K.H. Chung and C.S. Pyun (1992). Size, price–earnings ratio, and seasonal anomalies in the Korean stock market, in: S.G. Rhee and R.P. Chang (eds.), *Pacific-Basin Capital Markets Research*, Vol. III, North Holland, Amsterdam.

Kishimoto, K. (1990). A new appraoch for testing the randomness of heteroscedastic time-series data, working paper, University of Tsukuba.

Kothari, S.P., J. Shanken and R.G. Sloan (1993). Another look at the cross-section of expected stock returns, working paper, University of Rochester.

Kuhn, T. (1970). *The Stucture of Scientific Revolutions*, University of Chicago Press, Chicago, IL.

Lakonishok, J., and E. Maberly (1990). The weekend effect: Trading patterns of individual and institutional investors. *J. Finance*, 45(1), 231–243.

Lakonishok, J., and M. Levi (1982). Weekend effects on stock returns: A note. *J. Finance*, 37, 569–588.

Lakonishok, J., and S. Smidt (1988). Are seasonal anomalies real? A ninety-year perspective. *Rev. Financ. Studies* 1, 403–25.

Lawrence, M. (1986). Weak-form efficiency in the Kuala Lumpur and Singapore stock markets. *J. Banking Finance* 10, 431–445.

Lee, I. (1992). Stock market seasonality: Some evidence from the Pacific-Basin countries. *J. Bus. Finance Account.* 19, 200–210.

Lehmann, B.N. (1990). Fads, martingales, and market efficiency. *Q. J. Econ.* 105, 1–28.

Lehmann, B.N. (1991). Asset pricing and intrinsic values. *J. Monetary Econ.* 28, 485–500.

Levis, M. (1985). Are small firms big performers? *Invest. Anal.* 76, 21–27.

Levis, M. (1989). Market size, P/E ratios, dividend yield and share prices: The UK evidence, in: R.C. Guimaraes, B.G. Kingsman and S.J. Taylor (eds.), *A Reappraisal of the Efficiency of Financial Markets*, Springer-Verlag.

Lintner, J. (1965). The valuation of risk assets and the selection of risky investment in stock portfolios and capital budgets. *Rev. Econ. Stat.* 47, 13–37.

Litzenberger, R., and K. Ramaswamy (1979). The effects of personal taxes and dividends on capital asset prices: Theory and empirical evidence. *J. Financ. Econ.* 7(2),163–195.

Lo, A.W., and A.C. MacKinlay (1988). Stock market prices do not follow random walks: Evidence from a simple specification test. *Rev. Financ. Studies* 1, 41–66.

Lo, A.W., and A.C. Mackinlay (1990a). An econometric analysis of non-synchronous trading. *J. Econometrics* 45, 181–211.

Lo, A.W., and A.C. MacKinlay (1990b). Data snooping biases in tests of financial asset pricing models. *Rev. Financ. Studies* 3, 431–468.

Loughran, T. (1993). NYSE vs NASDAQ returns: Market microstructure or the poor performance of IPO's? *J. Financ. Econ.* 33, 241–260.

Louvet, P., and O. Taramasco (1991). The day-of-the-week effect on the Paris Stock Exchange: A transactional effect (in French), working paper, École Superieure des Affaires, Université des Sciences Sociales de Grenoble.

Ma T., and T.Y. Shaw (1990). The relationships between market value, P/E ratio, trading volume and the stock return of Taiwan Stock Exchange, in: S.G. Rhee and R.P. Chang (eds.), *Pacific-Basin Capital Markets Research*, Vol. I, North Holland, Amsterdam.

Mayers, D. (1972). Nonmarketable assets and capital market equilibrium under uncertainty, in: M.C. Jensen (ed.), *Studies in the Theory of Capital Markets*, Praeger, New York, NY.

Merton, R. (1973). An intertemporal capital asset pricing model. *Econometrica* 41, 867–887.

Merton, R. (1985). On the current state of the stock market rationality hypothesis, in: R. Dornbusch and S. Fischer (eds.), *Macroeconomics and Finance*, MIT Press, Cambridge, MA.

Miller, M., and M. Scholes (1982). Dividend and taxes: Some empirical evidence *J. Polit. Econ.* 90, 1118–41.

Mossin, J. (1966). Equilibrium in a capital asset market. *Econometrica* 34, 768–783.

Nakamura, T., and N. Terada (1984). The size effect and seasonality in Japanese stock returns, paper presented at the Institute for Quantitative Research in Finance (The Q Group).

Nelson, C. (1976). Inflation and rates of return on common stocks. *J. Finance*, 31, 471–483.

Nicholson, S.F. (1960). Price-earnings ratios. *Financ. Anal. J.* July/August, 43–50.

Niederhofer, V., and M.F.M. Osborne (1966). Market making and reversal on the stock exchange. *J. Am. Stat. Assoc.* 61, 897–916.

Peavy, J.W., and D.A. Goodman (1983). Industry-relative price-earnings ratios as indicators of investment returns. *Financ. Anal. J.* 39(4), 60–66.

Poon, S.H., and S.J.Taylor (1992). Stock returns and volatility: An empirical study of the U.K. stock market. *J. Banking Finance* 16, 37–59.

Poterba, J.M., and L.H. Summers (1988). Mean reversion in stock prices: Evidence and implications. *J. Financ. Econ.* 22, 27–60.

Reinganum, M. (1981). A misspecification of capital asset pricing: Empirical anomalies based on earnings yields and market values. *J. Financ. Econ.*, 9, 19–46.

Reinganum, M. (1982). A direct test of Roll's conjecture on the firm size effect. *J. Finance* 37, 27–35.

Reinganum, M. (1983). The anomalous stock market behavior of small firms in January: Empirical tests for tax-loss selling effects. *J. Financ. Econ.*, 12, 89–104

Reinganum, M. (1990). Market microstructure and asset pricing: an empirical investigation of NYSE and NASDAQ securities. *J. Financ. Econ.* 28, 127–148.

Reinganum, M., and A. Shapiro (1987). Taxes and stock return seasonality: Evidence from the London Stock Exchange. *J. Bus.*, 60(2), 281–295.

Richardson, M. (1991). Temporary components of stock prices: A skeptic's view, working paper, Wharton School.

Ritter, J. (1988). The buying and selling behavior of individual investors at the term of the year. *J. Finance*, 43, 701–717.

Ritter, J., and N. Chopra (1989). Portfolio rebalancing and the turn-of-the-year effect. *J. Finance*, 44(1), 149–166.

Roberts, H.V. (1959). Stock-market 'patterns' and financial analysis: Methodological suggestions. *J. Finance* 14, 1–10.

Rogalski, R. (1984). New findings regarding day of the week returns over trading and nontrading periods: A note. *J. Finance*, 29, 1257–1292.

Roll, R. (1977). A critique of the asset pricing theory's test: Part 1: On past and potential testability of the theory. *J. Financ. Econ.* 4, 129–176.

Roll, R. (1981). A possible explanation of the small firm effect. *J. Finance* 36, 879–888.

Roll, R. (1983). The turn of the year effect and the return premia of small firms, *J. Portfolio Manage.* 9, 18–28.

Roll, R. (1984). A simple implicit measure of the effective bid–ask spread in an efficient market. *J. Finance* 39, 1127–1139.

Rosenberg, B., and V. Marathe (1979). Tests of the capital asset pricing hypotheses, in: H. Levy (ed.), *Research in Finance*, JAI Press, Greenwich, CT.

Rosenberg, B., K. Reid and R. Lanstein (1985). Persuasive evidence of market inefficiency. *J. Portfolio Manage.* 11(3), 9–17.

Rozeff, M., and W. Kinney (1976). Capital market seasonality: The case of stock returns. *J. Financ. Econ.*, 3, 379–402.

Rozeff, M. (1984). Dividend yields are equity risk premiums. *J. Portfolio Manage.* 11, 68–75.

Rozeff, M. (1986). Tax-loss selling: Evidence from December stock returns and share shifts, in: *Proc. CRSP Seminar on the Analysis of Security Prices*, pp. 9–45.

Ross, S. (1976). The arbitrage theory of capital asset pricing. *J. Econ. Theory*, 13, 341–360.

Rubio, G. (1986). Size, liquidity and valuation, working paper.

Rubio G. (1988). Further international evidence on asset pricing: The case of the Spanish capital market. *J. Banking Finance*, 12, 221–242.

Samuelson, P. (1965). Proof that properly anticipated prices fluctuate ramdomly. *Ind. Manage. Rev.* 6, 49.

Santesmases, M. (1986). An investigation of the Spanish stock market seasonalities. *J. Bus. Finance Account.*, 13, 267–276.

Scholes, M., and J. Williams (1977). Estimating betas from non-synchronous data. *J. Financ. Econ.*, 5, 309–328.

Schultz, P. (1985). Personal income taxes and the January effect: Small firm stock returns before the War Revenue Act of 1917. *J. Finance* 40, 333–343.

Senchack, A., and J. Martin (1987). The relative performance of the PSR and the PER investment strategies. *Financ. Anal. J.* March–April, 46–56.

Sharpe, W. (1964). Capital asset prices: A theory of market equilibrium under conditions of risk. *J. Finance*, 19, 425–442.

Shiller, R.J. (1981). Do stock prices move too much to be justified by subsequent changes in dividends? *Am. Econ. Rev.* 71, 421–436.

Shiller, R.J. (1984). Stock prices and social dynamics. *Brookings Pap. Econ. Act.* 2, 457–510.

Smirlock, M., and L. Starks (1986). Day-of-the-week and intraday effects in stock returns. *J. Financ. Econ.* 17, 197–210.

Solnik, B. (1973). A note on the validity of the random walk for European prices. *J. Finance* 28, 1151–1159.

Stambaugh, R. (1982). On the exclusion of assets from the two-parameter model: A sensitivity analysis. *J. Financ. Econ.* 17, 237–268.

Stambaugh, R. (1986). Discussion of Summers paper. *J. Finance* 41, 601–602.

Stattman, D. (1980). Book values and expected stock returns, unpublished MBA Honors paper, University of Chicago.

Stehle, R. (1992). The size effect in the German stock market, unpublished manuscript, University of Augsburg.

Stoll, H., and R. Whaley (1983). Transactions costs and the small firm effect. *J. Financ. Econ.* 12, 57–80.

Summers, L.H. (1986). Does the stock market rationally reflect fundamental values?. *J. Finance* 41, 591–601.

Theobald, M., and V. Price (1984). Seasonality estimation in thin markets. *J. Finance*, 39, 377–392.

Treynor, J. (1961). Toward a theory of market value of risky assets, unpublished manuscript.

Wahlroos, B., and T. Berglund (1986). Risk, return and equilibrium returns in a small stock market. *J. Bus. Res.*, 14, 423–440.

Wilson, J.W., and C. Jones (1987). A comparison of annual common stock returns. *J. Bus.* 60, 239–58.

Wong, P.L., S.K. Neoh, K.H. Lee and T.H. Thong (1990). Seasonality in the Malaysian stock market. *Asia Pac. J. Manage.*, 7, 43–62.

Zarowin, P. (1989). Does the stock market overreact to corporate earnings information? *J. Finance*, 44, 1385–1399.

Ziemba, W.T. (1991). Japanese security market regularities. monthly, turn-of-the-month and year, holiday and Golden Week effects. *Japan World Econ.*, 3(2), 119–146.

Ziemba, W.T. (1992). Comment on 'Why a weekend effect?'. *J. Portfolio Manage.*, 93–99.

Ziemba, W.T., and S.L. Schwartz (1991). *Invest Japan*, Probus Publishing, Chicago, IL.

R. Jarrow et al., Eds., *Handbooks in OR & MS, Vol. 9*
1995 Elsevier Science B.V.

Chapter 18

Efficiency of Sports and Lottery Betting Markets

Donald B. Hausch
School of Business, University of Wisconsin, Madison, WI 53706, U.S.A.

William T. Ziemba
Faculty of Commerce and Business Administration, University of British Columbia, Vancouver, B.C. V6T 1Y8, Canada

1. Introduction

Economists have long been interested in the efficiency of financial markets.[1] In the 1960s the focus was on defining efficiency and performing tests for a range of efficiency notions. Roberts [1967] defined *weak*, *semi-strong*, and *strong* form efficiencies as holding when stock market prices reflect all price information, all publicly available information, and all information, respectively. Most financial markets have generally been shown to be efficient in the weak and semi-strong form, although not necessarily so in the strong sense (see Fama [1970] for a survey of this work). The exceptions, termed anomalies, include seasonal patterns such as the small firm January effect, turn-of-the-month and year effects, holiday effect, day of week, time of day, the Value Line enigma, and cross-sectional regularities that apply to stocks with low price to earnings ratios or with earnings surprises, etc. See the surveys by Hawawini & Keim [1995, chapter 17 in this volume] and Ziemba [1994] for more details.

Fama [1991] updated his earlier survey. Tests for return predictability focus on forecasting returns using variables such as interest rates and dividend yields. Event studies formalize the semi-strong form idea by testing whether or not there are adjustments of prices to specific public announcements. Finally, the strong form concept is studied through tests for private information. The evidence is that future returns are predictable from past returns, dividend yields and term structure variables. On the face of it, this is a violation of weak form efficiency. But, as suggested by Roll [1977], since every test of efficiency must be a joint one with a maintained equilibrium hypothesis of price formation (e.g., the capital asset or arbitrage pricing models), this violation is confounded by the joint hypothesis

[1] Academic work began with Kendall [1953], who examined the behavior of industrial share prices and spot prices for cotton and wheat. On the basis of an analysis of serial correlations, prices appeared to follow a random walk.

problem of whether there is a rational variation over time in expected returns or systematic deviations from fundamental value. While arguments can be made that increased returns may be occurring because of increased risk, which is difficult or impossible to measure accurately, there is very strong evidence that most or all of the gains in securities markets occur during the seasonally anomalous periods. Ritter & Chopra [1989] and Cadsby [1992] show, for example, that the only periods where risk as measured by the capital asset pricing model is rewarded with equity returns is precisely at the anomalous periods such as the day before holidays, the turn of the month, in the first two weeks of January for small stocks, etc. Ariel [1987], Lakonishok & Smidt [1988], and Hensel, Sick & Ziemba [1993] showed that all the stock market's gain during the 20th century in the U.S. occurred in the first half of the month. Event studies are more straightforward and less controversial since they are able to provide more clear cut evidence of the effect of new information. Regarding strong form tests there is considerable evidence that corporate insiders have private information that is not fully reflected in current prices.

Although sports and betting markets have received little attention relative to financial markets, they are well suited for testing market efficiency and bettor rationality. This is because vast amounts of data are available, in the form of prices (for devising *technical* systems) and other information (for devising *fundamental* systems), and each bet has a specified termination point when its final asset value is determined. For rationality tests, markets with this latter property offer an advantage over markets, like securities markets, where current value depends upon future events and current expectations of future values. Also, some wagering markets have characteristics that reduce the problematic nature of the aforementioned joint hypothesis test. For instance, Dana & Knetter [1994] note that pointspread bets on National Football League games all have identical risk and return characteristics, as well as similar horizons. This allows a test of efficiency without specifying the bettors' utility functions.

The special properties of sports betting and lotteries might lead one to speculate that they are even more efficient than financial markets. However, there is another aspect to these markets that confounds the notion of rationality: for them to be offered, the average bettor must lose. Indeed, given the transactions costs involved in these markets (e.g., about 20% for horseracing and about 50% for lotteries), the average losses are large. This has not stopped the search for profitable wagering systems, though, and there are some notable successes. For example, Thorp [1961, 1962] demonstrated that card-counters can win playing blackjack. This survey of research on horseracing, sports betting on football and basketball, and lotteries reports numerous studies of efficiency in these markets. Several profitable systems are also described, though.[2] The continued success of these winning systems tends to be related to some complicating factor in its development or execution. For instance, the system may involve short odds and complex probability estimation

[2] Beyond the academic work surveyed here, anecdotal evidence abounds of individuals who have successfully beaten the odds. See, for example, Akst [1989] and Beyer [1978].

(e.g. place and show wagering at the racetrack), it may rely on syndicates of bettors (e.g., cross-track horserace betting), it could require extremely long time horizons (e.g., lotteries), or extensive data collection and statistical work (e.g., fundamental handicapping systems for horseracing). The winning systems described are, of course, just a subset of the winning systems used in practice. The incentives to disclose details of a winning system may not be sufficient in some cases given that such an action typically reduces the system's profitability as others employ it. Finally, we also discuss optimal betting strategies for exploiting inefficiencies when they are present.

As mentioned, sports betting and lotteries involve substantial transactions costs. Because it directly affects prices, the *take* — what the gambling establishment keeps for its operation — is properly accounted for in all of the analyses discussed in this survey. Another cost in these markets is for information (e.g., tip sheets at the racetrack). Costly information requires a redefinition of efficiency, one where prices are said to reflect information to the point where the cost of additional information just equals the benefit of acting on that information. But because they are difficult to measure, this survey ignores information costs (and other transactions costs beyond the take). Thus, our general findings of efficiency gain further support with the introduction of these other costs.

Figure 1 provides a taxonomy for the types of games that we discuss. Games are classified by: 1) whether the chance of winning is purely luck or can be influenced with skill; and 2) whether the payoff upon winning is predetermined or can be improved with skill. Luck–luck games allow no possibility of discovering a profitable strategy, and so as markets are trivially efficient. On the other hand, there need not be a guarantee of efficiency for luck–skill games such as lotto (where we discuss a strategy of betting unpopular numbers, which does not affect the probability of winning but does affect the payoff upon winning) and skill–luck

		CHANCE OF WINNING	
		COMPLETE LUCK	SKILL INVOLVED
PAYOFF	COMPLETE LUCK	Scratch lottery games with fixed payment	Example: Pay $1 for a chance to pick all winners of hockey games on a particular day. From those who have all correct selections, one name is randomly drawn and awarded $100,000.
	SKILL INVOLVED	Lotto, such as 6/49, with some or all parimutuel payoffs	Sports pool games Horseracing Blackjack Sports betting

Fig. 1. Taxonomy of games. Source: adapted from Ziemba, Brumelle, Gautier & Schwartz [1986].

games (which are relatively uncommon). Blackjack, a skill–skill game, allows a profitable strategy. For horseracing, another skill–skill game, we review findings that certain forms of wagers are efficient while others are not.

Unlike most financial securities markets, the average lottery and sports betting participant must lose. We may, indeed, choose to differentiate gambling and investing by their expected returns, using the terms 'gambling' when the expected profit is negative and 'investing' when the expected profit, including all transactions costs and risk adjustments, is positive. Obviously a willingness to assume risk in the face of negative expected returns is inconsistent with the traditional assumptions that 1) individuals maximize the expected utility of wealth and 2) utility functions are concave, i.e., risk aversion. Instead of the second assumption, Friedman & Savage [1948] assumed a utility function that is convex in a neighborhood of the individual's present wealth but concave over higher and lower wealths. Given their different payoff distributions, simultaneously purchasing lottery tickets and insurance can be consistent with this form of a utility function. Markowitz [1952] offered a functional form that eliminates some behavior admitted by Friedman and Savage's form that is not generally observed. He also pointed to the possibility of a utility function that recognizes the 'fun' of gambling. Conlisk [1993] formalized this notion and found his model to be largely consistent with actual risk-taking behavior.

Other surveys on this topic include Clotfelter & Cook [1991] on lotteries, Thaler & Ziemba [1988] on horseracing and lotteries, Hausch & Ziemba [1992] on sports betting and lotteries, and Hausch, Lo & Ziemba [1994a] on horseracing.[3]

2. Extent of gambling in USA

The level of gambling in the U.S. is enormous. Welles [1989] estimates $240 billion as the total annual wagering by Americans, both legal and illegal; an amount that is growing at 10% per year. By 1992, the estimate is $329.9 billion including $29.9 billion of gross revenue for governments and gaming institutions, more than six times annual movie ticket sales in the U.S. [Kleinfield, 1993]. Table 1 presents gross gambling revenues from various gambling from 1985 to 1992. Parimutuel betting revenues have grown slowest while revenues from Indian gaming have dramatically risen.

Lotteries account for about one third of gross gambling revenues over this period. Table 2 provides, on a state-by-state basis, lottery sales, administrative costs, payback fraction, and average lottery sales per adult.

On average, the lottery returns only about 54% of sales. For parimutuel wagering, the average payback is about 80%, with the state government collecting usually only a few percent. That tax rate can vary across the tracks within a state, though. For example, the three major thoroughbred tracks in south Florida have

[3] Lane & Ziemba [1992] study hedging strategies for jai alai, a sport not considered in this survey.

Table 1

Gross gambling revenues from various gambling activities ($billions)

Year	Lotteries	Casinos [a]	Pari-mutuels [b]	Bingo [a]	Indian gaming	Total [c]
1985	5.2	5.5	3.1	0.91	0.09	15.4
1986	6.3	5.7	3.2	0.94	0.10	16.9
1987	6.6	6.4	3.3	0.90	0.11	18.3
1988	8.4	7.1	3.5	0.88	0.10	21.5
1989	9.6	7.7	3.6	0.95	0.30	24.0
1990	10.3	8.7	3.7	1.0	0.48	26.2
1991	10.2	9.0	3.7	1.1	0.72	26.7
1992	11.5	10.1	3.7	1.1	1.5	29.9

Source: Kleinfield [1993].
[a] Does not include Indian gaming.
[b] Includes horse and greyhound racing, jai alai, and off-track betting.
[c] Because of other forms of gambling, columns sum to less than the total column.

long feuded over the prime winter racing season when tourism is at a peak. Florida recently passed a bill that in 1994 granted the prime season to Gulfstream Park with a 3.0% state tax. Hialeah Park's season was taxed by the state at 1.15%, while Calder's tax was 2.4%. Thalheimer & Ali [1995] found that demand for racetrack betting is price elastic, which suggests that track take revenue should increase with a reduction in the track take fraction. By 1990, 34 states were offering parimutuel betting on thoroughbred or standardbred horses, or on greyhounds. Thalheimer & Ali [1995] also found that the presence of a state lottery lowered both attendance and the average bettor's wager.

Sports betting in Nevada was estimated at $1.3 billion in 1988, and illegal action nationwide at more than $26 billion [see Akst, 1989], with the largest event being the Super Bowl for the championship of NFL Football. Super Bowl wagering in 1994 was estimated to be $4 billion. A recent study in Ontario (see Abbate [1995]) found that 69% of adults played the lottery in the last month. For other forms of gambling, the corresponding percentages were 12% for sports gambling, 9% for card gambling, 7% for bingo, 3% for casinos, and 2% for horse racing.

3. Racetrack betting markets

3.1. Introduction to racetrack betting

The racetrack is a market in miniature in which wagering, odds, the outcome of the race, and payoffs all occur over a period of 20–30 minutes, followed by a new market, the next race. The number of horses in a race usually ranges from 6 to 12 in the United States, 3 to 14 in Hong Kong, 6 to 18 in Japan, and 4 to 20 in England. A variety of wagers is available to bettors. The simplest is a wager to

Table 2

Lottery revenues, by state

State	Total sales excluding commissions [a] ($millions)	Breakdown [a] (%)			Average lottery sales per adult [b] ($)	Lottery net proceeds per capita [c] ($)
		Prizes	Admin-istration	Proceeds available from ticket sales		
Arizona	217	51	10	40	94	23
California	2,012	53	9	39	66	26
Colorado	174	55	13	32	99	17
Connecticut	504	56	5	39	224	60
Delaware	62	55	4	41	154	37
Florida	2,043	52	6	42	194	64
Idaho	51	50	18	31	71	16
Illinois	1,414	55	4	41	188	51
Indiana	412	56	7	37	102	27
Iowa	143	61	13	27	88	14
Kansas	67	49	17	33	49	9
Kentucky	200	63	10	27	153	15
Maine	96	54	11	36	127	28
Maryland	772	53	4	43	218	69
Massachusetts	1,474	64	4	32	404	78
Michigan	1,041	54	4	41	181	46
Minnesota	303	59	19	22	98	15
Missouri	204	57	11	32	58	13
Montana	23	52	29	20	52	6
New Hampshire	99	56	10	34	133	31
New Jersey	1,174	52	4	45	228	68
New York	1,949	49	3	48	168	52
Ohio	1,569	54	6	41	226	58
Oregon	139	57	17	26	112	12
Pennsylvania	1,423	55	3	42	155	50
Rhode Island	59	53	5	42	105	25
South Dakota	44	24	9	67	43	42
Vermont	44	57	14	29	124	22
Virginia	749	56	9	35	176	41
Washington	259	48	14	38	89	20
West Virginia	76	54	14	33	64	14
Wisconsin	371	60	8	33	128	24
Total	19,167	54	6	40	–	–

[a] 1991 figures [source: *Statistical Abstract of the United States*, 1993].
[b] 1992 figures [source: Kleinfield, 1993].
[c] 1991 figures [source: *The State Policy Reference Book*, 1993].

win, which involves picking the horse that finishes first. A *place* (*show*) bet involves picking a horse that is at least second (third). *Exotic* wagers are based on two or more horses, such as the *daily double* — picking the winners of two consecutive races; *quinellas* — picking the top two finishers in a race; and *exactas* — picking the top two finishers in a race in the correct order. As in securities markets, the public directly establishes the odds in a parimutuel betting market; the more the public bets on a horse, the lower its odds and the lower its return upon winning. The track pools the public's wagers and returns a fraction Q — the *track payback* — of that total to the winners. The remainder — the *track take* — is shared by the track owners, the state government, jockey's fund, race purses, etc. An additional transactions cost is *breakage* where the track rounds down returns to the nearest nickel or dime on the dollar.

Weak form efficiency means that, with access only to the public's odds, no bet allows a positive expected profit. A profitable betting system based on the public's odds is possible only if weak form efficiency is violated [see Epstein, 1977]. We also consider a stricter version — *strictly-weak form* efficiency — which requires that with access to the public's odds, all bets have equal expected return, namely Q, for a loss of $1 - Q$.

There is an extensive literature on horserace betting. We begin in Section 3.2 with studies of win betting; they point to a weak form efficient win market but one that is not strictly-weak form efficient given a strong and stable betting bias by the public against favorites and for longshots. Section 3.3 discusses the evidence against weak form efficiency of the place and show markets. It also describes theoretical and implementation aspects of wagering schemes that have been devised to exploit this inefficiency. Exotic markets and cross-track betting are discussed in Sections 3.4 and 3.5, respectively.[4]

3.2 Win market

Define W_i as the public's wager to win on horse i and $W \equiv \sum_i W_i$ as the public's win pool. Then, ignoring breakage, QW/W_i is the payoff per dollar wagered on horse i to win if and only if horse i wins. Let $O_i \equiv QW/W_i - 1$. The odds on horse i are expressed as O_i to one, or $O_i - 1$, and the return on a \$1 wager to win on horse i is the original \$1 plus another $\$O_i$ in profit.[5] The quantity W_i/W can be interpreted as the public's subjective probability that horse i will win. If these subjective probabilities are indeed correct then the gross expected return on a win bet on any horse i is Q, i.e., strictly-weak form efficiency. Based on data on over 50,000 races and 300,000 horses collected from numerous studies, Figure 2 shows the actual expected returns for various odds categories. (This extends the analysis of Snyder [1978].) Expected returns are plotted against odds using transactions costs of 0.1533 ($= 1 - Q$) which applies in California. The horizontal line indicates the point at which returns are the expected 0.8467 ($= Q$). While objective odds (actual outcomes) and the public's subjective odds

[4] This survey of horseracing is restricted to parimutuel betting, i.e., where the payoffs are directly determined by the public's betting. In many countries outside of North America, betting is handled by bookies who offer fixed odds. This literature is compiled and discussed in Hausch, Lo & Ziemba [1994a].

[5] Similarly, odds of x to y (or $x - y$) means that a $\$y$ wager will pay $\$x + y$, the original wager plus $\$x$.

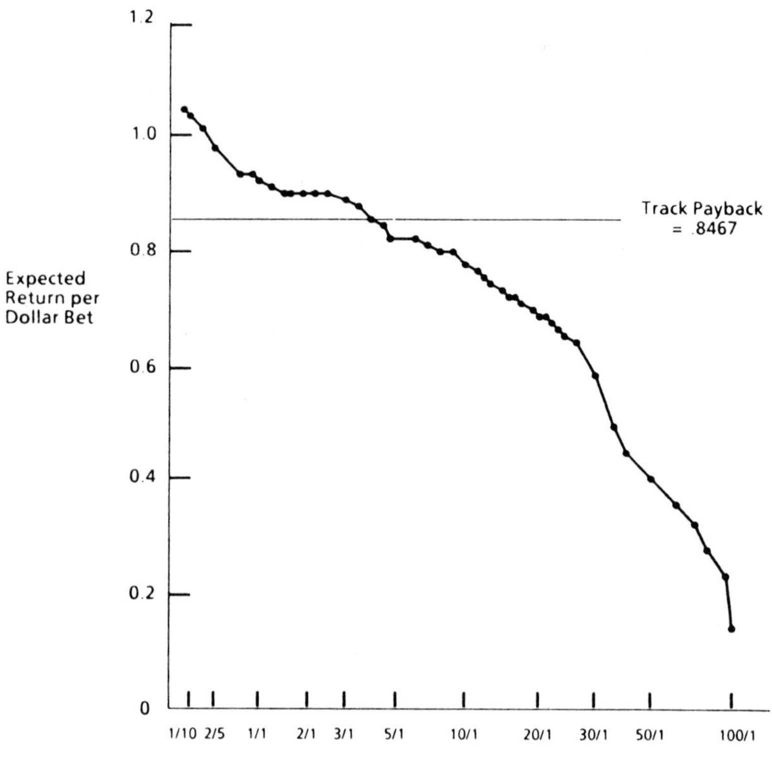

Fig. 2. Effective track payback less breakage for various odds levels in California. Source: Ziemba & Hausch [1986]

are highly correlated, actual returns departing from the horizontal line indicates that strictly-weak form efficiency is violated.

Figure 2 exhibits a clear favorite-longshot bias, with expected returns falling as odds lengthen, down to only 13.7¢ per dollar wagered at odds exceeding 100–1. This bias is strong and stable, having appeared in data sets collected over several decades and from tracks of all sizes and throughout the world. (Early studies include Griffith [1949], McGlothlin [1956], and Fabricand [1965].) In England, a similar graph [see Ziemba & Hausch, 1986] obtains even for fixed odds systems where bookies construct this risk preference situation to mirror bettors' desires to overbet longshots and underbet favorites. Exceptions to this bias are Busche & Hall [1988] and Busche [1994] for Hong Kong and Japan.

While clearly violating strictly-weak form efficiency, Figure 2 illustrates that the favorite-longshot bias is insufficient to allow for profitable wagers except on odds below 3–10. In this range, expected returns are positive and are about 4–5% for horses with the shortest odds. Such short odds are relatively rare; hence, for practical purposes the win market, while not strictly-weak form efficient, is weak form efficient. This supports the notion that bettors, at least in aggregate, behave rationally in the sense that few profitable wagers remain. Rosett [1965] finds additional support for bettor rationality with evidence that a bettor will not make a simple bet over a more complicated one (a parlay) that is preferred in terms of overall probability or payoff.

McGlothlin [1956] studied the favorite-longshot bias over the course of a racing day, finding interesting departures from the usual bias for the last two races of the day. The penultimate race is frequently the feature race of the day, involving horses with well-documented records that have received more public scrutiny than usually occurs, and this is particularly so for the favorites. Interestingly, McGlothlin found little underbetting of these favorites. For the final race, McGlothlin calculated significantly positive expected returns for short-odds horses, atypically low returns for mid-range odds horses, and small but positive expected returns for the longest-odds horses. An explanation offered for these returns is that bettors who are losers — which describes the average bettor by the beginning of the last race of the day — use an end-game strategy to recover their day's losses. Such a strategy will tend to overlook favorites because of their low payoff, key in on mid-range odds horses because of their adequate returns together with a reasonable probability of success, and perhaps even involve underbetting of extreme longshots given their low probability of success. Metzger [1985] also found a loose pattern of increased underbetting on the favorite as the racing day progressed.

The favorite-longshot bias may be insufficient to allow for a practical and profitable technical betting scheme, but its existence is still worthy of explanation. Two approaches based on rational betting behavior have considered risk-seeking bettors and differences of opinion. The first of these generates the bias because risk-seeking bettors will demand a higher expected return for favorites which have a lower variance of return than do longshots. Weitzman [1965] and Ali [1977] estimated the utility function of the representative bettor and showed it to be convex. Quandt [1986] proved that locally risk-seeking bettors are a necessary condition for the bias if the bettors have homogeneous beliefs, since a loss to the bettors in aggregate follows from a positive track take. Ali [1977] offered the second approach for generating the favorite-longshot bias. He considered races with two horses and assumed that the risk-neutral bettors hold heterogeneous beliefs about the likelihood of each horse winning, and all bettors wager an identical amount (say $1) on the horse with the highest expected return on the basis of their belief. Ali defined π_1 as the true probability that horse 1 wins and supposed that each bettor's belief about that probability is a draw from a distribution that has π_1 as its median value. Suppose that $\pi_1 > 1/2$, i.e., horse 1 truly is the favorite. Since each bettor wagers $1, a parimutuel market belief of π_1 would require that a fraction π_1 of the bettors have beliefs exceeding π_1. This would be unexpected, though, since π_1 is the median belief. The parimutuel market payoff must be lower on average to attract the additional bettors needed to sustain that payoff. The parimutuel result is that horse 1 will tend to be the betting favorite but it will be underbet relative to its true probability. The reverse occurs with the other horse, the longshot, resulting in the favorite-longshot bias.[6] Blough's [1994] model incorporated both nonlinear utility and heterogeneous beliefs, and with a restriction on the beliefs of bettors he extended Ali's analysis beyond two horses to an arbitrary number. He also developed an econometric test to distinguish between these two causes of the favorite-longshot bias but, as his data did not exhibit the bias, neither cause appeared to be present.

Behavioral explanations have also been offered for the favorite-longshot bias. Thaler & Ziemba [1988] mentioned several, including: 1) overestimation of small probability events; 2) exaggerating a longshot's contribution to expected utility (from prospect theory; see Kahneman & Tversky [1979]); and 3) 'bragging rights' that are available to those who win with longshots but not to those winning with favorites. They also suggest that mental accounting [see Kahneman & Tversky, 1984] may be a promising way of modeling racetrack betting. It allows the bettor to be risk seeking in one domain while risk averse in another. The notion is that bettors have mental accounts and act as if the funds in these accounts are not fungible. Suppose bettors A and B have the same betting behavior. If A just lost her \$100 on a horserace while B just read in the newspaper's financial section of a \$100 loss in his stock portfolio, then mental accounting predicts different subsequent wagering behavior because B's loss is unrelated to racetrack betting.

Figure 2 is based on final odds — the odds on which win payoffs are determined. The public's odds can vary considerably over the betting period, though. Such price movements are of interest if they themselves reveal information. Asch, Malkiel & Quandt [1982] concluded that bettors late in the betting period do achieve higher returns than early bettors but were unable to devise a profitable strategy exploiting this. Asch, Malkiel & Quandt [1984, 1986] and Asch & Quandt [1986], using new data, showed that wagering on the horse with the highest win probability, when that probability is partially based on the public's 'marginal' odds (i.e., odds calculated using only wagering late in the betting period), did not provide statistically significant profits.

Assuming that a bettor knows perfectly the true win odds of the horses in a race, Isaacs [1953] determined the betting scheme that maximizes expected profit. Isaacs accounted for the effect of one's bets on the odds and determined an algorithmic solution to the nonlinear optimization problem.[7] Rosner [1975] extended Isaacs by introducing logarithmic utility and a budget constraint, but ignored one's effect on the odds. Levin [1994] also extended Isaacs in several ways, e.g., by introducing nonlinear utility and a budget constraint.

The public's win odds are just one source of information at the track. Others include the racing form which provides past performances on all the horses entered

[6] This clearly is not a rational expectations equilibrium since bettors are not revising their estimates on the basis of the price that is offered.

[7] Section 3.3.2 develops a similar optimization problem for place and show betting.

in a race, predictions of expert handicappers that appear in local newspapers, and 'tip sheets' that can be purchased at the track. Semi-strong form efficiency can be studied by considering this information. Using a multinomial logit model to measure the information content of the forecasts of professional handicappers, Figlewski [1979] found their forecasts to contain considerable information but the public's odds discount almost all of it, in support of semi-strong efficiency. Snyder [1978] and a reanalysis of Losey & Talbott [1980] also showed that following the advice of professional handicappers is generally unprofitable. For harness racing, Ludlow [1994] tested a fundamental system. He considered several classification schemes for separating winners and nonwinners in one data set, and then cross-validated them on another data set.

Bolton & Chapman [1986] developed another fundamental system using a multinomial logit model to estimate win probabilities with ten factors such as weight, post position, past performances and jockey. They were essentially unable to demonstrate any significantly positive profits, though; in support of semi-strong form efficiency. Chapman [1994] extended this work to a 20-variable model and increased the data set to 2,000 races from 200 in Bolton & Chapman [1986]. Despite a very simple scheme of betting $1 on the horse with the highest expected return as long as that return was positive, some evidence of profits was shown. Chapman also showed that the public's win odds contained considerable information beyond that contained in his 20 factors, but he did not investigate how its inclusion in his model would improve profits.

Benter [1994] provided some details of a very elaborate implementation of a multinomial logit model that is reported to have been successfully employed in Hong Kong for a number of years. Benter described the importance of defining factors that extract as much information as possible, stating that 'a model involving only simplistic specifications of factors does not provide sufficiently accurate estimates of winning probabilities'. An example of the complexity of the factors that Benter uses is seen in his discussion of a 'distance preference' factor to indicate the horse's demonstrated preference for a race of the distance that it will run in the upcoming race. He notes that for predicting races of 1–1.25 miles, Bolton & Chapman [1986] deal with the distance preference factor through a variable that 'equals one if a horse had run three or four of its last four races at distance levels of less than one mile, and zero otherwise' [p. 1047]. Benter [1994], as a 'result of a large number of progressive refinements' uses a variable defined as follows:

> [F]or each of a horse's past races, a predicted finishing position is calculated via multiple regression based on all factors except those relating to distance. This predicted finishing position in each race is then subtracted from the horse's actual finishing position. The resulting quantity can be considered to be the unexplained residual which may be due to some unknown distance preference that the horse may possess plus a certain amount of random error. To estimate the horse's preference or aversion to today's distance, the residual in each of its past races is used to estimate a linear relationship between performance and similarity to today's distance. Given the statistical uncertainty of estimating this relationship from the usually small sample of past races, the final magnitude of the estimate is

standardized by dividing it by its standard error. The result is that horses with a clearly defined distance preference demonstrated over a large number of races will be awarded a relatively larger magnitude value than in cases where the evidence is less clear.

A horse's post position is further information that is available to the bettor. Horses with inside post positions typically have an advantage in gaining positions near the rail during the race, a benefit that increases with the number of turns in the race; in fact, horses lose about one length every turn for each horse between them and the rail. Canfield, Fauman & Ziemba [1987] demonstrated that a post position bias exists favoring the inside posts and showed that the market correctly adjusted odds to reflect it, both in the win market and other markets. An exception is when the situation is nonobvious and the bet is complex, such as exacta wagering on rainy days when the inside bias may not be present.[8] Such situations may allow profitable betting strategies. Betton [1994] also demonstrated a post position bias that was only partially reflected in the market's odds. She did not consider whether the bias was sufficient for profitable betting strategies.

Numerous trade publications purport to offer profitable systems that violate semi-strong form efficiency. Among the more 'scientific' are Mitchell [1986], Quinn [1986, 1987, 1992], Quirin [1979, 1984], and Ziemba & Hausch [1986, 1987]. Tests of strong form efficiency are more difficult to conduct as they involve data that is generally not publicly available. Self-proclaimed accounts of successful gambling exploits do exist, though [e.g. Beyer, 1978, 1993]. Also, Schnytzer & Shilony [1995] show that observing inside information in the odds can be beneficial. (See also Shin [1992, 1993].)

3.3 Place and show markets

In the place and show markets, bets are profitable if the horse is at least second and third, respectively. Define P_j as the amount bet by the public on horse j to place and $P \equiv \sum_j P_j$ as the place pool. Similarly S_k is the public's show bet on horse k and $S \equiv \sum_k S_k$ is the show pool. Then the payoff per dollar bet on horse j to place is

$$1 + \frac{QP - P_i - P_j}{2P_j} \tag{1}$$

if horses i and j are the first two finishers (in either order). Otherwise the payoff is zero. The first term of (1) is the return of the dollar that was wagered. The second term recognizes that the track returns only QP of the pool, and from that amount the original wagers on horses i and j are returned. Of the remainder, $PQ - P_i - P_j$, half goes to the bettors of j, who share it on a per-dollar-wagered basis. The payoff on j is independent of whether j finishes first or second, but does depend on which horse it finishes with. A bettor on j to place generally prefers that a longshot, not a favorite, finishes with horse j. The payoff per dollar bet

[8] Because tracks are beveled, rain may collect in the inside post positions.

on horse k to show is similar:

$$1 + \frac{QS - S_i - S_j - S_k}{3S_k} \tag{2}$$

if horses i, j and k are the top three finishers.[9]

One approach to place and show betting is to study whether profitable rules for those markets can be devised based on information in the win market. For instance, given the win market's bias for favorites, perhaps place and show bets on favorites — which are more likely to pay off than win bets — allow positive profits. Asch, Malkiel & Quandt [1984, 1986] studied this possibility using a logit model to estimate win probability based on the win odds, the 'marginal' win odds (odds based on late betting only), and the morning line. Betting to win, place and show on the horse with the highest win probability (together with additional screens), returns far exceeded those of the average bettor but were not positive with statistical significance. Betting to place or show based just on information in the win market can only be improved with some attention to information in the place and show markets, since it is the public's wagering in those markets that alone determine place and show payoffs. This was the approach of Hausch, Ziemba & Rubinstein [1981] (hereafter HZR), who demonstrated that weak form inefficiencies can be identified in the place and show markets. There are three distinct aspects to their model: i) determining place and show probabilities which together with (1) and (2) allow expected returns to be calculated; ii) using the optimal capital growth model for wagering; and iii) using approximations for implementation in real time. All three aspects will be described.

3.3.1. Place and show probabilities

Suppose that horse i's true win probability is q_i (which could be determined on the basis of fundamental handicapping or, as HZR assumed, be derived from the public's wagering as W_i/W). Then Harville's [1973] formulas estimate the probability that horse i is first and horse j is second as:

$$q_{ij} \equiv \frac{q_i q_j}{1 - q_i}. \tag{3}$$

Equation (3) follows from assuming that the likelihood that j will be second conditional on i being first is the probability that j would be first if i were not in the race, which can be estimated to be $q_j/(1 - q_i)$. Similarly, Harville estimated the probability that horses i, j and k finish first, second, and third, respectively, to be:

$$q_{ijk} \equiv \frac{q_i q_j q_k}{(1 - q_i)(1 - q_i - q_j)}. \tag{4}$$

[9] Equations (1) and (2) ignore breakage, which is incorporated by rounding down a payoff to the nearest nickel or, more typically, dime on the dollar. A further consideration is that U.S. tracks generally guarantee winners a minimum profit of 5%. So, even if $(SQ - S_i - S_j - S_k)/3S_i < 0.05$, which is termed a *minus pool*, show bettors on i receive a 5% return. Minus pools are most common when there is an extreme favorite. In that event, Hausch & Ziemba [1990b] show how risk-free arbitrage may be possible in the place and show markets.

Harville's formulas have also been discussed by Savage [1957] and Plackett [1975]. With these ordering probabilities, place and show probabilities can be calculated. The probability that i places is the probability that i finishes first or second, which is:

$$q_i + \sum_{j \neq i} q_{ji},$$

and the probability that i shows is:

$$q_i + \sum_{j \neq i} q_{ji} + \sum_{k \neq i,j} \sum_{j \neq i} q_{kji}.$$

Dansie [1983] and Henery [1981] demonstrated that Harville's formulas, (3) and (4), are implied when horses' running times are independently and exponentially distributed. If horse i's running time, T_i, is exponentially distributed with mean $1/\lambda_i$, then (3) and (4) follow with $q_i = \lambda_i / \sum_j \lambda_j$. An alternative derivation supposes that T_i has the extreme value distribution with location parameter θ_i, i.e., i's running time has density function:

$$f_i(t_i) = \exp(t_i - \theta_i) \exp\big(-\exp(t_i - \theta_i)\big), \qquad -\infty < t_i < \infty.$$

Then, if $T_1, \ldots, T_n$ are independent, (3) and (4) follow with $q_i = \exp(-\theta_i)/\sum_j \exp(-\theta_j)$. These two derivations are related because the extreme value distribution is the logarithm of an exponential distribution, and the logarithm preserves orders.

Underlying probability distributions not generating (3) and (4) have been considered, too. Henery [1981] considered running times, T_i, that are independent and normally distributed as $N(\theta_i, 1)$. Then

$$\begin{aligned} q_{ij} &= P\big(T_i < T_j < \min_{k \neq i,j}\{T_k\}\big) \\ &= \int_{-\infty}^{\infty} \Phi(t + \theta_j - \theta_i) \prod_{k \neq i,j} \big[1 - \Phi(t + \theta_j - \theta_k)\big]\, \phi(t)\, \mathrm{d}t, \end{aligned}$$

where $\Phi(\cdot)$ and $\phi(\cdot)$ are the standard normal cdf and density function, respectively. A similar expression holds for q_{ijk}. Thus, with $\{\theta_i\}$, the ordering probabilities involve numerical integration. With $\{q_i\}$, possibly on the basis of the public's win bets or from handicapping, $\{\theta_i\}$ is the solution of the following nonlinear system of equations:

$$\begin{aligned} q_i &= P\big(T_i < \min_{j \neq i}\{T_j\}\big) \qquad i = 1, \ldots, n \\ &= \int_{-\infty}^{\infty} \prod_{j \neq i} \Phi(t + \theta_i - \theta_j)\, \phi(t)\, \mathrm{d}t. \end{aligned}$$

Stern [1990] proposed another alternative to Harville's formulas. He assumed that running times are independent and gamma distributed with fixed shape parameter r. Such an underlying distribution is descriptive of a game where players score points according to independent Poisson processes and the winner is the first to score r points. With $r = 1$, Stern's model is Harville's model, and as $r \to \infty$, it converges to Henery's model.

Several empirical studies have considered these various models. Henery [1984] fit running times to the extreme value distribution, finding that it best fit the faster running times. Harville [1973] showed that his formulas tend to overestimate the probability that favorites finish second or third and underestimate these same probabilities for longshots. This reverse favorite-longshot bias for the likelihood that horses finishes second and third was also observed by HZR. The betting data in these two papers exhibit the favorite-longshot bias. One might conjecture that a natural consequence of this bias for first position is the reverse favorite-longshot bias for other positions, like second and third, as probabilities over a horse's finish positions must sum to one. However, Benter [1994] using Hong Kong data that does not exhibit the favorite-longshot bias, showed this conjecture to be incomplete at best. Table 3 shows his results. Table 3a categorizes horses by the public's estimate of their win probability (through the win odds) and compares that estimate to the actual win frequency. There is no obvious bias. Tables 3b and 3c calculate Harville's estimate of finishing second and third, respectively, and compare those with actual frequencies. The reverse favorite-longshot bias is clearly exhibited, and is more pronounced for third position than for second. Benter's explanation of this bias is that Harville's formula 'does not recognize the increasing randomness of the contests for second and third place'.

Lo [1994] provided a theoretical basis for this bias, demonstrating that Harville's formulas produce such a bias if the underlying distribution of running times is

Table 3a

Public's estimate of expected win probability versus actual win frequency (based on 3198 races, Royal Hong Kong Jockey Club, September 1986–June 1993)

Range of estimated probabilities	# Horses falling within a range	Mean expected win probability	Actual win frequency observed	Z-statistic
0.000–0.010	1343	0.007	0.007	0.0
0.010–0.025	4356	0.017	0.020	1.3
0.025–0.050	6193	0.037	0.042	2.1
0.050–0.100	8720	0.073	0.069	−1.5
0.100–0.150	5395	0.123	0.125	0.6
0.150–0.200	3016	0.172	0.173	0.1
0.200–0.250	1811	0.222	0.219	−0.3
0.250–0.300	1015	0.273	0.253	−1.4
0.300–0.400	716	0.339	0.339	0.0
>0.400	312	0.467	0.484	0.6

Source: Benter [1994].

Table 3b

Harville calculation of expected probability of finishing second versus actual frequency (based on 3198 races, Royal Hong Kong Jockey Club, September 1986–June 1993)

Range of estimated probabilities	# Horses falling within a range	Mean Harville probability of finishing second	Actual second position finish frequency	Z-statistic
0.000–0.010	962	0.007	0.010	0.9
0.010–0.025	3449	0.018	0.030	5.3
0.025–0.050	5253	0.037	0.045	2.8
0.050–0.100	7682	0.073	0.080	2.3
0.100–0.150	4957	0.123	0.132	1.9
0.150–0.200	3023	0.173	0.161	−1.8
0.200–0.250	1834	0.223	0.195	−3.0
0.250–0.300	1113	0.272	0.243	−2.3
0.300–0.400	1011	0.338	0.317	−1.4
>0.400	395	0.476	0.372	−4.3

Source: Benter [1994].

Table 3c

Harville calculation of expected probability of finishing third versus actual frequency (based on 3198 races, Royal Hong Kong Jockey Club, September 1986–June 1993)

Range of estimated probabilities	# Horses falling within a range	Mean Harville probability of finishing third	Actual third position finish frequency	Z-statistic
0.000–0.010	660	0.007	0.009	0.5
0.010–0.025	2680	0.018	0.033	4.3
0.025–0.050	4347	0.037	0.062	6.8
0.050–0.100	6646	0.073	0.087	4.0
0.100–0.150	4325	0.123	0.136	2.5
0.150–0.200	2923	0.173	0.178	0.7
0.200–0.250	1831	0.223	0.192	−3.4
0.250–0.300	1249	0.273	0.213	−4.9
0.300–0.400	1219	0.341	0.273	−5.3
>0.400	601	0.492	0.333	−8.3

Source: Benter [1994].

indeed independent Gamma. HZR described a special type of late-charging horse that tends to either win or finish far back in the field, making a second or third place finish unlikely. For such horses, this 'Silky Sullivan' phenomenon (named after a horse that displayed this racing pattern) provides another explanation of the probability bias for second and third. Stern [1994] described this as a type of 'information contained in the horse's failure to win [that] is not used to adjust the probabilities', and related it to the memorylessness property of the exponential distribution for running times. Stern [1990] analyzed 47 races and found that ordering probabilities estimated using $r = 1$ (Harville's model) were less accurate than those estimated using $r = 2$. Using a likelihood approach and Japanese wagering data, Lo [1994] found $r = 4$ to be best for Stern's model. He reported that $r = \infty$ (Henery's model) was best on his Meadowlands and Hong Kong data, though. Thus, while one running time distribution model does not appear to hold universally, there is limited empirical support for Harville's model. (Other empirical studies include Bacon-Shone, Lo & Busche [1992a, b], Lo [1994] and Lo & Bacon-Shone [1993].)

While Henery's [1981] and Stern's [1987] ordering probabilities are superior to Harville's, the complex numerical calculations that they both require essentially precludes them from being used on-track (unless one determines one's own odds in advance of the race). Henery suggested using a first order Taylor series approximation, but Bacon-Shone, Lo & Busche [1992b] demonstrated its inaccuracy. Stern [1994] also mentioned that this simplification does not seem to improve upon Harville's model.

Thus, Harville's model still is useful; in particular for place and show probabilities at tracks where the favorite-longshot bias is exhibited in the win market. The probability of place, say, involves adding the probability of first, for which there is a favorite-longshot bias, and the probability of second, which has a reverse bias when calculated using Harville's formula. These biases tend to cancel each other, as HZR demonstrated. Lo & Bacon-Shone's [1993] 'discount' model retains the simplicity of the Harville's model but attempts to directly correct its bias for ordering probabilities. They define $LO(i, j \mid k) \equiv$ logarithm of the odds that horse i beats j for the kth position given neither i nor j finish in the top $k - 1$ positions. For Harville this is simply $\log(q_i/q_j)$, independent of k. Lo and Bacon-Shone assumed instead that

$$LO(i, j \mid k) = \lambda_k LO(i, j \mid 1),$$

and further assumed that λ_k is decreasing in k, presuming that the relative abilities of the horses matters less as the finish position worsens and the prize money decreases. The parameters λ_2 and λ_3 can be estimated to best fit with Henery's or Stern's models, or estimated to best fit data from a particular track, from which simple ordering probabilities q_{ijk} can be calculated. For example, Benter's [1994] Hong Kong data generated values of $\lambda_2 = 0.81$ and $\lambda_3 = 0.65$, and Lo, Bacon-Shone & Busche [1995] used $\lambda_2 = 0.88$ and $\lambda_3 = 0.81$ for their Japanese data. They reported an improved fit between actual and expected frequencies.

For any of these ordering probability models, the expected return on a bet on horse i to place and show can, respectively, be calculated using (1) and (2) as:

$$EXP_i = \sum_{j \neq i} (q_{ij} + q_{ji}) \left[1 + \frac{QP - P_i - P_j}{2P_i} \right], \tag{5}$$

and

$$EXS_i = \sum_{k \neq j,i} \sum_{j \neq i} (q_{ijk} + q_{jik} + q_{jki}) \left[1 + \frac{QS - S_i - S_j - S_k}{3S_i} \right]. \tag{6}$$

Table 4

Results of betting $1 at Exhibition Park and Santa Anita to place and show on horses with a theoretical expected profit of at least a specified minimum level

	Place			Show		
Minimum level	Number of bets	Total net profit ($)	Rate of return (%)	Number of bets	Total net profit ($)	Rate of return (%)
Exhibition Park						
1.04	225	5.10	2.3	612	33.20	5.4
1.08	126	−10.10	−8.0	386	53.50	13.9
1.12	69	11.10	16.1	223	40.80	18.3
1.16	40	5.10	12.8	143	26.30	18.4
1.20	18	5.30	29.4	95	21.70	22.8
1.25	11	−2.70	−24.5	44	11.20	25.5
1.30	3	−3.00	−100.0	27	10.80	40.0
1.50	0	–	–	3	6.00	200.0
Santa Anita						
1.04	103	12.30	11.9	307	−18.00	−5.9
1.08	52	12.80	24.6	162	6.90	4.3
1.12	22	9.20	41.8	89	3.00	3.4
1.16	7	2.30	32.9	46	12.40	27.0
1.20	3	−1.30	−43.3	27	6.20	23.0
1.25	0	–	–	9	6.00	66.7
1.30	0	–	–	5	5.10	102.0
1.50	0	–	–	0	–	–

Source: Hausch, Ziemba & Rubinstein [1981].

Using Harville's model and equations (3) and (4), HZR studied (5) and (6) with data from the 1978 summer season at Exhibition Park (1065 races and 9037 horses over 110 days) and the 1973/74 winter season at Santa Anita Racetrack (627 races and 5895 horses over 75 days). Table 4 shows the results of wagering on bets that, through (5) and (6), are identified as having certain minimum levels of positive expected return.[10] The results strongly suggest that inefficiencies can be identified in the place and show markets. Furthermore, HZR found that such inefficiencies appear about 2–4 times per racing day. Additional calculations along these lines appear in Harville [1973].

3.3.2. *Optimal capital growth*

The previous section showed evidence of inefficiencies in the place and show markets. The second aspect of HZR's model is to determine the bet size upon identifying a profitable wager. HZR employ the optimal capital growth model, or the 'Kelly criterion', which maximizes the expected logarithm of wealth on a race-by-race basis. It was developed by Kelly [1956] for information transmission,

[10] See HZR for (5) and (6) adjusted for 'breakage'. Table 4 correctly accounts for the adverse effects of breakage.

independently developed by Latané [1959], extended by Breiman [1961] who provided rigorous proofs of the main results, and is described in detail by Hakansson & Ziemba [1995, chapter 4 in this volume].[11] Among its properties are: 1) it maximizes the asymptotic growth rate of capital; 2) asymptotically, it minimizes the expected time to reach a specified wealth goal; and 3) it outperforms in the long run any other essentially different strategy almost surely. While these are impressive asymptotic properties, Aucamp [1993] asked: how many periods are required to be reasonably confident that the Kelly criterion will be superior? Both theoretical and experimental evidence point to the need for only a moderate number of plays when the risk is low but a large number generally when the risk is high. See also Ziemba and Hausch [1986] for empirical calculations.

Using (5) and (6), assuming the appropriateness of Harville's formulas, introducing bets to place and show as decision variables, and accounting for one's effect on the odds (but ignoring breakage), the optimal capital growth model solves optimization problem 1 (OP1).[12] Notice that OP1 considers each possible 1-2-3 finish of the horses, determines the logarithm of final wealth in that event, and averages over all possible 1-2-3 finishes. For convenience, OP1 defines $P_{ij} \equiv P_i + P_j$ and $S_{ijk} \equiv S_i + S_j + S_k$. OP1 also involves a budget constraint with w_o representing current wealth.

$$\underset{\{p_l\}\{s_l\}}{\text{Maximize}} \sum_{i=1}^{n} \sum_{\substack{j=1\\ j\neq i}}^{n} \sum_{\substack{k=1\\ k\neq i,j}}^{n} \frac{q_i q_j q_k}{(1-q_i)(1-q_i-q_j)} \log \left[\begin{array}{l} \dfrac{Q(P+\sum_{l=1}^{n} p_l)-(p_i+p_j+P_{ij})}{2} \\ \quad \times \left[\dfrac{p_i}{p_i+P_i}+\dfrac{p_j}{p_j+P_j}\right] \\ + \dfrac{Q(S+\sum_{l=1}^{n} s_l)-(s_i+s_j+s_k+S_{ijk})}{3} \\ \quad \times \left[\dfrac{s_i}{s_i+S_i}+\dfrac{s_j}{s_j+S_j}+\dfrac{s_k}{s_k+S_K}\right] \\ \quad + w_o - \sum_{\substack{l=1\\ l\neq i,j,k}}^{n} s_l - \sum_{\substack{l=1\\ l\neq i,j}}^{n} p_l \end{array} \right]$$

$$\text{s.t.} \quad \sum_{l=1}^{n}(p_l+s_l) \le w_o, \qquad p_l \ge 0, \qquad s_l \ge 0, \qquad l=1,\ldots,n,$$

Optimization problem 1: Place and show betting with optimal capital growth model.

3.3.3. *Implementing the system and empirical results*

HZR and Hausch & Ziemba [1985] provided tests of OP1 on data from three North American racetracks. Figures 3–5 show, respectively, the wealth level histories for the 1978 season at Exhibition Park (Vancouver, B.C.), the 1973/74 winter season at Santa Anita (Arcadia, CA), and the 1981/82 winter season at

[11] See also Algeot & Cover [1988] for a more general mathematical treatment, and MacLean, Ziemba & Blazenko [1992] for fractional Kelly strategies and a comparison of its properties.

[12] Kallberg & Ziemba [1994] described OP1's generalized concavity properties.

Aqueduct (Jamaica, NY). Given the many approximations involved in the system, the authors established cutoffs on a bet's expected return [see (5) and (6)] that were necessary for wagering, cutoffs that decrease with the size of the track and one's confidence with the accuracy of the public's win odds. Specifically, Figure 3 for Exhibition Park, a relatively small track, uses an expected return cutoff of 1.20. Figure 4 for Santa Anita, a much larger track, uses a 1.16 cutoff, and Figure 5 for Aqueduct uses 1.14. The track take is generally established by the state or province, and varied across these three tracks. For the seasons studied, the track takes were 18.9% for Exhibition Park, 17.5% for Santa Anita, and 15% for Aqueduct. To appreciate the dramatic longrun effect of the take, Figure 5 also considers takes of 14 and 17%.

Figures 3–5 are based on OP1's use of *final* public wagers, i.e., the presumption was that our bettor could wager last. In practice, that is not possible because of three time-consuming activities necessary for implementing OP1 in real time. First is the input of the required data — the public's win, place and show bets on all horses in a race. This data is on the order of three four- or five-digit numbers for, perhaps, ten horses. Second is the solution of the nonlinear optimization problem OP1. And third is the time necessary to make one's bets before the end of the betting period. Since the public's wagering can and commonly does change over the betting period, these three activities mean that one must work with data that only imperfectly forecasts the eventual payoffs. To reduce the time involved in the

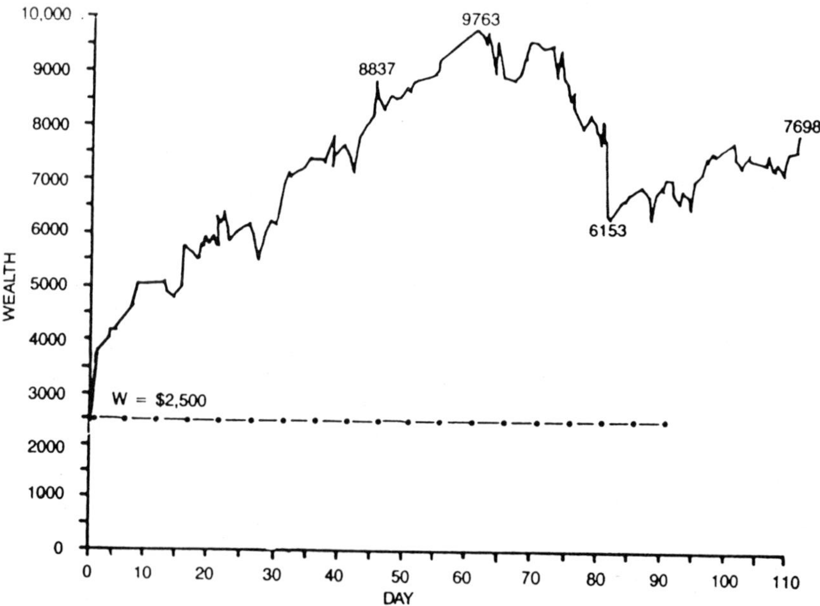

Fig. 3. Wealth level history, Exhibition Park, 1978 season. Results from expected log betting to place and show when expected returns $\geq$1.20. Initial wealth is $2,500, track payback is 81.9%, and breakage is accounted for. Source: Hausch, Ziemba & Rubinstein [1981].

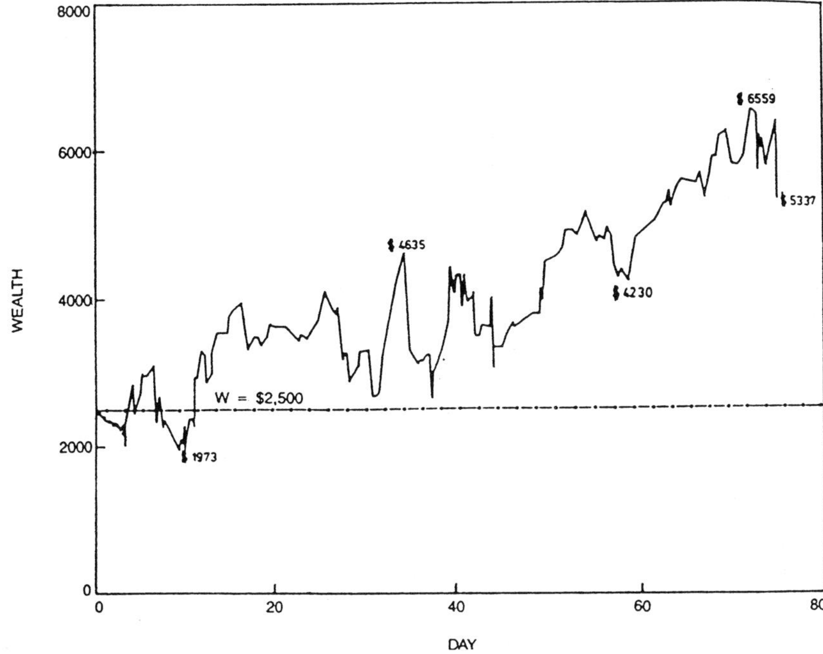

Fig. 4. Wealth level history, Santa Anita, 1973/74 season. Results from expected log betting to place and show when expected returns $\geq$1.16. Initial wealth is \$2,500, track payback is 82.5%, and breakage is accounted for. Source: Hausch, Ziemba & Rubinstein [1981].

first two activities, HZR developed regression approximations to the solution of OP1 that, once a horse was identified as being a possible bet, required as inputs only the public's win and place (or show) wagers on that horse as well as the win and place (or show) pools. Analyzing a small sample of races with data two minutes prior to the end of betting, HZR found that the problem of using such data is limited — bets identified as profitable based on odds two minutes before the end of the betting period generally remained profitable based on the eventual final odds. Hausch & Ziemba [1985] and Ziemba & Hausch [1987] improved upon HZR's regression approximations and introduced additional approximations for multiple horse entries and multiple bets. Programmed into calculator, entry of the required data and calculations takes about 30 seconds.

Hausch, Bain & Ziemba [1995] tested these approximations on 62 runnings of the Kentucky Derby (1934–1995). The anomaly was present during this period and \$2,500 grew to \$8,002. With a breeding filter (based on dosage theory), wealth increased to \$12,508.

Ritter [1994], in a revision of work predating HZR, also considered place and show betting. Instead of computing expected returns, Ritter used various filter rules to select place and show bets. He achieved positive profits using final odds, but not when wagers were based on the odds 1.5 minutes from the end of betting.

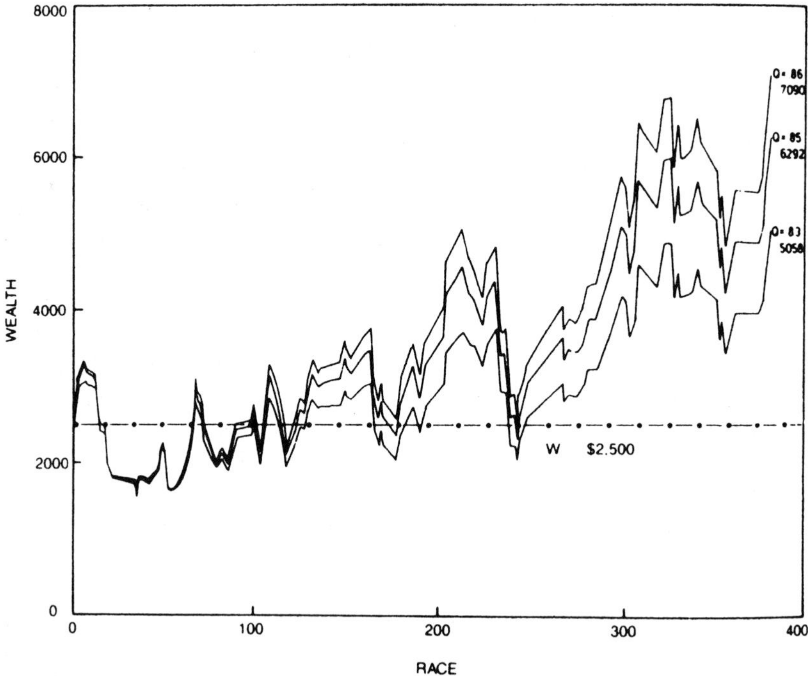

Fig. 5. Wealth level history, Aqueduct, 1981/82 season. Results from expected log betting to place and show when expected returns ≥1.14. Initial wealth is $2,500, breakage is accounted for, and track paybacks considered are 83%, 85% (actual), and 86%. Source: Hausch & Ziemba [1985].

Lo, Bacon-Shone & Busche [1995] demonstrated that OP1's performance can be improved by replacing Harville's model with Lo & Bacon-Shone's [1993] discount model that corrects for biases in Harville's model.

3.4. Exotics market

For at least two reasons, exotic bets are typically more complicated to assess than bets to win, place or show: 1) they involve the outcome of two or more horses; and 2) one often has poor access to information about the public's exotic wagering (in fact, some tracks display no exotic wagering data). The reason for not fully displaying exotic data is entirely due to the large quantity of it. For example, in a ten horse race, the public's win, place, and show bets involve 30 numbers. By comparison, there are 45 quinella numbers, 90 exacta numbers, and 720 trifecta numbers.

Exotic wagers tend to be popular with the public. One attraction is their low probability and high payoff characteristics. In view of the favorite-longshot bias for win bets, it is not surprising that longer-odds events than win bets will be heavily wagered. To illustrate a second attraction, consider the daily double. Bettors can create for themselves a daily double by wagering to win on a horse and then, if successful, betting all the proceeds to win on a horse in the next race. This self-constructed daily double, called a parlay, differs from a daily double in an important way. The parlay is subjected to the track take twice while the daily double pays it only once. Thus, transactions costs are higher with the sequence of win bets. A successful handicapper need skills significantly better than those of the average bettor. As transactions costs decrease, though, success demands less of a skill advantage or, for the same skill advantage, profits are greater.[13] Most tracks appreciate this and charge a higher track take on exotic wagers, reducing its advantage.

While a parlay that is a self-constructed version of a daily double pays the track take twice, it does allow the bettor more information. Since the daily double must be wagered before either race, the bettor has little information about the public's view of the second race (other than any information that can be gleaned from the payoffs that are offered on daily double combinations, but that information is usually difficult to access). The parlay allows one to wager on the second race with a better sense of the public's impressions of the horses. Ali [1979] found that returns of parlays and double bets were not significantly different. Asch & Quandt [1987], however, found that doubles are statistically more profitable than parlays. When parlay payoffs are adjusted as if parlay bettors paid the track take just once, then returns on parlays and doubles are not significantly different. Lo & Busche's [1994] conclusions were similar for Hong Kong data.

Asch & Quandt [1987] found some support for the notion that 'smart money' is in the exotic pools. The basis for this notion is that the informational content of smart money is more difficult for the public to discern in the exotic market than it would be if it were wagered in the win market. Their analysis ignores the systematic biases of the Harville [1973] model, though. Also, Dolbear [1993] described a further bias in their comparison of the theoretical and subjective probabilities of exacta outcomes. Bacon-Shone, Lo & Busche [1992b] addressed these concerns and concluded that the public's exacta betting provides more accurate estimates of ordering probabilities (the probability that i wins and j finishes second) than does the win market, and this is so using any of the probability models offered by Harville [1973], Henery [1981] or Stern [1990]. Similarly, the trifecta market provides more accurate estimates of their ordering probabilities than does the win market.

Asch & Quandt [1988] analyzed the unbiasedness of the probabilities implied by exacta and trifecta bet fractions. Using simple linear regressions on the relationship between objective probabilities (estimated by win frequencies) and subjective probabilities (average bet fractions), they drew different conclusions for the two pools. Exacta pools implied probabilities that appeared to be unbiased while the trifecta bet fractions more weakly approximated the objective probabilities and some clear over/underbetting bias was exhibited.

Ziemba & Hausch [1986] adapted for exotic wagering the techniques developed by HZR for place and show wagering: win probabilities from the efficient win market, Harville's [1973] model to price other wagers and the Kelly criterion to determine wagers. Hausch, Lo & Ziemba [1994b] developed general formulas for

[13] For more details on this effect and a numerical example, see Benter [1994].

optimal wagering on exotic bets, allowing ordering probabilities based on Harville [1973], Henery [1981] or Stern [1990] with the help of approximations developed by Lo & Bacon-Shone [1993]. Quinella data on 369 Hong Kong races was used to illustrate the system.

Kanto & Rosenqvist [1994] developed a betting system for quinella bets (called double bets in Finland) at a Finnish racetrack. Instead of using the win odds data directly, they used maximum likelihood estimation and Harville's [1973] model to estimate the win probabilities and the probabilities associated with a quinella bet by assuming that the quinella bet amounts for different combinations follow a multinomial distribution. Using the Kelly criterion for wagering and 111 races, they showed some evidence of positive profits.

3.5. Cross-track betting

Cross-track betting allows bettors to wager at their track (a cross track) on a race being run at another track (the home track). Since each track operates a separate pool, the payoffs at the tracks can differ. And, in fact, they do often differ, sometimes quite dramatically. For instance, a $2.00 win ticket on Ferdinand, the winner of the 1986 Kentucky Derby, paid $16.80 at Hollywood Park in California, $79.90 at Woodbine in Toronto, and $90.00 at Evangeline in Louisiana. Using data from Triple Crown races, Hausch & Ziemba [1990a] developed and tested optimal betting strategies for cross-track betting to exploit different odds across tracks. One strategy identified whether a risk-free hedge could be developed by betting each horse at the track where its offered odds was longest in relative amounts that guarantee a profit. Examples where the variance in odds across tracks was sufficient were provided. Also analyzed was the optimal capital growth strategy. This latter strategy was studied in two environments: 1) a single bettor at a cross track observing (perhaps by television) the home track's odds; and 2) a syndicate of bettors, one at each track, communicating with each other.

Leong & Lim [1994] also found evidence of profits using cross-track betting that exists between races in Singapore and Malaysia. Both papers showed profits but neither had sufficient data for statistically significant profits. Thus, further work is needed to understand cross-track betting, particularly as it is becoming more popular. Tracks have been facing declining attendances, due in part to the increase in other forms of gambling, e.g., lotteries. Cross-track betting helps attendance by offering bettors the opportunity to wager on prestigious horses in races at large tracks. Since the cross track does not need to stage an expensive race and the home track receives a portion of the cross track's revenues, both tracks can benefit from this arrangement.

4. The football betting market

Bettors on National Football League (NFL) games are offered a point spread. For example, suppose team A is a 10 points favorite over team B. Then a bet on A pays only if A wins by at least 11 points while a wager on B pays only if B either wins or loses by fewer than 10 points. If A wins by exactly 10 points then wagers are usually refunded. Typically bettors pay \$11 for a \$10 profit when they win. This provides the bookmaker a commission and means that a bettor has to beat the spread 52.4% of the time to break even. When the actual point spread equals the offered point spread, the bookmaker receives no return. Otherwise, by perfectly balancing the wagers, a bookmaker can guarantee a profit of 4.55% (since \$21 is paid for each \$22 wagered). The Las Vegas sports books, which dominate the market, offer opening point spreads on the coming week's game. These spreads may change over the week, but bettors receive the spread offered at the time they placed their bet.[14]

The efficiency of NFL betting rests on the accuracy of the point spreads. An obvious and common approach to study their accuracy is to regress actual point spread on the offered point spread. If, say, bettors tend to wager on underdogs then, to balance the books, the bookmaker has to offer point spreads lower than unbiased expectations about actual point spreads. Bettor biases should be reflected in the point spread offered and, if they are sufficiently large, should allow profitable betting opportunities, which would reject efficiency.

Let A_i be the actual point spread in game i and let P_i be the point spread offered. The following equation can be estimated:

$$A_i = \beta_1 + \beta_2 P_i + \epsilon_i, \tag{7}$$

where ϵ_i is the error term. The efficiency test is the joint hypothesis that $\beta_1 = 0$ and $\beta_2 = 1$. Pankoff [1968], Zuber, Gandar & Bowers [1985] and Sauer, Brajer, Ferris & Marr [1988] all found significant support for the hypothesis. Gandar, Zuber, O'Brien & Russo's [1988] results are similar for both opening and closing point spreads (the point spread can change over the betting period as bookmakers attempt to balance their books). Their large t-statistic on β_2 and low R^2 (3.4% for closing data) suggest that while the point spread for any particular game is a poor predictor of the actual point spread, it is a good predictor of the average actual point spread for a group of games with this point spread.

While these results support market efficiency, they are not directly useful in answering whether there might be technical rules that are economically profitable. Vergin & Scriabin [1978] used NFL data from 1969–1972 to consider various rules, such as betting on the underdog when the point spread exceeds some specified level, and identified several profitable strategies. Using 1975–1981 data, Tryfos, Casey, Cook, Leger & Pylypiak [1984] demonstrated that most of these strategies were unprofitable or, if profitable, not at the 5% significance level. Those that were significantly profitable all required a syndicate taking advantage of different

[14] These dynamics are also present in horserace wagering against bookies. Wagering on jai alai is similar [see Lane & Ziemba, 1992], too, but its odds change during the contest as points are scored rather than before the contest as with sports betting. Parimutuel betting is different, though; its odds change over the course of the betting period as betting patterns change, but payoffs to all bettors are based only on the final odds.

point spreads in different cities. Gandar, Zuber, O'Brien & Russo [1988] found similar negative results for these strategies using their 1980–1985 data.

Golec & Tamarkin [1991] discussed how a model such as (7) can mask specific biases: 'consider that β_1 measures the average of the biases that do not change with the magnitude of the point spread. If half the observations in a data sample include a positive bias and the other half a negative bias of equal magnitude, then $\beta_1 = 0$' [p. 314]. The problem is that (7) can deal with only one bias. For instance, a bias in favor (or against) the home team can be considered by defining the data, P_i, relative to the home team. But if there is also a bias for (or against) the favored team, that can confound measuring the home team bias. To specifically test for possible biases for the favorite and the home teams, Golec and Tamarkin used the following model:

$$A_i = \beta_1 + \beta_2 P_i + \beta_3 H_i + \beta_4 F_i + \epsilon_i,$$

where H_i is a dummy variable that is one for home teams and zero otherwise, and F_i is another dummy variable that is one if the team is favored and zero otherwise. Here the test of efficiency is that $\beta_1 = \beta_3 = \beta_4 = 0$ and $\beta_2 = 1$. Their empirical results for NFL games from 1973–1987 indicated that bettors tend to underestimate the home field advantage and overestimate the distinction of being the favorite. Interestingly, they showed that the home field bias is disappearing over time while the underdog bias is actually growing. Despite demonstrating these biases, profits are shown to be slim at best in the face of the bookmaker's commission. Neither bias is present in college football.

Sauer, Brajer, Ferris & Marr [1988] considered explanatory variables beyond the point spread, such as the number of wins prior to this game, fumbles, interceptions, penalties, yards passed, etc. Regressing these variables on the difference between the offered and the actual point spreads, they were unable to reject the hypothesis that their coefficients are all jointly zero. They concluded that these variables add essentially no information beyond that already in the point spread. Dana & Knetter [1994] allowed two modifications. Since fumbles, interceptions and penalties affect the game but are relatively uninformative about a team's ability, they accounted for these unsystematic sources of noise. Further, they used a nonlinear function of past point spreads. There is scant support for any of their models achieving the minimum 52.4% winners needed for profitable wagering.

What is the probability that a team favored to win a football game by p points does win the game? Stern [1991] showed that the margin of victory for the favorite is approximately normally distributed with mean equal to the point spread and standard deviation estimated at 13.86. The probability of winning a game is then:

$$\Pr(F > U \mid P = p) = 1 - N\left(\frac{-p}{13.86}\right) = N\left(\frac{p}{13.86}\right),$$

where F and U represent actual points scored by the favorite and the underdog, respectively, and $N(\cdot)$ is the standard normal's cumulative distribution function. A linear approximation to the probability of winning is:

$$\Pr(F > U \mid P = p) = 0.50 + 0.03p.$$

This formula is accurate to within 0.0175 for $|p| < 6$ and is based on data from the 1981, 1983, and 1984 NFL seasons. Data from 1985 and 1986 indicate that the normal approximation is valid outside of the original data set. This approximation is useful for a variety of applications, e.g., estimating the probability distribution of games won by a team, the probability a team makes the playoffs, and the probability distribution of season or playoff outcomes for particular teams.

5. The basketball betting market

Do athletes have performances that run in streaks? Gilovich, Vallone & Tversky [1985] using data from the 1980–81 season for the Philadelphia 76ers found that consecutive shots, if anything, were negatively autocorrelated. Hence there is no hot hand. They also let college players take shots while the players and other observers bet on the outcomes. Both players and observers made larger bets after players had just made shots, although bet size and actual performance were uncorrelated.[15] Camerer [1989, p. 1257] argued that '[b]elief in the hot hand is a mistake generated by persistent misunderstanding of randomness. People usually expect more alternations and fewer long streaks than actually occur in random series.'

If the hot hand is believed to exist within a game, then bettors might also believe in hot and cold streaks across games. And if point spreads reflect mistaken belief in hot hands then winning-streak teams should do worse than expected. For NBA regular season games from 1983–1986, Camerer [1989] found this effect to be very weak. The effect for losing streaks is slightly stronger, but in neither case is the bias sufficient to overcome the bookmaker's transactions costs. Camerer's test is premised on the myth of the hot hand. Using more data and a test that can also detect the presence of the hot hand, Brown & Sauer [1993b] demonstrated that the market believes in the hot hand. Neither the hypothesis that the hot hand is real nor that it is a myth could be rejected, though.

Brown & Sauer [1993a] examined the error term in a point spread pricing model. While the model's ex ante predictions explained 85% of the variation in point spreads, the error term has significant predictive power. Hence the error term contains unobserved fundamentals, not just noise.

Sauer [1991] showed that the Las Vegas Market point spreads offered at 5 p.m. Eastern time on the day of 5636 NBA games are an unbiased estimate of the actual difference in scores. In a subsample of 700 games that involved injuries to star players, the teams with the injured stars performed more than a point worse than the point spread. Obviously this is a nonrepresentative sample, though, because it consists of the games in which the injured star did not play, but not the games where the injured player decided after 5 p.m. to play. Accounting for the likelihood that a star with a nagging injury will play, the point spreads provided unbiased estimates of actual outcomes.

[15] Albright [1993] studied hitting streaks of baseball players and found no evidence of streaks beyond those expected by a statistical model of randomness. Comments on Albright's work and a rejoinder follow the article in the journal.

6. Lotteries

6.1. Introduction to lotteries

For thousands of years choosing by lots has been used as one means of resolving disputes. The first lottery of a more traditional form, where one pays for a chance to win, dates at least to the Middle Ages in Italy (Ziemba, Brumelle, Gautier & Schwartz [1986], hereafter ZBGS). Prior to this century lotteries were successfully used in the United States for local and state governments, and to fund numerous causes, such as universities. Corruption, fraud and moral opposition together with lottery restrictions imposed by Congress ended legalized lotteries by the end of the 19th century, with 35 states going so far as to explicitly prohibit them in their constitutions [Clotfelter & Cook, 1991, p. 38]. State lotteries continued to be nonexistent [16] until 1964 when New Hampshire introduced its lottery. Since then the United States has seen an explosive resurgence of lotteries. In 1991, the District of Columbia and 32 states offered lotteries. Furthermore, ticket sales across states exceeded $19 billion. Of that amount, prizes were $10.4 billion, administration including advertising was $1.1 billion, and net revenue was $7.6 billion.[17] Clotfelter & Cook [1990] mention that in the course of a year, 60% of the adults who live in lottery states play the lottery at least once [p. 105]. They also report that per capita sales in lottery states has increased from (in 1989 dollars) $22 in 1975 to $108 in 1989 [p. 105]. The present popularity of lotteries is more widespread than just the United States; in 1986, over 100 countries offered legalized lotteries [ZBGS, 1986, p. 2]. See ZBGS for more on the history and on the practice of lotteries.

Despite their popularity, with expected returns typically of 40–60%, lotteries are usually a poor investment.[18] This range is even lower (10–20%) if prizes are not tax-free or if they are paid in installments over say twenty years, as they typically are in the U.S. Canadian and U.K. prizes are paid in cash and are tax free. (See ZBGS for calculations on the effects of tax and payment in installments.)

Lotteries take several forms. A simple version has players buy pre-numbered tickets followed by a random drawing. Instant scratch-off games allow one to determine immediately if a prize has been won. Another form is the numbers game that requires players to match a randomly generated three- or four-digit number. Lastly, players of lotto games attempt to match five to seven numbers (with six most common) drawn from 50 or so numbers (with 49 most common), with the actual choice of the parameters varying state by state. A feature distinguishing the numbers and lotto games from the other two forms is the player's act of choosing

[16] Other lottery possibilities were available, though; such as charity raffles, foreign lotteries like the Irish Sweepstakes, and illegal lotteries.

[17] See *State Government Finances in 1991* (Washington, D.C., Government Printing Office), Table 35.

[18] An exception was the inaugural offering of a new lottery in British Columbia. To create a keen interest in its game, participants received six tickets for the price of one, for an expected return of $0.385 times 6 or $2.31, a 131% edge. See Ziemba (1995).

his or her numbers. For reasons not easily explained by traditional economics, the feature of choice is of tremendous importance. This was illustrated by Langer [1975] who conducted two lotteries where tickets cost $1 and all the money collected was awarded to the winner, i.e., the payback was 100%. Players in the first lottery were assigned their tickets while those in the second lottery chose theirs. As the winner was randomly drawn, subjects in both lotteries had the same chance of winning. However, Langer found that ticket holders in the two lotteries viewed their situations differently. When individually approached to sell their tickets before the drawing, those in the first lottery demanded a mean payment of $1.96, while in the second lottery the mean was $8.67. Langer referred to this phenomenon as the 'illusion of control', that choosing one's ticket improves in some way the likelihood one will win. States seem to appreciate this phenomenon and lotteries involving choices are very common.

The pre-numbered and instant scratch-off games allow a state to establish winning payoffs that exactly conform to any payback percentage. For instance, if the instant scratch-off game has $1 tickets and a $100 prize, then a 40% payback can be guaranteed by printing 0.4% winning tickets. The numbers game can also involve fixed payoffs. For instance, if the game is to pick the three-digit number that is randomly drawn from the 1000 possible three-digit numbers, then a prize of $400 is a 40% payback. The difference here is that the state averages a 60% return, but it is not guaranteed. If the winning number has disproportionately many bettors then the state's return will be less than 60% and the possibility exists that it could even be negative. Despite this difference to the state, the advice to bettors remains: no profitable betting scheme exists for lottery games of this sort and each bet's expected return equals the state's payback percentage.

For the numbers game, Clotfelter & Cook [1993] document a tendency for the public to choose numbers relatively less often immediately after they have been drawn. They describe this pattern as a form of the 'gambler's fallacy', the belief that if an event just occurred, then the likelihood that it will occur again falls.[19]

6.2. *Inefficiencies with unpopular numbers*

Fixed payoffs for lotteries are not the only possibility. Parimutuel payoffs are used by all states for lotto games and by Massachusetts for its numbers game. The parimutuel method allows a state to guarantee its percentage take by having the payoff to winners decreasing in the number of winners. Given that all numbers are equally likely[20], no system can be developed that will improve the likelihood

[19] Metzger [1985] considered the 'gambler's fallacy' at the racetrack, and found support for the hypothesis that betting on the favorite should be more attractive after a series of longshots have won than after a series of wins by favorites.

[20] Johnson & Klotz [1993], on the basis of 200 Lotto America winning combinations, suggest that each number may not be equally likely. They find that, roughly, small numbers are drawn more frequently than large numbers. They suggest that it may be a consequence of the mechanical mixing process, that small-numbered balls are dropped into the urn first.

of winning any of the lotteries that have been described. But, if a numbers or lotto game employs parimutuel payoffs, then by choosing unpopular numbers, upon winning one is likely to share the given prize with fewer other winners. If some numbers are sufficiently unpopular, bets with positive expected return may exist despite the lottery's low payout rate. Chernoff's [1980, 1981] study of the Massachusetts number game, where players pick a number from 0000 to 9999, found that numbers with 0s, 9s and to a lesser extent 8s tended to be unpopular. He showed that by concentrating on the unpopular numbers, bets with a positive expected return were possible. Clotfelter & Cook [1991] provided some evidence of this, too, with three days of 1986 data from Maryland's three-digit numbers game. The most popular three-digit choice was 333 which was 9.93 times more common than the average. The seven most popular choices were all triples — 333, 777, 555, 444, 888, 666, 999 — and all were at least five times more popular than the average number. The least popular was 092, picked 0.23 times as often as the average number, and was followed in unpopularity by 086, 887, 884, and 968, all 0.25 times as popular as the average.

Lotto with its possibility of prizes of tens of millions of dollars is one of the most popular games and it has received the most media attention. It involves matching six numbers drawn without replacement from fifty or so total possible numbers. If T is the total possible numbers and D is the number drawn, then the probability of matching is one in $T!/(D!(T-D)!)$. So, for example, the probability of winning when six numbers are drawn from 49 is one in 13,983,816. Most games have prizes for matching fewer than all the drawn numbers, too, but it is common for half the prize money to go to the grand prize. The long odds mean that none of the perhaps millions of bettors might win in a given week (the usual period over which lotto is played). In this event, the grand prize jackpot is carried over to the next week. ZBGS studied whether unpopular numbers and the carryover can allow a profit. Using several methods, they determined that there were unpopular numbers, they were virtually the same ones year to year, and they tended to be high numbers (non-birthdays, etc.) and those ending in 0s, 9s and 8s. For instance, a regression method based on actual payoffs generated the following as the twelve most unpopular numbers: 32, 29, 10, 30, 40, 39, 48, 12, 42, 41, 38 and 18. They were 15–30% less popular than average. The most popular number, 7, was selected nearly 50% more often than the average number. Using a maximum entropy distribution approach, Stern & Cover [1989] identified 20, 30, 38, 39, 40, 41, 42, 46, 48 and 49 as the ten most unpopular numbers while 3, 7, 9, 11, 25, and 27 were the six most popular.[21]

ZBGS showed that expected returns of \$1.50 without carryover and up to \$2.25 with carryover per dollar bet are possible. Does this imply that lotto games can be

[21] See also Joe [1987]. Clotfelter & Cook [1991] provided another example of popular numbers from Maryland's lotto, which has 40 total possible numbers. On the particular day they analyzed, players picked the 1-2-3-4-5-6 combination over 2000 times more frequently than the average pick. Had this been the winning combination (at a chance of one in 3,838,380), winners would have collected only \$193.50!

profitable, though? To see that it may not, consider a hypothetical game where you pay $1, choose a number between 1 and one million, and if your number matches the one that is randomly selected then you win $2 million. In spite of your edge, you are likely to go bankrupt before winning the jackpot. A reduced wager will increase the likelihood that you will eventually hit the correspondingly-reduced jackpot before you go bankrupt, but your expected wealth will suffer. MacLean, Ziemba & Blazenko [1992] analyzed this problem using a model contrasting growth of wealth and security of wealth and found that lotteries are an impractical way for modestly endowed investors to enhance their long-term wealth. For instance, by wagering an optimally small amount each round, one's initial stake can be increased tenfold before losing half the stake with a probability arbitrarily close to one. However, millions of years of wagering are required on average.

Rather than make optimally small wagers in the face of small probability gambles, growth may be improved by increasing the probability of success. For lotteries, this can be accomplished by buying more than one combination of numbers. It may even be possible in the face of a substantial carryover to profitably purchase most, or perhaps all, of the combinations. There have been times when this would have been profitable. In practice, though, the transactions costs are enormous because tickets must be purchased one at a time. Furthermore, there is the worry that others might also be covering all the numbers, to your joint detriment.[22]

Lotto typically involves drawing six numbers. Different states have different total possible numbers, though, resulting in very different probabilities of winning. In 1990 the extremes were one chance in 974,000 (36 numbers and 2 picks per ticket) in Delaware and one chance in 22,957,480 (53 total numbers and 1 pick per ticket) in California [Cook and Clotfelter, 1993, p. 635]. Cook & Clotfelter [1993] explain this as a tradeoff states must make between the size of the jackpot and a player's estimate of the likelihood that he or she will win. The former is easily learned through advertisements and the media. The latter, according to Cook and Clotfelter, is generally not well understood but tends to be 'based on the frequency with which someone wins' [p. 634]. Thus, Delaware could increase its total possible numbers to 53 like California but, given its population, on average there would be many weeks between winners. This would lower the public's view of the likelihood of winning and the attractiveness of purchasing a ticket. On the other hand, given California's population, even with 53 total possible numbers there will usually be a winner each week. This nonrational means of probability assessment causes a scale effect whereby per capita expenditure increases with the population base of the lottery. Smaller states cannot exploit this scale effect themselves but can through forming consortia with other states, as happens with the Tri-State lottery (involving Maine, New Hampshire and Vermont) and the states constituting Lotto America.

[22] A related opportunity arises with horseracing pick-sixes (pick the winners of six consecutive races) if there are substantial carryovers. Covering all pick-six possibilities is easily accomplished at the track and may be profitable if few others behave likewise.

Acknowledgements

We thank Werner De Bondt, Victor Lo and Raymond Sauer for their helpful comments and suggestions.

References

Abbate, G. (1995). Gambling afflicts Ontarians, study says, The Globe and Mail, August 11, A1.

Akst, D. (1989). This is like stealing, *Forbes* November 13, 142–144.

Albright, C. (1993). A statistical analysis of hitting streaks in baseball, *J. Am. Stat. Assoc.* 88(424), 1175–1183.

Algeot, P., and T. Cover (1988). Asymptotic optimality and asymptotic equipartition properties of log-optimum investment, *Ann. Probab.* 16, 875–898.

Ali, M. (1977). Probability and utility estimates for racetrack bettors, *J. Polit. Econ.* 85, 803–815.

Ali, M. (1979). Some evidence of the efficiency of a speculative market, *Econometrica* 47, 387–392.

Ariel, R. (1987). A monthly effect in stock returns, *J. Financ. Econ.* 18, 161–174.

Asch, P., B. Malkiel and R. Quandt (1982). Racetrack betting and informed behavior, *J. Financ. Econ.* 10, 187–194.

Asch, P., B. Malkiel and R. Quandt (1984). Market efficiency in racetrack betting, *J. Bus.* 57, 65–75.

Asch, P., B. Malkiel and R. Quandt (1986). Market efficiency in racetrack betting: Further evidence and a correction, *J. Bus.* 59, 157–160.

Asch, P., and R. Quandt (1986). *Racetrack Betting: The Professors'Guide to Strategies*, Auburn House, Dover, MA.

Asch, P., and R. Quandt (1987). Efficiency and profitability in exotic bets, *Economica* 59, 278–298.

Asch, P., and R. Quandt (1988). Betting bias in 'exotic' bets. *Econ. Lett.* 28, 215–219.

Aucamp, D. (1993). On the extensive number of plays to achieve superior performance with the geometric mean strategy, *Manage. Sci.* 39(9), 1163–1172.

Bacon-Shone, J., V. Lo and K. Busche (1992a). Modelling winning probability, working paper, University of Hong Kong.

Bacon-Shone, J., V. Lo and K. Busche (1992b). Logistic analyses for complicated bets, working paper, University of Hong Kong.

Benter, W. (1994). Computer based horse race handicapping and wagering systems: A report, in: D. Hausch, V. Lo and W. Ziemba (eds.), *Efficiency of Racetrack Betting Markets*, Academic Press, San Diego, 183–198.

Betton, S. (1994). Post position bias: An econometric analysis of the 1987 season at Exhibition Park. in: D. Hausch, V. Lo and W. Ziemba (eds.), *Efficiency of Racetrack Betting Markets*, Academic Press, San Diego, pp. 511–521.

Beyer, A. (1978). *My $50,000 Year at the Races*, Harcourt, Brace and Jovanovich, New York, NY.

Beyer, A. (1993). *Beyer on Speed*, Houghton Mifflin.

Blough, S. (1994). Differences of opinions at the racetrack, in: D. Hausch, V. Lo and W. Ziemba (eds.), *Efficiency of Racetrack Betting Markets*, Academic Press, San Diego, pp. 323–341.

Bolton, R., and R. Chapman (1986). Searching for positive returns at the track: A multinomial logit model for handicapping horse races, *Manage. Sci.* 32, 1040–1060.

Breiman, L. (1961). Optimal gambling systems for favorable games, in: *Proceedings of the Fourth Berkeley Symposium*, University of California Press, Berkeley, CA, pp. 65–85.

Brown, W., and R. Sauer (1993a). Fundamentals or noise? Evidence from the point spread betting market, *J. Finance* 48(4), 1193–1209

Brown, W., and R. Sauer (1993b). Does the baseball market believe in het hot hand? Comment. *Am. Econ. Rev.* December, 1377–1386.

Busche, K. (1994). Efficient market results in an Asian setting, in: D. Hausch, V. Lo and W. Ziemba (eds.), *Efficiency of Racetrack Betting Markets*, Academic Press, San Diego, pp. 615–616.

Busche, K., and C. Hall (1988). An exception to the risk preference anomaly, *J. Bus.* 61, 337–346.

Cadsby, C. (1992). The CAPM and the calendar: Empirical anomalies and the risk–return relationship, *Manage. Sci.* 38(11) 1543–1561.

Camerer, C. (1989). Does the basketball market believe in the 'hot hand'? *Am. Econ. Rev.* December, 1257–1261.

Canfield, B., B. Fauman and W. Ziemba (1987). Efficient market adjustment of odds prices to reflect track biases, *Manage. Sci.* 33, 1428–1439.

Chapman, R. (1994). Still searching for positive returns at the track: Empirical results from 2,000 Hong Kong races, in: D. Hausch, V. Lo and W. Ziemba (eds.), *Efficiency of Racetrack Betting Markets*, Academic Press, San Diego, pp. 173–181.

Chernoff, H. (1980). An analysis of the Massachusetts numbers game, MIT Department of Mathematics, Tech. Report No. 23, Cambridge, MA.

Chernoff, H. (1981). How to beat the Massachusetts number game: An application of some basic ideas in probability and statistics, *Math. Intell.* 3(4), 166–172.

Clotfelter, C., and P. Cook (1990). On the economics of state lotteries, *J. Econ. Perspect.* 4(4), 105–119.

Clotfelter, C., and P. Cook (1991). *Selling Hope: State Lotteries in America*, Harvard University Press, Cambridge, MA.

Clotfelter, C., and P. Cook (1993). The 'gambler's fallacy' in lottery Play, *Manage. Sci.* 39(12), 1521–1525.

Conlisk, J. (1993). The utility of gambling, *J. Risk Uncertainty* 6, 255–275.

Cook, P., and C. Clotfelter (1993). The peculiar scale economies of lotto, *Am. Econ. Rev.* 83(3), 634–643.

Dana, J.D., and M. Knetter (1994). Learning and efficiency in a gambling market, *Manage. Sci.* 40(10), 1317–1328.

Dansie, B. (1983). A note on permutation probabilities, *J. R. Stat. Assoc.* 68, 312–316.

Dolbear, F. (1993). Is racetrack betting on exactas efficient? *Economica* 60, 105–111.

Epstein, R. (1977). *The Theory of Gambling and Statistical Logic*, Academic Press.

Fabricand, B. (1965). *Horse Sense*, McKay, New York, NY.

Fama, E. (1970). Efficient capital markets: A review of theory and empirical work, *J. Finance* 25, 383–417.

Fama, E. (1991). Efficient capital markets: II, *J. Finance* 46, 1575–1617.

Figlewski, S. (1979). Subjective information and market efficiency in a betting model, *J. Polit. Econ.* 87, 75–88.

Friedman, M., and L. Savage (1948). The utility analysis of choices involving risk, *J. Polit. Econ.* 56, 279–304.

Gandar, J., R. Zuber, T. O'Brien and B. Russo (1988). Testing rationality in the point spread betting market, *J. Finance* September, 995–1008.

Gilovich, T., R. Vallone and A. Tversky (1985). The hot hand in basketball: On the misperception of random sequences, *Cogn. Psychol.* 17, 295–314.

Golec, J., and S. Tamarkin (1991). The degree of inefficiency in the football betting market, *J. Financ. Econ.* 30, 311–323.

Griffith, R. (1949). Odds adjustments by American horse race bettors, *Am. J. Psychol.* 62, 290–294.

Hakansson, N., and W. Ziemba (1995). Capital growth theory, in: R. Jarrow, V. Maksimovic and W.T. Ziemba (eds.), *Finance*, Handbooks in Operations Research and Management Science, Vol. 9, North Holland, Amsterdam, pp. 123–144 (this volume).

Harville, D. (1973). Assigning probabilities to the outcome of multi-entry competitions, *J. Am. Stat. Assoc.* 68, 312–316.

Hausch, D., R. Bain and W. Ziemba (1995). Betting with the Dr. Z system at the Kentucky Derby, 1934–1995, working paper, University of Britich Columbia.

Hausch, D., V. Lo and W. Ziemba, eds. (1994a). *Efficiency of Racetrack Betting Markets*, Academic Press, San Diego.

Hausch, D., V. Lo and W. Ziemba (1994b). Pricing exotic racetrack wagers, in: D. Hausch, V. Lo and W. Ziemba (eds.), *Efficiency of Racetrack Betting Markets*, Academic Press, San Diego, pp. 469–483.

Hausch, D., and W. Ziemba (1985). Transactions costs, extent of inefficiencies, entries and multiple wagers in a racetrack betting model, *Manage. Sci.* 31, 381–394.

Hausch, D., and W. Ziemba (1990a). Arbitrage strategies for cross-track betting on major horse races, *J. Bus.* 63, 61–78.

Hausch, D., and W. Ziemba (1990b). Locks at the racetrack, *Interfaces* 20, 41–48.

Hausch, D., and W. Ziemba (1992). Efficiency of sports and lottery betting markets, in: P. Newman, M. Milgate and J. Eatwell (eds.), *The New Palgrave Dictionary of Money and Banking*, Macmillan, London, pp. 735–739.

Hausch, D., W. Ziemba and M. Rubinstein (1981). Efficiency of the market for racetrack betting, *Manage. Sci.* 27, 1435–1452.

Hawawini, G., and D. Keim (1995). On the predictability of common stock returns: World-wide evidence, in: R. Jarrow, V. Maksimovic and W.T. Ziemba (eds.), *Finance*, Handbooks in Operations Research and Management Science, Vol. 9, North Holland, Amsterdam, pp. 497–544 (this volume).

Henery, R. (1981). Permutation probabilities as models for horse races, *J. R. Stat. Soc.* Ser. B, 43, 86–91.

Henery, R. (1984). An extreme-value model for predicting the results of horse races, *Appl. Stat.* 33, 125–133.

Hensel, C., G. Sick and W. Ziemba (1993). The turn-of-the-month effect in the S&P 500 (1928–1993), mimeo, Frank Russell Company.

Isaacs, R. (1953). Optimal horse race bets, *Am. Math. Monthly* 60, 310–315.

Joe, H. (1987). An ordering dependence for distribution of k-tuples, with applications to lotto games, *Cana. J. Stat.* 15(3), 227–238.

Johnson R., and J. Klotz (1993). Estimating hot numbers and testing uniformity for the lottery, *J. Am. Stat. Assoc.* 88(422), 662–668.

Kahneman, D and A. Tversky (1979). Prospect theory: An analysis of decision under risk, *Econometrica* 47, 263–291.

Kahneman, D and A. Tversky (1984). Choices, values, and frames, *Am. Psychol.* 39, 341–350.

Kallberg, J., and W. Ziemba (1994). Parimutuel betting models, in: D. Hausch, V. Lo and W. Ziemba (eds.), *Efficiency of Racetrack Betting Markets*, Academic Press, San Diego, pp. 99–107.

Kanto, A., and G. Rosenqvist (1994). On the efficiency of the market for double (quinella) bets at a Finnish racetrack, in: D. Hausch, V. Lo and W. Ziemba (eds.), *Efficiency of Racetrack Betting Markets*, Academic Press, San Diego, pp. 485–498.

Kendall, M. (1953). The analysis of economic time-series, part I: Prices, *J. R. Stat. Soc.* 96(I), 11–25.

Kelly, J. (1956). A new interpretation of the information rate, *Bell Syst. Tech. J.* July, 917–926.

Kleinfield, N. (1993). Legal gambling faces higher odds, *New York Times,* August 29, E3.

Lakonishok, J., and S. Smidt (1988). Are seasonal anomalies real? A ninety-year perspective, *Rev. Financ. Studies* 1, 403–426.

Lane, D., and W. Ziemba (1992). Jai alai hedging strategies, working paper, University of British Columbia.

Langer, E. (1975). The illusion of control, *J. Pers. Social Psychol.* 32(2), 311–328.

Latané, H. (1959). Criteria for choice among risky projects, *J. Polit. Econ.* 67, 144–155.

Leong, S., and K. Lim (1994). Cross-track betting: Is the grass greener on the other side?, in: D. Hausch, V. Lo and W. Ziemba (eds.), *Efficiency of Racetrack Betting Markets*, Academic Press, San Diego, pp. 617–629.

Levin, N. (1994). Optimal bets in pari-mutuel systems, in: D. Hausch, V. Lo and W. Ziemba (eds.), *Efficiency of Racetrack Betting Markets*, Academic Press, San Diego, pp. 109–125.

Lo, V. (1994). Application of running time distribution models in Japan, in: D. Hausch, V. Lo and W. Ziemba (eds.), *Efficiency of Racetrack Betting Markets*, Academic Press, San Diego, pp.

237–247.

Lo, V., and J. Bacon-Shone (1993). An approximation to ordering probabilities of multi-entry competitions, working paper, University of Hong Kong.

Lo, V., J. Bacon-Shone and K. Busche (1995). The application of ranking probability models to racetrack betting, *Manage. Sci.*, forthcoming.

Lo, V., and K. Busche (1994). How accurately do bettors bet in doubles? in: D. Hausch, V. Lo and W. Ziemba (eds.), *Efficiency of Racetrack Betting Markets*, Academic Press, San Diego, pp. 465–468.

Losey, R., and J. Talbott (1980). Back on the track with the efficient markets hypothesis, *J. Finance* 35, 1039–1043.

Ludlow, L. (1994). An empirical cross-validation of alternative classification strategies applied to harness racing data for win bets, in: D. Hausch, V. Lo and W. Ziemba (eds.), *Efficiency of Racetrack Betting Markets*, Academic Press, San Diego, pp. 199–212.

MacLean, L., W. Ziemba and G. Blazenko (1992). Growth versus security in dynamic investment analysis, *Manage. Sci.* 38(11), 1562–1585.

Markowitz, H. (1952). The utility of wealth, *J. Polit. Econ.* 60, 151–158.

McGlothlin, W. (1956). Stability of choices among uncertain alternatives, *Am. J. Psychol.* 63, 604–615.

Metzger, M. (1985). Biases in betting: An application of laboratory findings, *Psychol. Rep.* 56(3), 883–888.

Mitchell, D. (1986). *Thoroughbred Handicapping as an Investment*, Cynthia Publishing, Los Angeles, CA.

Pankoff, L. (1968). Market efficiency and football betting, *J. Bus.* 41, 203–214.

Plackett, R. (1975). The analysis of permutations, *Appl. Stat.* 24, 193–202.

Quandt, R. (1986). Betting and equilibrium, *Q. J. Econ.* 101, 201–207.

Quinn, J. (1986). *The Handicapper's Condition Book*, William Morrow, New York, NY.

Quinn, J. (1987). *The Best of Thoroughbred Handicapping (1965–1986)*, William Morrow, New York, NY.

Quinn, J. (1992). *Figure Handicapping*, William Morrow, New York, NY.

Quirin, W. (1979). *Winning at the Races: Computer Discoveries in Thoroughbred Handicapping*, William Morrow, New York, NY..

Quirin, W. (1984). *Thoroughbred Handicapping: State of the Art*, William Morrow, New York, NY.

Ritter, J. (1994). Racetrack betting –an example of a market with efficient arbitrage, in: D. Hausch, V. Lo and W. Ziemba (eds.), *Efficiency of Racetrack Betting Markets*, Academic Press, San Diego, pp. 431–441.

Ritter, J., and N. Chopra (1989). Portfolio rebalancing and the turn-of-the-year effect, *J. Finance* 44, 149–166.

Roberts, H. (1967). Statistical versus clinical prediction of the stock market, mimeo, University of Chicago.

Roll, R. (1977). A critique of the asset pricing theory's tests, *J. Financ. Econ.* 4, 129–176.

Rosner, B. (1975). Optimal allocation of resources in a pari-mutuel setting, *Manage. Sci.* 21(9), 997–1006.

Rosett, R. (1965). Gambling and rationality, *J. Polit. Econ.* 73, 595–607.

Sauer, R. (1991). An injury process model of forecast bias in NBA point spreads, working paper, Clemson University.

Sauer, R., V. Brajer, S. Ferris and W. Marr (1988). Hold your bets: Another look at the efficiency of the gambling market for national football league games, *J. Polit. Econ.* February, 206–213.

Savage, I. (1957). Contributions to the theory of rank order statistics — the Trend case, *Ann. Math. Stat.* 28, 968–977.

Schnytzer, A. and Y. Shilony (1995). Inside Information in a betting market, *Economic J.* 105, 963–971.

Shin, H. (1992). Prices of state contingent claims with insider traders, and the favorite-longshot bias, *Economic J.* 102, pp. 426–435.

Shin, H. (1993). Measuring the incidence of insider trading in a market for state contingent claims, *Economic J.* 103, pp. 1141–1153

Snyder, W. (1978). Horse racing: Testing the efficient markets model, *J. Finance* 33, 1109–1118.

Stern, H. (1987). Gamma processes, paired comparisons and ranking, Ph.D. dissertation, Stanford University Department of Statistics.

Stern, H. (1990). Models for distributions on permutations, *J. Am. Stat. Assoc.* 85, 558–564.

Stern, H. (1991). On the probability of winning a football game, *Am. Stat.* 45(3), 179–183.

Stern, H. (1994). Estimating the probabilities of outcomes on a horse race (Alternatives to the Harville formulas), in: D. Hausch, V. Lo and W. Ziemba (eds.), *Efficiency of Racetrack Betting Markets*, Academic Press, San Diego, pp. 225–235.

Stern, H., and T. Cover (1989). Maximum entropy and the lottery, *J. Am. Stat. Assoc.* 84(408), 980–985.

Thaler, R., and W. Ziemba (1988). Parimutuel betting markets: Racetracks and lotteries, *J. Econ. Perspect.* 2, 161–174.

Thalheimer, R., and M. Ali (1995). The demand for parimutuel horse race wagering and attendance, *Manage. Sci.* January, 41(1), 129–143.

Thorp, E. (1961). A favorable strategy for twenty-one, *Proc. Nat. Acad. Sci.* 47(1), 110–112.

Thorp, E. (1962). *Beat the Dealer*, Blaisdell Publishing, New York, NY/Revised edition Random House, New York, NY, 1966.

Tryfos, P., S. Casey, S. Cook, G. Leger and B. Pylypiak (1984). The profitability of wagering on NFL games, *Manage. Sci.* January, 123–132.

Vergin, R., and M. Scriabin (1978). Winning strategies for wagering on national football league games, *Manage. Sci.* April, 809–818.

Welles, C. (1989). America's gambling fever, *Business Week* April 24, 112–120.

Weitzman, M. (1965). Utility analysis and group behavior: An empirical study, *J. Polit. Econ.* 73, 18–26.

Ziemba, W. (1994). World wide security market regularities, *Eur. J. Oper. Res.* 74, 198–229.

Ziemba, W. (1995). Collection of Dr. Z Columns on Racing, Lotteries, Sports and Casino Gambling, Mimeo, Dr. Z Investments, Los Angeles, CA.

Ziemba, W., S. Brumelle, A. Gautier and S. Schwartz (1986). *Dr. Z's Lotto 6/49 Guidebook*, Dr. Z Investments, Los Angeles, CA.

Zuber, R., J. Gandar and B. Bowers (1985). Beating the spread: Testing the efficiency of the gambling market for NFL games, *J. Polit. Econ.* 93(4), 800–806.

Ziemba, W., and D. Hausch (1986). *Betting at the Racetrack*, Dr. Z Investments, Los Angeles, CA.

Ziemba, W., and D. Hausch (1987). *Dr. Z's Beat the Racetrack*, William Morrow, New York, NY.

R. Jarrow et al., Eds., *Handbooks in OR & MS, Vol. 9*

Chapter 19

Performance Evaluation

Mark Grinblatt
Anderson Graduate School of Management, University of California, Los Angeles, CA 90095-1481, U.S.A.

Sheridan Titman
W.E. Carroll School of Management, Boston College, Chestnut Hills, MA 02167, U.S.A.

1. Introduction

Trillions of dollars are invested in stocks worldwide by institutional portfolio managers. From a social perspective it is important to know whether these investors as a group add value to the portfolios they manage or whether they merely generate wasteful transaction costs through their active management. At the micro level it is important to know how to select a portfolio manager with the ability to add value to the portfolio he manages. Performance evaluation is a topic in financial economics that seeks to address both of these issues. In particular, it studies whether superior returns can be generated by active managers who are better able to collect and interpret information that helps forecast securities returns.[1]

To evaluate whether a manager has generated superior returns we need to adjust his portfolio return for risk. Since the mean returns of securities are positively related to their risk, performance measures are based on techniques that adjust for priced risk. Some performance measures use the diversification of a portfolio as an additional criterion for evaluation. This requires an adjustment for both priced risk and unpriced risk, typified by the performance measure known as Sharpe's ratio [Sharpe, 1966]. Sharpe's ratio is the excess return of the portfolio (above the risk-free return) divided by the standard deviation of the return of the portfolio.

Adjusting for performance based on the total risk of a portfolio rather than the priced risk of a portfolio is no longer popular and we think inappropriate. This is

[1] Many investors assert that they make money by 'arbitraging' mispriced derivatives. For example, they may buy a European call option that is underpriced relative to the Black-Scholes model and short the underlying stock in appropriate amounts so as to achieve a riskless return that exceeds the current riskless rate available in the fixed income markets. This type of performance is based on model failure, rather than asymmetric information. Indeed, in the effectively complete markets world of derivatives pricing, no asymmetric information about the mean returns of securities is permitted. Since there is no available performance methodology that addresses the issue of performance based on model failure, we do not discuss the issue here.

because the managers whose performance is typically evaluated rarely manage the entire savings of an investor. Investors in mutual funds, for example, typically hold a number of funds and may personally manage a large portion of their wealth. They may also hold a substantial fraction of their wealth in the home they own or the human capital they possess. Even if we argue that for some individuals, most of their wealth is held in their pension fund, most pension funds farm out the management of their assets to a number of different firms. It therefore seems more important to focus on the marginal contributions of a managed portfolio to the risk and expected return of an investor. This necessarily involves adjusting for risk with a marginal risk measure, like beta.

There are two basic classes of performance measures analyzed in this chapter. An intuitive way to think about both classes of performance measures is that they compare the returns of the actively managed portfolio that is being evaluated with a passive (i.e. buy and hold) portfolio with the same level of risk. The first class requires the observation of the returns of the evaluated portfolio as well as the returns of a benchmark that consists of one or more portfolios along with a risk-free asset. The second class utilizes information about the composition of the evaluated portfolio but does not necessarily require a benchmark portfolio(s). In most cases the first class of measures assumes that stock returns are normally distributed. This assumption is not needed for the second class of measures. However, both classes of measures require that stock returns be drawn from a stationary distribution.

The stationarity requirement is considered by some to be a serious weakness of the performance evaluation literature. Given the recent literature on the nonstationarity of expected stock returns, as found, for example, in Ferson [1995, chapter 5 in this volume] and Hawawini & Keim [1995, chapter 17 in this volume], this concern seems particularly valid. However, this assumption is needed because it is generally impossible for an observer to empirically distinguish between the performance of informed investors and the 'performance' of uninformed investors who optimally respond to changes in the parameters of the return generating process. Indeed, a fair 'philosophical' distinction between an economy with informed investors and an economy with changing parameters is one of magnitude. In the former, only a few investors observe the nonstationarities, whereas in the latter, virtually all investors observe the nonstationarities (and only the evaluator is naive). A more sophisticated evaluation technique that models the nonstationarities known to uninformed market participants can in principle avoid this problem, but modelling what is known by 'the market' is speculative at best.

2. Measures based solely on returns

2.1. *Treynor's ratio, Jensen's alpha, and the Treynor–Black appraisal ratio*

A number of measures of performance are based on the capital asset pricing model, a theory relating expected return to a measure of risk known as 'beta'.

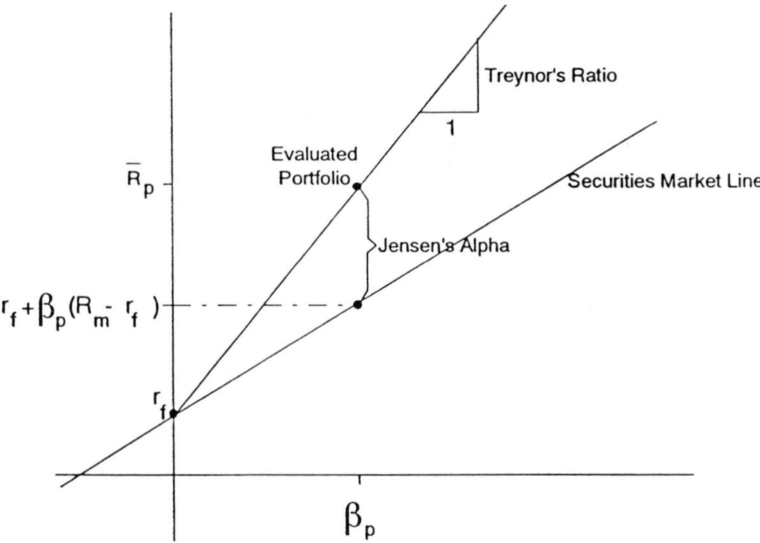

Fig. 1. The distinction between Treynor's ratio and Jensen's alpha.

Beta is the slope coefficient in a regression of the return of the portfolio being evaluated against the return of a proxy for the market portfolio. The relation between between beta and expected return is graphically represented by the securities market line, observed in Figure 1 (and discussed in Ferson [1995, chapter 5 in this volume]). The true mean returns and betas (as opposed to their estimated values) of all securities and all passive portfolios of securities lie on this line if the Capital Asset Pricing Model (CAPM) is true.

2.1.1. Treynor's ratio

Treynor's ratio [Treynor, 1965] was the first academic attempt to adjust returns with betas in order to measure performance. It is computed as

$$\frac{\bar{R}_{\mathrm{p}} - r_{\mathrm{f}}}{\beta_{\mathrm{p}}},$$

the average return of the portfolio in excess of the risk-free return divided by the portfolio's beta. It is thus the slope of a line connecting the risk-free return to the evaluated portfolio in mean–beta space, as illustrated in Figure 1.

2.1.2. Jensen's alpha

A variation of the Treynor approach, known as Jensen's alpha, is the arithmetic difference of the portfolio's return from the return of a portfolio on the securities-market line with the same beta, as illustrated in Figure 1. Since all securities are expected to lie on the securities market line if the CAPM holds, the alphas of passively managed portfolios (with returns measured before transaction costs, fees, and expenses), are expected to be zero. An actively managed portfolio with a significantly positive Jensen's alpha is therefore interpreted as a portfolio that is managed with superior forecasts. We will later examine the conditions under which this interpretation is correct.

Jensen's alpha is a more commonly used measure of performance than Treynor's ratio. One reason for its popularity is that it is easily computed by finding the intercept in the regression,

$$\tilde{R}_{\mathrm{p}} - r_{\mathrm{f}} = \alpha_{\mathrm{p}} + \beta_{\mathrm{p}}(\tilde{R}_{\mathrm{M}} - r_{\mathrm{f}}) + \tilde{\epsilon}_{\mathrm{p}} \tag{1}$$

The intercept, α_{p}, computed as

$$\alpha_{\mathrm{p}} = \bar{R}_{\mathrm{p}} - r_{\mathrm{f}} - \beta_{\mathrm{p}}(\bar{R}_{\mathrm{M}} - r_{\mathrm{f}}), \tag{2}$$

is the average excess return of the portfolio less the product of the portfolio's beta and the average excess return of the market portfolio. Intuitively, Jensen's alpha is the difference between the return of the evaluated portfolio and the return of the passive portfolio consisting of beta units of the benchmark portfolio and one minus beta units of the risk-free asset.

2.1.3. *Ranking of forecasting ability and the Treynor–Black appraisal ratio*

Treynor's ratio was designed to rank portfolios and does not determine whether a particular portfolio was managed by someone with superior abilities. However, if 'uninformed managers' have portfolios (absent fees, expenses, and transaction costs) that plot on the securities market line, any manager with forecasting ability is expected to have a Treynor ratio (absent these same frictions) that is significantly in excess of the slope of the securities market line, $\bar{R}_{\mathrm{M}} - r_{\mathrm{f}}$, where $\bar{R}_{\mathrm{M}}$ is the average return of the proxy for the market portfolio.

A manager's aggressiveness in using information will alter the expected return of a portfolio. Hence a manager with low risk aversion and good information may outperform a manager with a high degree of risk aversion and great information. Measures like Treynor's, that involve a ratio of return to risk mitigate this problem. However, there is no a priori reason to believe that the beta adjustment suggested by Treynor is the correct one for a cardinal ranking of managerial information precision. For example, a manager with the ability to forecast the epsilon in a market model regression

$$\tilde{r}_i - r_{\mathrm{f}} = \alpha_i + \beta_i(\tilde{R}_{\mathrm{M}} - r_{\mathrm{f}}) + \tilde{\epsilon}_i \tag{3}$$

might hedge out the market risk associated with the acquisition of large positions in the security. This requires shorting β_i dollars of the market portfolio for each \$1 invested in the ith security. If these forecasts are imperfect, so that $\tilde{\epsilon}_i$ conditioned on the manager's information still has some variability, a less risk averse manager will generally take a larger position in security i. In this case, simple division by the portfolio beta will not capture the relatively higher unsystematic risk of the less risk averse manager.

A measure derived from Jensen's alpha can rank managers according to information precision. Connor & Koraczyk [1986] describe a case in which the Treynor & Black [1973] appraisal ratio,

$$\frac{\alpha_{\mathrm{p}}}{s_{\mathrm{p}}},$$

which is Jensen's alpha divided by the standard deviation of the error term in the regression used to obtain alpha, properly ranks managers according to their forecasting abilities. However, this result requires a number of assumptions before it is valid, including: no ability to forecast the market, multivariate normal returns, exponential utility as the criterion for investment for all managers, and the tradability of all assets for all managers. These restrictions appear to be stringent enough to preclude the usefulness of this ratio as a tool for ranking

While the ability to rank managers according to the precision of their forecasting ability is an ideal, we must generally content ourselves with the separation of portfolio managers into two classes: those with superior forecasting ability and those without it. One cannot be greatly disappointed that ranking is probably impossible because of differences in managerial (and ultimately client) risk aversion. However, the ability to forecast securities returns is rare if one largely accepts the common academic view of the efficient markets hypothesis. A measure of performance that merely identifies the few managers with forecasting ability would then be quite useful.

2.2. Asset pricing, performance measurement, and Roll's critique

The measures of performance that we discussed in the last section used the Capital Asset Pricing Model as the theoretical basis for their construction. As a result, the benchmarks originally used to compute these measures are proxies for the value-weighted market portfolio. However, other benchmarks have been used to estimate Jensen's alpha, Treynor's ratio, and the Treynor–Black ratio. One can also use a multiple portfolio benchmark with Jensen's alpha. The summed product of the multiple regression betas and the average excess returns of the benchmark portfolios is then subtracted from the average excess return of the portfolio being evaluated. The alphas obtained from a multiple portfolio benchmark are equivalent to the alphas that would be obtained from using the ex-post efficient combination of the portfolios in the benchmark.[2]

The choice of a benchmark portfolio is probably the most controversial issue in performance evaluation. The debate about benchmarks was initiated by Roll [1978] who noted that different benchmark portfolios provide different risk adjustments and hence different assessments of abnormal performance. He showed that two benchmark portfolios lying inside the mean–variance efficient frontier

[2] Grinblatt & Titman [1987] show that the mean-variance efficient combination of a set of multiple benchmarks will be itself mean-variance efficient if and only if the Jensen's alphas derived from these multiple portfolio benchmarks are all zero.

could reverse the rankings of a group of passive portfolios. Portfolios lying above the securities market line with one benchmark lie below the securities market line with the other benchmark and vice versa. On the other hand, a benchmark portfolio that is mean–variance efficient cannot distinguish between passive portfolios. Passive portfolios, like all securities, lie on the securities market line in this case.

The reason for this is a mathematical relation. The equation of the securities market line,

$$\bar{r}_i = r_\mathrm{f} + \beta_i(\bar{R}_\mathrm{E} - r_\mathrm{f}), \qquad \text{for all } i$$

where

$$\beta_i = \frac{\mathrm{cov}\,(\tilde{r}_i, \tilde{R}_\mathrm{E})}{\mathrm{var}\,(\tilde{R}_\mathrm{E})},$$

is merely the (necessary and sufficient) first order condition for the mean–variance efficiency of the benchmark (portfolio E) used to compute beta. Because of this mathematical property of mean–variance efficiency, it would seem that a proper benchmark portfolio needs to be both mean–variance efficient and mean–variance inefficient at the same time. It needs to be mean–variance efficient so that the portfolios of uninformed managers and all passive portfolios will have Jensen's alphas of zero. It needs to be mean–variance inefficient for the portfolios of managers with forecasting ability so that these portfolios can have nonzero alphas.

This would seem to be an impossible task for a portfolio, but for the fact that the information sets of managers with forecasting ability differ from those without forecasting ability. Two managers with different information sets would necessarily draw different mean–standard deviation diagrams. In particular, the manager with forecasting ability would have mean–variance frontiers that are improved by dynamic portfolio strategies — strategies that weight more heavily those securities that are forecasted to have unusually high returns in a period. Managers lacking this ability cannot achieve a better mean–variance tradeoff by dynamically changing their portfolio weights. Hence, their efficient frontier plots inside the efficient frontier of informed managers, as in Figure 2. This insight implies that portfolio performance evaluation may escape Roll's critique if we use a benchmark that lies on the line connecting points A and B in Figure 2. This benchmark is mean–variance efficient with respect to passive portfolios but not with respect to the dynamic portfolios chosen by managers with forecasting ability.

The performance obtained with a benchmark having this property is analyzed in models developed by Mayers & Rice [1979], Dybvig & Ross [1985a, b], and Grinblatt & Titman [1989b]. In these models, investors with superior information about individual securities returns (i.e. selectivity information) but with no information about the return on the benchmark (i.e. timing information) achieve positive alphas if the benchmark is mean–variance efficient from the perspective of

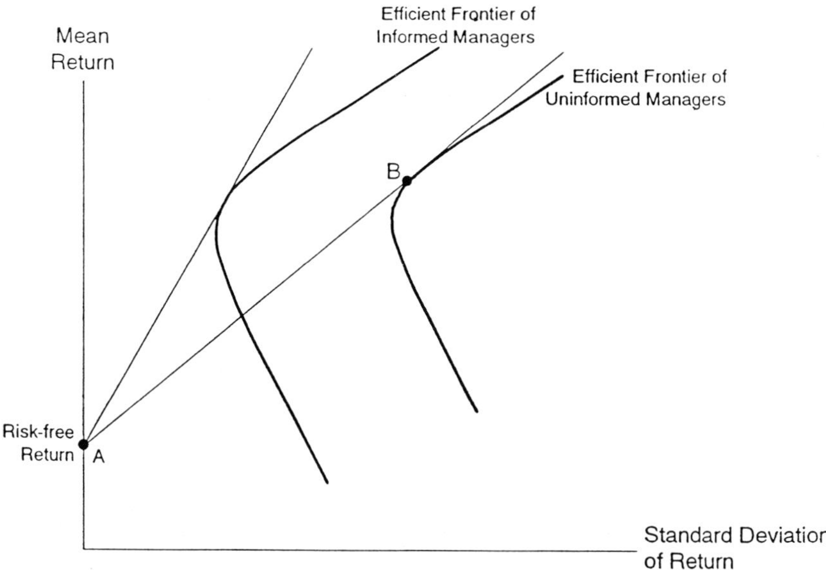

Fig. 2. Differences between the efficient frontiers of informed and uninformed portfolio managers.

an investor without forecasting ability. For investors with timing information, this result does not necessarily hold. We will defer discussion of this timing problem until later.

A practical complication still remains. Figure 2 is based on the ex-ante means and standard deviations of portfolios rather than their estimated means and standard deviations. It suggests that we employ a benchmark portfolio on the ex-ante efficient frontier, but finding such a portfolio is not an easy task. Motivated by the CAPM, early empirical studies of mutual fund performance made use of value-weighted portfolios as benchmarks. These studies were undertaken prior to the late 1970s, when a number of CAPM anomalies were discovered.[3] Given the more recent empirical evidence, the benchmarks used in these studies appear to be inappropriate for studying portfolio performance, since they can be gamed by managers aware of CAPM-related anomalies, like the well-known firm size or dividend yield effects. In the next section, we outline the results from empirical studies of fund performance with techniques that are based on securities market line analysis. We can see how benchmarks have evolved as we analyze these studies in chronological order.

[3] While there was evidence in the early 1970s of a beta-related anomaly, this anomaly was small for stocks with betas close to 1 (e.g. portfolios with betas from 0.85 to 1.1 deviated by at most 0.5% per year from the securities market line, which is well within levels of statistical tolerance). Since most mutual funds, and certainly the average mutual fund, have betas close to 1, early empirical studies of mutual fund performance felt that CAPM proxies were appropriate benchmarks.

2.3. Empirical studies that employ securities market line analysis

2.3.1. Studies that employ a single portfolio benchmark

Jensen's doctoral dissertation, summarized in articles in the *Journal of Finance* [1968] and the *Journal of Business* [1969], was one of the earliest and most influential studies of mutual fund performance. The study used Jensen's alpha to evaluate the yearly returns of 115 mutual funds over the 1945–1964 period. The sample included all of the funds that were followed by Wiesenberger's *Investment Companies* over the entire 1955–1964 period. The benchmark used to evaluate these funds was the S&P composite index which is a value-weighted portfolio (consisting of 500 stocks after March 1, 1957 and 90 stocks prior to this date).

Jensen concluded that over the 1955–1964 period, mutual funds, on average, achieved a risk-adjusted performance of about −0.9% per year.[4] When the various commissions and expenses of the funds were added back to the funds' returns, the risk-adjusted performance was virtually zero. Thus, the average returns of the funds were consistent with what would be expected in an efficient market. Similar results were found by McDonald [1974] using the equally-weighted NYSE index as his benchmark.

For a smaller sample of 56 funds, Jensen also examined whether funds that did relatively well (poorly) from 1945–1954 also did well (poorly) from 1955–1964. The correlation between the first half returns and second half returns was 0.64 indicating that the performance of some mutual funds persists over time. This would be evidence against market efficiency if it were the positive performers that did well persistently. However, the evidence suggests that it is primarily the bad performers that exhibit persistent performance. These persistently bad performance numbers could have been generated by funds that generated very high commissions and other expenses. The study failed to find evidence of persistently positive performance.

In a comment on Jensen's study, Mains [1977] argued that the mutual fund returns used by Jensen were biased downwards. Jensen assumed that the dividends of the fund were paid out at the end of the year which was in fact not true. As a result, the interest income on the dividend payments was ignored in Jensen's analysis. The way in which Jensen added back expenses and commissions produced a similar bias in his estimates of gross returns. Mains also questioned Jensen's estimates of systematic risk.

To reassess the Jensen results, Mains analyzed the monthly returns of 70 of the 115 funds examined by Jensen over the same 1955 to 1964 time period. The use of monthly returns, rather than the yearly returns used by Jensen, eliminates the bias associated with the assumption that the dividends were paid at the end of the year and provides superior estimates of the betas and alphas of the funds.

[4] While some funds achieved positive abnormal returns, it is difficult to ascertain the implications of this for the efficient markets hypothesis because of the multiple comparison being made. That is, even if no superior fund management ability existed, we would expect some funds to achiever superior risk-adjusted returns by chance.

Mains concluded that, on average, the net risk-adjusted returns of mutual funds were about zero. However, after adding back expenses, their gross risk-adjusted returns were about 1% per year. Although the study did not report the statistical significance of that 1% abnormal return, it is unlikely that a 1% return significantly differs from zero.

A more recent application of the securities market line methodology was undertaken by Ippolito [1989]. Using the S&P 500 benchmark, Ippolito found slightly positive average alphas (0.83% per year) for his sample of mutual funds in a later period (1965–1984). Ippolito interprets his findings as indicating that mutual funds are able to use their superior information to generate abnormal returns. However, as we discuss in the next subsection, such conclusions are highly dependent on the choice of benchmark portfolios.

2.3.2. *Studies with multiple portfolio benchmarks*

More recent studies have examined the sensitivity of performance inferences to the choice of the benchmark portfolio, examining multiple as well as single portfolio benchmarks. There are a number of advantages to using multiple portfolio benchmarks. First, unless stock returns are generated by only one common factor, it is unlikely that an arbitrarily chosen diversified portfolio will be mean–variance efficient. However, as Grinblatt & Titman [1987] emphasize, if securities returns are generated by at most k factors, then in the absence of arbitrage, any k well-diversified portfolios will sum to the mean–variance efficient frontier. For this reason we generally feel more comfortable with multiple portfolio benchmarks than with single portfolio benchmarks. Moreover, there is an alternative asset pricing theory, the Arbitrage Pricing Theory (APT), summarized by Connor & Korajczyk [1995, chapter 4 of this volume], that makes use of a multiple portfolio benchmark and which provides guidance on how to select a multiple portfolio benchmark.

Empirical investigations of mutual fund performance with multiple portfolio benchmarks can be found in papers by Lehmann & Modest [1987], Grinblatt & Titman [1989a, 1994], Connor & Korajczyk [1991], and Elton, Gruber, Das & Hlavka [1993]. The study by Lehmann and Modest was the first to adapt the APT to performance evaluation. The benchmarks considered by Lehmann and Modest included the CRSP value-weighted index of all NYSE and AMEX listed stocks (VW), the CRSP equally-weighted index of all NYSE and AMEX listed stocks (EW), and 5, 10, and 15 portfolio benchmarks formed using a variety of factor analysis methods. Over the 1968 to 1982 time period they found that benchmarks formed with the various factor analysis methods produced similar performance numbers. However, the performance numbers with the EW and VW benchmarks differed from each other as well as from the numbers generated with the factor analysis benchmarks. The factor analysis benchmark that they examined in the greatest detail generated very negative performance numbers on average, approximately −4% per year. The EW index generated performance numbers of similar magnitude while the VW index generated performance numbers that were close to zero on average.

Although the factor analysis benchmark has strong theoretical motivation, the extreme negative average performance numbers it generates indicate that the benchmark may not be appropriate. Given that the 4% negative performance greatly exceeds the level of expenses and commissions, the performance numbers suggest that the funds must, on average, be systematically selecting bad stocks, which does not seem plausible. Lehmann and Modest provide two possible explanations for this perverse finding: one is that the mutual funds exhibit timing ability, which biases the beta estimates upwards and the intercepts downwards (see Section 2.4); the second is that the benchmark portfolios cannot be combined to form a point on the mean–variance efficient frontier.

Lehmann and Modest's earlier work[5] suggests that the second explanation is very plausible. The factor analysis benchmark, like the EW benchmark, exhibits a strong size-related bias. In particular, the stocks of large firms exhibit negative alphas when evaluated by this benchmark. Since mutual funds generally select larger than average stocks, it follows that they are likely to exhibit negative performance when measured against this benchmark. Lehmann & Modest [1987] also examined the possibility that the negative performance estimates result from the mutual funds timing the market. They did this by employing a Treynor & Mazuy [1966] quadratic regression, but failed to find evidence of pervasive timing behavior.[6]

Connor & Korajczyk [1991], using a five factor model, analyzed the same sample of mutual funds over the same time period as did Lehmann and Modest. To derive their five portfolio benchmark they first constructed five portfolios using principal components analysis. Four linear combinations of these five portfolios that best mimic a set of four prespecified macroeconomic factors are then formed to yield four new factor portfolios that correspond to the four macro-factors. A fifth factor, the residual of the regression of the value-weighted index on the previously described four macro-factor portfolios, was also used. (The performance results generated with this residual are the same as those that would have been generated by including the value-weighted index itself as the fifth factor.) Because of the inclusion of this fifth factor, Connor and Koraczyk did not find the same evidence of negative performance found by Lehmann and Modest.

Grinblatt & Titman [1989a] provided further evidence that the negative abnormal return generated with Lehmann and Modest's factor analysis benchmark is the result of the inefficiency of the benchmark. In addition to examining performance with the equally-weighted and value-weighted indices and the Lehmann and Modest 10 factor benchmark, they developed a second multiple portfolio benchmark, referred to as 'P8', that is formed on the basis of securities character-

[5] Lehmann & Modest [1989], which developed the factor analysis technique used in Lehmann & Modest [1987], was published later than their mutual fund study.

[6] Even if timing ability were pervasive, it is unlikely that it would result in negative intercepts. Under reasonable parameter values, the intercept is likely to be positive for positive timers. It is more plausible that the negative intercepts are caused by perverse timers. For example, mutual funds might choose to be very conservative when return variances and expected returns are unusually high.

istics. This eight portfolio benchmark consisted of four size-based portfolios, three dividend-yield-based portfolios, and the lowest past returns portfolio. The rationale for forming benchmark portfolios based on securities characteristics is that these characteristics may be better proxies for the true factors than factors formed with statistical factor analysis. In their sample period, the P8 benchmark could not be gamed by simple strategies based on well-known CAPM and APT anomalies, such as firm size, dividend yield, beta, skewness, interest rate sensitivity, or past performance.[7] In addition, the benchmark did not generate significantly different alphas for portfolios grouped by industry.[8]

In addition to examining the actual returns of the mutual funds, Grinblatt & Titman [1989a] analyzed what they called 'hypothetical portfolios', formed from the quarterly holdings of the mutual funds. In contrast to the actual portfolios of the funds, the hypothetical portfolios consisted entirely of equity. Since a mutual fund manager's decisions to allocate assets between cash, bonds and stocks do not affect these hypothetical returns, their betas are likely to vary much less than the betas of the actual fund returns. Hence, performance measurement biases arising because of timing the market are substantially lower with these hypothetical returns. In addition, the hypothetical portfolio returns include no expenses or transaction costs and thus should generate zero performance under the null hypothesis that fund managers have no special information.

The Grinblatt & Titman [1989a] findings confirmed the Lehmann and Modest conclusion that benchmark choice does matter. For the actual mutual fund returns, the EW index and the factor analysis benchmark generated very negative performance numbers on average. In contrast, the performance numbers generated by the VW index and the P8 benchmark yielded performance numbers that were close to zero on average. The various benchmarks also ranked the mutual funds differently, [Grinblatt & Titman, 1988]. The P8 benchmark ranked funds very differently than the EW index and the 10 factor benchmark. However, the 10 factor benchmark provided performance scores that were similar to the EW index on a fund by fund basis. The cross-sectional correlation coefficient [from Grinblatt & Titman, 1994] was 0.86.[9]

An evaluation of the hypothetical returns of the portfolios formed from the quarterly holdings revealed slightly positive performance with the VW index (1.9% per year) and the P8 benchmark (1.1% per year) but negative average

[7] See Hawawini & Keim [1995, chapter 17 of this volume) and De Bondt & Thaler [1995, chapter 13 of this volume] for more detail.

[8] A recent paper by Sharpe [1992] forms benchmarks in a similar manner. Sharpe postulates that the 'style' of each managed portfolio can be characterized as a linear function of 12 prespecified passive portfolios that represent the various dimensions of investment style. To find the combination of these 12 portfolios that has the same style as the managed portfolio that is being evaluated, he regresses the managed portfolio's return on the returns of the 12 style portfolios. The estimated betas from this regression are then used as portfolios weights to construct a passive portfolio with the same style as the managed portfolio.

[9] This distinction from the Lehmann and Modest results can be explained by differences in the sample period.

performance with both the EW index (−3.0% per year) and the factor analysis benchmark (−2.4% per year). The positive performance was statistically significant with the VW index but not with the P8 benchmark. The negative performance was statistically significant with the factor analysis benchmark but not with the EW index. Since we can rule out timing and expenses as an explanation for the negative performance numbers generated with the equally-weighted index and the factor analysis benchmark, we must conclude that these benchmarks are not mean–variance efficient and are thus inappropriate for the evaluation of fund performance.

Grinblatt & Titman's [1989a] analysis of the aggressive growth funds is especially useful for understanding the suitability of the different benchmarks. The hypothetical returns of these funds generated significant positive performance (3.3% per year) when measured relative to the P8 benchmark. However, the performance is substantially negative (−3.7%) when measured relative to the factor analysis benchmark. To understand this, consider the fact that aggressive growth funds invest heavily in relatively large firms with low dividend yields. Since the returns of large firms with low dividend yields do poorly relative to the factor analysis benchmark (as shown in Grinblatt & Titman [1988]), mutual funds that follow such a strategy will also exhibit poor performance when measured with respect to this benchmark even if some of the funds really do have superior abilities. However, when these biases are eliminated with the P8 benchmark, the hypothetical returns of the aggressive growth funds exhibit positive performance on average.

The positive performance of the hypothetical returns of the aggressive growth funds does not imply that investors can realize abnormal returns by holding shares directly in these funds. The abnormal performance of the actual fund returns is close to zero on average. The difference in the performance of the hypothetical returns and the actual returns can be attributed to the expenses of the funds and the costs of trading (e.g. brokerage commisions and the bid–ask spread). The estimates of these costs that are derived from this difference is about 2.5% per year for the average mutual fund in the sample (and about 3% for the average aggressive growth fund).

The work of Elton, Gruber, Das & Hlavka [1993], punctuates this evidence on the importance of the benchmark portfolio in drawing performance evaluation conclusions. They propose a 3-index benchmark that includes bond portfolios as well as stock portfolios. Specifically, their benchmark is comprised of the S&P 500 index, a small stock index, and a bond index. They used this benchmark to reevaluate Ippolito's conclusions about mutual funds generating abnormal returns. They found that with their benchmark, Ippolito's sample of mutual funds generated insignificant negative abnormal performance, attributing Ippolito's 'performance' to fund holdings of non-S&P 500 stocks and bonds.

The importance of the choice of a benchmark portfolio is nicely illustrated by the contradictory results on average fund performance between single portfolio and multiple portfolio benchmarks and between different multiple portfolio benchmarks. The lesson of Roll [1978] could not be more clear: When evaluating the performance of a fund manager, the benchmark must be ex-ante efficient with respect to the mean–variance set generated by the passive investment strategies that the fund manager considers feasible.

2.3.3. *Is there differential performance?*

The positive abnormal performance of the hypothetical mutual fund returns in the Grinblatt & Titman [1989a] study suggests that at least some funds have superior selection ability. Given this, it is natural to ask whether some funds realize better performance than do other funds. We will discuss two ways to test this proposition: The most general test is to simultaneously estimate the market model regressions for each of the mutual funds and to jointly test the restriction that their Jensen's alphas are equal to each other. This test does not quantify differential performance. It merely rejects or fails to reject the hypothesis that all funds have the same risk-adjusted returns. A second test, which analyzes whether the past performance of a mutual fund is a good indicator of its future performance, has the ability to quantify differences in performance.

Within the first class of tests, Grinblatt & Titman [1989a] estimated a series of joint F-tests to determine whether mutual funds with the same investment objectives all generate the same performance.[10] These tests revealed evidence of differential performance for the actual as well as the hypothetical returns of the aggressive growth and growth funds. There was no evidence of differential performance among the funds with other investment objectives.

Tests of the persistence of mutual fund performance may be somewhat less general, but they more directly address the question that is of most interest to mutual fund investors. Is the past performance of a fund a good indicator of its future performance?

Direct tests of this proposition are found in Grinblatt & Titman [1992] and Hendricks, Patel & Zeckhauser [1993]. Grinblatt and Titman examined the actual returns of a sample of 279 funds over the 1975 to 1984 time period using their P8 benchmark. They divided the sample into 1975–1979 and 1980–1984 subperiods and examined whether better than average performance in the earlier half is indicative of better than average performance in the later half. Their results provide weak support for the hypothesis that better than average performance persists over time. For example, the subsample of funds that achieved performance in the top decile in the first subperiod did not realize abnormal performance on average in the second subperiod (although the performance would be positive if expenses were added to the returns). In contrast, funds that performed in the bottom decile in the first subperiod realized abnormal performance of −3.6% per year. The difference between the performance of these groups of funds is statistically significant at the 5% level.

The Hendricks, Patel, and Zeckhauser study, which looks at no-load growth-oriented mutual funds from 1974–1988, provides stronger evidence that funds

[10] Because their sample included 157 mutual funds, but only 120 monthly observations, they did not have enough degrees of freedom to jointly test the equality of all of the intercepts.

that do well in the past do well in the future. In their study, funds in the top octile of past performers over the past year (as measured with raw returns), outperformed the lowest octile past performers in the following year, by 10–16% per year (as measured by risk-adjusted returns, with the variation depending on the benchmark). Their analysis suggests that the best way to profit from this persistence is to focus on the raw returns of funds in the prior four quarters.[11] Information about performance beyond the previous four quarters does not seem to predict future performance. In contrast to Grinblatt & Titman [1992], they find profits from buying the winners as well as from selling the losers. While the profits from buying the past performers in the top octile are large for some benchmarks, they generally are not statistically significant.[12]

2.4. *Timing, selectivity and biases in Jensen's alpha*

We now analyze how timing and selectivity ability affect performance and discuss methods to separate these two types of performance ability. The distinction between timing and selectivity is important in that it is generally more difficult to evaluate performance when there is any timing ability contributing to it.

[11] The persistence of abnormal performance for only about four quarters is not consistent with the idea that some fund managers have superior ability. Ability should last more than four quarters. In addition, four quarters of historical returns is not a sufficiently long time series to draw proper statistical inferences about ability, given the volatility of mutual fund returns. Hence, the fund rankings of Hendricks, Patel & Zeckhauser [1993] are largely due to noise in stock returns. Their evidence on persistence may be related to recent evidence of persistence in individual stock returns [e.g. Jegadeesh & Titman, 1993]. Funds that happen to hold stocks that do well, and continue to hold those stocks, will continue to do well because of the persistence in the individual stock returns. While Hendricks, Patel & Zeckhauser [1993] employ simulations to conclude that persistence in stock returns is not driving their hot-hands effect, their simulations are based on randomly held equally-weighted portfolios of 100 stocks. Relative to actual fund strategies over this time period, this approach may be biased against finding a stock persistence effect.

[12] A recent paper by Brown, Goetzmann, Ibbotson & Ross [1992] argues that results of persistence will appear spuriously in samples limited to surviving mutual funds. Their argument is that funds that choose high risk strategies and survive in the first half of the sample period are likely to have above average returns. If these funds continue their high risk strategy and continue to survive, they are also likely to achieve above normal returns in the second half of the sample. This bias in favor of finding persistence is offset somewhat by the fact that funds which do poorly in the first half of the sample are more likely to exit the sample in the test period (because of poor performance in the test period) than those funds that did well in the first half. Survivorship bias of this type is therefore more severe for the past losers than for the past winners, biasing our tests against finding persistence. Apparently, these two effects are either unimportant in practice, or alternatively, they cancel each other out. Tests of the persistence of mutual fund performance on samples that are not subject to a survival requirement [e.g. Grinblatt & Titman, 1993, footnote 13], provide evidence that is similar to tests on samples that require survival for the entire sample period. Malkiel's [1995] work, however, suggests that conclusions about the unimportance of survivorship may be sensitive to the time period studied. In particular, he finds that there is no evidence of persistence among a sample of surviving and non-surviving funds in the 1980s (but there is persistence in the 1970s). Brown & Goetzmann [1995], using data on non-surviving funds, similarly find that survivorship bias plays some role (albeit a modest one) in the hot hands persistence findings.

We can more formally classify these two types of ability with a simple regression. Let

$\tilde{r}_j$ = excess return of asset j

$\tilde{x}_j$ = the investor's portfolio weight on asset j, which is random, since the investor may alter his portfolio in response to (real or imagined) information.

$\tilde{R}_{\mathrm{p}}$ = the summed product of $\tilde{r}_j$ and $\tilde{x}_j$

= excess return of the investor's portfolio of the N risky assets

$\tilde{R}_{\mathrm{E}}$ = the excess return of the portfolio of risky assets that is mean–variance efficient from the perspective of an uninformed observer.

A regression of the excess return of security i on the excess return of a mean–variance efficient benchmark portfolio implies that the excess return of each asset is

$$\tilde{r}_j = \beta_j \tilde{R}_{\mathrm{E}} + \tilde{\epsilon}_j \tag{4}$$

where

$$\beta_j = \frac{\operatorname{cov}(\tilde{r}_j, \tilde{R}_{\mathrm{E}})}{\operatorname{var}(\tilde{R}_{\mathrm{E}})}$$

and, given the efficiency of the benchmark, the mean of $\tilde{\epsilon}_j$ is zero. It follows that the excess return of the investor's portfolio is

$$\tilde{R}_{\mathrm{p}} = \tilde{\beta}_{\mathrm{p}} \tilde{R}_{\mathrm{E}} + \tilde{\epsilon}_{\mathrm{p}} \tag{5}$$

where

$$\tilde{\beta}_{\mathrm{p}} = \sum_{j=1}^{N} \tilde{x}_j \beta_j \qquad \text{and} \qquad \tilde{\epsilon}_{\mathrm{p}} = \sum_{j=1}^{N} \tilde{x}_j \tilde{\epsilon}_j .$$

Taking the expected value of both sides of equation (5) yields

$$E(\tilde{R}_{\mathrm{p}}) = E(\tilde{\beta}_{\mathrm{p}}) E(\tilde{R}_{\mathrm{E}}) + \operatorname{cov}(\tilde{\beta}_{\mathrm{p}}, \tilde{R}_{\mathrm{E}}) + E(\tilde{\epsilon}_{\mathrm{p}}) \tag{6}$$

The first term on the right hand side of equation (6) is the expected excess return of the portfolio conditional on knowing the portfolio's target risk level. The second term, the covariance between the portfolio beta and the return of the benchmark, is the contribution of timing to the excess return. The third term, which is the sum of the covariances between the portfolio holdings and the residuals, is the contribution of selectivity to the excess return. Total abnormal performance, the sum of the latter two terms, can be shown to be the sum of the covariances between the portfolio weights and the returns,

$$\sum_{j=1}^{N} \operatorname{cov}(\tilde{x}_j, \tilde{r}_j). \tag{7}$$

Grinblatt & Titman [1989b] have shown that this covariance should be positive for investors with the ability to forecast returns.[13]

It is often difficult to properly capture performance with Jensen's alpha, Treynor's ratio, or the Treynor–Black appraisal ratio if betas change. For example, if the beta of the portfolio increases as the forecasted benchmark return increases, the single portfolio beta estimated with Jensen's regression will overestimate the average beta, $E(\tilde{\beta}_{\mathrm{p}})$. The resulting intercept is then underestimated and under certain conditions can be negative for investors with timing information.[14] Figure 3, drawn from Grinblatt & Titman [1989b], provides a binomial illustration of this phenomenon. Popular examples in the literature illustrate that this phenomenon can also occur for certain parameter values when the portfolio beta is a linear function of a normally distributed timing signal.[15]

The large sample value (or probability limit) of Jensen's alpha can be decomposed to better analyze this phenomenon and to point out the relation of this performance measure to timing and selectivity. Grinblatt & Titman [1989b] showed that Jensen's alpha can be decomposed into the sum of three terms:

$$\begin{aligned}\alpha = \operatorname{plim}\left[\frac{1}{T}\sum_{t=1}^{T}(\tilde{\beta}_{\mathrm{p}t} - b_{\mathrm{p}})\right]\hat{R}_{\mathrm{E}} \\ + \operatorname{plim}\left[\frac{1}{T}\sum_{t=1}^{T}\tilde{\beta}_{\mathrm{p}t}(\tilde{R}_{\mathrm{E}t} - \hat{R}_{\mathrm{E}})\right] \\ + \operatorname{plim}\left[\frac{1}{T}\sum_{t=1}^{T}\tilde{\epsilon}_{\mathrm{p}t}\right],\end{aligned} \tag{8}$$

where

b_{p} = the probability limit of the least squares slope coefficient from the time-series regression of excess returns of the evaluated portfolio against the excess returns of the efficient benchmark portfolio and

$\hat{R}_{\mathrm{E}}$ = the probability limit of the sample mean of the excess returns of the benchmark portfolio.

[13] Verrecchia [1980] devised an example where betas were properly measured and where performance was negative for an investor with timing information. Grinblatt & Titman [1989b] showed that this was due to a wealth effect. Investors with positive information about the market reduced their betas because their information made them wealthier. The particular utility function used by Verrecchia, quadratic utility, is one where increased wealth make the investor's risk aversion arbitrarily large at large wealth levels. Hence, this was an risky assets were Giffen goods–wealth effects dominated substitution effects.

[14] See Jensen [1972], Dybvig & Ross [1985a], Admati & Ross [1985], Admati, Bhattacharya, Pfleiderer & Ross [1986], and Grinblatt & Titman [1989b] for other conditions that lead to this result.

[15] See, for example, Grant [1977], Dybvig & Ross [1985a], and Grinblatt & Titman [1989b].

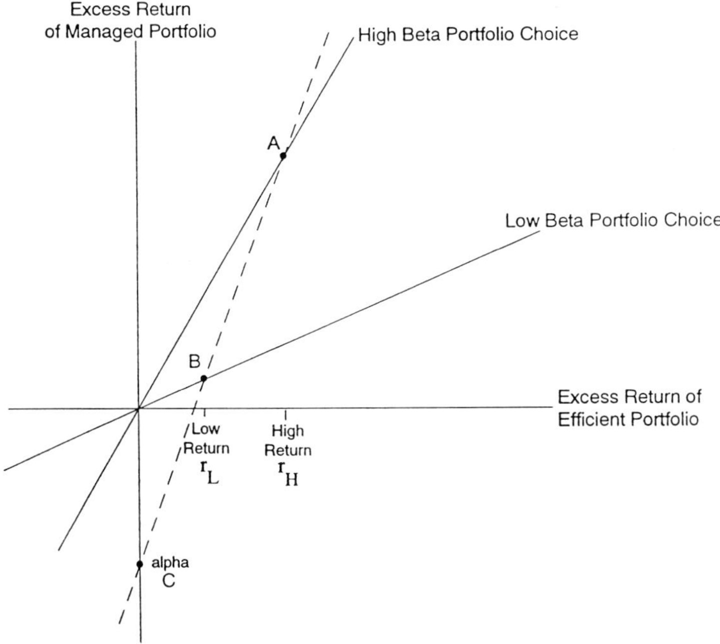

Fig. 3. An example of a negative Jensen measure for a market timer. The two solid lines plot the excess return of a managed portfolio of a risk-free investment and an investment in the risky efficient portfolio against the latter's excess return for two different choices of beta. A market-timing strategy, constrained to choose between the two betas, would plot at point A (point B) if information indicated that the excess return of the efficient portfolio was expected to be r_H (r_L). The slope of the dotted line is the estimated beta in the Jensen regression, and the intercept is the Jensen measure.

The three terms in equation (8) are respectively the component of performance that results from large sample biases in estimated beta, the component that results from timing, and the component that results from selectivity. If the first term is zero, Jensen's alpha aggregrates the sum of the timing and selectivity components. However, this is only the case in the absence of timing information [Grinblatt & Titman, 1989b, Lemma 1].

2.5. Regression-based timing measures

There are several procedures that have been proposed to correct for the bias in Jensen's alpha induced by the effect of timing ability on the estimate of beta. The first is a quadratic regression, proposed by Treynor & Mazuy [1966]. This regression,

$$\tilde{R}_p - r_f = \alpha_p + \beta_{0p}(\tilde{R}_E - r_f) + \beta_{1p}(\tilde{R}_E - r_f)^2 + \tilde{\epsilon}_p, \tag{9}$$

is identical to the regression used to compute Jensen's alpha, except that an additional term, the squared excess return of the benchmark portfolio is included. Admati, Bhattacharya, Pfleiderer & Ross [1986] developed conditions under which the coefficient on the quadratic term can be used to detect the precision of the manager's timing forecasts. Like Connor & Koraczyk, Admati, Bhattacharya, Pfleiderer & Ross assume exponential utility and multivariate normality. It is easy to show that these assumptions imply that the portfolio beta is a linear function of the timing signal.

Under the Admati, Bhattacharya, Pfleiderer & Ross conditions, one can relate the parameters of the Treynor–Mazuy regression to the timing and selectivity components discussed above. In this case, $\beta_{1\mathrm{p}} var(\tilde{R}_{\mathrm{E}})$ is the timing component of performance and α_{p} is the selectivity component of performance. Total performance is the sum of the two terms. There is no mismeasurement of beta in this case. However, the moment we depart from beta linearity, we can no longer assert this. This makes the application of this regression somewhat narrow.

To see that timing and selectivity are represented by these terms under the narrow set of assumptions, imagine that the manager observes the excess return of the benchmark plus noise, $\tilde{r}_{\mathrm{E}} + \tilde{\delta}$. His forecast of the benchmark return is a linear function of this signal and his portfolio beta is a linear function of the optimal forecast. This implies that

$$\tilde{\beta}_{\mathrm{p}} = \gamma_0 + \gamma_1(\tilde{R}_{\mathrm{E}} + \tilde{\delta})$$

and the excess return of the portfolio is

$$[\gamma_0 + \gamma_1(\tilde{R}_{\mathrm{E}} + \tilde{\delta})]\tilde{R}_{\mathrm{E}} + \tilde{\epsilon}_{\mathrm{p}}.$$

From this expression, let us regard

$$\gamma_1\tilde{\delta}\tilde{R}_{\mathrm{E}} + (\tilde{\epsilon}_{\mathrm{p}} - E(\tilde{\epsilon}_{\mathrm{p}}))$$

as the regression residual in the Treynor–Mazuy regression. Given exponential utility and the independence of the signals, we know that the portfolio weights that determine $\tilde{\epsilon}_{\mathrm{p}}$ are independent of $\tilde{R}_{\mathrm{E}}$ because of their independence from both the forecast of the benchmark return and of the expected wealth that is tied to this forecast. In addition, $\tilde{\delta}$, being noise, is independent of $\tilde{R}_{\mathrm{E}}$, making the regression residual, $\gamma_1\tilde{\delta}\tilde{R}_{\mathrm{E}} + (\tilde{\epsilon}_{\mathrm{p}} - E(\tilde{\epsilon}_{\mathrm{p}}))$, uncorrelated with both of the independent variables in the quadratic regression [equation (9)]. γ_0, which multiplies the first variable in the Treynor–Mazuy regression, must therefore equal the asymptotic value of β_1, while γ_1, which multiplies the quadratic term, must equal the asymptotic value of β_2. $E(\tilde{\epsilon}_{\mathrm{p}})$, which is the large sample expectation of what is left, must equal the asymptotic value of α_{p} in the quadratic regression.

Empirical work with quadratic regressions has been limited and somewhat disappointing. Work by Grinblatt & Titman [1988], and Cumby & Glen [1990] finds that a large proportion of mutual funds have negative coefficients on the quadratic term. Lehmann & Modest [1987] and Lee & Rahman [1990] also examine the Treynor–Mazuy regression, however neither of these papers report whether the significance of the coefficients is due to their being positive or negative.

Another returns-based approach for estimating timing performance is the option approach developed by Merton [1981] and Henriksson & Merton [1981]. The regression used is similar to the Treynor–Mazuy regression, except that $\max(0, r_{\mathrm{f}} - \tilde{R}_{\mathrm{E}})$ is used in place of the quadratic term on the right hand side of the regression. This term is the end-of-period value of a put option on the benchmark portfolio with a strike price equal to the risk-free return. Like the Treynor–Mazuy regression, the model used to develop this regression is based on a narrow set of behavioral assumptions. In contrast to the linear beta adjustment of the Treynor–Mazuy framework, the portfolio beta in the Henriksson and Merton study is assumed to switch between two betas: a high beta corresponding to a large forecasted benchmark return and a beta of zero, corresponding to a forecasted benchmark return that is less than the risk-free return.

Chang & Lewellen [1984] and Henriksson [1984] applied the Henriksson & Merton technique to samples of mutual funds and did not find evidence that funds were sytematically timing the market. If anything, there seems to be evidence of negative timing. The application of this technique to a multi-portfolio benchmark in Connor & Korajczyk [1991] reveals similar results.

In a similar spirit, Kon [1983] and Kon & Jen [1979] have used switching regression techniques to estimate performance. Rather than forcing one of the betas to be zero, the Kon & Jen and Kon approaches assume that one of two (or more) unknown betas is selected and use econometric techniques to infer estimates of them and of their contribution to performance. The more sophisticated of the two papers, Kon [1983], concludes that there is no evidence of timing performance within funds as a group.

Although the adjustment for performance developed with either the option approach or quadratic regression approach provide a reasonable estimate of whether timing exists or not, the actual contribution of timing ability to the portfolio return as well as the contribution of selectivity ability will generally be estimated with a bias. This is because investment behavior is unlikely to conform to the rather narrow behavioral assumptions used in these models.

In addition to having restrictive behavioral assumptions, the Treynor–Mazuy and Henriksson–Merton approaches require that stock returns not be co-skewed with the benchmark return. We know, however, from Kraus & Litzenberger [1976] that many stocks are co-skewed with the market return. They illustrated this by examining slope coefficients in quadratic regressions that are identical to the regression specified in equation (9). Since individual stocks exhibit 'timing' performance with these regressions, the Treynor–Mazuy approach will falsely classify passive investors who select stocks with returns that are co-skewed with the benchmark return as successful timers. For similar reasons, the Henrikkson & Merton and Kon & Jen approaches will lead to misclassifications when stock returns are co-skewed with the benchmark. Moreover, even if stock returns are multivariate normally distributed, dynamic portfolio strategies (e.g. synthetic put options or portfolio insurance on the market) generate co-skewness.[16] Hence, the

[16] See Jagannathan & Korajczyk [1986].

coefficient, β_{1p}, in the quadratic regression, as well as the binomial estimates of timing, will be positive for managers who follow such strategies even though they do not possess any real timing ability.

2.6. The positive period weighting measure

Grinblatt & Titman [1989b] developed an alternative performance measure that they describe as a weighting of the evaluated portfolio's time series of excess returns. They showed that if these period weights are nonnegative, and if the weighted average of the time series of excess returns of the benchmark portfolio is zero when using these weights, then the weighted-average of the excess returns of an evaluated portfolio will be positive if and only if it is managed by an investor with forecasting ability that enables him to time the market or select individual stocks to achieve a superior risk-return tradeoff.

Algebraically, the positive period weighting measure is

$$\sum_{t=1}^{T} w_t R_{pt}, \tag{10}$$

where

$$w_t \geq 0, \quad \sum_{t=1}^{T} w_t = 1, \quad \text{and} \quad \sum_{t=1}^{T} w_t R_{Et} = 0.$$

To understand the measure, consider the case where the period weights equal the marginal utilities of an investor who holds the benchmark portfolio. The measure then represents the marginal amount that the investor's expected utility will increase from adding a small amount of the evaluated portfolio to his existing portfolio. If the evaluated portfolio is managed with no special information, then adding it to the mean–variance efficient portfolio creates no improvement so the measure would be zero in that case. However, if the evaluated portfolio is managed with special information, its addition does lead to an increase in utility.

Jensen's alpha has implicit weights that satisfy two of the three conditions in (11). These weights correspond to the marginal utilities of a quadratic utility investor. They do not satisfy the constraint that the weights be nonnegative because quadratic utility functions exhibit satiation for sufficiently high wealth levels, making the marginal utilities (the weights) negative for benchmark returns that are very high. What this means is that successful timers that have very high betas when market returns are high may be penalized rather than rewarded by Jensen's alpha for this astute behavior. This gives an additional interpretation for why Jensen's alpha can provide misleading inferences for successful timers.

There are reasons to believe that the positive period weighting measure may be more robust to different behavioral assumptions than the other measures that develop timing adjustments. First, it is very flexible. Any set of weights satisfying the conditions (11) above will reward rather than penalize timing ability. This means that we are not restricted to the somewhat implausible binomial or linear beta adjustment behavior as being behavior that is properly adjusted for by the measure. If we select a plausible utility function to represent the behavior of the portfolio, then the measure is tailor made for that form of beta adjustment. Moreover, Grinblatt & Titman [1989b] have shown that irrespective of the monotone concave utility function used to compute the weights, the measure will reward timing behavior provided that (i) the portfolio's beta is monotonically related to the forecast of the benchmark return and (ii) returns are multivariate normal.

Grinblatt & Titman [1994] computed a positive period weighting measure using the marginal utilities from a power utility function. They found that the positive period weighting measure was highly correlated with Jensen's alpha when the same benchmark is used (e.g. the correlation coefficient with the equal-weighted index was 0.99). Since the two measures are asymptotically identical in the absence of market timing, the high correlation between these two measures suggests that there is at best a negligible amount of market timing prevalent in their sample. They also found a statistically significant relation between the difference between the positive period weighting measure and the quadratic term slope coefficient in the Treynor–Mazuy regression. This implies that the positive period weighting measure differentiated itself from Jensen's alpha when market timing did appear to exist.

Cumby & Glen [1990] also used the positive period weighting measure to study a small sample of international mutual funds. They found no evidence of superior performance within the fifteen funds that they looked at. Consistent with Grinblatt & Titman [1994], they found that the positive period weighting measure and Jensen's alpha provided virtually identical inferences.

3. Computing performance when portfolio weights are observable

3.1. Stationarity and measures based on portfolio holdings

When portfolio weights are observable, performance measures can be developed that substantially reduce or eliminate the problems relating to timing and benchmark choice. Although benchmark portfolios can be used with these measures to increase power and to test for robustness, they are not required. However, the requirement that asset return distributions be stationary is probably more important for the measures that utilize portfolio weights than for those that rely on a benchmark portfolio. For this reason, the addition of a benchmark portfolio may enhance the robustness of these measures with respect to certain nonstationarities.

The assumption that return distributions are stationary implies that the portfolio holdings of an investor with no special abilities or information cannot be correlated with future asset returns. However, since an informed investor can predict when certain assets will tend to have higher than average and lower than average returns, asset returns are nonstationary from his perspective. His percentage holdings for a particular investment, x_j, will tend to be large in periods when the investment's subsequent return, r_j, is large and vice versa implying that the covariance between the percentage holdings and the subsequent returns will be positive.

3.2. The event study measure and the Grinblatt–Titman measure

Grinblatt & Titman [1989b] have shown that the total contribution of timing and selectivity to an increased return is identical to the summed covariances between the portfolio weights and the returns of the securities in the portfolio:

$$\mathrm{Cov} = \sum_{j=1}^{N} \left(E[\tilde{x}_j \tilde{r}_j] - E[\tilde{x}_j] E[\tilde{r}_j] \right). \tag{12}$$

This sum equals the expected return of the investor's portfolio, given his information, less what the portfolio's expected return would be if his portfolio weights and asset returns were uncorrelated. Rewriting the expression in (12) in two equivalent ways leads to two alternative performance measures that have been implemented in the literature:

$$\mathrm{Cov} = \sum_{j=1}^{N} E\left[\tilde{x}_j \left(\tilde{r}_j - E[\tilde{r}_j]\right)\right] \tag{13a}$$

$$\mathrm{Cov} = \sum_{j=1}^{N} E\left[(x_j - E[x_j]) r_j\right] \tag{13b}$$

Expression (13a) is the foundation for the event study measure used by Copeland & Mayers [1982] to evaluate Value Line rankings. Implementing the event study measure requires a proxy for the expected return of each investment included in the evaluated portfolio. Expression (13b) is the foundation for the measure used by Grinblatt & Titman [1993] to evaluate the performance of mutual funds. Intuitively, this measure compares the return of a managed portfolio in each month with a 'passive' portfolio formed in an earlier time period. Implementing this measure requires an estimate of the expected portfolio weight for each of the investments in the evaluated portfolio.

In practice, Grinblatt & Titman [1993] use an investment's portfolio weight in an earlier period as the proxy for the expected portfolio weight of an investment.[17] Similarly, a reasonable proxy for the expected return in a given period is the investment's actual return in a later period. (Future average returns were the benchmarks implemented by Copeland & Mayers in their Value Line study.)

[17] The critical assumption is that the proxy for the expected portfolio holding be independent of the security return. This assumption is not necessarily valid if future holdings are used as a proxy for the expected holding. For example, in this case, an investor that selects past winners for his portfolio will induce a positive correlation between 'expected holdings' and returns, which will in turn downwardly bias the measure. Similarly, if past returns are used as a benchmark for expected returns, the event study measure will be downwardly biased.

Hence, to simplify a comparison of the two measures we will assume that the period $t+k$ return for each asset is used as a proxy for its period t expected return in the event study measure and that its period $t-k$ portfolio holding is used as a proxy for its expected holdings for the Grinblatt & Titman [1993] measure. The event study measure and the Grinblatt–Titman measure can thus be expressed as follows:

$$\text{The event study measure} = \sum\sum \frac{x_{jt}(r_{jt} - r_{j,t+k})}{T} \tag{14a}$$

$$\text{The Grinblatt–Titman measure} = \sum\sum \frac{r_{jt}(x_{jt} - x_{j,t-k})}{T} \tag{14b}$$

For a constant universe of risky assets, the two measures are asymptotically identical. (In finite samples they differ at the k first and k last time series entries.) However, there are several advantages to the measure described in equation (14b). One advantage is statistical. This measure is the average dollar return (i.e. end-of-period value per unit of investment) of a zero-cost, zero-systematic risk portfolio. Under the null hypothesis that asset returns are serially uncorrelated, the returns of this zero-cost portfolio are serially uncorrelated, which makes computation of test statistics for the significance of the average return a trivial exercise. In contrast, the event study measure uses future returns to calculate excess returns. As a result, serial correlation is induced in the time series of excess returns, which makes tests of statistical significance more difficult.

Another weakness of the event study measure is its sensitivity to the future survival of assets currently in the evaluated portfolio. If a particular asset fails to exist shortly after it is included in an evaluated portfolio, the investor's holding of that asset cannot be used to assess the portfolio's performance. This creates a bias in large samples as well as small samples. The problem is especially critical for evaluating portfolio managers who hold near bankrupt stocks or stocks in takeover plays. Grinblatt and Titman's measure, (14b), which for each time period applies current and past portfolio weights to returns in the coming period, cannot have survivorship bias by construction.

Both measures are sensitive to the stationarity of the returns of the individual assets in the evaluated portfolio. A portfolio will spuriously generate positive performance using either measure if it systematically selects assets that temporarily have high risk (and thus high expected return). An example would be a portfolio that buys either near bankrupt stocks or takeover plays. With the Grinblatt–Titman measure, however, it is possible to test whether or not this is a problem by regressing the time-series of return differences on the returns of various market indexes. The intercepts from these regressions are also performance measures. These intercepts will be as robust to various nonstationarities as Jensen's alpha.

3.3. Empirical work using performance measures that require portfolio weights

In practice, portfolio performance evaluators restrict their attention to portfolio returns and ignore information about the portfolio holdings of the evaluated funds. This is unfortunate since the timing related and benchmark related problems of the performance measures that do not require the observation of portfolio holdings can be substantially reduced with measures that employ portfolio holdings.

Although data on portfolio holdings are available to professional portfolio evaluators, the data is relatively expensive for academics to obtain. For this reason there are a limited number of academic articles that empirically examine measures that require portfolio holdings. We are aware of only three. The first was an article by Copeland & Mayers [1982] that examined the performance of portfolios formed on the basis of Value Line rankings. This article uses two measures similar to that in equation (14a). The first measure, as suggested by equation (14a), uses the difference in the raw returns of a stock between two time periods. The second looks at the difference over time between the Jensen's alphas of the stocks. There is also a follow up article by Chen, Copeland & Mayers [1987] that uses the same data set but employs APT-based alphas, rather than CAPM alphas for this subtraction. The third article, by Grinblatt & Titman [1993], examined the quarterly holdings of a sample of mutual funds.

Copeland and Mayers' sample included the rankings for each stock covered by Value Line at 26 week intervals for the 1965 to 1978 period. These rankings range from 1 to 5 with stocks ranking 1 considered the best choices and those ranked 5 considered the worst choices. In the past, those stocks ranked 1 have realized higher returns on average than those stocks ranked 5. In the Copeland and Mayers sample period, the stocks ranked 1 yielded average yearly returns of 17.7% while those ranked 5 yielded average yearly returns of 3.6% per year for portfolios formed on a six month basis. The average betas with respect to a market proxy for both groups were close to one, indicating that a Jensen's alpha would reveal an excess return of about 14% per year from a strategy of buying stocks ranked 1 and shorting stocks ranked 5.

The event study measure reveals somewhat reduced performance measures for this strategy. For example, Copeland and Mayers comparison of the Jensen measure of each stock in the 6 month holding period to its Jensen measure in the following 6 month period revealed a yearly risk-adjusted return of 0.7% for the rank 1 stocks and −6.1% for the rank 5 stocks. The measure that compares the raw returns in the holding period to the raw returns in the benchmark period reveals a risk-adjusted return of 4.3% per year for the rank 1 stocks and −4.7% per year for the rank 5 stocks.

Grinblatt & Titman [1993] used the measure described in equation (14b) to examine the performance of the quarterly mutual fund holdings considered in their earlier [1989a] paper. They considered two measures. The first, based on quarterly changes in portfolio holdings ($k = 1$), calculates the mean return of a zero cost portfolio that includes a long position in the current quarter's portfolio holdings and is short in the previous quarter's holdings. The second, based on yearly changes in portfolio holdings ($k = 4$), is the same as the first except that the short position in the zero cost portfolio is the previous year's, rather than the previous quarter's, holdings. If mutual fund managers have superior information that gets revealed to the market within one quarter, the quarterly measure provides the most power. However, if the information is incorporated into market prices more slowly, the quarterly measure may be biased downwards, (due to the correlation between the past holdings and current returns), making the yearly measure the preferred alternative.

Grinblatt and Titman found that the yearly change measure revealed statistically significant abnormal performance, (2% per year on average). However, the quarterly change measure revealed insignificant performance on average. These findings were consistent with the superior information used by the funds being revealed beyond one quarter following the initial purchase decision. With the yearly change measure, the magnitude of the average abnormal performance for the funds categorized by investment objectives were very similar to Grinblatt & Titman's [1989a] earlier results that used the Jensen measure with P8 benchmark. Specifically, the aggressive growth and growth funds revealed significant abnormal performance with both measures. The income funds, which did not exhibit significant superior performance in the earlier study, showed small (1.19% per year), but statistically significant, performance with the yearly change measure. The performance of funds with other investment objectives did not achieve significant abnormal performance in either study.

Grinblatt & Titman [1993] also used their measure to analyze whether or not differential performance existed within the various investment categories. They did this with the joint intercept tests and the persistence tests described earlier. The joint intercept tests revealed differential performance for the Aggressive Growth, Growth, Growth–Income and the Venture Capital/Special Situation funds. They also found evidence of persistence for the entire sample of funds; the second subperiod abnormal returns of funds that did well in the first subperiod exceeded the abnormal returns of the funds that did poorly in the first subperiod by a statistically significant 2.6% per year. These differences in excess returns were also found for subsamples of funds grouped by investment objective, however, the differences were statistically significant only for the Growth–Income funds.

4. Conclusions and directions for future research

In this chapter, we have described various methods for evaluating the performance of a managed portfolio. These methods assess whether the investment strategy of the managed portfolio achieves a higher return than a passive strategy with the equivalent risk. The major difficulty in implementing these techniques, and the source of most of the debate and criticism about them, revolves around the identification of the relevant passive portfolio.

When portfolio holdings are unobservable, it is necessary to make use of an asset pricing theory to derive a benchmark portfolio(s) that in combination with a risk-free security determines this passive portfolio. The passive portfolio estimated with the asset pricing methodology should maximize expected returns given its level of risk. The empirical evidence suggests that the equally-weighted index and the value-weighted index are not mean–variance efficient and thus would not be appropriate benchmark portfolios. Multiple portfolio benchmarks should be more reliable than single portfolio benchmarks and our own research suggests that forming factor portfolios based on the characteristics of stocks (like dividend yields and size) may be more reliable than using factor analysis to form benchmarks. However, the formation of benchmark portfolios is likely to remain controversial. It is always difficult to verify that your factor portfolios adequately capture all relevant factors. Perhaps future research that combines the various approaches will develop factor portfolios that are more widely accepted.

Although portfolio weights may not always be available to academic researchers, they are available to practitioners who are in the business of evaluating performance. In the past, this information may have been ignored because of the costs of handling such large data bases. However, computing power is now very cheap and the necessary software is now readily available so we would expect portfolio holdings data to be utilized more in the future. When portfolio holdings are used, a unique passive portfolio, based on the evaluated portfolio's past holdings, can be constructed for each point in time and each fund. We think that these individualized benchmarks are more reliable than the single benchmarks used in the more traditional approach.

Other issues also tend to favor the portfolio holdings methodology. If the evaluated investor has the ability to successfully time the benchmark portfolio, evaluation techniques based on the asset pricing methodology may generate biased estimates of risk. Although a number of asset pricing based measures have been developed that account for timing, each require that returns be normally distributed. The basic problem is that it is difficult to distinguish a managed portfolio with returns that are positively co-skewed with the benchmark portfolio from one that really can time the market. The portfolio holdings methodology cannot be subject to this timing-related bias because it does not require a benchmark portfolio.

Given the problems associated with evaluating timing performance it is not surprising that at this point there is no convincing evidence of mutual funds systematically timing the market. However, there is evidence that some mutual funds consistently achieve abnormal returns by systematically picking stocks that subsequently do well. How should we interpret this evidence?

One view is that there are certain skilled investors who are very good at uncovering and interpreting fundamental information. This view would suggest that the market is only weakly efficient; smart investors are earning what looks like a lot of money, but they have to be talented and they have to earn it. The second view is that the abnormal performance was generated by technical trading rules that exploit what we will call time-series anomalies. The performance measures examined in this chapter are designed to eliminate the possibility that abnormal performance is generated by exploiting what we call cross-sectional anomalies, like the size effect. However, since the techniques essentially compare managed returns to equivalent passive returns, abnormal performance can be generated by active trading if return distributions are not stationary, i.e., stocks with high past returns also have high future returns.[18]

For a variety reasons, it is important to understand the extent to which abnormal performance is generated as a result of technical trading rules rather than fundamental analysis. First, if the abnormal performance is generated by very simple technical rules rather than fundamental analysis, we would be less willing to attribute the performance to skill rather than luck. In addition, if the nonstationarities observed in past studies are due to market inefficiencies, they are likely to disappear over time. For these reasons, we would probably be less willing to hire a portfolio manager based on his past performance if we thought the performance was generated from exploiting simple technical rules. We would think that performance generated by careful fundamental analysis would be more likely to persist over time.

Grinblatt, Titman & Wermers [1995] examines the extent to which mutual funds generated abnormal performance by exploiting momemtum strategies.[19] The paper shows that mutual funds on average do have a tendency to buy stocks that did well in the past, and that this tendency is greatest among the Aggressive Growth funds, which was the category that showed the best performance. Moreover, the study shows that mutual funds that did not show this tendency to buy past winners did not realize significant abnormal performance. This evidence suggests that at least part of the abnormal performance of these funds comes from their tendency to buy past winners.

Research on portfolio performance evaluation has clearly progressed over the past 10 years, benefiting tremendously from the recent advances in the asset pricing literature. We expect similar strides to be made in the next 10 years. This area of research should benefit from the availability of much better mutual fund data sets that are both broader, in terms of the number of funds included, and longer, in terms of the length of the time-series. This literature should also benefit from our increased understanding of both the cross-sectional and time-series properties of stock returns which should enable us to develop new performance measures that account for both. With improved data and improved measures researchers should be able to achieve a very good understanding of what determines superior portfolio performance.

References

Admati, A., and S. Ross (1985). Measuring investment performance in a rational expectations equilibrium model. *J. Bus.* 58, 1–26.

Admati, A., S. Bhattacharya, P. Pfleiderer and S. Ross (1986). On timing and selectivity. *J. Finance* 41, 715–30.

[18] The P8 benchmark mitigates this somewhat by using a low past returns portfolio for estimating risk.

[19] Jegadeesh & Titman [1993] shows that strategies that buy stocks that performed well over the past 3, 6, 9 or 12 months continue to outperform the market over the subsequent 12 months.

Beebower, G., and G. Bergstrom (1977). A performance analysis of pension and profit-sharing portfolios: 1966–1975. *Financ. Anal. J.* (May/June), 31–38.

Brown, S., and W. Geotzmann (1995). Performance persistence, *J. Finance* 50, 679–98.

Brown, S., W. Goetzmann, R. Ibbotson and S. Ross (1992). Survivorship bias in performance studies. *Rev. Financ. Studies* 5, 553–580.

Chang, E., and W. Lewellen (1984). Market timing and mutual fund investment performance. *J. Bus.* 57, 57–72.

Chen, N.-f., T. Copeland and D. Mayers (1987). A comparison of single and multifactor portfolio performance methodologies. *J. Financ. Quant. Anal.* 22, 401–17.

Connor, G., and R. Korajzcyk (1986). Performance measurement with the arbitrage pricing theory: A new framework for analysis. *J. Financ. Econ.* 15, 374–94.

Connor, G., and R. Korajzcyk (1991). The attributes, behavior and performance of U.S. mutual funds. *Rev. Quant. Finance Account.* 1, 5–26.

Connor, G., and R. Korajzcyk (1995). The arbitrage pricing theory and multifactor models of asset returns, in: R. Jarrow, V. Maksimovic and W.T. Ziemba (eds.), *Finance*, Handbooks in Operations Research and Management Science, Vol. 9, North-Holland, Amsterdam, pp. 87–144 (this volume).

Copeland, T., and D. Mayers (1982). The Value Line enigma (1965–1978): A case study of performance evaluation issues. *J. Financ. Econ.* 10, 289–321.

Cornell, B. (1979). Asymmetric information and portfolio performance measurement. *J. Financ. Econ.* 7, 381–390.

Cumby, R., and J. Glen (1990). Evaluating the performance of international mutual funds. *J. Finance* 45, 497–521.

De Bondt, W.F.M., and R.H. Thaler (1995). Financial decision-making in markets and firms: A behavioral perspective, in: R. Jarrow, V. Maksimovic and W.T. Ziemba (eds.), *Finance*, Handbooks in Operations Research and Management Science, Vol. 9, North Holland, Amsterdam, pp. 385–410 (this volume).

Dybvig, P., and S. Ross (1985a). Differential information and performance measurement using a security market line. *J. Finance* 40, 383–399.

Dybvig, P., and S. Ross (1985b). The analytics of performance measurement using a security market line. *J. Finance* 40, 401–16

Elton, E., M. Gruber, S. Das and M. Hlavka (1993). Efficiency with costly information: A reinterpretation of evidence from managed portfolios. *Rev. Financ. Studies* 6(1), 1–22.

Ferson, W.E. (1995). Theory and empirical testing of asset pricing models, in: R. Jarrow, V. Maksimovic and W.T. Ziemba (eds.), *Finance*, Handbooks in Operations Research and Management Science, North Holland, Vol. 9, Amsterdam, pp. 145–200 (this volume).

Grant, D. (1977). Portfolio performace and the 'cost' of timing decisions. *J. Finance* 32, 837–46.

Grinblatt, M., and S. Titman (1987). The relation between mean–variance efficiency and arbitrage pricing. *J. Bus.* 60, 97–112.

Grinblatt, M., and S. Titman (1988). The evaluation of mutual fund performance: An analysis of monthly returns, working paper, University of California.

Grinblatt, M., and S. Titman (1989a). Mutual fund performance: An analysis of quarterly portfolio holdings. *J. Bus.* 62, 393–416.

Grinblatt, M., and S. Titman (1989b). Portfolio performance evaluation: Old issues and new insights. *Rev. Financ. Studies* 2(3), 393–421.

Grinblatt, M., and S. Titman (1992). The persistence of mutual fund performance. *J. Finance* 47, 1977–1984.

Grinblatt, M., and S. Titman (1993). Performance measurement without benchmarks: An examination of mutual fund returns. *J. Bus.* 66, 47–68.

Grinblatt, M., and S. Titman (1994). A study of monthly mutual fund returns and performance evaluation techniques. *J. Financ. Quant. Anal.* 29, in press.

Grinblatt, M., S. Titman and R. Wermers (1995). Momentum investment strategies, portfolio performance and herding: A study of mutual fund behavior, *Am. Econ. Rev.*, forthcoming.

Hawawini, G., and D.B. Keim (1995). On the predictability of common stock returns: World-wide evidence, in: R. Jarrow, V. Maksimovic and W.T. Ziemba (eds.), *Finance*, Handbooks in Operations Research and Management Science, Vol. 9, North Holland, Amsterdam, (this volume).

Hendricks, D., J. Patel and R. Zeckhauser (1993). Hot hands in mutual funds: The persistence of performance, 1974–88. *J. Finance* 48, 93–130.

Henriksson, R. (1984). Market timing and mutual fund performance. *J. Bus* 57, 73–96.

Henriksson, R., and R. Merton (1981). On market timing and investment performance II: Statistical procedures for evaluating forecasting skills. *J. Bus.* 54, 513–33.

Ippolito, R. (1989). Efficiency with costly information: A study of mutual fund performance, 1965–84. *Q. J. Econ.* 104, 1–23.

Jagannathan, R., and R.A. Korajczyk (1986). Assessing the market timing performance of managed portfolios. *J. Bus.* 59, 217–235.

Jegadeesh, N., and S. Titman (1993). Returns to buying winners and selling losers: Implications for stock market efficiency. *J. Finance* 48, 65–91.

Jensen, M. (1968). The performance of mutual funds in the period 1945–1964. *J. Finance* 23, 389–416.

Jensen, M. (1969). Risk, the pricing of capital assets, and the evaluation of investment portfolios. *J. Bus.* 42, 167–247.

Jensen, M. (1972). Optimal utilization of market forecasts and the evaluation of investment performance, in: G.P. Szego and K. Shell (eds.), *Mathematical Methods in Investment and Finance*. Elsevier, Amsterdam.

Kon, S. (1983). The market-timing performance of mutual fund managers. *J. Bus.* 56, 323–48.

Kon, S., and F. Jen (1979). The investment performance of mutual funds: An empirical investigation of timing, selectivity, and market efficiency. *J. Bus.* 52, 263–89.

Kraus, A., and R. Litzenberger (1976). Skewness preference and the valuation of risk assets. *J. Finance* 311, 1085–1100.

Lee, C.-f., and S. Rahman (1990). Market timing, selectivity, and mutual fund performance: An empirical investigation. *J. Bus.* 63, 261–78.

Lehmann, B., and D. Modest (1987). Mutual fund performance evaluation: A comparison of benchmarks and benchmark comparisons. *J. Finance* 42, 233–265.

Lehmann, B., and D. Modest (1989). The empirical foundations of the arbitrage pricing theory. *J. Financ. Econ.* 21, 213–54.

Mains, N. (1977). Risk, the pricing of capital assets, and the evaluation of investment portfolios: Comment. *J. Bus.* 50, 371–84.

Malkiel, B. (1995). Returns from investing in equity mutual funds 1971–1991, *J. Finance* 50, 549–72.

Mayers, D., and E. Rice (1979). Measuring portfolio performance and the empirical content of pricing models. *J. Financ. Econ.* 7, 3–28.

McDonald, J. (1974). Objectives and performance of mutual funds, 1960–1969. *J. Financ. Quant. Anal.* 9, 311–33.

Merton, R. (1981). On market timing and investment performance I: An equilibrium theory of value for market forecasts. *J. Bus.* 54, 363–406.

Roll, R. (1978). Ambiguity when performance is measured by the securities market line. *J. Finance* 33, 1051–69.

Sharpe, W. (1966). Mutual fund performance. *J. Bus.* 39, 119–38.

Sharpe, W. (1992). Asset allocation: Management style and performance measurement. *J. Portfolio Manage.* 18, 7–19.

Treynor, J. (1965). How to rate management of investment funds. *Harvard Bus. Rev.* 43, 63–75.

Treynor, J., and F. Black (1973). How to use security analysis to improve portfolio selection. *J. Bus.* 46, 66–86.

Treynor, J., and K. Mazuy (1966). Can mutual funds outguess the market? *Harvard Bus. Rev.* 44, 131–36.

Verrecchia, R. (1980). The Mayers–Rice conjecture. A counterexample. *J. Financ. Econ.* 8, 87–100.

R. Jarrow et al., Eds., *Handbooks in OR & MS, Vol. 9*

Chapter 20

Market Manipulation

Joseph A. Cherian
School of Management, Boston University, Boston, MA 02215, U.S.A.

Robert A. Jarrow
Johnson Graduate School of Management, Malott Hall, Cornell University, Ithaca, NY 14853-4201, U.S.A.

1. Introduction

A recent area of analysis in financial economics has been in the area of market manipulation. Roughly speaking, market manipulation occurs when an individual (or a group of individuals) trades a firm's shares in a manner such that the share price is influenced to his advantage. An immediate implication of market manipulation is the inappropriateness of the standard, perfect competition Walrasian equilibrium as a description of United States capital markets.

From a chronological perspective, research on market manipulations in futures markets predates that in U.S. equity and bond markets. There is also substantial regulation in futures markets which restricts the ability of individuals to influence futures prices. Admittedly, although the problem has not been entirely eliminated, traditional forms of manipulation in futures markets have been significantly reduced. In contrast, a literature investigating manipulations in the primary equity and bond markets has only recently been evolving. Part of the reason for this is the long-held belief that the Securities Exchange Act of 1934 had virtually eliminated manipulation in these markets. However, recent incidents of manipulation in equity and Treasury markets have dispelled this misconception.

This paper generates an analytical classification scheme for surveying the recent papers on market manipulations in primary markets, specifically equity markets. The model generating the classification scheme draws primarily from the paper by Jarrow [1992]. A sub-class of classifications is also derived using the model of Cherian & Kuriyan [1995], which extends Jarrow's work by introducing an intermediary akin to the market makers of U.S. capital markets. The survey is not meant to be exhaustive. Instead, the aim of the present work is to provide a definition of manipulation and enough theory so that the reader understands the issues and key results of the literature. Furthermore, the insights generated by viewing market manipulation in this context should, hopefully, spawn ideas for subsequent research. For the interested reader, a review of market manipulation in the context of corporate finance is provided in an article by Chatterjea, Cherian, & Jarrow [1993]. A new perspective on firm corporate policy is obtained by viewing the corporation as an active, strategic manipulator of its shares. The purpose of such corporation behavior is twofold: (i) to maximize its share price, and (ii) to prevent its shares from being manipulated by others. The analysis generated within this framework provides insights into a number of frequently occurring phenomena in the corporate world.

An outline of the paper is as follows. The next section provides the classification scheme for market manipulation. This includes the necessary definitions, assumptions, and conditions leading to known results. Section 3 surveys a selected subset of papers, which in the context of the classification scheme, unifies much of the burgeoning literature on market manipulations in primary markets. Section 4 presents an additional example and briefly reviews models of manipulation with derivative markets. Section 5 summarizes and concludes the paper.

2. A classification scheme

As stated in the introduction, the classification scheme draws heavily on the paper by Jarrow [1992]. In his paper, Jarrow examines the conditions under which a large trader, whose trades affect prices, can risklessly profit by implementing certain trading strategies. While Jarrow restricts his attention to manipulation in the absence of any proprietary or inside information on the intrinsic value of the asset, we generalize the model to include additional categories of manipulation. The purpose of such a generalization is to provide a unifying, classification scheme for studying the literature on market manipulation in primary markets. We exclude from our analysis market manipulation strategies involving a *market corner* and *short squeeze*. A market corner occurs when a trader controls more than the actual or floating supply of the securities available. A short squeeze happens when the trader calls in the shorts. In such a typical squeeze, the short sellers have to cover their positions at inflated prices. Our understanding of such market manipulating trading strategies is reasonably complete. As the analysis is straightforward, it is not considered here. On the other hand, manipulation in the presence of derivative securities is not well understood. It significantly complicates the current analysis, and is briefly discussed in Section 4.2 below.

2.1. The model

This section presents a description of the economy under which market manipulation trading strategies (to be defined) are considered. The approach taken herein parallels that of the options literature in that we exogenously specify a price process. The merit of such an approach is that the price process can be chosen to be consistent with a number of different equilibrium price constructs.

The reasonableness of this approach lies in the richness of the results obtained, without being bogged down by intricate, microeconomic details. The price process we specify depends, among other things, upon the manipulator's trades over time.

We examine a multi-period economy with discrete trading dates denoted by the set $\tau = \{0, 1, 2, \ldots, T\}$. Uncertainty in the economy at date T is represented by a measurable space $(\Omega, \mathbf{F})$ where Ω is the state space and $\mathbf{F}$ is a sigma-algebra of subsets of Ω. Information prior to date T about the 'true' state is represented by the filtration $(\mathcal{F}_t)_{t\in\tau}$, which is an increasing sequence of sub-σ-algebras of $\mathbf{F}$ satisfying the *usual conditions*.[1]

Let one risky security of limited liability, called a stock, and a riskless security, called a money market account, trade in this economy. The stock price process is represented by the non-negative stochastic process $\{S_t : t \in \tau\}$ *adapted* to $(\mathcal{F}_t)_{t\in\tau}$. This means that the stock price is part of the information set $\mathcal{F}_t$ available at date t. The money market account is represented by a stochastic process $\{B_t : t \in \tau\}$ *predictable* with respect to $(\mathcal{F}_t)_{t\in\tau}$. This means that the value of the money market account at time t is known at time $t-1$. This captures the notion that the money market account provides a riskless return over the 'next' trading interval. Assume that it is initialized with a dollar investment, i.e., $B_0 \equiv 1$ for all $\omega \in \Omega$, and that 'interest rates' are non-negative, i.e., $B_t \geq B_{t-1}$ for all $t \in \tau$ and $\omega \in \Omega$. For convenience, the remaining analysis is in terms of relative prices, with the money market account serving as the numeraire. Define

$$Z_t(\omega) = \frac{S_t(\omega)}{B_t(\omega)}, \qquad \forall t \in \tau \text{ and } \omega \in \Omega$$

as the relative stock price. By definition, the relative price of the money market account is 1 for all $t \in \tau$ and $\omega \in \Omega$. In order to reduce notation in the subsequent analysis, we require that dates, t, are always drawn from the set τ, and elements of the state space, ω, are always drawn from the set Ω, unless otherwise specified.

The economy is made up of one potentially manipulative trader called the manipulator and the 'rest' of the market, represented by an index set I. The manipulator could be a single trader or a cohort of traders acting in concert. He is characterized by the pair $(P, (\mathcal{F}_t)_{t\in\tau})$ where $P : \mathbf{F} \rightarrow [0, 1]$ is his probability belief and $(\mathcal{F}_t)_{t\in\tau}$ is his information set. The rest of the market could be a singleton or an interval (a continuum of atomistic traders). Each trader $i \in I$ is endowed with a probability belief $P^i : \mathbf{F} \rightarrow [0, 1]$, and an information set $(\mathcal{F}^i_t)_{t\in\tau}$.

The manipulator's holdings of the stock and money market account are given by a two-dimensional $(\mathcal{F}_t)_{t\in\tau}$-adapted stochastic process $\{\alpha_t, \beta_t : t \in \tau\}$ where α_t is the number of shares of stock held at time t and β_t is the number of shares of the money market account held at time t. Under the assumed information structure, $(\mathcal{F}_t)_{t\in\tau}$ corresponds to the information set of the manipulator. We emphasize that the information sets of the manipulator and the rest of the market

[1] See chapter 1 of Karatzas & Shreve [1991] for a description of the use of probability spaces in financial economics.

need not coincide. To simplify notation, let the vectors $\alpha^t \equiv (\alpha_t, \alpha_{t-1}, \ldots, \alpha_0)$ and $\beta^t \equiv (\beta_t, \beta_{t-1}, \ldots, \beta_0)$ represent the history of the manipulator's holdings of the two traded assets up to time t. Our notational convention is this: a superscript corresponds to a history and a subscript corresponds to a particular date t.

In order to obtain a reasonable price process in the context of market manipulation, we need to introduce two additional parameters. The first is a broadly-defined *action* parameter, a, which consists of a particular set of nontrade related and observable actions taken by the manipulator that can alter the perceived or intrinsic value of the stock. The second is the intrinsic value of the stock, v, which will only be revealed at time T, when the 'true' state is known. By the preceding considerations, v could be a function of a. The importance of the information parameter will be obvious when the price process is specified. In order for the price process to respond to the manipulator's trades, it must be the case that the price response is either due to the size of the trade or to the fact that the 'rest' of the market believes (with some probability) that the manipulator is informed about v. The possibility that it could be due to both is not ruled out.

We proceed under the general assumption that the manipulator operates under frictionless markets. This means he faces no transaction costs or short sale restrictions. The more formal assumptions are delineated as follows and invoked as needed in the subsequent analysis.

Assumption 1 (The relative stock price process). *There exists a sequence of functions $\{G_t\}_{t\in\tau}$ with $G_t : \Omega \ X \ [R]^{2(t+2)} \to R$ such that for any trading strategy $\{\alpha_t, \beta_t : t \in \tau\}$ of the manipulator, the composition mapping $Z_t : \Omega \ X \ \tau \to R$ defined by*

$$Z_t(\omega) = G_t(\omega, v(\omega), \alpha^t(\omega), \beta^t(\omega), a) \tag{1}$$

represents the stochastic process for the relative stock price, with $v : \Omega \to R$ an **F**-*measurable function representing the stock's intrinsic value, and $a \in R$ an action selection by the manipulator.*

This assumption summarizes the relationship between relative prices and the manipulator's trades, his set of non-trade related actions which are perfectly observable by the market, and the intrinsic value of the asset. The specific functional form $\{G_t\}_{t\in\tau}$ assumes depends on the particular economy under consideration. Two justifications for the assumed relationship in expression (1) are as follows. First, the manipulator, due to sizeable wealth, may affect the demand and supply curves of the market, thus causing prices to react to his trades. Second, he could also affect prices because he is informed or the rest of the market believes he is informed about v.

To motivate the next assumption, we introduce the concept of a *self-financing trading strategy* for the manipulator. For convenience, assume that the manipulator enters the market with zero holdings of both securities, i.e., $\alpha_{-1} \equiv 0$, $\beta_{-1} \equiv 0$. A self-financing trading strategy is one where there are no net cash inflows or outflows from the portfolio, except, perhaps, at time T. In the context of our economy, this implies that

$$\beta_{t-1}(\omega) + \alpha_{t-1}(\omega)Z_t(\omega) \equiv \beta_t(\omega) + \alpha_t(\omega)Z_t(\omega) \quad \text{a.e. } P \tag{2}$$

The above identity indicates that the manipulator finances his portfolio rebalancing from time $t-1$ to t solely through the realization of his gains and losses in the stock and money market account. The self-financing relationship (2) implies that β_t can be explicitly expressed as a function of α^t. Hence, for self-financing trading strategies we can define a new function $g_t : \Omega \; X \; [R]^{t+3} \rightarrow R$ such that

$$g_t(\omega, v(\omega), \alpha^t(\omega), a) = G_t(\omega, v(\omega), \alpha^t(\omega), \beta^t(\omega), a) \tag{3}$$

Define Φ to be the set of all self-financing trading strategies of the manipulator. To capture the notion that the manipulator's trades dominate the price setting process, we impose:

Assumption 2 (Manipulator has market power). *For all* $\{\alpha_t, \beta_t : t \in \tau\} \in \Phi$, $a \in R$, *and a.e.* P,

(a) if $\alpha_t(\omega) > \alpha_{t-1}(\omega)$
then $g_t(\omega, v(\omega), \alpha^t(\omega), a) > g_t(\omega, v(\omega), \alpha_{t-1}(\omega), \alpha^{t-1}(\omega), a)$

(b) if $\alpha_t(\omega) < \alpha_{t-1}(\omega)$
then $g_t(\omega, v(\omega), \alpha^t(\omega), a) < g_t(\omega, v(\omega), \alpha_{t-1}(\omega), \alpha^{t-1}(\omega), a)$.

Condition 2a states that relative prices increase with increases in the manipulator's holdings (or equivalently with manipulator demands), while condition 2b states that relative prices decrease with decreases in the manipulator's holdings (or equivalently with manipulator sales), everything else held constant. This assumption can be justified under two common economic settings. In the first, the standard Walrasian equilibrium concept of aggregating supply and demand curves is used to determine the market clearing price. Excess demand due to the manipulator increasing his holdings causes an upward shift in the aggregate demand curve, thus increasing the price of the security. A symmetric argument holds on the sell side. In the second, prices are set by a market maker in the standard manner of the market microstructure literature [see Easley & O'Hara's review in this volume]. In the *information-effects* model of market making, the size and sign of a trade may reflect informed trading; a net buy order is either information-based or a noise trade. If the market maker assigns a positive probability to the former event, then a buy order is transacted at a higher price than the previous transaction, with large orders being executed at less favorable prices than small orders. Since the market maker cannot distinguish between traders, the manipulator will find that his buy orders are executed at higher prices, as depicted in Assumption 2a.[2] Again, a similar argument holds on the sell side.

The next assumption is invoked only when dealing in situations of *informationless manipulation*. That is, when the manipulator has no proprietary information

[2] This second argument is central to the analysis of Cherian & Kuriyan [1995].

on the intrinsic value of the firm, v. It captures the condition that given the manipulator's information set, the market contains no arbitrage opportunities.

Assumption 3 (No arbitrage opportunities based on the manipulator's information).

(a) For all $A \in F$ *and* $i \in I$, $P^i(A) = 0$ *if and only if* $P(A) = 0$.

(b) There exists a probability measure $\bar{P} : \mathbf{F} \to [0, 1]$ *equivalent to* P *(i.e.,* P *and* $\bar{P}$ *have the same null sets on* $\mathbf{F}$*) such that for all* $\{\alpha_t, \beta_t : t \in \tau\} \in \Phi$, $a \in R$, *if* $\alpha_{t+1} = \alpha_t$ *a.e.* P *then,*

$$\bar{E}\{g_{t+1}(v, \alpha^{t+1}, a) \mid \mathcal{F}_t\} = g_t(v, \alpha^t, a) \quad \text{a.e. } \bar{P}. \tag{4}$$

Condition 3b says that for constant manipulator holdings over $[t, t+1]$, relative stock prices are a martingale with respect to his information set, thus making short-term buy and hold strategies a fair game. The mutual absolute continuity condition of 3a rules out the possibility of the manipulator being specially informed as it ensures that all traders agree on zero probability events.

To complete our set of assumptions, we include,

Assumption 4 (Price process independence of the manipulator's past holdings). *For all* $\{\alpha_t, \beta_t : t \in \tau\}, \{\alpha_t^*, \beta_t^* : t \in \tau\} \in \Phi$, $a \in R$, *if* $\alpha_t(\omega) = \alpha_t^*(\omega)$ *then* $g_t(\omega, v(\omega), \alpha^t(\omega), a) = g_t(\omega, v(\omega), \alpha^{*t}(\omega), a)$.

This assumption states that prices are independent of the history of the manipulator's trades. Equivalently, the price process is only a function of his current position, α_t, i.e.,

$$g_t(\omega, v(\omega), \alpha^t(\omega), a) = g_t(\omega, v(\omega), \alpha_t(\omega), a). \tag{5}$$

Assumption 5 (Price process independence of the manipulator's actions). *For all* $\{\alpha_t, \beta_t : t \in \tau\} \in \Phi$, $a \in R$,

$$g_t(\omega, v(\omega), \alpha^t(\omega), a) = g_t\big(\omega, v(\omega), \alpha^t(\omega)\big). \tag{6}$$

This assumption imposes the condition that the manipulator cannot undertake an observable action $a \in R$ which will change the equilibrium price process. Assumptions 1–5 are the possible assumptions. These are not maintained hypotheses, but only invoked when needed.

We now introduce the concept of a *market manipulation trading strategy*. First, we need to distinguish between *paper wealth* and *real wealth*. This is necessary when evaluating the profits (or wealth) of imperfectly competitive traders. The manipulator's paper wealth is defined to be the value of his holdings evaluated using the price of the last trade. This is common practice in market efficiency studies of profitable trading strategy rules, in the market value accounting procedure used by accountants, and in a financial risk management technique called 'marking-to-market'. Real wealth, in contrast, is defined to be the value of the manipulator's portfolio in the terms of the numeraire (money market account) upon liquidation of his stock holdings.

Definition 1 (Paper wealth). *The time t paper wealth of the portfolio position $\{\alpha_t, \beta_t : t \in \tau\} \in \Phi$ and action $a \in R$ is defined by*

$$W_t(\omega) = \alpha_{t-1}(\omega) g_t(\omega, v(\omega), \alpha_{t-1}(\omega), \alpha^{t-1}(\omega), a) + \beta_{t-1}(\omega) \tag{7}$$

This corresponds to the manipulator's time $t-1$ holdings evaluated at time t relative prices and given that he has not altered his holdings over $[t-1, t]$.

Definition 2 (Real wealth). *The time t real wealth of the portfolio position $\{\alpha_t, \beta_t : t \in \tau\} \in \Phi$ is defined by*

$$V_t(\omega) = \alpha_{t-1}(\omega) g_t(\omega, v(\omega), 0, \alpha^{t-1}(\omega), a) + \beta_{t-1}(\omega) \tag{8}$$

This corresponds to the manipulator's time $t-1$ holdings evaluated at time t relative prices and given that he has liquidated his stock holdings, i.e., $\alpha_t = 0$ a.e. P.

The relationship between real wealth and paper wealth is easily derived by subtracting equations (7) from (8).

$$\begin{aligned} V_t(\omega) = W_t(\omega) + \alpha_{t-1}(\omega)\big[& g_t(\omega, v(\omega), 0, \alpha^{t-1}(\omega), a) - \\ & - g_t(\omega, v(\omega), \alpha_{t-1}(\omega), \alpha^{t-1}(\omega), a)\big] \end{aligned} \tag{9}$$

The following lemma follows directly from Assumption 2 and equation (9).

Lemma 1. *Given Assumptions 1 and 2 and $\{\alpha_t, \beta_t : t \in \tau\} \in \Phi$, $a \in R$,*

$$V_t(\omega) < W_t(\omega) \text{ if and only if } \alpha_{t-1}(\omega) \neq 0 \text{ a.e. } P.$$

Lemma 1 demonstrates that real wealth and paper wealth are distinct for a large trader (as defined in Assumption 2). In some situations, it will be more convenient to analyze market manipulation trading strategies by calculating the manipulator's cumulative capital gain in the risky asset.

Definition 3 (Gains process). *The time t gains process of the portfolio position $\{\alpha_t, \beta_t : t \in \tau\} \in \Phi$ and action $a \in R$ is defined by*

$$\begin{aligned} \mathcal{G}_t(\omega) &= \alpha_{t-1}(\omega)\big[g_t(\omega, v(\omega), \alpha^t(\omega), a) - \\ &\qquad - g_{t-1}(\omega, v(\omega), \alpha^{t-1}(\omega), a)\big] + \mathcal{G}_{t-1}(\omega) \\ &= \sum_{j=1}^{t} \alpha_{j-1}\big[g_j(\omega, v(\omega), \alpha^j(\omega), a) - \\ &\qquad - g_{j-1}(\omega, v(\omega), \alpha^{j-1}(\omega), a)\big] + \mathcal{G}_0 \end{aligned} \tag{10}$$

where $\mathcal{G}_0 \equiv 0$ and $t > 0$.

The following result dictates that, under the right conditions, the gains process can be used to calculate paper wealth and real wealth.

Lemma 2. *Given Assumption 1 and* $\{\alpha_t, \beta_t : t \in \tau\} \in \Phi$, $a \in R$
1. *if* $\alpha_t = \alpha_{t-1}$ *then* $W_t(\omega) = \mathcal{G}_t(\omega)$ *a.e.* P, *and*
2. *if* $\alpha_t = 0$ *then* $V_t(\omega) = \mathcal{G}_t(\omega)$ *a.e.* P.

Proof. For the first part, note that if $\alpha_t = \alpha_{t-1}$, then $\alpha^t = (\alpha_{t-1}, \alpha^{t-1})$. This implies that

$$\alpha_{t-1}(\omega)[g_t(\omega, v(\omega), \alpha_{t-1}(\omega), \alpha^{t-1}(\omega), a)] = W_t(\omega) - \beta_{t-1}(\omega)$$

by Definition 1. Furthermore, by the self-financing condition (2),

$$\begin{aligned}\alpha_j(\omega)[g_j(\omega, v(\omega), \alpha^j(\omega), a)] &= \\ &= \beta_{j-1}(\omega) + \alpha_{j-1}(\omega)[g_j(\omega, v(\omega), \alpha^{j-1}(\omega), a)] - \beta_j(\omega)\end{aligned}$$

for $0 < j \leq t-1$. Substitution of the above into $\mathcal{G}_t(\omega)$ results in the telescoping sum on the right hand side of equation (10) collapsing to $W_t(\omega)$. The second part of the proof is similar except that Definition 2 ($\alpha_t = 0$) is used instead of Definition 1. □

Armed with the above definitions and results, a market manipulation trading strategy can now be defined.

Definition 4 (A market manipulation trading strategy). *A market manipulation trading strategy is defined to be any zero initial wealth, self-financing trading strategy* $\{\alpha_t, \beta_t : t \in \tau\} \in \Phi$, *such that*

$$V_T \geq 0 \text{ a.e. } P, \tag{11}$$

and

$$P(V_T > 0) > 0. \tag{12}$$

Hence, we define a market manipulation trading strategy to be an arbitrage opportunity in real wealth. An arbitrage opportunity, as common to option valuation, is any self-financing trading strategy such that the paper wealth at liquidation, W_T, is non-negative for sure, and strictly positive with positive probability. The distinction in this definition lies in the fact that we replaced paper wealth, W_T, with real wealth, V_T. As Lemma 1 reveals, the distinction can be quite important.

2.2. Main results

The primary aim of this section is to investigate the existence of market manipulation trading strategies under various economic scenarios. The analysis will be carried out by either invoking or violating some of the assumptions spelled out in the previous section. We first show the strength of Assumptions 3 and 5 in eliminating market manipulation for price takers. This generates Proposition 1. This is the standard setting used in the construction of competitive equilibrium models for asset pricing, like the CAPM. Then we show the existence of three types of market manipulations under the relaxation of these assumptions: Example 1 gives an information-based manipulation, Example 2 a trade-based manipulation, and Example 3 an action-based manipulation. This is consistent with the categorization scheme for market manipulations proposed by Allen & Gale [1992]. Finally, Proposition 2 shows that Assumptions 1–5 are sufficient to simultaneously rule out all three types of manipulation when the manipulator has market power. This is a generalization of the standard setting in Proposition 1, useful for game theoretic models of asset pricing, like in the market microstructure literature.

Given the absence of information-based arbitrage (Assumption 3), market manipulations can only exist, if at all, either because of the manipulator's market power (Assumption 2) or because of his non-trade based actions, a. We exclude action-based manipulation by imposing Assumption 5. This is standard practice in equilibrium asset pricing models. Next, for a *price taking based* manipulator, Assumption 2 is replaced by the condition that $g_t(v, \alpha_t, \alpha_{t-1}, \ldots, \alpha_0)$ is independent of $(\alpha_t, \alpha_{t-1}, \ldots, \alpha_0)$ i.e.,

$$g_t\big(\omega, v(\omega), \alpha^t(\omega)\big) = g_t\big(\omega, v(\omega)\big) \tag{13}$$

From equation (9), this implies that real wealth is equal to paper wealth, i.e., $V_t = W_t$ for all $t \in \tau$. The price taking condition (13) used in conjunction with Assumption 3 and 5 implies that no market manipulation trading strategies exist. We formalize this in the next result.

Proposition 1 (Nonexistence of manipulation for price takers). *Under Assumptions 1, 3, and 5 where for all $t \in \tau$, $\{\alpha_t, \beta_t : t \in \tau\} \in \Phi$, $a \in R$, and given the price taking condition*

$$g_t\big(\omega, v(\omega), \alpha^t(\omega)\big) = g_t\big(\omega, v(\omega)\big),$$

no market manipulation trading strategies exist.

Proof. This follows from the well-known result that the existence of an equivalent martingale measure implies the non-existence of arbitrage opportunities for price takers. □

This proposition provides the standard setting for most equilibrium asset pricing models, e.g., the CAPM. Under this scenario, manipulation cannot occur. However, by relaxing any of these assumptions, manipulation is possible.

The existence of market manipulation trading strategies based on the possession of inside information is possible if Assumption 3 is relaxed. This is probably the most profitable form of manipulation and is, judging from recent newspaper

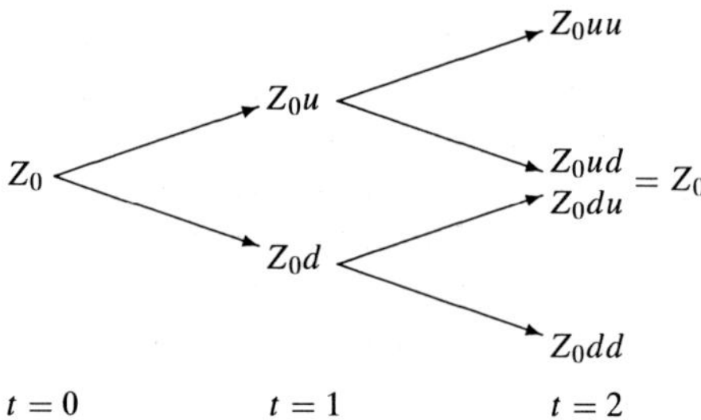

Fig. 1. Sample path of the price process of the stock where $u > d$ and $ud = 1$.

accounts, still rife in equity markets. A simple example is provided to illustrate this form of manipulation.[3] This example relaxes Assumption 3.

Example 1 (Information-based manipulation). Consider a three period economy with $T = 2$. Let the state space $\Omega = \{uu, ud, du, dd\}$. Assume that the stock price process follows a multiplicative binomial process with recombination, i.e., that the rate of return on the stock over each period could either be $u - 1$ with probability p, or $d - 1$ with probability $1 - p$, where u, d are positive constants, with $u > d$ and $d = 1/u$.[4] This implies that the price taking, non-action based condition (13) for the stock price process holds. Hence, if the stock price at time 0 is Z_0, the stock price at time 1 is given by either Z_0u or Z_0d. Proceeding in a similar manner, the possible stock prices at time 2 is given by $\{Z_0uu, Z_0ud, Z_0du, Z_0dd\}$ where $Z_0ud = Z_0du = Z_0$. The reader is referred to Figure 1 for a diagram of the price process. Further assume that the intrinsic value of the stock, v, is revealed at time 2 and has the structure $\{v(uu), v(ud), v(du), v(dd)\}$. By construction we have,

$$\begin{aligned} v(uu) &= Z_2(uu) = Z_0uu \\ v(ud) = v(du) &= Z_2(ud) = Z_2(du) = Z_0 \\ v(dd) &= Z_2(dd) = Z_0dd. \end{aligned}$$

The information structure is modelled as follows. The manipulator's information set evolves as:

$$\begin{aligned} \mathcal{F}_0 = \mathcal{F}_1 &= \{\{uu, ud\}, \{du, dd\}\} \\ \mathcal{F}_2 &= \{\{uu\}, \{ud\}, \{du\}, \{dd\}\}. \end{aligned}$$

The rest of the market's information set is given as:

$$\begin{aligned} \mathcal{F}_0^{\text{market}} &= \{\{uu, ud, du, dd\}\} \\ \mathcal{F}_1^{\text{market}} &= \mathcal{F}_0 = \mathcal{F}_1 \\ \mathcal{F}_2^{\text{market}} &= \mathcal{F}_2. \end{aligned}$$

[3] This example parallels the one found in Cherian & Kuriyan [1995].

[4] We use u and d as possible stock returns and as elements of Ω for notational convenience. The distinction in use should be obvious.

It is obvious that the manipulator has a more refined information set than the rest of the market. The manipulator knows at time 0 whether an up (u) or a down (d) will occur at time 1. The market knows nothing. This is a violation of the mutual absolute continuity condition in Assumption 3. A manipulator with the information set $(\mathcal{F}_t)_{t\in\tau}$ as specified will make arbitrage profits by buying the stock (at time 0) at the market price Z_0 if $\mathcal{F}_0$ reveals that the stock price is going up the next period or selling if $\mathcal{F}_0$ reveals that it is going down.

Example 1 shows that even a price taking (or non-strategic) informed trader can make arbitrage profits by trading on proprietary information. Some may argue that an informed trader is not considered a manipulator unless he trades *strategically* on his private information. This occurs for example when, like a typical monopolist, he takes into account the price impact of his trades by scaling down his orders in order to obtain more favorable prices. Example 1 can easily be generalized to incorporate this scenario. But, as it necessarily involves the introduction of additional notation, we leave it to the reader as a healthy exercise.

The next example incorporates a price process where the manipulator has market power, thereby relaxing the price taking assumption. The example simultaneously satisfies Assumptions 1–3 and 5. It is then shown that for specific parameter values, an asymmetric price response condition can generate profitable manipulation.

Example 2 (Trade-based manipulation). Let $c : \Omega \; X \; \tau \to R$ and $v : \Omega \to R$ be **F**-measurable. Define

$$g_t(\omega, v(\omega), \alpha^t(\omega), a) = \exp\left\{\sum_{j=0}^{t} c_j(\omega)[\alpha_j(\omega) - \alpha_{j-1}(\omega)]\right\} + v(\omega) \quad (14)$$

for $\{\alpha_t, \beta_t : t \in \tau\} \in \Phi$, $a \in R$, where $\{c_t : t \in \tau\}$ is adapted and strictly positive a.e. P, and v is **F**-measurable and non-negative a.e. P.

The coefficient process, $\{c_t : t \in \tau\}$, determines the price sensitivity to the manipulator's orders. It is easy to see that this specification is consistent with Assumptions 1–3 and 5. Assumptions 1, 2, and 5 are true by inspection as $\{c_t : t \in \tau\}$ is strictly positive. Next, assuming that there exists a probability $\bar{P}$ making $v(\omega)$ a martingale and with $\bar{P}$ and P mutually absolutely continuous guarantees the satisfaction of Assumption 3 (using the linearity of the expectation operator). The existence of such a probability $\bar{P}$ is easy to obtain. For example, the process in Figure 1 (if defined to be $v(\omega)$) has such a probability and it is

$$\frac{1-d}{u-d}.$$

To illustrate the market manipulation trading strategy, it is sufficient to consider only a three period economy ($T = 2$). We further specialize the price process of expression (14) as follows. For any $\{\alpha_t, \beta_t : t \in \tau\} \in \Phi$ and $t \in \tau$,

(a) if $\alpha_t(\omega) > \alpha_{t-1}(\omega)$ then $c_j(\omega) = c_+(\omega)$
(b) if $\alpha_t(\omega) < \alpha_{t-1}(\omega)$ then $c_j(\omega) = c_-(\omega)$

where $c_+ > c_- > 0$. For convenience, set $c_+ \equiv 1$ and $0 < c_-(\omega) < 1$. This says that the price sensitivity to a manipulator purchase is higher than for a sale. The rationale behind such a specification draws from the information-based models of market microstructure, i.e., uninformed buys are more likely to occur when traders can minimize their losses to insiders, whereas uninformed sellers, due to pressing cash needs, do not share this luxury. This tends to increase the perceived information content of purchases. The price process specified is also consistent with trend creating strategies such as finite horizon bubbles, price destabilizing speculation, and positive feedback trading. Under this specification, the manipulator can potentially generate manipulative profits by bidding the price up ($0 < \alpha_0 < \alpha_1$) before liquidating his position ($\alpha_2 = 0$). To see this, we evaluate the gains process for the manipulator when $\alpha_0 = 1, \alpha_1 = 3, \alpha_2 = 0$, and $c_- = 1/30$. Further assume that $v(\omega) \equiv 0$. From Definition 3,

$$\begin{aligned}\mathcal{G}_2 &= \sum_{j=1}^{2} \alpha_{j-1}[g_j(\omega, v(\omega), \alpha^j(\omega), a) - g_{j-1}(\omega, v(\omega), \alpha^{j-1}(\omega), a)] \\ &= \alpha_0[g_1(\omega) - g_0(\omega)] + \alpha_1[g_2(\omega) - g_1(\omega)].\end{aligned}$$

By construction

$$\begin{aligned}g_0(\omega) &= \mathrm{e}^{\alpha_0} = 2.718 \\ g_1(\omega) &= \mathrm{e}^{\alpha_1} = 20.086 \\ g_2(\omega) &= \mathrm{e}^{c_-(\alpha_2-\alpha_1)+\alpha_1} = 18.174\end{aligned}$$

Substitution into the gains process gives $\mathcal{G}_2 = 23.10 > 0$.

The following example shows how market manipulation trading strategies can arise when the manipulator takes certain actions which affect the price process. This example relaxes Assumption 5.

Example 3 (Action-based manipulation). We retain the three period economy and the basic functional form of the price process as in Example 2, except that we add that the manipulator's publicly observable action parameter, $a \in R$, has a linear effect on prices, i.e.:

$$\begin{aligned}&g_t(\omega, v(\omega), \alpha^t(\omega), a) = \\ &= \exp\left\{\sum_{j=0}^{t} c_j(\omega)[\alpha_j(\omega) - \alpha_{j-1}(\omega)]\right\} + v(\omega) + a \cdot I_{\{t=2\}}\end{aligned} \tag{15}$$

where I_Θ is the indicator function over the set Θ and such that

$$\exp\left\{\sum_{j=0}^{2} c_j(\omega)[\alpha_j(\omega) - \alpha_{j-1}(\omega)]\right\} + v(\omega) \geq |a|.$$

The latter condition ensures that prices are nonnegative. Notice that, by construction, the manipulator takes a publicly observable action which is reflected in prices at time 2. Although the manipulator knows the timing of his action in advance, we assume the rest of the market is aware of it only when it becomes public knowledge. For simplicity, assume that $c_j(\omega) \equiv 1$ for all $j \in \tau$ and $v(\omega) \equiv 0$. Hence, there isn't an asymmetric price response condition in this example. A positive action parameter effect ($a > 0$) temporarily induces a 'premium' in the price process, while a negative action parameter effect ($a < 0$) temporarily induces a 'discount'. It is now easy to construct trading strategies where a manipulator can make manipulative profits by taking advantage of the effect his action has on prices. Let the strategy he follows be $\alpha_0 = \alpha_1 > 0$, and $\alpha_2 = 0$. By evaluating the gains process as in Example 2, it is easy to see that manipulative profits are available when the action the manipulator takes is such that $a > \mathrm{e}^{\alpha_1} - 1 > 0$.

We now study conditions sufficient to rule out market manipulation trading strategies given that the manipulator has market power and is not a price taker. As such, this is a generalization of Proposition 1. Before doing that, we need the following result.

Lemma 3 (Prices are martingales for constant manipulator holdings). *Given Assumptions 1–5 and any self-financing trading strategy* $\{\alpha_t, \beta_t : t \in \tau\} \in \Phi$ *then,* $\bar{E}(g_t(\alpha_s) \mid \mathcal{F}_s) = g_s(\alpha_s)$ *a.e* $\bar{P}$ *for all* $0 \le s \le t \le T$.

Proof. This follows from Assumption 4 by taking conditional expectations and using the law of iterated expectations, see Jarrow [1992]. □

This lemma states that, for constant manipulator holdings, the expected future price is the same as the current price, in other words, the market provides a fair gamble to the manipulator. This precludes market manipulation trading strategies, as a tedious proof in Jarrow [1992] shows.

Proposition 2 (Nonexistence of manipulation where traders have market power). *Given Assumptions 1–5 and self-financing trading strategies* $\{\alpha_t, \beta_t : t \in \tau\} \in \Phi$, *there exist no market manipulation trading strategies.*

This proposition extends the competitive equilibrium setting to one where traders have market power. As such, it is a sufficient set of conditions useful for excluding manipulation in the game theoretic models common to the market microstructure literature. This completes the presentation of the model. In the next section we review a selected set of the market manipulation literature and relate them to our results and examples. As stated in the introduction, an exhaustive survey is not provided. Instead, we focus on models which illustrate the previous results by deriving the price process endogenously within the context of equilibrium constructs.

3. A review

The categorization scheme employed by Allen & Gale [1992] is useful for the subsequent survey. We have already used this earlier. They divide market manipulations into three categories:

1. *Information-based manipulation*: Manipulation based on trading strategically on inside information or spreading false rumours (our Example 1);

2. *Trade-based manipulation*: Manipulation due to buying or selling stocks without taking any actions or possessing any special information. This category also excludes trading on the release of false information (our Example 2); and

3. *Action-based manipulation*: Manipulation based on actions that change the actual or perceived value of the stock price (our Example 3).

The distinctions between the three different categories of manipulation are not always obvious, but are nonetheless useful.

Strategic, information-based manipulation of the sort described in Example 1 include the models by Kyle [1985] and Easley & O'Hara [1987].[5] In the Kyle model, the monopolistic, informed trader acting optimally, submits orders which increase with noise trading, as noise helps diffuse the information content of his trades. In a slightly different setting, Easley & O'Hara [1987] also allows the informed trader to strategically choose between small market orders and large block trades. In both models, the strategic component to an informed manipulator's trading strategy tends to make prices less informationally-revealing, thus enabling him to extract higher monopolistic information rents from the rest of the market. The reader is referred to the review of market microstructure in this volume by Easley & O'Hara [1995] for further examples of strategic, information-based manipulation.

In an example of trade-based manipulation akin to our Example 2, Allen & Gorton [1992] argue that an asymmetric price response to order flows can generate market manipulation trading strategies, even if the manipulator does not possess any proprietary information. In their example, a higher price sensitivity to purchases than sales, due to the presence of asymmetric noise traders, enables the manipulator to repeatedly buy stock, causing a relatively large effect on prices, and then sell, having relatively little effect on prices, and generating a profit. In a similar model, Allen & Gale [1992] demonstrate how an uninformed trader mimics an informed trader with positive information about the stock to raise the stock price and then sell his shares at a profit.

In another example of trade-based manipulation, Fishman & Hagerty [1991] demonstrate how an uninformed insider can take advantage of the mandatory disclosure (or post-announcement) requirement for insiders as found in the Securities Exchange Act. They find that the manipulator can take advantage of the market's inability to infer the information content of his disclosed trade. For example, al-

[5] As stated in Example 1, the strategic dimension to the example can be easily incorporated by adjusting the price process to be a function of the manipulator's holdings, as in the subsequent examples.

though he has no information, he discloses his sale causing the stock price to drop because the market believes he may be informed. The uninformed manipulator then buys his shares back at the lower price. Assumptions 1 and 2 and Example 2 succinctly describe a price process which is susceptible to this form of manipulation.

As stated, the definitions provided for the three different categories of manipulation may sometimes be confusing, especially when categorizing the models. A case in point is the paper by Gerard & Nanda [1993]. In their model, strategic informed traders short sell a firm's stock just prior to a seasoned equity offering in order to cause downward price pressures on the stock. The manipulators will then more than cover their positions by purchasing stocks in the offering at a reduced price. The discount available at the offering is assumed to be a function of the 'winner's curse' problem faced by new shareholders. The aggressive pre-issue short selling tends to exacerbate the size of the induced discounts. When the stock is eventually restored back to its fair value, the manipulators liquidate their positions at a profit. The model can either be viewed as trade-based manipulation as in Example 2 adjusted for pricing sensitivities, or as action-based manipulation with a negative action parameter effect ($a < 0$) which induces temporary discounts (see Example 3).

Vila [1989] has two models of action-based manipulation (our Example 3). In the first, Vila considers an equilibrium where a 'raider's' purchase of a stock before a takeover attempt increases the price of the stock. Even if the raider is not actually in the market and a takeover is not forthcoming, a manipulator can mimic the raider by purchasing the stock under similar conditions with the intent of misleading the market into thinking that he is genuinely bidding for the firm. He liquidates his position just in time with the profits obtained from the resulting appreciation on the share price. In a more elaborate model of takeovers, Bagnoli & Lipman [1990] have a situation where a large trader announces a takeover bid to manipulate the target corporation's shares. It differs from Vila's model in the sense that Vila doesn't incorporate such an announcement. The bidder-manipulator imitates a serious bidder by taking a substantial position in the stock. This causes an appreciation in share prices as the market cannot tell if the bid is serious. The manipulator then sells his holdings at a profit and drops the bid. Such actions are profitable because the manipulator credibly pools his trades with the raider's trades. Example 3 is consistent with this form of manipulation. When the action-based parameter of Example 3 has a positive effect on the price process ($a > 0$), it temporarily induces a premium in the price process, thus enabling profitable manipulation.

In the second model, Vila [1989] considers the opposite effect. A manipulator first short sells the stock, then releases false information which temporarily depresses the stock price, and then buys back the stock at the reduced price. This sort of manipulation, again, was covered in the negative action parameter effect of Example 3. Famous market manipulation incidents involving 'trading pools' and 'bear raids' during the 1920s lend credibility to Vila's example.

Benabou & Laroque [1992] consider a situation where possessors of private information can manipulate the market through strategically distorted announcements. Insiders, market gurus, and even journalists can manipulate stock prices through misleading forecasts or announcements, earning a profit in the process. The credibility of such announcements hinges on the fact that the manipulator intertemporally varies his forecasts, blaming the incorrect ones on honest mistakes. Thus a privately informed manipulator stands to gain more by speculating and making false announcements than by just trading on his private information. This could either be the premiums or discounts story of Example 3, depending on the circumstance.

4. Further examples

We study one more example of a market manipulation trading strategy in primary markets which is similar to Example 2 and then review briefly the more complicated topic of market manipulation with derivative markets. The following examples do not necessarily satisfy the assumptions of the previous section. They are included to illustrate other possible scenarios of manipulation.

4.1. Equity markets — a reprise

We consider an economy where there exist 'positive feedback' traders. These are traders who submit trades in the direction of current price movements, hence the term positive feedback. This trading strategy is not alien in financial markets. Strategies like stop-loss orders, portfolio insurance, technical analysis, etc., are examples of the positive feedback type.

Example 4 (Market maker economy). This simple example draws on Cherian & Kuriyan [1995].[6] In their model, the price process responds to the entire order flow processed by an intermediary like a market maker as opposed to just the manipulator's trades. However, by assuming that the manipulator (as a large trader) dominates the order flow, they derive a price process condition similar to Assumption 2.

Let the entire order flow be defined as ν_t, the manipulator's position be α_t, and the rest of the market's, u_t. We thus have

$$\nu_t = \alpha_t + u_t.$$

The modified relative stock price process for self-financing trading strategies is defined by

$$Z_t(\omega) = g_t(\omega, v(\omega), \nu_t(\omega), \nu_{t-1}(\omega), \ldots, \nu_0(\omega), a)$$

Based on the information-effects model common to market microstructure [see Easley & O'Hara, 1995], Assumption 2 is replaced by the condition that a net buy order cannot lower relative prices, while a net sell order cannot raise prices, i.e.,

[6] For the sake of brevity we skip notational complexities and concentrate on the results.

(a) if $\nu_t(\omega) > \nu_{t-1}(\omega)$
then $g_t(\omega, v(\omega), \nu^t(\omega), a) > g_t(\omega, v(\omega), \nu_{t-1}(\omega), \nu^{t-1}(\omega), a)$

(b) if $\nu_t(\omega) < \nu_{t-1}(\omega)$
then $g_t(\omega, v(\omega), \nu^t(\omega), a) < g_t(\omega, v(\omega), \nu_{t-1}(\omega), \nu^{t-1}(\omega), a)$.

The market power assumption 2 still holds depending on who is dominating the order flow. For example, if the rest of the market is dominating the order flow around time t, the above condition becomes

(a) if $u_t(\omega) > u_{t-1}(\omega)$
then $g_t(\omega, v(\omega), \nu^t(\omega), a) > g_t(\omega, v(\omega), \nu_{t-1}(\omega), \nu^{t-1}(\omega), a)$

(b) if $u_t(\omega) < u_{t-1}(\omega)$
then $g_t(\omega, v(\omega), \nu^t(\omega), a) < g_t(\omega, v(\omega), \nu_{t-1}(\omega), \nu^{t-1}(\omega), a)$.

Consider a three period economy ($T = 2$) where the manipulator dominates the order flow at time 1, whereas the rest of the market takes control of the order flow at time 2 due to the positive feedback effect. A simple way to capture positive feedback trading formally is to define

$$u_t \equiv d_t\,(Z_{t-1} - Z_{t-2})$$

where d_t is a positive proportionality constant. Assume that the positive feedback trading is 'explosive', i.e.,

$$d_2\,|\,Z_1 - Z_0\,| > |\,\alpha_1\,|. \tag{16}$$

The manipulator can make arbitrage profits by choosing to buy a large quantity of the stock at time 1 and immediately liquidating his position at time 2. Thus, his sequence of holdings $\{\alpha_0, \alpha_1, \alpha_2\}$ is given by $\{0, \alpha_1, 0\}$ where $\alpha_1 > 0$. To see this, we look at the gains process for the manipulator. From Lemma 2, the gains process is equivalent to the manipulator's real wealth if he liquidates his position ($\alpha_2 = 0$). Thus, we have

$$\begin{aligned}\mathcal{G}_2 &= \sum_{j=1}^{2} \alpha_{j-1}\big[g_j\big(\omega, v(\omega), \nu^j(\omega), a\big) - g_{j-1}\big(\omega, v(\omega), \nu^{j-1}(\omega), a\big)\big] \\ &= \alpha_0\big[g_1(\omega) - g_0(\omega)\big] + \alpha_1\big[g_2(\omega) - g_1(\omega)\big] \;>\; 0\end{aligned}$$

as $g_2(\omega) > g_1(\omega)$ by Condition (16). This is a market manipulation trading strategy.

4.2. Manipulation with derivative markets

In a second paper, Jarrow [1994] studies the profitability of manipulation when a third asset, like a derivative security, trades. He finds that riskless arbitrage profits are possible in derivative markets with imperfect information flows. For example, if the stock price process does not respond instantaneously to the manipulator's position in the derivative security by the equivalent synthetic amount in stock, riskless profitable strategies can exist.

In a recent paper, Chatterjea & Jarrow [1993] develop an equilibrium model of U.S. Treasury auctions where there are profitable manipulation opportunities by trading across the primary auction and the secondary *when-issued* markets. Their model captures the alleged 1991 Salomon Brothers Treasury scandal where Salomon ended up controlling a substantial portion of the May 1991 auction of two-year notes as well as the secondary when-issued market, resulting in a squeeze on the short sellers of those instruments.

Kumar & Seppi [1992] use a Kyle [1985] variant to demonstrate how uninformed traders can manipulate futures markets which have 'cash-settled' contracts. The manipulator, who has a substantial long futures contract position, is willing to take a temporary loss in the spot market by aggressively bidding up the spot price in order to end up with a more favorable settlement price. In the two period model they employ, the manipulator can earn positive expected profits at the settlement date, as the market cannot distinguish his trades from the informed trader's. In order to illustrate this form of manipulation within the context of our model, we present the next example.

Example 5 (Manipulation with derivatives). Consider the self-financing trading strategy $\{\alpha_0, \alpha_1, \alpha_2\}$ with $\alpha_0 < \alpha_1$ and $\alpha_2 = 0$, in a three period model with a futures contract on the stock trading. We assume conditions 1–3 hold even in the presence of the futures contract. The manipulator enters into a long futures contract agreement at time 0, with settlement at time 1. Let his futures position be represented by γ_0 and the futures price be $F(\omega)$. For convenience, assume $F(\omega) \equiv g_0(\omega)$ a.e. P. For

$$\gamma_0 > \alpha_1 \frac{g_1(\omega) - g_2(\omega)}{g_1(\omega) - g_0(\omega)} - \alpha_0 \quad \text{a.e. } P, \tag{17}$$

it can be shown that there are market manipulation trading strategies possible. To see this, consider the manipulator's modified gains process:

$$\begin{aligned} \mathcal{G}_2 = \sum_{j=1}^{2} \alpha_{j-1}\big[g_j(\omega, v(\omega), \alpha^j(\omega), a) - \\ - g_{j-1}(\omega, v(\omega), \alpha^{j-1}(\omega), a)\big] + \gamma_0[g_1(\omega) - F] \\ = \alpha_0[g_1(\omega) - g_0(\omega)] + \alpha_1[g_2(\omega) - g_1(\omega)] + \gamma_0[g_1(\omega) - F]. \end{aligned}$$

The additional term in the expression reflects the futures settlement which takes place at time 1. Since $\alpha_0 < \alpha_1$, this implies by Assumption 2 and Condition (17) that manipulation is profitable in this case.

5. Summary and conclusion

We generate an analytical classification scheme for surveying the recent papers on market manipulations in primary markets, specifically equity markets. The focus has been to illustrate the types of market manipulation trading strategies possible, with examples similar in spirit to equilibrium models contained in the literature. We also briefly illustrated the possibility of additional market manipulations in markets with derivative securities.

There are many ways to combat undesirable manipulation of the forms described in this paper. As Gerard & Nanda [1993] observe, disallowing manipulators to cover their short positions in the pre-issue market with stock purchased at the offering reduces manipulation around seasoned equity offerings. In the Jarrow [1994] and Kumar & Seppi [1992] models, better information flows between markets would curtail manipulation as prices act as a natural market-based safeguard against it. Furthermore, all three models agree that free, unrestricted competition between the manipulators tends to drive their profits to zero. A similar suggestion arises in the paper by Holden & Subrahmanyam [1992] who discover that competition between informed traders causes prices to be more informationally-efficient, thus alleviating information-based manipulation.

The firm can also prevent an accrual of unfair informational advantage within certain segments of the market by releasing information in a systematic and timely fashion. Fishman & Hagerty's [1991] results are especially important as mandatory disclosure of trades by insiders may be counter-productive as it could lead to manipulation. They suggest two approaches to circumvent manipulation around disclosures. If disclosure is mandatory, then the 'short-swing profit' rule, which currently only requires corporate insiders to give up profits from short-term trading profits, should be applied to all insiders who face disclosure requirements. Alternatively, they suggest removing the mandatory disclosure requirement since their analysis reveals that voluntary disclosure is generally not forthcoming. We go a step further by either requiring insiders to pre-announce (or pre-disclose) all their trades or, in the face of mandatory post-announcement disclosure, requiring them to do it more promptly so that prices can reflect insiders' trades, motives, and information.

The different approaches just suggested will not entirely eliminate profitable manipulation. However, it would make it more difficult for traders to mischievously indulge in manipulatory tactics. Since regulation can be cumbersome and costly, market-based safeguards should be encouraged to protect against manipulation.

References

Allen, F., and D. Gale (1992). Stock price manipulation. *Rev. Financ. Studies* 5, 503–529.

Allen, F., and G. Gorton (1992). Stock price manipulation, market microstructure, and asymmetric information. *Eur. Econ. Rev.* April, 624–630.

Bagnoli, M., and B.L. Lipman (1990). Stock price manipulation through takeover bids, working paper, Carnegie Mellon University.

Benabou, R., and G. Laroque (1992). Using privileged information to manipulate markets: Insiders, gurus, and credibility. *Q. J. Econ.* August, 921–958.

Chatterjea, A., J.A. Cherian and R.A. Jarrow (1993). Market manipulation and corporate finance: a new perspective. *Financ. Manage.* Summer, 200–209.

Chatterjea, A., and R.A. Jarrow (1993). Market manipulations and a model of U.S. Treasury Securities Market, working paper, Cornell University.

Cherian, J.A., and V.J. Kuriyan (1995). Informationless manipulation in a market-type economy, working paper, Boston University.

Easley, D., and M. O'Hara (1987). Price, trade size, and information in securities markets. *J. Financ. Econ.* 19, 69–90.

Easley, D., and M. O'Hara (1995). Market microstructure, in: R. Jarrow, V. Maksimovic and W.T. Ziemba (eds.), *Finance*, Handbooks in Operations Research and Management Science, Vol. 9., North Holland, Amsterdam, pp. 357–384 (this volume).

Fishman, M.J., and K. Hagerty (1991). The mandatory disclosure of trades and market liquidity, working paper, Northwestern University.

Gerard, B., and V. Nanda (1993). Trading and manipulation around seasoned equity offerings. *J. Finance* 48, 213–245.

Holden, C.W., and A. Subrahmanyam (1992). Long-lived private information and imperfect competition. *J. Finance* 47, 247–270.

Jarrow, R.A. (1992). Market manipulation, bubbles, corners, and short squeezes. *J. Financ. Quant. Anal.* September, 311–336.

Jarrow, R.A. (1994). Derivative security markets, market manipulation, and option pricing theory, *J. Finance. Quant. Anal.* June, 241–261.

Karatzas, I., and S. Shreve (1991). *Brownian Motion and Stochastic Calculus*, Springer-Verlag, New York, NY.

Kumar, P., and D.J. Seppi (1992). Futures manipulation with cash settlement. *J. Finance* 47, 1485–1502.

Kyle, A.S. (1985). Continuous auctions and insider trading. *Econometrica* 53, 1315–1335.

Vila, J.-L. (1989). Simple games of market manipulation. *Econ. Lett.* 29, 21–26.

R. Jarrow et al., Eds., *Handbooks in OR & MS, Vol. 9*

Chapter 21

Real Options

Gordon Sick
Faculty of Management, University of Calgary, Calgary, AB T2N 1N4, Canada

1. Introduction

A *real option* is the flexibility a manager has for making decisions about real assets. These decisions can involve adoption, abandonment, exchange of one asset for another or modification of the operating characteristics of an existing asset. In many cases, real options amount to American options on an underlying asset, so the real option literature has been viewed by some as a subset of the much larger financial option literature. On the other hand, the analysis of real options is closely related to dynamic programming in the operations research literature and to optimal control theory in the mathematics literature. Below, I argue that real options have some special characteristics that give them a special growing niche in the finance and capital budgeting literature.

1.1. Real vs. financial options

A *call option* is the right to acquire an underlying stock or asset (of price P) on a specific exercise or maturity date T at a pre-determined exercise price K. Similarly, a real option to develop a project at some future date provides a call option to acquire the underlying asset, which is the value of a going-concern operating project. The acquisition is done by paying an exercise price, which is the capital cost of developing the project. For example, the underlying asset could be developed urban property, while the option is agricultural land that can be converted to urban use.

1.2. Term

Financial options typically have a finite term to maturity, whereas many real options have a perpetual term to maturity. Many financial options and essentially all real options are *American options*. This means that they can be exercised early or at maturity. The determination of optimal exercise policy is central to the real options analysis and somewhat tangential to financial options analysis. Much of the financial options analysis involves modifying the Black–Scholes option pricing formula to suit special situations. The beauty of the Black–Scholes formula is that it provides an easy-to-compute analytic formula that is based on observable financial data. However, it provides the value of *European options*, which cannot be exercised prior to maturity. Its value in real options analysis is to provide a lower bound to the value of an American real option that has comparable payoff characteristics plus the value of flexibility of choice of exercise date.

1.3. Who will use real options first?

Real options analysis is not nearly as common in either academia or practice as is the analysis of financial options. The main reason for this is the availability of data. Academics have a wealth of data with which to build and test contingent claim models. Practitioners have many markets on which to trade, and the same data with which to parameterize their trading models. The deep and broad contingent claims markets of the 1980s and 1990s are based on the sophisticated models developed by academics.

Real options analysis is similar to financial options analysis insofar as practice will follow academic theory and empirical study. However, there is less data available for real options analysis. Thus, the first areas to adopt real options analysis will be those involving commodity production, such as resource and agricultural industries because of the wealth of data on commodity prices. Many leading-edge petroleum and mining companies are analyzing their developments with the help of real options analysis.

The next areas to adopt real options analysis will be those with a great deal of data, but data that is unfortunately of lower quality. The real estate industry has many databases but nonuniform products. Thus, data on average resale prices are widely available but not useful. Data on a standardized three bedroom bungalow or a square foot of class-A downtown office space are not direct data but data synthesized from a hedonic model of supply and demand. The quality of the data is reduced by the statistical error. Nevertheless, some useful theoretical and empirical models have been built to analyze real estate from a real options perspective.

The area to adopt real options last will probably be the broad area of research and development and strategic planning that is important to almost all firms. Past experience on the risky payoffs to research and development is difficult to codify into an empirical model. However, real options analysis does provide some very helpful comparative statics that will help guide the decision maker. This is a refreshing improvement over the cavalier strategic planning models that are so popular in business and business schools.

For example, the pharmaceutical company Merck uses Monte Carlo simulation to assess research and development strategy, and Black–Scholes option analysis to assess the merits of a joint venture.[1] It also uses game theory to analyze competitive responses to introduction of new products. While these may not

[1] See Nichols [1994].

be the perfect analytic tools for the problems at hand, they will give useful quantitative measures of value and optimal decisions. More importantly, they yield useful comparative statics, such as the notion that the ability to limit downside risk makes a real option more valuable than NPV analysis would suggest. Also, structuring an option to allow for delay enhances value.

Many more firms will come to see their strategic planning in a more sophisticated light, using financial analysis, including real options analysis. Merck is just an early adopter of these techniques.

1.4. The relative importance of real asset decisions

A great deal of research and analysis goes into making financing decisions, such as decisions involving capital structure, dividend policy and the management of exotic securities such as warrants, convertibles, caps, collars and futures or forward contracts. Under Modigliani–Miller theory, these decisions, as a first approximation, are all irrelevant because financial markets can be used to readily undo or replicate any financial decisions the firm may make. Thus, a firm cannot create significant value by its financing policies.

However, a firm can create significant value by its operating or capital budgeting policy, because it can have proprietary access to a portfolio of projects that it may undertake. This arises because of market power, patents, special corporate expertise and operating synergy. Real options analysis is directed toward managing this value-creating activity. Clearly, it makes sense to devote as many resources (academic and applied) to analyzing real options as it does to analyzing financial options. The field of real options has a great deal of catching up to do.

1.5. Real options and the traditional NPV rule

The traditional net-present-value (NPV) rule says 'develop as soon as NPV exceeds zero'. This is also true for real options, as long as we understand that the NPV of an option is the NPV of development minus the opportunity cost that consists of the loss in value of killing the option. To think of this in a different way, the traditional NPV rule for mutually exclusive projects advocates adopting the most valuable project (in order to maximize firm value). In a real options setting, what initially appears to be one project is an infinite number of projects. There is one project for each starting date of the basic project — the Year-0 project, the Year-1-start project, and so forth. The traditional NPV rule then says that we should select the start date that maximizes the value of the firm. This is what real options analysis is all about. The problem is in calculating the value gained or lost by delaying the project.

1.5.1. Random beta and cost of capital

The development cost of a project tends to be fixed, while the benefits of development tend to be random. The fixed cost tends to provide operating leverage for the option, which affects the beta and hence the cost of capital at which one would discount the option payoffs. The degree of this leverage is random, since it increases as the underlying project value falls toward the cost of development. Offsetting this is the risk-reducing effect from the option flexibility. The option passes through upside potential while protecting its owner from significant downside risk. Overall, there is no guarantee that the beta or cost of capital of an option is constant, so we will see that a certainty-equivalent approach is more appropriate. Once an option is analyzed, a cost of capital can be calculated, but this is of no benefit, since the value of the option will have been determined before its cost of capital is determined.

1.6. Real options vs. dynamic programming in operations research

Real options analysis bears a significant resemblance to the dynamic programming literature in operations research. Both deal with the flexibility of future decision making by a backward induction process. The critical difference is that real options analysis takes advantage of and requires an assessment of market risk. Markets are an important source of data for the real options analyst, but the presence of economic markets also imposes some discipline upon the analyst. Financial economists distinguish between systematic risk, which commands a risk premium, and unsystematic risk, which does not. The real options approach is to model these risk premia and adjust the probability distribution for them by calculating a 'risk-neutralized' probability distribution. This distribution can be determined by arbitrage analysis or by fundamental economic analysis.

Financial markets provide other valuable data about stochastic processes and their parameters, which are essential to real options analysis.

2. Primary principles in valuation

2.1. General asset-pricing models

There are two major approaches that can be taken to option pricing. Fortunately, the approaches are compatible, but their intuition is slightly different. One approach involves replicating the option payoffs with the payoffs of a portfolio which has a dynamically updated composition. In the absence of an arbitrage opportunity, the option value equals the value of the portfolio. This approach is popular in the financial option pricing literature and was made popular by Black & Scholes [1973].

Consider the valuation of a call option by the following Black–Scholes *replication approach*. The only random factor in the payoff to the call option is the random value of the underlying asset at the maturity date. The random portfolio that replicates the call option will thus take a long investment position in the underlying asset. It will also take a short position in the riskless asset (borrowing), since the fixed exercise price of the option provides leverage. The portfolio weights must be continuously updated to ensure that the portfolio replicates the option. The updates are done on a self-financing basis — the value of asset purchases equals the value of asset sales in the update procedure. If someone offers to pay more for the option than the value of the replicating portfolio, then an arbitrageur could sell the option short and use the proceeds to purchase the replicating portfolio, for an immediate net cash inflow or *arbitrage profit*. Since the dynamic portfolio strategy would not require any intermediate cash flows and would replicate the option cash flows at maturity, this would result in a riskless profit to the arbitrageur. Similarly, if someone were willing to sell the option for less than the value of the replicating portfolio, an arbitrageur could earn a riskless profit by going long on the option and short on the replicating portfolio. Arbitrage opportunities should be exhausted by trading in financial markets, so we conclude that the value of the option must equal the value of the replicating portfolio.

While this line of analysis is very useful for financial options because there are many arbitrageurs on the floors of options exchanges trading with strategies of this type, many people find this approach to be less compelling with real options, because it is so difficult to sell a real asset short. One can construct a dynamic portfolio strategy of riskless borrowing and ownership of the underlying asset that replicates the payoff of the option, as in the Black–Scholes analysis. However, the underlying asset may not exist as a tradeable asset if such assets only exist as a result of the exercise of real options. Thus, it may not be feasible to form the replicating portfolios needed to validate the arbitrage analysis. Even if the underlying asset exists, it may not be very liquid and could be hard to sell short. For example, when the underlying asset is developed urban property, agricultural land owners have a real option to convert their land to urban use. Neither urban nor agricultural land are so liquid that the replicating dynamic portfolio strategies are very realistic.

Unfortunately, these difficulties lead some people to discard all of the systematic analysis and resort to some very crude rules of thumb when dealing with real options. For example, they may ignore risk, they may accept a hurdle NPV of zero, or they may introduce arbitrary 'fudge factors' into the analysis. Clearly these people need something to grasp in order to make consistent value-maximizing decisions.

To serve these people, I advocate pricing real options with the capital asset-pricing model (CAPM) and all of its variations and extensions. The variations include arbitrage pricing theory, the consumption capital asset-pricing model, the intertemporal capital asset-pricing model, and martingale pricing theory. These linear pricing operators are the most general pricing operators that are consistent with the absence of arbitrage opportunities. This class of pricing operators will stand the test of time in financial economics. The only things we can expect to learn are details about the characterization and parameters of the pricing operators.

The popularity of the CAPM and its variants make them easy to accept for many financial decision makers, even though their proofs often rely on assumptions about perfect markets, absence of arbitrage or optimizing behavior on the part of economic agents. Indeed, most financial decision makers are prepared to accept the present-value approach to making decisions about riskless cash-flow streams, even if these streams are illiquid. If they are offered an illiquid stream at a price less than its present value, they will still acquire it even if they do not intend to earn an immediate arbitrage profit by offsetting it with a riskless stream of outflows. Similarly, if someone offers to buy from them an illiquid stream at a price greater than its present value, they will sell, even if the stream offered a suitable time pattern of future cash inflows. Buying and selling these illiquid streams merely amount to portfolio adjustments that can ultimately be offset by future trades in other assets.

More generally, these same decision makers are willing to use the CAPM to value the risk coming in or out of their portfolio by buying and selling risky assets. If they are offered the opportunity to buy or sell assets at favorable prices that are inconsistent with the CAPM, they will do so. If they want to offset the change in risk exposure, they can do so by trading broad and liquid stock portfolios. They are not forced to conduct their risk offsets with the illiquid or nontraded underlying asset. Indeed, decision makers may manage their own nontraded human wealth by trading financial assets to hedge their own personal risk. The only limitation would arise if there are incomplete markets (for the risk of human wealth), or compelling agency reasons for an owner-manager of a firm to not become well-diversified. Even in these situations, the CAPM provides a suitable starting point for risk analysis.

2.1.1. Martingale and state-space pricing

Although martingale valuation is also discussed by Carr & Jarrow [1995] elsewhere in this volume, I will review these ideas below to help keep this chapter self-contained. Readers who are only interested in applications can skim this material for the notation and refer back only as needed to interpret the later material. The applied material starts with the Section 2.2 on Hotelling valuation.

More rigorous discussions of martingale pricing appear in Harrison & Kreps [1979] and Harrison & Pliska [1981]. The ideas are also discussed succinctly in Ross [1989]. The broad extensions to the CAPM are discussed in Cox, Ingersoll & Ross [1985a]. An overall discussion of these issues appears in Ingersoll [1987] and Jarrow [1988].

First, I will discuss the martingale pricing operators, and interpret them in the context of state-preference theory, the consumption CAPM, and the CAPM. I will discuss the restrictions necessary to ensure that the operator is positive in the sense that it will always assign a nonnegative value to a nonnegative cash flow.

Suppose the riskless rate of interest r is known and constant. Consider the *valuation* today of risky cash-flow payoffs T periods hence. That is, we wish to determine the price[2] $V_t[\tilde{X}_T]$ to be paid at time t for the right to receive the risky cash flow $\tilde{X}_T$ at a future time $T > t$. The *risky cash flow* $\tilde{X}_T$ is a real-valued

[2] The future cash flow $\tilde{X}_T$ could be positive or negative. Thus, the value at time t could be positive, negative or even zero.

function $\tilde{X}_T$: $\Omega_T \to \Re$ on the state space Ω_τ that describes what amount of cash in $\tilde{X}_T(s)$ is paid in each state $s \in \Omega_T$. Suppose the probability distribution of this state space Ω_τ is $\pi = \pi_0$. Over time, information arrives, and this distribution is updated by all agents in the economy to the conditional distribution π_t at time t. Under *martingale valuation*, there exists a (martingale) probability measure $\hat{\pi}$ on the payoff space Ω_T such that the time-t value or price $V_t[\tilde{X}_T]$ of any time-T cash flow $\tilde{X}_T$ is given by the present value of the expected payoff under this martingale measure:

$$\begin{aligned} V_t[\tilde{X}_T] &= \mathrm{e}^{-r(T-t)} \int_{\Omega_T} \tilde{X}_T(s)\, \mathrm{d}\hat{\pi}_t(s) \\ &= \mathrm{e}^{-r(T-t)} \hat{E}_t[\tilde{X}_T] \qquad (0 \le t \le T) \end{aligned} \tag{1}$$

where $\hat{\pi}_t$ and $\hat{E}_t[\cdot]$ are, respectively, the distribution and expectation conditional on information available at time t with respect to the martingale measure.

The sequence of valuation measures over time forms a martingale in the sense that the stochastic process of discounted asset values $\{\mathrm{e}^{-rt} V_t[\tilde{X}_T]\}_{t=0}^{T}$ forms a martingale under the distribution $\hat{\pi}$:

$$\tau \le t \le T \Rightarrow \mathrm{e}^{-r\tau} V_\tau[\tilde{X}_T] = \hat{E}_\tau[\mathrm{e}^{-rt} V_t[\tilde{X}_T]]$$

This can be verified by an application of the law of iterated expectations:

$$\begin{aligned} \mathrm{e}^{-r\tau} V_\tau[\tilde{X}_T] &= \mathrm{e}^{-r\tau} \mathrm{e}^{-r(T-\tau)} \hat{E}_\tau[\tilde{X}_T] = \mathrm{e}^{-rT} \hat{E}_\tau\big[\hat{E}_t[\tilde{X}_T]\big] = \\ &= \mathrm{e}^{-rt} \hat{E}_\tau\big[\mathrm{e}^{-r(T-t)} \hat{E}_t[\tilde{X}_T]\big] = \mathrm{e}^{-rt} \hat{E}_\tau\big[V_t[\tilde{X}_T]\big]. \end{aligned}$$

This is just a consistency condition on the pricing operator. For example, setting $\tau = 0$, we can interject an intermediate time period and compute the same value: $V_0[\tilde{X}_T] = V_0\big[V_t[\tilde{X}_T]\big]$.

The martingale measure or expectation is sometimes called *risk-neutral* or *risk-neutralized* since values are computed by taking the present value of expected payoffs as though no risk-premium is required. In fact, we shall see that any risk-premium is embodied in the transition from the true probability distributions π_t to the martingale distributions $\hat{\pi}_t$.

To see that $\hat{\pi}_t$ must be a probability distribution, first note that a riskless security paying \$1 for certain at time T must have a value $\mathrm{e}^{-r(T-t)}$, so

$$\mathrm{e}^{-r(T-t)} = V_t[1] = \mathrm{e}^{-r(T-t)} \int_{\Omega_T} 1\, \mathrm{d}\hat{\pi}_t(s) = \mathrm{e}^{-r(T-t)} \hat{\pi}_t(\Omega_T)$$

and hence the probability measure integrates to unity over the probability space. Moreover, the measure should be positive in the sense that the probability of any event must be nonnegative. If we have a security or contingent claim that pays \$1 if an event A occurs and nothing otherwise, this security has a nonnegative payoff, and should have a nonnegative price to prevent arbitrage. The risk-neutral expected payoff of the security is the risk-neutral probability, $\hat{\pi}_t(A)$, and the price of this security is the present value of this amount, so the measure $\hat{\pi}_t$ itself must be positive. Thus, the risk-neutral measure $\hat{\pi}_t$ is nonnegative and assigns a value of 1 to the whole state space, so it must be a probability measure.

To make things more concrete, suppose we have a discrete state space, and replace the continuous discounting factor $e^{-r(T-t)}$ with the discrete discounting factor $(1+r)^{-(T-t)}$, recycling the discount rate r with this new meaning. Then the present value of the martingale probability of a state s at date T is simply the date-t *Arrow–Debreu state-space price* for a claim to \$1 contingent on occurrence of that state,

$$p_{s,t} = (1+r)^{-(T-t)}\hat{\pi}_t(s). \tag{2}$$

If markets are not complete, the Arrow–Debreu prices are not unique, but we do know that in the absence of arbitrage, there exists a set of positive Arrow–Debreu prices such that the value of a risky cash flow is the sum of its payoffs in each state times the price of an Arrow–Debreu claim to \$1 in that state. This is consistent with (1):

$$V_t[\tilde{X}_T] = (1+r)^{-(T-t)} \sum_{s\in\Omega_T} \hat{\pi}_t(s)\tilde{X}_T(s) = \sum_{s\in\Omega_T} p_{s,t}\tilde{X}_T(s). \tag{3}$$

Note that, if we are given a set of Arrow–Debreu prices of basic state-contingent claims, we can solve (2) for the martingale probabilities $\hat{\pi}_t$, so the martingale approach can be regarded as an outcome of Arrow–Debreu state-space theory with complete markets.

We can also relate the martingale measure to the true probability measure. First, observe that, if a state has a probability of 0, a claim to a payoff of \$1 in that state should also have a price of zero. The rationale is that nobody would pay anything for a security that pays nothing with probability 1. This means that $\pi_t(s) = 0 \Rightarrow p_{s,t} = 0$. For pricing purposes, we can restrict ourselves to discrete states that have positive probability. We can define the ratio of time-t price to the present value of the probability as the random variable:

$$\tilde{g}_{t,T}(s) = \frac{P_{s,t}}{(1+r)^{-(T-t)}\pi_t(s)}. \tag{4}$$

The outcome of the random variable $\tilde{g}_{t,T}$ is learned at time $T \geq t$, when state s is revealed. The date-t value of a risky payoff $\tilde{X}_T$ is the present value of the expected product of the risky payoff times $\tilde{g}_{t,T}$:

$$V_t[\tilde{X}_T] = (1+r)^{-(T-t)} E_t[\tilde{g}_{t,T}\tilde{X}_T]. \tag{5}$$

Note from (2) and the fact that $\hat{\pi}_t$ has the properties of a probability distribution implies that the random variable $\tilde{g}_{t,T} \geq 0$ and $E_t[\tilde{g}_{t,T}] = 1$.

2.1.2. Capital asset-pricing model and its relatives

In a utility-optimization model such as the *consumption CAPM* of Breeden [1979] the random variable $\tilde{g}_{t,T}(s) = U'(s)$ is the marginal utility[3] of date-T consumption for a representative investor in a market equilibrium, conditional on information available at time t about the probability of state s. Assuming that the investor is risk averse, the utility function is concave, so that its derivative (marginal utility) is positive. From (2) and (4),

$$\hat{\pi}_t(s) = \tilde{g}_{t,T}(s)\pi_t(s) = U'(s)\pi_t(s). \tag{6}$$

This means that the risk-neutral probability distribution $\hat{\pi}_t$ differs from the true distribution π_t by an adjustment factor equal to the marginal utility of consumption at the final payoff date. Since $E_t[\tilde{g}_{t,T}] = 1$, the average adjustment factor is 1. If the marginal or representative investor is risk-neutral, this adjustment factor is a constant, and must be 1. Thus, the risk-neutral probability distribution $\hat{\pi}_t$ is the one that is consistent with market prices being set by risk-neutral investors.

If the marginal investor is risk averse, then marginal utility is less than 1 for high-consumption states and more than 1 for low-consumption states. Thus, a security is relatively more valuable if it pays off when investors need the consumption the most (in the low-consumption states).

There is another important condition on the payoffs to a security that allow it to be priced as if the marginal investor were risk-neutral. For example, if the random payoff $\tilde{X}_T$ is distributed independently of marginal utility $\tilde{g}_{t,T}$, then the expectation of their product in (5) can be written as a product of expectations. Since $E_t[\tilde{g}_{t,T}] = 1$, this means that the value or price of the random payoff is the present value of its expected payoff under the true conditional probability distribution π_t. This result can be generalized slightly by characterizing the pricing operator in terms of returns to resemble the more traditional versions of the CAPM or arbitrage pricing theory (APT).

Using the fact that a covariance between two random variables is the mean of their product minus the product of their means, we can replace (5) with

$$\begin{aligned} V_t[\tilde{X}_T] &= (1+r)^{-(T-t)}E_t[\tilde{g}_{t,T}\tilde{X}_T] \\ &= (1+r)^{-(T-t)}\big(E_t[\tilde{g}_{t,T}]E_t[\tilde{X}_T] + \text{cov}_t[\tilde{X}_T\tilde{g}_{t,T}]\big) \\ &= (1+r)^{-(T-t)}\big(E_t[\tilde{X}_T] + \text{cov}_t[\tilde{X}_T\tilde{g}_{t,T}]\big). \end{aligned} \tag{7}$$

Up to this point, we have allowed the cash flow $\tilde{X}_T$ to be positive or negative. Thus, the valuation equation (7) is useful for valuing general contracts, such as

[3] We have scaled prices relative to current consumption as a numeraire. The investor's Von Neumann–Morgenstern utility function U is unique up to a linear transformation, so the marginal utility U' is unique only up to a positive scale factor. We also choose, for simplicity, a scaling of the utility function so that, for investment decisions made at time t about the date-T consumption in state s, $U'(s) = \tilde{g}_t(s)$.

futures and forward contracts for which future net cash flows can be positive or negative. Thus, it could impose future liabilities on the owner.

Now, suppose the cash flow imposes no future liability on the individual who is to receive it. There is limited liability and $\tilde{X}_T \geq 0$. The claim to such a cash flow is a fully paid-up capital asset, and has a nonnegative value $V_t[\tilde{X}_T] \geq 0$. An investment strategy of paying $V_t[\tilde{X}_T]$ at time t to acquire a claim to the future cash flow $\tilde{X}_T$, is self-financing in the sense that no other cash injections are required to maintain ownership of the asset. Thus, $V_t[\tilde{X}_T] > 0$ is the value of a capital asset.

Now, take $T - t = 1$ to be one year. We can rewrite (7) to resemble the CAPM in its rate of return form on the capital asset by defining

$$\tilde{z}_T \equiv \frac{\tilde{X}_T}{V_{T-1}[\tilde{X}_T]} - 1.$$

to be the one-period rate of return realized at time T on the investment in cash flow $\tilde{X}_T$. Then from (7), the expected rate of return is

$$E_{T-1}[\tilde{z}_T] = r + \text{cov}_{T-1}[\tilde{z}_T, \tilde{f}_{T-1,T}] \tag{8}$$

where we define the systematic risk factor

$$\tilde{f}_{T-1,T} \equiv -\tilde{g}_{T-1,T}. \tag{9}$$

More generally, we have the following *certainty-equivalent valuation* equation[4], which applies for a contingent contract that is not fully paid up and may incur future outflows:

$$V_{T-1}[\tilde{X}_T] = \frac{E_{T-1}[\tilde{X}_T] - \text{cov}_{T-1}[\tilde{X}_T \tilde{f}_{T-1,T}]}{1+r}. \tag{10}$$

This is the *consumption CAPM*, since $\tilde{f}_{T-1,T}$ is minus the marginal utility of consumption at date T. The measure of systematic risk of the security paying a rate of return $\tilde{z}_T$ is the 'consumption beta' $\text{cov}_{T-1}[\tilde{z}_T, \tilde{f}_{T-1,T}]$. This measure is normalized so that the return premium per unit risk is 1. Since marginal utility is decreasing in consumption, the marginal utility $\tilde{g}_{T-1,T}$ tends to be low in high-wealth states. Thus, $\tilde{f}_{T-1,T}$ is positively correlated with the marginal investor's consumption or aggregate wealth. As in the CAPM, the expected rate of return of a security is higher if the security payoff varies positively with aggregate wealth. If the expected rate of return is uncorrelated with marginal utility $\tilde{g}_{T-1,T}$, then the expected rate of return is the riskless return, and hence the risk-neutralized probability is the true probability. The difference between the true probability distribution of the rate of return on a security and the risk-neutralized probability distribution is the adjustment for systematic risk.

The standard CAPM also has the form (8) or (10), but the systematic risk factor $\tilde{f}_{T-1,T}$ is replaced by a factor that is proportional to the rate of return on the

[4] The numerator is the certainty equivalent of the risky cash flow $\tilde{X}_T$ because discounting such a certain payment at the riskless rate of interest gives the value of the cash flow.

market index security $\tilde{r}_{m,T}$, with the constant of proportionality chosen to make the relation correctly fit the expected return on the market index:

$$\tilde{\phi}_{T-1,T} \equiv \left(\frac{E_{T-1}[\tilde{r}_{m,T}]-r}{\operatorname{var}_{T-1}[\tilde{r}_{m,T}]}\right)\tilde{r}_{m,T}. \tag{11}$$

Let us relate $\tilde{\phi}_{T-1,T}$ to $\tilde{f}_{T-1,T}$, to see what restrictions this places on $\tilde{\phi}_{T-1,T}$. Applying (9) we must have $E_t[\tilde{f}_{t,T}] = -1$ and $\tilde{f}_{t,T} \leq 0$. Since covariance is not affected by adding a constant to a random variable, define

$$\tilde{f}_{T-1,T} \equiv \tilde{\phi}_{T-1,T} + A,$$

and choose the constant A so that $E_t[\tilde{f}_{t,T}] = -1$. This means that

$$A \equiv -\left[1+\left(\frac{E_{T-1}[\tilde{r}_{m,T}]-r}{\operatorname{var}_{T-1}[\tilde{r}_{m,T}]}\right)E_{T-1}[\tilde{r}_{m,T}]\right].$$

Ensuring that $\tilde{f}_{t,T} \leq 0$ is equivalent to the following upper-bound condition[5]:

$$\tilde{r}_{m,T} \leq E_{T-1}[\tilde{r}_{m,T}]+\left(\frac{\operatorname{var}_{T-1}[\tilde{r}_{m,T}]}{E_{T-1}[\tilde{r}_{m,T}]-r}\right). \tag{12}$$

In general, we do not model market rates of return to be bounded from above in discrete time, so the traditional CAPM does not give a positive operator. The CAPM can still correctly price the universe of (existing) assets that lead to the mean–variance optimization, such as joint normally distributed payoffs. However, once we start requiring that our pricing operator also correctly price assets with more general payoffs, then we must take care to ensure that we are using a positive pricing operator. For example, if (12) fails, then the value of a deep-out-of the money call option on the market index that only pays off when (12) is violated will have a negative price under the CAPM, even though it has nonnegative payoffs. To ensure that we have a consistent valuation operator for call options on such joint normally distributed payoffs, we could assume that the marginal investor has negative exponential utility, where $\tilde{g}_{T-1,T}$ is proportional to $\exp(-a\tilde{W}_T)$, where $\tilde{W}_T$ is the aggregate payoff to all risky assets. This will still give the CAPM for the joint normally distributed assets (because the expected utility functions are monotone transformations of a linear combination of mean and variance of payoff), and it will give meaningful nonnegative prices to call options on these assets since the pricing factor $\tilde{g}_{T-1,T}$ is nonnegative.

These techniques can be generalized to the continuous state space, where $\tilde{g}$ is the Radon–Nikodym derivative of the martingale measure $\hat{\pi}$ with respect to the true probability measure π. The martingale measure $\hat{\pi}$ and the pricing factor $\tilde{g}$ are uniquely determined if the markets are *complete*.[6] In general, markets will

[5] Assuming that $E_{T-1}[\tilde{r}_{m,T}] \geq r$, which is to say that the risk of the market index commands a positive risk premium.

not be complete, so the pricing operator is not unique. Moreover, it is possible that introducing a new *unspanned security* (one that does not pay off like a portfolio of existing securities), such as an option, will change the prices of existing securities. This could invalidate earlier choices of the martingale measure or the pricing factor. This can make it difficult to use some of the option-pricing techniques of this chapter and other papers with absolute impunity. Indeed, there may fail to be unanimity in such a situation, so that different investors may rank different investment strategies of the firm differently. In these situations, all of our existing capital budgeting techniques can fail, and choosing an optimal investment program can come down to game theory, which is not the focus of this paper.[7] Thus, we will assume, as do other authors in this field, that markets are either complete, or that the payoffs of any project under consideration can be spanned by the payoffs of existing securities.

2.1.3. *Steps to finding a martingale valuation operator*

Harrison & Pliska [1981] show that, even if markets are incomplete, all the martingale measures that correctly price traded assets give identical prices for claims to risky payoffs that are *attainable* by trading strategies for existing assets.[8] Call options on traded assets are attainable claims, using the standard Black & Scholes [1973] replication technique whereby the option payoff is synthesized by a dynamic portfolio strategy of investments in the underlying risky and riskless assets.

This creates a useful technique for valuing options and other claims that are attainable by dynamic trading strategies in existing assets:

1. Find a 'risk-neutral' or 'martingale' probability measure $\hat{\pi}$ on the same probability space[9] as the true probability measure π such that the stochastic

[6] The market is complete if, given a random scalar variable defined on the probability space, there exists a priced security that pays off according to the values of the random variable. If the state space is finite, then the market is complete if, given state s, it is possible to find a security or portfolio of securities that pays \$1 if state s occurs, and nothing otherwise. The prices p_s of such securities define the martingale measure and pricing factor uniquely, as above.

[7] Here is an example of how incomplete markets can break down unanimity. Suppose a pharmaceutical firm is trying to decide whether to develop a treatment for a very rare disease, with no existing treatment. Given the rarity of the disease, analysts in the firm conclude that the research and development program will be more costly than the potential sales revenue from the treatment. On a net present value basis, the R&D program has a negative value and would be rejected. However, if some of the shareholders of the firm are afflicted by this disease, they may find personal benefits to the research that exceed their share of the negative NPV.
This is the classic agency problem. If these shareholders can control the firm's decisions, they will undertake the project, even though the other shareholders disagree. The market failure here is the absence of a market for treatment in the rare disease. If treatments were available, then all shareholders would agree to make decisions based on value maximization, since even the ill shareholders would prefer to be wealthier, in order to be able to buy more of the existing treatment.

[8] For discrete-time processes, this is Harrison and Pliska's Proposition 2.9. In continuous time, see their Proposition 3.31.

[9] By 'same space' we mean that both the true probability distribution π and the martingale distribution $\hat{\pi}$ assign a zero probability to the same events. In this sense, these distributions are 'equivalent'.

process of discounted values of the underlying traded assets $\{e^{-rt}\tilde{P}_t\}_{t=0}^T$ form a martingale under $\hat{\pi}$. Thus, if the probability space is a continuous process over time that achieves the values on the interval $(0, \infty)$, the martingale process shall achieve values on the same interval. Or, if the true process is a sequence of Bernoulli trials over time, with increments drawn from a two-point set $\{z_1, z_2\}$ the martingale process must be also be a sequence of Bernoulli trials drawn from $\{z_1, z_2\}$. The probability of selecting the two points will be different for the martingale process and the true process, but the state space is the same for both. Note that we only need the marginal probability distribution for events defined by the payoff levels of the asset that we wish to value.

2. Value any payoff that is attainable by a trading strategy involving the underlying assets by the present value of the expected payoff under the selected martingale probability measure. The choice of the martingale measure may not be unique, but for any attainable payoff (i.e., one that can be replicated by a trading strategy in underlying assets), all such martingale processes will agree on the value of the new claim to this payoff as the present value of the expected payoff under the martingale probability.

To state this more mathematically, suppose $\tilde{X}_T$ is a risky payoff at date T that is a function of the date-T values of some existing, traded assets $(i = 0, 1, 2, \dots, n)$, which have price processes $\{\tilde{P}^i\}_{t=0}^T$. Also, suppose that there is a dynamic trading strategy in these traded assets that generates the payoff $\tilde{X}_T$. This is the case, for example, if $\tilde{X}_T$ is a call or put option on the traded assets. Then, we only need to find a way to adjust the parameters of the stochastic processes for the traded assets to get a risk-neutral martingale process for the values of these assets. That is, if the assets $i = 0, 1, 2, \dots, n$ pay no dividends[10], then letting ^ denote expectations with respect to this martingale distribution, we have

$$\tilde{P}^i(t) = e^{-r(T-t)}\hat{E}_t[\tilde{P}^i(T)]$$

whenever $0 \le t \le T$. Even if the joint probability distribution giving these marginal martingale distributions is not unique, the value of the claim to $\tilde{X}_T$ is the present value of the expected payoff under such a joint distribution, in the sense that (1) holds.

Often it is relatively simple to determine an eligible martingale probability, since under the martingale probability, the expected rate of return on each of the traded assets if the riskless rate of return. For example, in discrete time,

$$\tilde{z}_t^i \equiv \frac{\tilde{P}_t^i}{\tilde{P}_t^i - 1} - 1$$

is the one-period rate of return realized at time t on asset i. From the consumption CAPM (8), the true expected rate of return is

$$E_{t-1}[\tilde{z}_t^i] = r + \mathrm{cov}_{t-1}[\tilde{z}_t^i, \tilde{f}_t]. \tag{13}$$

[10] We will see how to adjust for dividends when they arise. The technique is straightforward, but merely makes the notation more clumsy at this point.

A suitable martingale distribution is one in which the expected rate of return on this asset is the riskless rate of return:

$$\hat{E}_{t-1}[\tilde{z}_t^i] = r.$$

To get such a risk-neutralized martingale process, we only need to subtract from the true mean rate of return the consumption CAPM risk premium $\text{cov}_{t-1}[\tilde{z}_t^i, \tilde{f}_t]$. This technique will also work if the underlying asset pays a dividend. In that case, we merely need to choose a martingale process for which the underlying asset pays an expected capital gain plus dividend at the rate r. Given this risk-neutral probability distribution, we can determine the value of a claim to the new cash flow as:

$$V_t[\tilde{X}_T] = (1+r)^{-(T-t)}\hat{E}_t[\tilde{X}_T]. \tag{14}$$

We will take the liberty of extending this technique to situations in which the risky payoff $\tilde{X}_T$ cannot be replicated or attained by a trading strategy in existing assets. As long as this new payoff occurs in sufficiently small quantities compared to the payoffs of existing assets, it is unlikely to change the parameters of the consumption CAPM, including the riskless rate of return r or the parameters of the marginal utility factor $\tilde{g}_{t,T}$. In this environment, the risk neutral probability distribution can be obtained by adjusting the drift to ensure that the value process $\{V_t[\tilde{X}_T]\}_{t=0}^T$ has an expected rate of return equal to the riskless rate under the risk-neutral probability $\hat{\pi}$.

This concludes our review of martingale pricing theory.

2.2. *Hotelling valuation of operating resource properties*

In many real options situations, we can relate the value of the underlying asset to the spot price of some commodity. For example, under the *Hotelling valuation principle* [11], the value of an optimally managed operating mineral property equals the current contribution margin per unit volume times the volume of reserves. Since the rate of resource extraction is optimally managed, the value today of extracting one unit of reserves must be the same as the value of reserves extracted at any later date. If not, value can be increased by shifting production ahead or back in time. Developing the property corresponds to exercising a call option. At the time of exercise, the *net proceeds from exercising* equal the net value of commencing production of a resource property, which is

$$\text{NPV} = Q(P - \text{VC}) - K. \tag{15}$$

where

P = spot price of commodity;

Q = quantity of reserves;

[11] See Hotelling [1931], Miller & Upton [1985a, b] or Sick [1989b, pp. 10–11] for more discussion.

VC = unit cost of production;
K = capital cost of development.

The net proceeds of exercise per unit of reserves is $P-(\mathrm{VC}+K/Q)$. This is the payoff to a call option that has an exercise price of $\mathrm{VC}+K/Q$, and the underlying asset is a unit of the commodity, with spot price P.

In more general problems, the spot price of the commodity is still a sufficient statistic for the random value arising from development of a property. In these situations, the net proceeds of exercise can be calculated by a discounted-cash-flow analysis of the NPV of development at a variety of spot prices. Bjerksund & Ekern [1990] develop models of this sort. Laughton & Jacoby [1991] suggest that the nonlinearity of tax and royalty structure, coupled with the uncertainty of future spot prices can best be modelled by Monte Carlo simulation of spot prices subsequent to the point at which the project is developed. The net proceeds of exercise is the expected present value of the after-tax net cash flows from the operating project, minus the cost of development.

2.3. Nature of financing (tax-adjusted discount rate)

Financial options are often priced by consideration of arbitrage opportunities amongst bonds, an underlying asset and the option. This arbitrage is typically conducted by a floor trader who trades in and out of arbitrage positions in just a few days. Thus, capital gains are not deferred, and become taxed at the same rate T_p as dividend income and debt income, in the hands of the arbitrageur. The after-tax net payoffs to arbitrage positions are simply the pre-tax net payoffs multiplied by the retention factor $(1-T_p)$. If taxation of gains and losses is linear and symmetric, this leads to the same arbitrage relations as in a pre-tax analysis. Thus, it is customary to ignore taxes in the analysis of financial options. The arbitrage analysis generates certainty-equivalents, which are simply discounted at the riskless rate of return r_f on debt.

On the other hand, real options are long-term in nature, so they fit naturally into the analysis of the capital budget of the firm. In capital budgeting analysis, it is customary to adjust for the differential taxation of long-term returns on debt and equity. This is accomplished by either adjusting the discount rate to get a weighted average cost of capital, or by adjusting a base-case value, corresponding to the value if all-equity financed, by the present value of the interest tax shields. This is discussed in most textbooks, such as Brealey and Myers [1991, chapter 19] or Ross, Westerfield & Jaffe [1993, chapter 17]. However, Sick [1990] and Taggart [1991] argue that the traditional treatment of interest tax shields is inconsistent with the modern literature on taxation and capital structure equilibrium stemming from Miller [1977]. Since real options are priced as certainty-equivalents of long-term cash-flow streams that will be taxed at a personal level when passed to investors, we do need to adjust for the differential taxation of debt and equity by using a tax-adjusted discount rate. In contrast, financial options are priced as certainty-equivalents of claims to underlying securities that are already priced in the market in a manner that already incorporates adjustments for personal taxation. In particular, Paddock, Siegel & Smith [1988] and Sick [1989b] advocate the use of a tax-adjusted bond return as the discount rate for the certainty-equivalents in real options.

First, let us review the arguments advanced by Miller and others regarding the integration of corporate and personal taxes into a capital structure equilibrium. Miller assumes there are different personal tax rates for various individuals but the same tax rate for all corporations τ_c. In equilibrium, the marginal investor faces a marginal tax rate of τ_{pb} on interest income and τ_{pe} on equity income. The after-all-tax cash flow on \$1 of riskless pre-tax debt income for the marginal investor is $(1-\tau_{pb})$ and the after-all-tax cash flow on \$1 of riskless pre-tax equity income for the same investor is $(1-\tau_c)\times(1-\tau_{pe})$. In equilibrium, the investor is indifferent between debt and equity, so

$$(1-\tau_c)\times(1-\tau_{pe})=(1-\tau_{pb}). \tag{16}$$

The claim to this cash flow would have the same value as debt or equity, so suppose it is $\$V$. The market rates of return on riskless debt, denoted r_f, and equity, denoted r_z, are after corporate tax and prior to personal tax. Thus,

$$r_f=\frac{1}{V}\quad\text{and}\quad r_z=\frac{1-\tau_c}{V}. \tag{17}$$

Substituting for V, from (17), we have:

$$r_z=(1-\tau_c)r_f. \tag{18}$$

There is a tax wedge $(1-\tau_c)$ between the market return on riskless debt and the return on riskless equity. The wedge arises because debt income is untaxed at the corporate level, but is taxed more heavily than equity income at the personal level. Under the Miller theory, the after-all-tax return on debt equals the after-all-tax return on equity for the marginal investor $(1-\tau_{pb})r_f=(1-\tau_{pe})r_z$.

Now, we can generalize the Miller theory to assume that not only do various individuals pay tax at different rates, but also assume that various corporations pay tax at different rates. Different firms or organizations can face different statutory tax rates, and a firms' effective tax rate will be lower than its statutory rate if it carries forward tax losses. In this case the effective tax rate τ_c is the present value of the statutory rate, discounted from the time the taxes are actually to be paid in the future. Now equilibrium in the debt and equity markets requires that the marginal firm and the marginal investor be indifferent between debt and equity flows. Let the marginal firm have tax rate τ_m. Then this generalized theory requires that

$$(1-\tau_m)\times(1-\tau_{pe})=(1-\tau_{pb}). \tag{19}$$

and that

$$r_z=(1-\tau_m)r_f. \tag{20}$$

2.3.1. Determination of the expected rate of return on riskless equity

In theory, the expected rate of return on riskless equity should be a composite rate of return on the dividends and capital gains on a riskless equity security. Unfortunately, such securities are hard to find. Thus we must search for a proxy.

A practical solution is to study the yield on high-grade preferred shares. Unfortunately such shares are not perfectly riskless, so they embody a small risk premium, and they provide dividend income, which may be taxed somewhat differently from capital gain income. One must also be careful to study a preferred share that has no conversion features, since these conversion features are valuable and substitute for yield. That is, convertible preferreds have lower yields than straight preferreds, even though their cost of capital is approximately the same, because they also provide some income in the form of capital gains from the conversion feature.

If straight high-grade preferred shares have a yield that is 70% to 80% of straight corporate bond yields, one can argue that the marginal firm's tax rate is approximately $\tau_m = 20\%$ to 30%.

Another approach to estimating r_z is to note that market-line asset-pricing theories, like the Capital Asset Pricing Model or Arbitrage Pricing Theory are typically estimated on equity securities, so the intercept or zero-beta rate of return in these models should be r_z. Unfortunately, most tests of these theories yield estimates of r_z that exceed the yield on riskless bonds, r_f, which would imply a negative tax rate for the marginal firm. This could be a result of misspecification of the market portfolio or errors in the measurement of beta. This debate is beyond the scope of this paper. However, a study by Breeden, Gibbons & Litzenberger [1989] does find $r_z < r_f$, and is consistent with marginal tax rates τ_m in the range of 20% to 30%.

If we assume that personal equity is untaxed, $\tau_{pe} = 0$, so that $\tau_m = \tau_{pb}$. This suggests estimating τ_m from the relationship between the yields on tax-exempt bonds (such as US municipal bonds) and taxable bonds. In this situation, r_z would be approximated by the yield on riskless tax-exempt bonds. More generally, let r_{mb} represent the yield on a riskless municipal bond. If the investor who is indifferent between municipal bonds and taxable bonds is also the investor who is indifferent between riskless debt and riskless equity, we have

$$r_{mb} = (1 - \tau_{pb})r_f. \tag{21}$$

Using (19) and (21), this implies that

$$r_z = \frac{r_{mb}}{1 - \tau_{pe}}. \tag{22}$$

Thus, if the marginal investor is taxable[12] and $\tau_{pe} > 0$, then $r_z > r_{mb}$.

[12] Paddock, Siegel & Smith [1988] advocate using a real after-tax return based on the real municipal bond yield.

To summarize the argument to this point, a firm with a tax rate (τ_c) equal to that of the marginal firm (τ_m), is indifferent between debt and equity on a tax basis, and should discount certainty-equivalents (for example, the risk-neutral expected payoffs to a real option) at the after-tax cost of riskless equity: $r = r_z$.

On the other hand, if the firm has a tax rate different from that of the marginal firm, ($\tau_c \neq \tau_m$), it should adjust for this in its valuation of a real option. If the firm maintains a constant or predictable debt level $\$D$, then the adjusted present value approach can be used, in which the base case value of the option consists of discounting the certainty-equivalents at the riskless rate for all-equity financing, which is r_z. To this should be added the present value of the interest tax shields. Sick [1990] shows that the certainty-equivalent of the net (risky) interest tax shield is the net tax shield $(\tau_c - \tau_m)$ on the rate of return to a riskless investment $(\mathrm{e}^{r_f} - 1)$. This certainty equivalent should be discounted at the all-equity riskless rate. To keep the notation simple, temporarily assume that the option will be financed with $\$D$ of debt in year t, the present value of the interest tax shield for year n is

$$\text{PV of ITS} = \mathrm{e}^{-(tr_z)}(\tau_c - \tau_m)(\mathrm{e}^{r_f} - 1)D. \tag{23}$$

An alternative case is the one in which the firm continually refinances as option or firm value changes, and keeps the debt ratio L constant. In this case, Sick shows that the appropriate discount rate for certainty-equivalents is

$$r = r_z - (\tau_c - \tau_m)r_f L. \tag{24}$$

This is equivalent to a weighted-average cost of riskless capital:

$$r = L(1 - \tau_c)r_f + (1 - L)r_z. \tag{25}$$

3. Derivative asset-pricing techniques

3.1. The stochastic process for the underlying asset

With real assets, there are so many uncertainties about precise asset values, and parameter values of stochastic processes that the analyst cannot hope to get precise values of real options and the critical values for decision making. Thus, the choice between continuous-time or discrete-time should be made to help the analyst understand the economics of the problem in order to be able to choose a meaningful model for the analysis. Real options analysis has not yet been adopted as widely in the practical world as has financial option analysis, so an important desideratum for the analyst is to make the model understandable by those who will have to make a decision with it. We find it convenient to develop intuition with both continuous-time and discrete-time representations for stochastic processes. We will prove some results, but merely reference a source of proof for more technical results, if the intuition can be made clear here.

3.2. Continuous-time processes for price

In continuous time, we will typically assume that the underlying asset price P follows the *diffusion process* [13]

$$\mathrm{d}P = \alpha(P,t)\mathrm{d}t + \sigma(P,t)\mathrm{d}\omega \tag{26}$$

where

α = expected growth in dollars per unit time of the underlying asset price P;

σ = annual standard deviation of underlying asset returns;

$\mathrm{d}\omega$ = Wiener process with zero drift and unit variance per unit time, i.e., $\omega(t) - \omega(t-1)$ is normally distributed with mean zero and variance one, and is independent of $\omega(\tau) - \omega(\tau - 1)$ for any time interval $[\tau - 1, \tau]$ that does not intersect the time interval $(t\text{-}1,t)$.

Suppose also that

$\delta(P,t)$ = The rate at which cash value is conveyed to the owner of the underlying asset (a 'dividend').

The expected rate of dollar return to the owner of the underlying asset is the sum of the capital gain and dividend:

$$E[\mathrm{d}P + \delta(P,t)\mathrm{d}t) = \alpha(P,t)\mathrm{d}t + \delta(P,t)\mathrm{d}t.$$

By the consumption CAPM (10) [14], this expected return is the risk-free rate of return on the investment P plus a premium dependent on the covariance between

[13] We will follow the custom in finance and denote risk in discrete time by a tilde, but drop the tilde in continuous time. Thus, the asset price could also be read as $\tilde{P}_t$.

[14] We have from (7) and (9) the discrete-time valuation model:

$$V_t[\tilde{X}_{t+1}](1+r) = E_t[\tilde{X}_{t+1}] - \mathrm{cov}_t[\tilde{X}_{t+1}\tilde{f}_{t,t+1}].$$

Let

$$\begin{aligned} t+1 &= t + \Delta t, \\ \tilde{X}_{t+\Delta t} &= \tilde{P}_{t+\Delta t} + \delta(P,t)\Delta t \\ V_t[\tilde{X}_{t+\Delta t}] &= P_t \\ \Delta\tilde{P}_{t+\Delta t} &= \tilde{P}_{t+\Delta t} - P_t. \end{aligned}$$

Also, replace r by $r\Delta t$, and $\tilde{f}_{T-1,T}$ by $\Delta\tilde{f}$ to allow for Δt to vary and approach 0. (These models were based on the assumptions that r was the interest rate for one period and $\tilde{f}_{t,t+1}$ is the accumulated systematic risk factor over one period.) Then, we have

$$P_t(1 + r\Delta t) = E_t[\tilde{P}_{t+\Delta t} + \delta(P,t)\Delta t] - \mathrm{cov}_t[(\tilde{P}_{t+\Delta t} + \delta(P,t)\Delta t, \Delta\tilde{f}].$$

Noting that $\delta(P,t)\Delta t$ and P_t are known at time t and can be removed or added without affecting the covariance, we can arrange and allow Δt to approach 0 getting

$$E[\mathrm{d}P + \delta(P,t)\mathrm{d}t] = rP\mathrm{d}t + \mathrm{cov}\,[\mathrm{d}P, \mathrm{d}f],$$

which is (26). Note that this derivation does not assume that the value of the claim is nonzero, so it can be used to describe the change in value of assets that do not have limited liability.

the price P and the pricing factor[15] $f(t)$:

$$\alpha(P,t)\mathrm{d}t + \delta(P,t)\mathrm{d}t = rP\,\mathrm{d}t + \operatorname{cov}[\sigma(P,t)\mathrm{d}\omega, \mathrm{d}f], \tag{27}$$

for some pricing factor df. We can write (27) as

$$\alpha(P,t) + \delta(P,t) = rP + \sigma(P,t)\sigma_f(f,t)\rho[\omega,\omega_f] \tag{28}$$

where

$\rho[\omega,\omega_f]$ = the unitless correlation between the Wiener processes $\mathrm{d}\omega$ and $\mathrm{d}f$;
$\sigma_f(f,t)\sqrt{\mathrm{d}t}$ = standard deviation of $\mathrm{d}f$.

Since Wiener processes have unit variance per unit time, the covariance is $\operatorname{cov}[\mathrm{d}\omega, \mathrm{d}f] = \rho[\omega,\omega_f]\mathrm{d}t$.

3.2.1. Pricing derivative assets: options

Now, we introduce the definitions for the option asset:

$W(P,t)$ = value of the real option or contingent claim. This real option could be the right to acquire, exchange or abandon the underlying asset under specified terms;
$D(t)$ = the rate at which cash value is conveyed to the owner of the option (e.g., net revenue on a property that must be exchanged for the underlying asset when the option is exercised).

We take the customary approach and assume that the option is a fully paid *capital asset* that generates no future liabilities and has a positive value. We will alter this restriction when we discuss futures and forward contracts.

Assuming the function $W(P,t)$ is twice differentiable, by Itô's lemma the stochastic process for the option is[16]

$$\begin{aligned}\mathrm{d}W &= W_P\,\mathrm{d}P + W_t\,\mathrm{d}t + \tfrac{1}{2}\sigma^2(P,t)W_{PP}\,\mathrm{d}t \\ &= W_P\alpha(P,t)\mathrm{d}t + W_P\sigma(P,t)\mathrm{d}\omega + W_t\,\mathrm{d}t + \tfrac{1}{2}\sigma^2(P,t)W_{PP}\,\mathrm{d}t.\end{aligned} \tag{29}$$

[15] From the martingale theory, we know that f can be represented as a scalar random variable. However, to write a diffusion equation for f, it may be necessary to use a vector of state variables. All we need here is that the risk premium depends on the product $\sigma_f(f,t)\rho[\omega,\omega_f]$. To see the full multivariate diffusion analysis, see Cox, Ingersoll & Ross [1985b].

[16] Itô's lemma is the chain rule for stochastic calculus. In ordinary calculus, the chain rule for a nonstochastic function $W(P,t)$ of two variables P and t is

$$\mathrm{d}W(P,t) = W_P\,\mathrm{d}P + W_t\,\mathrm{d}t.$$

When P is a random variable, we get an extra term $(1/2)\sigma^2(P,t)W_{PP}$, which is the drift in the option value induced by the combination of risk ($\sigma^2(P,t)$) and nonlinearity of the option price as a function of the underlying asset price. For example, if the option price is a convex function of the underlying asset price, then $W_{PP} > 0$ and by Jensen's inequality, the expectation of the option price (at the next instant of time) is higher than the option value at the expected underlying price: $E[W(P+\mathrm{d}P, t+\mathrm{d}t)] > W(P+E[\mathrm{d}P], t+\mathrm{d}t)$. This drift is represented by $(1/2)\sigma^2(P,t)W_{PP}$. Itô's lemma comes from a Taylor series expansion of $E[W]$ to order $\mathrm{d}t$ around the point (P,t). For a further discussion, see Ingersoll [1987, chapter 16], for example.

The expected return (capital appreciation plus dividend) to the option owner, per unit time, is then

$$\big(W_P\alpha(P,t) + W_t + \tfrac{1}{2}\sigma^2(P,t)W_{PP} + D(t)\big)\,\mathrm{d}t. \tag{30}$$

But, by the consumption CAPM and Itô's lemma, this expected return must also equal

$$rW\,\mathrm{d}t + \operatorname{cov}[\mathrm{d}W, \mathrm{d}f] = \big(rW + W_P\sigma(P,t)\sigma_f(f,t)\rho[\omega,\omega_f]\big)\,\mathrm{d}t. \tag{31}$$

Equating (30) and (31), noting the CAPM relation for the underlying asset (28), and simplifying, yields the fundamental partial differential equation for valuation of options:

$$\tfrac{1}{2}\sigma^2(P,t)W_{PP} + W_t + W_P[rP - \delta(P,t)] + D(t) = rW. \tag{32}$$

This pricing equation was derived by equating the return required by investors for an investment in the option (bearing in mind its risk) to the expected capital gain plus dividend payable to the owner of the option. These returns are dollar returns per unit time. The option inherits the systematic risk of the underlying asset through the factor W_P, and this generates a return premium for the option in the consumption CAPM. However, the option also inherits the same extra return from the underlying asset, through Itô's lemma. Equal terms in the consumption beta of the option appear on both sides of the equation and drop out. Thus, the option valuation equation (32) does not reference the consumption beta of the option or the underlying asset. The equation would be the same whatever the risk preferences of investors.

Indeed, equation (32) readily admits the following 'risk-neutral' interpretation: The right side represents the required return (per unit time) of a risk-neutral investor for an investment in the option. The left side represents the expected return to ownership of the option (per unit time), assuming the underlying asset is priced by a risk-neutral investor. The first term on the left side is the drift in option price induced by nonlinearity of the function $W(P,t)$ and the random variation of P. The second term on the left side is the direct dependence of the option value on time. The third term is the drift in the option price induced by drift in the underlying asset price, assuming that the underlying asset is priced by a risk-neutral investor who demands a total return of rP per unit time, but against this gets an amount $\delta(P,t)$ in the form of a dividend. Finally, the option holder also is compensated with a direct payment of a dividend in the amount $D(t)$.

While (32) does admit this risk-neutral interpretation, it does not necessarily require that investors be neutral towards risk. Adjustments for systematic risk are still embodied in the equation through the price of the underlying asset P. What is important from the risk-neutral analysis is the fact that, so long as P is the price of an asset, the value of P contains all the information about systematic risk that is necessary to determine the value of any asset whose value is contingent on future values of P. Equation (32) still directly depends on the total risk of the underlying asset $\sigma(P,t)$, because the underlying asset price does not have to reflect the level of total risk under the consumption CAPM.

We have derived this equation from the consumption CAPM, but it is the same equation that is commonly derived by no-arbitrage techniques. The no-arbitrage analyses of Black & Scholes [1973] and Cox & Ross [1976] were originally presented with risk-neutral interpretations. The appealing aspect of the approach we use here is that it does not require an assumption of the ability to perform short sales or continuous trading of the underlying asset, which may be very hard to justify if the underlying asset is a real asset that is not traded. For example, the outcome of research and development would be a call option to acquire an underlying operating project of uncertain value P, in exchange for a fixed construction cost of K. If we would like to use (32) to calculate the value of the real option, it is useful to know that the validity of the equation does not require any assumptions about liquidity of the underlying asset. Such an asset is very illiquid if it does not exist until the option is exercised! The option inherits its systematic risk from the systematic risk of the underlying asset through the *hedge ratio* W_P. This allows us to use the consumption CAPM to adjust for the systematic risk of the option. The martingale pricing operators adjust for this systematic risk in pricing assets, so all we need to know is how much systematic risk is conveyed to the option at various points in its life. If any hedging or arbitrage is done to price the option (or the underlying asset), the hedging can be done by transactions in liquid assets, matching the level of systematic risk in a portfolio of liquid assets to the level of systematic risk of the option. No trading in illiquid assets is required.

Indeed, this pricing approach can be readily extended to price options on assets that don't exist or never would be held. For example, suppose we have an option with a payoff that is a function of a random variable P. This function could be the standard payoff to a call option: $\max\{0, P-K\}$. Alternatively, it could be any nonlinear function representing the net payoff of some production process as a function of some basic economic variable[17] P. In the latter case, there is no asset that always has the value P, and we cannot directly infer the value of the dividend accruing to ownership of an asset with this value. However, given the process (26) for the variable P, we can use the consumption CAPM (27) to *impute* a dividend:

$$\delta(P,t) = rP + \sigma(P,t)\sigma_f(f,t)\rho[\omega,\omega_f] - \alpha(P,t). \tag{33}$$

Substituting into (32):

$$\begin{aligned}&\tfrac{1}{2}\sigma^2(P,t)W_{PP} + W_t + \\ &\quad + W_P\big(\alpha(P,t) - \sigma(P,t)\sigma_f(f,t)\rho[\omega,\omega_f]\big) + D(t) = rW.\end{aligned} \tag{34}$$

This equation can be used instead of (32) to derive the option value. It does require knowledge of the drift $\alpha(P,t)$ and a risk premium $\sigma(P,t)\sigma_f(f,t)\rho[\omega,\omega_f]$,

[17] Later, we will see that options analysis can be driven by uncertain interest rates, so we can replace P by r.

in order to compute value. In particular, it does require an explicit modelling of the pricing factor f, unlike equation (32). In a risk-neutral context, the factor $\alpha(P,t) - \sigma(P,t)\sigma_f(f,t)\rho[\omega,\omega_f]$ of (34) is the risk-neutralized drift for the random variable P. This is the true drift minus the risk premium that would be commanded by an asset whose price is perfectly correlated with P.

3.2.2. *Pricing derivative assets: forward and futures contracts*

It is useful to have an understanding of the pricing of forward and futures contracts because price data on these contracts provide useful information on the imputed *convenience dividends* on commodities as well as on their spot prices.[18]

A *forward contract* is a contract for the future delivery of a commodity. The contract is formed between two agents — the *long agent* agrees to take delivery against receipt of the forward price, and the *short agent* agrees to make delivery at time T in exchange for payment of the forward price. Since both agents could engage in spot market transactions at time T, the net swap payment is a gain to one and a loss to the other. The contract is a zero-sum game. No money changes hands at the time of negotiation, nor prior to delivery. Unlike options, forward contracts are not fully paid up and hence are not capital assets.

More formally, the forward price $F_{t,T}$ negotiated at time t for delivery of the commodity at time $T > t$ is the certain payment to be made at time T that has the same time-t value as the claim to the risky future spot price $\tilde{P}_T$. That is,

$$0 = V_t[F_{t,T} - \tilde{P}_T]. \tag{35}$$

Here it is understood that the net swap payment $F_{t,T} - \tilde{P}_T$ takes place at time T. Thus, the forward price $F_{t,T}$ is the certainty-equivalent set at time t of the risky future spot price $\tilde{P}_T$. Defining the *certainty-equivalent operator* set at time t by $\mathrm{CE}_t[\cdot]$, we have

$$F_{t,T} = \mathrm{CE}_t[\tilde{P}_T]. \tag{36}$$

The certainty-equivalent operator is the risk-neutral expectations operator. That is, the certainty-equivalent formed at time t of a claim to a risky payoff $\tilde{X}_T$ to be received at a future date T is the time-t risk-neutral expectation of that claim:

$$\mathrm{CE}_t[\tilde{X}_T] = \hat{E}_t[\tilde{X}_T]. \tag{37}$$

To see this, note that (35) and (36) implies (for $\tilde{X}_T = \tilde{P}_T$)

$$V_t[\tilde{P}_T] = \mathrm{e}^{-r(T-t)}F_{t,T} = \mathrm{e}^{-r(T-t)}\mathrm{CE}_t[\tilde{P}_T],$$

while (1) establishes that

$$V_t[\tilde{P}_T] = \mathrm{e}^{-r(T-t)}\hat{E}_t[\tilde{P}_T].$$

[18] Carr & Jarrow [1995] also take the view that futures markets are a practical source of information for contingent-claim valuation.

A forward contract does not convey a capital asset, because the contract is not fully prepaid. Money is exchanged between the contracting agents only at the maturity date T, and not at the earlier negotiation date t, so the forward price is not the prepaid price paid to acquire a capital asset.

A *futures contract*, like a forward contract, is a contract between two agents to purchase a commodity at a future date. However, the futures contract is resettled or *marked to market* by having payments from the losing agent to the gaining agent on a daily basis that keeps the value of the swap contract at \$0 every day[19]. That is, the futures price $\hat{F}_{t-1,T}$ set at time $t-1$ for delivery at time $T \geq t$ is the price that is the certainty equivalent of the next-period futures price, $\tilde{\hat{F}}_{t,T}$:

$$\hat{F}_{t-1,T} = \mathrm{CE}_t[\tilde{\hat{F}}_{t,T}]. \tag{38}$$

Analogous to (35), we can write:

$$0 = V_{t-1}[\hat{F}_{t-1,T} - \tilde{\hat{F}}_{t,T}]. \tag{39}$$

At maturity, the futures contract settles at a value equal to the prevailing spot price, so the time-$T-1$ futures price is set to reflect this:

$$0 = V_{T-1}[\hat{F}_{T-1,T} - \tilde{P}_T]. \tag{40}$$

Iterating applications of (38), and using (40), we see that the futures price equals a nest of certainty-equivalent operators applied to the final spot price:

$$\tilde{\hat{F}}_{t,T} = \mathrm{CE}_t[\mathrm{CE}_{t+1} \cdots \mathrm{CE}_{T-1}[\tilde{P}_T] \cdots]. \tag{41}$$

If interest rates are certain, futures and forward prices are identical[20]. If interest rates are stochastic and changes in interest rates are correlated with changes in

[19] This mark-to-market feature, combined with interest-earning margin requirements, removes the incentive of a losing agent to default on a futures contract. This facilitates exchange trading of futures contracts. In contrast, forward contracts are traded over the counter by direct negotiation between buyer and seller.

[20] From (35) and (40), it is clear that forward and futures prices are the same at time $T-1$. More generally, suppose for simplicity that the continuously compounded interest rate every period is the constant r. The value at time t of a claim to receive the spot price at time $T > t$ is the present value of the forward price:

$$V_t[\tilde{P}_T] = \mathrm{e}^{-r(T-t)}\mathrm{CE}_t[\tilde{P}_T] = \mathrm{e}^{-r(T-t)} F_{t,T}.$$

But an agent could also acquire the same payoff by purchasing a contract that will pay at time $t+1$ an amount equal to the time-$t+1$ value of a claim to the spot price at time T. Thus,

$$V_t[\tilde{P}_T] = V_t[V_{t+1}[\tilde{P}_T]] = \mathrm{e}^{-r}\mathrm{CE}_t[V_{t+1}[\tilde{P}_T]].$$

Iterating this process, we have that

$$\begin{aligned} V_t[\tilde{P}_T] &= \mathrm{e}^{-r} CE_t[\mathrm{e}^{-r} CE_{t+1} \cdots \mathrm{e}^{-r}\mathrm{CE}_{T-1}[\tilde{P}_T] \cdots] \\ &= \mathrm{e}^{-r(T-t)}\mathrm{CE}_t[\mathrm{CE}_{t+1} \cdots \mathrm{CE}_{T-1}[\tilde{P}_T] \cdots] \\ &= \mathrm{e}^{-r(T-t)} \tilde{\hat{F}}_{t,T}. \end{aligned}$$

the futures price, then forward prices can be different from futures prices because intermediate cash inflows and outflows on the futures contract are correlated with the interest rate at which they can be invested (or borrowed). Empirically, the difference between these does not seem to be large, however. For more information on these distinctions between futures and forward prices, see Cox, Ingersoll & Ross [1981], Jarrow & Oldfield [1981] and Richard & Sundaresan [1981]. We will use forward and futures prices interchangeably in the remainder of this article.

In continuous time, forward and futures contracts will still satisfy the fundamental pricing equations (32) or (34) that govern option assets, but with one important variation to account for the fact that the futures price is always marked to market in order to keep the contract value at \$0.

Define the futures price as a function of the underlying commodity spot price P as $F(P,t) = F_{t,T}$. Then the futures price function satisfies the analogue of (32):

$$\tfrac{1}{2}\sigma^2(P,t)F_{PP} + F_t + F_P\big(rP - \delta(P,t)\big) = 0. \tag{42}$$

or, equivalently, analogous to (34):

$$\tfrac{1}{2}\sigma^2(P,t)F_{PP} + F_t + F_P\big(\alpha(P,t) - \sigma(P,t)\sigma_f(f,t)\rho[\omega,\omega_f]\big) = 0. \tag{43}$$

These equations differ from their option analogues because they are missing the terms $D(t)$ and rW. Intuitively[21], one can ascribe this to two facts. First, a forward contract pays no intermediate dividends $D(t) = 0$. Second, the value of the futures contract is zero at the start of the period[22], so that the risk-neutral required dollar return $rF = 0$. That is, these equations describe the risk-neutralized expected payoff to an agent who goes long one futures contract (for a cost of \$0) and marks it to market at the next instant of time (for a net cash flow of $\mathrm{d}F$). Since there is no investment, the risk-neutral expected dollar payoff is \$0, which is the right-hand side of (42) or (43). The futures contract only generates capital gains,

Thus, the futures price must equal the forward price. Note that we needed interest rates to be nonstochastic to be able to float the present value factors into and out of the certainty-equivalent operators.

[21] More rigorously, we can develop (42) and (43) from (32) and (34), respectively, by considering the pricing of a portfolio strategy that consists of holding a fully-margined futures contract. At time t, such a portfolio consists of a long position in a futures contract (costing \$0), plus an investment in a bond worth $\$F_t$. The risk-neutral expected return on such a contract is $r(0 + F_t)\mathrm{d}t$. The mark-to-market generates a capital gain or loss of $\mathrm{d}F_t$. The portfolio strategy is self-financing because, at the end of the period, the agent has exactly the level of wealth required to acquire the portfolio prescribed by the strategy for the next period, plus a dividend equal to the interest earned on the margin. Thus, the portfolio cost is the value of a fully paid-up capital asset for which equations (32) and (34) apply. In these equations, the dividend $rF_t\,\mathrm{d}t$ paid to the portfolio equals the risk-neutral required return on the portfolio, so these terms cancel on either side of the equations, resulting in (42) and (43). The remaining terms in these equations are a result of the futures contract rather than the bond contract, so these equations apply equally well to the portfolio strategy as to the futures contract.

[22] Agents must also post margin to engage in futures markets to guarantee against default. Since they earn market rates of interest on the margin, the margin has no effect on the pricing of the contracts.

and no dividend payments, so the risk-neutral expected returns are the capital gains as identified in the left sides of (42) and (43).

3.3. Boundary conditions

Equations (32), (34), (42) and (43) describe the motion of the price W of any option asset or the futures contract, so long as its risk is derived from an underlying random variable P. Typically these differential equations have a general solution, with several parameters that must be determined to get a specific option value function. To determine a value for a specific option, boundary conditions must be specified to describe how the option price behaves in certain limiting circumstances. In practice, there are 3 types of boundary conditions:

1. Payoff boundaries describe the value of the option at the time the option is converted into another asset, which is often the underlying asset. Sometimes the option is a compound option, and exercising the option gives rise to another option or operating state of an asset. In these cases, the boundaries describe the transition between such states.
2. Free boundary conditions describe the freedom the option owner has to decide when to exercise the option. The owner acts to optimize the value of the option, so this condition often becomes a first-order condition of optimality. This typically is the *high-contact* or *smooth-pasting* condition, and says that at exercise or transition into another state, the option function is tangent to the payoff boundary described above.
3. Technical conditions are often necessary to preclude meaningless solutions to the differential equations. For example, the option may be expected to increase or decrease in value with the value of the underlying asset. Or the option may reasonably be expected to converge to a specific value as the underlying asset value becomes arbitrarily large or small.

3.4. Example: perpetual American call option on a log-normal asset

Consider a perpetual option to convert farm land earning income at the fixed rate $\$D$ per year to urban land with uncertain value $\$P$ by paying a fixed development cost K. This is a call option with an exercise price of K and dividend paid to the option owner of D. As with most real options, a key issue is to determine when to exercise the option, so the option is an American option. Suppose the standard deviation of the price of the underlying asset (urban land) is $\sigma(P,t) = \sigma_0 P$ for a one-year period. The dividend paid to the underlying asset is the net annual rental rate earned by the owner of developed urban land, which we assume to be $\delta(P,t) = \delta_0 P$. Thus, the underlying asset price follows a log-normal diffusion with a constant dividend yield δ_0. Equation (32) becomes:

$$\tfrac{1}{2}\sigma_0^2 P^2 W_{PP} + W_t + W_P(r - \delta_0)P + D = rW. \tag{44}$$

To exercise the call option, the owner pays a conversion cost K, so the net payoff if the option is exercised when the value of the underlying asset $P = P^*$ is

$$W(P^*, t) = \max\left\{\frac{D}{r}, P^* - K\right\}. \tag{45}$$

This says that the owner has the right to walk away from the option and receive the value of pure nonconvertible agricultural land, D/r, or exercise the option and receive the net present value of conversion, $P^* - K$. The owner chooses the larger of the two values. Condition (45) is a payoff boundary, as discussed above. The owner of the option must decide on an optimal exercise policy. There are two state variables in this problem — the underlying asset value P and the time t. Since the option is perpetual and the dividends and exercise prices do not change over time, the exercise decision should not depend on the state variable t. That is, the exercise decision is time-invariant — it can depend on P but not t. The optimal exercise policy is characterized by a region of values for P, such that exercise occurs the first time the underlying asset value enters the region. Let P^* be a boundary point of the region. Then (45) must hold whenever the underlying asset value passes into the region for the first time, at price $P = P^*$. After the underlying asset price passes into the exercise region the first time, there is no further exercise decision in this problem, since the option is not reversible. Later, we shall see that there is only one boundary point for the exercise region. So far, we have seen that all the characteristics of the model are invariant to time, since the dividends, drift, boundaries, and exercise price do not vary with time. Thus, the option value should not be dependent on time and we can write $W(P, t) = W(P)$ and set $W_t = 0$. We can rewrite (44) as

$$\tfrac{1}{2}\sigma_0^2 P^2 W_{PP} + W_P(r - \delta_0)P + D = rW. \tag{46}$$

This second-order ordinary differential equation is the Euler equation. A particular solution to (46) is $W = D/r$. The general solution is obtained by adding the general solution to the homogeneous equation, to obtain:

$$W(P) = A_+ P^{\gamma+} + A_- P^{\gamma-} + \frac{D}{r} \tag{47}$$

where

$$\gamma_{+,-} = \frac{1}{2} + \frac{\delta_0 - r}{\sigma_0^2} \pm \sqrt{\left(\frac{1}{2} + \frac{\delta_0 - r}{\sigma_0^2}\right)^2 + \frac{2r}{\sigma_0^2}}. \tag{48}$$

The constants A_+, A_- are to be determined by the boundary conditions. Note that $\gamma_{+,-} > 0$ if and only if

$$\pm\sqrt{\left(\frac{1}{2} + \frac{\delta_0 - r}{\sigma_0^2}\right)^2 + \frac{2r}{\sigma_0^2}} > -\left(\frac{1}{2} + \frac{\delta_0 - r}{\sigma_0^2}\right).$$

Thus, $\gamma_+ > 0$ and $\gamma_- < 0$. To determine signs for the constants A_+, A_- and B, we need to apply technical boundary conditions that consider the limiting behavior of (47) for large and small P. The option can be exercised at any time so (45) places a floor under the value of the option. Also, the option cannot provide any more value than the value of its perpetual dividend stream and the value of the underlying asset into which it can be converted. Thus, we must have $D/r \leq W(P) \leq P + D/r$. Since $P^{\gamma-}$ becomes unbounded as $P \to 0$, this means that $A_- = 0$. We would expect $W(P)$ to be increasing in P, so $A_+ > 0$. We would expect the owner to exercise into the underlying asset only if the proceeds of exercise $(P^* - K)$ exceed the value obtained by discarding the option and only maintaining the pure agricultural land value (D/r), so $(P^* - K) \geq D/r$. In (45), then:

$$W(P^*) = P^* - K. \tag{49}$$

Using this with (47) and the fact that $A_- = 0$, we have that

$$A_+ = P^{*(-\gamma+)}\left(P^* - K - \frac{D}{r}\right). \tag{50}$$

We can determine the values of A_+ and P^* jointly in either one of two equivalent ways. One way is to note that, with $A_- = 0$ in (47), the value of W is globally maximized if we maximize the value of the constant A_+. Thus, the owner of the option should choose P^* to maximize A_+ as defined by (50). This occurs at the unique value

$$P^* = \frac{\gamma_+}{\gamma_+ - 1}\left(K + \frac{D}{r}\right) \tag{51}$$

If the dividend yield on the underlying asset, δ_0, is positive, then $\gamma_+ > 1$ and the boundary value P^* is positive.[23]Substituting into (50) and (47), and simplifying, we have

$$W(P) = \frac{1}{\gamma_+ - 1}\left(K + \frac{D}{r}\right)\left(\frac{P}{P^*}\right)^{\gamma+} + \frac{D}{r}. \tag{52}$$

There are several observations to make about this solution and our derivation. First, note that if ownership of the option conveys no dividends $(D = 0)$ then (52) gives the well-documented solution for a perpetual call option on a log-normal asset. This allows an alternative derivation of this model by regarding convertible farm land to be a portfolio of two assets. One asset is pure nonconvertible land of value D/r. The other asset is an option to exchange the farmland for urban land by paying an exercise price of $K + D/r$, which consists of a conversion cost K plus

[23] Note that

$$\gamma_+ > 1 \leftrightarrow \sqrt{\left(\frac{1}{2} + \frac{\delta_0 - r}{\sigma_0^2}\right)^2 + \frac{2r}{\sigma_0^2}} > \frac{1}{2} - \frac{\delta_0 - r}{\sigma_0^2}.$$

But this latter inequality holds if $\delta_0 > 0$, for then

$$\frac{\delta_0 - r}{\sigma_0^2} + \frac{2r}{\sigma_0^2} > -\frac{\delta_0 - r}{\sigma_0^2} \Rightarrow \left(\frac{1}{2} + \frac{\delta_0 - r}{\sigma_0^2}\right)^2 + \frac{2r}{\sigma_0^2} > \left(\frac{1}{2} - \frac{\delta_0 - r}{\sigma_0^2}\right)^2,$$

as desired.

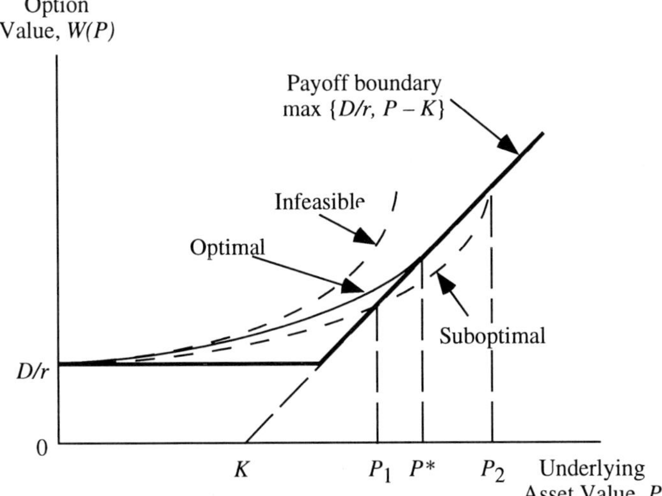

Exhibit A. At the optimal exercise price P^*, the option value graph is tangent to the payoff boundary.

the value of surrendering the pure nonconvertible farm land of value D/r. The pure option value is

$$\frac{1}{\gamma_+ - 1}\left(K + \frac{D}{r}\right)\left(\frac{P}{P^*}\right)^{\gamma}$$

in this interpretation.

This solution is illustrated in Exhibit A, which shows various solutions to the pricing differential equation (46), along with the payoff boundary $W(P) \geq \max\{D/r, P - K\}$. The lowest solution shown cuts the exercise boundary twice. It corresponds to a policy of exercising the option when the underlying asset price reaches one of the two intersection points P_1 or P_2, since at those points $W(P_i) = \max\{D/r, P_i - K\} = P_i - K$ (for $i = 1, 2$). Setting the value of A_+ to satisfy either of these boundary conditions results in the lower graph. But this solution is suboptimal, since we could clearly increase the function values everywhere by selecting an exercise price between P_1 and P_2. The highest solution to (46) shown is infeasible because it never intersects the exercise boundary. Its 'option' values are only hypothetical. The optimal solution is the graph that is tangent to the exercise boundary. The point of tangency is the optimal exercise price P^*.

This tangency condition is the smooth-pasting or high-contact condition. For a heuristic derivation of it, see Merton [1973]. In general, the condition is that the option value function (regarded as a function of underlying asset price) is tangent to the boundary at the point of exercise:

$$W_P(P^*, t) = \left.\frac{\partial(P - K)}{\partial P}\right|_{P=P^*}. \tag{53}$$

Since the slope of the exercise boundary is 1 in this call option, we have

$$W_P(P^*, t) = 1. \tag{54}$$

One can verify that this is the same as the first order condition that led to (53) in this particular example.

So far, we have not been particularly careful to describe the exercise region. Instead, we have merely studied the option behavior at an exercise point P^*. In the perpetual call option we have just seen, the exercise region only has one boundary point, and it is the interval $[P^*, \infty)$. This can be seen, for example, by noting that the global maximum of the coefficient A_+ is attained at one point only.[24] In other real option models, to be discussed below, there can be multiple critical or exercise points.

Finally, we can set the dividend yield on the underlying asset $\delta_0 = 0$, to note that $\gamma_+ = 1$ in (48). Thus in (51), P^* approaches $+\infty$ as δ_0 approaches 0. There is no incentive to exercise an American call option early, if the underlying asset does not pay a dividend. The option is exercised in order to capture the dividend on the underlying asset. In other situations, we may have other reasons to exercise an American call option early. These could be changing exercise prices, the arrival of a maturity date in finite time, or stochastic interest rates.

We can calculate the cost of capital for the option by dividing the right side of equation (31) by W and dropping the differential $\mathrm{d}t$:

$$\begin{aligned} r &+ \frac{W_P \sigma(P, t)\sigma_f(f, t)\rho[\omega, \omega_f]}{W} \\ &= r + \frac{W_P \sigma_0 P}{W}\sigma_f(f, t)\rho[\omega, \omega_f] \\ &= r + (\gamma_+)\left(\frac{W - D/r}{W}\right)\sigma_0\sigma_f(f, t)\rho[\omega, \omega_f]. \end{aligned}$$

We are assuming that the risk premium on the underlying asset (namely, $\sigma_0\sigma_f(f, t)\rho[\omega, \omega_f]$) is constant, so the cost of capital for the option is nonrandom if and only if the ratio $(W - D/r)/W$ is nonrandom, which is to say that $D = 0$. That is, D/r is the value of the perpetual deterministic dividend to the owner of the unexercised call option. If there is no such dividend, the cost of capital of the option is constant. When $D/r \neq 0$, the option value consists partly of the riskless dividend value and partly of the risky pure option to exchange this riskless asset and the exercise price for the risky underlying asset.

The fact that the cost of capital for the option is constant when $D = 0$, is the result of a knife-edge condition arising from the log-normal distribution of the underlying asset and the perpetual nature of the option. As the underlying asset price falls toward the fixed exercise price, the option cost of capital tends

[24] The only zero of the derivative of the function $A_+(P^*)$, is the solution (51), where it is positive. Noting that $A_+(P^*)$ is continuously differentiable on $(0, \infty)$ and that $\lim_{P^* \to \infty} A_+(P^*) = 0$ and $\lim_{P^* \to 0} A_+(P^*) = -\infty$, we can conclude that the maximum of $A_+(P^*)$ is unique.

to increase because of the higher operating leverage. However, this is mitigated by the way the option limits downside risk. As the underlying asset price falls, the right to allow the option to die worthless becomes more valuable, and this absorbs risk. As long as $\delta_0 > 0$, one can prove that $\gamma_+ > 1$, so that the cost of capital of the option is larger than that of the underlying asset, when $D = 0$. In this situation, the call option does lever up the risk of the underlying asset.

For other stochastic processes on the underlying asset price, the cost of capital on the underlying asset is random, so that of the option is random as well.

This example illustrates many of the important features of real options.

3.5. *Modelling the dividend on the underlying asset*

In the previous example, we saw that the dividend payout to the underlying asset is an important determinant of optimal exercise policy and call option value. In a financial option analysis, it is easy to determine the dividend on the underlying asset, since it is a cash payout that goes to the owner of the underlying asset but not to the owner of the option. In a real option setting, the dividend is a more elusive concept, since the underlying asset may not even exist until the option is exercised. Alternatively, the underlying asset may not be a capital asset that is held for capital appreciation and cash dividend income. The underlying asset is simply the value of an operating project after the initial construction cost has been sunk. In some situations, it may be convenient to think of the underlying asset as a unit of a commodity, such as petroleum, lumber or copper.

In other situations, the value of the underlying asset may be a function of a risky economic variable, such as an interest rate. It is still useful to think of the option value as being a function of this risky variable. At first it is not obvious how to impute a dividend to a risky economic variable that does not represent an asset price. We now turn to the problem of modelling this dividend, which can be called a *convenience value* or *convenience yield*.

3.5.1. *Commodity convenience dividend*

The convenience dividend may arise because there is value to being able to quickly use the spot commodity to meet an emergency demand. The convenience dividend we define here is net of the storage costs of the spot commodity. If these costs are larger than the benefit of being able to use the spot commodity in an emergency, then the convenience dividend could have a negative value.

If P is a risky future payoff, we define the commodity convenience dividend by the imputed dividend in (33). This imputed dividend is the difference between the expected dollar return under the CAPM (if the payoff were a capital asset) and the actual expected rate of dollar return. This is just a reexpression of the identity:

$$\text{Convenience dividend} + \text{Capital appreciation} = \text{Return on investment.}$$

For commodities, it is possible to determine the convenience dividend from market data on forward prices. For example, suppose that the spot price of a commodity P follows a log-normal diffusion so that $\sigma(P, t) = \sigma_0 P$ for some volatility σ_0, and the convenience dividend is proportional to the underlying asset value for some yield δ_0. Thus, $\delta(P,t) = \delta_0 P$. Then (42) provides a differential equation in the futures price F:

$$\tfrac{1}{2}\sigma_0^2 P^2 F_{PP} + F_t + F_P(rP - \delta_0 P) = 0. \tag{55}$$

The futures contract converges to the underlying spot price at maturity, providing the boundary condition:

$$F(P,T) = P. \tag{56}$$

This equation is solved by[25]

$$F(P,t) = e^{(r-\delta_0)(T-t)} P. \tag{57}$$

This assumes a constant convenience yield and a constant interest rate. If convenience yields and interest rates vary deterministically over time, so that r_τ and $\delta_{0,\tau}$ are the forward interest rates and forward convenience yields that will prevail at time τ, then we can generalize (58) and examine contracts with adjacent maturities $T = \tau$ and $T = \tau + \Delta\tau$ to get the approximation:

$$\delta_{0,\tau} = r_\tau + \frac{1}{\Delta\tau} \ln\left(\frac{F_{t,\tau}}{F_{t,\tau+\Delta\tau}}\right). \tag{58}$$

This model assumes that the (forward) interest rates and (forward) convenience yields are deterministic, and a test of this assumption is to examine the variation in the forward yields and rates implied by (58) at various points in time t. If they do vary, then we must consider one of the stochastic convenience yield models below. However, if the variation is not significant, real option models can be safely built by assuming them to be constant.

If we assume that convenience yields are deterministic and that the cost of capital for discounting the spot commodity is constant, then we can also calculate the convenience yields from a vector of forecasts of future spot prices. This is important, because in many practical situations, the value of the underlying project will be computed by a present-value analysis in which expected future cash flows are discounted at a cost of capital or risk-adjusted discount rate. By imposing a consistency between the convenience yields implied by the forecasts (typically made within the corporation) and the convenience yields implied by the market in forward prices, the analyst can get more economically relevant valuation models.

In order to get a constant discount rate for a future spot price, one has to assume a constant risk premium for the expected rate of return to an investment

[25] This is equivalent to $e^{-r(T-t)}F = e^{-\delta_0(T-t)}P$. This common value is the price at time t of a claim to the delivery of the spot commodity at time T. The left side is the present value of the certainty-equivalent of this claim. The right side is the value of the spot commodity today, discounted for the convenience dividends that will not be received.

in the project.[26] In the notation of (28) or (33), the expected rate of growth in the spot price of the commodity is

$$\frac{\alpha(P,t)}{P} = \frac{rP + \sigma(P,t)\sigma_f(f,t)\rho[\omega,\omega_f] - \delta(P,t)}{P}.$$

The discount rate for the spot price at time $\tau > 0$ is $k_\tau = r_\tau + \sigma(P,\tau)\sigma_f(f,\tau)\rho[\omega,\omega_f]/P$. In (33), this means that the 'beta' of the spot price cash flow $\sigma(P,\tau)\sigma_f(f,\tau)\rho[\omega,\omega_f]$ must be proportional to the spot price P. Thus, we assume that $\sigma(P,\tau)\sigma_f(f,\tau) = \sigma_{0,\tau}P\sigma_f$ and $\alpha(P,\tau) = \alpha_{0,\tau}P$ for some constants $\alpha_{0,\tau}$, $\sigma_{0,\tau}$ and σ_f, so that $\alpha_{0,\tau} = r_\tau + \sigma_{0,\tau}\sigma_f\rho[\omega,\omega_f] - \delta_{0,\tau}$. The discount rate then becomes $k_\tau = r_\tau + \sigma_{0,\tau}\sigma_f\rho[\omega,\omega_f]$. The time-0 forecasts of future spot prices are compounded at this growth rate net of the convenience dividend:

$$E_0[\tilde{P}_t] = \exp\left[\int_0^t (k_\tau - \delta_{0,\tau})\,\mathrm{d}\tau\right] P_0. \tag{59}$$

Analogous to (58), we can then approximate the forward convenience yield for time τ by comparing price forecasts for adjacent future points in time, τ and $\tau + \Delta\tau$:

$$\delta_{0,\tau} = k_\tau + \frac{1}{\Delta\tau}\ln\left(\frac{E_0[\tilde{P}_\tau]}{E_0[\tilde{P}_{\tau+\Delta\tau}]}\right). \tag{60}$$

3.5.2. *Stochastic convenience models*

The previous section modelled the convenience dividend as a constant proportion of the spot price. If the convenience dividend and yield are both stochastic, we need some useful models. Gibson & Schwartz [1990] and Garbade [1993] suggest modelling the convenience dividend by a mean-reverting process. Others, such as Pindyck [1991] and Laughton & Jacoby [1993] suggest modelling the commodity price itself as a mean-reverting process.

A commodity price can be mean-reverting to the extent that there are imperfect substitutes for it in various product markets and various sources of the commodity that can be brought on stream (with a capital cost or time lag) at different production costs. A mean-reverting commodity price could be a good representation if a cartel, such as OPEC, controls a significant fraction of the supply. If prices fall below some target, the cartel will cut back production to increase revenue. If prices rise above the target, the cartel produces more to preclude the development of alternative supplies. The strength of the cartel's response increases as the prices deviate more strongly from the mean.

The intuition for a mean-reverting convenience dividend or yield is more indirect, and perhaps less compelling. With many commodities, there is a seasonal

[26] See Myers & Turnbull [1977], Fama [1977] and Sick [1986, 1989a] for a discussion of environments in which expected cash flows can be discounted at a deterministic risk-adjusted discount rate. Little useful generalization can be made beyond the assumptions made here.

convenience yield induced by costly storage and either seasonal supply (particularly agricultural commodities) or seasonal demand (particularly energy sources). Since the period of the seasonality is one year or less, there should be little impact upon real option decisions that have a longer term. Alternatively, the short-run elasticity of supply could be much smaller than the long-run elasticity of supply.[27] If using a mean-reverting convenience model amounts to using the level of the convenience to proxy for the time of the season, a more efficient explanatory variable for the time of the season is the actual date!

Models of mean-reverting commodity prices amount to making choices of the functional form $\alpha(P,t)$ and $\sigma(P,t)$ in (26), which is reproduced here for convenience:

$$\mathrm{d}P = \alpha(P,t)\mathrm{d}t + \sigma(P,t)\mathrm{d}\omega \tag{61}$$

Mean-reverting processes are just continuous-time analogues of basic auto-regressive and integrated auto-regressive processes. The simplest such process is the Ornstein–Uhlenbeck process, in which the change in price level has a mean-reverting drift that elastically depends on a strength of mean-reversion λ, and the distance between price level and the long-run mean $\bar{P}$:

$$\mathrm{d}P = \lambda(\bar{P} - P)\mathrm{d}t + \sigma_0\mathrm{d}\omega. \tag{62}$$

This process is the analogue of the discrete-time AR(1) process:

$$P_t = \lambda\bar{P} + (1-\lambda)P_{t-1} + \Delta\omega_t. \tag{63}$$

To keep the process stationary, one would normally require that $\lambda > 0$, and to keep the process from overshooting the target, one would normally require $\lambda < 1$. Iterative substitution in (63) for P_{t-1}, P_{t-2}, etc. yields the infinite moving average process in the disturbances $\Delta\omega_{t-n}$:

$$\begin{aligned} P_t &= \lambda\bar{P} + (1-\lambda)P_{t-1} + \Delta\omega_t = \\ &= \lambda\bar{P} + (1-\lambda)\big(\lambda\bar{P} + (1-\lambda)P_{t-2} + \Delta\omega_{t-1}\big) + \Delta\omega_t = \cdots = \\ &= \sum_{n=0}^{\infty}\big(\lambda(1-\lambda)^n\bar{P} + (1-\lambda)^n\Delta\omega_{t-n}\big) \end{aligned} \tag{64}$$

Thus, the effect of a disturbance $\Delta\omega_t$ on the future price P_τ is reduced at an exponentially declining rate by the factor $(1-\lambda)^{\tau-t}$. The half-life of the process is the time required for this weight to decline to 1/2, which is $n = -\ln 2/[\ln(1-\lambda)]$.

Clearly, (63) can be easily be estimated by a multiple regression model, where $\Delta\omega_t$ could either be pure white noise or some function of the systematic risk factor $\tilde{f}$. This process could become negative, but the probability of this is small if σ_0 is small compared to λ and $\bar{P}$.

[27] It is also possible to model production decisions by the real option to start or stop production as a short-term planning measure after the capital investment has been made. This is discussed by Brennan & Schwartz [1985], Pindyck [1991] and Cortazar & Schwartz [1993].

To ensure that P never becomes negative, one could take the exponential of a random variable that follows an Ornstein–Uhlenbeck process [28]:

$$\mathrm{d}P = \lambda(\bar{L} - \ln P)P\,\mathrm{d}t + \sigma_0 P\,\mathrm{d}\omega. \tag{65}$$

It is convenient to assign a new constant $\bar{P}$, such that $\bar{L} = \ln \bar{P} + \sigma_0^2/2\lambda$. This is the analogue of the time-series technique of taking the logarithm of the price and modelling the transformed variable as following an auto-regressive process.

These processes imply a convenience dividend or yield by equation (33). Denote $\rho = \rho[\omega, \omega_f]$ and $\sigma_f = \sigma_f(f, t)$. Thus, the convenience dividend consistent with (62) is

$$\delta(P, t) = rP + \sigma_0\sigma_f\rho - \lambda(\bar{P} - P). \tag{66}$$

The basic pricing equation (32) or (34) for a real option with value $W(P, t)$ becomes:

$$\tfrac{1}{2}\sigma_0^2 W_{PP} + W_t + W_P\big(\lambda(\bar{P} - P) - \sigma_0\sigma_f\rho\big) + D(t) = rW. \tag{67}$$

Similarly, when the commodity follows (65), the convenience yield is

$$\frac{\delta(P, t)}{P} = r + \sigma_0\sigma_f\rho - \lambda\left(\ln \bar{P} + \frac{\sigma_0^2}{2\lambda} - \ln P\right) \tag{68}$$

and the basic pricing equation is

$$\begin{aligned} &\tfrac{1}{2}\sigma_0^2 P W_{PP} + W_t + \\ &\quad + W_P P\left[\lambda\left(\ln \bar{P} + \frac{\sigma_0^2}{2\lambda} - \ln P\right) - \sigma_0\sigma_f\rho\right] + D(t) = rW. \end{aligned} \tag{69}$$

In both of these models, the size of the convenience dividend increases with P. This is consistent with the notion that the value of ready access to the commodity rises as the commodity becomes more valuable.

Moreover, in (65) and (68), we see that the convenience yield rises with P. This is consistent with the notion of a temporary shortage (low inventories) driving up price and a sufficiently inelastic demand in the short run that the convenience dividend of a spot supply rises at an even faster rate. This model also implies that the convenience yield follows an Ornstein–Uhlenbeck process itself, since there is

[28] That is, assume that $P = \mathrm{e}^p$ where $\mathrm{d}p = \lambda(\ln \bar{P} - p)\mathrm{d}t + \sigma_0\mathrm{d}\omega$. By Itô's lemma,

$$\mathrm{d}P = \frac{\mathrm{d}P}{\mathrm{d}p}\mathrm{d}p + \frac{1}{2}\frac{\mathrm{d}^2P}{\mathrm{d}p^2}\sigma_0^2\,\mathrm{d}t = \lambda(\bar{L} - \ln P)P\,\mathrm{d}t + \sigma_0 P\,\mathrm{d}\omega.$$

This is the process proposed by Laughton & Jacoby [1993]. There are other variations on this, such as that which Pindyck [1991] proposes:

$$\mathrm{d}P = \lambda(\bar{P} - P)P\,\mathrm{d}t + \sigma_0 P\,\mathrm{d}\omega$$

or the process Trigeorgis [1995] proposes:

$$\mathrm{d}P = \lambda(\bar{P} - P)\mathrm{d}t + \sigma_0 P\,\mathrm{d}\omega.$$

an invertible linear relationship between $\ln P$ and δ_0 by (68), and $\ln P$ follows an Ornstein–Uhlenbeck process.

As we did earlier for the log-normal price process, we can infer the mean-reverting parameters from the futures markets by determining the futures prices that are consistent with the spot process. If the spot price follows (62), we can modify (67) as in (43) to get the partial differential equation for the futures price $F_{t,T}$:

$$\tfrac{1}{2}\sigma_0^2 F_{PP} + F_t + F_P\big(\lambda(\bar{P} - P) - \sigma_0\sigma_f(f,t)\rho[\omega,\omega_f]\big) = 0 \tag{70}$$

subject to the boundary condition (56).

The solution to this is the futures price term structure (assuming that the systematic risk measure $\rho[\omega,\omega_f]\sigma_f(f,t)$ is constant):

$$F_{t,T} = \bar{P} + \mathrm{e}^{-\lambda(T-t)}(P_t - \bar{P}) - \frac{\sigma_0\sigma_f\rho}{\lambda}\left(1 - \mathrm{e}^{-\lambda(T-t)}\right). \tag{71}$$

The futures price consists of the long-run mean price $\bar{P}$, plus a revision in expectations $\mathrm{e}^{-\lambda(T-t)}(P - \bar{P})$ arising from the difference between current spot price P and $\bar{P}$, minus a systematic risk term $[(\sigma_0\sigma_f\rho)/\lambda](1 - \mathrm{e}^{-\lambda(T-t)})$. The expectations revision term vanishes as the term of the futures contract increases to ∞. The systematic risk term increases to a maximum asymptotic value of $(\sigma_0\sigma_f\rho)/\lambda$ as the futures maturity approaches ∞. Setting this latter term to zero (for example, by setting $\sigma_f\rho = 0$) gives the term structure of expected future spot prices.

If the spot price follows (65), the fundamental pricing equation is the modification of (69):

$$\frac{1}{2}\sigma_0^2 P F_{PP} + F_t + F_P P\left[\lambda\left(\ln\bar{P} + \frac{\sigma_0^2}{2\lambda} - \ln P\right) - \sigma_0\sigma_f\rho\right] = 0. \tag{72}$$

The solution to this is the futures price term structure (assuming that $\rho[\omega,\omega_f]$ $\sigma_f(f,t)$ is constant):

$$F_{t,T} = \bar{P}\left(\frac{P_t}{\bar{P}}\right)^{\exp[-\lambda(T-t)]} \exp\left[\frac{\sigma_0^2}{4\lambda}(1 - \mathrm{e}^{-2\lambda(T-t)}) - \frac{\sigma_0\sigma_f\rho}{\lambda}\left(1 - \mathrm{e}^{-\lambda(T-t)}\right)\right]. \tag{73}$$

Again, by setting $\sigma_f\rho = 0$, we obtain the term structure of expected future spot prices.

Gibson & Schwartz [1990] assume that the spot price and the convenience yield follow joint stochastic processes. The spot price follows a log-normal diffusion and the convenience yield follows an Ornstein–Uhlenbeck process. This does not generalize our mean-reversion models, because their spot price is assumed to follow a log-normal diffusion rather than a mean-reverting process. Their convenience yields are estimated from futures market data. Since futures markets have maturities measured in months, while real options have maturities measured in years, care must be taken in extrapolating their convenience yield models to real option situations. They also find that the market price of convenience yield risk seems to vary over time.

Their model is

$$\begin{aligned} \mathrm{d}P &= \alpha_0 P\,\mathrm{d}t + \sigma_1 P\,\mathrm{d}\omega_1 \\ \mathrm{d}\delta &= \lambda(\bar{\delta} - \delta_0)\mathrm{d}t + \sigma_2 \mathrm{d}\omega_2 \\ \rho_{12} &= \mathrm{corr}\,[\mathrm{d}\omega_1, \mathrm{d}\omega_2]. \end{aligned} \tag{74}$$

Here, the convenience yield $\delta_0 = \delta(P, t)/P$ is measured from futures prices by the continuous-time analogue of (58), and is assumed to be independent of term to maturity of the contract.

Any contingent claim on future delivery of oil prices will have a value $W(P, \delta_0, t)$ that depends on oil price, convenience yield and time. Since both oil price and convenience yield are stochastic, the fundamental pricing equations (32) and (34) are expanded to incorporate a multivariate Itô's lemma:

$$\begin{aligned} &\tfrac{1}{2}\sigma_1^2 P^2 W_{PP} + P\delta_0\sigma_1\sigma_2\rho_{12} W_{P\delta} + \tfrac{1}{2}\sigma_2^2 W_{\delta\delta} + W_t + W_P(r - \delta_0) + \\ &\quad + W_\delta\left(\lambda(\bar{\delta} - \delta_0) - \frac{\mathrm{cov}\,[\sigma_2\mathrm{d}\omega_2, \mathrm{d}f]}{\mathrm{d}t}\right) + D(t) = rW. \end{aligned} \tag{75}$$

where $\mathrm{cov}[\sigma_2\mathrm{d}\omega_2, \mathrm{d}f]/\mathrm{d}t$ is the market price of convenience risk per unit time. The right side of this equation represents the risk-neutral return required for an investment of W in the contingent claim. The term $D(t)$ represents any payout to the owner of the contingent claim at time t. If we instead want to determine the time-t price $F_{t,\tau}$ of a futures or forward contract for delivery at time $\tau > t$, there is no initial payment, so the risk-neutral expected return is zero. The fundamental pricing equation for a futures contract becomes

$$\begin{aligned} &\tfrac{1}{2}\sigma_1^2 P^2 F_{PP} + P\delta_0\sigma_1\sigma_2\rho F_{P\delta} + \tfrac{1}{2}\sigma_2^2 F_{\delta\delta} + F_t + \\ &\quad + F_P(r - \delta_0) + F_\delta\big(\lambda(\bar{\delta} - \delta_0) - \mathrm{cov}\,[\sigma_2\mathrm{d}\omega_2, \mathrm{d}f]/\mathrm{d}t\big) = 0. \end{aligned} \tag{76}$$

Gibson and Schwartz estimate the convenience yield (once per week), using (58) for the two New York Mercantile Exchange (NYMEX) crude oil price contracts nearest to maturity. They then estimate a discretized version of the stochastic processes (74) for the spot oil price and the near-term convenience yield. They find, for example, that the long-run mean convenience yield $\bar{\delta}$ is approximately 18% per year. They also test for mean reversion in oil prices, but find none.[29] The resulting parameter estimates are then used to determine the value of the market price of convenience-yield risk by fitting the whole term structure of

[29] The failure to find mean reversion in oil prices is probably an artifact of the weekly sampling and short 5-year time interval they use. Monthly sampling over longer time periods does seem to suggest mean reversion in oil prices, with a half life of disturbances of less than 1 year.

actual futures prices to theoretical prices derived from (76) with the terminal boundary condition $F_{\tau,\tau} = P_\tau$. They find that the market price of convenience yield risk is quite variable, which could be interpreted as a misspecification of their model. They also determine risk-adjusted present value factors for long-term future delivery of oil, that are consistent with their estimates of the short-term processes.

Their results should be regarded as preliminary, since they use an inefficient two-step procedure for estimating the parameters of (76) and the market price of convenience-yield risk. Moreover, if they cannot find the riskless rate of interest used by commodity traders, they will make corresponding errors in their estimate of the convenience yield. Nevertheless, their model does share the following stylized fact with models (71) and (73): spot oil prices are more volatile than forward oil prices. This is because the short-term convenience yield is quite random.

Laughton & Jacoby [1993] find three general effects of mean reverting spot prices on the valuation of real options. First, because the mean reversion tends to reduce long-term uncertainty it can increase underlying asset value. Second, the reduced risk can reduce option value for a given underlying asset value. Finally, the future reversion of cash flow can have direct valuation effects. Thus, ignoring mean reversion can lead to early or to late project adoption, as well as under- or over-estimates of the value of the real option. The nature of the error depends on the particular circumstances of the problem, which can only be assessed by a full analysis of the real option.

3.6. *Discrete-time economic analysis of real options*

It is often the case that the continuous-time partial differential equations like (44) do not admit analytic solutions. In such a case, numerical methods [such as in Schwartz, 1977, or Brennan & Schwartz, 1978] can be employed to solve the partial differential equation, subject to the boundary conditions. These techniques convert the continuous-time economic problem into a discrete mathematical problem, and then allow the analysis to be done with mathematics.

An alternative approach is to regard the economic problem as a discrete-time problem in the first place. This allows the analysis to be done with economic reasoning backing up all the mathematical steps. Little, if anything, is given up by taking a discrete-time approach to analyzing real options, because accurate determination of value and optimal exercise hurdles is not as important as development of a consistent, economically meaningful model. The primary problem for the practitioner is to have analytic tools that are reliable and unlikely to result in bizarre normative prescriptions. By keeping the economic intuition in the problem as long as possible, there is less likelihood of a serious modelling error.[30]

[30] The situation is similar to a traditional capital budgeting setting in which determination of NPV consists of discounting expected cash flows at a cost of capital. It is often possible to calculate a cost of capital to a reasonable degree of accuracy using accepted financial techniques that make

Consider the discrete points in time $\{0, h, 2h, \ldots, nh, \ldots\}$ for some increment of time $h > 0$. A representative time from this set is t. The discrete-time analogue of the process (26) is:

$$\Delta \tilde{P}_{t+h} \equiv \tilde{P}_{t+h} - P_t = \alpha(P_t, t)h + \sigma(P_{th}, t)\sqrt{h}\tilde{z}_{t+h} \tag{77}$$

where

$\tilde{z}_{t+h}$ = independent, identically distributed error term, with mean zero and unit variance[31].

For each point in time, t, one can calculate the net value of an immediately adopted project as a function of the underlying asset price as discussed, for example, in Section 2.2 (Hotelling valuation of resource properties). Denote this by $\mathrm{NPV}(\tilde{P}_t, t)$. Denote by $W(\tilde{P}_{t+h}, t+h)$ the value of the option at the next point in time, $t+h$. Viewed from time t, the price $\tilde{P}_{t+h}$ is random, and the value at time $t+h$ of the policy of keeping the option alive at least for one more period is the present value of the risk-neutral expected value of the option next period, or

$$\mathrm{e}^{-rh}\hat{E}_t[W(\tilde{P}_{t+h}, t+h)]. \tag{78}$$

Since we have a Markov process in two state variables (underlying asset price and time), the risk-neutral conditional expectation operator $\hat{E}_t[\cdot]$ and the value in (78) are functions of P_t and t.

By the *Bellman equation* (or *principle of optimality* in dynamic programming), the value of the option at time t is the larger of these two values:

$$W(P_t, t) = \max\left\{\mathrm{NPV}(P_t, t), \mathrm{e}^{-rh}\hat{E}_t[W(\tilde{P}_{t+h}, t+h)]\right\}. \tag{79}$$

If the option has a finite maturity date $T = Nh$ by which the option must be exercised, then we have

$$W(\tilde{P}_{T+h}, T+h) = 0. \tag{80}$$

This allows us to analyze the option value and optimal exercise decisions by recursively working backwards from date T, using the principle of optimality (79). That is, from (80) in (79) for $t = T$, we can evaluate the function $W(\cdot, T)$, as a function of P. Given $W[\cdot, T]$, we use (79) to evaluate $W(\cdot, T-h)$. This process is continued until the function $W(\cdot, 0)$ is evaluated. Along the way, all the option price functions for various intermediate times have been evaluated, and all the optimal exercise decisions have been made, by remembering which element of

reference to various market relationships. The job of forecasting cash flows is often done outside a market context, and it is easy for an analyst to glibly extend historic start-up growth rates into a forecast of unrealistically high growth rates for a mature project. By recognizing that NPV is an economic rent, and noting that economic rents are scarce, the analyst with economic insight can provide more useful estimates of project NPV.

[31] For such increments, the variance and mean of increments to the process increase proportionally to the time increment h. Thus, the standard deviation, $\sigma(P_{t+nh}, t+nh)\sqrt{h}$ increases proportionally to $\sqrt{h}$.

the maximand (79) has been selected.[32] This is the standard backward-induction analysis of a decision tree.

If there is no maturity date and the real option is perpetual, then there is no starting boundary point for the induction, and dependence on time will vanish (unless the terms of exercise are still time-dependent). To solve the problem one must find an option function W that solves the Bellman equation (79), with the dependence on t dropped. The solution is a fixed point in some function space, and can be an intractable problem to solve. In practice, it is often simplest to approximate the problem by one with the maturity date T taken to be in the distant future.

By letting the time increment h shrink towards zero, the discrete process usually converges towards the continuous process. We have to be careful to say 'usually' since convergence depends on the nature of the distribution and the behavior of the drift and the variance as functions of the underlying asset price. At the level of real options, convergence might not be a critical issue, if the analyst feels that the economic representation of the problem in discrete terms is itself a good approximation to reality. That is, economic events do occur in discrete time, so a discrete model may have direct validity, rather than needing to inherit validity as an approximation to a continuous-time model.

The convergence of various discrete-time models to continuous-time models (typically when the discrete-time model also has a discrete state space) is discussed in greater detail by Boyle, Evnine & Gibbs [1989], He [1990], Nelson & Ramaswamy [1990] and Amin [1991]. The general methodology is to assume that the true underlying asset price follows a diffusion process, such as (26) with disturbances that are locally normally distributed: $\mathrm{d}\omega \sim N(0, \mathrm{d}t)$. By approximating the diffusion process with a discrete process (77) that locally has the same mean and variance as the diffusion, it is often possible to show that the distribution of the discrete process (even when the distribution of price increments is a discrete Bernoulli process) converges to the distribution of the diffusion process.[33] Then, the probability distribution for the discrete price process is replaced by

[32] This feature makes the recursion very efficient, because no analysis is done of suboptimal exercise policies. In general, the optimal exercise policy is a function of time — for example, a call option at maturity is optimally exercised when the underlying asset price exceeds the exercise price, but when the call option has an infinite time to maturity, the optimal exercise price is much higher. If we were to use Monte Carlo simulation to analyze a real American option, we would have to simulate the whole model for all possible exercise functions, and then choose the function that provides the highest option value. This is computationally inefficient, because the analyst (or her computer) must consider the myriad of wrong answers before finding the right answers.

[33] If the volatility and drift are reasonably well-behaved functions of the underlying asset price, convergence can often be proven. Problems occur if these functions grow too quickly as the asset price increases or drop to zero at prices that are attainable. In this respect, the normal, log-normal and mean-reverting processes discussed here are well-behaved. One of the most straightforward approaches, as discussed by Boyle, Evnine & Gibbs [1989] is to borrow from the proofs of the central limit theorem, and analyze the convergence of the characteristic function of the discrete distribution to the characteristic function of the normal distribution, after some appropriate transformation of variables. The characteristic functions can be approximated by a second order Taylor series, which depends on the first and second moments of the distribution. The question is whether the error term of the Taylor series vanishes as $h \to 0$.

the martingale distribution, as discussed in the Section 2.1.3 (Steps to finding a martingale valuation operator). Since this typically only amounts to subtracting a risk premium from the drift of the true probability distribution, the convergence properties carry over to the discrete martingale distribution. That is, the discrete martingale distribution will converge to the continuous martingale distribution. Since an asset price (such as an option price) is the present value of the risk-neutral expectation of the (continuous) payoff functions, the asset prices calculated for the discrete approximations will converge to the asset price for the continuous diffusion process.

Of course, this discussion is rather informal and heuristic. The real options analyst desiring more rigor could go to the literature cited above and go through the convergence proofs for the particular model of interest. Not only does this tend to dampen the enthusiasm of many who would want to analyze a real option, but it does not even address the important question of speed of convergence. How many steps are needed to get a good approximation? To get a practical grip on all these problems at once, the following checklist is useful:

1. Does the discrete approximation seem to be economically meaningful in the sense that it fits the important stylized facts known to the analyst?
2. In some problems, analytic solutions can be obtained for problems that bound the real option. Are these bounds are satisfied by the approximation? If not, shorten h and add more steps to the problem. If this doesn't address the violation of the bound, it may be that the process doesn't converge, or a modelling error has been made by the analyst. Useful bounds include:
   a. European options are less valuable than otherwise-similar real American options.
   b. Finite-lived American options are less valuable than perpetual American options.

Often it is possible to model a contract payoff so that the discrete solution should approximate that of a known analytic solution. Thus, if the Bellman equation (79) for an American option is replaced by

$$W(P_t, t) = \mathrm{e}^{-rh} \hat{E}_t[W(\tilde{P}_{t+h}, t + h)], \tag{81}$$

and the terminal condition (80) is replaced by

$$W(\tilde{P}_T, T) = \mathrm{NPV}(P_T, T), \tag{82}$$

we get a European option, for which there may be a known analytic solution for the continuous diffusion. Similarly, if we replace the Bellman equation by the certainty-equivalent characterization of the futures contract (37), and replace the terminal condition by futures-spot convergence (56), we get the futures price, which can be compared to the analytic formulas for futures prices given earlier for various processes. To obtain analytic formulas, one can determine a risk-neutral probability distribution of the terminal payoff (option payoff or spot price in the case of futures). The European option value is the present value of the risk-neutral expectation of the option payoff. The futures price is the risk-neutral expectation of the future spot price.

3.6.1. Choosing an approximating process

Consistent with the diffusion process, one could model $\tilde{z}_{t+h}$ as a normally distributed random variable, with mean 0 and variance 1. This could make the backward induction analysis unwieldy, since it might not be possible to parametrize the functional form of intermediate option values $W(\cdot, t)$. In general, this is a nonlinear function of P_t for underlying asset prices below the critical value at which the option is optimally exercised.

Alternatively, one can model $\tilde{z}_t$ as a discrete random variable taking on only two or three different values in its domain. Instead of needing a parametric representation of $W(P_t, t)$, as a function of P_t, one only needs the actual values of the function at a finite number of discrete points in time and at discrete underlying asset prices. The option values are only calculated for a tree-like lattice structure of discrete points (P, t). If the incremental process takes only two different values at each point in time, it is a *Bernoulli process*. Since Bernoulli processes can be made to converge to many useful continuous processes, such as normal, log-normal, and Poisson processes[34], little is lost by using a Bernoulli process as the main analytic tool. In a real options context, very useful analysis can be conducted with as few as 50 or 100 time steps, which can often be conveniently represented on a spreadsheet, as discussed in Sick [1989b].

3.6.2. Discrete Bernoulli approximations of continuous processes

For simplicity, we will restrict ourselves to discrete Bernoulli processes. At each time t, the random variable $\tilde{z}_{t+h}$ can assume only two values:

$$\tilde{z}_t = \begin{cases} \epsilon_+(P, t), & \text{with probability } \pi(P, t), \\ \epsilon_-(P, t), & \text{with probability } 1 - \pi(P, t) \end{cases} \tag{83}$$

These processes can be represented by a simple tree structure, and they can be analyzed with familiar decision-tree methods. By allowing π to depend on P, the increments of the z_t process may not be independent, as were the increments in the Wiener process ω in (26). However, the process is still a Markov process, and this extra freedom is needed to approximate some processes, such as a mean-reverting process. We will discuss various approaches selecting functional representations of the coefficients for the discrete process to approximate the continuous process.

We are only interested in the true probability distribution π in so far as knowing that it will converge to the true continuous distribution. Our analysis only involves the risk-neutral probability distribution $\hat{\pi}$. We find it convenient to rewrite the risk-neutral versions of (77) and (83) as:

$$\begin{aligned} \Delta\tilde{P}_{t+h} &\equiv \tilde{P}_{t+h} - P_t = \\ &= \begin{cases} u(P_t, t, h), & \text{with probability } \hat{\pi}(P - t, h), \\ d(P_t, t, h), & \text{with probability } 1 - \hat{\pi}(P - t, h), \end{cases} \end{aligned} \tag{84}$$

where $u(P_t, t, h) = \alpha(P_t, t)h + \epsilon_+(P, t)$ and $d(P_t, t, h) = \alpha(P_t, t)h + \epsilon_-(P, t)$.

[34] See, for example Madan, Milne & Shefrin [1989].

We have 3 general objectives in this approximation:

1. The drift of the price should equal the riskless return, adjusted for the convenience dividend[35]:

$$\hat{E}_t[\Delta \tilde{P}_{t+h}] = \mathrm{e}^{rh} P_t - \delta(P_t, t)h \tag{85}$$

In (84), this implies that

$$\hat{\pi}(P_t, t, h) = \frac{[\mathrm{e}^{rh} P_t - \delta(P_t, t)h] - d(P_t, t, h)}{u(P_t, t, h) - d(P_t, t, h)}. \tag{86}$$

Equivalently, we could use the CAPM, as in the transition from (32) to (34) to write:

$$\mathrm{e}^{rh} P_t - \delta(P_t, t)h = (\alpha(P_t, t) - \sigma(P_t, t)\sigma_f(f, t)\rho[\omega, \omega_f])h. \tag{87}$$

2. The variance of the price changes should equal the variance of the continuous distribution. In practice, we will see that this is often harder to achieve, and sometimes it is only necessary to have this condition hold as a limit when $h \to 0$. Simplifying the notation by suppressing the arguments of the functions, the strictest form of this becomes:

$$\begin{aligned}\sigma^2 h &= \mathrm{var}_t[\Delta \tilde{P}_{t+h}] \equiv \hat{E}_t\left[(\Delta \tilde{P}_{t+h})^2\right] - \left(\hat{E}_t[\Delta \tilde{P}_{t+h}]\right)^2 \\ &= \hat{\pi}(u^2 - d^2) + d^2 - (\alpha - \sigma\sigma_f\rho)^2 h^2.\end{aligned} \tag{88}$$

Using (86) and (87), this simplifies to

$$\sigma^2 h + (\alpha - \sigma\sigma_f\rho)^2 h^2 = (\alpha - \sigma\sigma_f\rho)(u + d) - ud. \tag{89}$$

Given u, equation (89) can be solved for d and (86) can be solved for $\hat{\pi}$.

The flexibility in choosing u gives one 'degree of freedom', which can be useful in meeting the final objective.

3. The tree of price levels over time must *recombine*, so that the state is fully described by the total number of up moves and down moves, and is independent of the order in which the moves occur. Thus, a down move followed by and up move must lead to the same underlying asset price as an up move followed by a down move. Mathematically, this means that the up and down operations must be commutative:

$$d\big(u(P_t, t, h), t + h, h\big) = u\big(d(P_t, t, h), t + h, h\big). \tag{90}$$

This basically forces us to use additive or multiplicative functional forms, or to use a transformation of price and time in which the up and down moves are

[35] In (85), we are taking a dividend that is analogous to simple interest but accruing the riskless interest at a compound rate. If h is sufficiently small, this distinction is not important. If we know more about the functional form of the dividend, a more accurate expression can be derived. For example, if $\delta(P, t) = \delta_0 P$ for a constant yield δ_0, then it is best to replace (85) with

$$\hat{E}_t[\Delta \tilde{P}_{t+h}] = \mathrm{e}^{(r-\delta_0)h} P_t.$$

additive.[36] It also limits our flexibility in allowing the parameters of the u and d functions to vary with price, because a sequence of $N/2$ ups followed by $N/2$ downs must lead to the same price as $N/2$ downs followed by $N/2$ ups. The former sequence resides in the high-priced portion of the tree, while the latter resides in the low-priced portion of the tree.

Similarly, the up and down functions cannot directly depend on time. However, if the variance function $\sigma^2(\cdot,\cdot)$ depends on price or time, it is often useful to transform the stochastic process to have constant variance over price and/or time. If we represent the underlying asset price and time as transformations of a stochastic variable and rescaled time, then there is an open question as to whether the first two criteria should involve the means and variances of the increments of the price process or of the transformed process. The two can be related by Itô's lemma and any resulting biases will generally vanish as $h \to 0$. The important question is the accuracy of the approximation for larger h.

3.6.3. Examples of discrete-time approximations

In the following examples, we will suppose that the underlying diffusion process has a constant risk premium $\sigma_0\sigma_f\rho$.

First, consider an *additive diffusion* in which $\alpha(P,t) = \alpha_0$ and $\sigma(P,t) = \sigma_0$, where α_0 and σ_0 are constants. Then the assignment

$$u(P,t) = -d(P,t) = \sqrt{\sigma_0^2 h + (\alpha - \sigma_0\sigma_f\rho)^2 h^2} \tag{91}$$

$$\hat{\pi} = \frac{1}{2} + \frac{\alpha - \sigma_0\sigma_f\rho}{2u} \tag{92}$$

satisfies our three criteria. It is also possible to verify that this gives $0 < \hat{\pi} < 1$. The resulting lattice structure has equal up and down jumps, from a starting point of P_0.

Next, consider a *log-normal diffusion* in which $\alpha(P,t) = \alpha_0 P$ and $\sigma(P,t) = \sigma_0 P$. By (33), this model implies a constant dividend yield $\delta_0 = r + \sigma_0\sigma_f\rho - \alpha_0$. For this popular model, Cox, Ross & Rubinstein [1979] (hereafter CRR) proposed using

$$\begin{aligned} u(P,t) &= P(\mathrm{e}^{\sigma_0\sqrt{h}} - 1), \\ d(P,t) &= P(\mathrm{e}^{-\sigma_0\sqrt{h}} - 1) \end{aligned} \tag{93}$$

and

$$\hat{\pi} = \frac{1}{2} + \frac{r}{2\sigma_0}\sqrt{h}. \tag{94}$$

They assumed that dividends were paid on discrete dates and adjusted the prices in the tree by the factor $(1-\delta_0)^\nu$, where $\nu \doteq$ the number of dividends paid in the amount $\delta_0 P$ per payment. This assignment satisfies our third criterion, but only satisfies the first two criteria in the limit as $h \to 0$. This assignment of values is

[36] If we take a logarithmic transformation, a multiplicative function becomes additive, so we generally only need to investigate additive functional forms.

based on a logarithmic transformation of prices, so that the diffusion is an additive diffusion, as in our first example. That is, the CRR assignment sets

$$\hat{\pi} = \frac{rh - \ln(1 + d/p)}{\ln(1 + u/p) - \ln(1 + d/p)}. \tag{95}$$

Also, this assignment sets the variance of the diffusion process equal to the second moment of the discrete process. That is instead of subtracting the mean square to get a central moment, in (88) CRR use the noncentral moment by setting:

$$\sigma^2 h \equiv \hat{E}_t\left[\left(\Delta \ln(\tilde{P}_{t+h})\right)^2\right]. \tag{96}$$

While the CRR approximation is simple and converges to the continuous model solution, it sometimes produces violation of some bounds for 'large' values of h. For example, it can result in discrete values of American options that are less than the Black–Scholes values of otherwise similar European options. Hull & White [1988] and Sick [1989b] suggest setting the mean and variance of the process for prices (rather than logarithms of prices) to be the same in the discrete and continuous models. This behaves better for large values of h, and one might wonder which of the two major changes gave most of the improvement — dealing with prices rather than logs, or measuring variance accurately, rather than as a second moment. Certainly a simple approach is to improve the accuracy of the mean and dividend approximation by setting

$$\hat{\pi} = \frac{e^{(r-\delta_0)h} - e^{-\sigma\sqrt{h}}}{e^{\sigma\sqrt{h}} - e^{-\sigma\sqrt{h}}} \tag{97}$$

while maintaining the volatility model of (93). This yields approximately the same results as the Hull–White model, but has a simpler formula.[37,38]

[37] If we desire to also have the logarithm of the price process have the same variance in the continuous and discrete cases, we must set

$$\sigma_0^2 h = u^2 - (\hat{E}_t[\Delta \ln(\tilde{P}_{t+h})])^2.$$

Using Itô's lemma or the properties of the log-normal distribution, we can see that this requires setting

$$u = \sqrt{h}\sqrt{\sigma_0^2 + \left(r - \delta_0 - \frac{\sigma_0^2}{2}\right)^2 h}.$$

The second term under the square root converges to 0 as $h \to 0$, so the expression is asymptotic to (93).

[38] Amin [1991] also uses the degrees of freedom in selecting u and d to model the mean price accurately, without addressing the volatility approximation:

$$\ln\left(1 + \frac{u(P,t)}{P}\right) = (r - \delta_0)h - \ln\left(\frac{e^{\sigma_0\sqrt{h}} - e^{-\sigma_0\sqrt{h}}}{2}\right) + \sigma_0\sqrt{h}$$

$$\ln\left(1 + \frac{d(P,t)}{P}\right) = (r - \delta_0)h - \ln\left(\frac{e^{\sigma_0\sqrt{h}} - e^{-\sigma_0\sqrt{h}}}{2}\right) - \sigma_0\sqrt{h}$$

and

$$\hat{\pi} = \frac{1}{2}.$$

Now, consider the *mean-reverting* diffusion (62). Using the information available at time t, the risk-neutral expected value of the spot price at time $t+h$ is the certainty equivalent or futures price $F_{t,t+h}$. Thus, by (71), the risk-neutral expected drift over the interval h is

$$\hat{E}_t[\Delta \tilde{P}_{t+h}] = F_{t,t+h} - P_t = (1 - \mathrm{e}^{-\lambda h})\left[(\bar{P} - P_t) - \frac{\sigma_0 \sigma_f \rho}{\lambda}\right]. \tag{98}$$

Thus, solving (84) for $\hat{\pi}$, we have[39]

$$\hat{\pi} = \frac{\hat{E}_t[\Delta \tilde{P}_{t+h}] - d}{u - d} = \frac{(1 - \mathrm{e}^{-\lambda h})\left[(\bar{P} - P_t) - (\sigma_0 \sigma_f \rho)/\lambda\right] - d}{u - d} \tag{99}$$

where we must select u and d to satisfy criteria 2 and 3. Consistent with the CRR analysis, we set

$$u = -d = \sigma_0 \sqrt{h}. \tag{100}$$

If the time to maturity is large and there are few steps so that h is large, (99) may give values of $\hat{\pi}$ that are outside the interval [0, 1]. In such cases, one could simply set the risk-neutral probability to 0 or 1 as the case may be. This has the effect of guaranteeing a risk-neutral up-move when the price is very low and guaranteeing a risk-neutral down-move when the price is very high, which is consistent with the notion of mean reversion. If this happens for substantial portions of the tree, however, more steps should be added to the tree.

Similarly, consider the mean-reverting process (65). By (73), the risk-neutral expected drift over the interval h is

$$\begin{aligned}\hat{E}_t[\Delta \tilde{P}_{t+h}] &= F_{t,t+h} - P_t = \\ &= P_t \left\{ \left(\frac{P_t}{\bar{P}}\right)^{\exp[(-\lambda h) - 1]} \right. \\ &\qquad \left. \exp\left[\frac{\sigma_0^2}{4\lambda}(1 - \mathrm{e}^{-2\lambda h}) - \frac{\sigma_0 \sigma_f \rho}{\lambda}(1 - \mathrm{e}^{-\lambda h})\right] - 1 \right\}. \end{aligned} \tag{101}$$

As in CRR, we set the up and down moves by (93). From (101) the risk-neutral

For general processes, including this one, Carr & Jarrow [1995] also advocate setting the risk-neutral probability equal to 1/2. They set the up and down moves (in a transformed process) equal to the instantaneous drift plus and minus $\sigma_0 \sqrt{h}$.

[39] A quicker but less accurate approximation results from assuming the convenience dividend is constant over the time interval $[t, t+h]$. In (66), this means that the risk-neutralized expected drift of the diffusion is

$$\hat{E}_t[\Delta \tilde{P}_{t+h}] = \left(\lambda(\bar{P} - P_t) - \sigma_0 \sigma_f \rho\right)h$$

and

$$\hat{\pi} = \frac{\left(\lambda(\bar{P} - P_t) - \sigma_0 \sigma_f \rho\right)h - d}{u - d}.$$

probability is [40]

$$\hat{\pi} = \frac{\left(\frac{P_t}{\bar{P}}\right)^{\exp[-\lambda h)-1]} \exp\left[\frac{\sigma_0^2}{4\lambda}(1-\mathrm{e}^{-2\lambda h}) - \frac{\sigma_0\sigma_f\rho}{\lambda}(1-\mathrm{e}^{-\lambda h})\right] - \mathrm{e}^{-\sigma_0\sqrt{h}}}{\mathrm{e}^{\sigma_0\sqrt{h}} - \mathrm{e}^{-\sigma_0\sqrt{h}}}. \tag{102}$$

In both of these mean-reverting models, the risk-neutral probability is a function of price. The magnitude of the up and down moves does not depend on price, in order that the tree should recombine.

Boyle, Evnine & Gibbs [1989] show how to use discrete processes to model multiple stochastic processes that are jointly correlated.

4. Examples

4.1. Interest-rate uncertainty

Ingersoll & Ross [1992] investigate the real option to delay the implementation of investment when the sole source of uncertainty is the real rate of interest. By using the martingale pricing operator $\hat{E}[\cdot]$, they can value an operating project as the present value of the certainty-equivalents of its cash flows. They show that a great deal of the practical analysis can be simplified to the simple case of project with a balloon payment to be received at time T after the implementation of the project. This case tends to generalize to projects that pay a stream of cash inflows because they find that the optimal deferral strategy is not sensitive to the project duration T, as long as the interest-rate uncertainty is not too large.

Suppose the spot real rate of interest r follows a square root process with no drift:

$$\mathrm{d}r = \sigma_0\sqrt{r}\,\mathrm{d}\omega \tag{103}$$

where ω follows a Wiener process.

Consider an interest-rate contingent claim with a value $W(r,t)$. The claim pays a cash dividend of $D(r,t)$ per unit time. Cox, Ingersoll & Ross [1985b], or CIR, show that the price of such a claim, satisfies

$$\tfrac{1}{2}W_{rr}\sigma_0^2 r + W_t + \lambda r W_r + D = rW, \tag{104}$$

[40] We could also use the quicker, but less accurate approximation from (68):

$$\hat{E}_t[\Delta\bar{P}_{t+h}] = \left(rP - \delta(P,t)\right)h = Ph\left[\lambda\left(\ln\bar{P} + \frac{\sigma_0^2}{2\lambda} - \ln P\right) - \sigma_0\sigma_f\rho\right]$$

and calculate

$$\hat{\pi} = \frac{h\left[\lambda\left(\ln\bar{P} + \sigma_0^2/2\lambda - \ln P\right) - \sigma_0\sigma_f\rho\right] + 1 - \mathrm{e}^{-\sigma_0\sqrt{h}}}{\mathrm{e}^{\sigma_0\sqrt{h}} - \mathrm{e}^{-\sigma_0\sqrt{h}}}.$$

where $-\lambda$ is the price of interest-rate risk. This can be obtained by substituting r for P in (34) and making two extra observations. First, in (103), $\alpha(r,t) = 0$. Second, we are setting the interest-rate risk premium to be $-\lambda r = \sigma(r,t)\sigma_f(f,t)\rho[\omega,\omega_f]$. Given that the volatility in (103) is $\sigma(r,t) = \sigma_0\sqrt{r}$, one might have expected the interest-rate risk premium to be $-\lambda\sqrt{r}$, for some constant λ. However, the interest rate variable upon which we price the option is a systematic risk variable for the whole economy. Thus, the component of the volatility of the market pricing factor that is related to interest-rate risk[41] is also proportional to $\sqrt{r}$. This gives the extra factor $\sqrt{r}$ for the risk-premium term.

For example, for a pure discount bond that matures at time T, set the price $P = W$ and the coupon dividend $D = 0$. Since $P_r < 0$ for a bond, examination of (104) establishes that $\lambda > 0$ corresponds to a positive term premium in the sense that the expected rate of return on the (long-term) bond exceeds the riskless rate of return by $-\lambda r P_r > 0$. CIR show that the price of the pure discount T-period bond in this situation is

$$P(r,T) = \mathrm{e}^{-b(T)r} \tag{105}$$

where

$$b(T) \equiv -\frac{2(\mathrm{e}^{\gamma T}-1)}{(\gamma-\lambda)(\mathrm{e}^{\gamma T}-1)+2\gamma} \quad \text{and} \quad \gamma \equiv \sqrt{\lambda^2+2\sigma_0^2} \tag{106}$$

Suppose the manager has the perpetual real option to select the time τ at which a project is implemented. Consider, first, a simple project with an investment I and a single cash inflow of \$1 to be received at time T after the investment. At the time τ of the investment, the value of the real option is the net present value of the project, which is the price of a discount bond with maturity T periods hence, when the spot interest rate is $r = r(\tau)$. That is, the project value at time τ when the spot interest rate $r = r(\tau)$ is:

$$W(r) = W\big(r(\tau),T,I\big) = P\big(r(\tau),T\big) - I. \tag{107}$$

The incentive to exercise early in this problem is the fact that the adopted project gives a predetermined dollar payoff (\$1) that does not grow with a delay in starting the project. By adopting early, the owner of the option can invest the NPV of the project in the bank and earn a market rate of interest. Thus, the market rate of interest to be earned by investing the proceeds of the NPV of the project is the dividend that motivates the owner of the option to exercise early.

Note that the interest rate process is Markov with the spot interest rate as the only state variable. Thus, the value of the real option to adopt the project does not

[41] In the martingale valuation or the consumption CAPM, there is only a single factor used for pricing. Arbitrage pricing theory decomposes this into multiple factors, one of which could reflect interest-rate risk. That is, if we project the interest rate r onto the market factor f, we get the interest rate variable itself. The CIR model is built on power or logarithmic utility and a single state variable Y that locally has volatility proportional to $\sqrt{Y}$. Since the only source of uncertainty in this problem comes from interest-rate risk, we can rederive the whole pricing theory for these problems using interest-rate risk as the pricing factor, and take Y to be proportional to r.

depend on the time t, although it does depend on the duration of the project, T. The optimal adoption policy specifies the boundary point(s) r^* for the adoption region in interest-rate space. The project is adopted the first time the interest rate hits r^* from outside the adoption region. If NPV is declining in the interest rate, this occurs at a random stopping time that depends on the interest-rate path:

$$\tilde{t}(r^*) \equiv \inf\{t \mid \tilde{r}(t) \geq r^*\}.$$

At this boundary, the value of the option satisfies (107):

$$W(r^*) = P(r^*, T) - I \tag{108}$$

Thus, the real option is an interest rate contingent claim that satisfies (104) with $W_t = C = 0$. At the boundary it satisfies (108). To eliminate a spurious term from the solution to the differential equation (104), we specify that the value of the option falls to zero as the interest rate becomes arbitrarily large: $\lim_{r\to\infty} W(r) = 0$. The general solution is

$$W(r) = A\mathrm{e}^{-\nu r} \tag{109}$$

where

$$A \equiv \mathrm{e}^{(\nu - b(T))r^*} - I\mathrm{e}^{\nu r^*} \quad \text{and} \quad \nu \equiv \frac{\lambda + \gamma}{\sigma_0^2} > 0. \tag{110}$$

Maximizing the value of the option is equivalent to selecting r^* to maximize the value of A. This is equivalent to the high-contact condition. This occurs when the critical interest rate is set at

$$r^* = r^*(T, I) = \frac{1}{b(T)} \ln\left(\frac{\nu - b(T)}{\nu I}\right). \tag{111}$$

The value of the option to adopt the project is, by (109) and (110):

$$W(r) = A\mathrm{e}^{-\nu r} = \left(\mathrm{e}^{[\nu - b(T)]r^*} - I\mathrm{e}^{\nu r^*}\right)\mathrm{e}^{-\nu r} = \mathrm{e}^{-\nu(r - r^*)}(\mathrm{e}^{-b(T)r^*} - I) \tag{112}$$

The second factor is the net present value of the adopted project at the time of exercise $W(r^*) = \mathrm{e}^{-b(T)r^*} - I$. Thus, the first factor is the risk-neutralized expected present value factor of waiting to adopt the project until the time $\tilde{t}(r^*)$ when the interest rate first drops to r^*, namely

$$\mathrm{e}^{-\nu(r - r^*)} = \hat{E}_0\left[\exp\left(-\int_0^{\tilde{t}(r^*)} \tilde{r}(s)\,\mathrm{d}s\right)\right] \tag{113}$$

The manager invests the first time that the interest rate r falls below the hurdle value r^*. In contrast, the internal rate of return of the project is calculated from

(105) and (107) as

$$\mathrm{IRR} = \mathrm{IRR}(T, I) = -\frac{\ln(I)}{b(T)}. \tag{114}$$

Thus,

$$r^* - \mathrm{IRR} = \frac{1}{b(T)} \ln\left(\frac{\nu - b(T)}{\nu}\right) < 0 \tag{115}$$

so that the real option is exercised at a lower interest rate than the IRR, which provides a break-even value of the NPV. However, Ingersoll & Ross make an interesting observation about the relationship between this difference $r^* - \mathrm{IRR}$ and the duration of the project T and the interest-rate volatility parameter σ_0. (Recall that interest-rate volatility is locally $\sigma_0\sqrt{r}$.) For small volatility levels (up to an annual standard deviation of the real rate of return of 20 to 30 basis points), the difference $r^* - \mathrm{IRR}$ is almost invariant to the project duration T. This leads them to suggest a practical method of calculating the approximate hurdle interest rate for adoption of projects that return a stream of cash flows, rather than just a single cash flow:

1. Calculate the internal rate of return of the project.
2. Calculate the duration T of the project.
3. For a project that pays a single cash flow at this duration, calculate the difference $r^* - \mathrm{IRR}$ in (115), noting that the difference is invariant to the investment level.
4. Add this difference to the IRR to get a good approximation to the hurdle real interest rate for the adoption of the project that has multiple cash flows.

This approximation can be improved by using the following technique for projects that have a net present value $N(r)$ that is declining in the interest rate. Using (112) and (113), the value of the real option to adopt the project when the critical interest rate is $\hat{r}$ is

$$\mathrm{e}^{-\nu(r-\hat{r})} N(\hat{r}) = \mathrm{e}^{-\nu r} \left(\mathrm{e}^{\nu \hat{r}} N(\hat{r})\right). \tag{116}$$

The task then reduces to one of selecting $\hat{r}$ to maximize the factor in brackets. This can be done analytically or numerically.

Ingersoll & Ross analyze the value of the option to adopt the project as a function of the term premium λ. As λ increases, long-term interest rates increase, and the value of an adopted project decreases. On the other hand, the higher (long-term) interest rates tend to increase the value of the option by increasing the benefit of deferring the date of incurring the investment cost. They show that the former effect dominates, so that the value of the option to invest in a project falls as the term premium increases and the yield curve steepens.

They also study a related question: Will an overall decrease in the level of interest rates stimulate an economy by causing real options to be exercised that would otherwise be deferred? If NPV is a declining function of the discount rate and investment decisions are made using the NPV rule, a decrease in interest rates will cause some projects to be accepted that were formerly rejected. Now, when we consider the option to delay a project, this answer does not always obtain. Ingersoll

& Ross show that a simple nonstochastic project with a declining term structure of interest rates can have the property that a decrease in short- and long-term interest rates makes it preferable to defer investment that otherwise would have been undertaken immediately. Intuitively, the declining term structure makes the NPV at the time of adoption more valuable when the project is deferred, which can tend to offset the loss due to discounting the NPV back to the present. When both long and short interest rates decline, the decline is proportionally more significant for the lower long rate, so the benefit of deferral becomes relatively more preferable. They go on to argue that this result is not simply an artifact of the declining term structure. In a stochastic model, they suggest that increasing risk over time could have the same effect.

Ingersoll & Ross also address the question of estimation error of the parameters and its resulting effect on estimation error of the hurdle rate r^*. The loss in option value for selecting the wrong hurdle is asymmetric for over- or under-estimating r^*. When interest rates are driven by the square-root process, significant losses occur when the project is adopted at too high an interest rate, while the losses are not so substantial for a policy of waiting too long and adopting at too low an interest rate. On the other hand, when they modify the analysis to the interest-rate process $\mathrm{d}r = \sigma_0 r^{3/2}\mathrm{d}\omega$, the asymmetry reverses direction, so the result is sensitive to the choice of interest-rate process.

In traditional capital budgeting, multiple IRRs, which are caused by reversals in signs of future cash flows, can create multiple project acceptance regions. That is, there can be unconnected sets of interest rates for which the project NPV is positive. Since the value of a real option to a project converges toward the NPV as the volatility of the interest rate falls, or as an expiration date approaches. Thus, with alternating cash flow signs, there can be multiple interest-rate acceptance regions. The regions are not characterized by the NPV graph crossing zero, as in the traditional IRR analysis, but they are caused by multiple high-contact points between the NPV graph and the graph of the value of the real option, as a function of interest rate. This requires that the NPV graph have sufficiently large swings that it comes into contact with the graph of the value of the option as shown in Exhibit B.

Ingersoll & Ross show how to use the existing bond-pricing literature to evaluate real options with more general risk-neutralized interest rate processes that have the general form:

$$\mathrm{d}r = \kappa r^{\beta}(\pi - r)\mathrm{d}t + \sigma_0 r^{\alpha}\mathrm{d}\omega$$

where $\kappa, \pi, \beta \geq 0$, and $\sigma_0 > 0$ are parameters. The procedure is to evaluate the risk-neutral expected present value of a claim to \$1 to be received at $\tilde{t}(r^*)$, which is the first time the interest rate falls to r^* from above. This is the general version of the right hand side of (113):

$$\phi(r, r^*) \equiv \hat{E}_0 \left[\exp\left(-\int_0^{\tilde{t}(r^*)} \tilde{r}(s)\,\mathrm{d}s \right) \bigg|_{r(0)=r} \right]. \tag{117}$$

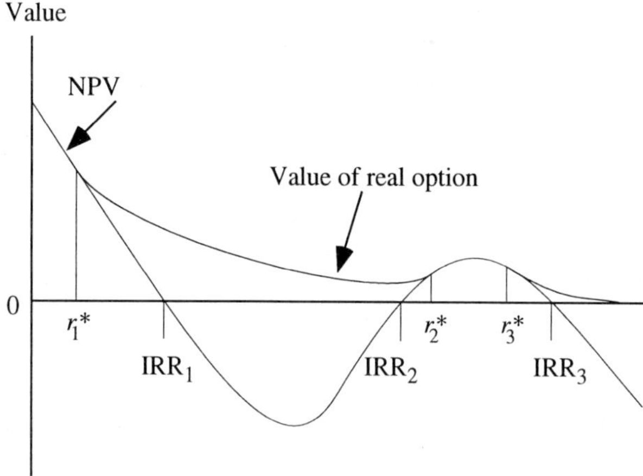

Exhibit B. Multiple internal rates of return occur when the NPV graph crosses the zero axis. Multiple acceptance rates for real option to adopt project occur when the graph of option value is tangent to the NPV graph. This is induced by large swings in the NPV graph.

This is multiplied by the NPV at the time of exercise to get the value today of the real option to adopt the project the first time the interest rate falls to r^*:

$$W|_{r^*} \equiv \phi(r, r^*)\mathrm{NPV}(r^*). \tag{118}$$

In general NPV(r) depends on the cash flow stream and the pricing structure of discount bonds for the chosen interest-rate process. The value of r^* is chosen to maximize the value of the real option $W|_{r^*}$. This can be done numerically or analytically, in some cases.

4.2. Further examples

4.2.1. Abandon and exchange

The option to adopt or abandon a project are options to exchange one asset for another. In the call option to adopt, an asset of certain value (construction cost) is exchanged for an underlying asset of uncertain value. In the put option to abandon, the risky underlying asset is exchanged for a certain scrap value, or a reduction in the present value of fixed operating costs. These two options can be generalized to options to exchange one risky asset for another. In general, this will involve two state variables and necessitates a multivariate analysis, such as used by Gibson & Schwartz in Section 3.5.2 on stochastic convenience value.

However, it is often possible to calculate a sufficient statistic that combines the two state variables into a single variable that is sufficient to characterize optimal exercise. This stems from the idea of Margrabe [1978] that one could cast the value of one of the assets in terms of the value of the other as a numeraire, thereby reducing the problem to the traditional option analysis with a single state variable.

McDonald & Siegel [1986] find that the sufficient statistic is the ratio of the two asset prices if they are joint log-normally distributed. Sick [1989b] shows that the sufficient statistic is the difference of the two asset prices if they are joint normally distributed.

4.2.2. Options to develop and redevelop property

Paddock, Siegel & Smith [1988] develop a three-stage model of exploration and development in the petroleum industry. At the first step, the firm is determining the value of a petroleum lease or right to explore for oil and gas. The probability distribution of the quantity of reserves, has a spike of mass at zero reserves (quantity of petroleum) and a continuous distribution for positive reserve levels. At the next step, the firm has proved up a quantity of reserves and determined a rate of exponentially declining production that can be sustained, and the uncertainty is about the price of oil and gas. The final step is the ownership of a developed operating petroleum property. At both of these transitions, the owner must analyze a real option. They also compare their estimates of the value of an exploration lease to that of the United States Geological Survey and the highest and mean bid posted by oil companies for several offshore leases. The average (across leases) highest bid was significantly larger than both the USGS and option valuation estimates.[42] Only at a high price of gas (compared to the prevailing spot price) was the option value greater the USGS discounted cash-flow valuation. The authors wondered whether their low estimates of option values were a function of the poor data they were forced to use on estimates of potential reserves. The petroleum companies would have more refined reserve estimates than the USGS reserve estimates used for the option analysis.

Capozza & Sick [1994] model an urban area as having uncertain rent at the center, with net rental revenue per unit density declining as distance increases from the center. Developers have the option to convert agricultural land (which earns rent at a possibly stochastic rate) into urban land by paying a fixed development cost. The optimal conversion policy determines the location of the urban boundary. An interesting aspect of the model is that the risk in the rental rate has systematic and unsystematic components. As systematic risk increases, the value of developed property falls, but the value of undeveloped property may either rise or fall. It will rise if the increased risk sufficiently increases option value, for any given level of value for the developed property. Up to this point, option models have always derived option value for a given value of the underlying asset, and had not explored the possibility that risk may be good or bad for the value of the option asset.

[42] For each lease, the mean bid is less than the highest bid, and is more in line with the estimate of option value. However, the best estimate of value is the winning bid, since each bidder should revise downward his or her estimate of the lease value to adjust for the 'winner's curse'. If the bidders have independent unbiased estimates of lease value, and bid according to their estimates, the winning bid will be an overestimate of lease value, conditional on winning, because the winner is more likely to have had positive valuation errors. This tendency for the winner to overestimate is the winner's curse.

One interesting use for models of this sort is to determine the option value lost to a farmer whose land is placed in a green belt by a government.

Capozza & Sick [1991], Capozza & Li [1994] and Williams [1991] examine another dimension of the option exercise decision: the choice of density of development. The value of a developed property equals the density times the price per unit of density. The development decision is made in two steps. First, for a given rental rate, the optimal development density is determined in a model of increasing costs to develop a unit of density. This gives a value of optimally developed property for each rental rate, which becomes the underlying asset in an option model. Second, given this payoff to optimal scale of development, the real option problem is solved to determine the development criterion in terms of a hurdle price for a unit of land.

The choice of process for the asset price and the functional cost of developing a unit of property is important in these models. For example, with log-normal asset prices and development cost that is a power function of density, the optimal density is often undefined, because setting a higher and higher density level, along with a higher and higher critical unit price of developed land delays development more and more into the future. The value gains in waiting exceed the loss in time value of money. Williams obtains a finite solution by imposing a maximum density (as in a zoning bylaw). Capozza & Sick get finite solutions by switching to an additive diffusion in underlying asset value.

The Capozza–Sick paper uses this variable density model to measure the loss in value to a lease 'ownership' contract (compared to a perpetual or fee-simple ownership contract) that arises from the distorted decisions to redevelop the property. That is, since redevelopment benefits are lost at the termination of the lease, the owner of a leasehold property has incentives to redevelop earlier and to a lower density than the owner of an otherwise identical fee-simple property. This model can be used to explain the significant discounts in the value of leased property without having to resort to high growth rates that lead to unrealistic rent multipliers.

The Williams paper also allows for stochastic development costs as well as income to a unit density of developed property. By expressing all prices and costs relative to a numeraire of the development costs, the model becomes the same as the log-normal model with one stochastic variable. He also examines the option to abandon property.

4.2.3. Production options

Various authors have modelled the flexibility a firm has to alter production rates as a real option. Brennan & Schwartz assume that there are three states of a mine or petroleum property: abandoned, shut in and operating. A transition cost (like an exercise price) is paid by the asset owner to go from one state to another. Only while operating does the property generate a positive net inflow or dividend. While shut in, the property incurs a cash outflow (to maintain the property). When abandoned, the property generates no cash flow. The manager must decide the critical points (in terms of spot commodity price, for example) at which to go from one state to another. An important characteristic of these optimal decision points is that they exhibit *hysteresis*. That is, the commodity price at which one would shut in an operating property is lower than the price at which one would put a shut-in property back on stream. This is analogous to setting the critical hurdle price of a real call option higher than the exercise price.

If there are no costs of opening or closing the operating property, then it is optimal to open when revenue exceeds cost and optimal to close otherwise. This decision can be made on a daily, weekly or annual basis, so it makes sense to view the flexible operating property as a portfolio of European call options on production, in which the exercise price is the operating cost. This approach was taken by McDonald & Siegel [1985].

In general, the net revenue from flexible production is some nonlinear function of an underlying risky variable (such as a commodity price). The function need not be piecewise-linear, as in an American call option. McDonald & Siegel [1985] show that a Cobb–Douglas production function leads to net profit function that is a power function of the commodity price. More generally, Sick [1989b] observes that the valuation of the claim to production for a given year in the future is the present value of the expected payoff under the martingale distribution. This can be determined by explicitly computing the expectation, or by approximating the payoff by a Taylor polynomial and using tabulated functions for the noncentral moments of the martingale distribution. Alternatively, the analyst could determine approximate payoff function values corresponding to ranges of values for the underlying risky variable. The present value of the risk-neutral probability of these ranges then becomes a price of a simple Arrow–Debreu claim, and the value of the property can be determined by state-space pricing methods. This method is developed by Breeden & Litzenberger [1978] and Banz & Miller [1978].

Mason & Baldwin [1988] also discuss the flexibility of the manager to alter short-term production as a feature of a larger model designed to assess the value of a government subsidy that is designed to encourage a nearly deployment of a project. In effect, the government is distorting the investment incentives of corporations in order to increase current economic activity or secure access to some critical national resource. By analyzing the situation as a real option, the government can determine the minimum subsidy needed to induce early development. The analysis will also provide a valuable measure of the cost of the distortion, so that policy makers can decide whether it was an effective way of developing jobs or achieving other social goals.

Cortazar & Schwartz [1993] model a firm as a two-stage production process in which the first stage has a bottleneck or maximum capacity constraint, and the second stage has no capacity constraint. Each stage has a constant unit production cost, and the only source of uncertainty is the unit selling price of output from the second stage, which follows a log-normal process. There is no cost of starting or stopping production. In this situation, production decisions are either all or nothing. If production is optimal at the second stage, all of the available output (including inventory) from the first stage is immediately processed, since there is no production constraint. Otherwise, nothing is processed. Similarly, at the first stage it is optimal to either produce nothing (the lower bound) or at capacity (the upper bound). The second stage provides a speculative opportunity to accumulate inventory, which is a perpetual option to sell a unit of commodity in exchange for the fixed production price, which works like an exercise price. The solution is the same as in Section 3.4 for the perpetual American call option on a log-normal asset. The first stage of production involves the production of these second-stage options. They find that it may be possible to have any of the following three situations:

1. the operation is closed, with no first- or second-stage production,
2. first-stage production occurs with inventory accumulation because no second-stage production occurs, or
3. both first- and second-stage production occurs, at a capacity constrained by the first-stage bottleneck.

They find that the model has some interesting properties. First, it is optimal to operate first-stage production at prices below marginal first-stage cost, because of the value of acquiring the speculative inventory option. Similarly, the optimal perpetual-option exercise decision means that the firm should wait until price substantially exceeds marginal second-stage cost before commencing second-stage production. Second, an increase in the risk-free interest rate or in the commodity price volatility[43] increases the value of the firm, and it also induces more first-stage output and less second-stage output. With sufficiently high interest rates and volatility, it is optimal to accumulate speculative inventories. Thus, optimal response to external economic variables is complex.

4.2.4. *Option to use excess capacity*

The traditional approach to assessing the opportunity cost of using excess capacity is the equivalent annual cost (EAC) method. The EAC is the annual rental payment that has the same present value as the capital cost of an asset. Suppose a capital asset is projected to have sufficient capacity to support the current (status quo) operations until year T, and suppose that a new project will use some of that excess capacity to the extent that it is expected that a new capital asset will be needed in year $t < T$. Then, the EAC approach charges to the project the opportunity cost of EAC for each of years $t, t+1, \ldots, T$.

By reviewing the rhetoric of the previous explanation of the EAC approach, we can see that the calculation requires a forecast of the starting and ending years of the period of binding capacity arising from the new project. But, these forecasts are subject to revision and the firm does not really have to make a decision until some time in the future. Thus, the EAC method overstates opportunity cost to the extent that it misses the flexibility option in determining years t and T. Moreover, the existing projects could be temporarily shut down, in the sense of the

[43] In their model, interest rates and volatilities are nonstochastic. Thus, a change in these variables would have to be a once-and-for-all surprise shock to the economy. In general, both of these variables are stochastic, and a full treatment would require combining the stochastic interest rate model of Ingersoll–Ross in Section 4.1 with a model of stochastic commodity prices and volatility.

production options discussed in the previous section. It may be that the capacity is not needed if it is optimal to not operate some of the current status quo projects in some of the future years in which capacity was thought to be binding. Again, the EAC method ignores this flexibility option and tends to overstate opportunity cost.

McLaughlin & Taggart [1992] suggest calculating the opportunity cost of using excess capacity with the formula

$$\text{Opportunity cost} = \sum_{\tau=0}^{T} W_\tau + I_T - I_0, \tag{119}$$

where W_τ is the value of a European option to produce the status-quo products in year τ with the equipment, I_T is the value of the option to invest the capital in T, and I_0 is the value of the option to invest the capital immediately. Using this approach, they assess the value of the opportunity cost of using excess capacity in a variety of situations, and find that the EAC method does generally overstate the true opportunity cost by understating the value of flexibility, which mitigates cost.

In more general situations, investing in a project now creates and destroys future investment options, and these options all interact with each other as discussed in Trigeorgis [1992]. Thus, the value of the portfolio of these options may not always be a simple sum of option values, as in (119).

4.2.5. Real options and industrial organization

While the fundamental risk that creates a real option is typically exogenous, other firms besides those of the analyst may also be responding optimally to this risk. They may be adopting projects that compete with or are synergistic to those of the analyst's firm. The analyst's firm may have market power, so that adopting a project affects the profitability of projects for the other firms. Baldwin [1982], McDonald & Siegel [1986], Dixit & Pindyck [1994] and Trigeorgis [1995] discuss various aspects of these oligopolistic and game-theoretic models.

5. Concluding remarks

In this paper we have summarized the basic techniques and ideas of real options analysis, as it extends the capital budgeting literature beyond the discounted cash flow technique. We reviewed the basic techniques in asset pricing, with a focus on the risk-neutral martingale and generalized CAPM approaches. These techniques are based on very broad economic principles, and are likely to stand the test of time. The only debate will concern the fine details of the market pricing factors or determination of an appropriate martingale measure. Little emphasis was placed on arbitrage analysis, because real assets often cannot be traded or sold short, as in financial option analysis. Indeed a real option can derive risk from an economic variable such as an interest rate that does not correspond to an asset price. We have also advocated discounting the certainty-equivalents in real options by a tax-adjusted riskless bond return.

We have studied real options from both a continuous-time-and-space approach, as well as from a discrete-time-and-space approach. Both approaches are useful and compatible with each other. The continuous-time approach is useful for modelling stochastic processes and for obtaining analytic solutions to option valuation problems in special limiting cases. It is based on a fundamental partial differential equation for the option value, coupled with boundary conditions that describe exercise payoffs amongst other things. An important boundary condition is the high-contact condition that characterizes optimal exercise or development policy. We applied these techniques to present the classic solution to the perpetual real American call option to develop an underlying project that has a log-normally distributed value.

We advocate an economic approach to option valuation that involves inferring price and convenience dividend information from futures markets by pricing futures contracts for common stochastic processes for spot prices. We also show how to relate the certainty-equivalents of futures markets to the expected cash flows and risk-adjustment techniques that are commonly used in discounted-cash-flow analysis. This imposes an extra consistency requirement that improves the quality of value estimates even for discounted cash-flow analysis.

The discrete-time approach is useful for analyzing finite-lived options or when the stochastic process has special characteristics such as mean reversion that make analytic solutions impossible to find. We have shown how to determine discrete processes (with a lattice or tree-like time and space structure) that approximate the economic characteristics of the continuous-time processes.

We concluded with a discussion of various real option models. The first model was of interest-rate uncertainty, which shows how the underlying economic variable need not be the price of a traded asset. In this model, the unusual (by classical economic standards) result can obtain in which a reduction in interest rates can deter rather than encourage the adoption of projects. A series of examples from the literature were then discussed of applications of real options analysis in the real estate and mineral industries. Real options can be used to analyze abandonment decisions, production decisions and to determine the opportunity cost of excess capacity.

Real options analysis will become a standard tool of capital budgeting analysis over the next one or two decades. Firms that ignore it will be missing out on value-creating opportunities. Moreover, they will find themselves trading these opportunities through asset restructuring with firms that do know their true value. The knowledgeable firms will use real options analysis to acquire undervalued assets and divest over-valued assets. The other side of these trades will be taken by firms that ignore real options analysis, and which will slowly but surely shrink in value.

Acknowledgements

The author gratefully acknowledges the research support of the Social Sciences and Humanities Research Council of Canada. Helpful comments have been provided by James Burns, and by participants in workshops at University of Connecticut and Baruch College.

References

Amin, K. (1991). On the computation of continuous time option prices using discrete approximations. *J. Financ. Quant. Anal.* 26, 477–495.

Baldwin, C. (1982). Optimal sequential investment when capital is not readily reversible. *J. Finance* 37, 763–782.

Banz, R., and M. Miller (1978). Prices for state-contingent claims: Some estimates and applications. *J. Bus.* 51, 653-672.

Bjerksund, P., and S. Ekern (1990). Managing investment opportunities under price uncertainty: From 'last chance' to 'wait and see' strategies. *Financ. Manage.* 19, 65–83.

Black, F., and M. Scholes. (1973). The pricing of options and corporate liabiities. *J. Polit. Econ.* 81, 637–659.

Boyle, P., J. Evnine and S. Gibbs (1989). Numerical evaluation of multivaríate contingent claims. *Rev. Financ. Studies* 2, 241–250.

Brealey, R.A., and S.C. Myers (1991). *Principles of Corporate Finance*, 4th edition, McGraw-Hill, New York, NY.

Breeden, D. (1979). An intertemporal asset pricing model with stochastic consumption and investment opportunities. *J. Financ. Econ.* 7, 295–296.

Breeden, D., M. Gibbons and R. Litzenberger (1989). Empirical tests of the consumption-oriented CAPM. *J. Finance* 44, 231–262.

Breeden, D., and R. Litzenberger (1978). Prices of state-contingent claims implicit in option prices. *J. Bus.* 51, 621–651.

Brennan, M., and E. Schwartz (1978). Finite difference methods and jump processes arising in the pricing of contingent claims: A synthesis. *J. Financ. Quant. Anal.* 13, 461–474.

Brennan, M. and E. Schwartz (1985). Evaluating natural resource investments. *J. Bus.* 58, 135–158.

Capozza, D., and Y. Li (1994). The intensity and timing of investment: The case of land. *Am. Econ. Rev.* September.

Capozza, D., and G. Sick (1991). Valuing long-term leases: The option to redevelop. *J. Real Estate Finance Econ.* 4, 209–223.

Capozza, D., and G. Sick (1994). The risk structure of land markets. *J. Urban Econ.* 35, 297–319.

Carr, P., and R. Jarrow (1995). A discrete time synthesis of derivative security valuation using a term structure of futures prices, in: R. Jarrow, V. Maksimovic and W.T. Ziemba (eds.). *Finance*, Handbooks in Operations Research and Management Science, Vol. 9, North-Holland, Amsterdam, pp. 225–250 (this volume).

Cortazar, G., and E.S. Schwartz (1993). A compound option model of production and intermediate inventories. *J. Bus.* 66, 517–540.

Cox, J.C., J.E. Ingersoll and S.A. Ross (1981). The relation between forward prices and futures prices. *J. Financ. Econ.* 9, 321–346.

Cox, J.C., J.E. Ingersoll and S.A. Ross (1985a). An intertemporal general equilibrium model of asset prices. *Econometrica* 53, 363–384.

Cox, J.C., J.E. Ingersoll and S.A. Ross (1985b). A theory of the term structure of interest rates. *Econometrica* 53, 385–407.

Cox, J.C., and S.A. Ross (1976). The valuation of options for alternative stochastic processes. *J. Financ. Econ.* 3, 145–166.

Cox, J.C., S.A. Ross and M. Rubinstein (1979). Option pricing: A simplified approach. *J. Financ. Econ.* 7, 229–263.

Dixit, A. and R. Pindyck (1994). *Investment underuncertainty*, Princeton University Press, Princeton, NJ.

Fama, E. (1977). Risk-adjusted discount rates and capital budgeting under uncertainty. *J. Financ. Econ.* 5, 3–24.

Garbade, K. (1993). A two-factor, arbitrage-free, model of fluctuations in crude oil futures prices. *J. Derivatives* 1(1), 86–97.

Gibson, R., and E.S. Schwartz (1990). Stochastic convenience yield and the pricing of oil contingent claims. *J. Finance* 45, 959–976.

Harrison, J.M., and D.M. Kreps (1979). Martingales and arbitrage in multiperiod securities markets. *J. Econ. Theory* 20, 381–408.

Harrison, J.M., and S.R. Pliska (1981). Martingales and stochastic integrals in the theory of continuous trading. *Stoch. Processes Appl.* 11, 215–260.

He, H. (1990). Convergence from discrete- to continuous-time contingent claims prices. *Rev. Financ. Studies* 3, 523–546.

Hotelling, H. (1931). The economics of exhaustible resources. *J. Polit. Econ.* 39, 137–75.

Hull, J. and A. White (1988). The use of the control variate techniquein option pricing. *J. Financ. Quant. Anal.* 23, 237–251.

Ingersoll, J.E., Jr. (1987). *Theory of Financial Decision Making*, Rowman & Littlefield, Totowa, NJ.

Ingersoll, J.E., Jr., and S.A. Ross (1992). Waiting to invest: Investment and uncertainty. *J. Bus.* 65, 1–29.

Jarrow, R. (1988). *Finance Theory*, Prentice-Hall, Englewood Cliffs, NJ.

Jarrow, R.A. and G.S. Oldfield (1981). Forward contracts and futures contracts. *J. Financ. Econ.* 9, 373–382.

Laughton, D.G., and H.D. Jacoby (1991). A two-method solution to the investment timing option, *Adv. Futures Options Res.* 5, 71–87.

Laughton, D.G., and H.D. Jacoby (1993). Reversion, timing options and long-term decision-making, *Financ. Manag.* 22, 225–240.

Madan, D., F. Milne and H. Shefrin (1989). The multinomial option pricing model and its Brownian and Poisson limits. *Rev. Financ. Studies* 2, 251–265.

Margrabe, W. (1978). The value of an option to exchange one asset for another, *J. Finance* 33, 177 –186.

Mason, S.P. and C.Y. Baldwin (1988). Evaluation of government subsidies to large-scale energy projects: A contingent claims approach. *Adv. Futures Options Res.* 3, 169–181.

McDonald, R., and D. Siegel (1985). Investment and the valuation of firms when there is an option to shut down. *Int. Econ. Rev.* 6, 331–349.

McDonald, R., and D. Siegel (1986). The value of waiting to invest, *Q. J. Econ.* 101, 707–727.

McLaughlin, R., and R. Taggart (1992). The opportunity cost of excess capacity. *Financ. Manage.* 20, 8–20.

Merton, R.C. (1973). Theory of rational option pricing. *Bell J. Econ. Manage.* 4, 141–83.

Miller, M. (1977). Debt and taxes. *J. Finance* 32, 261–275.

Miller, M., and C. Upton (1985a). A test of the Hotelling valuation principle. *J. Polit. Econ.* 93, 1–25.

Miller, M., and C. Upton (1985b). The pricing of oil and gas: some further results. *J. Finance* 40, 1009–1018.

Myers, S., and S. Turnbull (1977). Capital budgeting and the capital asset pricing model: good news and bad news. *J. Finance* 32, 321–333.

Nelson, D., and K. Ramaswamy (1990). Simple binomial processes as diffusion approximations in financial models, *Rev. Financ. Studies* 3, 393–430.

Nichols, N.A. (1994). Scientific management at Merck: An interview with CFO Judy Lewent. *Harvard Bus. Rev.* January, 89–99.

Paddock, J., D. Siegel and J. Smith (1988). Option valuation of claims on real assets: The case of offshore petroleum leases. *Q. J. Econ.* 103, 479–508.

Pindyck, R. (1991). Irreversibility, uncertainty, and investment. *J. Econ. Lit.* 29, 1110–1148.

Richard, S.F., and M. Sundaresan (1981). A continuous time equilibrium model of forward prices and future prices in a multigood economy. *J. Financ. Econ.* 9, 347–371.

Ross, S.A. (1989). Information and volatility: The no-arbitrage martingale approch to timing an resolution irrelevancy. *J. Finance* 44, 1–17.

Ross, S.A., R. Westerfield and J. Jaffe (1993). *Corporate Finance*, 3rd edition, Richard D. Irwin, Burr Ridge, IL.

Schwartz, E.S. (1977). The valuation of warrants: Implementing a new approach. *J. Financ. Econ.* 4, 79–93.

Sick, G.A. (1986). A certainty-equivalent approach to capital budgeting. *Financ. Manag.* 15(4), 23–32.

Sick, G.A. (1989a). Multiperiod risky project valuation: A mean–covariance certainty-equivalent approach. *Adv. Financ. Planning Forecasting* 3, 1–36.

Sick, G.A. (1989b). Capital budgeting with real options, monograph 1989-3, Salomon Brothers Center for the Study of Financial Institutions, Leonard N. Stern School of Business, New York University.

Sick, G.A. (1990). Tax-adjusted discount rates. *Manage. Sci.* 36, 1432–1450.

Taggart, R.A. (1991). Consistent valuation and cost of capital with corporate and personal taxes. *Financ. Manage.* 20, 8–20.

Trigeorgis, L. (1992). The nature of option interactions and the valuation of investments with multiple real options. *J. Financ. Quant. Anal.* 25, 1–20.

Trigeorgis, L. (1995). *Options in Capital Budgeting: Managerial Flexibility and Strategy in Resource Allocation*, MIT Press, Cambridge, MA.

Williams, J. (1991). Real estate development as an option. *J. Real Estate Finance Econ.* 4, 191–208.

R. Jarrow et al., Eds., *Handbooks in OR & MS, Vol. 9*

Chapter 22

Corporate Financial Structure, Incentives and Optimal Contracting

Franklin Allen
Wharton School, University of Pennsylvania, Philadelphia, PA 19104, U.S.A.

Andrew Winton
J.L. Kellogg School of Management, Northwestern University, Evanston, IL 60208-2006, U.S.A.

1. Introduction

The dominant paradigm in modern corporate finance views the firm as a nexus of contracts between various economic agents, particularly managers and investors. Beginning with Jensen & Meckling [1976], an ever-increasing volume of papers has addressed optimal corporate financial structure within this basic framework. These papers can be divided into two groups: those (*security design*) which derive optimal financial contracts as optimal mechanisms for overcoming various frictions between agents, and those (*capital structure*) which take certain contracts such as debt and equity as given and analyze the optimal mix of these contracts that firms should issue — again, in the face of frictions between agents.

Although our survey focuses on the design of optimal financial contracts,[1] the distinction between the two groups is not always clear-cut: some papers on security design make assumptions which immediately guarantee the use of specific contract types, while some papers on capital structure model the optimal choice of specific features of debt or equity securities. We have tended to err on the side of inclusion rather than exclusion. Nonetheless, a large literature on optimal capital structure is excluded; these papers are covered in other chapters of this handbook and in other recent surveys [Harris & Raviv, 1991, and Hart, 1991].[2]

We have divided our survey into five sections by topic. These include costly state verification and agency, when investors find it costly or impossible to verify or contractually control certain outcomes and actions relating to the firm; adverse selection, when investors cannot identify certain innate characteristics of the firm

[1] The early work on asymmetric information and incentives from which this literature developed is surveyed in Ross [1978].

[2] More recently, Harris & Raviv [1992] links the optimal financial contracting literature surveyed here and the optimal capital structure literature surveyed in their 1991 paper.

or manager; the allocation of control and ownership rights among investors; the allocation of risk between different types of investors; and the acquisition of information.

2. Costly state verification and agency

The models in this section assume that investors find it costly or impossible to verify ex-post features of firms such as output or managerial actions. Borrowers can make an announcement about the features in question, and the contract's terms are based on this announcement. In equilibrium, the contracts must be incentive compatible — that is, borrowers act as investors expect them to act. Since these models are typically partial equilibrium in nature, one agent (usually the borrower) maximizes his or her return subject to incentive compatibility and reservation return constraints for other agents (usually investors). Papers almost invariably assume that the utility of consumption is separable from the disutility of any direct costs of verification.

In models of costly state verification, the characteristic which cannot be freely observed is the borrower's income or return. Early work in this area focuses on contracting between a single investor and borrower within a single period, when one or both parties are risk neutral. Recent work has generalized this in two ways. The first involves broadening technical assumptions: allowing for more general preferences, contracting over multiple periods, and so forth. The second set of papers looks at changing the underlying asymmetry to better reflect institutional features of large modern firms which restrict management's ability to appropriate returns. We address each of these areas in turn.

Townsend [1979] is the first paper to use the costly state verification framework. There are two agents, one risk averse but endowed with risky income, the second risk neutral with constant income. The agents would like to enter into a risk-sharing agreement, but the first agent's income is costly to verify. Assuming that verification must be a deterministic function of announcements by the first agent, and that the cost of verification is constant, Townsend shows that an optimal incentive compatible contract will have the following features: income is verified whenever reported income is below a certain level, payments to the second agent are constant when income is not verified, and payments are strictly lower than this constant when income is verified.[3]

If the contracting situation is viewed as a loan to a risky borrower, this implies

[3] The intuition for these results is as follows. Suppose that income of y is verified, but income of x is not. If payments from the first agent to the second in state y exceed those in state x, the first agent would never report y. Similarly, if both x and y were unverified, and payments in y were higher than those in x, the first agent would never report y. Thus verified payments are lower than unverified payments, and unverified payments are effectively constant. Because the first agent is risk averse, he prefers to make the lowest payments in those regions where his marginal utility is highest — that is, where his income is lowest. Thus verified (low) payments are optimally made when the first agent's income is low.

that the optimal contract has some of the features of debt. In fact, if both agents are risk neutral, Gale & Hellwig [1985] prove that the optimal contract gives all of the borrower's income to the lender whenever this income does not exceed the fixed (nonverified) payment; this is precisely the arrangement specified by a simple single period debt contract. They also show that, whenever there is a chance of default, there will be less borrowing and investment than there would be with symmetric information.

Diamond [1984] also derives debt as the optimal borrowing contract, but with a somewhat different approach. In his model, agents are risk neutral and borrower returns are unobservable, but lenders can inflict potentially unlimited nonpecuniary penalties on the borrower. The optimal contract is debt, enforced by penalties which impose disutility equal to the amount by which the borrower's payment falls short of the debt's face value. While this view of debt contracts seems most applicable to early Victorian Britain with its debtors' prisons, the model has been generalized by Lacker [1990]. He shows that, for certain restrictions on utility functions,[4] a risky borrower with a good that always has higher marginal utility to her than to the lender will find it optimal to borrow under a debt contract collateralized by this good. Debt is optimal because it minimizes the expected amount of good transferred, which is a deadweight loss under the model's assumptions. In Diamond's model, the 'collateral' takes the form of the borrower's freedom from pain and suffering, which has no value to the lender; other examples include home mortgages, car loans, or loans backed by a new business' assets, where individual tastes, lemons market effects, or specialized managerial skills may make the collateral more valuable to the borrower than to the lender.

While these models motivate the use of debt-like contracts, they use a number of simplifying technical assumptions: risk neutrality, single period contracting with one investor, deterministic verification, and one type of borrower. In reality, people exhibit risk averse behavior, firms typically exist for many years and borrow from multiple investors, agents may be able to randomize their decision of whether or not to verify and there are many different types of borrowers; in addition, returns may be observable yet difficult to verify in court. We now turn to papers that allow for these complications.

Krasa & Villamil [1994] and Winton [1995] examine the impact of more general preferences. Both papers show that Townsend's results extend to the case where both agents are risk averse: basically, for any distribution of payments to the lender, the borrower still prefers to make the lowest (verified) payments in states where the borrower's income is lowest. Krasa and Villamil show that this also holds for contracting with multilateral information asymmetries and costly public state verification.

Chang [1990] addresses multi-period contracts in a setting where a firm produces independent returns in each of two periods. Assuming that the firm only borrows once and is not allowed to make interim dividend distributions to its

[4] Risk neutrality satisfies the restrictions on the utility function.

owner, the optimal contract has some resemblance to a bond with interim coupon or sinking fund payment and final principal repayment; in addition, the borrower may have the option to call part of the bond in the first period at a fixed price. Verification will only occur when the fixed (coupon or sinking fund) payment is missed in the first period, or when the final payment is missed in the last period. Although allowing additional borrowing or interim dividend payments would change these results, the firm would prefer to precommit to avoiding these actions.[5] In fact, debt contracts commonly include covenants which restrict both borrowing and dividends.

Mookherjee & Png [1989] and Krasa & Villamil [1994] both address contracting when stochastic verification is feasible. The first paper observes that, if penalties for lying can be imposed, verifying with certainty is generally not optimal: in equilibrium, the borrower wouldn't lie at all, and so the lender can verify less often. While risk aversion on the borrower's part will typically lead to a contract in which borrower consumption doesn't always increase with returns (Winton [1995] shows this is true even with deterministic verification), Krasa & Villamil show that payments to the *lender* will weakly increase with returns. These authors also prove that the probability of verification weakly decreases with reported returns. Thus, with randomized verification, optimal contracts look much less like simple debt, but still retain a certain amount of monotonicity. Whether randomized verification is credible in actual financial contracts remains an open question.

If more than one investor is needed to fund the borrower's project, and verification is private information, use of a symmetric debt-like contract will result in duplication of monitoring effort. This has been used by Diamond [1984] and Williamson [1986] to obtain the optimality of well-diversified financial intermediaries when all agents are risk neutral and borrowers' projects are stochastically independent of one another. However, these results assume that there are no diseconomies of scale — one lender can monitor large numbers of loans at constant marginal cost. To the extent this isn't the case, investors (institutional or otherwise) may optimally have imperfectly diversified portfolios, and multiple lenders may lend to the same borrower.

Analyzing the case where several investors lend directly to the same borrower, Winton [1995] shows that the borrower prefers issuing debt-like contracts with varying degrees of seniority rather than symmetric debt-like contracts. In the case where investors are risk neutral, priority among investors of different seniority is absolute — that is, more junior investors receive nothing until more senior investors are paid in full. This corresponds with actual practice, in which the absolute priority rule is the basic standard and firms issue securities with multiple levels of seniority — senior debt, subordinated debt, or preferred stock. The intuition for the result is that, when investors are risk neutral, reducing total verification costs is paramount. By giving senior investors their fixed (unverified)

[5] If dividends cannot be restricted ex ante, the optimal contract has a similar form, but with a more complicated call price. Chang does not explicitly analyze the optimal contract that results when interim borrowing is allowed.

payment as often as possible, their verification costs are made as small as possible.[6]

Boyd & Smith [1993] consider the case where borrower return distributions are completely unobservable, so that there is adverse selection as well as costly state verification. Provided verification costs are positive, debt is an optimal contract. Credit rationing where loans are granted randomly allows good borrowers to separate from bad ones. To see this, consider a pooling contract which breaks even: good borrowers effectively subsidize bad ones. A decrease in the interest rate benefits good borrowers relatively more, because bad borrowers have more chance of defaulting and losing any benefit from a lower interest rate. Thus, in order to obtain a lower interest rate, good borrowers are more willing to endure random rationing than are bad borrowers. In the separating equilibrium, good borrowers face credit rationing but pay a lower interest rate than bad borrowers, who are always granted loans.

Hart & Moore [1989] consider a problem which is somewhat different from the usual costly state verification setting. An entrepreneur wishes to raise funds to undertake a project when contracting possibilities are incomplete: both the entrepreneur and the outside investor can observe the project payoffs at each date, but they cannot write contracts based on these payoffs because third parties such as courts cannot observe them. The focus of Hart & Moore's analysis is the problem of providing an incentive for the entrepreneur to repay the borrowed funds. Among other things, it is shown that the optimal contract is a debt contract and incentives to repay are provided by the ability of the creditor to seize the entrepreneur's assets.

Lacker [1989] pursues a more complex form of this problem. As in Hart & Moore [1989], returns are observable to both borrower and lender (sometimes the lender incurs a cost), but now contracts based on returns can be enforced in a court of law — at a cost. He shows that optimal contracts resemble debt so long as enforcement is used deterministically; however, as in the costly state verification literature, mixed strategies may dominate deterministic contracts.

Thus, relaxing the technical assumptions of the basic costly state verification model leads to optimal contracts which still have certain features in common with real debt or debt-like securities: fixed maximum payments, interim coupon payments, multiple levels of seniority, and credit rationing. Nevertheless, the application of these models to modern corporations is still open to question: all assume the firm is effectively owned by a single insider, who can costlessly lie and appropriate all of the firm's returns if verification does not occur. Although this may be appropriate for closely-held firms, many corporations in the United States actually issue equity to large numbers of outside investors, most of whom cannot be thought of as insiders in any sense. To some extent, this difficulty is caused by the single period assumed in much of the analysis: if the firm operates over multiple periods,

[6] The model also offers an explanation for why managers (as employees) become general creditors of the corporation for any unpaid salary when it enters into bankruptcy: when investors are risk neutral and the manager is risk averse, it is generally optimal to give the manager some compensation in states where junior investors receive nothing.

excessive managerial consumption might affect future returns, leading to eventual discovery and penalties. In addition, accounting systems and outside auditors are used to control such behavior. Several papers have attempted to incorporate some of these institutional features into the design of optimal financial contracts.

Lacker & Weinberg [1989] develop a model in which the borrower can only falsify reported earnings at a cost which increases in the amount of the discrepancy, reflecting costs of physical concealment, keeping two sets of books, and so forth. If it is required that no falsification occur, optimal contracts look like outside equity for the investors, and a combination of fixed salary plus equity for the borrower. The falsification cost places an upper bound on the rate at which the borrower's compensation can increase with reported income, since steeper increases would make lying profitable; thus, the lenders' claim increases with reported earnings. The authors show that, under certain conditions on the cost of falsification, contracts that are optimal under the requirement of no falsification are optimal over all incentive compatible contracts.

In Chang [1993], a firm exists for two periods. After first period output is realized, it is optimal for a random fraction of output to be reinvested in the firm, with the remainder paid out to investors. The manager observes the optimal payout while investors do not. If the payout is less than this optimal amount, the difference is diverted into projects which yield the manager some utility but give below average returns to investors in the second period. The manager reports the optimal payout level, which results in an interim payment to investors and to herself by contract. In the absence of a bankruptcy mechanism, optimal incentive compatible contracts resemble equity with dividends — the interim payments to both the manager and the investors increase in reported optimal payout, and there is corporate slack invested in inefficient projects. Chang defines the bankruptcy mechanism as a costly liquidation of the firm which deprives the manager of her utility from corporate slack. Once contracts are allowed to include this mechanism, the optimal contract resembles debt plus the equity contract described previously.

A related body of work adopts principal-agent theory to financial contracting between an investor and the manager of a firm. In classic models of this sort, firm output is observable, but its distribution or realization is influenced by the manager's effort, which is hidden. In the absence of limited liability constraints or risk aversion, the first-best solution is to give the manager the entire risk of the project; the investor gets a fixed payment, and the manager maximizes the return from the project because it all accrues to her [see Harris & Raviv, 1979]. Thus the manager's position corresponds to unlimited liability equity, while that of the investor corresponds to riskless debt.

Since the manager's wealth is usually limited, a more realistic model is that of Innes [1990].[7] Here the manager's costly effort improves the distribution of firm

[7] Yet another difficulty with the Harris & Raviv model is that it assumes the manager is risk neutral. However, the presence of risk aversion complicates principal-agent models considerably [see for example Grossman & Hart, 1983]; not surprisingly, there has been little work applying results from this literature to optimal financial contracting.

returns according to the monotone likelihood ratio property of Milgrom [1981], but the manager has no wealth and his effort cannot be observed by the investor. If the investor's compensation is constrained to be monotone increasing in firm returns, the optimal contract will in fact be debt; however, without monotonicity, optimal contracts have a 'live or die' form that gives the manager the firm's entire output when firm returns are equal to or above a given level, and nothing otherwise.[8]

Innes defends monotonicity by showing that it is necessary when either the investor can sabotage the firm ex post or the manager can borrow risklessly on the side and merge the amount raised with the firm's output. Both situations seem somewhat unlikely. A more plausible approach is that of Dionne & Viala [1992], who combine unobservable managerial effort with costly return verification. Although monotonicity is not always an optimal outcome, sufficiently high verification costs do make the standard debt contract of Gale & Hellwig [1985] optimal.

In a setting similar to that of Innes, Chiesa [1992] investigates the effect of having a random state of nature determined before the effort decision is made. She shows that standard debt is not optimal; instead a debt contract with warrants for the lender and cash/equity settlement options for the borrower is optimal. This contract shifts payments on the debt to the good states and helps provide incentives to supply effort when the state of nature turns out to be bad. Under a standard debt contract the borrower would have little incentive to provide effort in bad states because the bondholder would receive most of the benefits.

Hart & Moore [1991] also consider the funding of an entrepreneurial firm, but focus more explicitly on the importance of the entrepreneur's skills in a dynamic setting. There is no uncertainty, and contracting possibilities are complete except that the entrepreneur cannot precommit to stay with the firm; she can always leave and withdraw her human capital. In an optimal contract, the investor lends a sum of money to finance the project, and the entrepreneur promises a series of payments in return. If a payment is made, the entrepreneur has the right to keep using the project's assets for another period; if a payment is missed, the lender obtains control and can liquidate the project. The entrepreneur's threat of leaving limits the payments, since she can threaten to leave if a payment is too high. As a result, some projects which would be undertaken in an ideal world are not undertaken here. As the project's assets become more durable or its cash flows come later, debt payments are pushed further into the future. These results correspond to practitioners' maxims 'lend long if the loan is supported by durable collateral' and 'match assets with liabilities'.

As with costly state verification, most agency models have focused on entrepreneurial firms. The next two papers investigate optimal solutions to agency problems in an institutional setting closer to that of a large corporation.

Williams [1989] investigates optimal contracting when the firm's output and the managerial effort that influences the distribution of output are both unobservable.

[8] The intuition is that, by being given everything in high output states and nothing in low output states, the manager has the greatest incentives to try to ensure high output and avoid low output.

'Ex-ante monitoring systems' (e.g., accounting controls, or security for debt) are assumed to prevent the manager from consuming the firm's output, but they do not reveal its true level. The manager announces current earnings and makes a distribution as per contract; residual claimants then receive the remaining value of the firm. Williams assumes investors are effectively risk neutral, and that the firm's value is revealed at some point in the future.[9] In this setting, optimal contracts resemble combinations of equity and up to three classes of debt. Williams' results do not require any special assumptions about the way in which the manager can affect the distribution of returns, although special cases lead to the use of fewer securities.

Although Hart & Moore [1990] take the use of debt contracts as given, they provide insight into how differential seniority can control managerial agency problems. In this model, managers wish to expand their firms so as to increase their power; as a result, they are willing to undertake projects with negative net present value as well as those with positive net present value. It is not possible for outsiders to observe whether or not a project is profitable ex ante, so managers' actions cannot be controlled directly by contract. Nevertheless, managers can be controlled indirectly by choosing an appropriate seniority structure. If a firm has outstanding senior debt, it will be unable to raise new funds unless its prospects are good because the senior debtholders have a prior claim to the output from any new investment. An optimal debt structure ensures that the firm can only obtain financing when prospects are good enough for new projects to have a positive NPV.

3. Adverse selection

While the previous section focused on models where investors could not freely observe the borrower's efforts or results ex post, models of adverse selection typically assume that the asymmetry involves innate characteristics of the borrower; that is, the asymmetry involves ex-ante information. Now the focus is on contracts that borrowers can use as credible signals of their type.[10] Since signalling models typically produce a multiplicity of equilibria, many of the models surveyed here attempt to narrow down the number of equilibria through the refinements of

[9] Strictly speaking, he assumes markets are complete, and cash flows are measured in state-contingent price terms. However, complete markets are incompatible with a firm-specific agency problem.

[10] In certain cases, adverse selection and moral hazard can produce observationally equivalent results. Hagerty & Siegel [1988] discuss this in the context of a managerial compensation setting. Their equivalence result requires that, just as the moral hazard setting assumes more effort is more costly, the adverse selection setting must assume that the manager's reservation wage increases in her ability. In other words, the manager has some method of capturing her ability's value outside of the firm, perhaps by starting a company of her own. Since most models in this section implicitly assume that different types of borrowers have the same reservation return, they will not meet this requirement.

sequentiality now standard in the signalling literature. This has been a particular focus of models seeking to use adverse selection to explain noncontingent financial contracts.[11]

Standard contract theory suggests that optimal contracts should be contingent on all relevant information, which generally implies they will be extremely complex [see Hart & Holmstrom, 1987]. However, an important feature of many existing financial contracts is that they are not contingent on easily available information which would appear to be relevant. For example, standard debt contracts are not contingent on the firm's earnings; this appears to be inconsistent with optimal risk sharing, which requires that borrowers and lenders have equal marginal rates of substitution between states. Although there are forms of debt such as income bonds where payments are contingent on the accounting earnings of the firm, these are rarely used. The next three papers show that, with adverse selection and certain refinements on beliefs, noncontingent securities like standard debt are optimal.

Allen & Gale [1992] develop a model where adverse selection interacts with measurement distortion and this leads to noncontingent securities being used. In practice, securities cannot be made contingent on 'states of nature'. Some type of measurement system such as an accounting system is necessary to generate the variables such as earnings that payoffs are contingent on. These measurement systems can be distorted at some cost by firms if they have sufficient incentive to do so. Allen and Gale argue that a case of interest is where the cost of distorting the measurement system is positively correlated with firm type so good firms have a high cost of distortion and bad firms have a low cost. In this case bad firms are more likely to offer securities such as income bonds where payments are contingent on earnings since the net benefits of distorting are greater for bad firms. The equilibrium where all firms offer a noncontingent contract is then Universally Divine [Banks & Sobel, 1987] since investors deduce that any firm offering a contingent contract is likely to be bad since they gain the most from the contingency.

Nachman & Noe [1994] consider a model where a firm issues a security to investors in order to undertake an investment which generates an uncertain output. The probability distribution of output depends on whether the firm is good or bad which is known to the firm but not to investors. A good firm's output conditionally stochastically dominates that of a bad firm. It is assumed that the security is monotonic in the sense that the payment to investors is nondecreasing in the firm's earnings. A good firm would like to signal its type by reducing the payment it makes when output is high and increasing it when output is low. Firms pool at a debt contract in the equilibrium which is stable according to the D1 version of Universal Divinity discussed by Cho & Kreps [1987]. A good firm cannot try to separate itself by increasing payments in low output states since this would violate feasibility or by reducing payments in the high output states since

[11] A related area concerns the role of reputation in financial contracting. For recent contributions in this area see Diamond [1989, 1991a] and Boot, Greenbaum & Thakor [1993].

this would violate monotonicity. The equilibrium contract is thus noncontingent in the sense that the payment is equal to a constant except when there are insufficient earnings to pay this amount.

In a related paper, De & Kale [1993] assume that a firm can use some combination of two types of contract, Fixed-Periodic-Obligation Debt (FD) and No-Periodic-Obligation Debt (ND). Standard debt is an example of an FD security and income bonds are an example of an ND security. Having offered the market its securities, they are priced by the market. Investors infer that firms that offer ND contracts are more likely to be bad firms since bad firms benefit more from the low payments if earnings are low. The unique equilibrium that is stable in the sense of Universal Divinity involves only FD being used by firms. As with Nachman & Noe's monotonicity condition, the restriction of contract forms to combinations of FD and ND prevents firms from signalling their type.

In a somewhat different vein, Ravid & Spiegel [1992] develop a theory of why small firms use debt and equity which combines adverse selection and agency concerns. They assume the number of entrepreneurs who have positive net present value investment projects is limited. Other entrepreneurs can provide an unlimited number of negative net present value projects if there is an incentive to do so. Given that the type of entrepreneur and quality of projects are unobservable, securities must be designed so there is no such incentive; in many circumstances, an appropriate mix of debt and equity accomplishes this. To see why, suppose initially that projects do not include any collateral. In this case, all financing is in the form of equity, and the entrepreneur is given a share of the equity equal to the proportion of costs he provides; given this structure, the entrepreneur prefers to invest in a risk free asset rather than accept negative net present value investments. When projects have collateral, debt can be used along with equity; the collateral ensures the entrepreneur's interests are aligned with those of shareholders.

Yet another use of adverse selection can be found in Diamond [1991b, 1993], who examines its impact on the choice of seniority and maturity in debt contracts. A manager runs a firm whose chance of success is private information; in addition to any share in the firm's proceeds, he obtains nontransferable rents from controlling the firm throughout its life. A noisy signal of firm type becomes public after initial investment but before output is realized. If the firm is liquidated at this point, it yields a fixed return which is better than the output of a failed firm but less than that of a successful firm; if the firm is liquidated after production, it yields its output. Control rents are high enough that no firm will willingly liquidate at the interim date.

Because cash payments and the signal are observable and output is not, liquidation must be used to enforce payments to investors; thus, optimal contracts resemble debt. Debt can either be short term, in which case it is refinanced at the interim date, or long term. The ability to refinance depends on the market's beliefs about the firm's type, which depend on the signal. Good firms have a better chance of getting a good signal and better refinancing terms, but they must trade this off against the chance of getting a (false) bad signal, being liquidated early, and losing control rents. Bad firms would never be financed if their type was known, so they must imitate the actions of good firms.

Diamond [1991b] focuses on the choice of debt maturity. If the market's prior beliefs are that the firm is very likely to be good, firms optimally issue short-term debt; good firms are reasonably certain of getting refinanced, and wish to take advantage of the chance to distinguish themselves from the bad firms. As this prior decreases, good firms prefer to issue more long-term financing so as to avoid an excessive chance of liquidation. However, if this prior is too low, only short-term debt is feasible: too many firms are likely to be bad to support long-term debt, but short-term debt allows early liquidation and a return independent of firm type.

Diamond [1993] allows the firm to choose debt seniority as well as maturity. It proves to be optimal for short-term debt to be senior, for long-term debt to be junior, and for long-term debt to allow the issue of additional senior short-term debt at the interim date. By allowing short-term debtholders to be refinanced at the expense of long-term debtholders, firms obtain a better price for short-term debt, and the firm is liquidated less often. This makes it cheaper for a good firm to take advantage of the information sensitivity of short-term debt.

As with most agency models, these adverse selection models generally assume that the manager is either the firm's sole owner or (equivalently) acts completely in the shareholders' interests. In this case capital structure choice and dividend policy matter because they affect the value of equity. A well-known example from the capital structure literature is Myers & Majluf [1984], who show that managers who know a firm's existing assets are undervalued are reluctant to use equity to finance new investments. The intuition is that, if equity is used, the eventual release of good information to the public will cause an increase in value which is shared between old and new shareholders. As a result, some profitable investments may be foregone.

Dybvig & Zender [1991] point out that a suitably chosen incentive scheme can avoid inefficiencies arising from asymmetric information. For example, in the Myers & Majluf [1984] model, a managerial compensation scheme which is insensitive to the fact that shareholders must share increases in value with new shareholders eliminates the incentives to forego profitable investments. Dybvig & Zender show that, in a wide range of circumstances where managers are better informed than investors, capital structure choice and dividend policy are irrelevant provided managerial compensation schemes are not tied to the interests of shareholders but instead are chosen optimally before there is any asymmetric information. This result would seem to rule out the use of adverse selection models to explain financial contracts used at large widely-held corporations.

Persons [1994] shows that Dybvig & Zender's result depends crucially on the absence of renegotiation. Ex post, shareholders and manager have incentive to renegotiate the manager's contract; once they have done so, management's interests are aligned with shareholders, and the adverse selection problems discussed by Myers & Majluf reappear. In addition, share-based compensation contracts are robust to such renegotiation, which may explain why such contracts are commonly used.

4. The allocation of ownership and control among investors

The papers in the previous two sections are primarily concerned with the allocation of cash flows to and among investors so as to resolve conflicts between the investors and the firm's manager. Another strand of the literature has focused on the allocation of ownership and control rights among different investors so as to improve firm performance. The difference between this literature and that on agency/costly state verification is that, where agency/costly state verification focuses mainly on managerial incentives, research on ownership and control focuses on investors' incentives as well.

As in the previous two sections, the starting point for work on control and ownership is the fact that the agents who control the large modern firm on a day-to-day basis (management) tend to be separate from those who own it (investors). In a series of articles, Fama & Jensen [1983a, 1983b, 1985] discuss factors that favor this separation, and use them to motivate a variety of ownership forms. Our survey considers more formal modeling of two general issues: the allocation of ownership and control rights among different securities such as debt and equity, and the structure of ownership (equity) claims per se.

Work on allocation of control among different securities typically focuses on the role of outside debt and equity. The basic role of outside debt in these models is illustrated by Aghion & Bolton [1992], who consider an entrepreneur with limited wealth who has a project that requires funding from outside investors. These outside investors are only interested in the monetary profits they receive whereas the entrepreneur is concerned about the effort required to produce the profits as well as the money he receives. The important feature of Aghion & Bolton's model is that contracting possibilities are incomplete so that the conflict of interests between the entrepreneur and the outside investors cannot be solved by a contract specifying entrepreneurial effort and reward. An efficient allocation of resources is achieved by allocating control appropriately using debt and the institution of bankruptcy. This ensures that when earnings and hence future prospects are good the entrepreneur decides whether or not the increased payoffs from expansion are worth the effort involved. However, when earnings and future prospects are bad the investor makes the liquidation decision and this is not frustrated by the entrepreneur who weights the effort of liquidation too highly.

In Kalay & Zender [1992], an entrepreneur needs additional funding from an outsider. Although the entrepreneur is better informed than the outsider about the cost of exerting effort to improve future firm performance, his limited stake in the firm distorts his incentives to exert effort. Thus, even though the outsider must pay a cost to become fully informed and run the firm, it may be optimal in lower productivity states to give the outsider control of the firm and rights to all future cash flows; this resembles debt with transfer of ownership in bankruptcy. Not surprisingly, the number of states in which the outsider takes control increases with the amount of outside funding required. The authors also show that, when liquidation is possible, different firms may prefer contracts with bankruptcy provisions resembling either chapter 7 or chapter 11; however, unlike reality, the type of bankruptcy is chosen ex ante rather than ex post.

Like the agency/costly state verification literature previously discussed, the last two papers motivate outside debt only. By contrast, Zender [1991] develops a model in which the use of both outside debt and outside equity is optimal. The project to be undertaken requires two investors to provide the financing; individually, neither has sufficient resources. In order for there to be the correct incentives to make the proper decisions efficiently, only one of the investors can be assigned control. One of the investors is therefore given equity and is made the residual claimant while the other receives debt and does not obtain control unless the initial decisions are not made properly and the firm goes bankrupt.

In Berglöf & Von Thadden [1994], the basic problem is that of Hart & Moore [1989]: an entrepreneur cannot commit to making payments to investors, who must rely on the threat of liquidation to obtain redress. An investor who provides long-term financing has a weaker bargaining position if the entrepreneur reneges on payments, since liquidation hurts the investor's position as well as that of the entrepreneur; this raises the firm's ex-ante cost of capital, and may prevent good projects from being undertaken. By contrast, an additional investor with a short-term claim secured by the firm's assets has stronger bargaining position, since the assets' liquidation value may be enough to satisfy his or her claims even if they are insufficient to satisfy all investors. Thus, a capital structure with both short-term secured debt and long-term claims such as debt or equity dominates having a single investor provide all financing.

Aghion, Dewatripont & Rey [1990] consider a model where managers must be given the correct incentives to provide effort. It is not possible to do this with the manager's compensation scheme because the manager has limited financial resources; this restricts the amount the manager can be penalized if the firm does badly. Introducing voting equity allows the correct incentives to the manager to be provided because there is then the possibility of a high payment to the manager (a 'golden parachute') when she exerts effort so the firm is valuable and is taken over. If the manager has private benefits of control, debt also enhances incentives: if the firm does badly, control is transferred to debtholders, eliminating the manager's private benefit — which gives the manager incentive to exert effort in the first place.

In Aghion, Dewatripont & Rey, debt serves to commit investors to a course of action ex post which provides ex-ante incentives for management. Dewatripont & Tirole [1994] and Berkovitch & Israel [1993] explore this issue in greater detail.

In Dewatripont & Tirole [1994], a firm's manager may not exert optimal amounts of effort in running the firm. Outside investors can intervene ex post, effectively liquidating the firm in whole or in part. This action reduces the manager's control rents, reduces the risk of the firm's return distribution (assets are replaced with cash), but reduces the mean of the distribution as well (there are costs to liquidation). The difficulty with financing the firm with outside equity alone is that, ex post, equityholders view any shirking on the manager's part as a sunk cost — they would rather keep the manager and earn a higher expected return. This leads to renegotiation ex post, weakening the manager's ex-ante incentives to work hard. By contrast, debtholders have a concave payoff function, so they prefer less risky return distributions. In an optimal financial structure, some debt is short-term, forcing the manager to try to refinance it at an interim date; if he has shirked, the debt cannot be refinanced, and control is given to the debtholders, who liquidate the firm. Some equity is necessary to maintain sufficient concavity of debtholder payoffs, and some long-term debt is necessary so that the refinancing requirement can be met when the manager does not shirk.

In a related paper, Berkovitch & Israel [1993] focus on the allocation of control rights between holders of debt and equity when control allows the replacement of an incumbent manager. The incumbent manager affects a firm's return distribution both through his effort, which he knows, and his ability, which becomes known to both manager and investors at an interim date. Threat of replacement at the interim date affects managerial effort, so commitment to various replacement schemes is necessary. Because a new manager is something of an unknown quantity, replacing an incumbent manager generates additional uncertainty over the firm's return distribution. Debtholders dislike uncertainty, and are more likely to retain below average incumbents; the opposite is true of equityholders. Thus, if it is desirable to retain below average managers, debtholders are given substantial control rights (covenants, seats on the board); otherwise, debt is only given the right of control in bankruptcy, and shareholders generally control the firm.

The next two papers serve to bridge the gap between research on the allocation of control between debt and equity and work on the design of ownership (equity) contracts. These papers also place more emphasis on an externality which the control rights literature tends to ignore: just as a firm's management and employees may use their day-to-day control of the firm to take advantage of investors, investors may use their own control rights in ways which take advantage of managers and employees.

In Garvey & Swan [1992], a firm has a hierarchy which, in simplest form, consists of a CEO and a divisional manager, whose joint effort influences firm output. The CEO can also devote effort to monitoring the divisional manager, and is responsible for administering the latter's compensation; however, the results of monitoring cannot be verified in court. Thus any contracts between the firm and the divisional manager must be implicit. This leads to the following problem: if the CEO has a (large) equity type stake in the firm, she will have incentive to breach the contract with the other manager ex post so as to increase the firm's profits. However, if she bears none of the firm's downside risk, she has no incentive to monitor or expend effort on the firm's output. Thus residual claims on the firm's profits should be given to outside (passive) investors, and the CEO's optimal compensation will be concave: flat in good states, and positively sloped in bad ones. In order to commit to hurting the CEO in bad times, the firm issues debt to outside investors, and the CEO is fired in the event of default.

Garvey & Swan's optimal contract motivates separation of ownership and control, the use of outside debt and equity, and the lack of large equity stakes for CEOs, all in the context of a firm which resembles the way large corporations are actually organized. One caveat is that real CEOs often receive options which give them much upside potential; such contracts might be useful in offsetting managerial risk aversion. Although such options might give CEOs incentives to breach subordinates' contracts, this might in part be offset by long-term reputational concerns. Since Garvey & Swan focus on single period contracting and risk neutral CEOs, these concerns are beyond the scope of their model.

Chang [1992] obtains somewhat similar results in a model where employees (modeled as a representative agent) run the firm for outside investors. All parties observe an unverifiable signal of future output; if the signal is low, restructuring will improve output at a noncontractable cost to the employees. Although the employees cannot directly commit to restructure, they can commit indirectly by funding the firm with a combination of short-term debt and equity. The output signal determines whether or not the debt can be refinanced in the open market; if the signal is low, the debt is not refinanced, the firm defaults, and debtholders seize control and restructure the firm. Since they are risk averse and investors are not, employees receive a fixed wage with priority, which accords with actual practice. Chang argues that it is necessary that outside shareholders be dispersed, so that employees make the financing decision; otherwise, the shareholders would ignore the employees' cost of restructuring and issue too much debt.

The remaining papers in this section focus on the design of ownership (equity) structure, which involves the allocation of shares to different investors, the allocation of liability to shareholders, and the allocation of control (voting rights) among shares. A relatively early piece in this area is that of Holmstrom [1982]. A team of workers jointly determine a firm's output through their individual efforts, which are unobservable. Holmstrom demonstrates that no sharing rule that divides up total firm output among the workers will induce first-best effort: free rider effects will always come into play. Incentive schemes that can break the firm's budget constraint — i.e., those that impose aggregate penalties — can enforce the first-best outcome. The problem is that the workers cannot enforce such a scheme, because ex post they will always prefer to divide up whatever is on hand. Introducing a principal (owner) provides a credible means of enforcing such penalties. Thus 'capitalistic' firms (those owned by investors) may dominate partnerships (those owned by workers).

When uncertainty is present, Holmstrom's result may require an extremely wealthy owner. To the extent individual investors can cooperate, this assumption presents no problems, since a large number of owners can pool their wealth. Cooperation seems reasonable enough if ownership simply involves pledging assets for an enforceable incentive scheme. However, to the extent ownership involves monitoring (addressed in the second half of Holmstrom's paper), which in turn requires individual effort, there may be free rider problems among multiple owners. Having a single owner monitor may dominate, but limited wealth will restrict that individual's incentives to monitor.[12] Thus, one important

[12] Note that monitoring costs may hurt working partnerships as well: to the extent partners monitor one another, costs will rise geometrically with the number of partners, and free rider effects may decrease each partner's incentive to monitor.

feature of optimal ownership structure is ownership concentration, including both the number of owners and the amount of wealth each commits to the firm.

Although there has been little work on optimal concentration per se, several papers touch tangentially on this issue. Shleifer & Vishny [1986], Huddart [1993], and Admati, Pfleiderer & Zechner [1994] all model equity-financed firms which have one large shareholder and a fringe of smaller ones. In all these models, distributional assumptions are such that more wealth commitment by owners increases monitoring and firm performance. Shleifer and Vishny find that firm value unambiguously increases in the large shareholder's holding; this needn't be true in Huddart and Admati et al., because the large shareholder is risk averse.

One difficulty discussed in all three papers concerns the large shareholder's incentives to acquire and maintain her share of the firm. As shown by Huddart and by Admati et al., if the large shareholder can trade shares piecemeal and anonymously, she will do so: in this fashion, she captures the perceived value of her monitoring without actually bearing the cost involved. Of course, in equilibrium this causes a breakdown in monitoring. The papers discuss various methods for mitigating this problem: Huddart shows that requiring the large shareholder to trade proportionately with other investors removes her incentives to sell out; Admati et al. show that diversification motives will lead the large investor to hold large stakes in each firm in the economy; Shleifer & Vishny discuss means for compensating the large investor for her efforts. The importance of the ability to 'trade away' from the optimal ownership structure suggests that future work on optimal ownership structure should examine the impact of varying degrees of market liquidity.

In a somewhat different vein, Winton [1993] describes a model in which a number of symmetric large investors own a firm which may require additional financing from other investors, and any owner can independently monitor the manager of the firm with some probability. In Winton's model, owners always weakly prefer to increase the amount of wealth they commit to the firm (effectively reducing the debt–equity ratio, but see below). The impact of increasing the number of owners depends on the nature of the monitoring cost function; for most functions, free rider effects dominate in the limit, and firm value decreases, but in some cases firm value may increase over some range.

Closely related to the issue of ownership concentration is the nature of the owners' financial commitment to the firm. Even if distributional assumptions are such that increasing the amount of the firm's risk that is borne by the owners increases both their incentive to monitor and firm value (a common thread in the last four papers), they can make their wealth commitment in two ways: initially, by investing their funds in the firm, or on a contingent basis, by raising additional firm debt which they guarantee with their outside wealth. This ties into the large (mainly legal) literature discussing the tradeoffs between limited and unlimited liability for owners.[13] While at first glance the difference between

[13] See for example Easterbrook & Fischel [1985] and Halpern, Trebilcock & Turnbull [1980], as well as Jensen & Meckling [1976].

these two regimes would seem to relate to risk aversion, these authors suggest this is more apparent than real. A limited liability shareholder could invest all of her wealth in the firm, and an unlimited liability shareholder can never lose more than her total wealth. Unlimited liability certainly reduces the choice set of the shareholder, but the shareholder could limit her liability to any desired amount by purchasing insurance. Furthermore, limited liability in British law merely means that there is an upper bound (set when shares are issued) on each shareholder's potential liability; this bound need not be zero. Thus the major difference between regimes seems more related to the contingent nature of shareholder commitments under any regime where their liability exceeds zero, unlimited liability being one extreme and zero liability (as in U.S. corporations) the other.

Several authors have pointed out drawbacks of regimes where shareholders bear significant contingent liabilities. Jensen & Meckling [1976] note that the extent of any one shareholder's own liability will depend on the wealth of each of the other shareholders, so that shareholders and creditors will have to monitor shareholder wealth. The costs of this will increase (geometrically, if monitoring is private information) with the number of shareholders, and firms with large numbers of owners will find such a system prohibitively expensive. Woodward [1985] points out that under contingent liability, the value of a share decreases in the holder's outside wealth, since poorer individuals have less they can lose in the event the firm defaults. Thus, if shares are freely traded, wealthy investors will tend to sell such shares and poorer investors will buy them; in the limit, adverse selection will lead to a firm owned by individuals with no remaining outside funds, and the shareholders' liability will be valueless.[14]

The difficulty with these arguments is that contingent liability is and has been used in a number of settings.[15] A possible explanation is given by Winton [1993]. As discussed earlier, firm owners in his model have incentive to use their wealth as a means of bonding themselves to monitor management. To the extent the bulk of their wealth is illiquid, they will prefer to commit wealth via a contingent guarantee rather than actual investment so as to minimize the probability of liquidation costs — just as in Lacker's [1990] model. The firm is then funded with liquid funds from a large number of other investors, whose claim is equivalent to debt backed by the shareholders' guarantee.[16] However, if shares are issued or traded freely, the adverse selection problem noted by Woodward [1985] occurs. Thus trading restrictions and wealth verification are necessary to enforce contingent liability regimes, and their cost tends to increase with the number of shareholders. Winton uses these results to motivate several actual ownership structures.

[14] This effect will be mitigated to the extent investors exhibit increasing relative risk aversion; see Winton [1993].

[15] Winton [1993] gives a number of examples.

[16] Winton assumes that payments to outsiders must be monotone. However, if owner wealth is sufficiently high, the optimal contract between owners and outside investors may take the form of higher payments in bad states than good ones, analogous to the result of Innes [1990]. As in that case, incorporation of costly output verification for outsiders might avoid this problem.

The last issue considered in this section concerns the allocation of voting rights among different investors. A particular focus of research on this issue has been identifying the circumstances under which the use of one vote per share and majority voting are optimal.

Grossman & Hart's [1988] starting point is the fact that when securities are widely held there is a free rider problem; individual shareholders do not have an incentive to expend sufficient resources to monitor management. The situation where voting rights matter most is when outside 'rivals' monitor the 'incumbent management' and make a takeover bid. Grossman & Hart consider the corporate charter an entrepreneur should adopt to maximize the initial value of the firm. The important determinant of the allocation of voting rights in their model is the distribution of the private benefits of control between the rival and the incumbent management. If there is an asymmetry so that one group has much larger benefits than the other, then one share one vote is optimal because it maximizes the amount that has to be paid to acquire control; concentrating votes makes it cheaper to acquire control because fewer shares have to be bought. If there are symmetric private benefits of control then concentrating votes is optimal since it makes rivals and incumbents compete and pay for the private benefits. Grossman and Hart argue that the asymmetric case is relevant because the extent to which incumbents can extract private benefits is limited by the law, and suggest that this is why one share one vote is so prevalent.

Harris & Raviv [1988] consider a model that is closely related to Grossman & Hart's. However, they distinguish between privately optimal arrangements where the corporate charter is chosen to maximize the initial value of the firm as in Grossman & Hart and the socially optimal arrangement which takes into account the private benefits accruing to rival and incumbent management teams. They show that one share one vote majority rule is socially optimal because it ensures that the team that generates the greatest total amount gains control; any deviation gives an advantage to the incumbent or rival that may allow them to gain control even though they generate a lower total amount. In contrast to Grossman & Hart, they focus on the case where both rivals and incumbents have private benefits of control. They therefore argue that issuing two sets of securities — one with all the voting rights and one with all the dividends — is privately optimal because it makes them compete for the right to extract the private benefits. This difference in results suggests that an important empirical issue in this area is the extent to which private benefits differ between incumbents and rivals.

Blair, Golbe & Gerard [1989] consider a model similar to that of Harris & Raviv [1988] except that they assume the rival and incumbent bid simultaneously whereas Harris & Raviv assume they bid sequentially. This difference in assumptions leads to a difference in results in that Blair, Golbe & Gerard [1989] find that in the absence of taxes, one share one vote majority rule and extreme securities that unbundle voting rights and cash flows are equivalent and both lead to social optimality. The main concern of Blair, Golbe & Gerard is to consider the effect of capital gains taxes on the allocation of voting rights and cash flows. If capital gains taxes are in effect then welfare is improved if extreme securities are used.

This is because a lock-in effect means capital gains taxes may prevent a superior rival from winning if there is one share one vote majority rule; tax liabilities may be higher when the rival wins than when the incumbent wins. Allowing separate trading of votes alleviates this effect.

Harris & Raviv [1989] consider the allocation of voting rights and cash flows when the firm is not restricted to issuing just equity. Using a model similar to that of Grossman & Hart [1988], they focus on private optimality and assume there are asymmetric private benefits of control. The problem of the entrepreneur who owns the firm initially is to design securities that prevent the incumbent management that has private benefits from maintaining control when a superior rival appears. This means that the cost of resisting takeovers must be maximized. As in the papers focusing only on equity, one share one vote among voting securities is an important component of this, since it means that control cannot be acquired cheaply by the party with private benefits. In addition, nonvoting risky securities should not be sold to outside investors; if nonvoting securities are sold to the outside investors they should be risk-free debt. The reason is that these maximize the cost of obtaining control and so tend to favor the superior rival.

Nagarajan [1995] uses a mechanism design approach to investigate what forms of takeover mechanism are generically efficient in the sense that the person or team that values the firm the most always acquires control. It is assumed that shareholders' valuations of the firm are private information but there are no private benefits to control. Among other things, it is shown that a pure proxy mechanism where there is no exchange of shares is not generically efficient. Also, there does not exist a takeover mechanism which involves the largest stockholder gaining control which is generically efficient. Finally, it is shown that if the initial owner's valuation is common knowledge there exists a mechanism which is generically efficient but if there are more than two shareholders it is not simple majority rule.

The approach of considering the allocation of voting rights when an incumbent management team is challenged by a rival team is not the only possible one. Bagwell & Judd [1989] instead consider the optimality of majority rule where control is concerned with payout and investment decisions. Initially in their model, all investors are identical, corporate charters are designed and securities are issued to finance firms' investments. Investors then discover whether they prefer early or late consumption and how risk averse they are. After this firms decide on how much to pay out and whether to invest in risky or safe projects. In an ideal world investors can acquire the shares of firms which adopt their preferred policies. In this case majority rule is optimal since, within firms, shareholders will be homogeneous. The problem is if investors face high costs of reallocating their portfolios such as capital gains taxes with lock-in effects, the reallocation of investors will not be optimal. In this case shareholders are no longer homogeneous within firms and majority rule is no longer optimal. Instead, when the costs of reallocation are high, the initial corporate charters should specify a utilitarian form of objective function where the weights assigned to each type correspond to their representation in the population.

Maug [1993] considers the important issue of the role of outside boards of directors. In his model, investment in firm-specific human capital by managers is necessary for the firm to be productive and the level of skill that managers attain cannot be contracted upon. The use of debt and liquidation when bankruptcy occurs has the drawback that managers' incentives to invest in firm-specific human capital are attenuated because bankruptcy may occur in states where in an ideal world it would not. Maug shows that by introducing an outside board of directors it is possible to reduce this inefficiency.

Bagwell & Judd's and Maug's models illustrate that the allocation of voting rights and control may be important in situations other than takeovers. They focus on two particular situations of this type but there are many others. For example, when there are differences in beliefs on the effects of various policies the firm might adopt, the allocation of control by appropriate design of securities and corporate charters is important.

5. The allocation of risk

Traditional financial theories suggest that one of the major advantages of having different types of securities is that they allow different groups of investors with different risk tolerances to bear the amount of risk they desire. This raises the question of how securities should be designed when risk sharing rather than control is the important issue. The Modigliani & Miller result, that capital structure is irrelevant when markets are complete, suggests that the form of securities are irrelevant in these circumstances. In order to develop a theory of optimal corporate financial structure in a risk sharing context, it is necessary that markets be incomplete. One possible reason for incompleteness that is suggested is transaction costs. Allen & Gale [1988, 1991, 1994], Madan & Soubra [1991], Pesendorfer [1995] and Bisin [1993] have considered models of this type.[17]

Allen & Gale [1988] consider a perfectly competitive, symmetric information model where different groups of investor have different degrees of risk aversion and there are transaction costs of issuing securities. It is shown that restrictions on short sales are necessary if an equilibrium is to exist. This is because a firm that issues multiple securities must be able to recoup the transactions costs of issuing the securities and so must be more valuable than a similar firm with fewer securities. If costless short sales were possible there would be an arbitrage opportunity; by going short in the multiple security firm and long in the firm with fewer securities it would be possible to make a profit equal to the difference in transaction costs. Hence for equilibrium to exist there must be short sale restrictions. These restrictions mean that different types of investors value securities differently on the margin and the price of a security is determined by

[17] For an analysis of security design by futures exchanges, see Duffie & Jackson [1989] and Cuny [1993], for security design by options exchanges see Allen & Gale [1990] and for security design by governments see Gale [1990].

the group that values it most. Among other things, it is shown that equilibrium is constrained efficient. Also, debt and equity are not optimal. Optimal securities are extreme in the sense that they allocate all of a firm's payoff in a particular state to one security or another. This allows the securities to be used most effectively in investors' portfolios to smooth consumption.

Madan & Soubra [1991] combine the approach of Allen & Gale [1988] with that of Ross [1989] to take into account the problem of marketing securities. The important transaction costs in their model are the costs of marketing securities. Widening the appeal of a security reduces the marketing costs. In this framework it is shown that optimal securities are no longer extreme. In some cases equity, debt and warrants are optimal.

Pesendorfer [1995] has also considered financial innovation in a model which is related to Ross [1989]. He assumes there are standard securities that can be traded with zero costs. Intermediaries purchase these and repackage them to create intermediated securities. These need to be marketed which is costly. As in Allen & Gale [1988], there are short sale constraints for intermediated securities; without these, short selling would be equivalent to issuing securities and avoiding marketing costs.

Three main results are obtained. It is shown that innovation can improve agents' utilities even if markets are as complete as before, because innovation can allow the costs of marketing to be reduced. The second result is that the level of innovation is not necessarily constrained efficient. This is because no intermediary has access to all standard security markets, so there is no mechanism to coordinate innovations. As a result it is possible to get stuck at equilibria where there is too little innovation. If two intermediaries were to innovate simultaneously in these equilibria everybody could be better off because of complementarities provided by the innovation. Since there is no mechanism to coordinate them, and it is not worthwhile for either of them to do it individually, they do not innovate. The final result concerns the role of innovation in eliminating indeterminacy. Balasko & Cass [1989] and Geanokoplos & Mas-Colell [1989], among others, have shown that if securities pay off in nominal units of account and markets are incomplete then there is an indeterminacy in real equilibrium allocations. The reason is that the payoffs to securities which are specified in nominal terms can have different values in different equilibria. With complete markets this does not happen since all that is changing is the numeraire; the set of real payoffs does not alter. Pesendorfer shows that as marketing costs tend to zero, the markets become complete and any real indeterminacy is eliminated.

Allen & Gale [1991] develop an approach to security design which does not rely on there being short sales restrictions. The crucial feature of this model is the assumption concerning the timing of events. Firms first choose the securities to issue and these securities are then traded on competitive markets. When there are short sale restrictions the results are essentially the same as those in Allen & Gale [1988]. However, when there are no short sales restrictions an equilibrium exists. This is consistent with there being no arbitrage opportunities because at the second stage, multiple security firms can have the same value as otherwise similar firms with fewer securities. The reason that there are still incentives to innovate is that instead of being price takers as in Allen & Gale [1988], firms take into account the fact that their actions will affect equilibrium prices in the second stage security markets. Thus they may be willing to innovate and issue costly securities even though ex post the value of their firms is the same as that of noninnovating firms; they compare their utilities in different second stage equilibria. The results here are somewhat different from those in Allen & Gale [1988]. Equilibrium is no longer constrained efficient. An example is given of too little innovation; the change in firm value across security market equilibria is such that firms fail to issue a security even though everybody could be made better off if such a security were issued. An example is also given of too much innovation; in this case firms issue securities even though everybody could be made better off if fewer securities were issued. The endogenous incomplete market structure that arises from profit maximizing behavior in this model is not necessarily efficient.

Bisin [1993] uses an imperfectly competitive model related to that in Allen & Gale [1991] to reconsider the Balasko & Cass [1989] and Geanokoplos & Mas-Colell [1989] real indeterminacy result. At the first stage intermediaries optimally design the pay-off structure of the securities they issue and choose the spread between the buying and selling prices. These intermediaries bear a transaction cost for each security issued that has a fixed component and a variable component that is proportional to the volume traded. At the second stage the securities are traded on Walrasian markets where investors are price takers. Intermediaries have rational expectations about the second stage equilibria when they design securities at the first stage. Bisin's main result is to show that the introduction of intermediaries that choose securities optimally removes the real indeterminacy result of Balasko & Cass [1989] and Geanokoplos & Mas-Colell [1989]. Unlike Pesendorfer's [1995] related result which depends on transaction costs being vanishingly small, it is shown that the real determinacy of equilibrium does not depend on the level of transaction costs.

6. Acquisition of information

One of the determinants of a security's value is the information that investors have. This raises the possibility that securities will be designed to affect the extent to which information is acquired in order to maximize value. Boot & Thakor [1993] have considered a noisy rational expectations model of this type. A firm, which can be high or low value, sells its securities to investors. The firm knows its own value but investors do not unless they pay to become informed. There is a group of liquidity traders whose demand for securities is exogenously determined and random; this ensures that asset prices are noisy and do not fully reveal firm type. The investors who do not choose to become informed are the residual holders of the security. All traders are risk neutral. The informed traders cannot borrow or sell short; if they find out the firm has high value they invest all their wealth in it and if it has low value they invest nothing in it. The price is determined by the residual holders who will only hold it if price is equal to the expected value of the stock conditional on the sum of the liquidity and informed traders' demands. In equilibrium the profits of the informed are just sufficient to cover the cost of buying the information.

Good firms want there to be as many informed investors as possible because this creates a high demand for their securities and increases the amount the firms receive. By splitting its cash flow into a safe and a risky portion, i.e. into debt and equity, a good firm provides better incentives for investors to become informed. The reason is that the fluctuations in price of the risky component are increased and this raises the profits an informed investor earns. As a result more investors become informed and the value of the firm is raised. Bad firms always find it worthwhile to mimic the good firms so they can receive the average value of the two. Thus in equilibrium all firms find it worthwhile to split.

One extension of the model is where the information informed investors receive does not perfectly signal firm type and there are many firms. In this case it is worthwhile to bundle the securities and then to split this portfolio into a safe and risky component. This allows the idiosyncratic risk associated with the signals to be eliminated and for the firms to receive more because people are better informed. This result is consistent with the fact that financial intermediaries such as collateralized mortgage obligations (CMOs) pool securities and then issue multiple claims against them.

In a related paper, DeMarzo & Duffie [1993] analyze the effect of information acquisition by intermediaries on the design of securities such as CMOs. Suppose that an intermediary finds out that the value of an asset they have acquired and plan to sell is below the expected market price that it will fetch. It will have an incentive to sell as much of the asset as possible. On the other hand, if it finds out the market value is above the expected market price it will have an incentive to retain some of the asset. This 'option' on the amount to trade means that the payoff from selling the asset is convex in the intermediary's private valuation. DeMarzo and Duffie show that this convexity makes it worthwhile to split the cash flows in ways which resemble CMOs. For example, rather than split marginal cash flows between securities, they should be allocated to one security or another as is done with different CMO tranches.

When a new security is introduced investors may face a kind of uncertainty which is different from that which they face when they buy a familiar security. They may be unsure what the characteristics of the security are and how it will operate in practice. To offset this they must gather information to discover how the security will help them increase their ability to hedge risks or increase the expected returns on their portfolio. If this information is costly they will demand a premium from the issuer so that the price the issuer can obtain is reduced. In contrast, standard securities whose operation investors are familiar with will not require this type of reduction in price. Gale [1992] has shown that this preference for standard securities can lead to a coordination failure because issuers can get stuck at an undesirable equilibrium. Any single firm will be reluctant to issue a new security with better characteristics but if all firms were to do this a Pareto superior equilibrium could result. The costs of gathering information about a new security mean that the privately optimal security does not necessarily correspond to the socially optimal one.

Demange & Laroque [1995] consider the relationship between private information and the design of securities in a noisy rational expectations model. Entrepreneurs who have a large stake in a single company will want to diversify their holdings. However if they have superior information investors will be reluctant to trade with them; in extreme cases they will not be able to diversify at all. Demange & Laroque show that entrepreneurs can overcome this problem to some extent by designing the securities they sell so they are uncorrelated with their information. The optimal security design trades off insurance opportunities with speculative gains. Rahi [1995] considers a model that is similar to Demange & Laroque's but without noise traders and is able to show that equity is the optimal security.

7. Concluding remarks

The existing research on optimal financial contracting has contributed greatly to our understanding of the situations under which actual securities are in fact optimal responses to various capital market imperfections. For example, from the viewpoint of risk-sharing, debt seems suboptimal, and costs of financial distress associated with bankruptcy should make debt even less attractive; yet, as our survey shows, debt-like contracts are often optimal responses to agency and adverse selection problems. Similarly, although equity has risk-sharing appeal, various institutional features need to be in place before equity can be used as an effective investment vehicle.

Nevertheless, despite the considerable amount of work on the role of incentives and optimal contracting in determining corporate financial structure, several important areas require further research. The first concerns the robustness of simple optimal contracts in different environments. In general in this literature, small changes in the assumptions of the underlying model can lead to an important change in the optimal contract. In practice, however, certain simple contracts and securities appear to be used in a wide variety of circumstances.

The second area for further research is to identify the effects of more complicated agency problems on ownership structure and financial contracting. At present most of the models involve relatively simple agency problems and the results focus on one or a few aspects of the resulting arrangements or contracts. The way in which different agency problems interact is an important issue. Along the same lines, many of these models essentially focus on entrepreneurial firms; more work needs to be done on firms which resemble large corporations with effective separation of ownership and control.

Finally, many securities issued by public corporations are liquid and can be easily traded. Most models abstract from this important feature and assume a signal period structure where security owners remain unchanged throughout time.

Allowing for the possibility that a security might be sold to a new investor with different risk aversion or information is an important step which may considerably extend our understanding of the phenomena we observe.

Acknowledgements

We thank an anonymous referee, Charles Calomiris, Darrell Duffie, Adam Dunsby, Gerald Garvey, Joseph Haubrich, Steven Huddart, Jeffrey Lacker, Vojislav Maksimovic, David Nachman, Thomas Noe, John Persons, Stephen Ross, and Yossi Spiegel for helpful comments. Franklin Allen gratefully acknowledges financial support from the National Science Foundation. Parts of this survey draw from Allen [1990] and Allen & Gale [1994].

References

Admati, A., P. Pfleiderer and J. Zechner (1994). Large shareholder activism, risk sharing, and financial market equilibrium, *J. Polit. Econ.* 102, 1097–1130.

Aghion, P., and P. Bolton (1992). An 'incomplete contract' approach to bankruptcy and the financial structure of the firm. *Review of Economic Studies* 59, 473–494.

Aghion, P., M. Dewatripont and P. Rey (1990). Optimal incentive schemes and the coexistence of debt and equity, working paper, ENSAE.

Allen, F. (1990). The changing nature of debt and equity: A financial perspective, in: R.W. Kopcke and E.S. Rosengren (eds.), *Are the Differences between Equity and Debt Disappearing?*, Conference Series No. 33, 1989, Federal Reserve Bank of Boston, Boston, MA, pp. 12–38.

Allen, F., and D. Gale (1988). Optimal security design. *Rev. Financ. Studies* 1, 229–263.

Allen, F., and D. Gale (1990). Incomplete markets and incentives to set up an options exchange. *Geneva Pap. Risk Insur.*, Spec. Issue, 15, 17–46.

Allen, F., and D. Gale (1991). Arbitrage, short sales and financial innovation. *Econometrica* 59, 1041–1068.

Allen, F., and D. Gale (1992). Measurement distortion and missing contingencies in optimal contracts. *Econ. Theory* 2, 1–26.

Allen, F., and D. Gale (1994). *Financial Innovation and Risk Sharing*. MIT Press, Boston, MA.

Bagwell, L.S., and K.L. Judd (1989). Transactions costs and corporate control, working paper 67, Kellogg Graduate School of Management, Northwestern University.

Balasko, Y., and D. Cass (1989). The structure of financial equilibrium with exogenous yields: I. Unrestricted participation. *Econometrica* 57, 135–162.

Banks, J., and J. Sobel (1987). Equilibrium selection in signaling games. *Econometrica* 55, 647–662.

Berglöf, E., and E.-L. von Thadden (1994). Short-term versus long-term interests: Capital structure with multiple investors, *Q. J. Econ.* 109, 1055–1084.

Berkovitch, E. and R. Israel (1993). The design of internal control and capital structure, working paper, Department of Finance, University of Michigan.

Bisin, A. (1993). General equilibrium economies with imperfectly competitive financial intermediaries, working paper, Department of Economics, University of Chicago.

Blair, D.H., D.L. Golbe and J.M. Gerard (1989). Unbundling the voting rights and profit claims of common shares. *J. Polit. Econ.* 97, 420–443.

Boot, A.W., S.I. Greenbaum and A.V. Thakor (1993). Reputation and discretion in financial contracting. *Am. Econ. Rev.* 83, 1165–1183.

Boot, A. and A. Thakor (1993). Security design. *J. Finance* 48, 1349–1378.

Boyd, J.H., and B.D. Smith (1993). The equilibrium allocation of investment capital in the presence of adverse selection and costly state verification. *Econ. Theory* 3, 427–451.

Chang, C. (1990). The dynamic structure of optimal debt contracts. *J. Econ. Theory* 52, 68–86.

Chang, C. (1992), Capital structure as an optimal contract between employees and investors. *J. Finance* 47, 1141–1158.

Chang, C. (1993). Payout policy, capital structure, and compensation contracts when managers value control. *Rev. Financ. Studies* 6, 911–933.

Chiesa, G. (1992). Debt and warrants: Agency problems and mechanism design. *J. Financ. Intermed.* 2, 237–254.

Cho, I.-K., and D.M. Kreps (1987). Signaling games and stable equilibria. *Q. J. Econ.* 102, 179–222.

Cuny, C.J. (1993). The role of liquidity in futures market innovations. *Rev. Financ. Studies* 6, 57–78.

De, S., and J. Kale (1993). Contingent payments and debt contracts. *Financ. Manage.* 22, 106–122.

Demange, G., and G. Laroque (1995). Private information and the control of securities, *J. Econ. Theory* 65, 233–257.

DeMarzo, P.M., and D. Duffie (1993). A liquidity-based model of asset-backed security design, working Paper, Graduate School of Business, Stanford University.

Dewatripont, M., and J. Tirole (1994). A theory of debt and equity: Diversity of securities and manager–shareholder congruence, *Q. J. Econ.* 109, 1027–1054.

Diamond, D.W. (1984). Financial intermediation and delegated monitoring, *Rev. Econ. Studies* 51, 393–414.

Diamond, D.W. (1989). Reputation acquisition in debt markets, *J. Polit. Econ.* 97, 828–862.

Diamond, D.W. (1991a). Monitoring and reputation: The choice between bank loans and directly placed debt, *J. Polit. Econ.* 99, 689–721.

Diamond, D.W. (1991b), Debt maturity structure and liquidity risk. *Q. J. Econ.* 106, 709–737.

Diamond, D.W. (1993), Seniority and maturity of debt contracts. *J. Financ. Econ.* 33, 341–368.

Dionne, G., and P. Viala (1992). Optimal design of financial contracts and moral hazard, working paper, Department of Economics, Universitè de Montrèal.

Duffie, D., and M.O. Jackson (1989). Optimal innovation of futures contracts. *Rev. Financ. Studies* 2, 275–296.

Dybvig, P.H., and J.F. Zender (1991). Capital structure and dividend irrelevance with asymmetric information. *Rev. Financ. Studies* 4, 201–219.

Easterbrook, F., and D. Fischel (1985). Limited liability and the corporation. *Univ. Chicago Law Rev.* 52, 89–117.

Fama, E., and M. Jensen (1983a). Separation of ownership and control. *J. Law Econ.* 26, 301–325.

Fama, E., and M. Jensen (1983b). Agency problems and residual claims. *J. Law Econ.* 26, 327–349.

Fama, E., and M. Jensen (1985). Organizational forms and investment decisions. *J. Financ. Econ.* 14, 101–119.

Gale, D. (1990). The efficient design of public debt, in: R. Dornbusch and M. Draghi (eds.),*Public Debt Management: Theory and History*, Cambridge University Press, Cambridge.

Gale, D. (1992). Standard securities. *Rev. Econ. Studies* 59, 731–756.

Gale, D., and M. Hellwig (1985). Incentive-compatible debt contracts: The one-period problem. *Rev. Econ. Studies* 52, 647 663.

Garvey, G., and P. Swan (1992). Optimal capital structure for a hierarchical firm. *J. Financ. Intermed.* 2, 376–400.

Geanokoplos, J., and A. Mas-Colell (1989). Real indeterminacy with financial assets. *J. Econ. Theory* 47, 22-38.

Grossman, S., and O. Hart (1983). An analysis of the principal-agent problem, *Econometrica* 51, 7-45.

Grossman, S.J., and O.D. Hart (1988). One share/one vote and the market for corporate control. *J. Financ. Econ.* 20, 175-202.

Hagerty, K., and D. Siegel (1988). On the observational equivalence of managerial contracts under conditions of moral hazard and self selection. *Q. J. Econ.* 103, 425-428.

Halpern, P., M. Trebilcock and S. Turnbull (1980). An economic analysis of limited liability in corporation law. *Univ. Toronto Law J.* 30, 117-50.

Harris, M., and A. Raviv (1979). Optimal incentive contracts with imperfect information. *J. Econ. Theory* 20, 231-259.

Harris, M., and A. Raviv (1988). Corporate governance: Voting rights and majority rules, *J. Financ. Econ.* 20, 203-235.

Harris, M., and A. Raviv (1989). The design of securities. *J. Financ. Econ.* 24, 255-287.

Harris, M., and A. Raviv (1991). The theory of capital structure. *J. Finance* 46, 297-355.

Harris, M., and A. Raviv (1992). Financial contracting theory, in: J.-J. Laffont (ed.), *Advances in Economic Theory*, Vol. 1, Cambridge University Press, Cambridge.

Hart, O.D. (1991). Theories of optimal capital structure: A principal-agent perspective, working Paper 91-2, Brookings Institution.

Hart, O.D., and B. Holmstrom (1987). Theory of contracts, in: T. Bewley (ed.), *Advances in Economic Theory*, Econometric Society Monographs, 5th World Congress, Cambridge University Press, New York, NY.

Hart, O.D., and J. Moore (1989). Default and renegotiation: A dynamic model of debt, working paper 89-069, Harvard Business School.

Hart, O.D., and J. Moore (1990). A theory of corporate financial structure based on the seniority of claims, working paper 560, Massachusetts Institute of Technology.

Hart, O.D., and J. Moore (1991). A theory of debt based on the inalienability of human capital, NBER working paper #3906.

Holmstrom, B. (1982). Moral hazard in teams. *Bell J. Econ.* 13, 324–340.

Huddart, S. (1993). The effect of a large shareholder on corporate value. *Manage. Sci.* 39, 1407–1421.

Innes, R. (1990). Limited liability and incentive contracting with ex-ante action choices. *J. Econ. Theory* 52, 45–67.

Jensen, M.C., and W.H. Meckling (1976). Theory of the firm: Managerial behavior, agency cost and ownership structure. *J. Financ. Econ.* 3, 305–360.

Kalay, A., and J.F. Zender (1992), Bankruptcy and state contingent changes in the ownership of control, working paper, School of Business, University of Utah.

Krasa, S., and A. Villamil (1994). Optimal contracts with costly state verification: The multilateral case. *Econ. Theory* 4, 167–187.

Lacker, J. (1989). Limited commitment and costly enforcement, working Paper 90-2, Federal Reserve Bank of Richmond.

Lacker, J. (1990). Collateralized debt as the optimal contract, working paper, Federal Reserve Bank of Richmond.

Lacker, J.M., and J.A. Weinberg (1989). Optimal contracts under costly state falsification. *J. Polit. Econ.* 97, 1345–1363.

Madan, D., and B. Soubra (1991). Design and marketing of financial products. *Rev. Financ. Studies* 4, 361–384.

Maug, E. (1993). Capital structure and organizational form: Alternative governance structures to force liquidation, working paper, London Business School.

Milgrom, P. (1981). Good news and bad news: Representation theorems and applications. *Bell J. Econ.* 13, 380–391.

Mookherjee, D., and I. Png (1989). Optimal auditing, insurance and redistribution. *Q. J. Econ.* 104, 399–416.

Myers, S.C., and N.S. Majluf (1984). Corporate financing and investment decisions when firms have information that investors do not have. *J. Financ. Econ.* 13, 187–221.

Nachman, D., and T. Noe (1994). Optimal design of securities under asymmetric information. *Rev. Financ. Studies* 7, 1–44.

Nagarajan, S. (1995). On the generic efficiency of takeovers under incomplete information, *J. Econ. Theory* 65, 522–556.

Persons, J.C. (1994). Renegotiation and the impossibility of optimal investment. *Rev. Financ. Studies* 7, 419–449.

Pesendorfer, W. (1995). Financial innovation in a general equilibrium model, *J. Econ. Theory* 65, 79–116.

Rahi, R. (1995). Optimal incomplete markets with asymmetric information, *J. Econ. Theory* 65, 171–197.

Ravid, S.A., and M. Spiegel (1992). Linear securities as optimal contracts in environments with an infinite number of bad projects, working paper, University of California, Berkeley.

Ross, S.A. (1978). Some notes on financial incentive-signalling models, activity choice and risk preferences. *J. Finance* 33, 777–792.

Ross, S.A. (1989). Institutional markets, financial marketing and financial innovation. *J. Finance* 44, 541–556.

Shleifer, A., and R. Vishny (1986). Large shareholders and corporate control. *J. Polit. Econ.* 94, 461–488.

Townsend, R.M. (1979). Optimal contracts and competitive markets with costly state verification. *J. Econ. Theory* 22, 265–293.

Williams, J. (1989). Ex-ante monitoring, ex-post asymmetry, and optimal securities, working paper, Faculty of Commerce, University of British Columbia.

Williamson, S. (1986). Costly monitoring, financial intermediation, and equilibrium credit rationing. *J. Monetary Econ.* 18, 159–179.

Winton, A. (1993). Limitation of liability and the ownership structure of the firm. *J. Finance* 48, 487–512.

Winton, A. (1995). Costly state verification and multiple investors: The role of seniority, *Rev. Finance. Studies* 8, 91–123.

Woodward, S. (1985). Limited liability in the theory of the firm. *Z. Gesamte Staatswiss. J. Inst. Theor. Econ.* 141, 601–611.

Zender, J.F. (1991). Optimal financial instruments. *J. Finance* 46, 1645–1664.

R. Jarrow et al., Eds., *Handbooks in OR & MS, Vol. 9*

Chapter 23

Financing Investment Under Asymmetric Information

Kent Daniel

Graduate School of Business, University of Chicago, Chicago, IL 60637, U.S.A.

Sheridan Titman

W.E. Carroll School of Management, Finance Department, Boston College, Chestnut Hill, MA 02167, U.S.A.

1. Introduction

When a firm has an opportunity to accept a positive net present value project that requires equity financing, it faces a dilemma. If its managers believe the firm's stock is underpriced, then taking the project forces the firm to issue underpriced stock and thereby dilutes the value of its existing stock. As Myers & Majluf [1984] point out, firms with underpriced stock may forego attractive investment projects for this reason. Given this, analysts and investors will believe that when firms do issue equity, their shares are more likely to be overpriced. Hence, announcements of equity offers are likely to be accompanied by share price declines.

The Myers & Majluf theory has been subject to extensive empirical testing. Chapter 31 in this volume reviews a number of empirical papers that confirm the Myers & Majluf prediction that stock prices will generally decline when firms announce equity issues. The basic theoretical framework provided by Myers & Majluf has also been extended in a variety of ways. Most of these extensions consider ways in which a firm that intends to issue equity can signal its value and thereby reduce adverse selection problem.

This chapter provides a simple framework for understanding the basic Myers & Majluf underinvestment model as well as the related literature that examines how financial decisions provide information to market participants. The financial decisions we analyze include dividend policy [John & Williams [1985] and Ambarish, John & Williams, 1987], the scale of the investment project (Krasker [1986]), the timing of the project's initiation [Choe, Masulis & Nanda, 1993], the underpricing of the issue [Allen & Faulhaber, 1989; Grinblatt & Huang, 1989; and Welch, 1989] and the overpricing of the issue [Giammarino & Lewis, 1988].

The information content of these financial decisions have typically been examined in isolation. For example, no one has examined whether or not it makes sense to underprice an equity issue if one could also provide information to the market by paying a dividend. To examine issues of this type, we analyze how efficiently the various financial decisions convey information to market participants. Our analysis suggests that only those decisions (or combinations of decisions) which provide the most efficient signals, (i.e., minimum cost), will be used in equilibrium.

A signal can generally be viewed as a certain action or decision that imposes greater costs on low valued firms (or individuals) than on high valued firms. For example, in the classic Spence [1973] model, more talented individuals can successfully signal their talents by acquiring more education, since doing so is less costly for them than for less talented individuals. In general, signals that impose the highest costs on the lower valued firms or individuals, relative to the costs imposed on the higher valued firms or individuals, are the most efficient since they prevent mimicry by the low valued firms at a minimum cost to the high valued firm. In the education example, talented individuals will want to study subjects which are both easiest for them and most difficult for those with less talent.

Our analysis of the signalling efficiency of the various financial decisions includes two forms of 'money burning' signals. A signal is typically referred to as a 'money burning' signal if it satisfies two conditions: (1) the signalling action must be purely dissipative, meaning that it provides no direct benefits to the signalling firm, and (2) the signalling action must be equally costly for all types. For example Milgrom & Roberts [1986] present a model where advertising is a money burning signal. In their model: (1) potential customers learn nothing from a firm's advertising other than that it is spending money, and (2) advertising is equally costly for all firm types, which is in contrast to the education signal suggested by Spence which imposed a higher cost on the less talented individuals. The effect of a money burning signal can always be duplicated by actually burning currency, which is why the signal is so designated.

Given that burning money imposes the same costs on all firms regardless of their types it provides a relatively inefficient signal. As we will show, the efficiency of a money burning signal depends on its timing. We analyze two types of these money burning signals; the first, which is much less efficient, requires burning money prior to the equity offering and the second requires a commitment to burn money subsequent to the equity offering when the project's cash flows are realized. Since we expect that something equivalent to both types of money burning signals should always be available to equity issuers,[1] our analysis of money burning signals provides a useful benchmark for judging the signalling efficiency of the financial decisions suggested in the literature.

When there is asymmetric information about the value of the firm's assets-in-place, but not about the value of the project, the overpricing and project scaling signals are shown to be the most efficient signals. However, when there is asymmetric information about the project's value and projects of high valued firms are worth considerably more than those implemented by lower valued firms, the overpricing and project scaling signals are much less efficient and are in fact dominated by signals that commit the firm to burn money subsequent to

[1] For example, the firm can spend an excessive amount promoting the equity issue or alternatively commit to overpay their investment banker.

the offering. The John & Williams dividend signal as well as the Choe, Masulis & Nanda project delay signal turn out to be equivalent to signalling with a commitment to burn money subsequent to the offering. Under some conditions, the most efficient signal will be a combination of committing to burn money, scaling the project, and overpricing the issue. Underpricing the issue, which is equivalent to burning money out of the proceeds of the issue, is the least efficient signal and is always dominated by commitments to burn money in the future.

Although most of this chapter is devoted to an analysis of how financial signals mitigate the adverse selection problem that arises when firms issue equity, we also briefly examine the choice between debt and equity financing in this setting. As Myers & Majluf discuss, when a firm can issue risk-free debt, there is no adverse selection problem and thus no need for costly signals. However, when the firm must issue risky debt, the problem becomes substantially more interesting. While we expect that in general the Myers & Majluf adverse selection problem will exist when firms are unable to issue risk-free debt, there are certain cases described in the literature where firms can costlessly signal their type with their financing choices and as a result invest efficiently.

The rest of this chapter is organized as follows: Sections 2 and 3 describe the basic Myers & Majluf model in the case where the more highly valued issuing firm can burn money to signal its type. The fourth and fifth sections expand the potential signals of the issuing firm to include price setting, dividends, project scaling and project delay. Section 6 analyzes the model when firms can issue debt as well as equity and Section 7 presents our conclusions.

2. Model description

Our basic model includes a group of risk-neutral investors and a firm that has the opportunity to take on a positive NPV project. We will initially assume that the project requires equity capital. Perhaps, the firm has existing debt covenants that prevents it from issuing additional debt. Alternatively, the firm may want to avoid issuing debt because of concerns about costs associated with financial distress and bankruptcy.

The firm's manager is assumed to maximize the intrinsic value of its shares or equivalently the wealth of its shareholders who choose to retain their shares and do not purchase any part of a new issue.[2] This assumption will be discussed in detail in Section 6.4. Initially, we assume that the firm is one of two types: high or low. The high type is characterized by a larger value of its assets-in-place and in some cases by a more valuable investment opportunity. In this model, the firm's management knows the firm's type, but investors do not.

To simplify notation, we assume that the risk-free interest rate is zero and that

[2] The model can easily be generalized to have a manager's objective function that includes the firm's current market price as well as its intrinsic value, though the conclusions will change somewhat.

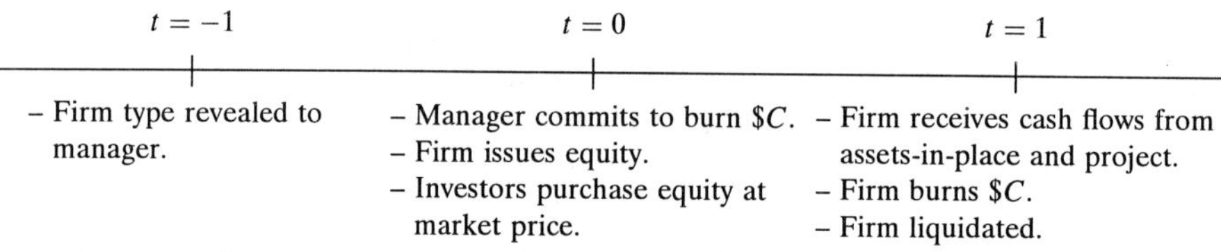

Fig. 1. Basic model timeline.

the competitive equity market purchases equity issues at a price equal to the expected future cash flows of the shares. If the issuer specifies a price, then the market will not purchase the issue if it is priced above this level, and at any issue price below this level there will be rationing of the issue. In one case we allow the investors to mix if the issue price is equal to the conditional expected value.

The timeline for the two type model is illustrated in Figure 1. At $t = -1$ the firm's type is revealed to its management. At $t = 0$, the firm's manager decides whether or not to take the project. If his decision is affirmative, he issues just enough equity to fund the project. At this point in time he can also commit to burn money at $t = 1$. Examples of mechanisms by which the manager can make this commitment are given later in this section.

We vary the strategy space of the model throughout the paper. In the first part of Section 4 we restrict the firm to either undertaking or foregoing the project; no other actions are possible. The model with this restriction is equivalent to the Myers & Majluf model and the conclusions are identical. In the second half of the section we extend the basic model's strategy space to allow the firm to commit to burn money, in Sections 4.1 and 4.2 we extend the strategy space to allow the firm's manager to specify an issue price [as in Giammarino & Lewis, 1988] and to scale the new project [as in Krasker, 1986]

The following notation is employed: θ denotes the value of the firm's assets-in-place. In our basic two type model when the manager's private information concerns the value of the firm's assets in place $\theta \in \{H, L\}$, where L denotes the value of the assets-in-place of the low value firm and H the value of the assets-in-place of high value firm. I is the cost of project and the size of the equity issue and V the revenue from project (so that $V - I$ is equal to the NPV of the project). In this section of the paper V is assumed to be common knowledge. In later sections of the paper, we will consider a setting where the manager has private information about the value of the project, in which case V will be a random variable observable only by the manager. C is the amount of money which the firm commits to burn as a signal.

3. Analysis of the model

In Sections 3.1 and 3.2 a model with two possible firm types is used to illustrate the Myers & Majluf model. We analyze the various equilibria that can arise in this setting and the effect on these equilibria of the addition of committing to burn money to the strategy space. In Section 3.3 these results are extended to a continuum of types.

3.1. The basic model

Table 1 illustrates the first example. The model parameters are listed at the top of the table. A high valued firm has assets-in-place worth $H = 100$, compared to $L = 50$ for a low valued firm. Both types have investment opportunities which cost $I = 20$ to undertake, and yield a cash flow at the end of the period of $V = 30$. The NPV of the project is thus $30 - 20 = 10$. Finally, the probability that the firm type is high is $\%H = 0.1$. The firm has no slack (or cash on hand), and therefore must issue equity to obtain the \$20. In this example we assume that the firm's managers maximize the wealth of the original shareholders.

In order to find the sequential equilibria [as defined by Kreps & Wilson, 1982] of the model we determine the payoffs to the firm for each strategy it might employ and for each possible set of investor beliefs *about* the firm's strategy. Based on the assumptions about the equity market stated in Section 2, the investors' purchase the issue at a price equal to the firm's expected value conditioned on all available information. If the firm's optimal strategy coincides with the investors' beliefs (i.e., if a fixed point is achieved), then neither the investors nor the firm wish to change their strategy knowing the strategy of the other, and the strategies form a sequential equilibrium. For example, if an investor believes that the strategy of both type H and type L is to take the project (Belief set A), and sets prices accordingly, then the payoffs to the high and low type firm are \$99.40 and \$61.20, respectively, if it issues equity and takes the project, and \$100 and \$50 if it does not. For these payoffs, it is optimal for the high type to *not* take the project, contrary to investor beliefs, and thus we see that there is no sequential pooling equilibrium for these parameter values.

Table 1

Separating equilibrium

Model parameters

$H = 100$ $L = 50$ $I = 20$ $V = 30$ $\%H = 0.1$

Belief set A			
Don't take:	None		
Take:	Both (pool)		
Payoffs			
		RESPONSE	
		Don't take	Take
TYPE	High	100	99.40
	Low	50	61.20

Belief set B			
Don't take:	Highs		
Take:	Lows		
Payoffs			
		RESPONSE	
		Don't take	Take
TYPE	High	100	97.50
	Low	50	60

The values in the payoff matrix are calculated in the following way: First, the payoff to either a high or low type firm if it doesn't take the project is just the value of that firm's assets-in-place (50 or 100 in this case). Note that in calculating these two payoffs the investors' beliefs do not matter because a firm doesn't issue equity if it doesn't take the project. Calculating the payoff for the high type firm when it takes the project is slightly more complicated. Now the firm must issue equity worth \$20 to finance the project. Investors, in return for their \$20, will receive a certain number of the firm's shares or, equivalently, a fraction of the firm's cash flows at the end of the period. The total cash flow for a given type of firm at date 1 is equal to the value of its assets-in-place plus the gross payoff of the new project:

$$\text{Total payoff for high firm:} \quad 100 + 30 = 130$$

$$\text{Total payoff for low firm:} \quad 50 + 30 = 80$$

Because investors are risk neutral they demand an expected payoff equal to the size of the equity issue, \$20. Because prior beliefs are that 10% of the firms are high type and 90% are low, investors will have an expected payoff of:

$$E(\text{Payoff}) = f \cdot (\overline{\theta} + V) = I \tag{1}$$

where f is the fraction of the firm's cash flow demanded by the investors and $\overline{\theta} + V$ is the average firm value, equal to $0.1(H + V) + 0.9(L + V)$. Inserting the values from Table 1 into Equation (1) we see that the value of f in this numerical example is:

$$f = \frac{20}{0.1(130) + 0.9(80)} = \frac{20}{85}$$

With investors demanding this fraction of the firm's cash flows, the original shareholders' payoff is:

$$\begin{pmatrix} \pi_H \\ \pi_L \end{pmatrix} = (1 - f) \cdot \begin{pmatrix} H + V \\ L + V \end{pmatrix} = \begin{pmatrix} 99.40 \\ 61.20 \end{pmatrix} \tag{2}$$

These are the entries in the right hand side of the payoff matrix for belief set A in Table 1.

Comparing the payoffs for the two types reveals that while the low type will take the project the high will not: their payoff is 100 if they don't take the project versus 99.40 if they do. This indicates that the investors' beliefs are not confirmed in equilibrium, showing that this is not a sequential equilibrium. So we must try another set of beliefs.

The right side of Table 1 shows the payoffs given the belief that only the low firms accept the project. The fraction f of the firm now demanded in return for the \$20 investment is:

$$f = \frac{20}{80} = 25\%$$

Substituting f into equation (2) gives payoffs of (97.50, 60) for taking the project, as shown in Table 1, right side. With these payoffs we see that the beliefs are now credible: the lows take the project and the highs do not. This separating equilibrium is the only sequential equilibrium.[3]

It is important to note that the separating equilibrium is not ex-ante efficient in the sense that if, before discovering its type, the firm could make a binding commitment to always issue and invest it would be better off. In the table, note that the original shareholders' expected payoff in the separating equilibrium is $0.1 \cdot 97.50 + 0.9 \cdot 60 = 63.75$. If, however, the manager could commit to always issuing, this payoff would be $0.1 \cdot 99.40 + 0.9 \cdot 61.20 = 65.02$. The reason why this payoff will always be higher is that if the new investors believe the firm's commitment to issue, and the firm does in fact issue regardless of type, than the firm will on-average sell equity which is properly priced. Since, in this case, the original shareholders always capture the full NPV of the project, they are better off than in the separating equilibrium, where the equity which is sold is always properly priced but where the project is passed up 10% of the time. Of course, the problem is that without a strong commitment mechanism the policy of always taking the project is time inconsistent: at time 0 the manager will always prefer to pass up the project if the firm turns out to be a high type even if investors believe that the firm will always issue.

Although the equilibrium given in Table 1 is unique, it is important to note that with different parameter values multiple equilibria can sometimes obtain. This is demonstrated in the Table 2 example where all parameters are the same except for the priors which have now been changed from 10% high to 90% high. In this case two equilibria exist:[4] a pooling equilibrium illustrated in the left side of Table 2, where both types take the project; and a separating equilibrium, illustrated in the right side of Table 2, where the lows accept the project and the highs do not.[5]

Both sets of beliefs are confirmed in equilibrium; if the investors believe the

[3] We have assumed in this analysis that the value of the project is equally well known by the firm manager and by investors, and have shown that under these conditions there will be 'underinvestment'. It is easily shown that if only the project value is asymmetric information then the firm will overinvest: firms with negative NPV projects will sometimes issue and invest to take advantage of overvalued shares. Myers & Majluf argue that this overinvestment problem should not be a problem since firms can always buy securities (a zero NPV investment) rather than taking a negative NPV investment.

[4] Additionally, for these parameter values a mixed strategy equilibrium exists in which the high firm takes the project with a probability α of approximately 0.17, and the payoff to a high firm whether or not he invests is 100. However, this equilibrium is unstable in the sense that if the investors behaved as if α were slightly higher than 0.17, the high firm would move from being indifferent to wanting to always take the project, which should cause the investors to revise their probability of α even further upwards, and if investors behaved as if α were slightly lower than 0.17, high type firms would never want to take the project, which should cause investors to revise the belief about α even further downwards.

[5] Cadsby, Frank & Maksimovic [1990] also note the existence of multiple equilibria. In their experiments, they demonstrate that markets tend to converge to the pooling rather than the separating equilibrium in these cases.

Table 2

Separating and pooling equilibrium

Model parameters				
$H = 100$	$L = 50$	$I = 20$	$V = 30$	$\%H = 0.9$

Belief set A	
Don't take:	None
Take:	Both (pool)

Payoffs

		RESPONSE	
		Don't take	Take
TYPE	High	100	109.20
	Low	50	67.20

Belief set B	
Don't take:	Highs
Take:	Lows

Payoffs

		RESPONSE	
		Don't take	Take
TYPE	High	100	97.50
	Low	50	60

highs will accept the project, they will, and vice-versa. Thus both equilibria are sequential.[6]

3.2. *Money burning*

In this section we extend the firm's strategy space to allow it to commit to burn money. We show that if this signal is available to the firm, then both the separating and the pooling equilibria of the last section will be 'broken' in that there will not exist beliefs satisfying the Cho & Kreps [1987] intuitive criterion which support either equilibrium. Specifically we show that for some parameter values a single equilibrium whose supporting beliefs satisfy Cho–Kreps exists. In this equilibrium both firms issue equity and finance the project and the high valued firm commits to burn money to signal its type.

We note here that when we refer to money burning we do not mean that the firm actually burns currency. Rather, we use money burning to refer to an irreversible action on the part of the firm which either causes the future revenues to drop by a fixed amount (whether the firm is a high or low type), or commits the firm or its shareholders to pay out some fixed dollar amount after project revenues are realized. We show in Section 5 that the John & Williams dividend signal and the Choe, Masulis & Nanda project delay signal fall into this category.

3.2.1. *Robustness of the underinvestment equilibrium*

In this section we describe why the underinvestment equilibrium will be broken when firms are able to signal their types with a commitment to burn money.

[6] Additionally, with the limited strategy space here, both equilibria survive the Cho & Kreps [1987] intuitive criterion. However the beliefs supporting the separating equilibrium are not part of a perfect sequential equilibrium [Grossman & Perry, 1986] if the manager's strategy space includes the possibility of somehow indicating that he is making an out-of-equilibrium move when he takes the project.

Consider again the example illustrated in Table 2. In the separating equilibrium, (on the right hand side of the table) an issuing firm (being revealed as a low type) must give up 25% of its firm to obtain equity financing for its project. If, however, a high valued firm could reveal its type, it would only have to issue 15.4% of its equity to obtain the $20 financing for the project. For the investor:

$$E(\text{Payoff}) = f' \cdot 130 = 20 \Longrightarrow f' = \frac{20}{130} = 15.4\%$$

Hence, by credibly signalling, a high type can reduce the percentage of the firm it offers by (25% - 15.4%) = 9.6%. This reduction has a value to the original shareholders of ($130 · 9.6%) = $12.48. But if a low firm were to mimic this signal, its gain would be only ($80 · 9.6%) = $7.68, because each share of the low firm is worth less. This asymmetric benefit means that by committing to burn only $7.68 a high type firm can credibly signal its type. Really, a high type must actually commit to burn slightly more than $7.68 because new investors will not demand $f' = 20/130$ as shown above, but rather $f' = 20/(130 - C)$, where C is the signalling cost. In signalling, the firm is dissipating part of its $130 value. When this factor is taken into account, the payoffs to the firm depending on their type (either H or L) and on their action (denoted by a superscript B if they commit to burn money) are:

$$\begin{aligned}
\pi_H^{\mathrm{B}} &= \left(1 - \frac{I}{H+V-C}\right)(H+V-C) \\
\pi_L^{\mathrm{B}} &= \left(1 - \frac{I}{H+V-C}\right)(L+V-C) \\
\pi_H &= \left(1 - \frac{I}{L+V}\right)(H+V) \\
\pi_L &= \left(1 - \frac{I}{L+V}\right)(L+V)
\end{aligned} \tag{3}$$

In order for committing to burn money to be a signal, incentive compatibility must be satisfied, meaning that there must exist a C for which $\pi_H^{\mathrm{B}} > \pi_h$ and $\pi_L^{\mathrm{B}} \leq \pi_L$,[7] with the equality holding for the most efficient signal level. The value of C which makes this an equality is:

$$C = \tfrac{1}{2}\left[(H+V) - \sqrt{(H+V)^2 - 4I(H-L)}\right] \tag{4}$$

Substituting C, which equals $8.21 in our numerical example, into equation (3), gives the values for the right side of Table 3. Inspection reveals that for this C, $\pi_H^{\mathrm{B}} > \pi_H$. Substituting equation (4) into equation (3) shows that this inequality holds for all parameter values. However, for some parameter values, $\pi_H^{\mathrm{B}} < H$, implying that a high would prefer to pass up the project rather than signal.

[7] Incentive compatibility requires that the payoff to the low valued firm if he mimics the high be no higher than his payoff if he does not mimic.

Table 3

Nonexistence of pooling and project choice-separating equilibria when the firm can commit to burn money

Model parameters				
$H = 100$	$L = 50$	$I = 20$	$V = 30$	$\%H = 0.9$

Belief set A

Don't take:	None
Take:	Both (pool)
Take & signal:	Highs

Payoffs — Signal cost: 0.52

		RESPONSE		
		Don't take	Take	Signal
TYPE	High	100	109.20	109.48
	Low	50	67.20	67.20

Belief set B

Don't take:	Highs
Take:	Lows
Take & signal:	Highs

Payoffs — Signal cost: 8.21

		RESPONSE		
		Don't take	Take	Signal
TYPE	High	100	97.50	101.79
	Low	50	60	60

3.2.2. *Robustness of the pooling equilibrium*

In this section we argue that the pooling equilibrium can never exist if firms have the opportunity to signal their types with a commitment to burn money. In the pooling equilibrium, the investors believe that both types take the project, and price the firm's equity accordingly. The question that we now ask is whether a high type firm can make an *out-of-equilibrium* move which will not be imitated by the low type and which gives it a higher payoff than what it receives in the pooling equilibrium. Consider again the example illustrated in Table 3. The high firm in this example can improve its value by \$0.28 by committing to burn \$0.52 to signal its type if investors consider this signal credible and value the firm accordingly. The signal should in fact be credible, since the low valued firm will not find it in its interest to mimic this money burning commitment. The signal level of \$0.52 is chosen because this is the level that just deters the low type from mimicking; the table shows that the low type's payoff does not increase from \$67.20 if it signals.

Under Kreps & Wilson's [1982] original sequential equilibrium concept, the pooling equilibrium would still be viable. It would be supported under the out of equilibrium belief that both types of firms are equally likely to commit to burn money. Given that under these beliefs neither type will burn money, the beliefs cannot be considered entirely unreasonable. Cho & Kreps [1987] analysis, however, suggests that a more reasonable out-of-equilibrium belief in this case is that the signalling firm's value is high: since it is not in the low type's interest to send this signal even if the signal results in the investor believing that the signalling firm is high, the signalling firm must be high.

The intuition behind the Cho & Kreps intuitive criterion is that a high valued firm could send a message to the investors spelling out this argument, and if the investors are rational they should believe it. The intuitive criterion essentially requires that such a message can be sent.[8] When uniform cost signalling is possible, the pooling equilibrium does not survive the intuitive criteria, but the illustrated example in which the highs pay \$0.52 to signal their type is also not a sequential equilibrium: if the highs signal, then firms that do not signal are revealed to be lows. Although a low type is only willing to pay \$0.52 to be treated as a high rather than a pool member, he is willing to pay up to \$8.21 to move from being considered a low to being considered a high.

Hence, in equilibrium, a high must commit to burn at least \$8.21 to credibly reveal his type. No other sequential equilibrium satisfies the intuitive criterion.[9] [10]

Also, note that although the sequential pooling equilibrium never survives the intuitive criterion if the firm can commit to burn money, the unique equilibrium which *does* survive need not involve committing to burn money. If, for example, V is reduced from 30 to 28, the 'no-mimic' signal level of \$8.26 is higher than the NPV of the project, so the highs prefer to pass up the project. The only equilibrium surviving the intuitive criterion is then one in which the high firm chooses to forego the project.

The results of this section are summarized in the following proposition:

Proposition 1. *In a setting where firms have the ability to commit to burn money and beliefs are governed by the Cho and Kreps intuitive criterion,*

1. A single equilibrium will exist in which the high type either commits to burn money, or passes up the project.

2. If, without money burning, a unique pooling equilibrium exists, then a high valued firm will commit to burn money, issue equity, and take the project.

3. If, without money burning, either a unique separating equilibrium or multiple equilibria exist, a high firm will commit to burn money, issue equity and take the project if $(H + I)(V - I) - I(H - L) > 0$,[11] *and pass up the project otherwise.*

[8] The essence of the intuitive criterion is that the beliefs supporting a sequential equilibrium should not be considered reasonable if the following message can be sent:

> I am sending you the message that my type is $t_i \in B$ and you should believe me. For I would *never* send this message if I were in $T - B$ (where T is the set of all possible types), regardless of your inference as to who is making the out-of equilibrium move. However, if sending this message convinces you that my type is any of the types in B, you can see that it is in my interest to send it.

If *any* player can send this message then the equilibrium fails the intuitive criterion. The pooling equilibrium here clearly fails when the manager's strategy space includes the ability to commit to burn money. The intuitive criterion also breaks the equilibrium in which the high firm chooses not to invest.

[9] Any equilibrium with a signalling cost higher than \$8.21 cannot survive because investors must believe that a signal of \$8.21 indicates a firm is high, and any equilibrium with a signalling cost lower than \$8.21, which must be a pooling equilibrium to be sequential, will fail because, based on the same belief, a high can and will signal his type by committing to burn \$8.21.

[10] Note that the money burning equilibrium is Pareto dominated by the sequential pooling equilibrium in this example. This means that the beliefs supporting the money burning equilibrium cannot be part of a perfect sequential equilibrium [Grossman & Perry, 1986]. Also, see footnote 6.

[11] This condition comes from the requirement that C in equation (4) be less than $V - I$.

3.2.3. The equilibrium when the manager has private information about the firm's investment opportunities

In order to conform to the literature, our analysis up to this point has assumed that the manager's private information concerns the value of the firm's asset's in place. However, Narayanan [1988] has suggested that managers are more likely to have private information about the value of the firm's investment opportunity than about the value of the firm's assets in place. In this setting, Narayanan shows that all firms with project's NPV is above a certain cutoff level will issue and invest.[12] Additionally, he shows that this cutoff level will be less than zero: in contrast to the Myers & Majluf equilibrium, this equilibrium will be characterized by 'overinvestment', or firms investing in negative NPV projects.[13]

To see the intuition behind this result, consider a candidate equilibrium in which only firms with positive NPV projects issue and invest. In this setting, a firm which had a slightly negative NPV project would still wish to issue, because even though the firm loses on taking on the negative NPV project, the original shareholders in the firm benefit when the firm sells overvalued securities; the securities will be overvalued for this firm because the market price of the securities is based on the fact that, in the candidate equilibrium, only firms with positive NPV projects issue. So we see that the candidate equilibrium is not, in fact, an equilibrium, and that the equilibrium must be one in which some firms with negative NPV projects issue and invest. Similar reasoning reveals that, in equilibrium, the average project NPV of the issuing firm must be positive.

A difficulty with Narayanan's analysis is its counterfactual implication that the firm's share price will rise on the announcement of an equity issue (provided there are some firms for which the project is sufficiently unprofitable that they pass it up).[14]

3.3. Generalization to a model with a continuum of types

Having developed the intuition for our model by examining the case with two types, we now extend the model to allow for a continuum of types with values of their assets-in-place denoted by θ, where $\theta \in [\underline{\theta}, \overline{\theta}]$. We derive the equilibrium signalling schedule and show that this equilibrium uniquely survives the intuitive criterion. In the proposed equilibrium the amount that the firm commits to burn, C, is a monotonic function of θ. By inverting this function, investors can infer the value of the firm's assets-in-place as $\hat{\theta}(C)$. The firm solves the problem choosing C to maximize the value of the original shares:

[12] Narayanan also shows that this result holds for either risky debt or equity

[13] Myers & Majluf challenge this conclusion on the basis that a firm can always invest any excess funds in securities (which are a zero NPV investment), and therefore would never need to take on negative NPV projects. They also show that under this assumption the share price reaction to an equity issue should always be negative.

[14] Actually, Narayanan shows that, given his assumptions the firm will not issue equity. However, were the firm constrained to issue equity, this would be the implication. We discuss these aspects of Narayanan's paper in Section 6.1

$$\max_{C} \quad \underbrace{\left(1 - \frac{I}{(\hat{\theta}(C) + V - C)}\right)}_{\text{fraction of the firm retained by the original shareholders}} \times \underbrace{(\theta + V - C)}_{\text{total value of the firm}}$$

Assuming that $\hat{\theta}(C)$ is differentiable, the sufficient first-order condition with respect to the signalling cost, after some manipulation, is:

$$[\hat{\theta}'(C) - 1]\frac{(\theta + V - C)I}{[\hat{\theta}(C) + V - C - I][\hat{\theta}(C) + V - C]} = 1 \tag{5}$$

To obtain the equilibrium solution, we set $\theta = \hat{\theta}(C)$, which yields:

$$\frac{\hat{\theta}'(C) - 1}{\hat{\theta}(C) - C + V - I} = \frac{1}{I}$$

which can be solved to yield:

$$\hat{\theta}(C) = K\mathrm{e}^{C/I} + C + I - V \tag{6}$$

where K is a constant of integration. Because a firm with the lowest θ has no incentive to signal, we have the requirement that $\hat{\theta}(0) = \underline{\theta}$, implying that $K = \underline{\theta} + V - I$. Additionally note that for the highest type firms with $\theta > \theta_c = (\underline{\theta} + V - I)\mathrm{e}^{(V-I)/I}$ the signalling cost C exceeds $V - I$, the NPV of the project. Hence, as in the Myers & Majluf model, these types pass up the project. Note that in this signalling equilibrium the cutoff value depends only on the lower bound of the type distribution $\underline{\theta}$, while in the Myers & Majluf equilibrium without signalling the cutoff depends on the actual shape of the type distribution.

Based on this development, we can state the following proposition:

Proposition 2. *Given that the value of a firm's assets-in-place, known by the firm's managers, is believed by investors to be distributed on $\theta \in [\underline{\theta}, \overline{\theta}]$ with a continuously increasing distribution function $F(\theta)$, the only sequential equilibrium in which each issuer is uniquely identified by his signal has the property that:*

1. The firm takes the project and commits to burn C dollars if $\theta < \theta_c$, where

$$\theta_c = (\underline{\theta} + V - I)\mathrm{e}^{(V-I)/I}.$$

2. C reveals the firm's θ and can be implicitly defined from the following signalling schedule:

$$\hat{\theta}(C) = (\underline{\theta} + V - I)\mathrm{e}^{C/I} + C + I - V. \tag{7}$$

This equilibrium uniquely satisfies the Cho–Kreps intuitive criterion.[15]

[15] It is also possible to show that no equilibrium, including the one here, is a perfect sequential equilibrium [Grossman & Perry, 1986] if $F'(\underline{\theta}) < \infty$.

Proof. See Appendix.

It is interesting to consider the efficiency of this signalling equilibrium relative to an equilibrium where signalling is prohibited. Without signalling a semi-separating equilibrium will usually obtain in which all types with assets-in-place worth less than a certain cutoff value will take the project, and all others will pass it up (i.e., a Myers & Majluf type equilibrium). However, depending on the distribution of types, there may be multiple equilibria of this type, just as in the discrete type example illustrated in Table 2. Hence the relative efficiency of the signalling and nonsignalling equilibria will depend on both the distribution of types and the particular nonsignalling equilibrium chosen.

Additionally, we state without proof the following proposition for a Narayanan [1988] type setting where the manager has private information about the value of the project (V), but where θ is common knowledge.

Proposition 3. *Given that the value of a firm's assets in place is common knowledge and that the value of a firm's investment opportunity, known by the firm's managers, is believed by investors to be distributed on* $V \in [\underline{V}, \overline{V}]$ *where* $\underline{V} \leq I$, *with a continuously increasing distribution function* $F(V)$, *the only sequential equilibrium in which each issuer is uniquely identified by his signal has the property that:*

1. The firm takes the project and commits to burn C dollars if and only if $V \geq I$,

2. C reveals the firm's V and can be implicitly defined from the following signalling schedule:

$$\hat{V}(C) = \theta \mathrm{e}^{C/I} + C + I - \theta. \tag{8}$$

This equilibrium also uniquely satisfies the Cho–Kreps intuitive criterion.[16]

Note that in this setting, the firm *always* issues and invests if the project NPV is greater than zero. Thus investment is perfectly efficient. The intuition for this result is as follows: First, since the equilibrium is fully revealing for all types which issue, it cannot be the case that a type with a negative NPV project would issue. Also, the lowest type which issues cannot be a firm with a positive NPV project, because then types with lower project values would mimic this firm.

What we conclude is that the overinvestment problem (when only project value is asymmetric information) is completely eliminated through money burning, but that money burning cannot completely solve the underinvestment problem (when only the value of the assets-in-place is asymmetric information). Additionally, one can show that a signalling schedule will obtain in the case where both θ and V are asymmetric information, and that this signalling schedule is described by $\hat{u}(C) = \underline{u}\mathrm{e}^{C/I} + C$ where $u = \theta + V$ is the firm value contingent on issuing and where $\underline{u}$ is the lowest u firm which will issue in equilibrium.[17] In this equilibrium,

[16] And again, it is possible to show that no equilibrium, including the one here, is a perfect sequential equilibrium if $F'(\underline{\theta}) < \infty$.

[17] Given certain distributional assumptions, this will be the lowest valuation firm with a positive NPV project.

firms will only issue if the project is positive NPV and if the signalling cost C is less than the NPV of the project $(V - I)$.

3.4. Equity financed money burning

In the preceding analysis the money that was burned as a signal came out of project revenues rather than from the equity issue. This distinction turns out to be critical. We now show that while an equilibrium in which money is burned from the proceeds of the equity issue is possible, such a signal is very inefficient. In such an equilibrium the high valued firm is indifferent between signalling and not, and the low valued firm is indifferent between mimicking and not. Why can't equity financed money burning be an efficient signal in this setting, while committing to burn money out of project revenues is? Burning money in the current period uses up resources and increases the amount of capital required by the firm to fund its investment and therefore the size of its equity issue. This larger equity issue increases the benefit to the low type because now, in mimicking, he can sell more overpriced stock, and as a result the high type must burn still more money to satisfy incentive compatibility. As we show in the proposition below, this extra benefit to the low type exactly offsets the above mentioned benefit to the high type from signalling. As a result, the amount that must be burned to prevent mimicking is such that a firm gains nothing and is thus indifferent between signalling and not signalling. We state this formally in the following proposition:

Proposition 4. *In an equilibrium in which equity financed money burning is used as a signal, the costs and benefits of signalling are equal for both high and low types. Both firm types are therefore indifferent between signalling and not signalling. A strong preference for signalling requires that burned money come out of project revenues.*

Proof. Again we can construct a payoff matrix for a two type model assuming a separating equilibrium. Here the subscript of either H or L indicates the firm type, and a superscript of U indicates that this is the payoff if the firm burns money raised through an equity issue:

$$\begin{aligned} \pi_H^U &= \left(1 - \frac{I+C}{H+V}\right)(H+V) & \pi_H &= \left(1 - \frac{I}{L+V}\right)(H+V) \\ \pi_L^U &= \left(1 - \frac{I+C}{H+V}\right)(L+V) & \pi_L &= \left(1 - \frac{I}{L+V}\right)(L+V) \end{aligned} \tag{9}$$

Again, incentive compatibility requires that $\pi_L^U \leq \pi_L$, and therefore that $(I + C)/(H + V) \geq I/(L + V)$. If C is large enough to satisfy this condition, the high firm's payoff from signalling is seen to be less than or equal to that from not signalling. The equilibrium signal level is therefore $C = I[(H - L)/(L + V)]$, and therefore $\pi_H^U = \pi_H$ and $\pi_L^U = \pi_L$. The high firm is indifferent between signalling and not and the low firm is indifferent between mimicking and not. □

Note that the proposition also implies that slack cannot be burned as a signal: high and low types equally benefit from this action because it increases the size of the equity issue. Another implication is that no pooling equilibrium can be broken by an equity financed money burning signal. Also, note that this signal is functionally equivalent to simply increasing the fraction of the firm given to the new shareholders from $I/(L+V)$ to $(I+C)/(H+V)$: instead of burning the money, the managers give it to the new investor by underpricing the issue. Proposition 2 implies that underpricing will not be an efficient signal. However we shall show in Section 5.1 that with a minor change in the assumptions we can obtain an equilibrium, similar to Welch [1989], in which firms with favorable information underprice.

4. Further extensions of the model strategy space

4.1. *The price setting signal*

If the Myers & Majluf strategy space is enlarged to allow the manager to set the offering price of the issue, an equilibrium arises in which the high type firm sets an offering price above the firm's ex-ante market price, but equal to the full-information value of the firm. In the two type model, high price offers have some probability of being rejected, but low price offers never fail. In equilibrium, the probability of rejection of a high price offer, α, is just high enough to keep the low type firms from setting a high price. The investor is indifferent between accepting and rejecting the offer because the equity issue is a zero-NPV investment, so any probability of acceptance is an optimal strategy for him.

The price setting equilibrium presented here is essentially the same as the equilibrium presented in Giammarino & Lewis [1988]. In the Giammarino & Lewis model, however, the firm proposes a price to an investment banker, who rejects the offer with a certain probability. In our model, the firm sets an issue price, and the *market* issue goes through (i.e., is fully subscribed) with a certain probability. In addition to the model differences, our analysis is slightly different. Giammarino & Lewis present a set of mixed strategy equilibria, each characterized by the probability that a low type mimics. We consider only one member of this set, that for which the low type never mimics. This equilibrium dominates the others in the sense that all others can be eliminated by a modified intuitive criterion which we will discuss in Section 4.1.1. Additionally this no-mimic equilibrium Pareto dominates the other members of the set.

In Section 4.1.1 we discuss the price setting model with observable project values and show that price setting dominates committing to burn money as a signal. However, we show in Section 4.1.2 that if the project's cash flow is significantly larger for the high type firm, committing to burn money is the more efficient signal.

4.1.1. *Price setting when project value is observable*

Equation (10) gives the payoffs to a firm of type t (either H or L) given that it sets an offering price p (either $h$igh or $l$ow), and given that the investor believes that a firm which sets a high price is indeed a high type firm:

$$\begin{aligned} \pi^{p=h}_{t=H} &= H + \alpha(V - I) \qquad & \pi^h_L &= L + \alpha\left(V - I\frac{L+V}{H+V}\right) \\ \pi^l_H &= H + V - I\frac{H+V}{L+V} \qquad & \pi^l_L &= (L + V - I) \end{aligned} \tag{10}$$

In equilibrium, α will be set so that $\pi^h_L = \pi^l_L$ and incentive compatibility is satisfied. This leads to the following equation for α:

$$\alpha = \frac{V - I}{V - I[(L+V)/(H+V)]} \tag{11}$$

Note that α is always between zero and one for $H > L$ and $V > I$. Additionally, substituting this definition for α into equation (10) reveals that $\pi^h_H > \pi^l_H$, and thus a mixed strategy equilibrium exists for all parameter values.

Unlike the money burning equilibrium, where for some parameter values the high type chooses to pass up the project, the high type in this equilibrium always signals and takes the project if he receives funding.

Table 4 shows the payoffs to the two types of firms for each possible action under two sets of investor beliefs. Notice that the payoffs in the columns labeled 'Reject', 'p = pool', and 'p = low', are the same as given in Table 3. The left side of the table shows that if a firm can set a price for its equity, a sequential pooling equilibrium will not exist if beliefs must satisfy the modified intuitive criterion which is discussed below. This will be true for any parameter values,

Table 4

Price setting as a signal

Model parameters

$H = 100$ $L = 50$ $I = 20$ $V = 30$ $\%H = 0.9$

Price setting		Price setting equilibrium	
Reject:	(Doesn't matter)	Reject:	(Doesn't matter)
High price:	Highs	High price:	High
Pool price:	Both (pool)	Low price:	Low

Payoffs, $\alpha = 0.972$ (price setting)

		RESPONSE		
		Reject	p = high	p = pool
TYPE	High	100	119.44	109.48
	Low	50	67.20	67.20

Payoffs, $\alpha = 0.565$ (price setting equilibrium)

		RESPONSE		
		Reject	p = high	p = low
TYPE	High	100	105.65	97.50
	Low	50	60	60

again provided the project's value is common knowledge. Comparing the payoffs here with the payoffs in Table 3 shows that the mixed strategy equilibrium Pareto dominates the money burning equilibrium.

As was discussed earlier, the viability of a sequential equilibrium is critically dependent on the admissibility of the investor's out-of-equilibrium beliefs. Section 3.2.2 showed that the out-of-equilibrium beliefs required to support a sequential pooling equilibrium do not satisfy the intuitive criterion when money burning is possible. However, the price setting signal will not break the pooling equilibrium if out-of-equilibrium beliefs are governed by the intuitive criterion.

For a signal to break an equilibrium under the standard intuitive criterion, the signal must pass a test: some type (the low, in this example) must never wish to send the signal *no matter what the investor's anticipated response to the signal,* provided the investor's response to the signal is optimal for *some* belief about who is signalling. In the preceding example, accepting the high price offer with certainty is an optimal response if the investor believes that only the high type would select the high price. However, the low type would have an incentive to also price high if this were the investor's response, so the pooling equilibrium cannot be broken with this signal.

It does seem reasonable that the pooling equilibrium should be eliminated by the price-setting signal since the issuing firm strictly prefers the signalling equilibrium to the pooling equilibrium, and would therefore take actions, if it can, to insure that the separating beliefs prevail. However, to kill the pooling equilibrium with the price setting signal, we need a stronger refinement which eliminates certain possible best-responses by the investor.

To eliminate the pooling equilibrium with the price-setting signal, we propose a refinement we call *the modified intuitive criterion*, which requires that the price-setting signal be met by a specific mixed response by the investor. The modified intuitive criterion we propose limits the investor's best responses but not his beliefs. If the investor believes the firm making the out-of-equilibrium move has a high value, and as a result of this belief he is indifferent between a set of best responses, he must if possible choose a best-response which would make the low not want to mimic.[18]

In this specific model, if the investor makes the inference that it is the high type that is setting a high price, *any* rejection probability is a rational response,

[18] The modified message analogous to that in footnote 8 is the following:

> I am sending you the out of equilibrium message m, indicating that my type is $t_i \in B$ and you should believe me. For I would never send this message if I were in $T - B$ regardless of your inference as to who is making the out of equilibrium move, assuming your response meets the condition specified below. However if sending this message convinces you that my type is any of the types in B, then you can see that it is in my interest to send it.
> The condition I place on your response is that if an inference that I was in B led you to be indifferent between a number of responses, but your utility would be lower were I in fact some type in $T - B$, then you must, if possible, choose a response which would make any member of $T - B$ not wish to send the message.

since the issue is properly priced and thus is a zero NPV investment.[19] However, a small rejection probability will not deter a low type from mimicking, and if the low type mimics, the investor will, on average, pay too much for the equity issue. The modified intuitive criterion therefore states that the investor *must* respond with a probability large enough to keep the low type from mimicking.

The price setting signal is somewhat less intuitive than the other signals considered here since it requires investors to reject issues at specific probabilities even though, within the equilibrium, they are indifferent between rejecting and accepting the issues. As a modeling convenience we assume that investors in a sense flip a coin in this equilibrium to decide whether to purchase an issue or not. Although this is clearly unrealistic, we think it approximates a more complex model where the issuing firm does not know investors' reservation price exactly. For example, the firm may not know the investors' full information set and may instead observe only some (common knowledge) distribution on the probability of the issue's success as a function of the issue price. In this setting, the high type firm would set a price high enough so that, even if the investors believe the firm is a high type, there is still some significant probability that the issue is rejected.[20] In this setting the firm is in essence specifying the desired probability of rejection by the price it sets. Therefore the standard intuitive criterion would suffice to eliminate other equilibria when the price setting signal is available. However, this model would be far less tractable and would add little additional insight to the problem. We therefore choose to model the investor's decision as a mixed strategy and consequently need the modified criterion.

To see why the price setting signal works, consider the costs and benefits it creates for each of the two types.[21] The benefit is asymmetric just as with committing to burn money since the firm gives up a fixed percentage of its cash flows in exchange for the required investment funds. If a high value firm signals its type, this percentage drops from $I/(L+V)$ to $I/(H+V)$. We have shown that a percentage drop is more valuable to a high value firm than to a low value firm. Of course, the high type firm only gets this benefit when the issue succeeds, which it does a fraction α of the time. The benefit from signalling is therefore:

$$\alpha\left(\frac{I}{L+V}-\frac{I}{H+V}\right)(\theta+V), \tag{12}$$

where θ is again the value of the firm's asssets-in-place (H or L). Recall that the cost of committing to burn money is the same for all types: the cost of burning a dollar of project revenues is a dollar whether you are a high or a low type. In the Giammarino & Lewis model though, the cost of signalling is asymmetric. With the benefit defined in equation (12), the cost of signalling for the low firm

[19] If the investor believes that it is the low type *with any probability*, the only rational response is to always reject the issue.

[20] This argument, in a slightly different context, is in the appendix of Hirshleifer & Titman [1990], and is similar to the intuition behind the model of Jegadeesh & Chowdhry [1994].

[21] Note that the absolute cost and benefit here are arbitrary and are defined to facilitate comparison with the money burning equilibrium. However the benefit minus the cost must equal $\pi_\theta^h - \pi_\theta^l$.

is $(1-\alpha)(V-I)$: the low firm, in mimicking, gives up the NPV of the project $(V-I)$ a fraction $(1-\alpha)$ of the time. For a high type though, the cost of signalling is lower since it has to sell undervalued equity and thus does not capture the full NPV of the project when it obtains financing without signalling. The cost of issuing undervalued equity to fund the project is $I[(H+V)/(L+V)]$, and the captured NPV is therefore $(V-I)[(H+V)/(L+V)]$. This makes the high type's cost of signalling:

$$(1-\alpha)\left(V - I\frac{H+V}{L+V}\right) \tag{13}$$

Since $H > L > 0$ and $V > 0$, this is less than the low type's cost of signalling. Extending this analysis of costs and benefits, it is clear that the price setting signal is more efficient than the money burning signal, meaning that a high type's payoff will be higher if he sets a high price than if he burns money. This means that if both money burning and price setting are included in the strategy space, and if beliefs are required to satisfy the modified intuitive criterion, no equilibrium in which money is burned will exist.[22] Formally, we have the following proposition:

Proposition 5. *Given that firms can specify a price for their equity or can commit to burn money, and given that project NPV is known to investors, a sequential mixed strategy equilibrium always exists in which all types sell equity at the full information price, the low type's offer is always accepted by the investor and the high type's is accepted with probability* $\alpha < 1$. *This equilibrium uniquely survives the modified intuitive criterion.*

Proof. See Appendix

4.1.2. The price setting signal when the project value is unobservable

As is indicated, the above proposition holds when the only asymmetric information concerns the value of the firm's assets-in-place. However, to the extent that the value of the firm's assets-in-place is better known by the firm's manager so should the NPV of the project. Also, it is reasonable to assume that the project NPV should be positively correlated with the value of the assets-in-place: to the extent that type is a proxy for management ability or for the general prospects of the firm, a higher type should have a higher value of both ongoing assets and new projects.

The following proposition demonstrates that if the NPV of the high type's project is sufficiently high relative to the NPV of the low type's project, committing to burn money will dominate price setting as a signal. The intuition for this result is that if the high type has a more valuable project, the cost of foregoing this project is higher. If the cost is high enough, the high prefers to commit to burn money rather than run the risk not obtaining financing. This result is formally stated in the following proposition:

[22] We also note that the price setting equilibrium Pareto dominates an equilibrium in which money is burned, since the high type's payoff is higher and the low type's payoff is the same.

Proposition 6. *If the NPV of the high type's project is sufficiently greater than the NPV of the low type's, committing to burn money will be a more efficient signal than price setting, and the price setting equilibrium will fail to survive the intuitive criterion.*

Proof. See Appendix

Note that if the project NPV is inversely related to the value of the firm's assets-in-place, the result will be reversed: the price setting signal will be even more efficient, in the sense that the cost to the high type of achieving separation from the low type is lower if the project scaling signal is employed. However, for the reasons discussed above, our intuition suggests the correlation is more likely to be positive.

4.2. The project scaling signal

Krasker [1986] extended the Myers & Majluf strategy space to allow the firm to scale back the size of the investment project and thus issue fewer shares. He showed that in this setting the amount of equity issued, or alternatively the amount by which the project is scaled back, serves as a signal of the value of a firm's assets-in-place. This section provides conditions under which the project scaling signal will be a more or less efficient signal than committing to burn money or price setting. As in Section 4.1, we begin by analyzing a model in which all project details are observable. With this restriction project scaling, like price setting, is a more efficient signal than committing to burn money because scaling the project decreases the size of the firm's equity issue and thus decreases the benefit to the low firm of mimicking. However if project value is related to the unknown value of the assets-in-place, project scaling will not be as efficient a signal.

In the following example, we assume that if the firm invests x fewer dollars [for a total investment of $(I - x)$], its payoff will be reduced by γx dollars, for a total cash flow from the project of $(V - \gamma x)$ dollars. Note that if γ is (less than, equal to, greater than) V/I, the project is (decreasing, constant, increasing) returns to scale. We again assume that everything is known except θ, the value of the firm's assets-in-place, which is known only to the managers.

The equilibrium payoffs to the high and low types, given a decrease in investment of x, are given in the following payoff matrix. The payoffs are calculated assuming that the investor believes that a firm which scales is a high type.

$$
\begin{aligned}
\pi^{S}_{t=H} &= \left(1 - \frac{I - x}{H + V - \gamma x}\right)(H + V - \gamma x) \\
\pi^{S}_{t=L} &= \left(1 - \frac{I - x}{H + V - \gamma x}\right)(L + V - \gamma x) \\
\pi_{H} &= \left(1 - \frac{I}{L + V}\right)(H + V) \\
\pi_{L} &= (L + V - I)
\end{aligned}
\tag{14}
$$

Subtracting π_L^S from π_L gives a benefit minus cost from signalling of:

$$I\left(1-\frac{L+V-\gamma x}{H+V-\gamma x}\right)-x\left(\gamma-\frac{L+V-\gamma x}{H+V-\gamma x}\right) \tag{15}$$

In equilibrium, x is chosen so that this is equal to zero. Similarly, the benefit minus cost for the high type is:

$$I\left(\frac{H+V}{L+V}-1\right)-x(\gamma-1)$$

The high type's benefit minus cost from signalling is seen by comparison with equation (3) to be equal to the cost of committing to burn $x(\gamma-1)$ dollars.[23] However, for the low type the cost is considerably higher,[24] indicating that at least for small values of γ, project scaling is more efficient than committing to burn money. In fact, for $\gamma=1$, when the marginal return on additional investment is zero the cost to the high type of reducing his investment is zero since decreasing the project size does not change the NPV of the project. The cost to the low is not zero, however, because as the project size is decreased, the low cannot sell as much overpriced equity.

If the project has constant returns to scale (i.e. $\gamma=V/I$), the scaling signal is similar to the price setting signal. The cost of the price setting signal is that the firm gives up the entire project NPV a certain fraction of the time in exchange for a higher price for its equity.[25] When project scaling is used as a signal, a fraction of the NPV of the project is given up all of the time. Although these signals appear to be equivalent, price setting in this case is slightly more efficient than project scaling.

The intuition for this is the following:[26] The high type's cost of signalling is lower if he can reduce the degree of asymmetric information about the firm, the value of which is composed of two parts: the cash flow from the assets-in-place, θ, which cannot be directly observed except by management, and the cash flow from the project, V, which is known. Scaling back the project reduces the portion of the firm's cash flow that investors are informed about, and therefore increases the asymmetry of information and increases signalling costs. While in the price setting equilibrium, the total firm value when the equity issue succeeds is $\theta+V$, in the scaling equilibrium the total firm value is $\theta+\alpha V$; a larger fraction of the firm is composed of the uncertain assets-in-place. Because of this more severe asymmetric information problem, the cost of signalling is higher, and the net payoff to the high firm is lower. As one would expect based on this

[23] From (3), $\pi_H^B-\pi_H=I[(H+V)/(L+V)-1]-C$.

[24] This is because the fraction $(L+V-\gamma x)/(H+V-\gamma x)$ is always less than one.

[25] In Section 4.1 we show that a fraction $(1-\alpha)$ of the time, the high's equity issue fails, in which case the firm fails to capture the NPV of the project. However, when the issue succeeds, the high value firm sells equity at a price which is a factor $(H+V)/(L+V)$ higher.

[26] Our thanks to David Hirshleifer for suggesting this interpretation.

intuition, the difference between the payoffs using the two signals approaches zero for $\theta \gg V$.

For large returns to scale, project scaling is a less efficient method of signalling firm value. Intuitively, this is because it is now more costly for the high type to reduce the size of the equity issue. However, as long as the project's value is known, project scaling is always more efficient than committing to burn money. As $\gamma \to \infty$, scaling the project by some infinitesimal amount reduces the cash flow from the project without appreciably decreasing the size of the equity issue, and hence, is equivalent to committing to burn money.

We can now state the following proposition. Note again that with any of the three signalling mechanisms in the strategy space, the equilibrium in which the most efficient signal is used will be the only one which will survive the modified intuitive criterion:

Proposition 7. *The following are characteristics of the project scaling equilibrium in the case where the project NPV is observable and where project scaling, price setting, and committing to burn money can be used as signals:*

1. For a constant returns to scale project, project scaling is a less efficient signal than price setting, and the project scaling equilibrium does not survive the modified intuitive criterion.

2. For $\gamma < \gamma^*$, project scaling dominates price setting as a signal, and the price setting equilibrium does not survive the intuitive criterion, where γ^* is defined by the system of equations:

$$\gamma^* x = (V - I)\left(1 - \frac{(V - I)}{V - I(L + V)/(H + V)}\right)$$

$$I\left(1 - \frac{L + V - \gamma^* x}{H + V - \gamma^* x}\right) = x\left(\gamma^* - \frac{L + V - \gamma^* x}{H + V - \gamma^* x}\right)$$

3. Project Scaling is always a more efficient signal than committing to burn money, and the money burning equilibrium never survives the intuitive criterion.

4. As $\gamma \to \infty$, the efficiency of project scaling approaches that of committing to burn money.

Proof. See Appendix

4.3. An optimal combination of signals

Until now we have made the assumption that a high firm would signal using only one of the three available signalling mechanisms. However, under certain conditions a combination of scaling, committing to burn money, and price setting will be the most efficient signal and hence the only signal observed in an equilibrium which satisfies the modified intuitive criterion.

As an example, when $H - L$ is large and the project's production function $V(I)$ is identical for the two types, and is everywhere concave with $V'(\infty) < 1$

and $V'(0) = \infty$, the optimal signal will be a combination of project scaling and price setting. The intuition for this is as follows: We have already shown that if the project's marginal return on investment is zero (i.e., if $V'(I) = 1$), then a marginal scaling of the project imposes a cost of mimicking on a low type, and no signalling cost on a high. Because of this, a high type will always do some scaling. But, as we showed in Section 4.2, as investment decreases, so does the efficiency of the scaling signal. Therefore, after some amount of scaling, the marginal cost to a high of further scaling becomes higher than the cost of increasing the probability of having the issue rejected.[27] In this case, a high can minimize its signalling cost if it utilizes a combination of scaling and price setting as a signal.

Similarly, Appendix B shows that if the project's production function is different for high and low type firms, then a combination of two of the three, or of all three signals may be the most efficient way for a high valued firm to convey its type. Based on the derivation presented in Appendix B, we present the following proposition.

Proposition 8. *In an equilibrium in which beliefs are governed by the modified Cho–Kreps intuitive criterion, there exist production functions for which the equilibrium signal is either price setting, committing to burn money or project scaling, or a combination of either two or three of the signals.*

Ambarish, John & Williams [1987] is a special case of this analysis in that they do not allow the firm to set its issue price, but do allow it to vary its investment level and commit to burn money (by paying taxable dividends). Based on their assumptions, they find that for small $H - L$, a high valued firm will signal by scaling, but for large $H - L$, a combination of the two signals will be optimal. Their model assumes that the high type's production function is everywhere more concave than the low type's, so that the high type's marginal return on investment changes faster with a change in investment than the low type's. Therefore, though the scaling signal is always more efficient at the high's full information investment level, if the high firm decreases its investment level far enough, scaling becomes a less efficient signal than committing to burn money.[28]

[27] Where 'marginal cost' is defined as the cost to the high of imposing an additional \$1 cost of mimicking on the low

[28] In Ambarish, John and Williams the present value of the investment opportunity for a type j firm, $F_j(I)$ is equal to $a_j + b_j G(I)$, where $G'(I) > 0$, $G''(I) < 0$, $G(O) = 0$, and $G'(0) = \infty$. They show that when $a_2 > a_1$ and $b_2 > b_1$ a type 2 firm will combine underinvestment with payment of a dividend as a signal of firm type. In their model, as the investment decreases, $b_j G'(I)$ (the marginal return on investment) increases, and project scaling becomes a less efficient signal. Also, because $b_2 > b_1$, scaling the project costs the high (type 2) firm more than it cost the low firm in revenues from the project. So below some investment level, project scaling is less efficient than burning money. Thus a high firm finds it optimal to signal its type through a combination of project scaling and money burning.Note that they also require that $a_2/a_1 > b_2/b_1$. If this condition is not satisfied the high firm will find overinvestment a superior signal to underinvestment.

5. Money burning models in the finance literature

As we stated in the introduction, a number of papers in the literature analyze signals that are either equivalent to burning money or committing to burn money. By 'equivalent' we mean that the cost and benefit for each type is the same. In this section we discuss a number of these models. These include the underpricing models of Allen & Faulhaber [1989], Grinblatt & Hwang [1989], and Welch [1989], which feature a signal that is equivalent to equity financed money burning, and the dividend signalling model of John & Williams [1985] and the project delay model of Choe, Masulis & Nanda [1993], which employ methods of committing to burn money.

5.1. IPO underpricing models

In equity financed money burning, firms must sell extra equity to get the money that they burn. If they were to take the extra money obtained from the equity issue and, instead of burning it, return it to the new shareholders, the effect would be the same. This latter action is equivalent to underpricing the issue.

The interpretation of equity financed money burning as underpricing yields insights into why equity financed money burning does not work as a signal. To satisfy incentive compatibility in a separating equilibrium, the high type would have to set a share price for his IPO which would be at or below the share value of the low type. However, this could not be an equilibirum because the high would always prefer pooling with the low, and receiving the average of the high and low share values.

In several recent papers, IPO underpricing does serve as a signal. However, these models either provide an additional benefit to the higher valued firms from signalling, or alternatively impose an additional cost on the low. In Welch [1989], for example, the project NPV is negative for the low type and it is assumed that to mimic, the low type must both issue equity and take on the project. The low thus incurs a cost by taking on the project. If this cost outweighs the benefit from selling overpriced equity, the low will choose to not take the project so that the high type will not have to signal. However, if the cost to a low is not quite high enough to induce separation in this way, a high can underprice slightly, and reduce the benefit to mimicking just enough so that a low would not be willing to mimic. This rationale for underpricing an issue can easily be illustrated within the context of our model as we do in the following proposition:

Proposition 9. *Assume that firms cannot commit to burn money and cannot scale back their projects. Then, if the project has a negative NPV for the low type ($V_L < I$) and a positive NPV for the high types ($V_H > I$), with assets-in-place of $\theta_H > \theta_L > 0$:*

1. If $V_L < I[\theta_L/(\theta_H + V_H - I)]$ a pure strategy equilibrium exists in which:

- *The high type issues equity at the market price, which is equal to the full information value, and takes the project.*

- *The low type does not issue equity and does not take on the project.*

2. If $\theta_L/(\theta_H + V_H - I) < V_L < V_H[(\theta_H + V_H)/(\theta_L + V_L)]$ *an equilibrium exists in which:* [29]

- *The high type issues equity at less than the full information value (underprices) and takes the project.*
- *The low type does not issue equity and does not take on the project.*

3. If $V_L > V_H[(\theta_H + V_H)/(\theta_L + V_L)]$ *an equilibrium exists in which:*

- *Neither high nor low type issues equity nor takes on the project.*

All of these are sequential equilibria, and satisfy the intuitive criterion if the firm is unable to commit to burn money. If the firm has the ability to commit to burn money, the second and third equilibria will not satisfy the intuitive criterion.

Proof. See Appendix.

In the Welch model V_L is constrained to be zero, so the project NPV is negative and an underpricing equilibrium can be obtained without a more complicated structure. In the Grinblatt & Hwang [1989] and Allen & Faulhaber [1989] models the project NPV is positive for both firm types, so these models also require somewhat more complicated structures to get underpricing results. However in all three models as in the above proposition, committing to burn money in the future, if feasible, would be a more efficient signal and would dominate underpricing.

It is important to note that, in terms of maximizing social welfare, the underpricing signal may be optimal, in that it is a simple transfer while the project scaling, and price-setting signals both result in a misallocation of resources. Burning money may also be optimal in this sense if the manager transfers money to some party rather than wasting resources. However, keep in mind that the notion of efficiency we are employing here is concerned only with the old shareholders' welfare.[30]

5.2. Dividend signalling models

As we mentioned earlier, dividends in the John and Williams model are paid out of the equity issue. This seems to contradict Proposition 2, which shows that the money burned, or in this case the taxes paid on the dividends, must come out of project revenues. However, in the John and Williams model both the firm and the shareholder sell shares: the firm sells new equity to raise money for the investment opportunity and the original shareholders sell shares to fulfill their liquidity needs. When a dividend is paid to the original shareholders, their liquidity needs decrease by the amount of the dividend, and thus the net amount of equity sold by the firm and the original shareholders does not change. It should be noted that this assumes that the shareholder's tax liability is not incurred until after the firm's

[29] We also note that, although this equilibrium satisfies the intuitive criterion, there always exists either a pooling or a mixed strategy equilibrium which Pareto domintes it.

[30] Perhaps, it is possible for the firm to ex ante sell the right to receive undervalued shares in the future. If they could do this, we might conclude that the underpricing signal is ex ante efficient as well as socially beneficial.

type is revealed. If the taxes were due immediately the shareholders would have to sell additional shares to raise the money necessary to pay the taxes on the dividend. This would mean that the total amount of equity sold would increase with the dividend, making the signal equivalent to equity financed money burning. As we showed earlier, dividends would not be an effective signal if that were the case. However, the taxes on the dividends in John and William's model are not required to be paid until after the project's revenues are realized. So the dividend tax is actually modeled as a commitment to burn money in the future, which as we have shown, is in fact an effective signal in this setting.[31]

5.3. A model of project delay

A recent paper by Choe, Masulis & Nanda [1993] proposes a theory to explain why there are more equity issues in economic expansions than in contractions. A crucial feature of the model is that all firms have the option to delay investment. Delay is costly in the sense that it reduces the present value of the project revenues, but does not increase the investment required to fund the project. What Choe, Masulis & Nanda show is that although high value firms may choose to delay the project to a good period, low value firms will issue and invest when the project first becomes available.

A somewhat modified version of the Choe, Masulis & Nanda model is as follows: Assume that all details of the model are the same as presented in Table 1 in Section 3.1, except that now the firm can issue and invest in the project at either $t = 0$ or $t = 1$, and the cash flow from both the assets-in-place and the project are realized at $t = 2$. If the firm invests at $t = 0$, then $V = 30$ (and NPV = 10), as in Table 1, but if the firm delays and invests at $t = 1$, V falls to 21 (i.e., the project *NPV* falls to \$1). It is easily shown that the only equilibrium whose beliefs satisfy the intuitive criterion is one in which the low valued firm issues and invests at $t = 0$ and the high valued firm issues and invests at $t = 1$.

This equilibrium can easily be understood in relation to the concept of burning money. Delaying the project in this model is precisely equivalent to committing to burn money in that it wastes future resources but costs nothing extra at the time of the equity issue. However, the way in which the delay affects the NPV of the project is crucial in the model. If instead of decreasing project revenues delaying the project increased the required investment and left the project's cash flows unchanged, the project delay would be equivalent to money burning in the current period (or underpricing), and delay would then not then be observed in equilibrium.

Additionally, it seems reasonable that delay should cost the high type more than it costs the low type; this will be the case if a high type's project is more valuable

[31] In Ambarish, John & Williams [1987], L denotes the after-tax demand for liquidity, and is an arbitrary function of the dividend D. AJW show that if $L_D = 0$, dividends cannot function as a signal of firm value, and the model becomes a Myers & Majluf like model in which high value firms underinvest.

and the cost of delay is proportional to the value of the project. If there is a substantial cost differential, project delay will not function as a signal.

6. Debt and the pecking order hypothesis

The literature that we have discussed so far assumes that the firm must issue equity. If the firm can issue debt, many of our earlier conclusions change significantly. Myers & Majluf consider the implications of adding the option of issuing debt to the firm's strategy space, and conclude that there exists a 'pecking order' in the issuance of securities;[32] the securities whose payoffs depend least on the manager's private information should be issued, because by issuing these securities the manager minimizes the adverse selection problem. Therefore, when the manager has private information about the level of the cash flows from the project, the firm will always issue riskless debt if possible. However, a more likely scenario is one in which there is some uncertainty, even from the manager's perspective, as to what the firm's future cash flows will be, and probably enough uncertainty so that the firm cannot issue perfectly risk-free debt. In this scenario, as we show below, the firm will sometimes find it optimal to issue equity instead of risky debt.

This section is divided as follows: In Section 6.1 we analyze the setting in which managers have information which investors do not about the mean of the project's cash flows distribution, and in Section 6.2 we explore the possibility that managers have extra information about the variance of the project's cash flows. In Section 6.3 we investigate the setting where the firm has outstanding risky debt. Brennan & Kraus [1988] shows that firms in this category can costlessly signal their type though their financing decisions. The final section discusses the relation between the Myers & Majluf pecking order hypothesis and the Modigliani & Miller capital structure irrelevance theorem.

6.1. Financing when the project's cash flows are uncertain

If a firm can issue riskless debt, the adverse selection problem disappears, and only firms with positive NPV projects issue riskless debt and invest. In the basic Myers & Majluf model where cash flows are certain, debt would be riskless and there would efficient investment. However, in a more realistic setting the firm manager will not know the firm's future cash flows with certainty but will know certain properties of the cash flow distribution better than investors. In this setting, there can be an adverse selection problem whether the firm issues equity or risky debt.

Narayanan [1988] suggests that in a setting where the manager has private information about the mean of the distribution of the cash flows from the firm's investment opportunity but where the variance of this distribution is common

[32] See also Myers [1984]

knowledge, the Myers pecking order will still apply in the sense that the firm will always issue risky debt rather than equity. Narayanan demonstrates his result by comparing a pooling equilibrium in which firms only issue risky debt to one in which firms only issue equity. In the debt equilibrium, security values are less affected by the manager's private information, so the higher value firms lose less due to adverse selection. Narayanan concludes from this that only debt would be issued in this setting.[33]

Noe [1988] extends Narayanan's model to a three type example, and shows that an equilibrium may obtain in which low (L) and high (H) value firms issue debt and medium (M) value firms issue equity. In this example, type L issues debt because there is a substantial probability that it will default, and since the debt is also issued by a type H firm, the yield on the debt is sufficiently low to make the type L prefer debt to equity. The type M firm is less likely to default on the debt, so the yield is too high from its perspective so it therefore prefers to issue fairly priced equity. For the type H firm, the debt yield is also too high, but the equity would be even more mispriced since the cost of pooling with the type M firm would be still higher.

6.2. Financing when managers have private information about cash flow variance

Both Noe and Narayanan assume that the mean of the distribution of project's cash flows is asymmetric information, but that the variance of the distribution is common knowledge. However as Giammarino & Neave [1982] have shown, if manager's have private information about only cash flow variance then the pecking order will be reversed: firms will never issue debt.

Table 5 provides a numerical example that illustrates this concept. Now, the assets-in-place for both the high and low type firms are worth 10. The firm has an investment opportunity which requires investment of 30 and has an (expected) NPV of 10. There are two equally probable states of nature, U and D, in which the cash flows from the project take on the values specified in Table 5. It is seen that the value of the assets in place as well as the expected value of the project's cash flows are the same for the two types. The only thing that now distinguishes high and low types is the variance of the project's cash flow: for type H's project cash flow variance is 100, and type L's is 1600. The probability that a firm is type H is 0.5.

It is straightforward to show that if the firm were to issue equity there would be no adverse selection problem because the full-information value of a share of a type L's equity would be the same as a type H's (given our assumption of risk neutrality). Therefore, the original shareholders of both types would issue equity

[33] To be somewhat more rigorous about Narayanan's argument, note that a sequential equilibrium may in fact exist in which only equity is issued: this equilibrium would have to be supported by the belief that a firm which issued debt was low valuation. Given this belief, an investor's response to the out-of-equilibrium move of issuing debt would be to pay only a low price for the debt, and based on this firms would therefore always issue equity. While this equilibrium would survive the Cho–Kreps refinement, it would not survive be a perfect sequential equilibrium [Grossman & Perry, 1986].

Table 5

Debt–issuance equilibria

Model parameters		
$H = L = 10$	$I = 30$	$E(V_H) = E(V_L) = 40$
$V_H^{\mathrm{u}} = 50,\ V_H^{\mathrm{d}} = 30$	$V_L^{\mathrm{u}} = 80,\ V_L^{\mathrm{d}} = 0$	$\%H = 0.5,\ \pi_{\mathrm{u}} = \pi_{\mathrm{d}} = 0.5$

Belief set A	
Don't take:	None
Take:	Both (pool)

Payoffs

		RESPONSE	
		Don't take	Take
TYPE	H	10	13.33
	L	10	26.67

Belief set B	
Don't take:	H (Low Variance)
Take:	L (High Variance)

Payoffs

		RESPONSE	
		Don't take	Take
TYPE	H	10	5
	L	10	20

at the full-information value and therefore capture the full NPV of the project, and the value of the original shares would be $V_{\text{old}} = 20$.

However, let's consider the situation where the firm chooses to issue debt. Here the full-information value of a type L bond would be lower because a type L would default more often. In this example, if the type were observable, a type L would have to incur a notional obligation of 50 to raise the 30 necessary to fund the project: this is because 50% of the time the low type would default on the bonds and the bondholders would only receive 10, giving the bonds a total value of $(0.5 \cdot 10 + 0.5 \cdot 50) = 30$.

In the setting where the investor does not know the firm's type there exists a pooling equilibrium (supported by Belief set A) in which the unknown type firm would have to incur a total debt obligation of 36.67 to raise the necessary \$30. To see that this is the equilibrium obligation, note that in the pooling equilibrium, if state d occurs a type L firm will default and the debtholders will receive only 10, otherwise a type L pays the full obligation. Since a type H never defaults, the value of the bonds is $(0.25 \cdot 10 + 0.75 \cdot 36.67) = 30$.

The right hand side of Table 5 shows that there also exist investor beliefs which support a separating equilibrium in which a type H firm does not issue. However, note that the payoff to the type H firm in both of the pooling and separating equilibria is lower than it would be if the firm issued debt. Thus, we can argue that, under reasonable restrictions on out-of-equilibrium beliefs, the type H firm would always issue equity: debt will be the dominated security.

6.3. *Signalling by choice of financing*

Brennan & Kraus [1987] examine the case where the firm has existing senior debt and the project's cash flows are uncertain. In this model in which firms can sometimes costlessly signal their type by appropriate choice of financing.[34] They show that when the firms' managers have private information about the mean of their projects' cash flow distributions and the variances are common knowledge, high value firms can signal their type by repurchasing outstanding risky debt. Additionally, they show that when the manager has private information about the variance (and the mean is common knowledge), high value (meaning high variance) firms will issue subordinated debt, and low value firms will issue equity.[35]

The intuition for Brennan & Kraus' first result is as follows: the low type's debt is less valuable because the low is more likely to default. Therefore a high can signal its type by repurchasing some of its outstanding debt at its full information value: this action is costless for the high type, but is costly for the low type. If the cost differential is large enough, it outweighs the gain from mimicking and a separating equilibrium will obtain.

The left side of Table 6 gives a two-type example of such a separating equilibrium. In this example types H and L both have assets-in-place worth 10 and outstanding debt with a face value (D) of 10. Each type has an opportunity to take on a project which requires an investment of 5. The payoff to the project (V_θ^s) is dependent on both the firm type ($\theta \in \{H, L\}$) and on the state of nature ($s \in \{u, d\}$). Type H's project has a NPV which is \$10 greater than that of the type L firm, but the variance of the project cash flow is the same for the either type. In this equilibrium, the type H firm sells 42.8% of the firm's equity for \$15; it uses \$10 to repurchase debt at face value and \$5 to fund the new project. The type H loses nothing by repurchasing the debt at face value since the face value is equal to the full information value, but a type L would lose \$5 by repurchasing debt (because the full information value of L's debt is only \$5). Since the cost of mimicking is less than the benefit, a type L does not mimic, and instead sells 25% of the firm's equity for \$5. The payoff diagram at the bottom of the table shows that the incentive compatibility conditions are satisfied.[36]

Brennan & Kraus' second result concerns a setting where the different types have the same expected cash flows, but where type H's cash flow variance is higher. In this setting, a type H wants to show that it is risky before it undertakes an equity issue, because the riskier it is, the lower the value of the outstanding debt and hence the greater the value of its equity. Here, the type H firm can

[34] Constantinides & Grundy [1989] present a model with many of these same features.

[35] Heinkel & Zechner [1990] combine elements of Narayanan [1988], Brennan & Kraus [1987], and Myers [1977] into a model in which in which firms have an opportunity to take on a risky project. As Narayanan shows, firms in this setting will overinvest in the project. However, in the Heinkel and Zechner model firms have an opportunity to issue risky debt before the firm's manager's know the project value (before they gain their information advantage). The reason they have an incentive to issue risky debt is in order to set up a Brennan & Kraus situation: with risky debt in place the firm can costlessly signal its type by repurchasing risky debt, and thus can avoid the over/underinvestment problem.

[36] We note that when the type distribution is continuous, a fully revealing equilibrium will obtain in which higher value firms will repurchase more debt, and all debt will be repurchased at the full-information value (i.e., at less than the face value).

Table 6

Brennan & Kraus equilibria

Costless signalling with outstanding debt

Model parameters

$H = L = 10 \quad I = 5 \quad D = 10$

$E(V_H) = 25 \quad E(V_L) = 15$

$V_H^{\mathrm{u}} = 50,\ V_H^{\mathrm{d}} = 0 \quad V_L^{\mathrm{u}} = 40,\ V_L^{\mathrm{d}} = -10$

$\pi_U = \pi_D = 0.5$

Belief set

Forgo:	None
Take:	Low
Take/repurchase debt:	High

Payoffs

		RESPONSE		
		Forgo	Take	Repurchase
TYPE	High	0	18.75	20
	Low	0	15	14.29

Costless signalling with junior debt

Model parameters

$H = L = 10 \quad I = 5 \quad D = 10$

$E(V_H) = E(V_L) = 10$

$V_H^{\mathrm{u}} = 25,\ V_H^{\mathrm{d}} = -5 \quad V_L^{\mathrm{u}} = 10,\ V_L^{\mathrm{d}} = 10$

$\pi_{\mathrm{u}} = \pi_{\mathrm{d}} = 0.5$

Belief set

Forgo:	None
Take/issue equity:	Low
Take/issue junior debt:	High

Payoffs

		RESPONSE		
		Forgo	Equity	Debt
TYPE	High	0	6.25	7.5
	Low	0	5	0

signal its type by issuing subordinated debt. Since the type H firm is characterized by higher cash flow variance and hence a higher probability of default (and lower price) on new subordinated debt, the type H can issue debt at this low price, and the low will be unwilling to mimic.

A simple numerical example of this equilibrium with two types is provided as the right side of Table 6. Here, the firm has assets in place with a value of 10, outstanding senior debt with a face value of 10, and a project with a required investment of 5 and an expected cash flow of 10. However if the firm is type L the project pays a *certain* 10, while if it is type H the project will pay either -5 or 25 (0.5/0.5 probability). In equilibrium, type H issues junior debt with a face value of 10, which sells at a price of 5. The only way that a type L can obtain financing in this setting is to sell undervalued subordinated debt, or to issue equity at the full information value, which it does.[37]

6.4. The pecking order hypothesis and capital structure irrelevance

Up to now, we have assumed that managers act to maximize the value of the firm's shares. Assuming that managers maximize share prices is equivalent to assuming that they act in the interests of 'passive' shareholders, who do not update

[37] For a continuum of types, this model extends to an equilibrium in which firms issue either a combination of more subordinated debt and less equity (higher types issuing more subordinated debt and less equity) or, as Brennan & Kraus suggest, convertible subordinated debt with a higher face value and a lower conversion ratio.

their portfolios in response to the firm's investment and financing decisions. While this type of behavior seems plausible, the passive shareholders are clearly not optimizing their portfolios. In this section we examine the implications of having managers act in the interests of 'active' shareholders who do optimize.

To begin this consideration it is instructive to compare the Myers & Majluf pecking order hypothesis with the original Modigliani & Miller irrelevance proposition. Like Modigliani & Miller, Myers & Majluf assume that there are no taxes and no transaction costs, yet the general conclusions of the two papers are very different: Modigliani & Miller conclude that the firm's capital structure choice is irrelevant while Myers & Majluf conclude that firms will prefer to issue debt.

To understand the difference between the two models, recall the well-known proof of the Modigliani & Miller theorem which demonstrates the equivalence of 'corporate' leverage (the firm borrowing on its own account) and 'homemade' leverage (the investors borrowing on their personal accounts). With perfect markets, shareholders are unaffected by increases or decreases in the debt ratio of a firm since they can 'undo' the leverage change in their personal portfolios, keeping both their fractional holdings of the firm's assets and their net debt level unchanged.

In contrast to the Modigliani & Miller framework, the Myers & Majluf pecking order hypothesis considers the capital structure choice from the perspective of 'passive' shareholders who do not rebalance their portfolios when the firm issues new securities. When the firm issues equity to finance investment, the passive shareholders' fractional holdings of the firm's assets decrease, causing them to suffer losses (from dilution) if the shares are undervalued. However, if the firm instead issues riskless debt, the shareholders' fractional holdings remain constant so that their interests are not diluted. Based on this logic, Myers & Majluf conclude that under these circumstances firms should undertake all positive NPV projects and should always use debt to finance them.

Myers & Majluf recognize that in theory, with frictionless markets, shareholders should be 'active' in the Modigliani & Miller sense: they should keep the risk of their portfolio constant and respond to a debt issue by selling equity and purchasing some of the newly issued debt. Such active shareholders' post-issue fractional holdings of the firm's assets would be independent of the financing choice: the shareholders would respond to a debt financed investment by selling shares and adding the risk-free asset to their portfolios, and as a result their fractional holdings of the firm's equity will not be a function of whether the firm uses debt rather than equity to fund the project. Managers acting in the interest of these shareholders might therefore pass up positive NPV debt financed investments, since doing so could lead the shareholders to sell undervalued shares.

Although Myers & Majluf consider the possibility that shareholders might be active with respect to capital structure changes they ignore the possibility that shareholders might also be active with respect to equity issues. They assume, as indeed we have throughout the chapter, that the original investors do not allocate additional funds to the firm when it undertakes a new investment that expands its capital base. This assumption is not consistent with most equilibrium models which suggest that the original investors will in fact purchase some of the new equity. For example, if the model were embedded into the capital asset pricing model (CAPM), each investor would purchase a pro-rata share of any new debt *or* equity issue, thereby eliminating the adverse selection costs associated with issuing underpriced shares to finance a new project. The implication of this is that a manager who wished to maximize the original shareholders' wealth would invest whenever the firm has a positive NPV investment opportunity, regardless of the firm's current share price, even if the investment required equity financing.

The question that arises at this point is which assumption is most reasonable? Do corporate managers act to maximize wealth for the passive shareholders, do they maximize wealth for what Myers & Majluf call the active shareholders who undo capital structure changes but do not add shares when the firm issues new equity, or do they maximize wealth for the even more active shareholders who buy the new equity on a pro-rata basis? The debate on this issue is quite important since it has implications for all of the signalling models discussed in this chapter. If managers act in the interests of shareholders that purchase new equity issues on a pro-rata basis, the incentive to take any of the costly actions described in this chapter for the purpose of increasing stock prices is eliminated.

Since maximizing the wealth of the passive shareholders is equivalent to maximizing the firm's share price one might argue that this is the most plausible objective function. Of course, the disadvantage with having managers act to maximize share price is that it either leads to underinvestment or dissipative signalling costs. Ex ante, shareholders would like their managers to have the incentive to accept all positive NPV projects that occur in the future since such a policy maximizes the current value of the firm. To give the managers this incentive, they should be compensated to act in the interests of the most active shareholders who purchase new equity issues on a pro-rata basis, as pointed out by Dybvig & Zender [1991].

As we have seen, compensating them in this way would, in theory, be straightforward: managers will take all positive NPV projects as long as they are paid a fixed salary and are required to keep their percentage ownership of the firm constant. However, in reality, managers have other considerations that might make a solution to the underinvestment problem more complex. Consider the situation where the perceived market value of a firm influences its full information intrinsic value. For example, Apple computer might find that its customers, who may be concerned about the future viability of the Macintosh operating system, will view the firm's products more favorably if Apple's stock price is higher.[38] As a result, there will be a tendency to take costly actions to signal favorable information even when managers are compensated in a way that makes them act in the interests of the most active shareholders. While it is still possible, in theory, to come up with a compensation package which induces the manager to take on all positive NPV projects, this compensation package would be very complex and may not be implementable in reality.

[38] See for example, Titman [1984] and chapter 27 in this volume.

6.4.1. The effect of a manager's shareholdings on the investment decision

We believe that future research on the topics considered in this chapter will take management incentive issues much more seriously. Rather than starting with the assumption that managers either maximize share prices or maximize the expected wealth of active shareholders, future work is likely to determine these incentives from more basic principles. A key issue that will have to be resolved in this work relates to the kinds of constraints that are placed on managers in regards to how they trade in their firm's shares. As a first step along these lines it makes sense to think about how an unconstrained owner/manager's portfolio choice interacts with project selection choices in a Myers & Majluf setting.

As we mentioned above, if the manager does not participate in equity issues, then there will be an underinvestment problem. However, if the manager is forced to buy additional stock in proportion to his original holdings, then there will be no underinvestment problem. The question that we wish to address in this section is what happens when managers are not constrained in the amount of their firm's stock they buy or sell, either before or after the investment is taken. In this case, as we argue below, the Myers & Majluf underinvestment problem may be eliminated.

To understand this, consider a firm that owns property on which a gold mine was recently discovered. Only the firm's manager knows about this gold mine, and as a result the firm's shares are undervalued (from his perspective) which means that he has an incentive to purchase shares for his own account. A risk-neutral manager would buy as many shares as possible, up to the point where he is financially constrained. At this point, for the risk-neutral manager, the marginal value of a share still exceeds the market price because the marginal value of a share to him is not affected by the size of his holdings.

However if the manager is risk-averse, this will not be true. Now, since each additional share the manager acquires increases the covariance between the returns of his portfolio and the firm's stock, the stock's marginal value to him decreases as he accumulates more shares. In the absence of financing constraints, the risk-averse manager will continue acquiring shares only up to the point where the marginal value to him of an additional share falls to the market price of a share of the firm's stock.[39] At this point, though the share price is equal to the a share's marginal value for the manager, other investors would still find them underpriced if they had the manager's information.

Consider now what happens when the manager has the opportunity to issue additional shares at the prevailing price to fund a risk-free positive NPV project. To the constrained, risk-neutral manager, the firm's stock is undervalued, so from his perspective when the firm issues shares it is giving away a positive NPV project to the new shareholders. For this reason the risk neutral manager might pass up a project that requires an equity issue.

However from the risk-averse manager's perspective, the shares that would be

[39] Note that we are assuming here both that the manager is risk averse and that markets are not complete. Both these conditions are necessary to obtain an interior optimum.

issued to fund the project would be priced at their fair value; they are a zero NPV investment. In contrast, the NPV of the project is positive. Therefore it would be in the manager's interest to sell some of his shares in the firm and use the proceeds to purchase shares in the new project. This is what the firm, in essence, does for him when it sells equity to fund the new project. What this means is that as long as the manager has optimized his portfolio, he will make appropriate choices with regards to the selection of risk-free projects.

When the project is risky the analysis becomes somewhat more complicated. If the returns of the project can be spanned by the returns of other traded securities the answer is the same. In essence, a positive NPV project that can be spanned by existing securities is equivalent to a risk-free positive NPV project since all of its risk can be effectively hedged. However, if the project contains risks that are specific to the firm's stock, then in taking on the project the manager would be increasing the riskiness of his own portfolio.[40] He would therefore pass up projects that (from the outside shareholders' perspective) have positive NPVs. An example of this would be a project that simply increased the firm's scale of operations. This would be a positive NPV project if it yielded, for example, 15% when its cost of capital (from the perspective of outside shareholders) was 12%. However, if the unknown gold mine implied that the shares would have an expected return of 18%, then the manager would prefer to pass up the project. Since most projects do have some firm specific component, one must conclude that in general there will be some tendency to underinvest.

On the other hand, if the project cash flows are negatively correlated with the firm specific cash flows, the manager might take on the project even if it has a negative NPV. Taking on such a project lowers the portfolio's expected return but also diversifies the portfolio. For these projects there could be a tendency to overinvestment.

All of this suggests that a manager who is unconstrained in his portfolio choice is likely to have a tendency, unless compensated otherwise, to overinvest in diversifying projects and underinvest in projects in the core business of the firm.

7. Conclusions

In this chapter we examined the incentives of firms to signal their values prior to making a new equity offering. By analyzing this issue within a simple framework that encompasses a number of models in the literature, we were able to judge the relative efficiency of various signals that have been proposed.

Although we believe that the signalling literature examined in this chapter offers valuable insights, our analysis suggests that in a number of respects the models are not robust. For example, a number of signals appear to be relatively inefficient, so that their use requires that more efficient signals be unavailable to the firm.

[40] What we mean by firm specific cash flows is that component of the cash flows out of the firm's assets-in-place which cannot be hedged by buying and selling other assets in the economy.

Additional required restrictions relate to the type of securities the firms can issue and the way in which management is compensated.

The limited robustness of these signalling models suggests that additional research is warranted. It is important to understand, for example, whether or not plausible conditions exist under which managers will be compensated in such a way that they will have the incentives described in Myers & Majluf and the related literature. Perhaps, compensation contracts with this feature arise endogenously as a result of other agency problems that may exist between managers and shareholders.

A second area of future research relates to motivating why firms issue equity in situations where debt financing greatly reduces the adverse selection problem. Presumably, other debt related costs (e.g. bankruptcy costs) can preclude the use of debt financing and force the firm to issue equity. In such a setting we would expect firms to issue securities that minimize both adverse selection costs as well as expected bankruptcy costs. This might explain, for example, the use of preferred stock, which receives a fixed dividend but which cannot trigger default. Signalling efficiency could be especially important in settings where bankruptcy is costly. Perhaps firms that can signal their values very efficiently will prefer raising capital with equity issues, while those firms that find signalling very costly will prefer the debt markets, running a greater risk of bankruptcy. We expect that in the future, these information issues will play a larger role in the literature on the determination of optimal capital structures.

Acknowledgements

Most of this work was completed while the two authors were at UCLA. We are indebted to Franklin Allen, James Ang, Bhagwan Chowdhry, Ron Giammarino, David Hirshleifer, Narasimhan Jegadeesh, Kose John, Raghu Rajan, John Riley, Ivo Welch, Jaime Zender, and the participants of the UCLA and UCI finance seminars for helpful discussions, comments and suggestions. We are responsible for all remaining errors. Daniel thanks the Center for Research in Security Prices for research support.

Appendix A — Proofs of propositions

Proof of Proposition 2. The proof that this equilibrium is the unique sequential equilibrium in which each issuer is uniquely identified by his signal level is partly taken from Riley [1979]. Riley shows that if six assumptions are met, then the only informationally consistent signalling schedule must be a solution to the differential equation (5).

Riley shows that the only admissible solutions are those for which $K \leq \underline{\theta}+V-I$. That K must be equal to $\underline{\theta}+V-I$ comes from the fact that the equilibrium must be sequential. If the equality did not hold the lowest type ($\underline{\theta}$) would have to signal to receive a fair price for his equity. Clearly this equilibrium is not sequential, because the investor *cannot* pay less than the value of the lowest type for shares of a firm which does not signal.

To prove that the equilibrium satisfies the intuitive criterion requires that we consider two cases:

1. All types signal and take the project. This is the case if $\overline{\theta} < \theta_c = (\underline{\theta} + V - I)\exp(VI/I)$.

2. All types $\theta < \theta_c$ take the project and signal according to the schedule in equation (7). All types for which $\theta_c < \theta < \overline{\theta}$ do not issue and pass up the project.

In case 1, the highest type burns some amount as a signal, say $\overline{C}$. No type is willing to burn more than this because, under the sequential equilibrium criterion, the highest value the investor could place on any firm which did this would be $\overline{\theta}$. Since they can achieve the same valuation by burning only $\overline{C}$, no type wishes to make this out-of-equilibrium move. The only other out-of-equilibrium move available to firms is to pass up the project, which we have already shown is not maximizing behavior in this case.

In case 2, the highest signal level is burning $\overline{C} = V - I$, in other words burning up the entire NPV of the project. Clearly no firm would be willing to make this out-of-equilibrium move if they are not willing to burn $\overline{C}$. Thus in both cases, the equilibrium satisfies the intuitive criterion. □

Proof of Proposition 4. Given that $V > I > 0$, $H > L > 0$, and that the signalling cost in the money burning equilibrium is always positive ($C > 0$), the following relationship must hold:

$$\frac{V - I}{V - I(L + V)/(H + V)} < 1 < \frac{H + V}{H + V - C}$$

Multiplying each side by $[I(H - L)]/(H + V)$, and noting that the left side of the above inequality is equal to α [by equation (11)] gives the following:

$$\alpha \frac{I(H - L)}{H + V} < \frac{I(H - L)}{H + V - C}$$

The left side of this inequality is equal to $(V - I)(1 - \alpha)$, using the definition of α given in equation (11). Multiplying each side by -1 and adding $(H - L)$ to each side gives the following:

$$(H - L) - (V - I)(1 - \alpha) > (H - L)\left(1 - \frac{I}{H + V - C}\right)$$

Equations (9) and (10) reveal that the left side of this inequality is equal to $\pi_H^h - \pi_L^h$, the difference between the high and low type's payoffs in the price setting equilibrium if the low mimics, and that the right side of the inequality is equal to $\pi_H^{\mathrm{B}} - \pi_L^{\mathrm{B}}$, the difference between the high and low types payoffs in the money burning equilibrium if the low mimics. By the fact that the incentive compatibility condition is binding in equilibrium, we have that $\pi_L^h = \pi_L^{\mathrm{B}} = L + V - I$ (the low's payoff must be the same whether he mimics or not), and therefore $\pi_H^h > \pi_H^{\mathrm{B}}$: the payoff to the high type in the price setting equilibrium is higher than in the money burning equilibrium. Therefore a high type firm would always want to overprice and, under the modified intuitive criterion, the investor would have to respond with a sufficiently high probability of rejection so that a low type would never mimic. The money burning equilibrium, as well as the Myers and Majluf pooling and separating equilibria, therefore fail the modified intuitive criterion. Note also that, since the payoff to the low type in each of the two equilibria is the same, the price setting equilibrium Pareto dominates the money burning equilibrium. □

Proof of Proposition 5. Let V_H and V_L denote the cash flow from the project for the high and low types, respectively. Appropriate modification of the payoffs given in equation (10) and application of the incentive compatibility condition gives the following equation for the fraction of the time the issue must be accepted in equilibrium, which we will denote α^*:

$$\alpha^* = \frac{V_L - I}{V_L - I(L + V_L)/(H + V_H)} \tag{16}$$

In the limit as $V_H \to \infty$, $\alpha^* \to (V_L - I)/(V_L)$, and the payoff to the high approaches $(V_L I/V_L)V_H$.

In the money burning equilibrium equation (4), which defines the amount of money that must be burned, becomes:

$$C^* = \tfrac{1}{2}\left[(H + V_H) - \sqrt{(H + V_H)^2 - 4I(H - L + V_H - V_L)}\right]$$

so that as $V_H \to \infty$, $C^* \to I$. Thus, as $V_H \to \infty$, the payoff to the high type approaches V_H, and for large enough V_H *the payoff is higher in the burning money equilibrium than in the price setting equilibrium.* It follows then that in an price setting equilibrium, the high could increase his utility by burning money rather than price setting. The low would not wish to mimic, no matter what the investor's response. Therefore the investor would accept the issue all the time, and the price setting equilibrium fails the intuitive criterion. To show that price setting is not a credible signal for high enough V_H, note that the payoff to the high type if he sets a low issue price is:

$$\left(1 - \frac{I}{L + V_L}\right)(H + V_H)$$

In the limit as $V_H \to \infty$, this is equal to:

$$\left(\frac{L + V_L - I}{L + V_L}\right) V_H$$

If he sets a high issue price, his payoff is $H + \alpha^*(V_H - I)$ which, using equation (16) above, is equal to

$$\left(\frac{V_L - I}{V_L}\right) V_H$$

as $V_H \to \infty$. Since $(L + V_L - I)/(L + V_L) > (V_L - I)/(V_L)$, the high type cannot use price setting as a credible signal as $V_H \to \infty$. □

Proof of Proposition 6.
Part 1: For constant returns to scale, if the project is cut back to a fraction β of its original size, the payoffs to the high and low type *if they scale* are:

$$\pi_H^S = \left(1 - \frac{\beta I}{H + \beta V}\right)(H + \beta V) = H + \beta(V - I)$$

$$\pi_L^S = \left(1 - \frac{\beta I}{H + \beta V}\right)(L + \beta V) = L + \beta\left(V - I\frac{L + \beta V}{H + \beta V}\right)$$

The payoffs to the high and low types *if they set a high price* are given by equation (10) as:

$$\pi_H^h = H + \alpha(V - I)$$

$$\pi_L^l = L + \alpha\left(V - I\frac{L + \beta V}{H + \beta V}\right)$$

Because the incentive compatibility condition will be binding in both equilibria, π_L^h must equal π_L^S (which equals $L + V - I$):

$$\alpha\left(V - I\frac{L + V}{H + V}\right) = \beta\left(V - I\frac{L + \beta V}{H + \beta V}\right)$$

Since $H > L > 0$ and $\beta < 1$, it follows that:

$$V - I\frac{L + \beta V}{H + \beta V} > V - I\frac{L + V}{H + V}$$

This implies that $\alpha > \beta$, and that $\pi_H^h > \pi_H^S$. Therefore the high, in a scaling equilibrium, can make the out of equilibrium move of setting a high price and be better off. The low would never want to set a high price because, under the modified intuitive criterion, the largest probability of acceptance the investor could respond with would be α. Therefore the scaling equilibrium does not survive the modified intuitive criterion. □

Part 2: The first of the two equation defines the γx for which the high firm is indifferent between scaling and price setting. Recall that γx is the decrease in the cash flow out of the project when the firm scales. This relation is derived from equations (10), (11), and (14). The second equation is just equation (15), the incentive compatibility condition for the scaling equilibrium. From the second equation, it is clear that if γ is large, then γx will be large, and the scaling equilibrium will be inefficient. So for $\gamma < \gamma^*$, the payoff to the high in the scaling equilibrium is greater than the payoff in the price setting equilibrium, and the price setting equilibrium will fail the intuitive criterion. By the same argument, the scaling equilibrium will fail the modified intuitive criterion for $\gamma > \gamma^*$. □

Part 3: Again by the fact that the incentive compatibility constraint is binding in both the money burning and scaling equilibria, we know that the payoff to the low firm in both equilibria must be the same:

$$\left(1 - \frac{I - x}{H + V - \gamma x}\right)(L + V - \gamma x) = \left(1 - \frac{I}{H + V - C}\right)(L + V - C)$$

This can be rearranged to yield:

$$\frac{H + V - I - C}{H + V - I - (\gamma - 1)x} = \left(\frac{L + V - \gamma x}{H + V - \gamma x}\right)\left(\frac{H + V - C}{L + V - C}\right)$$

Given the usual parameter restrictions, we can see that the left side of the above equation is greater than one if and only if $C < (\gamma - 1)x$, and the right side of the equation is greater than one if and only if $C > \gamma x$. These two conditions are incompatible, since $x > 0$, and therefore both sides of the equation must be less than one, and the following condition must hold:

$$(\gamma - 1)x < C < \gamma x$$

Based on this inequality, it is clear that:

$$\frac{H + V - I - (\gamma - 1)x}{H + V - \gamma x} > \frac{H + V - I - C}{H + V - C}$$

and that:

$$\left(1 - \frac{I - x}{H + V - \gamma x}\right)(H - L) = \left(1 \frac{I}{H + V - C}\right)(H - L)$$

Adding the left and right sides of equation (15) to the same sides of the equation directly above gives the following:

$$\left(1 - \frac{I - x}{H + V - \gamma x}\right)(H + V - \gamma x) > \left(1 - \frac{I}{H + V - C}\right)(H + V - C)$$

The left side of this equation is π_H^S and the right side is π_H^B. So we see that, for $\gamma \in [1, \infty)$, the payoff to the high type is higher in the scaling equilibrium, and by the binding incentive compatibility constraint the payoff to the low type in the two equilibria is the same, therefore the money burning equilibrium fails to satisfy the intuitive criterion in the presence of the money burning equilibrium. □

Part 4: Following the argument above (Part 2 of this proof), and then taking the limit as $\gamma \to \infty$ shows that $\gamma x \to C$ and $\pi_H^S \to \pi_H^B$ as $\gamma \to \infty$. □

Proof of Proposition 9.

Part 1: The payoffs to the two types of firm, depending on whether they issue equity (and take the project) or not, are:

$$\pi^{I}_{t=H} = \left(1 - \frac{I}{\theta_H + V_H}\right)(\theta_H + V_H)$$

$$\pi^{I}_{t=L} = \left(1 - \frac{I}{\theta_H + V_H}\right)(\theta_L + V_L)$$

$$\pi^{NI}_{H} = \theta_H \qquad \pi^{NI}_{L} = \theta_L$$

In order for the low to choose to issue in equilibrium, π^{NI}_{L} must be greater than π^{I}_{L}. This will only be the case if $V_L < I[\theta_L/(\theta_H + V_H - I)]$. The belief which supports this equilibrium as a sequential equilibrium is that any firm which issues is high. This belief is admissible under the intuitive criterion. □

Part 2: If $V_L > \theta_L/(\theta_H + V_H - I)$, then the low will have an incentive to mimic if the high simply issues. Therefore, the high has to burn money as well as issue to credibly signal his type. The payoffs to the two types, if they (1) burn C, issue and invest or (2) don't burn money and don't invest, are:

$$\pi^{\mathrm{B}}_{t=H} = \left(1 - \frac{I + C}{\theta_H + V_H}\right)(\theta_H + V_H)$$

$$\pi^{\mathrm{B}}_{t=L} = \left(1 - \frac{I + C}{\theta_H + V_H}\right)(\theta_L + V_L)$$

$$\pi^{NI}_{H} = \theta_H \qquad \pi^{NI}_{L} = \theta_L$$

Again, the amount burned is set so that the incentive compatibility constraint is binding. This will be the case when:

$$C = \left(\frac{\theta_H + V_H}{\theta_L + V_L}\right) - I \tag{17}$$

Substituting this into the payoff equation for the high and rearranging, we see that the high still wishes to issue if:

$$V_L < V_H\left(\frac{\theta_H + V_H}{\theta_L + V_L}\right)$$

This two inequalities define the condition in Part 2. The beliefs which support this sequential equilibrium are that any firm which burns less than C and issues is low type, and any firm which burns C or more is high type. These beliefs are admissible under the intuitive criterion. □

Part 3: The development above shows that if the specified condition is met, the high type must burn so much to satisfy the incentive compatibility constraint that he no longer wishes to issue. Therefore a sequential equilibrium exists in which neither type issues in equilibrium. The investor beliefs which support this are that a type which issues and burns less than C [as defined in equation (17)] is low, and that any type which burns C or more is high. These beliefs are admissible under the intuitive criterion. □

Appendix B — The efficient combination of signals

In this appendix we present the maximization problem the solution of which is the optimal signal. We prove, by example, that parameter values exist for which any combination of the three signals may be optimal.

The choice of the high type's optimal signal is represented by the following maximization problem:

$$\max_{\alpha,C,I} H + (1-\alpha)(V_H(I) - I - C)$$

subject to the incentive compatibility constraint for the low type:

$$\alpha L + (1-\alpha)\beta = L + V_L(I^*) - I^*$$

where β is defined as the profit to the low type if he mimics and the equity issue is successful:

$$\beta \equiv \left(1 - \frac{I}{H_V}\right) L_V$$

and H_V and L_V are defined as the value of the high and low type firms given that the firm issues and invests I and burns C]*i.e.*, $H_V \equiv H + V_H(I) - C$ and $L_V \equiv L + V_L(I) - C$). I^* is the full-information investment level for the low type (*i.e.*, $I^* = \text{argmax}(V_L(I) - I)$].[41] Additionally, the three constraints which define the firm's strategy space are $0 \le \alpha \le 1$, $C \ge 0$, and $I \ge 0$. Note that both $I = 0$ and $\alpha = 0$ are equivalent to the high not taking the project.

The Lagrangian for this problem is:

$$\begin{aligned} \mathrm{L}(\alpha, C, I, \lambda) = H + (1-\alpha)[V_H(I) - I - C] \times \\ \times \lambda[\alpha L + (1-\alpha)\beta - L - V_L(I^*) - I^*] \end{aligned}$$

The first-order conditions for an interior solution result in the following restrictions:

$$\frac{\partial \mathrm{L}}{\partial \alpha} = -(V_H(I) - I - C) - \lambda(L - \beta) = 0 \quad \to \lambda = \frac{V_H(I) - I - C}{\beta - L} \qquad (18)$$

[41] Although we assume that the high type underinvests as a signal, our analysis here does not preclude overinvestment. If the full-information investment level for the high type is considerably higher than for the low, and if $V_L(I)$ is sufficiently concave, the high will choose to overinvest as a signal. (see Ambarish, John & Williams [1987]).

$$\frac{\partial \mathrm{L}}{\partial C} = -(1-\alpha) - \lambda(1-\alpha)\frac{\partial \beta}{\partial C} = 0 \qquad \rightarrow \lambda = \frac{-1}{\partial \beta / \partial C} \tag{19}$$

$$\frac{\partial \mathrm{L}}{\partial I} = (1-\alpha)[V_H'(I) - 1]\lambda(1-\alpha)\frac{\partial \beta}{\partial I} = 0 \rightarrow \lambda = \frac{V_H'(I) - 1}{\partial \beta / \partial I} \tag{20}$$

$$\frac{\partial \mathrm{L}}{\partial \lambda} = \alpha L + (1-\alpha)\beta - LV_L(I^*) - I^* = 0 \rightarrow$$

$$\alpha L + (1-\alpha)\beta = LV_L(I^*) - I^*$$

where

$$\frac{\partial \beta}{\partial C} = I\frac{H_V - L_V}{H_V^2} - 1$$

$$\frac{\partial \beta}{\partial I} = V_L'(I) - \frac{L_V}{H_V} + I\frac{L_V V_H'(I) - H_V V_L'(I)}{H_V^2}$$

A necessary condition for an interior solution (*i.e.,* for a three signal combination to be optimal) is that all first-order conditions be binding. If a two signal combination is optimal then two of the first-order conditions (18), (19), or (20) will be satisfied, and if only one signal is optimal then only one of the FOC's (18), (19), or (20) will be satisfied.

To verify that the second-order conditions are satisfied, the bordered Hessian matrix can be evaluated as described in Varian [1984]. The condition that there be an interior solution can be reduced to the following two inequalities:

$$\lambda(\beta - L)^2(1-\alpha)\frac{\partial^2 \beta}{\partial C^2} > 0 \tag{21}$$

and

$$\lambda(\beta - L)^2\left[\frac{\partial^2 \beta}{\partial C^2}\left(V_H''(I) - \lambda\frac{\partial^2 \beta}{\partial I^2}\right) + \lambda\left(\frac{\partial^2 \beta}{\partial I \partial C}\right)^2\right] < 0 \tag{22}$$

where:

$$\frac{\partial^2 \beta}{\partial C^2} \quad - 2I\frac{H_V - L_V}{H_V^3}$$

$$\frac{\partial^2 \beta}{\partial I^2} = \frac{1}{H_V^2}\left\{2\left(1 - I\frac{V_H'(I)}{H_V}\right)\left[L_V V_H'(I) - H_V V_L'(I)\right] + \right.$$
$$\left. + I\left[L_V V_H''(I) - H_V V_L''(I)\right] + H_V^2 V_L''(I)\right\}$$

$$\frac{\partial^2 \beta}{\partial I \partial C} = \frac{1}{H_V^2}\left\{(H_V - L_V) + I\left[\left(2\frac{L_V}{H_V} - 1\right)V_H'(I) - V_L'(I)\right]\right\}$$

The conditions (21) and (22) are necessary and sufficient condition for the matrix of second derivatives of the Lagrangian to be negative definite subject to the constraint.

Table 7 gives the parameters of a numerical example in which a three signal combination is optimal. The upper part of the table gives the signal levels, the first-order conditions corresponding to (18), (19), and (20), and second-order conditions corresponding to (21) and (22). For this example, the production function for both high and low firms is defined only in terms of the function's value, first and second derivatives at $I = 20$. For the value of $V''_H(I)$ given, the determinant of the bordered Hessian is zero. For $V''_H(I)$ greater than the tabulated value, the three signal combination is a saddle point, not a true maximum. But when the high type's project's production function is more concave than specified (*i.e.*, when $V''_H(I)$ is less than the specified value), the signal levels specified will be a local maximum and, assuming proper behavior of the production function away from this point, a global maximum. Similar examples show for some set of parameter values, any of the three two-signal combinations can be the most efficient signal.

Table 7

Three signal example

Signal levels					
		First-order conditions		Second-order conditions	
α	0.3596	λ_α	1.083003385	$\|H_2^B\|$	0.018903489
C	7.891955805	λ_C	1.083003385	$\|H^B\|$	0.0
I	20	λ_I	1.083003385		
Parameters					
High firm		Low firm		Derived values	
H	100	L	50	λ	1.083003385
$V_H(I)$	33.0000025	$V_L(I)$	23.02	$\frac{\partial \beta}{\partial C}$	−0.923358148
$V'_H(I)$	1.479425617	$V'_L(I)$	1	$\frac{\partial^2 \beta}{\partial C^2}$	0.001225211
$V''_H(I)$	−0.010069594	$V''_L(I)$	0	$\frac{\partial^2 \beta}{\partial C \partial I}$	0.00263209
Π_H	103.2711931	I^*	25	$\frac{\partial^2 \beta}{\partial I^2}$	−0.003643387
		$V_L(I^*)$	28.0204828	$\frac{\partial \beta}{\partial I}$	0.44268155
		Π_L	53.0204828		

References

Allen, F., and G.R. Faulhaber (1989). Signalling by underpricing in the IPO market. *J. Financ. Econ.* 23, 303–324.

Ambarish, R., K. John and J. Williams (1987). Efficient signalling with dividends and investments. *J. Finance* 42, 321-343.

Brennan, M. and A. Kraus (1988). Efficient financing under asymmetric information. *J. Finance* 42, 1225–1243.

Cadsby, C.B., M. Frank, and V. Maksimovic (1990). Pooling, separating, and semiseparating equilibria in financial markets: Some empirical evidence. *Rev. Financ. Studies* 3, 315-342.

Choe, H., R.W. Masulis and V. Nanda (1993). Common stock offerings across the business cycle: Theory and evidence. *J. Empirical Finance* 1, 3–31.

Cho, I.-K. and D.M. Kreps (1987). Signaling games and stable equilibria. *Q. J. Econ.* 102, 179–221.

Constantinides, G., and B. Grundy (1989). Optimal investment with stock repurchase and financing as signals. *Rev. Financ. Studies* 2, 445–466.

Dybvig, P.H., and J.F. Zender (1991). Capital structure and dividend irrelevance with asymmetric information. *Rev. Financ. Studies* 4, 201–219.

Giammarino, R.M., and T. Lewis (1988). A theory of negotiated equity financing. *Rev. Financ. Studies* 1, 265–288.

Giammarino, R.M., and E.H. Neave (1982). The failure of financial contracts and the relevance of financial policy, working paper, Queen's University.

Grinblatt, M., and C.Y. Hwang (1989). Signalling and the pricing of new issues. *J. Finance* 44, 393–420.

Grossman, S.J., and M. Perry (1986). Perfect sequential equilibrium. *J. Econ. Theory* 39, 97–119.

Heinkel, R., and J. Zechner (1990). The role of debt and preferred stock as a solution to adverse investment incentives. *J. Financ. Quant. Anal.* 25, 1–24.

Hirshleifer, D., and S. Titman (1990). Share tendering strategies and the success of hostile takeover bids. *J. Polit. Econ.* 98, 295–324.

Jegadeesh, N., and B. Chowdhry (1994). Optimal pre-tender offer share acquisition strategy in takeovers. *J. Financ. Quant. Anal.*, 117–130.

John, K., and J. Williams (1985). Dividends, dilution and taxes: A signalling equilibrium. *J. Finance* 40, 1053–1070.

Krasker, W.S. (1986). Stock price movements in response to stock issues under asymmetric information. *J. Finance* 41, 93-105.

Kreps, D., and R. Wilson (1982). Sequential equilibria. *Econometrica* 50, 863–894.

Milgrom, P., and J. Roberts (1986). Price and advertising signals of product quality. *J. Polit. Econ.* 94, 796–821.

Myers, S.C. (1977). Determinants of corporate borrowing. *J. Financ. Econ.* 9, 147–176.

Myers, S.C. (1984). The capital structure puzzle. *J. Finance* 39, 575–592.

Myers, S.C. and N.S. Majluf (1984). Corporate financing and investment decisions when firms have information that investors do not have. *J. Financ. Econ.* 13, 187–221.

Narayanan, M.P. (1988). Debt versus equity under asymmetric information. *J. Financ. Quant. Anal.* 23, 39-51.

Noe, T.H. (1988). Capital structure and signalling game equilibria. *Rev. Financ. Studies* 1, 331- 355.

Raymar, S. (1989). The financing and investment of a levered firm under asymmetric information, working paper, Indiana University.

Riley, J. (1979). Informational equilibrium. *Econometrica* 42, 331–360.

Spence, M. (1973). Job market signalling. *Q. J. Econ.*, 87, 355–374.

Titman, S. (1984). The effect of capital structure on a firm's liquidation decision. *J. Financ. Econ.* 13, 137–152.

Varian, H.R. (1984). *Microeconomic Analysis*, W.W. Norton and Co., New York, NY.

Welch, I. (1989). Seasoned offerings, imitation costs, and the underpricing of initial public offerings. *J. Finance* 44, 421–449.

R. Jarrow et al., Eds., *Handbooks in OR & MS, Vol. 9*

Chapter 24

Financial Structure and the Tax System[1]

Peter Swoboda

Institut für Industrie und Fertigungswirtschaft, Karl-Franzens-Universität, Hans-Sachs-Gasse 3/III, A-8010 Graz, Austria

Josef Zechner

Institute of Management, University of Vienna, Brünner Straße 72, A-1210 Wien, Austria

1. Introduction

It is the general consensus among practitioners as well as financial economists that taxes are important factors influencing an economy's financing patterns. Since the pathbreaking work by Modigliani & Miller [1958, 1963], researchers have made steady progress in deriving more comprehensive, detailed, and realistic models of the relationship between tax systems and capital structure decisions. In this chapter we present a unified framework within which different aspects of taxation can be analysed and summarize major results from the literature on taxes and capital structure.

The tax systems currently adopted by most industrialized countries can be classified into classical systems and imputation systems. Classical tax systems are characterized by the fact that interest payments are tax deductible at the corporate level whereas dividends are not. At the personal level dividends and interest are taxed at the same rate. Imputation systems reduce or eliminate double taxation of dividends by granting a tax credit to recipients of dividends equal to some fraction of the corporate tax paid on the dividends.

In Section 2 we derive securities and capital structure equilibria for the main tax systems. Since income from different securities is taxed differently, capital structure decisions are generally relevant under all currently implemented tax systems — at least at the macro-level.[2] If there exists an investor who is marginal on all securities, then capital structure may be irrelevant for individual firms

[1] This chapter reflects the literature and tax code features up to 1992.

[2] While differential taxation is a necessary condition for relevance, it is not a sufficient condition. As Litzenberger & Talmor [1989] point out, if the market is sufficiently complete and investors have traded to their optimal portfolios, then taxes are irrelevant. The underlying idea is that investors are perfectly hedged so that, in their model, the only relevant state variable is aggregate consumption. Since the government's total share of GNP is independent of individual firms' tax payments (the government offsets any surplus or deficiency of tax revenues by choosing the appropriate inflation

but the aggregate amounts of debt and equity in the economy generally matter. Under some currently adopted tax systems such a marginal investor does not exist. For example, under the current US tax system, if only taxes are considered, debt dominates equity and there do not exist securities prices at which firms would be willing to supply and investors would be willing to hold both debt and equity.

Section 3 derives a capital structure equilibrium in a multinational setting. It is shown that firms in countries with relatively higher corporate tax rates and inflation rates have a comparative advantage issuing debt and should therefore be more highly levered. In Section 4 we identify and analyse two distinct effects of uncertainty. First, stochastic earnings tend to make interest tax shields risky and may therefore lead to firm-specific interior optimal debt levels. The conclusions depend on whether or not a distinction between principal repayments and interest payments is made and on the assumed priority structure for tax payments, principal repayments and interest payments. The second effect of uncertainty implies that different bonds are not perfect substitutes. High-risk high-coupon bonds offer an expected mix of taxable versus nontaxable income that differs from that of low-risk low-coupon bonds. This introduces bondholder tax clienteles such that investors in low tax brackets hold high-risk bonds and investors in higher tax brackets prefer low-risk bonds.

Section 5 deals with multiperiod aspects of taxes and capital structure. In particular we analyse the effects of retrading, intertemporal capital structure adjustments, and debt maturity choice. Finally, in Section 6 we discuss the effects of taxes other than the corporate and personal income tax that are relevant in some countries as well as the effect of investment tax credits and tax evasion.[3]

2. Tax systems and capital structure equilibria under certainty

Some of the main effects of taxes on capital structure can be best illustrated in a one-period certainty framework. We therefore postpone the analysis of the effects of uncertainty and multiperiod aspects to Sections 4 and 5. In this section we introduce a simple model to derive a securities market and capital structure equilibrium for the classical tax system and the imputation system. We use the

rate) aggregate consumption is independent of individual firms' tax payments as well. Furthermore, since each investor is assumed to hold a portfolio that pays off a constant amount for each level of aggregate consumption, individual firms' capital structure decisions are irrelevant. In this setting, investors do not object if a firm does not minimize tax payments, since the payoff of investors' portfolios is independent of each individual firm's tax payments. However, it seems unlikely that markets can be sufficiently complete such as to enable investors to hold portfolios that pay off a constant amount for each level of aggregate consumption if firms are allowed to randomly change their capital structure, thereby affecting their after-tax payments to investors.

[3] For the purpose of this paper we assume that firms have fixed their investment decisions. It should be recognized, however, that in general taxes can influence firms' investment decisions. For an analysis of the effect of taxes on investment decisions see [Dammon & Senbet, 1988; Masulis & Trueman, 1988; Scholes & Wolfson, 1992; and Sinn, 1987].

following notation:

E_j, D_j	=	market value of firm j's equity and debt, respectively, at time 0;
V_j	=	firm j's total market value at time 0;
X_j	=	firm j's before tax cash flow at time 1;
I_j	=	firm j's nondebt tax shields;
r_D, r_E	=	before personal tax rate of return on debt and equity, respectively;
t_c	=	corporate tax rate;
t_{pi}, t_{gi}	=	investor i's constant tax rate on ordinary income and on capital gains income respectively;
$\bar{\alpha}_i, \alpha_i$	=	J-vector of investor i's fractional equityholdings before and after the trade at time 0 respectively, i.e. $\bar{\alpha}_i = (\bar{\alpha}_{i1}, \bar{\alpha}_{i2}, \ldots, \bar{\alpha}_{iJ})^{\mathrm{T}}$ where J is the total number of firms in the economy;
$\bar{\beta}_i, \beta_i$	=	J-vector of investor i's fractional debtholdings before and after the trade at time 0 respectively, i.e. $\bar{\beta}_i = (\bar{\beta}_{i1}, \bar{\beta}_{i2}, \ldots, \bar{\beta}_{iJ})^{\mathrm{T}}$;
c_i	=	investor i's consumption at time 1;
$U_i(c_i)$	=	investor i's utility derived from consumption at time 1.

2.1. The classical tax system

Among the countries which have adopted versions of the classical tax system are Australia, Austria, Belgium, Netherlands, Portugal, Sweden, Switzerland, and the US [Mennel, 1991]. This tax system is characterized in the following way. Interest payments are tax deductible at the corporate level and are taxable at the personal level at the rate for ordinary income. Dividends are not tax deductible at the corporate level and are taxable at the rate for ordinary income at the personal level. Finally, capital gains are taxed at the capital gains tax rate which is less than or equal to the tax rate on ordinary income. If only taxes are considered, it is therefore suboptimal for firms to pay dividends since capital gains are taxed less heavily than dividends. If equity returns are assumed to be taxed at the capital gains tax rate, then investor i's consumption at time 1 is given by

$$c_i = \sum_j \alpha_{ij} E_j[1 + r_E(1 - t_{gi})] + \sum_j \beta_{ij} D_j[1 + r_D(1 - t_{pi})]. \tag{1}$$

Securities market equilibrium

A securities market equilibrium is defined by investors' portfolio holdings, α_i and β_i, and rates of return, r_E and r_D, such that each investor's portfolio holdings solve the problem

$$\max_{\alpha_i, \beta_i} U_i(c_i) \tag{2}$$

$$\text{s.t.} \quad \sum_j (\alpha_{ij} - \bar{\alpha}_{ij}) E_j + \sum_j (\beta_{ij} - \bar{\beta}_{ij}) D_j \le 0 \tag{3}$$

and markets clear,

$$\sum_i \alpha_{ij} = 1 \quad \forall j \tag{4}$$

and

$$\sum_i \beta_{ij} = 1 \quad \forall j. \tag{5}$$

For reasons that will be discussed below, most tax models also impose short sale constraints. Thus, we also require that, in equilibrium,[4]

$$\alpha_{ij} E_j \geq 0 \quad \forall i, j \tag{6}$$

$$\beta_{ij} D_j \geq 0 \quad \forall i, j. \tag{7}$$

Given our certainty framework, we can simplify $U_i(c_i) = c_i$. The resulting first-order conditions for investor i are then

$$\frac{\partial c_i}{\partial \alpha_{ij}} = E_j[1 + r_E(1 - t_{gi})] - \lambda_i E_j - \eta_{ij}^{\mathrm{E}} E_j = 0 \quad \forall j \tag{8}$$

$$\frac{\partial c_i}{\partial \beta_{ij}} = D_j[1 + r_D(1 - t_{pi})] - \lambda_i D_j - \eta_{ij}^{\mathrm{D}} D_j = 0 \quad \forall j \tag{9}$$

and

$$\left.\begin{array}{llll} \lambda_i > 0, & \alpha_{ij} E_j \geq 0, & \beta_{ij} D_j \geq 0, & \\ \eta_{ij}^{\mathrm{D}} \beta_{ij} D_j = 0, & \eta_{ij}^{\mathrm{E}} \alpha_{ij} E_j = 0, & \eta_{ij}^{\mathrm{D}} \leq 0, & \eta_{ij}^{\mathrm{E}} \leq 0 \end{array}\right\} \forall j$$

where λ_i, η_{ij}^{D} and η_{ij}^{E} are Kuhn–Tucker multipliers associated with the budget constraint and the short sales constraints for debt and equity securities, respectively.

Dividing equations (8) and (9) by E_j and D_j respectively, and noting that the multipliers η_{ij}^{E} and η_{ij}^{D} are negative if the short sales constraint is binding and zero otherwise, it can be verified that each investor only holds the securities with the highest after-tax rate of return. Under certainty it then follows that the equity market can only clear if all stocks offer the same before-tax rate of return. Similarly, for bond markets to clear all bonds must offer the same before-tax rate of return.

Capital structure equilibrium

If securities markets are competitive, then the objective of the firm is to maximize its market value. The market value of the firm can be written as

$$V_j = D_j + \frac{X_j - D_j(1 + r_D) - t_c(X_j - r_D D_j - I_j)}{1 + r_E}. \tag{10}$$

[4] It turns out to be more convenient to write the short sales constraints in the form of inequalities (6) and (7) rather than just $\alpha_{ij} \geq 0$ and $\beta_{ij} \geq 0$.

The second expression in equation (10) represents the market value of equity, i.e. firm cash flow minus payments to debtholders minus corporate tax payments, discounted at the appropriate discount rate, r_E. For simplicity we assume that debt is issued at par such that the required interest payment at the end of the period is given by $r_D D_j$.[5] It can be verified that

$$\frac{\partial V_j}{\partial D_j} = \begin{cases} > 0 & \text{if } r_D < \dfrac{r_E}{1-t_c} \\ = 0 & \text{if } r_D = \dfrac{r_E}{1-t_c} \\ < 0 & \text{if } r_D > \dfrac{r_E}{1-t_c}. \end{cases} \tag{11}$$

Thus, if an interior equilibrium with both debt and equity exists, firms issue debt until $r_D = r_E/(1 - t_c)$ at which point each individual firm is indifferent between debt and equity. Using this relationship it follows from the investor's first-order conditions that

$$\text{investor } i\text{'s demand} = \begin{cases} \text{debt} & \text{if } (1-t_{pi}) > (1-t_c)(1-t_{gi}) \\ \text{debt and equity} & \text{if } (1-t_{pi}) = (1-t_c)(1-t_{gi}) \\ \text{equity} & \text{if } (1-t_{pi}) < (1-t_c)(1-t_{gi}). \end{cases} \tag{12}$$

According to equation (12), in an equilibrium with both debt and equity, all debt securities are held by investors with tax rates on ordinary income less than or equal to the combined effect of the corporate tax and capital gains tax. Investors with high tax rates hold equity. This minimizes the total taxes paid. This result was first derived by Miller [1977]. A critical assumption underlying the above equilibrium is that short sales are not allowed, which implies that investors cannot borrow. Relaxing this assumption is equivalent to allowing investors to borrow at an after tax cost of either $r_D(1 - t_{pi})$ or $r_E(1 - t_{gi})$. In this case one can verify that first-order conditions imply that, for each investor, $r_E(1 - t_{gi}) = r_D(1 - t_{pi})$, i.e. the after tax rate of return on debt and equity must be equal for all investors. If this is not the case, then investors could make arbitrage profits by short selling the security with the lower after tax rate of return and investing the proceeds in the security with the higher after tax rate of return. For a discussion of equilibrium and heterogeneous tax rates see Hamada & Scholes [1985], Stiglitz [1985], Kim, Lewellen & McConnell [1979], Schaefer [1982], and Dammon & Green [1987].

We will now briefly discuss whether or not currently adopted classical tax systems are likely to support a Miller equilibrium. First, recall that equation (11) implies that firms issue both debt and equity if the interest rate is given by $r_D = r_E/(1 - t_c)$. This can only be an equilibrium if, at these interest rates, there are some investors who demand debt and other investors who

[5] In a riskless one-period setting original issue discounts would not alter any of the following results since discounts must be amortized and are therefore equivalent to coupon payments.

demand equity. As shown in equation (12), this is the case if there are some investors for which $(1 - t_{pi})/(1 - t_{gi}) > (1 - t_c)$ and other investors for which $(1 - t_{pi})/(1 - t_{gi}) < (1 - t_c)$. The first condition will generally hold, since in most tax systems there are some investors or corporations with zero income tax rates. The second condition requires that there are investors with personal tax rates which exceed the combined effect of the corporate tax rate and the capital gains tax rate.

In most of the countries listed above, the highest personal tax rate exceeds the corporate tax rate. In addition, the capital gains tax rate for private investors is frequently zero if the capital gain is realized after some minimum holding period.[6] These tax systems therefore clearly support the Miller equilibrium derived in Section 2.[7]

Note that a Miller equilibrium might be supported in a tax system even if $(1 - t_{pi}) < (1 - t_c)(1 - t_{gi})$ for all investors if t_{gi} is the effective tax rate on capital gains. This is the case because investors can postpone the realization of capital gains and thereby reduce the present value of the capital gains tax. This reduction is even more significant if investors are able to postpone the realization of capital gains to periods when their marginal tax rate is low. The optimal timing of realizations of capital losses can further reduce the effective capital gains tax rate and we discuss this aspect in more detail in Section 5. Thus, even if the last inequality in expression (12) does not hold for any investor using the statutory capital gains tax rate, this inequality may still hold for the effective capital gains tax rate so that the Miller equilibrium can still be obtained.

In the US, since the Income Tax Reform Act 1986, realized capital gains are taxed at the tax rate for ordinary income and the highest personal tax rate on ordinary income is reduced to 30%. Since in the absence of state or county income taxes, the corporate tax rate at 34% exceeds the highest personal tax rate, a Miller equilibrium is currently not supported by the US tax system. There are no investors for which the personal tax on interest income exceeds the combined effect of corporate tax and capital gains tax, that is $(1 - t_{pi})/(1 - t_{gi}) > (1 - t_c)$ for all i. This is true even if the effective capital gains tax rate is assumed to be zero. This implies that debt financing is advantageous in equilibrium and firms should maximize their financial leverage.[8]

[6] In some countries, e.g. in the Netherlands and Switzerland, the capital gains tax is zero without restrictions on the holding period.

[7] The classical tax systems of Austria and Switzerland show some special features. In Austria the income tax rate for dividends is reduced to one half of the average tax rate of the investor. In spite of this, it can be shown that firms should not pay dividends since the capital gains tax is zero after a minimum holding period of one year. Switzerland has also chosen a classical tax system. A unique feature of the Swiss tax system is that the corporate tax rate is an increasing function of the rate of return on equity.

[8] Consistent with this result a significant increase in leverage of US firms over the recent years has been observed. For example, Hodder & Tschoegl [1991] show that for manufacturing corporations in the US shareholders' equity has decreased from 49.5% in 1980 to 40.2% in 1990. For a discussion of the effects of the US tax reform of 1986 on capital structure decisions see Auerbach [1990] and Scholes & Wolfson [1992].

2.2. Imputation systems

Canada, Japan and most European countries have implemented tax systems that mitigate or eliminate double taxation of dividends [Mennel, 1991]. A minority of these countries (for example Greece and Norway) allow dividends to be deducted from corporate taxable income and thus treat interest payments and dividends symmetrically. The majority of countries has adopted tax systems where dividends are taxed at the corporate level but the corporate tax on dividends is either fully or partly credited to the personal income tax (for example Canada, Denmark, Finland, France, Germany, Italy, Japan, Spain, UK). Some of these countries apply different corporate tax rates to distributed and retained profits. There are two distinct variations of the imputation system, depending on whether or not the credited corporate tax is taxable at the personal level.

2.2.1. The credited corporate tax is taxable at the personal level

Examples of countries that have adopted this tax system are Canada, France, Germany, Italy and UK.[9] In the analysis below we simultaneously derive firms' optimal dividend and debt policy. To capture the effect of dividend policy on firm value we assume that the firm can issue two different types of shares. Owners of type A shares receive cash dividends whereas type B shares offer a return in the form of capital gains, for example via stock dividends. For simplicity, we assume a zero capital gains tax rate.[10]

Define:

E_{Aj}, E_{Bj} = time 0 market value of firm j's type A and type B shares, respectively;
Div_j = firm j's dividends after corporate tax (i.e. dividends before corporate tax are given by $Div/(1-t_{cd})$);
t_{cd} = corporate tax rate for distributed profits;
TCR = dividend tax credit.

E_{B_j} can be written as:

$$E_{Bj} = \frac{X_j - D_j(1+r_D) - E_{Aj} - \mathrm{Div}_j/(1-t_{cd})}{1+r_E} - \frac{t_c[X_j - r_D D_j - I_j - \mathrm{Div}_j/(1-t_{cd})]}{1+r_E}. \tag{13}$$

The right hand side of equation (13) represents the return realized by holders of type B shares consisting of the firm's cash flow minus payments to debtholders and minus payments to type A shareholders minus corporate tax payments.[11] Since

[9] In Canada dividends are first grossed up by 25% and then investors receive a tax credit of $13\frac{1}{3}\%$

[10] For results with a positive capital gains tax rate see Zechner [1989].

[11] Note that $\mathrm{Div}_j/(1-t_{cd})$ consists of the dividend paid to shareholders, Div_j, and the corporate tax on the dividend, $t_{cd}\mathrm{Div}_j/(1-t_{cd})$.

the return is realized in the form of tax free capital gains, the discount rate r_E corresponds to an after-tax rate.

The value of type A shares, E_{Aj}, can be derived from the following relation:

$$E_{Aj} = \frac{E_{Aj} + \text{Div}_j + TCR}{1 + r_D} \tag{14}$$

or

$$E_{Aj} = \frac{\text{Div}_j + TCR}{r_D} \tag{15}$$

where r_D is the rate of return on taxable securities and TCR is the (taxable) dividend tax credit.

The value of the firm is

$$V_j = E_{Aj} + E_{Bj} + D_j. \tag{16}$$

In order to derive the capital structure and dividend equilibrium, we need to specify how the corporate tax credit, TCR is defined by the tax code. In Germany and Italy the corporate tax on dividends is fully credited to the income tax. Therefore the credited corporate tax is given by $TCR = t_{cd}\text{Div}_j/(1 - t_{cd})$. The resulting value of type A shares is $E_{Aj} = \text{Div}_j/r_D(1 - t_{cd})$. To illustrate the implications of a fully credited corporate tax we derive the equilibrium for the German tax system where the corporate tax rates on retained and distributed earnings are given by $t_c = 0.50$ and $t_{cd} = 0.36$.

The first step is to show that debt financing is equivalent to issuing type A shares. This follows from differentiating equation (16) with respect to D_j, holding dividends constant, and with respect to E_{Aj}, holding debt constant,

$$\frac{\partial V_j}{\partial D_j} = \frac{\partial V_j}{\partial E_{Aj}} = \frac{r_E - r_D(1 - t_c)}{1 + r_E}. \tag{17}$$

In the second step we observe from equation (17) that firms find it optimal to issue debt or dividend paying equity if $r_E > r_D(1 - t_c)$. Alternatively, if $r_E < r_D(1 - t_c)$, then firms optimally issue equity and retain earnings. Thus, an equilibrium where all three types of securities are issued exists only if $r_E = r_D(1 - t_c)$.[12] This requires that there exist a marginal investor with tax rate $t_{pm} = t_c$.

Investors with tax rates $t_{pi} < t_c$ buy debt or shares that pay dividends; investors with tax rates such that $t_{pi} = t_{pm} = t_c$ are indifferent between debt and both types of shares; investors with tax rates $t_{pi} > t_c$ buy shares of firms that retain earnings.

So far we have analysed tax systems where the corporate tax on distributed earnings is fully credited to the personal income tax. In France and in the UK, for example, only a part of the corporate tax is credited against the personal income tax. In France, the corporate tax rate $t_c = t_{cd} = 0.42$. The tax credit is 50% of the after corporate tax dividend. With the French data, E_{Aj} and E_{Bj} are:

[12] For general conditions for simultaneous tax irrelevance of debt and dividend policies see Haugen, Senbet & Talmor [1986].

$$E_{Bj} = \frac{X_j - D_j(1+r_D) - E_{Aj} - \mathrm{Div}_j/(1-t_c)}{1+r_E} - \\ - \frac{t_c[X_j - r_D D_j - I_j - \mathrm{Div}_j/(1-t_c)]}{1+r_E} \tag{18}$$

$$E_{Aj} = 1.5\,\frac{\mathrm{Div}}{r_D}. \tag{19}$$

We again compare debt financing with issuing type A shares:

$$\frac{\partial V_j}{\partial D_j} = \frac{r_E - r_D(1-t_c)}{1+r_E} \tag{20}$$

$$\frac{\partial V_j}{\partial E_{Aj}} = \frac{r_E - r_D/1.5}{1+r_E}. \tag{21}$$

The right hand sides of equations (20) and (21) are equal at $t_c = 0.33$. Since in France $t_c = 0.42$, debt financing is preferred to equity financing with dividend payments.

Next, equation (20) shows that an equilibrium where firms are indifferent between debt and shares of type B exists if $r_E = r_D(1 - t_c)$. This requires a marginal investor with tax rate $t_{pm} = t_c$. Investors who are not marginal either buy debt or shares of firms which retain earnings, depending on their personal income tax rates.[13]

2.2.2. The credited corporate tax is not taxable at the personal level

This system has been introduced, for example, by Japan and Spain. For these tax systems the market value of type *B* shares, E_{Bj}, is again given by equation (13) whereas the market value of type *A* shares, E_{Aj} now becomes:

$$E_{Aj} = \frac{\mathrm{Div}_j}{r_D} + \frac{TCR}{r_E}. \tag{22}$$

Equation (22) reflects the fact that dividends are taxable at the personal level and are thus discounted at the before-tax rate r_D. The credited corporate tax is realized tax-free and is therefore discounted at the after-tax rate r_E.

In Japan, for example, the corporate tax rate including state and municipal taxes is $t_c = t_{cd}$ = approximately 0.45. The dividend tax credit varies between 7.4% and 12.8% of the dividend, depending on the taxable income of the investor. Going through the same analysis as in Section 2.2.1., we find that the results are identical to the case where the corporate tax is only partly credited to the personal tax on dividends. If there is a marginal investor with a personal income tax rate equal to the corporate tax rate, firms are indifferent between debt and equity. To pay out dividends is suboptimal and investors decide between shares and debt according to their personal income tax rate.

[13] It should be mentioned that the Commission of the European Community advocates a tax system where the corporate tax rate is credited to the personal income tax only to an extent of 45% to 55% [Herzig, 1990].

3. Taxes and international equilibrium

Sofar the analysis has focused on a single economy with a homogeneous tax system. However, it becomes increasingly important to recognize that investors can invest and firms can issue securities in foreign capital markets which are possibly subject to different tax systems. In this section we specifically analyse securities market and capital structure equilibria in a multinational setting. In particular we develop the analysis for two countries with classical tax systems where corporate tax rates and inflation rates differ across countries. For simplicity the capital gains tax rates are assumed to be zero.

3.1. Differences in corporate tax rates

Consider two countries with different corporate tax rates. Without loss of generality assume that $t_c < t_c^*$ where t_c and t_c^* denote the corporate tax rate in the domestic and in the foreign country respectively. In a closed economy, the analysis in Section 2 implies that national equilibria are reached when $r_D = r_E/(1 - t_c)$ and $r_D^* = r_E^*/(1 - t_c^*)$. Now consider an international equilibrium when investors can hold securities issued in foreign capital markets and firms can issue securities both domestically and internationally. If there are no barriers to international investment, the rate of return on equity must be the same across countries, i.e. $r_E = r_E^*$. Then, since firms in the foreign country supply debt at rates $r_D^* = r_E^*/(1 - t_c^*) > r_D = r_E/(1 - t_c)$, all investors with tax rates $t_{pi} < t_c^*$ maximize their after-tax rate of return by holding foreign debt. One possible equilibrium is reached when the supply of debt by foreign firms is sufficient to satisfy the demand by all investors in tax brackets $t_{pi} \leq t_c^*$. In this case the equilibrium interest rate is $r_D^* = r_E/(1 - t_c^*)$, firms in the foreign country are indifferent between debt and equity but firms in the domestic country are equity financed since they could only supply debt at the lower rate $r_D = r_E/(1 - t_c)$.

Alternatively, if foreign firms are already fully levered and there exist investors with unsatisfied demands for debt, then interest rates drop to $r_D = r_E/(1 - t_c)$ and firms in the domestic country i.e. the low-tax country also supply debt. In this case foreign firms are fully debt financed and domestic firms are indifferent between debt and equity.

Thus, ceteris paribus, firms in the high-tax country are relatively more highly levered than firms in the low-tax country. The reason for this result is that firms in the high-tax country can deduct their interest expenses against a higher corporate tax-rate and can thus afford to pay higher before-tax interest rates. The analysis so far is based on a model developed in Lee & Zechner [1984]. Hodder & Senbet [1990] extend this analysis and allow firms to set up foreign subsidiaries. Firms in the low-tax country would borrow through their subsidiaries in the high-tax country and then subtract interest against the higher corporate tax rate t_c^*. In this framework all firms can supply debt at interest rates $r_D^* = r_E/(1 - t_c^*)$ and an international version of the Miller equilibrium obtains where the highest corporate tax rate determines the equilibrium. This result, however, hinges on the assumption that firms can always deduct their interest expenses against the highest corporate tax rate, for example through unlimited loss-offset provisions.

3.2. Differences in inflation rates

In this section we discuss the effects of differences in inflation rates across countries on capital structure and securities market equilibria.[14] Let i and i^* denote the inflation rates in the domestic and in the foreign country respectively. For simplicity assume that $i^* = 0$. Define the exchange rate at time t, S_t, as domestic currency units per foreign currency unit. The law of one price then requires that the exchange rate at time one is equal to $S_0(1+i)$. For investors to be indifferent between holding domestic or foreign equity, the required rates of return are

$$r_E = r_E^* + i + i r_E^*. \tag{23}$$

If equation (23) holds, then the real rate of return on equity in the two countries is the same. Assuming that corporate tax rates are the same in the two countries, national equilibria are reached if $r_D = r_E/(1-t_c)$ and $r_D^* = r_E^*/(1-t_c)$. Given these equilibria, suppose we allow a firm in the domestic country to issue debt in the foreign country with face value D_j, denominated in the foreign currency. The value of such a firm, expressed in domestic currency, is given by

$$V_j = D_j S_0 + \frac{X_j - D_j S_1(1+r_D^*) - t_c[X_j - I_j - D_j(S_1 - S_0) - D_j S_1 r_D^*]}{1 + r_E^*(1+i) + i}. \tag{24}$$

The first term in the right hand side of equation (24) represents the market value of foreign currency debt and the second term defines the market value of equity. Note that the firm can deduct not only the interest payment on foreign debt, $D_j S_1 r_D^*$, from taxable income but also the foreign exchange loss, equal to $D_j(S_1 - S_0)$. Partially differentiating the value of the firm yields

$$\frac{\partial V_j}{\partial D_j} = S_0 - \frac{S_1(1+r_D^*) - t_c(S_1 - S_0) - t_c S_1 r_D^*}{1 + r_E^*(1+i) + i}. \tag{25}$$

After some simplification this can be rewritten as

$$\frac{\partial V_j}{\partial D_j} = \frac{t_c i S_0}{1 + r_E^*(1+i) + i}. \tag{26}$$

Thus, if yields are initially determined by national equilibria, firms in the high inflation country have an incentive to issue debt denominated in the currency of the low inflation country. The intuition for this result is the following. If firms in the high inflation country issue debt denominated in the currency of the low inflation country, the issuing firms expect to realize a foreign exchange loss. If

[14] The following analysis is based on Lee & Zechner [1984].

realized, this loss is tax deductible under most tax codes. This additional tax advantage of foreign debt allows firms in the high inflation country to offer higher interest rates on foreign currency debt.[15]

As in the case where corporate tax rates were allowed to differ, two equilibria are possible. In one equilibrium the interest rate is determined by firms in the high inflation country issuing foreign currency debt. In this case firms in the high inflation country are indifferent between debt and equity and firms in the low inflation country are all equity financed. In the other possible equilibrium, the interest rates are determined by firms in the low inflation country. In this case firms in the low inflation country are indifferent between debt and equity and firms in the high inflation country are all debt financed. Which equilibrium obtains depends on the relative sizes of the two economies.

The analysis so far assumes that corporations' abilities to engage in international tax arbitrage are limited. Hodder & Senbet [1990] analyze different inflation rates with unrestricted tax arbitrage and show that in this case all corporations issue debt in the high-inflation country — possibly through subsidiaries — and an international version of the Miller equilibrium obtains again.

Summarizing, the main results in this section on international equilibrium are that, under restricted international tax arbitrage, firms in countries with higher corporate tax rates and higher inflation rates have a comparative advantage in issuing debt and should be relatively more highly levered than firms in countries with low corporate tax rates and low inflation rates.

4. The effects of uncertainty

In the previous sections we have simplified the analysis by assuming certainty. This assumption has allowed us to focus on some important effects of different tax systems on optimal financial structure in a simple framework. However, there are some effects of tax systems that can only be captured in models that specifically allow for uncertainty. In this section we introduce a state preference framework which enables us to analyse these effects. In particular we identify two main effects which are due to uncertainty. First, if the firm's taxable income is stochastic, then the corporate tax savings due to interest deductions generally become uncertain as well. This affects the present value of debt-related corporate tax savings. Second, under uncertainty different bonds are no longer perfect substitutes. As we show below, high-risk bonds offer higher expected coupon payments than low-risk bonds. This introduces clientele effects among investors since low-tax investors have a comparative advantage holding high coupon bonds and high-tax investors

[15] Note that high inflation does not make domestic debt more advantageous. In the case of domestic debt the high inflation leads to high interest rates which are tax deductible at the corporate level but are taxable at the personal level. Thus, when the personal tax rate equals the corporate tax rate, then inflation has no effect on the net tax advantage of debt [see Schall, 1984, and Hochman & Palmon, 1985].

prefer low-coupon bonds. In Sections 4.1 and 4.2 we explore these two effects. We base the analysis on the classical tax system and assume for simplicity that the capital gains tax is zero and that investors are risk neutral.[16]

4.1. Uncertain debt tax shields

It has been shown in Section 2 that under certainty the equilibrium relationship between yields on debt and equity is given by $r_E = r_D(1 - t_c)$. Given this relationship, firms' after-tax cost of debt and equity is the same. Under uncertainty, however, the firm's before-tax income might be insufficient to utilize all interest deductions. Ignoring tax loss carry forwards, the after tax cost of the marginal unit of debt in states in which the firm's taxable income is negative then rises from $r_D(1-t_c)$ to r_D. This effect has first been analysed by DeAngelo & Masulis [1980]. We will briefly summarize their analysis.

4.1.1. Uncertain debt tax shields without distinction between interest and principal

To simplify the analysis, DeAngelo and Masulis ignore the distinction between interest and principal and assume that all payments to debtholders are tax deductible to firms and taxable to bondholders. The firm's taxable income is then given by $\max[X_j - B_j - I_j, 0]$ where X_j is the firm's random cash flow before taxes, B_j denotes the total promised payment to bondholders, i.e. principal plus interest and I_j denotes non debt tax shields. Define the following critical cash flow levels: $X_j^a = B_j$ and $X_j^b = B_j + I_j$. If the firm's cash flow exceeds X_j^a, then the firm can meet all its obligations to bondholders and is thus solvent. If the firm's cash flow exceeds X_j^b, then the firm is not only solvent but its taxable income is positive as well. The values of debt and equity are given by

$$D_j = \frac{1}{1+r_D} \int_0^{X_j^a} X_j \pi(X_j)\,\mathrm{d}X_j + \frac{1}{1+r_D} \int_{X_j^a}^{X_j^{\max}} B_j \pi(X_j)\,\mathrm{d}X_j \tag{27}$$

$$\begin{aligned} E_j = {} & \frac{1}{1+r_E} \int_{X_j^a}^{X_j^b} (X_j - B_j)\pi(X_j)\,\mathrm{d}X_j + \\ & + \frac{1}{1+r_E} \int_{X_j^b}^{X_j^{\max}} [X_j - B_j - t_c(X_j - B_j - I_j)]\pi(X_j) dX_j \end{aligned} \tag{28}$$

where $\pi(X_j)$ is the probability density of cash flow realization X_j. Let t_{pm} denote the tax rate of the marginal investor who is indifferent between debt and equity

[16] For an analysis of uncertainty with risk averse investors in complete and incomplete markets see Taggart [1980].

such that $(1+r_D)(1-t_{pm}) = 1+r_E$. Substituting from this relationship for $1+r_D$ in equation (27) we can partially differentiate $V_j = E_j + D_j$ with respect to B_j. Noting that the partials with respect to the limits of integration drop out this yields

$$\frac{\partial V_j}{\partial B_j} = \frac{1-t_{pm}}{1+r_E}\int_{X_j^a}^{X_j^{\max}} \pi(X_j)\,\mathrm{d}X_j - \frac{1}{1+r_E}\int_{X_j^a}^{X_j^b} \pi(X_j)\,\mathrm{d}X_j - \\ - \frac{1-t_c}{1+r_E}\int_{X_j^b}^{X_j^{\max}} \pi(X_j)\,\mathrm{d}X_j. \tag{29}$$

It can be verified that the derivative in equation (29) is zero if

$$t_{pm} = t_c \frac{\int_{X_j^b}^{X_j^{\max}} \pi(X_j)\,\mathrm{d}X_j}{\int_{X_j^a}^{X_j^{\max}} \pi(X_j)\,\mathrm{d}X_j}. \tag{30}$$

The left hand side of equation (30), ie. t_{pm}, represents the personal tax on interest income paid by the marginal investor. The right hand side represents the effective corporate tax rate against which the marginal dollar of debt payments can be applied. If the firm's taxable income is always positive, then $X_j^a = X_j^b = X_j^{\min}$ and the effective corporate tax rate is equal to the statutory rate, t_c. If the probability of a loss is positive, i.e. if $X_j^a < X_j^b$, then the effective corporate tax rate is less than t_c. If the firm has issued so much debt that the probability of realizing taxable earnings is zero, i.e. if $X_j^b = X_j^{\max}$, then the effective corporate tax rate is zero.

If t_{pm} is less than (greater than) the right hand side of equation (30), then $\partial V_j / \partial B_j$ is positive (negative) and firms should increase (decrease) their debt level until equation (30) holds. Thus, each firm has an interior, tax-motivated optimal capital structure. Each particular firm's optimal leverage level is determined by the firm's nondebt tax shields, I_j, and its cash flow distribution. If in equilibrium firms face some probability of not being able to utilize debt tax shields, then the marginal investor's personal tax rate reflected in the interest rate is less than the corporate tax rate.

4.1.2. Uncertain debt tax shields with distinction between principal and interest

The main result in DeAngelo & Masulis [1980] is that the marginal tax advantage of debt decreases monotonically with the amount of debt issued [see equation (30)]. As discussed above, this result has been derived under the assumption that all debt payments are tax deductible. In practice, only interest payments are deductible expenses but principal repayments are not. The effect of the distinction between interest and principal has first been analysed by Talmor, Haugen & Barnea [1985] and Zechner & Swoboda [1986]. In this section we summarize how uncertainty of debt tax shields affects optimal capital structure given the distinction between principal and interest.[17]

Once principal and interest payments are distinguished, it becomes necessary to specify priority rules that determine how partial payments in default are allocated to (i) tax payments, (ii) principal repayments and (iii) interest payments. According to most tax codes the tax authority's claims precede debtholders' claims. After taxes owed have been paid, partial payments to debtholders are first considered principal repayments and then, after principal has been repaid in full, interest payments. The following analysis is based on this priority structure.

Without loss of generality we assume that debt is issued at par. In this case tax deductible interest payments to debtholders are given by

$$b_j^T(X_j) = \max[b_j(X_j) - D_j, 0] \tag{31}$$

where $b_j(X_j)$ and $b_j^T(X_j)$ denote firm j's total payments and interest payments to debtholders, respectively. Given this definition of interest payments, it can be shown that the corporate tax savings due to the marginal dollar of debt do not go to zero, as in the DeAngelo Masulis analysis. To see this, consider a highly levered firm with debt level $D_j > I_j$. Note that interest payments can only be made if the firm's cash flow exceeds the face value of debt, i.e. if $X_j > D_j$. Given this condition, interest payments are then less than or equal to $\min[X_j - D_j, B_j - D_j]$ whereas the firm's taxable income before interest is $X_j - I_j$.[18] Since we analyse a firm for which $D_j > I_j$, its taxable income before interest always exceeds the amount of interest paid: $X_j - I_j > \min[X_j - D_j, B_j - D_j]$. Thus, if a firm is highly levered such that $D_j \geq I_j$, then it has no redundant interest tax shields.

The intuition of the above result is straightforward. If a firm is highly levered, then it defaults when its earnings are low. In these states the firm partly repays the principal amount but makes no interest payments such that there are no debt tax shields. It can only make interest payments in those states in which taxable earnings are high enough such that all debt tax shields can be utilized.[19]

The following capital structure equilibrium obtains. If the marginal investor's personal tax rate is below the corporate tax rate, then all firms would choose maximum leverage. If it is equal to the corporate tax rate, then firms are indifferent between all equity, low leverage ratios and very high leverage ratios (i.e. $D_j > I_j$). If investors' tax rates are higher than the corporate tax rate, firms are optimally all equity financed.

Zechner & Swoboda [1986] also extend the analysis to the case where interest

[17] We base this discussion on the analysis in Zechner & Swoboda [1986].

[18] Note that interest payments are always less than $X_j - D_j$ since tax payments precede interest payments.

[19] In the above analysis very risky debt achieves that tax-deductible payments are made only when taxable income before interest is high. As Scholes & Wolfson [1988, p.170] point out, there are other possibilities to obtain this result. Examples are income bonds, leases tied to revenue, employee bonus plans tied to profitability.

precedes principal. In this case interest payments are given by

$$b_j^T(X_j) = \min[X_j, B_j - D_j]. \tag{32}$$

It is shown that, even under this alternative priority structure, the marginal corporate tax advantage of debt does generally not go to zero as the firm increases its leverage. Thus, independent of the assumed priority structure of principal versus interest, uncertainty of debt tax shields is insufficient to generate interior optimal capital structures for all firms.

Uncertainty with progressive personal taxes

The analysis so far has assumed that investors' marginal tax rates are constant. In reality most tax schedules are progressive in the sense that additional increments to taxable income are taxed at higher marginal tax rates. One important implication of progressive taxes is the fact that marginal tax rates will generally be correlated with aggregate consumption. In states in which aggregate consumption is high, the representative investor's marginal tax rate is likely to be higher than in states in which aggregate consumption is low. As a result, the net-tax subsidy of interest payments may be positive in states in which aggregate consumption is low but negative in states with high aggregate consumption. The choice of an optimal capital structure therefore involves a tradeoff between states with a net-tax advantage and those with a net-tax disadvantage of debt. Dammon [1987] & Ross [1985] show that this may lead to interior optimal capital structures. The analysis is based on the assumptions that all payments to debtholders are taxable/tax-deductible and that no nondebt tax shields are available. Both authors find that the higher the firm's unlevered asset beta with respect to aggregate consumption, the lower its optimal debt level. More specifically, Ross [1985] finds that interior optimal leverage ratios may obtain only in the 'positive beta case'. To gain intuition for this result, consider a firm with risky debt outstanding. If this firm issues an additional unit of debt, then additional payments to debtholders can only be made in states in which the firm's cash flow is high. In the case of a positive beta firm, these are the states with high aggregate consumption and therefore high marginal tax rates. Such an increase in debt may lower firm value. In the 'negative beta case' Ross [1985] finds that corner solutions are optimal. Both papers identify a tax motive for spin-offs or mergers which may be used to transfer debt payments to those states in which the tax-subsidy of debt is positive.

4.2. Clientele effects

Dybvig & Ross [1986] define tax clientele effects in quantities and in prices. Tax clienteles in quantities exist if there is an investor who is marginal on all securities and inframarginal investors plunge and strictly prefer to hold only a subset of securities. The Miller equilibrium discussed in Section 2 is an example for tax clienteles in quantities. All investors with tax rates less than the corporate tax rate hold only debt and all investors with tax rates greater than the corporate tax rate hold only equity. However, there exists a group of marginal investors with tax rates exactly equal to the corporate tax rate who are indifferent between debt and equity.

Tax clienteles in prices are defined by a securities market equilibrium where there is no investor who is marginal on all securities. Zechner [1990] shows that uncertainty generally introduces tax clientele effects in prices among bondholders.[20] In other words, given uncertainty, there is no single investor who is marginal on all bonds. In this section we summarize the intuition underlying this result. Following Zechner [1990] we simplify the analysis by assuming risk neutrality, a zero capital gains tax and certain debt-tax shields.

An example

It is easiest to demonstrate the intuition underlying the bondholder clientele effect with a numerical example. Consider 3 risky bonds, each bond issued at par for $100. There are two equiprobable states of the world. The bonds' payoffs in these two states are summarized in the following table.

Bond	State 1	State 2
Bond 1	110	110
Bond 2	90	134
Bond 3	85	140

Note that Bond 1 is riskless, Bond 2 exhibits a capital loss of $10 in state 1 and Bond 3 exhibits a capital loss of $15 in state 1. Loosely speaking, Bond 1 is the least risky security, Bond 2 is of intermediate risk and Bond 3 is the riskiest security. We can now calculate the expected interest payment received from the three bonds. For Bond 1 the expected interest payment is $10. Bond 2 pays no interest in state 1 and pays $34 of interest in state 2, yielding expected interest payments of $17. Bond 3 pays no interest in state 1 and $40 in state 2, implying expected interest payments of $20. Thus, the riskier the bond, the higher its expected interest payment. This is the case even if the expected before tax rate of return were the same across bonds since riskier bonds must compensate investors for higher possible capital losses in the default states through higher coupon payments in the solvency states.

The clientele effect

Investors in different tax brackets rank the three bonds summarized in the table above differently. Investors with personal tax rates $t_{pi} \leq 0.167$ realize the highest after-tax rate of return if they invest in Bond 3; investors in tax brackets $0.167 < t_{pi} \leq 0.286$ prefer Bond 2 and investors in tax brackets $t_{pi} > 0.286$ optimally invest in Bond 1. Thus, there is no single investor who is marginal on all three bonds. Investors in high tax brackets prefer low-risk, low-coupon bonds,

[20] Park & Williams [1985] analyse bondholder tax clienteles in a model where the mix of taxable versus nontaxable payments to debtholders can be essentially chosen by the firm independently of the bond's risk.

even if their before-tax rate of return is slightly lower than that of high-risk, high-coupon bonds. Investors in low tax-brackets prefer high-risk, high-coupon bonds with high before-tax yields.

Implicit tax rates

To analyse tax clienteles it is useful to introduce the concept of 'implicit tax rates'. We define a bond's implicit tax rate as the personal tax rate that would make an investor indifferent between holding the bond and holding tax-exempt equity. Continuing the above example, suppose that the expected rate of return on equity is 7%. Then it can be verified that the implicit tax rate, as defined above, is 30% for Bond 1, 29.4% for Bond 2 and 27.5% for Bond 3.[21]

Thus, we see that the implicit tax rate is highest for the riskless bond and lowest for the riskiest bond, i.e. Bond 3. As shown in Zechner [1990], this is necessary for an equilibrium to exist. To obtain a contradiction, conjecture that the implicit tax rate of Bond 3 is higher than the implicit tax rates on the other two bonds. In this case investors in all tax brackets find that their after-tax rate of return is highest if they invest in Bond 3. Thus, the market would not clear, contradicting the original conjecture that Bond 3 is the bond with the highest implicit tax rate.

Equilibrium

The discussion above has established the following results. First, high risk bonds offer high *expected* interest payments per dollar of market value. Second, in equilibrium, bonds with higher expected interest payments are priced at lower implicit tax rates i.e. for risky bonds interest payments are 'grossed up' by a smaller amount. Now we can discuss how these two effects influence firms' optimal capital structure decisions. As a firm increases its leverage, its debt becomes riskier. As a consequence, the expected interest payments per dollar of debt issued increases and the implicit tax rate at which debt is priced, decreases. Note that the net tax advantage of debt to the corporation is reflected in the difference between the corporate tax rate and the implicit tax rate. Since the implicit tax rate decreases with leverage, firms either issue the maximum amount of debt or remain all equity financed. The latter is optimal if the implicit tax rate on the firm's debt given maximum leverage, exceeds the corporate tax rate. The tax clientele effect therefore generates incentives for firms to choose extreme capital structures.

5. Multiperiod models

Most of the literature on taxes and optimal financial structure is based on single period models. However, some important questions regarding the relationship

[21] For example, the implicit tax rate for Bond 2, t_{i2}, is given by

$$\frac{(90 + 134 - t_{i2}34)0.5 - 100}{100} = 0.07.$$

Solving for t_{i2} yields the result in the text, i.e. $t_{i2} = 29.4\%$.

between taxes and optimal financial structure cannot be addressed in static models. The main questions that can only be analyzed in multiperiod models are: How does investors' ability to retrade affect firms' capital structure choice? What is the effect of firms' ability to adjust their capital structures over time? Do taxes generate an optimal debt maturity structure? In this section we discuss papers that address these questions.

5.1. Intertemporal trading and optimal capital structure

Intertemporal trading can have two distinct effects on optimal financial structure. First, as new information about a bond's riskiness becomes available, it may become optimal for one investor clientele to sell a particular bond to another clientele. This can change a bond's implicit tax rate and can also affect the firm's initial choice of capital structure. Second, if capital gains taxes are nonzero, investors may exercise their tax timing options by selling securities which exhibit capital losses and holding on to bonds with capital gains. The first effect has been analyzed by Zechner [1990] and the second by Constantinides [1983, 1984], Dammon, Dunn & Spatt [1989] and Mauer & Lewellen [1988].

We first focus on the effect due to intertemporal trades across investor clienteles. Consider a three-date model where investors are allowed to trade before the final period. Firms issue debt and equity securities at time 0. At time 1 investors receive new information about the final payoffs that are realized at time 2 and are allowed to rebalance their portfolios. The possibility to retrade at time 1 allows a more efficient allocation of taxable income across investors. To see this, one must recognize that the expected portion of taxable income generated by a bond can change over time. If investors learn that a given firm will default on its interest payments at time 2, it becomes optimal for investors in low tax brackets to sell this firm's debt. This is the case because such a bond takes on equity characteristics and the wealth of investors in low tax brackets is optimally invested in securities with high portions of taxable income. By contrast, if an initially risky bond becomes riskless, then the bond generates high coupon payments with certainty and should therefore be passed on to low tax investors. This leads to the result that bonds trading at large discounts (premia) should be priced at high (low) implicit tax rates.

Investors' ability to retrade also affects firms' optimal capital structure decisions. Since, with retrading, a bond's implicit tax rate generally differs across future states, the distribution of interest payments across states becomes important.[22] This can give rise to interior optimal capital structures where firms optimally design their financial structures to attract bondholder clienteles to maximize the expected net-tax subsidy of debt.

We now turn to the second effect of retrading which is based on the tax timing option. Since capital gains are only taxed when realized, there is an incentive to

[22] The effect of stochastic marginal tax rates has been analyzed in a one-period framework by Dammon [1987] and Ross [1985].

realize losses and to defer gains [Constantinides, 1983, 1984; and Dammon, Dunn & Spatt, 1989]. This may be relevant for the financial policy of the firm since the value of tax timing options can be influenced by capital structure decisions. As Mauer & Lewellen [1988] show, a partly debt financed firm offers more possibilities for loss realizations than a purely equity financed firm if prices for equity and debt do not move in the same direction in each state of the world. The following example briefly demonstrates this argument.

Consider a firm that will be liquidated at time 1. Suppose that at time 0^+ two events happen: the total value of the firm increases by ΔV and there is an unexpected increase in interest rates of Δr. If the firm is all equity financed then investors cannot realize any capital losses at time 0^+ and the optimal strategy is simply to defer their capital gains until the end of the period. Now consider an otherwise identical firm that has issued riskless debt with initial market value of D_j. At time 0^+ debtholders suffer a capital loss equal to $D_j[\Delta r/(1+r+\Delta r)$ which they can realize immediately. Thus, compared to a fully equity financed firm, a firm that issues several different securities with values that are imperfectly correlated gives investors more opportunities to realize their capital losses early and therefore makes the tax timing option more valuable. This should be reflected in a higher initial firm value.

5.2. *The effect of intertemporal capital structure adjustments*

Most capital structure models ignore firms' optimal restructuring choices in response to fluctuations in asset values over time. One exception is the model developed by Brennan & Schwartz [1984] who analyze a firm's intertemporal investment and capital structure policy. In their model, capital structure decisions are driven by a tax advantage and agency costs created by debt. Since there are no transactions costs in their model, firms recapitalize continuously and the results focus on the optimal rate of change in the face value of debt.

Fischer, Heinkel & Zechner [1989] derive a continuous time model where firms can adjust their leverage at each point in time. If the capital structure adjustment is instantaneous and costless, then firms can be all debt financed without losing tax shields or risking bankruptcy. If it is costly to adjust the firm's financial structure, then firms have an optimal range within which their leverage ratio can lie. If stochastic changes in firm value push the firm's leverage ratio to these bounds, then the firm adjusts its capital structure back to some optimal level. In equilibrium, firms with low corporate tax rates, high variance of asset values and high transactions costs allow wide swings in their debt ratios.

Thus, summarizing, the firm's ability to adjust its capital structure over time reduces the effect of uncertainty. When recapitalizations are costless, firms could be highly levered but adjust their financial structure over time thereby avoiding lost debt tax shields and bankruptcy. If recapitalizations are costly, some of the effects of uncertainty are reintroduced. Firms then choose interior initial debt levels to avoid too frequent recapitalizations. The meaning of optimal capital structure must be redefined for this case since firms then define ranges of leverage levels which are 'optimal' and recapitalization occurs only if leverage reaches an upper or a lower bound. The higher the net-tax advantage of debt the tighter are these bounds.

5.3. Taxes and debt maturity

Kane, Marcus & McDonald [1984] analyse the tax advantage of debt in a continuous time framework where debt maturity is endogenous. The optimal maturity of debt is determined by the tradeoff between costs of issuing debt and the probability of going bankrupt. In this model firms cannot adjust their debt levels before the bonds mature which implies that the probability of going bankrupt increases with the maturity of the debt. Since bankruptcy is assumed to be costly and also triggers the loss of some debt tax shields there exists an optimal interior solution to the firm's debt maturity choice.

Lewis [1990] constructs a discrete multi-period model of optimal capital structure that explicitly allows firms to issue debt with different maturities. To simplify the analysis it is assumed that payments are made in the following order: (1) interest payments, (2) corporate tax payments, (3) principal payments. This priority structure together with the existence of nondebt related tax shields leads to an equilibrium where each firm has an interior optimum of state and time dependent interest payments per period. It is shown that each combination of capital structure and maturity structure which leads to the desired interest payments is equally optimal. For example, given an increasing term structure, the firm can reach its optimum by choosing a lower leverage and issuing long term debt or by a higher leverage but issuing short term debt.[23]

6. Extensions

6.1. Other taxes

In some European countries, notably Germany, Austria and Switzerland, the tax system comprises not only a corporate tax and an income tax, but also other taxes which may be relevant for capital structure decisions. In the following the effects of these additional taxes will be demonstrated for Germany.

[23] Barnea, Talmor & Haugen [1987] present a multi-period model which does not directly fit into the structure of this section. Their model allows for uncertain cash flows but assumes that debt is riskless and is paid back in the last period. In all periods except the last one operating earnings can be lower than interest payments, which are the only tax shield. If this happens new shares are issued to make up the difference between operating earnings and interest. In such a framework the probability that the marginal dollar of interest can be immediately offset against taxable income is less than one, even without nondebt tax shields. As more debt is issued, the marginal value of the expected tax benefit diminishes. In this scenario, an interior optimal capital structure exists for most firms and the equilibrium annual interest rate on debt, r_D, will be lower than $r_E/(1 - t_c)$, reflecting the fact that taxable income can be insufficient to use all interest payments as tax shields.

First, in Germany there is a general property tax (Vermögensteuer). Not only the property of individuals is subject to this tax (shares, bonds, savings accounts, real estate) but also the equity of corporations. While the property tax of individuals is essentially irrelevant for the financing decisions of corporations since both shares and bonds are taxable, the property tax for corporations is not: Since only the equity is taxed, the property tax can be reduced by increasing the debt level. The property tax is not deductible from the taxable income and its rate is currently 0.006 of 75% (= 0.0045) of the equity, valued according to special tax rules.

To evaluate the combined effect of the corporate and property tax, it is not adequate to simply add the two tax rates. One has to take into account that the property tax must be paid on the value of equity which is generally significantly higher than the firm's profit. If a value to earnings relation of 10 : 1 is assumed then the combined corporate and property tax is 0.50 ($= t_c$) + 0.045 (= property tax rate times 10) = 0.545. Since the highest marginal income tax rate in Germany is only 0.53, a Miller equilibrium does not exist in Germany!

Second, in Germany there is an additional relevant tax, the business tax (Gewerbesteuer). It consists of the business profit tax and the business capital tax. The base of the business profit tax is the firm's profit plus half of the interest paid on long term debt. The interest paid on short term debt is not subject to this tax. The tax rate is about 0.16, (the exact rate depends on the municipality) and is deductible from the corporate tax. The business capital tax is levied on the firm's equity and on 50% of the long term debt. The tax rate is about 0.008. The tax is deductible from any profit tax.

The business tax clearly makes debt still more advantageous in relation to equity since short term debt is not subject to this tax and only half of long term debt is taxable. Therefore, this tax enforces the conclusion that a Miller equilibrium should not exist in Germany. Moreover, the business tax clearly favors short term debt against long term debt.

Third, there is still another relevant tax in Germany, the church income tax. The federal tax authorities collect an additional surtax from members of officially recognized churches. This surtax (Kirchensteuer) amounts to 8% or 9% of the income tax but is a deductible expense. The inclusion of the church income tax at a rate of 9% increases the highest marginal tax rate of an investor from 0.53 to 0.5514. Therefore, the church tax makes debt financing less profitable. Nevertheless, the rate of 0.5514 is still lower than the combined corporate tax rate, property tax rate plus the additional business tax on equity. Therefore the result remains valid that a Miller equilibrium is not supported by the German tax system.[24]

[24] See Swoboda [1991]; this contradicts Fung & Theobald [1984] and Bay & Stehle [1988] who do not include the property tax, the business tax and the church income tax into their analysis. It is interesting to note, however, that church members have potentially different optimal portfolios than nonchurch members. If there was a Miller-equilibrium in Germany with a marginal tax rate of 0.54, only church members would buy shares! The acquisition of shares of companies who do

6.2. The influence of investment tax credits

In many countries, the corporate tax can be reduced by investment credits, accelerated depreciations and similar provisions. To realize the advantage of those deductions the firm must not be wholly debt financed since then 100% of the profit is paid out as interest. Therefore, the more generous the possibilities are to generate investment tax credits, the more equity should firms issue. For example, for the classical tax system the following result obtains: The firm should issue at least as much equity as is needed in order to generate profits that are greater than or equal to the investment credit (plus tax deductible contributions to pension funds etc).[25] In Chapter 3 we have analysed a tax system where the corporate tax is fully credited to the income tax. With this tax system the capital structure as well as the dividend policy is irrelevant. With investment credits and similar positions, this statement must be refined. Again, firms need a minimum amount of equity to make use of investment credits etc. Moreover, this tax free 'profit' must not be distributed since the resulting dividend would otherwise be taxable at the personal level [see also Cooper and Franks, 1983].

6.3. Tax evasion and capital structure

Tax evasion is a common problem in most countries. The General Accounting Office (Bundesrechnungshof) of Germany estimates that 65% to 70% of privately received interest income is not reported to tax authorities [see Bay & Stehle, 1988, p. 13]. In other countries the degree of tax evasion should be still higher. Tax evasion on investment income is made easy in most European countries since banks and other financial institutions are not required to report the investment income of their customers to tax authorities. Tax authorities, on the other hand, are ordered to inquire about the investment income of taxpayers only in exceptional circumstances. In some countries, financial institutions have to withhold a rather low percentage of the interest income as an advance income tax payment (for example, in Germany 30%). In most cases, however, the amount withheld is the only tax paid.

Assume that without tax evasion a Miller equilibrium would exist. Then, if all investors are tax evaders, the equilibrium would break down. All investors would hold bonds, evade the tax on interest income or pay only the amount withheld. Firms would be exclusively debt financed.

If only some investors cheat — which is the more realistic assumption — those investors who do demand interest payments. Honest investors divide into buyers of shares and buyers of debt instruments, depending on their marginal tax rate.

not pay out dividends is the only legal possibility to avoid the payment of the church income tax.

[25] This is similar to the problem analysed by DeAngelo & Masulis [1980] or Zechner & Swoboda [1986]. However, in these studies debt tax shields may be lost due to stochastic variation of earnings. With investment tax credits, however, this problem arises even under certainty. In a DeAngelo & Masulis [1980] or Zechner & Swoboda [1986] framework investment tax credits would increase the nondebt tax shields, I_j.

This again leads to a Miller equilibrium. The amount of equity in the economy, however, is considerably smaller.

This result holds irrespective of the tax system. When tax evasion is introduced even into a tax system where the corporate tax is fully credited to the income tax, dishonest investors clearly would hold only debt instruments. (For a formal analysis of tax evasion in the context of the German tax system — also in the context of the DeAngelo Masulis approach — see Bay & Stehle [1988]).

Concluding, one might argue that the high average leverage in most countries of continental Europe — compared to the USA, Canada and Great Britain —is consistent with a high degree of tax evasion. This is confirmed by the observation that the average leverage ratios in these countries seem to be quite independent of the tax system [see OECD, 1989].

References

Auerbach, A.J. (1990). Debt, equity, and the taxation of corporate cash flow, in J.B. Shoven and J. Waldfogel (eds.), *Debt, Taxes, and Corporate Restructuring*, The Brookings Institution, Washington, D.C.

Barnea, A., E. Talmor and R.A. Haugen (1987). Debt and taxes. A multiperiod investigation. *J. Banking Finance* 11, 79–97.

Bay, W., and R. Stehle (1988). Elimination of the double taxation of dividends: Is the German experience relevant for the USA?, working paper, University of Augsburg.

Brennan, M., and E.S. Schwartz (1984). Optimal financial policies and firm valuation. *J. Finance* 39, 593–607.

Constantinides, G.M. (1983). Capital market equilibrium with personal tax. *Econometrica* 51, 611–636.

Constantinides, G.M. (1984). Optimal bond trading with personal taxes. *J. Financ. Econ.* 13, 299–335.

Cooper, I.A., and J.R. Franks (1983). The interaction of financing and investment decisions when the firm has unused tax credits. *J. Finance* 38, 571–583.

Dammon, R.M. (1987). A security market and capital structure equilibrium under uncertainty with progressive personal taxes, in: A. Chen (ed.), *Research in Finance,* Vol. 7, Jai Press, Greenwich, CT.

Dammon, R.M., K.G. Dunn and C.S. Spatt (1989). A reexamination ot the value of tax options. *Rev. Financ. Studies* 2, 341–372.

Dammon, R.M., and R.C. Green (1987). Tax arbitrage and the existence of equilibrium prices for financial assets. *J. Finance* 42, 1143–1166.

Dammon, R.M., and L.W. Senbet (1988). The effect of taxes on the interaction between production and finance. *J. Finance* 42, 357–73.

DeAngelo, H. (1991). Payout policy and tax deferral. *J. Finance* 46, 357–368.

DeAngelo, H., and R.W. Masulis (1980). Optimal capital structure under corporate and personal taxation. *J. Financ. Econ.* 8, 3–29.

Dybvig, P.H., and S.A. Ross (1986). Tax clienteles and asset pricing. *J. Finance* 41, 751–763.

Fischer, E.O., R. Heinkel and J. Zechner (1989). Dynamic capital structure choice: Theory and tests. *J. Finance* 44, 19–40.

Fung, K.H., and M.F. Theobald (1984). Dividends and debt under alternative tax systems. *J. Financ. Quant. Anal.* 19, 59–72.

Hamada, R.S., and M.S. Scholes (1985). Taxes and corporate financial management, in: E.I. Altman and M.G. Subrahmanyam (eds.), *Recent Advances in Corporate Finance*, Richard D.

Irwin, Homewood Illinois, pp. 187–226.
Haugen, R.A., L.W. Senbet and E. Talmor (1986). Debt, dividends and taxes: Equilibrium conditions for simultaneous tax neutrality of debt and dividend policies, in: A.H. Chen (ed.), *Research in Finance*, Vol. 6, Jai Press, Greenwich/London, pp. 1–27.
Herzig, N. (1990). Nationale und internationale Aspekte einer Reform der Koerperschaftsteuer. *Steuer Wirtsch.*, 22–39.
Hochman, S., and O. Palmon (1985). The impact of inflation on the aggregate debt–asset ratio. *J. Finance* 40, 1115–1125.
Hodder, J.E., and L.W. Senbet (1990). International capital structure equilibrium. *J. Finance* 45, 1495–1516.
Hodder, J.E., and A.E. Tschoegl (1991). Corporate finance in Japan, working paper, Stanford University.
Kane, A., A.J. Marcus and R.L. McDonald (1984). How big is the tax advantage to debt? *J. Finance* 39, 841–853.
Kim, E.H., W.G. Lewellen and J.J. McConnell (1979). Financial leverage clienteles: Theory and evidence. *J. Financ. Econ.* 7, 83–109.
Lee, M., and J. Zechner (1984). Debt, taxes and international equilibrium. *J. Int. Money Finance* 3, 343–359.
Lewis, C.M. (1990). A multiperiod theory of corporate financial policy under taxation. *J. Financ. Quant. Anal.* 25, 25–43.
Litzenberger, R.H., and E. Talmor (1989). Tax policies and corporate decisions: Incongruity of value maximization with shareholder utility maximization, working paper, University of Pennsylvania.
Masulis, R.W., and B. Truemann (1988). Corporate investment and dividend decisions under differential personal taxation. *J. Financ. Quant. Anal.* 23, 369–385.
Mauer, D.C., and W.G. Lewellen (1988). Tax options and corporate capital structure, working paper, University of Purdue.
Mennel, A., ed. (1991). *Steuern in Europe, USA, Kanada und Japan*, Verlag Neue Wirtschafts-Briefe — Herne, Berlin.
Miller, M.H. (1977). Debt and taxes. *J. Finance* 32, 261–275.
Modigliani, F., and M.H. Miller (1958). The cost of capital, corporation finance and the theory of investment. *Am. Econ. Rev.* 48, 261–297.
Modigliani, F., and M.H. Miller (1963). Corporate income taxes and the cost of capital: A correction. *Am. Econ. Rev.* 53, 433–443.
OECD, ed. (1989). Non-Financial Enterprises–Financial Statements, Paris.
Park, S.Y., and J. Williams (1985). Taxes, capital structure, and bondholder clienteles. *J. Bus.* 58, 203–224.
Ross, S.A. (1985). Debt and taxes and uncertainty. *J. Finance* 40, 637–658.
Schaefer, S. (1982). Tax-induced clientele effects in the market for British government securities: Placing bounds on security values in an incomplete market. *J. Financ. Econ.* 10, 121–159.
Schall, L.D. (1984). Taxes, inflation and corporate financial policy. *J. Finance* 39, 105–126.
Scholes, M.S., and M.A. Wolfson (1988). The cost of capital and changes in tax regimes, in H.J. Aaron, H. Galper and J.A. Pechmann (eds.), *Uneasy Compromise: Problems of a Hybrid Income-Consumption Tax*, Brookings Institute, Washington D.C., pp. 157–190.
Scholes, M.S., and M.A. Wolfson (1992). *Taxes and Business Strategy*, Prentice Hall, Englewook Cliffs, NJ.
Sinn, H.W. (1987). *Capital Income Taxation and Resource Allocation*, North Holland, Amsterdam.
Stiglitz, J.E. (1985). The general theory of tax avoidance. *Nat. Tax J.* 38, 325–337.
Swoboda, P. (1991). Irrelevanz oder Relevanz der Kapitalstruktur und Dividendenpolitik von Kapitalgesellschaften in Deutschland und Oesterreich nach der Steuerreform 1990 bzw. 1989? *Z. Betriebswirtsch. Forsch.* 43, 851–866.
Taggart, R. (1980). Taxes and corporate capital structure in an incomplete market. *J. Finance* 35, 645–660.

Talmor, E., R. Haugen and A. Barnea (1985). The value of the tax subsidy on risky debt. *J. Bus.* 58, 191–202.

Zechner, J. (1989). *Der Einfluss von Steuern auf die optimale Kapitalstruktur von Unternehmungen*, Verlag der Oesterreichischen Akademie der Wissenschaften, Wien.

Zechner, J. (1990). Tax clienteles and optimal capital structure under uncertainty. *J. Bus.* 63, 465–491.

Zechner, J., and P. Swoboda (1986). The critical implicit tax rate and capital structure. *J. Banking Finance* 10, 327–341.

R. Jarrow et al., Eds., *Handbooks in OR & MS, Vol. 9*

Chapter 25

Dividend Policy

Franklin Allen
Wharton School, University of Pennsylvania, Philadelphia, PA 19104-6367, U.S.A.

Roni Michaely
Johnson Graduate School of Management, Malott Hall, Cornell University, Ithaca, NY 14853-4201, U.S.A.

1. Introduction

Why is dividend policy so interesting? One reason is that deciding on the amount of earnings to pay out as dividends is one of the major financial decisions that a firm's managers face. Another is that a proper understanding of dividend policy is crucial for many other areas of financial economics. In particular, theories of asset pricing, capital structure, mergers and acquisitions, and capital budgeting all rely on a view of how and why dividends are paid.

Five empirical observations have played an important role in discussions of dividend policy:

1. Corporations typically pay out a significant percentage of their earnings as dividends.
2. Historically, dividends have been the predominant form of payout; share repurchases were relatively unimportant until the mid 1980s.
3. Individuals in high tax brackets receive large amounts in dividends and pay substantial amounts of taxes on these dividends.
4. Corporations smooth dividends.
5. The market reacts positively to announcements of dividend increases and negatively to announcements of dividend decreases.

The first observation that corporations pay a substantial portion of their after-tax profits out as dividends is illustrated by Table 1. This shows the after-tax profits (with inventory valuation and capital consumption adjustments) and dividends for all U.S. corporations from 1971 through 1992. It shows that in recent years, U.S. corporations have paid between 50 and 70% of their profits out as dividends. This compares with a range of 40 to 60% in earlier years.

The second observation is illustrated in Table 2. Using data from the Compustat database, which includes the largest and most significant market participants from the major stock exchanges, Table 2 shows the net income, dividends, and share repurchases for these firms for the period 1973 through 1991. The first thing to

Table 1

After-tax profits and dividends for all corporations 1971–1992

Year	After-tax corporate profits [a] ($Billion)	Dividends ($Billion)	Dividends/ profits (%)
1971	53	24	45
1972	61	26	42
1973	67	30	45
1974	53	30	58
1975	71	30	42
1976	83	36	43
1977	103	41	40
1978	116	46	40
1979	115	52	46
1980	93	59	64
1981	101	69	69
1982	88	70	79
1983	135	81	60
1984	170	83	49
1985	184	92	50
1986	165	110	67
1987	193	106	55
1988	228	115	51
1989	221	135	61
1990	242	153	63
1991	240	137	57
1992	261	150	57

Source: Based on table B-88 from the 1994 Economic Report of the President.

[a] After-tax corporate profits with inventory valuation and capital consumption adjustments.

notice is that for large firms, the percentage paid out is somewhat lower and also somewhat more stable when payout is measured as a percentage of net income (as opposed to after-tax corporate profits). In the 1980s, it was usually between 40 and 50%, compared to 30 and 40% in the 1970s. As Bagwell & Shoven [1989] stress, there was an important change in 1984 and 1985 in the repurchases made by corporations. Before that time, the amount repurchased was usually around 5% of net income. Since then, it has ranged between 25 and 47% of net income. An important question concerns why this change in repurchases occurred. The data in Table 2 suggests that dividends as a proportion of net income did not decrease to compensate for the increase in repurchases. In a careful study, Dunsby [1993] finds some evidence of a small substitution of repurchases for dividends, but this does not appear to be very significant. Instead, the increase in repurchases appears to correspond to an increase in the overall level of payouts. It is notable that the other major form of payout from the corporate to private sector, namely

Table 2

Aggregate share repurchases and dividends. Data is from the 1,000 largest firms (by book value of assets) from the combined industrial and research files on Compustat for each year. Repurchases is cash spent on common equity and preferred shares. Dividends is cash dividends declared on common equity. Earnings is earnings before extraordinary items. Amounts are in millions of 1991 dollars (except for ratios).

Year	Repurchase	Dividends	Assets	$\frac{\text{Repurchases}}{\text{Dividends}}$	$\frac{\text{Repurchases}}{\text{Earnings}}$	$\frac{\text{Dividends}}{\text{Earnings}}$
1973	8,050	48,373	2,103,711	0.166	0.061	0.365
1974	3,992	47,794	2,171,683	0.084	0.030	0.363
1975	2,168	46,576	2,208,012	0.047	0.019	0.403
1976	3,506	50,516	2,285,521	0.069	0.026	0.374
1977	6,886	56,979	2,381,092	0.121	0.049	0.405
1978	7,263	58,260	2,477,665	0.125	0.048	0.383
1979	8,676	59,778	2,603,041	0.145	0.050	0.348
1980	9,844	61,759	2,694,689	0.159	0.061	0.382
1981	7,788	57,584	2,585,671	0.135	0.053	0.392
1982	13,090	59,888	2,695,448	0.219	0.114	0.522
1983	11,711	60,331	2,739,986	0.194	0.095	0.490
1984	34,974	55,255	2,670,838	0.633	0.260	0.410
1985	51,239	60,438	3,028,599	0.848	0.445	0.524
1986	46,523	65,461	3,167,161	0.711	0.446	0.627
1987	56,608	67,330	3,315,037	0.840	0.413	0.491
1988	51,931	77,454	3,322,015	0.670	0.322	0.481
1989	46,751	68,106	3,438,869	0.686	0.323	0.470
1990	39,187	66,697	3,514,739	0.588	0.306	0.521
1991	21,742	64,181	3,488,678	0.339	0.247	0.730

Source: Based on tables 1 and 2 of Dunsby [1993].

mergers and acquisitions, also increased dramatically during the mid 1980s. This is documented in Table 3, which shows the total dollar value of mergers and acquisitions from 1971 to 1992.

The third observation is that individuals pay substantial taxes on the large amounts they receive in dividends. Peterson, Peterson & Ang [1985] conducted an extensive study of the tax returns of individuals in 1979. More than \$33 billion was included in gross income that year. Table 1 shows that the total amount of dividends paid out by corporations in 1979 was \$52 billion, so individuals received over two-thirds of the total. The average marginal tax rate on these dividends received by individuals (weighted by dividends received) was 40%. Most dividends were received by individuals in high tax brackets.

The fact that individuals pay large amounts of taxes on dividends has been particularly important in the dividend debate, because there is a substantial tax disadvantage to dividends compared to repurchases. When dividends are received by shareholders, they are taxed as ordinary income. Before the implementation of the 1986 Tax Reform Act (TRA), share repurchases were taxed on a capital gains basis. Since the tax rate on capital gains was significantly lower than the tax rate on ordinary income, this meant there was a substantial advantage to

Table 3

Value of mergers and acquisitions 1971–1992

Year	Total dollar value (Billions)	Year	Total dollar value (Billions)
1971	12.6	1982	53.8
1972	16.7	1983	73.1
1973	16.7	1984	122.2
1974	12.5	1985	179.8
1975	11.8	1986	173.1
1976	20	1987	163.7
1977	21.9	1988	246.9
1978	34.2	1989	221.1
1979	43.5	1990	108.2
1980	44.3	1991	71.2
1981	82.6	1992	96.7

Source: Grimm's Mergerstat Review [1993]

repurchasing. Even after the 1986 TRA, which equalized the tax rate on capital gains and dividend income, there was a tax disadvantage to dividends: the basis of repurchased shares is not taxed, so the tax liability is effectively postponed. If stocks are held for the long term, this advantage can be substantial. Under the current tax code, individual investors' marginal tax rate on capital gains income is at most 28%, while the highest marginal tax rate on dividend income is 39.6%. The fact that large amounts of taxes are paid on dividends despite the existence of another, relatively untaxed, payout method has been termed the 'dividend puzzle' by Black [1976].

The fourth observation is that corporations smooth dividends. Table 4 shows the dividend behavior of five large corporations from 1950 through 1990. It can be seen that dividends were stable for long periods of time, particularly in the 1950s and 1960s. For example, USX's dividend was unchanged from 1957 to 1960. Dividends are usually increased gradually and are rarely cut. Table 5 shows the number of dividend increases and decreases for over 13,000 publicly-held issues, for the years 1971 to 1993. In each year, the number of dividend cuts is much smaller than the number of dividend increases. For example, in 1992, there were 1,437 dividend increases or initiations and only 395 cuts or omissions.

In a classic study, Lintner [1956] showed that this behavior was fairly widespread. He started with over 600 listed companies and selected 28 to survey and interview. These companies were not selected as a statistically representative sample, but were chosen to encompass a wide range of different situations. Lintner made a number of important observations concerning the dividend policies of these firms. The first is that firms are primarily concerned with the stability of dividends. They do not set dividends de novo each quarter. Instead, they first consider whether any change from the existing rate is necessary. Only when they have decided a change is necessary do they consider how large it should be. Managers appear to believe strongly that the market puts a premium on firms with a stable dividend policy.

Table 4

Dividend histories for five corporations 1950–1990 ($Million)

Year	Dow Chemical	GE	GM	IBM	USX
1950	12	97	539	11	118
	17	86	363	12	104
	18	86	362	12	104
	22	122	362	13	104
	24	131	450	16	111
1955	23	146	606	16	148
	25	172	566	20	170
	30	173	568	25	187
	31	174	572	31	187
	31	174	575	37	187
1960	37	176	577	55	187
	40	176	720	63	188
	47	178	863	83	161
	47	183	1,149	118	133
	53	198	1,279	166	134
1965	54	217	1,510	211	134
	60	235	1,311	231	119
	66	234	1,097	243	130
	73	235	1,240	293	130
	77	235	1,240	408	130
1970	79	235	984	548	130
	81	250	985	598	98
	82	255	1,286	626	87
	90	273	1,514	654	92
	111	291	986	819	119
1975	139	293	701	969	152
	176	333	1,603	1,204	173
	212	477	1,958	1,488	182
	237	570	1,726	1,685	136
	272	624	1,533	2,008	138
1980	302	670	874	2,008	140
	342	715	731	2,023	178
	348	760	750	2,053	188
	352	852	892	2,251	187
	347	930	1,524	2,507	260
1985	341	1,020	1,617	2,703	282
	364	1,081	1,663	2,698	361
	411	1,209	1,668	2,654	395
	486	1,314	1,658	2,609	398
	578	1,537	1,964	2,752	403
1990	711	1,696	1,956	2,774	360

Source: From corporate annual reports.

Table 5

Comparative annual dividend changes 1971–1993 (based on data from approximately 13,200 publicly held issues)

Year	Type of dividend change			
	Increase	Decrease	Resume	Omit
1971	794	155	106	215
1972	1,301	96	124	111
1973	2,292	55	154	95
1974	2,529	100	162	225
1975	1,713	215	116	297
1976	2,672	78	133	153
1977	3,090	92	135	168
1978	3,354	65	127	144
1979	3,054	70	85	115
1980	2,483	127	82	122
1981	2,513	136	82	226
1982	1,805	322	97	319
1983	2,006	137	183	172
1984	2,085	95	162	199
1985	1,898	104	99	231
1986	1,685	148	93	257
1987	1,822	84	114	186
1988	1,858	83	62	175
1989	1,869	89	65	218
1990	1,433	195	52	328
1991	1,135	204	44	412
1992	1,364	133	73	294
1993	1,622	137	113	258

Source: Moody's Dividend Record [1993].

Second, Lintner observed that earnings were the most important determinant of any change in dividends. Management needed to explain to shareholders the reasons for its actions, and needed to base its explanations on observable indicators. The level of earnings is the most important of these. Most companies appeared to have a target payout ratio; if there was a sudden unexpected increase in earnings, firms adjusted their dividends slowly. Firms were very reluctant to cut dividends.

Lintner's third finding was that dividend policy was set first. Other policies were then adjusted, taking dividend policy as given. For example, if investment opportunities were abundant and the firm had insufficient internal funds, it would resort to raising outside funds.

Lintner suggested the following model captured the most important elements of firms' dividend policies. For firm i,

$$D_{it}^{*} = \pi_i E_{it},$$

$$D_{it} - D_{i(t-1)} = a_i + c_i(D_{it}^{*} - D_{i(t-1)}) + u_{it},$$

where for firm i

D^*_{it} = desired dividend payment during period t,
D_{it} = actual dividend payment during period t,
π_i = target payout ratio,
E_{it} = earnings of the firm during period t,
a_i = constant relating to dividend growth,
c_i = partial adjustment factor,
u_{it} = error term.

This model was able to explain 85% of the dividend changes in his sample of companies. Fama & Babiak [1968] undertook a more comprehensive study of the Lintner model's performance, using data for 392 major industrial firms over the period 1946 through 1964. They also found the Lintner model performed well. Over the years, other studies have confirmed this.

The fifth observation is that the market reacts positively to announcements of dividend increases and negatively to announcements of dividend decreases. This phenomenon was documented by many studies such as Pettit [1972], Charest [1978], and Aharony & Swary [1980]. This evidence is consistent with markets in which managers know more than outside shareholders [e.g., Bhattacharya, 1979, or Miller & Rock, 1985], or when contracts are incomplete as suggested by Grossman & Hart [1982], Jensen [1986] and Easterbrook [1984].

The challenge to financial economists has been to develop a dividend policy framework based on firms maximizing profits and investors maximizing utility, that is consistent with these observations and is not rejected by careful empirical tests. The seminal contribution to research on dividend policy was Miller & Modigliani [1961]. Prior to their paper, it was widely accepted that the more dividends a firm paid, the more valuable the firm would be. This view was derived from an extension of the discounted dividends approach to firm valuation, which says that the value V_0 of the firm at date 0, if the first dividends are paid one period from now at date 1, is given by the formula:

$$V_0 = \sum_{t=1}^{\infty} \frac{D_t}{(1+r_t)^t}$$

where

D_t = the dividends paid by the firm at the end of period t,
r_t = the investors' opportunity cost of capital for period t.

Gordon [1959] argued that the investor's required rate of return r_t would increase as a result of increased retention of earnings. Although the future dividend stream would presumably be larger as a result of the increase in investment (i.e., D_t would grow faster), he felt that higher r_t would overshadow this effect. The reason for the increase in r_t would be the higher uncertainty concerning cash flows due to delaying the dividend stream.

Miller & Modigliani pointed out that this view of dividend policy was flawed, and they developed a rigorous framework for analyzing dividend policy. This framework has formed the foundation of subsequent work on dividends. Section 2 characterizes their analysis. Subsequent sections recount the literature that has relaxed their assumptions in various ways.

2. The Miller–Modigliani dividend irrelevance proposition

Miller & Modigliani [1961] showed that with perfect and complete capital markets, a firm's dividend policy will not affect its value. The basic premise of their argument is that firm value is determined by choosing optimal investments. The net payout is the difference between earnings and investment, and is simply a residual. Because the net payout consists of dividends and share issues/repurchases, a firm can adjust its dividends to any level with an offsetting change in shares outstanding. From the perspective of investors, dividend policy is irrelevant, because any desired stream of payments can be replicated by appropriate purchases and sales of equity. Thus, investors will not pay a premium for any particular dividend policy.

To illustrate the argument behind the theorem, suppose there are perfect and complete capital markets (with no taxes). At date t, the value of the firm is

$$V_t = \text{present value of payouts}$$

where payouts includes dividends and repurchases. For ease of exposition, it is simplest to initially consider the case with two periods, t and $t+1$. At date t a firm has

- earnings, E_t, (earned previously) on hand.

It has to decide on

- the level of investment, I_t,
- the level of dividends, D_t,
- the amount of shares to be issued, ΔS_t (or repurchased if ΔS_t is negative).

The level of earnings at $t+1$, denoted $E_{t+1}(I_t, \theta_{t+1})$, depends on the level of investment I_t and a random variable θ_{t+1}. Since $t+1$ is the final date, all earnings are paid out at $t+1$. Given complete markets, let

$$p_t(\theta_{t+1}) \;=\; \text{time } t \text{ price of consumption in state } \theta$$

Then it follows that

$$V_t = D_t - \Delta S_t + \int p_t(\theta_{t+1}) E_{t+1}(I_t, \theta_{t+1})\, \mathrm{d}\theta_{t+1}$$

The sources and uses of funds identity says that in the current period t:

$$E_t + \Delta S_t = I_t + D_t$$

Using this to substitute for current payouts, $D_t - \Delta S_t$, gives

$$V_t = E_t - I_t + \int p_t(\theta_{t+1}) E_{t+1}(I_t, \theta_{t+1})\, \mathrm{d}\theta_{t+1}$$

The first insight from Miller & Modigliani's analysis can be seen immediately from this equation. Since E_t is given, the only determinant of the value of the firm is current investment I_t.

This analysis can be easily extended to the case with more than two periods. Now

$$V_t = E_t - I_t + V_{t+1}$$

where

$$V_{t+1} = E_{t+1}(I_t, \theta_{t+1}) - I_{t+1} + V_{t+2}$$

and so on, recursively. It follows from this extension that it is only the sequence of investments $I_t, I_{t+1}, \ldots$ that is important in determining firm value. Firm value is maximized by an appropriate choice of investment policy.

The second insight from the Miller–Modigliani analysis concerns the firm's dividend policy which involves setting the value of D_t each period. Given that investment is chosen to maximize firm value, the firm's payout in period t, $D_t - \Delta S_t$, must be equal to the difference between earnings and investment, $E_t - I_t$. However, the level of dividends, D_t, can take any value, since the level of share issuance, ΔS_t, can always be set to offset this. It follows that dividend policy does not affect firm value at all; it is only investment policy that matters.

The above analysis implicitly assumes 100% equity financing. It can be extended straightforwardly to include debt financing. In this case, dividends can be financed by debt issues as well as equity issues. This added degree of freedom does not affect the result. As with equity-financed dividends, no additional value is created by debt-financed dividends, since capital markets are perfect and complete.

The third and perhaps most important insight of Miller & Modigliani's analysis is that it identifies the situations in which dividend policy may affect firm value. It may matter, not because dividends are 'safer' than capital gains as was traditionally argued, but because one of the assumptions underlying the result is violated. In particular, perfect and complete capital markets have the following elements:

1. No taxes.
2. Symmetric information.
3. Complete contracting possibilities.
4. No transaction costs.
5. Complete markets.

It is easy to see the role played by each of the above assumptions. The reason for assumption 1 is clear. In the no-taxes case, it is irrelevant whether a firm pays out dividends or repurchases shares; what is important is $D_t - \Delta S_t$. If dividends and share repurchases are taxed differently, this is no longer the case. Suppose, for example, dividends are taxed at a higher rate than capital gains from share repurchases. Then it is optimal to pay no dividends and instead to pay out any residual funds by repurchasing shares. The issues raised by relaxing assumption 1 are considered in Section 3.

Assumption 2 is that all participants (including the firms) have exactly the same information set. In practice, this is rarely the case. Managers are insiders and are likely to know more about the current and future prospects of the firm than outsiders. Dividends may reveal some information to outsiders about the value of the corporation. Moreover, insiders may even use dividends deliberately to change the market's perception about the firm's value. Again, dividend policy may affect firm value. Section 4 considers the effect of asymmetric information.

The complete contracting possibilities specified in assumption 3 mean that there is no agency problem amongst managers and security holders. In this case, motivating the decisions of managers is possible through the use of forcing contracts. Without complete contracting possibilities, dividend policy may, for example, help to ensure that managers act in the interest of shareholders. A high payout ratio may force the management to be more disciplined in the use of the firm's resources and consequently increase firm value. These issues are considered in Section 5.

Assumption 4 concerns transaction costs. These come in a variety of forms. For example, firms can distribute cash through dividends and raise capital through equity issues. If flotation costs are significant, every trip to the capital market reduces the firm's value. By the same token, transaction costs incurred by investors when selling securities and making decisions about such sales may also result in an optimal dividend policy. Section 6 develops several transaction-cost-related theories of dividend policy.

Finally, assumption 5 is that markets are complete. To see why this is important, assume that because trading opportunities are limited, there are two groups with different marginal rates of substitution between current and future consumption. By adjusting its dividend policy, a firm may be able to increase its value by appealing to one of these groups. Explanations along these lines for dividend policy have received very little attention in the literature.[1] Nevertheless, they may be important if some investors desire stocks with a steady income stream, and markets are incomplete because of high transaction costs. Further analysis in this area may provide some insights into dividend policy.

3. Taxes

A large part of the literature on dividend policy has focused on the importance of taxes, and has tried to reconcile the first three empirical observations discussed in the introduction. Firms pay out a large part of their earnings as dividends and many of the recipients are in high tax brackets. Firms have not traditionally used repurchases as a method of payout. The basic aim of the tax-related literature on dividends has been to investigate whether there is a tax effect: Other things being equal, are firms that pay out high dividends less valuable than firms that pay out low dividends?

Two basic ideas are important to understanding how the results of these investigations should be interpreted:

[1] One exception is Bagwell & Judd [1989].

1. *Static clientele models*:

(i) Different groups, or 'clienteles', are taxed differently. As Miller & Modigliani [1961] argued, firms have an incentive to supply stocks that minimize the taxes of each clientele. In equilibrium, no further possibilities for reducing taxes will exist and all firms will be equally priced.

(ii) A particular case (labeled as the simple static model), is when all investors are taxed the same way, and capital gains are taxed less than dividend income. In this case, the optimal policy is not to pay dividends. Firms with high dividend yield would be worth less than equivalent firms with low dividend yield.

2. *Dynamic clientele model*: If investors can trade through time, tax liabilities can be reduced even further. The dividend-paying stock will end up (just before the ex-dividend day) in the hands of those who are taxed the least when the dividend is received. Such trades will be reversed directly after the ex-day.

The empirical studies of dividend policy have tried to distinguish between the different versions of these models by trying to identify one or more of the following:

(i) Is there a tax effect so that low-dividend-paying stocks are more valuable than high dividend stocks?

(ii) Do static tax clienteles exist so that the marginal tax rates of high-dividend stockholders are lower than those of low-dividend stockholders?

(iii) Do dynamic tax clienteles exist so that there is a large volume around the ex-dividend day, and low-tax-rate investors actually receive the dividend?

This literature has traditionally been divided into CAPM-based studies and ex-dividend day studies. In our view, more insight is gained by considering *static* versus *dynamic* models. In the static models, investors trade only once. Thus, investors have to make a long-term decision about their holdings with the objective of minimizing taxes (keeping all else constant). The buy-and-hold CAPM studies, such as Litzenberger & Ramaswamy [1979], and Miller & Scholes [1982], fall into this category. The Elton & Gruber [1970] study is also in this category: Investors are allowed to trade only once, either on the cum-day or on the ex-day, but not on both. As we shall see shortly, a static view is appropriate when transaction costs are exceedingly high, or when tax payments have been reduced to zero in the static clientele model.

In contrast, in dynamic models investors are allowed to take different positions at different times taking into account risk, taxes, and transaction costs. In particular, just before the ex-day, dividend paying stocks can flow temporarily to investors who value them the most.

In Section 3.1, we describe the setting for the formation of a static or holding tax clientele. We then discuss the structure and the findings of the static models. In Section 3.2, we proceed to the dynamic models.

3.1. Static models

The static clientele model

First consider the special case where all investors are taxed in the same way and the tax rate on dividend income is higher than the tax rate on capital gains income.

The optimal policy, in otherwise perfect capital markets, is to pay no dividends. Equity holders are better off receiving profits through capital gains rather than dividends. If corporations do not have enough positive (or nonnegative) NPV projects to exhaust earnings, profits should be distributed through other means, such as share repurchases. As Table 2 shows, this prescription has not been followed by U.S. corporations: Most firms have paid dividends regularly and have rarely repurchased their shares. On the face of it, this behavior is puzzling, especially if we believe that agents in the market place behave in a rational manner.

The basic assumption of this simple static model is that all investors are taxed such that there is a substantial tax disadvantage to dividends because they are taxed (heavily) as ordinary income, while share repurchases are taxed (lightly) as capital gains. In reality, of course not all investors are taxed as individuals. Many financial institutions, such as pension funds and endowments, do not pay taxes. They have no reason to prefer capital gains to dividends, or vice versa. Not only do individuals hold stocks directly or indirectly, corporations do also. One of the principal reasons corporations hold dividend-paying stocks as a form of near-cash assets as well as an investment is because, under the U.S. tax code, a large fraction of intercorporate dividends are exempt from taxation, while intercorporate (or government) interest payments are not. Under the old tax code, only 15% of dividends, deemed taxable income, were taxed so the effective tax rate on dividends received was 0.15×0.46 (marginal corporate tax rate) $= 6.9\%$. But corporations had to pay the full amount of taxes on any realized tax gains. Under the current tax code, 30% of dividends are taxed.[2]

In a clientele model, taxpayers in different groups hold different types of assets, as illustrated in the stylized example below. Low-dividend-payout stocks are held by individuals. Medium-dividend-payout firms are owned by people who can avoid taxes, or by tax-free institutions. High-dividend-payout stocks are owned by corporations. Firms must be indifferent between the three types of stock; otherwise, they would increase their value by issuing more of the type that they prefer.

How are assets priced in this model? Since firms must be indifferent between the different types of assets, they must be priced so they are equally desirable. To see how this works, consider the following example:

Suppose there are three groups that hold stocks:

(i) Individuals who have high tax brackets and pay high taxes on dividend-

[2] Prior to the 1986 Tax Reform Act (TRA), individual investors who held a stock for at least six months paid a lower tax on capital gains (20%) than on ordinary dividends (50%). The TRA eliminated all distinction between capital gains and ordinary income. However, it is still possible to defer taxes on capital gains by not realizing the gains. Before the 1986 TRA, a corporation that held the stock of another corporation paid taxes on only 15% of the dividend. Therefore, the effective tax rate for dividend income was $0.15 \times 0.46 = 0.069$. After the TRA, the corporation income tax rate was reduced to 34%. The fraction of the dividend exempted from taxes was also reduced to 70%. The effective tax rate for dividend income was therefore increased to $0.3 \times 0.34 = 0.102$. In both time periods, the dividend exemption could be as high as 100% if the dividend-paying corporation was a wholly-owned subsidiary of the dividend-receiving corporation.

paying stocks. In particular, these investors are subject to a 50% tax rate on dividend income and a 20% tax rate on capital gains.

(ii) Corporations whose tax situation is such that they pay low taxes on stocks that pay dividends. In particular, their tax rate on dividend income is 10% and is 35% on capital gains.

(iii) Institutions that pay no taxes.

Group	Asset holdings
High tax bracket	Low-dividend-payout assets
Corporations	High-dividend-payout assets
Tax-free institutions	Any assets

Assume that these groups are risk neutral, so risk is not an issue; all that matters is the after-tax returns to the stocks.[3]

There are three types of stock. For simplicity, each stock is assumed to have earnings per share of $100. The only difference between these shares are the form of payout. We describe below the after-tax cash flow for each group if they held each type of stock:

	High dividend payout	Medium dividend payout	Low dividend payout
Before-tax earnings/share	$100	$100	$100
Payout policy:			
Dividends	$100	$50	$0
Capital gains	$0	$50	$100
After-tax payoff/share for group:			
(i) Individuals	$50	$65	$80
(ii) Corporations	$90	$77.5	$65
(iii) Institutions	$100	$100	$100
Equilibrium price/share	$1000	$1000	$1000

In this situation, individuals with high tax brackets will hold low-payout shares, corporations will hold the high-payout shares, and institutions will be prepared to hold all three. Let's suppose that in equilibrium, the total dollar value of holdings of each group in each type of stock are as below:

	High payout	Medium payout	Low payout
(i) Individuals	$0	$0	$320M
(ii) Corporations	$110M	$0	$0
(iii) Institutions	$500M	$730M	$220M
Total	$610M	$730M	$540M

[3] Note that in this stylized market, a tax clientele is a result of both the risk neutrality assumption *and* the trading restrictions.

To see why the shares must all have the same price, suppose the price of low-payout shares was \$1050 and the prices of the high- and medium-payout stocks was \$1000, what would happen? High- and medium-payout firms would have an incentive to change their dividend policies and increase the supply of low-payout stocks. This would put downward pressure on the price of low payout stock. What amount of stock do investors demand? Individuals would still be prepared to buy the low-payout stock, since \$80/\$1050 = 7.62%, which is greater than the 6.5% (\$65/\$1000) they would obtain from holding medium-payout stocks, or the 5% (\$50/\$1000) they would obtain from holding low-payout stocks. What about institutions? They won't be prepared to hold low-payout stocks, since the return on them is \$100/\$1050 = 9.52%. This is less than the 10% (\$100/\$1000) they can get on the other two stocks, and they will try to sell. Again, there is downward pressure on the price of low-payout stock. Hence the price must fall from \$1050 to \$1000 for equilibrium to be restored. A similar argument explains why the prices of other stocks are also \$1000. Thus, in equilibrium the price is independent of payout policy and dividend policy is irrelevant, as in the original Miller & Modigliani theory.

Simple ways of distinguishing between the static models' theories

A number of studies have attempted to distinguish between the case of the static model, where everybody is taxed the same and the static clientele model where investors are taxed differently. Perhaps the easiest way to make the distinction is to investigate the relationship between the marginal tax rates of stockholders and the amount of dividends paid.

Blume, Crockett & Friend [1974] find some evidence from survey data that there is a modest (inverse) relationship between investors' tax brackets and the dividend yield of the stocks they hold. In a more recent study, Lewellen, Stanley, Lease & Schlarbaum [1978], using individual investor data supplied by a brokerage firm, find very little evidence of an effect of this type. Both studies indicate that investors in high tax brackets hold substantial amounts of dividend-paying stock. According to the clientele theory, this should not occur; firms should be able to increase their value by switching from a policy of paying dividends to repurchasing shares.

Elton & Gruber [1970] sought to identify the relationship between marginal tax rates and dividend yield using an ex-dividend date price data. They argue that when people are about to sell a stock around its ex-dividend date, they will calculate whether they are better off selling just before it goes ex-dividend, or just after. If they sell before the stock goes ex-dividend, they get a higher price, and their marginal tax liability is on the capital gain, represented by the difference between the two prices. If they sell just after, the price will have fallen because the dividend has been paid. They will receive the dividend plus this low price, and their marginal tax liability will be their personal tax rate times the dividend. In equilibrium, stocks must be priced so that individuals' marginal tax liabilities are the same for both strategies.

Assuming investors are risk-neutral and there are no transaction costs, it is necessary that

$$P_B - t_g (P_B - P_0) = \bar{P}_A - t_g \left(\bar{P}_A - P_0\right) + D (1 - t_d)$$

where

P_B = stock price cum-dividend (the last day the stock is traded with the dividend),

$\bar{P}_A$ = expected stock price on the ex-dividend day (the first day the stock is traded without the dividend),

P_0 = stock price when purchased initially,

D = dividend amount,

t_g = personal tax rate on capital gains,

t_d = personal tax rate on dividends.

The left-hand side represents the after-tax receipts the seller would receive if he sold the stock cum-dividend and had bought it originally for P_0. The right-hand side represents the expected net receipts from sale on the ex-dividend day. Rearranging,

$$\frac{P_B - \bar{P}_A}{D} = \frac{1 - t_d}{1 - t_g}.$$

If there are clienteles with different tax brackets, the tax rates implied by the ratio of the price change to the dividend will differ for stocks with different levels of dividends. It will be greater the higher the dividend yield, and, hence, the lower the tax bracket of investors. Elton and Gruber found strong evidence of a clientele effect that was consistent with this relationship.

The role of risk

In the simplest versions of the theories presented above, risk has been ignored. In practice, risk is likely to be of primary importance, and so needs to be explicitly incorporated in the analysis.

As Long [1977] points out, implicit in the argument of a tax clientele when there is risk, is the assumption that there are redundant securities in the market. An investor can achieve the desired portfolio allocation in risk characteristics, without regard to dividend yield. In other words, investors can create several identical portfolios in all aspects but dividend yield. Indeed, Keim [1985] presents evidence that indicates that stocks with different yields also have different risk characteristics.[4] Zero-dividend-yield stocks and stocks with low-dividend-yield have significantly higher beta than high-yield stocks. This finding implies that it may be a nontrivial task to freely choose the optimal risk-return tradeoff while ignoring dividend yield.

Depending on the precise assumptions made, some models that incorporate risk are similar to the simple static model in that there is a tax effect and dividend policy affects value. On the other hand, others are similar to the static clientele

[4] See also Blume [1980].

model in that there is no tax effect and dividend does not affect value. Most of the literature has therefore focused on the issue of whether or not there is a tax effect.

Brennan [1970] was the first one to develop an after-tax version of the CAPM. Litzenberger & Ramaswamy [1979, 1980] extend the model to incorporate borrowing and short-selling constraints. In both cases, however, the basic result is that for a given level of risk, the compensation for higher dividend yield is positively related to the differential taxes between dividends and capital gains:

$$E\,(R_{it} - R_{\mathrm{f}t}) = a_1 + a_2\beta_{it} + a_3\,(d_{it} - R_{\mathrm{f}t}) \tag{1}$$

Equation (1) describes equilibrium relationships between a security expected return $E(R_{it})$, its expected dividend yield (d_{it}), and its systematic risk (β_{it}). Finding a significantly positive a_3 is interpreted as evidence of a tax effect.

Tests of such relationship were carried out by several researchers, including Black & Scholes [1974], Blume [1980], Morgan [1982], Poterba & Summers [1984], Keim [1985], Rosenberg & Marathe [1979], Miller & Scholes [1982], Chen, Grundy & Stambaugh [1990], and Kalay & Michaely [1993]. The empirical results are mixed. Several of these authors find a positive yield coefficient, which they attribute to differential taxes.

The earliest (and one of the more influential) test was done by Black & Scholes [1974]. Using annual data, and a slightly different version than that stated in equation (1) they test the tax effect hypothesis.

$$\tilde{R}_i = \gamma_0 + \left[\tilde{R}_{\mathrm{m}} - \gamma_0\right]\beta_i + \frac{\gamma_1\,(d_i - d_{\mathrm{m}})}{d_{\mathrm{m}}} + \varepsilon_i, \qquad i = 1, \ldots, N \tag{2}$$

where

$\tilde{R}_i$ = the rate of return on the ith portfolio,

γ_0 = an intercept term that should be equal to the risk-free rate, R_{f}, according to the CAPM,

$\tilde{R}_{\mathrm{m}}$ = the rate of return on the market portfolio,

β_i = the systematic risk of the ith portfolio,

γ_1 = the dividend impact coefficient,

d_i = the dividend yield on the ith portfolio, measured as the sum of dividends paid during the previous year divided by the end-of-year stock price,

d_{m} = the dividend yield on the market portfolio measured over the prior 12 months,

ε_i = the error term.

The null hypothesis is that the dividend yield coefficient is not significantly different from zero. This hypothesis can not be rejected for the entire time period [1936 through 1966] or for any of the 10-year subperiods. Black & Scholes concluded that '...it is not possible to demonstrate that the expected returns on high yield common stocks differ from the expected return on low yield common stocks either before or after taxes'.

In a series of papers, Litzenberger & Ramaswamy [1979, 1980, 1982] reexamined this issue.[5] Their experimental design differs from that of Black & Scholes in several important aspects: They use individual instead of group data; they correct for the error in variables problems in the beta estimation by using maximum likelihood procedures; and perhaps most importantly, they classify stock into yield classes by using a monthly definition of dividend yield rather than a long-term dividend yield definition as in Black & Scholes [1974].

The Litzenberger & Ramaswamy experiment involves three steps. First, the systematic risk of each stock is estimated for each one of the test months. The estimation uses the market model regression. Formally,

$$R_{it} - R_{\mathrm{f}t} = a_{it} + \beta_{it}\left(R_{\mathrm{m}j} - R_{\mathrm{f}j}\right) + \epsilon_j \qquad j = t - 60, \dots, t - 1, \tag{3}$$

where $R_{\mathrm{m}j}$ is the return on the market portfolio during period j, R_{ij} is the rate of return on stock i during period j, β_{it} is the estimated beta for stock i for period t, the riskless rate of interest during period t is $R_{\mathrm{f}j}$, and ϵ_{it} is a noise term. The second stage uses the estimated beta for stock i during month t, β_{it}, and an estimate of stock i's expected dividend yield for month t, d_{it}, as independent variables in the following cross-sectional regression for month t:

$$R_{it} - R_{\mathrm{f}t} = a_{1t} + a_{2t}\beta_{it} + a_{3t}\left(d_{it} - R_{\mathrm{f}t}\right) + \epsilon_i \qquad i = 1, \dots, N \tag{4}$$

The experiment requires an ex-ante estimate of the test month dividend yield. The estimate of expected dividend yield for month t is obtained from past observations. For cases in which the dividends were announced at month $t - 1$, the estimate is simply d_t/p_{t-1}. When announcement and ex-date occur in month t, Litzenberger & Ramaswamy have to estimate the market's time t expected dividend as of the end of month $t - 1$. The estimate they chose is the last dividend paid during the previous 12 months. If no dividends were paid during this period, the expected dividend is assumed to be zero.

The second step is repeated for every month included in the period 1936 to 1977. β_{it+1} is estimated using the previous 60 months of data. An updated estimate of the expected dividend yield for each stock is provided for each one of the test months.

This sequence of cross-sectional regressions results in time series of a_3's. The estimate of a_3 is the mean of this series. The standard error of the estimate is computed from the time series of the a's in a straightforward manner. Litzenberger & Ramaswamy [1979, 1980] find a_3 to be positive and significantly different from zero. Using MLE and GLS procedures, Litzenberger & Ramaswamy corrected for the error in variables and heteroskedasticity problems presented in the data. However, the empirical regularity they document — a positive and statistically significant dividend yield coefficient — is not sensitive to the methodology employed. The various methodologies yielded similar estimated coefficients with

[5] The econometric technique used by Litzenberger & Ramaswamy to correct for the errors in variables problem represents a significant contribution to the empirical asset pricing literature. It will not be reviewed here, however, given the focus of this chapter.

minor differences in the significance level. Litzenberger & Ramaswamy interpret their finding as consistent with Brennan's [1970] after-tax CAPM. That is, the positive dividend yield coefficient is evidence of a dividend tax effect.

Miller & Scholes [1982] argue that the positive yield coefficient found by Litzenberger & Ramaswamy is not a manifestation of a tax effect, but an artifact of two information biases. First, Litzenberger & Ramaswamy's estimate of next-month dividend yield can be correlated with month t information. Of the firms paying dividends, about 40% announce and pay the dividend (i.e., the ex-dividend day) at the same month. The use of the Litzenberger & Ramaswamy yield definition assumes that the ex-dividend month is known a priori even for ex-months in which dividends were not declared in advance.

Second, Litzenberger & Ramaswamy ignore the potential effect of dividend omission announcements. An omission announcement, which is associated with bad news, will tend to bias upward the dividend yield coefficient, since it reduces the return of the zero yield group. The effect of these informational biases has been the center of the debate between Litzenberger & Ramaswamy [1982] and Miller & Scholes [1982].

Miller & Scholes show that when only dividends declared in advance are included in the sample, or when the dividend yield is defined as the dividend yield in month $t - 12$, the yield coefficient is statistically insignificant. Based on these results, Miller & Scholes attributed the Litzenberger & Ramaswamy results to information rather than tax effects. Responding to this criticism, Litzenberger & Ramaswamy [1982] constructed a dividend yield variable that incorporated only information that investors could possess at the time. The sample contained only stocks that either declared in month $t - 1$ and paid in month t, or stocks that paid in month $t - 1$ and therefore were not likely to repay in the current month. Using the 'information-free' sample, Litzenberger & Ramaswamy find the yield coefficient to be positive and significant.

The question still remains whether the positive yield coefficient found by Litzenberger & Ramaswamy can be attributed to taxes. Kalay & Michaely [1993] argue that while the single-period model derived by Brennan [1970] and Litzenberger & Ramaswamy [1979] predicts cross-sectional return variation as a function of dividend yield, the Litzenberger & Ramaswamy test of Brennan's model, in contrast, is inadvertently designed to discover whether the ex-dividend period offers unusually large risk-adjusted returns (i.e., time-series return variation). Time-series return variation, per se, is not evidence of a tax effect. As mentioned above, the Litzenberger & Ramaswamy experiment categorizes stocks as having positive dividend yield only in the ex-dividend month. Hence, two-thirds of the time (assuming quarterly dividend payments), a dividend-paying stock is categorized as a zero-yield stock. This experimental design makes it very difficult to relate the dividend yield coefficient to taxes, since these static models predict cross-sectional variation in returns, not time-series variation. In fact, this experiment's design can even result in a rejection of the tax effect hypothesis when it is true. For example, assume that a tax effect exists and that the tax-related premium is evenly spread throughout the year. By putting stocks in the zero-yield group two-thirds of the time (in all the non-ex-dividend months), the yield coefficient may become insignificant despite the fact that cross-sectional variation in returns exists. Thus, their experiment is not designed to uncover cross-sectional return variations. It is therefore important to identify whether the positive yield coefficient arises because of time series or cross-sectional return variation.[6] Separating the time series from the cross-sectional return variations, Kalay & Michaely cannot detect any cross-sectional return variation across stocks with different yields. This is inconsistent with the Brennan's and Litzenberger & Ramaswamy's buy and hold models.

Another potential problem is whether some omitted risk factors (other than beta) that are correlated with dividend yield, rather than taxes, can explain the positive yield coefficient. As a first indication of the potential importance of some omitted risk factors, Miller & Scholes [1982] demonstrate that when the reciprocal of price, $(1/P)$, is incorporated in the regression equation instead of the dividend yield, (D/P), its coefficient is still positive and significant. The issue was thoroughly investigated by Chen, Grundy & Stambaugh [1990]. Categorizing all dividend-paying stocks into 20 portfolios according to size and yield, they find that: (1) when a single risk factor is used, large firms with high dividend yield are the only ones to experience positive yield coefficient; (2) when two risk factor models are used, the yield coefficient is significant for only one of the 20 portfolios.

As also suggested by Miller & Scholes [1982] and Hess [1983], Chen, Grundy & Stambaugh [1990] present evidence that dividend yield and risk measures are cross-sectionally correlated. When they allowed the risk measures to vary, the yield coefficient was found to be positive but insignificant. Chen, Grundy & Stambaugh show that the positive association between yield and their portfolios' returns can be explained by a time-varying risk premium that is correlated with yield. Thus, they conclude that there is no reliable relationship between cross-sectional variation in returns and dividend yield that is a consequence of tax penalty.

Summing up, a growing body of evidence shows that within static, single-period equilibrium models, there is no convincing evidence of a significant cross sectional relationship between stocks' returns and their dividend yields. Perhaps a more promising avenue for investigating this issue is to examine a model that allows for dynamic trading around the ex-dividend day.

3.2. *Dynamic models*

An important development in the literature on taxes and dividends was the realization that investors could trade dynamically to reduce their tax liability. The first paper to emphasize this aspect was Miller & Scholes [1978]. They argued that there were a number dynamic strategies that allowed taxes to be avoided.

[6] It should be noted that since the Black & Scholes study uses a long-term definition of dividend yield, a finding of positive yield coefficient is indicative of cross-sectional variation in return due to dividend yield. However, as noted earlier, Black & Scholes did not find a significant yield coefficient.

In particular, with perfect capital markets all taxes could be avoided, bringing us back to the case where dividend policy is irrelevant. In practice, however, the transaction costs of pursuing these strategies appear to be too high to make them empirically significant. An area where dynamic strategies appear to be more empirically relevant is trading around the ex-date. A number of studies, starting with Kalay [1982a], have considered the implications of this. We consider the two types of approach in turn.

Dynamic tax avoidance strategies

Miller & Scholes [1978] suggested an ingenious strategy for avoiding taxes. By borrowing and investing the proceeds with tax-free institutions, such as insurance companies or pension funds, it is possible to create an interest deduction that allows taxes to be avoided. Since there are assets that are held to offset the borrowing, the position can be closed out at an appropriate point.

A number of other dynamic tax avoidance strategies have been suggested by Stiglitz [1983]. If individuals can easily launder dividends so they don't have to pay taxes on them, we're essentially back in a Miller & Modigliani world, and dividend policy is irrelevant. However, there is little evidence that this or other such strategies are actually being used by investors. Peterson, Peterson & Ang [1985], for example, show that the marginal tax on dividend income faced by individual investors has been about double the marginal tax rate they pay on capital gains income. This evidence is not consistent with a widespread use of tax avoidance strategies of the type described by Miller & Scholes. It suggests that the transaction costs of such strategies are too high to be useful to investors.

Dynamic ex-dividend day strategies

A number of studies have considered dynamic trading strategies around the ex-dividend day. The basic idea is that investors may change their trading patterns around the ex-dividend day to capture or avoid the upcoming dividend. As first argued by Kalay [1982a], in a risk neutral world, without any restrictions or imperfections such as transaction costs, dynamic arbitrage may eliminate a tax effect in prices. Traders with a zero-tax rate on dividends and capital gains will buy the stock before it goes ex-dividend and sell it just after. Without risk or transaction costs, the arbitrage will ensure the price drop is equal to the dividend, i.e., $(P_B - \bar{P}_A)/D = 1$. If there are transaction costs, and no price uncertainty, then $(P_B - \bar{P}_A)/D$ must lie within a range around 1. This range will be larger the greater are transaction costs.

Kalay [1982a], however, did not explicitly account for the risk involved in the ex-day trading. In what follows, we describe the framework used by Michaely & Vila [1993] to describe the ex-day price formation within a dynamic equilibrium framework in which agents have heterogeneous valuation of a publicly traded asset. The intuition behind this model is as follows: An investor equates the marginal benefit of trading arising from being more (less) heavily invested in the dividend-paying stock with the marginal cost which arises from the deviation from optimal risk sharing.

Agents trade because they have heterogeneous valuation of dividends relative to capital gains (on an after-tax basis). This framework incorporates short-term, corporate, and individual investors' desires to trade around the ex-dividend day. It differs from other models in several ways: First, it explicitly accounts for the risk involved in the trade, and therefore concludes that it is not arbitrage, but equilibrium, that determines prices and volume.[7] Consequently, no trader will attempt to take an unlimited position in the stock, regardless of his or her tax preference. Second, while two-period models like those of Brennan [1970] or Litzenberger & Ramaswamy [1979], adequately describe the effect of taxes on portfolio holdings in a static equilibrium, they mask a qualitative difference between models of financial markets with and without taxation, namely, optimal tax-induced trading. Because of the dynamic nature of the model, it is possible to derive volume as well as price behavior implications. As it turns out, the second moment of the heterogeneity distribution (i.e., the dispersion in the after-tax valuation of dividends) can be extracted from the trading volume around the ex-day.

Using this framework, it is possible to show that in equilibrium, the expected price drop in relation to the dividend reflects the average preference of *all* traders, weighted by their risk tolerance and wealth, and the risk involved in the ex-dividend day transaction.

Specifically,

$$E(Pr) = \frac{\{P_c - E(P_e \mid P_c)\}}{D} = \bar{\alpha} - \frac{X(\sigma_e^2/K)}{D} \tag{5}$$

where

$E(Pr)$ = the expected price drop in relation to the dividend amount (hereafter, 'the premium'),

P_c = the cum-day price,

P_e = the ex-day price,

D = the dividend amount,

σ_ε^2 = the ex-day variance,

K = the after-tax weighted average of investors' risk tolerance,

X = the supply of securities,

$\alpha_i = \dfrac{1 - T_d^i}{1 - T_g^i}$ = the relative tax preference of dividend relative to capital gains,

$\bar{\alpha} = \dfrac{\sum_{i=1}^{N} k_i \alpha_i}{\sum k_i}$ = the average of investors tax preferences weighted by their risk tolerance.

As it turns out, unless a perfect tax clientele exists, in which different groups hold different stocks rather than just different quantities of the same stock, it

[7] This point was first noted by Heath & Jarrow [1988].

is not possible to infer tax rates from price alone. However, the cross-sectional distribution of tax rates can be inferred by using both price and volume data. By observing the premium alone, we can infer only the weighted-average relative tax rates, not the entire distribution of tax rates for the trading population. As shown in Michaely & Vila [1993], the second moment of the distribution can be extracted from the volume behavior on the ex-dividend day.

This point can be illustrated by using the following stylized example: Assume that there are three groups of traders in the marketplace with a marginal rate of substitution between dividends and capital gains income of 0.75, 1.0, and 1.25, respectively. Assume further that the average price drop relative to the dividend amount is 1.0. Using the standard analysis, we may conclude that the second group dominates the ex-dividend day price determination. However, this may not be the case. For example, suppose that half of the traders are from the first group and half are from the third group, and both have the same effect on prices. This market composition will also result in a relative price drop equal to the dividend amount. The only way to distinguish between the two scenarios is by incorporating volume into the analysis. In the first case, there are no gains from trade, and, consequently, no excess volume will be observed on the ex-dividend day. In the second case, there are gains from trade, excess volume is observed, and the particular equilibrium point is at a relative price drop equal to one. The model presented here allows us to distinguish between such cases.

More formally,

$$AV = \frac{1}{2}\left\{D\sum_{i=1}^{N}\left|(\alpha^i - \bar{\alpha})\left(\frac{K^i}{\sigma^2}\right)\right|\right\}, \tag{6}$$

where AV is the abnormal trading volume on the ex-dividend day.

The Elton & Gruber [1970] and Kalay [1982a] analyses are also incorporated in equation (5). Both assume an arbitrage framework in the sense that the last term in equation (5) is zero, i.e., there is no risk involved in the trade. Elton and Gruber assume that for some exogenous reason (e.g., transaction costs), the only trade around the ex-day will be done by investors within the same tax clientele group. In other words, if a perfect holding clientele exists and all trading is intra-group, then the relative price drop will reflect the marginal value of dividends relative to capital gains. (Note that in this scenario, the marginal and the weighted average values are the same.) There are two reasons why, in this case, there will be no abnormal trading volume around the ex-dividend day. First, since all trades are within the same clientele group, all relevant traders value the dividend equally, and there are no gains from trade. Second, there are no incentives for investors within the clientele group to delay or accelerate trades because of the upcoming dividends as Grundy [1985], for example, suggested. In other words, Elton & Gruber suggest that taxes affect price, but do not locally affect investors' behavior [no extra trading, as in equation (6)]. Kalay, on the other end of the spectrum, takes the opposite view: Taxes affect behavior but not prices, i.e., the arbitrageurs will make sure (through their tradings) that the price drop equals the dividend amount. Since Kalay uses the arbitrage framework, he can show that short-term investors may take an unlimited position in the stock as long as the expected price drop is not equal to the dividend amount.

Tests of these propositions have taken several forms. Most studies have examined the price behavior and infer investors' preferences and behavior from prices. With only a few exceptions [Grundy, 1985; Lakonishok & Vermaelen, 1986; and Michaely & Vila, 1993, 1994], much less attention has been devoted to a direct examination of the effect of differential taxes on investors' trading behavior through volume.

Researchers have almost always found the average price drop between the cum- and the ex-day to be lower than the dividend amount [see Elton & Gruber, 1970; Kalay, 1982a; Eades, Hess & Kim, 1984; and Poterba & Summers, 1984, among others].[8] Another finding across many of these studies is that the average premium increases with dividend yield [see, for example, Elton & Gruber, 1970; Kalay, 1982a; Lakonishok & Vermaelen, 1986; and Boyd & Jagannathan, 1994]. The latter findings are consistent with tax clientele: corporations, which prefer dividends over capital gains, and tax free institutions, which are indifferent to the form of payment, hold high-yield stocks. The ex-day premium reflects those preferences.[9]

Eades, Hess & Kim's [1984] findings of a premium greater than one for preferred stock is also consistent with this notion. That is, this group of stocks pays a high dividend yield, and the dominant traders of these stocks (at least around the ex-day) are the corporate traders, who prefer dividends.

Another way to examine the effect of taxes on ex-day price behavior is to examine the effect of tax changes. If taxes affect investors' decisions on buying or selling stocks around the ex-day, a change in the relative taxation of dividends to capital gains should affect prices. Poterba & Summers [1984] looked at the British market before and after tax changes and found evidence consistent with the existence of a tax effect. Barclay [1987] compared the ex-day price behavior prior to the introduction of federal taxes in 1913 with its behavior in the years 1962 to 1985. He found that the average premium was not significantly different from one before the enactment of the federal taxes, and significantly below one after. Barclay concluded that the higher taxes on dividends after 1913 caused investors to discount their value.

Michaely [1991] examined the effect of the 1986 Tax Reform Act (TRA) on ex-day stock price behavior. The 1986 TRA eliminated the preferential tax treatment of long-term capital gains that had been adopted in 1921; dividend income and realized capital gains were taxed equally after the reform. If taxes are at work, we would expect the premium to be closer to one after the 1986 TRA. Surprisingly,

[8] For international evidence, see Kato & Loewenstein [1995] for the Japanese market, Lakonishok & Vermaelen [1983] for the Canadian market, and Michaely & Murgia [1995] for the Italian market.

[9] It is important to note that the tax clientele we are alluding to can be either a holding clientele or a trading clientele. Only examination of trading volume can separate the two.

Table 6

Ex-dividend day premiums [a]. Average premiums (price drop relative to dividend paid) is calculated for three time periods. The first period, 1966 and 1967, is in Elton & Gruber [1970] and Kalay [1982a]; the second and third periods, 1986 and 1987, are the periods before and after the implementation of the 1986 TRA. Premiums are adjusted to the overall market movements using the OLS market model, and are corrected for heteroskedasticity.

Period	Mean premium	S.D.	Z value [b]	% above one	Fisher test
1966–67	0.838	1.44	−7.23	46.1	−4.94
1986	1.054	1.32	2.32	49.9	−0.03
1987	1.028	1.229	1.33	50.7	0.80
1988	0.998	0.821	0.168	NA	NA

[a] Results are taken from Michaely [1991, tables 2 and 3].
[b] Test the null hypothesis that the mean premium equals one.

this was not the case. The average premium, both before and after the TRA, is not lower than one. Comparing his results to the Elton and Gruber study, which uses data from the 1960s, Michaely concludes that the change in the relative pricing of dividends between the 1960s and the 1980s is not because of taxes, but because of the change in weights of the various trading groups. Facing lower transaction costs in the equity, options, and futures markets, institutional and corporate investors seem to trade more around the ex-day in the latter period. Thus, their preferences have a greater effect on the price formation. These results are summarized in Table 6.

While in static models, such as Brennan [1970] or Elton & Gruber [1970], transaction costs can be safely ignored (since investors trade only once), they are potentially much more important in the dynamic models. If investors trade in and out of stocks because of taxes, the multiple rounds of trades may result in a nontrivial cost of transacting. Disregarding risk, Kalay shows that the 'arbitrage' by the short-term traders will take place as long as the level of transaction costs is low enough. Indeed, Karpoff & Walkling [1988, 1990] show that excess returns are lower for stocks with lower transaction costs. This is especially pronounced for stocks with high dividend yields, both on the NYSE/AMEX and for NASDAQ stocks. In other words, corporations and short-term traders have a greater effect on the ex-day prices in stocks with lower levels of transaction costs.[10]

When the risk involved in the ex-day trading is accounted for, the effect of transaction costs on trading is not as straightforward. Michaely & Vila [1994] develop a formal model that incorporates the effect of both transaction costs and risk on ex-day prices and trading. As expected, transaction costs are predicted to reduce the volume of trade. More interesting is the interaction between transaction costs and risk. First, with or without transaction costs, risk reduces

[10] See also Boyd & Jaganathan [1994].

volume. Unlike prices, however, volume is negatively affected by the level of idiosyncratic risk. As the level of transaction costs increases, systematic risk negatively affects the volume of trade. The reason is simple: Without transaction costs, investors can afford to hedge all of the systematic risk. In the presence of transaction costs, the systematic risk is not completely hedged; consequently, it affects the amount of trading.

Empirical evidence supports these results. As documented in Grundy [1985], Lakonishok & Vermaelen [1986], and Michaely & Vila [1995b], the abnormal volume on and around the ex-day is significant. This evidence indicates that a perfect tax clientele where investors hold strictly different stocks, does not exist. (In a perfect clientele, no ex-day trading will take place.) Moreover, it questions the notion that the marginal tax rate can be inferred from prices alone.

Michaely & Vila [1995b] provide evidence that both risk and transaction costs affect volume. They show that: (i) stocks with lower transaction costs experience higher abnormal volume; (ii) idiosyncratic risk significantly affects trading volume; (iii) market risk has a greater effect (negative) on trading volume when the level of transaction costs is higher.

Koski [1991] reports that ex-day trading volume increases by more than ten times when traders are able to arrange the cum-day/ex-day trading using non-standard settlement days. That is, by reducing the risk exposure and transaction costs, volume increases significantly. In particular, Koski examines very large block trades around the ex-day. Those trades involve a large purchase and subsequent sale of the dividend-paying stock within minutes (with a different settlement day for each transaction). These trades are done through bilateral bargaining between the two parties involved, usually Japanese insurance companies on the buying side and a U.S. institution on the selling side. This procedure substantially reduces the risk exposure (and transaction costs) relative to 'conventional' dividend-capture trading.[11]

3.3. Dividends and taxes — conclusions

Differential taxes affect both prices (at least around the ex-dividend day) and investors' trading decisions. On average, in most periods examined the price drop is less than the amount of dividend paid, implying a negative effect on value. Thus, the evidence from the ex-day studies seems to indicate that from a tax perspective, dividends should be minimized. The volume of trade around these events is much higher than usual, indicating that the shares change hands from one investors' group to the other. This evidence tells us that taxes affect behavior. The facts also indicate that a perfect holding clientele does not exist: There is clear evidence for inter-group ex-day trading that is motivated by taxes. It is also

[11] Consistent with the notion that low transaction costs enhance ex-day trading, Michaely & Murgia [1995] show that the trading volume of both block trades and nonblock trades (on the Milan stock exchange) increases substantially for stocks with high dividend yield and low transaction costs.

apparent that ex-day trading volume increases as the degree of tax heterogeneity among investors increases [Michaely & Vila, 1995a,b; and Michaely & Murgia, 1995], indicating that as the benefits of trading increase, so does trading volume. Also, a direct examination of portfolio holdings by the various tax groups shows that even investors in the highest tax brackets hold high dividend-paying stocks.

While in perfect and complete capital markets dividends may not affect value, this is much less clear in incomplete markets with transaction costs. The theory and some of the empirical evidence indicate that taxes do matter and dividends reduce value when risk cannot be fully hedged and transactions are costly.

In light of the above discussion, it may be less surprising that tests of the static models with taxes have not proven successful: These tests cannot accommodate dynamic trading strategies, which seem to be important in this context. In addition, as shown by Chen, Grundy & Stambaugh [1990], time-varying risk may result in spurious positive yield coefficients. Indeed, the ex-dividend day studies that account for these have been more successful in identifying the extent to which taxes affect prices and traders' behavior.

4. Asymmetric information — signaling and adverse selection models

4.1. *Theory*

The clientele model is not the only approach to understanding the dividend policy suggested by Miller & Modigliani [1961]. Another possibility is that capital markets are informationally imperfect. In particular, Miller & Modigliani suggested that dividends might convey information about a firm's prospects. However, it was not until the late 1970s and early 1980s that any signaling models were developed. The best known of these are Bhattacharya [1979], Miller & Rock [1985], and John & Williams [1985]. The basic intuitive idea in all these models is that firms adjust dividends to signal their prospects. A rise in dividends typically signals the firm will do better, and a decrease suggests that it will do worse. These theories may explain why firms pay out so much of their earnings as dividends, and thus consistently prove the first empirical observation. However, one of the central questions that arises in this context is why firms use dividends and not share repurchases, or some other less costly means of signaling, to convey their prospects to investors.

Bhattacharya [1979] considers a two-period model where the firm's managers act in the original shareholders' interests. At time zero, the managers invest in a project. The expected profitability of this investment is known to the managers, but not to investors. At this time, the managers also 'commit' to a dividend policy. At time 1, the project generates a payoff that is used to pay the dividends committed to at time zero. A crucial assumption of the model is that if the payoff is insufficient to cover the dividends, the firm must resort to outside financing and incur transaction costs in doing so. Just after the dividends are paid, the firm is sold to a new group of shareholders, who receive the payoff generated by the project at time 2. The payoffs in the two periods are independent and identically distributed. The price that the new shareholders are prepared to pay at time 1 clearly depends on their beliefs concerning the profitability of the project. At time zero, the managers can signal that the firm's project is good by committing to a large dividend at time 1. If a firm does indeed have a good project, it will usually be able to pay the dividend without resorting to outside financing and, therefore, will not have to bear the associated transaction costs. It is not worthwhile for a firm with a bad project to do this, because it will have to resort to outside financing more often and thus will bear higher transaction costs. If the dividends are high enough, these extra costs will more than offset the advantage gained from the higher price received at time 1. Since the critical trade-off in the model is between the transaction costs incurred by committing to a large dividend and the price paid at time 1, it follows that similar results hold when the dividends are taxed.

Bhattacharya's model is a significant step forward. It is apparently consistent with the observation that firms pay dividends even when these are taxed. However, it has been criticized on the grounds that it does not explain why firms use dividends to signal their prospects. It would seem that firms could signal better by using share repurchases instead. This would result in the same tradeoff between the transaction costs of resorting to outside finance and the amount received when the firm is sold but would result in lower personal taxes than when dividends are used.

A number of Bhattacharya's assumptions are also the subject of criticism. For example, it is not clear precisely what is meant by firms '... committing to a certain level of dividends.'

The dissatisfaction with early models led to the development of a number of alternative signaling theories. Miller & Rock [1985] also consider a two-period model. Initially, at time zero, firms invest in a project, the profitability of which cannot be observed by investors. At time 1, the project produces earnings, and the firm uses these to finance its dividend payment and its new investment. Neither earnings nor the new level of investment can be observed by investors. Some shareholders sell their holdings in the firm at time 1. At time 2, the firm's investments again produce earnings. A critical assumption of the model is that the firm's earnings are correlated through time. This means that the firm has an incentive to make shareholders believe that the earnings at time 1 are high so that the shareholders who sell then receive a high price. Since both earnings and investment are unobservable, a bad firm can pretend to have high earnings by cutting its investment and paying out high dividends instead. A good firm must pay a level of dividends that is sufficiently high to make it unattractive for bad firms to reduce their investment enough to achieve the same level.

The Miller & Rock theory has a number of attractive features. The basic story — that firms shave investment to make dividends higher and signal high earnings — is a plausible one. Unlike the Bhattacharya [1979] model, it does not rely on assumptions that are difficult to interpret, such as firms being able to commit to a dividend level. What are its weaknesses? It is vulnerable to the standard criticism of signaling models; it is not clear that if taxes are introduced, dividends remain the best form of signal. It would seem that share repurchases could again achieve the same objective, but at a lower cost.

In Bhattacharya [1979], the dissipative cost that allowed signaling to occur was the transaction cost of having to resort to outside financing. In Miller & Rock [1985], the dissipative costs arise from the distortion in the firm's investment decision. John & Williams [1985] present a theory in which the taxes themselves are the dissipative cost. The theory thus meets the criticism that the same signal could be achieved at a lower cost if the firm were to repurchase shares instead.

What is the reasoning behind this result? John & Williams' starting point is the assumption that the shareholders in a firm have liquidity needs they must meet by selling some of their shares. The firm's managers, who act in the interest of the original shareholders, know the true value of the firm; outside investors do not. If the firm is undervalued when the shareholders must meet their liquidity needs, then they would be selling at a price below the true value. However, suppose the firm pays a dividend, which is taxed. If outside investors take this to be a good signal, then the share price will rise; the shareholders will have to sell less equity to meet their liquidity needs and will maintain a higher proportionate share in the firm.

Why is it that bad firms do not find it worthwhile to imitate the good ones? When the dividends are paid it is costly to shareholders because they must pay taxes on them. But there are two benefits: First, a higher price is received for the shares that are sold. Second, and more importantly, a higher proportionate share in the firm is retained. If the firm is actually undervalued, this higher proportionate share is valuable to the shareholder. If the managers' information is bad and the firm is overvalued, the reverse is true. It is this difference that allows separation. Only firms that are actually good will benefit enough from the higher proportionate share to make it worthwhile bearing the cost of the taxes on the dividends.

John & Williams' model thus avoids the objection to most theories of dividends. Firms do not repurchase shares to avoid taxes, because it is precisely the cost of the taxes that makes dividends desirable. This is clearly an important innovation.

What are the weaknesses of the John & Williams' theory? [12] In terms of assumptions, they take it as a given that shareholders must meet their liquidity needs by selling their shares. The use of debt, either by the firm or the shareholders themselves, is ruled out. One question asks why the firm does not borrow and use the proceeds to repurchase its shares. Again, this would meet the liquidity needs of investors and would only be worthwhile if the firm's shares were undervalued. It would seem that it should be possible to signal the firm's value costlessly. Even if, for some reason, corporate borrowing is not possible, an alternative is for the investors to borrow on their personal accounts instead of selling shares. Again, this would allow them to meet their liquidity needs without incurring the cost of signaling.

A more important criticism of the John & Williams model is that it is not obvious that its empirical implications are consistent with the smoothing of

[12] See also the chapter by Daniel & Titman [1995] in this book.

dividends. The best way to extend it over a longer time is not entirely clear. If firms' prospects do not change over time, then once a firm has signalled its type, no further dividend payments will be necessary and payouts can be made through share repurchases. If firms' prospects are constantly changing, which seems more plausible, and if dividends signal these, we would expect the dividends to constantly change, also. This prediction of the model is difficult to reconcile with the fourth observation, that corporations smooth dividends and in many cases do not alter them at all for long periods of time. A similar criticism of the other signaling models can also be made.

After the Miller & Rock [1985] and John & Williams [1985] papers, a number of other theories with multiple signals were developed. Ambarish, John & Williams [1987] develop a single-period model with dividends, investment, and stock repurchases. Williams [1988] develops a multiperiod model with these elements. He shows that in the efficient signaling equilibrium, firms typically pay dividends, choose their investments in risky assets to maximize net present value, and issue new stock. Constantinides & Grundy [1989] focus on the interaction between investment decisions and repurchase and financing decisions in signaling equilibria. With investment fixed, a straight bond issue cannot act as a signal but a convertible bond issue can. When investment is chosen optimally rather than being fixed, this is no longer true; a straight bond issue can act as a signal.

The signaling models presented are important contributions. However, they do not provide an entirely satisfactory explanation of firms' dividend behavior. They are either difficult to reconcile with the evidence on smoothing, or they do not meet the objection that firms could do better by repurchasing shares.

Two recent theories make progress in meeting these criticisms. Kumar [1988] provides a 'coarse signaling' theory that is consistent with the fact that some firms do not vary their dividends for long periods of time. This does not explain why firms use dividends rather than repurchases. However, building on work by Ofer & Thakor [1987] and Barclay & Smith [1988], Brennan & Thakor [1990] suggest that repurchases have a disadvantage in that informed investors are able to bid for undervalued stocks and avoid overvalued ones. Thus, there is an adverse selection problem. Dividends do not suffer from this problem because they are pro rata.

In Kumar's [1988] model, managers have better information about their firm's productivity than outside investors. The sequence of events is that the managers learn the firm's productivity type, signal it to investors through the level of dividend payments, and the shareholders then decide how much to invest. Both managers and investors own shares in the company proportional to their respective investments in it. Firms' production functions have a diminishing marginal product of capital. Since managers' resources are fixed, increasing outside shareholders' investment has two effects: It increases output, but reduces the share of the managers. When the marginal product of capital is large, managers are made wealthier as the amount of investment increases, but eventually there comes a point where the fall in the managers' shares offsets this.

If the managers and outside shareholders have the same degree of risk aversion, they agree on this optimal level of investment. However, if the managers are more risk-averse than the shareholders, they require a higher level of output to compensate them for a given level of risk. This means their preferred level of investment is smaller than that of the outside shareholders. Therefore, to get closer to their desired investment level, the managers have an incentive to pay a dividend that corresponds to a lower level of productivity than their true one. As a result, a fully revealing equilibrium cannot exist: Given any set of common beliefs, the shareholders can always deduce the managers' true productivity type. This, however, is inconsistent with managers' desire to underreport. Although no fully revealing equilibrium exists, Kumar shows that a coarse signaling equilibrium is possible. Within any given interval of productivity, the different types cluster at a particular dividend level. If a firm's managers deviated from the cluster that corresponds to their true productivity level, they would be worse off, because they would get a share of the firm at a significantly different level from their desired level.

Kumar's theory is consistent with smoothing, since small changes in productivity will not lead to changes in dividends. It thus provides an interesting explanation of the smoothing phenomenon. In particular, it is consistent with the fact that many firms leave dividends unchanged for long periods of time. Kang & Kumar [1991] have looked at the empirical relationship between firm productivity and the frequency of dividend changes. Their results are consistent with Kumar's analysis.

One drawback of Kumar's model is that it uses dividends as the only vehicle for signaling. It would appear that share repurchases could be used instead of dividends, and would be superior because they are taxed less. In an important paper, developing on an insight of Ofer & Thakor [1987] and Barclay & Smith [1988], Brennan & Thakor [1990] provide an explanation for why firms may prefer dividends to share repurchases despite the differences in tax treatment. Moreover, this explanation is consistent with Kumar's model.

When some shareholders are better informed about the prospects of the firm than others, they will be able to take advantage of this information when there is a repurchase. They will bid for stock when it is worth more than the tender price, but will not bid when it is worth less. Uninformed buyers will receive only a portion of their order when the stock is undervalued, but will receive the entire amount when it is overvalued. This adverse selection means that they are at a disadvantage in a share repurchase. When money is paid out in the form of dividends, the informed and the uninformed receive a pro rata amount, so there is no adverse selection. As a result, uninformed shareholders prefer dividends to repurchases; this preference will persist even if dividends are taxed more heavily than repurchases, provided the tax disadvantage is not too large. On the other hand, the informed will prefer repurchases because this allows them to profit at the expense of the uninformed.

Brennan & Thakor argue that the method of disbursement chosen by firms will be determined by a majority vote of the shareholders. If the uninformed have more votes than the informed, dividends will be used, but if the informed predominate, repurchases will be chosen. When there is a fixed cost of obtaining information, the number of informed will depend on the distribution of shareholdings and the amount paid out. For a given payout, investors with large holdings will have an incentive to become informed. When a small amount is paid out, only the investors with the largest holdings will become informed; most shareholders will remain uninformed and will prefer dividends. When a larger amount is paid out, more shareholders become informed, so repurchases may be chosen.

The Brennan & Thakor model is an intriguing explanation of the preference firms appear to have for dividends. It answers the question of why firms prefer to use dividends even though they are taxed more heavily. Unlike the John & Williams' theory, it is consistent with dividends being smoothed. It is not above criticism, however. The range of tax rates for which dividends are preferred to repurchases because of adverse selection is usually small. In order to explain the predominance of dividends, they must use another argument that relies on shareholders being homogeneous. For tax rates above the level where adverse selection can explain the preference for dividends, everybody will tender in a repurchase, so it will be pro rata. The tax code specifies that if repurchases are pro rata they will be treated the same as dividends, so firms might as well pay dividends. It is critical to this argument that shareholders are the same, so that they all tender. In practice, Bagwell [1991] has provided evidence that there is considerable shareholder *heterogeneity* so this part of the explanation for dividends is not very convincing. Another criticism is that if adverse selection were a serious problem, firms could gather the relevant information and publicly announce it. Nevertheless, Brennan & Thakor's theory, particularly when combined with that of Kumar, comes closest to being able to explain the empirical regularities of dividends that have been focused on.

4.2. Empirical evidence

In their original article, Miller & Modigliani suggested that if management's expectations of future earnings affect their decision about current dividend payouts, then changes in dividends will convey information to the market about future earnings. This notion is labeled 'the information content of dividends'. As discussed earlier in this section, this notion has been formalized in two ways: In the first, dividends are used as an ex-ante signal of future cash flow as, for example, in Bhattacharya [1979]. In the second, dividends provide information about earnings as a description of the sources and uses of funds identity as, for example, in Miller & Rock [1985]. The latter alternative can be interpreted as claiming that the fact that dividends convey information does not necessarily imply that they are being used as a signal. This distinction may be subtle, but it is crucially important in interpreting the empirical tests as supporting the signaling theory. Most, if not all, of the empirical tests we are aware of cannot help us in distinguishing between these two alternatives.

The information/signaling hypotheses contain three important implications that have been tested empirically:

(i) Dividend changes should be followed by subsequent earnings changes in the same direction.

(ii) Unanticipated changes in dividends should be followed by revisions in the market's expectations of future earnings in the same direction as the dividend change.

(iii) Unanticipated dividend changes should be accompanied by stock price changes in the same direction.

It is important to note that all of the above implications are necessary, but insufficient, conditions for dividend signaling. The condition that earnings changes will follow dividend changes is perhaps the most basic one. If this condition is not met, we may conclude that dividends do not even have the potential to convey information, let alone to signal. The evidence about the relationship between dividend changes and subsequent earnings changes is mixed. Watts [1973] was among the first to test the proposition that the knowledge of current dividends improves the predictions of future earnings, over and above knowledge of current and past earnings. Using 310 firms with complete dividend and earnings information for the years 1946–1967, and annual definitions of dividends and earnings, Watts tests whether earnings in year $t+1$ can be explained by current (year t) and past (year $t-1$) levels of dividend and earnings. For each firm in the sample, Watts estimates the current and past dividend coefficients (while controlling for earnings). While the average dividend coefficients across firms were positive, the average t-statistic was very low. In fact, only the top 10% of the coefficients were marginally significant. Using change in levels yielded similar results. He concludes that: '... in general, if there is any information in dividends, it is very small'. Gonedes [1978] reaches a similar conclusion.[13]

Recent evidence, such as Healy & Palepu [1988], however, indicates that extreme dividend changes contain some information about future changes in earnings. Healy & Palepu show that earnings changes following dividend initiations and omissions are at least partially anticipated at the dividend announcement. Using a cross-sectional regression, Benartzi [1993] shows that dividend changes have some predictive power about subsequent quarterly earnings changes.

The overall accumulated evidence lends, at best, only weak support to the assertion that dividend changes convey information about future changes in earnings. The important point is that such a relationship is a crucial initial condition for any dividend signaling model. As Miller & Rock [1985] suggested, dividends may convey information about current earnings through the sources and uses of funds identity, and not because of signaling.[14]

More encouraging news is found in the second implication of the information/signaling hypothesis. These tests examine the relationship between dividend changes and analysts' forecasts of future earnings. Ofer & Siegel [1987], for

[13] Penman [1983] shows that managements' earnings forecasts are a better predictor of future earnings than dividend announcements. After accounting for these earnings forecasts, there is not much information conveyed in the dividend announcements themselves. Another interesting point in this study is the finding that many firms with improved future earnings do not adjust their dividends accordingly.

[14] It is important to note that most firms declare their quarterly dividends several days before they report their quarterly earnings.

example, find that analysts revise their earnings forecast by an amount that is positively related to the size of the announced dividend change. They also provide evidence that their revision is positively correlated with the market reaction to the announced dividend. The result of this study is consistent with the information/signaling hypothesis. It is also consistent with the agency explanation of why firms pay dividends. If higher dividend payouts discipline management, then we may expect better performance by those firms in the future, hence positive price reaction and a like revision in analysts' forecasts.[15]

The third set of tests questions whether the market perceives changes in dividends as conveying new information about the value of the firm (or the value of the equity).[16] The answer to this question is almost uniformly 'yes'. There are numerous studies that show that dividend changes cause a like change in security prices. For example, Pettit [1972] shows that announcements of dividend increases are followed by a significant price increase, and announcements of dividend decreases are followed by a significant price drop. Aharony & Swary [1980] show that these relationships hold even after controlling for contemporaneous earnings announcements. Most studies find an average excess return of about 0.4% around dividend increase and −1.3% for a dividend decrease. Focusing on extreme changes in dividend policy, Asquith & Mullins [1983] (dividend initiations), Healy & Palepu [1988], and Michaely, Thaler & Womack [1995] (dividend omissions) show that the market reacts quite severely to those announcements. The average excess return is around 3% for initiation and −7% for omissions.[17] All in all, there seems to be an overall agreement that dividend changes are associated with like changes in stock price.

In summary, the empirical evidence is far from conclusive. The relationship between dividend changes and subsequent earnings changes is positive, but not significant. Given these, it is rather hard to interpret any of the evidence as supporting the information signaling hypothesis. Researchers find that significant market reaction to dividend changes is positively related to the size of the dividend change and that analysts revise their expectation in the direction of the dividend change. The latter evidence deepens the puzzle. How can it be that analysts interpret dividend changes as a good proxy for subsequent earnings changes, but we cannot detect strong empirical relations between dividends and subsequent earnings? It is safe to say that more research is needed on this topic.

[15] The findings of revisions in earning expectations following analysts' forecasts are not consistent with the wealth transfer hypothesis [e.g., Handjinicolaou & Kalay, 1984]. We discuss the agency explanations in more detail in the next section.

[16] The new information can be about the firm value, or about the equity value alone. The latter may be the case if the change in dividend payments represents a wealth transfer from bondholders to equity holders. We address this issue in the next section.

[17] The apparent asymmetry between the market reaction to announcements of increases and decreases can be partially explained by the magnitude of the dividend change: Reductions in dividends are less frequent and more dramatic in magnitude. Also, Michaely, Thaler & Womack [1995] show that when the dividend yield is defined as the dividend amount over the beginning-of-the-year price, and the magnitude of the change is accounted for, the market reacts in the same way to initiations and omissions (in absolute value).

5. Incomplete contracts — agency models

Relaxing the assumption of complete (and fully enforceable) contracts comes from the realization that a firm is more than just a black box. The different forces that operate within a firm may, at different points in time, pull it in different directions; the interests of different groups within a firm may conflict. In particular, the three groups that may be affected the most by a firm's dividend policy are stockholders, bondholders, and management.

The first potential conflict of interest that may be affected by dividend policy is between stockholders and bondholders. As Myers [1977] and Jensen & Meckling [1976] have so persuasively argued, there are some situations in which equity holders may try to expropriate wealth from debtholders. This wealth expropriation may come in the form of excessive (and unanticipated) dividend payments. Shareholders can reduce investments and thereby increase dividends (investment-financed dividends), or they may raise debt to finance the dividends (debt-financed dividend). In both cases, if the shareholders' action is not anticipated by debtholders, the market value of debt will go down, and the market value of equity will rise.

To test this proposition empirically, Handjinicolaou & Kalay [1984] examine the effect of dividend change announcements on bond prices as well as on the prices of equity. They contrast two competing hypotheses. The agency hypothesis implies that in the event of dividend increase (decrease), stock prices should go up (down) and bond prices should go down (up). The alternative is the information content of dividends hypothesis. Dividend increases (decreases) convey good (bad) news about the firm. Consequently, both debt and equity prices will move in the direction of the unanticipated dividend change. Handjinicolaou & Kalay find that bond prices drop significantly at the announcement of dividend decreases, and do not change significantly at dividend increase announcements. These results do not lend support to the wealth expropriation hypothesis, but are consistent with the information content of dividends.[18]

As suggested by Myers [1977] and Jensen & Meckling [1976], both equity holders and bondholders may a priori agree on restricting dividends. Indeed, most bond covenants contain constraints that limit both investment-financed dividends and debt-financed dividends. Kalay [1982b] examines these constraints. He finds that firms hold significantly more cash (or cash equivalents) than the minimum they should hold, according to the bond covenants. This finding can be interpreted as a reverse wealth transfer. That is, if debt were priced under the assumption that only the minimum cash will be held by the corporation, then a positive reservoir would increase the market value of debt at the expense of equity holders.

There are several possible reasons for this finding. First, it may be that given the covenants, dividend policy is not driven by the desire to expropriate bondholders.

[18] The asymmetry in the bond price reaction may be explained by several factors. Among them is the fact that dividend decreases are larger in absolute value than dividend increases and therefore have a more significant impact on both bond and stock prices.

The positive reservoir is consistent with Myers & Majluf's [1984] argument that because of adverse selection, a firm is better off having some cash in hand, rather than being forced to the capital market each time it has an opportunity to invest. Second, most, if not all, of the models that allude to this potential conflict of interests, are single-period models. Much of the problem will disappear if equity holders and debtholders have to interact on a continual basis, which is the case in practice: Corporations issue new debt on an ongoing basis.

We can readily see how a one-time wealth transfer from existing bondholders to equityholders may result in a long-run loss because of the increase in the cost of capital. When would the problem arise? In precisely those cases where there is a large probability that the firm's time horizon is short, e.g., the firm is in financial distress, or is about to be taken private. The evidence documented by DeAngelo & DeAngelo [1990] is consistent with this assertion. They show that firms in financial distress are reluctant to cut their dividends. In these cases, not cutting dividends may constitute a significant wealth transfer from debtholders to equity holders. This is still an open question that is worth further consideration.

The other potential conflict of interest that may affect dividend policy is between management and stockholders. As suggested by Jensen & Meckling, managers of a publicly held firm may allocate resources to activities that benefit them, but are not in the shareholders' best interest. These activities can range from lavish expenses on corporate jets to unjustifiable acquisitions and expansions. In other words, too much cash in the firm may result in overinvestment. Grossman & Hart [1982], Easterbrook [1984] and Jensen [1986] have suggested a partial solution to this problem. If equity holders can minimize the cash that management controls, it will make it much harder for management to go on (unmonitored) spending sprees. The less discretionary cash management has, the harder it is for them to invest in negative NPV projects. One way to take unnecessary cash from the firm is to increase the level of dividend payouts.[19]

This 'free-cash flow' problem is likely to be more pronounced in stable, cash-rich companies in mature industries without many growth opportunities. Lang & Litzenberger [1989] exploit this feature to test the free-cash flow hypothesis, and to contrast it with the information-signaling hypothesis. The basic idea is that, according to the free-cash flow hypothesis, an increase in dividends should have a larger (positive) price impact for firms that overinvest than for firms that do not. Empirically, they have identified overinvesting firms as ones with Tobin's Q less than unity.[20] Considering only dividend changes that are greater than 10% (in absolute value), they find that for dividend increase announcements, firms with Q less than unity experience a larger price appreciation than firms with Q greater than one. For dividend decrease, firms with Q lower than one experience a more dramatic price drop. The larger effect (in absolute value) of dividend

[19] As Grossman & Hart [1982] and Jensen [1986] argue, a more effective mechanism to achieve this goal is to increase the level of debt. It is harder for management to renege on a debt commitment relative to a dividend commitment.

[20] Tobin's Q is defined as market value over replacement value.

changes on firms with lower Q is consistent with the free-cash flow hypothesis. The information-signaling hypothesis, on the other hand, would have predicted a symmetric effect regardless of the ratio of market value to replacement value.

Repeating the experiment for a longer time period, Yoon & Starks [1993] find that the reaction to dividend decrease is the same for high and low Tobin-Q firms. The fact that the market reacts negatively to dividend decrease announcements by the value-maximizing (high Q) firms is not consistent with the free-cash flow hypothesis. Like Lang & Litzenberger, they find a differential reaction to announcements of dividend increases. However, controlling for other factors such as the level of dividend yield, firm size and the magnitude of the change in the dividend yield (through a regression analysis) Yoon & Starks find symmetric reaction to dividend changes (both increases and decreases) between high and low Tobin's Q firm. This evidence is inconsistent with the free-cash flow hypotheses.

Bernheim & Wantz [1995] investigate the market reaction to dividend changes during different tax regimes. In periods when the relative taxes on dividends are higher than taxes on capital gains, the signaling hypothesis implies that the market reaction to dividend increases should be stronger because it is more costly to pay dividends. Since it is more expensive to signal, it is more revealing for those who choose to use it. The free-cash flow hypothesis has the opposite prediction. Since it is more expensive to pay dividends and the benefit presumably does not change, in periods of higher relative taxes on dividends the market should react less favorably to dividend increases. These results are consistent with the dividend signaling hypothesis: in periods of higher relative taxes on dividends, the market reaction to dividend payments is more favorable.[21]

To summarize, the last two sections presented two opposing views of why dividends are paid. The first view is that dividends convey good news. The alternative view is that dividends are good news (they resolve agency problems). There is, at best, weak empirical support for the former explanation and practically no support for the latter. A priori, we expect that the different incentives in the firm will interact more strongly with dividend policy. As we mentioned earlier, we believe this is an important area for future research.

6. Transaction costs and other explanations

Under certain circumstances, it is possible that, despite the tax disadvantage of dividends relative to capital gains, investors would prefer dividends. In this section we describe four potential reasons for such a preference.

The first explanation of why firms pay dividends is because of 'prudent man' roles. Various institutions are constrained to hold only dividend-paying stocks.

[21] In a recent article, Bernhardt, Robertson & Farrow [1994] account for the nonlinear properties common to many of the dividend-signaling models. Applying nonparametric techniques to an experiment similar to Bernheim & Wantz, they find no evidence to support dividend signaling.

This role may be in place because it may seem like a simple rule of thumb of how to constrain the agents (the fund managers for example) not to take too much risk. Also, some trust and endowment funds are constrained to only spend income and not capital gains. Such a constraint will create a preference for dividends on the part of these market participants. If these constraints are binding and if those institutions who are subject to those constraints represent a significant portion of the market wealth, then dividend payment on the part of the corporation is optimal.

The second is the transaction costs argument. If investors want a steady flow of income from their capital investment (say, for consumption reasons), then it is possible that dividend payments would be the cheapest way to achieve this goal. This may be the case if the cost of the alternative (i.e., to sell a portion of the holdings and receive capital gains) involves nontrivial costs. These costs may be the actual transaction costs for selling the shares, which can be quite high for retail investors, or the time and effort spent on these transactions.

If this effect is in fact substantial, it will lead to an optimal dividend policy on the aggregate level. As Black & Scholes [1974] argue, however, firms will adjust their dividend policy such that the demand for dividends by this clientele would be fulfilled. Thus, in equilibrium, any specific firm should be indifferent to dividend policy. So, while this explanation can account for positive payouts despite the adverse tax consequences, it cannot explain why in equilibrium firms care about the level of dividends paid.

The third explanation as to why investors may prefer dividend-paying stocks is suggested by Shefrin & Statman [1984]. Rather than developing an economic model based on maximizing behavior, they eliminate the maximizing assumptions that are the cornerstone of neoclassical economics, and which we have maintained throughout. Instead, Shefrin & Statman develop a theory of dividends based on a number of recent theories of behavior. The basic idea is that even if the eventual cash received is the same, there is a significant difference in whether it comes in the form of dividends, or as share repurchases. In other words, form is more important than substance. We will illustrate Shefrin & Statman's approach with the theory they develop, based on Thaler & Shefrin's [1981] theory of self-control.

Thaler & Shefrin have suggested that people have difficulties behaving rationally when they want to do something but have problems carrying it through. Examples that illustrate this suggestion are the prevalence of smoking clinics, credit counselors, diet clubs, and substance abuse groups. Individuals wish to deny themselves a present indulgence, but find that they yield to temptation. Thaler & Shefrin represent this conflict in a principal-agent form. The principal is the individual's internal planner, which expresses consistent long-run preferences. However, the responsibility for carrying out the individual's action lies not with the planner, but with the doer, the agent.

There are two ways the planner can control the agent. The first is will power. The problem is that this causes disutility. The second is to avoid situations where will power has to be used. This is accomplished by adopting rules of behavior that make it unnecessary for people to question what they are doing most of the time.

Shefrin & Statman suggest that by having money in the form of dividends rather than capital gains, people avoid having to make decisions about how much to consume. Thus, they avoid letting the agent in them behave opportunistically. They postulate that the benefit of doing this is sufficient to offset the taxes on dividends.

As with the transaction costs story, the self-control explanation can account for an aggregate positive payout policy, but not an individual firm optimal payout policy. That is, in equilibrium, firms will adjust their dividend policy such that the marginal firm is indifferent to the level of dividend paid out. Thus, neither the transaction costs explanation nor the behavioral explanation can account for the positive price reaction to dividend increases and the negative price reaction to dividend decreases.

It should also be noted that both explanations rely heavily on the effect individual investors have on market prices. The need for a steady stream of cash flow combined with significant transaction costs (the transaction costs story) may be adequate to describe small retail investors, but this argument may not hold when applied to corporate and institutional investors. Likewise, self control as an explanation for why firms pay dividends is more persuasive when individual investors are the dominant force in the marketplace. An immediate implication of these explanations is that the amount of dividends paid by corporations should decline as the market share of individual investors declines (as we have experienced in the past two decades). As the evidence in Table 1 indicates, the level of dividend payout did not decrease through time, which is inconsistent with the self-control and transaction costs explanations.

Consistent with these explanations, however, is Long's [1978] study of Citizens Utilities (CU). CU stocks are an almost perfect medium for examining the effect of dividend policy on prices. The reason is that this company had, from 1955 until 1989, two types of common stocks that differed only in their dividend policy. Series A stock paid a stock dividend and series B stock paid a cash dividend.[22] The company's charter required that the stock dividend on series A stock be of equal value with series B cash dividends. In practice, however, the board of directors have chosen stock dividends that average 10% higher than the cash dividends. Even without taxes, we would expect the price ratio of series A stock to series B stock to be equal to the dividend ratio, i.e., to 1.1. Long finds that the price ratio was consistently below 1.1 in the period considered. This price ratio implies a preference for cash dividends over stock dividends despite the tax penalty.

Poterba [1986] revisited the Citizens Utilities case. For the period 1976–1984, he found that the price ratio and the dividend ratios were comparable: the average price ratio was 1.134 and the average dividend ratio was 1.122. Roughly speaking, this evidence implies indifference between dividend and capital gains income. Poterba also examined the ex-dividend day behavior of CU for the period 1965–1984, and found that, on average, the ex-day price decline was less than the

[22] CU received a special IRS ruling so that for tax purposes, the series A stock dividends would be taxed in the same way as proportionate stock dividends are treated for firms having only one series of common stock outstanding. The special ruling expired in 1990.

dividend payment. This is consistent with the ex-dividend day studies discussed previously. It is hard to reconcile the ex-day evidence of the CU stocks with the relative prices of the two stocks on ordinary days.

Hubbard & Michaely [1995] examined the relative prices of these two stocks after the passage of the 1986 TRA. Since the 1986 TRA substantially reduced the advantage of receiving stock dividends rather than cash dividends, they hypothesized that the price ratio should decrease. Indeed, they found that during 1986, the price ratio was considerably lower than in the previous years. However, in the years 1987 through 1989, the price ratio rose and stayed consistently above the dividend ratio.

It seems that the evidence from the price behavior of Citizens Utilities deepens the dividend mystery, rather than enlightening us. It is difficult to know just how to interpret it.

Another rationale for paying dividends (that is not consistent with efficient markets), is as follows: If managers know more about their firm than the market does, and they can time their equity issues decisions to periods when their firm is highly overvalued, then a positive payout is optimal. That is, if investors prefer constant cash flow and managers can sell additional equity when it is overvalued, investors will be better off receiving a steady stream of dividends and leaving the timing of the sales to the firm. However, in efficient markets, outside investors will realize that when a firm sells its securities, it implies that the firm is overvalued [see Myers & Majluf, 1984, for example], and its price (post announcement) will reflect that. In such a case, current equity holders are not better off, even if the managers know more about the firm's value than the market does. The attempt to raise equity will result in a reduction in the existing equity value; the new shares will be sold at fair value, which renders dividend policy irrelevant.

A growing number of studies present evidence that is not consistent with the market rationality described above. Specifically, the evidence presented is consistent with the notion that: (i) managers can time the market; and (ii) the market underreacts to some financial policy decisions, such as seasoned equity issues [Loughran & Ritter, 1995], Initial Public Offerings [Ritter, 1991; Michaely & Shaw, 1994], and repurchases [Ikenberry, Lakonishok & Vermaelen, 1994]. While it is well established that announcements of seasoned equity issues are associated with a price decline [e.g., Masulis & Korwar, 1986], and share repurchases announcements are associated with price increase [e.g., Vermaelen, 1981], these studies show that a significant price movement in the same direction continues several years after the event. Hence, one may argue that paying dividends is the optimal policy.[23]

The literature on dividend policy is plentiful. Due to a lack of space, many contributions have not been covered in detail. One theory that has received considerable attention in the economics literature, but not in the finance literature,

[23] None of the above studies directly relates equity issues (and subsequent performance) to dividend policy. The relationship between the timing of issuance, repurchase decisions, and dividend policy should receive a closer look before arriving at any definite conclusions.

was developed by King [1977], Auerbach [1979], and Bradford [1981]. They have developed a framework where it is assumed that the prohibition on repurchasing shares is binding, and paying dividends is the only way firms can distribute cash to investors. The market value of corporate assets is therefore equal to the present value of the after-tax dividends firms are expected to pay. Because dividend taxes are capitalized into share values, firms are indifferent to the margin between policies of retaining earnings or paying dividends. Thus, the model is consistent with the fact that a significant portion of corporate earnings is paid out as dividends. The reason the theory has not received much attention in the finance literature is its assumption that dividends are the only way the firm can pay out money to shareholders.[24] This is an appropriate assumption in some countries, such as the U.K., where repurchases have historically been illegal. It is not appropriate for the U.S., where they are legal, provided some justification other than tax avoidance can be given. It is usually argued that this can be done fairly easily.

7. Concluding remarks

In perfect and complete capital markets, firms can not alter their value by changing dividend policy. Because markets are less than perfect, dividends, or more generally, payout policy, represents one of the most important financial decisions faced by corporate financial managers. The theoretical work on this issue tells us that there are five potential imperfections to be considered when dividend policy is determined.

(i) *Taxes*. If dividends are taxed more heavily than capital gains, and investors can not avoid this higher taxation by dynamic trading strategies, then minimizing dividends is optimal.

(ii) *Asymmetric information*. If managers know more about the true worth of their firm, dividends may be used to convey that information to the market, despite the costs associated with paying those dividends.[25]

(iii) *Incomplete contracts*. If contracts are incomplete or are not fully enforceable dividends may, under some circumstances, be used by equityholders to discipline managers or to expropriate wealth from debtholders.

(iv) *Institutional constraints*. If various institutions avoid investing in nondividend (or low dividend) paying stocks because of legal restrictions, it may be optimal to pay dividends despite the tax burden it causes to individual investors.

(v) *Transaction costs*. If dividend payments minimize transaction costs to equityholders (either direct transaction costs or the efforts of self control), positive dividend payout may be optimal.

[24] Some models have been criticized on the grounds that they implicitly assume that dividends cannot be financed by equity or debt issues. See Hasbrouck & Friend [1984] and Sarig [1984].

[25] It should be noted that with asymmetric information, dividends can also be viewed as bad news: firms that pay dividends are the ones without positive NPV projects to invest in.

The empirical evidence on the importance of dividend policy is, unfortunately, very mixed. Much work remains to be done before there are definite conclusions on prescriptions for managers.

At this stage, we cannot recommend an optimal dividend policy. There are, however, several general (and, admittedly, somewhat speculative) suggestions we can come up with:

1. To the greatest extent possible, firms that are associated with a high degree of information asymmetry and large growth opportunities should avoid paying dividends. The significant costs associated with raising equity capital for these firms makes payment of dividends even more costly. Stated differently, in periods when a firm faces many good investment opportunities, a dividend reduction may not be such a bad idea.

2. Firms that, for whatever reason, are primarily interested in institutional investors for shareholder base should pay higher dividends than otherwise. First, these shareholders are not affected by the adverse taxes associated with dividends. Second, various 'prudent man' roles constrain some institutions to hold only dividend-paying stocks.

3. Given the restrictive dividend-related covenants and the fact that firms interact with bondholders more than once, the use of dividends to extract wealth from debtholders should be avoided. Most times, it does not work. And even when it does, the long-run result can be detrimental to equity holders.

4. Repurchases should be used much more frequently than they have been historically. Investment and repurchase policies should be coordinated to avoid the transaction costs of financing. When there are positive NPV investments, repurchases should be avoided. In years where they are low, unneeded cash should be paid out by repurchasing shares.

5. We can not think of a good reason why most U.S. firms pay dividends on a quarterly basis instead of on an annual basis. Longer intervals between payments would allow investors that are interested in long-term capital gains to sell the stock before the ex-day, avoid paying tax on the dividend, and maintain the long-term tax status of the stock. It would also allow corporations who may be interested in dividend income to minimize transaction costs and deviation from optimal asset allocation while capturing the dividend. Finally it will save the dividend paying corporation administrative and mailing costs associated with dividend payments.

6. Avoid costly 'signals'. Hopefully, the firm is going to stay alive for a long time. Managers can find cheaper and more persuasive ways to credibly convey the company's true worth to the market.

7. The differential taxes between dividends and capital gains make high-yield stocks less attractive to individual investors in high tax brackets. Such investors should try to hold an otherwise identical portfolio with low-yield stocks.

Other people might disagree with these suggestions. However, until our understanding of the subject is improved, they represent a logical way for managers and investors to proceed. Much more empirical and theoretical research on the subject of dividends is required before a consensus can be reached.

Acknowledgements

We would like to thank Laurie Simon Bagwell, Adam Dunsby, Jerry Hass, Bob Jarrow and John Long for their comments and suggestions. The first author is grateful to the NSF for financial support. Remaining errors are ours.

References

Aharony, J., and I. Swary (1980). Quarterly dividend and earnings announcements and stockholders' returns: An empirical analysis. *J. Finance* 35(1), 1–12.

Ambarish, R., K. John and J. Williams (1987). Efficient signaling with dividends and investments. *J. Finance* 42(2), 321–343.

Asquith, P., and D.W. Mullins, Jr. (1983). The impact of initiating dividend payments on shareholders' wealth. *J. Bus.* 56(1), 77–96.

Auerbach, A.J. (1979). Wealth maximization and the cost of capital. *Q. J. Econ.*, 93(3), 433–446.

Bagwell, L.S. (1991). Shareholder heterogeneity: Evidence and implications. *Am. Econ. Rev.* 81(2), 218–221.

Bagwell, L.S., and K. Judd (1989). Transaction costs and corporate control, working paper, Northwestern University.

Bagwell, L.S., and J. Shoven (1989). Cash distributions to shareholders. *J. Econ. Perspect.* 3(3), 129–140.

Barclay, M. (1987). Dividends, taxes, and common stock prices: The ex-dividend day behavior of common stock prices before the income tax. *J. Financ. Econ.* 14, 31–44.

Barclay, M.J., and C.W. Smith, Jr. (1988). Corporate payout policy: Cash dividends versus open-market repurchases. *J. Financ. Econ.* 22(1), 61–82.

Bernhardt, D., J.F. Robertson and R. Farrow (1994). Testing dividend signaling models, working paper, Queen's University.

Bernheim, D., and A. Wantz (1995). A tax-based test of the dividend signaling hypothesis, *Am. Econ. Rev.* 85(3), 532–551.

Benartzi, S. (1993). Evidence that investors underreact to the implications of dividend changes for subsequent earnings, working paper, Cornell University.

Bhattacharya, S. (1979). Imperfect information, dividend policy, and 'the bird in the hand' fallacy. *Bell J. Econ.* 10(1), 259–270.

Black, F. (1976). The dividend puzzle. *J. Portfolio Manage.* 2, 5–8.

Black, F., and M. Scholes (1974). The effects of dividend yield and dividend policy on common stock prices and returns. *J. Financ. Econ.* 1, 1–22.

Blume, M.E. (1980). Stock return and dividend yield: Some more evidence. *Rev. Econ. Stat.* 62, 567–577.

Blume, M.E., J. Crockett and I. Friend (1974). Stock ownership in the United States: Characteristics and trends. *Surv. Current Bus.* 54(11), 16–40.

Boyd, J., and R. Jagannathan (1994). Ex-dividend price behavior of common stocks: Fitting some pieces of the puzzle. *Rev. Financ. Studies* 7(4), 711–741.

Bradford, D.F. (1981). The incidence and allocation effects of a tax on corporate distributions. *J. Public Econ.* 15, 1–22.

Brennan, M.J. (1970). Taxes, market valuation and financial policy. *Nat. Tax J.* 23, 417–429.

Brennan, M.J., and A.V. Thakor (1990). Shareholder preferences and dividend policy. *J. Finance* 45(4), 993–1019.

Charest, G. (1978). Dividend information, stock returns and market efficiency — II. *J. Financ. Econ.* 6, 297–330.

Chen, N.F., B. Grundy and R.F. Stambaugh (1990). Changing risk, changing risk premiums, and dividend yield effects. *J. Bus.* 63, S51–S70.

Christie, W. (1990). Dividend yield and expected returns: The zero-dividend yield puzzle. *J. Financ. Econ.* 28, 95–125.

Constantinides, G.M., and B.D. Grundy (1989). Optimal investment with stock repurchase and financing as signals. *Rev. Financ. Studies* 2(4), 445–466.

Daniel, K., and S. Titman (1995). Investment under asymmetric information, in: R. Jarrow, V. Maksimovic and W.T. Ziemba (eds.), *Finance*, Handbooks in Operations Research and Management Science, Vol. 9, North-Holland, Amsterdam, pp. 721–766 (this volume).

DeAngelo, H., and L. DeAngelo (1990). Dividend policy and financial distress: An empirical investigation of troubled NYSE firms. *J. Finance* 45(5), 1415–1431.

Dunsby, A. (1993). Share repurchases and corporate distributions: An empirical study, working paper, University of Pennsylvania.

Eades, K., P. Hess and H.E. Kim (1984). On interpreting security returns during the ex-dividend period. *J. Financ. Econ.* 13, 3–34.

Easterbrook, F.H. (1984). Two agency-cost explanations of dividends. *Am. Econ. Rev.* 74(4), 650–659.

Elton, E., and M. Gruber (1970). Marginal stockholders' tax rates and the clientele effect. *Rev. Econ. Stat.* 52, 68–74.

Elton, E., M. Gruber and J. Rentzler (1984). The ex-dividend day behavior of stock prices: A re-examination of the clientele effect. *J. Finance* 39, 551–556.

Fama, E.F., and H. Babiak (1968). Dividend policy: An empirical analysis. *J. Am. Stat. Assoc.* 63(324), 1132–1161.

Fama, E.F., and J.D. Macbeth (1973). Risk, return and equilibrium: Empirical tests. *J. Polit. Econ.* 81, 607–636.

Gonedes, N.J. (1978). Corporate signaling, external accounting, and capital market equilibrium: Evidence on dividends, income, and extraordinary items. *J. Account. Res.* 16(1), 26–79.

Gordon, M. (1959). Dividends, earnings and stock prices. *Rev. Econ. Stat.* 41, 99–105.

Gordon, R.J., and D.F. Bradford (1980). Taxation and the stock market valuation of capital gains and dividends: Theory and empirical results. *J. Public Econ.* 14, 109–136.

Grossman, S.J., and O.D. Hart (1982). Corporate financial structure and managerial incentives, in: J. McCall (ed.), *The Economics of Information and Uncertainty*, University Press, Chicago, IL.

Grundy, B. (1985). Trading volume and stock returns around ex-dividend dates, working paper, University of Chicago, Chicago, IL.

Handjinicolaou, G., and A. Kalay (1984). Wealth redistributions or changes in firm value: An analysis of returns to bondholders and the stockholders around dividend announcements. *J. Financ. Econ.* 13(1), 35–63.

Hasbrouck, J., and I. Friend (1984). Why do companies pay dividends? Comment. *Am. Econ. Rev.* 74, 1137–1141.

Healy, P.M., and K.G. Palepu (1988). Earnings information conveyed by dividend initiations and omissions. *J. Financ. Econ.* 21(2), 149–176.

Heath, D., and R. Jarrow (1988). Ex-dividend stock price behavior and arbitrage opportunities. *J. Bus.* 61, 95–108.

Hess, P.J. (1982). The ex-dividend day behavior of stock returns: Further evidence on tax effects. *J. Finance*, 37, 445–456.

Hess, P.J. (1983). Test of price effects in the pricing of financial assets. *J. Bus.* 56, 537–554.

Hubbard, J., and R. Michaely (1995). Do investors ignore dividend taxation? A re-examination of the citizens utilities case.

Ikenberry, D., J. Lakonishok and T. Vermaelen (1994). Market underreaction to open market share repurchases, working paper, University of Illinois at Urbana-Champaign.

Jensen, M.C. (1986). Agency costs of free cash flow, corporate finance, and takeovers. *Am. Econ. Rev.* 76(2), 323–329.

Jensen, M.C., and W.H. Meckling (1976). Theory of the firm: Managerial behavior, agency costs and ownership structure. *J. Financ. Econ.* 3(4), 305–360.

John, K., and J. Williams (1985). Dividends, dilution, and taxes: A signaling equilibrium. *J. Finance* 40(4), 1053–1070.

Kalay, A. (1982a). The ex-dividend day behavior of stock prices: A re-examination of the clientele effect. *J. Finance* 37, 1059–1070.

Kalay, A. (1982b). Stockholder–bondholder conflict and dividend constraint. *J. Financ. Econ.*, 10, 211–233.

Kalay, A., and U. Loewenstein (1985). Predictable events and excess returns: The case of dividend announcements. *J.Financ. Econ.* 14, 423–449.

Kalay, A., and U. Loewenstein (1986). The information content of the timing of dividend announcements. *J. Financ. Econ.* 16, 373–388.

Kalay, A., and R. Michaely (1993). Dividends and taxes: A reexamination, working paper, Cornell University.

Kang, S.H., and P. Kumar (1991). Determinants of dividend smooting: Evidence from dividend changes, working paper, Carnegie Mellon University.

Karpoff, J.M., and R.A. Walkling (1988). Short-term trading around ex-dividend days: Additional evidence. *J. Financ. Econ.* 21(2), 291–298.

Karpoff, J.M., and R.A. Walkling (1990). Dividend capture in NASDAQ stocks. *J. Financ. Econ.* 28(1/2), 39–66.

Kato, K., and U. Loewenstein (1995). The ex-dividend-day behavior of stock prices: The case of Japan, *Rev. Finance. Studies* 8(3), 819–850.

Keim, D. (1985). Dividend yields and stock returns: Implications of abnormal January returns. *J. Financ. Econ.* 14, 473–489.

King, M. (1977). *Public Policy and the Corporation*, Chapman and Hall, London.

Koski, J.L. (1991). Market segmentation and the identification of marginal traders on ex-dividend days: A microstructure analysis, working paper, Stanford University.

Kumar, P. (1988). Shareholder–manager conflict and the information content of dividends. *Rev. Financ. Studies* 1(2), 111–136.

Lakonishok, J., and T. Vermaelen (1983). Tax reform and the ex-dividend day behavior. *J. Finance* 38, 1157–1179.

Lakonishok, J., and T. Vermaelen (1986). Tax induced trading around ex-dividend dates. *J. Financ. Econ.* 16, 287–319.

Lang, L.H.P., and R. Litzenberger (1989). Dividend announcements: Cash flow signaling vs. free cash flow hypothesis. *J. Financ. Econ.* 24(1), 181–192.

Lewellen, W.G., K.L. Stanley, R.C. Lease and G.G. Schlarbaum (1978). Some direct evidence on the dividend clientele phenomenon. *J. Finance* 33(5), 1385–1399.

Lintner, J. (1956). Distribution of incomes of corporations among dividends, retained earnings, and taxes. *Am. Econ. Rev.* 46(2), 97–113.

Litzenberger, R., and K. Ramaswamy (1979). The effects of personal taxes and dividends on capital asset prices: Theory and empirical evidence. *J. Financ. Econ.* 7, 163–195.

Litzenberger, R., and K. Ramaswamy (1980). Dividends, short selling restrictions, tax induced investor clientele and market equilibrium. *J. Finance* 35, 469–482.

Litzenberger, R., and K. Ramaswamy (1982). The effects of dividends on common stock prices: Tax effects or information effects?. *J. Finance* 37, 429–443.

Long, J.B. (1977). Efficient portfolio choice with differential taxation of dividend and capital gains. *J.Financ. Econ.* 5, 25–53.

Long, J.B., Jr. (1978). The market valuation of cash dividends: A case to consider. *J. Financ. Econ.* 6(2/3), 235–264.

Loughran, T., and J. Ritter (1995). The new issues puzzle. *J. Finance* 50(1), 23–51.

Masulis, R.W., and A.N. Korwar (1986). Seasoned equity offerings: An empirical investigation. *J. Financ. Econ.* 15(1/2), 91–118.

Michaely, R. (1991). Ex-dividend day stock price behavior: The case of the 1986 Tax Reform Act. *J. Finance* 46, 845–860.

Michaely, R., and M. Murgia (1995). The effect of tax heterogeneity on prices and volume around the ex-dividend day: Evidence from the Milan Stock Exchange, *Rev. Finance. Studies* 8(2), 369–399.

Michaely, R., R.H. Thaler and K. Womack (1995). Price reactions to dividend initiations and omissions: Overreaction or drift? *J. Finance* 50, 573–608.

Michaely, R., and W.H. Shaw (1994). The pricing of initial public offerings: Tests of the adverse selection and signaling theories. *Rev. Financ. Studies* 7(2), 279–319.

Michaely, R., and J.-L. Vila (1995a). Investors' heterogeneity, prices and volume around the ex-dividend day, *J. Financ. Quant. Anal.* 30, 171–198.

Michaely, R., and J.-L. Vila (1995b). Trading volume with private valuations: Evidence from the ex-dividend day, *Rev. Financ. Studies*.

Miller, M., and F. Modigliani (1961). Dividend policy, growth and the valuation of shares. *J. Bus.* 34, 411–433.

Miller, M., and K. Rock (1985). Dividend policy under asymmetric information. *J. Finance* 40(4), 1031–1051.

Miller, M., and M. Scholes (1978). Dividends and taxes. *J.Financ. Econ.* 6, 333–264.

Miller, M., and M. Scholes (1982). Dividends and taxes: Empirical evidence. *J. Polit. Econ.* 90, 1118–1141.

Morgan, I.G. (1982). Dividends and capital asset prices. *J. Finance* 37, 1071–1086.

Myers, S.C. (1977). Determinants of corporate borrowing. *J.Financ. Econ.* 5(2), 147–175.

Myers, S.C., and N.S. Majluf (1984). Corporate financing and investment decisions when firms have information that investors do not have. *J. Financ. Econ.* 13(2), 187–221.

Ofer, A.R., and D.R. Siegel (1987). Corporate financial policy, information, and market expectations: An empirical investigation of dividends. *J. Finance* 42(4), 889–911.

Ofer, A.R., and A.V. Thakor (1987). A theory of stock price responses to alternative corporate cash disbursement methods: Stock repurchases and dividends. *J. Finance* 42(2), 365–394.

Penman, S.H. (1983). The predictive content of earnings forecasts and dividends. *J. Finance* 38(4), 1181–1199.

Peterson, P., D. Peterson and J. Ang (1985). Direct evidence on the marginal rate of taxation on dividend income. *J. Financ. Econ.* 14, 267–282.

Pettit, R.R. (1972). Dividend announcements, security performance, and capital market efficiency. *J. Finance* 27(5), 993–1007.

Poterba, J. (1986). The market valuation of cash dividends: The citizens utilities case reconsidered. *J. Financ. Econ.* 15, 395–406.

Poterba, J., and L.H. Summers (1984). New evidence that taxes affect the valuation of dividends. *J. Finance* 39, 1397–1415.

Ritter, J.R. (1991). The long run performance of initial public offerings. *J. Finance* 46(1), 3–28.

Rosenberg, B., and V. Marathe (1979). Tests of capital asset pricing hypotheses. *Res. Finance* 1, 115–224.

Sarig, O. (1984). Why do companies pay dividends? Comment. *Am. Econ. Rev.* 74, 1142.

Shefrin, H.M., and M. Statman (1984). Explaining investor preference for cash dividends. *J. Financ. Econ.* 13(2), 253–282.

Stiglitz, J.E. (1983). Some aspects of the taxation of capital gains. *J. Public Econ.* 21, 257–296.

Thaler, R.H., and H.M. Shefrin (1981). An economic theory of self-control. *J. Polit. Econ.* 89(2), 392–406.

Vermaelen, T. (1981). Common stock repurchases and market signaling: An empirical study. *J. Financ. Econ.* 9(2), 138–183.

Watts, R. (1973). The information content of dividends. *J. Bus.* 46(2), 191–211.

Williams, J. (1988). Efficient signaling with dividends, investment, and stock repurchases. *J. Finance* 43(3), 737–747.

Yoon, P.S., and L. Starks (1993). Signaling, investment opportunities, and dividend announcements, *Rev. Financ. Studies* 8(4).

R. Jarrow et al., Eds., *Handbooks in OR & MS, Vol. 9*
1995 Elsevier Science B.V.

Chapter 26

Mergers and Acquisitions: Strategic and Informational Issues

David Hirshleifer
School of Business Administration, University of Michigan, 701 Tappan, Ann Arbor, MI 48109-1234, U.S.A.

1. Introduction

A merger is a transaction that combines two firms, leaving one surviving entity. An acquisition is the purchase of one firm by another individual or firm. Both transactions fall under the more general heading of *takeovers*. Takeovers can play a constructive economic role, for example by removing inefficient management or by achieving economies of scale and complementarity. On the other hand, they can have the possibly less desirable effect of redistributing wealth, as in takeovers that exploit tax benefits or expropriate bondholders or stakeholders. Finally, takeovers may reduce efficiency if they reflect agency problems on the part of bidding managers, or result simply from misjudgments.

There are many important conflicts of interest and informational differences among parties to takeovers: bidding shareholders who only want an acquisition if the price of the target is not too high compared to underlying value, bidding management who may seek self-aggrandization through takeover, target shareholders who wish to obtain a price that fully reflects any possible takeover improvements, target management who wish to retain private benefits of control, and potential competing bidders deciding whether to make their own offers.

This essay describes the relationships between different models of the takeover process, and where possible provides analytical syntheses to integrate major trends in the literature. I focus mainly on three types of models: (1) models of tender offers, which examine the decisions of individual shareholders whether to tender (sell) their shares to a bidder, (2) models of competition among multiple bidders, and (3) models that examine the voting power of target managers who own shares.[1]

Beginning with (1), tender offers to purchase shares directly from shareholders are a crucial mechanism for overcoming management opposition to takeover,

[1] These categories are neither mutually exclusive nor exhaustive. In practice, however, most theoretical papers on takeovers have fallen into one of these categories. Many of the insights from these papers would also apply to other cases, such as the analysis of merger bid when there is little competitive threat, or the analysis of tender offers when there is competitive threat.

as contrasted with merger bids which require management approval. Models of the tender offer process may be classified according to whether (i) all parties are identically informed, or alternatively the bidder has superior information about the post-takeover value of the target; and whether (ii) individual target shareholders take the probability of offer success as given, or else recognize the influence of their individual tendering decisions upon offer success or failure.

Issues (i) and (ii) are important for understanding target managers' defensive measures and bidders' incentives to undertake mergers and acquisitions, and so for the design of regulatory policy. With regard to (i), superior bidder information presents target shareholders with an inference problem. One would expect that this informational disadvantage could lead target shareholders to be skeptical about the adequacy of the offer, and thus reluctant to tender their shares. I therefore examine the effect of bidder information on its probability of success and expected profits, and how defensive measures affect the informational advantage.

With regard to (ii), if target shareholders take probability of success as given, then their tendering decisions will be nonstrategic — being based on a simple comparison of gains from tendering or not. If a shareholder's decision influences the probability of success, however, she has a stronger incentive to tender in order to bring about success. This essay will therefore examine the determinants of how likely it is that individual shareholders will be pivotal in determining offer success, and the effect of this probability on the expected profitability of takeovers for bidders.

Turning to point (2), models of competition, any attempt to understand competitive takeover auctions must address the anomaly that bidding in takeover contests generally occurs in a few large jumps, rather than many small increments as predicted by the conventional analysis of bidding in costless English auctions. This essay therefore examines models of costly investigation and costly bid revision, wherein successive bids may increase by large increments when bidders try to intimidate their competitors into quitting. Since the intimidated bidder may be able to increase value more than the intimidator, this may not be a good thing. This leads to consideration of the effects of regulations that influence the cost of investigation and the ease of preemption. I will also consider how the choice of means of payment (cash, equity, or other securities) can signal information, and thus can be used as a tool for preempting competitors.

Finally, with regard to point (3) above, the share ownership and voting power of target management that values control can be important for the outcome of a tender bid and for the bidder's decision whether to undertake a tender offer or a proxy fight. It is therefore important to understand how a manager may be able to alter his effective control of voting rights either directly through share purchases or indirectly through changes in capital structure.

This essay mainly covers topics that have been the focus of several related models that yield divergent results. It is for these topics that integrated discussion and analysis seems most valuable and feasible. The cost of this approach is that many other important topics are not addressed here or are only briefly touched upon. Such topics include the analysis of why takeover occur, bidder/target bargaining, the effect on competition of bidding by well-informed target managers (as in leveraged buyouts), winner's curse effects when bidders with common valuations compete, and the effect of takeover threats on directorial oversight of managers and on investment and operating decisions. Section 7 discusses these issues briefly and gives some literature references.

The remainder of this essay is structured as follows. Section 2 gives a synopsis of empirical material. Section 3 discusses tender offers and share tendering decisions. Section 4 analyzes competitive bidding. Section 5 discusses the means of payment in takeover contests. Section 6 discusses target financing, managerial voting power and private benefits of control. Section 8 concludes.

2. An empirical synopsis

This section lays out some empirical evidence relevant for the theories discussed in this review. The summary will by no means be comprehensive, even for this limited purpose.

Target shareholders on average earn large positive abnormal returns from tender offers, while bidding shareholder abnormal returns are on average close to zero; see, e.g., Weston, Chung & Hoag [1990] for summary of empirical evidence. High target returns reflect remarkably high and rising premia in successful contests. Nathan & O'Keefe [1989] report average successful premia for cash tender takeovers that rose from 41% to 75% in the 1963–1973 and 1974–1985 periods, and a rise from rose from 29% to 70% for cash merger premia.

The Williams Act of 1968 and associated legislation requires disclosure and delays completion of tender offers. Tender offer premia decreased after the Williams Act [Nathan & O'Keefe, 1989].[2]

Bradley, Desai & Kim [1988] provide evidence that the joint market value increase of bidder and target is on average positive. Bradley, Desai & Kim [1983] find that target stock market gains on average vanish in failed offers where the target is not later acquired by another bidder. Roll [1986] emphasized that stock returns may not accurately measure value improvements to the extent that making a takeover bid reveals information about the stand-alone value of the bidder (e.g., that the bidder has enough funds to afford the offer). However, Bhagat & Hirshleifer [1995] estimate value improvements to be on average positive and substantial using a method that disentangles value improvements from revelation effects.

Bradley, Desai & Kim [1988] also find that U.S. bidder abnormal stock returns were on average lower in the 1980s than in the 1960s and 1970s. They report that multiple bidder contests provide higher average abnormal target stock returns, and lower bidder returns (close to zero).

[2] A persistent upward trend in takeover premia and target abnormal returns began five years after the Williams Act. This timing suggests that the change was not related to the Williams Act. A similar increase occurred in the UK [Franks & Harris, 1989] during the 1970s and 80s.

Tender offer success versus failure is often highly uncertain, as evidenced by the negative reaction of the target stock price to offer failure [see Bradley, Desai & Kim, 1983; Samuelson & Rosenthal, 1986; Ruback, 1988] and by the positive bidder stock price reaction to success and negative reaction to failure [see Bradley, 1980]. Offer success is positively related to the bid premium and to the initial shareholding of the bidder in the target [Walkling, 1985].

Target management defensive measures on average reduce the probability of a takeover occurring [Walkling, 1985; Pound, 1988]. The target stock price reaction to greenmail is on average negative [Bradley & Wakeman, 1983; and Dann & DeAngelo, 1983], as is the average reaction to antitakeover amendments, poison pills, defensive restructurings, and several other defensive measures [see, e.g., Bhagat & Jefferis, 1991; Malatesta & Walkling, 1988; Ryngaert, 1988; and Dann & DeAngelo, 1988].

There is evidence that target managers can position their firms in ways that alter bidder behavior. Stulz, Walkling & Song [1990] provide evidence that the bid level is on average higher when target management owns a greater share of the target. Palepu [1986] finds that the probability of a hostile takeover attempt is decreasing with the target's debt–equity ratio.

Certain items of evidence have provided sharp empirical challenges to theories of the takeover transaction process. The traditional solution to the English auctions model with multiple buyers involves many small bid increments. This has faced a glaring challenge from the evidence that takeover bidding occurs by small numbers of enormous jumps, a challenge taken up in Section 4. In Jennings & Mazzeo [1993] the majority of *initial* bid premia were over 20% of the market value of the target 10 days prior to the offer. Since price runup may occur earlier, this is likely to be an underestimate of premia relative to non-takeover value.

A second challenge is provided by the often puzzlingly low ownership in target firms accumulated by bidders prior to making a takeover bid. Given the very high premia paid in tender offers, we would expect bidders to buy up shares at the open market price prior to the bid up to the limits of market liquidity. In fact, the majority of tender offer bidders own no target shares [Bradley, Desai & Kim, 1988],[3] and even among those that do, the potential profit on these holdings appears to be modest compared to bidding costs [Bhagat & Hirshleifer, 1995]. This challenge is taken up by theories discussed in Section 3.1.5.

A third empirical challenge is the mixed evidence regarding the effect of means of payment (stock versus fixed payments) on bidder and target stock abnormal stock returns. There is evidence, consistent with the Myers & Majluf [1984] adverse selection problem with equity issuance, that bidder and target returns for stock offers are on average lower than for cash offers (see, e.g., Huang & Walkling [1987] on target returns). However, the U.S. result that average abnormal bidder returns are negative in stock offers does not apply in France, the UK or Canada

[3] In a sample of successful post-1968 offers, Stulz, Walkling & Song [1990] find a positive median bidder share ownership of 2.35% among successful offers, and a 4.75% ownership in successful single bidder contests.

(Eckbo, Giammarino & Heinkel [1990] and citations therein). Furthermore, Lang, Stulz & Walkling [1991] report that the effect of means of payment in the U.S. is subsumed by a cash flow variable. The associated theoretical issues are discussed in Section 5.

3. Tender offers and share tendering decisions

A tender offer can be either conditional or unconditional. A conditional offer is not binding on the bidder unless a given number of shares are tendered. An offer may require acceptance of all tendered shares (an unrestricted offer), or alternatively the bidder may not be obliged to purchase more than a prespecified number of shares (a restricted offer). An offer that is unconditional and unrestricted is often called an 'any-or-all' offer.

Consider a bidder who can increase the value of the target only if he obtains control. Except where otherwise specified, in this essay the non-takeover value of the target firm is normalized to zero. Also, I assume that the bidder obtains no control unless he succeeds in buying a given fraction of target shares, in which event he obtains complete control. Let v be the post-takeover value of a firm's shares. Ignoring taxes, a risk-neutral target shareholder i should tender if the price offered for the firm's shares, b, exceeds the expected value of her share if she retains it:

$$\text{Tender if } b > \Pr(\text{Success} \mid i \text{ Retain})v. \tag{1}$$

A target shareholder will be more willing to tender if she believes that post-takeover value v is low, and if she believes that her individual decision not to tender will reduce the takeover's probability of succeeding.

Section 3.1 presents a model (due to Grossman & Hart [1980], Shleifer & Vishny [1986a], and Hirshleifer & Titman [1990]) in which each shareholder believes he will not be pivotal. This model allows for possible informational superiority of the bidder. Section 3.2 discusses models (by Bagnoli & Lipman [1988] and Holmstrom & Nalebuff [1992]) which allow for the fact that individual shareholders are sometimes pivotal, but assume symmetric information.

3.1. A nonpivotal shareholder model

3.1.1. The model under complete information

Consider a bidder who can increase the value of the target to \$100 per share if he obtains control, which requires >50% of the target's shares. Assume the offer is conditional upon obtaining control. Under some circumstances, he will be unable to profit on the shares that he purchases owing to a free-rider problem among target shareholders [Grossman & Hart, 1980; Bradley, 1980]. Suppose he makes a rather generous offer of \$80 per share. Each shareholder reasons that if the offer fails, the value of her retained shares remains the same regardless of whether she tenders; while if the offer succeeds, she is better off receiving the post-takeover value of \$100 than the offered price of \$80. Thus each shareholder will retain her shares, and the offer will fail, even though its success would be jointly profitable for shareholders. The paradoxical conclusion is that a bidder cannot succeed in a tender offer except at a price that gives all the potential profits to the target shareholders. If there is any cost of investigation or bidding, the bidder actually loses money. Empirically, the evidence cited earlier on bidder and target stock returns are fairly consistent with this conclusion, particularly in the 1980s.

Nevertheless, bidders may reap a profit if they can dilute the value of minority shares after a takeover (Grossman and Hart).[4] The threat of dilution may induce target shareholders to tender at a price low enough for the bidder to profit. Alternatively, if the bidder himself owns shares in the target prior to the offer, he can reap a profit even without dilution. By improving firm value, he increases the value of his own shares [Shleifer & Vishny, 1986a].[5]

To illustrate these points, let the post-takeover value of the target be v, the fraction that can be diluted be δ, the initial fractional shareholding of the bidder in the target be α, the level of the conditional tender offer be b, and the cost of bidding be c^{B}.[6] Under complete information, a risk neutral target shareholder will tender if the price offered exceeds the diluted post-takeover value, i.e.:

$$\text{Tender if } b > (1-\delta)v. \tag{2}$$

Assume that the bidder needs to buy an additional fraction of at least ω of the firm's shares, over and above his initial fraction α, to obtain control. The equilibrium strategy pair for the bidder is to offer just above $(1-\delta)v$, and for all shareholders to tender at this price. If the offer is unrestricted (so that all tendered shares are purchased), he therefore purchases all $1-\alpha$ shares, for a profit of

$$\alpha v + (1-\alpha)(v-b) - c^{\mathrm{B}}. \tag{3}$$

Combining (2) with (3) gives the following proposition.

Proposition 1. *Under complete information, the bidder's profit in a conditional unrestricted offer is*

$$\alpha v + (1-\alpha)\delta v - c^{\mathrm{B}}.$$

[4] In other words, the bidder can exclude (nontendering) minority target shareholders from part of the post-takeover value of the target firm. For example, the bidder, having obtained control, may be able to choose the price in a merger with the target (subject to legal constraints). Or the bidder may be able to buy assets of the target at a below-market price. A restricted two-tier offer can be profitable if nontendering minority shareholders can be forced to accept less than tendering shareholders. This will be the case if there is a credible dilution threat.

[5] Since this internalizes only a fraction of the value improvement, the bidder still has a suboptimal incentive to make a bid.

[6] Since the non-takeover value has been set to zero, the possibility that the bidder can extract value from the target's assets-in-place (rather than just appropriating part of the takeover improvement) has been excluded.

The first term is the improvement in value of the bidder's initial shareholding. The second term is the profit on the shares purchased in the tender offer. If follows trivially (letting α and δ approach zero) that:

Proposition 2. *Under complete information, if a bidder's initial shareholding (α) in the target and dilution opportunities (δ) are sufficiently small, then a conditional unrestricted tender offer is unprofitable.*

Four further points are worth noting. First, diluting target value may be costly, in the sense that the bidder's gain is less than target shareholder's loss. If so, then it is a dominant strategy for the bidder to make an unrestricted offer as assumed above.[7] Second, the second term in Proposition 1 shows that having an initial shareholding reduces the value of the dilution threat, because to some extent the bidder would be diluting his own holdings. Third, the profit deriving from initial shareholdings tends to be fairly small because of low shareholdings (see empirical synopsis). Fourth, if a shareholder may be pivotal, or if the offer is unconditional, then a threat by the bidder to reduce the target's *non*-takeover value would also encourage shareholders to tender.[8]

3.1.2. Share tendering decisions under asymmetric information

A bidder usually knows what he plans to do with the target better than target shareholders. Superficially, it might appear that a bidder could on average profit even without dilution or an initial shareholding, based on superior information about the post-takeover value of the target (v). However, rational expectations (or in game-theoretic terminology, perfect Bayesian equilibrium) implies that if the bidders were on average offering less than post-takeover value in tender offers, shareholders would be aware of this and would refuse to tender. Thus, the free-rider problem remains when asymmetric information is introduced.

In such a generalized model, two equilibria are of interest. In one, the price offered is uninformative, and offers always succeed [Shleifer & Vishny, 1986a]. In the other, the level of the offer reveals the bidder's valuation, and the probability of offer success increases with the amount offered [Hirshleifer & Titman, 1990].[9]

3.1.2.1. Uninformative offer levels. If a bidder's information about post-takeover value or about potential dilution is superior to that of target shareholders, then shareholders must draw some inference about the bidder's valuation from the level of the offer. Shleifer & Vishny [1986a] provide a model in which the level of

[7] If there is no wastage, then whether the offer is restricted is a matter of indifference. Even if wastage is arbitrarily close to 100%, as Proposition 1 shows, the bidder benefits substantially from the threat of dilution since it allows him to buy shares cheaply.

[8] Gilbert & Newbery [1988] examine a model in which a bidder acquires cheaply because he can threaten to enter an industry and reduce the profits of a member of an oligopoly.

[9] In what follows, it is assumed that the only information asymmetry is about post-takeover value v; information is symmetric about the initial shareholding α. Regulations require the bidder to file information about share ownership with the S.E.C. at the time of the bid.

the offer is uninformative in equilibrium, because shareholders foresee perfectly the price that will be offered if a bid occurs. Since it is assumed that at any offer level the bidder knows with certainty whether shareholders will tender, the equilibrium price offered is set to be just high enough to induce shareholders to accept the offer. When indifferent, it is assumed that target shareholders tender. For simplicity, assume that there is no dilution ($\delta = 0$), that bidding is costless ($c^{\mathrm{B}} = 0$), and that (possibly owing to financing costs) the offer is restricted to the minimum additional fraction of the firms shares needed for control, ω.

Then to persuade target shareholders to tender, a bidder must offer target shareholders at least

$$b^* = E[v \mid \text{Offer}], \tag{4}$$

where the RHS is the expected valuation of the bidder given that he makes an offer. In the proposed equilibrium, a bidder with low valuation cannot reduce the amount offered, because if he bid any less, $b < b^*$, shareholders would infer that his valuation was higher than the amount offered, $v > b$, and so would retain their shares. Thus, the probability of success $P(b)$ is a step function of the level of the offer, i.e., $P(b) = 0$ if $b < E[v]$, and $P(b) = 1$ if $b \geq E[v]$ (as illustrated by the dark line segments in Figure 1).

Proposition 3. *Under asymmetric information, there is an equilibrium in which a bidder who makes an offer pays a price equal to the expected post-takeover valuation of the shares he purchases. His gain on the shares he buys is positive if the improvement v is high, and is negative if v is low. He derives an expected profit from the increase in value of his initial shareholding in the target.*

On average a bidder does not profit on the shares purchased in a tender offer. (If he did, shareholders would not want to tender!) A bidder with valuation v close to zero will not make an offer, because he takes a loss on the shares purchased in the offer of $v - b^*$, and his initial holding profit αv is low. For larger v, the bidder's profits both on shares purchased and on the initial holding increase. There is a critical value v^* such that profits are zero. The bidder makes an offer if and only if $v > v^*$. Thus, the bid in (4) is $b^* = E[v \mid v > v^*]$.[10]

3.1.2.2. Revealing offer levels. The bidder's gain from succeeding is increasing with its valuation of the target. Since a low offer reduces the probability of offer success [Walkling, 1985], a low-valuation bidder has a stronger incentive to save money by defecting to a low offer than a high-valuation bidder.[11] The probability

[10] If bidding is costly, the critical value increases. An empirical implication is that if the cost of bidding decreases, the critical level for bidding decreases, so premia on average decrease.

[11] A low-valuation bidder who makes a lower bid will profit under a wider set of shareholder responses than a high-valuation bidder. This suggests that investors should believe his valuation is low, and should accept his offer. Thus, the pooling equilibrium of the preceding section is removed by the strong refinement criterion of Banks & Sobel [1987]. However, the pooling equilibrium survives several other criteria, such as those of Grossman & Perry [1986] and Cho & Kreps [1987].

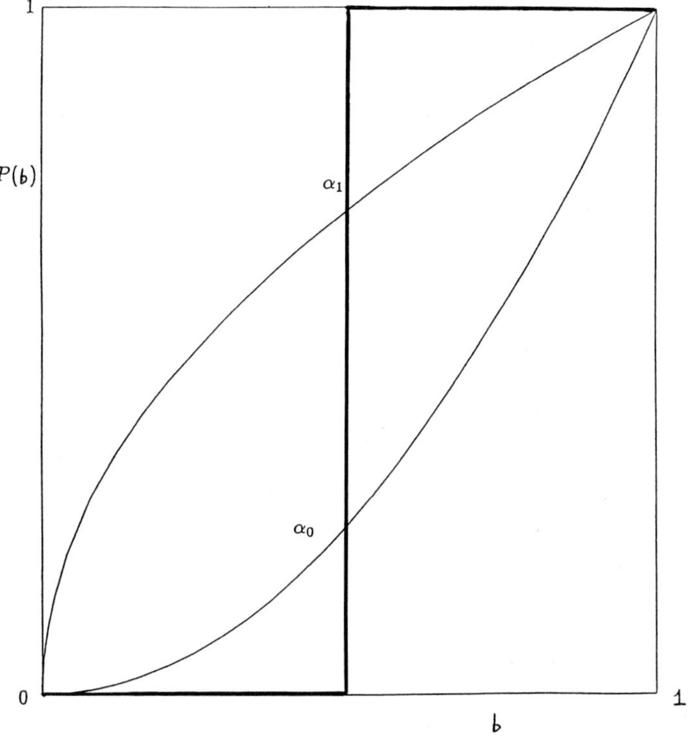

Fig. 1.

of a low offer succeeding is greater to the extent that the bidder can persuade shareholders that his improvement is small, since this encourages shareholders to tender [equation (1)]. Since high-valuation bidders have a stronger incentive to bid high, a bidder can reveal a lower valuation credibly by bidding less.

In order to examine the revealing equilibrium of the tender offer model, let $P(b;\alpha,\omega)$ be an offer's probability of success given a bid of b by a bidder with initial shareholding of α who needs a further ω shares to obtain control. The bidder chooses a bid level to maximize his expected profit, so he solves

$$\max_b \, [\alpha v + (v-b)\omega] P(b;\, \alpha, \omega). \tag{5}$$

The first order condition for this problem is

$$P'(b)[\alpha v + (v-b)\omega] = P(b)\omega. \tag{6}$$

Assuming an interior solution for b, and parametrically differentiating (6) with respect to v, implies the following proposition [see Hirshleifer & Titman, 1990].

Proposition 4. *Suppose that a bidder faces an exogenous probability of offer success function that is twice differentiable and increasing with the amount bid. If an interior* *optimal level of the bid exists for each bidder valuation, then the level of the bid is increasing in the bidder's valuation of the target* ($\mathrm{d}b/\mathrm{d}v > 0$). *Therefore, the bidder's information is fully revealed by his bid.*

This proposition takes shareholder behavior as exogenous, so we cannot yet conclude that there is a revealing equilibrium. One is displayed later. Proposition 4, however, shows that almost any reasonable model of tender offers will lead to separation for at least a range of bidder types. For example, in a model in which target management can take defensive action but cannot with perfect effectiveness 'just say no', we expect the intensity of opposition to the takeover to decrease with the amount bid, so the probability of offer success should increase smoothly. Such a model leads to full revelation. A steadily increasing probability of success as a function of the bid can also be derived from a model where shareholders have different capital gains bases [Stulz, 1988; Bagwell, 1991].[12] In the pooling equilibrium of the previous section, there is no revelation because it violates the assumption of a continuous probability of success.

In the model developed here, there is a unique equilibrium in which the level of the bid is a fully revealing signal of the bidder's valuation. In this equilibrium, the bidder offers his valuation, the minimum amounted needed to have a chance of succeeding, $b = v$ [compare with equation (4)]. Instead of assuming that indifferent shareholders always tender, let us now (consistent with evidence cited earlier) allow for the possibility that the outcome of the offer is uncertain from the viewpoint of the bidder. This uncertainty is modelled as arising from randomization by shareholders as to whether to tender in a mixed strategy equilibrium.[13] In the mixed strategy equilibrium, the bidder's uncertainty about his probability of success at different bid levels is such that he optimally makes a bid that leaves shareholders indifferent as to whether to tender. Imposing the indifference condition ($b = v$) in (6) leads to a differential equation that determines the probability of success,

$$\frac{P'(b)}{P(b)} = \frac{\omega}{\alpha b}. \tag{7}$$

The relevant boundary condition is that the highest possible bid (made by the highest valuation bidder) always succeeds, $P(\bar{v}) = 1$. The solution,

$$P(b; \alpha) = \left(\frac{b}{\bar{v}}\right)^{\omega/\alpha}, \tag{8}$$

is illustrated by the dark curves in Figure 1. The probability of an offer's success increases with the bid premium and with the initial holding α (consistent with

[12] Pooling among the highest valuation types, however, remains a possibility because if a very high offer is sure to succeed, above this bid level $P(b)$ is no longer increasing.

[13] A mixed strategy equilibrium is a way of modeling the fact that, owing to small amounts of uncertainty about payoffs, the behavior of some players (target shareholders) seems uncertain from the point of view of another player (the bidder) [see Harsanyi, 1973]. For example, the bidder may not know the liquidity or capital gains tax considerations that affect shareholders' tender decisions.

evidence cited earlier) of Walkling [1985], and decreases with the number of additional shares needed for control ω.[14] Offer failure is caused by the informational superiority of the bidder. Shareholders recognize the bidder's temptation to offer less than the post-takeover value of their shares, and are therefore reluctant to tender at low prices (i.e., they tender with lower probability). The model therefore predicts that actions that improve the information of target shareholders will (by shifting the upper bound $\bar{v}$ in (8) downward toward the true value $v < \bar{v}$) increase the probability of offer success.[15]

Like an initial shareholding, proportional dilution increases the benefit to achieving success. It therefore increases the incentive to bid high. This reduces shareholders' skepticism of the offer, and increases the probability of offer success.[16]

This model assumes that if the offer fails, the bidder does not acquire the target and hence loses a valuable profit opportunity. In reality, if an offer fails, the bidder can revise his offer upward. This opportunity can potentially eliminate the separating equilibrium. In order for a separating equilibrium to survive, it is crucial that failure impose an opportunity cost on the bidder that is increasing in the size of the potential value improvement. This can occur for several reasons: (1) initial failure gives entrenched managers more time to mobilize blocking defensive strategies, (2) failure may give target management time to announce changes that preempt the potential takeover improvement, (3) loss of time can involve the loss of a window of opportunity to exploit a synergy between the firms, and (4) rejection may give a competing bidder time to enter. The arrival of a competitor is costly to a bidder who hopes to profit by diluting minority shareholders [see Hirshleifer & Titman, 1990, section I.D]. In evaluating defensive measures in the next section, it should be kept in mind that the efficiency consequences of failure of an initial offer depend on which of the costs of failure listed above are relevant.

3.1.3. Management defensive strategies

We focus in this section on the revealing equilibrium, since it permits analysis of how defensive strategies affect the information revealed by the bid and the probability of offer success.

[14] Thus, a supermajority antitakeover amendment reduces the probability of offer success. An untested implication of the model is that the ratio of the target stock price increase at the announcement of the bid to the bid premium is increasing in both the bid level and α, and decreasing in ω. The model also implies that average premia are lower when the initial shareholding α is higher (consistent with evidence of Walkling & Edmister [1985]), and when the required number of shares ω is lower.

[15] This is consistent with Walkling's [1985] evidence that share solicitation activity increases the probability of success.

[16] Asquith [1991] extends this model by allowing for a probability that the bidding manager is afflicted with 'hubris' [see Roll, 1986] in the sense that he incorrectly believes he can increase target value (i.e., he believes that $v > 0$ when actually $v = 0$). Asquith shows that the presence of hubristic bidders allows nonhubristic bidders to profit, even without dilution and without initial shareholdings. Target shareholders become willing to tender even if rational bidders offer below post-takeover value owing to the chance that the offer is from a hubristic bidder. Thus hubris can improve efficiency despite the obvious cost of inefficient takeovers.

3.1.3.1. Effects on incentive to bid high. A manager who values control may oppose takeover for his own purposes. As an extreme example, if a target manager is expected to be able to block any reasonable offer, then no offer will be made. The Grossman & Hart model without dilution (Section 3.1.1) suggests that defensive measures are undesirable, as there is already too little incentive to make an offer. They suggest that target shareholders, in order to attract later takeovers, will write corporate charters that encourage dilution, e.g., the absence of defensive antitakeover provisions such as 'fair price' amendments or classified boards [see Jarrell & Poulsen, 1987]. However, the incentive of target shareholders to permit dilution is too weak, because extracting a high price from the bidder provides shareholders with a redistributive gain.

On the other hand, if a bidder has substantial opportunities for dilution, then target shareholders can benefit from defensive activity to force a higher bid [DeAngelo & Rice, 1983]. There is a time-inconsistency problem here, however, in that the ex-post benefit to shareholders of forcing a higher price conflicts with the ex-ante benefit of encouraging potential bidders to investigate the target.

In practice, U.S. courts have allowed firms to reject takeover offers at will based upon the 'business judgement' of target management. Target management's incentive to block low-priced offers is greater when management's share ownership is high. The key exception in which the target management may be coerced into selling is if it has already begun negotiating sale of the firm to another buyer. Once the firm has been put in play in this fashion, management is obligated to auction the firm and attempt to get the best deal for shareholders.

Since a defensive measure can induce a high offer, when information is asymmetric defensive measures can reduce shareholders' skepticism, and thereby increase the probability of offer success. Consider a threat to block the offer unless an offer of over $\bar{v}$ is made. Since the bidder must then offer $b > \bar{v}$, shareholders should always tender, and the offer will always succeed. More generally, if the cost or risk of failure imposed on the bidder by the defensive strategy is greater when the bid is lower, then the bidder is encouraged to bid higher, so that shareholders probabilistically become more willing to tender [Hirshleifer & Titman, 1990].

These results are summarized as follows.

Proposition 5. *A management defensive strategy, by blocking takeover, can harm target shareholders and reduce efficiency. However, by increasing the incentive to bid high, such a measure can also increase the probability of offer success and improve efficiency.*

Other defensive measures reduce the incentive to bid high, and therefore reduce the probability of success. A poison pill, by increasing the value of nontendered shares after a successful offer, acts as the opposite of dilution (see Section 3.1.1 earlier). Thus, it reduces the incentive to ensure success by bidding high. More generally, strategies that impose greater costs on the bidder when his offer succeeds than when it fails reduce the incentive to bid high, since they reduce the gain from success. For example, an antitakeover amendment ('shark repellent') such as staggered board terms that delays transfer of control to the bidder in the event of offer success will reduce bid levels, and so the probability of success. Evidence cited earlier indicating that defensive measures tend to prevent takeover from occurring [Walkling, 1985; Pound, 1988] suggests that target managers may often be acting against shareholder interest by adopting those strategies that prevent takeovers.

3.1.3.2. Effects on asymmetry of information. A subtler effect of defensive strategies is to change the informational advantage of the bidder over target shareholders. Consider a value-reduction strategy, defined as a defensive activity that reduces the post-takeover value of the target. An example would be the sale of an asset that, as part of the target, could be improved by the bidder ('sale of the crown jewels', also known as the 'scorched earth defense'.). A value-reducing defensive measure can reduce or increase informational asymmetry. Suppose that the bidder can increase the value of the target by $v = x + y$, where x is an improvement that is known to shareholders perfectly while y is known to the bidder but not the target. If a value-reduction strategy eliminates the possibility of the unknown improvement y, then the informational asymmetry is removed, and the bidder can ensure success by offering just above x. Thus, a value-reduction strategy can reduce informational asymmetry and promote success.

Conversely, if a value-reduction strategy eliminates the known improvement x, then the probability of success is

$$P(b; \alpha) = \left(\frac{b}{\bar{y}}\right)^{\omega/\alpha}. \tag{9}$$

The probability of success at any level of the bid b is higher than in (8).[17] However, the probability of success is reduced for a given bidder because he bids less when his valuation is reduced.[18]

Proposition 6. *A value-reduction defensive strategy, by decreasing (increasing) the importance of publicly known improvements relative to improvements known privately by the bidder, can decrease (increase) the probability of tender offer success.*

3.1.4. Target private information

The target as well as the bidder may have private information. If the target is undervalued by the market, then by signalling high value, managers can make shareholders less willing to tender. Increasing leverage and repurchasing shares, actions which can signal high value, are often used defensively. Ofer & Thakor [1987] analyze signalling through repurchase; Bagnoli, Gordon, & Lipman [1989] analyze repurchase signalling as a defensive strategy.

[17] This is not surprising, since a given level of the bid becomes more attractive when compared to a smaller post-takeover value.

[18] Without the value-reduction measure, the probability of a bidder with valuation v succeeding is $(v/\bar{v})^{\omega/\alpha}$. With the defensive measure, the probability is $[(v - x)/(\bar{v} - x)]^{\omega/\alpha}$.

3.1.5. *Pre-tender offer share acquisition*

Prior to announcing his offer, a takeover bidder has private information about an event that will increase the market price of the target's stock. This leads to an incentive to acquire shares of the target quietly at a lower price. Pre-takeover share acquisition is limited by disclosure requirements and by the depth of the market, because in a thin market a large purchase of shares will more quickly reveal the information of an informed trader. Kyle & Vila [1991] point out that if the possibility of a takeover is foreseen, then a potential bidder can profit by either buying shares secretly before making a takeover bid or selling shares short and not making a bid.

In any case, the evidence mentioned in the empirical synopsis that the majority of actual tender offer bidders do not accumulate *any* target shares is puzzling. One explanation has to do with the desire to signal low-valuation to target shareholders. Since a high valuation bidder has an incentive to bid higher (see Section 3.1.2.2), he has a stronger incentive to accumulate shares prior to the offer. But this means that the disclosure of the initial shareholding required at the time of an offer for a U.S. firm reveals the bidder's valuation. It follows that there is an incentive to accumulate fewer shares in order to persuade target shareholders to tender their shares at a lower price [Chowdhry & Jegadeesh, 1994].[19]

3.1.6. *The general free-rider problem*

The free-rider problem has been discussed in the context of conditional tender offers. However, the conclusion that in the absence of dilution and initial holdings the bidder cannot profit holds very generally, so long as target shareholders do not perceive themselves to be pivotal.

Let us define a *tender offer* as an offer to buy shares in which the same prespecified price is offered for all purchased shares, no share is purchased unless it is tendered by the shareholder, and if it is tendered, whether it is purchased is a function of the tendering decisions of all shareholders.[20] Suppose that there are two control states, bidder control and target control, leading to target firm values of v or 0 respectively. The state is determined by whether the critical fraction of shares is tendered.

If a shareholder is virtually never pivotal, then she perceives herself as being in a virtually constant-sum game with the bidder. Shareholders as a whole are in a nonconstant sum game with the bidder, but any individual shareholder partakes of only a vanishingly small fraction of the joint benefit derived from her decision to tender. Thus, any offer that gives the individual shareholder an expected profit will give the bidder an expected loss on purchases from that shareholder.

[19] Another possible explanation for low initial holdings is that the bidder wishes to keep the preoffer share price low, if the legally permissible amount of dilution in a freeze-out merger is constrained by this price [Ravid & Spiegel, 1991].

[20] These conditions hold for both conditional and unconditional offers, for either restricted or unrestricted offers, and for offers in which oversubscription leads to pro-rationing, first-come-first-serve, or to discrimination by the bidder amongst different shareholders in acceptance of shares.

Let the cost of bidding be $c^{\mathrm{B}} > 0$. For brevity and clarity of notation, let it be assumed that shareholders tender all or none of their shares; the result does not depend on this assumption.

Definition. A shareholder is *pivotal* if, given the actions of the other shareholders, her decision of whether to tender determines whether the bidder obtains control.

The word 'pivotal' might seem to suggest that there is always exactly one pivotal shareholder. This is far from the case. For example, if there are three identical shareholders, and if all (or if none) tender, then none of them are pivotal. If one or two tender, then two are pivotal. One might expect that in a very widely held firm with small shareholders, shareholders will be very unlikely to be pivotal because it is unlikely that the number of shares tendered will be close to the borderline. The following result, which is in the spirit of Grossman & Hart [1980], shows that such a situation leads to zero gross profits for a takeover bidder. Net of bidding costs, the bidder's profit becomes negative, so no offer occurs.

Proposition 7. *Holding constant the value improvement v but allowing the distribution of target share ownership to vary, as the probability of any shareholder being pivotal approaches zero the bidder's expected gross profit becomes arbitrarily close to zero.*

Proof. See Appendix

The conclusion of this proposition is not at all surprising given the critical premise that the probability of a shareholder being pivotal is small. This assumption is not valid in all models, as discussed in Section 3.2. If an individual shareholder's decision can cause an offer to succeed when otherwise it will fail or *vice versa*, i.e., if he may be pivotal, then he should tender if the price offered exceeds the expected value of her shares *given that she does not tender*. This latter quantity may be below the expected value given that she does tender. This wedge allows the bidder to make a profit on purchased shares.

3.2. When are shareholders pivotal?

This section discusses the conditions under which pivotality can be important. Section 3.2.1 points out that large shareholdings lead to pivotality. Sections 3.2.2 and 3.2.3 discuss equilibria in which pivotality is important even in widely held firms. Section 3.2.4 examines the effect on bidder profits of the ability to bid repeatedly. In Section 3.2.5, I argue that pivotality in widely held firms may not provide a plausible solution to the free-rider problem.

3.2.1. Block size

The larger the blocks held by target shareholders, the larger the probability of being pivotal, and so the greater the incentive to tender. Since in reality there are large blockholders even in many large firms, this is an important escape from the free-rider problem.[21]

Holmstrom & Nalebuff [1992] point out that the increased probability of offer success resulting from the tender of one share by a blockholder increases the expected value of retaining her other shares. A large blockholder therefore has a greater incentive to tender some of her shares than a small one, leading to an equilibrium that gets close to equalizing the number of nontendered shares by larger stockholders. By tendering only a fraction of her shares, a blockholder partly internalizes the benefit accruing to nontendering shareholders.

3.2.2. *Pure strategy equilibria with pivotal shareholders*

Under complete information, in either a conditional or an unconditional tender offer, there are many equilibria in which just enough shares are tendered to cause a transfer of control. Consider a conditional tender offer for 20,000 shares in a takeover that will increase value. Consider a set of shareholders whose shares total to exactly 20,000. An equilibrium is for these shareholders to tender all their shares, and for the others to retain their shares. In the equilibrium, If any shareholder were to tender one less share, the offer would fail, reducing the value of her nontendered shares. Thus, a bidder can succeed with a very small premium [Bagnoli & Lipman, 1988], apparently solving the free-rider problem.

Proposition 8. *Under complete information, and in the absence of management defensive measures, in both an unconditional tender offer and a conditional offer for the minimum number of shares required to shift control, there exist strong Nash equilibria in which the bidder offers just above zero and receives exactly enough shares to transfer control. Therefore the bidder can effect any desirable change in the target even if he owns no shares in the target and cannot dilute.*

3.2.3. *Mixed strategy equilibria with pivotal shareholders*

There are also many mixed strategy equilibria in which shareholders are sometimes pivotal. Continuing the assumption of complete information, let us focus on any-or-all offers. Intuitively, if other shareholders tender with high probability, then the offer is likely to succeed, in which case a given shareholder would do better to retain her shares; while if other shareholders tender with low probability, then the offer is likely to fail, in which case a given shareholder does better by tendering. Thus, there is a stable outcome in which shareholders tender with intermediate probability (see Bagnoli & Lipman, 1988; Holmstrom & Nalebuff, 1992].[22]

[21] This is related to the general principle, important in the theory of political pressure groups, that the small free-ride on the large [see Olson, 1965].

[22] Intuitively, if an individual shareholder does not know the precise liquidity or capital gains situation of other shareholders, from her point of view their behavior is random. The logic described in the text causes shareholders to be near indifference, so that small uncertainties about payoffs lead to substantial uncertainty about behavior.

To develop this point, I follow the presentation of Holmstrom & Nalebuff [1992]. Consider a firm with N risk neutral shareholders each of whom owns a single share. Suppose that the bidder needs exactly K shares to obtain control. It is informative to focus on the symmetric equilibrium in which shareholders randomize with identical probabilities. Let the improved value of the target be $v = 1$. Shareholder i's tendering decision will be based on a comparison of the certainty of receiving the per-share offer price b/N versus a probability $P(b \mid i \text{ does not tender})$ of the per-share improved value of the firm $1/N$. She will be indifferent if

$$b = P(b \mid i \text{ does not tender}). \tag{10}$$

Let $p(b)$ be the probability that a single shareholder tenders, and let $P(b)$ be the probability that the offer succeeds given equilibrium behavior by all shareholders. Then the bidder's expected surplus is the difference between the total expected surplus, $P(b)$, and the expected surplus going to shareholders, b. Thus, the bidder's expected surplus is

$$P(b) - b = P(b) - P(b \mid i \text{ does not tender}). \tag{11}$$

On the RHS, $P(b)$ is the probability that at least K shareholders tender, and $P(b \mid i \text{ does not tender})$ is the probability that at least K shareholders other than i tender. The difference is therefore the probability that the other shareholders tender exactly $K - 1$ shares, and shareholder i also tenders, i.e.,

$$_{N-1}C_{K-1}\ p(b)^K[1 - p(b)]^{N-K}, \tag{12}$$

where $_{N-1}C_{K-1}$ is the number of combinations by which $K - 1$ tendering shareholders other than shareholder i can be selected from the $N - 1$ possible shareholders. Maximizing this quantity over p (which the bidder controls through b) gives the following proposition.

Proposition 9. *In the symmetric equilibrium of the any-or-all tender offer game of this section, the tendering probability is $p^* = K/N$, and the bidder's expected profit is positive. This profit approaches zero,* ceteris paribus, *as the number of shareholders N becomes large.*

By making the expected number of shares tendered equal to the number of shares needed for success, the bidder maximizes the probability that a given shareholder will be pivotal. The proposition's last statement is shown in Bagnoli & Lipman [1988].

Holmstrom and Nalebuff examine a more general setting in which shareholders hold any number of shares. They find an equilibrium in which all sufficiently large shareholders tender down to a common range of either m or $m + 1$ shares. Large shareholders randomize between these two possibilities, the offer sometimes succeeds and sometimes fails, and the bidder makes a positive gross profit. Those with less than m shares do not tender. Since each large shareholder randomizes over just a single share, if the number of outstanding shares is large compared to the number of shareholders, the fraction of the firm tendered is always very close to the minimum needed to shift control.

If the number of shares is increased through stock splits, in the limit, even if the firm is widely held, the takeover almost surely succeeds, and the bidder's gross profit approaches fraction f of the takeover improvement, where f is the fraction of the shares needed to obtain control.[23] This equilibrium becomes very similar to the pure strategy equilibria of Section 3.2.2, in which just enough shares are tendered to ensure success and make shareholders pivotal. Here, the probability of failure must approach zero, because in equilibrium each shareholder can ensure success at low cost by tendering a vanishingly small additional fraction of her shares. Thus, they are always pivotal.

An implication of the Holmstrom–Nalebuff analysis is that if each shareholder holds a single share, then a supermajority antitakeover amendment, which increase the number of shares needed for control, increases the probability of offer success by increasing the probability that shareholders will be pivotal. The reason for this is that the probability that a shareholder is pivotal decreases with the variance in the total number of shares tendered. A supermajority rule corresponds to a higher probability of tendering in the mixed strategy equilibrium, which (with a tendering probability of greater than 1/2) corresponds to a lower variance.[24]

3.2.4. *The effects of offer revision with pivotal shareholders*

The ability of a bidder to make repeated offers for a given target may be very important for the strategic structure of the takeover auction (see, e.g., the discussion at the end of Section 3.1.2.2). The option to bid a second time after failing to obtain control in an initial bid must benefit the bidder ex post, because he may obtain control on his second try. However, the possibility of a later offer reduces a shareholder's incentive to tender initially. The balance between these effects is not obvious. Harrington & Prokop [1993] find that with discounting, as the time between offers approaches zero, the expected gross profit to a tender offer bidder approaches zero. Their numerical simulations based on reasonable parameter values imply that bidders can obtain less than 1% of the takeover surplus.

3.2.5. *Plausibility of equilibria with pivotal shareholders*

The equilibria described in Sections 3.2.3 and 3.2.4, in which bidders profit on shares purchased because shareholders are often pivotal, are based on delicate coordination amongst shareholders. Realistically, in a firm with many small share-

[23] In a widely held firm, notwithstanding the fact that shareholders retain some of their shares, each internalizes only a small fraction of total value improvement arising from takeover. This is offset by the fact that there are many such shareholders, and each has a significant chance of being pivotal.

[24] Empiricists should note that this implication is the opposite of that of Hirshleifer & Titman [1990] discussed in Section 3.1.2, in which supermajority amendments reduce the probability of offer success by reducing the incentive to bid high (see footnote 15).

holders, it seems unlikely that shareholders perceive themselves to have a significant chance of being pivotal. Why don't the models match the *a priori* intuition?

In general, in games with many players, a plausible equilibrium (I contend) should be robust with respect to 'misbehavior' by a small (though not necessarily infinitesimal) fraction of individuals. Consider a widely held firm of N shareholders, and suppose that h of the shareholders will not tender their shares in the relevant range of offer prices, where h is a discrete random variable, $0 \leq h \leq H$, and H/N is 'small', but not infinitesimal (say $1/50$).[25]

I make the quantitative conjecture that under mild conditions on the distribution of h, there will be no equilibrium in which shareholders have a significant chance of being pivotal. The reason is that, not knowing h, strategic shareholders have no way of knowing how many shares they must jointly tender in order to make the offer succeed. Suppose shareholdings are identical, for example, with $H = 100$, and $N = 5,000$. Substantial exogenous uncertainty about the characteristics of even 100 shareholders would seem to make it exceedingly unlikely that the decision of a single shareholder will determine success or failure.

In experiments in which shareholders can tender all or none of their shares, Kale & Noe [1991] provide evidence that is only partly consistent with the argument provided here. They found that the probability of success in conditional tender offers to 41 shareholders was at some prices substantially below that predicted by a mixed strategy equilibrium with pivotal shareholders. However, the probability of success in any-or-all offers to 32 shareholders was greater than the equilibrium prediction.

4. Competitive bidding

Most models of the free-rider problem assume only one bidder for a given target. The models of competing bids discussed here generally makes the assumption that the target will always accept the highest offer made by any bidder, so long as it is above some minimum reservation price.

The analysis in this section should thus be viewed as referring to merger bids, or else to tender offers in which the threat of dilution limits free-riding. We focus on models of competitive bidding in which bidders have differing private valuations of a target, and examine the effects of investigation costs and bidding costs on auction outcomes.

Perhaps the simplest model of takeover bidding is the standard analysis of English auctions. In this model, bidders *costlessly* make offers and counteroffers, each bid incrementally higher than the previous one, until the bidder with highest valuation wins at a price equal to the valuation of the second highest bidder. I will call this outcome the *ratchet solution*.

[25] This 'misbehavior' could be rational, if their are costs of tendering such as locked in capital gains of size known only to the individual. The upper bound H could be quite low, e.g., $1/50$ of outstanding shares, but the argument may fail if probability bunches too close to zero. Thus, the plausibility concept suggested here differs in this respect from Selten's trembling hand equilibrium.

In the conventional English auction analysis, rather than paying a substantial initial premium, an initial bidder should bid the minimum reservation price, and increase the offer only if a competitor actually arrives. Suppose that the first bidder (*FB*) has a known valuation of $v_1 = \$80$, and a potential competing bidder (*SB*) has a valuation of $v_2 = \$0$, \$30 or \$100 with equal probability. Normalize the reservation price of the target to zero. Then *FB* will begin with a bid of zero. If $v_2 = 0$, *FB* buys the target at this price. If $v_2 = \$30$, *FB* still wins, but the price is driven up to \$30. If $v_2 = \$100$, then *SB* buys the target at a price of \$80. Competition in the bidding process not only helps target shareholders, it increases total surplus, because of the possible realization of a larger improvement (\$100).

The ratchet solution illustrates the potential gain to the target and society of competition. It is, however, not descriptive of actual takeover contests, in which initial bids are typically made at a substantial premium to the market price (see the empirical synopsis), and each successive bid typically involves a significant increase over the previous outstanding bid.

4.1. *Costly investigation and preemptive takeover bidding*

A possible explanation for a high initial bid in a takeover contest derives from the fact that takeover benefits are partly specific to the acquirer (e.g., complementarities), but partly common (e.g., gains derived from replacing inefficient target management). Owing to correlated valuations, an initial bid will alert potential competitors to the potential desirability of the target.[26] This suggests that in planning its initial offer, an initial bidder will consider the incentives created for potential competitors.

Specifically, such a bidder may wish to offer a substantial premium on his initial bid in order to deter potential competitors [Fishman, 1988; Png, 1985]. In Fishman's model, an initial bid alerts a second potential bidder to a state of the world in which the target is potentially profitable. However, the model assumes that conditional upon this state of the world, the valuations of the first and second bidder are independent. *FB* and *SB* can acquire information about the target at a cost of c^{I}. By investigating, a bidder learns his private valuation of the target.[27] If both bidders enter, it is assumed that a costless English auction ensues, so that the target is sold to the highest valuation bidder at a price equal to the valuation of the second highest bidder, $min(v_1, v_2)$ (i.e., the ratchet solution).

In the unique equilibrium in this game (applying the equilibrium concept of Grossman & Perry [1986]), the bidder offers the minimum reservation price for the target if his valuation is below a critical threshold level v^*. In this event *SB* investigates, and the target is sold in a costless English auction. If $v > v^*$, *FB* makes a high bid b^{D} that deters *SB* from investigating. The initial bid is therefore a coarse signal of the first bidder's valuation.

[26] See, e.g., Grossman & Hart [1981].

[27] Low valuations are assumed to be so likely that it does not pay to bid without investigating.

Suppose that the valuations of *FB* and *SB* are independent and uniform on the unit interval [0, 1]. I assume directly that *SB* only arrives if *FB* bids. *FB*'s payoff after a bid of b_1 is $v_1 - b_1$ if *SB* does not investigate. If *SB* does investigate, *FB* makes:

$$\begin{aligned} &v_1 - b_1 && \text{if } v_2 \le b_1, \\ &v_1 - v_2 && \text{if } b_1 < v_2 \le v_1, \\ &0 && \text{if } v_2 > v_1. \end{aligned} \tag{13}$$

SB's payoffs are zero unless he investigates. If he does, he makes:

$$\begin{aligned} &-c_2^{\mathrm{I}} && \text{if } v_2 \le v_1, \\ &v_2 - v_1 - c_2^{\mathrm{I}} && \text{if } v_2 > v_1. \end{aligned} \tag{14}$$

SB as well as *FB* follows threshold behavior. If *FB* bids $b_1 < b_1^{\mathrm{D}}$, *SB* infers that $v_1 < v^*$, so *SB* investigates and a costless English auction ensues. If *FB* bids $b_1 \ge b_1^{\mathrm{D}}$, *SB* infers that $v_1 \ge v^*$, so *SB* quits.

To understand the equilibrium, first note that if *FB* offers less than b_1^{D}, he should bid zero, because *SB* will investigate and bid up to v_2 in any case. There is no gain to *FB* from bidding $b_1 > b_1^{\mathrm{D}}$, because he can already win with certainty at b_1^{D}. The gain to *FB* of bidding b_1^{D} instead of 0 is increasing in v_1, because his cost of bidding zero is greater when his valuation is higher. This is because *FB* with a larger v_1 values certainty of victory more highly, and because paying v_2 to beat the competitor whenever $v_2 < v_1$ has a greater expected cost when v_1 is higher.

The high deterring bid does *not* deter *SB* through the direct means of forcing him to pay at least b_1^{D}. Since $b_1^{\mathrm{D}} < v_1$, *SB* knows that if he investigates he must pay *more* than b_1^{D} to win. Rather, high b_1 *signals* to *SB* that $v_1 > v_1^*$, which makes *SB* pessimistic about his potential profit. Thus, it is reasonable for *SB* to follow a threshold rule in which he investigates if and only if the initial bid is below a critical value.

Specifically, *SB* is deterred if his expected profit from investigating is zero or negative, i.e.,

$$E\left[\Pi_2(v_1, v_2) \mid v_1 > v_1^*\right] \le 0, \tag{15}$$

where Π_2 is *SB*'s profit as a function of the two valuations, and where *SB* believes that *FB* has valuation of at least v_1^*. *SB*'s profit does not depend directly on b^*, the level of the initial bid, only on the minimum valuation v_1^* communicated by the offer. Direct substitution from (14) and differentiation with respect to v_1^* shows that the LHS of this inequality is decreasing with v_1^*, because higher v_1^* makes *SB* more likely to lose and makes him on average pay more when he wins. This monotonicity leads to the threshold rule for *SB*.

To make expectations and actions consistent, the deterring bid b_1^D is set as a function of v_1^*, $b_1^D(v_1^*)$, defined as the maximum amount that *FB* with $v_1 = v_1^*$ would be willing to bid in order to preempt competition. This just prevents mimicry by any *FB* with $v_1 < v_1^*$.

There are multiple equilibria of this type, based on a value of v_1^* and the implied deterring bid value b_1^d. The lowest possible value of v_1^* consistent with this equilibrium sets (15) to zero so that *SB* is *just* deterred.[28]

To calculate v_1^*, set (15) to zero. Under the uniform assumption, this yields

$$c^{\mathrm{I}} = \int_{v_1^*}^{1} \int_{v_1}^{1} \left(\frac{v_2 - v_1}{1 - v_1^*} \right) \mathrm{d}v_2 \, \mathrm{d}v_1, \tag{16}$$

so

$$v_1^* = 1 - \sqrt{6c^{\mathrm{I}}}. \tag{17}$$

The deterring bid b_1^{D} makes *FB* with $v_1 = v_1^*$ indifferent between bidding to deter or to accommodate investigation. If he bids to deter, he gets

$$1 - \sqrt{6c^{\mathrm{I}}} - b_1^{\mathrm{D}}. \tag{18}$$

If he bids 0, he receives $v_1^* - v_2$ if $v_1^* > v_2$, and zero otherwise, for an expected gain of

$$\int_{0}^{v_1^*} (v_1^* - v_2) f(v_2) \, \mathrm{d}v_2 = \tfrac{1}{2}(v_1^*)^2. \tag{19}$$

Equating and solving for b_1^{D} gives

$$b_1^{\mathrm{D}} = \tfrac{1}{2} - 3c^{\mathrm{I}}. \tag{20}$$

The model has the following properties.

Proposition 10. *In the Fishman model, SB investigates only after a low-premium bid, not after a high bid. The level of the bid needed to deter competition is decreasing with the investigation cost* c^{I}. *The expected profit of FB is increasing and SB decreasing with* c^{I}.

The expected profit of *FB* is increasing and *SB* decreasing with c^{I}, because it is more expensive for *SB* to compete and thus cheaper for *FB* to preempt competition.

As discussed in Spatt [1989], the Fishman model has the excessively strong implication that an initial bid at a premium will always deter competition. Fishman suggests that if *SB* has private information about his investigation costs or valuation, then attempts to deter will sometimes fail (as analyzed by Bhattacharyya [1992]).

[28] Note that if *FB* is going to bid, he would prefer to pay the low $b_1^{\mathrm{D}}(v_1^*)$ rather than some higher amount. This equilibrium is the sole one consistent with the 'credibility' criterion of Grossman & Perry [1986].

Evidence consistent with the implication that a second bidder is less likely to compete after a high-premium bid than a low one has been provided by Jennings & Mazzeo [1993]. A further implication of the model is that a reduction in *SB*'s cost of investigation leads to a higher expected price of the target. This results from two reinforcing effects. First, if the investigation cost is low, then higher value must be signalled to deter competition, and hence a higher preemptive bid b^{D} is needed by (20). Thus the bid is higher in single-bidder contests. Furthermore, since deterring competition is more costly, *FB* makes the deterring bid over a smaller range of valuations, so that the higher expected price associated with competition is more often realized.

Lower investigation cost also increases efficiency. The social cost of competition comes from *SB*'s investigation cost c^{I}. The social benefit from competition is $max(0, v_2 - v_1)$, derived from the possible realization of a higher valuation than that of *FB*'s. Since in the ratchet solution a victorious *SB* profits by difference between his valuation and *FB*'s *SB*'s decision of whether to investigate is socially as well as privately optimal. Therefore, taking the occurrence of the initial bid as given, lower investigation cost improves efficiency by permitting realization of higher valuations. However, there is a crucial countervailing effect on the incentive of *FB* to investigate in the first place. A greater threat of competition can lead to too little initial investigation, and the loss of takeover gains.

Proposition 11. *Taking FB's investigation as given, a reduction in SB's cost of investigation* c^{I} *leads to a higher expected price of the target and greater social efficiency.*

4.2. Costly bidding

Fishman's and Bhattacharyya's models show that predictions that are more realistic than those derived from the costless English auction model can be derived when there are investigation costs associated with an initial offer. However, both authors assume that once both bidders have investigated, the game reverts to a costless English auction and the ratchet solution ensues. Several more recent papers extending the Fishman model for different purposes have made a similar assumption.

The ratchet solution may at first seem appealing in post-entry subgames, because of its tractability and because the costs of revising a bid upward are likely to be smaller than the setup and investigation costs needed for an initial offer. However, the conventional English auction analysis is extremely sensitive to small costs of bidding [Hirshleifer & Png, 1990]. To see this, suppose that *FB*'s valuation is known to be \$80, and *SB*'s is known to be \$30. In the ratchet solution, *SB* has nothing to lose by bidding up to \$30, which becomes the price paid by *FB*. Suppose now that there is a cost of bidding and of revising a bid of $c^{B} = \$.01$. Then the target will be sold at a price of *zero*, because *SB* quits rather than wasting bid costs in a contest he must lose. Thus, even an extremely low bid cost drastically reduces the price paid for the target.

A possible justification for the ratchet solution is imperfect information. If *SB* does not know whether *FB*'s valuation is higher or lower, then he should be willing to incur some bid cost to preserve his chance of winning. There are two important limitations to this argument.

First, *FB*'s offer may signal his valuation. If so, a *SB* who knows his own valuation can make a well-informed decision as to whether to bid again or to quit immediately [see Daniel & Hirshleifer, 1993].[29]

Second, there are costs associated with revising an offer that may be far from trivial. First is the extension of the period during which managers must devote time to the takeover contest. Second are possible costs of obtaining further financing. Third, if takeovers will be associated with restructuring of the bidder and target, then real investment and operating decisions of the bidder may continue to be influenced by uncertainty over whether merger will occur. Fourth, some mandated filings may have to be repeated.[30]

By changing auction strategies, bidding costs can crucially affect the implications of takeovers models (see, e.g., the discussion of target defensive strategies in Section 4.3). When bid revision costs are added to Fishman's preemptive bidding model, it is still the case that *FB* can preempt competition through a high initial bid. However, Hirshleifer & Png [1990] show that a reduction in the cost of investigation c^{I} can *reduce* both the expected price paid for the target and efficiency. With regard to price, the difference arises from the much lower gains to the target when a second bidder investigates. Instead of a price of $\min(v_1, v_2)$, the premium may go up by little. Because of this, even though lower c^{I} raises the price that must be offered when *FB* deters investigation, the greater frequency of low offers that do not deter competition can lead to a lower target price on average. The welfare advantage of greater competition is also ambiguous since, with costly bidding, *SB* may sometimes succeed even if his valuation is below that of *FB*.

The Williams Act of 1968 and associated legislation discussed in the empirical synopsis has been widely viewed as reducing the cost to competitors of investigating after an initial bid [see, e.g., Jarrell & Bradley, 1980]. Evidence discussed earlier that average tender offer premia decreased after passage of the Williams Act is consistent with the costly-bidding analysis.[31]

An unrealistic implication of the assumption of costless bid revisions is that after a single initial jump, offers increase by infinitesimal increments. Daniel & Hirshleifer [1993] examine a model of costly sequential bidding in which the offered price jumps on each successive bid. In this model, since the initial bid signals *FB*'s valuation, *SB* either quits (if his valuation is below some critical value

[29] Note that even if the bid cost is small, more than a small amount of residual uncertainty about *FB*'s valuation may be required to induce *SB* to bid, because *FB*'s valuation must be sufficiently variable that it may be below *SB*'s valuation.

[30] Investigation as well as pure bid costs may be positive even after the initial bid, since more investigation may be required to justify the risk of a higher offer.

[31] Even in the costless bid revision model, a decrease in average premia could be predicted since initial bids will be observed from a lower valuation pool of bidders.

determined by *FB*'s signalled valuation), or else jumps to a bid high enough to induce *FB* to withdraw. Since *FB*'s offer reveals his valuation, any less conclusive response by *SB* would be wasteful of bidding costs without any corresponding gain. Daniel and Hirshleifer argue that the only plausible equilibrium in a sequential bidding model with bid costs has bids revealing valuation and substantial bid increments until the auction ends.

To understand why, consider the Fishman model with the investigation cost c^{I} replaced with a cost of bidding c^{B} that is incurred by a bidder *each time he bids*. This is a pure transaction cost (such as those described a few paragraphs earlier); paying c_B does not directly yield any information about valuations. It is simplest to analyze a limiting case of the Daniel–Hirshleifer model in which the bid cost is very close to zero. As the numerical example at the start of Section 4 suggests, the outcome will be very different from the conventional ratchet solution outcome with costless bidding.[32] Let $b_1(v_1)$ denote *FB*'s equilibrium bid as a function of his valuation. If this schedule is strictly monotonic, then the inverse function $\hat{v}_1 = \hat{v}(b_1) \equiv b_1^{-1}(v_1)$ is single-valued. This function is the inference schedule for *FB*, that is the valuation signalled by a bid of b_1.

Figure 2 illustrates the equilibrium geometrically when both bidders' valuations are drawn from a uniform distribution on [0, 1]. The horizontal axis represents *FB*'s valuation v_1 and his bid b_1. The vertical axis represents the inferred valuation of *FB*, $\hat{v}\,(b_1)$. In this example the inference schedule is a straight line. In equilibrium *SB* quits if $v_2 < \hat{v}_1$, so *FB*'s probability of winning with his first bid is $\Pr\,(v_2 < \hat{v}_1) = \hat{v}_1$. The bold line is the inference schedule. Inscribed in the large triangle is a rectangle with width $v_1 - b_1$, *FB*'s gain if he wins, and height $\hat{v}\,(b_1)$, *FB*'s probability of winning with his first bid. Suppose (as will be verified later) that in equilibrium *FB* will make only a single bid. Then the area of the inscribed rectangle is *FB*'s expected profit, and *FB*'s maximization problem is to set b_1 so as to maximize the area of this rectangle. Thus *FB* solves

$$\max_{b_1}\,(v_1 - b_1)\hat{v}(b_1) = \max_{\hat{v}_1}\,[v_1 - b_1(\hat{v}_1)]\hat{v}_1.$$

This problem is identical to that solved by a bidder in a first price symmetric sealed bid auction [see, e.g. Riley & Samuelson, 1981]. Differentiating with respect to $\hat{v}_1$ gives the first order condition of the latter problem. In equilibrium $\hat{v}_1 = v_1$, which gives the differential equation

$$v_1 b_1'(v_1) + b_1(v_1) - v_1 = 0, \tag{21}$$

with the initial condition that a low valuation leads to a low bid, i.e., $\lim_{v_1 \to 0} b_1\,(v_1) = 0$. The solution is $b_1(v_1) = v_1/2$, so the inference schedule is $\hat{v}(b_1) = 2b_1$, the straight line in Figure 2.

[32] Daniel & Hirshleifer describe a hitherto unrecognized weak signalling equilibrium of a costless English auction game ($c^{\mathrm{B}} = 0$). However, this is best viewed as a limit of strong equilibria as $c^{\mathrm{B}} \to 0$. Suppose (as will be shown) that the initial bid signals the true valuation v_1. If there is a positive bidding cost, however small, then after v_1 is revealed, *SB* with $v_2 < v_1$ strongly prefers to quit. Hence, bidding ends at a price below $\min(v_1, v_2)$, the price under the ratchet solution.

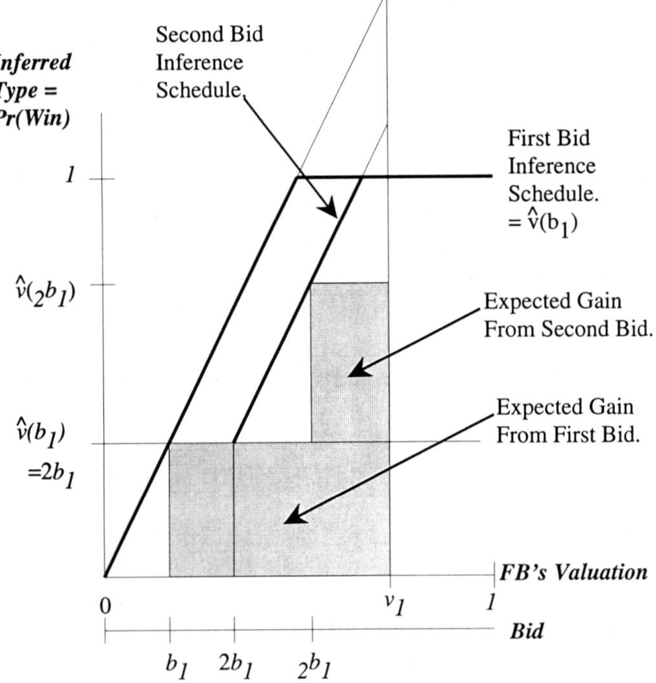

Fig. 2. Geometric interpretation of the signalling equilibrium.

Interestingly, the bid is equal to the expected price paid by *FB* conditional on his winning in the ratchet solution,

$$E\left[\tilde{v}_2 \mid \tilde{v}_2 < v_1\right] = \frac{v_1}{2}. \tag{22}$$

Thus, *FB*'s expected profit as a function of his valuation,

$$\left(v_1 - \frac{v_1}{2}\right) \Pr\left(\tilde{v}_2 < v_1\right) = \frac{(v_1)^2}{2}, \tag{23}$$

is the same as in the ratchet solution.[33]

In response to the initial bid, *SB* withdraws if $v_2 \leq \hat{v}_1$, and wins with a bid of $b_2 = \hat{v}_1$ if $v_2 > \hat{v}_1$. *SB* does not bid less than $\hat{v}_1$ because in this equilibrium *FB* always infers skeptically that *SB*'s bid is virtually as high as *SB*'s valuation.[34] Thus

[33] *FB*'s bidding schedule in (22) depends not on the distribution of his own valuation, but on the distribution of his *opponent's* valuation. This is because the differential equation (21) derives from *FB*'s choice problem, which weighs the extent to which raising his bid will reduce the probability that his opponent's valuation will lead to a competing bid.

[34] *FB* would top any bid below $\hat{v}_1$ in order to force out *SB*. Thus, *SB* will never bid below $\hat{v}(b_1)$. There are other equilibria in which *FB* is less skeptical about *SB*'s valuation; these are broadly similar to the equilibrium discussed here.

SB's expected price paid and expected profit as a function of this valuation are respectively as given in (22) and (23) with subscripts 1 and 2 reversed.

Before analyzing *FB*'s possible defections in more detail, it is useful to summarize some implications.

Proposition 12. *If two risk neutral bidders have valuations that are uniformly distributed on the interval* $[0, 1]$ *and the bid cost* $c^B = 0$*, then there exists a weak equilibrium in which the FB offers half his valuation as his initial offer. This offer is the same as FB's expected payment, given that he wins, in the ratchet solution. SB, if he wins, pays FB's valuation, the same amount as in a ratchet solution.*

In this special case of zero bid costs, the first bidder's bid schedule is the same as that in a conventional first price sealed bid auction, and the bid schedule in Bhattacharyya [1992] (as the one-shot entry fee approaches zero). The *realized* price in the sealed first price auction differs, since the winning bid in this auction essentially never matches the ratchet solution outcome.

To see that this is an equilibrium when *FB* can bid repeatedly, note first that *FB* would never bid higher than the proposed bidding schedule because, if he did, and *SB* followed with his equilibrium response $b_2 = \hat{v}_1 > v_1$, *FB* would quit. As was already shown, if *FB* plans to bid at most once, he will bid on the proposed schedule.

So consider instead a defection by *FB* of initially bidding low ($b_1 < v_1/2$), and if *SB* responds with a higher bid, bidding a second time to signal his true valuation v_1. The initial offer signals his type to be $v(b_1) < v_1$. SB's equilibrium response to the initial offer is either to withdraw or else to win with a bid of $v(b_1)$. If *SB* bids, and *FB* responds, then SB's bidding decision will depend on his inference after observing this off-equilibrium occurrence. Let us assume that *SB* interprets *FB*'s second bid as a new and (this time) truthful separating bid.[35] *FB*'s two-bid maximization problem is illustrated in Figure 2. *FB* expected profit derived from states of the world in which *SB* quits immediately after the initial bid is $2b_1\,(v_1 - b_1)$, the large lower rectangle. *SB*'s equilibrium responses are either to quit or to bid *FB*'s signalled valuation of $v(b_1) = 2b_1$. If *SB* bids, *FB* infers that *SB*'s type is distributed uniformly on $[2b_1, 1]$. Analogous to the equilibrium schedule on the first bid, to signal his type as v_1, *FB* must bid $b_1' = (v_1 + 2b_1)/2$. *FB*'s expected profit derived from states of the world in which he makes a second bid is therefore $(v_1 - 2b_1)^2/2$, the smaller upper rectangle. Thus the *total* expected profit from both bids, the sum of the rectangular areas, is $v_1^2/2$, which is *independent of the amount bid*, and the same as if *FB* did not defect. This confirms the proposed (weak) equilibrium.

By defecting to a low-bid strategy, *FB* pays less than with the truth-revealing strategy if *SB* quits. However, he pays considerably more if he wins on a second

[35] This is a conservative assumption. If, once convinced by the first signal that $v_1 = \hat{v}_1$, *SB* would never change his mind, he would be less willing to withdraw, making *FB*'s defection even less profitable.

bid, so his expected profit is no higher with the low-bid strategy than with the truth-revealing strategy. As Daniel & Hirshleifer show, with a strictly positive bidding cost, his profit from the low-bid defection is *strictly* lower.[36]

Proposition 12 implies that the signalling equilibrium leads to a surprising identity of expected payoffs between the bidders, and with other auction mechanisms.

Proposition 13. *Both unconditionally and conditional on his own valuation, each bidder is indifferent between the signalling equilibrium and the ratchet solution. If target shareholders are risk neutral, then they are also indifferent. The two bidders earn the same expected profits, so who moves first is a matter of indifference.*

Thus, the revenue equivalence of optimal auctions [see Myerson, 1981; Riley & Samuelson, 1981] extends to the sequential bidding game (when bid costs approach zero). Since the ratchet solution provides the bidders and stockholders with the same expected revenue as a sealed bid first or second price auction, the signalling equilibrium described here provides the same expected revenues as well.[37]

When a specific level of the bid cost is considered (instead of the limit approaching zero), the Daniel–Hirshleifer model implies that a bidder with low valuation may wait one or several rounds before bidding. Suppose the game continues until one player makes a positive offer and the other player quits. If neither bidder makes an offer in the first round, *FB* gets another chance to bid in the second round. In this setting, a low valuation bidder will wait rather than bid. To illustrate, consider the uniform example with a bid cost of 0.01. A bidder with valuation of 0.1 has a 0.1 probability of winning. If he bids zero and wins, his gross profit is 0.1, so his expected gross profit is $0.1 \cdot 0.1 = 0.01$, leaving him zero net profits. By waiting, he can obtain positive expected profits, so no type with $v_1 \leq 0.1$ will bid in the first round. If *SB* similarly passes, *FB* learns that *SB* valuation is low, which raises *FB*'s chance of winning. At this point *FB* may submit a bid. Each further round of waiting reveals lower valuations, increasing the incentive to bid. Eventually any bidder whose valuation exceeds the bid cost c^B will submit a bid, but he may need to wait many rounds before doing so.

Prices jump either once or twice in the version of the Daniel–Hirshleifer model discussed here. They also suggest when there will be a greater number of bids. First, further information disclosed during the contest can alter bidder valuations. Second, the target may undertake defensive measures that shift bidders' valuations (see Sections 3.1.3.2 and 4.3). Third, when there are n bidders, the price jumps up to n times, as each of the first $n - 1$ bidders either signals his type or quits.

[36] *FB* could also contemplate a low bid followed by a contingency plan involving several possible further bids. It can be shown by similar reasoning that such defections are not profitable.

[37] Although the bidding process and strategic reasoning is different, the final outcome with arbitrarily small bid costs in every round is identical to a game with only a small entry fee (followed by the ratchet solution if *SB* enters). However, if there is a significant investigation cost or entry fee, the first bid will not fully reveal the bidder's valuation [Fishman, 1988; Bhattacharyya, 1992]. In such settings, the introduction of small bid costs in later rounds drastically affects final outcomes as well as the bid process.

Their signalling equilibrium suggests that bidders will make substantial bid jumps in order to drive out unmotivated competitors not just initially (as in Fishman & Bhattacharyya), but at every stage of a sequential auction. However, the existence of a signalling equilibrium does not rule out alternative equilibria in which pools of bidder types are gradually revealed through small bid increments. Daniel & Hirshleifer argue that reasonable equilibria in costly sequential bidding games have the property that bidders bid in substantial increments in order to signal in the minimum number of moves enough information to determine the contest winner. In this view, the outcomes of sequential bidding games with even modest bid costs will not resemble the conventional ratchet solution to the English auction.

The intuition is roughly as follows. If in equilibrium pooling disappears with certainty within a given number of rounds of bidding, then a backwards recursion argument indicates that it pays to bid to win earlier rather than risk incurring extra bid costs. Suppose instead the equilibrium calls for 'dueling pools' that potentially last any number of rounds, gradually shrinking as offers grow. Then a bidder whose valuation is near the top of a pooling interval foresees a chance that, after his current bid, he will need to bid again. To avoid the extra bid cost, he will defect to a higher bid in the current round. If a high valuation bidder has a stronger incentive to signal in this fashion than a low valuation bidder, this defection can credibly deter the competitor. Profitable defection unravels the dueling pools from the top.

4.3. Managerial defensive measures and bidder elimination

In Subsection 3.1.3, management defensive measures were analyzed in single-bidder contests. In multiple-bidder contests, the possibility exists of using defensive measures as means of discriminating among bidders. The extreme case of discrimination between bidders is to take an action that eliminates one bidder but not others. Shleifer & Vishny [1986b] show that it is possible for a target firm to profit from payment of greenmail to a bidder, in order to signal to other potential bidders that the target does not have a hidden 'white knight' bidder ready to top all offers.[38] This encourages investigation by other bidders. Since the fact that the target does not have a hidden white knight can be bad news for shareholders, the stock price reaction to greenmail can be negative (consistent with evidence cited earlier) even if it benefits target shareholders.[39]

Spatt [1989] describes and generalizes an example due to Sudipto Bhattacharya in which several potential bidders decide simultaneously whether to pay an entry fee in order to participate in bidding. Spatt concludes that even under full

[38] Greenmail is the repurchase at a premium of the shareholdings of a potential takeover bidder, often combined with a standstill agreement that prevents the bidder from further purchases of target shares.

[39] This last implication is shared by the model of Giammarino & Heinkel [1990], which is based on greenmail signalling that the target has greater value under current management than if investment levels are cut by an acquirer.

information the elimination of some members of a group of potential bidders can increase the expected profit of the target when an increase in the entry fee does not. The example assumes the conventional ratchet solution among those bidders that enter.

In summary, several models have demonstrated the theoretical possibility that the elimination of potential bidders can sometimes improve efficiency and help target shareholders. But since the conditions needed for elimination to be in shareholders' interests seem to be restrictive, it would be desirable to develop empirical tests to distinguish these models from the common view that greenmail promotes undesirable entrenchment of target management.

As these models show, even a defensive strategy that is good for target shareholders can reveal bad news. However, there are perhaps stronger reasons to expect defensive measures to convey favorable information (even if they are undesirable). One expects management to be more likely to oppose a takeover at a given price if it has favorable information about firm value, or about the likelihood of other bidders arriving. Furthermore, a defensive strategy can be good for shareholders given the arrival of a bid, and yet undesirable ex ante because it deters investigation. The negative average stock price reactions associated with various kinds of defensive measures cited earlier suggests that these actions are often undesirable for target shareholders.

Instead of buying off the bidder, the target can raise the cost to a bidder by repurchasing shares from other investors. Aside from signalling effects (see Section 3.1.4), a repurchase can forces the bidder to offer more if the supply curve of shares slopes upward [Bagwell, 1991]. For example, if different investors have different capital gains bases, repurchase takes out the shareholders with lowest reservation prices. Thus, the greater is shareholder heterogeneity, the more effective is repurchase in blocking takeover.

As emphasized by Jensen [1986], the distribution of cash through repurchase can be a good thing if management would otherwise be inclined to overinvest, and can reduce the gain from takeover. More generally, a management can help preserve its control by preempting the improvements that might otherwise be effected through a hostile takeover. The issue of whether the threat of takeover on the whole improves efficiency (by giving managers a 'kick-in-the-pants') or harm it (by inducing risk avoidance and 'short-termism') is a topic of current debate.[40]

Uncertainty about how much a firm's management values control affects the information conveyed by target resistance activity [Baron, 1982]. If the manager is a shareholder, then he may reject an offer if he has private information indicating that the target is worth more than the price offered, or because he places high value on retaining control. In Baron's model, the expected value of making an offer to a manager who values control is negative because of an associated adverse selection problem, that the offer will only be accepted if it is too high. The rejection of an offer leads outsiders to revise upward their beliefs about the

[40] See, e.g., Stein [1988] and other models reviewed in Hirshleifer [1993a]

manager's value of control, discouraging further offers and causing bidders to shade their offers downward.

As with the analysis of takeover auctions in general, it is important to take into account bidding costs to arrive at robust conclusions about the effects of defensive strategies (see Section 4.2). Berkovitch & Khanna [1990] examine a model in which a target takes an action that reduces its value more to an initial bidder than to a potential second bidder. An example would be selling an asset that can be improved more by *FB* than *SB*. The advantage of this is that it encourages *SB* to compete, despite an entry cost, and forces the first bidder to make a higher offer to deter value reduction and competition.[41]

The following numerical example illustrates their model under full information. Suppose that *FB*'s valuation is \$80, and *SB*'s valuation is \$30. Suppose that *SB* has a cost of \$5 for its *initial* bid only, and that if *SB* enters, the ratchet solution of a costless English auction ensues thereafter. Assume no defensive measures. Then *FB* will succeed with an offer just above zero. Now allow the target, after the first bid, to reduce *FB*'s valuation by an arbitrary amount without changing *SB*'s valuation. *FB* will now win at a price of \$25.[42]

The outcome is very different when bid revision is slightly costly. Suppose that after *SB* enters, there is a further cost of bidding of \$0.01 for either bidder. Suppose in addition there is a cost of \$0.01 to the target of value reduction. (For example, value reduction is likely to be costly if there is a slight chance that no acquisition will take place.) Now, even with value-reduction strategies, *FB* will win at a price of \$0.[43] More generally, the gains from stimulating a competing bid are greatly reduced by even small bid costs in later rounds of bidding.

4.4. *Bidder debt as a strategic positioning device*

Debt can play an important strategic role in takeover contests. The role of target debt is discussed in Section 6; here I discuss the bidding side. Merging has a risk-combination effect that can benefit either bidder debt- or equity-holders, depending on capital structures, the probability distributions for separate and combined firm cash flows, and the means of payment. To disentangle other effects, consider acquisitions without merger.

High leverage increases the bidder's incentive to prefer risky investments (especially if financed by further debt). This increases the incentive to bid high. Thus, an initial bidder may obtain a strategic advantage by leveraging his firm, thereby

[41] Giammarino & Heinkel [1986] provide a related model in which an uninformed bidder is reluctant to compete against an informed bidder when valuations are common. This leads to a gain to the target of committing to resist counteroffers by the informed bidder.

[42] If *FB* offered any less, \$20 say, then the target would reduce *FB*'s valuation of the target to just below \$25. *SB* would win the English auction at a price of just under \$25, to make a small profit.

[43] If the target responds to a first bid of \$0 by reducing *FB*'s valuation to below \$25, then *SB* will enter, *FB* will quit, and *SB* will win at a price just above \$0. But this means that the target has lost \$.01 from its value reduction strategy. Hence, the threat to reduce value is not credible.

committing to bidding aggressively. While this reduces the cost of deterring competition, if the first bidder is imperfectly informed about potential competition, in equilibrium a competitor will still sometimes investigate and bid. In such cases, an equity-value-maximizing bidder may buy the target above its value to the bidding firm as a whole [Chowdhry & Nanda, 1993].

Chowdhry and Nanda's conclusion that debt helps a bidder commit to aggressive bidding conflicts with the popular view that a bidder with high debt is 'strapped for cash', hence unable to afford a high offer. The popular view is consistent with the underinvestment problem with debt [Myers, 1977]; if debtholders absorb part of the value-improvement from takeover, shareholders may have insufficient incentive to undertake it.

Which view is correct? The advantage of issuing new debt to expropriate old debtholders (which does not occur in the Chowdhry/Nanda model) can be achieved without an acquisition, and so is not a benefit to bidding high. If the bid is financed internally, shareholders are sacrificing dividends to make the purchase, so the underinvestment problem will normally apply. However, some acquisitions probably create substantial risk of generating losses greater than the purchase price (reducing the value of the bidder's assets-in-place). In this case part of the potential loss from the investment is borne by debtholders, so overbidding may be profitable for equityholders. Finally, the risk-combination effects of merger in redistributing wealth between debt and equity can operate in either direction.

4.5. *Initial shareholdings as a strategic positioning device*

Another way to commit to aggressive bidding in takeover contests is to accumulate an initial shareholding in the target [Burkart, 1994]. A simple numerical example (developed independently of Burkart's paper) illustrates these incentives. Suppose there are two bidders with valuations known to be \$100 and \$200. If there are no initial shareholdings, the high-valuation bidder will win at a low price: \$0 if there is even a small transaction cost of bidding (or \$100 in the costless English auction solution). Suppose now that the low-valuation bidder owns an initial fraction $\alpha > 0$ of the target firm. He will now bid up to $\$200 - \epsilon$, ($\epsilon > 0$ small), in order to sell his stake to the winning bidder at the highest possible price. Thus, initial shareholdings can lead to drastic overbidding.

This threat of overbidding can deter potential new bidders from investigating. If the initial bidder has a low valuation, he may prefer not to deter competitors, since he would rather sell out at a higher profit. His initial offer may attract competition by conveying information about possible value improvements. Some corporate 'raiders' have in fact been accused of making bids to put companies 'in play', with the intention of selling out.

An initial bidder with a high valuation would like to deter low-valuation competitors. But deterrence may be incomplete, because it may be profitable for another bidder to accumulate a stake (even at prices elevated by takeover speculation), drive up the price further, and sell out to the first bidder. This possibility reduces the expected value to investigating and becoming an initial bidder. Thus, ironically, it seems that the potential to accumulate initial shareholdings may *reduce* takeover activity.

If the bidder does not know the valuation of his competitor, his incentive to overbid is weakened, because he runs the risk of driving out the competitor. A critical strategic factor then is whether the bidder is contractually committed to following through with an acquisition offer. Another limit to overbidding is the difficulty of obtaining financing for an offer that is likely to either lose money or just lose.

4.6. Bidding for multiple targets

Some bidders, such as corporate 'raiders' or firms building conglomerates, have engaged in programs of repeated acquisition. In general, when a repeating player has private information about some strategically relevant characteristic, there can be an incentive to select actions in early rounds that help to build reputation [see, e.g., Kreps, Milgrom, Roberts & Wilson, 1982; Fudenberg & Levine, 1989]. A repeated takeover bidder may want to bid relatively low in early contests, because if later targets believe he can bring about large improvements, they may insist on higher prices [Leach, 1992]. Leach provides evidence which suggests that repeat bidders bid lower than nonrepeaters.

5. Means of payment

The means of payment (cash versus debt or equity securities) in takeover contests has important consequences for the information revealed by the bidder and the target and the efficiency of the transaction outcome. Four key factors have been emphasized by recent theoretical research:

(i) *Value of equity in limiting overpayment* [Hansen, 1987; Eckbo, Giammarino & Heinkel, 1990]. If the target has some private information about its value or the value of the takeover, then the bidder faces a tradeoff between the likelihood of paying too much, or of offering too little and being rejected. The latter case is inefficient. Equity makes the terms contingent on the target's value, mitigating adverse selection.

(ii) *Cash as an indicator of high value or valuation, and equity as an indicator of low value or valuation* [Myers & Majluf, 1984; Hansen, 1987; Fishman, 1989; Eckbo, Giammarino & Heinkel, 1990; Berkovitch & Narayanan, 1990]. Equity (or risky debt) is cheaper for a bidder that is overvalued, or whose valuation of the target is low, so the offer of cash instead signals high value or valuation. For example, a bidder can preempt competitors by offering cash. However, empirically cash does not seem to be associated with less competition [Jennings & Mazzeo, 1993]. With mixed offers value can be revealed fully. If the target has bargaining power, a bidder may offer equity to signal low valuation and induce the target to accept less.

(iii) *The use of equity to exploit the target's information* [Fishman, 1989]. If the bidder is not sure whether a merger will create or destroy value, it is valuable to exploit the target's information. An equity offer gives the target a share of takeover gains or losses, so it will tend to reject undesirable transactions.

(iv) *Tax advantages of equity* [Brown & Ryngaert, 1991]. In the U.S., tax-free status depends on at least 50% of consideration being in the form of equity; many offers occur at or near 50%.

A stimulus to this theoretical research has been evidence (discussed in the empirical synopsis) of lower bidder and target returns for stock offers than for cash offers (see point (ii) above). The failure of the U.S. result of negative average abnormal bidder returns to carry over to other countries is puzzling.[44] Further research will help clarify the source of the inconsistency between theory and evidence.

The use of securities as a means of payment is a case of what Riley [1988] refers to as use of ex-post information to set auction payoffs. Riley shows that a *seller* who can set the payoff function, will want to use ex-post information. This suggests that sellers may insist upon an appropriate debt–equity bundle in order to reduce the problems of asymmetric information about buyers' valuations. Applications of these ideas to takeovers may be of interest for further research.

6. Target financing, managerial voting power and private benefits of control

6.1. Debt as a means of preempting takeover benefits

Debt is frequently increased by potential takeover targets either before or after the arrival of a bidder. A possible explanation is that the purpose of hostile takeovers is to cut expenses and investment. If there are agency problems associated with free cash flow that are reduced by debt [see Jensen, 1986], then the target can commit to preempting the bidder's planned cutbacks by increasing debt.[45] Alternatively, if managers who value control are reluctant to risk financial distress to exploit heavily the tax advantage of debt, they may shift to higher debt when a takeover threat appears.

6.2. Debt as a means of capturing takeover benefits

An alternative theory is that high leverage allow the target to capture a greater fraction of a bidder's improvement through increases in the value of debt [Israel, 1992]. The greater the improvement in firm value associated with a takeover,

[44] Since stock is associated with mergers, and cash with tender offers, it is hard to distinguish acquisition form from means of payment. Since cash tender offers can be consummated more rapidly than stock offers, returns may also be related to the mood of the takeover and prospects for competition.

[45] However, on average investment was not reduced following successful hostile takeovers in the mid-1980s [see Bhide, 1989; Bhagat, Shleifer & Vishny, 1990].

ceteris paribus the lower the probability of default on target debt. If the possibility of takeover-related improvement in debt value can be foreseen by purchasers of debt in advance, target shareholders can absorb this gain at the time of debt issuance. A limit to debt issuance is that this reduces the incentive of potential bidders to investigate the target [Israel, 1991],[46] consistent with evidence cited earlier that high debt targets are less likely to receive hostile tender offers. Similarly, going public can have the advantage of introducing a free-rider problem in tendering [Zingales, 1991]. If dilution opportunities are limited, then public shareholders, by virtue of the free-rider problem, are effectively committed to bargaining tough with the bidder, allowing them to absorb more of the takeover gain than would a single firm owner. The owner can absorb these potential profits at the time of equity issuance.

6.3. Use of resistance strategies to influence contest form

Harris & Raviv [1988] describe how target management, through its resistance strategy, can influence the form of the takeover contest and the likelihood that control changes. They focus on the relationship between target debt levels and two alternative corporate control mechanisms: proxy fights and tender offers.[47] In their model, shifts in capital structure at the time of a control contest affect management's voting power and gains from a control change. Management's resistance strategy is based on a trade-off between value improvements brought about by control changes, and management's private interest in retaining control benefits.

Their model focuses on the behavior of incumbent management (I), a rival management team (R), and passive investors (P). Passive investors may vote in a proxy fight for I or R, but do not seek control for themselves. Both I and R may have either high or low ability. If ability is high, the NPV of the firm (Y_H) is greater than if ability is low (NPV= Y_L). Managers do not have any superior information about their ability. When R arrives, all agents assess a probability p that I is better than R, $1-p$ that R is better than I, and 0 that they are equally able. Prior to R's arrival, p is distributed uniformly on $[0, 1]$. Each passive investor receives an i.i.d signal about the relative abilities of I and R. If a proxy fight occurs, each passive investor votes for the control candidate he believes is better based on p and her signal. If I is actually of ability $i = H, L$, then $\pi_i(p)$ is the probability that a passive investor will vote for I, with $\pi_H(p) > \pi_L(p)$. With many small passive investors, $\pi_i(p)$ is also the fraction of small investors voting for I.

I and R have limited amounts of wealth available to invest in the firm's equity, W_I and W_R. When a potential rival for control of a firm appears, target management may initiate a debt-for-equity exchange to increase its voting power.

[46] It is also possible that an acquirer can expropriate target debt by shifting dividend or investment policy.

[47] A third mechanism of corporate control is dismissal of top executives by the board of directors.

Let D be the face value of debt issued when a takeover threat begins. Debt affects firm value only through its effect on who ends up managing the firm. Higher D reduces I's benefit from control, $K_i(D)$, as it increases the probability of bankruptcy. For any level of debt D, control benefits are greater for a high than for a low ability manager, $K_1(D) > K_2(D)$.

The sequence of events is as follows. Before R appears, the firm makes an initial investment of \$1, financed by \$ W_I from I and \$ $1 - W_I$ from passive investors. I initially selects zero debt. When R appears, I decides on the size of a debt-for-equity exchange in order to maximize the sum of the value of his shares and his expected benefit from control. After any such exchange, R decides whether to purchase equity. Passive investors then observe their signals about managerial ability. A shareholder vote then determines control of the firm.

The value of the firm if no control change is possible is

$$Y_I \equiv pY_1 + (1-p)Y_2. \tag{24}$$

Let α_I be the initial fraction of the firm owned by the incumbent. After issuing debt in exchange for nonmanagement equity, I's equity share becomes

$$\alpha_I(D) = \frac{\alpha_I Y(D)}{E(D)}, \tag{25}$$

where $Y(D)$ and $E(D)$ are the market values of the firm and of the firm's equity when the face value of the debt is D. The numerator is the value of the manager's old shares when it becomes known that debt will be increased, and the denominator is the total value of the firm's equity after recapitalization. Y and E depend on D because D, by affecting ownership fractions, affects the outcome of the control contest.

If the rival appears, he invests his wealth W_R in equity. An upper bound on his purchases is that he can buy no more than $1 - \alpha_I$, the holdings of passive shareholders. Thus, his purchase is

$$\alpha_R(D) = \min\left[\frac{W_R}{E(D)}, 1 - \alpha_I(D)\right]. \tag{26}$$

The remaining fraction of the firm's equity is held by P.

The incumbent's problem is then to set debt to solve

$$\max_{D \geq 0} \alpha_I Y(D) + K(D), \tag{27}$$

where $K(D)$ denotes the expected control benefit to the incumbent given debt level D. There are three possible cases:

1. R acquires enough shares to guarantee he obtains control.
2. Neither R nor I is certain of control.
3. I increases his fractional ownership so much that he is certain to retain control.

These three cases are suggestively termed *successful tender offer*, *proxy fight*, and *unsuccessful tender offer*, respectively. In a successful tender offer, R obtains control even if he is inferior to I. In an unsuccessful tender offer, I retains control even if he is inferior to R. In a proxy fight the superior candidate always wins, because passive investors in the aggregate always cast more votes in favor of the superior candidate.

I's total vote in a control contest is

$$\alpha_I(D) + \pi_i \alpha_P(D), \tag{28}$$

where $i = 1$ if I is better and $i = 2$ if R is better. Thus, an unsuccessful tender offer corresponds to a level of debt such that (28) is at least 1/2 even when $i = 2$. A successful tender offer corresponds to a level of debt such that (28) is less than 1/2 even when $i = 1$. A proxy fight corresponds to debt levels such that (28) is less than 1/2 if $i = 2$, but at least 1/2 when $i = 1$.

If I selects a given case, he will optimally select the lowest debt level consistent with that case. This is because debt affects the control outcome only when it changes the case, while higher debt always reduces I's expected benefit of control. Thus, if I chooses to permit a successful tender offer, he will choose a debt level $D = 0$. It is assumed that a positive level of debt is needed to bring about an unsuccessful tender offer. A positive level of debt may be needed to force a proxy fight.

Because of the role of leverage in blocking control change, greater debt issuance is associated with those types of transactions that maintain incumbent control. Some implications of the model for leverage are now summarized.

Proposition 14. *In the Harris–Raviv model, leverage-increasing shifts in financial structure occur during control contests. Since greater incumbent shareholdings are required to prevent a control shift than to allow one, leverage increases are predicted to be on average smaller for targets of successful tender offers than for firms involved in proxy contests (in which control may not shift) or unsuccessful tender offers. So long as passive shareholders are sufficiently well-informed, the average increase in debt is lower among firms involved in proxy contests than in the unsuccessful tender offer case.*

The analysis also has implications for stock price reactions to control contests, summarized as follows.

Proposition 15.

(1) The average target abnormal stock return associated with successful tender offers (in which control change is certain) is larger than the abnormal returns associated with a proxy fight (in which a change in control is uncertain).

(2) The target stock price does not increase on average, in an unsuccessful tender offer.

(3) Thus, even an unsuccessful proxy fight is associated with positive abnormal stock return.

(4) The abnormal return associated with a successful proxy fight is higher than for an unsuccessful one

(1) holds because incumbent management will risk relinquishing control if the likelihood that the rival is more efficient is sufficiently large, since this increases the potential capital gain on management-owned shares. (2) holds because no value improvement is effected; it is consistent with the evidence of Bradley, Desai & Kim [1983] discussed earlier. (3) holds because the winner of a proxy fight is the more efficient management team. (4) holds because success is associated with a lower ex-ante probability that incumbent management is efficient, and thus a lower prior stock price.

6.4. *Target management ownership and resistance when the supply of shares is upward sloping*

Stulz [1988] offers related arguments concerning the defensive role of target management share ownership and capital structure in a model that focuses on tender offers. He considers an incumbent manager who wishes to retain control and owns shares of the firm. The greater his holdings, the smaller the remaining share fraction available for purchase by a potential bidder. (The incumbent's shareholding can be adjusted through changes in leverage and other means.) Under the assumptions of an upward sloping supply curve for shares, and that the target manager values control so much that he never tenders, it follow that the bidder must pay a larger premium for a given probability of success. (For a related argument, see Bagwell [1991].)

Under these more adverse circumstances, the bidder will in fact offer more. To see this, consider a slightly modified equation (5), so that the bidder's expected profit is

$$E[\Pi] = P(b;\, m)(v - b), \tag{29}$$

where $P(b;\, m)$ is the bidder's probability of success as a function of the amount offered b and target management share ownership m, and where v is the bidder's valuation of the target. The first order condition is

$$P'(b;\, m)(v - b) = P(b;\, m). \tag{30}$$

Suppose that the probability of offer success is linearly increasing in the bid and is linearly decreasing in the level of target management share ownership,

$$P(b;\, m) = a_0 + a_1 b - a_2 m. \tag{31}$$

This simplified equation reflects two considerations in Stulz's analysis. First, a higher offer increases the probability that the bid will exceed the unknown reservation prices of a large enough fraction of shareholders that the offer will succeed. Second, an increase in the fraction of shares not available for tendering m decreases the probability of success. Then substituting (31) into (30) and solving for b gives

$$b(v;\, m) = \frac{v}{2} - \frac{a_0}{2a_1} + \frac{a_2 m}{2a_1}. \tag{32}$$

By (32), this argument implies the following proposition.

Proposition 16. *The level of the bid is increasing with target management share ownership, m.*

This result may seem surprising, because with an upward sloping supply curve for shares, a higher target management ownership raises the cost of purchasing shares. One might suppose that this higher cost could induce the bidder to reduce his offer and accept a lower expected number of tendered shares. The reason this does not occur is that, for any given offered price, the lower probability of success reduces the expected marginal cost of increasing the level of the bid (the price increment multiplied by the probability of success). Thus, the bid increases. The evidence of Stulz, Walkling & Song [1990] discussed earlier that supports the prediction of Proposition 16, particularly for multiple bidder contests.

The paper goes on to examine the consequences of target management shareholding for firm value. Stulz finds that increased managerial ownership does not necessarily improve shareholder welfare because it facilitates the entrenchment of the incumbent manager in control contests. As the incumbent management's shareholding increases, the target loses from a reduction in the probability of a successful takeover, but benefits from a higher premium in the event of success. Private benefits of control in effect serve as a commitment not to tender. In general, such commitment can have strategic value [Schelling, 1960]. Here, the manager is strategically positioned to force the bidder to raise the premium. This leads to an interior optimum from shareholders' point of view.

A number of different kinds of corporate actions can lead to effective increases in management control of voting rights. First, as in Harris and Raviv, shifts in capital structure can effect this end. Thus, the model predicts that the probability of a hostile takeover attempt is decreasing with the target's debt–equity ratio (consistent with evidence cited earlier). Another way of maintaining high management control of voting rights may be to delay the call of a convertible debt. The negative common stock price reaction to the announcement of forced conversion of debt into common stock could then be due to the fact that this reveals to the market that the firm is unlikely to be a takeover target. Since a supermajority rule make takeover more costly for the bidder, Stulz predicts that these can either increase or decrease firm value, but that a decrease is more likely when managerial shareholdings are high (consistent with evidence of Alexander [1986] and Jarrell & Poulsen [1987]). Differential voting rights of stock and the purchase of shares by a firm's ESOP provide ways for managers to increase voting power at low personal cost.

7. Omitted topics and further references

With its focus on the transaction process, this essay has not addressed in detail the reasons that mergers and acquisitions occur. Some value-improving motives for takeovers include scale economies and complementarities, and remedying inefficient target management behavior. Some reasons for value-reducing takeovers include bidder agency problems, bidder overconfidence, and redistribution of wealth from target securityholders or other stakeholders. Hirshleifer [1993b] reviews these issues and provides references.

I have by no means exhausted the application of economic theories of bargaining and of auctions to takeover modelling. Spatt [1989] provides an insightful survey that deals further with these issues. When target management has the power to reject a bidder, there is room for bargaining over the price. If delay is costly, there is pressure on both sides to reach agreement. This suggests the application of a Rubinstein-type model of bargaining between a bidder and a target in which an alternating sequence of offers determines the division of gains [see Tiemann, 1985; Berkovitch & Narayanan, 1990]. Bulow & Klemperer [1993] examine the expected-price-maximizing choice between selling the company in an English auction versus negotiating with a bidder, and find that under mild conditions the public auction is superior. When the valuations of different competing bidders contain a common component, auction theory suggests a need for bidders to shade their offers downward to account for the winner's curse effect; see the evidence of Giliberto & Varaiya [1989].

Takeover threats can influence the behavior of a firm's top executives and its board of directors. Top executives may be forced to work harder, or may make investment or other operating decisions which are unprofitable but make the firm appear successful temporarily. A growing literature on such managerial reputational concerns has been stimulated by Holmstrom [1982]; for a recent review, see Hirshleifer [1993a]. Takeover markets can also interact with internal supervision by boards of directors, because arrival or nonarrival of a bid conveys information about how potential bidders view the manager [see Hirshleifer & Thakor, 1994].

8. Conclusion

Certain central ideas emerge from the models discussed here:

1. *The free-rider problem in tender offers*. A free-rider problem occurs among shareholders of a tender offer target whose value can be improved by the bidder. This occurs because an individual shareholder does not take into account that tendering his shares to the bidder increases the expected wealth of the other shareholders and the bidder. Since the free-rider problem encourages shareholders to retain their shares, it leads to higher prices in successful tender offers, and deters potential bidders. In the extreme case, a bidder cannot capture any of the takeover surplus. Free-riding is more severe if shareholders are small, hence less likely to be individually pivotal in determining the success or failure of an offer (Grossman & Hart [1980]; but see Bagnoli & Lipman [1988] and Holmstrom & Nalebuff [1992]), and if a bidder can revise his offers [Harrington & Prokop, 1993].

2. *The effect of noise on the likelihood of shareholders being pivotal.* Models in which shareholders overcome the free-rider problem are based on tendering strategies that are coordinated so that each shareholder has a substantial probability of being pivotal. It was conjectured that this degree of coordination may not be possible when plausible noise is added in the form of a fraction of the shareholders who are influenced by costs and benefits that are not observed by the others. Thus, there remains reason to expect the free-rider problem to be effective.

3. *Means of profit in tender offers.* Despite the free-rider problem, there exist means by which a value-improving bidder can profit in a tender offer. First, the bidder can succeed at a price below post-takeover value if he has a credible threat to dilute the post-takeover value of nontendered shares [Grossman & Hart, 1980]. Second, the improvement in target value will increase the value of shares owned by the bidder or accumulated secretly prior to the offer [e.g., Shleifer & Vishny, 1986; Kyle & Vila, 1991; Chowdhry & Jegadeesh, 1994]. However, in many tender offers, profits derived from initial shareholdings do not justify the costs of bidding.

4. *Adverse selection among targets.* A disadvantage of cash tender offers is that there is an adverse selection problem arising from the information possessed by targets of merger bids: they will accept offers that are too generous, and reject offers that are too stingy [Hansen, 1987]. This leads to a problem of efficiency as well as distribution, because potential bidders may be deterred from making offers, and because targets may accept offers even when their information indicates that the takeover will not increase underlying value [Fishman, 1989].

5. *Offer success and informational superiority of the bidder.* Informational superiority does not necessarily benefit the bidder, because this increases the skepticism of the target about the adequacy of the offer in comparison with the post-takeover value the bidder can generate. Thus, an informational advantage of the bidder can cause offer failure, and steps taken to reduce asymmetry of information can increase the probability of offer success [Hirshleifer & Titman, 1990].

6. *Communication and structuring of offers.* The terms of takeover bids (level of bid and the choice of means of payment) communicate part or all of the bidder's information about the target, and can be designed to mitigate inefficiencies that arise from informational advantages of the bidder or target [e.g., Hansen, 1987; Fishman, 1988, 1989; Hirshleifer & Titman, 1990; Berkovitch & Narayanan, 1990; Eckbo, Giammarino & Heinkel, 1990]. Communication occurs through both the level of the bid and the means of payment chosen. A high offer generally indicates high valuation, because it indicates that the bidder places high value on increasing his probability of success. The use of equity rather than cash indicates low valuation, because of adverse selection problems with equity issuance [Myers & Majluf, 1984]. Payment with equity makes the target partake in the bidder's gains and losses, so that overpayment by the bidder can be limited and the target's information can be exploited in determining whether the takeover will be completed.

7. *Information costs, bid costs and the efficiency of auction outcomes.* Costs of investigation and of bidding cause takeover auctions to proceed by a few jumps

rather than many small increments, and can reduce the expected price at which the target is sold. The advantage of increasing the bid substantially is that this can communicate a high valuation, inducing a competitor to withdraw. Since both investigation and costs of bid revision limit the information conveyed in the auction process, the winner need not be the bidder with highest valuation of the target [e.g., Fishman, 1988, 1989; Bhattacharyya, 1992; Hirshleifer & Png, 1990; Daniel & Hirshleifer, 1993]. The conventional analysis of competitive takeover auctions based on zero bid costs is extremely delicate; very different results emerge with positive but small costs. This is because in a costly auction, as information is communicated a bidder withdraws as soon as he believes he will lose; this can occur at an offer level well below the lowest bidder valuation.

8. *Ambiguous nature and effects of managerial defensive strategies.* Certain measures ordinarily regarded as defensive can promote bidder success by reducing asymmetry of information, and by driving the price up to a level that encourages shareholders to tender [Hirshleifer & Titman, 1990]. Most target defensive measures and takeover regulations imposed upon bidders have theoretically ambiguous effects on the expected price paid and efficiency, because they (i) drive up price, (ii) cause failure, (iii) deter investigation of targets by initial bidders, and (iv) sometimes encourage competition by higher valuation bidders (numerous papers).

9. *Managerial voting rights as a takeover defense.* Target managerial control of voting rights provides a defense against tender offers by reducing the pool of voting shares available for purchase by the bidder [Harris & Raviv, 1988; Stulz, 1988]. It therefore affects whether a rival for control will attempt a tender offer, a merger bid or a proxy fight (Harris–Raviv).

10. *The effect of target capital structure on managerial voting power.* Managerial control of voting rights and the fraction of gains appropriated by the bidder are influenced by target capital structure and other corporate decisions. A debt-for-equity exchange in which managers do not participate will increase managers' fractional equity holdings [Harris & Raviv, 1988; Stulz, 1988]. Thus, capital structure can be used as a strategic device to position the firm to absorb takeover gains.

11. *Other uses of capital structure as a device for strategic positioning.* A bidder can position himself to bid aggressively by adjusting his debt levels or his initial shareholdings in the target, deterring potential competitors [Chowdhry & Nanda, 1993; Burkart, 1994]. A target can issue risky debt so that a value improvement effected by takeover will accrue partly to its debtholders rather than the acquirer [Israel, 1991].

I will conclude by mentioning three directions for further research. A problem that will require a combination of analytics and empiricism is to select among various possible explanations why bidders on average pay such high premia [see Nathan & O'Keefe, 1989; and Berkovitch and Narayanan, 1991], and why average combined bidder-target equityholder value gains from takeover appear to be so large. (The much-noted phenomenon of high average target abnormal stock returns associated with takeover is of course a result of the high premia paid.)

A second direction is to explore the consequences of bid costs for the analysis of competitive bidding when there are management defensive measures, and when there is strategic commitment through capital structure or bidder share ownership. Our understanding of these topics is based on models in which bidding is costless (except possibly for the initial bid), and the first bidder's valuation is imperfectly revealed by his bid. In these models bidders ratchet up price a little at a time, instead of the large jumps in price actually observed in most takeovers. Auction outcomes in such settings will be sensitive to the inclusion of arbitrarily small bid costs. Thus, more realistic assumptions about bid costs are likely to lead to different conclusions about various corporate control issues.

A third direction is to explore more thoroughly the consequences of strategic target management behavior, in contrast with the passive or mechanistic assumptions of many models. It would be interesting to study the most dangerous competitor to a takeover bidder, the target management itself. Target management can use inside information about target value and potential improvements either indirectly, by encouraging a white knight (friendly) acquirer to make an offer, or directly by making an offer to purchase the company in a leveraged buyout. It seems possible that the threat of target management competition with potential bidders could be so intense that the feasibility of buyouts would *decrease* aggregate takeover activity, and the disciplinary power of takeover threats.

Appendix: Pivotality and bidder profits

Proof of Proposition 7. Let shareholder i own fraction θ_i of the target. Let v_R be the target firm value if a given shareholder retains her shares, for given actions by the other shareholders, and let v_T be the firm value if she tenders her shares. Let Π^i_S be the gain to a shareholder from tendering her share fraction given the actions of all other shareholders, i.e., the difference in the share value if he retains her shares $\theta_i v_R$ and her revenue if she tenders (bid price b, if her share is purchased; $\theta_i v_R$ if not). Let Π^i_B be the profit made by a bidder from his transaction with given shareholder i, i.e., zero if the shareholder retains her share, zero if the shareholder tenders but her share is not purchased, and the difference between the bid price and v_T if the share is purchased. The shareholder will not tender unless $E[\Pi^i_S] \geq 0$.

I will show that as the probability that any shareholder is pivotal becomes small, the bidder's expected profits can be reduced below any given positive ϵ,

$$E\left[\sum_i \Pi^i_B\right] < \epsilon. \tag{33}$$

Thus, for a sufficiently low probability that shareholders are pivotal, if there is any positive bidding cost, no bid will occur. In obtaining this 'sufficiently low' probability, we are allowing the ownership distribution (number of shareholders and sizes of θ_i's) to vary. I now verify that the tendering condition implies the no-bid condition (33). $\Pi_S^i = 0$ unless the shareholder actually sells her share, in which case $\Pi_S^i = \theta_i(b - v_R)$. The bidder's profit from the shareholder Π_S^i is zero unless the shareholder sells her share, in which case it is $\theta_i(v_T - b)$. Hence, the sum $\Pi_B^i + \Pi_S^i$ is zero if the shares are not purchased, and is $\theta_i(v_T - v_R)$ if they are. Taking the expectation over the probability distribution of the equilibrium actions of the other players and summing over i, and recalling that the θ_i's sum to 1,

$$E\sum_i [\Pi_B^i] = \Pr(\text{Sale})\, E\big[v_T - v_R \mid \text{Sale}\big] - E\left[\sum_i \Pi_S^i\right]. \tag{34}$$

As the probability that shareholder i is pivotal becomes arbitrarily small,

$$E\big[v_T - v_R \mid \text{Sale}\big] \to 0, \tag{35}$$

because $v_T = v_R$ unless the shareholder is pivotal. Since the target shareholder expected profit is nonnegative, it follows that the bidder's expected gross profit is arbitrarily close to zero. Therefore he never makes an offer. □

Acknowledgements

I thank the anonymous referee for extremely insightful comments, and James Ang, Mark Bagnoli, Henry Cao, Bhagwan Chowdhry, Kent Daniel, Michael Fishman, Milton Harris, Jack Hirshleifer, Barton Lipman, Rene Stulz, Sheridan Titman, Ralph Walkling, and J. Fred Weston for very helpful comments and discussions.

References

Alexander, C. (1986). Ownership structure, efficiency and entrenchment and antitakeover charter amendments, manuscript, UCLA .

Asquith, D. (1991). Are bad bidders good?, working paper, Tulane University.

Bagnoli, M., and B. Lipman (1988). Successful takeovers without exclusion. *Rev. Financ. Studies* 1, 89–110.

Bagnoli, M., R. Gordon and B.L. Lipman (1989). Stock repurchase as a takeover defense. *Rev. Financ. Studies* 2(3), 423–43.

Bagwell, L.S. (1991). Share repurchase and takeover deterrence. *Rand Journal of Economics* 22(1), 72–88.

Banks, J.S., and J. Sobel (1987). Equilibrium selection in signalling games. *Econometrica* 55, 647–64.

Baron, D. (1982). Tender offers and management resistance. *J. Finance* 38, 331–42.

Berkovitch, E., and N. Khanna (1990). How target shareholders benefit from value-reducing defensive strategies. *J. Finance* 45, 137–56.

Berkovitch, E., and M.P. Narayanan (1990). Competition and the medium of exchange in takeovers. *Rev. Financ. Studies* 3, 153–74.

Berkovitch, E., and M.P. Narayanan (1991). Negative acquirer returns in takeovers: Agency or error?, working paper No. 91-22, School of Business Administration, University of Michigan.

Bhagat, S., and D. Hirshleifer (1995). Do takeovers create value? An intervention approach, working paper #9505-03, School of Business Administration, University of Michigan.

Bhagat, S., and R. Jefferis (1991). Voting power in the proxy process: The case of antitakeover charter amendments. *J. Financ. Econ.* 30(1), 193–226.

Bhagat, S., A. Shleifer and R. Vishny (1990). Hostile takeovers in the 1980's: The return to corporate specialization. *Brookings Pap. Econ. Activity*. Microeconomics, 1–72.

Bhattacharyya, S. (1992). The analytics of takeover bidding: Initial bids and their premia, working paper, Carnegie Mellon University.

Bhide, A. (1989). The causes and consequences of hostile takeovers. *J. Appl. Corp. Finance* 2, 36–59.

Bradley, M. (1980). Interfirm tender offers and the market for corporate control. *J. Bus.* 53, 345–76.

Bradley, M., A. Desai and E.H. Kim (1983). The rationale behind inter-firm tender offers: Information or synergy? *J. Financ. Econ.* 11, 141–53.

Bradley, M., A. Desai and E.H. Kim (1988). Synergistic gains from corporate acquisitions and their division between the stockholders of target and acquiring firms. *J. Financ. Econ.* 21, 3–40.

Bradley, M., and L. Wakeman (1983). The wealth effects of targeted share repurchases *J. Financ. Econ.* 11, 301–28.

Brown, D.T., and M.D. Ryngaert (1991). The mode of acquisition in tender offers: Taxes and asymmetric information. *J. Finance* 46(2), 653–670.

Bulow, J., and P. Klemperer (1993). Auctions vs. Negotiations, Stanford University.

Burkart, M. (1994). Overbidding in takeover contests, discussion paper No. 180, London Business School.

Cho, I.-K. and D. Kreps (1987). Signaling games and stable equilibria. *Q. J. Econ.* 102, 179–221.

Chowdhry, B. and N. Jegadeesh (1994). Optimal pre-tender offer share acquisition strategy in takeovers. *J. Financ. Quant. Anal.* 29, 117–129.

Chowdhry, B., and V. Nanda (1993). The strategic role of debt in takeover contests. *J. Finance* 48(2), 731–46.

Daniel, K., and D. Hirshleifer (1993). A theory of costly sequential bidding, manuscript, Anderson Graduate School of Management, UCLA.

Dann, L., and H. DeAngelo (1988). Corporate finance policy and corporate control: A study of defensive adjustments in asset and ownership structure. *J. Financ. Econ.* 20, 87–127.

DeAngelo, H., and E. Rice (1983). Antitakeover amendments and stockholder wealth. *J. Financ. Econ.* 11, 329–60.

Eckbo, B.E., R. Giammarino and R. Heinkel (1990). Asymmetric information and the medium of exchange in takeovers: Theory and evidence. *Rev. Financ. Studies* 3, 651–76.

Fishman, M.J. (1988). A theory of pre-emptive takeover bidding. *Rand J. Econ.* 19(1), 88–101.

Fishman, M.J. (1989). Preemptive bidding and the role of medium of exchange in acquisitions. *J. Finance* 44, 41–58.

Franks, J., and R. Harris (1989). Shareholder wealth effects of corporate takeovers: The U.K. experience 1955–85. *J. Financ. Econ.* August, 225–250.

Fudenberg, D., and D.K. Levine (1989). Reputation and equilibrium selection in games with a patient player. *Econometrica* 57(4), 759–78.

Giammarino, R.M., and R.L. Heinkel (1986). A model of dynamic takeover behavior. *J. Finance* 41, 465–81.

Giammarino, R.M., and R.L. Heinkel (1990). The evolution of firm value and the allocative role of green mail, School of Commerce, University of British Columbia.

Gilbert, R.J., and D.M. Newbery (1988). Entry, acquisition, and the value of shark repellents, working paper #8888, University of California, Berkeley.

Giliberto, S., and N. Varaiya (1989), The winner's curse and bidder competition in acquisitions: evidence from failed bank auctions. *J. Finance* 44(1), March, 59–76.

Grossman, S.J., and O.D. Hart (1980). Takeover bids, the free-rider problem and the theory of the corporation. *Bell J. Econ.* 11, 42–64.

Grossman, S.J., and O.D. Hart (1981). The allocational role of takeover bids in situations of asymmetric information. *J. Finance* 36, 253–270.

Grossman, S.J., and O.D. Hart (1988). One share–one vote and the market for corporate control. *J. Financ. Econ.* 20(1/2), 175–202

Grossman, S.J., and M. Perry (1986). Perfect sequential equilibrium. *J. Econ. Theory* 39, 97–119.

Hansen, R.G. (1987). A theory for the choice of exchange medium in mergers and acquisitions. *J. Bus.* 60, 75–95.

Harrington, J.E., Jr., and J. Prokop (1993). The dynamics of the free-rider problem in takeovers. *Rev. Financ. Studies* 6(4), 851–882.

Harris, M., and A. Raviv (1988). Corporate control contests and capital structure. *J. Financ. Econ.* 20(1/2), 55–86.

Harsanyi, J.C. (1973). Games with randomly disturbed payoffs: A new rationale for mixed-strategy equilibrium points. *Int. J. Game Theory* 2(1), 1–23.

Hirshleifer, D. (1993a). Reputation, incentives and managerial decisions, in: P. Newman, M. Milgate and J. Eatwell (eds.), *The New Palgrave Dictionary of Money and Finance*, Stockton Press, New York.

Hirshleifer, D. (1993b). Takeovers, in: P. Newman, M. Milgate and J. Eatwell (eds.), *The New Palgrave Dictionary of Money and Finance*, Stockton Press, New York.

Hirshleifer, D., and I.P.L. Png (1990). Facilitation of competing bids and the price of a takeover target. *Rev. Financ. Studies* 2(4), 587–606.

Hirshleifer, D., and A. Thakor (1994). Managerial performance, boards of directors and takeover bidding. *J. Corp. Finance* 1(1), 63–90.

Hirshleifer, D., and S. Titman (1990). Share tendering strategies and the success of hostile takeover bids. *J. Polit. Econ.* 98(2), 295–324.

Holmström, B., and B. Nalebuff (1992). To the raider goes the surplus? A reexamination of the free-rider problem. *J. Econ. Manage. Strategy* 1(1).

Huang, R., and R. Walkling (1987). Target abnormal returns associated with acquisition announcements: Payment, acquisition form, and managerial resistance. *J. Financ. Econ.* 19(2), 329–350.

Israel, R. (1991). Capital structure and the market for corporate control: The defensive role of debt financing. *J. Finance* 46(4), 1391–1410.

Israel, R. (1992). Capital and ownership structures and the market for corporate control. *Rev. Financ. Studies* 5(2), 181–198.

Jarrell, G., and M. Bradley (1980). The economic effects of federal and state regulations of cash tender offers. *J. Law Econ.* 23, 371–407.

Jarrell, G., and A. Poulsen (1987). Shark repellents and stock prices: The effects of antitakeover amendments since 1980. *J. Financ. Econ.* 19, 127–68.

Jennings, R.H., and M.A. Mazzeo (1993). Competing bids, target management resistance and the structure of takeover bids. *Rev. Financ. Studies* 6(4), 883–910.

Jensen M. (1986). Agency costs of free cash flow, corporate finance and takeovers. *Am. Econ. Rev.* 76, 323–39.

Kale, J.R., and T.H. Noe (1991). Unconditional and conditional takeover offers: Theory and experimental evidence. Department of Finance, Georgia State University.

Kreps, D., P. Milgrom, J. Roberts and R. Wilson (1982). Rational cooperation in the finitely repeated prisoners' dilemma. *J. Econ. Theory* 27, 245–52, 486–502.

Kyle, A.S., and J.-L. Vila (1991). Noise trading and takeovers. *Rand J. Econ.* 22(1), 54–71.

Lang, L.H.P., R.M. Stulz and R.A Walkling (1991). A test of the free cash flow hypothesis: The case of bidder returns. *J. Financ. Econ.* 29(2), 315–36.

Leach, C. (1992). Repetition, reputation and raiding. *Rev. Financ. Studies* 5(4), 685–708.

Malatesta, P., and R. Walkling (1988). Poison pill securities: Stockholder wealth, profitability and ownership structure. *J. Financ. Econ.* 20(1–2), 347–76.

Myers, S.C. (1977). Determinants of corporate borrowing. *J. Financ. Econ.* 5, 147–175.

Myers, S.C., and N. Majluf (1984). Corporate financing and investment decisions when firms have information that investors do not have. *J. Financ. Econ.* 13, 187–222.

Myerson, R. (1981). Optimal auction design. *Math. Oper. Res.* 6(1), 58–73.

Nathan, K.S. and T.B, O'Keefe (1989). The rise in takeover premiums: An exploratory study. *J. Financ. Econ.* 23(1), 101–19.

Ofer, A.R. and A.V. Thakor (1987). A theory of stock price responses to alternative corporate cash disbursement methods: Stock repurchases and dividends. *J. Finance* 42, 365–94.

Olson, M. (1965). *The Logic of Collective Action*, Harvard University Press, Cambridge.

Palepu, K. (1986). Predicting takeover targets: A methodological and empirical analysis. *J. Account. Econ.*, 3–37.

Png, I.P.L. (1985). The information conveyed by a takeover bid, working paper #3-85, UCLA AGSM.

Pound, J. (1988). The information effects of takeover bids and resistance. *J. Financ. Econ.* 22(2), 207–28.

Ravid, A., and M. Spiegel (1991). On toeholds and bidding contests, working paper, Columbia University.

Riley, J. (1988). Ex-post information in auctions. *Rev. Econ. Studies*. 55, 409–30.

Riley, J., and W. Samuelson (1981). Optimal auctions. *Am. Econ. Rev.* 71, 381–92.

Roll, R. (1986). The hubris hypothesis of corporate takeovers. J. Bus., 59(2), Part 1, 197–216.

Ruback, R.S. (1988). Do target shareholders lose in unsuccessful control contests?, in: A.J. Auerbach (ed.), *Corporate Takeovers: Causes and Consequences*, University of Chicago Press (for NBER), Chicago.

Ryngaert, M. (1988). The effect of poison pill securities on shareholder wealth. *J. Financ. Econ.* 20(1/2), 377–417.

Samuelson, W., and L. Rosenthal (1986). Price movements as indicators of tender offer success. *J. Finance* 41, 481–99.

Schelling, T. (1960). *The Strategy of Conflict*, Harvard University Press, Cambridge.

Shleifer, A., and R.W. Vishny (1986a). Large shareholders and corporate control. *J. Polit. Econ.* 94(3), Part 1, 461–88.

Shleifer, A., and R.W. Vishny (1986b). Greenmail, white knights, and shareholders' interest. *Rand J. Econ.* 17, 293–309.

Spatt, C.S. (1989). Strategic analyses of takeover bids, in: S. Bhattacharya and G. Constantinides (eds.), *Financial Markets and Incomplete Information*, Rowman and Littlefield, Totowa, NJ, pp. 106–21.

Stein, J. (1988). Takeover threats and managerial myopia. *J. Polit. Econ.* 96(1), 61–80.

Stulz, R.M. (1988). Managerial control of voting rights: Financing policies and the market for corporate control. *J. Financ. Econ.* 20, 25–54.

Stulz, R.M., R.A., Walkling and M.H. Song (1990). The distribution of target ownership and the division of gains in successful takeovers. *J. Finance* 45, 817–33.

Tiemann, J. (1985). Applications of bargaining games in mergers and acquisitions, working paper, Harvard Business School.

Walkling, R. (1985). Predicting tender offer success: A logistic analysis. *J. Financ. Quant. Anal.* 20(4), 461–78.

Walkling, R., and R. Edmister (1985). Determinants of tender offer premiums. *Financ. Anal. J.* 27, 27–37.

Weston, J.F., K.S. Chung and S.E. Hoag (1990). *Mergers, Restructuring, and Corporate Control*, Prentice Hall, Englewood Cliffs, NJ.

Zingales, L. (1991). Insider ownership and the decision to go public, working paper, MIT.

R. Jarrow et al., Eds., *Handbooks in OR & MS, Vol. 9*

Chapter 27

Financial Structure and Product Market Competition

Vojislav Maksimovic
College of Business and Management, University of Maryland, College Park, MD 20742, U.S.A.

1. Introduction

The corporate finance literature has devoted a great deal of attention to the analysis of the implications of firms' financial structure choices on their incentives to produce and invest.[1] Starting with the work on agency costs by Jensen & Meckling [1976] and Myers [1977], researchers have shown how the split between ownership and control and the existence of multiple classes of claimants on the firm's cash flow introduce conflicts of interest. As a result of these conflicts, the firm's equityholders or managers may have an incentive to choose investment projects that reduce the total value of the firm. The literature on agency costs has identified financial policies that can mitigate these incentives, thereby maximizing the value of the firm.

Analytical models in this literature take the firm as the unit of analysis. The firm's environment is usually not specified. Instead, the cash-flows from alternative investment choices are exogenous. The models are usually solved to yield financial structures that maximize the value of the firm, taking the payoffs from different investment choices as given and recognizing the conflicts of interest between different classes of stakeholders.[2]

Because agency models normally do not specify the firm's industry environment, the reactions of the firm's customers and suppliers and of rival firms to changes in its incentives are not addressed. There is therefore a danger that the analysis may miss some of the consequences of firm's financial decisions. In particular, it is possible that if the reactions of other product market participants to firm's policies are analyzed, then the effects of some financing decisions may differ from those that obtain in single firm models.

In this chapter we review some recent contributions that have attempted to address this issue. These contributions specify the firm's product market environment and analyze the relationship between financing decisions and product

[1] See Allen & Winton [1995, this volume].

[2] See, for example, Myers [1977] or Barnea, Haugen & Senbet [1985].

market behavior. The literature that we review begins with Titman's [1984] analysis of the effect of financial structure on contracts between sellers and customers and with the analysis of financing choices on product market competition by Allen [1986], Brander & Lewis [1986] and Maksimovic [1986].

In common with the earlier literature on agency, the contributions reviewed here posit a potential conflict of interests between the equityholders (or managers) who control the firm and other stakeholders. For some choices of financial structure, this conflict may result in inefficient production or investment incentives. However, instead of analyzing the interaction between financial structure choices and incentives of a single firm in isolation, these papers explore how financial structure choices interact with the firm's environment to affect incentives. In most contributions analyzed here, the object is to describe financial structures that minimize the loss of firm value from conflicts of interest. However, in contrast to single-firm models, it is shown that when the firm's product market environment is taken into account, the firm may sometimes benefit from a perceived conflict of interest between stakeholders.

Product market environments differ from each other in many dimensions.[3] As a result, financial structures that unfavorably affect incentives in one industry may be optimal in other industries. It is therefore important to identify 'mechanisms' that have the potential to affect the interaction between financial structure choices and incentives in different product market environments. Whether or not a specific mechanism is important for any individual industry is an empirical question.

In this chapter we focus on four mechanisms that have been identified in the literature as determining how financial structure affects value in product markets. These mechanisms are: (i) the effect of investment choices of other firms in the industry on the interaction between the firm's financial structure and its investment incentives; (ii) the effect of debt on a firm's ability to enter into advantageous implicit and explicit contracts with competitors or customers; (iii) the effects of changes in leverage firms' incentives and on industry equilibrium in oligopolies and (iv) the exploitation by competitors of conflicts of interest caused by the firm's need to finance its investments externally. Below we characterize in turn each of the mechanisms and describe recent work that attempts to ascertain their empirical relevance.

The rest of the chapter is organized as follows. Section 2 discusses models that directly extend the single firm paradigm by analyzing financial structure choice in the context of an industry equilibrium that takes into account the investment decisions of all firms in the industry. These models are referred to in this chapter as *industry equilibrium* models (IE). These models show how the riskiness of firms' investment strategies is endogenously determined in industry

[3] For example, in some industries the quality of output is an important decision variable for the firm, whereas in other industries there is less opportunity for deviations from the industry standard. More generally, industries differ in the number of firms, cost structures of firms, demand elasticity, importance of research and development and marketing, barriers of entry, among other factors. See Tirole [1988] for an overview of models of product market rivalry.

equilibrium. As a result, the effect of financial structure on firms' investment incentives also depends on the equilibrium number of firms in the industry and their investment choices. Using these insights, the papers show how several familiar results about the relationship between financial structure and firm value derived from single firm models must be modified when industry equilibrium is taken into account. The models also generate empirical predictions about how the distributions of financial structures and technology choices depend on industry characteristics, such as cost structures and availability of alternative technologies.

Section 3 discusses how financial structure affects the firm's ability to make credible implicit or explicit contracts with customers and rival firms. The papers reviewed in this section analyze two consequences of leverage. First, high debt levels increase the probability that the firm will become bankrupt and cannot be compelled to fulfil its obligations. Second, debt may decrease both the profits that the firm's equityholders receive from complying with the contract and the cost that they bear if they act opportunistically. Both these effects decrease the firm's ability to enter into credible contracts.

Section 4 discusses papers that address the effect of financial structure choices on the firm's incentives in the product market when firms act strategically. These papers show that particular financing choices may credibly commit to higher output levels and thereby influence market equilibrium outcomes in the firm's favor. A theme of these contributions is that it is individually rational for the firm to adopt financial structures that do this. However, when all firms try to gain advantage in this way their values are reduced.

Financial structures that mitigate conflicts of interest within the corporation may make the firm more vulnerable to competitive moves by rivals or simply to bad outcomes in the product market. The papers in Section 5 analyze different trade-offs that arise between avoiding internal conflicts and increased costs in the product market.

The chapter emphasizes theoretical papers because much of the recent work on the interactions between product and financial markets belongs to this category. Empirical testing of the theoretical models is difficult and that literature is only just beginning to take shape. Several promising recent papers are reviewed in Section 6.

To keep the survey manageable I have omitted entirely several important topics about which much has been written. In particular, as there have been very few contributions that have focused solely on taxes and market equilibrium since Ravid's [1988] earlier survey of the product and financial markets literature, I have not attempted to add to his review of that literature.[4] Also, I do not discuss mergers and product market competition. Finally, this, like every such survey, reflects the current world view of the author.

[4] I have also not been able to include several important papers that do not fit easily into the classification adopted or would require more lengthy exposition. Among the papers that are not discussed are Bhattacharya & Ritter [1983] and Gertner, Gibbons & Scharfstein [1988].

2. Conflicts of interest and industry equilibrium

The IE models that we review in this section explore the consequences of directly embedding the single firm agency model in an industry environment. The models, Maksimovic & Zechner [1991] (MZ) and Williams [1995], differ from the usual single firm agency models in three important respects. First, it is assumed that the potential conflict of interest between different classes of stakeholders is over the choice of which technology to use for producing the firm's output in a single industry.[5] Second, the number of firms in the industry and their investment choices are endogenously determined in equilibrium. Third, the cash-flows generated by investing in each of the available technologies are not exogenous. Instead, the cash-flows depend on the number of firms competing in the industry, their investment technology choices and on the demand function for the firms' products.[6]

The endogeneity of cash-flows generated by different technologies introduces a key difference between single firm agency models and the IE models. In single firm models it is clear which investment choice maximizes the net present value of the firm and the models are usually constructed so that other choices reduce the value of the firm. By contrast, in IE models the net present value of a technology depends on the number of firms choosing it. As a result, in equilibrium the number of firms choosing each project may adjust so that several seemingly different investment choices may have the same value. Thus, changes in incentives that cause the firm to choose different investments may not change the firm's value.

These issues were first explored by MZ in the context of a two technology model. They show more formally how the risk of a firm's cash flows is endogenously determined and depends on the efficiency of the firm's technology. In equilibrium, the returns of the less efficient technology are a mean preserving spread of the returns of the more efficient technology. As in the single firm models, MZ show that financial structures may create incentives to choose a technology that appears less efficient from a nonequilibrium single firm viewpoint. They also show that over certain parameter ranges the equilibrium number of firms choosing each technology adjusts, so that firm value is unaffected by these apparently perverse incentives. However, the equilibrium distribution of financial structures across firms in an industry depends on the number of firms choosing each technology and is not arbitrary.[7]

[5] Thus, it implicitly assumed that debt covenants can constrain the firm to invest in a specific industry.

[6] This contrasts with the single firm models in which the cash-flows from alternative investment choices are exogenous.

[7] A parallel can be drawn between these results and the literature on taxes and financial structure. Focusing on one firm in isolation, it can shown that in simple models it is optimal for firms to be either fully leveraged or for firms to have no debt. However, Miller [1977] shows that once firms and investors adjust fully to tax incentives, individual firms do not lose value by arbitrarily picking financial structures. Similarly, MZ show that incentives which appear to lower value do not do so once industry adjustments are taken into account.

This framework can be adjusted to allow for tax advantages of debt. In this case the equilibrium is asymmetric. As before, the riskiness of a project's cash flows is endogenous. An endogenously determined number of firms have a high level of debt and have riskier earnings before interest and taxes. Others issue less debt and have less risky earnings before interest and debt. In equilibrium firms are indifferent between low leverage and the choice of a project with higher expected pre-tax cash flows and high leverage and the choice of a project with lower expected pre-tax cash flows.

Interestingly, it can be shown that when industry equilibrium is taken into account, determinants of capital structure (such as corporate tax rates) not only have a direct effect on firm decisions but also change the distribution of projects in the industry. This, in turn, affects the cash flows generated by each project, and indirectly the firm's capital structure choice. Thus, for example, increases in the corporate tax rate lead more firms to select financial structures that provide equityholders with incentives to pick riskier projects. However, as more firms do so they change the project's cash flow distribution, and lower this project's debt capacity.

A simple numerical example may help clarify the relationship between single firm and IE analysis. We consider at the incentive to 'risk-shift' in context of a simple model in which all investors are risk-neutral and the interest rate is zero. The sequence of events is that (1) a firm's financial structure is chosen, (2) the firm chooses to invest in a particular project, and (3) the state of the world is revealed and the output is produced and sold. Consider first an all-equity firm in isolation choosing between two projects. A nonstochastic project *NS* always yields a cash flow of 100 and does not require any investment. A stochastic project *S* yields either 120 or 80, depending on which of two equiprobable states occurs. In addition, it requires an initial investment of $I_S = 2.5$.

It is clear that the optimal choice is that of Project *NS*. However, if the firm has sufficient preexisting debt outstanding and the firm's decisions are taken in the interests of the firm's equityholders only, then the firm will choose Project *S* providing that it has enough cash on hand to invest.[8] In this example this results in a lower value for the firm as a whole whenever the firm has preexisting debt with a face value above 80.

The example suggests several intuitions. All other things being equal, a zero debt policy is optimal in this case. Second, we can predict that only the stochastic technology will be subject to risk shifting. Finally, risk shifting only requires attention when the stochastic technology is less efficient.

Each of these intuitions may have to be modified in an IE model if the analysis is expanded to take into account market clearing in product markets. We illustrate the differences with a numerical example based on MZ. To do so we specify an

[8] We make the standard assumption that the firm's owners and creditors are distinct. The importance of the conflict of interest between different classes of investors in the firm has been analyzed by Jensen & Meckling [1976] and Myers [1977]. See also the monograph by Barnea, Haugen & Senbet [1985].

inverse demand function for the firm's output and we explicitly assume that the marginal cost of output depends on the quantity produced.

Specifically, consider the following simple market environment in which all firms are price-takers.[9] Let there be 100 firms facing a linear market demand

$$p = 250 - \sum_{i=1}^{100} q_i,$$

where q_i is the output of firm i. As before, there are two projects. If a firm selects project NS it pays no initial fixed cost and can produce q_i units at an increasing marginal cost $MC_{NS} = 15 + q_i$. If a firm selects the stochastic technology, it pays an initial fixed cost $I_S = 2.5$. The marginal cost of output is $MC_S^L = 5 + q_i$ in the state of the world denoted by L and $MC_S^H = 25 + q_i$ in the state of the world denoted by H.

Once each of the hundred firms has chosen its project, we can determine the industry supply curve in each of the two states by summing the firms' individual supply functions. The aggregate supply function together with the demand curves yields an equilibrium price for each state (p^L and p^H). From these it is possible to determine the operating revenues in each state for a firm that chooses Project NS (π_{NS}^L and π_{NS}^H) or one that chooses Project S (π_S^L and π_S^H).

First, we explore how the riskiness of a firm's cash-flows depends on the investment choices of other firms in the industry. Assume that all the firms have chosen Project NS. In that case there is no uncertainty and it can be shown that $p^L = p^H = 17.3$ and that $\pi_{NS}^L = \pi_{NS}^H = 2.71$. Consider now the revenues that a price-taking firm that enters the market and adopts Project S might expect. In accordance with the intuition from single firm analysis, the firm would be much riskier ($\pi_S^L = 76$ and $\pi_S^H = 24.43$). Perhaps less obvious, its expected value is 47.71 [$v_S = 0.5(\pi_S^L + \pi_S^H) - I_S$], considerably more than that of a firm that has adopted Project NS, which is 2.70 [$v_{NS} = 0.5(\pi_{NS}^L + \pi_{NS}^H)$] by inspection.[10]

Consider next the opposite case, where all the firms have chosen Project S. It can be shown that $p^L = 7.42$ and $p^H = 27.23$ and that $\pi_S^L = 2.94$ and $\pi_S^H = 2.48$. Given these market prices, a price-taking firm that enters the market and adopts Project NS realises $\pi_{NS}^L = 28.68$ and $\pi_{NS}^H = 74.75$. Thus, the nonstochastic project now has riskier cash flows. Moreover, it is now more valuable than the stochastic project, $v_{NS} = 51.72 > v_S = 0.22$. Hence, high leverage would induce the firm's equityholders to choose Project NS.

Neither of these two examples is an equilibrium because $v_{NS} \neq v_S$. As a result, all-equity firms would not all choose Project S or Project NS. For the same reason, financial structures that induced all firms to choose the same project would not be equilibrium financial structures.

[9] The assumption that firms are price-takers is made for convenience only. Similar considerations apply if firms act strategically.

[10] The difference in values occurs because in this example the firm adopting technology S has a valuable option to adjust output once the state of the world is revealed. This point is further discussed in MZ where all the formulas used to calculate the examples are derived.

To find the equilibrium it is necessary to make the number of firms adopting each technology endogenous and solve for this quantity in the following equilibrium equation,

$$0.5\left(\pi_{NS}^{L}+\pi_{NS}^{H}\right)-I_{NS}=0.5\left(\pi_{S}^{L}+\pi_{S}^{H}\right)-I_{S}$$

where I_{NS} is the initial fixed cost of Project *NS*, if any. Solving for the equilibrium number of firms choosing each project, we find that 48 firms will chose Project *S* and the reminder will choose Project *NS*. $p^L = 12.58$ and $p^H = 22.08$. Project *NS* is in equilibrium less risky than project *S*: $\pi_{NS}^{L} = 2.94$ and $\pi_{NS}^{H} = 25.04$ compared to $\pi_{S}^{L} = 28.70$ and $\pi_{S}^{H} = 4.27$.

Note that in equilibrium a highly leveraged financial structure would induce a firm to choose the project with the riskier cash flows, Project *S*. However, in equilibrium the value of the firm is equal regardless of the choice of projects. Thus, a single firm would be indifferent in its choice of financial structure. However, if all firms adopt highly levered financial structures the equilibrium would break down. Thus, the analysis places restrictions on the industry wide distribution of financial structures that support the first-best equilibrium allocation of projects.

In the last example, Project *S* had more volatile cash flows than Project *NS*. This accords with the single firm intuition, but is not a necessary outcome of equilibrium analysis. If $I_{NS} = 2.5$ and $I_S = 0$, then 53 firms will chose Project *S*. For these parameter values, $\pi_{S}^{L} = 25.05$ and $\pi_{S}^{H} = 2.93$, while $\pi_{NS}^{L} = 4.27$ and $\pi_{NS}^{H} = 28.7$. Highly levered firms will now chose the less efficient Project *NS*. Thus, the riskiness of the project's cash flows is endogenous, and depends on its efficiency, in this case measured by I.

Williams [1994] extends the MZ analysis in four key respects. First, in his model firms can be financed by both external debt and external equity. Second, an agency problem is introduced by assuming that entrepreneurs who raise funds by issuing equity and/or debt cannot commit themselves to invest the proceeds. If they wish, they may instead consume the proceeds themselves. Third, firms are not price-takers but act strategically.[11] Fourth, in his model demand is uncertain (it is 'high' or 'low') and all technologies are nonstochastic. Instead, firms have a choice of investing in 'labor intensive' technologies or 'capital intensive' technologies. Labor intensive technologies require no initial investment and can produce quantity q at a variable cost of αq. Capital intensive technologies require a initial investment of γ and can produce quantity q at a variable cost of $(\alpha - \beta)q, \alpha > \beta > 0$. Thus, capital intensive firms always produce more than labor intensive firms. Taking γ into account, they are more efficient at high levels of output whereas labor intensive technologies are more efficient at low levels of output.[12]

If financial contracting issues were not material (e.g., if all firms were internally financed), then for a range of parameter values the model would yield a market

[11] The principal insights of the model would be equally valid in an industry where all firms are pricetakers.

[12] The paper introduces a number of other assumptions that generate numerous results that are interesting but not central to this review.

equilibrium in which some firms are capital intensive and some labor intensive.[13] This is the first-best equilibrium in which the number of firms adopting each technology adjusts so that the net present values of firms adopting the two technologies are equal. Let the number of firms choosing the capital intensive technology in first-best equilibrium be n^*. The central questions in the Williams paper are: Can the first-best product market equilibrium be supported by equilibrium choices of financial structures once the agency problems are recognized? If not, what configuration of technology and financial structure choices occurs?

The agency problem arises because if an entrepreneur elects to raise funds for the capital intensive technology from outside investors, he or she must be motivated to invest rather than consume the proceeds. This requires that the entrepreneur's net returns from investing in this technology be greater than the sum of the benefits of immediate consumption of the proceeds and the profits from selecting the labor intensive technology.[14]

For some parameter values, appropriate choices of outside debt and equity can remove the entrepreneur's incentive to substitute the labor intensive technology for capital intensive technology and to consume the investment funds. Consider first the incentive to substitute the labor intensive technology. Suppose that there exists a debt level that exceeds the operating profit of the labor intensive technology in any state of the world but is smaller than the profit of the capital intensive technology in some state. If so, this level of debt solves the substitution problem because an entrepreneur whose firm has issued that much debt will not have an incentive to adopt the labor intensive technology. Next, consider the incentive to consume investment funds. The entrepreneur does not wish to consume the investment funds when the capital intensive technology generates sufficiently high net returns and when his share of these returns is sufficiently high.

As in the numerical examples above, the fewer capital intensive firms there are in the industry the higher is their return and the greater the amount by which their highest operating profit exceeds that of labor intensive firms. As a result, the number of firms that can successfully solve the financial contracting problem and obtain financing for the capital intensive technology is endogenous.

Two types of market outcomes occur in the Williams model. The first best equilibrium occurs if parameters are such that n^* entrepreneurs can successfully solve their financial contracting problem and raise γ externally. The properties of this equilibrium are similar to those in MZ.

A second-best equilibrium occurs if parameters are such that fewer than n^* entrepreneurs can satisfy the financial contracting constraints permitting them to raise γ externally. In this equilibrium the NPV of the capital intensive technology will exceed the NPV of the labor intensive technology.[15] As a result, more

[13] As in MZ, the diversity arises because each type of firm has a comparative advantage in one state of the world.

[14] Recall that the labor intensive technology does not require an initial investment.

[15] Specifically, the NPV of the labor intensive firms is zero and the NPV of capital intensive firms is positive.

entrepreneurs would like to select the capital intensive technology. However, their marginal investment in the capital intensive technology would reduce the returns of this technology. This reduced rate of return makes it rational for entrepreneurs to consume the proceeds of security sales instead of investing them. As a result, they cannot credibly commit to invest in the capital intensive technology and will not be able to obtain external financing to do so.

The Williams model yields interesting empirical predictions. To avoid technology substitution, each capital intensive firm must issue debt obligations with a higher face value than a labor intensive firm could issue. Thus, in the second-best equilibrium profitable, large capital intensive firms with high debt levels can coexist with small marginally profitable labor intensive firms that issue a smaller absolute quantity of debt securities.

The IE papers in this section suggest that once industry equilibrium is taken into account, predictions drawn from the analysis of a single firm in isolation may need to be modified or reversed. For example, an important conclusion of equilibrium analysis is that a diversity of financial structures may exist within the same industry even when debt financing has a tax advantage. This suggests that the observed diversity in financial structures within industries does not imply that even simple tax based models of leverage fail to identify the relevant trade-offs facing firms. Thus, the prospect that we might explain financial structures with such models may not be as bleak as it may have seemed.[16]

The IE framework is capable of making predictions about the joint determination of industry structure and the set of optimal financial contracts appropriate for each class of firms. Because of the large number of potential predictions about the combination of profitability, size distributions, riskiness and choice of technology these predictions are likely to be testable.

3. Financial structure and implicit contracts

In many cases it is advantageous for firms to enter either explicit or implicit contracts with customers, rival firms or with suppliers. Examples are contracts committing the firm to producing output of a certain quality, guaranteeing to repair any deficiencies or implicit contracts with rivals controlling the amount of competition in the marketplace. Many such contracts have the following two characteristics: (i) if the opposing party believes them to be credible they increase the value of the firm at the time of their inception, and (ii) there exist circumstances in which it is advantageous for firms to renege on their contracts unless there is sufficient punishment for doing so. Since financial structure affect a firm's incentives, it will also affect the firm's ability to enter into credible agreements with other product market participants. As a result, financial structure choices affect the value of the firm and the outcomes in the product market.

[16] See Myers [1984] for a discussion of within industry variation of financial structures.

The literature has focused on two ways in which financial structure affects the implicit or explicit commitments that the firm enters into. Titman [1984] has studied the effect of the possibility of insolvency on the firm's ability to make optimal contracts with customers or other stakeholders in the firm. Maksimovic [1987, 1988] and Maksimovic & Titman [1991] (MT) have analyzed the effect of financial structure on the firm's incentives to renege on implicit agreements.

Insolvency and contracts with customers

Buyers of durable goods often require spare parts or servicing for a prolonged period after purchase. To the extent that these services are more efficiently provided by the original manufacturer, it may be efficient for the seller to enter into a long term contract to supply these services at the time of purchase.[17] A seller who can credibly enter into such a contract may command a higher price for his or her product than one who cannot. As a result, the ability to enter into credible contracts may be valuable for the firm even after making provisions for the expected costs of the services to be provided.

While entering into this type of long term contract creates value for the seller at the contract's inception, the seller may have an incentive to renege on the contract at a later date. This may occur if performance of contractually agreed services is costly. Therefore, if a contract is to be credible, it must contain provisions that remove the incentive to renege by penalizing a firm that does so.

Such penalties fail as enforcement devices if the seller becomes bankrupt between the inception of the contract and the time that the agreed services are to be performed. The new owners of a bankrupt firm cannot be compelled to fulfill its contractual obligations made by the previous owners. Thus, the higher the probability that the firm will become insolvent, the less likely it is that the firm will fulfill its contractual obligations.

Titman [1984] analyzes a model in which the firm's probability of bankruptcy increases with leverage. Hence, in his model debt financing lowers the value of a seller by reducing the price that can be obtained for the output. The significance of this effect will depend on the nature of the firm's business. Thus, Titman is able to make predictions relating the firm's equilibrium financial structure to the characteristics of the relationship between it and its customers.[18]

Financial structure and the incentive to renege

An implicit contract between a firm and its customers or rivals cannot be enforced by legal penalties. This does not mean that such contracts will always be broken. A firm will not renege on a contract if the benefits of complying with the terms of the contract exceed the cost of opportunistic behavior. The benefits

[17] Similar considerations apply to some nondurable products. A person purchasing an airline ticket or booking a holiday enters into a forward agreement for the supply of services. Such an agreement will only be honored if the supplier has not gone out of business in the interim.

[18] Titman & Wessels [1988] provide evidence that firms that produce more specialized products for which the manufacturer's support is likely to be a significant feature, have lower leverage then firms that do not.

of complying will typically include the profits from future business and the value of maintaining its reputation. Costs of reneging may include legal sanctions and 'punishment' that customers may inflict by withholding their business and rivals may inflict by engaging in a price war. Both benefits and costs are affected by such factors as the number of rival firms in the industry, opportunities for secretly varying the quality of the product and the growth in demand over time.

Changes in financial structure alter the share of future cash flows that belongs to equityholders, thereby affecting their incentive to comply with the terms of the contract. For example, as leverage increases, a greater proportion of future cash flows are assigned to debtholders. This reduces the value to the equityholders of complying with implicit or explicit contracts limiting opportunistic behavior. As a result, for high enough leverage the equityholders will prefer to engage in opportunistic behavior.

Consider the consequences of a large increase in leverage by the firm. Because other parties understand the incentives of equityholders to renege, they will expect opportunistic behavior by the firm if its leverage increases sufficiently. Accordingly, they will take actions to protect themselves.[19] In turn, these actions will be predicted by the firm's equityholders. The resulting market outcome in which both parties predict a breakdown of the contract, and plan for it, will in general be less favorable to the firm then if leverage had not increased.

These considerations suggest that to avoid such outcomes the firm should limit its leverage. The level at which leverage should be limited depends on the details of the debt contract and the type of market interaction between rival firms. This relationship between market structure, leverage and the firm's ability to enter into implicit contracts has been explored by Maksimovic [1988] and is examined next.

For simplicity, assume that there are two identical firms with access to a product market opportunity that repeats in each future period.[20] Industry demand and costs are known and are constant over time. To realize maximum total profits, each firm should set its output at a fraction of the monopoly level in each period. However, in the absence of a binding contract or threat of future punishment it is individually rational for firms to produce more in each period. If they maximize profits without coming to an understanding to limit output each firm will produce its Nash equilibrium output. The profits at this equilibrium are generally lower than would be the case if firms produced less. As a result, it is advantageous for the firms to devise a way to enforce a tacit agreement to limit output.

Output can only be limited below the Nash equilibrium level if a firm can credibly impose costs on a rival that breaks a tacit agreement. The ways in which firms can commit themselves to punish violators have been studied extensively in the industrial organization literature. A class of output strategies that have been shown to sustain understandings to limit output in some imperfectly competitive industries is the class of trigger strategies, investigated by Friedman [1971], Green

[19] For example, rival firms will increase output or customers may expect the firm to cut the quality and will therefore not be willing to pay as much for the product.

[20] The generalization to the case of more than two firms is immediate.

& Porter [1984], Porter [1983a], and Brock & Scheinkman [1985].[21] A firm following a trigger strategy will commence by producing at some output level, and will maintain that output unless one of its rivals deviates. Should this occur, the firm produces at the Nash level in each subsequent period.[22] The threat of increased production in the future (i.e., a price war) provides incentives to limit output. The threat is credible because if one of the firms is producing at the Nash equilibrium level, then it is also optimal for its rival to produce the Nash equilibrium output. Such an equilibrium is subgame perfect. The price war that occurs if a tacit agreement breaks down is both the result of the breakdown and the 'punishment' which the transgressor firm brings down on itself.

If firms collude and limit output in each period the present value of each firm's profit is $\pi^c + \pi^c/r$, where π^c is the profit realized in each period and r is the interest rate. If a firm cheats, its total profit is $\pi^d + \pi^{nc}/r$, where π^d is the one-period profit from deviating if the other firm adheres to the agreement and π^{nc} is the profit realized in each period in a Nash equilibrium.[23] For

$$\pi^c + \frac{\pi^c}{r} > \pi^d + \frac{\pi^{nc}}{r},$$

an implicit agreement to limit output to the monopoly level is sustainable since firms will find it in their interest to abide by that agreement. If $\pi^c + \pi^c/r < \pi^d + \pi^{nc}/r$, an agreement is not feasible and the firms will realize the Nash equilibrium profits π^{nc} in each period. Thus, in both cases the output (and profit levels) are constant over time.[24]

By issuing financial claims against future income, however, the equity holders may alter the trade-off between their *net* payoffs from maintaining the long term relationship and their *net* payoffs from deviating. As a result, industry output and firm value can be affected by a firm's capital structure. If the financial market is efficient, this will be factored into the price of debt and the price of shares at the time debt is issued.

Suppose that the equityholders of all previously all-equity firms simultaneously issue debt. For each debt instrument sold equityholders receive a lump sum cash payment in return for an obligation to pay \$1 per period forever. Let Firm i issue b_i debt instruments. At the end of each period the equityholders pay the debtholders \$$b_i$ and are then free to declare and pay out a dividend.[25] If the

[21] For applications of trigger strategies in other contexts see, for example, Klein & Leffler [1981], Shapiro [1982], Dybvig & Spatt [1983] and Allen [1984]. For an empirical application to the railroad industry see Porter [1983b].

[22] In practice firms may be able to reestablish cooperation over time. For trigger strategies to be effective in regulating rivalry it is only required that, once broken, an agreement cannot be reestablished in the short run.

[23] Note that $\pi^d > \pi^c > \pi^{nc}$.

[24] There will in general be many collusive levels of output that can be sustained over time [see Friedman, 1971]. The results below are not affected the choice of a particular sustainable output level (and hence π^c).

[25] The coupon payment per period cannot exceed π^c. The maximum value of debt issued cannot exceed π^c/r, the value of the firm if the tacit agreement is sustained.

firm cannot meet its obligations, then, in accordance with contractual obligations, the debtholders gain control of the firm and its resources. In that case the equityholders receive nothing. Debt obligations are common knowledge. The payoff to equityholders consists of the cash receipt from the sale of financial instruments and dividends paid by the firm. The payoff to the debtholders of firm i is $\$b_i$ in each period in which the firm is solvent and the firm itself if bankruptcy is declared.

If the firm is leveraged the profit to the equityholders from maintaining an agreement is $\pi^c - b_i + (\pi^c - b_i)/r$. If the equityholders break the agreement they can realize $\pi^d - b_i + \max[(\pi^{nc} - b_i)/r, 0]$. It is clear that no choice of debt level can increase the total profit realized in the trigger strategy equilibrium. However, as $b_i \to \pi^c$ it becomes rational for the firm's equityholders to deviate from the agreement. Thus, high levels of debt may make a previously self-enforcing tacit agreement unsustainable.[26]

Let the maximum coupon payment for which the agreement is sustainable be b^*. In the absence of any tax advantage of debt the financial structure will be chosen so that the coupon payment of each firm is below b^*. In equilibrium, output, and thus the total value realized, will not be affected by the existence of debt.[27]

This approach can be generalized to take into account production capacity constraints by firms. It can also be adapted to analyze the interaction between a firm and its customers when the firm can vary the quality of its output.[28] In the preceding analysis it has been assumed that the quantity produced by each firm is known to its rival. In a more general setting, pertinent information such as the rival's output or technology may not be directly observable. Firms have to use publicly available information to infer whether their rival is breaking the tacit agreement. As shown by Green & Porter [1984], if a firm cannot observe its rival's output directly it will base its response on a noisy signal, such as the market price of output.

The basic approach can be adapted to analyze cases where the firm wants to commit not to enter into implicit contracts. For example, by selecting a high level of debt an incumbent firm may be able to deter a potential entrant to the industry. On observing the incumbent firm's debt level, the entrant would know that the incumbent's equityholders would have an incentive to renege on any implicit agreement between the two firms. Without an implicit agreement the most profit that the entrant could earn is π^{nc}. Thus, the incumbent high leverage would deter an entrant whose the initial cost of is entry is greater than π^{nc}/r and less than

[26] An implicit assumption of the model is that equityholders can extract sufficient opportunistic gains, either through stock repurchases or dividend payments, before the firm is forced into bankruptcy. As $b_i \to \pi^c$, the payout that the equityholders would need to extract in order for it to be advantageous to deviate tends to zero.

[27] If there is a tax advantage to debt, firms may tradeoff some restriction on output in equilibrium in return for a greater tax subsidy from higher leverage. This will alter the output level in the implicit agreement but will not alter the nature of the equilibrium.

[28] For example, by introducing financial structure in the quality model of Dybvig & Spatt [1983].

π^c/r.[29] In the preceding analysis it has been assumed that the quantity produced by each firm is known to its rival. In a more general setting, pertinent information such as the rival's output or technology may not be directly observable. Firms have to use publicly available information to infer whether their rival is breaking the tacit agreement. As shown by Green & Porter [1984], if a firm cannot observe its rival's output directly it will base its response on a noisy signal, such as the market price of output. Although optimal, this policy will result in unintended breakdowns of the implicit agreement. Thus, it is in the interest of firms to find a mechanism that maintains cooperation without exposing them to the risk of a costly price war.

MT extend the analysis of the firm's incentives to maintain a reputation for honoring implicit contracts in three ways. First, they allow the future demand for the firm's product to be stochastic — in their case it follows a random walk. This makes the incentive to deviate from an implicit agreement vary with demand. Second, they investigate the incentive to renege when dividends and repurchases are not permitted. These restrictions on payouts to equityholders prevent them withdrawing any cash from the firm after reneging on an implicit agreement to produce high quality goods.[30] Third, they extend Titman's [1984] analysis to industries in which suppliers and customers do not have a relationship beyond the point of sale.

MT examine incentives to maintain a reputation in the context of a firm selling a good of variable quality. The customers cannot observe the quality of the good until they purchase it. It is more costly to produce the high quality good than the low quality good. However, customers would be willing to pay a premium that exceeds the additional production cost for a good that they knew was of high quality. As a result, the firm can increase its value if it can credibly commit to produce the high quality good.

Because it is more costly to produce the high quality good, firms have an incentive to renege on their implicit commitments and to substitute low quality output. However, if the firm does this it destroys its reputation for producing a high quality product. Thus, the incentive to deviate may be counterbalanced by the present value of the additional future cash flows that arise from maintaining a reputation for high quality. If the present value of the reputation is sufficiently high and the firm has, or can raise, enough cash to finance the production of high quality goods, it can credibly commit to producing a high quality good. Because the commitment is credible the customers will be willing to pay a premium in the current period.

A firm can only maintain its reputation if it is able to finance the additional cost of producing high quality goods. A firm in financial distress is thus not able

[29] Maksimovic [1987] discusses this case and its generalization to the case when potential entrants may be of two types, one that can be deterred and one that cannot.

[30] By contrast to the previous paper, MT analyze the effect of financial incentives within a finite period model. See Tirole [1988] for a discussion of different ways of modelling the incentive to acquire reputation.

to maintain its reputation. As a result, policies that increase the probability that the firm encounters financial distress in the future also increases the probability that the firm will not be able to benefit fully from investment in building up its reputation. Thus, an increase in the probability of financial distress in the *future* reduces the value of maintaining a reputation *today*. For a sufficiently large the reduction in value of maintaining a reputation, the firm lose its incentive to produce high quality output today. If customers are rational, the change of incentives will translate into an immediate reduction in the amount that they will pay for the firm's goods and thus its value.

High leverage increases the probability of financial distress. By increasing leverage, firms in industries where implicit contracts are important reduce their value. MT's model predicts that these firms will have lower leverage than firms in industries in which implicit contracts are not important. The model also predicts that failures in implicit contracts and price-wars are most likely to occur in industry downturns, when firms are facing financial distress.

4. Conflicts of interest and commitment

In many industries firms interact with a small number of rivals in the product market or with a small number of suppliers. In those instances the interaction between the firm and its rivals can be modeled as a strategic game. A change in the incentives of the agents who control the firm may then cause rivals or suppliers to change their production or pricing decisions, thereby affecting the firm's value. This occurs because the rivals' outputs will in general depend on some action of the firm, such as its choice of quantity produced.

Interestingly, in some cases a change in incentives that creates a conflict of interests between different classes of investors in the firm's securities may increase the value of the firm. This will happen if the new incentives enable the firm to commit credibly to product market strategies that move the industry to a more advantageous equilibrium.[31]

The effect of conflicts between equityholders and debtholders on the firm's incentives and value in an oligopoly is examined in contributions by Brander & Lewis [1986](BL) and Maksimovic [1986]. Rotemberg & Scharfstein [1990] (RS) consider another conflict, that between the firm's current investors and potential new investors. They show that a firm's incentives and value in an oligopoly can also be affected by varying its firm's dependence on external financing.

Before discussing conflicts of interest between equityholders and debtholders it is helpful to proceed by first examining an inherently simpler setup in which the effect of changes of incentives on a product market equilibrium is explored.

[31] Commitment has received a great deal of attention in both the finance and industrial economics literature. In many strategic interactions in the product market it is to the firm's advantage to credibly commit to a profitable course of action. See Tirole [1988] for a discussion and references on the role of commitment in strategic product market games.

Accordingly, we first show how optimal loan commitments may affect market outcomes in an oligopoly, and how to derive equilibrium loan commitment terms.

To illustrate the issues consider a standard Nash–Cournot duopoly in which the firm chooses the quantity it produces.[32] Thus, each firm strategically chooses the quantity it must produce to maximize its profits, taking the other's output as given. In equilibrium, each firm's output is its best response to the other's equilibrium output. Firms do not collude and there is perfect information.

The event sequence is as follows: At time t_0 firms arrange financing for the output that they plan to produce in equilibrium. At time t_1, they produce the output at a constant and identical marginal cost of production, c, and take it to market. There is no uncertainty.

Let the demand function in the industry be linear

$$p = \alpha - \beta(q_1 + q_2), \qquad \alpha, \beta > 0,$$

where p is the price and q_i the output of firm i.

The profits of firm i, $i = 1, 2$ are

$$\pi_i(q_1, q_2) = \big(a - b(q_1 + q_2)\big)q_i - rq_i,$$

where r is one plus the market rate of interest, $a = \alpha/c$ and $b = \beta/c$. Differentiating π_i, $i = 1, 2$, with respect to q_i, setting each to zero and solving jointly yields the standard expressions for output $q_i = q_j = (a - r)/(3b)$ and profits $\pi_i = \pi_j = (a - r)^2/(9b)$.

Consider now how the situation would change if instead of obtaining a loan for cq_i at time t_0 firm i obtained a larger loan commitment at a rate $r_i < r$. Such a transaction would require a fixed initial fee to be paid. We assume that the banks are willing to provide such commitments at zero economic profit and determine the terms below. Can firms benefit from such an arrangement? How should r_i be set?

Having received a loan commitment, the marginal cost of financing a unit of output for firm i is, at r_i, less than it would be without the commitment. All other things being equal, the firm will be a more aggressive competitor. If the marginal financing cost for other firms remained unchanged, this would alter the product equilibrium. In the new equilibrium firm i would produce more than before and firm j would produce less. As a result, the value of firm i would increase and the value of firm j would decrease. Thus, it is to the advantage firm i to obtain a loan commitment with $r_i < r^*$.

In equilibrium both firms will attempt to take advantage of loan commitments to increase value. Repeating the steps above, the equilibrium outputs at time t_1 are now $q_i = (a - 2r_i + r_j)/(3b)$ and $q_j = (a - 2r_j + r_i)/(3b)$. Thus, industry equilibrium in the product market at time t_1 depends on the terms of the loan commitment at time t_0. To see how the value of firm i depends on the loan

[32] The exposition is based on Maksimovic [1990].

commitment we substitute the expressions for q_i and q_j in the expression for π_i. This yields

$$\pi_i(r_1, r_2) = \frac{(a - 2r_i + r_j)(a - 3r + r_i + r_j)}{9b}.$$

From this expression one can determine the optimal r_i for each r_j. Differentiating the expression with respect to zero and solving for r_i we obtain the reaction function for firm i,

$$r_i = -\frac{r_j}{4} + \frac{6r - a}{4}.$$

Note that each firm will prefer to take a loan commitment because it increases its output at the expense of the rival. We can derive a similar expression for r_j as a function of r_i. Nash equilibrium choices of r_i and r_j occur when the reaction functions intersect at $r_i = r_j = r^* = (6r - a)/5$.

It can be verified by direct calculation that the bank will supply the required loan commitment in return for a flat fee of $(r - r^*) \times (a - r^*)/(3b)$. In equilibrium each firm now produces $q = (a - r^*)/(3b)$, which exceeds the equilibrium output in the absence of loan commitments. This occurs because the lower marginal cost of financing makes each firm a more aggressive competitor.

The equilibrium of this simple model illustrates the following propositions. First, financial contracts can affect equilibrium in the product market by providing incentives for firms to act more aggressively. Second, it is individually rational for each firm to obtain loan commitments that guarantee loans at a rate below the spot rate r, thereby credibly committing itself to produce more than in the absence of loan commitments. Third, because in the new equilibrium each firm produces more than before, taken together the firms are worse off than in the absence of the loan commitments.

Conflicts of interest between debtholders and equityholders

The intuition that the firm's financial structure can commit it to advantageous product market strategies has received has been explored in contemporaneous contributions by BL and Maksimovic [1986]. As a commitment device, debt has two important features. First, the payoff to debt holders is a function of the total value of the firm rather than the level of output. Second, the standard debt contract results in a transfer of ownership from one class of investors to another if the firm is insolvent.

The contingent transfer of ownership in bankruptcy is central for constructing leverage policies that credibly change industry equilibrium to the firm's advantage. In states that are favorable to the firm, the firm will be solvent and the residual cash flows will belong to the firm's equityholders. By contrast, in states of the world which are sufficiently unfavorable to the firm, the firm will be bankrupt. In this case the residual right to the firm's cash flows will belong to the debtholders. The key insight is that the agents controlling the firm's actions will chose output levels to maximize the expected profits in those states in which they are the residual owners of the firm and *not* the unconditional expected value of the firm. By altering the firm's financial structure, its equityholders can alter the states in which the transfer from themselves to debtholders will occur. Hence the firm's optimal output level will in general change as the firm's financial structure changes.

As in the model above, if the firm increases output as a result of changed incentives, its rivals may decrease their output in equilibrium. The reduction in the rivals' output, combined with the increase in the firm's output, may result in an increase in the value of the firm taken as a whole.[33]

The firm increases output as a result of changed incentives if the output that maximizes expected profits only over the states in which the firm's equityholders retain control exceeds the output that maximizes expected profit over all states. In that case leverage provides incentives for the equityholders to increase output in excess of that of a profit maximizing all-equity firm.

The role of debt in affecting the states in which the firm maximizes profits can be seen by examining the firm's objective function in the BL model. They focus on the case of a Nash–Cournot duopoly in which firms use their output levels as strategic variables. In BL the product market is modeled at a high degree of abstraction. The operating profit (revenue *minus* variable costs) of firm i is $R^i(q_i, q_j, z_i)$, where q_i and q_j are the outputs of firms i and j respectively. The random variable z_i reflects the stochastic shocks to the operating profit and is distributed over an interval $[z_1, z_2]$. It is assumed that larger values of values of z_i denote a better state of the world (i.e., $R^i_z > 0$) and that R^i satisfies the usual properties relating output to operating profits, such as $R^i_{ii} < 0$ and $R^i_j < 0$. For most of the analysis Brander and Lewis also assume that $R^i_{iz} > 0$, so that a better state of the world is associated with higher marginal operating revenues.[34]

The sequence of decisions is that first firms simultaneously choose a debt level, D_i. The equityholders of each firm then choose an output level, q_i to maximize the value of equity, taking the debt levels of both firms as given. Finally, uncertainty is resolved and cash flows are realized.

The debt levels are chosen initially by the owners of each firm so as to maximize the total value of the debt securities they sell and the expected value of equity. The expected total value of equity depends on the equilibrium values of q_i and q_j. These equilibrium values are the Nash strategies of the product market game between the firms and depend on the equityholders' payoff functions of both firms.

The key insight is that as the debt level of a firm changes, the equityholders' objective function changes. As a result, the equilibrium values of q_i and q_j change. Hence, it is possible to express the values of the firms as functions of the debt levels D_i and D_j and the interaction between firms as a game in which each firm's

[33] By contrast, in a single firm setting it is optimal to take into account the firm's cash flows in all states of the world in determining the quantity produced. Financial structures that induce the equityholders to ignore the payoffs in some states of the world would therefore lower the firm's value.

[34] BL show that if the sign of this partial derivative is reversed, many of the results are also reversed.

debt level is its strategic variable. BL characterize the equilibrium debt choices in this game.

The change in equityholders' incentives introduced by issuing debt can be seen by comparing the payoff function of the equityholders at the time that they choose the quantity produced with the value of the firm as a whole. After debt is issued, the value of equity is given by

$$E_i = \int_{z*}^{z_2} \left(R_i^i(q_i, q_j, z_i) f(z_i) - D_i\right) f(z_i)\,\mathrm{d}z_i,$$

where $f(z_i)$ is the density of z_i and z^* is the level of z_i at which bankruptcy occurs, defined by

$$R_i^i(q_i, q_j, z_i^*) - D_i = 0.$$

This is contrasted with the value of the firm as a whole

$$V_i = \int_{z_1}^{z_2} R_i^i(q_i, q_j, z_i) f(z_i) f(z_i)\,\mathrm{d}z_i.$$

By varying the level of debt, the firm's owners can alter the firm's objective function at the time that the output is selected. Note that this introduces a conflict of interests between the firm's equityholders and debtholders. The rationale for the use of debt critically depends on this conflict of interests. It is precisely because the firm's equityholders do not take the value of the firm's debt into account that their new payoff function is credible.

Given debt levels, the equilibrium outputs are obtained by differentiating the expressions for E_i and E_j above with respect to q_i and q_j respectively and equating them to zero, and solving the resulting first order conditions for output levels. The relationship between a firm's debt level and the equilibrium outputs of the two firms can then be derived by totally differentiating the first order conditions and using Cramer's rule to solve for $\mathrm{d}q_i/\mathrm{d}D_i$ and $\mathrm{d}q_j/\mathrm{d}D_i$. This yields

$$\frac{\mathrm{d}q_i}{\mathrm{d}D_i} = \frac{-E^i_{iD_i} E^j jj}{E^i_{ii} E^j_{jj} - E^i_{ij} E^j_{ji}}$$

and

$$\frac{\mathrm{d}q_j}{\mathrm{d}D_i} = \frac{E^i_{iD_i} E^j ji}{E^i_{ii} E^j_{jj} - E^i_{ij} E^j_{ji}}.$$

BL assume further that $E^i_{ii} E^j_{jj} - E^i_{ij} E^j_{ji} > 0$, $E^j_{jj} < 0$ and that $E^j_{ji} < 0$. With these assumptions, an exogenous increase in a firm's debt level leads to an increase in its equilibrium output and a decrease in the equilibrium output of the rival firm. It can be shown that these considerations imply that in equilibrium it is optimal for firms to have at least some debt in their financial structures.

BL provide a convincing rationale for the existence of a linkage between financial and product markets based on the intuition that changes in debt levels can commit a firm to a more aggressive product market strategy. However, it is a feature of their modeling approach that the product market is not modeled directly. Instead, it is described by a reduced form function $R_i^i(q_i, q_j, z_i)$. Signs of certain endogenous variables are assumed rather than derived from first principles. While this has the advantage of making the model general, it leaves room for further research to characterize the parameter values for which the model holds in any particular application.

A key assumption for deriving the specific result that leverage causes the firm's equityholders to be more aggressive and the rival's equityholders to be less aggressive is that $E_{ji}^j < 0$. This is a fairly common assumption in the analysis of Cournot oligopolies. As pointed out by Sundaram & John [1992], it implies that the product market game are strategic substitutes in the sense of Bulow, Geanakoplos & Klemperer [1985]. However, it is easy to come up with specifications of product market games in which this assumption is violated. In those cases leverage would not be advantageous for firms.

As is common in models of oligopoly, it also assumed that the conditions for the equilibrium modeled to exist are satisfied. This could be a problem in the application of the model to some industries because the usual existence theorems for oligopolistic games assume that the decision-maker's payoff function is concave in the strategic variable i.e., ($E_{jj}^j < 0$). It is not clear in the present context under what conditions the value of equity is concave in the quantity produced over the relevant ranges.

One of the models in Maksimovic [1986] also investigates the use of leverage to create a commitment in the product market. His approach is to introduce uncertainty into the framework of the loan commitment model discussed above by allowing demand to be either high or low. The level of demand is revealed only after the quantity produced is chosen and paid for by the equityholders.

For some parameter values the firm will produce more if the equityholders maximize profits in the high state only. However, if the firm has no debt the equityholders cannot credibly commit to produce only for the high state. The equityholders of a leveraged firm can commit to do so. By taking on a sufficiently large debt burden the firm will be bankrupt if the low state occurs. As a result, the equityholders of a sufficiently leveraged firm receive no profits in the low state and their commitment to maximize profits in the high state only is credible. Hence, leverage is a commitment device. Results about value dissipation similar to those derived in the loan commitment model then follow.

A conceptual issue in both BL and Maksimovic [1986] relates to the timing of the decision on the quantity to produce. In BL equityholders decide on the level of output before the state of the world is revealed, but production costs are paid only out of revenues. This timing sequence is important in determining the effect of leverage on incentives. It raises issues of limited liability. It is in general not possible for the original equityholders to commit the new owners of a bankrupt firm to pay for predetermined output levels. If, as in Maksimovic [1986], production costs are paid by the firm's owners before the state of the world is revealed, then leverage may create incentives to *decrease* the level of output.[35]

The papers reviewed so far in this section suggest that it may be optimal to create a conflict of interests between the firm's claimants because the conflict induces the firm's rivals to lower output. However, once the rivals are committed to their reduced output levels it would be optimal for the firm to revert to an all-equity structure and reduce its own output levels. Thus, there is an incipient tension between the profitability of committing to a high output level to induce the rival to reduce his output and an incentive to remove that conflict of interest.

If the firm is financed with public debt, so that a recapitalization is observable, then this incipient tension does not pose a difficulty for the model. However, the incentive to revert to an all-equity financial structure is a problem if the firm is private and if it tries to effect the commitment using private debt. In that case, the initial commitment could be undone secretly, and would therefore not be credible to rivals. For the commitment to be credible in this case, another imperfection that makes the reduction of leverage costly is required. One such case is explored in Fulghieri & Nagarajan [1992]. In their model the firm's equityholders have proprietary information about the value of the firm. The lower the value of the firm, the greater is the equityholders' incentive to reduce leverage and to issue additional equity. This adverse selection problem makes it costly to undo the change in incentives from the increase in leverage. As a result, the initial commitment may be credible even if it can be reversed secretly.

Several papers have used the BL framework to explore the changes of financial structure on market equilibrium. Glazer [1994] analyzes the effect of a fixed level of long term debt on production incentives. With limited liability, the more valuable the firm's other assets, the less aggressively the firm will compete in the product market. Thus, a firm that makes and retains lower profits this year will be a more aggressive competitor next year than a firm that has made and retained higher profits. Glazer argues in this context, that rival's financial leverage may in some cases induce firms to be less aggressive competitors. The reason is that an increase in output today will not only lower market prices today but will lead to lower prices tomorrow as rivals react to their depleted bank accounts.

Brander & Lewis [1988] suggest that leverage may favorably alter the incentives of the firm's managers even if it does not create a conflict of interest. They show that there may a commitment value of bankruptcy costs even when managers do not act only in the interest of the shareholders. To show this they introduce bankruptcy costs into a framework very similar to that of the BL model above. The main differences are that (i) the managers maximize the total value of the firm, and (ii) there is a cost of bankruptcy. The expected cost of bankruptcy is modeled by subtracting $BF(z^*)$ from the expected value of the firm, where B is the bankruptcy cost, $F(z)$ is the cumulative distribution of stochastic shock and, as before, z^* is the level of the shock at which the firm becomes insolvent. Thus,

[35] See Kim & Maksimovic [1991] for a discussion of technologies for which the level of output would increase if the equityholders pay for the output before the state of the world is revealed.

Brander & Lewis [1988] the managers maximize

$$V_i = \int_{z_1}^{z_2} R_i^i(q_i, q_j, z_i) f(z_i) f(z_i)\,\mathrm{d}z_i - BF(z^*).$$

Thus, in Brander & Lewis [1988] bankruptcy costs punish low profits. Interestingly, they show that if B is a fixed cost, then the firm may become a more aggressive competitor as B increases.[36]

Conflicts of interest between current and future investors

RS analyze the product-market incentives of a firm when the managers are interested in maximizing the expected value of a combination of future profits and the market price of the firm's stock in the short term. They show that if the two differ, then managers have an incentive to increase the market price of stock in the short term by manipulating output levels.[37] The optimal manipulation depends on industry parameters and may result in an increase or decrease in the firm's output.

RS characterize parameters for which firms that adopt the objective of market price maximization become more aggressive competitors. In this case the firm's short term objective acts as a credible commitment to increase output. This commitment moves the industry to an equilibrium more advantageous to the firm. As a result, financial policies that induce managers to maximize short term stock price increase the value of the firm. However, as in all models in this section, if financial policies that promote aggressive competition are adopted by enough firms, the value of all firms in the industry declines.

As in many other models in corporate finance, investors have less information than managers of firms. The managers know the firm's output level but the investors do not. This asymmetry of information drives the difference between the stock price and the managers' expectation of future profits. However, the information structure of the RS model is somewhat unusual in corporate finance in that neither the managers nor the investors knows the firm's true costs precisely.[38]

Each firm's costs depend on four components unknown to managers or investors: a permanent and a temporary industry wide component and a permanent and temporary firm-specific component. Thus, firms' costs are correlated over time and across firms. Information about one firm's current costs improves estimates of its own and other firms' future costs.

[36] Brander and Lewis also obtain interesting results for the case in which B is a function of the difference between the firm's new revenues and its debt obligations.

[37] More precisely, RS consider a two period model. The stock price that enters the managers' objective function is the price at the end of the first period. The firm's managers maximize $E[\alpha(\pi^1 + p) + (1-\alpha)(\pi^1 + \pi^2)]$, where π^i is the profit in period i and p is the market price of the stock at the end of the first period.

[38] Because managers do not know costs, they cannot signal costs to investors. Instead, as in the signal-jamming models, such as Holmstrom [1982], they attempt to change the market's beliefs to their advantage by taking hidden actions.

The firm's stock price depends on the investors' estimate of both the absolute level of future costs and its future costs relative to the costs of rival firms. Since investors do not observe costs directly, they must infer them from the profits realized by all firms in the industry. This provides a potential incentive for each firm to vary its output so as to increase the stock market's assessment of its price.

RS focus on the inference drawn by the stock market from observing the first period profits of rival firms relative to those of the firm. Two competing effects are involved. Suppose, for example, that the rival firms' profits are high relative to those of the firm. The high profits of rival firms may lead the investors to conclude that the firm's costs are high compared to those of rival firms. If the market believes this, the price of the firm's shares will fall. Alternatively, investors may conclude that the industry wide costs are low. If this occurs, the price of the firm's shares will increase.

If the first effect is stronger, then the firm will try to reduce its rivals' profits by increasing its own output. If the second is stronger, then the firm will try to increase its rivals' profits by cutting its own output. In the former case the firm becomes a more aggressive competitor and its expected profits will increase in industry equilibrium. In the latter case it becomes a less aggressive competitor and its expected profits will decrease in industry equilibrium.

By altering its payout policy a firm can determine the extent to which it will need to go to the market at the end of the first period. Increased dependence on market financing increases firm value if increased concern with the stock price leads the firm to become a more aggressive competitor, i.e., if the first effect described above predominates. Similarly, if the second effect predominates, a smaller dependence on the market will make the firm more aggressive. As a result, the firm's payout policy is determined by the inferences investors draw from relative profits and is set to maximize the firm's incentive to produce.

5. Agency costs and product market strategies

Corporate finance literature has devoted a great deal of attention to devising financial contracts to mitigate perceived agency problems within the firm. Less attention has been devoted to analyzing how contracts designed to mitigate specific conflicts of interest within the firm affect the firm's ability to compete in product markets. By contrast, many of the models that have focused on the effect of debt on product market competition have an opposite bias. They do not address the effect of financial policies designed to gain product market advantage on the firm's internal incentives. Relatively few contributions have considered both problems jointly.

One problem naturally arises when the firm's financial contracting problem and its product market are considered together: do solutions to firms' internal agency problems leave them open to aggressive competition or predation from rivals? If so, financial structures that mitigate conflicts of interest between different classes of investors may lower the value of the firm. This has important empirical consequences in view of the claims made for high leverage as a way of improving managers' incentives [e.g., Jensen, 1986].[39]

Allen [1986] is an early contribution that addresses these issues. More recently Bolton & Scharfstein [1990] and Phillips [1993] show how rivals can exploit the conflicts of interest within the firm to deny it access to outside financing. Schleifer & Vishny [1992] (SV) analyze how financial structures designed to prevent managers from dissipating the firm's resources can in downturns impel the firm to liquidate its assets at loss.

Allen considers a two period duopoly where demand is stochastic. The two firms compete on an equal footing as Nash–Cournot duopolists in the first period. If neither of the firms becomes insolvent at the end of the first period, then they compete similarly in the second period. Similarly, if they both become insolvent, they both undergo costly reorganization between periods and compete on an equal basis in the second period. However, if only one firm becomes insolvent, the process of reorganization causes it to set its second period output after its rival has done so. As a result of this strategic disadvantage, the firm is less profitable and its rival is more profitable than would otherwise be the case.

Allen considers a case where debt financing provides a corporate tax shield. Firms face a trade-off between increasing debt to take advantage of the tax shield and at the same time increasing the probability of bankruptcy and the associated strategic disadvantage in the second period. An equilibrium may then exist in which one firm adopts high leverage while the second firm foregoes the tax advantages of debt in order to increase the probability of strategic dominance in the second period.

In Allen's model the financial market imperfection that drives trade-off arises from the costs of reorganizing a bankrupt firm's assets. Costly contracting at the point at which the firm initially tries to acquire assets in order to compete can also affect industry equilibrium. Bolton & Scharfstein [1990] bring out these issues is sharp relief. They analyze a model in which an initial solution to a firm's internal agency problem leaves it open to aggressive competition from rivals. They also consider how the contract between the firm and its investors can be amended to deter predation by rivals.

Bolton and Scharfstein model the firm's agency problem by assuming that only the firm and not outside investors observe profits in each period. As a result, the firm's owners have an incentive to under report profits, thereby keeping more for the firm's cash flow for themselves. If the incentive to misrepresent profits is not corrected, the firm will not be able to raise external financing. The firm's financial contract with investors is therefore designed to mitigate the conflict of interest between the firm and investors.

In the formal model two firms compete over two periods. To stay in business each firm incurs a fixed cost, F per period. One of the firm's can finance the

[39] Some of the papers discussed above, for example, Williams [1995] fall into this broad category. The papers discussed here differ in that the interaction between the product market and the financial market develops over time, allowing different equilibrium outcomes.

investment of F internally, whereas the other firm must obtain funding from the capital market. Bolton and Scharfstein focus first on the latter firm and examine how financial contracts designed to mitigate agency problems of external financing can provide incentives for the rival firms to become a more aggressive competitor. Bolton and Scharfstein assume that the firm's gross profit per period is either π_l or π_h, where $\pi_l < \pi_h$ and $\pi_l < F$.[40] At the beginning of each period both the firm and investors expect that the probability of profits being π_l is ω, where $\pi = \omega\pi_l + (1-\omega)\pi_h > F$. For simplicity we assume that profit levels at the two dates are statistically independent.

The investors initially have to decide whether or not to finance the firm's first period production. If the firm is financed it reports profits of either π_l or π_h. If the firm reports $\pi_l(\pi_h)$ it pays the investor R_l (R_h) at this time. The investors then decide whether or not to fund production in the second period. Let β_i, where $i = h, l$ be the probability that the firm is funded in the second period if it reports profits π_i. If the firm is funded investors receive $R^l(R^h)$ at the end of the second period, depending on the state that they had reported in the first period.[41]

The optimal contract maximizes the expected profits of the investor subject to (i) an incentive compatibility constraint that the firm truthfully reveals profits at the end of the first period, (ii) limited liability constraints and (iii) the individual rationality constraint that the firm wishes to enter into the contract. Thus, the firm's problem is

$$\max_{\{\beta, R^i, R_i\}} \; -F + \omega\left(R_l + \beta_l(R^l - F)\right) + (1-\omega)\left(R_h + \beta_h(R^h - F)\right),$$

subject to the incentive compatibility constraint

$$\pi_h - R_h + \beta_h(\pi - R^h) \geq \pi_h - R_l + \beta_l(\pi - R^l),$$

and the limited liability constraints $\pi_i \geq R_i$ and $\pi_i - R_i + \pi_l \geq R^i$ for $i = h, l$.[42]

Bolton and Scharfstein show that if the firm is funded, the optimal contract between it and investors requires that $R_l = \pi_l$, $\beta_l = 0$, $R_h = \pi$ and $\beta_h = 1$. A key feature of this contract is that the firm is not funded in the second period if low profits are realized in the first period (since $\beta_l = 0$). This provision provides an incentive for a rival firm to become a more aggressive competitor in the first period by producing more than its the profit maximizing output. By overproducing in the first period the internally financed rival firm can lower the profits of the outside financed firm, ensuring that outside investors will not finance operations in the second period. As a result, the internally financed firm will benefit from increased market power in the second period achieved by predation in the first period.

[40] The paper discusses several different information structure regimes and parameter ranges. In this exposition we focus on an illustrative 'base' case.

[41] Since investors cannot observe the profit level the firm has no incentive to make the final report contingent on the state.

[42] The individual rationality constraint has been suppressed.

Bolton and Scharfstein consider how the contract between the cash constrained firm and investors can be amended to deter predation by the rival firm. The rival firm's incentive to predate in the first period is determined by the difference $\beta_h - \beta_l$. As this difference decreases, the rival firm's benefit from predation in the first period also decreases. Predation can therefore be deterred by reducing β_h or by increasing β_l sufficiently.

Increasing β_l sufficiently to deter predation is in general costly because it creates incentives for the firm to misrepresent the firm's profits to investors. Bolton and Scharfstein show that the optimal contract that deters predation requires that $R_l = \pi_l$, $\beta_l = 0$, that R_h be less than π and that β_h be less than one. This modified optimal contract is less efficient than the contract derived in the absence of the rival firm because to deter predation investors *reduce* their probability of funding the firm if it is successful in the first period. Thus, the investor and the externally financed firm have a choice of either adopting the modified optimal contract that deters predation and is less efficient or of adopting the previously derived contract and accepting predation by the rival firm.

These results suggest that external financing may be costly for the firm by encouraging aggressive competition and reducing the likelihood that the firm will be able to obtain capital for its continuing its operations. Several strong assumption are made in order to obtain these results so cleanly. For example, it is assumed that the investors can commit to enforceable choices of β_h and β_l at the beginning of the first period, that profits may be unobservable (or observable but unverifiable, so that contracts cannot be written contingent on the realized profits) and that the investors have all the bargaining power in determining the firm's financial contract. It is a strength of the analysis that the implications of the assumptions are discussed extensively and defended in the paper.

Phillips [1993] also analyses the effect of another informational imperfection in the financial markets on product market competition. However, in contrast to Bolton and Scharfstein, in his model profits are observable and contracts drawn on the firm's cash flows are enforceable. Efficient financial contracting is impeded by an informational asymmetry between investors and the entrepreneur: Investors cannot observe the firm's profit potential at the time when the firm must invest in order to take advantage of a product market opportunity.

Phillips [1993] considers a game-theoretic model of oligopolistic competition. Firms have a two period horizon. They must make an investment at the end of the first period in order to stay in business in the second period. Phillips assumes that the investment project at the end of the first period can be financed either with the firm's internal cash or borrowed funds. The informational asymmetry between investors and the entrepreneur creates an incentive for the entrepreneur to borrow to invest even if the expected net present value of the project is negative. To resolve this adverse selection problem, optimal contracts between firms and investors will require some portion of the new investment to be financed by internal cash.

Because a firm that wants to invest is required to partially finance the project internally, the amount of cash that the firm has on hand at the end of the first period is a critical variable. This creates incentives for a rival producer to compete more aggressively in the first period, thereby depleting the firm's cash reserves and forcing it to forego the investment. The rival producer benefits from the resulting reduction in competition.

The strength of the incentive to predate in the first period depends on the firm's initial financial structure in the first period. If the firm enters the first period with very little debt, then the cost to a rival producer of depleting the firm's resources sufficiently to prevent it from investing is very high. On the other hand, if the firm enters the first period with high leverage, then the rival producer may be able to drive it out at little cost.

Phillips [1993] derives equilibrium financial structures of firms in both periods and equilibrium product market strategies. His model predicts that firms with good second period profit potential have low leverage in the first period. This financial structure deters predation. Interestingly, firms with low second period profit potential may adopt very high leverage. The high level of leverage makes it impossible for them to obtain sufficient loans for new investment at the end of the first period. Accordingly, it commits them to exiting the industry at the end of the first period, depriving rival producers of any incentive to predate. Phillips also explores a case in which firms with good second period profit potential have an incentive to adopt high leverage. In that equilibrium product market high quality firms have an incentive to show that they will not invest in the future.

SV explore a different trade-off: between financial structures that are designed to avoid agency problems within the firm, and the value of the firm's assets if the firm is liquidated due to financial distress. The agency problem that they are interested in is the manager's incentive to use the firm's cash surplus on projects that do not benefit the shareholders. This incentive may be avoided in some cases by a financial structure that combines short-term and long-term debt. As discussed by Hart [1991], short-term debt forces the firm to go to the capital market for investment funds. Long-term debt creates a debt-overhang that limits the managers' ability to finance the undesirable projects by borrowing.

Highly leveraged financial structures that reduce the manager's discretion to undertake undesirable investments when the firm has surplus cash may also expose it to financial distress in market downturns. This is not a concern if the liquidation value of the firm's assets equals the value of the firm. The firm's assets can simply be sold and the proceeds paid out to securityholders.

The key claim in SV is that any firm's assets are worth more to industry insiders than to outside investors. Insiders, such as rival producers, have superior information about the value of a firm's assets. Often they have specialized skills necessary to exploit the assets optimally. Thus, if a firm is to be liquidated it may be worth more to an industry insider than to an outside investor.

The comparative advantage of insiders for running firms in an industry has implications for financial structure choice. If all firms in an industry adopt highly leveraged financial structures, then it is likely that all firms will be in financial distress at the same time. As a result, the assets of distressed firms will be purchased by outsiders. Since outsiders cannot operate the assets as well as insiders, the price obtained in these sales should be less than the value that the sellers could have realized by continuing to operate the asset. This difference is a loss that can be attributed to forced sales of assets that result from the choice of a financial structure designed to prevent managers from undertaking unprofitable investments in good times.

The trade-off between agency costs and loss of value in liquidation can be used to generate predictions about financial choices of firms in an industry. SV discuss numerous scenarios and their dependence on parameter values. For example, in a duopoly, one firm may adopt a highly leveraged financial structure. This prevents unprofitable investments in good times but leads to losses when assets are liquidated in downturns. The second firm may instead chose low leverage. By doing so it positions itself to acquire assets of the distressed firm in a downturn. However, this option is may be costly because low leverage permits the manager to waste cash when the firm is profitable.

More generally, the SV suggest that optimal debt levels are limited by asset illiquidity. SV partially attribute the increases in leverage in the 1980s to an increase in liquidity of the market for corporate divisions. They see the increase as having been driven both by exogenous factors such as relaxed antitrust enforcement and an influx of foreign buyers, and as having been partially self-reinforcing.

6. Empirical tests

The preceding sections suggest several mechanisms by which financial structure could affect product market equilibrium. It is therefore important to sort out which, if any, of these mechanisms can explain financial and product market decisions in specific product market environments. In this section we describe three contributions that have attempted to do this: Titman & Wessels [1988] (TW), Chevalier [1994a,b] and Phillips [1995]. [43]

Of the models reviewed in this chapter perhaps the easiest to test empirically are Titman's [1984] model of the indirect costs of bankruptcy. Because this model focuses on the transaction between the firm and customers it does not require the specification of an econometric model of industry equilibrium or the analysis of interactions between firms. Instead, much can be learned by regressing the firm's leverage on measures of the costs that firms can impose on customers by liquidating or by breaking implicit contracts.

One paper that includes variables measuring these costs in a more extensive study of capital structure choice is TW. TW begin by specifying eight determinants of firms' financial structure choice. We focus on one of these hypothesized determinants: the extent to which the firm produces unique products or its

[43] See also the recent papers by Kovenock adn Phillips [1995a,b]. See Spence [1985] for an early study of financial-product market interactions. For a broader perspective on empirical research on product markets see Schmalensee's [1989] survey of empirical findings in the industrial organization literature.

'uniqueness'. Following Titman [1984], they argue that the cost borne by customers when a firm liquidates is positively related to 'uniqueness'. Hence, firms that produce 'unique' products should have lower leverage than firms that do not.

TW's model of capital structure choice is

$$y = \Gamma\xi + \varepsilon, \tag{1}$$

where y is a vector of measures of capital structure, ξ the vector of eight determinants, Γ is an unknown matrix of coefficients and ε is a Gaussian error term. In addition to 'uniqueness' the other determinants ξ are the collateral value of assets, nondebt tax shields, growth, industry classification, firm size, volatility of earnings and profitability. TW use six measures of capital structures: ratios of long-term, short-term and convertible debt to market value and book value of equity.

There do not exit direct measures of some of the determinants of capital structure identified by TW. Instead, they assume that there exists a linear relationship between the unobserved determinants and fifteen observed indicators or firm characteristics. This relationship is given by

$$x = \Lambda\xi + \delta, \tag{2}$$

where x is a vector of indicators, Λ an unknown matrix of coefficients and δ is a Gaussian error term.The specification in equation (2) permits some of the indicators to be related to more than one determinant. For example, TW assume that a firm's 'uniqueness' is measured by an unknown linear function of the ratio of the firm's R&D expenditures to sales, the ratio of sales expenditures to sales and the proportion of the industry's total workforce that voluntarily quits its job in the sample year.[44]

TW estimate equations (1) and (2) using LISREL on a single cross-section of 469 firms from the Compustat annual file using data from 1974–1982. By using LISREL, TW are able to estimate the coefficients of Γ using observed indicators x instead of the unobserved determinants ξ specified in the model of capital structure choice (1).[45]

TW find that both the ratio of long-term and short-term debt to equity are negatively related to 'uniqueness'. This relationship holds both when equity is measured as book value and when it is measured at market value. It also appears stronger than other, more traditional determinants of financial structure. TW interpret this finding as providing support for Titman's [1984] model discussed in Section 3 above.[46]

[44] Quit rates were only available at the industry level.

[45] LISREL requires that the researcher places sufficient a priori restrictions on the parameters of Λ. Each of these restrictions either precludes or restricts a possible relationship between an indicator x_k and a determinant ξ_i. For a lucid introduction to structural equation estimation using LISREL see Bollen [1989].

[46] For an alternative interpretation of the relationship between R&D and leverage see Long & Malitz [1987].

In contrast to Titman [1984], in most models reviewed in this chapter both debt levels and product market interactions between firms are endogenously determined. As a result of this added complexity, it is often possible to obtain very different predictions about the covariation between debt and competitive levels as the values of the exogenous variables change.[47] General tests of these models call for a structural estimation approach in which both output and financial structures are endogenous. Unfortunately, such structural models at the industry level would be difficult to estimate and have not been attempted. Instead, researchers have attempted to obtain evidence on the links between financial structure choices and product market interactions by tracing out the product market consequences of significant recapitalizations in several industries. Phillips [1995] and Chevalier [1994a, b] represent alternative approaches to this problem.

Phillips [1995] examines the association between financial structure and industry output in four industries: fiberglass, tractor trailer, polyethylene and gypsum. These industries were chosen because in each the largest firms used leveraged recapitalizations to increase debt ratios by at least twenty five percent. In each industry the largest four firms have a high market share. The first three industries are relatively concentrated. Gypsum differs from the industries in the sample because the minimum efficient scale is small relative to the size of the market and there are few barriers to entry.

Phillips [1995] finds that in all cases except gypsum the major firms that increased leverage either lost market share or did not increase their market share when other firms exited the industry. Instead, in these industries the firms that recapitalized experienced sales decreases, but operating margins increases. In gypsum these results are reversed.

Phillips also investigates whether the debt level in the industry affects the intensity of competition using output and cost data for each industry. His approach is based on Porter [1983b] and Bresnahan [1989]. The starting point is the observation that the difference between the price p and marginal cost mc is an indicator of the intensity of competition. In a perfectly competitive industry $p = mc$. More generally, in a Cournot–Nash oligopoly where demand and cost function satisfy certain aggregation conditions, the following supply relationship can be obtained,

$$p_t = mc_t - \theta D_q(q_t)q_t,$$

where the subscript t stands for time t, q_t is the industry and $D_q(q_t)$ is the derivative of the inverse demand function with respect to industry output. The parameter θ measures the level of competition. In a perfectly competitive industry $\theta = 0$, whereas in a monopoly $\theta = 1$. In Nash–Cournot oligopolies, θ takes on intermediate values. Phillips tests whether the term θ is affected by the average debt ratio in that industry.

To derive an equation that can be estimated it is necessary to make some assumptions about specific functional forms. A key assumption made by Phillips

[47] For example, in RS external financing is predicted to cause the firm to be either a more or less aggressive competitor, depending on whether a condition is satisfied or not.

is that firms have Cobb–Douglas production functions. Cobb–Douglas production functions yield a relatively simple functional form for the term mc_t. It is also assumed that each industry faces a loglinear demand function,

$$\log q_t = \alpha_0 + \alpha_1 \log p_t + \alpha_2 \log y_t + \alpha_3 r_t, \tag{3}$$

where y_t is a exogenous shift in demand parameter and r_t measures the relative price of substitute products. Substituting for q_t and mc_t in the demand function, and solving for p_t, the following modified supply relationship can be obtained

$$p_t = \beta_0 + \beta_1 q_t + \sum_{j=1}^{n} \beta_j w_{jt} - \log\left(1 + \frac{\theta_t}{\alpha_1 + \alpha_3}\right), \tag{4}$$

where the w_j are the prices of inputs. If the average leverage in the industry determines the level of competition, then the last term in the preceding equation is a function of average leverage.[48] With this motivation, Phillips replaces the last term of the supply relationship (4) by $\gamma \times LEV_t$ where γ is a constant and LEV_t is measure of the average leverage in the industry. This supply function for each industry is jointly estimated with the demand function (3) on monthly data over the period 1980–1990 using two-stage least squares.

Phillips finds that in all the industries with the exception of gypsum the average industry debt ratio is positively correlated with industry price and negatively correlated with industry supply. In the gypsum industry the reverse occurs — high leverage is associated with intensified competition. Phillips attributes this contrast to differences in industry structure: the gypsum industry is more fragmented and has lower barriers of entry than the other industries in his sample.

Chevalier [1994a, b] also examines the relationship between market structure and industry pricing following leveraged buyouts (LBOs). In contrast to Phillips, she focuses on a shorter time period [1985–1988] and one industry — supermarkets — in which firms interact in many local submarkets. This approach has the advantage of generating multiple observations from one industry and thereby controlling for shifts in demand or firms' production functions without specifying parametric forms. The approach has a potential disadvantage in that the observations in the approximately eighty submarkets in her sample may not be independent, making cross-sectional comparisons more difficult to interpret.

Chevalier finds that LBOs are good news for rival firms. When a LBO is announced rival supermarket chains that share some of the local markets with the firm undergoing the LBO experience a significant positive share price response. She also examines supermarket prices in local markets in which one of the participating supermarket chains has undergone a LBO. Chevalier finds price decreases in local markets in which rival firms have not undergone LBOs and one of the rivals has a large market share. She finds that price increases are likely

[48] Equation (4) is estimated for each industry. Thus, it is assumed that the production functions of firms in an industry can only differ by a multiplicative constant.

if some rival firms have undergone LBOs and if there does not a rival that has undergone an LBO and has a large market share.

Chevalier [1994a,b] and Phillips [1994] are important both for the evidence they provide about the relationship between leveraged recapitalizations and market competition and because they adopt innovative approaches to estimating that relationship. What is not yet clear is whether their findings on the relationship between leverage and competition can be generalized or are specific to industries that undergo leveraged recapitalizations. The latter might occur if the factors that make the industry attractive for leveraged recapitalizations also directly affect industry equilibrium. Equally important, leveraged recapitalizations are frequently accompanied by changes in incentives that cannot be measured by changes in leverage and that are specifically intended to reduce the conflicts of interest between the equityholders and debtholders.[49] Such changes in incentives are difficult to quantify but are at the heart of agency models.

Acknowledgements

I would like to thank Murray Frank, Gordon Phillips and Sheridan Titman for their helpful comments, and the Faculty of Commerce at UBC for their hospitality while this chapter was being written.

References

Allen, F. (1986). Capital structure and imperfect competition in product markets, discussion paper, University of Pennsylvania.

Allen, F., and A. Winton (1995). Corporate financial structure and incentives, in: R. Jarrow, V. Maksimovic and W.T. Ziemba (eds.), Finance, Handbooks in Operations Research and Management Science, Vol. 9, North-Holland, Amsterdam, pp. 693–720 (this volume).

Barnea, A., R.A. Haugen and L.W. Senbet (1985). *Agency problems of financial contracting*, Prentice Hall, Englewood Hills, NJ.

Bhattacharya S. and J.R. Ritter (1983). Innovation and communication, signalling with partial disclosure. *Rev. Econ. Studies* 50, 331–346.

Bollen, K.A. (1989). *Structural equations with latent variables*, John Wiley, New York, NY.

Bolton, P., and D. Scharfstein (1990). A theory of predation based on agency problems in financial contracting. *Am. Econ. Rev.* 80, 93–106.

Brander, J.A., and T. R. Lewis (1986). Oligopoly and financial structure: the limited liability effect. *Am. Econ. Rev.* 76, 956–970.

Brander, J.A., and B. Spencer (1989). Moral hazard and limited liability: implications for the theory of the firm. *Int. Econ. Rev.* 30, 833–849.

Bresnahan, T.F. (1989). Empirical studies of industries with market power, in: R. Schmalensee and R.D. Willg (eds.), *Handbook of Industrial Organization*, North-Holland, Amsterdam.

Brock, W.A. and J.A. Scheinkman (1985). Price Setting Supergames with Capacity Constraints, *Rev. Econ. Studies* 52, 371–382.

[49] For example, Phillips [1994] shows that sales growth is significantly associated with executive compensation before, but not after recapitalizations.

Bulow, J., J. Geanakoplos and P. Klemperer (1985). Multimarket oligopoly: strategic substitutes and complements. *J. Polit. Econ.* 93, 488–511.

Chevalier, J.A. (1994a). Capital structure and product market competition: an examination of supermarket LBOs, Harvard University, working paper, unpublished.

Chevalier, J.A. (1994b). Capital structure and product market competition: an empirical study of supermarket pricing, Harvard University, working paper, unpublished.

Dotan, A., and S. Ravid (1985). On the interaction of real and financial decisions of the firm under uncertainty. *J. Finance* 40, 501–517.

Dybvig, P. and C. Spatt (1983). Does it pay to maintain a reputation, Yale University, working paper.

Fershtman, C., and K. L. Judd (1987). Equilibrium incentives in oligopoly. *Am. Econ. Rev.* 77, 927–40.

Friedman, J. (1971). A non-cooperative equilibrium for supergames. *Rev. Econ. Studies* 28, 1–12.

Fulghieri, P. and S. Nagarajan (1992). Financial contracts as lasting commitments: the case of leveraged oligopoly, *J. Financ. Intermed.* 2, 2–32.

Gertner, R., Gibbons, R. and D. Scharfstein (1988). Simultaneous signalling to the capital and product markets, *Rand J. Econ.* 19, 173–190.

Glazer, J. (1994). The strategic effects of long-term debt in imperfect competition. *J. Econ. Theory* 62, 428–443.

Green, E.J., and R.H. Porter (1984). Non-cooperative collusion under imperfect price information. *Econometrica* 52, 87–100.

Harris, M.A., and A. Raviv (1991). The theory of capital structure. *J. Finance* 46, 297–355.

Hart, O. (1991). Theories of optimal capital structure: a principal-agent perspective, in: M. Blair (ed.), *The Deal Decade*, Brooking Institution, Washington D.C.

Holmström, B. (1982). Moral hazard in teams, *Bell J. Econ.* 13, 324–340.

Jensen, M. (1986). Agency costs of free cash flow, corporate finance and takeovers. *Am. Econ. Rev.* 76, 323–39.

Jensen, M., and W. Meckling (1976). The theory of the firm: managerial behavior, agency costs and ownership structure. *J. Financ. Econ.* 3, 305–360.

Kim, M. and V. Maksimovic (1991). Technology, debt and the exploitation of growth options, *J. Bank. Finance* 14, 1113–1131.

Klein, B., and K.B. Leffler (1981). The role of market forces assuring contractual performance. *J. Polit. Econ.* 89, 615–641.

Kovenock, D. and G. Phillips (1995a). Capital structure and product market rivalry: How do we reconcile theory and evidence? *Am. Econ. Rev.* 85, 403–408.

Kovenock, D. and G. Phillips (1995b). Capital structure and product market behavior, Center for Economics Studies, working paper No 95-4, US Bureau of Census.

Long, M.S., and I.B. Malitz (1985). Investment patterns and financial leverage, in: B.M. Friedman (ed.), *Corporate Capital Structures in the United States*, National Bureau of Economic Research Project Report, University of Chicago Press, Chicago and London, pp. 325–48.

Maksimovic, V. (1986). Optimal capital structure in oligopolies, Ph.D. dissertation, Harvard University, unpublished.

Maksimovic, V. (1987). Oligopoly, price wars and bankruptcy, UBC, working paper, unpublished.

Maksimovic, V. (1988). Optimal capital structure in repeated oligopolies. *Rand J. Econ.* 19, 389–407.

Maksimovic, V. (1990). Product market imperfections and loan commitments. *J. Finance* 45, 1641–1653.

Maksimovic, V., and S. Titman (1991). Financial reputation and reputation for product quality. *Rev. Financ. Studies* 2, 175–200.

Maksimovic, V., and J. Zechner (1991). Agency, debt and product market equilibrium. *J. Finance* 46, 1619–1643.

Miller, M. (1977). Debt and taxes. *J. Finance* 32, 261–275.

Myers, S., and N. Majluf (1984). Corporate financing and investment decisions when firms have information that investors do not have. *J. Financ. Econ.* 13, 187–221.

Myers, S. (1977). Determinants of corporate borrowing, *J. Financ. Econ.* 5, 147–175.

Myers, S. (1984). The capital structure puzzle. *J. Finance* 39, 572–592.

Phillips, G. (1995). Increased debt and product markets: an empirical analysis, *J. Financ. Econ.* 37, 189–238.

Phillips, G. (1993). Financing investment and product market competition, Purdue University, working paper, Krannert Graduate School of Management, unpublished.

Porter, R.H. (1983a). Optimal cartel trigger-trice strategies. *J. Econ. Theory* 29, 313–328.

Porter, R.H. (1983b). A study of cartel stability: The joint executive committee 1880–1886. *Bell J. Econ.* 14, 301–314.

Ravid, S.A. (1988). On the interactions of production and financial decisions. *Financ. Manage.* 17, 87–89.

Rotemberg, J., and D. Scharfstein (1990). Shareholder value maximization and product market competition. *Rev. Financ. Studies* 367–393.

Schmalensee, R. (1980). Inter-industry studies of structure and performance, in R. Schmalensee and R.D. Willig, Handbook of Industrial Organization, Vol. 2., North-Holland, Amsterdam, Oxford, Tokyo.

Shapiro, C. (1982). Consumer information, product quality and seller reputation, *Bell J. Econ.* 13, 20–35.

Shapiro, A., and S. Titman (1985). An integrated approach to corporate risk management, *Midland Corp. Finance J.* 3, 41–56.

Shleifer, A., and R.W. Vishny (1992). Liquidation values and debt capacity: a market equilibrium approach. *J. Finance* 47, 1343–1365.

Spence, A.M. (1985). Capital structure and the corporation's product market environment, in: B. Friedman (ed.), *Corporate Capital Structures in the United States*, University of Chicago Press, Chicago, IL, pp. 353–382.

Sundaram, A., and K. John (1992). Product market games and signaling models in finance: do we know what we know?, New York University, mimeo.

Tirole, J. (1988). *The theory of industrial organization*, MIT Press, Cambridge, MA.

Titman, S. (1984). The effect of capital structure on the firm's liquidation decision. *J. Financ. Econ.* 13 137–152.

Titman, S., and R. Wessels (1988). The determinants of capital structure choice. *J. Finance* 42, 1–19.

Williams, J.T. (1995). Financial and Industrial Structure with Agency, *Rev. Financ. Studies* 8, 431–475.

R. Jarrow et al., Eds., *Handbooks in OR & MS, Vol. 9*

Chapter 28

Financial Distress, Bankruptcy and Reorganization

Lemma W. Senbet
College of Business and Management, University of Maryland, University Park, MD 20742, U.S.A.

James K. Seward
Amos Tuck School of Business Administration, Dartmouth University, Hanover, NH 03755, U.S.A.

1. Introduction and overview

The decade of the 1980s saw some dramatic events in corporate finance, leading to wide attention to the role of corporate debt in public policy debates. Among these events are: (a) the increased reliance on the use of debt financing in corporate takeovers, restructurings and reorganizations; (b) the popularity (and subsequent collapse) of the 'junk' bond or original issue high yield bond market; and (c) the savings and loan crisis. These debates have been recently fueled by the arrival and severity of an economic recession, raising public concerns about the possibility of massive bankruptcies and their adverse consequences on the overall performance of the economy.[1] Correspondingly, the subject matter of financial distress and workouts has received a great deal of attention in the academic literature by finance and legal scholars.

The purpose of this survey article is to synthesize the recent developments in the topics of financial distress, bankruptcy and reorganization. We focus primarily on developments in the corporate finance literature, although we summarize some important contributions by legal scholars that bear on the issue. Where appropriate, we also suggest research avenues of high promise. The subject matter is quite extensive with many important features that cannot be instructively included in a single, general model. Consequently, we refrain from attempting to work through a single structure that would have yielded no clear insights. Rather we organize the contributions around some unifying theoretical themes, and where available, we provide corresponding empirical evidence.[2]

[1] Recent experience indicates that the number of corporations undergoing distress has increased substantially. For example, White [1990] reports that 86,000 businesses, with aggregate liabilities of $36 billion, filed for bankruptcy in 1987.

[2] This approach is similar to the organization of the survey on capital structure by Harris & Raviv [1991].

We begin by setting forth the legal and economic ramifications of the U.S. Bankruptcy Code, focusing on the Bankruptcy Reform Act of 1978. It is important to have a deep appreciation of the main provisions of the Code in studying the economic implications of financial distress and formal bankruptcy procedures. Formal bankruptcy proceedings entail a liquidation process (*Chapter 7*) and a reorganization process (*Chapter 11*). Under Chapter 7, the firm is shut down by a court-appointed trustee, the firm's assets are sold, and the liquidation proceeds are distributed in accordance with the absolute priority rule (APR). Absolute priority establishes a strict hierarchy of distribution according to the seniority of claims held against the firm. While the procedure seems rather straightforward, it begs important issues of conflicts among claimholder groups with diverse interests, valuation of assets under asymmetrically informed parties, and related inefficiencies. Chapter 11 is intended primarily for a rehabilitation of a financially distressed firm, and the incumbent management team plays a crucial role in the reorganization process. We describe the economic implications of the main reorganization provisions, such as the automatic stay provision, the exclusivity privilege of management in filing a reorganization plan, and new financing by a 'debtor-in-possession'. In evaluating the legal ramifications, we also underscore the impact of the bankruptcy provisions on the behavior of corporate stakeholders outside of the formal bankruptcy process.

Our next item on the survey agenda is a theoretical examination of the relationship between financial distress and economic distress. We do so by way of synthesizing the literature on bankruptcy and corporate financial policy. An important corollary of the Modigliani–Miller [1958] theorem, as generalized by Stiglitz [1974], is that corporate bankruptcy is immaterial to firm value. This important insight is often missed in discussions relating to the economic consequences of corporate bankruptcy, which often casually link economic distress with financial distress. As a related mater, it is also important to gain a clear appreciation of the dichotomy between bankruptcy and liquidation (the process of dismantling the firm's assets and selling them — either piecemeal or in their entirety); otherwise liquidation costs may be mistakenly attributable to bankruptcy costs. Indeed, at the heart of the contemporary literature on financial distress is the determination of costs *relevant* to bankruptcy. These costs depend on the efficiency of resolution of financial distress.

Thus, an important component of this survey is a synthesis of the theoretical and empirical evidence on private and formal resolutions of financial distress. At the outset, we recognize that these alternative methods for resolving financial distress are related in the sense that the incentives which various claimant groups have to reorganize a financially distressed firm depend on the relative costs and benefits conferred by each method. We discuss various private methods of resolving financial distress through debt restructurings, workouts, and informal reorganizations in the capital and real asset markets.

There are, however, potential impediments to the privatization of financial distress. Foremost among these frictions are (a) the free rider problem, (b) informational asymmetry, and (c) inter- and intra-group conflicts of interest.

We believe that it is important to recognize that these potential impediments do not necessarily engender significant bankruptcy costs. Consequently, apart from examining these potential impediments in detail, the survey emphasizes innovations in the design of corporate financial contracts and capital structures which endogenize these impediments in the contracting process. We provide examples of bond indenture (and corporate charter) provisions and innovations in financial contracting designed to mitigate, or even eliminate, potential problems in the resolution of financial distress. We recognize, however, that other legal and regulatory restrictions might preclude full utilization of certain private contracting mechanisms. There is now a gradual accumulation of empirical literature which provides evidence on the determinants of relative utilization of private debt restructurings and formal bankruptcy proceedings. In our survey of this literature, we have found that the nature and degree of the complexity of corporate financial structures is a crucial determinant between informal and formal restructurings.

Continuing with our survey, we discuss court-supervised methods of financial distress (or formal reorganizations), focusing on the efficiency characteristics of such methods of resolving bankruptcy disputes (and the available evidence) as well as the role of market mechanisms in formal reorganizations. While these methods of bankruptcy resolution serve as an alternative when private workouts fail, we also recognize that innovations in the legislative reform of the bankruptcy processes can facilitate or discourage private resolution methods. As an example, the nonunanimity requirement and automatic stay provisions of Chapter 11 reorganization serve as a threat against the free rider problem in private workouts. Thus, the formal bankruptcy process, as it is structured under the 1978 Bankruptcy Code, may entail benefits as well as costs. The inefficiency issues discussed stem mainly from bargaining and coordinating problems among claimant groups and from judicial discretion in the firm valuation and claimholder wealth allocation problems.

We review the available empirical evidence on court-supervised methods of resolution, focusing on deviations from absolute priority rule, and the direct and indirect costs of formal bankruptcy proceedings. There is consistent evidence suggesting that direct bankruptcy costs, such as fees to bankruptcy lawyers, tax accountant, and trustees, are unlikely to be significant determinants of the firm's capital structure when the debt was originally issued. The evidence on the indirect costs of bankruptcy is inconclusive. These costs are difficult to conceptualize, let alone measure empirically. They are presumed to arise in the form of opportunity costs, resulting from suboptimal actions by corporate stakeholders, including customers, suppliers, and employees, in response to financial distress. The fundamental difficulty in empiricism arises from an inability to distinguish these costs form those that would have arisen form pure business dislocation and distress. We believe that none of the papers reviewed here has met this test satisfactorily, and hence this problem represents a challenging avenue for future research. Nonetheless, there is an important groundwork established, which we review in this survey.

There is now an increasing utilization of capital market data in empirical investigations of formal bankruptcies through share price reactions surrounding bankruptcy processes and announcements. These studies have expanded to include the effects of bankruptcy on competing firms to see if there are industry effects of bankruptcy announcements.[3] The use of capital market data has also helped to demonstrate efficient securities pricing of deviations from the absolute priority rule. Recent empirical evidence suggests that the APR is frequently violated in Chapter 11 reorganizations, but that the equity markets generally anticipate and price these deviations, as documented by the relationship between share price reactions and subsequent APR violations.

Our survey turns attention to the role of asset and financial market mechanisms in resolving financial distress under court-supervised reorganizations and liquidations. A market approach to formal bankruptcy proceedings has received little attention in corporate finance, but it is an exciting subject matter of debate in the legal literature. At the heart of debate is the relative efficiency of market valuations and judicial valuations in the appraisal of the firm and allocation of claims under formal bankruptcy.[4] There are some imaginative suggestions of the design of new financial instruments to minimize conflicts of interest under asymmetric information. A theme that runs through the available proposals is that market mechanisms and innovations can be employed to improve the efficiency and fairness of formal bankruptcy proceedings. We present the perspectives of legal scholars in this survey, and hope that the debate on the market approach to formal bankruptcy proceedings will also interface with the domain of finance scholars.

This survey has a limited purpose and cannot incorporate all the facets of the subject matter — financial distress, bankruptcy and reorganization. As an example of the richness of the facets, we conclude the survey with a discussion of the impact of financial distress on the behavior of top corporate management, governance structures, and the firm's dividend policy. The literature here is sparse and primarily empirical. It faces the same challenges as the literature on the measurement of indirect costs of bankruptcy in the sense of not clearly disentangling real financial costs from those that would have been attributable to pure operational inefficiencies. However, this is also an example of a challenging avenue for further research. In closing, we wish to emphasize some general areas of research that are underdeveloped: the dichotomy between economic distress and financial distress; the increasing use of capital market data in evaluating the relative efficacy of Chapter 11 and private workouts; interface between legal and financial research, particularly on the use of market mechanisms under formal, court-supervised bankruptcy proceedings; the design of innovative financial contracts and capital structures in enhancing efficiency in private workouts and formal reorganizations.

[3] As an example, there is now considerable debate within the airline industry and the retail industry about how bankruptcy court protection can be strategically utilized to alter a financially distressed firm's cost structure. Healthy firms in the industry argue that this process, in turn, weakens their own financial condition as they seek to remain competitive with the court-protected bankrupt firms.

[4] There is also a continuing debate on the efficiency of Chapter 11 in the legal literature. Moreover, our survey gives some attention to 'pre-packaged' bankruptcies which, we think, can be viewed as a 'convex combination' of Chapter 11 and private workouts.

It is our hope that this survey facilitates an understanding of the principal issues and stimulates further research on this topic.

2. Legal and economic ramifications of the U.S. Bankruptcy Code

The process of resolving the disputes that arise in formal corporate bankruptcy is currently governed by the Bankruptcy Reform Act of 1978 (hereinafter, the 'Code').[5] The role of a formal bankruptcy proceeding is to provide a collective procedure for the resolution of impaired contractual claims held against the firm. A bankruptcy filing may be voluntary or involuntary, depending on whether the procedure is initiated by the incumbent management or by the firm's creditors. The majority of bankruptcy filings by U.S. corporations are voluntary. The Code alters the powers, duties and responsibilities of the firm's contractual claimants relative to the normal operation of a solvent, ongoing entity under current commercial and tax law. Since bankruptcy law supercedes the commercial code, it seems likely that the incentives and behavior of the claimants may be affected by the opportunity to enter formal bankruptcy. Consequently, an understanding of the main provisions of the Code is necessary in order to determine the economic implications of financial distress and formal bankruptcy procedures.

For the majority of the corporations that enter formal bankruptcy proceedings, the 1978 Code provides a liquidation process (*Chapter 7*) and a reorganization process (*Chapter 11*). Chapter 7 liquidations are relatively straightforward procedures. The court appoints a trustee who then shuts down the firm. The trustee sells or abandons the firm's assets, and the proceeds are then turned over to the court for distribution to the firm's claimants. The seniority of payment distribution is well-defined according to the *absolute priority rule* (*APR*). According to this rule, once the court establishes the hierarchy of claimants, a junior claim can receive no payment until all senior claims are fully paid. Thus, payoffs to the firm's claimants depend directly on the values which the trustee obtains by liquidating all of the firm's assets, as well as the assigned seniority of the claim.

In principle, the design of an equitable and efficient bankruptcy law is relatively straightforward. Ideally, the Code would be structured so that efficient firms (i.e., asset values are highest in their current use, and going concern value exceeds liquidation value) would be reorganized and continue to survive, while only

[5] Bankruptcy laws date back centuries in other advanced countries. A quotation from the *Economist* [February 24, 1990] provides a glimpse of an historical perspective on bankruptcy laws: 'The word *bankruptcy* comes from *banca rotta*, Italian for broken bench. The custom was that when a medieval trader failed to pay his creditors his trading bench was broken. Since bankruptcy was taken off the streets and put into the statute book it has become rather complicated... England's first bankruptcy law, signed by Henry VIII in 1542, was an "Act against such persons as do make bankrupt". For centuries British bankrupts went to debtor's prison: Charles Lamb, an essayist, thought they should be hanged... In contrast, one of America's attractions to immigrants was its very lack of a debtor's prison. Bankruptcy is still viewed in America as a side-effect of entrepreneurship.'

inefficient firms would be liquidated. White [1989], however, argues that it may not be possible to construct a bankruptcy law which provides this outcome. The difficulty is that conflicts of interest between claimant classes lead to diverse preferences for the resolution of financial distress. In general, senior claimants favor premature shutdown and the loss of going concern value in order to preserve the value of their claims. The residual nature of junior claims, such as common equity, implies that its value is increased by maintenance of the firm as an ongoing entity. As a consequence, formal bankruptcy law leads to one of two undesirable outcomes: either the Code allows *inefficient* firms to reorganize and survive, or the Code leads to inefficient liquidation of viable firms. The provisions of the 1978 Act effectively lead to the former outcome.

The inefficiencies created by the transfers of wealth among the firm's distinct claimant classes are further complicated by the problem of *asymmetric information.* The presence of asymmetric information induces disagreement over the aggregate value of the assets to be distributed among the firm's claimant classes. Furthermore, since bankruptcy law encourages the resolution of impaired claims through a bargaining process, claimant groups may intentionally misrepresent their opinion of aggregate firm value. For example, if firm value is small, senior claimant entitlements will generally ensure that they are allocated a larger proportion of the corporation's assets. Conversely, junior claimants have an incentive to present inflated estimates of firm value.

The primary purpose of Chapter 11 is rehabilitation of a financially distressed firm. Once the firm enters Chapter 11, the incumbent management prepares a reorganization plan which proposes an allocation of firm value among the existing claimants. Although formal reorganization procedures are somewhat complicated, we can describe the economic implications of the major provisions of Chapter 11. (A summary of these features appears in Table 1.)

First, an *automatic stay provision* stops all principal and interest payments due to creditors. In addition, interest ceases to accrue on all outstanding unsecured debt. This effectively extends the maturity of the firm's debt obligations and reduces the market value of the debtholders' claim on the firm's assets. The provision also prevents secured creditors from seizing their collateral. Finally, the automatic stay precludes creditors from cancelling contracts and halts lawsuits against the firm. Relatedly, the court may void certain transfers and contracts that occurred prior to the bankruptcy filing. Thus, for example, Chapter 11 may allow the firm to eliminate costly labor or lease contracts.

The 1978 Act also mandated that the incumbent management team remain in control of the firm's assets, except in extreme cases such as fraud. Interestingly, mere incompetence is not a sufficient motive to remove incumbent management under Chapter 11. Beyond simple entrenchment, Chapter 11 also conveys important additional advantages to management. First, for the initial 120 day period after filing, incumbent management retains the exclusive right to file a reorganization plan. Since this plan often forms the basis for subsequent bargaining among the diverse claimant groups, this *exclusivity* represents a valuable power. Extensions of the exclusivity period beyond the initial 120 day period are quite

Table 1

Basic Chapter 11 reorganization features

1. *The automatic stay*
   - Stops principal and interest payments to unsecured creditors.
   - Secured creditors lose the right to take possession of collateral, but may receive 'adequate protection' payments;
   - Executory contracts can be assumed or rejected. If rejected, these claims then become unsecured creditors.
2. *The debtor-in-possession*
   - Typically the current management and board of directors retain control.
   - Management initially maintains exclusive right to file a plan of reorganization and solicit acceptances by the committees. Exclusivity period extends for 120 days to file the plan and an additional 60 days to seek approval. Extensions are common.
   - Debtor-in-possession financing effectively allows the court to strip seniority covenants and collateral from existing debt. Allows incremental senior borrowing.
3. *Reorganization*
   - Plan must be approved by all classes of creditors and the court. Exception is the cramdown procedure.
   - Threat of delay of reorganization plan by management. Transfers wealth from some creditor classes to equity.
   - Bargaining powers favor debtors, but creditors can
     (i) propose an alternative cramdown;
     (ii) ask for a lift of the automatic stay;
     (iii) request conversion to Chapter 7 liquidation;
     (iv) refuse to lend new funds;
     (v) block asset sales.

common, especially in the case of large, complex bankruptcies. In addition, once the firm has filed for bankruptcy, the debtor-in-possession can obtain new debt financing and those creditors will be provided senior status. This provision is intended to encourage new lending and protect the integrity of any new loans as the firm reorganizes. As we shall discuss in detail later, in the absence of such a provision, new funds may not be forthcoming, thereby diminishing the likelihood that the firm can emerge from bankruptcy as a viable entity.

Finally, the voting process for the approval of a reorganization plan may be advantageous to the incumbent management and the shareholders. Restructuring of public debt outside of the bankruptcy process (i.e., informal or private workouts) is governed by the *Trust Indenture Act of 1939*. The Act mandates that any changes to an outstanding public bond's interest, principal, or maturity can be made only if approved by 100% of the issue's holders. In practice, this virtually precludes any change in these terms directly. Consequently, informal restructuring of public debt generally takes the form of an *exchange offer*. In bankruptcy, however, the voting process for approval of a debt restructuring plan is different. First, approval of a reorganization plan requires an affirmative vote by two-thirds in face value and one-half of the number of holders in each class. Thus, Chapter 11 would be especially advantageous to firms with complex capital structures or a small group of obstinate holdouts. Moreover, the bankruptcy court has the power to bind dissenting parties to a reorganization through the cramdown procedure. This procedure allows the court to confirm a reorganization plan that has been vetoed by one of the claimant classes. Although the voting process for the approval of a reorganization plan favors a Chapter 11 filing, one important disadvantage of the bankruptcy process is that it is a collective procedure. This effectively accelerates the due date for all of the firm's liabilities. Thus, relative to the case of a private restructuring with a single class of creditors, formal bankruptcy substantially increases the number of diverse claimant classes involved in the plan of reorganization.

Related to the voting process is the provision in the Code that encourages the parties to bargain during the reorganization process. This, in conjunction with the other powers bestowed upon management, allows equity claimants to retain some fractional ownership in many reorganized firms, despite the fact that senior claimants do not receive their full entitlement (i.e., absolute priority is violated). Because the incumbent management remains in control of the firm, the ability to extract economic concessions from senior claimants can be viewed as compensation for extinguishing the option to delay the process and to invest funds in excessively risky projects.

Thus, the Bankruptcy Code impacts the balance of power among managers, equityholders, and the firm's remaining stakeholders in economically important and identifiable ways. Since the Code specifies the set of rules under which claimants bargain for their entitlements, it also influences the behavior of the various stakeholders outside of the formal bankruptcy process. This point is important because it suggests that any reform of the Code must also consider its impact on the behavior of corporate stakeholders outside of the formal bankruptcy process. Next, we consider the linkage between a firm's capital structure policies and the firm's decision to enter formal bankruptcy. As we shall see, the importance of this link to the theory of capital structure depends upon the costliness of bankruptcy. An understanding of this relationship is crucial in distinguishing between economic distress and financial distress.

3. Bankruptcy and corporate financial policy

The origin of the early literature on the relationship between bankruptcy and corporate capital structure decisions can be found in the seminal work of Modigliani & Miller [1958, 1963]. Their initial analysis establishes that, in perfect and frictionless capital markets, firm value is unaffected by financial policy. The original proof of the celebrated Modigliani–Miller theorem is predicated on the assumption of riskless debt. The theorem was later generalized by Stiglitz [1974] and others who argued that, in perfect and frictionless markets, the irrelevance of corporate financial policy extends beyond the issuance of riskless debt and equity securities to other forms of securities, including risky debt, preferred stock, and all kinds of hybrid securities. The theorem holds both in a single period and multiperiod framework so that firm value is also independent of debt maturity structure decisions.

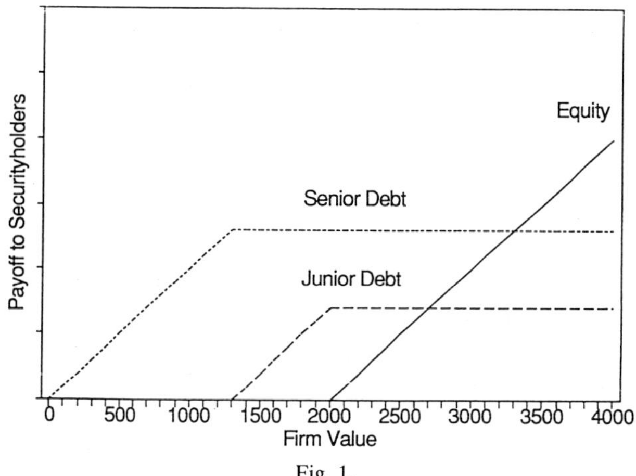

Fig. 1.

The corollary of the MM theorem is that corporate bankruptcy is inconsequential to firm value, since the operating or investment decisions are completely separable from the financing decisions. Figure 1 provides an intuitive illustration of this result. Consider the allocation of the firm's aggregate cash flows between the equity claimants and bondholders on the maturity date of the firm's debt securities. In the Modigliani–Miller framework, the amount of corporate indebtedness has no effect on the value of the firm's assets nor on the riskiness of the total cash flow stream generated by the firm's assets. Debt financing simply partitions the cash flows so that greater financial leverage alters the amount of risk borne by the bondholders. While obvious, this important insight is often missed in discussions relating to the economic consequences of corporate bankruptcy. There is no necessary linkage between bankruptcy and the firm's operating performance; *bankruptcy does not cause economic distress or poor performance.* We will consider the distinction between financial distress and economic distress later in this chapter, but wish to emphasize here that a clear appreciation of this dichotomy greatly enhances an appreciation of the voluminous debate surrounding the consequences of corporate bankruptcy. For instance, it is tempting to point to news stories of distressed firms as evidence of a causal relationship between impending bankruptcy and a deterioration in profitability or a decrease in product demand. The crucial consideration is whether an identical but otherwise nondistressed firm (due to low financial leverage) would face a similar deterioration in its operating performance.

Moreover, *liquidation and bankruptcy* are often discussed in the literature as though they are related. Liquidation is the process of dismantling the firm's assets and selling them (either piecemeal or in their entirety) to new management teams. Liquidation is optimal when the value of the firm's existing resources is higher in alternative uses. Hence liquidation should be viewed as a capital budgeting decision which is independent of the way in which the firm is financed. Liquidation and bankruptcy are separate, independent events. (See Haugen &

Senbet [1978] for further discussion on this issue.) A highly profitable firm with high leverage may remain viable as a going concern, irrespective of bankruptcy, while an unprofitable firm may be liquidated even if it has no debt in its capital structure. It is important to resist the temptation of confounding bankruptcy and liquidation, because liquidation costs may be mistakenly characterized as bankruptcy costs. The latter, if significant, are determinants of the firm's capital structure, but liquidation costs are inconsequential to corporate financial policies or debt decisions.

In the event that bankruptcy is costly, it fills an important void between the corner result of the Modigliani–Miller tax adjusted model and the observed limitations on the amount of debt financing employed in practice. Although the costliness of bankruptcy and financial distress is not the primary subject of this paper, it is appropriate to highlight what has come to be known as the 'trade-off theory'. Modigliani & Miller [1963] argue that the tax code favors debt over equity financing by allowing the firm's interest expense to be deducted from gross income for corporate tax purposes. Since an additional dollar of debt generates the marginal benefit of a tax deduction without any offsetting cost in this framework, firm value is maximized by utilizing as much debt as possible to finance corporate investment decisions. Other financial economists, such as Kraus & Litzenberger [1973], Scott [1976], and Kim [1978], suggest that the costs of bankruptcy might provide a reconciliation between the observed limits on the usage of debt and the predictions of the tax-adjusted Modigliani–Miller analysis of financial policy. The intuition provided for the existence of finite, optimal capital structures is straightforward. Debt capacity is limited, because corporations trade-off the tax savings generated by the deductibility of interest payments against the expected value of the costs incurred in the event of bankruptcy. Unfortunately, these early models failed to provide any rigorous economic justification for the existence of these bankruptcy costs.

Thus, at the heart of the contemporary literature on the relationship between corporate financing decisions and financial distress is the issue of whether bankruptcy is costly. Bankruptcy costs may potentially emerge *directly* in the form of court fees involving third party advisors to the firm, such as lawyers, tax accountants, trustees, etc., or *indirectly* in the form of costly disruptions in the relationship of the firm with customers, suppliers, and employees. If market mechanisms exist, such as those described in Haugen & Senbet [1988], which allow firms to escape the deadweight costs of bankruptcy, then bankruptcy has no impact on corporate capital structure decisions. If, however, bankruptcy costs are not always avoidable, then virtually all dimensions of the firm's financial contracting decision are impacted. This latter result follows because the characteristics of the firm's financial contracts influence the likelihood of bankruptcy as well as the magnitude of the costs incurred. Consequently, for example, financial contract characteristics such as maturity, seniority, complexity, collateral, covenants, and public vs. private are likely to influence the firm's bankruptcy decision.

The next two sections consider the theoretical and empirical evidence on private and formal resolutions of financial distress. It is useful to recognize that these alternative methods for resolving distress are related, so that the incentives which various claimant groups have to reorganize the firm depend on the relative costs and benefits conferred by each method. The costliness of financial distress depends on the design of resolution procedures which facilitate maintenance of maximum firm value. We shall argue that, currently, a number of factors exist which potentially impede costless formal or informal reorganization of financially distressed firms. We also suggest a number of market mechanisms which might be utilized to enhance the efficiency of formal and informal resolution procedures.

4. Private methods of resolving financial distress

In this section, we examine various methods of resolving financial distress outside the bankruptcy court system. Our discussion focuses on three alternatives which are available to corporate managers for dealing with financial distress. In particular, we consider the following: (1) financial restructurings; (2) asset sales; (3) infusions of new capital from outside sources. The academic literature focuses principally on the restructuring of the firm's financial claims which, for reasons we discuss below, are typically implemented through an exchange offer. Generally, these informal, or private, reorganization mechanisms are designed to mitigate, or possibly even eliminate, the costs of bankruptcy. We also discuss conditions under which these informal reorganization methods may be impeded, possibly giving rise to significant costs of financial distress. We then generalize our discussion to consider additional market mechanisms and innovations that may reduce, or eliminate, the potential impediments to the informal resolution of financial distress.

4.1. Debt restructurings and private workouts

An actual or impending default on the firm's existing debt obligations is typically the event that initiates the process of resolving financial distress. This does not imply that default causes financial distress, but rather that it provides creditors with the contractual right to renegotiate certain aspects of their claim against the firm. A default can occur either because the firm fails to make a scheduled payment to the creditors, or because the firm violates one or more of the restrictive provisions contained in the indenture. In the following discussion, we do not distinguish between the causes of a default, but rather focus on its consequences. There is an abundance of attention in both the academic literature and the popular press about informal reorganization of corporate financial structures through *debt restructurings and private workouts.* We define a debt restructuring as an agreement by the firm's creditors to modify any term(s) of an outstanding financial claim currently held against the firm. We view the term broadly so as to encompass both public and private loan agreements. We note, however, that publicly-held credit arrangements are subject to different disclosure and regulatory constraints than private debt. As a result, the set of feasible debt restructuring techniques outside of formal bankruptcy proceedings will depend on who holds the firm's credit obligations. Common restructuring techniques include exchange offers, tender offers, covenant modification, and (in the case of private debt) maturity extension or interest rate adjustments.

Haugen & Senbet [1978] provide an early theoretical analysis of the linkage between informal debt restructurings and bankruptcy costs, and the firm's financial policy decisions. They utilize the spirit of the Modigliani and Miller no-arbitrage approach to argue that the costs of financial distress are insignificant to the theory of capital structure. To understand their argument, consider a firm that encounters financial distress and must restructure its financial contracts. Haugen and Senbet note that the firm can elect to resolve financial distress through (1) a formal reorganization involving the court system, or (2) informal reorganization through the financial markets. Hence, the costs of resolving financial distress must be *bounded* by the least costly of these two alternative resolution mechanisms. In addition, they argue that, in general, the present value of the transaction costs of informal reorganization are likely to be small, or even insignificant, at the time of the firm's initial capital structure decisions. Hence, all rational claimholders will agree to restructure in this manner. Since capital market participants recognize that it is in the interests of all claimholders to support the more efficient method of restructuring, bankruptcy costs should not be sufficiently large to offset the tax subsidy generated by debt financing. Hence, they argue, bankruptcy costs do not explain the corporate decision to limit the amount of debt financing utilized to fund real investments decisions. The intuition for this result is to recognize that informal restructurings represent an alternative to formal bankruptcy proceedings and it pays claimants to 'privatize' bankruptcy away from the court system, if the informal route of resolving financial distress is cost-efficient. Jensen [1989, 1991] provides a similar argument in support of the privatization of bankruptcy. Similar viewpoints were also expressed forcefully in the legal literature by Roe [1983].

The preceding discussion focuses on the incentives and opportunities for corporate insiders to restructure a distressed firm's financial claims through the capital markets. However, the privatization of the bankruptcy process can also be initiated by outside *arbitrageurs*. To see this, suppose that the market values of a distressed firm's publicly-traded securities reflect the expectation that significant bankruptcy costs would be incurred as a result of the claimants' failure to successfully implement an informal reorganization. Outside arbitrageurs can buy up the outstanding securities at prevailing market values to prevent the costly alternative of a formal reorganization. The potential arbitrage profit would be the bankruptcy costs, net of the transactions costs, of informal reorganization. Once the old debt is eliminated in its entirety so as to prevent any windfall gain to the remaining bondholders, new debt can be issued to take optimal advantage of the corporate tax subsidy. The expedient of outside takeover, as an alternative to private workout and recapitalization by the original claimants, is also discussed in Haugen & Senbet [1978]. The main implication of this analysis is that the capital markets provide a more efficient forum for the resolution of financial distress, and hence one would not expect to observe a substantial amount of court-supervised reorganization activity. However, it seems clear that a large and growing number of corporations elect to forgo the alternative of a private workout. As Haugen & Senbet [1978] recognize, failure to utilize cost-effective private mechanisms for resolving financial distress must be predicated upon: (1) outright irrationality by the firm's financial claimants or market participants, or (2) impediments to the arbitrage or private workout processes. Much of the subsequent literature on informal debt restructurings focuses on attempts to identify the potential impediments to informal reorganizations[6] The next two sections examine the theoretical and empirical evidence which focuses on the implications of these impediments.

4.2. *Potential impediments to privatization of financial distress*

In this section, we examine the impact of the following impediments to the resolution of financial distress through private reorganization mechanisms: (1) free rider problem; (2) asymmetric information; (3) inter- and intra-group conflicts of interest. Although we discuss these impediments in detail, it is important to note that their existence does not necessarily render bankruptcy costs significant to the theory of optimal capital structure. We describe how these impediments, particularly the free rider problem, can be eliminated by inclusion of simple provisions into corporate charters and bond indentures. More generally, we would expect to observe *innovations* in the design of corporate financial contracts and capital structures which endogenize the potential impediments in the contracting process. We suggest that corporate decision-makers should recognize the benefits of adopting financing arrangements that mitigate, or even eliminate, potential problems in the resolution of financial distress in the bankruptcy process. A case in point is an increased usage of the *strip financing* technique which allows the financial claimants to hold both the debt and the equity claims issued by the firm. We recognize, however, that other legal and regulatory restrictions might preclude full realization of certain solutions. For example, current limitations on the ability of U.S. banks to hold long-term corporate equity stakes may inhibit the range of feasible resolution mechanisms. We discuss the implications of some of these restrictions in more detail below.

4.2.1. *The free rider problem*

A financial restructuring of the firm's existing debt obligations is typically intended to relax the firm's cash flow problems by: (1) reducing interest payment obligations, or (2) extending the maturity date. Informal renegotiation of creditor claims depends on whether the debt obligation is public or private. The restructuring of public debt is governed primarily by the Trust Indenture Act of 1939. This Act requires *unanimous* consent by the holders of a particular class of debt secu-

[6] Senbet & Seward [1991] propose an indifference proposition for the equivalence of three private workout mechanisms — informal reorganization initiated by corporate insiders (equity-holders), informal reorganization initiated by bondholders, and informal reorganization initiated by outside arbitrageurs — in well-functioning markets. They examine the relative efficacy of these reorganization procedures in more general settings characterized by frictions.

rities in order to change the debt obligation's maturity, principal, or coupon rate of interest. These stringent voting rules effectively preclude a debt restructuring in which the holders of any outstanding public bonds agree to alter these terms. As a result, virtually all informal public debt restructurings are accomplished through an *exchange offer.*

In a typical exchange offer, the firm allows the holders of a particular class of the firm's debt securities the right to exchange their existing claims for a new class of securities. A successful exchange offer generally enhances the firm's credit quality, thereby enhancing the value of the remaining bonds which are not tendered. Since exchange offers grant holders the right (but not the obligation) to participate, some bondholders may elect to *'hold-out'* in the expectation that the post-exchange offer value of their existing claim will exceed the value of participation in the exchange. Since all bondholders have similar incentives, the exchange offer is likely to fail. This problem could be solved if the issuer induces the required level of participation by sufficiently increasing the value of the claims offered in the exchange. Unfortunately, the firm may find that the costs of resolving the free rider problem in this way can be sufficiently large so as to eliminate all of the economic benefit created by a successful debt restructuring. Green & Juster [1992] study the structure and timing of debt restructuring decisions by financially distressed firms. They show that the firm's decision to exchange or repurchase outstanding debt is a separable, two-part decision. First, the firm must decide on the amount of debt to repurchase. Then, the firm can determine the price to offer in the exchange. They also show that it is oftentimes optimal for the firm to delay the exchange or repurchase in order to efficiently reduce the role of free riders in the restructuring process.

At least two other approaches towards mitigating the hold-out problem should be mentioned: (1) endogenize the impediment at the time of the firm's initial capital structure decision; (2) coercive participation. The first approach is analyzed by Haugen & Senbet [1988]. They suggest that the bondholder free rider problem can be eliminated through simple, innovative bond indenture provisions, such as (a) granting the bond trustee the right to accept or reject tender and exchange offers on behalf of *all* bondholders; (b) by making tender offers binding on all holders within the class, once a majority of bondholders have tendered their holdings; (c) including a 'continuous' call provision, which allows the firm to call the bonds at the price registered in the most recent trade. These suggestions highlight the fact that the potential impediments to a successful financial restructuring often assume that the form of the firm's debt finance is *exogenously* specified. Here, we argue that security design and corporate capital structure decisions should be endogenized in order to redress the problems that may arise in the bankruptcy process.

In practice, corporations have relied upon coercive techniques in order to successfully implement exchange offers. Although the Trust Indenture Act requires unanimous approval by all holders within a particular class of public debt in order to change the maturity, interest, or principal features of the security, covenants can be changed or waived by a simple majority or super-majority vote. The modification of bond covenants is typically accomplished through a technique known as consent solicitations or *exit consents*.

The combination of exit consents and exchange, or tender, offers works as follows. A distressed firm announces an exchange offer, but conditions the offer on a bondholder vote to change or eliminate the issue's covenant(s). The issuer also conditions its acceptance of the exchanged debt on approval of the consent solicitation by the requisite majority. The loss in value for those bondholders who elect to retain their original, stripped debt claim generally outweighs the benefits of electing to not participate. As a result, financially distressed firms can design financial restructuring programs which simultaneously strip the protection of existing bond indentures and coerce participation in tender or exchange offers. Coffee & Klein [1991] argue that participation in the exchange offer should be separate from, not conditional on, the vote to strip covenants. This separation of the vote and the exchange decision would mitigate the coercive element of this technique.

Gertner & Scharfstein [1991], building upon an earlier work which analyzes the investment distortions created by risk shifting [Jensen & Meckling, 1976] and underinvestment [Myers, 1977], show how: (1) the possibility of debt restructurings affects the investment decisions of financially distressed firms and (2) the use of consent solicitations alters investment decisions. One of their principal findings is that informal debt restructurings typically do not restore efficient investment incentives. Rather, exchange offers may serve to reduce the burden of debt obligations by simply extracting wealth from the participating creditors.

The impact of exchange offers on investment incentives depends on the presence or absence of *seniority* covenants. A seniority covenant is a provision in debt contracts, which precludes the firm from issuing new securities with a more senior claim. This provision is intended to protect the seniority position of a firm's outstanding securities against the dilutive effects of subsequent financing decisions. The use of a consent solicitation allows the firm to strip the seniority covenant, thereby allowing the firm to offer a more senior security in the exchange. Gertner and Scharfstein find that a separation of the vote to strip covenants and the decision to participate in an exchange offer does enhance the efficiency of corporate investment decisions.

More generally, these findings offer some new evidence on the ability of bond covenants to protect creditors against expropriative behavior by managers and stockholders. Divergent views on this issue are offered by Smith & Warner [1979] & McDaniel [1986]. The use of consent solicitations to strip covenant protection in distressed exchange offers is more consistent with the view advocated by McDaniel. He argues that bond covenants provide the least protection at precisely the time when they are most needed. The use of exit consents by distressed firms in order to implement coercive exchange offers suggests that even well-thought-out covenants can be circumvented under certain conditions, thereby reducing their value as an integral limitation on the opportunistic behavior of equityholders. These findings suggest that additional research on the role of bond covenants in controlling agency problems between bondholders and stockholders is necessary.

4.2.2. Information asymmetry

The problem of designing and completing an informal debt restructuring is exacerbated in the case of financially distressed firms by information asymmetries. Asymmetric information exists in any transaction where one party knows more about true value than another party. In order to understand the role of asymmetric information in different financial transactions, corporate managers are typically assumed to possess *private* information about the true economic value of the firm. For example, a substantial number of models in the capital structure literature assume that insiders have private information about the firm's cash flow stream or its future investment opportunities. The existence of asymmetric information in the case of financially distressed firms emanates from two possible sources. First, corporate insiders and outside investors may, based upon their differential information, simply disagree about the value of the firm. Second, when the firm is financially distressed, insiders may have an incentive to intentionally misrepresent value in order to convince bondholders to agree to exchange their existing claims for lower valued securities.

In this connection, even the state of financial distress can be misrepresented by a privately informed entrepreneur, depending on the nature of the debt contract, as recently demonstrated by Heinkel & Zechner [1993]. They show that informational asymmetry may prevent contract renegotiation prior to maturity if the debt outstanding is a pure discount bond. The insiders of a firm with poor prospects may hide the default state and hence their worthless position, and those with good prospects may declare default with the expectation of favorable debt renegotiation. The inefficiencies resulting from not declaring default prior to maturity may be mitigated by an alternative design of debt contract with risky intermediate payments, such as a coupon or sinking fund payments and bankruptcy institutional arrangements permitting deviations from absolute priority rules (APRs). (We will have more to say about APRs in the next section.)

The asymmetric information effect of financial distress suggests that a greater proportion of the securities offered in a distressed exchange offer should contain *contingent* payment features. The reason why contingent payment securities are useful is that their future values will adjust more readily to the revelation of information about the true value of the firm.[7] There are, of course, different types and classes of financial securities with different degrees and forms of payment contingencies — common equity, warrants, contingent value rights, and call provisions, to name just a few. Franks & Torous [1989] indicate that a few financially distressed firms, in fact, issued debt with warrants or convertible securities in exchange for defaulted debt. Ultimately, then, the resolution of this issue involves a *security design* problem.[8]

There are, however, various legal, regulatory and institutional restrictions that limit the types of securities that debtholders may be able or willing to accept in exchange for their claims. These restrictions may impede the completion of an ex-

[7] A more complete discussion of this issue is contained in Senbet & Seward [1991].

[8] Heinkel & Zechner [1993]

change offer if the optimal security does not conform to these requirements. This suggests one of two outcomes: (1) holding the restrictions constant, the firm will be able to complete the debt restructuring only if the existing claimants accept a new security which is suboptimal; or (2) in order to distribute the appropriate security, the applicable restrictions must somehow be loosened. Unfortunately, while the latter outcome would seem more desirable, the former is more likely to happen.

Giammarino [1988], however, shows how the structure of a normal bankruptcy procedure may, in the presence of asymmetric information, induce financial claimants to forgo an informal debt restructuring. Thus, his analysis provides an explanation for the 'rational' decision by claimholders to incur significant bankruptcy costs by entering the formal reorganization process in order to resolve financial distress. Successful formal reorganization in Chapter 11 involves a substantial amount of judicial discretion and latitude. The presence of asymmetric information may cause debtholders to prefer the uncertain allocation outcome of a formal bankruptcy procedure rather than to trust the claims of equityholders/management in an informal reorganization. Hence, Giammarino's analysis suggests that there are conditions under which a formal reorganization may be preferred even when the process involves deadweight costs.[9] Future analyses of the role of security design in mitigating asymmetric information problems in an informal debt restructuring should explicitly consider the alternative outcome(s) offered by a formal bankruptcy proceeding.

Although the outcome of financial distress depends on imperfect information and, as we discuss in the following section, conflicts of interest among claimants, this does not necessarily imply that the use of debt financing should be minimized to avoid such problems. Wruck [1990] suggests that debt may serve as an important and valuable catalyst for operational and organizational change, and that reducing leverage may obviate this service. For example, she argues that financial distress may entail benefits such as precipitating changes in management, corporate governance, and organization strategy and structure. Evidence which supports this view is contained in Warner, Watts & Wruck [1988] and Gilson [1989], who show that poor stock performance *per se* is generally not sufficient to motivate the replacement of the incumbent management. Hence, although lower financial leverage may reduce the costs of financial distress due purely to asymmetric information problems, important benefits are foregone by the suboptimal use of debt financing.

Indeed, a recent literature on optimal security design [e.g. Aghion & Bolton, 1988; Zender, 1991; Dewatripont & Tirole, 1992; Harris & Raviv, 1993] empha-

[9] A similar argument is made by Webb [1987] who proposes two different informational scenarios under which bankruptcy costs may be incurred, namely (a) uncertainty about court valuation of bankruptcy settlement, and (b) heterogeneous beliefs of bondholders and equityholders about firm value. The court settlement uncertainty problem, though, may be resolved by avoiding the court system to begin with via informal reorganization. The second informational issue assumes that information can be segmented on the basis of security ownership types. At any rate, arguments based on asymmetric information confound bankruptcy and informational problems, because the latter exist even under all-equity financing.

sizes the efficiency gains from debt financing attributable to transfer of control rights in bankruptcy. Financial contracts are mechanisms that distribute the firm's cash flows and control rights. In Zender [1991], an optimal security design that implements efficient investment decisions results in debt-like and equity contracts through joint distribution of cash flows and control rights. Bankruptcy implements a state-contingent transfer of control and mitigates opportunistic behavior by the controlling investor, since the marginal return from investment is realized by these investors. Likewise, control is vested in the hands of shareholders in those states where the payments to debtholders are fixed. In either case, the return to passive (or noncontrolling) investors is insensitive to performance. Thus, Zender's analysis endogenizes the beneficial role of bankruptcy as a mechanism for state-contingent transfer of control, with the resultant efficiency gain. Likewise, Aghion & Bolton [1988] argue that, bankruptcy as a state-contingent transfer of control, facilitates contract renegotiation based on information revealed concerning the prospects of the firm. Dewatripont & Tirole [1992] show how to generalize the notion of control transfer into efficient design of managerial contracts, along with the design of capital structure. An optimal financial structure exists by virtue of trading off excessive interference of debtholders in managerial decisions and passivity of equityholders.

4.2.3. Conflicts of interest and coalition formation

Different reorganization plans, whether formal or informal, allocate wealth across management, creditors and shareholders differently. Hence, at least two concerns will govern the design and advocacy of any reorganization plan: (1) how does the plan affect the aggregate value of the firm's assets; (2) how is the value of the firm under alternative reorganization plans distributed among the different claimants. Since the latter consideration is largely a problem in bargaining, several studies examine the linkage between conflicts of interest, coalition formation and the resolution of financial distress. Not surprisingly, conflicts of interest can reduce overall economic efficiency because coalitions of claimants can be formed to extract concessions (i.e., wealth transfers) from other nonaligned claimants. For example, Bulow & Shoven [1978] and White [1989] investigated the impact of coalition formation on the firm's liquidation vs. continuation decision. In both cases, private gains from the restructuring process interfere with the efficient resolution of financial distress.

Brown [1989] examines the way in which conflicts of interest among claimholders can inhibit the resolution of financial distress through an informal reorganization. These conflicts may either be inter- or intra-claimant class. Intergroup conflicts arise because allocations under any given reorganization plan can always be increased at the expense of a separate claimant class. Intragroup conflicts can emerge when a restructuring allows members of a particular reorganization plan to decide whether to participate or not. This creates the incentive to holdout, or free ride, if successful reorganization would enhance the value of the old claims. Brown [1989] demonstrates that the structure provided by the Bankruptcy Code pares down the feasible set of outcomes otherwise available in a voluntary, informal workout. This distinction arises because the set of rules and procedures which govern informal reorganizations (such as the Trust Indenture Act) differ from those which apply in a formal reorganization. Effectively, the relative bargaining strengths of the various claimant classes are altered once a firm enters the bankruptcy process.

4.3. Empirical evidence on debt restructurings

An empirical study by Gilson, John & Lang [1990] provides extensive evidence on the incentives of financially distressed firms to choose between private debt restructurings and formal bankruptcy proceedings. Their findings suggest that asset and financial characteristics *jointly* affect the firm's choice between these alternative reorganization mechanisms. In particular, the firms in their sample are more likely to resolve financial distress through private workouts under the following conditions: (1) a greater proportion of the firm's assets are intangible; (2) the firm has fewer distinct classes of debt outstanding; (3) the firm relies more heavily on bank debt than public debt.

The economic intuition which explains these findings is consistent with the theories discussed earlier. In essence, these asset and financial characteristics make the privatization of financial distress more cost-effective and/or minimize the role of costly impediments in the informal resolution process. Intangible assets proxy for the likelihood that the failure to renegotiate the firm's impaired credit obligations will result in the destruction of going concern firm value. The aggregate value of firms which have a larger proportion of intangible assets will be higher if the firm maintains operating continuity through private resolution mechanisms. Presumably, then, the private renegotiation process ensures that the creditors' impaired share of the larger going concern value exceeds what they would receive by forcing the firm into formal bankruptcy reorganization or liquidation. Capital structure characteristics (i.e., role of bank lenders, number and complexity of firm's financial contracts) matter, because they impact the efficiency of the bargaining process in a private renegotiation. Smaller numbers of distinct creditor classes, with fewer claimants in each, facilitate informal restructurings by reducing the potential problems created by asymmetric information and conflicts of interest. Gilson, John & Lang also provide evidence of the *relative* indirect costs of financial distress for formal and informal reorganizations. They examine stock market price reactions around the time that investors become aware that the firm is experiencing financial distress, and find that: (1) the market is capable of predicting whether a private workout will be successful or not; (2) private workouts are a more efficient form of reorganization than Chapter 11. Indeed, they find that the costs of private restructuring are only a fraction of the cost of a bankruptcy court-supervised workout.[10]

[10] Of course, this is not to suggest that the firms that ended up in Chapter 11 would have been better off under private workouts. It may well be that such firms found it more cost-efficient to enter formal bankruptcy (under court supervision) due to their complex financial structures.

A subsequent study by Asquith, Gertner & Scharfstein [1991] sheds further light on the costs of financial distress. They examine the restructuring activities of 102 companies which issued *high yield debt* and then subsequently encountered financial distress. In particular, they find that: (1) banks rarely forgive principal on outstanding loans or provide new financing in an informal restructuring; (2) public debt restructurings through exchange offers are a crucial determinant of the success of an informal reorganization; (3) the complexity of a firm's contractual claims is a key determinant of whether a firm will enter formal bankruptcy; (4) there is no evidence that firms with better operating performance deal more successfully with financial distress; (5) asset sales and capital expenditure reductions are commonly utilized by financially distressed firms. These findings conflict somewhat with the evidence and conclusions described in Gilson, John & Lang [1990]. In particular, Asquith, Gertner & Scharfstein conclude that 'banks do not play much of a role in resolving financial distress'. They attribute this to the presence of subordinated public debt in the capital structures of many of the firms in their sample. Thus, although much of the literature emphasizes the unique role of bank debt in the resolution of financial distress, these findings suggest that this issue requires further study.

An alternative avenue of future research which promises to shed light on these issues is to examine the structure of bankruptcy laws and financial systems in other economies. Hoshi, Kashyap & Scharfstein [1990] provide empirical evidence on the relationship between financial distress and firm performance for a sample of Japanese industrial firms. They discuss how several unique features of the Japanese product and financial markets — i.e., *the keiretsu and the main bank system* — are structured to economize on the costs of financial distress. Their findings demonstrate how those firms with close ties to a main bank are able to invest more and increase sales, following the onset of financial distress. Hoshi, Kashyap & Scharfstein interpret their results as evidence that certain financial structures and creditor relationships reduce the costs of financial distress and facilitate better firm performance. Problems of free ridership and asymmetric information are internalized by the close main bank relationships, concentration of financial claims among financial institutions, and by the strengthening of product market ties through cross-holding equity relationships.

4.4. The interfirm asset sale market

As an alternative to the informal restructurings of its debt obligations, the firm may attempt to sell assets in an attempt to relieve its financial distress. A partial sell-off of the firm's existing assets generates cash which can be used to reduce outstanding debt or to undertake new investment opportunities. There are several reasons why asset sales by financially distressed firms may differ from asset sales by healthy firms, and hence may be difficult to implement on a favorable basis. Shleifer & Vishny [1992] suggest that the secondary market for interfirm asset sales may be subject to adverse *liquidity* problems. They argue that there are several factors which determine market liquidity in the case of interfirm asset sales, such as fungibility (i.e., the number of uses and users for a particular asset), participation restrictions (e.g., regulations on foreign acquisitions or antitrust considerations), and credit constraints. If such liquidity problems occur, then the price which the seller is likely to receive in a distress sale will be adversely affected. Hence, the main consequence of an illiquid secondary market for interfirm asset sales is that it increases the costs of dealing with financial distress through this mechanism.

A second distinguishing characteristic of this market is that purchasers of assets from distressed firms face some *unique* risks when assets are acquired outside of formal bankruptcy proceedings. First, the transaction must be structured to ensure that the acquiror does not subsequently become unintentionally liable for the debts and obligations of the seller. In addition, if the selling firm subsequently files for bankruptcy, the court may void the sale as a fraudulent transfer or a voidable preference. Typically, this would occur if the price received by the seller is deemed insufficient consideration for the value of the assets sold. In such a case, the acquiror risks the possibility of subsequently having to return the assets to the seller. Finally, the sale of assets can limit, or even eliminate, the use of net operating losses (NOLs) to shield future income from taxation. To the extent that these loss carry forwards represent a valuable firm asset, financially distressed firms must ensure that the sale of assets is structured to preserve their tax benefits.

The price obtained by the seller in an asset sale is ultimately determined by the outcome of a bargaining negotiation between the acquiror and the seller. The poor financial condition of the seller may weaken the firm's bargaining position, thereby reducing the price it receives for the assets. Furthermore, if the sale is conducted under duress from the firm's creditors, the outcome may be that the price received is less than the value of the asset under continued ownership and operation by the distressed firm. Creditors may favor the asset sale, however, because it effectively accelerates receipt of the future cash flow stream that would otherwise be generated by continued ownership. Hence, the net result of the transaction could entail a *wealth transfer* from stockholders to bondholders as well as a reduction in aggregate firm value.

Brown, James & Mooradian [1992b] provide empirical evidence on this issue in their study of asset sales by financially distressed firms. They find that asset sales are frequently conducted by the financially distressed firms in their sample, and that the distinguishing characteristic of the firms which sell assets is that they operate *multiple* divisions or subsidiaries. Conversely, most of the sample firms that don't sell assets operate only a single division. Thus, to the extent that asset sales help reduce the firm's expected costs of bankruptcy, corporate diversification may provide important economic benefits. They find that, on average, shareholder abnormal wealth effects are insignificant on the announcement date of the asset sale. However, further partitioning of the sample suggests that stockholder returns are positive if the firm subsequently avoids bankruptcy. This finding also suggests that, at least in some cases, asset sales are implemented to the benefit of creditors and the detriment of shareholders. Thus, although asset sales do provide an alternative mechanism to deal with financial distress, the impediments described above may inhibit the flow of benefits to shareholders.

4.5. Infusions of new capital

Assuming that the firm in financial distress still has positive net present value projects available, one alternative for enhancing firm value is to attract new investment capital. In the event of financial distress, however, additional funding may be difficult to obtain due to problems described in Myers [1977]. Essentially, this *'underinvestment'* problem arises because a disproportionate amount of the economic gain from the incremental investment accrues to the pre-existing (especially senior) financial claimants. This problem is likely to be greater the more junior the incremental source of funding.

These observations suggest two general approaches to the problem of attracting new investment capital. First, the firm should try to make the new claim as senior as possible. Oftentimes, however, covenants in the firm's outstanding debt securities explicitly preclude this form of financing. One alternative to circumvent this problem is to utilize asset-based and *secured* debt financings [see, e.g., Stulz & Johnson, 1985]. In general, the feasibility of this form of financing depends upon the availability of collateral to pledge, as well as an understanding of the additional encumbrances imposed by the new creditors. We are unaware of any empirical study of this issue.

The second alternative is to combine junior financing with a certain amount of senior debt restructuring. For example, the Southland Corporation was privately reorganized in 1990 by arranging an equity infusion by Ito-Yokado Co. and Seven-Eleven Japan. The equity investment was made contingent upon the successful completion of a *conditional exchange offer.* Although we are unaware of any empirical study of this issue, our impression is that new equity infusions are not frequently utilized to resolve distress. Apparently, the problems which discourage new investment described by Myers [1977] and Gertner & Scharfstein [1991] make this form of distress resolution unattractive. Relatedly, perhaps, the availability of debtor-in-possession financing in Chapter 11 may limit the amount of control which equity claimants are willing to forgo in a private restructuring.

5. Court-supervised methods of resolving financial distress or formal reorganizations

Court-supervised methods of bankruptcy resolution serve as an alternative when private workouts fail. However, we take a view here that the innovations in the legislative reform of the bankruptcy processes can facilitate or discourage private resolution methods. For instance, the nonunanimity requirement and Automatic Stay provisions of Chapter 11 reorganization serve as a threat against the free rider problem discussed earlier, and hence facilitate private workouts. On the negative side, we already saw how the Trust Indenture Act of 1939 could inhibit private informal reorganization. In this section we shall examine the efficiency characteristics of court-supervised methods of resolving bankruptcy disputes and the available evidence.

5.1. The efficiency characteristics of the Bankruptcy Code

The formal bankruptcy process, as it is currently structured under the 1978 Bankruptcy Code, may entail *benefits as well as costs*. Recent studies by Gertner & Scharfstein [1991] and Wruck [1990] provide evidence on these benefits. Gertner and Scharfstein adopt a coalition view of financial distress, and argue that coordination problems among public debtholders create investment inefficiencies which may not be mitigated by private restructurings. They show how three particular features of existing reorganization law (the automatic stay, voting rules for the reorganization plan, and the retention of equity value) affect investment decisions by financially distressed firms. In particular, these provisions increase the level of investment both inside and outside of Chapter 11.

However, while these provisions increase investment incentives, economic efficiency may not necessarily be enhanced. Gertner & Scharfstein show that the net benefit of the increased investment depends on the incentives generated by various characteristics of the firm's financial contracts, such as maturity structure, covenants, and the priority of private vs. public debt. They conclude that Chapter 11 has ambiguous effects on efficiency, but will provide the greatest economic benefit when underinvestment is a problem. All else equal, this is most likely to happen when the firm has shorter-term public debt, senior bank debt, and the public debt has seniority covenants.

The additional inefficiencies may arise from bankruptcy *judges overstepping* their legal jurisdiction and interfering with rational wealth allocation among the conflicting parties in the bankrupt firm. Weiss [1991] cites several such incidents: a refusal of the judge to liquidate Eastern Airlines when it appeared optimal to do so in the judgment of the creditors and other outside observers, and an interference of the judge with private restructuring of the LTV and hence forcing a costly negotiation under court supervision. Weiss also observes lack of uniformity in extensions of the exclusivity period of 120 days, since judges have considerable latitude in deciding to extend the period. For instance, Florida judges rarely extend while judges in the Southern District of New York often extend the period for years. This creates an incentive for migration of bankruptcy cases from Florida to New York, since bankruptcy falls under federal law (e.g., the filing of Eastern in New York rather than Miami, its principal place of business). Shopping for the right bankruptcy court judge presumably favors management and engenders cost to society, apart from the direct cost of case overloads.[11]

Wruck [1990] suggests that Chapter 11 provides gross benefits for certain firms.

[11] There is also a problem relating to arbitrariness in appraisals by judges. Consider a question from Fortgang & Mayer [1985] regarding Judge Winner in Canadian Arctic: 'With all of these things, to say that you can appraise the values of Canadian Arctic is to say you can attend the county fair with your crystal ball, because that is the only possible way you can come up with a result ... my final conclusion ... is that it is worth somewhere between $90 million and $100 million as a going concern and to satisfy the people who want precision on value, I will fix ... $96,856,850, which, of course, is a total absurdity that anybody would fix a value with that degree of precision, but for the lawyers who want to make that *fool* estimate, I have just made it.'

She identifies the ability to deal with diffuse creditors as a single class, the ability to renegotiate or void burdensome lease or labor contracts, and debtor-in-possession financing as valuable rights contained in Chapter 11. Also, Chapter 11 protects against a race to the assets of the firm by diverse creditors [Easterbrook, 1990].

Berkovitch & Israel [1992] analyze a strategic choice of a financially distressed firm between a private workout and bankruptcy declaration under Chapter 11. The firm's choice is dictated by the two standard incentive problems arising from bondholder–stockholder conflict, namely the underinvestment problem associated with valuable growth opportunities and the risk-shifting problem. The optimal choice is one which minimizes the loss in value due to the investment distortions resulting from the incentive problems. It is argued that a private workout can eliminate the underinvestment distortion by creating an incentive for debtholders to accept a renegotiated contract that compensates shareholders for undertaking value-increasing projects. However, the converse is argued for the problem of overinvesting in risk. Since the risk-shifting incentive decreases debt value and debtholders would seek to block such investments if they are disclosed, shareholders may lose incentive to engage in private methods of resolving financial distress. It is argued that the 'automatic stay' provision of Chapter 11 extinguishes the blocking power of debtholders and leads to renegotiation.

5.2. Empirical evidence

In this section, we review the available evidence on the direct and indirect costs of formal bankruptcy proceedings. In principle, bankruptcy costs matter because they impose dead weight costs on the firm which are borne by the shareholders through an *ex ante* compensation to the creditors for the possibility of incurring these costs ex post. In addition, bankruptcy may impose costs on *stakeholders* other than the firm's capital contributor. For example, Titman [1984] examines the financing implications of bankruptcy-related costs borne by employees, supplies, and/or customers. To the extent that the bankruptcy process itself is costly, and if these costs are not avoidable, then capital structure decisions will be affected.

5.2.1. Direct costs

A study of railroad bankruptcies by Warner [1977] provides evidence of the magnitude of direct bankruptcy costs. Direct bankruptcy costs are the legal, administrative and advisory fees that the firm bears as a direct result of entering the formal bankruptcy process. Warner finds that these direct costs average about four percent of the firm's aggregate market value measured just prior to declaring bankruptcy. Warner notes that costs of this magnitude are unlikely to affect the pricing of debt claims and optimality of capital structure at the time of debt issuance. The reason is that it is the *present value* of bankruptcy costs that matter at the time of capital structure decisions. The ex-ante costs of bankruptcy in Warner's study are insignificant when adjusted for the ex-ante probability of bankruptcy.

The time period for Warner's study [1933–1955] predates the adoption of the current Bankruptcy Code, and hence may not be applicable under existing practice. Weiss [1990] provides evidence on the direct costs of bankruptcy in the period 1980–1986. His results are comparable, but somewhat lower, than the estimate provided by Warner.[12] This, again, suggests that direct bankruptcy costs are unlikely to represent a significant determinant of security pricing prior to the entry into formal bankruptcy and of the capital structure decision when debt was originally issued.

5.2.2. Indirect costs

Potentially more significant and substantial are the indirect costs of bankruptcy. These costs can be viewed as opportunity costs, in that they collectively represent the outcome of suboptimal actions by corporate stakeholders. Thus, costs that arise because of inter- or intra-group conflicts of interest, asymmetric information, free-rider problems, lost sales and competitive position, higher operating costs, and ineffective use of management's time all potentially represent the indirect costs of bankruptcy. A common sentiment seems to be that the indirect costs are substantially larger than the direct costs, but they may also be confounded with costs that would have arisen with pure business dislocation and distress. Moreover, these costs are difficult to observe and measure. As a result, the empirical evidence on the magnitude of the indirect costs of bankruptcy is derived primarily from specific cases.

Altman [1984] measures the indirect costs of bankruptcy as the difference between the earnings realized in each of the three years prior to the firm's bankruptcy and the earnings that could have been expected at the beginning of each of those years. In essence, this procedure measures the *deviation* of actual profits from their expected counterparts and attributes it indirect bankruptcy costs. A second test examines deviations from what security analysts were predicting for up to two years. The immediate danger is that the deviations are not distinguishable from a mere forecasting error in the event that the market or security analysis makes rational and unbiased forecasts about earnings. The more fundamental issue, though, is that the procedure *confounds* the costs of liquidation with the indirect costs associated with bankruptcy. To see this, consider the example in Haugen & Senbet [1988] whereby the firm is confronted with the introduction of a dominant product by a competing firm. This event has an adverse impact on the economic viability of the firm as a going concern with the consequent impact on the realized earnings through reductions in sales and increases in costs. The unanticipated event is not reflected in the expected profits at the beginning of the year, leading to negative surprises at the end of the year. Altman's procedure measures such negative deviations as part of indirect bankruptcy costs, but they are unrelated to the way the firm is financed. The above problem cannot be alleviated by splitting the sample into those firms that are reorganized and those that are liquidated. Liquidation costs can be incurred even when the firm is not liquidated ex post. In the above example the increased

[12] See also Altman [1984], Morse & Shaw [1988], Macmillan, Nachtman & Phillips-Patrick [1990] for similar results.

probability of liquidation stemming from the firm's strategic disadvantage in its product market triggers adverse reactions from its suppliers, customers, and employees. Thus, *indirect costs of liquidation* could have been incurred by firms that were reorganized. These issues are once again illustrations of how difficult it is to empirically measure indirect costs of bankruptcy without confounding economic and financial distress.

Lang & Stulz [1992] study the intra-industry effects of bankruptcy announcements by investigating the reactions of share prices of *competing* firms. The study is based on the notion that bankruptcy announcements convey information about the cash flow characteristics of similar firms in the industry and their competitive position. They find evidence that the equity value of competing firms in the industry of the bankrupt firm decreased, on the average, by 1% at the time of the bankruptcy announcement. However, for competing firms in highly concentrated industries and low leverage, the stock price reaction was positive with an increase in the equity value of 2.2%. The positive competitive effect is attributable to the possibility that the competitive position of the nonbankrupt firms is enhanced by the misfortunes of the bankrupt firm. If these industry effects are merely informational, they cannot be used as evidence of bankruptcy leading to investment inefficiency and indirect bankruptcy costs. It is interesting, though, that such magnitudes of industry effects of bankruptcy announcements are detected for concentrated industries.[13]

Cutler & Summers [1988] study abnormal share price reactions surrounding various events in the Texaco–Pennzoil litigation. They argue that the amount of the award represents a pure wealth transfer, so that fluctuations in the joint value of the firms would likely represent the direct and indirect costs of the litigation process. Their estimates indicate that, upon settlement of the litigation, shareholder wealth had declined by approximately one *billion* dollars. They note that this amount significantly exceeds most estimates of direct bankruptcy costs, and hence may reflect the economic value lost due to the disruptive effects of the formal proceedings. Here there is an asymmetry between price reaction of Texaco and Pennzoil shares. However, this analysis fails to deal with an ever-present thorny issue of separating economic distress from financial distress. It is very likely that the impact is related to the adverse effects of lost reputation with the stakeholders resulting from information release surrounding the award. This is reflected in the asymmetric stock price reaction of Texaco and Pennzoil.

[13] There are other studies dealing with announcement effects of bankruptcy, but they don't investigate intra-industry effects directly. Clark & Weinstein [1983] document a significant informational content of bankruptcy filings; so do Eberhart, Moore & Roenfeldt [1990]. Aharony & Swary [1983] provide evidence for bankruptcy announcements where the industry effect is negligible due to the bankruptcy filings being made for idiosyncratic purposes. Bankruptcy announcement effects of risk measures have been investigated by Baldwin & Mason [1983], Johnson [1989], Aharony & Swary [1983], and Morse & Shaw [1988]. In general, the authors report negligible announcement effects of systematic or beta risk but significantly positive effects of the unsystematic risk component. However, Baldwin & Mason [1983] show a decrease in beta as the firm approached bankruptcy, and they suggest an expected violation in APR as a possible explanation.

5.3. Deviations from absolute priority rule (APR)

Traditionally, financial economists have assumed that the value of a bankrupt firm is allocated among its claimants by strict adherence to the absolute priority rule (APR). APR is an allocation rule based upon the relative seniority of the contractual entitlements held by all of the firm's claimants. According to the APR, the value of a bankrupt firm is distributed so that senior claimants receive their full contractual entitlement before any class with a more junior claim receives anything. In a Chapter 7 liquidation, the trustee sells the assets of the firm, and distributions of the proceeds are made according to the APR.

Recent empirical evidence contained in studies by Franks & Torous [1989], Eberhart, Moore & Roenfeldt [1990], and Weiss [1990] suggests that the APR is frequently *violated* in a Chapter 11 reorganization. Deviations from APR in formal reorganization are primarily attributable to various features and provisions of the Bankruptcy Code, which effectively provide the debtor with substantial protection and bargaining powers against creditors. Relatedly, sanctions of APR violations by the courts in *formal* reorganization procedures increase the likelihood of similar violations in *informal* debt restructurings. This is because formal reorganization can be viewed as an alternative to informal workouts, and hence forms the basis for negotiations with creditors outside of the protection of formal bankruptcy.

Franks & Torous [1989] suggest that the institutional features of Chapter 11, which grant the debtor-in-possession valuable rights, effectively provide management with a *valuable option*. This option provides management the opportunity to adopt investment and financing decisions which can diminish the value of the claims held by the firm's creditors. For example, Chapter 11 allows management to obtain new senior financing and to exclusively propose a plan of reorganization for the first 120 days. These rights can be used to diminish the value of the pre-existing creditors' claims by effectively decreasing the exercise price and extending the maturity of the firm's pre-bankruptcy liabilities. As a result, deviations from the APR can be viewed as compensation by senior claimants to the junior claimants in order to extinguish this option.

The documentation of frequent and economically significant deviations from the APR raises a number of related issues. First, if market participants are rational and anticipate the frequency and magnitude of deviations from the APR, then security prices should reflect these violations. Eberhart, Moore & Roenfeldt [1990] examine the relationship between share price reactions and subsequent APR violations, and find that the equity markets generally anticipate and price these deviations. Frank & Torous [1989] provide numerical examples to show how deviations from the APR affect risk premiums on corporate bonds. They adjust Merton's [1974] model for valuing risky debt for APR violations, and then show how their results are closer to observed spreads between risky and default-free interest rates.

Thus, ex-ante deviations from the APR raise the interest cost of debt financing for corporations as might be expected in an efficient market. Weiss [1990] shows that it is primarily unsecured creditors who bear a disproportionate amount of this transfer, so that the pricing of junior level debt should reflect a high premium for APR violations. Note that if bonds are priced correctly and efficiently in the manner discussed above, there is no wealth transfer among bondholders and equityholders as APR violations are fully *internalized*. In addition, Eberhart & Senbet [1992] argue that APR violations have the potential to mitigate the risk shifting agency costs of debt financing. The incentives of corporate insiders to engage in excessive risk taking are typically magnified by the increased probability of bankruptcy which cannot be readily controlled by traditional incentive compatible contracts, such as convertible debt. Eberhardt & Senbet show how APR violations serve as an implicit contract to control the risk incentives in the vicinity of bankruptcy. In a related context, Berkovitch & Israel [1992] rationalize APR violations as part of a strategic debt renegotiation both under private workout as motivated by a desire to eliminate the underinvestment problem and under Chapter 11 as motivated by a desire to reduce the investment distortion resulting from riskshifting incentives. Note we have earlier provided a more detailed discussion of Berkovitch and Israel under Section IV(B).

Among a growing literature on efficiency rationale for deviations from absolute priority rule is an interesting paper by Harris & Raviv [1993], which proposes an optimal design of Chapter 7 — like bankruptcy procedure. Harris & Raviv consider an environment with suboptimal liquidation under financial distress and with noncontractible project returns. The entrepreneur has an incentive to make payments to outside capital contributors only to avoid costly liquidation; otherwise he can appropriate funds not paid out. This environment is akin to Hart & Moore [1989]. Moreover, private workouts and privatization of bankruptcy through informal reorganization and takeover markets are precluded. It is interesting that this environment then rationalizes a debt-like contract with a bankruptcy court. The role of the court is to impose limits on the extent of liquidation via involuntary debt forgiveness in states with high costs of liquidation. In this sense, deviations from absolute priority rule are *endogenous* to an optimal design of bankruptcy procedure, since the court's role is precisely to enforce these deviations.

5.4. The role of market mechanisms in formal reorganizations

The resolution of financial distress through a formal court proceeding is typically accomplished via a process of bargaining among the claimants and the application of judicial discretion by the presiding bankruptcy judge. As a result, formal bankruptcy proceedings currently forgo the opportunity to utilize asset and financial market mechanisms to resolve financial distress. In this section, we examine various proposals which have been advanced to enhance the role of market forces in efficiently resolving financial distress in formal bankruptcy proceedings. Although financial economists have not yet studied this issue in detail, legal scholars have provided some important insights into the question of whether *market* valuations or *discretionary* judicial valuations provide more efficient estimates of aggregate firm value in formal bankruptcy proceedings. Baird [1986], for example, views the two forms of bankruptcy (i.e., reorganization and liquidation) as the sale of a firm's assets and the distribution of proceeds among the existing claimants. He suggests, however, that Chapter 7 involves the actual sale of assets while Chapter 11 is a 'hypothetical' sale, where judicial discretion establishes a 'fictitious' value for the firm. Baird argues that claimants collectively would benefit from elimination of the formal reorganization option since it is a costlier procedure than the actual sale of assets. Thus, the market mechanism supported by Baird is to utilize only the market for asset sales.

As an alternative to the forced liquidation of all firms that file formal bankruptcy, Roe [1983] and Bebchuck [1988] suggest that *the innovative* design of new financial instruments might mitigate the valuation problems in the existing formal bankruptcy process. Essentially, their argument is that, by designing and distributing claims whose structure minimizes conflicts of interest and whose value is not particularly sensitive to asymmetric information, firm value can be efficiently allocated to claimants in accordance with their contractual entitlements. Roe, for example, criticizes the existing Chapter 11 reorganization process because the current practice reconstitutes the firm's capital structure as the outcome of an interclass bargaining process and the determination of firm value by judicial discretion. Thus, the capital structures confirmed in reorganization plans are quite disparate, and unlikely to represent a decision which maximizes the value of the firm. The solution proposed by Roe is to require that the bankruptcy courts approve only those reorganizations with *all-equity* capital structures. The allocation of firm value among the claimant classes would then be determined by the initial sale of a small amount of equity (Roe mentions 10%) in the capital markets, the use of this sale to infer the aggregate value of the firm, and then the distribution of the equity claims according to the absolute priority rule.

The role of the initial sale of equity in Roe's proposal is that it is necessary to establish the aggregate value of the reorganized firm in order to then distribute claims according to each participants contractual entitlements. Bebchuck [1988] argues that Roe's proposal is predicated on the correct market pricing of the initial equity sale. The role of the equity sale in Roe's proposal is that it is necessary to infer the aggregate value of the reorganized firm in order to then allocate claims according to contractual entitlements. Bebchuck proposes a modification of the Chapter 11 process which utilizes claims whose value does not depend on knowing the true value of the firm. He suggests that the distribution of *rights*, or warrants, whose exercise prices and seniority are based upon the seniority and contractual entitlements of the firm's existing claimants. He shows how these rights can be designed and distributed to provide claim holders with values that are consistent with their contractual entitlements.

One later addition to the stock of bankruptcy reform proposals is an anti-Chapter 11 extension of Bebchuck by Aghion, Hart, & Moore [1992]. The proposal adopts Bebchuck's allocation mechanism for claims in bankruptcy under Chapter 7, but it curtails the role of management in the bankruptcy process. A judge (or a reorganizer) is appointed to solicit cash and noncash bids for the bankrupt firm, and distributions are made under a strict APR rule. Aghion, Hart & Moore view management as pro-Chapter 11, and their proposal is intended to eliminate all the inefficiencies associated with managerial handling of the bankruptcy process. The paper sidesteps the issue of correctly identifying the priority and the size of individual entitlements and the judge has considerable discretion in deciding who gets what (or who gets which options). In order to be successful, the allocation of the bidding process has to be done in a short period of time; Aghion, Hart & Moore propose a three-month period. Longer periods would engender managerial intention problems.[14, 15]

A common theme in each of these proposals is that market mechanisms, either asset or financial, can be employed or developed to improve the efficiency and fairness of formal corporate bankruptcy proceedings. A countervailing viewpoint is provided in Easterbrook [1990], who suggests that the costs of judicial valuation errors may be less than the costs of market mechanisms (in particular, the costs of conducting an auction for the firm). Thus, he argues that the judicial system may operate with lower transactions costs than markets. The question of whether market mechanisms can enhance the resolution of financial distress in formal bankruptcy proceedings remains important but largely unanswered.

A related matter is the extent to which the rules and structure of the formal bankruptcy process influences the efficiency of informal reorganizations and private workouts. As reported earlier, there is strong evidence that the costs of informal reorganizations are much less than the costs of formal bankruptcy. Consequently, an important role of any reform of the formal bankruptcy process should be to introduce innovations that facilitate the role of markets and informal reorganizations in privatizing bankruptcy outside the court system. As an example of the beneficial effect of the 1978 reform, the nonunanimity requirement and automatic stay provisions of Chapter 11 should serve as an important threat against the free rider problem in private reorganization. On the other hand, the detrimental effect of the legislative rules is reflected in the Trust Indenture Act of 1939, which inhibits private workouts.

5.5. *Pre-packaged bankruptcies*

Section 1126(b) of the Bankruptcy Code allows a financially distressed firm to simultaneously file a bankruptcy petition and a plan of reorganization. A

[14] There is a continuing debate on the efficiency of Chapter 11 in the legal literature. For instance, Eisenberg [1992] challenges reformer proposals that call for the abolition of Chapter 11 on the ground that its costs are overstated ad confounded with the costs of reorganization that would have been incurred even in the absence of Chapter 11. He points out that the *real* costs of Chapter 11 are unknown. From historical perspective, Eisenberg argues that Chapter 11 reorganization proceedings took roughly the same length of time, on average, as the traditional receivership reorganizations and pre-Chapter 11 proceedings. In addition, even deviations from the APR are not inherent in Chapter 11, since they too occurred in receivership reorganizations that preceded Chapter 11.

[15] A provocative article by Bradley & Rosenzweig [1992] proposes a complete repeal of the current Chapter 11 process. They provide empirical evidence to support their contention that stakeholder welfare is reduced under the existing bankruptcy procedure. Altman [1993], however, questions some of their findings.

pre-negotiated bankruptcy reorganization allows the firm to combine the cost efficiency of an *informal* debt restructuring with certain benefits afforded by a *formal* bankruptcy proceeding. In particular, the less stringent voting requirements in Chapter 11 can be utilized to bind all creditors to a reorganization plan. Thus, a pre-packaged bankruptcy effectively circumvents the holdout problem by allowing the court to force dissenting creditors to accept the proposed reorganization plan.

Two other considerations also enhance the relative benefits of a pre-packaged bankruptcy. The first arises from a January 1990 ruling by a bankruptcy judge in the LTV bankruptcy case. The judge ruled that creditors who participate in an informal debt restructuring are, if the firm subsequently files for bankruptcy, entitled to a claim equal to the value of the securities received in the exchange offer. Since exchange offers typically involve some amount of debt relief, this ruling further discourages participation by creditors in a private restructuring of the firm's liabilities. This, in turn, is likely to enhance the attractiveness of a pre-packaged bankruptcy.

The other factor to consider is the tax consequences that arise from the cancellation of indebtedness. For a firm which reorganizes outside of bankruptcy, the taxability of the 'income' generated by debt forgiveness depends upon whether the firm is deemed to be solvent or insolvent. To the extent that the firm is made solvent by the cancellation of debt through an informal exchange offer, the income is taxable. However, if the firm reorganizes within a formal bankruptcy proceeding, the debt discharge is exempt from corporate income taxation. Thus, all else equal, certain tax benefits may be available to the firm if it reorganizes within a formal bankruptcy proceeding that would otherwise not be allowed. Moreover, the maintenance of net operating loss carry-forwards depends upon the retention of at least a 50% ownership position by the pre-existing equity claimants. There are, however, special rules that may apply in a bankruptcy case that preserve these valuable tax shields even if a substantial change in ownership occurs. Thus, asymmetric tax treatment in formal and informal debt restructurings will likely encourage more frequent use of pre-packaged bankruptcies in the future.

6. An assessment of the impact of financial distress on the behavior of corporate managers

6.1. *Top management turnover and corporate governance structures*

Managerial ability and decision-making are important determinants of the value of the firm. The managerial labor market can be viewed as an arena where corporations compete to acquire and retain the services of top management. Fama [1980] argues that a competitive managerial labor market is an important mechanism to control the behavior of opportunistic professional corporate managers. In effect, a well-functioning managerial labor market disciplines the behavior of corporate executives in two ways. First, compensation schemes are structured to reward decisions that enhance shareholder wealth, and penalize outcomes that diminish shareholder wealth. Second, shareholders, through their representatives elected to the Board of Directors, hire and fire top managers.

The behavior and decision-making of top corporate managers are likely to be influenced by financial distress for a number of reasons. First, the wealth of top managers is usually affected directly by stock price performance through equity ownership positions in their firms. To the extent that shareholders bear any costs of financial distress, managerial welfare is likely to be affected as well. Secondly, financial distress may also impose costs directly on top management. For example, Gilson [1989] notes that financial distress may entail significant personal costs to corporate managers through: (1) loss of future income; (2) loss of firm-specific human capital; (3) loss of power, prestige, or other nonpecuniary benefits; (4) adverse reputation effects. Since top managers make major corporate policy decisions that can influence firm value, these costs can directly influence firm performance and efficiency.[16]

In assessing the significance of management-borne costs, it is important again to distinguish between economic distress and financial distress. Thus, management-borne costs are associated with the increased probability of the firm going out of business or being liquidated rather than financial distress or the way that the assets are financed. Of course, the economic viability of the firm is affected by managerial performance and competence so that management-borne costs, such as the loss of future income, may be appropriately attributable to managerial efficiency both in the reorganized firm and alternative employment opportunities.

Is the performance and decision-making of top management responsible for the onset of financial distress, or is deterioration due to systematic economic or industry factors? This distinction, while difficult to make in practice, is crucial to understand in order to enhance the likelihood that a distressed firm will remain viable in the future. If management is inefficient or incompetent, then a well-functioning managerial labor market would simply replace the incumbent with a new, qualified manager. The problem is that managerial ability is difficult to observe, and that performance proxies (such as stock price returns) are, at best, noisy indicators of the manager's ability.

In general, it is the responsibility of the Board of Directors to monitor top management, design and implement compensation packages, and make hiring and firing decisions. However, as financial distress approaches, the membership of the Board experiences higher turnover [see, e.g., Gilson, 1990]. Thus, the legal appara-

[16] There is considerable interest in the legal literature on the impact of financial distress on the firm's *stakeholders* beyond financial claimholders. For instance, Triantis [1992] suggests that bankruptcy may lead to a debtor's unilateral abrogation of contracts involving various stakeholders. The argument is based on the notion that, unlike the nondebt party, a debtor may not be disciplined by social norms and reputational considerations. In addition, the debtor enjoys moral legitimacy for the rehabilitation of the firm through an abrogation of burdensome contracts. This opportunistic behavior may not be fully internalized at the time of debt issuance due to an incomplete contracting environment. However, the inefficiency suggested by Triantis is more relevant for the bankruptcy case with an endgame (or liquidation) because a bankrupt, but economically viable firm, would be concerned about market sanction and reputation.

tus which is designed to monitor top management performance may be ineffective at precisely the time that its fiduciary role is most important. This suggests that ineffectiveness on the part of the Board of Directors may also be a contributing factor to the onset or acceleration of financial distress. Walsh & Seward [1990] argue that poor decision-making by top management may not necessarily reflect managerial inability or incompetence. The economic foundation of agency models is that managerial actions can be directed and motivated by appropriately designed incentive mechanisms. But suppose that these incentives are inappropriately designed. Then poor firm performance may be due to poorly designed incentive mechanisms by the Board rather than poor management per se. In this case, management turnover is unlikely to resolve the firm's performance problem.

In light of the *ambiguity* about the relationships between firm performance, top management, and board membership, consideration of the empirical evidence on the linkage between them is important. Gilson [1989] examines the incidence of senior management turnover in 381 unprofitable firms between 1979 and 1984. He separates the sample into distressed and nondistressed firms, and finds that the top management of financially distressed firms are almost three times as likely to experience turnover as those in nonfinancially distressed firms. Since the sampling procedure selects only poorly performing firms, this finding suggests that the onset of financial distress is itself an important determinant of management turnover. Interestingly, Gilson [1989] also finds that a larger fraction of managers keep their jobs when firms restructure privately rather than through the formal chapter 11 process. This finding is somewhat surprising because of the debtor-in-possession provisions that effectively entrench incumbent management under the Bankruptcy Code. Although Gilson provides no explanation for this result, it does suggest that other factors influence management turnover in financially distressed firms. In particular, financial distress may just be a signal for poor economic performance and managerial inefficiency or incompetence leading to managerial turnover. Since private restructuring is less costly, as documented empirically, it may be associated with more efficient management and hence lower turnover. Again, the available evidence is insufficient in documenting that financial distress, rather than economic misfortunes and the associated managerial inefficiency, that leads to management turnover.

Gilson [1990] provides an extensive empirical analysis of changes in the corporate governance structures of 111 firms that defaulted on a creditors' claim between 1979 and 1985. He finds evidence of substantial changes in directors' roles and responsibilities when the firm restructures its liabilities. Turnover among the pre-default board members is high, and their monitoring role is largely replaced by two sources. First, creditor influence increases by obtaining stock ownership and board representation in exchange for the agreement to forgo their entitlements under their debt contracts. Relatedly, new credit agreements often contain explicit covenant restrictions on corporate investment and financing policies. These covenants enhance the creditors' ability to constrain managerial decision-making. The second source of monitoring in restructured firms is the substantial increase in large blockholdings that occurs when firms become financially distressed. The greater degree of equity concentration among fewer holders improves the net benefits attainable from greater monitoring.

Although these two studies provide extensive evidence on the impact of financial distress on top management turnover and corporate governance structures, the literature still lacks a unified study of these issues. That is, when firm performance is poor, and some change in the management, governance and control of the corporation is necessary, how do we know which should be changed? Is poor performance and financial distress due to the inability or incompetence of management, or is a quality manager simply led to poor decisions through an ineffective, inefficient or unqualified governance structure? Despite the difficulty in disentangling these separate effects, the distinction is crucial if we are to understand how public and private initiatives can improve the process of rehabilitating or liquidating distressed firms.

6.2. Dividend policy

Smith & Warner [1979], in their analysis of bond covenants, note that restrictions on dividend payments help to control the agency conflict between bondholders and stockholders. In the absence of such a restriction, shareholder wealth could be maximized by simply expropriating bondholders through the payment of as large a dividend as possible. This view, however, ignores the possibility that this policy may precipitate the onset of financial distress, which may in turn be personally costly for corporate managers. Since dividend policy is controlled by the latter, and managers may be more interested in job preservation than maximizing shareholder wealth, empirical evidence on the link between cash distributions to equity claimants and financial distress is necessary to understand these conflicting incentives.

DeAngelo & DeAngelo [1990] investigate the link between dividend policy and financial distress in a sample of 80 financially distressed firms from 1980 through 1985. The authors find that dividend growth during the pre-distress period was high (approximately 11% per year for the ten year period prior to the onset of distress), but that managers substantially decreased dividends during the distress period. Moreover, they find that, on average, managers reduce dividends quite early in reaction to the onset of financial distress. Their findings suggest that binding debt covenants are an important motivation for the reduction of dividends. They also find, however, that many distressed firms which are not constrained by binding debt covenants, nonetheless, voluntarily reduce dividends. This finding suggests that other factors beyond restrictive covenants are likely to influence the dividend policy decision of distressed firms. DeAngelo & DeAngelo [1990] find evidence that the history of the firm's dividend record is important, and strategic motivations also matter. Examples of the latter are bargaining situations with organized labor or other stakeholder groups. This suggests that some managers may view dividend omissions as a credible signal of impending financial distress.

Since dividend policy decisions represent observable events, it would be interesting to examine the relationship between dividends and management turnover.

Stated differently, do dividend policy decisions convey information to market participants about the quality of management, and hence signal whether the incumbent team should be replaced? An investigation of the linkage between observable policy decisions, management turnover, and subsequent firm performance represents a fruitful area of future research.

Appendix

A.1. Financial distress: theory

AUTHORS [a]	MAIN FINDINGS
	1. *Bankruptcy and corporate financial policy*
Modigliani & Miller [1958, corollary], Stiglitz [1974]	Bankruptcy is inconsequential to firm value under perfect and frictionless capital markets.
Kraus & Litzenberger [1973], Scott [1976], Kim [1978]	The costs of bankruptcy serve as a countervailing force against the corner solution of the Modigliani–Miller [1963] tax-adjusted model, giving rise to optimal capital structure and the observed limits on the usage of debt.
	2. *Liquidation and bankruptcy*
Haugen & Senbet [1978, 1988]	Liquidation, the process of dismantling the firm's assets and selling them (either piecemeal or in their entirety) to new management teams, is independent of the way the firm is financed, and hence bankruptcy and liquidation are independent events. A highly profitable firm with high leverage may remain viable as a going concern, irrespective of bankruptcy, while an unprofitable firm may be liquidated even if it has no debt in its capital structure.
Titman [1984]	Because of costs imposed on customers when the firm liquidates, equityholders may promote a capital structure that results in a (binding) suboptimal liquidation policy.
White [1989]	Because of agency conflicts where claimants act in their own best interest, some profitable firms may get liquidated while some unprofitable firms may not get liquidated.
	3. *Debt restructurings and private workouts*
Haugen & Senbet [1978, 1988]	The costs of resolving financial distress must be bounded by the lower of (a) costs of formal reorganization involving the court system, or (b) transaction costs of informal reorganization through financial markets or private workouts. It is argued that the present value of transaction costs are insignificant at the time of capital structure decisions, and hence bankruptcy costs, that affect capital structure choices, are insignificant.
Jensen [1989, 1991]	Bankruptcy will be taken out of the courts and 'privatized', because large potential costs of formal reorganization provide incentives for the parties to accomplish informal reorganization more efficiently outside the courtroom.

[a] Not all authors are included. See the text for more writers on the subject matter.

Berkovitch & Israel [1992]	The choice between a private workout and bankruptcy declaration under Chapter 11 is a strategic decision. The optimal choice minimizes the value loss due to investment distortions from underinvestment and risk-shifting problems.
	4. *Potential impediments to privatization of financial distress*
Grossman & Hart [1980]	*The free rider problem*: Claimants may not be willing to tender their claims in an informal reorganization so as to capture the potential increase in value that would occur in an informal reorganization. This may preclude an exchange offer or market-based solution.
Green & Juster [1992]	The firm's decision to exchange or repurchase outstanding debt is separable in terms of the amount of debt to repurchase, and the price to offer in the exchange. Also, delaying the timing of renegotiation can reduce the free rider problem.
Bulow & Shoven [1978], Brown [1989], White [1989]	*Coalition formation*: Conflicts of interest can reduce overall economic efficiency, because coalitions of claimants can be formed to extract concessions (e.g., wealth transfers) from other nonaligned claimants. For instance, coalition comprising equity/bank will have an incentive to reorganize, whereas senior claimants will have an incentive to force liquidation. This conflict may prevent private workouts.
Giammarino [1989]	*Information asymmetry*: Because insiders know more about the true value of the company, outsiders (senior claimants) may find it in their best interest to use a court-imposed solution that results in deadweight costs even if private reorganization is costless.
Heinkel & Zechner [1993]	A firm's insiders may attempt to misrepresent the company's solvency position. This informational problem can be mitigated by debt features such as the repayment schedule, and institutional features such as deviations from APR.
Gertner & Scharfstein [1991]	Exchange offers may not restore efficient investment incentives as a result of coordination problems between public debtholders. Underinvestment occurs with senior bank debt and short-term public debt protected by covenants. Formal bankruptcy helps to solve the coordination problem.
	5. *The role of markets and complex financial securities in the resolution of financial distress*
Roe [1983]	A sale of 10% of equity can be used to calculate aggregate value. A reorganized capital structure should be all-equity to overcome the problem of valuing reorganized claims.
Baird [1986]	Since reorganization is a hypothetical sale, while auctions are an actual sale, an auction of company assets is preferable in a formal reorganization.
Bebchuck [1988], Aghion, Hart & Moore [1992]	Option contracts can be issued to claimants in a company that enforces absolute priority rule and avoids strategic actions. It will also be insensitive to the valuation problem.
Easterbrook [1990]	Auctions or private reorganizations may be used when they are superior to a legal solution. Likewise, the converse is true as 'legal rules endure because they are efficient (or transfer wealth)'.
Haugen & Senbet [1988], Senbet & Seward [1991]	Simple (ex-ante) features in corporate charters and bond indentures can mitigate the free-rider problem. The provisions in the existing bankruptcy code may enhance or impede private workouts or market-based solutions.

Zender [1991]	Bankruptcy is a means to transfer decision-making power from debtors to creditors. Such control right transfers can improve the efficiency of investment decisions.
Dewatripont & Tirole [1992]	Generalize the concept of control transfer into the design of capital structure and managerial contracts. An optional financial structure exists by trading-off excessive interference of debtholders in managerial decisions against the passivity of equity claimants.

A.2. Financial distress: empirical

AUTHORS	MAIN FINDINGS
	1. *Debt restructurings*
Gilson, John & Lang [1990]	The larger the proportion of assets that were intangible, of debt held by banks, and less the number of classes of debtholders then the greater the chance that a private restructurings would be successful. Successful private restructuring were associated with an abnormal positive stock price performance relative to stock price reactions associated with formal restructurings.
Asquith, Gertner & Scharfstein [1991]	Examined the restructuring activities of companies which issued high yield bonds.
	2. *Direct costs of bankruptcy*
Warner [1977]	Direct costs of 5.3% (average) of market value at announcement of bankruptcy of firm for 11 large railway companies. Economies of scale in direct costs appears to exist.
Altman [1984]	Direct costs of 4% of market value of equity plus book value of debt at announcement of bankruptcy for a retailing sample and 6% for an industrial sample.
Weiss [1990]	A sample of 31 firms from 1980–1986 reported a mean of 20.6% (range 2.0–63.6%) of equity value or 3.1% of the book value of debt plus equity value (range 1.0–6.6%). This was 2.9% of book value of assets.
Gilson, John & Lang [1990]	The direct costs of exchange offerings was found to be, on average, 0.65% of the book value of assets (median 0.32%) with a range of 0.01%–3.4%. Economies of scale appeared to exist for direct exchange costs. See the text for a comprehensive discussion.
	3. *Indirect costs of financial distress*
Altman [1984]	By using unexpected losses as a proxy for indirect costs it was found that 11–17% of firm value as measured up to 3 years before bankruptcy was consumed as indirect costs.
Lang & Stulz [1992]	Intra-industry effects of bankruptcy announcements were studied by investigating the share price reactions of competing firms. The positive competitive effect was detected for concentrated industries.
Cutler & Summers [1988]	In the Texaco–Pennzoil litigation the shareholders wealth declined by $3 billion, significantly exceeding most estimates of direct costs and hence consistent with indirect costs.
	4. *Management, governance, and ownership*
Gilson [1989]	Selecting the bottom 5% of companies on the NYSE and AMEX (ranked by returns) as a sample of economically distressed firms,

	those that were also financially distressed experienced management (including directors) turnover of 52%. This was significantly greater than the nonfinancially distressed firms. Companies that restructured privately had lower turnover.
DeAngelo & DeAngelo [1990]	78.6% of 42 firms that were financially distressed cut dividends, even when covenants were nonbinding.
Gilson [1990]	Of 111 financially distressed firms only 46% of incumbent directors and 44% of CEOs remained after 4 years. Other changes included more covenants and larger block shareholders (which included creditors).
	5. *Deviations from the absolute priority rule*
Weiss [1990]	APR violations were reported in 29 out of 37 cases examined. The deviations were mainly at the expense of unsecured creditors for the benefit of equityholders and other junior security. APR deviations were worst in the case of large firms with complex capital structures.
Franks & Torous [1989]	Of a sample of 39 firms in Chapter 11, 21 firms exhibited deviations from APR. In some cases the deviations were substantial.
Eberhart, Moore & Roenfeldt [1990]	23 APR deviations were reported for 30 cases examined. The mean violation was 7.5% (range 0–35.71%) of total awards to claimants. Evidence was presented for the equity markets anticipating subsequent deviations and pricing them efficiently.
Harris & Raviv [1993]	Demonstrate that the role of the court in an efficient bankruptcy procedure is to impose limits on the extent of liquidation via involuntary debt forgiveness in high liquidation cost states. Hence, deviations from APR are endogenous in their bankruptcy procedure recommendation.

Acknowledgements

We thank Philip O'Connor for research assistance. Comments on an earlier version of the paper by Edward Altman, David T. Brown, Stuart Gilson, and Rick Green are gratefully acknowledged.

References

Aghion, P. and P. Bolton (1988). An 'incomplete contract' approach to bankruptcy and the financial structure of the firm, unpublished manuscript, MIT.

Aghion, P., O. Hart, and J. Moore (1992). The economics of bankruptcy reform, unpublished manuscript, MIT.

Aharony, J., C. Jones, and I. Swary (1980). An analysis of risk and return characteristics of corporate bankruptcy using capital market data. *J. Finance* 35, 1001–1016.

Aharony, J. and I. Swary (1983). contagion effects of bank failures: Evidence from capital markets. *J. Bus.* 56, 305–322.

Altman, E. (1984). A further empirical investigation of the bankruptcy cost question. *J. Finance* 39, 1067–1089.

Altman, E. (1993). *Corporate Financial Distress and Bankruptcy* John Wiley and Sons, Inc., New York, NY.

Ang, J., J. Chua, J. McConnel (1982). The administrative costs of corporate bankruptcy: A note. *J. Finance* 37, 219–226.

Asquith, P., R. Gertner, and D. Scharfstein (1991). Anatomy of financial distress: An examination of junk-bond issuers, unpublished manuscript, MIT and University of Chicago.

Baird, D. (1986). The uneasy case for corporate reorganizations. *J. Legal Studies* 15, 127–147.

Baldwin, C. and S. Mason (1983). The resolution of claims in financial distress: The case of Massey Ferguson. *J. Finance* 38, 505–516.

Bebchuck, L. (1988). A new approach to corporate reorganizations. *Harvard Law Rev.* 101, 775–804.

Bergman, Y., and J. Callen (1991). Opportunistic underinvestment in debt renegotiation and capital structure. *J. Financ. Econ.* 29, 137–171.

Berkovitch, E. and R. Israel (1992). The bankruptcy decision and debt contrat renegotiations, unpublished manuscript, University of Michigan.

Betker, B. (1990). An analysis of the returns to stockholders and bondholders in a Chapter 11 reorganization, unpublished manuscript, UCLA.

Bradley, M. and M. Rosenzweig (1992). The untenable case for Chapter 11. *Yale Law J.* 101, 1043–1095.

Brown, D. (1989). Claimholder incentive conflicts in reorganization: The role of bankruptcy law. *Rev. Financ.Studies* 2(1), 109–123.

Brown, D., C. James and R. Mooradian (1992a). The information content of distressed restructurings involving public and private debt claims, unpublished manuscript, University of Florida.

Brown, D., C. James and R. Mooradian (1992b). Asset sales by financially distressed firms, unpublished manuscript, University of Florida.

Bulow, J. and J. Shoven (1978). The bankruptcy decision. *Bell J. Econ.* 9, 437–456.

Clark, T. and M. Weinstein (1983). The behavior of the common stock of bankrupt firms. *J. Finance* 38, 489–504.

Coffee, J. and W. Klein (1991). Bondholder coercion: The problem of constrained choice in debt tender offers and recapitalizations, unpublished manuscript, Columbia Law School and UCLA Law School.

Cutler, D. and L. Summers (1988). The costs of conflict resolution and financial distress: Evidence from the Texaco–Pennzoil litigation. *Rand J. Econ.* 19, 157–172.

DeAngelo, H. and L. DeAngelo (1990). Dividend policy and financial distress: An empirical investigation of troubled NYSE firms. *J. Finance* 45, 1415–1431.

Dewatripont, M. and J. Tirole (1992). A theory of debt and equity: Diversity of securities and manager–shareholder congruence, unpublished manuscript, MIT.

Easterbrook, F. (1990). Is corporate bankruptcy efficient? *J. Financ. Econ.* 27, 411–417.

Eberhart, A., W. Moore, and R. Roenfeldt (1990). Security pricing and deviations from the absolute priority rule in bankruptcy proceedings. *J. Finance* 45, 1457–1470.

Eberhart, A., and L. Senbet (1992). Absolute priority rule violations and risk incentives for financially distressed firms, unpublished manuscript, Georgetown University and University of Maryland.

Eberhart, A., and R. Sweeney (1992). Bond prices as unbiased forecasts of bankruptcy settlements, *J. Finance* 47, 943–980.

Eisenberg, T. (1992). Baseline problems in assessing Chapter 11, unpublished manuscript, Cornell University.

Fama, E. (1980). Agency problems and the theory of the firm. *J. Polit. Econ.* 88, 288–307.

Fortgang, C. and T.M. Mayer (1985). Valuation in bankrutpcy. *UCLA Law Rev.* 32, 1061–1132.

Franks, J. and W. Torous (1989). An empirical investigation of U.S. firms in reorganization. *J. Finance* 44, 747–770.

Gertner, R. and D. Scharfstein (1991). A theory of workouts and the effects of reorganization law. *J. Finance* 46, 1189–1222.

Giammarino, R. (1989). The resolution of financial distress. *Rev. Financ. Studies* 2(1), 25–47.

Gilson, S. (1989). Management turnover and financial distress. *J. Financ. Econ.* 25, 241–262.

Gilson, S. (1990). Bankruptcy, boards, banks and blockholders: Evidence on changes in corporate ownership and control when firms default. *J. Financ. Econ.* 27, 355–388.

Gilson, S., K. John, and L. Lang (1990). Troubled debt restructurings: An empirical study of private reorganization of firms in default. *J. Financ. Econ.* 27, 315–353.

Gilson, S. and M. Vetsuypens (1993). CEO compensation in financially distressed firms: An empirical analysis. *J.Finance* 48, 425–458.

Green, R. and A. Juster (1992). The structure and timing of debt renegotiations by financially distressed firms, unpublished manuscript, Carnegie-Mellon University.

Grossman, S. and O. Hart (1980). Takeover bids, the free-rider problem and the theory of the corporation. *Bell J. Econ.* 11, 42–64.

Harris, M. and A. Raviv (1990). Capital structure and the informational role of debt. *J. Finance* 45, 321–349.

Harris, M. and A. Raviv (1991). The theory of capital structure. *J. Finance* 46, 297–356.

Harris, M. and A. Raviv (1993). The design of bankruptcy procedures, unpublished manuscript, University of Chicago.

Hart, O. and J. Moore (1989). Default and renegotiation: A dynamic model of debt, unpublished manuscript, MIT.

Haugen, R. and L. Senbet (1978). The insignificance of bankruptcy costs to the theory of optimal capital structure. *J. Finance* 33, 383–392.

Haugen, R. and L. Senbet (1988). Bankruptcy and agency costs: Their significance to the theory of optimal capital structure. *J. Financ. Quant. Anal.* 23, 27–38.

Heinkel, R. and J. Zechner (1993). Financial distress and optimal capital structure adjustments, unpublished manuscript, University of British Columbia.

Hoshi, T., A. Kashyap and D. Scharfstein (1990). The role of banks in reducing the costs of financial distress in Japan. *J. Financ. Econ.* 27, 67–88.

Jensen, J. (1991). Corporate control and the politics of finance. *J. Appl. Corp. Finance* 4, 13–33.

Jensen, M. (1989). Active investors, LBOs, and the privatization of bankruptcy. *J. Appl. Corp. Finance* 2, 35–44.

Jensen, M. and W. Meckling (1976). Theory of the firm: Managerial behavior, agency costs, and ownership structure, *J. Financ. Econ.* 3, 305–360.

Johnson, D. (1989). The risk behavior of equity of firms approaching bankruptcy. *J. Financ. Res.* XII(1), 33–50.

Kim, E.H. (1978). A mean–variance theory of optimal capital structure and corporate debt capacity. *J. Finance* 33, 45–64.

Kraus, A. and R. Litzenberger (1973). A state-preference model of optimal financial leverage. *J. Finance* 28, 911–922.

Lang, L. and R. Stulz (1992). Contagion and competitive intra-industry effects of bankruptcy announcements: An empirical analysis, New York University and Ohio State University, unpublished manuscript.

McDaniel, M. (1986). Bondholders and corporate governance. *Bus. Lawyer* 41, 413–460.

McMillan, H., R. Nachtmann and F. Phillips-Patrick (1990). Costs of reorganizing under Chapter 11: Some evidence from the 1980's, SEC working paper.

Merton, R. (1974). Theory of rational option pricing, *Bell J. Econ. Manage. Sci.* 4, 141–183.

Merton, R. (1990). The financial system and economic performance. *J. Financ. Serv. Res.* 4, 263–300.

Miller, M. (1977). Debt and taxes. *J. Finance* 32, 261–275.

Miller, M. (1991). Leverage. *J. Finance* 46, 479–488.

Modigliani, F. and M. Miller (1958). The cost of capital, corporation finance, and the theory of investment. *Am. Econ.Rev.* 48, 261–297.

Modigliani, F. and M. Miller (1963). Corporate income taxes and the cost of capital. *Am. Econ. Rev.* 53, 433–443.

Morse, D. and W. Shaw (1988). Investing in bankrupt firms. *J. Finance* 43, 1193–1206.

Myers, S. (1977). Determinants of corporate borrowing. *J. Financ. Econ.* 5, 147–176.

Roe, M. (1983). Bankruptcy and debt: A new model for corporate reorganization. *Columbia Law Rev.* 83, 527–602.

Roe, M. (1987). The voting prohibition in bond workouts. *Yale Law J.* 97, 232–279.

Rohman, M. and M. Policano (1990). Financing Chapter 11 companies in the 1990s. *J. Appl. Corp. Finance* 5, 96–101.

Schwartz, A. (1981). Security interests and bankruptcy priorities: A review of current theories. *J. Legal Studies* 10, 1–37.

Scott, J. (1976). A theory of optimal capital structure. *Bell J. Econ.* 7, 33–54.

Senbet, L. and J. Seward (1991). A market-based reform of the bankruptcy process, unpublished manuscript, University of Maryland and Dartmouth College.

Shleifer, A. and R. Vishny (1992). Liquidation values and debt capacity: A market equilibrium approach. *J. Finance* 47, 1343–1366.

Smith, C. and J. Warner (1979). On financial contracting: An analysis of bond covenants. *J. Financ. Econ.* 7, 117–161.

Stiglitz, J. (1974). On the irrelevance of corporate financial policy. *Am. Econ. Rev.* 64, 851–866.

Stulz, R. and H. Johnson (1985). An analysis of secured debt. *J. Financ. Econ.* 14, 501–521.

Titman, S. (1984). The effect of capital structure on a firm's liquidation decision. *J. Financ. Econ.* 137–152.

Triantis, G. (1992). Relational stakeholder contracts in bankruptcy, University of Toronto, unpublished manuscript.

Walsh, J. and J. Seward (1990). On the efficiency of internal and external corporate control mechanisms. *Acad. Manage. Rev.* 15, 421–458.

Warner, J. (1977). Bankruptcy, absolute priority, and the pricing of risky debt claims. *J. Financ. Econ.* 4, 239–276.

Warner, J., R. Watts and K. Wruck (1988). Stock prices and top management changes. *J. Financ. Econ.* 20, 461–492.

Webb, D. (1985). The importance of incomplete information in explaining the existence of costly bankruptcy, unpublished manuscript, London School of Economics.

Webb, D. (1987). The importance of incomplete information in explaining the existence of costly bankruptcy. *Economica* 54, 279–288.

Weiss, L. (1990). Bankruptcy resolution: Direct costs and violation of priority of claims. *J. Financ. Econ.* 27, 285–314.

Weiss, L. (1991). Bankruptcy judges overstepping their bounds: Commentary, unpublished manuscript, Tulane University.

White, M. (1989). The Corporate bankruptcy decision. *J. Econ. Perspect.* 3, 129–151.

White, M. (1990). Bankruptcy liquidation and reorganization, in: D.E. Logue (ed.), *Handbook of Modern Finance*, Warren, Gorham & Lamont, New York.

Wruck, K. (1990). Financial distress, reorganization, and organizational efficiency. *J. Financ. Econ.* 27, 419–444.

Zender, J. (1991). Optimal financial instruments. *J. Finance* 46, pp. 1645–1663.

R. Jarrow et al., Eds., *Handbooks in OR & MS, Vol. 9*

Chapter 29

Empirical Methods of Event Studies in Corporate Finance

Rex Thompson
Cox School of Business, Southern Methodist University, Dallas, TX 75275, U.S.A.

1. Introduction

Empirical work in corporate finance is directed toward three primary topic areas: how various decisions and events affect the value of existing corporate debt and equity claims; how corporations choose the mix of financial claims that comprises their capital structure; and the effect of capital structure on a corporation's future decisions. While empirical work in all of the three topic areas is important, this review focuses on the methodology of event studies, the common expression given for the first category. I have chosen this focus because finance distinguishes itself from other branches of applied economics by its emphasis on the role of security markets and the underlying security pricing process. Many empirical investigations into capital structure choice and how capital structure affects future decisions also rely on the use of security prices and are, therefore, indirectly contained in the first topic area [1].

Although experimental research in finance is gaining popularity, particularly in the area of how markets assimilate information [see Cadsby, Frank & Maksimovic, 1990, and references], virtually all corporate empirical work to date revolves around the actual experiences of existing corporations, with data collected ex post. While this type of empirical work does not have the benefit of a control experiment, in this review I will call the collection and processing of observational

[1] The branch of corporate empirical work that will not be discussed involves correlating economic and financial decisions with capital structure variables and other, exogenous variables hypothesized to influence these decisions. This type of empirical analysis is done both cross-sectionally and in time series. Logit models are popular estimation methods to infer, say, the importance of ownership structure in determining whether a firm is involved in a control contest [Mikkelson & Partch, 1989], or engages in management turnover [Gilson, 1989; Warner, Watts & Wruck, 1988]. Logit has been used for estimating the importance of financial variables in predicting bankruptcy [Ohlson, 1980; Zmijewski, 1984], takeovers [Palepu, 1986] or the existence of particular bond covenants [Begley, 1990]. The econometric methods chosen by researchers are similar to those chosen in other areas of applied economics in which there is a focus on the correlation between decision variables and exogenous variables.

data on corporations an experiment, and treat the lack of control over the independent variables as an inherent limitation of the experimental design.

In event studies the design of experiments follows the traditional structure underlying the scientific method as applied in positive economics. A theory of decision-making within the corporation is proposed that contains a set of refutable predictions for observed phenomena. An experiment is contrived that involves the collection of observational data from past experience. Classical hypothesis tests are performed to determine the conformity between the data and the predictions of the theory. The theory is either supported or rejected according to the results.

Conclusions about competing theories are often couched in terms of which has the best descriptive validity. The concept of descriptive validity is intuitive but somewhat informal as applied in corporate finance [2]. Most researchers acknowledge that all parsimonious theories are to some extent false. Therefore, the goal is to find the best among available theories.

Because the complex environment surrounding the modern corporation can create a gulf between what theory is able to model and what data are generated by actual experience, many empirical investigations involve aggregating data and summarizing empirical regularities without the clear direction of theory. Empirical regularities, however, form a pool of stylized facts that serves to motivate new theoretical modeling. Thus the empirical work in corporate finance serves two functions: first, to identify the most descriptive among competing theories and, second, to provide motivation for new theoretical analysis. This second function is served, for example, by research into empirical regularities that are considered unexplainable by existing theory. Further, because the researcher is not testing a formal hypothesis when the objective is to identify stylized facts about the corporate experience, this latter area of empirical work is justifiably less formal, less structured and less rigorous in its experimental design.

There is a final issue concerning the design of experiments in corporate finance that deserves mentioning before the details surrounding specific applications are explored in later sections. As in all empirical modeling, refinements in methodology frequently come through the careful specification of underlying assumptions about both economic behavior and the nature of the stochastic processes that generate observable variables. Where the assumptions are valid, refinements improve the power of tests and the efficiency of parameter estimates. Where assumptions are invalid or incapable of being tested directly, researchers are forced to evaluate tradeoffs between simple and sophisticated econometric methods. The criterion of what works best becomes a matter of judgement and experience. In later sections, I discuss several tradeoffs that have received attention in the literature. In my conclusions, I also offer some thoughts on the potential costs of adopting an informal notion of what works best as a guide to careful empirical modeling.

[2] Formal Bayesian constructs for discriminating among competing theories, such as the posterior odds ratio, are only recently gaining attention in corporate finance. See Malatesta & Thompson [1993] for an application.

2. Sources of data for empirical investigations

Many machine readable data sets covering information about corporations are sold by private vendors. In this review, I will highlight only the most commonly available at research Universities. Perhaps the most frequently cited are the files available from the Center for Research in Security Prices (CRSP) and Standard and Poor's. As the name implies, CRSP specializes in data relating to the transactions prices of publicly traded corporate common stock and government securities. On the corporate side, CRSP provides daily transactions prices for all securities traded on the New York and American Stock Exchanges. These data are available from July 2, 1962 along with various types of 'header' information about the securities, including dividends per share and number of shares outstanding. CRSP also provides a data base of monthly transactions prices on all NYSE and AMEX securities, starting in December 1925. Daily price quotations for securities traded through NASDAQ are available from CRSP starting in January, 1973. Rate of return files, derived from the price and dividend information are available as are the returns on various security market indexes [3].

The primary source for detailed accounting information about major corporations is the Standard and Poor's Compustat Service, started in 1962. Compustat provides a number of files containing financial, statistical and market information on over 7,100 US and Canadian industrial and nonindustrial companies. The most important for empirical work in corporate finance is the Industrial Full-coverage File, containing approximately 4,800 companies that file reports with the SEC. The annual format has up to 20 years and 320 data items per firm year compiled from annual reports, 10K and 10Q filings, various Standard & Poor's Publications, and other data vendors. Compustat attempts to reproduce major portions of each firm's annual report in a consistent machine readable structure. Footnotes are not included. There is also a 12 year, quarterly format and extensive industry summary information. The existence of data on Compustat is often a screen for firms to be included in empirical studies [4].

Among sources of financial information that are not machine readable, Moody's manuals are frequently referenced for firm and security information as are SEC filings and the audited financial statements published directly by public corporations. The 10K version of the annual report is available at the SEC in Washington DC and in several regional reading rooms. Since the 10K reports

[3] While other security price data bases are available, CRSP is clearly dominant. For example, I could not find an exception to the use of CRSP for some aspect of the experimental design in the over forty-five empirical studies using American companies published in the Journal of Financial Economics in volumes 16–26 between 1986 and 1990. There are several exceptions in later volumes and exceptions involving foreign companies.

[4] One oddity of Compustat is that their files contain only the most recent 20 or 12 year history. Older information is dropped from the files when new information is added. To my knowledge there is no systematically compiled source of information deleted from the Compustat tapes. There are over 20 years of data, once compiled by Compustat and in circulation at research universities, but now no longer available from the company. Many universities keep back files informally.

can be purchased, many Universities maintain files on sets of firms such as the S&P 500.

The Wall Street Journal is a standard source for identifying the first public announcement of corporate activities. Securities laws and listing requirements mandate the timely disclosure of material news that may affect the market for a firm's securities. The Wall Street Journal has become the most prominent reporting vehicle for corporations, partly because news reported there is considered to be publicly disclosed by the SEC and other securities regulators. For events covered by the Journal, it is rare that the first public disclosure is not well approximated by a two day window ending on the day the event is reported in the Journal.

The Wall Street Journal exercises some discretion over what it considers to be material news. Therefore, it is possible that the Journal does not report certain corporate events of interest to researchers. Barclay & Litzenberger [1988] discuss the advantages of using the Dow Jones News Service as an alternative to the Wall Street Journal.

Obviously, many investigations require extensive hand collected data. Accepted practice in published studies is to report detailed collection procedures, leaving the author latitude over whether or not to make data available upon request. Some authors are more generous than others but the profession is sensitive to the tradeoff between the private benefits of maintaining a proprietary data set and the public benefits of independent verification of empirical results. *The Journal of Money Credit and Banking* is the only journal of which I am aware that requires authors to submit their data for distribution by the journal to interested readers.

Several institutions and individuals have compiled specialized data sets for general use such as the University of Rochester's Merc Database on tender offers and Professor Jay Ritter's Database on Initial Public Offerings. A number of studies contain appendices listing, for example, firm names and key event dates.

3. The conceptual foundation of empirical methods used in event studies

A typical event study starts with hypotheses about how a particular corporate event should affect the value of some of the claims issued against the corporation. Define the valuation effect of an event as the difference between firm or security value conditional upon the event occurring and value conditional upon the event not occurring. Empirical methods used to estimate the valuation effect involve the details of experimental design. Before examining these details, it is important to review three conceptual issues.

3.1. A limitation in the design of experiments involving management decisions

The market values of corporate securities are derived from a combination of the exogenous environment and the corporate decision process acting within the environment. In testing valuation issues, we would like to separate these forces so as to infer the equivalent of partial derivatives of the value function. What we observe in the data, however, are a collection of financial decisions, all chosen presumably through optimizing processes, in conjunction with the exogenous market structures that are causing firms to make different decision choices. As a result, it is often difficult to disentangle the valuation effects of a management decision, holding constant the economic environment within which the decision is made, from the valuation effects of a change in the economic environment itself. Suppose, for example, that we wish to test a model of dividend irrelevance. To measure the relation between firm value and dividends we would like to have an experiment containing many firms that differ only in the amount of dividends paid. Real data, however, will typically contain observations in which dividend payments are correlated with cash flow. The separate effects of dividends and cash flow can be difficult to untangle.

One way to hold some of the exogenous forces constant is to direct attention to the change in market value associated with a change in corporate policy, or a change in economic environment. This is the approach chosen by the vast majority of empirical studies in corporate finance dealing with valuation issues. Structuring the empirical model in terms of value changes simplifies the empirical model because any factors that do not change drop out of the equation. Most empirical work, then, looks at the impact of changes in the exogenous environment and changes in corporate decisions on changes in firm value and changes in the partitioning of firm value among various claimants [5].

Adopting an approach based on changes rather than levels of variables requires the accurate identification of event dates. With accurate event dates it is possible to disentangle various influences on security value as long as changes in these influences are temporally separate. This proviso leads to the second conceptual issue underlying event study methods.

3.2. *The role of information arrival*

An efficient capital market sets prices based on expectations of the future, and it is difficult to identify when the market forms and changes expectations, particularly about corporate policy. At the time a corporate decision is announced, for example, the price response will be based on the change in expectations that this decision would be made. Any partial anticipation must somehow be accounted for to avoid underestimating the value implications. Define the announcement effect as the change in value resulting from the announcement of a corporate event. In simple environments with only a single possible event, the announcement effect equals the valuation effect times one minus the probability that the event would occur. It is thus attenuated toward zero. For inquiries designed to test the

[5] Christie [1987] discusses the link between what he calls levels models and returns models in the Accounting literature. He identifies situations where the models are equivalent conceptually. Long [1978] looks at the difference in price between two classes of claims in the same corporation that differ in the amount of dividends received. Differencing serves to control for factors that are the same across the two types of securities.

null hypothesis of no effect, attenuation creates a bias against rejection and is not critical to the interpretation of a study that successfully rejects.

The concept of rational prior anticipation opens an important final issue about information arrival. To say that a decision made within a corporation is not perfectly anticipated requires that something about the decision be uncertain in the eyes of investors. There are two possibilities. The first is that investors do not understand the objective function of the decision-maker. But, if the market learns something about the decision-making process, this presumably affects market perceptions of the probabilities of future decisions made within the firm. The second possibility is that investors do not know as much about the exogenous environment surrounding the corporate decision as the corporate decision-maker. In this case the market learns something about private information simultaneously with the decision. In both situations, the implications of theory must be couched in terms of everything that the market learns from a corporate event. Myers & Majluf [1984] have an early discussion of this issue in the context of equity offerings.

3.3. A tradeoff in estimation error

The security price reaction to a corporate event involves several sources of estimation error. I will discuss errors induced by both prior anticipation of the event and failing to identify the event period precisely. The simultaneous arrival of extraneous information about market wide factors and other unrelated firm specific events also induce security price changes that create estimation error. Finally, even in the absence of these other influences, the stock price reaction at the time of announcement represents only an expectation of the ultimate valuation effect. While this estimate is presumably unbiased ex ante, there could be a large difference between what investors expected and what actually happens. The ultimate relevance of a particular event for security holders may not be revealed for a number of years. Over large samples of firms and long time periods, these estimation errors tend to cancel out because they are uncorrelated across the sample. On the other hand, if investors are unfamiliar with an event and a sample of similar events occurs over a short interval of time, the announcement period estimation errors could be very highly correlated. Examples include the market reaction to junk bond issuances and the adoption of anti-takeover defenses in the mid 1980s and the cluster of LIFO adoptions in 1974. Under these circumstances, an argument can be made for examining stock return performance over intervals that include a learning period for investors.

An alternative approach to estimating the cash flow effects of corporate decisions is to abandon the market reaction to the announcement and focus on changes in cash flow directly. These changes can be estimated relative to a number of benchmarks. In the absence of a financial market to price securities, this approach would be the most natural, but it is fraught with difficulties arising from the openendedness of such a forward looking exercise. Nevertheless, the approach has been used with satisfactory results in a few instances. McNichols [1990] looks at changes in earnings after the announcement of corporate dividend increases with the goal of verifying that the favorable stock price reaction to such increases is a rational response to future expected cash flow increases. Jarrell [1991] and Healey, Palepu & Ruback [1990] look at the future earnings effects of successful corporate acquisitions to ascertain the existence of benefits from acquisitions activity. Even if an event is perfectly anticipated such an exercise can, in principle, uncover the effects of the event[6]. In practice, however, adequately controlling for unrelated influences over long estimation periods makes the forward looking approach of working with realized cash flows difficult to implement. It is used primarily when the evidence based on stock price reactions is considered insufficient to discriminate among competing hypotheses.

4. Details of the empirical model

As mentioned previously, event studies start with hypotheses about how corporate events should affect the value of claims issued against the corporation. If one is interested in the sign of the effect, it is typical to structure the hypothesis in terms of the event's impact on the rate of return process for the corporation's securities. Most investigations focus on common stock returns; occasionally the returns to publicly traded corporate bonds and preferred stock are investigated. The hypothesis that the value of a security has increased consequent on a particular event translates into the hypothesis that the rate of return earned on that security over an interval spanning the first public announcement of the event is more positive than normal. Coupled with the notion that securities markets assimilate new information almost instantaneously, the concept of an abnormal return measured over an event interval is the grist of event study methods.

The empirical model is generally stated as follows. For each security j, let returns follow a stationary stochastic process in the absence of the event of interest. When the event occurs, market participants revise their value of the security, causing a shift in the return generating process.[7] Thus, the conditional return generating process can be written as

$$r_t = x_t B + e_t \tag{1a}$$

for nonevent time periods, and

$$r_t = x_t B + FG + e_t \tag{1b}$$

in an event period,

[6] It is important to distinguish between future cash flows and future security price appreciation over long periods. There is no reason to expect a correlation between, say, a good management decision and future *abnormal* security returns unless there is systematic mispricing of the kind mentioned in the previous paragraph. Future abnormal cash flows relative to a benchmark of normal cash flows is a viable metric of performance regardless of the market pricing process.

[7] A corporate event might also cause other changes in the return generating process besides a discrete change in security valuation. Several possibilities are discussed below.

where

r_t = the return to the security in period t,

x_t = a vector of independent variables not related to the event of interest, such as the return earned on one or more index portfolios in period t,

B = a vector of parameters, such as the security beta, measuring the comovement between the security return and the independent variables,

F = a row vector of firm characteristics or market conditions hypothesized to influence the impact of the event on the return process,

G = a vector of parameters measuring the influence of F on the impact of the event,

e_t = a mean zero disturbance having variance possibly differing in event and nonevent periods, and

The subscript j has been omitted from r, B, F and e.

Hypotheses usually center on G. Where an event spans several periods or takes several periods to be reflected in security prices, FG represents the cumulative shift in the return process and (1b) can be written as

$$\sum_{t=1}^{T} r_t = \sum_{t=1}^{T} (x_t B) + FG + \sum_{t=1}^{T} e_t \tag{1b$'$}$$

where T is the number of event periods (usually days) required to incorporate FG into prices.

In a simple application, the experiment involves estimating the return process for securities having a particular characteristic or set of characteristics (e.g. common stock in those firms announcing a new equity issue). F is set to unity for each sample firm during the event period and the event's impact is measured by G, a one dimensional event parameter. The null hypothesis is that such an announcement has no impact on the return process, or that $G = 0$.

The event's impact for a single firm is captured by F times G. It is not possible to disentangle the joint effect of several firm characteristics with data from a single announcement. If, for example, the effect of an event is hypothesized to be a function of leverage and firm size, grouping or regression procedures are required. These involve the aggregation of a sample of firms or of several events within the same firm if firm characteristics are time varying. Aggregation techniques are discussed in Section 5.3.

5. Issues in event study methods

Event study methods are the econometric techniques used to estimate and draw inferences about G. The issues are covered in four sections: (1) modeling and estimating the return process for a single security, (2) modeling and estimating the event's impact, (3) aggregation across securities, and (4) hypothesis testing.

Interest in the profession vacillates across the topics, with new ideas and suggestions implemented by researchers according to their needs. Latitude is given researchers to determine the balance between simplicity and sophistication that is appropriate for their specific applications.

5.1. *Modeling the return generating process*

5.1.1. *Preliminaries*

The return generating process for nonevent periods is estimated over a time period that does not contain the event. Conventions for choosing this period, called the nonevent period, are discussed below. As will also be discussed, conventions for how the process is parameterized varies greatly across applications, creating some confusion as to which is best in any particular case. Generally, researchers choose processes that can be defended as providing forecast errors (unconditional on an event) that have zero means. Tradeoffs between expediency and forecast error variance are frequently made, particularly when large samples will be aggregated.

The general structure of the empirical model in nonevent periods is

$$r = xB + e \tag{2}$$

where r, e and x are the stacked vectors and matrix with typical rows r_t, e_t and x_t. The parameters in B are estimated through regression.

5.1.2. *The return interval*

It is common to use daily data for the measurement of rates of return. The primary motivation for daily data is that it is readily available and provides an acceptable range of event periods from one to several days. The use of weekly and monthly data are common where a shorter event period is unnecessary. Intraday data are also used occasionally where an extremely short event period is deemed desirable. It is good methodology to maintain a consistent return interval across any particular application because the parameters of the return process can depend upon the return interval. For example, market model betas estimated with daily data can differ from those estimated with monthly data for the same securities.

5.1.3. *Mean adjusted returns*

Many event studies include no information in x, using only a column of 1's. G is measured by the difference or cumulative difference between event period returns and the average nonevent period return. This mean adjusted returns approach or comparison period returns approach is used by Masulis [1980], for example, in his study of exchange offers.

5.1.4. *The market model and control portfolios*

Most event studies include some information in x, commonly the contemporaneous rate of return on a market index. When a market index and a column of 1's are used, the result is the market model, in which an intercept and slope or beta coefficient are estimated using return data from nonevent periods. The announcement effect, FG, is estimated by the market model forecast error cumulated over the event period(s).

x may also include the return on a similar firm or portfolio of similar firms that do not have the event of interest. The purpose of control firms or control portfolios is to reduce sampling variation of the forecast error. To properly interpret the forecast error, it is important that the control firms chosen not be affected by the event under study. As an example, Eisenbeis, Harris & Lakonishok [1984] use the return on an index of bank securities as a control for the returns on banks that elect to become one bank holding companies.

The Center for Research in Security Prices (CRSP) provides an excess returns tape that is used by a number of researchers such as Vermaelen [1981] in his study of common stock repurchases. For each firm, the tape contains a time series of the difference between the return earned on the firm's stock and the return earned on a portfolio of stocks with similar betas.

In principle, adding explanatory variables to the forecast model reduces forecast error variance relative to a mean adjusted returns approach. On the other hand, in applications where security events are not clustered in calendar time and thus can be viewed as independent, the reduction in error variance is often not material, particularly when a large sample of firms is aggregated.

5.1.5. Multivariate models

In multivariate extensions to the market model, several portfolio return series are used as regressors to further reduce the sampling variability of the forecast error. Langetieg [1978] considers these issues in his study of mergers. Industry indexes and firm size based portfolios can be used as well as portfolios selected to represent other, unrelated stochastic variation in the economy. Again, the researcher must make the assumption that the regressors chosen are uncorrelated with the timing of the event and its price effect.

5.1.6. Excess returns

Some researchers define the return process in excess of the risk free rate available on Treasury Bills. It is more defensible to assume that excess returns follow a fixed stochastic process than to assume the same for raw returns [8]. The reason is that raw returns are typically characterized as containing the risk free return plus a risk premium. Since the former varies over time, raw returns will follow a time varying stochastic process unless the expected value of the risk

[8] Recent evidence in the asset pricing literature shows mean excess returns on market indexes to vary over time and hence the assumption of a fixed stochastic process is not entirely descriptive [see, for example, Fama & French, 1989; and Campbell, 1987]. Market model forecast errors and other measures of abnormal returns to individual securities can still conform to a fixed stochastic process, however, even if mean returns to the market index are time varying. In the context of equilibrium models such as the CAPM, the same cannot generally be said of market model forecast errors in raw returns when the risk free rate is time varying.

premium is perfectly negatively correlated with the risk free rate. Evidence shows this assumption to be counter-factual for market indexes. While, the distinction is trivial for daily data because daily risk free returns are so small, the time variation in T-Bill returns can exert a measurable influence over monthly data, although rarely a material one.

5.1.7. Projection errors versus deviations from an equilibrium model

Occasionally, researchers distinguish between forecast models that involve simple projections of security returns on other return variables and models that specify an equilibrium relation between security returns and the returns on, for example, the market index. An equilibrium model imposes restrictions on the intercept of the projection. For example, the traditional Capital Asset Pricing Model implies that the intercept in the unconditional market model measured in excess returns has expected value equal to zero [see Gibbons, 1982, and references]. Incorporating such a restriction reduces estimation error when the equilibrium model is true.

5.1.8. Estimation window

There is discretion over the choice of nonevent estimation period for most empirical investigations. Typically, prior periods of about 250 days for daily data or 60 months for monthly data are used [9]. Alternatives are to use post event period data or to center the nonevent period around the event. Once the nonevent period is chosen, the relevant parameters of the return generating process are estimated.

The primary concern with using prior period data is that the event could be caused in part by prior period return performance. In such cases, forecast errors in event periods based on prior period parameter estimates can contain biases because the nonevent period does not provide an unbiased estimate of what the security return would have been absent the event. Post event period data are preferred in these cases. For example, Mikkelson [1981, footnote 13] in his examination of the effects of calling convertible debt uses post announcement returns to estimate the normal return on equity because debt is typically called after a period of positive stock price performance.

5.2. Modeling the Event Effect

5.2.1. Forecast errors versus multiple regression event parameters

Most event studies use a nonevent period to estimate a forecast model and estimate the event's impact from forecast errors in the event period. An alternative characterization of the conditional return generating process under the same

[9] The predominant use of prior data probably results from two influences. Prior data were used by the first event studies published; for example by Fama, Fisher, Jensen & Roll [1969] in their study of stock splits. These early studies were concerned with the possibility of forming a trading rule to beat the market by investing in securities after corporate events. Therefore, they were careful to base their analysis on information known to the market before the event. In addition, using prior data allows researchers to process the greatest number of recent events.

assumptions combines the event and nonevent periods into a single model for security j of the form

$$r_j = xB_j + D_j \otimes F_j G + e_j$$

where now the vectors r, e and x contain both the event and nonevent data while D is a column of indicators having zeros for nonevent periods and $1/T$ in the event periods [10]. The model can be written more compactly as

$$r_j = X_j B_j^* + e_j \tag{3}$$

where $X_j = [x, D_j \otimes F_j]$, and

$$B_j^* = [B_j, G]'$$

This characterization will be referenced later during the discussion of aggregation across firms because it is a convenient econometric format. Binder [1985] and Thompson [1985] discuss the versatility of models like equation (3).

5.2.2. Risk changes during and after the event

Events may influence the return process other than through a shift in the level of security prices. For example, theory might imply an increase in beta risk or residual risk for a sample of firms. Both permanent and transitory changes have been investigated. Permanent changes in risk parameters can be estimated by comparing pre and post event return data, either estimating two separate market models or combining pre and post event data into a switching regimes model. Mandelker [1974], and Dodd & Ruback [1977] contain two of the first estimates of risk shifting around mergers and successful tender offers. More recently, Dann, Masulis & Mayers [1991], Hertzel & Jain [1991] and Bartov [1991] estimate risk changes around stock repurchases.

Transitory risk changes involve a shock to risk parameters during the event period itself. If the event period is just a few days, it is difficult to estimate risk parameters for individual firms unless the event recurs periodically. For example, Kalay & Loewenstein [1985] document increases in both total risk and beta risk during dividend announcement periods by comparing risk parameters estimated during nondividend announcement periods and risk parameters estimated over a set of sequential dividend announcements. In a slightly different context, Brown, Harlow & Tinic [1988] examine transitory risk changes around major corporate events. Where each firm has only a single event, the approach taken involves cross-sectional aggregation of individual firm events. Cross-sectional risk estimation is discussed in Section 3.3.3.

[10] Another characterization would be to view D as a matrix of zero-one variables, letting each column indicate a single event period (say, day). G equals the sum of the individual event period effects. This approach maintains an algebraic equality between forecast errors from a two step approach and the individual event period multiple regression event parameters.

5.2.3. Security value changes versus abnormal rates of return

Some economic theories focus more directly on firm value changes than on rates of return. While the two processes are closely tied, the distinction is most relevant when the researcher wishes to average or aggregate results across a sample of securities. The sign of the average abnormal security value change can differ from the sign of the average abnormal security return when the sample securities vary in market values. For example, testing whether mergers create value across bidders and targets involves aggregating effects across firms that likely differ in size. Based on average abnormal returns, the estimated effects are positive, but based on average abnormal value changes, the results are less supportive of an increase in combined value. The difference in inference is caused by the fact that targets have large average positive abnormal returns but small size, while bidders have small average abnormal returns but large size. Malatesta [1983] evaluates abnormal value changes for combinations of merging firms, while Bradley, Desai & Kim [1988] look at tender offer pairs. Dann [1981] combines the abnormal value change of debt and equity in considering the effects of corporate common stock repurchases.

5.2.4. Multiple events and multiple event dates

Some research considers several events within a single return generating process. Most researchers, such as Mikkelson & Ruback [1985] in their examination of interfirm equity investments, assume that a single nonannouncement period applies to all events; each event is then compared to the same forecast model.

Where multiple events share common event dates an additional complexity is introduced. Schipper & Thompson [1983] discuss the effects of several regulatory changes on a common sample of corporations. In their problem, each regulatory change evolves over a set of dates, some of which are common with the dates of other regulatory changes. If the impact of the regulatory changes are estimated singly, the impact of one regulatory change may affect the estimate of the impact of another wherever the two changes share a common event date. The solution to this problem is a multivariate extension to model (3) above in which the event indicators are a set of columns with each column pertaining to a single regulatory change. The model is estimated jointly with each event parameter estimated holding constant the effects of the other regulatory changes.

5.2.5. Inaccurate event dates

Precise identification of event dates is important because the standard deviation of cumulative forecast errors increases with about the square root of the number of time periods over which the errors are cumulated [11]. Detecting an effect when one is present is facilitated by identifying the shortest possible interval containing

[11] For example, a typical common stock daily return forecast error (residual) from the market model might have a standard deviation of about 2.5% [see Brown & Warner, 1985, table 1]. Since security returns are almost serially uncorrelated, the cumulated forecast error for, say, 10 days would have a standard deviation of about the square root of 10 times 2.5%, or about 8%. An empirical study with 100 independent firms would detect a 1% average event effect rather easily

the event. Where an event unfolds through a series of announcements or potential information leaks, there is a tradeoff between reducing estimation error by focussing on the most important information dates and attenuation caused by missing some of the true market reaction. Attempting to trace a slow diffusion of information about an event is the exception rather than the rule unless a series of event dates can be identified objectively such as in Mikkelson & Ruback's [1985] investigation of corporate control contests.

The highest signal to noise ratio is often found in extremely short time intervals. For example, Barclay & Litzenberger [1988] use intraday data to examine the effects of new equity issues. Their investigation focusses on the first fifteen minutes to a few hours of trading, so an accurate announcement time is required. They use the Dow Jones News Service, which time stamps each announcement.

At the other logical extreme is the case where the actual event date falls within an interval of time, but the exact date is uncertain. This situation is examined by Ball & Torous [1988] in studying stock splits and stock dividends. They contrast the standard approach of cumulating abnormal returns in an event window with a maximum likelihood procedure based on the assumption that the event takes place on a single, but unknown, day within the event window. Forecast errors are assumed to be mean zero on all days except the true event day. The procedure estimates the event effect and the probabilities that each day in the interval is the true event day. Maximum likelihood provides more efficient estimates of the event effect than cumulating forecast errors when the underlying assumptions are true.

5.2.6. *Infrequent trading*

The low trading frequency of some securities introduces new complexities into the measurement of the event's impact. In general, it is desirable to measure the impact over an interval that includes significant trading volume on both sides of the event because transactions represent market clearing phenomena and are thus most likely to reflect information accurately. Bid-asked spreads with no volume may be stale relative to the market's assessment of value. In some data sets (e.g. CRSP), it is not possible to tell whether a particular closing price represents a transaction made after an announcement. In cases where low volume exists the event window is typically widened, although for common stock traded on the organized exchanges, it is rare that a two day event window would not capture sufficient volume to include the announcement effect. In markets with infrequent

if the exact event day could be pinpointed for each firm. The average forecast error would have a standard deviation of about 0.25%, making a 1% average event effect about 4 standard deviations from the null hypothesis. On the other hand, with a 10 day event window, the average forecast error would have a standard deviation of about 0.8%, making a 1% average event effect only 1.25 standard deviations from the null hypothesis. Reference to the cumulative normal distribution reveals that a t-statistic greater than 2 would occur only about 23% of the time if projection errors are roughly normal. With a two day event window, a 1% average event effect would be detected about 79% of the time.

Estimation error in parameters of the forecast model is also more important with longer event windows. Estimation error in the intercept of the market model, for example, cumulates additively over the event window.

trading, the forecast model can include leading and lagging values of the return on the market index in the spirit of Scholes & Williams [1977] and Dimson [1979].

The greatest concern over infrequent trading involves the use of bond and preferred stock returns where transactions can be separated by several days, even up to a month. In these cases, researchers view multiple day returns as the aggregation of several single day returns with care taken to determine over what interval each return is measured. Handjinicolaou & Kalay [1984] compute a premium between their bond returns and the returns on comparison Treasury Bonds measured over identical time intervals. The mean of the underlying daily premium series is then used to compute abnormal premiums in the event periods [12]. Marais, Schipper & Smith [1989] estimate a forecast model and work with forecast errors by assuming that multiple day returns are the summation of independently and identically distributed daily returns. Where an event day has no trade, the forecast error cumulates until the next trade.

5.2.7. Market microstructure issues.

Although event study methods presume that transactions are made at equilibrium prices, the distinction between transactions made at the bid and the asked can exert an influence in applications where an event creates an order flow imbalance. Normally, one would expect a bid-asked bounce to cancel out across a sample of firms but some events create a bias. Grinblatt, Masulis & Titman [1984] discuss the market for stock that has recently announced a split. Trading off the exchange in the 'when issued' market causes the predominance of exchange trades to take place at the bid during periods shortly before the ex date. This can cause an apparent positive market reaction at the ex date as the stock resumes trading at both bid and asked prices. Lease, Masulis & Page [1991] consider the role of order imbalances in measuring the effect of seasoned equity offerings. They argue that some purchase orders are temporarily diverted to a primary market causing a preponderance of sell orders to be observed in the secondary market. The effect is to create an artificial negative impact on offering day returns. One solution is to use the average of the closing bid and asked quotes, assuming that the specialist uses volume between the event and the close to set equilibrium spreads.

5.2.8. Partial anticipation

The potential importance of partial anticipation of events was discussed in Section 3.2. In an early effort to formally model the effects of partial anticipation, Malatesta & Thompson [1985], assumed that market participants hold constant beliefs about the likelihood that a merger will occur each month. In their model, a merger announcement engenders a surprise equal to $(1 - p)$ times the true valuation effect of a merger, where p is the prior probability that a merger will occur. Nonannouncement months, on the other hand, are associated with a

[12] The premium between a corporate bond and Treasury Bond controls for term structure variation. Their model could be extended to control for other market information such as the return on a stock market index.

surprise of $-p$ times the valuation effect of a merger. The difference between returns in announcement and nonannouncement periods provides an unbiased estimate of the event's full valuation effect.

Subsequent researchers such as Acharya [1988, 1993] have extended the logic of prior anticipation to include models of the prior probability formation process. Observable firm characteristics are used to build a forecast model of event announcements and their probability. In his discussion, Acharya makes an important point about the effects of partial anticipation when the probability of an event is not constant over time. If a researcher simply differences the returns in announcement and nonannouncement periods, in general a downward biased estimate of the valuation effect results. This is because events typically occur in periods where they are more likely and do not occur in periods where they are less likely. Thus the average surprise in event periods is less than one minus the average surprise in nonevent periods and the difference in surprises is less than one.

5.3. Aggregating results across firms

5.3.1. General considerations

In order to streamline the discussion, I first treat concepts in aggregation that apply to cases in which prior anticipation is not of paramount importance. Either the researcher is interested in modeling the announcement effect specifically rather than the valuation effect or the event is sufficiently unanticipated that the difference between the two measures is immaterial. Where I do not wish to distinguish between valuation effects and announcement effects, I will use the term 'event effect' to capture both concepts. Prior anticipation is introduced again in Section 5.3.3.4.

Aggregation across firms can be viewed as a mechanism for estimating G within a pooled system of equations with a typical equation for firm j as in (3). Most studies use a two step process. First, the separate models in (3) are estimated on a firm by firm basis, ignoring the separate influences of the elements in each F_j. The first step estimates the event effect for each firm, typically with a forecast error, and also provides residual variance and covariance information from the nonevent periods. Next, viewing each separate firm as an observation, the event effect is modeled as

$$\gamma = FG + \epsilon \tag{4a}$$

where

γ = a column vector of length J with typical element γ_j,
γ_j = an estimate of the event effect for firm j [13]
F = a matrix of firm characteristics with typical row F_j as defined in equation (3),

[13] Using the notation from equations (1b) and (3), γ_j is an estimate of F_jG. Where a single event period (month or day) is used, γ_j would be the forecast error for that period. Where a series of periods are included, γ_j would generally be estimated by the cumulative forecast error over the

G = the influence of F on the event effect as defined in (3),
ϵ = a column of estimation errors of γ around FG.

To help visualize the second step, suppose there are J firms that have undergone a stock repurchase and K $(K < J)$ firm characteristics such as leverage and ownership concentration that are hypothesized to explain the effect of stock repurchases on equity values. Equation (4a) then has the following representation:

$$\begin{bmatrix} \gamma_1 \\ \vdots \\ \gamma_J \end{bmatrix} = \begin{bmatrix} f_{1,1} & \cdots & f_{K,1} \\ & \vdots & \\ f_{1,J} & \cdots & f_{K,J} \end{bmatrix} \begin{bmatrix} g_1 \\ \vdots \\ g_K \end{bmatrix} + \begin{bmatrix} \epsilon_1 \\ \vdots \\ \epsilon_J \end{bmatrix} \tag{4b}$$

The simplest way to estimate equation (4) is with OLS cross-sectional regression, letting the regression provide an estimate G and its covariance matrix. Such an approach can be enhanced, however, by recognizing that the error variance and covariance in the estimates of the individual event effects result from variability and covariability in the time series of individual security returns.

5.3.2. A digression on time series measures of variability.

In an ideal experiment, created in the laboratory, it would be natural for firms to have constant residual variance across event and nonevent periods. A model of the event's impact would be added to the system in the form of FG. Security returns and regression coefficients generated in repeated simulations of the experiment, holding F and G constant, would have sampling variability consistent with the residual variance–covariance matrix estimated in nonevent periods. The perspective of such an ideal experiment is the one taken by most researchers in the field.

As noted by Christie [1993], however, a number of researchers have observed that forecast errors seem to have higher variance in event periods than otherwise. In fact, a comparison of variance between event and nonevent periods is an approach to testing whether or not an event has information content [see Beaver, 1968]. How to incorporate increased variance during event periods into the inference problem is an interesting issue that is not altogether completely resolved in the literature. For example, Christie [1993] advocates including increased variance while Sefcik & Thompson [1986] describe a scenario where increased variance should be ignored. Many different arguments have been offered as motivation for particular variance estimation procedures and empirical evidence shows that the choice can affect inferences.

To clarify the issues, reconsider the ideal experiment described above. If data generated by such an experiment were studied, ex post, it is likely that a researcher

event periods. An alternative estimation approach is to estimate the model in equation (3) directly, with the event indicator variable, D, having the value $1/T$ for each of the T announcement days in the event window.

would find increased variance in event periods. Increased variance will be observed whenever the researcher omits explanatory variables from F. These variables enter the residual of the event periods.

Viewing the inference problem in terms of omitted variables is quite general; the issues center on what statistical properties the omitted variables are assumed to possess. To focus on significance measures, assume that the omitted variables are uncorrelated with the included variables so the remaining regression coefficients are still unbiased. In this sense the model is correctly specified.

If the omitted variables are orthogonal to the included variables, regression coefficients are unaffected by whether or not the omitted variables are in the model. It is clear in such a case that increased variability should be ignored in assessing the estimation error of coefficients on the included variables. This is because the increased variability does not contribute estimation error. An important application is where inferences are to be drawn about the mean impact of an event on a particular sample of firms. The mean impact across a sample is, in a trivial sense, always orthogonal to any other potential explanatory variables [14]. Therefore, a test of the mean impact should not include increased variance in the event period because this increased variance does not contribute to the estimation error of the mean.

There is a second, equally interesting, perspective, however, that argues in favor of accounting for the increased variance caused by omitted variables. Suppose the realizations of the omitted variables are viewed as drawings from an underlying population of possible realizations such that any sample is orthogonal only in expectation. In this case we might wish to draw inferences unconditionally, treating the omitted variables as additional error that may be spuriously correlated with the included variables in this particular realization of the experiment. If we assume that the omitted variables are drawn independently across the sample from a common population, then the increased variance in the event periods captures the noise added by the sampling variability of the omitted variables.

In any case, the use of nonevent time series variability is a common feature of event study methods and I will discuss it carefully. One approach to combining time series information with increased variability in event periods is suggested by Collins & Dent [1984]. They suggest scaling the covariance matrix estimated in nonevent periods, say S, by the factor $(J\text{-}1)^{-1}\ \epsilon' S^{-1}\epsilon$, where ϵ is the vector of estimated residuals in the event periods for the sample of J firms. In the discussion that follows I will ignore this scalar for convenience although in specific applications such an adjustment can be defended.

5.3.3. *When firm events are dispersed in time (no event clustering)*

The assumption that security returns are serially uncorrelated simplifies both the forecast model of nonevent returns and the cross-sectional aggregation of

[14] If a model is structured with an intercept and any other variables defined in terms of deviations from means, the intercept will always be the mean of the sample regardless of which variables are included in the regression.

results [15]. If security returns are serially uncorrelated, forecast errors across firms are essentially cross-sectionally uncorrelated whenever the events of interest are dispersed in calendar time. Except when events are clustered in calendar time, a cross-sectional independence assumption is virtually universal in the literature. Interest in residual variance–covariance information in nonevent periods centers on heteroscedasticity adjustments.

Measures of individual firm variances are typically estimated in the nonevent periods under the assumption of stationarity [16]. Where heteroscedasticity is small or uncorrelated with the (squared) explanatory variables in the model of the event effect, OLS cross-sectional regression can be defended as an unbiased procedure. In richer contexts, accounting for heteroscedasticity is commonly included in the experimental design.

5.3.3.1. Tests for an average effect. The average event effect is couched within (4) by setting F as a column of ones, ignoring all other firm characteristics. Such a model is usually not a complete specification of (4) but rather a simple model of inherent interest. Time series estimates of variability are combined with estimates of individual firm event effects in a number of ways. I will discuss the three most common approaches, giving each a cross-sectional regression interpretation.

The first approach is to estimate the mean effect and its significance through a weighted least squares regression (WLS) of the individual firm estimates on the column of ones. Let σ_j be an estimate of the standard error of γ_j around the true event effect for firm j [17]. Then the weighted least squares regression coefficient, which is an estimate of the mean event effect [18], is

$$\frac{\sum_{j=1}^{J} \gamma_j/\sigma_j^2}{\sum_{j=1}^{J} 1/\sigma_j^2} \tag{5}$$

[15] The critical assumption is that security residuals (forecast errors) are serially uncorrelated. There is some evidence of serial correlation in daily forecast errors, primarily due to serial correlation in index returns (see Scholes & Williams [1977] for reasons why). Researchers such as Ruback [1982] have proposed corrections to standard errors for the slight serial correlation that exists.

[16] A process for residual variance can also be incorporated. For example, Christie [1987] discusses a model in which residual variance is a function of leverage and, indirectly, a function of firm size. Where forecast errors are used to compute γ_j, Patell [1976] suggests a correction for the increased variability of forecast errors but this is typically not material.

[17] If equation (3) is used to calculate γ, the standard error of γ would come from the same regression and be used for σ. Where a forecast model is used, σ would come from the standard error of the residuals, adjusted for the number of forecast errors cumulated to compute γ with a possible correction for the fact that it is an out of sample forecast error.

[18] Weighted least squares does not generally lead to an unbiased estimate of the average event effect because the individual abnormal returns are weighted. A sufficient condition for unbiasedness, however, is that the deviations of the true individual firm effects from the true mean effect are uncorrelated with the inverse of the residual variances.

The standard error of the coefficient is the square root of the inverse of the denominator and thus a t-ratio is often based on the ratio of the numerator to the square root of the denominator. The standard deviation of residuals from the WLS cross-sectional regression could also be used to estimate the standard error of the coefficient. This measure includes the increased variance created by the omitted explanatory variables discussed earlier.

A second approach is to test significance of the average event effect by using the time series estimates of variability to construct an estimate of variability for the arithmetic mean. This is equivalent to an OLS regression of forecast errors on a column of ones. To test for significance of the mean event effect, compute the statistic

$$\frac{\sum_{j=1}^{J} \gamma_j}{\left(\sum_{j=1}^{J} \sigma_j^2\right)^{1/2}} \tag{6}$$

The standard errors from OLS cross-sectional regressions are often ignored in actual applications because they fail to account for heteroscedasticity.

A final approach is to compute standardized residuals by dividing the forecast error for each firm by the time series estimate of its standard error as in weighted least squares. These standardized residuals are then averaged and inferences drawn under the assumption that each standardized residual is a mean zero, t-distributed random variable; an assumption that follows from the null hypothesis that there is no event effect for any firm. Estimation is analogous to an OLS regression of standardized residuals on a column of ones. The average standardized residual, has standard deviation approximately equal to $1/\sqrt{J}$ if there is no time series heteroscedasticity in the event periods. Some researchers use the standard deviation from the cross-sectional regression for hypothesis tests rather than the theoretical standard deviation of $1/\sqrt{J}$. This latter measure includes any increased variation in the event periods caused by omitted explanatory variables as discussed above.

The three test procedures just described combine the same information in slightly different ways and thus can lead to different inferences. Which statistic is emphasized depends on what assumptions about the event effect are being maintained and what specifically is being tested or estimated. Suppose, for example, that the event effect is assumed to be the same for all firms and the hypothesis being tested is that this common event effect is zero. Then weighted least squares (the first procedure) is the natural choice because it provides an unbiased and efficient estimate of the common event effect. OLS (the second procedure) provides an unbiased estimate, but is less efficient than WLS.

Alternatively, suppose we do not wish to maintain the assumption that the event effect is the same for all firms but we wish an unbiased estimate of the mean effect and a test for significance. Then OLS is the obvious choice, although WLS might be more efficient under some assumptions [19].

The third procedure provides a statistic with a convenient sampling distribution under the null hypothesis that all firms have a zero event effect. While the two previous procedures also provide test statistics with convenient sampling distributions under this null hypothesis, the relative power of the three procedures to reject the null hypothesis when it is false depends on the nature of the alternative. Many empirical studies report more than one of these procedures because the economic hypotheses are not sharpened to the point where the procedures can be clearly ranked on the basis of efficiency or power.

5.3.3.2. Tests for general cross-sectional relationships. Inquiries into general cross-sectional models involve extending (4) to include more information in F. The researcher provides a model relating the event effect to firm specific characteristics such as leverage, firm size, or beta. Equation (4b) represents such a structure. Estimation is by regression. As in tests for a mean effect, weighted least squares based on the residual variance in the first step forecast model is a common approach to control for heteroscedasticity across firms. It is also common to use a heteroscedasticity consistent estimator for the cross-sectional covariance matrix of residuals as suggested in White [1980]. Dann, Masulis & Mayers [1991], for example, adopt both procedures.

Where general models are estimated, typically the residuals from the cross-sectional regression are used to estimate the covariance matrix of the model's coefficients, ignoring the time series variability measures available from the forecast models for each firm. As discussed above, cross-sectional variance measures include variation that time series measures do not: the variation caused by omitted explanatory variables in the cross-sectional model of the event effect. The researcher has to decide whether the increased variation should be included during hypothesis testing.

5.3.3.3. Event specific market risk measures. When events are temporally separated, it is possible to estimate a beta coefficient for the event returns apart from the individual beta coefficients of the firms during nonevent periods. A cross-sectional regression is run of forecast errors or raw security returns on a market index return that is matched pair-wise in calendar time. If forecast errors from a market model are used, such a cross-sectional beta identifies the average increase in beta during the event for the firms under investigation. The concept of a cross-sectional beta was first suggested by Ibbotson [1975] in his study of new stock issues and was later adopted by Clarkson & Thompson [1990] to study the question of how beta changes as securities season.

[19] See the previous footnote for conditions under which WLS is unbiased. Where it is unbiased, the efficiency of WLS relative to OLS depends on how large the differences are across the true individual firm event effects relative to the amount of heteroscedasticity in the residuals across firms.

5.3.3.4. Incorporating prior anticipation. Most economic models that link event effects to firm characteristics focus on the complete valuation effect including any partial anticipation component. Inferences drawn from cross-sectional econometric models often rely on the assumption that there is no correlation between the degree of surprise in the event and the firm characteristics used in the second step of the model [20]. Rational market participants, however, will use firm characteristics to help forecast the likelihood of corporate events. If, for example, events are more likely for firms with high leverage, the announcement effect will be more attenuated for highly levered firms. The forecast error for these firms may be lower even though the economic importance of the event is higher [21].

Lanen & Thompson [1988] give several examples where rational prior anticipation destroys the relation between a firm characteristic and the announcement effect even though there is a linear relation between the same firm characteristic and the valuation effect. Their first example [p. 314] clearly shows the problem: 'As a stylized example, consider the association between the stock reaction to LIFO adoptions and the firm specific tax benefits as assumed here to be known by investors prior to the adoptions. If the tax benefits are large, the likelihood of a LIFO adoption is also large and thus the market surprise will be small. Obviously, there will also be a small market reaction to a LIFO adoption if the tax benefits are small. Our model shows that the association between stock reaction and tax benefits depends upon where, between these extreme tax benefits, the sample is drawn.'

Careful modeling of the information arrival process can incorporate partial anticipation. Eckbo, Maksimovic & Williams [1990] develop a model of mergers that includes formal recognition of partial anticipation. The model has three essential parts, which, in a simplified form are as follows: First, observable firm characteristics, which, to be consistent with the notation in equation (4), I will denote as F, and a characteristic observable only to the manager, denoted η, summarize the effect of a merger. η enters directly while F enters through coefficients, denoted G. Second, the objective function of the manager is such that the merger takes place iff $y = FG + \eta$ exceeds zero. Third, investors, are assumed to know the probability distribution of η and thus by observing F and knowing G they can determine the probability of a merger, prob $(y > 0)$. The linear structure in equation (4) is replaced by a nonlinear model of the form

$$\gamma = [1 - \text{prob}\,(y > 0)] \cdot E(y \mid y > 0) + \epsilon. \tag{7}$$

As before, the researcher is interested in estimating G. This can be accomplished by assuming a distribution for η and fitting (7) with nonlinear optimization [22].

[20] Another obviously critical assumption underlying cross-sectional regression is that the right hand side variables are measured without error.

[21] Researchers are careful to state the necessary assumptions for their estimation approaches. For example, Holthausen [1981 p. 80] and Barclay & Litzenberger [1988, footnote 11] state sufficient econometric conditions to interpret their cross-sectional regressions. It is often more difficult to provide good economic justification for these conditions.

[22] Eckbo, Maksimovic and Williams assume that η is mean zero and normal, allowing maximum likelihood estimation.

5.3.4. Events clustered in calendar time

5.3.4.1. Introduction. When firms share common event dates, any cross-correlation of security returns transfers to the security forecast errors in the event period. Cross-correlation has often been found to be important, particularly for studies with industry clustering. The covariance matrix or a quadratic form in the covariance matrix can be estimated from data in the nonevent periods. It is much more important to include common sources of variation in the specification of the return generating process, such as a market index, when there is event clustering.

Once the major sources of common variation are included in the return generating process, there is a potential tradeoff to be considered in using additional residual covariance information. Where covariances are expected to be small, the estimation error involved in estimating a large covariance matrix can outweigh the asymptotic benefits. This issue is discussed carefully by Bernard [1987] who offers a nice synthesis and relevant references. In my discussion, I will assume that the researcher wishes to incorporate covariance information because it is felt to be material in the application at hand. I will also emphasize portfolio approaches to estimation where the amount of covariance information explicitly estimated can be greatly reduced.

In one of the first applications, Collins & Dent [1979] couched their hypothesis in terms of the difference between the impact of a common event on two types of firms. To estimate the significance of the difference in average event period forecast errors, they identified a pre-test period within which a time series of average differences in forecast errors could be computed. The event period difference was then compared to the distribution so estimated in order to assess statistical significance [23].

Most studies involving common event *dates* also involve common *events* such as regulatory changes, macroeconomic changes, or, as in the case of Eckbo [1985] and Eisenbeis, Harris & Lakonishok [1984], the effect of firm specific events on other firms in the same industry. In such cases, it is possible to combine the individual firms into a seemingly unrelated regressions (SUR) framework and estimate the entire system jointly. This is the approach advocated by Binder [1985] and Schipper & Thompson [1983] in the case of regulatory changes and French, Ruback & Schwert [1983] for studying macroeconomic effects.

One useful fact about the firms affected by a common event is that the degree of surprise is constant across the sample. This is not to say that a common event affects all firms equally; the attenuation due to partial anticipation is, however, constant across the sample. An example will clarify the issues.

Let there be three firms, i, j, and k that are potentially affected by events a, b, and c. The events are mutually exclusive and equally likely, for example, the three possible outcomes from the resolution of a control contest. Assume a structure as

[23] This logic can be extended to the investigation of various kinds of cross-sectional relationships. Hughes & Ricks [1984] use a prior period to determine the significance of a regression coefficient by running the same regression repeatedly in nonevent periods and ascertaining the likelihood of observing the regression coefficient estimated in the event period.

Table 1

The structure of a common event

Event	Firm	Payoff ($)	Economic impact ($)	Announcement effect ($)
a	*i*	20	20– 5	20–10
	j	6	6–12	6–10
	k	0	0–15	0–10
b	*i*	10	10–10	10–10
	j	4	4–13	4–10
	k	20	20– 5	20–10
c	*i*	0	0–15	0–10
	j	20	20– 5	20–10
	k	10	10–10	10–10

indicated in Table 1, where the third column shows the possible payoffs and the example is constructed so each firm has the same market value of $10 prior to the announcement of which event is chosen.

Suppose event b is the outcome. For each firm, what is the valuation effect of event b and what is the announcement effect? Earlier we defined the valuation effect as the difference between firm value conditional upon the event occurring and value conditional upon the event not occurring. In this context, then, the valuation effect of event b is the payoff minus the expected payoff from the other two events. These are shown in column four of Table 1. For event b, the valuation effect is $0 for firm i, –$9 for firm j, and $15 for firm k. The announcement effect was defined as the change in value resulting from the announcement of an event. Column five in Table 1 shows the announcement effect to be $0 for firm i, –$6 for firm j, and $10 for firm k. For each firm, prior anticipation has attenuated the announcement effect toward zero by 1/3. This is the prior probability that the event would occur, and since the prior probability is the same for all firms, the attenuation is also the same.

With common events, cross-sectional relationships will be preserved in the following sense: Let G represent the true influence of a particular firm characteristic on the valuation effect of the event, as described in equation (1) above. Let p represent the prior probability that the event would occur. Then the cross-sectional relation between firm characteristics and the announcement effect will be $(1 - p)G$. The sign of the relation is preserved[24].

SUR systems become very large in typical applications involving several hundred

[24] As indicated in the example of Table 1, both the valuation effect and the announcement effect of an event involve the relation between that particular event and any other events whose probabilities are changed. A clean interpretation of announcement effects requires modeling the prior probability and consequences of all affected events. Obviously this is an extremely difficult task and many topics in corporate finance are studied over and over as new refinements to the event possibilities are modeled.

firms. If the individual firm parameters are of little interest in themselves because the researcher is focussing on hypotheses about G, the size of the models can be reduced to the number of parameters in G, typically on the order of one to five, regardless of the number of firms. This is accomplished through portfolio aggregation.

5.3.4.2. Portfolio approaches. A popular and powerful estimation approach for large systems of firms is to group firms into portfolios. For a given sample of firms, the average forecast error is equivalent to the forecast error from an equally weighted portfolio of the sample. This equivalence also applies to other forecast model parameters such as the average beta. Thus a simple approach to estimating the average effect of a common event is to create a portfolio of firms and compute the portfolio forecast error. Moreover, the residual variance of a portfolio includes any effects of cross-correlation of individual firm residuals. Thus a simple approach to estimating the statistical significance of a mean effect is to create a portfolio of firms and compare the portfolio forecast error in the event period to the portfolio's estimated standard error derived from the nonevent periods.

Portfolio approaches can be used to test various hypotheses for samples of firms all influenced by a common event. For example, assume a sample of J firms conforming to equation (3) above, each with K different firm characteristics in F_j for the jth firm. As before, the elements in G represent the importance of the K firm characteristics in determining the impact of the event across the sample. With common events, the researcher would typically like to include information about the full covariance matrix of the residuals. This can be accomplished by creating K portfolios that separate the effects of each type of characteristic.

Let W equal a matrix of portfolio weights with K rows and J columns, chosen by the researcher to satisfy the constraint

$$WF = I_{K \times K} \tag{7}$$

where, as in equation (4), F is a $J \times K$ matrix of firm characteristics with typical row F_j. The kth portfolio created with these weights has all of its characteristics summing to zero except the kth, which sum to unity. K seemingly unrelated regressions can be run in the form

$$R_k = XB^* + \mathrm{e}_k \tag{8}$$

where the notation is the same as in equation (3) except that R_k is the column of rates of return to the portfolio constructed with weights equal to the kth row in W. For the kth portfolio, the influence of everything but the kth characteristic is zeroed out, leaving only the kth element in G to be estimated. The distribution of the residuals in (8), e_k, incorporates all relevant variance–covariance information about the original sample. X is the same for each portfolio, so the system involves identical explanatory variables.

Popular portfolio weighting schemes come from the regression literature. OLS weights would set $W = (F'F)^{-1}F'$ while GLS weights would set $W = (F'S^{-1}F)^{-1}F'S^{-1}$ with S the estimated covariance matrix of residuals for the original sample of firms, typically estimated over the same sample period. Notice that OLS weights do not require any covariance information about the sample firms. The only covariance information necessary to test hypotheses about G is contained in the covariance matrix of the K portfolios. Portfolios can be based on WLS weights as well. WLS represents an appealing compromise between the non-stochastic, but inefficient, weights implicit in OLS and the asymptotic efficiency of full GLS. Sefcik & Thompson [1986] discuss portfolio approaches in more detail.

5.4. A final hypothesis testing issue: normality of estimation errors

Evidence dating back to Fama [1965] indicates that daily security return distributions have fatter tails than the normal and studies such as Brown & Warner [1985, table 1] show daily abnormal returns to be generally skewed right. Various nonparametric statistical procedures are included in empirical examinations to confirm that results are not sensitive to outliers; for example, a percent positive or percent negative test based on the assumption of cross-sectional independence. Hite & Vetsuypens [1989] use several simple nonparametric tests in their study of divisional management buyouts. Corrado [1989] discusses more elaborate nonparametric procedures based on ranks. Where inferences are reversed with nonparametric tests, researchers focus on outliers to better understand which test is preferred.

An alternative approach is to explain outliers and eliminate them from the sample, then base inferences on normal theory applied to the rest of the sample. Where sample trimming has occurred, most researchers point it out and leave the interpretation up to the reader. For example, Weinstein [1977] treats the influence of an outlier in his study of bond rating changes by reporting all results but emphasizing his interpretation on a sample that omits an influential outlier.

6. Concluding remarks

I have attempted, within a unified framework, to show the spectrum of experimental designs adopted by empiricists who employ event studies methods. In concert with the variety of detail, several investigations into empirical methods have concluded that minor variations have little impact on inferences [e.g. Brown and Warner, 1980, 1985; and Malatesta, 1986]. Researchers are left with discretion over the choice of estimation window, projection model, raw versus excess returns, forecast error versus event parameter and the form of hypothesis tests. Where these decisions are made ex ante, this discretion seems harmless although latitude can be manipulated, however unintentionally, to generate significant results in any specific application. If a researcher can choose an estimation window between 200 and 300 days, choose an event window between 1 and 5 days, select a projection model with 3 or 4 different types of explanatory variables, use raw or excess returns, pick parametric or nonparametric tests and exercise judgement over modeling how the event affects different firms, it is likely that something of interest will turn up in the data. Credibility is added to the findings of empirical investigations when the methods chosen can be defended on the basis of objective econometric or economic criteria, however minor the improvement in the estimation method on average.

Notwithstanding the concern over latitude in experimental design, there has been little debate over design details, possibly because there is little abuse in practice. Sensitivity analysis is usually requested by reviewers and routinely provided by researchers to minimize the chance that an extremely unusual set of results, based on a particular research design will be reported. One is left with the problem of how to interpret conflicting results across methods, however. Generally it is agreed that all results are reported and the interpretation of conflicting results left to the reader.

Acknowledgements

I would like to thank K. Schipper, E. Eckbo and an anonymous reviewer for comments on earlier drafts and also apologize to the empiricists whose ideas I have incorporated (some might say stolen) without adequate references.

References

Acharya, S. (1988). A generalized econometric model and tests of a signalling hypothesis with two discrete signals. *J. Finance* 43, 413–429.

Acharya, S. (1993). Value of latent information:Alternative event study methods. *J. Finance* 48, 363–386.

Ball, C., and W. Torous (1988). Investigating security-price performance in the presence of event-day uncertainty. *J. Financ. Econ.* 22, 123–154.

Barclay, M., and R. Litzenberger (1988). Announcement effects of new equity issues and the use of intraday price data. *J. Financ. Econ.* 21, 71–100.

Bartov, E. (1991). Open-market stock repurchases as signals of earnings and risk changes. *J. Account. Econ.* 14, 275–294.

Beaver, W. (1968). The information content of annual earnings announcements, in: *Empirical Research in Accounting: Selected Studies, J. Account. Res.* (Supp.) 6, 67–92.

Begley, J. (1990). Debt covenants and accounting choice. *J. Account. Econ.* 12, 125–139.

Bernard, V. (1987). Cross-sectional dependence and problems in inference in market-based accounting research. *J. Account. Res.* 25, 1–48.

Binder, J. (1985). On the use of the multivariate regression model in event studies. *J. Account. Res.* 23, 370–383.

Bradley, M., A. Desai and H. Kim (1988). Synergistic gains from corporate acquisitions and their division between the stockholders of target and acquiring firms. *J. Financ. Econ.* 21, 3–40.

Brown, K., W. Harlow and S. Tinic (1988). Risk aversion, uncertain information, and market efficiency, *J. Financ. Econ.* 22, 355–386.

Brown, S., and J. Warner (1980). Measuring security price performance. *J. Financ. Econ.* 8, 205–258.

Brown, S., and J. Warner (1985). Using daily stock returns. *J. Financ. Econ.* 14, 3–31.

Cadsby, C., M. Frank and V. Maksimovic (1990) Pooling, separating and semiseparating equilibria in financial markets: some experimental evidence. *Rev. Financ. Studies* 3, 343–366.

Campbell, J. (1987). Stock returns and the term structure. *J. Financ. Econ.* 18, 373–340.

Christie, A. (1987). On cross-sectional analysis in accounting research. *J. Account. Econ.* 9, 231–258.

Christie, A. (1993). On information arrival and hypothesis testing in event studies, working paper, University of Rochester.

Clarkson, P., and R. Thompson (1990). Empirical estimates of beta when investors face estimation risk. *J. Finance* 45, 431–453.

Collins, D., and W. Dent (1979). The proposed elimination of full cost accounting in the extractive petroleum industry: An empirical assessment of the market consequences. *J. Account. Econ.* 1, 3–44.

Collins, D., and W. Dent (1984). A comparison of alternative testing methodologies used in capital market research. *J. Account. Res.* 22, 48–84.

Corrado, C. (1989). A nonparametric test for abnormal security-price performance in event studies. *J. Financ. Econ.* 23, 385–396.

Dann, L. (1981). Common stock repurchases: an analysis of returns to bondholders and stockholders. *J. Financ. Econ.* 9, 113–139.

Dann, L., R. Masulis and D. Mayers (1991). Repurchase tender offers and earnings information. *J. Account. Econ.* 14, 217–252.

Dimson, E. (1979). Risk measurement when shares are subject to infrequent trading. *J. Financ. Econ.* 14, 197–226.

Dodd, P., and R. Ruback (1977). Tender offers and stockholder returns. *J. Financ. Econ.* 5, 351–373.

Eckbo, E. (1985). Mergers and the market concentration doctrine: Evidence from the capital market. *J. Bus.* 58, 325–349.

Eckbo, E., V. Maksimovic and J. Williams (1990). Consistent estimation of cross-sectional models in event studies. *Rev. Financ. Studies* 3, 343–365.

Eisenbeis, R., R. Harris and J. Lakonishok (1984). Benefits of bank diversification: The evidence from shareholder returns. *J. Finance* 39, 881–892.

Fama, E. (1965). The behavior of stock market prices. *J. Bus.* 38, 34–105.

Fama, E., L. Fisher, M. Jensen and R. Roll (1969). The adjustment of stock prices to new information. *Int. Econ. Rev.* 10, 1–21.

Fama, E., and K. French (1989). Business conditions and expected returns on stocks and bonds. *J. Financ. Econ.* 25, 23–50.

French, K., R. Ruback and W. Schwert (1983). Effects of nominal contracting on stock returns. *J. Polit. Econ.* 91, 70–96.

Gibbons, M. (1982). Multivariate tests of financial models: A new approach. *J. Financ. Econ.* 10, 3–28.

Gilson, S. (1989). Management turnover and financial distress. *J. Financ. Econ.* 25, 241–262.

Grinblatt, M., R. Masulis and S. Titman (1984). The valuation effects of stock splits and stock dividends. *J. Financ. Econ.* 13, 461–490.

Handjinicolaou, G., and A. Kalay (1984). Wealth redistributions or changes in firm value: An analysis of returns to bondholders and stockholders at dividend announcements. *J. Financ. Econ.* 13, 35–63.

Healey, P., K. Palepu and R. Ruback (1990). Does corporate performance improve after mergers, working paper, Harvard.

Hertzel, M., and P. Jain (1991). Earnings and risk changes around stock repurchase tender offers. *J. Account. Econ.* 14, 253–275.

Hite, G., and M. Vetsuypens (1989). Management buyouts of divisions and shareholder wealth. *J. Finance* 44, 953–970.

Holthausen, R. (1981). Evidence on the effect of bond covenants and management compensation contracts on the choice of accounting techniques. *J. Account. Econ.* 3, 37–109.

Hughes, J., and W. Ricks (1984). Accounting for retail land sales: analysis of a mandated change. *J. Account. Econ.* 6, 101–132.

Ibbotson, R. (1975). Price performance of common stock new issues. *J. Financ. Econ.* 2, 235–272.

Jarrell, S. (1991). Do takeovers generate value? Evidence of the capital market ability to assess takeovers, Ph.D. dissertation, University of Chicago.

Kalay, A., and U. Loewenstein (1985). Predictable events and excess returns: The case of dividend announcements. *J. Financ. Econ.* 14, 423–449.

Lanen, W., and R. Thompson (1988). Stock price reactions as surrogates for the net cash flow effects of corporate policy decisions in cross-sectional studies. *J. Account. Econ.* 10, 311–334.

Langetieg, T. (1978). An application of a three-factor performance index to measure stockholder gains from merger. *J. Financ. Econ.* 6, 365–383.

Lease, R., R. Masulis and J. Page (1991). An investigation of market microstructure impacts on event study returns. *J. Finance* 46, 1523–1536.

Long, J. (1978). The market value of cash dividends: A case to consider. *J. Financ. Econ.* 6, 235–264.

Malatesta, P. (1983). The wealth effect of merger activity and the objective functions of merging firms. *J. Financ. Econ.* 11, 155–182.

Malatesta, P. (1986). Measuring abnormal performance: the event parameter approach using joint generalized least squares. *J. Financ. Quant. Anal.* 21, 27–38.

Malatesta, P., and R. Thompson (1985). Partially anticipated events: A model of stock price reactions with an application to corporate acquisitions. *J. Financ. Econ.* 14, 237 250.

Malatesta, P., and R. Thompson (1993). Government regulation and structural change in the corporate acquisitions market: The impact of the Williams Act. *J. Financ. Quant. Anal.* 28, 363–381.

Mandelker, G. (1974). Risk and return: The case of merging firms. *J. Financ. Econ.* 1(4), 303–335.

Marais, L., K. Schipper and A. Smith (1989). Wealth effects of going private for senior securities. *J. Financ. Econ.* 23, 155–191.

Masulis, R. (1980). The effects of capital structure change on security prices: A case study of exchange offers. *J. Financ. Econ.* 8, 139–178.

McNichols, M., and A. David (1990). Stock dividends, stock splits and signaling. *J. Finance* 45, 857–880.

Myers, S., and N. Majluf (1984). Corporate financing and investment decisions when firms have information that investors do not have. *J. Financ. Econ.* 13, 187–222.

Mikkelson, W. (1981). Convertible calls and security returns. *J. Financ. Econ.* 9, 237–264.

Mikkelson, W., and M. Partch (1989). Managers' voting rights and corporate control. *J. Financ. Econ.* 25, 263–290.

Mikkelson, W., and R. Ruback (1985). An empirical analysis of the interfirm equity investment process. *J. Financ. Econ.* 14, 523–554.

Ohlson, J. (1980). Financial ratios and the probabilistic prediction of bankruptcy. *J. Account. Res.* 18, 109–131.

Palepu, K. (1986). Predicting takeover targets: A methodological and empirical analysis. *J. Account. Econ.* 8, 3–36.

Patell, J. (1976). Corporate forecasts of earnings per share and stock price behavior. *J. Account. Res.* 14, 246–275.

Ruback, R.S. (1982). The effect of discretionary price control decision on equity values. *J. Financ. Econ.* 10(1), 83–105.

Schipper, K., and R. Thompson (1983). The impact of merger-related regulations on the shareholders of acquiring firms. *J. Account. Res.* 21, 184–221.

Scholes, M., and J. Williams (1977). Estimating betas from nonsynchronous data. *J. Financ. Econ.* 5, 309–328.

Sefcik, S., and R. Thompson (1986). An approach to statistical inference in cross-sectional models with security abnormal returns as dependent variable. *J. Account. Res.* 24, 316–334.

Thompson, R. (1985). Conditioning the return-generating process on firm-specific events: a discussion of event study methods. *J. Financ. Quant. Anal.* 20, 151–168.

Warner, J., R. Watts and K. Wruck (1988). Stock prices and top management changes. *J. Financ. Econ.* 20, 461–492.

Weinstein, M. (1977). The effect of a rating change announcement on bond price. *J. Financ. Econ.* 5, 329–350.

White, H. (1980). A heteroskedasticity-consistent covariance matrix estimator and a direct test for heteroskedasticity. *Econometrica* 48, 817–838.

Vermaelen, T. (1981). Common stock repurchases and market signalling: An empirical study. *J. Financ. Econ.* 9, 139–184.

Zmijewski, M. (1984). Methodological issues related to the estimation of financial distress prediction models. *J. Account. Res.* 22 (Supp.), 59–82.

R. Jarrow et al., Eds., *Handbooks in OR & MS, Vol. 9*

Chapter 30

Initial Public Offerings

Roger G. Ibbotson
School of Organization and Management, Yale University, Box 1A, Yale Station, New Haven, CT 06520, U.S.A.

Jay R. Ritter
College of Commerce, University of Illinois, 1206 South Sixth Street, Champaign/Urbana, IL 61820-6271, U.S.A.

1. Introduction

Most companies start out by raising equity capital from a small number of investors, with no liquid market existing if these investors wish to sell their stock. If a company prospers and needs additional equity capital, at some point it generally finds it desirable to 'go public' by selling stock to a large number of diversified investors. Once the stock is publicly traded, this enhanced liquidity allows the company to raise capital on more favorable terms than if it had to compensate investors for the lack of liquidity associated with a privately-held company. With these benefits, however, come costs. In particular, there are certain ongoing costs associated with the need to supply information on a regular basis to investors and regulators for publicly-traded firms. Furthermore, there are substantial one-time costs associated with initial public offerings (IPOs) that can be categorized as direct and indirect costs. The direct costs include the legal, auditing, and underwriting fees. The indirect costs are the management time and effort devoted to conducting the offering, and the dilution associated with selling shares at an offering price that is, on average, below the price prevailing in the market shortly after the IPO. These direct and indirect costs affect the cost of capital for firms going public.

Because initial public offerings involve the sale of securities in closely-held firms in which some of the existing shareholders may possess nonpublic information, some of the classic problems caused by asymmetric information may be present. In addition to the adverse selection problems that can arise when firms have a choice of when and if to go public, a further problem is that the underlying value of the firm is affected by the actions that the managers can undertake. This moral hazard problem must also be dealt with by the market. These features make the initial public offering market an interesting area to study. This chapter describes some of the mechanisms that are used in practice to overcome the problems created by information asymmetries. In addition, evidence is presented on three anomalies associated with IPOs: (i) new issue underpricing, (ii) cycles in the extent of underpricing, and (iii) long-run underperformance. These patterns have generated a large empirical literature, which this chapter surveys. Various theories that have been advanced to explain these patterns are also discussed.

While this chapter focuses on operating companies going public, the IPOs of closed-end mutual funds are also briefly discussed. A closed-end fund raises money from investors, which is then invested in other financial securities. The closed-end fund shares then sell in the public market. In the U.S. during 1985–1993, a large proportion of the money raised in IPOs went to closed-end funds.

The structure of the remainder of this chapter is as follows. First, evidence and explanations for the three anomalies mentioned above are presented. Second, an analysis of the costs and benefits of going public is presented in the context of the life cycle of a firm, from founding to its eventual ability to self-finance. This includes a short analysis of venture capital. Some of the contract design issues that arise with IPOs are discussed. We do not discuss many of the 'how to go public' issues that are described in a number of books by practitioners. A useful book covering this material is Zeune [1994].

2. New issues underpricing

The best-known anomaly associated with the process of going public is the frequent incidence of large initial returns (the price change measured from the offering price to the market price within a few weeks of the offering date) accruing to investors in IPOs of common stock. A large empirical literature exists documenting the phenomenon. This literature can be traced back to a 1963 study by the U.S. Securities and Exchange Commission that finds positive average initial returns on companies going public. Academic studies followed, including studies by Logue [1973] in which cross-sectional patterns are documented for 250 IPOs during 1965–1969, and Ibbotson [1975] in which numerous statistical tests are performed on a sample of 120 IPOs during 1960–1969 (one issue per month). Ibbotson finds that the distribution of initial returns is highly skewed, with a positive mean and a median near zero. He also examines the performance of IPOs during their first five years of seasoning, concluding that beyond the first month or two of seasoning, the hypothesis of market efficiency cannot be rejected.

Using data from the 1970s and 1980s, numerous studies have confirmed the new issues underpricing anomaly. (In this chapter, we use the term 'new issue' to refer to unseasoned security offerings, although the term is frequently applied to seasoned security offerings as well. Furthermore, we focus on IPOs of equity securities, even though many security offerings involve fixed-income securities.) Among the studies using U.S. data are papers by Barry, Muscarella & Vetsuypens [1991]; Carter & Manaster [1990]; Hanley [1993]; James & Wier [1990]; Michaely & Shaw [1994]; and Miller & Reilly [1987]. The underpricing phenomenon exists in every nation with a stock market, although the amount of underpricing varies from country to country.

Table 1 gives a summary of the equally-weighted average initial returns on IPOs in a number of countries around the world. This is an updated version of Loughran, Ritter & Rydqvist's [1994] table 1.

Various empirical studies using U.S. data find that smaller offerings are underpriced by more, on average, than larger offerings. Indeed, the common practice of computing average initial returns using equal weights on all IPOs tends to overstate the amount of short-run underpricing that exists in the U.S., since smaller and lower-priced issues tend to be underpriced by more in the short-run. (This difference between value-weighted and equally-weighted average initial returns, however, is not present in all countries.) Ibbotson, Sindelar & Ritter [1994] report that for 2439 U.S. IPOs in 1975–1984, the average initial return on IPOs with an offering price of less than $3.00 is 42.8%, whereas the average initial return on IPOs with an offering price of $3.00 or more is only 8.6%. Similar results are reported in Chalk & Peavy [1987].

3. Reasons for new issues underpricing

A number of reasons have been advanced for the new issues underpricing phenomenon, with different theories focusing on various aspects of the relations between investors, issuers, and the investment bankers taking the firms public. In general, these theories are not mutually exclusive. Furthermore, a given reason can be more important for some IPOs than for others.

3.1. The winner's curse hypothesis

An important rationale for the underpricing of IPOs is the 'winner's curse' explanation introduced by Rock [1986]. Since a more or less fixed number of shares are sold at a fixed offering price, rationing will result if demand is unexpectedly strong. Rationing in itself does not lead to underpricing, but if some investors are at an informational disadvantage relative to others, some investors will be worse off. In the model, issuing firms are assumed to be unable to forecast the market price with certainty. For simplicity, Rock groups all investors into two categories: perfectly informed, and completely uninformed with respect to knowledge of the future market price of the shares being sold. In the model, informed investors will only attempt to buy shares when an issue is underpriced. Uninformed investors, on the other hand, do not know which issues will be underpriced or overpriced, and so will be allocated only a fraction of the most desirable new issues, while they are allocated all of the least desirable new issues. They face a winner's curse: if they get all of the shares which they demand, it is because the informed investors don't want the shares. Faced with this adverse selection problem, the uninformed investors will only submit purchase orders if, on average, IPOs are underpriced sufficiently to compensate them for the bias in the allocation of new issues.

Table 1

International evidence on short-run IPO underpricing

Country	Sample size	Time period	Average initial return (%)
Australia	266	1976–89	11.9
Belgium	28	1984–90	10.2
Brazil	62	1979–90	78.5
Canada	258	1971–92	5.4
Chile	19	1982–90	16.3
Finland	85	1984–92	9.6
France	187	1983–92	4.2
Germany	172	1978–92	11.1
Greece	79	1987–91	48.5
Hong Kong	80	1980–90	17.6
India	98	1992–93	35.3
Italy	75	1985–91	27.1
Japan	472	1970–91	32.5
Korea	347	1980–90	78.1
Malaysia	132	1980–91	80.3
Mexico	37	1987–90	33.0
Netherlands	72	1982–91	7.2
New Zealand	149	1979–87	28.8
Portugal	62	1986–87	54.4
Singapore	128	1973–92	31.4
Spain	71	1985–90	35.0
Sweden	213	1970–91	39.0
Switzerland	42	1983–89	35.8
Taiwan	168	1971–90	45.0
Thailand	32	1988–89	58.1
United Kingdom	2,133	1959–90	12.0
United States	10,626	1960–92	15.3

Initial returns are generally defined as the percentage increase from the offer price to a closing market price shortly after public trading begins. The length of this period varies from study to study, with one day to several weeks being the usual time frame. The studies using only a day or two generally report raw returns, whereas those using a week or more generally adjust for market movements during the measurement interval. The average initial returns are generally not very sensitive to the length of the interval used or whether market movements are accounted for, since all of the measurement intervals are short. The average initial returns are computed as equally-weighted averages of the initial returns. The data are from various studies, including those by Lee, Taylor & Walter [1994a] for Australia; Aggarwal, Leal & Hernandez [1993] for Brazil, Chile, and Mexico; Jog & Srivastava [1995] for Canada; Dawson [1987] for Hong Kong; Dimson [1979] and Levis [1993] for the U.K.; Husson & Jacquillat [1989] and Leleux & Muzyka [1993] for France; Ibbotson, Sindelar & Ritter [1994] for the U.S.; Jenkinson [1990], and Hebner & Hiraki [1993] for Japan; Kazantzis & Levis [1994] for Greece; Keloharju [1993] for Finland; Kim, Krinsky & Lee [1993] for Korea; Krishnamurti & Kumar [1994] for India; Isa [1993] for Malaysia; Lee, Taylor & Walter [1994b] for Singapore; Rydqvist [1993] for Sweden; Kunz & Aggarwal [1994] for Switzerland; Uhlir [1989] and Ljungqvist [1993] for Germany; Vos & Cheung [1992] for New Zealand; Chen [1992] for Taiwan; Wethyavivorn & Koo-smith [1991] for Thailand; and Wessels [1989] for the Netherlands. Additional references are listed in Loughran, Ritter & Rydqvist [1994].

Numerous studies have attempted to test Rock's winner's curse model, both for the U.S. and other countries. A cross-sectional implication of the model, developed in Beatty & Ritter [1986], is that riskier issues should have greater underpricing, on average. While the evidence is consistent with this prediction, other explanations of the underpricing phenomenon also make this prediction. A direct test of the model by Koh & Walter [1989] using data from Singapore, supports the model.

3.2. *The costly information acquisition hypothesis*

Investment bankers may underprice IPOs to induce regular investors to reveal information during the pre-selling period, which can then be used to assist in pricing the issue. This argument has been developed by Benveniste & Spindt [1989]. In order to induce regular investors to truthfully reveal their valuations, the investment banker compensates investors through underpricing. Furthermore, in order to induce truthful revelation for a given IPO, the investment banker must underprice issues for which favorable information is revealed by more than those for which unfavorable information is revealed. This leads to a prediction that there will only be a partial adjustment of the offer price from that contained in the preliminary prospectus to that in the final prospectus. In other words, those IPOs for which the offer price is revised upwards will be *more* underpriced than those for which the offer price is revised downwards. This pattern is in fact present in the data, as documented by Hanley [1993].

3.3. *The cascades hypothesis*

Welch [1992] presents an equilibrium model in which he argues that the IPO market is subject to 'cascades'. In the model, potential investors pay attention not only to their own information about a new issue, but also whether other investors are purchasing. If an investor sees that no one else wants to buy, he may decide not to buy even when he has favorable information. To prevent this from happening, an issuer may want to underprice an issue to induce the first few potential investors to buy, and induce a cascade in which all subsequent investors want to buy irrespective of their private information.

An interesting implication of the Benveniste & Spindt [1989] dynamic information acquisition explanation, in conjunction with the Welch [1992] cascades model, is that positively-sloped demand curves can result. In Benveniste and Spindt, the offering price is adjusted upwards if regular investors indicate positive information. Other investors, knowing that this will only be a partial adjustment, correctly infer that these offerings will be underpriced. These other investors will consequently want to purchase additional shares, resulting in a positively sloped demand curve. The inferences of investors, however, will change if a given underwriter opportunisticly exploits investors. In other words, in an intertemporal equilibrium, the inferences that investors make will be affected by the track record of an underwriter. If this is not the case, any underwriter could create a cascade and sell an issue for more than its fundamental value. This, indeed, is what Shiller [1990] refers to as the 'impresario' hypothesis, discussed below in the section on the long-run performance of IPOs.

3.4. The investment banker's monopsony power hypothesis

Another explanation for the underpricing phenomenon focuses on information asymmetries between issuing firms and their investment bankers. Baron & Holmström [1980] and Baron [1982] hypothesize that investment bankers take advantage of their superior knowledge of market conditions to underprice offerings, which permits them to expend less marketing effort and ingratiate themselves with buy-side clients. While there is undoubtedly some truth to this, especially with less sophisticated issuers, Muscarella & Vetsuypens [1989] find that when investment banking firms go public, they underprice themselves by as much as other IPOs of similar size.

3.5. The lawsuit avoidance hypothesis

Since the Securities Act of 1933 makes all participants in the offer who sign the prospectus liable for any material omissions, one way of reducing the frequency and severity of future lawsuits is to underprice. Tinic [1988] develops this hypothesis, and presents evidence that is consistent with it. Just as with tests of Rock's winner's curse hypothesis, however, the evidence is also consistent with alternative explanations. Hughes & Thakor [1992] develop several models for the pricing of IPOs in which there is a threat of litigation. Under some conditions, underpricing results; under other conditions, no underpricing results. Simon [1989] also examines the impact of the Securities Act of 1933.

Drake & Vetsuypens [1993] examine 93 IPOs from 1969–1990 that were subsequently involved in lawsuits. They find that these IPOs had average initial returns that are similar to control firms that did not subsequently get sued. Drake & Vetsuypens conclude that whether there is short-run underpricing or not has little influence on whether there is a subsequent lawsuit. Alexander [1991, 1993] presents additional evidence, focusing on lawsuits following IPOs of computer firms in 1983. She reports that every firm in which the total decline in the market value of the offering was over $20 million during the subsequent several years was sued; and that almost all of the suits were settled, independent of the merits of the individual case, for approximately 25% of the decline in market value. Alexander points out [in footnote 256 of her 1991 article] that the cost to law firms of bringing suits deters lawsuits following small offerings, so that legal liability considerations would imply less underpricing of small issues; and that underwriters rarely contribute to part of the settlement. The evidence presented by Drake & Vetsuypens and by Alexander suggests that legal liability considerations are, at best, a minor reason for the underpricing of large IPOs. Furthermore, legal liability considerations suggest that smaller offerings should be underpriced less, contrary to the evidence. In addition, as Ljungqvist [1993] notes, there is underpricing in other countries where securities lawsuits are unknown.

3.6. The signalling hypothesis

Underpriced new issues 'leave a good taste' with investors, allowing the firms and insiders to sell future offerings at a higher price than would otherwise be the case. This reputation argument has been formalized in signalling models by Allen & Faulhaber [1989], Welch [1989], and Grinblatt & Hwang [1989]. In these models, issuing firms have private information about whether they have high or low values. They follow a dynamic issue strategy, in which the IPO will be followed by a seasoned offering. There is some probability that investors will become aware of the true value before the seasoned offering, in which case any actions undertaken at the time of the IPO will have little consequence for the seasoned offering. Depending upon parameter values, the high-value firms may choose to underprice their IPOs as a way of signalling that they are high value. In order for this to be worthwhile, they must benefit sufficiently at the time of the seasoned offering. If the probability of an exogenous revelation of the true value is too high, a pooling equilibrium may instead result, in which case the high-value issuers wind up subsidizing the low-value issuers at the time of the IPO.

Welch [1989] presents evidence that roughly one-third of the firms going public conduct a seasoned equity issue within the next few years, a proportion that is much higher than one would find among a random sample of New York Stock Exchange firms. Many more issuing firms undoubtedly are subject to open-market sales by insiders as well. Garfinkel [1993], Jegadeesh, Weinstein & Welch [1993], and Michaely & Shaw [1994], however, find that the hypothesized relation between initial returns and subsequent seasoned new issues is not present, casting doubt on the empirical relevance of signalling as a reason for underpricing.

3.7. The regulatory constraint hypothesis

Underpricing in IPOs may be caused by regulators who require offer prices to be set lower than they otherwise would be. This argument has limited relevance for the U.S., where the Securities and Exchange Commission is concerned with full disclosure, rather than 'fairness'. In some other countries, however, regulators require that offer prices be set based upon book values. For companies with valuable growth opportunities that are not reflected in their book values, this results in underpricing. In Japan, prior to reforms introduced in 1989, issuing firms were required to have their offer prices based upon the multiples (price-to-earnings, market-to-book, and dividend yields) of three comparable companies. In principle, this does not cause underpricing, but in practice comparable firms with low multiples were chosen. The extremely high average initial returns that exist in some countries, as reported in Table 1, are due to government regulation of offering prices.

3.8. The wealth redistribution hypothesis

Because being allocated shares in underpriced IPOs is valuable, issuers/investment bankers may be able to use these allocations to pursue other goals. In Japan, the Recruit Cosmos IPO led to the resignation of Prime Minister Takeshita in April 1989. The Recruit Company sold off a real estate subsidiary, Cosmos, in an initial public offering that was severely, and intentionally, underpriced. Many of the shares were allocated to politicians. When the details came to light, several prominent politicians resigned, for the scheme was only a tiny step away from handing over envelopes filled with cash.[1] The scandal also led to a change in the Japanese regulations for selling IPOs, with much less underpricing in 1989 than previously.

In some denationalizations, or privatizations, the value of underpriced shares has been recognized by the government. In 1979, when Margaret Thatcher became Prime Minister of Britain, the government owned many firms, including British Airways and British Steel. To give British voters a positive experience with capitalism as the government denationalized businesses, issues were both intentionally underpriced and allocated to as many voters as possible. Due largely to this campaign, the number of shareholders in Britain increased from three million in 1979 to 11 million in 1990. As a byproduct of the $57 billion raised in the denationalizations during the Thatcher regime, the British government ran a budget surplus during the latter part of the 1979–1990 period.

In both Japan and the UK, denationalizations, which are typically very large offerings, are also underpriced more than the IPOs of other companies. For the 36 British IPOs involving privatizations during the Thatcher regime, the average initial return was 41%. The Nippon Telegraph and Telephone (NTT) denationalization, a $13 billion (U.S.) IPO, jumped from its ¥1.2 million offering price to over ¥3 million within three months of its early 1987 offering date.

3.9. The stabilization hypothesis

Ruud [1993] argues that the practice of 'stabilization' by investment bankers results in average initial returns that are substantially overstated. Stabilization is the practice of buying large numbers of shares in the immediate aftermarket in an effort to prevent the price from falling. New issues typically include overallotment options whereby an investment banker can sell 115% of the issue size, and then retire the incremental 15% if these shares are immediately resold ('flipped') by investors without other buyers being willing to pay a price at or above the offer price. Direct evidence, however, does not support Ruud's hypothesis that, after adjusting for the effect of underwriter support, the average initial return is close to zero. Using a sample of 510 firm commitment IPOs from 1982–83, Miller & Reilly [1987] report that 30% of the sample has non-positive market-adjusted one-day returns. These issues underperform by an average of 3.9% during the next four

[1] For a more detailed description, see Ziemba & Schwartz [1992].

weeks, whereas the other 70% of issues outperform the market by 1%. Given that the average initial return for the sample is 9.9%, the effect of stabilization activities is to decrease the average initial return to about 9% at worst. (Ruud uses a virtually identical sample of 463 firm commitment IPOs from 1982–83 in her empirical work, without acknowledging Miller & Reilly's evidence. She also uses logarithmic returns, which, given the skewness of initial return distributions, results in a lower mean than when more conventional return computations are used.)

3.10. The ownership dispersion hypothesis

Issuing firms may intentionally underprice their shares in order to generate excess demand and be able to have a large number of small shareholders. This disperse ownership will both increase the liquidity of the market for the stock, and make it more difficult for outsiders to challenge management.

Booth & Chua [1995] argue that investors will be willing to price a stock using a lower discount rate if they expect a liquid market for their shares. Thus, the aftermarket price depends upon the dispersion of ownership.

Brennan & Franks [1995] also argue that firms may want to underprice in order to have a diffuse ownership base. They do not assume that this is necessarily in shareholders' best interests, however, in that an entrenched management may result in a lower firm value.

Presumably, the managers of some firms are willing to underprice for these control reasons, to the detriment of shareholders. Other managers may want to underprice in order to enhance liquidity, to the benefit of shareholders.

3.11. The market incompleteness hypothesis

Another explanation for underpricing, which may have some relevance for companies in new industries, is that investors in IPOs may have to be compensated for 'market incompleteness'. If there is some segmentation between the market for IPOs and the broader capital market, purchasers of IPOs may receive some premium to compensate them for bearing diversifiable risk. Mauer & Senbet [1992] provide a model with segmented markets in which this occurs. They also present evidence that is consistent with their model, although in common with most of the empirical work on IPOs, the evidence is also consistent with alternative explanations.

All of the above explanations involve rational strategies by buyers. Several other explanations involving irrational strategies by investors have been proposed. These irrational strategies are discussed below under the heading of the long-run performance of IPOs, for any model implying that investors are willing to overpay at the time of the IPO also implies that there will be poor long-run performance.

Many of the above explanations for the underpricing phenomenon can be criticized on the grounds of either the extreme assumptions that are made or the unnecessarily convoluted stories involved. Still, the underpricing phenomenon has persisted for decades with no signs of its imminent demise.

4. 'Hot issue' markets

A second anomaly is that cycles exist in both the volume and the average initial returns of IPOs. This is illustrated using U.S. data in Figures 1 and 2. The periods of high average initial returns are known as 'hot issue' markets, and were first documented in the academic literature by Ibbotson & Jaffe [1975].

Rational explanations for the existence of hot issue markets are difficult to come by. Ritter [1984a] hypothesizes that 'changing risk composition' might be able to account for the dramatic swings in average initial returns, since cross-sectionally, riskier issues tend to be underpriced to a greater extent. If there are some periods in which the firms going public are riskier than in other periods, the periods with the riskier firms will have higher average initial returns. Ritter finds that although there is some evidence that the hot issue periods are characterized by riskier issues, the amplitude of the cycles in average initial returns is far larger than can be accounted for by the changing risk composition hypothesis. Instead, the high average initial returns for the 15-month period starting in January 1980 are primarily due to the effect of a single industry: oil and gas stocks. Many of these oil and gas offerings were 'penny stocks', with offering prices of less than $1.00. These offerings generally had low market capitalizations, so that if the average initial

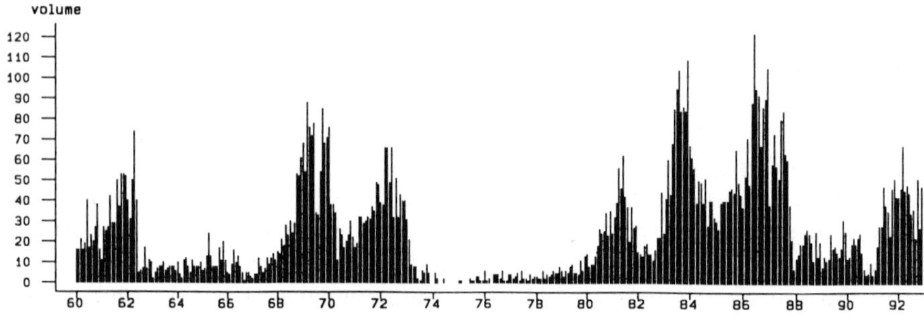

Fig. 1. Average initial returns by month for S.E.C.-registered IPOs in the U.S. during 1960–1992. Source: Ibbotson, Sindelar & Ritter [1994].

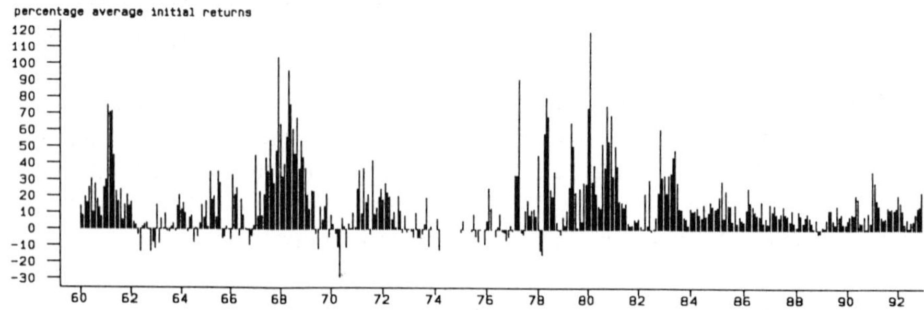

Fig. 2. The number of IPOs by month in the U.S. during 1960–1992, excluding closed-end fund IPOs. Source: Ibbotson, Sindelar & Ritter [1994].

returns were calculated as a value-weighted average, rather than equally-weighted, the cycles would have a smaller amplitude.

A second possible explanation for the existence of hot issue markets is that some investors follow 'positive feedback' strategies, in which they assume that there is positive autocorrelation in the initial returns on IPOs. These investors are willing to bid up the price of an issue once it starts trading if other recent issues have risen in price. If enough investors follow such a strategy, they may induce the positive autocorrelation of initial returns that they assumed. The difficulty of taking a short position in an IPO immediately after the offering may prevent other investors from making money at the expense of these positive feedback traders. See Rajan & Servaes [1993] for a further discussion.

Hot issue markets exist in other countries as well as the U.S. For example, there was a hot issue market in the United Kingdom between the 'Big Bang' (the end of fixed commission rates) in October 1986 and the crash a year later. In South Korea, there was a hot issue market in 1988 that coincided with a major bull market. Uhlir [1989] reports the existence of hot issues markets in Germany during 1982–83 and 1985–86.

The volume of IPOs, both in the U.S. and other countries, shows a strong tendency to be high following periods of high stock market returns, as documented by Loughran, Ritter & Rydqvist [1994].

5. Long-run performance

The third anomaly associated with IPOs is the poor stock price performance of IPOs in the long run. Ritter [1991] documents a −15.08% average cumulative matching firm-adjusted return (measured from the offering price) after 36 months of seasoning for 1526 IPOs during 1975–1984. Measured from the market price at the end of the first day of trading, the underperformance is even more dramatic. Ritter reports that the long-run underperformance is concentrated among firms that went public in the heavy-volume years of the early 1980s, and for younger firms. Indeed, for more established firms going public, and for those that went public in the light-volume years of the mid- and late-1970s, he finds no long-run underperformance. Aggarwal & Rivoli [1990], using a sample that includes the heavy-volume years of 1985–86, find poor performance during the first year of seasoning.

Loughran [1993] analyzes the long-run performance of 3,656 firms going public on Nasdaq from 1967–1987.[2] He reports that the underperformance of Nasdaq-listed IPOs continues for approximately six years after the offering date. Loughran & Ritter [1995] examine the long-run performance of 4,753 U.S. IPOs going public from 1970–1990 and subsequently listed on either Nasdaq or the American or New

[2] Nasdaq did not start until February of 1971, and CRSP does not report prices prior to December of 1972. Consequently, the results in Loughran's paper involve returns only since December of 1972, even for firms going public in the late 1960s.

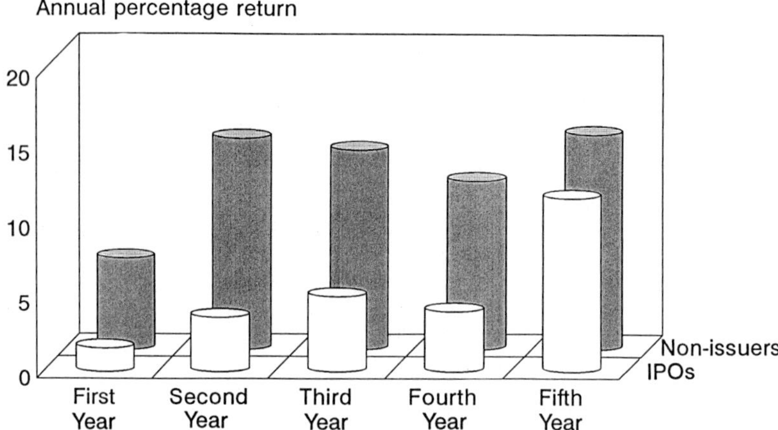

Fig. 3. Average annual returns for the five years after the offering date for 4,753 IPOs in the U.S. from 1970–1990, and for nonissuing firms of the same market capitalization that are bought and sold on the same dates as the IPOs. The returns (dividends plus capital gains) exclude the first-day returns. Source: Loughran & Ritter [1995].

York Stock Exchanges. They report economically significant underperformance, as illustrated in Figure 3. Loughran and Ritter report that the companies going public produced an average return of just 5% per year for the five years after the offering, using the first closing market price as the purchase price. A control group of nonissuing firms, matched by market capitalization, produced average annual returns of 12%. The very low returns in the aftermarket for IPOs partly reflect the pattern that IPO volume is high near market peaks.

The international evidence on the long-run performance of IPOs is limited. Uhlir [1989] reports that German IPOs underperform in the year after going public. Aggarwal, Leal & Hernandez [1993] report that Brazilian and Chilean IPOs underperform the market in the three years after going public, although the relatively small number of offerings and the huge variability of stock returns raise questions about the reliability of the patterns. Levis [1993] reports that 712 IPOs in the UK in 1980–1988 had average initial returns of 14.1%, but then underperformed market indices during the next three years. Keloharju [1993] reports that 79 Finnish IPOs also underperformed during the 36 months after the IPO. The results of these and other studies are summarized in Table 2.

Weiss [1989] finds that the long-run underperformance of IPOs is not limited to firms going public. She reports a −15.05 cumulative index-adjusted return through the first six months of seasoning for a sample of 64 closed-end funds that went public from 1985 to 1987. These findings are illustrated in Figure 4. Given that closed-end funds typically sell at a discount to net asset value (the market value of the securities that the fund holds), it is difficult to explain why investors are willing to purchase the shares at a premium in the IPO. A premium over net asset value at the time of the IPO exists because commissions equal about 7% of the offering

Table 2

International evidence on long-run IPO overpricing

Country	Sample size	Time period	Length of aftermarket period	Total abnormal return from	
				Offer price (%)	Early market price (%)
Australia	266	1976–89	3 years	n.a.	−46.5
Brazil	62	1980–90	3 years	n.a.	−47.0
Chile	28	1982–90	3 years	n.a.	−23.7
Finland	79	1984–89	3 years	−10.6	−21.1
Germany	119	1974–89	3 years	n.a.	−12.8
Sweden	162	1980–90	3 years	n.a.	+1.2
U.K.	712	1980–88	3 years	n.a.	−8.1
U.S.	4753	1970–90	3 years	n.a.	−17.0

Total abnormal returns are measured as $100 \cdot [(1 + R_{\mathrm{ipo},T})/(1 + R_{\mathrm{m},T})] - 100$, where $R_{\mathrm{ipo},T}$ is the average total return on an IPO from either the offer price or the market price shortly after trading commences until the earlier of the delisting date or T; $R_{\mathrm{m},T}$ is the average of either the market return or matching-firm returns over the same interval. n.a. refers to not available, based upon the numbers reported in the paper. Data comes from Lee, Taylor & Walter [1994a] for Australia; Aggarwal, Leal & Hernandez [1993] for Brazil and Chile; Keloharju [1993] for Finland; Levis [1993] for the U.K. (using the Hoare Govett Smaller Companies Index as the market); Loughran, Ritter & Rydqvist [1994] for Sweden; and Loughran & Ritter [1995] for the U.S. (using seasoned size-matched firms).

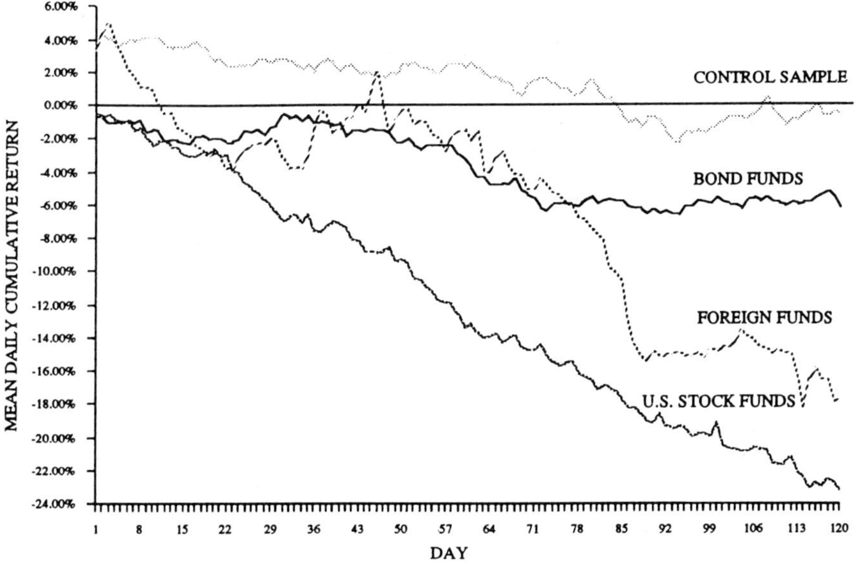

Fig. 4. Cumulative average adjusted returns during the 120 trading days (approximately 6 months) after the offering date for 64 closed-end mutual funds going public in 1985–1987. The domestic equity funds are compared with the S&P 500, the foreign equity funds are compared with foreign stock indices, and the bond funds are compared with a long-term bond index. Source: Weiss [1989].

price, so that every \$10.00 invested at the offering price buys only \$9.30 of net asset value. Perhaps it is no surprise that practitioners say that 'closed-end funds are sold, not bought'. Almost all closed-end fund shares are sold to individuals, rather than more sophisticated institutional investors, at the time of the IPO. Peavy [1990] reports results that are consistent with Weiss. Furthermore, new issues of closed-end funds are highly cyclical, as documented in Lee, Shleifer & Thaler [1991].

Wang, Chan & Gau [1992] investigate the price performance of the initial public offerings of Real Estate Investment Trusts (REITs). REITs are similar to closed-end funds, but they invest in property and mortgage-related securities. They find that the average initial return on 87 REIT IPOs in 1971–1988 is −2.8%, with a further −8.9% cumulative average market-adjusted return during the next 189 trading days (approximately 9 months). They also report that the REIT shares are overwhelmingly purchased by individual investors, consistent with Weiss' findings for closed-end funds.

Three theories have been proposed to explain the phenomena of the long-run underperformance of IPOs.

5.1. The divergence of opinion hypothesis

Miller [1977] argues that investors who are most optimistic about an IPO will be the buyers. If there is a great deal of uncertainty about the value of an IPO the valuations of optimistic investors may be much higher than those of pessimistic investors. As time goes on and more information becomes available, the divergence of opinion between optimistic and pessimistic investors will narrow, and consequently, the market price will drop. Thus, Miller predicts that IPOs will underperform in the long run.

There is survey evidence that many investors are periodically overoptimistic about the earnings potential of young growth companies. Shiller [1990] provides evidence via a survey of investors in IPOs, that only 26% of the respondents in his sample did any fundamental analysis of the relation between the offer price and the firm's underlying value. Jain & Kini [1994] provide evidence that the earnings per share of companies going public typically grows rapidly in the year prior to going public, but then actually declines in the first few years after the IPO.

5.2. The impresario hypothesis

Shiller [1990] presents an 'impresario' hypothesis in which he argues that the market for IPOs is subject to fads and that IPOs are underpriced by investment bankers (the impresarios) to create the appearance of excess demand, just as the promoter of a rock concert attempts to make it an 'event'. Shiller's hypothesis predicts that companies with the highest initial returns should have the lowest subsequent returns. There is some evidence of this relation in Ritter [1991].

5.3. The windows of opportunity hypothesis

If there are periods when investors are especially optimistic about the growth potential of companies going public, the large cycles in volume may represent a response by firms attempting to 'time' their IPOs to take advantage of these swings in investor sentiment. Of course, due to normal business cycle activity, one would expect to see some variation through time in the volume of IPOs. The large amplitude of the cycles displayed in Figure 2 of this chapter, however, seems difficult to explain as merely normal business cycle activity.

Ritter [1991] and Loughran & Ritter [1995] argue that the low long-run returns on IPOs are consistent with issuers taking advantage of 'windows of opportunity' in which the market is willing to overpay for their equity. This framework can be viewed as a dynamic version of Myers' [1984] financing hierarchy, or pecking order, framework. In the static financing hierarchy model, external equity is always the last choice for financing. In the dynamic financing hierarchy, or windows of opportunity, model, external equity is sometimes the first choice for financing, because sometimes a firm can issue overvalued equity. The windows of opportunity framework predicts that there will be low long-run returns on firms conducting IPOs and on firms conducting seasoned equity offerings (SEOs). Loughran & Ritter [1995] provide evidence that this is indeed the case.

A caveat is in order regarding the long-run performance evidence. Because, by definition, long-run returns involve long holding periods, the evidence involves firms with overlapping observations. Thus, the number of independent observations is limited. Consequently, it is possible that the patterns reported in the literature may be the result of common factors that are unlikely to be repeated. Thus, the long-run performance evidence should be viewed as more tentative than the evidence on short-run underpricing and hot issue markets, where a large number of studies using nonoverlapping data finds similar results.

6. Going public as a stage in the life cycle of a firm's external financing

Most startup companies seeking external financing do not immediately utilize the public capital markets, but instead raise capital from private sources. Because young firms frequently have much of their value represented by intangibles such as growth opportunities, rather than assets in place, outside investors face a difficult job of valuing them. Usually, the value of these opportunities is dependent upon the actions taken by the entrepreneur (the moral hazard problem). Self-selection in terms of which firms seek external financing may also create an adverse selection problem for potential investors.

The source of capital for an entrepreneur that is least subject to problems caused by information asymmetries is self-financing: entrepreneurs contribute their own money. With limited resources, however, the ability to grow rapidly will be constrained if external sources of capital are not used. Because of the discipline imposed by social networks, friends and relatives might be the next source of capital. If a firm approaches potential external investors for financing when the entrepreneur and closely associated individuals have not invested a substantial fraction of their own assets in the venture, suspicions will be aroused. Only when these sources have been tapped will nonaffiliated sources of capital become readily available. Even then, the ability to disclose proprietary information to potential investors encourages the use of private financing, either from banks or venture capitalists. If potential investors are unable to differentiate high-value firms from low-value firms, an adverse selection problem may result. If firms are pooled together, some of the high-value firms may choose to not seek external financing. This is an example of the problem discussed by Akerlof [1970] in his famous 'lemons' analysis.

In the U.S., a venture capital industry exists to assist in the financing of private firms in their early stages of growth. As described by Sahlman [1988, 1990], venture capitalists typically specialize by industry or region, developing a network of contacts that can assist them in evaluating potential investment opportunities. Adverse selection and moral hazard considerations are of paramount importance in deciding what deals to finance, and how to structure the deals.

Typically, venture capitalists do not make passive financial investments in young firms. Instead, they typically insist on board membership, and provide advice. This advice-giving role is one of the reasons for industry specialization. Thus, the returns to the venture capitalist are partly a return on capital, and partly a return on the other services provided. Of course, there can be disagreements between entrepreneurs and their financiers, for the interests of the various parties will not be identical. Venture capitalists typically provide capital in stages, with further commitments contingent upon performance up to that time.

While there are advantages to raising capital from a small number of investors who actively monitor the firm and to whom proprietary information can be disclosed, there are disadvantages as well. As long as the firm is private, any equity investment is illiquid, and investors will have to be compensated both for the lack of liquidity and the lack of diversification associated with a blockholding. As a firm becomes larger, these disadvantages may come to outweigh the advantages of private financing. This is the point in the life cycle of a firm's financing at which it is optimal to go public, even though there are agency costs associated with 'outside' equity. IPOs are one of the mechanisms by which the market allocates capital to its highest valued uses.

Among those firms that do go public, if investors are unable to fully distinguish the high-value firms from low-value firms, wealth transfers will result. A number of mechanisms are employed, by high-value firms to minimize this.

Leland & Pyle [1977] present a model in which the amount of equity retained by insiders signals their private valuation. In their model, risk-averse entrepreneurs achieve a higher expected utility level by holding a diversified portfolio, rather than having a large part of their wealth comprised of a stake in their own firm. Entrepreneurs, however, are assumed to have private information about their true firm value. The high-value firm entrepreneurs will be willing to forego more of the benefits of diversification in order to avoid selling undervalued stock. Investors will realize these incentives, and thus will be willing to pay more for stock in firms where the entrepreneur is retaining a large holding. After making some auxiliary assumptions, Leland and Pyle derive an equilibrium signaling model in which the amount of equity retained by entrepreneurs signals their private information.

Downes & Heinkel [1982] present evidence consistent with the Leland–Pyle model. They find that firms with a larger fraction of the equity retained by pre-issue shareholders have higher market valuations. Alternative explanations, however, could account for this empirical regularity. Ritter [1984b] argues that the positive empirical relation between firm value and insider holdings may be due to agency, rather than signaling, explanations. Alternatively, it may just be a manifestation of the fact that a firm with a high market capitalization can raise a given amount of money by selling a smaller fraction of the equity than if it had a low market capitalization. Ritter attempts to distinguish among these alternative hypotheses with limited success. Since these hypotheses are not mutually exclusive, it is likely that all three have some merit.

In practice, sophisticated investors do look at whether major shareholders are selling some of their stock in the IPO. (These are known as secondary shares; primary shares are those sold by the firm.) Cho [1992] reports that 98% of best efforts offerings, which tend to be young firms, contain no secondary shares. Furthermore, insiders frequently agree to retain any stock not sold at the time of the IPO for a specified length of time, known as the lock-up period. This lock-up period is mandated by law to be at least 90 days in the U.S., but frequently insiders agree to a longer time period. For example, when Morgan Stanley went public in 1986, the insiders agreed not to sell any of their other shares for a full two years after the offering. Investors are willing to pay more for a firm where the insiders have agreed to retain their shares for a long period of time for two reasons: i) any negative information being withheld is likely to be divulged before the shares can be sold, reducing the benefit of withholding the information, and ii) as long as the insiders retain large shareholdings, their incentives will be more closely aligned with those of outside equityholders.

Another observable variable that is used by practitioners to address adverse selection and moral hazard problems is the structure of compensation contracts: entrepreneurs who are willing to accept low base salaries and stock have their incentives more closely aligned with outside equityholders than entrepreneurs who demand large amounts of noncontingent compensation.

Since most theories of new issue underpricing imply that firms with greater uncertainty about the value per share will be underpriced more, issuing firms have incentives to reduce the amount of uncertainty. One method by which an issuer may reduce the degree of information asymmetry surrounding its initial public offering is to hire agents who, because they have reputation capital at stake, will have the incentive to certify that the offer price is consistent with inside information. A growing body of literature examines the role of the underwriter as a certifying agent. Beatty & Ritter [1986], Booth & Smith [1986], Smith [1986], and James [1992] all argue that the need to have repeat business gives underwriters a role that issuing firms cannot credibly duplicate. Chemmanur &

Fulghieri [1994] present a formal model in which the multi-period business of underwriters allows them to develop a reputation for accurately pricing issues. Michaely & Shaw [1994] make a similar argument, and present evidence that less-prestigious underwriters underprice their offerings to a greater extent than do more prestigious underwriters. Carter & Manaster [1990] document a significant inverse relationship between the reputation of the underwriter and the level of initial returns. Reputation, in this case, is measured by the location of the underwriter's name in advertisements about the offerings, known as tombstones. Investment bankers that are listed highest in the announcement are considered to have the highest prestige or reputation.

In addition to the certification role played by underwriters, Titman & Trueman [1986] argue that auditors play a similar role. Beatty [1989] empirically examines the relation between auditor reputation and initial returns, and Balver, McDonald & Miller [1988] examine the relation between initial returns and both auditor and investment banker reputation. In a related fashion, Barry, Muscarella, Peavy & Vetsuypens [1990] and Megginson & Weiss [1991] find evidence that venture capitalists can also serve to credibly convey information about the issuing firm and lower the level of initial returns. James & Wier [1990] examine the role of commercial banks as monitoring and certifying agents as well.

7. Contractual forms and the going public process

In the U.S., firms issuing stock use either a firm commitment or best efforts contract. With a firm commitment contract, a preliminary prospectus is issued containing a tentative offering price range. After the issuing firm and its investment banker have conducted a marketing campaign and acquired information about investors' willingness to purchase the issue, and after the Securities and Exchange Commission (S.E.C.) approves the offering, a final offering price is set. The final prospectus is then issued, and the firm goes public. Under a firm commitment contract, the underwriter agrees to bear the risk of the issue by purchasing the shares of the offer, less an underwriting discount, at the time of the offer. Only when the final prospectus is issued does the investment banker guarantee to deliver the proceeds (net of commission) to the issuing firm, whether or not the offer is fully subscribed. If demand for the issue is weak, the investment banker is permitted to sell any unsold shares at a lower price. This is referred to as 'breaking the syndicate', for normally the managing or comanaging investment bankers have formed a syndicate that attempts to 'stabilize' or 'support' the market price by buying shares that investors are immediately reselling. The investment banker must sell all of the shares in the offering at a price no higher than the offering price once the offer price has been set. This one-price feature constrains the ability of investment bankers to price discriminate among various classes of investors. Benveniste & Wilhelm [1990] analyze this.

With a best efforts contract, the issuing firm and its investment banker agree on an offer price as well as a minimum and maximum number of shares to be sold. Following S.E.C. approval, a 'selling period' commences. During the selling period, the investment banker makes its 'best efforts' to sell the shares to investors. If the minimum number of shares are not sold at the offer price within a specified period of time, usually 90 days, the offer is withdrawn and all investors' monies are refunded, with the issuing firm receiving no money. As documented in Ritter [1987], best efforts offerings are used almost exclusively by smaller, more speculative issuers. Essentially all larger IPOs (raising more than $10 million) use firm commitment contracts. Furthermore, the average initial return is higher on best efforts offerings than on firm commitment offerings. In contrast to the diversity of contracts used with IPOs, or unseasoned new issues, publicly-traded firms issuing additional shares of stock in a seasoned new issue invariably use a firm commitment contract in the U.S.

The key differences between best efforts and firm commitment contracts are as follows: i) a firm commitment contract permits information to be acquired during the preselling period that can be used for setting the final offering price and the number of shares to be sold, ii) a best efforts contract allows for a greater range of shares to be sold (i.e., a firm commitment contract only allows for a 15% overallotment option, whereas a best efforts contract can have a maximum number of shares much larger than the minimum number), iii) with a firm commitment contract, the underwriter assumes risk by guaranteeing the proceeds to the issuing firm, whereas if there is insufficient demand to fully subscribe the minimum number of shares in a best efforts offering, the issue is withdrawn.

Several papers have attempted to explain the choice between best efforts and firm commitment contracts. The risk-bearing aspect of the contract choice decision is emphasized in Mandelker & Raviv [1977], while the variable number of shares aspect is analyzed in Welch [1991]. Ritter [1987], Benveniste & Spindt [1989], and Benveniste & Wilhelm [1990] all argue that the ability of investment bankers to sell more shares when demand is strong than when it is weak can result in less underpricing than would otherwise be the case. Ritter emphasizes that this reduces the adverse selection problem facing uninformed investors, while Benveniste and Wilhelm emphasize that this permits underwriters to reward regular investors with a large number of shares (underpriced a little bit) when positive information is indicated, rather than having to reward them with a small number of shares that are underpriced a lot. Spatt & Srivastava [1991] also discuss the information acquisition process.

One of the explicit costs of going public is the compensation paid to underwriters. The National Association of Securities Dealers (NASD) limits underwriter compensation to 'reasonable' amounts. In addition to regulation by the NASD, state regulations may also limit the amount of underwriter compensation. These state regulations are known as 'blue sky' laws, allegedly to prevent the selling of companies whose assets are nothing but 'the big blue sky'. Many states, however, grant automatic regulatory clearance to IPOs qualifying for listing on the New York or American Stock Exchanges, or on Nasdaq's National Market System. There are substantial economies of scale in underwriting costs for both best efforts and firm commitment offers. Ritter [1987] documents that the average underwriting fee is 8.7% for firm commitment and 10.3% for best efforts offers. The percentage commission paid to underwriters is positively related to the risk of the issue and inversely related to the size of the offering.

One way that underwriters may overcome the limits on direct compensation set by the NASD and state regulators is by including warrants to purchase additional shares as part of the compensation of the investment banker. Barry, Muscarella & Vetsuypens [1991] document that underwriter warrants tend to be associated with riskier issues. They argue that the warrants are a mechanism for the circumvention of 'otherwise binding regulatory constraints for those issues that are most costly to market'.

In other countries, various institutional arrangements exist for marketing IPOs. The practice in Japan is similar in some regards to that in the U.S.: an offer price is set, and underwriters have considerable latitude in the allocation of shares. In the United Kingdom, most firms going public use either an 'offer for sale' or a 'placing'. In an offer for sale, the offering price is generally set 10 days before the date of the offering, and the investment banker involved bears the risk that market demand may fall before the offering is consummated. Normally, in an offer for sale, much of the stock is sold to individual investors. In a placing, which is very similar to a firm commitment offering in the U.S., the shares are generally sold to institutional investors. In France, IPOs are underpriced by less than in many other countries. This is of interest because the contractual mechanisms for going public in France, as described by Husson & Jacquillat [1989], are much more explicitly auctions than is true in the U.S. Indeed, Wessels [1989] reports that in the Netherlands firms that use a procedure similar to that used in France are not underpriced at all, whereas those using a fixed price offering (similar to a firm commitment offering in the U.S.) have average initial returns of 12.3%.

8. Summary

Companies going public offer an excellent opportunity to examine how the market deals with some of the problems created by information asymmetries between closely-held firms, underwriters, and external investors. To deal with these potential problems, market participants and regulators insist on the disclosure of material information.

Three anomalies have also been documented for IPOs in many countries: i) new issue underpricing, ii) cycles in volume and the extent of underpricing, and iii) long-run underperformance. In some respects, the poor performance of IPOs in the long run makes the new issues underpricing phenomenon even more of a puzzle. Whether or not IPOs underperform in the long run, the question of why issuers set their IPO price at a level that is lower on average than the market price at the end of the first day has generated a large literature. While no one model can provide a definitive explanation of these anomalies, collectively the theories can account for many of the patterns that are observed.

Acknowledgements

This chapter draws heavily on 'The Market's Problems with the Pricing of Initial Public Offerings', coauthored by Roger G. Ibbotson, Jody Sindelar and Jay R. Ritter in the 1994 *Journal of Applied Corporate Finance*, and 'Going Public', coauthored by Kathleen Weiss Hanley and Jay R. Ritter, in *The New Palgrave Dictionary of Money and Finance*. We thank our coauthors for permission to draw on material from this earlier work.

References

Aggarwal, R., R. Leal and F. Hernandez (1993). The aftermarket performance of initial public offerings in Latin America. *Financ. Manage.* 22, 42–53.

Aggarwal, R., and P. Rivoli (1990). Fads in the initial public offering market? *Financ. Manage.* 19, 45–57.

Akerlof, G.A. (1970). The market for "lemons": Quality uncertainty and the market mechanism. *Q. J. Econ.* 84, 488–500.

Alexander, J.C. (1991). Do the merits matter? A study of settlements in securities classactions. *Stanford Law Rev.* 43, 497–597.

Alexander, J.C. (1993). The lawsuit avoidance theory of why initial public offerings are underpriced. *UCLA Law Rev.* 41, 17–71.

Allen, F., and G. Faulhaber (1989). Signalling by underpricing in the IPO market. *J. Financ. Econ.* 23, 303–323.

Balver, R.J., B. McDonald and R.E. Miller (1988). Underpricing of new issues and the choice of auditor as a signal of investment banker reputation. *Account. Rev.* 63, 605–622.

Baron, D. (1982). A model of the demand of investment banking advising and distribution services for new issues. *J. Finance* 37, 955–976.

Baron, D., and B. Holmström (1980). The investment banking contract for new issues under asymmetric information: Delegation and the incentive problem. *J. Finance* 35, 1115–1138.

Barry, C., and R. Jennings (1993). The opening price performance of initial public offerings of common stock. *Financ. Manage.* 22, 54–63.

Barry, C., C. Muscarella, J. Peavy and M. Vetsuypens (1990). The role of venture capital in the creation of public companies: Evidence from the going public process. *J. Financ. Econ.* 27, 447–471.

Barry, C., C. Muscarella and M. Vetsuypens (1991). Underwriter warrants, underwriter compensation and the costs of going public. *J. Financ. Econ.* 29, 113–135.

Beatty, R.P. (1989). Auditor reputation and the pricing of initial public offerings. *Account. Rev.* 64, 693–709.

Beatty, R.P., and J.R. Ritter (1986). Investment banking, reputation, and the underpricing of initial public offerings. *J. Financ. Econ.* 15, 213–232.

Benveniste, L., and P. Spindt (1989). How investment bankers determine the offer price and allocation of new issues. *J. Financ. Econ.* 24, 343–361.

Benveniste, L., and W. Wilhelm (1990). A comparative analysis of IPO proceeds under alternative regulatory environments. *J. Financ. Econ.* 28, 173–207.

Booth, J., and L. Chua (1995). Ownership dispersion, costly information, and IPO underpricing, unpublished working paper, Arizona State.

Booth, J., and R. Smith (1986). Capital raising, underwriting and the certification hypothesis. *J. Financ. Econ.* 15, 261–281.

Brennan, M., and J. Franks (1995). Underpricing, ownership and control in initial public offerings of equity securities in the U.K., unpublished working paper, London Business School.

Carter, R., and S. Manaster (1990). Initial public offerings and underwriter reputation. *J. Finance* 45, 1045–1067.

Chalk, A., and J. Peavy (1987). Initial public offerings: Daily returns, offering types and the price effect. *Financ. Anal. J.*, 65–69.

Chemmanur, T.J. (1993). The pricing of initial public offerings: A dynamic model with information production. *J. Finance* 48, 285–304.

Chemmanur, T.J., and P. Fulghieri (1994). Investment banker reputation, information production, and financial intermediation. *J. Finance* 49, 57–79.

Chen, H.-L. (1992). The price behavior of IPOs in Taiwan, unpublished working paper, University of Illinois.

Cho, S. (1992). The possibility of failure and the pricing of best efforts offerings. *Q. Rev. Econ. Finance* 32, 30–45.

Dawson, S.M. (1987). Secondary stock market performance of initial public offers, Hong Kong, Singapore, and Malaysia: 1978–1984. *J. Bus. Finance Account.* 14, 65–76.

Dimson, E. (1979). The efficiency of the British new issue market for ordinary shares, unpublished Ph.D. dissertation, University of London.

Downes, D., and R. Heinkel (1982). Signaling and the valuation of unseasoned new issues. *J. Finance* 37, 1–10.

Drake, P.D., and M.R. Vetsuypens (1993). IPO underpricing: Insurance against legal liability? *Financ. Manage.* 22, 64–73.

Garfinkel, J. (1993). IPO underpricing, insider selling and subsequent equity offerings: Is underpricing a signal of quality? *Financ. Manage.* 22, 74–83.

Grinblatt, M., and C.Y. Hwang (1989). Signalling and the pricing of new issues. *J. Finance* 44, 393–420.

Hanley, K.W. (1993). Underpricing of initial public offerings and the partial adjustment phenomenon. *J. Financ. Econ.* 34, 231–250.

Hanley, K.W., and J.R. Ritter (1992). Going public, in: P. Newman, M. Milgste and J. Eatwell (eds.), *The New Palgrave Dictionary of Money and Finance*, MacMillan, London.

Hebner, K.J., and T. Hiraki (1993). Japanese initial public offerings, in: I. Walter and T. Hiraki (eds.), *Restructuring Japan's Financial Markets*, Business One/Irwin, Homewood, IL.

Hughes, P.J., and A.V. Thakor (1992). Litigation risk, intermediation, and the underpricing of initial public offerings. *Rev. Financ. Studies* 5, 709–742.

Husson, B., and B. Jacquillat (1989). French new issues, underpricing, and alternative methods of distribution, in: R. Guimaraes et al. (eds.), *A Reappraisal of the Efficiency of Financial Markets*, Springer-Verlag, Berlin.

Ibbotson, R.G. (1975). Price performance of common stock new issues. *J. Financ. Econ.* 2, 235–272.

Ibbotson, R.G., and J.F. Jaffe (1975). 'Hot issue' markets. *J. Finance* 30, 1027–1042.

Ibbotson, R.G., J. Sindelar, and J. Ritter (1994). The market's problems with the pricing of initial public offerings. *J. Appl. Corp. Finance* 6, 66–74.

Isa, M. (1993). List of Malaysian IPOs, unpublished working paper, University of Malaya.

Jain, B.A. and O. Kini (1994). The post-issue operating performance of IPO Firms. *J. Finance* 49, 1699–1726.

James, C. (1992). Relationship specific assets and the pricing of underwriter services. *J. Finance* 47, 1865–1885.

James, C., and P. Wier (1990). Borrowing relationships, intermediation, and the costs of issuing public securities. *J. Financ. Econ.* 28, 149–171.

Jegadeesh, N., M. Weinstein and I. Welch (1993). An empirical investigation of IPO returns and subsequent equity offerings. *J. Financ. Econ.* 34, 153–175.

Jenkinson, T. (1990). Initial public offerings in the UK, USA, and Japan. *J. Jap. Int. Econ.* 4, 428–449.

Jog, V.M., and A. Srivastava (1995). Underpricing in Canadian IPOs 1971–1992 — An update, *FINECO* 5.

Kazantzis, C., and M. Levis (1994). Price support and initial public offerings: Evidence from the Athens Stock Exchange, unpublished working paper, Piraeus University.

Keloharju, M. (1993). The winner's curse, legal liability, and the long-run price performance of initial public offerings in the Finland. *J. Financ. Econ.* 34, 251–277.

Kim, J., I. Krinsky and J. Lee (1993). Motives for going public and underpricing: New findings from Korea. *J. Banking Finance Account.* 20, 195–211.

Koh, F., and T. Walter (1989). A direct test of Rock's model of the pricing of unseasoned issues. *J. Financ. Econ.* 23, 251–272.

Krishnamurti, C., and P. Kumar (1994). The initial listing performance of Indian IPOs, unpublished working paper, Indian Institute of Science, Bangalore.

Kunz, R.M., and R. Aggarwal (1994). Why initial public offerings are underpriced: Evidence from Switzerland. *J. Banking Finance* 18, 705–723.

Lee, C., A. Shleifer and R. Thaler (1991). Investor sentiment and the closed-end fund puzzle. *J. Finance* 46, 75–109.

Lee, P., S. Taylor and T. Walter (1994a). Australian IPO underpricing in the short andlong run, unpublished working paper, University of Sydney.

Lee, P., S. Taylor and T. Walter (1994b). Expected and realized returns of Singaporean IPOs, unpublished working paper, University of Sydney.

Leland, H., and D. Pyle (1977). Informational asymmetries, financial structure and financial intermediation. *J. Finance* 32, 371–387.

Leleux, B.F., and D.F. Muzyka (1993). The demise of European IPO markets: A post-issue performance study, unpublished working paper, INSEAD.

Levis, M. (1993). The long-run performance of initial public offerings: The UK experience 1980–88. *Financ. Manage.* 22, 28–41.

Ljungqvist, A.P. (1993). Underpricing and long-term performance of German IPOs, 1978–92, unpublished working paper, Nuffield College, Oxford.

Logue, D. (1973). On the pricing of unseasoned equity issues: 1965–69. *J. Financ. Quant. Anal.* 8, 91–103.

Loughran, T. (1993). NYSE vs NASDAQ returns: Market microstructure or the poor performance of IPOs? *J. Financ. Econ.* 33, 241–260.

Loughran, T., and J.R. Ritter (1995). The new issues puzzle. *J. Finance* 50, 23–51.

Loughran, T., J.R. Ritter and K. Rydqvist (1994). Initial public offerings: International insights. *Pac.-Basin Finance J.* 2, 165–199.

Mandelker, G., and A. Raviv (1977). Investment banking: An economic analysis of optimal underwriting contracts. *J. Finance* 32, 683–694.

Mauer, D., and L. Senbet (1992). The effect of the secondary market on the pricing of initial public offerings: Theory and evidence. *J. Financ. Quant. Anal.* 27, 55–79.

Megginson, W.L., and K.A. Weiss (1991). Venture capitalist certification in initial public offerings. *J. Finance* 46, 879–903.

Michaely, R., and W., Shaw (1994). The pricing of initial public offerings: Tests of adverse selection and signaling theories. *Rev. Financ. Studies* 7, 279–317.

Miller, E. (1977). Risk, uncertainty, and divergence of opinion. *J. Finance* 32, 1151–1168.

Miller, R., and F. Reilly (1987). An examination of mispricing, returns, and uncertainty for initial public offerings. *Financ. Manage.* 16, 33–38.

Muscarella, C., and M. Vetsuypens (1989). A simple test of Baron's model of IPO underpricing. *J. Financ. Econ.* 24, 125–135.

Myers, S. (1984). The capital structure puzzle. *J. Finance* 39, 575–592.

Peavy, J.W. (1990). Returns on initial public offerings of closed-end funds. *Rev. Financ. Studies* 3, 695–708.

Rajan, R., and H. Servaes (1993). The effect of market conditions on initial public offerings, unpublished working paper, University of Chicago.

Ritter, J.R. (1984a). The 'hot issue' market of 1980. *J. Bus.* 57, 215–240.

Ritter, J.R. (1984b). Signaling and the valuation of unseasoned new issues: A comment. *J. Finance* 39, 1231–37.

Ritter, J.R. (1987). The costs of going public. *J. Financ. Econ.* 19, 269–281.

Ritter, J.R. (1991). The long-run performance of initial public offerings, *J. Finance* 46, 3–27.

Rock, K. (1986). Why new issues are underpriced. *J. Financ. Econ.* 15, 187–212.

Ruud, J. (1993). Underwriter price support and the IPO underpricing puzzle. *J. Financ. Econ.* 34, 135–151.

Rydqvist, K. (1993). Initial public offerings in Sweden and other small markets, unpublished working paper, Stockholm School of Economics.

Sahlman, W. (1988). Aspects of financial contracting in venture capital. *J. Appl. Corp. Finance* 1, 23–36.

Sahlman, W. (1990). The structure and governance of venture capital organizations. *J. Financ. Econ.* 27, 473–521.

Schultz, P. (1993). Unit initial public offerings: A form of staged financing. *J. Financ. Econ.* 34, 199–229.

Shiller, R.J. (1990). Speculative prices and popular models. *J. Econ. Perspect.* 4, 55–65.

Simon, C. (1989). The effect of the 1933 securities act on investor information and the performance of new issues. *Am. Econ. Rev.* 79, 295–318.

Smith, C. (1986). Investment banking and the capital acquisition process. *J. Financ. Econ.* 15, 3–29.

Spatt, C., and S. Srivastava (1991). Preplay communication, participation restrictions, and efficiency in initial public offerings. *Rev. Financ. Studies* 4, 709–726.

Tinic, S. (1988). Anatomy of initial public offerings of common stock. *J. Finance* 43, 789–822.

Titman, S., and B. Trueman (1986). Information quality and the valuation of new issues. *J. Account. Econ.* 8, 159–172.

Uhlir, H. (1989). Going public in the F.R.G., in: R. Guimaraes et al. (eds.), *A Reappraisal of the Efficiency of Financial Markets*, Springer-Verlag, Berlin.

Vos, E.A., and J. Cheung (1992). New Zealand IPO underpricing: A reputation based model. *Small Enterprise Res.* 1, 13–22.

Wang, K., S.H. Chan and G.W. Gau (1992). Initial public offerings of equity securities: Anomalous evidence using REITs. *J. Financ. Econ.* 31, 381–410.

Weiss, K. (1989). The post-offering price performance of closed-end funds. *Financ. Manage.* 18, 57–67.

Welch, I. (1989). Seasoned offerings, imitation costs, and the underpricing of initial public offerings. *J. Finance* 44, 421–449.

Welch, I. (1991). An empirical examination of models of contract choice in initial public offerings. *J. Financ. Quant. Anal.* 26, 497–518.

Welch, I. (1992). Sequential sales, learning, and cascades. *J. Finance* 47, 695–732.

Wessels, R. (1989). The market for IPOs: An analysis of the Amsterdam stock exchange, in: R. Guimaraes et al. (eds.), *A Reappraisal of the Efficiency of Financial Markets*, Springer-Verlag, Berlin.

Wethyavivorn, K., and Y. Koo-smith (1991). Initial public offerings in Thailand, 1988–89: Price and return patterns, in: S.G. Rhee and R.P. Chang (eds.), *Pacific-Basin Capital Markets Research, Vol. II*, North-Holland, Amsterdam.

Zeune, G.D. (1994). *Going Public: What the CFO Needs to Know*, AICPA, forthcoming.

Ziemba, W.T., and S.L. Schwartz (1992). *Power Japan*, Probus Publishing, Chicago, IL.

R. Jarrow et al., Eds., *Handbooks in OR & MS, Vol. 9*

Chapter 31

Seasoned Equity Offerings: A Survey

B. Espen Eckbo

Faculty of Commerce and Business Administration, University of British Columbia, Vancouver, B.C. V6T 1Y8, Canada

Ronald W. Masulis

Owen Graduate School of Management, Vanderbilt University, Nashville, TN 37203, U.S.A.

1. Introduction

Corporate securities are issued through a wide variety of methods, often involving complex contractual arrangements. While we do not yet have a unified theory of the capital acquisition process, our understanding of these contractual arrangements and their impact on firm value has progressed substantially over the past decade. In this paper, we review the theory and statistical evidence concerning the causes and effects of seasoned public offers (SPOs) of common stock,[1] with particular emphasis on results and findings that post-date the well known survey by Smith (1986) up to 1994. In fact, recent studies now provide at least partial answers to several of the 'unresolved issues' listed by Smith at the end of his survey. These include (i) to what extent does the market reaction to issue announcements depend on the flotation method; (ii) the conditions that lead issuers to select uninsured rights or rights with standby underwriting over a firm commitment underwritten offer; (iii) why rights issues continue to be the predominant flotation method in many foreign jurisdictions while they have become virtually extinct in the U.S.; and (iv) the determinants of direct and indirect flotation costs across flotation methods. In addition, we review (v) recent trends in aggregate issue activity; (vi) the timing of individual equity issues; and (vii) market microstructure effects of equity offers.

We begin in Section 2 by showing trends in aggregate issue activity across common stock, preferred stock, and corporate bonds in the U.S. over the last 50 years. This serves to place the relative importance of seasoned common stock issues in its proper historical perspective. Section 2 also compares recent trends in equity issue activity in the U.S. with those of Canada, Europe and Japan.

Section 3 describes the most frequently used flotation methods and shows their relative aggregate frequencies beginning in 1935. Section 3 then goes on to

[1] *Initial* public offers (IPOs) are discussed in Ibbotson & Ritter [1995, this volume].

examine available evidence on direct and indirect costs for three major flotation methods: uninsured rights, standby rights and firm commitment underwritten offers. Multivariate regressions strongly indicate that rights issues have the lowest *direct* flotation cost, firm commitment underwritten offers the highest, while standby rights offers are in between. In light of this, the overwhelming preference for the apparently expensive firm commitment flotation method must reflect either additional indirect costs which decrease the attractiveness of rights and standbys or, alternatively, a managerial incentive problem in choosing the optimal flotation method. Section 3 discusses a number of indirect costs, including personal taxes, shareholder borne transaction costs of selling rights, costs of rights offering failure, and anti-dilution clause mandated wealth transfers to convertible security holders triggered by rights issues. However, there is insufficient evidence to conclude that these indirect costs explain the low frequency of rights in the U.S.

Section 4 discusses the valuation effects of seasoned equity offers across flotation methods. The major theoretical arguments are based on adverse selection and signalling effects associated with information asymmetries, agency costs of free cash flow, wealth transfers between classes of security holders, as well as moral hazard problems in lowering managerial stock ownership. We review the large body of empirical evidence in this area, including stock price effects of SPO announcements by: flotation method, type of securities issued, and classified by offer completion or withdrawal. Available evidence on nonpublic seasoned equity offers is also integrated into the analysis of this section.

Section 5 discusses models of the flotation method choice (rights vs. underwriting, best effort vs. firm commitment) which explicitly recognize information asymmetries between the issuer and the market. Section 6 surveys recent theories and evidence on the correlation between issue activity, the stock price pattern prior to the issue announcement, and the business cycle, while Section 7 discusses potential market microstructure effects of SPOs. Concluding remarks are made in Section 8.

2. Trends in aggregate corporate financing activity

2.1. Debt vs. equity

Corporations raise capital through internal sources of equity (retained earnings plus depreciation) and external sales of securities and other financial claims. Table 1 shows the proportions of total funds accounted for by internal equity and external equity and debt sources for U.S. nonfinancial corporations after World War II. The table strongly indicates that retained earnings is the dominant funding source, followed by debt security issuance.[2]

It should be noted that since debt must be refinanced at maturity, and part of the debt is convertible into equity, Table 1 is biased in favour of finding a higher

[2] This trend persists also when debt values are reduced to take into account the effect of inflation.

Table 1

Sources of funds for U.S. nonfarm, nonfinancial corporate business, 1946–1991 [a]

Year	Total funds	Retained earnings		Depreciation		Bonds & mortgages		Short-term debt		Other debt		Equity offers	
	($ bill.)	($ bill.)	(%)	($ bill.)	(%)	($ bill.)	(%)	($ bill.)	(%)	($ bill.)	(%)	($ bill.)	(%)
1946	19.3	8.8	45.6	−0.2	−1.0	2.6	13.5	3.3	17.1	3.8	19.7	1.0	5.2
1947	27.6	13.1	47.5	0.3	1.1	4.3	15.6	3.0	10.9	5.8	21.0	1.1	4.0
1948	29.4	14.4	49.0	5.2	17.7	5.7	19.4	−0.2	−0.7	3.3	11.2	1.0	3.4
1949	20.5	9.8	47.8	10.2	49.8	3.7	18.0	−1.8	−8.8	−2.6	−12.7	1.2	5.9
1950	42.5	14.4	33.9	4.1	9.6	2.9	6.8	3.9	9.2	15.9	37.4	1.3	3.1
1951	37.0	11.4	30.8	9.4	25.4	4.3	11.6	4.1	11.1	5.7	15.4	2.1	5.7
1952	3.04	9.7	31.9	12.8	42.1	5.7	18.8	1.5	4.9	−1.6	−5.3	2.3	7.6
1953	28.7	9.8	34.1	12.6	43.9	4.4	15.3	−0.4	−1.4	0.5	1.7	1.8	6.3
1954	30.0	9.5	31.7	14.9	49.7	5.1	17.0	−0.3	−1.0	−0.8	−2.7	1.6	5.3
1955	53.4	14.2	26.6	15.7	29.4	4.9	9.2	3.8	7.1	13.1	24.5	1.7	3.2
1956	45.1	13.7	30.4	16.2	35.9	5.1	11.3	5.3	11.8	2.5	5.5	2.3	5.1
1957	43.5	12.7	29.2	19.3	44.4	7.6	17.5	1.8	4.1	−0.3	−0.7	2.4	5.5
1958	42.3	9.0	21.3	21.6	51.1	8.5	20.1	0.0	0.0	1.2	2.8	2.0	4.7
1959	56.6	13.3	23.5	23.0	40.6	6.2	11.0	4.2	7.4	7.8	13.8	2.1	3.7
1960	48.8	11.1	22.7	24.7	50.6	6.0	12.3	4.4	9.0	1.2	2.6	1.4	2.9
1961	56.1	10.5	18.7	26.5	47.2	8.4	15.0	1.7	3.0	6.9	12.3	2.1	3.7
1962	60.2	13.3	22.1	29.9	49.7	8.6	14.3	3.5	5.8	4.5	7.5	0.4	0.7
1963	68.6	15.1	22.0	31.9	46.5	8.5	12.4	3.9	5.7	9.5	13.8	−0.3	−0.4
1964	74.1	19.1	25.8	33.3	44.9	6.7	9.0	5.9	8.0	8.0	10.8	1.1	1.5
1965	93.0	23.8	25.6	35.4	38.1	7.6	8.2	11.4	12.3	14.8	15.9	0.0	0.0
1966	98.3	25.7	26.1	37.6	38.3	13.0	13.2	9.5	9.7	11.2	11.4	1.3	1.3
1967	95.0	22.8	24.0	41.5	43.7	16.8	17.7	8.1	8.5	3.4	3.6	2.4	2.5
1968	114.5	22.7	19.8	43.0	37.6	15.1	13.2	13.0	11.4	20.9	18.3	−0.2	−0.2
1969	117.9	19.9	16.9	45.3	38.4	11.2	9.5	19.2	16.3	18.9	16.0	3.4	2.9
1970	102.5	14.6	14.2	48.3	47.1	20.7	20.2	7.9	7.7	5.3	5.2	5.7	5.6
1971	126.4	20.4	16.1	54.3	43.0	21.4	16.9	4.3	3.4	14.5	11.6	11.4	9.0
1972	153.2	27.4	17.9	58.9	38.4	15.5	10.1	17.4	11.4	23.1	15.1	10.9	7.1
1973	195.7	43.3	22.1	50.6	25.9	12.9	6.6	36.9	18.9	44.1	22.5	7.9	4.0
1974	194.2	51.1	26.3	38.2	19.7	22.3	11.5	43.9	22.6	34.6	17.8	4.1	2.1
1975	158.3	50.8	32.1	74.0	46.7	28.6	18.1	−11.5	−7.3	6.5	4.1	9.9	6.3
1976	219.1	65.1	29.7	76.9	35.1	37.8	12.7	16.7	7.6	22.1	10.1	10.5	4.8
1977	261.4	76.7	29.3	88.3	33.8	33.3	12.7	36.1	13.8	24.3	9.3	2.7	1.0
1978	328.7	89.1	27.1	93.2	28.4	33.4	10.2	51.8	15.8	61.3	18.6	−0.1	0.0
1979	352.7	105.2	29.8	92.4	26.2	28.8	8.2	66.9	19.0	67.2	19.1	−7.8	−2.2
1980	337.2	104.2	30.9	111.9	33.2	17.5	5.2	40.7	12.1	52.5	15.6	10.4	3.1
1981	409.3	93.4	22.8	160.6	39.2	55.7	13.6	67.2	16.4	46.0	11.2	−13.5	−3.3
1982	371.9	58.5	15.7	205.2	55.2	36.2	9.7	54.7	14.7	15.4	4.1	1.9	0.5
1983	452.9	6.9	13.4	243.1	53.7	35.5	7.8	35.5	7.8	57.9	12.8	20.0	4.4
1984	532.4	77.6	14.6	270.2	50.8	95.6	18.0	105.5	19.8	62.5	11.7	−79.0	−14.8
1985	484.9	52.6	10.8	310.5	64.0	89.4	18.4	57.0	11.8	59.9	12.4	−84.5	−17.4
1986	597.8	30.9	5.2	322.7	54.0	205.4	34.4	65.8	11.0	58.0	9.7	−85.0	−14.2
1987	569.2	80.9	14.2	309.9	54.4	112.5	19.8	35.4	6.2	106.0	18.6	−75.5	−13.3
1988	652.0	122.7	18.8	310.9	47.7	152.8	23.4	75.9	11.6	199.2	18.3	−129.5	−19.9
1989	603.1	102.3	17.0	320.9	53.2	118.0	19.6	83.8	13.9	102.3	17.0	−124.2	−20.6
1990	489.3	84.8	17.3	313.7	64.1	51.3	10.5	29.9	6.1	72.6	14.8	−63.0	−12.9
1991	469.1	69.0	14.7	337.1	71.9	62.1	13.2	−58.0	−12.4	41.4	8.8	17.5	3.7

[a] Source: Flow of Funds, Board of Governors of the Federal Reserve Accouts, Seasonally Adjusted Flows, 'Non-Financing Corporate Business Excluding Farms'.

Table 2

Leverage ratios for U.S. corporations, 1926–1986 [a]

Year	All U.S. corporations			Manufacturing corporations	
	Debt/ total assets	Long-term debt/ long-term capital	Debt/ total assets	Long-term debt/ long-term capital	Debt/ total assets
1926	–	0.21	–	0.09	–
1927	–	0.22	–	0.09	–
1928	–	0.23	–	0.10	–
1929	0.13	0.23	–	0.09	–
1930	0.18	0.24	–	0.10	–
1931	0.25	0.25	–	0.10	–
1932	0.39	0.26	–	0.11	–
1933	0.37	0.26	–	0.10	–
1934	0.32	0.26	–	0.10	–
1935	0.36	0.26	–	0.10	–
1936	0.24	0.26	–	0.10	–
1937	0.27	0.26	0.53	0.10	0.26
1938	0.41	0.27	0.54	0.11	0.25
1939	0.32	0.27	0.55	0.11	0.25
1940	0.33	0.26	0.57	0.11	0.27
1941	0.38	0.26	0.58	0.11	0.31
1942	0.44	0.24	0.61	0.10	0.35
1943	0.28	0.23	0.63	0.09	0.36
1944	0.28	0.23	0.64	0.09	0.34
1945	0.25	0.21	0.65	0.09	0.30
1946	0.16	0.21	0.64	0.10	0.30
1947	0.17	0.22	0.63	0.11	0.31
1948	0.17	0.23	0.62	0.12	0.32
1949	0.23	0.23	0.62	0.12	0.28
1950	0.18	0.23	0.63	0.11	0.31
1951	0.19	0.23	0.63	0.13	0.35
1952	0.21	0.24	0.65	0.15	0.36
1953	0.21	0.25	0.64	0.15	0.36
1954	0.22	0.25	0.65	0.15	0.34
1955	0.16	0.24	0.66	0.15	0.35
1956	0.15	0.25	0.65	0.16	0.36
1957	0.17	0.26	0.65	0.17	0.37
1959	0.16	0.27	0.66	0.17	0.38
1960	0.18	0.27	0.66	0.17	0.38
1961	0.16	0.28	0.66	0.18	0.43
1962	0.21	–	–	–	–
1963	0.18	0.28	0.68	0.17	0.38
1964	0.17	0.28	0.68	0.18	0.39
1965	0.17	0.28	0.69	0.19	0.40
1966	0.22	0.29	0.69	0.21	0.43
1967	0.19	0.29	0.69	0.21	0.42
1968	0.18	0.30	0.70	0.23	0.45
1969	0.22	0.31	0.70	0.23	0.45

Table 2 (cont'd)

Year	All U.S. corporations			Manufacturing corporations	
	Debt/ total assets	Long-term debt/ long-term capital	Debt/ total assets	Long-term debt/ long-term capital	Debt/ total assets
1970	0.27	0.32	0.71	0.26	0.49
1971	0.26	0.33	0.72	0.27	0.69
1972	0.24	0.33	0.72	0.26	0.49
1973	0.31	0.34	0.73	0.26	0.51
1974	0.38	0.34	0.74	0.27	0.53
1975	0.32	0.34	0.74	0.28	0.52
1976	0.32	0.34	0.74	0.28	0.53
1977	0.34	0.34	0.74	0.27	0.53
1978	0.35	0.34	0.75	0.28	0.54
1979	0.36	0.33	0.74	0.28	0.55
1980	0.32	0.33	0.74	0.28	0.56
1981	0.29	0.32	0.73	0.28	0.56
1982	0.29	0.33	0.73	0.29	0.56
1983	0.26	0.33	0.74	0.28	0.57
1984	0.27	0.34	0.74	0.29	0.57
1985	0.30	0.33	0.74	0.29	0.58
1986	0.31	0.35	0.74	0.34	0.62
1987	–	0.35	0.74	0.35	0.62
1988	–	0.36	0.75	0.37	0.63

[a] Source: Masulis [1988, updated]. The sources in the original study include Taggart [1985], Holland & Myers [1979], and the Statistics of Income, Corporation Returns, Table 2. All figures are in book value terms except for column 2 (Debt/total assets) which is an estimate of the leverage ratio using market value data.

proportion of debt than equity issues. A firm issuing $100 worth of equity to finance the next fifty years of investment will appear as having issued equity once at the level of $100 over the 50-year period. In contrast, if the same firm rolls over five 10-year bonds, Table 1 will record five debt issues each worth around $100 over the same time period. While it is difficult to control for the resulting double counting, Eckbo [1986] reports that approximately 40% of a sample of 650 corporate debt issues by publicly traded firms over the period 1963–1981 were for the purpose of refunding old debt (including retirement of outstanding bonds and conversion of bank loans and commercial paper to bonds). Based on this, a rough adjustment would be to reduce the debt proportion by one half, which would leave unalterred the conclusion that debt constitutes the predominant external funding source in the post-war period.

The evidence in Table 1 can be summarized as follows:

Observation 1 *Corporate funding sources.*

(i) Internal equity has remained the dominant funding source for U.S. nonfinancial corporations after the second world war.

(ii) Debt dominates equity as an external funding source, with a net retirement of equity in the 1980s.
(iii) In periods with low internally generated equity, the proportion of debt financing tends to increase to finance the shortfall. In periods with high internal equity, debt issues tend to be used to retire external equity.

The relative increase in debt financing witnessed since the second world war is also apparent from the time series of debt to asset ratios in Table 2:

Observation 2 *Leverage ratios.* Leverage (debt to total asset) ratios for U.S. manufacturing companies have increased steadily over the post-war period from a low of 30% in 1946 to approximately 60% in 1984.

Models of optimal capital structure predict that a number of economy wide variables will effect the debt to asset ratio, including tax rates, interest rates and business cycles. Consistent with this, Taggart [1985] also observes that corporate debt appears to rise in periods of rising corporate tax rates, especially when not offset by rising personal tax rates and in periods when corporate nondebt deductions were falling due to inflation. Increases in equity appear to be deterred by increased volatility in economic conditions.

2.2. Public security offerings for cash

Table 3 presents the dollar volume of annual public and private offerings of common stock, preferred stock and corporate bonds in the U.S. from 1938 through 1991. An interesting aspect of the data is the low average frequency of common stock and especially preferred stock offers. The table also shows substantial variation across time in both the size of aggregate security offerings and the proportion of total funds raised by equity. What are the sources of this variability? Based on U.K. data, Marsh [1982] reports that the debt–equity choice can partially be predicted by the tendency of firms' short term and long term debt and retained earnings levels to move toward their historical levels. In the U.S., Taggart [1977] and Choe, Masulis & Nanda [1993] report that equity issues are more frequent in upswings of the business cycle and when stock price volatility is relatively low. In contrast, nonconvertible debt tends to be relatively more frequent in downturns of the business cycle and when stock market volatility is relatively high.

Table 3 also indicates that the proportion of public sales of securities has historically been substantially higher than the proportion of private placements in the U.S.. This trend appears to have changed towards the end of the 1980s, as the dollar volume of private sales has approached the volume of public offers for both debt and equity.

Observation 3 *Offer frequencies.*
(i) The ratio of public equity to public debt issues tends to increase during business cycle expansions and to decrease during business cycle contractions.

Table 3

U.S. corporate securities offerings for cash, 1938–1991 ($ millions) [a]

Year	Total issues	Corporate bonds					Prfd. stock		Common stock			
		Total bonds	% of total	Public domestic	Private domestic	Sold abroad	Public	% of total	Total common	% of total	Public	Private
1938	2,155	2,044	94.9	1,353	691	0	86	4.0	25	1.2	25	0
1939	2,164	1,979	91.5	1,276	703	0	98	4.5	87	4.0	87	0
1940	2,677	2,386	89.1	1,628	758	0	183	6.8	108	4.0	108	0
1941	2,666	2,389	89.6	1,578	811	0	167	6.3	110	4.1	110	0
1942	1,063	917	86.3	506	411	0	112	10.5	34	3.2	34	0
1943	1,170	990	84.6	621	369	0	124	10.6	56	4.8	56	0
1944	3,202	2,670	83.4	1,892	778	0	369	11.5	163	5.1	163	0
1945	6,010	4,855	80.8	3,851	1,004	0	758	12.6	397	6.6	397	0
1946	6,898	4,881	70.8	3,019	1,862	0	1,126	16.3	891	12.9	891	0
1947	6,574	5,035	76.6	2,888	2,147	0	761	11.6	778	11.8	778	0
1948	7,079	5,973	84.4	2,963	3,010	0	492	7.0	614	8.7	614	0
1949	6,049	4,889	80.8	2,434	2,455	0	424	7.0	736	12.2	736	0
1950	6,362	4,920	77.3	2,360	2,560	0	631	9.9	811	12.7	811	0
1951	7,740	5,690	73.5	2,364	3,326	0	838	10.8	1,212	15.7	1,212	0
1952	9,535	7,602	79.7	3,645	3,957	0	564	5.9	1,369	14.4	1,369	0
1953	8,899	7,084	79.6	3,856	3,228	0	489	5.5	1,326	14.9	1,326	0
1954	9,516	7,487	78.7	4,003	3,484	0	816	8.6	1,213	12.7	1,213	0
1955	10,240	7,420	72.5	4,119	3,301	0	635	6.2	2,185	21.3	2,185	0
1956	10,939	8,002	73.2	4,225	3,777	0	636	5.8	2,301	21.0	2,301	0
1957	12,884	9,957	77.3	6,118	3,839	0	411	3.2	2,516	19.5	2,516	0
1958	11,557	9,652	83.5	6,332	3,320	0	571	4.9	1,334	11.5	1,334	0
1959	9,747	7,189	73.8	3,557	3,632	0	531	5.4	2,027	20.8	2,027	0
1960	10,154	8,081	79.6	4,806	3,275	0	409	4.0	1,664	16.4	1,664	0
1961	13,164	9,420	71.6	4,700	4,720	0	450	3.4	3,294	25.0	3,294	0
1962	10,705	8,969	83.8	4,440	4,529	0	422	3.9	1,314	12.3	1,314	0
1963	12,236	10,872	88.9	4,714	6,158	0	342	2.8	1,022	8.4	1,022	0
1964	13,957	10,866	77.9	3,623	7,243	0	412	3.0	2,679	19.2	2,679	0
1965	15,992	13,720	85.8	5,570	8,150	0	725	4.5	1,547	9.7	1,547	0
1966	18,073	15,560	96.1	8,018	7,542	0	574	3.2	1,939	10.7	1,939	0
1967	24,798	21,954	88.5	14,990	6,964	0	885	3.6	1,959	7.9	1,959	0
1968	21,966	17,383	79.1	10,732	6,651	0	637	2.9	3,946	18.0	3,946	0
1969	26,743	18,347	68.6	12,734	5,613	0	682	2.6	7,714	28.8	7,714	0
1970	38,945	30,315	77.8	25,384	4,931	0	1,390	3.6	7,240	18.6	7,240	0
1971	45,090	32,129	71.3	24,775	7,354	0	3,670	8.1	9,291	20.6	9,291	0
1972	40,226	26,131	65.0	17,425	8,706	0	3,370	8.4	10,725	26.7	10,725	0
1973	32,025	21,046	65.7	13,244	7,802	0	3,337	10.4	7,642	23.9	7,642	0
1974	38,310	32,063	83.7	25,903	6,160	0	2,253	5.9	3,994	10.4	3,994	0
1975	53,618	42,755	79.7	32,583	10,172	0	3,458	6.4	7,405	13.8	7,405	0
1976	53,488	42,380	79.2	26,453	15,927	0	2,803	5.2	8,305	15.5	8,305	0
1977	54,206	42,193	77.8	24,186	18,007	0	3,878	7.2	8,135	15.0	8,135	0
1978	47,230	36,872	78.1	19,815	17,057	0	2,832	6.0	7,526	15.9	7,526	0
1979	51,533	40,208	78.0	25,814	14,394	0	3,574	6.9	7,751	15.0	7,751	0
1980	73,695	53,206	72.2	41,587	11,619	0	3,631	4.9	16,858	22.9	16,858	0
1981	70,441	45,092	64.0	38,103	6,989	0	1,797	2.6	23,552	33.4	23,552	0
1982	84,638	54,076	63.9	44,278	9,798	0	5,113	6.0	25,449	30.1	25,449	0
1983	120,074	68,495	57.0	47,369	21,126	0	7,213	6.0	44,366	36.9	44,366	0
1984	132,311	109,683	82.9	73,357	36,326	0	4,118	3.1	18,510	14.0	18,510	0
1985	239,055	203,540	85.1	119,559	46,200	37,781	6,505	2.7	29,010	12.1	29,010	0
1986	423,725	355,292	83.8	231,936	80,760	42,596	11,514	2.7	56,919	13.4	50,316	6,603
1987	392,671	326,166	83.1	209,790	92,070	24,306	10,123	2.6	56,382	14.4	43,225	13,157
1988	410,893	353,092	85.9	202,215	127,699	23,178	6,544	1.6	51,257	12.5	35,911	15,346
1989	378,760	320,889	84.7	180,618	177,420	22,851	6,194	1.6	51,677	13.6	26,030	25,647
1990	340,126	229,959	88.2	189,917	86,988	23,054	3,998	1.2	36,169	10.6	19,433	16,736

[a] Source: Federal Reserve Bulletin, New Security Issues.

(ii) Until the second half of the 1980s, only a small fraction of security issue volume in the U.S. was sold privately. However, recent years have seen a substantial increase in private placement volume.

2.3. International trends

Table 4 shows the major financing sources for nonfinancial companies in Canada, Finland, France, Germany, Italy, Japan, the U.K. and the U.S. over the 1970–1985 period. The table, which originally appeared in Mayer [1990], indicates several interesting aspects concerning the corporate financing strategies across these countries.

Table 4

Average financing of nonfinancial enterprises, in percent of total financing sources, 1970–1985 [a]

	Canada [b]	Finland [c]	France	Germany [d]	Italy [e]	Japan [f]	United Kingdom [g]	United States [h]
Retentions	54.2	42.1	44.1	55.2	38.5	33.7	72.0	66.9
Capital transfers	0.0	0.1	1.4	6.7	5.7	0.0	2.9	0.0
Short-term securities	1.4	2.5	0.0	0.0	0.1	N.A.	2.3	1.4
Loans	12.8	27.2	41.5	21.1	38.6	40.7	21.4	23.1
Trade credit	8.6	17.2	4.7	2.2	0.0	18.3	2.8	8.4
Bonds	6.1	1.8	2.3	0.7	2.4	3.1	0.8	9.7
Shares	11.9	5.6	10.6	2.1	10.8	3.5	4.9	0.8
Other	4.1	6.9	0.0	11.9	1.6	0.7	2.2	−6.1
Statistical adjustment	0.8	−3.5	−4.7	0.0	2.3	N.A.	−9.4	−4.1
Total	99.9	99.9	99.9	99.9	99.9	100.0	99.9	100.1

[a] Source: Mayer [1990]. The original data are constructed from OECD flow-of-funds statistics. The footnotes below are from the original table.

[b] For Canada, mortgages are included in loans, foreign investments are included in other, and capital transfers are included in retentions.

[c] Data on Finland refer to the period 1969–1984. Errors in the OECD statistics have required that the statistical adjustment be altered as follows: 1971, DM 2 billion and 1973, +DM 89 billion.

[d] There is no statistical adjustment in German accounts. Funds placed with insurance companies and building and loans associations are included in loans.

[e] The Italian statistical adjustment has been reduced by Lit 2.070 billion in 1974 to make accounts balance. Trade credit is not recorded as a separate item in Italian flow-of-funds.

[f] Japanese flow-of-funds do not report retentions. The ratio of external to internal financing of Japanese enterprises was obtained by applying proportions recorded in aggregate company accounts for the period 1972–1984, as shown in Table 12 (IV and V). The Japanese figures therefore have to be treated with particular caution. Short-term securities are included in bonds.

[g] United Kingdom statistics refer to private enterprises only; were public enterprise to be included then entries would read as follows: retentions, 91.9; capital transfers, 5.7; short-term securities, 1.3; loans, 11.7; trade credit, −0.7; bonds, −0.9, shares, −2.5; other, 2.1; statistical adjustment, −8.5.

[h] The following modifications have been made to the U.S. statistical adjustment to make accounts balance (in millions of dollars): 1970, −1; 1971, −3; 1973, +3; 1975, +1; 1976, −2; 1979, +2; 1981, −1; 1982, +1; 1983, −2; 1984, −1. Capital transfers are included under retentions in U.S. accounts. Acquisitions of central government short-term securities are not shown separately from bonds.

Observation 4 *International funding sources.*

(i) Retained earnings are the major source of finance in all the industrial countries studied.

(ii) The proportion of external funding is largest in Finland, France, Japan and Italy.

(iii) Banks are the dominant source of external finance in all countries, representing approximately 40% of gross sources in France, Italy and Japan.

(iv) Companies in Canada, France and Italy are the largest users of external capital markets, with short-term securities, bonds and shares representing 19%, 13% and 13% of gross financing, respectively.

(v) Canadian, French and Italian firms raise approximately 10% of their gross financing by issuing equity, while the corresponding proportion is less than 5% in Germany, Japan and the U.S..

Over the 1970–1985 period, there was a trend towards increased use of securities markets to finance corporate activity. This trend was accelerated by the announcement of the European Single Act in 1985, which set the stage for a more complete financial integration of the European Community. Walter & Smith [1989] show that, at the end of 1987, the total volume of new security issues by European corporations in the intra-European capital market had reached approximately 70% of the comparable corporate financing activity in the U.S., and 78% of the level of comparable activity in Japan (reproduced here in Table 5, panel A). In part, this trend reflects the large privatization programs in France and the U.K. in 1986 and 1987.

Interestingly, as shown in panel B of Table 5, while the Eurobond and Euroequity markets are the largest European securities markets, European nonfinancial corporations sell most of their new issues in their respective domestic markets. The largest players in the Eurobond and Euroequity markets are governments and multinational corporations, particularly of Japanese origin.

Observation 5 *Volume of European SPOs.* By 1987, the dollar volume of new security issues made by European nonfinancial corporations had reached approximately three-quarters of the corresponding issue volume in the U.S. and Japan. The 1987 total issue volume in European domestic markets was approximately four times the combined volume in the Eurobond and Euroequity markets. European equity issues by nonfinancial institutions had grown to more than twice the volume of equity issues in the U.S. and in Japan.

3. Flotation methods and costs

3.1. Frequency of major flotation methods

SPOs of common stock are sold through a wider array of alternative flotation methods than is the case for IPOs. This reflects the fact that IPO stocks lack an

Table 5

Volume of equity and bond issues in the U.S., Europe and Japan [a]

Panel A: Volume of domestic corporate security issues in 1987 ($ billion)

	United States			Europe			Japan		
	Financial	Non-financial	Total	Financial	Non-financial	Total	Financial	Non-financial	Total
Equities	25.3	28.1	53.4	13.8	75.8 [c]	89.6	14.0	28.5	42.5
Bonds [d]	143.2	220.1	363.3	170.1	31.5	201.6	227.9 [b]	103.1	331.0
Total [e]	168.5	248.2	416.7	183.9	107.3	291.2	241.9	131.6	373.5

Panel B: Security issues by European nonfinancial corporations, 1985–1987 ($ million) [f]

	Nonfinancial debt issues			Nonfinancial equity issues			Total nonfinancial issues		
	Euro and foreign	Domestic bonds	Total bonds	Euro and foreign	Domestic	Total equities	Euro and foreign	Domestic	Total issues
1985	11,779	12,249	24,028	2,660	23,610	26,270	14,439	35,859	50,298
1986	25,314	19,122	44,436	13,112	45,886	58,998	38,426	65,008	103,434
1987	13,576	23,894	37,470	9,873	64,113	73,986	23,449	88,007	111,456
1988	31,996	n.a.		6,351	n.a.		38,347	n.a.	

[a] Source: Walter & Smith [1989]. Their original data sources include Securities Data Co. for Euro and foreign data, and OECD for domestic data. The footnotes below are from the original table.
[b] Includes discount notes issued by banks, many of which can be considered short term.
[c] Total gross shares sold through public distributions, including privatization issues.
[d] Includes private placements where reported, as well as local government and revenue bonds.
[e] Issues by domestic firms outside their home regions are excluded, for example, U.S. corporate issues of Eurobonds. However, the total includes European corporate sales of Euro-issues and foreign issues estimated at $ 35.7 billion in 1987.
[f] The volume of nonfinancial issues is 29.9%, 38.3%, 38.3% of the total issue volume in 1985, 1986, 1987, and 1988, respectively.

active secondary market where current prices for the stock are easily obtainable and have a small number of current stockholders. Alternative methods of floating seasoned common stock include firm commitment offers which can be either privately negotiated or competitively bid or by shelf registration, best efforts offers, rights offers, rights offers with standby underwriting, direct issues (e.g. to securityholders of acquired firms) and private placements. Common stock is also sometimes sold to the issuer's own senior securityholders through exchange offers and swaps. In addition, stock is sold through the issuance of convertible securities, warrants and stock options and through the establishment of dividend reinvestment, employee stock ownership and management compensation plans.

In a rights offer, current shareholders are given short-term warrants on a pro rata basis, allowing shareholders the option to either purchase the new shares or sell the warrants in the market before expiration (typically 20 days). Unsubscribed shares are offered to shareholders who wish to purchase more than their pro rata share of the issue (overallotment option or green shoe). The rights subscription price is typically 15–20% below the current market price of the stock. In the U.S., Canada and Europe, corporate law typically dictates that the corporate charter grant current shareholders the first right of refusal to purchase a new issue of voting stock. Thus, the issuer must amend its charter, eliminating the preemptive rights requirement, before a flotation method other than a rights issue can be used. Such charter amendments were particularly popular among NYSE- and AMEX-listed industrial firms in the late 1960s and the early 1970s [Bhagat, 1983].

Since current shareholders capture the full value of the rights by either subscribing or selling the rights in the secondary market, it is often argued that the issuer can costlessly increase the rights subscription price discount until the offer is virtually guaranteed to succeed. However, as discussed later, this argument does not necessarily hold in a world of asymmetric information, which may explain why rights issuers often hire an underwriter to guarantee the proceeds on any unsubscribed shares. We refer to this flotation method as 'rights with standby underwriting' or simply as 'standbys'. Rights offers in the U.S. are typically fully subscribed [Eckbo & Masulis, 1992], and the typical underwriter takeup in standbys is 15% of the issue [Singh, 1992].

If rights are not used, the firm can attempt to sell the issue directly to the market with no financial intermediary, place the issue with a private group of investors (a private placement), or employ an intermediary, usually an investment banker or underwriting syndicate. There are several forms of investment banking contracts. In a best efforts offer, the investment banker simply acts as a marketing agent for the issuer, and the issuer bears the risk of offer failure. In contrast, in a firm commitment underwriting agreement, the investment banker guarantees the proceeds from the entire issue, bearing the responsibility for selling the shares to the public.

In the U.S., a firm formally starts the issuance process by filing a registration statement with the SEC. In the case of a firm commitment offer, the issuing firm and the investment banker then issue a preliminary prospectus in order to elicit interest in the offer from potential investors. This prospectus states minimum and maximum offer prices and the maximum number of shares to be sold (including overallotments). Following SEC approval of the issue, the actual offer price and number of shares to be sold are determined at a pricing meeting of the issuer and the underwriter. Normally, the issue is offered to the public within 24 hours of the pricing meeting. Common stock offers are typically made near the stock market open but also occur in late afternoon after the close of exchange trading. The underwriter's guarantee of the offer proceeds becomes effective only after the offer price is set; up to this point the firm itself bears the proceeds risk. In the case of a best efforts underwritten offer, the prospectus issued following SEC approval contains a definite minimum sales level, and the issuer precommits to withdrawing the entire issue if this minimum is not met during the specified offer period. Because of the downward pressure that the offering places on the secondary market price, syndicates typically execute price support activities in the secondary market during the public offering.

Since the early eighties, the public offering process has been simplified by the SEC which introduced an expedited registration procedure as well as the so-called 'shelf registration' procedure for large well known firms. The expedited registration procedure speeds up SEC approval of a specific issue, while the shelf registration procedure allows the issuer to preregister potential equity offerings where a number of alternative underwriters can be specified. Under the latter procedure, the firm can sell part or all of the issue to an underwriter or syndicate on a moment's notice any time over the two year life of the shelf registration filing.

The possibility for rapid sale of new equity has also been enhanced by the emergence of the 'bought deal'. In a bought deal, a development caused by competition among underwriters, an investment bank or securities firm quickly purchases the entire stock issue for a minimum fee, with no further obligations on the part of the issuer. This flotation method, which has been particularly popular in Canada and in Euroequity markets in the 1980s, is seen as a way for relatively unknown securities firms to compete for underwriting business in a market where it is often difficult to break the existing relationship between the issuer and its traditional choice of investment banker.

Table 6 shows the frequencies of common stock issues by the firm commitment, standby and uninsured rights methods for NYSE and AMEX listed stocks since 1935. The time series trends of these three flotation methods are noteworthy. As shown, from the mid 1930s through the mid 1950s, rights plus standby offers tended to exceed firm commitment offers. However, over the 1960–1983 period rights have declined in frequency, virtually disappearing by 1980. Standby offers have shown a similar but less precipitous decline in recent years. The causes for these declines are addressed later in this essay.

Table 7 shows that straight debt as well as securities which involve a contingent equity sale, such as convertible bonds and convertible preferred stock, are also typically issued by a firm commitment contract.[3] The information, which is based on the SEC's Registered Offerings Statistics Tape for the 1977–1982 period as compiled by Booth & Smith [1986], also indicates that more than 90% of the common stock firm commitment underwriting arrangements are 'negotiated' as opposed to 'competitive', while 25% of the straight bond firm commitments are competitive.

Observation 6 *SPO flotation method trends in the U.S.*

(i) Over the past 60 years, publicly traded U.S. companies have gradually switched from the uninsured rights and standby flotation methods to the firm commitment method. By 1980, the rights method has virtually disappeared in the group of large publicly traded industrial firms.

(ii) U.S. firms also show an overwhelming preference for the firm commitment method when offering securities other than common stock, including mortgage bonds, straight bonds, convertible debt, convertible preferred and warrants.

[3] Eckbo [1986] finds that in a large sample of corporate debt issues by publicly traded firms over the period 1964–1981 less than 5% were sold using the rights offer method.

Table 6

Primary offers of seasoned common stock by NYSE and AMEX-listed firms, classified by the flotation method (FC = firm commitments, Stand = standby rights), over the periods 1935–1955 and 1963–1981

	Total issues				Industrial issues				Utility issues			
	Total	FC	Stand	Right	Total	FC	Stand	Right	Total	FC	Stand	Right
Source: Stevenson [1957][a]												
1935	6	1	3	2	5	–	3	2	1	1	–	–
1936	37	11	17	9	37	11	17	9	–	–	–	–
1937	40	15	18	7	39	15	17	7	1	–	1	–
1938	5	2	–	3	4	1	–	3	1	1	–	–
1939	13	6	3	4	8	5	3	–	2	1	–	1
1940	18	9	4	5	13	7	4	2	3	2	–	1
1941	9	1	3	5	9	5	3	1	6	2	–	4
1942	1	1	–	–	1	1	–	–	–	–	–	–
1943	14	8	5	1	13	7	5	1	1	1	–	–
1944	23	13	9	1	22	12	9	1	1	1	–	–
1945	52	23	18	11	45	20	15	10	7	3	3	1
1946	110	73	24	13	96	65	21	10	14	8	3	3
1947	53	27	12	14	29	19	5	5	24	8	7	9
1948	61	20	20	21	28	11	9	8	33	9	11	13
1949	79	27	30	22	14	7	5	2	65	20	25	20
1950	84	35	31	18	30	16	9	5	54	19	22	13
1951	131	61	49	21	63	40	16	7	68	21	33	14
1952	131	66	43	22	71	41	20	10	60	25	23	12
1953	120	55	47	18	43	28	11	4	77	27	36	14
1954	101	51	33	17	51	36	11	4	50	15	22	13
1955	113	44	56	13	56	29	25	2	57	15	31	11
Source: Eckbo and Masulis [1992][b]												
1963	12	2	6	4	5	1	3	1	7	1	3	3
1964	17	8	6	3	8	4	3	1	9	4	3	2
1965	20	5	9	6	11	5	4	2	9	0	5	4
1966	27	12	12	3	17	7	8	2	10	5	4	1
1967	26	12	9	5	17	9	4	4	9	3	5	1
1968	44	26	9	9	31	20	4	7	13	6	5	2
1969	42	24	15	3	22	13	7	2	20	11	8	1
1970	49	36	10	3	22	18	2	2	27	18	8	1
1971	84	65	15	4	44	40	2	2	40	25	13	2
1972	81	68	11	2	29	27	1	1	52	41	10	1
1973	58	50	6	2	12	10	1	1	46	40	5	1
1974	53	47	4	3	6	5	0	1	47	42	3	2
1975	89	79	8	1	20	19	1	0	69	60	8	1
1976	93	88	3	1	30	29	1	0	63	59	3	1
1977	65	62	3	0	2	2	0	0	63	60	3	0
1978	90	86	3	1	25	23	2	0	65	63	1	1
1979	85	81	2	2	21	20	0	1	64	61	2	1
1980	162	157	2	3	87	86	0	1	75	71	2	2
1981	152	149	1	2	64	63	0	1	88	86	1	1

[a] Stevenson [1957] lists common stock issues with proceeds over $ 1 million. Original data sources include Sullivan and Cromwell Issuer Summaries 1933–1950, and The Commercial and Financial Chronicle 1950–1955.

[b] Original data sources include the Wall Street Journal Index, the Investment Dealer's Digest, and Moody's Industrials and Utilities Manuals. The sample excludes simultaneous offers of debt/preferred stock/warrants, combination primary/secondary stock offerings, cancelled or postponed offers, and non-U.S. issues.

Table 7

Alternative methods of security issuance by type of security, U.S. 1977–1982[a]

Method of security issuance	Type of security					
	Mortgage bonds	Straight bonds	Preferred stock	Convertible bonds	Convertible preferred stock	Common stock
Use of underwriters						
Noninitial registered offerings (NIR)[b]						
firm commitment[c]	454	896	221	240	70	1,008
best efforts	2	128	0	5	1	27
rights with standby	0	7	1	4	0	29
rights without standby	1	2	3	3	1	67
self-registered[d]	2	205	7	2	2	106
% firm commitment	98.9	72.4	95.3	94.5	94.6	81.5
Initial registered offerings (IR)						
firm commitment[c]	29	68	1	14	4	396
best efforts	3	22	0	2	0	470
rights with standby	0	0	1	0	0	5
rights without standby	1	0	1	1	0	14
self-registered[d]	1	28	3	3	3	106
% firm commitment	87.9	57.6	16.7	70.0	57.1	40.0
Types of firm commitment underwriting arrangements						
Noninitial registered offerings (NIR)[b]						
Utilities						
negotiated	201	58	122	5	7	413
competitive	199	12	61	0	0	43
% negotiated	50.2	82.9	67.7	100.0	100.0	90.6
Other industries						
negotiated	35	816	36	235	63	551
competitive	19	25	2	0	0	1
% negotiated	64.8	97.0	94.7	100.0	100.0	99.8

[a] Source: Booth & Smith [1986]. The footnotes below are from the original table. The table summarizes data from the Registered Offering Statistics Tape provided by the Securities and Exchange Commission. Data include all issues listed on the tapes where type of underwriting arrangement could be identified. Rule 415 security issues are excluded. The type of underwriting arrangement varies based on security type and whether the offering is an initial registration. Firm commitment is the most common arrangement. Among firm commitment issues, choice of competitive versus negotiated offering is related to the priority of the security claim. Competitive underwriting is less common despite its lower level of underwriter compensation.

[b] Includes initial offers of securities by firms already registered with the SEC.

[c] Data set includes all firm commitment offerings that could be identified as being underwritten either competitively or on a negotiated basis for the 1977–1982 period.

[d] Includes issues where no underwriter was utilized. Self-registration tends to occur between issuers and investors with much in common and where an active securities market is of little value. For example, shares of cooperative ownership such as a grocery cooperative are often issued without use of an investment banker.

In contrast, Table 7 confirms that IPOs are primarily sold through best effort and firm commitment contracts, with approximately 40% of the IPOs sold using the best efforts method. The popularity of best efforts and firm commitment contracts for IPOs reflect several factors specific to this offer category: IPO stocks have no secondary market price information prior to the issue, no stock analyst following, little publicly available information about the firm, and high share ownership concentration with management generally being a major holder. These factors all contribute to a more severe informational asymmetry between existing shareholders and outside investors, increasing the uncertainty over the stock's true value.

Observation 7 *IPO flotation methods.* In the U.S., IPOs are sold almost exclusively by means of the firm commitment method (approximately 60%) and the best efforts underwritten method (approximately 40%).

As documented by Eckbo & Masulis [1992], concurrent with the disappearance of rights and standby offers in the U.S., these same firms have increasingly relied on new methods of raising equity capital from shareholders and employees such as dividend reinvestment plans (DRIPs) and employee stock ownership plans (ESOPs). In a DRIP, shareholders can elect to receive shares of common stock in lieu of cash dividends. The shares sold through these plans can be purchased in the secondary market by the firm or, if the DRIP is registered with the SEC, the firm can issue new shares. When new shares are issued through DRIPs, it is common to allow shareholders to purchase additional shares in excess of their dividends up to some maximum dollar amount on the ex-dividend date [Scholes & Wolfson, 1989]. Thus, given the well-documented inflexibility of dividend payouts, DRIPs are in many ways similar to a periodic rights offer.

In an ESOP, employees are vested with shares of stock after fulfilling a specific period of service in the firm. This represents an alternative to a higher wage or retirement benefit. In addition, employees often can elect to purchase for cash a specified number of additional shares at a discount from the current market price. The periodic purchase or crediting of shares through the ESOP is similar to a predictable sale of stock by the firm which raises new capital or reduces other employee expenses. As such, it is similar to a DRIP even though the purchasers are employees rather than existing shareholders and the plan falls under more restrictive tax and retirement regulations.[4]

Observation 8 *DRIPs and ESOPs.* There is evidence that DRIPs and ESOPs, which in many ways are similar to periodic rights offers, to some extent have replaced rights issues as a means of raising capital from shareholders and employees.

Several researchers have found that equity issuers in smaller capital markets, which generally have a small equity capitalization, tend to rely on rights offers, private placements and dividend reinvestment plans to sell common stock. For

[4] See Chang [1990] for a further description.

example, the current low frequency of rights issues in the U.S. contrasts sharply with that in Canada where in recent years almost half of all equity issues are sold through rights offers. Furthermore, in Europe, with the exception of issues in the Eurobond and the Euroequity markets, the majority of all issues are sold through rights or standby offers, though recent trends toward greater firm commitment and standby use have occurred in a number of these countries as well.[5] This is also the case in most Pacific Basin countries. For example, while approximately 80% of SPOs on the Tokyo Stock Exchange were sold through rights in the 1950s, as shown in Table 8, this percentage had decreased to approximately 20% by 1990, with 80% of the SPOs currently issued through firm commitments.

Observation 9 *International flotation method trends.* Domestic issues in the Canadian, the European and most Pacific Rim capital markets are predominantly sold through rights. There is a trend towards increased use of underwriters and the firm commitment method in the larger of these markets as well. In Japan, one of the largest stock markets, a majority of equity issues is now sold through the firm commitment method.

3.2. Direct flotation costs

Table 9 lists average direct flotation costs for uninsured rights, standbys and firm commitment offers from a sample of 1249 SPOs compiled by Eckbo & Masulis [1992]. In a rights offer, the direct costs of issuing equity are limited to fees for legal- and accounting services, trustees' fees, listing fees, printing and engraving expenses, SEC registration fees, Federal Revenue Stamps, and state taxes. Firms issuing rights typically obtain subscription precommitments from large shareholders for a significant portion of the issue (on average 60%), and the rights are typically fully subscribed by the end of the subscription period. Thus, any expected rights offer failure costs for these firms are small.[6] As shown in Table 9, the average direct costs of uninsured rights as a percent of total issue proceeds is 1.8% for industrial issuers and 0.5% for utility issuers.

In a standby offer, the firm also pays a fee to the underwriter. The underwriter compensation typically consists of two components: a fixed commitment fee and a takeup fee on all rights exercised by the underwriter at the rights offer expiration. The typical subscription or exercise rate in a standby offer exceeds 70%. Thus, the risk to the standby underwriter from this commitment appears limited. The average cost of standbys is 4.0% of gross proceeds for industrials and 2.4% for utilities, respectively. In best efforts and firm commitment offers, the underwriter receives a fixed fee (which, as noted above, typically is established through

[5] For international evidence on equity issues, see Bøhren, Eckbo & Michalsen [1992] (Norway), Dehnert [1991] (Australia), Hietala & Löyttyniemi [1991] (Finland), Kato & Schallheim [1991] (Japan), Loderer & Zimmerman [1987] (Switzerland), MacCulloch [1990] (New Zealand), and Marsh [1979] (the UK).

[6] Firms issuing shares through DRIPs and ESOPs generally absorb commissions and other expenses associated with the sale of stock.

Table 8

Equity security issues by firms listed on the Tokyo Stock Exchange, 1956–1990 [a]

	Rights offerings		Public offerings		Private placements		Exercise of warrants		Total	
	No. of issues	Amount raised (¥bils.)	No. of issues	Amount raised (¥bils.)	No. of issues	Amount raised (¥bils.)	No. of issues	Amount raised (¥bils.)	No. of issues	Amount raised (¥bils.)
1956	294	157	36	4	11	2	–	–	341	164
1957	292	199	40	5	10	1	–	–	342	205
1958	147	160	30	5	3	0	–	–	180	165
1959	158	153	60	10	3	0	–	–	211	183
1960	275	331	100	35	4	1	–	–	379	387
1961	465	632	224	80	6	1	–	–	695	712
1962	554	587	171	20	9	3	–	–	734	609
1963	508	410	157	38	8	7	–	–	673	453
1964	434	623	85	4	14	3	–	–	533	631
1965	95	115	19	1	8	3	–	–	122	117
1966	173	202	34	1	24	8	–	–	231	212
1967	190	194	68	5	13	4	–	–	261	202
1968	201	303	80	10	12	2	–	–	293	315
1969	300	447	145	55	14	5	–	–	469	506
1970	316	538	203	138	18	5	–	–	537	681
1971	220	409	147	84	24	44	–	–	391	637
1972	180	284	275	665	43	92	–	–	498	1,041
1973	177	344	256	565	45	30	–	–	478	939
1974	214	244	193	277	31	23	–	–	438	544
1975	166	771	103	222	16	8	–	–	285	1,001
1976	102	180	181	500	11	9	–	–	294	689
1977	120	291	238	604	48	29	–	–	406	923
1978	86	267	195	565	62	84	–	–	313	897
1979	64	262	229	629	42	63	–	–	325	953
1980	34	90	218	881	28	81	–	–	280	1,052
1981	67	494	249	1,396	20	37	–	–	336	1,928
1982	45	224	209	1,103	14	21	4	2	272	1,349
1983	18	135	72	472	23	165	18	30	131	802
1984	23	91	128	821	18	68	39	66	208	1,043
1985	40	183	103	506	18	33	70	137	231	859
1986	27	69	76	400	18	30	118	373	235	673
1987	26	436	99	1,394	22	109	241	1,074	388	3,013
1988	40	787	157	2,582	23	104	316	1,309	536	4,782
1989	32	726	227	5,830	22	102	436	2,190	718	8,849
1990	39	825	121	1,975	21	315	397	678	578	3,792

[a] Source: The Tokyo Stock Exchange Fact Book, multiple years. The table includes foreign issues.

negotiations but sometimes by competitive bids). Average firm commitment costs are 6.1% for industrials and 4.2% for utilities.

While not shown in Table 9, flotation costs as a percentage of the gross proceeds are also found to be higher for common stock offers than convertible debt offers of

Table 9

Mean (median) underwriter compensation and other flotation expenses for the sample of seasoned common stock offers by U.S. firms, classified by the type of firm and method of offering, 1963–1981[a]

Flotation costs	Firm commitments		Standby rights		Uninsured rights	
	Ind	Utl	Ind	Utl	Ind	Utl
Number of observations	351	639	42	89	26	23
Underwriter compensation ($ millions)	1.47 (1.03)	1.78 (1.32)	1.20 (0.47)	0.56 (0.34)	–	–
Other expenses ($ millions)	0.16 (0.15)	0.14 (0.12)	0.36 (0.19)	0.38 (0.29)	0.11 (0.09)	0.45 (0.19)
Total costs ($ millions)	1.72 (1.28)	1.92 (1.45)	1.59 (0.68)	0.94 (0.72)	0.11 (0.09)	0.45 (0.19)
Total costs/ gross proceeds (%)	6.09 (5.53)	4.23 (3.82)	4.03 (3.32)	2.44 (2.07)	1.82 (0.94)	0.51 (0.22)
Total costs/ market value common (%)	1.05 (0.68)	0.49 (0.41)	0.93 (0.57)	0.22 (0.18)	0.80 (0.30)	0.05 (0.02)

[a] Source: Eckbo & Masulis [1992]. 'Ind' denotes industrial issues, and 'Utl' denotes public utility. Data sources are the SEC Registered Offerings Statistics data tape and issue prospectuses. The cost of the offer price discount in firm commitment offers is not included, nor is the value of any 'Green Shoe' options. In the standby rights category, the underwriter's compensation is computed using the actual takeup fee based on subscription information.

comparable size. In turn, convertible debt offers are found to have higher flotation costs than nonconvertible debt offers, controlling for issue size. This suggests that the debt–equity issuance decision can be influenced by the lower flotation costs associated with debt issues. It is also consistent with the proposition that flotation costs are positively related to the variability of the security's price (shown below).

Furthermore, examining firm commitment offers by public utilities, Bhagat & Frost [1986] document that the total underwriter compensation is significantly higher for negotiated contracts than in contracts where the terms have been determined through competitive bidding by underwriters. Despite this fact, utilities almost exclusively rely on negotiated contracts. Also, Bhagat, Marr & Thompson [1985] report that total underwriter compensation has decreased with the shelf registration procedure. Denis [1993], however, presents contradictory evidence that shelf issues are not less costly, but appeared so due to selection biases and the inclusion of zero underwriting fee 'bought deals' in the shelf sample. Denis [1991] also finds more negative announcement effects for shelf issues, which is consistent with a greater adverse selection effect due to the less complete 'due diligence' investigation that occurs in the shelf process. Denis [1991] also observes that the shelf registration procedure has not gained widespread popularity among equity issuers.

In sum,

Observation 10 *SPO flotation costs.* The empirical evidence indicates that direct flotation costs on average

(i) are higher for common stock offers than for debt offers of comparable size, and higher for convertible debt than for nonconvertible debt;
(ii) are higher for industrial issuers than for public utilities;
(iii) are lowest for uninsured rights and highest for firm commitments, with standbys in between; and
(iv) are higher for negotiated than for competitive underwritten contracts.

Several studies have identified issue characteristics which are correlated with direct flotation costs. Examples of such studies are Smith [1977], Hansen & Pinkerton [1982], Smith & Dhatt [1984], Bhagat, Marr & Thompson [1985], Bhagat & Frost [1986], Booth & Smith [1986], Ritter [1987], Hansen [1989], Hansen & Torregrosa [1992], Eckbo & Masulis [1992], and Bøhren, Eckbo & Michalsen [1992]. Table 10 shows the coefficient estimates in cross-sectional regressions on such characteristics (Table 10A for industrial issuers and Table 10B for utility issuers). The regressions, which are highly significant, are based on the sample of SPOs in Eckbo & Masulis [1992]. The dependent variable is direct flotation cost as a percent of offer proceeds, while the explanatory variables include offer size, percentage change in shares outstanding, issuer's regulatory status, stock systematic and unsystematic risk, shareholder concentration, and binary variables for the flotation method.

The regression intercept is positive and significant indicating a fixed component to flotation expenses. Furthermore, the significance of the natural log of the issue's gross proceeds (PRO), and PRO^2 indicate that the flotation cost function is decreasing and convex in the gross proceeds of the offer (i.e., economies of scale). The log of equity capitalization per shareholder ($SCON$) is significantly negative, indicating that shareholder concentration lowers flotation costs.[7] The standard deviation of the issuer's daily stock return (ST) is positive and statistically significant for firm commitment issues, probably because greater stock risk increases underwriting risk and therefore the underwriter fee. This effect is to a smaller degree reflected in the standby rights issues. In the pure rights category, ST is

[7] Firms with concentrated ownership tend to obtain subscription precommitments which lowers flotation costs. However, Eckbo & Masulis [1992] find that the statistical impact of the ownership concentration variable is not fully explained by the presence of subscription precommitments. Hansen & Pinkerton [1982] use a nonlinear flotation cost function that includes ownership concentration to estimate the hypothetical flotation cost of a rights offer for a sample of firms that choose the firm commitment method, and conclude that rights offers would have entailed higher costs. However, their t-statistics are conditional on the functional form used to generate the flotation cost structure and are therefore difficult to assess. Also, Smith & Dhatt [1984] argue that the Hansen–Pinkerton shareholder concentration parameter is biased, and that correction for this bias leaves rights offers as the cheapest flotation method.

Table 10A

OLS parameter estimates in cross-sectional regressions of percentage flotation costs against issue characteristics and offering method, for *industrial* issuers in the U.S., 1963–1981[a] (t-statistics in parentheses)

	Const. α_0	*PRO* α_1	PRO^2 α_2	*SCON* α_3	*ST* α_4	ΔSHR α_5	D_1 α_6	D_2 α_7	$\overline{R^2}$	F value
I. Firm commitments ($N = 334$)										
(1)	0.588	−0.093	0.004	−0.003	0.504	0.024	–	–	0.73	179.5
	(11.09)	(−8.74)	(7.41)	(−3.44)	(5.87)	(3.49)				
(2)	0.584	−0.091	0.004	0.004	0.573	–	–	–	0.72	214.1
	(10.83)	(−8.42)	(7.12)	(−5.00)	(6.74)					
II. Standby rights ($N = 41$)										
(3)	0.427	−0.070	0.003	−0.005	0.368	0.003	–	–	0.75	25.2
	(6.60)	(−5.28)	(4.63)	(−2.03)	(1.53)	(0.23)				
(4)	0.427	−0.070	0.003	−0.005	0.393	–	–	–	0.75	32.3
	(6.68)	(−5.35)	(4.69)	(−2.11)	(1.85)					
III. Pure rights ($N = 26$)										
(5)	0.351	−0.069	0.003	−0.003	0.421	−0.007	–	–	0.84	28.9
	(6.39)	(−5.56)	(4.88)	(−1.50)	(2.64)	(−0.92)				
(6)	0.340	−0.067	0.003	−0.002	0.371	–	–	–	0.84	36.2
	(6.36)	(−5.51)	(4.82)	(−1.19)	(2.48)					
IV. All three flotation methods ($N = 403$)										
(7)	0.336	−0.057	0.002	−0.003	0.451	0.010	0.026	0.044	0.76	181.5
	(9.43)	(−7.93)	(6.20)	(−4.32)	(5.56)	(1.95)	(12.16)	(14.08)		
(8)	0.339	−0.057	0.002	−0.004	0.496	–	0.026	0.043	0.76	209.7
	(9.47)	(−7.88)	(6.17)	(−5.33)	(6.35)		(12.03)	(13.9)		

[a] The data underlying these regressions are from Eckbo & Masulis [1992]. The flotation cost in firm commitment offerings includes underpricing relative to the market price on the day prior to the offering day.

Variable definitions:

PRO = natural log of gross proceeds of offering,

PRO^2 = square (PRO),

SCON = natural log of share value at the offering divided by number of shareholders (based on offering price),

ST = standard deviation of issuer's daily stock return over 450 trading days starting 60 days prior to the Wall Street Journal offering announcement,

ΔSHR = percentage change in shares outstanding due to the offering (new shares divided by old plus new shares),

D_1 = indicator variable of offering method (standby or firm commitment offering = 1),

D_2 = 2nd indicator variable of offering method (firm commitment offering = 1),

significant for industrial issuers but not for utilities.[8] Finally, the percent change in shares (ΔSHR) is statistically significant only for the sample of industrial firm commitments, where it receives a positive coefficient. As discussed later in this

[8] Since a rights offer requires a minimum 14-day subscription period, it is possible that *ST* represents a proxy for the risk of offer failure due to random changes in stock price over the

Table 10B

OLS parameter estimates in cross-sectional regressions of percentage flotation costs against issue characteristics and offering method, for *utility* issuers in the U.S., 1963–1981[a] (t-statistics in parentheses)

	Const. α_0	PRO α_1	PRO^2 α_2	$SCON$ α_3	ST α_4	ΔSHR α_5	D_1 α_6	D_2 α_7	$\overline{R^2}$	F value
I. Firm commitments ($N = 629$)										
(1)	0.500	−0.083	0.004	−0.006	1.717	0.0001	–	–	0.34	65.3
	(9.19)	(−7.98)	(7.39)	(−5.43)	(9.82)	(0.009)				
(2)	0.500	−0.083	0.004	−0.006	1.719	–	–	–	0.34	81.7
	(9.20)	(−7.99)	(7.40)	(−5.89)	(9.83)					
II. Standby rights ($N = 85$)										
(3)	0.470	−0.080	0.004	−0.008	0.683	0.010	–	–	0.57	23.9
	(6.62)	(−5.72)	(5.20)	(−3.85)	(2.00)	(0.28)				
(4)	0.474	−0.081	0.004	−0.008	0.679	–	–	–	0.58	30.3
	(6.83)	(−5.86)	(5.35)	(−3.93)	(2.00)					
III. Pure rights ($N = 22$)										
(5)	0.156	−0.024	0.001	−0.003	0.198	0.001	–	–	0.73	13.0
	(3.67)	(−3.02)	(2.77)	(−2.14)	(0.90)	(0.03)				
(6)	0.155	−0.024	0.001	−0.003	0.198	–	–	–	0.75	17.2
	(3.86)	(−3.19)	(2.93)	(−2.21)	(0.93)					
IV. All three flotation methods ($N = 738$)										
(7)	0.433	−0.078	0.003	−0.005	1.573	0.003	0.023	0.013	0.48	99.5
	(10.10)	(−9.29)	(8.59)	(−6.08)	(10.05)	(0.29)	(13.04)	(3.53)		
(8)	0.433	−0.078	0.003	−0.006	1.574		0.023	0.013	0.48	116.2
	(10.12)	(−9.30)	(8.60)	(−6.60)	(10.07)		(13.22)	(3.52)		

[a] See Table 10A for variable definitions.

survey, it is possible that larger percentage changes in shares subject shareholders to greater costs of adverse selection, raising the underwriter fee for the more risky industrial firm commitment issues.

The indicator variables D_1 and D_2 in the pooled regressions adjust for the flotation method and support the earlier evidence from Table 9 that rights offers have the lowest direct flotation costs. D_1 separates underwritten offers (standbys and firm commitments) from nonunderwritten offers (uninsured rights), while D_2 separates firm commitments from all rights offers. The positive and statistically significant impact of both D_1 and D_2 for industrial issuers suggests that the choice of an underwritten offer (standby or firm commitment) increases the flotation costs, and that the choice of a firm commitment offer increases these costs further. For utilities, the D_1 parameter is significant and positive indicating again that underwritten offers are more costly. However, the D_2 parameter is insignificant, indicating that

rights subscription period (where failure involves higher costs of alternative sources of capital). The greater the expected failure costs, the greater the issuer's distributional/selling effort which in turn translates into higher 'other' expenses in the sample of industrial rights issues.

firm commitment and standby fees in utility offers are close in magnitude after controlling for the other explanatory variables in the regression model.

Note that the coefficient estimates in Table 10 are remarkably similar across flotation methods and across issuer types. Furthermore, while not shown in the table, the coefficient estimates do not change much if one reestimates the model excluding post-1975 offers (as shown in Table 6, 90% of the rights offers took place before 1976). Thus, the results in Table 10 strongly indicate that the respective issue characteristics represent fundamental determinants of direct flotation costs.[9]

Observation 11 *Flotation costs and offer characteristics.* The empirical evidence indicates that direct flotation costs depend on issuer characteristics such as gross proceeds (scale economies), stock risk (value of underwriter guarantee), and shareholder concentration (rights distribution costs). Direct flotation costs remain lowest for uninsured rights and highest for firm commitments after controlling for these issue characteristics.

It has become common for an issuer to grant the underwriter an *overallotment option* which allows the underwriter to purchase additional shares at the offer price to the extent that the issue is oversubscribed, up to a maximum of 15% of the offer size. The value to the issuer of granting this option lies in its positive effect on the underwriter's selling effort in the period prior to the public offer date. Aggressive selling reduces the risk of offer failure but increases the risk of oversubscription. Thus, the cost to the underwriter of unmet oversubscription (in terms of disappointed clients) is reduced by allowing additional shares to be issued ex post. Overallotment options are very common in firm commitment IPOs and less frequent in firm commitment SPOs. Hansen, Fuller & Janjigian [1987] report that the value of the overallotment options represents a very small fraction of a typical seasoned stock issue's gross proceeds.

In a rights issue, and in shares offered through DRIPs, the subscription price discount acts as a stock dividend paid to current shareholders. This discount is defined as the difference between the offer price and the closing secondary market price the day before or after the offer, divided by that same secondary market price. In the U.S., this discount is typically 15–20% for rights, and 3–5% for new share DRIPS. The offer price discount represents a wealth transfer to the purchasers and if these are outside investors, this represents as an additional flotation cost component. The discount in underwritten IPOs is substantial, on average 15–20% and largest in best efforts offers [Ibbotson, 1975; Ritter, 1984, 1987]. In contrast, there is very little evidence of underpricing in underwritten SPOs when compared to the prior trading day's opening, closing, high or low prices [Loderer, Sheenan & Kadlec, 1991; Eckbo & Masulis, 1992].

[9] For evidence on the determinants of rights offer flotation costs in the U.K. and in Norway, see Marsh [1980] and Bøhren, Eckbo & Michalsen [1992]. Also, see Hansen & Torregrosa [1992] who examine underwriter spread determinants for common stock offers and find a negative relation to firm size, the log of offering size, managerial stock ownership and institutional ownership and a positive relation to residual stock risk and offer size.

When adding direct flotation expenses, underwriter fees and underpricing costs, it is clear that the average IPO is more expensive than the average SPO. Total flotation costs in the U.S. as a percent of offering proceeds in IPOs average 21% for firm commitments and 32% for best efforts [Ritter, 1987], compared to the average 6% cost for industrial issuers shown in Table 9. In both IPOs and SPOs, there are significant scale economies.[10] But IPOs have a much smaller average size, which is one explanation why the average SPO has lower percent flotation costs. Another reason is a SPO has lower price uncertainty due to the existence of an active secondary market prior to the offering which implies lower risk of offer failure. For IPOs, the offer failure rate is quite high [Ritter, 1987], while cancellations or postponements of SPOs occur only rarely [Mikkelson & Partch, 1988]. Offer failure causes issuers additional costs of obtaining funds from alternative sources, or of abandoning promising investment projects.

Observation 12 *Issue underpricing and overallotment options.* Underpricing, while large in IPOs, is negligible in firm commitment SPOs. Overallotment options, which are common in firm commitment IPOs, are much less frequent in SPOs, and the average value of this option is a very small percent of the SPO's gross proceeds. Overall, flotation costs as a percent of offering proceeds, and the risk of offer failure, are substantially higher for IPOs than for SPOs.

3.3. Additional costs of rights

As highlighted by Smith [1977], Hansen [1989], and Table 9–10 above, the preference by U.S. managers for the relatively expensive firm commitment flotation method over rights offers is puzzling. In particular, since the value of the right increases with the subscription price discount, the rights issuer can virtually guarantee success of the offer by properly adjusting the subscription price. So why not select the cheaper rights method?

Smith [1977] suggests that the overwhelming preference for firm commitment SPOs may reflect an agency problem. For example, managers may receive personal benefits from underwriters who are selected to handle the equity issue. Second, there may be pressure from the boardroom; Herman [1981] finds that 21% of the 200 largest nonfinancials and 27% of the 100 largest industrial companies have one or more investment bankers on their board of directors. The resulting conflict of interest may lead to an excessive use of the underwritten flotation methods. Third, while a rights offer is unlikely to substantially change the distribution of voting rights, a sale to the public through an underwriter can increase shareholder dispersion and therefore reduce shareholder monitoring of managers, thereby enhancing potential manager welfare.

[10] Evidence of scale economies is shown in Table 10, above. SEC staff reports, Smith [1977], and Smith & Dhatt [1984] also find that flotation costs as a percent of the gross proceeds for the typical offer falls significantly as the dollar value of the offerings rises, but at a decreasing rate.

An alternative explanation for the apparent demise of the rights offer is that other important shareholder borne costs of the rights offer method have been ignored or underestimated, which value-maximizing managers have taken into account. Examples of such costs are given below, and include capital gains taxes, transaction costs of selling rights in the secondary market, wealth transfers due to anti-dilution clauses which are a standard feature in convertible securities and warrants, and costs due to asymmetric information.

(i) Capital gains taxes: In a rights offer, shareholders who do not wish to purchase shares of the issue must sell their rights (or subscribe and sell the shares) in order to avoid losing the value of the subscription price discount. These sales are subject to capital gains taxes, which are increasing in the subscription price discount, discouraging large discounts.

(ii) Stock liquidity and transaction costs of reselling rights: The resale of rights by current shareholders takes place on organized exchanges, entailing dealer spreads and brokerage fees. Since shareholders avoid these costs when the firm employs an underwriter to sell its new shares, a rights offer carries a transaction cost disadvantage for shareholders uninterested in subscribing to the issue. This relative cost disadvantage is exacerbated if the efforts of the investment bankers tend to increase stock liquidity and reduce bid–ask spreads when underwritten methods are used.

(iii) Arbitrage activity and the risk of rights offer failure: Investors can use rights as warrants to hedge their short sale positions in a firm's stock. This encourages increased short selling of the stock, but as additional short positions are opened, the stock price will tend to be depressed as resulting sell orders rise (at least within the bid–ask spread). Thus, between the announcement of rights offer terms and offer expiration, this short-selling activity tends to keep the stock price down, reducing the attractiveness of exercising rights for most stockholders. This creates additional uncertainty for issuers as to the ultimate rights offer subscription level, which can cause the issuer to extend the expiration of the rights offer, increasing flotation costs and creating continued downward pressure on stock price for the extended life of a rights offer.

(iv) Anti-dilution clauses and wealth transfers to convertible security holders: If a firm has convertible securities or warrants outstanding with anti-dilution clauses in place, then issuing rights at discounts can trigger automatic reductions in conversion rates of these securities as discussed in Kaplan [1965] and Myhal [1990]. These anti-dilution clauses are likely to result in improved positions for the convertible security holders, shifting wealth away from the common stock holders who are the residual claimants. As a result, there is an added incentive for firms with convertible securities outstanding to avoid issuing rights at deep discounts.

Observation 13 *Additional costs of rights*. Additional shareholder-borne costs which tend to reduce the attractiveness of rights arise from capital gains taxes, reduced stock liquidity, transaction costs of selling rights, arbitrage activity which affects the risk of offer failure, and anti-dilution clauses which induce wealth transfers to convertible security holders.

There is currently insufficient empirical evidence to dismiss these additional costs of rights offers as immaterial, or to argue that any single one is the primary reason for the demise of the rights issue. Smith [1977] estimates that the capital gains tax disadvantage of rights, in a worst-case scenario, is at most 2% of offering proceeds in the U.S., but this was before the capital gains tax rate was raised. Hansen [1989] presents some evidence of selling pressure in the secondary market for rights.[11] Kothare [1993] documents a negative effect of rights offers on stock liquidity and bid–ask spreads over the rights period, while Lease, Masulis & Page [1992] find bid–ask spreads to fall subsequent to firm commitments. Third, Eckbo & Masulis [1992] find some evidence that the total number of convertible security issues has risen over the period when firms have switched from rights to firm commitment offers.

As reviewed in Section 4 below, the literature on the valuation effects of seasoned equity announcements strongly suggests the presence of important information asymmetries in the primary market for common stock. Perhaps the most promising approach to resolve the rights offer puzzle is to explicitly recognize the role of information asymmetries on the flotation method choice. Recent attempts to capture this role are reviewed in Section 5.

4. Valuation effects of SPO announcements

4.1. Summary of evidence

A large number of studies provide estimates of the valuation effects of security issue announcements by exchange listed firms. Table 11 summarizes the main findings of the literature on SPOs in the U.S., classified by type of security issued (common stock, straight/convertible preferred stock/bonds), by flotation method (uninsured rights offers, standby rights, firm commitments), and by issuer type (industrial firm, public utility). Table 12 summarizes the evidence on other types of common stock and convertible security issue announcements by U.S. firms (private placements, repurchase/exchange offers, conversion-forcing calls, DRIPs/ESOPs, and offer cancellations/withdrawals), as well as on announcement effects of common stock SPOs in other countries.[12]

The well known negative price impact of firm commitment SPO announcements in the U.S. (on average -3% industrial issuers over the two-day announcement interval) has fascinated financial economists since its was documented in studies

[11] Also, see Table 4 of Marsh [1979] for some U.K. evidence.

[12] A thorough discussion of the econometrics of event studies is provided by Rex Thompson in another chapter of this volume. In the following, statistical inferences are made on the basis of average announcement-induced abnormal returns and of parameters estimated in cross-sectional regressions with announcement returns as dependent variable. While potentially important, we make no attempt to adjust the conclusions of the various studies reviewed for the impact on announcement returns of partial anticipation of the event [e.g., Malatesta & Thompson, 1985] or of selection bias due to managerial private information [Eckbo, Maksimovic & Williams, 1990].

Table 11

Average two-day abnormal common stock returns and average sample size (in parenthesis) from studies of announcements of SPOs by NYSE/AMEX listed U.S. companies. Returns are weighted averages by sample size of the returns reported by the respective studies (all returns *not* marked with a '*' are significantly different from zero at the 5% level).

Type of security offered	Flotation method	Type of issuer	
		Industrial	Utility
Common stock	Firm commitment	−3.1 [a] (216)	−0.8 [b] (424)
	Standby rights	−1.5 [c] (32)	−1.4 [d] (84)
	Rights	−1.4 [e] (26)	0.2 [e] (27)
Preferred stock	Firm commitment	−0.78* [f] (14)	0.1* [g] (249)
Convertible preferred stock	Firm commitment	−1.4 [g] (53)	−1.4 [g] (8)
Convertible bonds	Firm commitment	−2.0 [h] (104)	n.a. [i]
	Rights	−1.1 [j] (26)	n.a. [i]
Straight bonds	Firm commitment	−0.3* [k] (210)	−0.13* [l] (140)
	Rights	0.4* [l] (11)	n.a.

[a] Asquith & Mullins [1986] (1963–1981, N = 128, −3.0); Masulis & Korwar [1986] (1963–1980, N=388, −3.3); Mikkelson & Partch [1986] (1972–1982, N = 80, −3.6); Bhaghat & Hess [1986] (1963–1978, N = 95, −4.3); Eckbo & Masulis [1992] (1963–1981, N = 389, −3.3).

[b] Asquith & Mullins [1986] (N = 264, −0.9); Masulis & Korwar [1986] (N = 584, −0.7); Bhaghat & Frost [1986] (N = 201, −1.0); Eckbo & Masulis [1992] (N = 646, −0.8).

[c] Hansen [1989] (1963–1985, N = 22, −2.6); Eckbo & Masulis [1992] (N = 41, −1.0).

[d] Hansen [1989] (N = 80, −2.3); Eckbo & Masulis [1992] (N = 87, −0.5).

[e] Eckbo & Masulis [1992].

[f] Linn & Pinegar [1988] (1962–1984, N = 14, −1.295*); Mikkelson & Partch [1986] (N = 14, −0.26*).

[g] Linn & Pinegar [1988].

[h] Dann & Mikkelson [1984] (1970–1979, N = 132, −2.3); Eckbo [1986] (1964–1981, N = 53, −1.9); Mikkelson & Partch [1986] (N = 33, −2.0); Jangigian [1987] (1968–1983, N = 234, −1.7); Hansen & Crutchley [1990] (1975–1982, N = 67, −1.5).

[i] Not available (virtually none are issued by utilities).

[j] Dann & Mikkelson [1984] (N = 38, −1.2); Eckbo [1986] (N = 14, −0.8*).

[k] Dann & Mikkelson [1984] (N = 150, −0.37*); Eckbo [1986] (N = 310, −0.1*); Mikkelson & Partch [1986] (N = 171, −0.23*).

[l] Eckbo [1986].

Table 12

Average two-day announcement period abnormal stock return associated with equity issues or retirements by means of nonstandard flotation methods, combination primary-secondary offerings, swaps, exchange and repurchase offers, conversion-forcing debt calls, cancellations and withdrawals, and international stock offerings. (All returns *not* marked with a '*' are statistically significant at the 5% level)

Study	Flotation method/ type of offer	Sample size	Two-day mean ann. ret. (%)
I. Primary issues of seasoned common stock, nonstandard flotation methods			
Bhagat, Marr & Thompson [1985]	Shelf registration	83	−1.2
Blackwell, Marr & Spivey [1990]	Shelf registration		
Denis [1991]	Shelf registration	343	−2.6
Wruck [1989]	Private placement	99	1.9*
Schipper & Smith [1986]	Equity carve-out	76	0.7*
Dubofsky & Bierman [1988]	Dividend reinvestment plan	53	0.8
Chang [1990]	Employee stock ownership plan	165	3.7*
II. Combination primary-secondary offerings of common stock			
Masulis & Korwar [1986]	firm commitment, no management sales	186	−2.2*
Korajczyk, Lucas & McDonald [1990]	firm commitment, with management sales	56	−4.6*
III. Swaps, exchange offers, and repurchases of common stock			
Masulis [1980a]	Exchange, common stock for debt	20	−9.9*
Masulis [1980a]	Exchange, common for preferred	30	−2.6*
Masulis [1980a]	Exchange, preferred for common	9	8.3*
Masulis [1980a]	Exchange, debt for common	52	14.0*
Lease & Pinegar [1986]	Exchange, common for preferred	30	−1.5*
Lease & Pinegar [1986]	Exchange, preferred for common	15	8.1*
Finnerty [1985]	Private swap, common for debt	113	−1.1*
Rogers & Owers [1985]	Private swap, common for debt	74	−1.1*
Israel, Ofer & Siegel [1989]	Swap, common stock for debt	125	−1.6
Lease & Pinegar [1986]	Exchange, preferred for common	15	8.1*
Masulis [1980b]	Tend. off. repurchase of common	199	16.4*
Masulis [1980b]	Debt. off. repurchase of common	45	21.9*
Dann [1981]	Tend. off. repurchase of common	142	15.4*
Vermaelen [1981]	Tend. off. repurchase of common	131	14.1*
Vermaelen [1981]	Open mkt. repurchases of common	243	3.4*
IV. Convertible debt and preferred stock calls			
Mikkelson [1981]	Calls forcing conversion of convertible debt	113	−2.1*
Mikkelson [1981]	Calls forcing conversion of convertible preferred stock	57	−0.4
Campbell, Ederington & VanKudre [1991]	Calls forcing conversion of bonds	167	−1.5
Singh, Cowan & Nayar [1991]	Call of convertible bonds (underwritten)	65	−2.0
Singh, Cowan & Nayar [1991], Janjigian [1987]	Call of convertible bonds (not underwritten)	64	−0.8

Table 12 (cont'd)

Study	Flotation method/ type of offer	Sample size	Two-day mean ann. ret. (%)
V. Cancellations and withdrawals of stock offers			
Officer & Smith [1986]	Withdrawals of nonconvertible debt	30	−0.4
Officer & Smith [1986]	Withdrawal of common stock offering	31	2.4
Mikkelson & Partch [1988]	Withdrawn equity offering	62	1.3
VI. Common stock issues, international evidence			
Marsh [1979]	U.K.; rights and standbys	997	2.1 (month)
Hietala & Loyttyniemi [1991]	Finland; rights and standbys	63	4.9*
Kang [1990]	Korea; rights and standbys	89	1.5
Loderer & Zimmerman [1987]	Switzerland; rights and standbys	99	2.0 (month)
Eckbo & Verma [1992]	Canada; all SPO methods	69	−4.0*
Bøhren, Eckbo & Michalsen [1992]	Norway; rights and standbys	206	0.80*
Dehnert [1991]	Australia, rights and standbys	158	−2.0*

by Asquith & Mullins [1986] and Masulis & Korwar [1986]. This fascination has been increased by the findings that there are no significant negative price impacts from announcements of (1) straight debt issues as reported by Eckbo [1986], (2) equity issues sold through rights offers as reported by Eckbo & Masulis [1992], and (3) private placements as reported by Wruck [1989].

The negative firm commitment evidence is further confirmed in Barclay & Litzenberger [1988] who study transaction data and pinpoint the minute that a common stock offer announcement crosses the Broad tape (but only examine equity offers over a short sample period). Also, as shown in Table 12, Officer & Smith [1986] and Mikkelson & Partch [1988] report that common stock offer *cancellations* are associated with a significantly positive average announcement effect of slightly smaller magnitude than the average negative effect associated with stock offer announcements.

Common stock can also be issued indirectly through a number of alternative financing mechanisms such as the issuance of convertible securities which can be viewed as a delayed stock offer. As seen from Table 11, the evidence from these event studies is that public offers of convertible debt are associated with significant negative announcement effects of a magnitude (on average −2%) close to that found for firm commitment stock offers, though the offering size tends to be much larger. As shown in Table 12, a similar result is obtained when estimating the market reaction to debt calls which force conversion into common stock [Mikkelson, 1981; Campbell, Ederington & Vankudre, 1991; Singh, Cowan & Nayar, 1991]. The conjecture that the market interprets a convertible security offer as equivalent to a stock offer might be questioned given that a number of studies conclude that managers do not call convertibles as soon as they can force conversion. However, Asquith [1992] finds that once the call protection clauses in these issues are taken into account, the evidence clearly favours the conclusion that managers do force conversion to common stock as soon as it is feasible.

Table 11 also reveals a systematic relationship between the two-day announcement effect and the choice of flotation method by industrial issuers. Firm commitment issue announcements command the largest negative market reaction and, while not shown in Table 11, the market reaction is more negative the larger the issue size. Standby rights issues result in a significantly negative effect which is approximately half of the firm commitment effect, while rights issues have an insignificant announcement effect. As shown in Table 12, nonnegative announcement effects are also reported by Dubofsky & Bierman [1988] and Chang [1990] for the adoption of DRIPs and ESOPs which, as noted earlier, in many ways are similar to periodic rights offers of stock.

The lack of a significant negative market reaction to the typical rights issue also characterizes much of the international evidence on seasoned equity offerings, as seen in Table 12, where rights/standby offers represent the primary flotation method. Studies of offer announcement effects by Marsh [1979] for standby rights issues in the UK, Loderer & Zimmerman [1987] for rights in Switzerland, Kang [1990] for rights and standbys in Korea, Hietala & Löyttyniemi [1991] for rights and standbys in Finland, and Bøhren, Eckbo & Michalsen [1992] for rights and standbys in Norway support this conclusion. Kato & Schallheim [1991] document insignificant two-day announcement effects for *firm commitment* offerings in Japan, while Dehnert [1991] and Eckbo & Verma [1992] find small negative announcement effects of rights and standby offers in Australia and Canada, respectively.

As shown in Table 12, studies of security exchange offers and swaps show that leverage-increasing transactions (debt in place of equity) on average produce significantly positive announcement returns, while leverage-decreasing transactions (equity in place of debt) cause significantly negative effects [Masulis, 1980a, 1983; McConnell & Schlarbaum, 1981]. Moreover, transactions with no change in leverage (debt for debt exchanges) produce insignificant announcement returns [Eckbo, 1986; Mikkelson & Partch, 1986].

Overall, from the evidence summarized in Tables 11 and 12, it appears that the market reaction to *public* offers is significantly different from zero *only* when the financing decision either increases or reduces the (potential) amount of outstanding common stock. Furthermore, the market reaction is negative when stock is increased and positive when stock is decreased. Thus, debt/preferred stock issues cause an insignificant market reaction unless exchanged for outstanding common stock, in which case the reaction is significantly positive. Stock issues cause a negative market reaction whether issued for cash or in exchange for more senior securities.

The above results for SPOs can be summarized as follows:

Observation 14 *Valuation effects of SPO announcements in the U.S.* For NYSE/AMEX listed firms, the average valuation effect (typically represented by the two-day announcement period abnormal stock returns) is

(i) nonpositive;
(ii) more negative the larger the size of the issue;
(iii) most negative for firm commitment offers, least negative (or zero) for uninsured rights, with standby rights in between;
(iv) most negative for common stock, least negative (zero) for straight debt/preferred stock, with convertible securities in between; and
(v) smaller for public utilities than for industrial issuers.

Furthermore,

Observation 15 *Valuation effects of SPO announcements internationally.* Internationally, where common stock is primarily issued using rights and standbys, the average market reaction is typically positive for uninsured rights and small but negative for standbys (Australia, Canada, Finland, Japan, Korea, Norway, Switzerland, UK).

Furthermore, the evidence on announcement effects of other (non-SPO) capital structure change announcements involving common stock is as follows:

Observation 16 *Valuation effects of other capital structure change announcements.* For exchange listed U.S. firms, the average valuation effect (typically represented by the two-day announcement period abnormal stock return) is

(i) positive for private placements of common stock;
(ii) positive when debt/preferred stock is exchanged for common and negative when common stock is exchanged for debt/preferred stock;
(iii) positive when common stock is repurchased (by tender offer/open market repurchase);
(iv) negative for convertible debt/preferred stock calls forcing conversion into common;
(v) positive for withdrawals or cancellations of common stock offerings; and
(vi) nonnegative for adoptions of DRIPs and ESOPs.

In the remainder of this section, we examine a number of competing hypotheses to explain this evidence. These hypotheses include (1) optimal capital structure effects, (2) asymmetric information and implied cash flow effects, (3) adverse selection effects, (4) effects of changes in ownership structure, and (5) effects of partial anticipation of SPOs.

4.2. Optimal capital structure effects

Theories of optimal capital structure generally imply a nonnegative market reaction to capital structure changes. These theories emphasize various debt and equity issuance trade-offs such as between the corporate tax advantage of debt and the costs of financial distress [Kraus & Litzenberger, 1973; Brennan & Schwartz, 1978], the personal tax disadvantage of debt and the impact of excess corporate tax deductions on the corporate tax advantage of debt [Miller, 1977; DeAngelo & Masulis, 1980], agency costs of debt and equity [Jensen & Meckling, 1976; Myers, 1977], and the effect of debt on the firm's competitive product market strategy [Brander & Lewis, 1987; Maksimovic, 1988]. In the presence of transaction costs, optimal capital structure adjustments (i.e., movements along a concave leverage-value function) are observed only when the benefit of the adjustment exceeds the required transaction cost [Fischer, Heinkel & Zechner, 1989], causing a nonnegative announcement effect.

The evidence of a nonpositive market reaction to SPO announcements of both debt and equity, and to equity-for-debt exchange offers and swaps, fails to support these optimal capital structure effects. However, as pointed out by Masulis [1983], tests of optimal capital structure effects using offer announcements are complicated because these announcements can also indicate to the market a shift in the issuer's economic situation which implies that the issuer's leverage-value function has shifted.[13] In addition, stock offers are often quickly offset by debt offers or additions of other types of debt. Thus, the long term leverage change is unlikely to be closely related to the equity issue induced leverage change. It is therefore unclear to what extent the theories of optimal capital structure can explain the evidence in Tables 11 and 12.

4.3. *Asymmetric information and cash flow effects*

In a world where managers have information about the firm that the market does not have, 'pure' capital structure changes are unlikely.[14] In this case, the announcement effect of a planned security offer will reflect the economic impact of the capital structure change conditional on the market's estimate of the change in managers' private information implied by the voluntary corporate decision.

Assuming it is prohibitively costly for low-quality firms to perfectly mimic high-quality firms, signalling models of Ross [1977], Leland & Pyle [1977], Heinkel [1982], and John & Williams [1985] imply that leverage-decreasing corporate events signal negative revisions in management expectations concerning the firm's future cash flows, thus causing a negative revaluation of the firm's shares. The Ross [1977] and Heinkel [1982] models symmetrically imply that leverage-increasing capital structure changes signal positive information about firm value, and result in positive announcement effects. The average market reaction to *exchange offers* shown in Table 12 is consistent with these predictions, while the nonpositive market reaction to public offers of *debt for cash* in Table 11 is inconsistent. Thus, the evidence regarding the relevance of the above signalling theories is mixed.

[13] See also Smith [1986] on this point.

[14] A 'pure' capital structure change is one which does not alter the market's perception of the issuing firm's real asset composition or investment policy.

Since SPOs for cash alter the issuer's *current* cash flow, these events provide insights concerning the empirical relevance of an alternative asymmetric information model of Miller & Rock [1985]. In their model, any larger-than-expected external financing by the firm reveals a smaller-than-expected current operating cash flow, which constitutes negative news to the market about current and expected future cash flows. Under this theory, the security offer announcement decreases the issuer's market price regardless of the direction of the implied leverage change. The significant negative market reaction to common stock and convertible debt issue announcements is consistent with this argument, while the insignificant market reaction to straight debt and preferred stock issue announcements is inconsistent. The Miller–Rock model also implies that the market reaction to external financing is more negative the greater the size of the offer. This prediction is supported by cross-sectional regressions of the market reaction to equity offers reported in Masulis & Korwar [1986] and Eckbo & Masulis [1992], but receives no support in the cross-sectional regressions of the market reaction to straight debt offers reported in Eckbo [1986].

Studies of post-issue changes in earnings provide additional perspective on the hypothesis that the negative valuation effect of firm commitment offers reflects expectations of lower future cash flows. Hansen & Crutchley [1990] examine abnormal earnings changes over several years subsequent to common stock, convertible debt and straight debt offerings. They report abnormal earnings declines following all three forms of financing. However, straight debt appears to be used after the abnormal earnings decline has been ongoing. In contrast, equity issuers finance in advance of earnings declines. Examining abnormal earnings declines over the subsequent three year period, they report that earnings are significantly more negative for common stock offerings and for relatively larger offerings of securities. Brous [1992] and Jain [1992] report that following common stock offers there are significant downward revisions in analysts' one year earnings forecasts and the size of the revisions is positively related to announcement returns.

Israel, Ofer & Siegel [1989] examine revisions in Valueline earnings forecasts following equity for debt swaps, which are an indirect method of equity issuance. They report that earnings forecasts are revised downward following the equity for debt swap. Furthermore, when firms repurchase shares in a tender offer, Hertzel & Jain [1991] report evidence that these announcements cause positive revisions in Valueline earnings forecasts. Investigating stock repurchases by tender offer, Dann, Masulis & Mayers [1991] report several forms of evidence of an increase in unexpected earnings. Overall, the evidence on post-offer earnings changes suggests that the market reaction to the issue announcement in part reflects market anticipation of future cash flow changes. This is supportive of the adverse selection model of the issuance process discussed below. However, direct evidence to support this conjecture is mixed as both Eckbo [1986] and Hansen & Crutchley [1990] fail to find a significant cross-sectional correlation between the announcement effect and future abnormal earnings, while Dann, Masulis & Mayers [1991] report a marginally significant relationship.

4.4. Adverse selection effects

In the adverse selection model of Myers & Majluf [1984], the issuing firm knows more than the market about the true value of the issuer's assets in place. Assuming managers have an incentive not to sell underpriced securities, the market now demands a price discount in order to hedge against the risk that the security offered is overvalued.[15] Krasker [1986] extends the Myers–Majluf analysis to allow managers to choose an offer's size and shows that firms with overpriced stock will have greater incentives to choose larger offers. Adverse selection effects are also caused by the underwriter's ability to allocate shares to its preferred clients in oversubscribed offers [Benveniste & Spindt, 1989], and by the presence of differentially informed investors which cause underpriced new issues to be oversubscribed while overvalued offers are not [Rock, 1986].

There are several potential solutions to the adverse selection problem which could in principle eliminate the cost borne by the high quality marginal issuer of stock. These include changing managerial incentives through compensation contracts [Dybvig & Zender, 1991]; issuing common stock through nontransferable rights to existing stockholders [Eckbo & Masulis, 1992]; communicating private information to the market through reliable financial intermediaries such as investment bankers who have built a reputation for truthful information disclosure [Booth & Smith, 1986; Titman & Trueman, 1986]; using private placements where sophisticated investors have access to proprietary firm information [Wruck, 1989]; maintaining excess financial slack (i.e., internally generated funds and a capacity to issue risk-free securities, as proposed by Myers & Majluf); and selling securities in separately incorporated subsidiaries termed 'equity carve-outs' in order to avoid some of the information asymmetry associated with buying residual claims in the parent company [Schipper & Smith, 1986; Nanda, 1991]. Also, Stein [1992] argues that issuing callable convertible debt instead of stock can lower the adverse selection problem, though not eliminate it.

The empirical evidence concerning the average market reaction to SPO announcements, summarized in Observation 14 above, is largely consistent with the adverse selection framework. That is, SPOs have nonpositive effects regardless of security type, and the average market reaction to equity issues is more negative the larger the issue and less negative the less risky the security issued. Moreover, the market reaction to equity issues is less negative for uninsured rights than for standbys, and is less negative for standbys than for firm commitment offers. This ordering of average announcement effects is consistent with the Eckbo & Masulis [1992] adverse selection model for the flotation method choice discussed in Section 5 below.

Furthermore, there is typically less adverse selection risk associated with a public utility issue than with an industrial issue. The investment and financing decisions of utilities are highly regulated, and public knowledge of regulatory policy lowers the probability that a utility announcing a stock offer is attempting to take advantage

[15] An extensive discussion of adverse selection models is presented in Kent Daniel and Sheridan Titman [1995, this volume].

of an informational asymmetry in the stock market. For example, stock offers may require state utility commission approval or SEC approval for utility holding companies. It also appears that state regulatory commissions often pressure utilities to make equity offers by withholding rate increase approval unless equity issues are made, which further lowers the anticipated adverse selection effect of such actions. Consequently, the adverse market reaction to a public sale of equity should be smaller for public utility issues than for industrial issues, as observed for firm commitment offers [Asquith & Mullins, 1986; Masulis & Korwar, 1986] and rights/standby offers [Eckbo & Masulis, 1992]. Similarly, the shelf registration procedure, which allows the issuer greater flexibility in terms of timing the equity offer, increases adverse selection effects and is found on average to cause larger negative announcement effects [Bhagat, Marr & Thompson, 1985; Denis, 1991].

4.5. Effects of changes in ownership structure

A large stock ownership position subjects the manager to the loss of significant diversification, so increasing management stock ownership acts as a credible signal of firm quality [Leland & Pyle, 1977; Grinblatt & Hwang, 1989]. On the other hand, owner/manager sales of equity in IPOs or SPOs creates greater incentives for managers to sell overvalued stock to outsiders.[16] This is one explanation for the finding of Masulis & Korwar [1986] that combination primary–secondary offers where management is lowering the dollar investment in the stock cause relatively large negative announcement returns.

Wruck [1989] examines announcements of private placement sales of common stock and finds a significantly positive 4.5% average announcement return. Unlike public stock offers, private placements tend to increase shareholder concentration. For firms with relatively low or high initial shareholder concentration, the offer-induced increase in shareholder concentration is positively related to the stock's announcement return. Private placements are also likely to minimize the potential asymmetry of information between the purchaser and the issuer of the stock since the private placement gives investors access to the issuer's operations and financial condition.

Using a sample of Canadian security issues, Eckbo & Verma [1992] test whether the market reaction to various forms of SPOs is driven by the implied change in the distribution of voting rights. Their tests are in part motivated by the theoretical work of, e.g., Harris & Raviv [1990], Stulz [1990], and Israel [1992], who link the firm's capital structure choice to corporate control considerations. For example, insiders may retain a certain fraction of the voting rights in order to maximize the value of the voting premium during a future takeover contest for the firm. Controlling for the distinction between equity and debt, Eckbo & Verma find some evidence that the market reaction to an offer announcement is more negative the greater the dilution of voting rights caused by the offering.

[16] Karpoff & Lee [1991] and Bøhren, Eckbo & Michalsen [1992] report that insiders on average sell stock prior to stock offers.

4.6. *Effects of partial anticipation*

To the extent that security offerings are predictable events, the announcement effects of SPOs listed in Table 11 reflect only the *unanticipated* component of the total valuation impact. This may not be a serious concern for most equity issues since these are relatively infrequent [Mikkelson & Partch, 1986]. However, some public utilities make frequent common stock offerings which should depress the likely market reactions to these events. On the other hand, debt issues are much more frequent than equity, and are in part predictable based on the known maturity structure of the firm's outstanding debt. Thus, it is possible that the generally insignificant announcement effect of debt offerings reflects an attenuation bias due to market anticipation of the issue rather than an inherently insignificant economic event per se.

Bayless & Chaplinsky [1991] provide some perspective on this question by developing a debt and equity offer prediction model. Their logit prediction model includes as explanatory variables stock risk measures, the firm's tax paying status, deviation of leverage from its long term level, proportion of intangible assets, the change in the stock's price, the change in stock market index and the change in interest rates. Using this model to classify announcements, they separately examine the price effects of debt and equity offer announcements according to whether or not the same type of security offer is predicted. They find that equity announcement effects are more negative when debt is predicted, while debt announcement effects are positive when equity is predicted and negative but close to zero when debt is predicted. Bayless & Chaplinsky also estimate cross-sectional regressions of the equity and debt offer announcements and find additional support for their event study results. Their findings are further evidence that firm commitment stock offers –but not debt offers– are greeted negatively by the market.[17]

Jung, Lee & Stultz [1992] also examine the predictability of debt versus equity offers. They report that Tobin's q, prior cumulative stock returns, tax payments divided by total assets and the index of leading indicators of economic activity are important predictive variables, which allow the debt–equity choice to be predicted with a large degree of accuracy once we condition on one of these securities issues being announced.

5. The choice of equity flotation method

5.1. *Rights vs. underwritten offers*

In Section 3, we observed that direct flotation costs of seasoned equity offers differ significantly across flotation methods, with the costs being highest for industrial firm commitment offers (on average 6% of offering proceeds for industrial

[17] Also see Jung, Kim & Stultz [1991].

issuers), lowest for uninsured rights (on average 1%), and with standby costs in between (on average 4%). Furthermore, the evidence in Section 4 indicates that the average market reaction to seasoned equity offers depends significantly on the flotation method. For example, the dollar value of the −3% average two-day announcement period price drop associated with firm commitment offers is equivalent to a loss of approximately 25% of the proceeds of the average issue. In contrast, there is no such economically significant price drop for the average rights issue, and only a moderate price drop for standby offers.

Thus, the choice between rights and underwritten offers significantly affects the total wealth effect of the equity issue decision. Heinkel & Schwartz [1986] and Eckbo & Masulis [1992] model this choice assuming the issuer is better informed than investors about the true value of the shares sold. In the Heinkel–Schwartz model, firms (1) sell the issue immediately to an *uninformed* underwriter for a nominal firm commitment fee, (2) select a standby rights offer where the underwriter charges an additional investigation cost in order to become sufficiently informed to correctly price the put option implicit in the standby underwriting contract, or (3) use uninsured rights and risk incurring a fixed failure cost if the issue is undersubscribed. In their model, the investigation cost associated with the standby contract helps separate high-quality from low-quality issuers. Thus, in equilibrium, only the highest quality issuers select the standby contract, the lowest quality firms select direct sale to the underwriter, while intermediate-quality issuers select uninsured rights.

The flotation cost structure assumed in the Heinkel & Schwartz model is, however, inconsistent with the evidence that firm commitment contracts are more expensive than standby contracts. Second, since only the highest quality firms elect to pay the investigation costs implied by a standby offerings the market reaction to the issue announcement is predicted to be most favorable for standby contracts, least favorable for firm commitments, with uninsured rights in between. This is also inconsistent with the evidence that uninsured rights issue announcements are associated with the most favorable market reaction.

Third, the Heinkel–Schwartz model implies that a rights issuer who privately expects the stock price to fall over the rights offer period will select a relatively low subscription price relative to the *current* market price in order to insure against offer failure. Consequently, market participants infer the issuer's private information from the magnitude of the offer price discount, with greater discounts causing larger downward adjustments in the stock's secondary market price. However, while this explanation for the apparent reluctance of managers to issue rights with a deep subscription price discount is interesting, it receives no direct support from cross-sectional regressions of the offer-day abnormal stock return on the offer price discount [Eckbo & Masulis, 1992].[18]

[18] Hietala & Löyttyniemi [1991] point to another signalling effect which can occur in an institutional setting such as the Finnish stock market, where firms apparently set their dividends as a percent of the *par* value of common stock. Since a stock issue does not change the par value, it implies a dividend increase unless the issuer simultaneously reduces the percentage dividend. If

Eckbo & Masulis [1992] present an alternative model for the flotation method choice which builds on the Myers & Majluf [1984] adverse selection model where a firm faces a profitable investment opportunity that requires a commonly known level of new equity capital. The firm's decision to issue and invest depends on the value of the project, b, the cost of selling under or overpriced stock, c, and direct flotation costs, f. Managers, who are assumed to maximize the intrinsic (full information) value of the firm's shares, elect to issue and invest if and only if the net issue benefit is nonnegative, that is, when $b - (c + f) \geq 0$. Thus, a decision to issue generally signals a truncation of the upper tail of the distribution of share intrinsic values.

The Eckbo–Masulis model differs from the Myers–Majluf framework in that managers can select from alternative flotation methods including rights offers where current shareholders can subscribe to the issue, and standby and firm commitment methods where underwriters have some ability to evaluate and credibly certify the true quality of the shares sold.[19] Stock sales to current shareholders are essentially treated as another source of 'financial slack' (i.e., exogenously given internal sources of funds), which reduces the size of the issue offered to outside investors. As in the Krasker [1986] model, a smaller sale of stock to outside investors lowers the expected adverse selection effect. Thus, the selection of a rights offer or standby offer method potentially allows for partial separation where higher quality issuers can pool together, provided that a significant portion of the issue is taken up by existing shareholders.

The expected takeup level, k, is assumed to be exogenously determined by individual shareholder considerations. Rights offers dominate underwritten offers only when k is high, i.e., when existing shareholder takeup substantially reduces the size of the issue sold to outside investors. Firms faced with low k can find costly certification to be attractive because some lowering of adverse selection is obtained as some overpriced issues are detected by the underwriter and forced to lower their offer prices or withdraw their issues. In addition, issuers of overpriced stock find firm commitments attractive because if they go undetected as overpriced, then the current shareholders realize greater wealth gains from the stock issue decision. Standbys dominate firm commitments for low-k firms as long as k is sufficiently large to justify the direct costs of distributing the shares to existing shareholders.

The model predicts that (1) issuers select uninsured rights only if k is high

managers are reluctant to cut the dividend (e.g., due to information effects), a stock issue under these conditions should provide a positive signal to the market, and the signal should be increasing in the offer price discount (a deeper discount necessitates issuance of more shares to raise a given amount of capital). Hietala & Löyttyniemi present evidence which supports this prediction.

[19] This is consistent with models such as Booth & Smith [1986], Beatty & Ritter [1986], and Titman & Trueman [1986], where the underwriter is given some ability to evaluate the extent to which the stock is over or underpriced and is given an incentive to use this information to avoid selling significantly overpriced stock to the public. In addition to reputation considerations, due diligence and legal liability also help induce the underwriter to avoid overpriced issues [Tinic, 1988; Blackwell, Marr & Spivey, 1990].

and the stock is not greatly overvalued; (2) issuers selecting standbys have both a higher value of k and are of a higher average quality than firms selecting firm commitments; and (3) the average market reaction to an offer announcement will be least negative for uninsured rights and most negative for firm commitments, with standbys in between.

These predictions of the Eckbo & Masulis model are supported by the empirical evidence summarized in Table 11. They are also supported by their evidence that uninsured rights, but not standbys or firm commitments, are typically accompanied by announcements of substantial shareholder subscription precommitments which serve to credibly signal the issuer's high k-value. Furthermore, Bøhren, Eckbo & Michalsen [1992] estimate the value of k and find that the probability that a rights offer is underwritten decreases significantly with the estimate of k, as predicted by Eckbo & Masulis.

Moreover, to the extent that the value of k decreases as the firm's equity capitalization and degree of share-ownership dispersion increase, the Eckbo & Masulis analysis suggests that the frequency of rights offers should be higher for relatively small, closely held firms. They present evidence on industrial issuers which supports this prediction. The fact that smaller, private companies use the rights method more frequently than publicly traded firms is also consistent with this size argument. This may also explain the greater use of rights in foreign jurisdictions (including Canada and most countries in Europe and the Pacific Basin) characterized by smaller and relatively closely held firms.

Furthermore, for a given value of k, the Eckbo & Masulis model suggests that the greater the information asymmetry between the issuer and the market, the greater the marginal benefit of quality certification, and the greater the probability that the issuer will employ an underwriter. Thus, issuers with a relatively transparent production technology, or a high level of mandated disclosure, which reduces information asymmetries between the firm and the market, are more likely to use rights. Thus, regulated utilities, with the greater level of public information and less discretion in terms of the timing of a new issue, are more likely to select rights. This prediction is supported by the evidence on offer frequencies across industrial and utility equity issuers in Table 6.

Since firms switching from rights to firm commitment offers must first eliminate corporate charter provisions granting shareholders preemptive rights to purchase new equity issues, the Eckbo–Masulis model also has implications for the timing of preemptive rights charter amendments. That is, as the value of k falls (perhaps because firm size grows with time), managers find it optimal to switch to firm commitment offers and therefore propose preemptive rights charter amendments. According to the sample of preemptive rights charter amendments in Bhagat [1983], there was a surge in such amendments early in the 1970s, just preceding the sharp reduction in rights issues shown in our Table 6. Moreover, the model predicts a negative market reaction to announcement of preemptive rights charter amendments. The charter amendment proposal signals management information on k, causing the market to capitalize the higher future expected costs of raising capital. The evidence in Bhagat [1983] is consistent with this prediction as well.

The above empirical observations can be summarized as follows:

Observation 17 *Rights vs. underwritten offers.* In Eckbo & Masulis [1992], a rights issue where current shareholders elect *not* to subscribe causes the market to infer that the firm is of relatively low quality, resulting in relatively large adverse selection costs of the type analyzed in Myers & Majluf [1984]. Current shareholder takeup reduces adverse selection costs, as does costly quality certification by underwriters. In this framework,

(i) expected shareholder takeup is an important determinant of the flotation method choice;
(ii) firms selecting uninsured rights sometimes use shareholder subscription precommitments to credibly signal a high shareholder takeup;
(iii) firms tend to switch to underwriting as the firm's ownership structure becomes dispersed (as with most publicly traded firms);
(iv) firms with less discretion over their issue policy, such as regulated utilities, tend to use rights more often than unregulated firms; and
(v) the market reacts most negatively to firm commitment offers, least negatively to uninsured rights, with the market reaction to standby offers in between.

All of these predictions are supported by empirical evidence.

5.2. Best efforts vs. firm commitment underwriting contracts

The Eckbo–Masulis analysis can be applied to other flotation methods. For example, low-k firms who derive only a small certification benefit from underwriting because the true quality of the issuer is relatively transparent to the market (there is little to certify) may select the cheaper best efforts underwriting contract over firm commitment underwriting. Interestingly, only regulated utilities, which have relatively low adverse selection effects, use the best efforts method for issuing SPOs with any frequency.

The choice between best efforts and firm commitment contracts has also been analyzed in the literature on IPOs where best efforts are much more frequent (approximately 40%). Building on the underpricing model of Rock [1986], Ritter [1987] argues that uninformed investors view the minimum investor takeup requirement that characterizes best efforts contracts as a substitute for underpricing. A minimum takeup requirement implies that the issuer precommits to withdrawing the issue if demand is insufficient to meet the requirement. Since informed investors do not subscribe to overpriced issues, the minimum takeup requirement tends to release uninformed investors from their obligation to accept their share allocation precisely when the issue is overpriced and likely to be partially sold.

Viewing a firm commitment contract as essentially a best efforts contract with a zero minimum sales requirement, the issuer in Ritter's model determines the optimal underwriting contract by trading off the cost of underpricing with the increased risk of offer failure caused by a minimum sales requirement. He shows that the most risky issuers are more inclined to select best efforts contracts, while less risky issuers select firm commitments. Intuitively, since the necessary winner's curse underpricing [Rock, 1986] is highest for the riskiest issuers, they benefit most by offering the minimum sales requirement as an insurance to uninformed investors.

Welch [1991] performs cross-sectional regressions with IPO underpricing as dependent variable and finds that the coefficient on the minimum sales requirement variable is significantly *positive*, and that proxies for the risk of the issue have no significant impact on underpricing. Both findings are inconsistent with Ritter's model. Welch interprets the positive impact of the minimum sales requirement as consistent with the model of Benveniste & Spindt [1989], where a larger investor takeup requirement induces greater preselling activity by the underwriter which in turn requires greater underpricing.

6. The timing of SPOs

Given that equity offers occur relatively infrequently for the typical industrial firm, it is also important to understand the determinants of the timing of these offers. A number of theories have been posited to explain the timing of equity offerings, several of which take into account the phase of the business cycle that exists or is expected. In Choe, Masulis & Nanda [1993], an adverse selection argument similar to Myers & Majluf [1984] is developed where firms choose between issuing debt and equity across business cycle expansions and contractions.

As discussed earlier, in the Myers & Majluf model, managers want to issue stock when it is overvalued and avoid issuing it when it is undervalued. However, profitable investment projects exist that would be lost if the equity issue is delayed or foregone. This causes some but not all firms with undervalued stock to issue equity, avoiding a market breakdown of the type explored by Akerloff [1970]. Nevertheless, firms with especially undervalued stock continue to find it optimal to forego the investment opportunity, and an adverse selection effect is generated.

Choe, Masulis & Nanda observe that since expansions involve more profitable investment opportunities, firms are less likely to forego investments because the stock is underpriced. Thus, they predict that adverse selection effects of equity offers will be smaller in economic expansions and, therefore, the frequency of equity offers greater. There is empirical support for these arguments in Moore [1980] and Choe, Masulis & Nanda who find that the frequency of equity offers relative to debt offers rises in expansions, while the magnitude of the negative stock price reaction to firm commitment equity offer announcements decreases. In contrast, debt issues are insensitive to this equity mispricing effect. The evidence in Choe, Masulis & Nanda, Taggart [1977] and Marsh [1982] indicates that the number of straight debt offers do not fall in economic contractions and may rise after interest rates have fallen. This latter effect may in part reflect debt refinancing activities in these periods.

The Choe–Masulis–Nanda model also predicts that the adverse selection effect increases as investor uncertainty concerning the value of assets in place rises. Schwert [1989] documents that stock price volatility varies over the business cycle, increasing during recessions.[20] Controlling for the effect of the business cycle, Choe, Masulis & Nanda find that the relative frequency of equity issues is significantly negatively related to the variance of issuer's daily stock returns, which gives further empirical support to their adverse selection framework.

Several other hypotheses concerning the timing of equity offers can be extended to a business cycle environment. For example, under Myers' [1984] 'pecking order' hypothesis, firms are viewed as preferring to finance projects internally if possible, otherwise to issue low risk debt and finally to issue equity only as a last resort. Imposing an arbitrary limit on firm leverage, the timing of equity issues is affected by business cycle downturns that reduce internal sources of funds and raise leverage by lowering asset values, thereby making equity offers more attractive. However, this scenario is inconsistent with the evidence found in Choe, Masulis & Nanda.

Another hypothesis is based on debt–equity wealth transfers occurring when leverage is unexpectedly revised. If a firm issues equity, thus lowering firm leverage, debtholders gain in that their risk bearing falls while their risk premium continues to be paid in full. This tends to discourage management seeking to maximize shareholder wealth from undertaking equity offers, except when leverage has become unacceptably high. In economic contractions, debtholders bear greater risk and expect greater risk premiums. So, in downturns equity offers cause leverage reductions resulting in larger reductions in debt riskbearing, which lead to greater debtholder wealth gains. Thus, there are greater costs to equity issues in economic downturns, leading to a lower predicted frequency of equity offers and a more negative stock price reaction. However, the positive price reaction of the issuer's outstanding debt to an equity offer announcement, predicted by the wealth transfer hypothesis, is not observed by Kalay & Shimrat [1987].

In the Stulz [1990] model of 'free cash flow', debt issuance becomes more attractive when free cash flow increases. In economic contractions, if earnings decline less sharply than capital spending, which is typically the case, free cash flow can increase, increasing the attractiveness of debt offers. The cost of debt issuance in the Stulz model is underinvestment in profitable projects which would tend to be less of a problem in economic downturns. Thus, debt issuance would appear to be predicted to rise in frequency, near contractions under the Stulz model, which is contrary to the Marsh [1982] and Taggart [1977] evidence but somewhat supported by the Choe, Masulis & Nanda [1993] evidence. It is also supported in a recent study by Jung, Lee & Stulz [1992] who report that firms with relatively good investment opportunities measured by Tobin's q, are significantly more likely to issue equity over straight debt.

Another hypothesis that predicts variation in equity and debt offers over time is the belief of many practitioners that management prefers debt issuance when interest rates are historically low and stock issuance when stock prices are historically high, provided that either risk premiums are relatively low or expected

[20] Schwert links this volatility increase to increases in operating leverage, which is likely to be positively related to investor uncertainty concerning the value of assets in place.

returns are high. Since stock market prices tend to reflect future economic prospects, this hypothesis tends to predict increases in equity offers in economic expansions and debt issues in economic contractions when interest rates tend to be lower. This is consistent with the Marsh and Taggart evidence but only partially consistent with the Choe, Masulis & Nanda evidence.

Lucas & McDonald [1990] develop a dynamic model of the equity issuance process that predicts a greater frequency of equity issuance following a general stock market increase. As in Choe, Masulis & Nanda, temporarily underpriced firms have an incentive to postpone the issue until the stock price is higher, which implies that the average preannouncement price path of these issuing firms will be upward sloping. On the other hand, temporarily overpriced firms will issue immediately as investment opportunities arise. If the arrival of investment projects is uncorrelated with the firm's price history, then the average preannouncement price path of temporarily overvalued firms will be flat. As a result, the average preannouncement price path of *all* issuing firms will be upward sloping, as is typically observed in samples of firm commitment offers [Asquith & Mullins, 1986; Masulis & Korwar, 1986; Choe, Masulis & Nanda, 1992; Taggart, 1977; and Marsh, 1982]. Also, the Lucas & McDonald argument implies that market reaction to the issue announcement will be more negative for firms with higher stock price rises over the preannouncement period, which is supported by the regression results of Masulis & Korwar [1986], Korajczyk, Lucas & McDonald [1990], Eckbo & Masulis [1992], and Jung, Lee & Stulz [1992].

Eckbo & Masulis [1992] note that the effect of increased shareholder participation in the equity issue is to reduce the incentive of undervalued firms to postpone equity issuance since current shareholders capture part of the underpricing. At the extreme, when current shareholders purchase the entire issue, the firm issues immediately regardless of its current degree of underpricing. Thus, in a sample of issuers where the average level of shareholder participation is known to be large, the Eckbo & Masulis model predicts that there should be little or no stock price runup prior to the issue announcement. This prediction is supported by their evidence of little or no prior runup in the sample of uninsured rights, and a smaller runup prior to the announcement of standby rights than prior to firm commitment underwritten offers.

Finally, Korajczyk, Lucas & McDonald [1992] propose a short run adverse selection model which predicts that equity issues will occur less frequently prior to accounting earnings releases and more frequently after these releases. This follows because the uncertainty about the value of the assets-in-place is lowered with the accounting releases, thereby lowering the market's concern over adverse selection effects. Dierkens [1991] and Korajczyk, Lucas & McDonald [1991] present evidence which supports this argument.

Observation 18 *Timing of equity issues*. Several models predict that the frequency of equity and debt offers will vary with the business cycle and with the prior stock price history of the security issued. Several pieces of evidence support these predictions:

(i) the frequency of equity issues tends to rise during economic expansions;
(ii) the magnitude of the negative market reaction to firm commitment offers of equity decreases in expansions;
(iii) equity issues occur more frequently after accounting earnings releases; and
(iv) on average, firm commitment issues of common stock occur after a significant runup in the issuer's secondary market price, while no such runup is observed prior to equity rights issues.

7. Market microstructure effects

Seasoned public offers of common stock have important impacts on the secondary market in which the common stock trades. The typical firm commitment offer involves a large increase in shares outstanding along with a large increase in the number of stockholders and a reduction in management and blockholder percentage ownership. As a result, one would anticipate that there would be major increases in trading volume, a lower percentage of insider trading and possibly major changes in price volatility after the public offering.

Theories of bid–ask spread determination are based on adverse selection and inventory cost considerations. These theories predict that if trading volume rises and price volatility falls, then bid–ask spreads will also fall since the expected costs of market making decline. The SPO announcement per se can also lower the asymmetric information about the firm's stock price borne by market makers, which would cause bid–ask spreads to drop further.

Amihud & Mendelson [1986] develop a valuation model of security pricing that assumes that investors have a positive preference for liquidity measured by percentage bid–ask spread. They derive a model of security pricing where the expected return is a positive and concave function of bid–ask spread. Amihud & Mendelson [1988] extend the implications of the model and present evidence that liquidity is an important determinant of security value. They argue that managers seeking to maximize current stockholder wealth should take market liquidity into account when making corporate financing decisions. Thus, in deciding whether to make an SPO and in choosing the flotation method, liquidity implications need to be taken into account. A further implication is that the negative adverse selection effect of the offer announcement can be partially offset by the positive liquidity effect.

Lease, Masulis & Page [1992] explore the market microstructure effects of firm commitment SPOs for NYSE and AMEX listed firms. They document that share trading volume on average rises substantially and that price volatility falls subsequent to the SPO. In exploring this question, Lease, Masulis & Page find that both dollar bid–ask spreads and percentage spreads fall significantly after the seasoned public offering, consistent with existing inventory cost and adverse selection cost models of bid–ask spread determination. They also investigate how these variables change between the announcement and the offer dates. They report that trading volume and price volatility fall in the interim. In addition, bid–ask spreads drop but not to the level observed subsequent to the public offer. This is suggestive of a modest lowering of the adverse selection effect borne by market makers following the SPO announcement.

In two related studies, Loderer & Sheehan [1992] and Tripathy & Rao [1992] examine the market microstructure effects of SPOs for NASDAQ listed firms. Loderer & Sheehan report that the number of shareholders, number of market makers and share trading volume rise, and bid–ask spreads rise slightly at the SPO announcement and fall subsequent to the public offering date.

Tripathy & Rao [1992] separate their NASDAQ SPO sample into large and small capitalization stocks. They find that larger stocks have increases in bid–ask spread over a 60-day period prior to the announcement followed by decreases in spread over the next 43 days. In contrast, small stocks experience increases in spread from 80 days prior to the announcement through 20 days after the announcement. Focusing on the public offering date, they find that the bid–ask spreads of large stocks decrease over the 20 days prior to the offering and decrease even more over the 20 days following the offer. Spreads of small stocks increase over the 20 days prior to the offering but then decrease from just before the offering through 20 days after. This suggests that information asymmetries decrease for large firms once the investment bankers begin their due diligence investigation. However, for smaller firms this information asymmetry does not appear to fall before the public offering date. The major results of these two NASDAQ studies are generally consistent with the findings of the prior NYSE/AMEX study.

Kothare [1993] examines the market microstructure effects of rights offers from the perspective that these offers have a stock split embedded in them. Since stock splits are known to have market microstructure effects [Copeland, 1979; Brennan & Copeland, 1988], rights offers are likely to have them as well. Kothare finds that rights offers result in higher bid–ask spreads both before and over the rights offer period, and a small reduction thereafter, unlike firm commitment offers which experience substantial declines in spread following the SPO.

Stock offers can also cause temporary biases in daily stock returns by disrupting normal buy–sell order flow in the secondary market. Lease, Masulis & Page [1991] document that around the public offer dates of SPOs stock returns are biased downward due to the loss of purchase orders to the temporary primary market in the stock. One result is that the transaction prices in the stock tend to occur at the lower ask quote, rather than at the midpoint of the bid and ask, which generates an apparent fall in the stock price. There is also evidence that market makers lower their quotes in this period due to a positive imbalance in their inventory position resulting from the predominance of sell orders at this time. Lease, Masulis & Page find that using the closing bid–ask average rather than the closing transaction prices eliminates the statistical significance of the drop and reduces by more than half the average negative offer date return.

Observation 19 *Effects of seasoned equity offers on bid–ask spreads.* Percentage bid–ask spreads of common stocks having firm commitment SPOs drop significantly before and after the public offering date. This post offer phenomenon in part reflects the increase in shareholders and trading volume which occurs after the SPO. Percentage bid–ask spreads of common stocks having equity rights offers increase before and during the rights offer period and decrease only slightly thereafter. A firm issuing by means of a rights offer can be viewed as experiencing a stock split which tends to increase percentage spreads, while the resulting increase in shareholders and trading volume is substantially less than in firm commitments. Also, the offering date return exhibits a significant negative bias due to the preponderance of sell orders received in the secondary market.

8. Conclusions

Over the past decade, our understanding of the various contractual arrangements in the corporate capital acquisition process, and the influence of this process on corporate financial and investment policy, has progressed substantially. As summarized in the Appendix, we have identified nineteen groups of empirical observations which form perhaps the core of our empirical understanding of *how*, by *how much* and *when* corporations make seasoned public offerings of equity.

The results indicate that, since World War II, internal equity (retained earnings including depreciation) has remained the dominant funding source for nonfinancial corporations in all the industrial countries studied. Debt has been the dominant external funding source, with a steady increase in leverage ratios in the U.S. from a low of 30% in 1946 to approximately 60% in 1984. The ratio of public debt to public equity issues tends to decrease during business cycle expansions and to increase during business cycle contractions. While the U.S. has traditionally been the country with the largest volume of equity issues, the volume of equity issues by European nonfinancial corporations had by 1987 grown to more than twice the corresponding volume in the U.S. and in Japan, in part due to major privatization programs of government owned firms.

Both in the U.S. and internationally, there is a trend towards selecting underwritten flotation methods when issuing equity as well as other more senior securities. In the U.S., this trend caused the rights offer method to virtually disappear by the early 1980s, while rights offers still count for the majority of domestic equity issues in the Canadian, the European and most Pacific Rim capital markets. In Japan, the majority of equity issues are now sold through the firm commitment underwritten method. In the U.S., the demise of the rights issue has coincided with a surge in DRIPs and ESOPs, which are in some ways similar to periodic rights offers.

The trend towards greater use of underwritten offers occurs despite substantial evidence that the direct flotation costs associated with the uninsured rights method are significantly lower than the underwriter fee. This 'rights offer paradox' may in part be resolved by considering shareholder-borne costs of the rights method which are not included in traditional measures of direct flotation costs but which tend to reduce the attractiveness of rights for value-maximizing managers of issuing firms. While the evidence here is relatively sparse, these additional costs include capital gains taxes, reduced stock liquidity and transaction costs of selling rights in the secondary market, risk of offer failure and wealth transfers to convertible security holders triggered by anti-dilution clauses in these contracts.

Eckbo & Masulis [1992] also point out potentially large *adverse selection costs* of the type analyzed by Myers & Majluf [1984] when a firm makes a rights offer in which current shareholders do *not* wish to participate and accordingly sell their rights in the secondary market. However, shareholder takeup is in part determined by factors such as personal wealth constraints and demand for diversification which are beyond an issuer's control. These factors tend to limit shareholder participation in equity issues by relatively large widely held firms. Thus, it is possible that issuers which anticipate a low shareholder takeup turn to underwriters for (imperfect) quality certification in order to avoid the high adverse selection cost of the rights offer method in the face of heavy sales of rights. The Eckbo & Masulis adverse selection framework also implies that firms with less discretion over issue policy, such as regulated utilities, bear lower adverse selection costs and so tend to use rights more often than unregulated firms, which is supported by the empirical evidence.

Recent studies have also established that while IPOs are substantially underpriced, SPO underpricing is negligible. This difference in underpricing accounts for the finding that IPOs are on average substantially more expensive than underwritten SPOs for issues of similar sizes. Flotation costs as a percent of underwritten SPOs' gross proceeds, consisting primarily of underwriter fees, decrease with issue size and increase with stock risk and share-ownership dispersion. Overallotment options, frequent in IPOs but less frequent in SPOs, typically account for a very small percentage of the SPO's gross proceeds.

The results of the growing literature on the valuation effects of SPO announcements, typically represented by the two-day announcement period abnormal stock return, give further support to theories of adverse selection in primary markets for securities. In particular, the announcement effect is nonpositive across both equity and debt issues, and significantly negative for issues of equity and convertible debt. Consistent with the adverse selection framework of Eckbo & Masulis [1992], the market reaction to equity issues is most negative for firm commitment offers, least negative (or zero) for uninsured rights, with standby offers in between. The international evidence also typically indicates a negligible market reaction to uninsured rights issues. Moreover, consistent with Krasker's [1986] extension of the Myers & Majluf [1984] model, the valuation effect of firm commitment equity offers is more negative the larger the relative issue size. Finally, equity issues by regulated utilities, which have smaller adverse selection effects due to the regulatory process, are consistently associated with smaller negative abnormal returns than equity issues by industrial firms.

Adverse selection arguments can also be extended to analyse the *timing* of SPOs. These arguments imply that the frequency of equity issues tends to rise during economic expansions, and thus, the negative market reaction to the typical issue tends to fall. Furthermore, equity issues are predicted to occur more frequently after major information releases (e.g., of accounting earnings) and, with the exception of uninsured rights offers, to follow significant runups in an issuer's stock price. All of these predictions receive substantial empirical support.

Finally, seasoned public offers of common stock have important impacts on the secondary market in which the common stock trades. The typical firm commitment offer involves a large increase in shares outstanding along with a large increase in the number of stockholders and a reduction in management and blockholder percentage ownership. As a result, one would anticipate that there would be major increases in trading volume, a lower percentage of insider trading and possibly major changes in price volatility after the public offering.

The growing literature examining these effects finds that percentage bid–ask spreads of common stocks having firm commitment SPOs drop significantly before and after the public offering date. This post offer phenomenon in part reflects the increase in shareholders and trading volume which occurs after the SPO. Percentage bid–ask spreads of common stocks experiencing equity rights offers increase before and during the rights offer period and decrease only slightly thereafter. A firm issuing common stock through a rights offer can be viewed as experiencing a stock split which tends to increase percentage spreads, while the resulting increase in shareholders and trading volume is substantially less than the changes which typically occur in firm commitments. Finally, the offering date return exhibits a significant negative bias due to the preponderance of sell orders received in the secondary market. This reflects the diversion of buy orders from the secondary market to the primary market during the offer period.

Appendix. Summary of empirical observations on seasoned public offerings

1. *Corporate funding sources.*

(i) Internal equity has remained the dominant funding source for U.S. nonfinancial corporations after the second world war.

(ii) Debt dominates equity as an external funding source, with net retirements of equity in the 1980s.

(iii) In periods with low internally generated equity, the proportion of debt financing tends to increase to finance the shortfall. In periods with high internal equity, debt issues tend to be used to retire external equity.

2. *Leverage ratios.* Leverage (debt to total asset) ratios for U.S. manufacturing companies have increased steadily over the post-war period from a low of 30% in 1946 to approximately 60% in 1984.

3. *Offer frequencies.*

(i) The ratio of public equity to public debt issues tends to increase during business cycle expansions and to decrease during business cycle contractions.

(ii) Until the second half of the 1980s, only a small fraction of security issue volume in the U.S. was sold privately. However, recent years have seen a substantial increase in private placement volume.

4. *International funding sources.*
   (i) Retained earnings are the major source of finance in all the industrial countries studied.
   (ii) The proportion of external funding is largest in Finland, France, Japan and Italy.
   (iii) Banks are the dominant source of external finance in all countries, representing approximately 40% of gross sources in France, Italy and Japan.
   (iv) Companies in Canada, France and Italy are the largest user of external capital markets, with short-term securities, bonds and shares representing 19%, 13% and 13% of gross financing, respectively.
   (v) Canadian, French and Italian firms raise approximately 10% of their gross financing by issuing equity, while the corresponding proportion is less than 5% in Germany, Japan and the U.S..

5. *Volume of European SPOs.* By 1987, the dollar volume of new security issues made by European nonfinancial corporations had reached approximately three-quarters of the corresponding issue volume in the U.S. and Japan. The 1987 total issue volume in European domestic markets was approximately four times the combined volume in the Eurobond and Euroequity markets. European equity issues by nonfinancial institutions had grown to more than twice the volume of equity issues in the U.S. and in Japan.

6. *SPO flotation method trends in the U.S.*
   (i) Over the past 60 years, publicly traded U.S. companies have gradually switched from the uninsured rights and standby flotation methods to the firm commitment method. By 1980, the rights method has virtually disappeared in the group of large publicly traded industrial firms.
   (ii) U.S. firms also show an overwhelming preference for the firm commitment method when offering securities other than common stock, including mortgage bonds, straight bonds, convertible debt, convertible preferred and warrants.

7. *IPO flotation methods.* In the U.S., IPOs are sold almost exclusively by means of the firm commitment method (approximately 60%) and the best efforts underwritten method (approximately 40%).

8. *DRIPs and ESOPs.* There is evidence that DRIPs and ESOPs, which in many ways are similar to periodic rights offers, to some extent have replaced rights issues as a means of raising capital from shareholders and employees.

9. *International flotation method trends.* Domestic issues in the Canadian, the European and most Pacific Rim capital markets are predominantly sold through rights. There is a trend towards increased use of underwriters and the firm commitment method in these markets as well. In Japan, one of the largest stock markets, a majority of equity issues is now sold through the firm commitment method.

10. *SPO flotation costs.* The empirical evidence indicates that direct flotation costs on average

(i) are higher for common stock offers than for debt offers of comparable size, and higher for convertible debt than for non-convertible debt;
(ii) are higher for industrial issuers than for public utilities;
(iii) are lowest for uninsured rights and highest for firm commitments, with standbys in between; and
(iv) are higher for negotiated than for competitive underwritten contracts.

11. *Flotation costs and offer characteristics.* The empirical evidence indicates that direct flotation costs depend on issuer characteristics such as gross proceeds (scale economies), stock risk (value of an underwriter guarantee), and shareholder concentration (rights distribution costs). Direct flotation costs remain lowest for uninsured rights and highest for firm commitments after controlling for these issue characteristics.

12. *Issue underpricing and overallotment options.* Underpricing, while large in IPOs, is negligible in firm commitment SPOs. Overallotment options, which are common in firm commitment IPOs, are much less frequent in SPOs, and the average value of this option is a very small percent of the SPO's gross proceeds. Overall, flotation costs as a percent of offering proceeds, and the risk of offer failure, are substantially higher for IPOs than for SPOs.

13. *Additional costs of rights.* Additional shareholder-borne costs which tend to reduce the attractiveness of rights arise from capital gains taxes, reduced stock liquidity, transaction costs of selling rights, arbitrage activity which affects the risk of offer failure, and anti-dilution clauses which induce wealth transfers to convertible security holders.

14. *Valuation effects of SPO announcements in the U.S.* For NYSE/AMEX listed firms, the average valuation effect (typically represented by the two-day announcement period abnormal stock returns) is

(i) non-positive;
(ii) more negative the larger the size of the issue;
(iii) most negative for firm commitment offers, least negative (or zero) for uninsured rights, with standby rights in between;
(iv) most negative for common stock, least negative (zero) for straight debt/preferred stock, with convertible securities in between; and
(v) smaller for public utilities than for industrial issuers.

15. *Valuation effects of SPO announcements internationally.* Internationally, where common stock is primarily issued using rights and standbys, the average market reaction is either positive (Finland, Japan, Korea, Switzerland, UK) or small but negative (Australia, Canada, Norway).

16. *Valuation effects of other capital structure change announcements.* For exchange listed U.S. firms, the average valuation effect (typically represented by the two-day announcement period abnormal stock return) is
(i) positive for private placements of common stock;
(ii) positive when debt/preferred stock is exchanged for common and negative when common stock is exchanged for debt/preferred stock;
(iii) positive when common stock is repurchased (by tender offer/open market repurchase);
(iv) negative for convertible debt/preferred stock calls forcing conversion into common;
(v) positive for withdrawals or cancellations of common stock offerings; and
(vi) non-negative for adoptions of DRIPs and ESOPs.

17. *Rights vs. underwritten offers.* In Eckbo & Masulis [1992], a rights issue where current shareholders elect *not* to subscribe causes the market to infer that the firm is of relatively low quality, resulting in relatively large adverse selection costs of the type analyzed in Myers & Majluf [1984]. Current shareholder takeup reduces adverse selection costs, as does costly quality certification by underwriters. In this framework,
(i) expected shareholder takeup is an important determinant of the flotation method choice;
(ii) firms selecting uninsured rights sometimes use shareholder subscription precommitments to credibly signal a high shareholder takeup;
(iii) firms tend to switch to underwriting as the firm's ownership structure becomes dispersed (as with most publicly traded firms);
(iv) firms with less discretion over their issue policy, such as regulated utilities, tend to use rights more often than unregulated firms; and
(v) the market reacts most negatively to firm commitment offers, least negatively to uninsured rights, with the market reaction to standby offers in between.
All of these predictions are supported by empirical evidence.

18. *Timing of equity issues.* Several models predict that the frequency of equity and debt offers will vary with the business cycle and with the prior stock price history of the security issued. Several pieces of evidence support these predictions:
(i) the frequency of equity issues tends to rise during economic expansions;
(ii) the magnitude of the negative market reaction to firm commitment offers of equity decreases in expansions;
(iii) equity issues occur more frequently after accounting earnings releases; and
(iv) on average, firm commitment issues of common stock occur after a significant runup in the issuer's secondary market price, while no such runup is observed prior to equity rights issues.

19. *Effects of seasoned equity offers on bid-ask spreads.* Percentage bid-ask spreads of common stocks having firm commitment SPOs drop significantly before and after the public offering date. This post offer phenomenon in part reflects the in-

crease in shareholders and trading volume which occurs after the SPO. Percentage bid-ask spreads of common stocks having equity rights offers increase before and during the rights offer period and decrease only slightly thereafter. A firm issuing by means of a rights offer can be viewed as experiencing a stock split which tends to increase percentage spreads, while the resulting increase in shareholders and trading volume is substantially less than in firm commitments. Also, the offering date return exhibits a significant negative bias due to the preponderance of sell orders received in the secondary market.

Acknowledgements

We appreciate the comments of the referee, Rex Thompson.

References

Akerlof, G.A. (1970). The market for 'lemons': Quality and the market mechanism. *Q. J. Econ.* 84, 488–500.

Amihud, Y., and H. Mendelson (1986). Asset pricing and the bid–ask spread. *J. Financ. Econ.* 17, 223–250.

Amihud, Y., and H. Mendelson (1988). Liquidity and asset prices: Financial management implications. *Financ. Manage.* 17, 5–15.

Asquith, P. (1992). Convertible debt: A dynamic test of call policy, working paper, Massachussetts Institute of Technology.

Asquith, P., and D.W. Mullins, Jr. (1986). Seasoned equity offerings. *J. Financ. Econ.* 15, 61–89.

Barclay, M.J., and R.H. Litzenberger (1988). Announcement effects of new equity issues and the use of intraday price data. *J. Financ. Econ.* 21, 71–99.

Bayless, M., and S. Chaplinsky (1991). Expectations of security type and the information content of debt and equity offers. *J. Financ. Intermed.* 1, 195–214.

Beatty, R., and J.R. Ritter (1986). Investment banking, reputation, and the underpricing of initial public offerings. *J. Financ. Econ.* 15, 213–232.

Benveniste, L.M., and P.A. Spindt (1989). How investment bankers determine the offer price and allocation of new issues. *J. Financ. Econ.* 24, 343–362.

Bhagat, S. (1983). The effect of pre-emptive right amendments on shareholder wealth. *J. Financ. Econ.* 12, 289–310.

Bhagat, S. (1986). The effect of management's choice between negotiated and competitive equity offerings on shareholder wealth. *J. Financ. Quant. Anal.* 21, 181–196.

Bhagat, S., and P.A. Frost (1986). Issuing costs to existing shareholders in competitive and negotiated underwritten public utility equity offerings. *J. Financ. Econ.* 15, 233–259.

Bhagat, S., M.W. Marr and G.R. Thompson (1985). The rule 415 experiment: Equity markets. *J. Finance* 40, 1385–1401.

Blackwell, D., M.W. Marr and M.F. Spivey (1990). Shelf registration and the reduced due diligence argument: Implications of the underwriter certification and the implicit insurance hypotheses. *J. Financ. Quant. Anal.* 25, 245–257.

Bøhren, Ø., B.E. Eckbo and D. Michalsen (1992). Why underwrite equity issues? working paper, Norwegian School of Management, Oslo.

Booth, J., and R. Smith (1986). Capital raising, underwriting and the certification hypothesis. *J. Financ. Econ.* 15, 2–20.

Brander, J.A., and T.R. Lewis (1987). Oligopoly and financial structure: The limited liability effect. *Am. Econ. Rev.* 76, 956–970.

Brennan, M.J., and T.E. Copeland (1988). Beta changes around stock splits: A note. *J. Finance*, 43, 1009–1014.

Brennan, M.J., and E.S. Schwartz (1978). Corporate income taxes, valuation, and the problem of optimal capital structure. *J. Bus.* 51, 103–115.

Brous, P. (1992). Common stock offerings and earnings expectations: A test of the release of unfavorable information. *J. Finance* 47, 1517–1536.

Campbell, C.J., L.H. Ederington and P. Vankudre (1991). Tax shields, sample-selection bias, and the information content of conversion-forcing bond calls. *J. Finance* 46, 1291–1324.

Chang, S. (1990). Employee stock ownership plans and shareholder wealth: An empirical investigation. *Financ. Manage.* 19, 48–58.

Choe, H., R. Masulis and V. Nanda (1993). Common stock offerings across the business cycle: Theory and evidence. *J. Empirical Finance* 1, 3–31.

Copeland, T.E. (1979). Liquidity changes following stock splits. *J. Finance* 34, 115–141.

Cowan, A.R., N. Nayar and A.K. Singh (1990). Stock returns before and after calls of convertible bonds. *J. Financ. Quant. Anal.* 25, 549–554.

Daniel, K., and Titman, S. (1995). Investment under asymmetric information, in: R. Jarrow, V. Maksimovic and W.T. Ziemba (eds.), *Finance*, Handbooks in Operations Research and Management Science, Vol. 9, North-Holland, Amsterdam, pp. 721–766 (this volume).

Dann, L.Y. (1981). Common stock repurchases: An analysis of returns to bondholders and stockholders. *J. Financ. Econ.* 9, 113–138.

Dann, L.Y., R.W. Masulis and D. Mayers (1991). Repurchase tender offers and earnings information. *J. Account. Econ.* 14, 217–251.

Dann, L., and W.H. Mikkelson (1984). Convertible debt issuance, capital structure change and financing-related information: Some new evidence. *J. Financ. Econ.* 13, 157–186.

DeAngelo, H., and R.W. Masulis (1980). Optimal capital structure under corporate and personal taxation. *J. Financ. Econ.* 8, 3–30.

Dehnert, J. (1991). The determinants of the size of equity issue announcement effects, unpublished Dissertation Proposal, Australian School of Management, University of New South Wales.

Denis, D.J. (1991). Shelf registration and the market for seasoned equity offerings. *J. Bus.* 64, 189–212.

Denis, D.J. (1993). The costs of equity issues since Rule 415: A closer look. *J. Financ. Res.* 16, 77–78.

Dierkens, N. (1991). Information asymmetry and equity issues. *J. Financ. Quant. Anal.* 26, 181–199.

Dubofsky, D.A., and L. Bierman (1988). The effect of discount dividend reinvestment plan announcements on equity value. *Akron J. Bus. Econ. Res.* 19, 58–68.

Dunn, K.B., and K.M. Eades (1989). Voluntary conversion of convertible securities and the optimal call strategy. *J. Financ. Econ.* 23, 273–301.

Dybvig, P., and J.F. Zender (1991). Capital structure and dividend irrelevance with asymmetric information. *Rev. Financ. Studies* 4, 201–220.

Eckbo, B.E. (1986). Valuation effects of corporate debt offerings. *J. Financ. Econ.* 15, 119–151.

Eckbo, B.E., V. Maksimovic and J. Williams (1990). Consistent estimation of cross-sectional models in event studies. *Rev. Financ. Studies* 3, 343–365.

Eckbo, B.E., and R.W. Masulis (1992). Adverse selection and the rights offer paradox. *J. Financ. Econ.* 32, 293–332.

Eckbo, B.E., and S. Verma (1992). Voting power and valuation effects of security offerings, working paper, University of British Columbia.

Finnerty, J.D. (1985). Stock-for-debt swaps and shareholder returns. *Financ. Manage.* 14, 5–17.

Fischer, E.O., R. Heinkel and J. Zechner (1989). Dynamic capital structure choice: theory and tests. *J. Finance* 44, 19–40.

Grinblatt, M., and C.Y. Hwang (1989). Signalling and the pricing of new issues. *J. Finance* 44, 393–420.

Hansen, R.S. (1989). The demise of the rights issue. *Rev. Financ. Studies* 1, 289–309.

Hansen, R.S., and C. Crutchley (1990). Corporate earnings and financing: An empirical analysis. *J. Bus.* 63, 349–371.

Hansen, R.S., B.R. Fuller and V. Janjigian (1987). The over-allotment option and equity financing flotation costs: An empirical investigation. *Financ. Manage.*, 24–32.

Hansen, R.S., and J.M. Pinkerton (1982). Direct equity financing: A resolution of a paradox. *J. Finance* 37, 651–665.

Hansen, R.S., J.M. Pinkerton and T. Ma (1987). On the rightholders' subscription to the underwritten rights offering. *J. Banking Finance* 10, 595–605.

Hansen, R.S., and P. Torregrosa (1992). Underwriter compensation and and corporate monitoring. *J. Finance* 47, 1537–1555.

Harris, M., and A. Raviv (1985). A sequential signalling model of convertible debt call policy. *J. Finance* 40, 1263–1282.

Harris, M., and A. Raviv (1990). Capital structure and the informational role of debt. *J. Finance* 45, 321–349.

Heinkel, R. (1982). A theory of capital structure relevance under imperfect information. *J. Finance* 37, 1141–1150.

Heinkel, R., and E.S. Schwartz (1986). Rights versus underwritten offerings: An asymmetric information approach. *J. Finance* 41, 1–18.

Herman, E. (1981). *Corporate Control, Corporate Power*, Cambridge University Press, New York, NY.

Hertzel, M., and P.C. Jain (1991). Earnings and risk changes around stock repurchase tender offers. *J. Account. Econ.* 14, 253–274.

Hess, A.C., S. Bhagat (1986). Size effects of seasoned stock issues: Empirical evidence. *J. Bus.* 59, 567–584.

Hietala, P., and T. Löyttyniemi (1991). An implicit dividend increase in rights issues: Theory and evidence, working paper, INSEAD.

Holland, D.M., and S.F. Meyers (1979). Trends in corporate profitability and capital costs, in: R. Lindsay (ed.), *The Nation's Captial Needs: Three Studies*, Committee of Economic Development, Washington, DC, pp. 103–188.

Ibbotson, R.G. (1975). Price performance of common stock new issues. *J. Financ. Econ.* 2, 235–272.

Ibbotson, R.G., and J.R. Ritter (1995). Initial public offerings. in: R. Jarrow, V. Maksimovic and W.T. Ziemba (eds.), *Finance*, Handbooks in Operations Research and Management Science, Vol. 9, North-Holland, Amsterdam, pp. 993–1016 (this volume).

Israel, R. (1992). Capital and ownership structures, and the market for corporate control. *Rev. Financ. Studies* 5, 181–198.

Israel, R., A.R. Ofer and D. Siegel (1989). The information content of equity-for-debt swaps: An investigation of analyst forecasts of firm cash flows. *J. Financ. Econ.* 25, 349–370.

Jain, P.C. (1992). Equity issues and changes in expectations of earnings by financial analysts. *Rev. Financ. Studies* 5, 669–683.

Janjigian, V. (1987). The leverage changing consequences of convertible debt financing. *Financ. Manage.* 15–21.

Jensen, M. (1986). Agency costs of free cash flow, corporate finance, and takeovers. *Am. Econ. Rev.* 76, 323–329.

Jensen, M.C., and W.H. Meckling (1976). Theory of the firm: Managerial behavior, agency costs and ownership structure. *J. Financ. Econ.* 3, 305–360.

John, K., R. Ambarish and J. Williams (1987). Efficient signalling with dividends and investments. *J. Finance* 42, 321–343.

John, K., and J. Williams (1985). Dividends, dilution, and taxes: A signalling equilibrium. *J. Finance* 40, 1053–1070.

Jung, K., Y.-C. Kim and R.M. Stulz (1991). Dynamic capital structure theories and new security issues: An empirical investigation, working paper, Baruch College.

Jung, K., H.-W. Lee and R.M. Stulz (1992). Management discretion, investment opportunities, and the security issue decision, working paper, Ohio State University.

Kalay, A., and A. Shimrat (1987). Firm value and seasoned equity issues price pressure, wealth redistribution, or negative information. *J. Financ. Econ.* 19, 109–126.

Kang, H. (1990). Effects of seasoned equity offerings in Korea on shareholder's wealth, in: S. Rhee and R. Chang (eds.), *Pacific-Basin Capital Markets Research*, North Holland.

Kaplan, S.A. (1965). Piercing the corporate boilerplate: Anti-dilution clauses in convertible securities. *Univ. Chicago Law Rev.* 33, 1–31.

Karpoff, J.M. and D. Lee (1991). Insider trading before new issue announcements. *Financ. Manage.* 20, 18–26.

Kato, K., and J.S. Schallheim (1991). Public and private placements of seasoned equity issues in Japan, unpublished paper, University of Utah.

Kidwell, D.S., M.W. Marr and G.R. Thompson (1984). SEC rule 415: The ultimate competitive bid. *J. Financ. Quant. Anal.* 19, 183–195.

Korajczyk, R.A., D.J. Lucas and R.L. McDonald (1990). Understanding stock price behavior around the time of equity issues, in: R. Hubbard (ed.), *Asymmetric Information, Corporate Finance and Investment*, University of Chicago Press, Chicago, IL.

Korajczyk, R.A., D.J. Lucas and R.L. McDonald (1991). The effect of information releases on the pricing and timing of equity issues. *Rev. Financ. Studies* 4(4), 685–708.

Korajczyk, R.A., D.J. Lucas and R.L. McDonald (1992). Equity issues with time-varying asymmetric information. *J. Financ. Quant. Anal.* 27, 397–417.

Kothare, M. (1993). The impact of equity issuance on stock liquidity: Rights versus public offers, working paper University of Texas at Austin.

Krasker, W.S. (1986). Stock price movements in response to stock issues under asymmetric information. *J. Finance* 41, 93–105.

Kraus, A., and R. Litzenberger (1973). A state preference model of optimal financial leverage. *J. Finance* 28, 911–922.

Lease, R.C., R.W. Masulis and J.R. Page (1991). An investigation of market microstructure impacts on event study returns. *J. Finance* 44, 1523–1536.

Lease, R.C., R.W. Masulis and J.R. Page, (1992). Impacts of seasoned equity offerings on market microstructure and the stock return generating process, working paper,Vanderbilt University.

Lease, R.C., and J.M. Pinegar (1986). The impact of preferred-for-common exchange offers on firm value. *J. Finance* 41, 795–814.

Leland, H., and D. Pyle (1977). Informational asymmetries, financial structure and financial intermediation. *J. Finance* 32, 371–387.

Linn, S.C., and J.M. Pinegar (1988). The effect of issuing preferred stock on common and preferred stockholder wealth. *J. Financ. Econ.* 22, 155–184.

Loderer, C.F., and D.P. Sheehan (1992). Seasoned stock offerings and the bid–ask spread, working paper, Pennsylvania State University.

Loderer, C.F., D.P. Sheehan and G.B. Kadlec (1991). The pricing of equity offerings. *J. Financ. Econ.* 29, 35–57.

Loderer, C.F., and H. Zimmermann (1987). Stock offerings in a different institutional setting, The Swiss case. *J. Banking Finance* 12, 353–377.

Lucas, D.J., and R.L. McDonald (1990). Equity issues and stock price dynamics. *J. Finance* 45, 1019–1043.

MacCulloch, E. (1990). The valuation of New Zealand underwriting agreements, unpublished working paper, University of Auckland.

Maksimovic, V. (1988). Capital structure in repeated oligopolies. *Rand J. Econ.* 19, 389–407.

Malatesta, P., and R. Thompson (1985). Partially anticipated events: A model of stock price reactions with an application to corporate acquisitions. *J. Financ. Econ.* 14, 237–250.

Marsh, P. (1979). Equity rights issues and the efficiency of the UK stock market. *J. Finance* 34, 839–862.

Marsh, P. (1980). Valuation of underwriting agreements for UK rights issues. *J. Finance* 35, 693–716.

Marsh, P. (1982). The choice between equity and debt: An empirical study. *J. Finance* 37, 121–144.

Masulis, R.W. (1980a). The effects of capital structure change on security prices: A study of exchange offers. *J. Financ. Econ.* 8, 139–177.

Masulis, R.W. (1980b). Stock repurchase by tender offer: An analysis of thecauses of common stock price changes. *J. Finance* 35,305–319.

Masulis, R.W. (1983). The impact of capital structure change on firm value: Some estimates. *J. Finance* 38, 107–126.

Masulis, R.W. (1988). *The Debt–Equity Choice* (Ballinger Press: Cambridge, MA).

Masulis, R.W., and A.N. Korwar (1986). Seasoned equity offerings, An empirical investigation. *J. Financ. Econ.* 15, 91–117.

Mayer, C. (1990). Financial systems, corporate finance, and economic development, in: R.G. Hubbard (ed.), *Asymmetric Information, Corporate Finance, and Investment*, NBER, University of Chicago Press, Chicago, IL.

McConnell, J.J., and G.G. Schlarbaum (1981). Evidence on the impact of exchange offers on security prices: The case of income bonds. *J. Bus.* 54, 65–85.

Mikkelson, W.H. (1981). Convertible calls and security returns. *J. Financ. Econ.* 9, 237–264.

Mikkelson, W.H., and M.M. Partch (1985). Valuation effects and costs of secondary distributions. *J. Financ. Econ.* 14, 165–199.

Mikkelson, W.H., and M.M. Partch (1986). Valuation effects of security offerings and the issuance process. *J. Financ. Econ.* 15, 30–60.

Mikkelson, W.H., and M.M. Partch (1988). Withdrawn security offerings. *J. Financ. Quant. Anal.* 23, 119–133.

Miller, M. (1977). Debt and Taxes. *J. Finance* 32, 261–276.

Miller, M., and K. Rock (1985). Dividend policy under asymmetric information. *J. Finance* 40, 1031–1051.

Moore, G.H. (1980). Business Cycles, Inflation, and forecasting, in: *National Bureau of Economic Research Studies in Business Cycles* No. 24, National Bureau of Economic Research, Inc., Ballinger Publishing Co., Cambridge, MA.

Myers, S.C. (1977). Determinants of corporate borrowing. *J. Financ. Econ.* 5, 147–175.

Myers, S.C. (1984). The capital structure puzzle. *J. Finance* 39, 575–592.

Myers, S.C., and N. Majluf (1984). Corporate financing and investment decisions when firms have information that investors do not have. *J. Financ. Econ.* 13, 187–221.

Myhal, P. (1990). Some observations on the "usual" anti-dilution provisions. *Canadian Business Law J.* 17, 283–302.

Nanda, V. (1991). "On the good news in equity carve-outs". *J. Finance* 46, 1717–1737.

Officer, D., and R. Smith (1986). Announcement effects of withdrawn security offerings: Evidence on the wealth redistribution hypothesis. *J. Financ. Res.* 9, 229–238.

Ritter, J.R. (1984). The "hot issue" market of 1980. *J. Bus.* 57, 215–241.

Ritter, J.R. (1987). The costs of going public. *J. Financ. Econ.* 19, 269–281.

Ritter, J.R. (1991). The long-run performance of initial public offerings. *J. Finance* 46, 3–27.

Rock, K. (1986). Why new issues are underpriced. *J. Financ. Econ.* 13, 187–212.

Rogers, R.C., and J.E. Owers (1985). Equity for debt exchanges and stockholder wealth. *Financ. Manage.* 14, 18–26.

Ross, S. (1977). The determination of financial structure: The incentive-signalling approach. *Bell J. Econ.* 8, 23–40.

Schipper, K., and A. Smith (1986). A comparison of equity carve-outs and equity offerings: Share price effects and corporate restructuring. *J. Financ. Econ.* 15, 153–186.

Schwert, G.W. (1989). Why does stock market volatility change over time? *J. Finance* 36, 15–29.

Scholes, M.S., and M.A. Wolfson (1989). Decentralized investment banking, the case of discount dividend-reinvestment and stock-purchase plans. *J. Financ. Econ.* 23, 7–35.

Singh, A.K. (1992). Common stock rights offering and the standby underwriting contract, working paper, Iowa State University.

Singh, A.K., A.R. Cowan and N. Nayar (1991). Underwritten calls of convertible bonds. *J. Financ. Econ.* 29, 173–196.

Smith, C.W., Jr. (1977). Alternative methods for raising capital rights versus underwritten offerings. *J. Financ. Econ.* 5, 273–307.
Smith, C.W., Jr. (1986). Investment banking and the capital acquisition process. *J. Financ. Econ.* 15, 3–29.
Smith, R., and M. Dhatt (1984). Direct equity financing: A resolution of a paradox: A comment. *J. Finance* 39, 1615–1618.
Stevenson, H.W. (1957). Common stock financing, Michigan Business Rep. No. 29, Bureau of Business Research, School of Business Administration, University of Michigan, Ann Arbor.
Stein, J. (1992). Convertible bonds as backdoor equity financing. *J. Financ. Econ.* 32, 3–21.
Stulz, R.M. (1990). Managerial discretion and optimal financing policies. *J. Financ. Econ.*, 26, 3–28.
Taggart, R.A., Jr. (1977). A model of corporate financing decisions. *J. Finance* 32, 1467–1485.
Taggart, R.A., Jr. (1985). Secular patterns in the financing of U.S. Corporations, National Bureau of Economic Research, No. 614.
Tinic, S. (1988). Anatomy of initial public offerings of common stock. *J. Finance* 43, 789–822.
Titman, S., and B. Trueman (1986). Information quality and the valuation of new issues. *J. Account. Econ.* 8, 159–172.
Tripathy, N., and R. Rao (1992). Adverse selection, spread behavior, and over-the-counter seasoned equity offerings. *J. Financ. Res.* 15, 39–56.
Vanthienen, L., and T. Vermaelen (1987). The effect of personal taxes on common stock prices. *J. Banking Finance* 11, 223–244.
Vermaelen, T. (1981). Common stock repurchases and market signalling. *J. Financ. Econ.* 9, 139–183.
Walter, I., and R.C. Smith (1989). *Investment Banking in Europe: Restructuring for the 1990s*, Basil Blackwell, New York, NY.
Welch, I. (1989). Seasoned offerings, imitation costs, and the underpricing of initial public offerings. *J. Finance* 44, 421–447.
Welch, I. (1991). An empirical examination of models of contract choice in initial public offerings. *J. Quant. Anal.*, 26, 497–518.
Wruck, K.H. (1989). Equity ownership concentration and firm value: Evidence from private equity financings. *J. Financ. Econ.* 23, 3–28.

R. Jarrow et al., Eds., *Handbooks in OR & MS, Vol. 9*

Chapter 32

Financial Intermediation and the Market for Credit

Anjan V. Thakor

School of Business, Indiana University, Bloomington, IN 47405, U.S.A.

1. Introduction

The main goal of this paper is to provide a brief review of the services produced by financial intermediaries and their role in the allocation of credit, a task made somewhat ambitious by the proliferation of new ideas in this literature.[1] Two developments have spurred impressive advances in the theory of financial intermediation over the last two decades. First, there has been an explosive growth in innovations in financial contracts, institutions and markets, so that there has been much for academic research to explain. Second, increasing sophistication in the analytical tools provided by option pricing, information economics and game theory has facilitated the adoption of a scientific approach to examining the economic issues raised by these developments in the credit markets.

Because of space limitations, I will not even attempt a complete review of all of the recent research in financial intermediation. Rather, I will organize my discussion around the main services provided by financial intermediaries, and hence review selected papers that have enhanced our understanding of these services. Figure 1 sketches these services. The traditional way of classifying financial intermediation services is to group them as 'asset services' and 'liability services'. I have avoided such a classification because it is somewhat artificial and because it gets blurred in many places. For example, 'guaranteeing' is usually listed as an asset service, and yet it includes the sale of contingent claims like loan commitments and letters of credit which impose a *contingent liability* on the bank.

In Figure 1, I have first classified financial intermediary services into *brokerage* and *qualitative asset transformation*, and then elaborated on the specific services provided in each group. A financial intermediary provides brokerage services when it intermediates in a financial transaction without affecting the nature

[1] See, for example, Bhattacharya & Thakor [1993] for a more comprehensive and critical survey of this literature. My discussions in this paper draw upon material in that paper as well as my work with Stuart Greenbaum [Greenbaum & Thakor, 1995]. My thanks to my co-authors for permission to utilize the fruits of these collaborations.

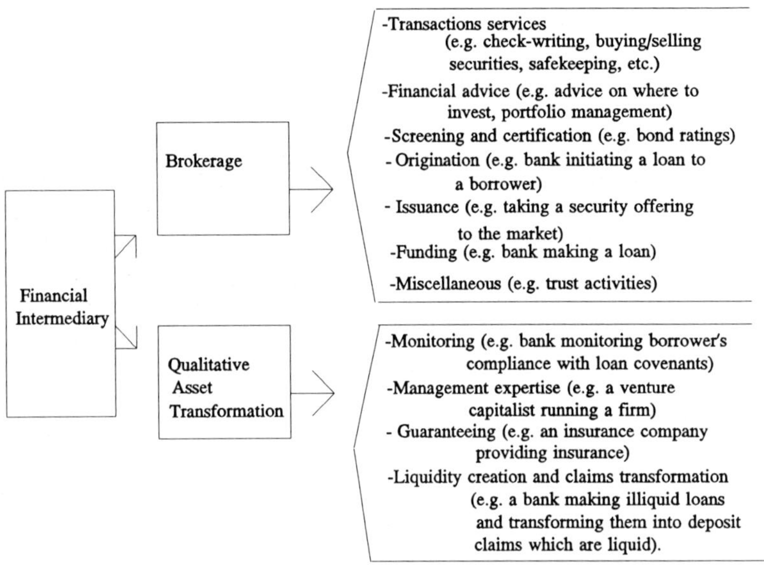

Fig. 1. Services provided by financial intermediaries.

of the claim being transacted. Qualitative asset transformation (QAT) takes place when the financial intermediary affects the nature of the claim whose exchange it facilitates through intermediation. Financial intermediaries often *specialize* in the provision of one or more of these services. Depository financial intermediaries — institutions that raise funds by accepting deposits and investing them in loans and securities — have traditionally provided almost all of these services, although with emphasis on specific services varying across different depository institutions. For example, commercial banks have traditionally focused more on guaranteeing and certain types of transactions services than credit unions and mutual savings banks. Nondepository financial intermediaries — institutions that produce financial services but do not raise funds through deposits — have traditionally specialized in subsets of these services. For example, rating agencies specialize in screening and certification, insurance companies specialize in guaranteeing, and financial counselors (as well as newsletters) specialize in financial advice. While the ensuing discussion is organized around the services provided by financial intermediaries, I will also refer to the types of intermediaries that provide these services.

The rest of the paper is organized as follows. Section 2 discusses brokerage services, and examines the incentives for financial intermediaries to arise as diversified information brokers. Section 3 takes up QAT and examines a model emphasizing the monitoring aspects of QAT. Guaranteeing is examined in Section 4. Section 5 looks at liquidity creation and claims transformation. Regulatory issues related to these various issues are briefly examined *en route*. Section 6 concludes.

2. Brokerage and financial intermediaries

2.1. General discussion of benefits of brokerage

A broker's stock-in-trade is information. A broker is often able to produce payoff-relevant information at lower cost than is possible in nonintermediated transactions. This relative advantage stems from two sources. First, a broker develops special skills in interpreting *subtle* signals, so that the value of brokerage is a function of the nature of information being sought. If the payoff-relevant attributes are trivially observable — telephone numbers, for instance — the broker's skills are not very important. On the other hand, if the relevant attributes are not readily observable — desired attributes in a chief executive officer or the desired attributes in a firm for a corporate merger — the broker's skills become important. Second, brokers can reduce information production costs due to *reusability of information*. Unlike many other commodities, the use of information does not necessarily result in its consumption. The extraordinary attribute of information applies both *cross-sectionally* (across customers) and *intertemporally* (through time on a given customer). The brokers considered in this section are like investment advisers, rating agencies and possibly auditors, rather than securities brokers per se.

2.2. Benefits of intermediaries consisting of many brokers

Thus far we have discussed the benefit of a single broker. Financial intermediaries typically consist of many individual brokers. For example, a rating agency has many individual information producers, as do financial newsletters and other information gathering agencies. That is, these firms are *diversified information brokers*. This suggests that there must be additional gains from brokerage which are created by the coalescing of individual brokers. What are these gains?

Asking this question is similar to the long-standing question in industrial organization about why firms exist. The existence of a firm means that some price-mediated market transactions are replaced by intrafirm arrangements. Williamson [1975] explains the reasons why this may be optimal. In the context of financial intermediation, this issue has been explored by Campbell & Kracaw [1980], Ramakrishnan & Thakor [1984], Millon & Thakor [1985], and Allen [1990].

Ramakrishnan & Thakor suggest that by coalescing into a group, individual information producers are confronted with two effects. First, they can pool individual payoffs and thus diversify away idiosyncratic risk; this is a positive externality. Second, payoff pooling engenders incentives for individual agents to 'free-ride' on each other's effort inputs; this is a negative externality. The extent to which the benefits from intermediation can be captured depends on the interaction of these two externalities in the formation of the intermediary.

The essential features of the Ramakrishnan–Thakor model are captured in the discussion below. Suppose the cost to an individual broker of producing payoff-relevant information about an asset is $c > 0$, and each broker is risk averse, with a strictly increasing and concave utility function of $U(\cdot)$ defined over monetary wealth. We assume that c is a nonmonetary cost to the information producer (i.p.); it does not figure in his utility over wealth. Moreover, it is incurred only if the i.p. actually produces information about the firm he specializes in. Also, each i.p. has a minimum level of expected utility, say $\bar{U}$, that must be guaranteed by his compensation package for producing information, or else he'll work in his best *alternative* occupation.

Now suppose that the firm that wishes to attract capital (or the investor who wants to decide whether he should invest in a particular asset) approaches an i.p. directly to produce information about it and release it to the market, i.e., the i.p. plays the role of a rating agency. If the i.p. is just paid a fixed fee, we have a moral hazard problem in that he will avoid actually producing information, thereby saving itself the effort-related cost c. He'll simply make a quick guess, collect his fee and send the firm on its way. Investors will recognize this and the firm's price will not move. The firm will have wasted its money.

But suppose the firm is able to monitor the i.p. to discover something about whether he actually invested c. This monitoring produces a signal which tells the firm about the i.p.s effort. However, this signal is noisy. Even if the i.p. invests c in information production, the signal says that he did only with probability p. With probability $1 - p$, the signal is erroneous and indicates that the i.p. did not produce information. If the i.p. did not produce information, then the signal says that he did with probability q and that he did not with probability $1 - q$. We assume $p > q$, so that the signal is informative. Now let the i.p.s compensation be as follows: pay him $\$H$ if the signal says he produced information and $\$L$ if it says he did not, with $H > L$. If the i.p. does produce information, he gets an expected utility of

$$EU(\text{produce information}) = pU(H) + [1 - p]U(L) - c \tag{1}$$

If he does not produce information, he gets an expected utility of

$$EU(\text{don't produce information}) = qU(H) + [1 - q]U(L) \tag{2}$$

If investors are to believe that the i.p. is credible, his compensation schedule should be incentive compatible. That is,

$$pU(H) + [1 - p]U(L) - c \geq qU(H) + [1 - q]U(L) \tag{3}$$

It will also be necessary to make sure that the i.p. is willing to work for the firm. This requires that

$$pU(H) + [1 - p]U(L) - c \geq \bar{U} \tag{4}$$

We can solve (3) and (4) to come up with H and L. We can show that in equilibrium (3) and (4) should hold as equalities, i.e., treating them as equalities leads to a solution that minimizes the expected cost for each firm. To illustrate, suppose $U(x) = \sqrt{x}$ for any number x, $\bar{U} = 20$, $p = 0.8$, $q = 0.2$ and $c = 10$. Solving (3) and (4) as a pair of simultaneous equations with these numbers, we get

$H = 10,000/9$ and $L = 10,000/36$. The i.p. earns an expected utility of exactly 20. The expected cost of information production for each firm is $0.8H + 0.2L = 944.44$ approximately.

Now suppose that there are two i.p.s, each like the i.p. in the preceding analysis, who coalesce and form a financial intermediary of two i.p.s. Each still deals with a separate firm. However, they now pool their payoffs to avail of diversification benefits. We assume that because the i.p.s are cooperating, they can costlessly observe each other's actions. This means neither i.p. has to be concerned about his partner free-riding off his effort. So now each i.p.s compensation becomes

$$\frac{2H}{2} = H \quad \text{if both signals are favorable}$$
$$\frac{H + L}{2} \quad \text{if only one signal is favorable}$$
$$\frac{2L}{2} = L \quad \text{if both signals are unfavorable}$$

Assuming that signals across firms are uncorrelated, the probabilities of different compensations for each i.p. are given in the table below.

Probability of compensation	Compensation of each i.p.
p^2 if both i.p.s produce information and q^2 if both don't	H
$2p[1 - p]$ if both i.p.s produce information and $2q[1 - q]$ if both don't	$\frac{[H + L]}{2}$
$[1 - p]^2$ if both i.p.s produce information and $[1 - q]^2$ if both don't	L

Note that both i.p.s will act in concert. The firms that give them compensation contracts realize that the rules of the game have changed. They must now solve the following pair of simultaneous equations.

$$\begin{aligned} p^2U(H) + 2p[1 - p]U\left(\frac{H + L}{2}\right) + [1 - p]^2U(L) - c = \\ = q^2U(H) + 2q(1 - q)U\left(\frac{H + L}{2}\right) + [1 - q]^2U(L) \end{aligned} \tag{5}$$

and

$$p^2U(H) + 2p[1 - p]U\left(\frac{H + L}{2}\right) + [1 - p]^2U(L) - c = \bar{U} \tag{6}$$

Generally, the solution to this will be different from the previous solution. Suppose, however, that firms continue to use the old contracts with $H = 10,000/9$ and $L = 10,000/36$. It can be checked in this case that (5) is satisfied exactly and that the left hand side of (6) is about 20.43. That is, each i.p. in the financial intermediary enjoys a higher expected utility than he did before. Note that the expected cost of having information produced for each firm will be exactly the same as before. Thus, the formation of a financial intermediary makes i.p.s better off if firms don't alter their contracts. Of course, firms may wish to write different contracts to remove the excess utility enjoyed by the i.p.s. In this case, expected information production costs of firms are lowered.

The reason why the formation of an intermediary helps is diversification. By pooling their payoffs, the i.p.s are able to reduce individual risks. This means that they can increase their expected utility and if at least some of the benefit of this increased utility is shared with the firms they are screening, the cost of information production will also reduce.

This argument can be taken to the limit. Ramakrishnan & Thakor show that an infinitely large intermediary can achieve the first best even though investors cannot observe any i.p.s effort. To see this, note that when the financial intermediary becomes infinitely large, by the law of large numbers, (loosely speaking) the probabilities become actual fractions. That is, if all i.p.s produce information, the intermediary knows almost surely that 80% of them will get H each and 20% will get L each. Thus, the intermediary knows that its payoff will be

$$0.8H + 0.2L = 0.8\left[\frac{40000}{36}\right] + 0.2\left[\frac{10000}{36}\right] = 944.44$$

per i.p. with probability one. Since the financial intermediary itself can monitor its own members, it does not have to worry about moral hazard. Thus, it can promise each of its member i.p.s a *fixed* payment of 944.44, knowing that even though on any given i.p., it could receive either more or less than this amount, the random fluctuations around 944.44 will cancel out for the intermediary as a whole. Thus, each individual i.p.s expected utility in this intermediary is $U(944.44) - 10 = 20.73$, which is higher than with the two-i.p. intermediary. If the intermediary passes along this gain to the firms it screens, then *information production costs are lowest with a very large intermediary*.

That is, we have shown that a *diversified information broker* can lower the cost of information production and hence the cost of exchanging capital. Once again, the pivotal function served by a financial intermediary is that of providing a more efficient resolution of informational problems.

Diversification in this model is achieved by letting each i.p. within the intermediary share the risk in the compensation of every other member i.p.. That is, as we add to the size of the group, each individual compensation risk is shared by an increasing number of i.p.s. Due to the risk aversion of the member i.p.s, such diversification helps to improve welfare. We shall call this 'diversification by subdividing risks'. Another type of diversification, considered by Diamond [1984], is 'diversification by adding risks'. In this case, a single i.p. bears 100% of N independent risks, with diversification occurring as N increases. This is quite different from the first form of diversification because the total wealth of the i.p. is growing as he adds more risks. That is, instead of spreading a given amount of wealth over a larger number of independent gambles, we are spreading an increasing amount of wealth over a larger number of independent gambles. Samuelson [1963] has called such diversification 'the fallacy of large numbers', because it is not generally true that, for all risk averse utility functions, the individual's risk aversion toward the Nth independent gamble is a decreasing function of N. However, there are sufficient conditions involving restrictions on utility functions such that such diversification is beneficial.

Of course, in practice we do not observe a single large bank or information broker, but rather lots of imperfectly diversified intermediaries. Why? Millon & Thakor [1985] attempted an answer by pointing out that an important assumption in Ramakrishnan & Thakor's analysis is that the i.p.s within the intermediary can monitor each other costlessly. That is, 'free-riding' problems within the intermediary are assumed away. This permits the intermediary to capture the full benefits from diversification. Millon & Thakor relax the costless internal monitoring assumption and show that, if the *only* benefit to group formation is risk sharing, the negative externality from intra-intermediary incentive problems more than offsets the positive externality from risk sharing. Hence, diversification is counterproductive. They suggest, however, that there may be *information-sharing* gains associated with group formation. In their model, in addition to idiosyncratic factors affecting the values of firms, there is a systematic risk factor which affects the values of all firms being screened, so that the group can delegate one i.p. to produce information about that factor and then share this information with others in the group. This cross-sectional information reusability provides another benefit of group formation in addition to diversification. They show that it is now worthwhile for a diversified intermediary to arise, but its size will be finite, as opposed to the infinitely large intermediary in Ramakrishnan & Thakor.

Allen [1990] tackles the question of the value of intermediation from a somewhat different perspective. As in Ramakrishnan & Thakor and Millon & Thakor, he too examines the direct sale of financial information. But rather than assuming the availability of noisy monitoring to ensure the reliability of the information being sold, he analyzes optimal contracts that make the information seller's payoff contingent on the realized return on the asset being screened. Allen explores a rich problem that involves the information seller having superior information about both the asset return and his own utility function. A key result in the paper is that the presence of uninformed sellers who have a propensity to mimic the informed sellers prevents the latter from fully capturing the surplus from being informed. This implies that, if a buyer of information has sufficient time before asset markets meet to act as an intermediary and *resell* the information, then it will be worthwhile for him to do so. The reason is simple. An agent who has purchased the information has paid less for it to the initially informed agent than he would have if the incentive compatibility constraint (ensuring nonmimicry by the uninformed) did not have to be satisfied. Moreover, the incentive compatibility constraint depends in part on the information seller's risk aversion, so that adding another seller (an intermediary) improves the amount of risk-taking by information sellers as a group, thus enhancing the gains from selling information. This makes it profitable for the buyer to resell the information and capture the residual gains. Allen's model too predicts that FIs which provide brokerage services will be large.

Examples of real-world diversified brokers are credit rating agencies like Moody's and S&P, information gathering agencies like Dun & Bradstreet, financial newsletters, investment counsellors, etc.

3. Qualitative asset transformation and financial intermediation

3.1. General discussion of benefits of qualitative asset transformation (QAT)

A financial intermediary (FI) typically achieves QAT by: (i) holding assets of longer duration than its own liabilities, (ii) reducing the unit size of its clients' claims by holding assets of larger unit size than its liabilities, (iii) enhancing the liquidity of client's claims by holding assets which are more illiquid than its liabilities, and (iv) reducing credit risk by monitoring borrowers and diversifying across borrowers.

An FI that performs QAT does more than what a pure broker does in that QAT subsumes brokerage as a component service. Examples of real-world FIs that perform QAT include banks, S&Ls, credit unions, venture capitalists, insurance companies, etc.

The 'standard' question posed in connection with the role of FIs in providing QAT is: why do we need FIs to provide QAT, i.e., why can't savers and users of capital engage in direct, nonintermediated transactions? A related question has to do with the size of the FI. Why do FIs need multiple agents coalescing to provide QAT? The next subsection is devoted to answering these questions.

3.2. Benefits of a diversified QAT

In an early paper on the subject, Leland & Pyle [1977] provided a glimpse at possible answers to the questions raised in the previous subsection. They crafted an asymmetric information model in which entrepreneurs signal their privately known mean project cash flows to investors (from whom they wish to raise capital) through the equity positions they personally take in their projects. The resulting equilibrium is dissipative in that risk-averse entrepreneurs end up with undiversified portfolio holdings due to the desire to signal. Moreover, the signaling cost for each entrepreneur is positively related to the riskiness inherent in project cash flows.[2] Leland & Pyle suggested that FIs could perhaps improve welfare by certifying project values to investors on behalf of individual entrepreneurs. This certification would involve the FI first becoming informed at a cost about project values itself, and then incurring an additional signaling cost to communicate this information to investors. The key is that the FI would be diversified across many projects, so that the portfolio would have lower cash flow risk, and hence a lower signaling cost in communicating the value of the *portfolio* to investors. It may

[2] Actually, Leland & Pyle made an error in their comparative statics analysis and came up with the opposite result. Diamond [1984] provided a corrected version of their analysis.

turn out that the sum of the FI's own cost of becoming informed and the cost of signaling to investors may be less than the total cost of entrepreneurs signaling themselves; in this case, intermediation would be valuable.

Leland & Pyle did not pursue this possibility formally, relying instead on raising the possibility and discussing it qualitatively. Diamond [1984] provided a formal model of a bank which funds entrepreneurs using debt contracts and finances these loans with deposits which are also debt contracts. These debt contracts arise endogenously in Diamond because of the assumption that only the entrepreneur can observe the cash flow realization from his project.[3] This assumption creates an incentive for the entrepreneur/borrower to misrepresent the realized cash flow to the lender. Diamond proposes solving this problem in one of two ways: (i) the lender can impose a sufficiently large nonpecuniary penalty on the borrower any time he reports a cash flow realization less than the promised repayment to the lender, or (ii) the lender can produce costly information about the cash flow realization; Diamond refers to such verification as 'monitoring'. Both alternatives are dissipative. Moreover, when there is no FI, *each* individual investor must produce costly information about each entrepreneur if alternative (ii) is preferred. This results in duplicated information production by multiple investors. Now, if an FI were to intermediate between entrepreneurs and investors, it could resolve the problem of ex-post privately observed cash flows by producing costly information just once per entrepreneur. Of course, the FI might be tempted to lie to depositors about this cash flow in order to reduce its payout to them. Suppose that depositors induce truth-telling by the FI by imposing a nonpecuniary penalty on it whenever it defaults on deposits, the expected value of which is D.

Let K represent the cost of discovering an entrepreneur's realized cash flow, and let there be m investors who provide (deposit) funds to each entrepreneur. Then, if $E(\phi)$ represents the expected value of the nonpecuniary penalty on an entrepreneur with alternative (i), an intermediary strictly improves welfare if

$$K + D < \min[E(\phi), mK]. \tag{7}$$

Diamond goes on to show that this inequality may be satisfied for a sufficiently large FI. The reason is as follows. Suppose that the only way to achieve incentive compatibility and motivate the FI to pay depositors when the aggregate cash flow is insufficient is to impose a nonpecuniary penalty on it for failing to make the promised repayment to depositors; recall D is the expected value of this nonpecuniary cost. Now, if individual entrepreneurs' project cash flows are identically and independently distributed (i.i.d.), then each depositor's share of the *sum* of these cash flows converges to a known value almost surely as the number of projects being financed (n) increases to infinity. Thus, *if* the FI does not engage in ex-post misrepresentation of aggregate cash flow realizations, it can avoid default and hence the nonpecuniary penalty with probability one. Consequently, $D \to 0$

[3] This result depends on the assumption that the ex-post state verification is deterministic. Mookherjee & P'ng [1989] show that the optimal verification strategy is randomized and that the optimal contract conditional on this optimal strategy is never a debt contract.

as $n \to \infty$. Then, at least in the case in which $\min[E(\phi), mK] = mK$, we have (7) being satisfied.

The bank in Diamond's model achieves QAT by reducing the riskiness of depositors' claims through diversification, and it provides the brokerage services associated with funding and avoiding the costs of duplicated verification by multiple depositors. Like Diamond, Boyd & Prescott [1986] also seek to explain the role of banks in the financial intermediation process, and like Ramakrishnan & Thakor, they consider intermediary coalitions. They consider an economy in which entrepreneurs have projects with differing payoff attributes and increasing returns to scale. The FI provides incentives for those with less valuable projects to become depositors and evaluators of other entrepreneurs' projects. Thus, investment is diverted from these less valuable projects to more highly valued projects, and aggregate investment is made more efficient. This implies that in providing the brokerage service associated with screening and funding projects, the FI performs a valuable QAT service because it transforms the claims of entrepreneurs with less valuable projects into higher-valued claims against a portion of the cash flows from the more valuable projects. In this model, the FI has an impact on the 'real' economy since aggregate investment is channeled into more productive uses.

4. Guarantees, QAT and financial intermediation

Thus far we have discussed QAT in terms of the traditional funding and monitoring activities of banks. These activities are 'on-balance sheet' in that their volume and nature impinge visibly on the FI's balance sheet. Banking, however, has changed considerably. Now it is very much a business of making contingent promises or guarantees or commitments; just over a decade ago, it was not. We will refer to these activities generically as *commercial bank contingent claims* (CBCC). These activities are *off-balance sheet* in that they are not reported as of yet as part of the bank's statement of assets and liabilities. It should also be noted that many other financial intermediaries are also significantly involved in the creation of contingent claims. For example, pension funds and insurance companies are significant players in the contingent claims arena.

4.1. General remarks on guarantees and QAT in nonbank financial intermediaries

According to Webster's dictionary, a 'commitment' is a promise to do something in the future. *Insurance companies* routinely make commitments in their normal course of business, since an insurance policy is basically a promise to pay in some future state of nature. Thus, contingent claims *define* the insurance business. This gives rise to a host of interesting adverse selection issues due to asymmetrically distributed information, and there is a rich literature on these problems [e.g. Rothschild & Stiglitz, 1976]. Moreover, because insurance companies bear contingent liabilities whose magnitude is affected by actions that the insured can take but the insurance company cannot observe, moral hazard arises. This is typically dealt with both contractually and through direct monitoring of the insured. In this sense, and also because they make loans, insurance companies are very much like banks in their QAT function. Indeed, the value of insurance-based monitoring as part of QAT may be one reason why shareholders of publicly-held corporations may want their firms insured despite their indifference to idiosyncratic risk [see Mayers & Smith, 1992].

Pension funds also make commitments. A pension fund is the cumulation of assets created from contributions and the investment earnings on these contribution, less any payments of benefits from the fund. There are two 'pure' types of pension plans: *defined contribution* and *defined benefit*. In a defined-contribution plan, a formula specifies contributions by the employee and the employer, but not the eventual benefit payments. In a defined-benefit plan, a formula specifies benefits, but not the manner, including contributions, in which these benefits are funded. With this plan, the employer has a contingent liability equal to the value of its aggregate obligation to employees minus the market value of the pension portfolio (it is a contingent asset if this difference is negative). In essence, the employees have loaned the firm the money it must pay them in benefits, using the assets in the pension fund as collateral. As with a bank's borrower, this creates incentives for the firm to increase the investment risk of the pension fund [see Bodie & Merton, 1992], although the employee is protected from investment risk (relative to a defined-contribution plan) as long as the value of the fund's assets exceeds the employer's obligation to the employees. Pension guarantees have arisen to protect investors against the default risk that arises from the possibility that investment risk could make the assets in the defined-benefit plan be worth less than the promised benefits. In the U.S., private-sector defined-benefit pension plans can be insured by the Pension Benefit Guaranty Corporation (PBGC), a federal agency within the Department of Labor. Despite the obvious benefits of a federal pension guarantee, as Bodie & Merton [1992] point out, these guarantees create a variety of moral hazard problems that have striking similarities to those encountered with federal deposit insurance (see Section 5 for a discussion of deposit insurance). For more on pension plans, see Merton [1983] and Bodie & Merton [1992].

4.2. General remarks on guarantees and QAT in banking

Once negligible in amount, CBCCs now amount to trillions of dollars in the U.S. They represent a variety of exposures across markets and credit risks — standby letters of credit, interest rate and currency swaps, note issuance facilities, options, fixed and variable rate loan commitments, futures and forward contracts on everything from Treasury bills to gold, and foreign currency transactions. Table 1 provides data on the volume of contingent claims.

We can expand Webster's definition of a commitment to say that an off-balance sheet contingent claim is a *promise* by the bank to purchase/sell a financial claim from/to the holder of the commitment at prespecified terms and at the *option* of the holder of the commitment. Thus, an off-balance sheet commitment imposes

Table 1

Outstanding volume of commercial bank contingent claims by quarter for 1988–1989

Quarter	Contingent claims in billions of dollars							
	Interest rate swaps	Foreign currency trans-actions	Loan commit-ment and guarantees	Loan sales	Options	Futures and forward contracts	Standby letters of credit	Total assets
I – 1988	501.15	595.61	616.49	217.22	90.07	273.06	135.86	1345.68
II – 1988	552.94	709.86	622.93	229.68	95.58	310.51	138.15	1324.67
III – 1988	527.03	597.62	621.51	245.02	102.49	328.12	135.34	1368.60
IV – 1988	597.10	675.11	643.29	168.57	92.83	384.02	141.46	1381.38
I – 1989	619.90	486.49	640.68	158.15	133.12	560.65	140.82	1400.93
II – 1989	539.28	715.86	663.15	158.28	157.42	506.29	159.11	1425.20
III – 1989	583.75	833.03	649.73	174.79	182.74	467.97	141.91	1431.65
IV – 1989	520.36	677.57	695.33	242.21	173.81	498.44	159.99	1498.20

Note: Quarter I – 198x means March 198x, Quarter II – 198x means June 198x, Quarter III – 198x means September 198x, and Quarter IV – 198x means December 198x.
Source: We thank Julapa Jagtiani for supplying this data to us.

a contingent liability on the bank (the seller) and endows the buyer of the commitment with an option. In a competitive market for contingent claims, the bank should be paid a fee at the time the contingent claim is sold that equals the value of the option contained in that claim.

Sales of contingent claims have proved to be a useful source of fee income for banks. They provide banks a way in which they can operate in *forward* credit markets. Thus our focus in this section is on credit transactions whose consummation depends on future, as-yet-unpredictable contingencies. We will confine our attention to a discussion of two CBCCs: loan commitments and interest rate swaps.

4.3. Loan commitments

4.3.1. Description

A loan commitment (or a line of credit) is a promise by the bank to lend to the customer up to a prespecified amount during a prespecified future time period at prespecified terms. The terms usually specify how the interest rate on the loan will be computed and the covenants the borrower must satisfy during the commitment period to ensure that the commitment will be honored. Commitments are usually exercised (taken down) when the commitment rate is lower than the customer's spot borrowing rate. The bank's compensation for selling the commitment comes in a variety of forms, used in various combinations. It can take the form of a *commitment fee* which is expressed as a percentage of the total commitment (or credit line) and paid up front by the borrower when the commitment is negotiated. Quite often, commitment and usage fees are employed simultaneously. Also frequently used in conjunction with loan commitments are *compensating balances* which are deposit balances the borrower must keep with the bank during the period of their commitment relationship. These balances are computed as fractions of the total commitment and commonly have associated with them below-market interest rates to be paid by the bank.

Formal loan commitments are used with many commercial and industrial loans, construction and land development loans, leveraged buyouts, mergers and acquisitions. Loan commitments also include backup lines of credit on commercial paper (the bank agrees to lend to the customer as an alterative to its issuing paper) and note issuance facilities (called NIF, in which the bank agrees to buy the short-term notes of a borrower if the latter is unable to sell them in the capital markets). Roughly 80% of all commercial lending in the U.S. is now done under commitments, and by June 30, 1990, outstanding (unused) loan commitments for U.S. corporations had grown to $743 billion. (see Duca & Vanhoose [1990]).

A loan commitment is a contingent claim. The contingency is the spot rate applicable to the specific borrower at the time of commitment takedown. If that spot rate is higher than the commitment rate, the customer will exercise the commitment and the bank will suffer a loss. If the spot rate is exceeded by the commitment rate, the customer will let the commitment expire unused and borrow instead in the spot market. Thus, the bank has an obligation and the customer has an option. The bank has a liability in those states of nature in which the customer will exercise the commitment, and this liability is contingent on the occurrence of those states of nature. We turn now to the question of why so much of commercial bank lending is done under commitments.

4.3.2. Supply side explanations for loan commitments

4.3.2.1. Regulatory taxes. It has been argued that loan commitments have been popular because they have permitted banks to generate fee revenue without having to keep additional capital to support the loan commitments that are sold. Moreover, until the commitment is actually taken down, there is no loan, which means no funding has actually taken place. Consequently, the bank needs no deposits until commitment takedown, which implies that reserve requirements don't affect the commitment until that time. In fact, if the bank is interested only in generating the fee income related to the loan commitment, it could sell the commitment and avoid funding the (potential) loan under the commitment altogether. This could be achieved by selling the loan to another bank if and when the customer decides to exercise the commitment. Alternatively, the bank could securitize the loan.

This 'supply side' explanation for the popularity of loan commitments relies on regulation as the driving force behind the growth in commitment volume. While reserve and capital requirements have certainly been influential in inducing banks to seek nonfunding revenue sources like loan commitments and other contingent claims, I believe that the story is incomplete. The reason is that the timing and magnitudes of changes in these so-called regulatory taxes are inadequate to explain the surge in the popularity of loan commitments and other contingent claims. For example, in 1971, regulators were still more than a decade away from getting Congressional approval to enforce minimum capital-asset ratios. And yet the per-year increases in the dollar volume of banks' contingent claims during the 1970s were nothing short of phenomenal.

4.3.2.2. Contractual discretion. There is another supply side explanation for the popularity of contingent claims, and its virtue is that it does not rely on regulatory taxes; it has recently been proposed by Boot, Greenbaum & Thakor [1993]. Simply put, it says that since contingent claims are promises to deliver something in the future, but invariably involve 'escape clauses' which give the bank the discretion to not honor its promises under 'extenuating' circumstances ('material deterioration', as judged by the bank, in the borrower's financial condition), issuing such claims gives the bank improved ability to manage its overall portfolio of *financial* and *reputational* capital. Consider a bank that has built up a reputation for honoring its contingent claims even in circumstances where provisions in the terms of its contract with the other party would give it the latitude not to. For example, a bank may have agreed to a \$10 million credit line at 10% interest, and yet it allows the customer to borrow \$12 million at 10% even though the customer's (spot) market borrowing rate is 10.75%. Such reputational capital is of value to the bank since it enables it to sell *future* contingent claims at higher prices. Now suppose a bank that has accumulated quite a bit of such reputational capital is faced with the decision of whether to honor a loan commitment to a borrower whose financial condition has deteriorated significantly since the commitment was sold. If it honors the commitment, it would end up lending \$12 million at 10% to a borrower whose spot borrowing rate may be 15%. The bank may well decide not to honor this commitment. This will result in some depreciation of its reputational capital, but it will conserve some financial capital. Thus, the decision to not honor the commitment can be seen as an optimal tradeoff by the bank between its reputational and financial capital, and it is essentially an act of *liquifying* its reputational capital; note that, unlike the bank's financial capital, its reputational capital cannot (with good reason) be *directly* traded.

4.3.3. Demand side explanations for loan commitments

4.3.3.1. Risk sharing considerations. Loan commitments provide banks with a way to increase expected profits by taking on interest rate risk. When a bank sells a fixed rate loan commitment, it agrees to absorb the interest rate risk that the customer would bear if it were to plan to borrow in the spot credit market instead. The customer should, of course, be willing to compensate the bank for taking this risk, and this compensation should be reflected in the price paid for the loan commitment. That loan commitment demand can be rationalized on these grounds was pointed out by Campbell [1978], whose argument is explained below.

Borrowers who are more risk averse than the bank will then be willing to pay the bank *more* for taking interest rate risk on their behalf than the bank would need to be indifferent between taking that risk and not taking it. In other words, the risk premium demanded by the bank for bearing interest rate risk will be lower than that demanded by the customer for bearing the same risk if the latter is more risk averse than the former. Such a disparity in risk preferences makes trade possible between the bank and the customer, and this trade involves the bank selling the borrower a fixed rate loan commitment that puts an upper bound on the customer's future borrowing cost. With a variable rate loan commitment, the bank still bears some interest rate risk relative to a spot lending situation, but the risk borne is less than with a fixed rate commitment. In essence, with a fixed rate commitment the bank bears both the 'systematic' component of interest rate risk (as reflected in unpredictable changes in the index rate, be it the prime rate or the bank's cost of funds), as well as the idiosyncratic component of that risk (as reflected in unpredictable changes in conditions *specific* to the borrower that affect its borrowing cost relative to the index rate), whereas with a variable rate commitment the bank bears only the latter component of interest rate risk. In either case, the risk averse borrower is transferring some interest rate risk from itself to the bank, and to the extent that the bank is willing to participate at a price that is acceptable to the borrower, we have an explanation for why loan commitments are demanded by the bank's customers.

4.3.3.2. Moral hazard. One drawback of the previous explanation is that many loan commitment customers are large, publicly owned firms with numerous shareholders. From portfolio theory we know that even risk averse shareholders should be neutral toward idiosyncratic (firm-specific) risk because they can diversify it away. Moreover, it is not at all clear why they should collectively demand a higher premium for bearing systematic risk than the bank's shareholders do. So we would like to know if there will be a demand for loan commitments even when the bank's customers are not motivated by the desire to purchase insurance against interest rate risk, for example, if they were risk neutral.

It has recently been suggested by Boot, Thakor & Udell [1987, 1991] and Boot & Thakor [1991] that loan commitments may be effective in deterring *moral hazard* stemming either from an incentive on the borrower's part to undersupply productive effort (relative to the case in which the borrower self-finances) or switch projects (in an undetected manner) to the bank's detriment. The intuition is as follows. We know from Stiglitz & Weiss [1981] that the loan interest rate is distortionary in the sense that the higher this rate, the lower is the net return accruing to the borrower, and hence the greater is the borrower's incentive to shirk in providing effort and/or switch to a riskier project. A loan commitment provides a means for the bank to circumvent the distortionary effect of the loan interest rate without relying on more costly alternatives such as collateral or rationing. This can be achieved by lowering the interest rate on the loan to a level sufficient to eliminate (or significantly diminish) moral hazard. This will generally mean that the bank will suffer an expected loss on the loan made under the commitment. Such a loss could arise because the bank may commit to lending at a rate below its own cost of funds, for instance, although it wouldn't be necessary to reduce the loan interest rate that much to make an expected loss on the loan. This loss can be recouped through the commitment fee paid by the customer at the time of purchasing the commitment.

They key is that the customer views the commitment fee as a sunk cost after it is paid, and hence it does not affect either its choice of effort or project. This way the loan commitment helps to attenuate moral hazard.

4.3.3.3. Liquidity guarantee for other creditors. When a firm purchases a loan commitment, suppliers of inputs to the firm know that the firm will have access to liquidity equal to the amount of the commitment. This would reassure these suppliers that the firm will have the funds necessary to service its debt obligations to them. Consequently, these suppliers may be willing to provide inputs to the firm at better credit terms than they would in the absence of the loan commitment. The result would be an overall lowering of the cost of debt for the firm, which would make the firm's *shareholders* better off. This intuition has been formalized by Berkovitch & Greenbaum [1990] who show that the Myers [1977] underinvestment problem facing levered firms can be mitigated with a loan commitment because a commitment — through its lower borrowing rate relative to the spot borrowing rate — can reduce the borrower's repayment obligation and hence his marginal return to equity investment. Recently, Shockley [1995] has developed a similar model to predict that a borrower's *non-commitment* debt would be increasing in its unused loan commitment size, and has also provided supporting empirical evidence.

4.3.3.4. Protection against future credit rationing. Another motive for loan commitments, closely related to the moral hazard argument presented earlier, is that it may protect the buyer against a 'credit crunch', assuring funds availability when credit market conditions are tight. Of course, the 'general nervous' or 'material adverse change' (MAC) clause in the loan commitment contract limits the usefulness of the commitment as insurance against rationing. However, the empirical evidence suggests that this motive is present in the purchase of many loan commitments. This possibility has yet to be formally modeled.

4.3.4. Loan commitments and QAT

When a bank sells a loan commitment, it provides three QAT services. First, it provides the customer an interest rate *guarantee* that its borrowing rate will not be higher than the commitment rate. Second, the loan commitment is a form of delegated monitoring. Third, by attenuating moral hazards of various kinds, a loan commitment reduces the customer's credit risk. This third function may well be the most important of the three principal QAT functions provided by banks.[4]

4.3.5. Regulatory concerns

Although off-balance sheet claims have not been subject to regulatory capital and reserve requirements until now, this is soon going to change. The *Basel Ac-*

[4] Thakor [1989] suggests that bank loan commitments may also improve the efficiency of credit contracting by providing for the implementation of less costly self-selection mechanisms. Maksimovic [1990] argues that loan commitments could also impact product market competition, and shows that competitive pressures could drive all competing firms to purchase loan commitments.

cord, reached under the auspices of the Bank for International Settlements (BIS), stipulates a new set of capital guidelines that are now applicable to commercial banks in virtually all industrialized countries. Under these guidelines, loan commitments with maturities under one year are still not subject to capital requirements, whereas longer maturity commitments have a 4% capital requirements (half that against most loans).

4.4. *Swaps*

4.4.1. *What are swaps?*

An *interest rate swap* is an arrangement between two parties that want to change their exposure to future interest rate fluctuations in opposite directions. The arrangement often involves an intermediating (swap) broker. Thus, a swap is a tool for managing interest rate risk.

Basically a swap involves exchanging interest payments. For example, suppose a firm has a floating rate liability and a fixed rate asset. Such a firm can suffer losses if interest rates were to rise sharply. Now suppose another firm has a fixed rate liability and a floating rate asset. This firm would suffer losses if interest rates were to fall sharply. These two firms could get together and arrange a swap to exchange their interest payments. In principle, they could do more. For instance, they could pool some of their assets and some of their liabilities and work out an arrangement in which each is responsible for making a predetermined fraction of the total interest payments on the pooled liabilities and receiving a predetermined fraction of the total cash flows from the pooled assets.

Interest rate swaps were first used in the Eurobond market during 1981. Large international banks, which lend mostly on a floating-rate basis, were the first to use swaps in which they exchanged the fixed-rate interest obligations on their liabilities for lower-cost floating-rate interest payments. The swap market came into existence in the U.S. in 1982 when the first domestic swap took place between Sallie Mae (Student Loan Marketing Association) and the ITT Financial Corp. Since then this market has experienced enormous growth, with volume reaching $3 trillion by 1991.

An interest rate swap typically works as follows. Suppose we have two firms. Firm A is a bank that lists as its assets loans which promise a floating interest rate of prime plus 25 basis points, and as its liabilities $150 million of 10-year bonds promising a fixed 10% interest rate. Firm B is an S&L whose assets are fixed rate mortgages, and whose liabilities are short-term MMFs (money market funds) and CDs with (floating) interest rates indexed to the T-bill rate. Each institution is exposed to interest rate risk that it wishes to hedge.

We could now arrange a $150 million, 10-year interest rate swap between the bank and the S&L. The swap may be structured as follows. The S&L agrees to pay the bank a fixed rate of 10% per year on $150 million, for ten years. In return, the bank agrees to make the S&L a floating rate payment at 25 basis points above prime, on a $150 million principal. In this way the bank and the S&L have basically exchanged their liabilities. Each has now hedged its interest rate

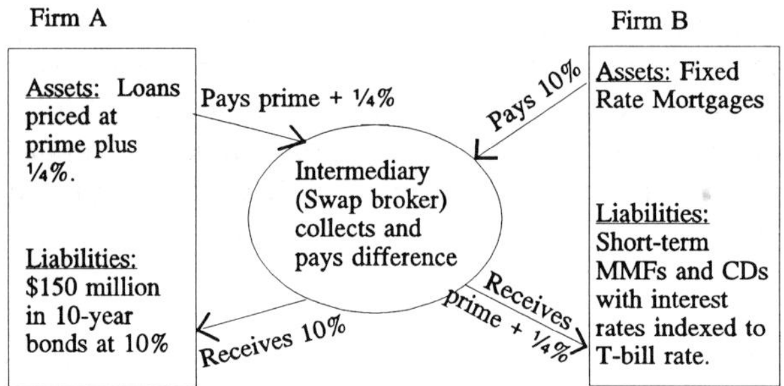

Fig. 2. An example of an interest rate swap.

exposure since the fixed rate liability more closely matches the S&L's fixed rate assets, whereas the floating rate liability more closely matches the bank's floating rate assets. Figure 2 is a pictorial depiction of this arrangement.

Deals such as this normally involve an intermediary (the swap broker) which computes the necessary payments and passes them along to the respective parties. The swap broker, often a bank or an investment banker, collects a substantial fee for its services.

In the early days of swaps, the swap intermediary was a pure broker which did *not* expose itself. Nowadays the intermediary acts more like an asset transformer as it backs up each party and assumes some interest rate risk itself. For example, if the bank in the above transaction defaults, the intermediary would collect the fixed 10% from the S&L and make payments to it at 25 basis points above prime. Thus, *it would assume the role of the bank*. And to the extent that it may not have the bank's balance sheet, it would expose itself to interest rate risk, e.g. if interest rates were to rise sharply, the intermediary would lose.

Traditionally the most common type of swap was the one described in our example, namely that involving a dollar fixed-rate loan swapped for a dollar floating-rate loan. Such a swap is called a 'plain vanilla' swap. However, recently several different types of swaps have become popular. One variation is a floating-to-floating swap where parties agree to swap floating rates based on different index rates. For example, a bank whose assets are floating rate loans at prime plus 20 basis points and whose liabilities are floating rate CDs at LIBOR minus 40 basis points may wish to swap the interest payments on its liabilities with those of an institution which has the interest rate on its liabilities indexed to the prime rate. Such swaps are also known as *basis swaps*. Another popular variation involves swapping currencies. For example, a bank may have foreign loans financed by domestic deposits, so that the interest payments on its loans may be denominated in Japanese yens, while the interest payments on its deposits may be denominated in dollars. Such a bank may wish to swap its yen-denominated loans for dollar-denominated loans (perhaps with a Japanese bank that has dollar-denominated loans financed by yen-denominated deposits raised in Japan).

There are two general types of currency swaps: traditional *fixed/fixed currency swaps* and *cross-currency interest rate swaps*. A fixed/fixed currency swap involves fixed interest rates in each currency. Exchange of principal may or may not be involved. If principal is exchanged, this kind of swap transforms a fixed coupon bond denominated in one currency into a fixed coupon bond in another currency. With a cross-currency interest rate swap one exchanges a fixed payment stream for a floating payment stream, as well as payments in different currencies. These arrangements are occasionally combined in a single transaction, and sometimes the currency and interest rate components are separated. There are other variations as well. For example, there are swaps in which the two parties exchange yields on assets of different maturities (or currency denominations), rather than interest payments on liabilities. The point is that a swap can be tailor-made to suit the needs of the swapping parties, so that a great variety of swaps can be expected to be observed.

4.4.2. The relative advantages of swaps and swap brokers

Campbell & Kracaw [1991] have recently provided an integrated theory of swaps and swap brokers. According to their model, arranging a swap transaction through an intermediating broker offers the following three distinct advantages to the firms involved:

4.4.2.1. Reduction of transactions costs. In order to hedge its interest rate exposure using a futures contract or other 'market-based' mechanisms, a firm needs to compute its 'minimum variance' hedge, i.e., the hedge position that minimizes its risk exposure. Campbell & Kracaw assert that the information needed for this computation is costly, involving both fixed and variable costs. By using a swap broker, both these costs can be reduced. The logic underlying the reduction in fixed costs is transparent — the swap broker does not need to duplicate his learning on repeated transactions. Cross-sectional informational reusability guarantees that the skills acquired in identifying the optimal hedging alternatives can be used across many customers. Variable transactions costs can also be reduced because the swap broker can pool many different cash flows and thereby *offset* the individual hedge positions of the counterparties in the swap.

4.4.2.2. Reduction of basis risk. Since a perfect hedge is usually unavailable, a firm that uses a futures contract to hedge will find that its optimal hedge still leaves it exposed to some interest rate risk. This risk is known as *basis risk*, and it can be reduced by a swap broker through diversification achieved by pooling many individual transactions with imperfectly correlated basis risks.

4.4.2.3. Reduction of agency costs. A firm can reduce its exposure to the risk of refinancing at possibly higher future interest rates by issuing long-term debt. However, long-term debt creates both asset substitution and underinvestment moral hazards. Thus, from an agency costs perspective, it would be preferable for the firm to issue debt of short maturity relative to the maturity structure of its asset payouts. But this exposes the firm to interest rate risk. This is where a swap transaction can help. The firm can issue debt of relatively short maturity to reduce agency costs, and then use a swap transaction to reduce its exposure to interest rate risk.

5. Liquidity creation and claims transformation

5.1. General remarks

Banks provide QAT by financing illiquid loans of relatively long maturities with more liquid deposits of shorter maturities. Indeed, demand deposits have an undefined maturity, i.e., an arbitrarily short maturity. Providing this kind of liquidity creation and maturity transformation exposes the bank to risks. Maturity transformation creates an interest rate risk exposure for the bank, and the bank can cope with this risk in the same manner as other (nonfinancial) firms. I will not discuss that further here. Liquidity creation exposes the bank to *liquidity risk*, which arises because of the possibility of unexpectedly large deposit withdrawals that could force the bank to prematurely call back its loans. In this section I discuss the optimal design of the deposit contract in an uninsured environment, and how this creates liquidity risk for the bank, thus leading to a rationale for deposit insurance to reduce this liquidity risk.

5.2. The nature of the deposit contract

Deposit contracts either have *defined maturities* like *certificates of deposit* (CDs), or are *withdrawable on demand*. I will focus on demand deposits since they provide the clearest characterization of the deposit contract.

The demand deposit contract has four important features:

- Its maturity is undefined.
- It is a debt contract.
- It is not traded.
- It is governed by a 'sequential service' constraint.

The undefined maturity of the contract simply means that the depositor can withdraw at any time, without penalty. Thus, a demand deposit is virtually as liquid as currency, the key difference being that currency carries no default risk, whereas an uninsured bank could default and thus not be able to fully satisfy a withdrawing depositor. Indeed, I will assume for now that there is no deposit insurance, so that we can focus on the characteristics of the deposit contract itself.

Because the deposit is a debt contract, the depositor in an uninsured bank confronts the same asset-substitution moral hazard in dealing with the bank as the bank does in dealing with its borrowers. That is, when a bank creates a deposit, it is simply borrowing from the depositor.

The fact that demand deposits are not traded implies that the depositor's payoff does not depend directly on how information about the bank is processed by other market participants, i.e., the depositor does not face market price risk. Unlike a person who plans to sell a traded security in the market at the (random) price prevailing at that future date, a demand depositor knows precisely (in nominal terms) how much he will receive at *any* future point in time when he withdraws from his account, subject to the condition that the bank is solvent then.

This last condition is not always satisfied, however. In fact, if things were believed to be going badly for the bank, we would expect those who suspected it to rush to the bank to withdraw their deposits. If you arrive late, it is possible that in paying off the earlier depositors the bank has run out of money by the time you get there. In this case, absent deposit insurance, the maximum amount you can withdraw would be less than what you had anticipated. In this sense, your payoff *does* depend on what other depositors believe about the bank, as it would if you were investing in a *traded* debt contract and were liquidating your holding prior to maturity.

This happens because the deposit contract satisfies a sequential service constraint (SSC). Hence, when a depositor seeks to withdraw, the amount the bank pays depends only on what was promised *and* on his place in the queue of depositors wishing to withdraw. In particular, *the depositor's payoff cannot depend on any information that the bank may have about depositors in the queue behind that depositor.* Thus, the bank pays depositors on a 'first come, first served' basis. This creates an incentive for depositors to rush to be first in line whenever they hear bad news.

These features of the deposit contract are worth delineating for two reasons. First, when *all* of the bank's liabilities are uninsured, these features have significant implications for the disciplining of bank management. This suggests that the details of the demand deposit contract are probably not an outcome of chance; they serve a purpose. Second, when deposits are insured, some of these features of the demand deposit contract *encourage* bank runs, thus increasing the liability of the deposit insurer.

5.3. *The demand deposit contract and economic incentives*

Consider first that demandable debt is not traded and that it is a debt contract. The presence of asset substitution moral hazard implies that the bank in this case has an incentive to increase asset risk to the detriment of the depositors. Similarly, depositors face moral hazard in that the bank has an incentive to shirk in monitoring the borrowers to whom it has extended loans. This too adversely affects the depositors' expected payoff. A third form of moral hazard is fraud. Deposits are essentially 'someone else's' money, so that managers may be tempted to pilfer some of that money for themselves. While these cases have recently been attributed to the weakening of efficiency motives due to federal deposit insurance, they were encountered even prior to the adoption of deposit insurance, and our theory predicts that incentives for managerial fraud exist with (nontraded) deposits. The fact that the deposit contract is not traded makes the moral hazard more severe. The reason is that there isn't the discipline imposed by market pricing.

Calomiris & Kahn [1991] and Calomiris, Kahn & Krasa [1991] argue, however, that the other two features of the demand deposit contract — its undefined maturity and the sequential service constraint — help to attenuate these different types of moral hazard. The intuition is as follows.

Suppose that there are numerous individuals who have deposited money in demand deposit accounts at a bank. It is natural to expect that some of these depositors are particularly skilled in analyzing the bank's financial health, whereas others are less able. Let us suppose that these skilled depositors monitor the bank's managers. Now, imagine that a few of these vigilant depositors discover that bank's risky loans are not doing well. Moreover, these depositors also discover that the bank has extended numerous loans to close friends of the top managers; this raises suspicion of fraud. This adverse information induces these depositors to withdraw their funds as quickly as possible.

When these informed depositors withdraw their funds from the bank, there are two possibilities. One is that the uninformed depositors do not react to the actions of the informed depositors. In this case, the total outflow of funds from the bank will depend on the size of the deposit holdings by the informed depositors. If these holdings are large, the bank will be compelled to attract significant new deposits. The second possibility is that some or all of the uninformed depositors observe the withdrawals of the informed depositors and decide to follow suit. In this case, there is a bank run. In either case, the bank will either need to attract new deposits to replace withdrawals, or liquidate. This liquidation will involve either an actual calling back of loans, with the associated disruptions in the productive activities of borrowers, or it will involve loan sales to other banks. The alternative of attracting new deposits will be difficult, for obvious reasons. Prospective depositors will see the large deposit withdrawals and will therefore be reluctant to entrust their money to the bank. And even if some deposit money flows in, the bank will have to pay higher interest rates on these deposits. Thus, deposit withdrawals by the informed depositors are likely to be costly to the bank. The anticipation of incurring these costs could deter the bank's managers from risky investments, or shirking on the monitoring of borrowers. It could also reduce the temptation to defraud the depositors.

This intuition tells us how the demandable nature of deposits helps to keep bank management on its toes.[5] There is a slight hitch in this disciplining process, however. If a depositor can rely on other depositors to monitor the bank, then all that such a depositor has to do is to keep an eye on the informed depositors. There is no need for the 'free-riding' depositor to expend personal resources to monitor the bank. This problem can subvert the depositor monitoring scheme. The reason is that *every* depositor may think that others will do the necessary monitoring, and in that case, no one monitors! This is where the SSC comes into play. Because a depositor's expected payoff is greater if he is at the front of the queue than if he is at the rear, he recognizes that by playing a 'follow the leader' strategy, his *expected* payoff is lower than if he monitors himself. This strengthens each individual depositor's incentive to monitor.

[5] Although the analysis is carried out in the context of demand deposits, it could also be applied to time deposits that mature before the bank's assets.

5.4. The need for deposit insurance

Thus far, I have discussed a bank's role in providing QAT with an uninsured deposit contract whose contractual features contribute to efficiency by ameliorating moral hazard. However, this observation, attributable primarily to Calomiris & Kahn [1991], is predicated on the strong assumption that the monitoring performed by the vigilant depositors is perfect. Interesting possibilities arise if this monitoring were assumed to be noisy. This is because noisy monitoring means that the vigilant depositors may sometimes be wrong, i.e., they may run the bank even though there is no fraud and the bank's assets are sound. This creates the likelihood of inefficient liquidations of loans, which is socially costly. The observation that deposit insurance may have an important role to play in such an environment was given formal structure by Bryant [1980] and Diamond & Dybvig [1983]. I will outline the essence of the Diamond & Dybvig argument below.

Suppose that we live in a two-period world with three points in time: $t = 0, 1, 2$. Individuals are risk averse. At $t = 0$, there are individuals who have endowments of wealth that they wish to invest in projects. Each of these projects requires a \$1 investment at $t = 1$, pays off \$R for sure at $t = 2$ if not liquidated before then, and has positive NPV, i.e., each offers a rate of return sufficiently higher than the riskless rate (which is zero) if continued until $t = 2$. Let $R > 1$. However, if the project is prematurely liquidated at $t = 1$, then there is a loss of productive efficiency and the project pays off only \$1. At $t = 0$, individuals are unsure of their future preferences for consumption. At $t = 1$, they receive a 'preference shock' and learn whether they are about to die or will live another period. If they are about to die, they want to withdraw the money they have invested and consume it immediately at $t = 1$. If they learn that they will live, then they want to leave their money in the projects and consume $\$R$ at $t = 2$. For the population as a whole, a (random) fraction, f, of individuals are 'diers' at $t = 1$ and a fraction, $1 - f$, are 'livers'.

What would happen without a bank? Let C_t^i be the consumption of a type-i agent at time t. Then, if you are a depositor and you discover at $t = 1$ that you are a dier, you will liquidate your investment and consume \$1 then. That is, your first-period consumption $C_1^{\mathrm{D}} = 1$, and your second-period consumption, $C_2^{\mathrm{D}} = 0$. If you discover that you are a 'liver', then you will choose to consume nothing at $t = 1$ (i.e., $C_1^{\mathrm{L}} = 0$) and you will consume an amount $C_2^{\mathrm{L}} = R$ at $t = 2$. Thus, the *nonbank outcome* is the pair $\{C_1^{\mathrm{D}} = 1, C_2^{\mathrm{D}} = 0\}$ or the pair $\{C_1^{\mathrm{L}} = 0, C_2^{\mathrm{L}} = R\}$, depending on the individual's type. Is this the best outcome from the standpoint of an individual at $t = 0$? The answer is obviously no! Since you are a *risk averse* individual, you would like some insurance at $t = 0$ against a random future shock to your own preference for consumption.

Suppose we form a bank $t = 0$ to provide insurance against future shocks to individuals' preferences. This bank is essentially a mutual organization owned by the depositors. It crafts a demand deposit contract which involves $C_1^* > 1$ and $C_2^* < R$ (where asterisks are used to denote first and second period consumptions in the banking case), with the stipulation that C_1^* and C_2^* are mutually exclusive.

Hence, every individual is made better off ex ante — prior to the arrival of the preference shock — by the existence of the bank whose role is to provide individuals with *consumption smoothing*.

The scheme I have just described is incentive compatible — no agent has an incentive to misrepresent his preferences — and represents a Nash equilibrium among depositors. Each type-D depositor's Nash equilibrium strategy is to withdraw at $t = 1$ since that gives him his highest utility (his utility from consumption at $t = 2$ is zero). If each type-L depositor *takes as given* the Nash equilibrium strategy of the *other* type-D depositors (to wait until $t = 2$ to withdraw), then it is clear that no type-L depositor can do better by withdrawing at $t = 1$ than withdrawing at $t = 2$. Thus, it is indeed a Nash equilibrium for all type-D depositors to withdraw at $t = 1$ and all type L-depositors to wait until $t = 2$.

Unfortunately, this 'good' outcome is not the only Nash equilibrium. There is also a 'bad' Nash equilibrium. To see how it might come about, suppose that, instead of assuming that a type-L depositor thinks that all the other type-L depositors will only withdraw at $t = 2$, we assume that a type-L depositor believes that all the other type-L depositors will withdraw at $t = 1$. In this case, what should our 'representative' type-L depositor do?

Suppose he decides to also withdraw at $t = 1$. In this case, the bank will observe that all depositors wish to withdraw. All projects will have to be liquidated to obtain the necessary funds to meet the deposit withdrawals at $t = 1$. The sequential service constraint means that if you are a type-L depositor who waits until $t = 2$ to withdraw (when all the other depositors withdraw at $t = 1$), you surely get nothing. If you rush to the bank at $t = 1$, then assuming that your position in the queue would be decided randomly (with equal probability of being at any position in the queue), you have a nonzero probability of receiving a positive amount. Clearly, your optimal strategy is to withdraw at $t = 1$ too. Thus, it is also a Nash equilibrium for *all* depositors to withdraw at $t = 1$. This equilibrium can be called a *bank run*.

Two points are worth noting. First, the bank run in this setup arises for no particular reason. We are not in a position to say whether the good or the bad Nash equilibrium will arise. Hence, while we can say that a bank run is a possibility, we cannot say *why* it might arise. Second, a simple way for the bank to eliminate a run in this model is to stipulate that withdrawers of demand deposits at $t = 1$ can receive only \$1. In this case, the bank does not need to liquidate more projects than there are withdrawers at $t = 1$, so that a depositor who waits until $t = 2$ will surely receive $\$R$. Thus, it is optimal for *every* type-L depositor to wait until $t = 2$, *regardless of what the other type-L depositors do*. But in this case the bank's demand deposit contract provides *no* risk sharing! Hence, the possibility of runs exists in this model whenever the bank itself has a reason to exist.

However, deposit insurance can eliminate the bad Nash equilibrium in this model *without* eliminating the optimal risk sharing provided by the demand deposit contract. To see this, imagine that a (federal) insurer were to *guarantee* that any individual withdrawing at $t = 1$ will receive less than any individual withdrawing at $t = 2$. In other words, the deposit insurer could guarantee that if the bank was unable to meet contractually specified payouts to depositors at any point in time, the insurer would provide the necessary funds to meet these payouts. In this case, a depositor's payoff would be independent of the strategies of other depositors and it is pretty obvious that only the good Nash equilibrium survives.

Because this theory does not tell us what triggers a bank run, we cannot explore means of stopping runs, *other than* deposit insurance. The message of this theory is this: in the absence of deposit insurance, even a perfectly healthy bank faces the threat of a run, *given* the sequential service constraint associated with demand deposits.[6] In other words, runs and panics are caused by shifts in the beliefs of individuals which are *unrelated* to the 'real' economy (the health of the banking system). Bank runs are simply random manifestations of 'mob psychology' or 'mass hysteria', and can be triggered even by 'sunspots'. This viewpoint makes banking panics a rather mysterious event and suggests that banks are inherently flawed. Moreover, it makes a compelling case for deposit insurance.

5.5. An adverse information theory of bank runs

Chari & Jagannathan [1988] provided a theory of bank runs in which runs are triggered by adverse information. Suppose now that we have three types of individuals. We still have the type-D individuals who *must* consume at the end of the first period. But among the type-L individuals, we now have a fraction who receive information about the terminal ($t = 2$) value of the bank's assets. In the previous theory, we assumed that this value, $\$R$, was known for sure to everybody. Assume now that this value is a random variable, $\tilde{R}$, with a commonly known expected value, $\bar{R}$. Let $\tilde{R} = H > 0$ with probability p and $\tilde{R} = 0$ with probability $1 - p$. At $t = 0$, nobody knows what value $\tilde{R}$ will take at $t = 2$; moreover, none of the individuals knows at $t = 0$ what his type will be at $t = 1$. However, at $t = 1$, each individual discovers whether he is a liver or a dier, and some fraction q of the livers also come to know the value $\tilde{R}$ will take at $t = 2$. Nobody knows how many individuals of each type there are at $t = 1$ (i.e., both the fraction f and the fraction q are *random*).

The choice problem faced by the diers and the informed livers at $t = 1$ is straightforward. All the diers will line up to withdraw their deposits. If the informed livers learn that $\tilde{R} = H$, then it is better for them to leave their money in the bank until $t = 2$ and thereby avoid premature liquidation of the investment projects. But if the informed livers learn that $\tilde{R} = 0$, then clearly it pays for them to withdraw whatever they can at $t = 1$.

Consider now the choice problem of the uninformed livers. They can decide to withdraw their money at $t = 1$ or keep it in the bank until $t = 2$. Their decision

[6] The sequential service constraint in Diamond & Dybvig can be viewed as a discrete-time approximation of the arrival-and-payout process in continuous time. That is, depositors arrive continuously at a random rate and the bank pays each depositor the contractually promised amount on demand as long as it has the resources to do so.

will be based on what they *believe* the value of the bank's assets will be at $t = 2$. Although they can't directly observe this value, they can draw an inference about this value by *observing* the length of the line of withdrawers at the bank at $t = 1$. In drawing this Bayesian inference, they realize that there will always be some people who wish to withdraw at $t = 1$ because they have discovered that they are diers. But they don't know *how many* such individuals there are. This means that when they observe the length of the queue at the bank at $t = 1$, they are never sure whether all the withdrawers are diers or whether there are some livers among them.

It is true, however, that if the queue is relatively long, it is *more likely* that it contains some informed livers who possess adverse information about the bank. Likewise, if the queue is relatively short, it is likely that it consists of only diers. In the perfect information case, if the uninformed livers could tell for sure that the queue contained only diers, they would leave their money in the bank until $t = 2$, and if they could tell for sure that the queue contained livers as well as diers, they would withdraw their money at $t = 1$. In the more realistic case in which they can't be sure, they use the queue length as a *noisy* signal of the information possessed by the informed livers. Thus, they rush to withdraw their deposits at $t = 1$ if they observe a relatively long queue, and they keep their money in the bank until $t = 2$ if they observe a relatively short queue.

Defining a run on the bank as a situation in which some livers end up withdrawing their deposits, we see now that a bank run is more likely when some depositors receive adverse information about the bank. The reason is that in that case the informed livers line up to withdraw their funds and this increases the queue length that induces the uninformed livers to also seek withdrawal of their deposits. Thus, a bank run comes about because some depositors attempt to learn something about the bank by looking at how many other depositors are withdrawing their money. However, since their learning is 'noisy' (they occasionally confuse liquidity-motivated withdrawals with informed withdrawals), they make both type-I and type-II errors in the statistical sense. That is, they sometimes don't run the bank when they should (i.e., when the queue is relatively short but consists of informed livers: a type-II error if the null hypothesis is that the bank is healthy), and they sometimes run the bank when they shouldn't (i.e., when the queue length is relatively long but consists only of diers: a type-I error). Because runs can sometimes occur when they shouldn't, deposit insurance may improve welfare by making it unnecessary for any liver to withdraw his deposits prematurely.

The adverse information theory of bank runs also raises questions about the desirability of using nontraded demand deposit contracts to insure individuals against random shocks to their consumption preferences. The analysis of Jacklin & Bhattacharya [1988] indicates that, when information-based bank runs are possible, less risky asset portfolios are better financed with deposit contracts and more risky ones with traded equity or debt contracts. Moreover, they show that, if investment is irreversible, the 'panic' equilibrium in Diamond & Dybvig [1983] can be ruled out.

5.6. Regulatory implications

The contemporary theories of bank runs suggest that deposit insurance is an important ingredient of banking. However, deposit insurance creates a host of issues, some of which I will touch upon very briefly here.

First, deposit insurance has been alleged to create moral hazard. Merton [1977] showed that deposit insurance is analogous to a put option in that the bank can 'put' the bank to the insurer whenever total asset value falls below the value of its liabilities. This creates an incentive for the bank to substitute riskier assets for safer assets, to the insurer's detriment. Given this risk-taking propensity, the insurer needs to regulate in a way to cope with this moral hazard. Merton's framework also suggests a way to compute the cost of deposit insurance to the insurer; for a more recent treatment in a multiperiod framework, see Cooperstein, Pennacchi and Redburn [1995]. Kahane [1977] suggests that any regulation aimed at curbing bank risk taking must impose portfolio restrictions *as well as* minimum capital requirements on banks. However, Boot & Greenbaum [1992] point out that what really creates moral hazard is the protection afforded the bank's shareholders by *limited liability*. Hence, risk-taking incentives would exist even in a regime with uninsured deposits. But they show that deposit insurance weakens a bank's desire to build a reputation for monitoring borrowers and making prudent asset choices. It therefore contributes to risk taking, but in a much more subtle manner than previously recognized.

Second, deposit insurance raises the question of how the insurance premium should be structured. Some have suggested the necessity of risk-sensitive deposit insurance premia to cope with asset substitution moral hazard. However, Chan, Greenbaum & Thakor [1992] have recently shown that an *incentive compatible* risk-sensitive deposit insurance pricing scheme is impossible in a completely deregulated competitive banking system. Their arguments, as well as the empirical work of Keeley [1990], suggest the need for restrictions on entry to augment bank charter values and retard risk taking.

Third, deposit insurance creates the need for regulatory monitoring to control bank risk taking and fraud. The more efficient this monitoring, the less likely are regulated banks to take undue risks and rely on federal deposit insurance to bail them out. Thus, when bank failures do occur, they reveal potential inefficiencies in regulatory monitoring. Boot & Thakor [1993] construct a model of regulatory reputation which shows that self-interested regulators will display a propensity to delay closures of troubled banks, relative to the social optimum, to protect their reputations.[7] The policy ramifications of this result have been discussed by Kane [1990] and others.

[7] See also Campbell, Chan & Marino [1992] who model the interplay between capital requirements and regulatory monitoring in a setting in which regulators are effort-averse.

6. Conclusions

This paper has provided a selective survey of the key services provided by financial intermediaries and the regulatory implications of these services. Clearly, the survey is not exhaustive. For further details as well as a more critical analysis of the issues, see Bhattacharya & Thakor [1993].

An important insight of the contemporary financial intermediation literature is this. For FIs to provide valuable QAT services, they must take on unavoidable risks. These risks create potential instabilities in the financial services industry and give rise to a rationale for regulatory intervention to stabilize the industry. However, the level of risks assumed by an FI is *manipulable*, and it is difficult to tell which risks are essential for QAT and which risks are speculative in nature. Moreover, regulation intended to enhance the stability of the industry can create perverse *private* incentives for individual FIs to take excessive risks, paving the way for further regulatory intervention to monitor/control these incentives. Hence, regulation and the *raison d'etre* for the existence of FIs are intertwined.

While this observation suggests that a completely unregulated banking system may be a myth, it does *not* make a case for highly intrusive regulation either. Recent work on a borrower's choice of financing source from a menu consisting of venture capitalists, banks and the capital market suggests that the manner in which these financing sources (banks in particular) are regulated is likely to affect the services they provide and hence the allocation of credit in the economy.[8] Experience with banking regulation in the U.S. has shown that the more complex and intrusive the regulation, the less predictable are its effects. This points to a potentially rich agenda for future research on the optimal design of bank regulation.[9]

Another promising topic for future research has to do with *nonbank* financial intermediaries. As the Introduction clarifies, financial intermediation is a concept that embraces a wide variety of institutions, not just banks. Much of the research on financial intermediation has dealt with banks, although there are exceptions.[10] There may be interesting research opportunities for those who wish to bring together ideas in the burgeoning market microstructure literature and the literature on financial intermediation.[11]

[8] Chan, Siegel & Thakor [1990] provide an analysis of venture capital contracting and explain why start-up firms are likely to go to venture capitalists. Diamond [1991] and Rajan [1992] explain a borrower's choice between the bank and the capital market. See also Thakor & Wilson [1995].

[9] Recent contributions on this score include Giammarino, Lewis & Sappington [1993] who address incentive compatibility issues in bank regulation, Besanko & Kanatas [1994] who explore time-consistency problems, and Besanko & Thakor [1992a, b] who address market structure issues in banking. Loewy [1991] highlights the difference between fiat currency and bank deposits in a model of bank runs to generate regulatory implications.

[10] For example, Allen [1990], Chan, Siegel & Thakor [1990], and Chan [1983].

[11] See Peck [1990] for a promising stab at such an integration. See also Yavas [1992] for a recent formalization of the choice between brokerage and QAT which joins together banking and market microstructure concepts.

Acknowledgments

I thank Arnoud Boot, Jimmy Wales and an anonymous referee for helpful comments.

References

Allen, F. (1990). The market for information and the origin of financial intermediation. *J. Financ. Intermed.* 1(1), 3–30.

Berkovitch, E., and S.I. Greenbaum (1990). The loan commitment as an optimal financing contract. *J. Financ. Quantit. Anal.* 26, 83–95.

Besanko, D., and G. Kanatas (1994). The regulation of bank capital: Time-consistency, hedging, and incentive compatibility, working paper, Northwestern University and Rice University.

Besanko, D., and A.V. Thakor (1992a). Banking deregulation: Allocational consequences of relaxing entry barriers. *J. Banking Finance* 16(5), 909–932.

Besanko, D., and A.V. Thakor (1992b). Relationship banking, deposit insurance and bank portfolio choice, discussion paper #511, Indiana University, forthcoming in: X. Vives and C. Mayer (eds.), *Capital Markets and Financial Intermediation* Cambridge University Press.

Bhattacharya, S., and A.V. Thakor (1993). Contemporary banking theory, *J. Financ. Intermed.* 3, 2–50.

Bodie, Z., and R.C. Merton (1992). Pension benefit guarantees in the united states: A functional analysis, working paper, presented at the Pension Research Council Annual Symposium.

Boot, A.W.A., and S.I. Greenbaum (1992). Financial intermediation, regulation and reputation: Theory and policy implications, working paper, Northwestern University.

Boot, A.W.A., S.I. Greenbaum and A.V. Thakor (1993). Reputation and discretion in financial contracting, *Am. Econ. Rev.* 83, 1165–1183.

Boot, A.W.A., and A.V. Thakor (1991). Off-balance sheet liabilities, deposit insurance and capital regulation. *J. Banking Finance* 15, 605–632.

Boot, A.W.A., and A.V. Thakor (1993). Self-interested bank regulation, *Am. Econ. Rev.* 83, 206–212.

Boot, A.W.A., A.V. Thakor, and G.F. Udell (1987). Competition, risk neutrality and loan commitments. *J. Banking Finance* 11, 449–471.

Boot, A.W.A., A.V. Thakor, and G.F. Udell (1991). Credible commitments, contract enforcement problems and banks: Intermediation as credibility assurance. *J. Banking Finance* 15, 605–632.

Boyd, J., and E.C. Prescott (1986). Financial intermediary coalitions. *J. Econ. Theory* 38, 211–232.

Bryant, J. (1980). A model of reserves, bank runs, and deposit insurance. *J. Banking Finance* 4, 335–344.

Calomiris, C., and C. Kahn (1991). The role of demandable debt in structuring optimal banking arrangements. *Am. Econ. Rev.* 81–83, 497–513.

Calomiris, C., C. Kahn, and S. Krasa (1991). Optimal contingent bank liquidation under moral hazard, working paper, Northwestern University.

Campbell, T.S. (1978). A model of the market for lines of credit. *J. Finance* 33, 231–244.

Campbell, T.S., Y. Chan and A.M. Marino (1992). An incentive-based theory of bank regulation, *J. Financ. Intermed.* 2, 225–276.

Campbell, T.S., and W. Kracaw (1980). Information production, market signalling, and the theory of financial intermediation. *J. Finance* 35, 863–882.

Campbell, T. S., and W. Kracaw (1991). Intermediation and the market for interest rate swaps. *J. Financ. Intermed.* 1(4), 362–384.

Chan, Y. (1983). On the positive role of financial intermediation in allocation of venture capital in a market with imperfect information. *J. Finance* 38, 1543–1568.

Chan, Y., S.I. Greenbaum, and A.V. Thakor (1992). Is fairly priced deposit insurance possible? *J. Financ.* 47, 227–246.

Chan, Y., D. Siegel, and A.V. Thakor (1990). Learning, corporate control and performance requirements in venture capital contracts. *Int. Econ. Rev.* 31, 365–381.

Chari, V., and R. Jagannathan (1988). Banking panics, information and rational expectations equilibruim. *J. Finance* 43, 749–761.

Cooperstein, R.L., G.G. Pennacchi, and F.S. Redburn (1995). The Aggregate Cost of Deposit Insurance; A Multipreriod Analysis. *J. Finac. Intermed.* 4, 242–271.

Diamond, D.W. (1984). Financial intermediation and delegated monitoring. *Rev. Econ. Studies* 51, 393–414.

Diamond, D.W. (1991). Monitoring and reputation: The choice between bank loans and directly placed debt. *J. Polit. Econ.* 99(4), 689–721.

Diamond, D.W., and P. Dybvig (1983). Bank runs, deposit insurance, and liquidity. *J. Polit. Econ.* 91, 401–419.

Duca, J., and D.D. Vanhoose (1990). Loan commitments and optimal monetary policy. *J. Money, Credit Banking* 22(2), 178–194.

Giammarino, R., T. Lewis, and D. Sappington (1993). An incentive approach to banking regulation, *J. Financ.* 48, 1523–1542.

Greenbaum, S.I., and A.V. Thakor (1995). *Contemporary Financial Intermediation*, Dryden Press.

Jacklin, C., and S. Bhattacharya (1988). Distinguishing panics and information-based bank runs: Welfare and policy implications. *J. Polit. Econ.* 96, 568–592.

Kahane, Y. (1977). Capital adequacy and the regulation of financial intermediaries. *J. Banking Finance* 1, 207–218.

Kane, E.J. (1990). Principal-agent problems in S&L salvage. *J. Finance* 45(3), 755–764.

Keeley, M.C. (1990). Deposit insurance, risk, and market power in banking. *Am. Econ. Rev.* 80, 1183–1200.

Leland, H., and D. Pyle (1977). Informational asymmetries, financial structure, and financial intermediation. *J. Finance* 32, 371–387.

Loewy, M.B. (1991). The macroeconomic effects of bank runs: An equilibrium analysis. *J. Financ. Intermed.* 1(3), 242–256.

Maksimovic, V. (1990). Product market imperfections and loan commitments. *J. Finance* 555, 1641–1653.

Mayers, D., and C.W. Smith, Jr. (1982). On the corporate demand for insurance. *J. Bus.* 55, 281–296.

Merton, R.C. (1977). An analytic derivation of the cost of deposit insurance loan guarantees. *J. Banking Finance* 1, 3–11.

Merton, R.C. (1983). On consumption indexed public pension plans, in: Z. Bodie and J.B. Shoven (eds.), *Financial Aspects of the U.S. Pension System*, University of Chicago Press, Chigago, IL.

Millon, M., and A.V. Thakor (1985). Moral hazard and information sharing: A model of financial information gathering agencies. *J. Finance* 40, 1403–1422.

Mookherjee, D., and I. P'ng (1989). Optimal auditing, insurance and redistribution. *Q. J. Econ.* 104, 399–415.

Myers, S.C. (1977). The determinants of corporate borrowing. *J. Financ. Econ.* 5, 147–175.

Peck, J. (1990). Liquidity without money: A general equilibrium model of market microstructure. *J. Financ. Intermed.* 1(1), 80–103.

Rajan, R. (1992). Insiders and outsiders: The choice between relationship and armslength debt, *J. Finance* 47, 1367–1400.

Ramakrishnan, R.T.S., and A.V. Thakor (1984). Information reliability and a theory of financial intermediation. *Rev. Econ. Studies* 51, 415–432.

Rothschild, M., and J.E. Stiglitz (1976). Equilibrium in competitive insurance markets: An essay on the economics of imperfect information. *Q. J. Econ.* 90, 629–649.

Samuelson, P. (1963). Risk and uncertainty: A fallacy of large numbers, *Scientia* 57, 1–6.

Shockley, R. (1995). Bank loan commitments and corporate leverage. *J. Financ. Intermed.* 4, 272–301.

Stiglitz, J.D., and A. Weiss (1981). Credit rationing in markets with imperfect information. *Am. Econ. Rev.* 71, 393–410.

Thakor, A.V. (1989). Competitive equilibrium with type convergence in an asymmetrically informed market. *Rev. Financ. Studies* 2, 49–71.

Thakor, A.V., and P. Wilson (1995). Capital requirements, loan renegotiation and the borrower's choice of financing source. *J. Banking Finance* 19, 693–712.

Williamson, O.E. (1975). *Markets and Hierarchies: Analysis and Antitrust Implications*, The Free Press, New York, NY.

Yavas, A. (1992). Market-makers vs. match-makers. *J. Financ. Intermed.* 2(1), 33–58.

R. Jarrow et al., Eds., *Handbooks in OR & MS, Vol. 9*

Chapter 33

The U.S. Savings and Loan Crisis

David H. Pyle

Haas School of Business, University of California, Berkeley, CA. 94708 and London Business School, Sussex Place, Regents Park, London, NW1 4SA, England

1. Introduction

Between 1980 and March 31, 1992, federal agencies disposed of over 1100 insolvent Savings and Loan (S&L) institutions and, as of March 31, 1992, an additional 408 S&Ls holding 29% of the industry's assets were classified as troubled.[1] Because the Federal Savings and Loan Insurance Corporation reserves have been exhausted, the vast majority of the past and future costs of these failures will be absorbed by U.S. taxpayers. As of May 1993, resolving these failures has cost taxpayers nearly $200 billion and the Resolution Trust Corporation (RTC) had an additional $69 billion of assets (net of cash and near cash assets) in receivership or operating as RTC conservatorships.[2] Most of the insolvencies occurred after 1988 and their cause is frequently attributed to the deregulation of the industry in 1980 and 1982. In fact, this crisis developed over a substantially longer period and had other significant contributory causes. The abysmal performance of Savings and Loan Associations (S&Ls) over the past decade is, in part, the consequence of a fundamental flaw in the structure of these institutions and is also attributable to regulatory and supervisory mistakes predating the events of the late 1980s and early 1990s.

2. A predisposition to failure

2.1. *The key roles of U.S. Savings and Loan Associations*

Until 1980, S&LS performed a narrowly defined role in the U.S. financial system. The bulk of their asset operations involved originating, investing in, and

[1] See Barth & Brumbaugh [1992] for data on failures and failure resolution costs. The data on the number of institutions classified as troubled was taken from Office of Thrift Supervision [1992] and includes 354 institutions 'considered by OTS to be troubled but not projected to require federal assistance' and 54 institutions that are projected to require federal assistance.

[2] See the *RTC Review*, Vol. IV, No. 7 (July 1993). As of May 1993, Resolution Trust Corporation outlays due to S&L closures totalled $191.1 billion. In addition, the RTC had incurred $7.5 billion in interest cost on borrowings from the Federal Financing Bank. The final cost of the S&L resolution appears likely to exceed $225 billion.

servicing home mortgages. On the liability side, they accumulated household savings plus some form of net worth to finance the mortgage portfolio.

As mortgage originators, S&Ls served the basic lending function of precontract monitoring of the mortgage borrower. They expended resources to evaluate individual investments in real estate properties and to determine the conditions under which a mortgage loan would be made. Leland & Pyle [1977], Diamond [1984], and others have observed that providing this monitoring service through a financial intermediary can only be sustained if the gains from collective monitoring exceed the costs of convincing the primary investors (mainly the depositors) that the screening process has correctly identified loan values. Models in which collective monitoring justifies the existence of depository and nondepository intermediaries are discussed in Bhattacharya & Thakor [1991].

Collective monitoring need not involve continuing investment by the monitoring firm in the loans it originates. In mortgage markets, brokers provide the precontract monitoring and pass the mortgage loans they originate on to other lenders. Until recently, S&Ls did not engage heavily in mortgage brokerage operations. Instead, they held most of the mortgage loans they originated in their own portfolios. This required them to engage in an asset transformation process. The nature of this transformation changed over time ultimately resulting in an asset/liability structure subject to significant interest rate risk. The maturity mismatch between long-term, fixed rate mortgage assets and short-term deposit liabilities was a major cause of the series of S&L crises that began in the mid-60s.

Diamond & Dybvig [1983] provide a theoretical analysis of maturity transformation by financial intermediaries. See Bhattacharya & Thakor [1991] for additional references and a review of this topic. In its most basic form, maturity transformation involves a mismatch between the contract length of an intermediary's assets and that of its liabilities. Typically, this mismatch involves holding illiquid assets with contract lengths greater than those of the intermediary's liabilities. The resulting risks to an intermediary's net worth come from two sources, default by the borrowers and untimely withdrawal or nonrenewal of the liabilities. The first of these risks is common to all intermediary structures; the second can occur only where there is an asset/liability liquidity mismatch. Until the advent of broad secondary markets for mortgage-backed securities, mortgage loans were illiquid.[3] In contrast, S&L liabilities became more liquid over time, i.e. available on demand or short notice without penalty.

Maturity transformation may also involve interest rate risk. Absent regulatory constraints, it is unnecessary for S&Ls to couple liquidity transformation with interest rate risk as their more recent reliance on adjustable rate mortgages demonstrates.[4] Until the late 1970s, when they were able to loan at variable

[3] There is an important link between the monitoring and liquidity creation functions of an intermediary. Even though an underlying asset is long-lived, as is the case for single-family homes, the loan that finances the asset will only be illiquid to the extent that reliable information on the loan's value cannot be efficiently transferred from one holder to another.

[4] See Bhattacharya & Thakor [1991] for a discussion of conditions under which the coupling of liquidity creation and interest rate risk would be necessary.

rates, S&Ls became increasingly short-funded and subject to interest rate risk.

The S&Ls' predisposition to failure involves their adoption of an asset/liability structure subject to significant interest rate risk. The next two sections of this chapter trace the events leading to that flawed structure.

2.2. *The evolution of U.S. Savings and Loan Associations: 1831–1930*[5]

The origin of U.S. Savings and Loan Associations has been traced to the Oxford Provident Society of Philadelphia founded in 1831 and to other local building societies.[6] These were mutual associations organized to provide a pool of funds to be loaned to members for home building. Regular contributions by members accumulated as shares and were used to finance mortgage loans. The return on the loans was paid to the holders of the shares. Initially, the shares were a form of equity neither entitled to a fixed dividend nor withdrawable on demand. The association had a limited life being dissolved when every member had obtained a loan and all loans had been repaid. These early S&Ls had two characteristics which provided strong support for their intermediary functions. As local, closed organizations, they provided a simple, efficient means for selecting and monitoring borrowers. Secondly, the equity-like nature of member shares solved the problem of financing illiquid, defaultable assets. Any shortfalls in mortgage payments were, of necessity, absorbed by share-holding members who did not have the option to withdraw their shares.

By 1870, a sharper division between borrowers and savers developed with the introduction of permanent associations and shares issued in series so that new members were permitted to enter the association over time. By the turn of the century, some S&Ls were financing mortgage loans with as many as three kinds of liabilities, the traditional permanent shares, shares that received fixed interest payments at stated intervals and matured on specific dates (similar to modern day CDs), and shares that could be withdrawn on short notice.[7]

An S&L liability structure including deposits available on short notice remained in place through the 1920s. Up to the Great Depression, however, S&Ls continued to rely chiefly on accounts that brought in funds likely to stay for several years. The possibility of withdrawal penalties help enforce saver discipline.

Turning to the asset side, there are few data on the contract terms of mortgage loans at S&Ls in the 19th century. The data in Morton's [1956] classic NBER study

[5] The following discussion of the early evolution of U.S. Savings and Loan Associations draws heavily on Schwartz & Vasconcellos [1989].

[6] Most of these institutions were called building societies and building and loan associations until the 1930s. In what follows, the name savings and loan associations (S&Ls) will be used to describe the institution in both the pre-Depression and the post-Depression periods.

[7] In the late 19th century, locally-based societies were challenged in deposit markets by competition from 'National Building & Loan Associations'. These 'national associations' grew rapidly until 1896 after which they fell into a steep decline apparently resulting from the depression of 1893–1996. Presumably, the local societies fared better because of the superior monitoring and contracting associated with their local focus.

of urban mortgage lending begin with 1920. These data show contract lengths for straight mortgages made on nonfarm homes by S&Ls averaging 11.2 years from 1920 through 1930 with only minor year-to-year variation. Significantly, from the perspective of interest rate risk, the realized maturities of mortgage loans at S&Ls were even shorter averaging 6.9 years over the same period.

S&L asset risk during the first three decades of the 20th century was mitigated further by stable mortgage interest rates. Conventional mortgage rates in Manhattan from 1900 through 1929 averaged 5.59% with a 26 basis point standard deviation.[8] Morton reported contract interest rates at S&Ls from 1920 through 1930 averaging 6.94% with only a 15 basis point standard deviation.

S&Ls are thus seen to have been immune from significant interest rate risk from their inception up to the Great Depression. Initially, this was due to the absence of a maturity mismatch in the design of the institution. Later, when there was a potential mismatch from increased use of short-term deposit liabilities, S&Ls were protected by a stable interest rate environment combined with a prudent avoidance of a reliance on short-term liabilities. Nonetheless, by 1930, the seeds of a serious problem had been planted. The significance of this was recognized by Lieber [1931] who said:

> The inconsistency of considering demand money, money that has been invested in mortgages repayable by amortization over a period of 15 to 20 years is apparent. Whatever the desires or preferences, however altruistic the attempt to have money invested in building and loan associations payable on demand, the theory of long-term mortgage and demand funds will no more work than will oil and water mix.

Lieber's concern centered on the liquidity mismatch resulting from financing long-term mortgages with demand funds. Ultimately, the problem he anticipated result more from the effects of a maturity mismatch than from illiquidity, though both played a role in the S&L crisis that began some 30 years after his warning.

2.3. *The transformation of U.S. Savings and Loan Associations under the new deal*

Property devaluations and the precipitous fall in incomes accompanying the Great Depression had a profoundly adverse effect on S&Ls and other mortgage lenders. Home owners could not meet their mortgage payments and the depressed state of real estate markets often made foreclosure a response of questionable worth. On the liability side, depositors pressed for immediate access to their savings because of personal liquidity needs and from fear of S&L failures. The federal response to the resulting crisis had a fundamental and persistent effect in changing the typical S&L asset/liability structure.

Beginning with the *Home Owners Loan Corporation Act of 1933* (HOLC), New Deal administrators took bold steps to stabilize the mortgage market. The Corporation was an emergency organization which took over more than $3

[8] Homer [1977, p. 399].

billion in mortgage loans from S&Ls, banks, and other mortgage lenders before its lending function ended in 1936. HOLC refinanced home owners' existing mortgage contracts using 5%, 15-year amortizing mortgages. The creation of the Federal Housing Administration (FHA) as part of the National Housing Act of 1934 was the next New Deal initiative in mortgage market stabilization. The FHA (later joined by the Veterans Administration), as a federally-backed insurer of mortgage contracts, set the standards for mortgage lending. Longer contract lengths on amortizing loans were attractive from the insurer's viewpoint and insured mortgages appealed to lenders. By 1947, the average contract length of a new mortgage at S&Ls had risen to 15.2 years from the 10.8-year average contract length prevailing in 1930.[9] This trend toward longer contract lengths continued through the postwar period so, by the late 1950s, the average maturity of mortgage loans at S&Ls was in excess of 20 years. Between the start of the Depression and 1960, S&L asset values became substantially more sensitive to interest rate fluctuations.

On the liability side, the consumer liquidity problems created by the drastic fall in incomes put pressure on the institutions to provide depositors their savings on demand. In an environment with unstable asset values, demand liabilities can and do result in depositor 'runs' and an unstable financial system. As early as the fall of 1931, many associations went 'on notice' paying withdrawals only as cash came into the institution. Withdrawal moratoria and withdrawal rotation systems enabled the association to stop a run, but at the cost of imposing illiquidity on depositors who had a legitimate need for the funds on deposit.[10] The establishment of the Federal Savings and Loan Insurance Corporation in 1934 put a federal commitment behind S&L deposits. This permitted S&Ls to make short-term deposits a permanent and, ultimately, a dominant feature of their liability structure without incurring the threat of depositor runs or the need for withdrawal moratoria.

The asset/liability mismatch that concerned Phillip Lieber in 1931 became the S&L norm through well-intentioned New Deal interventions. By 1947, S&Ls were financial intermediaries backed by a federal guarantee of their major liabilities and predisposed to net worth losses given adverse interest rate movements. This predisposition was further exacerbated between 1947 and 1960 by a secular rise in the average asset maturity at S&Ls. However, the interest rate environment remained reasonably benign over most of the 1950s. From 1947 through 1956, the annual average interest rate on conventional mortgage loans in Manhattan rose by 39 basis points. This increase came as a steady secular rise; the maximum year-to-year change was an 11 basis points increase between 1947 and 1948. The

[9] See Morton [1956].

[10] See Ewalt [1962, pp. 14–17] and Prather [1970, pp. 58–60, 411–412]. State banking laws provided (and to the best of my knowledge still provide) for withdrawal moratoria (i.e., a period of time during which withdrawal requests need not be met) and withdrawal rotation systems (i.e., a system under which withdrawal lists are maintained and depositors paid according to a rotation scheme as funds became available). I am grateful to an anonymous referee for this point.

situation on the liability side of the typical S&L was similar, but less benign. The average annual yield on savings accounts increased steadily over the 1947–1956 period. The total increase was 70 basis points resulting in a 31 basis point erosion on the net interest spread on new mortgage loans and, of course, an erosion in the interest spread on older loans.

2.4. U.S. Savings and Loan Associations and interest rate risk

Entering the 1960s, the interest rate sensitivity of the market value of a typical S&L's assets was substantially greater than the interest rate sensitivity of its liabilities, subjecting S&Ls to market net worth losses given interest rate increases. For example, the Macaulay duration of a 25-year, 6% yield, amortizing loan is just over 10 years. If taken as a reasonable estimate of the interest elasticity of loan value, this measure implies that a mortgage loan with the stated characteristics will lose (gain) 1% of its value for a 10-basis-point change in the market yield on 25-year mortgages. If the economic value of depositor claims had remained unchanged in the process, the 1% decline in asset value would have translated into more than a 14% decrease in the association's economic net worth given the approximately 7% net worth to asset ratio at the typical S&L.

The typical association's economic net worth in 1960 was somewhat less interest sensitive than this simple duration measure suggests. S&L asset portfolios included seasoned as well as new mortgages so, by the standard Macaulay measure, the average duration of its assets was about 7 years instead of 10 years. Secondly, borrowers had the option to prepay their mortgage loans in whole or part and, since some borrowers used this option, the interest sensitivity of the assets was further reduced.[11] Finally, changes in association net worth also reflect the effect of changes in market interest rates on the liability side of the net worth equation. If the interest paid on savings deposits does not respond as rapidly to changes in market rates as the interest rates on loans, the effect on association net worth will be lessened.

Unfortunately for S&L managers, regulators, and especially for U.S. taxpayers, the stable interest rate environment of 1947–1956 did not persist. Mortgage interest rates rose rapidly from 1956 to 1961. The Manhattan conventional mortgage loan rate rose by 178 basis points over this period.[12] This upward shift in mortgage interest rates wiped out a significant fraction, perhaps 5%, of the market value of the typical S&L asset portfolio while having little effect on the value of its liabilities. From an income perspective, the accompanying 90 basis point rise in the interest rate paid to S&L savers sharply reduced the S&Ls' interest margins on seasoned mortgages and resulted in an increase in the faction of net operating

[11] Although prepayments reduce the interest rate sensitivity of prepayable mortgage loans relative to an otherwise equivalent loan not subject to prepayment, this effect is perversely affected by market interest rate changes. As rates rise, prepayments tend to fall and as rates fall prepayments tend to rise.

[12] Homer [1977].

income paid out as interest from 72.3% in 1956 to 78.6% in 1961.[13] Aggregate association net worth to total assets which stood at 7.6% in 1950 was less than 7% by 1961.[14]

In 1962, mortgage interest rates fell by over 100 basis points and stabilized at around 5.8% for the next three years. Unfortunately for anyone concerned with S&L soundness, the average cost of savings deposits at S&Ls rose by an additional 33 basis points between 1961 and 1965 so that income paid out as interest rose to 84.5% of net operating income in 1965. In December 1965, the Federal Reserve Board responded to rising money market interest rates and the higher deposit account interest rates being offered by S&Ls by sharply increasing the maximum rate payable on bank time deposits (from 4% (for less than 90 day maturities) and 4.5% (for 90 days and over) to 5.5% across the board).[15] Money market interest rates rose sharply during the first half of 1966 (e.g. the federal funds rate rose by 85 basis points) and banks used their new deposit interest rate powers to bid aggressively for time deposit balances. Most S&Ls, saddled with the income consequences of below-market fixed rate mortgage portfolios and facing higher loan losses in a depressed real estate market, found it difficult to compete. The S&L deposit growth rate fell to less than 2% annually over the first six months of 1966.

The resulting crisis over the vitality of S&Ls and their ability to supply funds to the housing construction industry led Congress to pass and President Lyndon Johnson to sign the *Interest Rate Adjustment Act of 1966*. The provisions of this Act fixed the deposit interest rates payable by S&Ls, lowered the maximum time deposit interest rates payable by commercial banks, and established a positive differential between the rates payable by S&Ls and those payable by commercial banks. The passing and signing of this Act was a tacit recognition that the S&L industry was unable to continue to function in a competitive market for deposits at existing interest rate levels with the typical S&L asset/liability structure. Rather than addressing the structural flaw, federal authorities tried to control the effects of the market by mandating cartel pricing across the regulated depository institutions. The seeds of the epidemic of S&L failures in the 1980s and 1990s and of the billions of dollars it has and will cost to resolve those failures were sown by the failure of the federal authorities to address the root causes of the 1966 crisis.

The immediate consequence of the *Interest Rate Adjustment Act*, aided substan-

[13] United States Savings and Loan League, *Savings and Loan Fact Book* [1973].

[14] The net worth used in calculating these ratios is a book value measure was taken from the Savings and Loan Fact Book of 1977. Given the substantial increase in mortgage interest rates between 1950 and 1961, the fall in the economic or market value net worth to total assets ratio is understated by the book value figures.

[15] Under the provisions of the *Banking Act of 1935*, the Federal Reserve Board was authorized to set maximum interest rates that could be paid on bank time and savings deposits. This authority was carried out through Federal Reserve Board Regulation Q. Until 1966, thrift regulators (e.g. the Federal Home Loan Bank Board) had no interest rate ceiling powers.

tially by a fall in money market interest rates, was the temporary stabilization of the S&L crisis. Predictably, this partial price control solution was not sustainable over the longer term.[16] The attempt to maintain S&L profitability through deposit interest rate ceilings might have worked had the need to do so been short-lived. However, the short-term interest rate levels of the 1960s were mild compared to those that followed, and the interest cost control strategy unraveled. Because of the interest rate ceilings, S&L interest expenses grew slowly through the mid-1970s, but increases in money market rates above the ceilings led to disintermediation into Treasury Bills, money market mutual funds, and other short-term investments not subject to interest rate controls. There were numerous, futile attempts by federal regulators to stabilize deposit flows at S&Ls without causing unduly adverse effects on their total deposit costs.[17] Despite these attempts, S&Ls were only able to grow at significant rates when short-term market interest rates were near the ceilings (in 1971–72 and 1975–1978). Growth during these periods of relatively lower mortgage interest rates proved to be dysfunctional from a long-run solvency perspective. Overall, the growth in savings between 1970 and 1981 barely kept up with the increase in housing prices.

By 1981, the strategy of housing construction support and S&L cost containment through the use of deposit interest rate ceilings was in complete disarray. Net savings flows at S&Ls were negative, the S&Ls' average interest cost had risen to 10.71%, aggregate S&L income after interest and taxes was negative, and aggregate book net worth had fallen to 4.3% of total assets. In market value terms, it has been estimated that aggregate S&L net worth which in 1966 was around –$2.8 billion fell to about –$100 billion by 1981.[18] By contrast, Federal Savings and Loan Insurance Corporation reserves were $1.8 billion in 1966 and $6.2 billion in 1981. The misguided and ultimately failed attempt to shelter the structurally defective S&L industry from the effects of interest rate risk had convert an unfunded federal liability from about $1.0 billion to one of over $90 billion. While the precise magnitude of this unfunded liability may be questioned,

[16] The interest rate controls were partial in that they did not apply to all instruments accessible by depositors. Cootner [1969] made a prescient comment on the potential for this legislation to achieve its goal:

> Whatever merits one may find in rate regulation, it cannot be accomplished by one sector of a highly competitive market. It is true that when the [interest rate] regulation was first attempted, neither the commercial banking sector nor the debt securities markets were as competitive as they gradually became, and so the prospects for success were more sanguine at the outset than they were in retrospect, but that is an outstanding characteristic of partial price regulation. ...There is some serious question about the merits of trying to control soundness ... by rate controls because of its tremendous impact on liquidity problems.

[17] These attempts included the introduction of the aborted 'wild-card' experiment in 1973, the six month money market certificate in 1978, and the small saver certificate in 1979.

[18] These estimates are taken from Kane [1985, p. 102], but adjusted to be consistent with the more conservative estimates in Brumbaugh [1988, p. 50]. The 1966 S&L net worth estimate was obtained by extrapolation from Kane's net worth estimate for mutual savings banks for that year.

there is no doubt that it increased dramatically over the 15 years of deposit interest rate ceilings.

The failure to address the fundamental structural problem of the S&L industry went beyond the misguided use of deposit interest rate ceilings. Variable interest rate mortgages (VRMs) provided an alternative method of reducing the maturity imbalance faced by S&Ls, one that was successfully adopted by some states for state-chartered S&Ls in the early 1970s. Despite periodic support for VRMs by the Federal Home Loan Bank Board, Congress throughout the 1970s steadfastly opposed VRMs for federally-chartered institutions, belatedly authorizing their use in 1979.[19]

Furthermore, as discussed in the sequel, the various legislative and regulatory steps taken to sustain the deposit interest rate cartel, including some consequences of the *Interest Rate Adjustment Act of 1966* for the structure of the industry, had significant and adverse effects on the magnitude and cost of the S&L failures in the 1980s and 1990s.

3. The role of legislation and regulation in worsening the S&L crisis

In addition their responsibility for the flawed design of S&Ls, federal and state regulators, supervisors, and legislators took actions that exacerbated the S&L crisis and failed to adopt measures that would have eased the crisis. The asset deregulation of 1980 and 1982 and the subsequent inadequate supervision of S&Ls are chief cases in point and are discussed in the sequel. However, the undertaking that contributed most to the scope and scale of the crisis was the adoption of an actuarially unsound savings and loan deposit insurance system and occurred over a half-century earlier.[20] It is inconceivable that either the broad-scale investment excesses that followed S&L asset deregulation or the rapid growth of deposits at under-capitalized S&L could have transpired without federal deposit guarantees. In the next subsection, I lay out a model of the deposit insurer's liability. The analysis highlights the determining factors of that liability. The implications of this model are then used in the analysis of other key actions by federal and state authorities.

3.1. Deposit insurance and the S&L crisis

The basic deficiencies of deposit insurance were well-known, in theory and in practice, well before federal deposit insurance was finally introduced.[21] The federal scheme, enacted for banks in 1933 and extended to S&Ls in 1934, imposed

[19] Between 1970 and 1978, federally chartered S&Ls accounted for almost 60% of the total asset growth at S&Ls.

[20] See Tobin [1989].

[21] The numerous attempts by Congress to introduce federal deposit guarantees in the late 19th and early 20th centuries and the experiences of the fourteen state deposit insurance schemes established between 1829 and 1917 are summarized in FDIC [1950, 1952].

a fixed premium per dollar of deposits on each insured institution in exchange for a guarantee of depositor claims up to a specified limit. For such a scheme to be actuarially sound, each insured bank must present the guarantor with the same risk of loss or, to put it more precisely, with the same contingent liability per dollar of deposits and the value of that liability must be equal to the insurance premium less the guarantor's operating expenses. Failure to meet this actuarial standard has a number of undesirable consequences including the accumulation by the guarantor of an unfunded liability (if the fixed fee does not prove to be large enough) and differential net subsidies or taxes across insured institutions (if the incidence of the difference between the actuarial fee and the actual fee is not uniform).

Furthermore, with the fee held constant, an actuarial sound scheme is subject to 'moral hazard' in the sense described by Mayers & Smith [1982], namely that the owners of an insured institution may have an incentive to restructure that institution in a way that increases the value to them of the guarantee. In large measure, the S&L crisis was the realization of these and other predictable consequences of an unsound deposit insurance system.

The defective nature of the deposit insurance system introduced in 1933 was apparent to critics at that time[22] and its deficiencies were periodically pointed out during the 1960s and 1970s.[23] As noted above, the consequences of the S&L deposit insurance flaws were not felt seriously until the mid-sixties because of the unusually benign interest rate environment that persisted until the early 1960s and because of pre-1980 asset and liability restrictions that limited the scope of S&L operations.[24] The fact that legislative action to deal with these consequences did not occur until 1989 resulted from a concerted effort by the authorities to deny the existence of an unfunded liability.[25] The ultimate cost of the crisis was greatly increased due, in large part, to dysfunctional actions to support that denial.

A more systematic theory of the value of the guarantor's contingent liability and its determinants became possible with the development of the analytical option pricing model of Black & Scholes [1973]. Merton [1977] showed that 'the properties of deposit insurance viewed as a security are isomorphic to those of a put option'. The essence of his demonstration follows.

Consider a bank with assets having market value V at a future date T, where T is the date of the next audit of the bank. These assets are financed with a combination of insured deposits, having a current value D and a future value $B = De^{rT}$ (where r is a riskless rate of return), plus equity. At T, the payoff to the various claimants are:

[22] In one of the first published critiques of the federal deposit insurance system, Emerson [1934] identified the fact that 'premiums are not graded according to the risks involved' and the absence of a 'provision for the accumulation of a reserve fund' as two of the major deficiencies in the scheme.

[23] See Gibson [1972], Horvitz [1975], Mayer [1965], and Scott & Mayer [1971].

[24] Interestingly, there is evidence that, in a less benign environment, the moral hazard consequences of federal deposit insurance were felt as early as 1939. See Grossman [1992].

[25] See Kane [1989] for a discussion of the political incentives driving this behavior.

$$\begin{aligned}
&\text{Payoff to equity at } T &&= \text{Max}\,(0, V - B)\\
&\text{Payoff to depositors at } T &&= B\\
&\text{Payoff to guarantor at } T &&= \text{Min}\,(0, V - B) = -\text{Max}\,(0, B - V)
\end{aligned}$$

The payoff structure for the guarantor is that of a short position in a put option on the bank's assets with an exercise price B and a maturity T. The present value of the guarantor's conditional liability is the present value of this put option. The gain to the bank equity holders from mispriced deposit insurance is that they are able to contract with the depositors at the riskless rate r rather than at $R(T)$, a promised yield necessarily in excess of r to compensate uninsured depositors for the risk that the bank would be unable to pay the promised rate. The present value of the equity holders' gain in this set-up is exactly equal to the value of the put. Using Black–Scholes option pricing, Merton is able to write the value of the put per dollar of insured deposits, $g(d, \tau)$, as

$$g(d, \tau) = \phi(h_2) - \frac{1}{d}\phi(h_1)$$

where:

$\phi(\cdot)$ = the cumulative normal density function,

$h_1 \equiv \dfrac{\ln(d) - \tau/2}{\sqrt{\tau}}$,

$h_2 \equiv h_1 + \sqrt{\tau}$,

$d \equiv \dfrac{D}{V}$ (the current deposit-to-asset value ratio),

$\tau \equiv \sigma^2 T$ (the variance in the log change in asset value over T).

As long as the deposit-to-asset value ratio and the volatility of the assets are fixed, the cost of the deposit guarantee remains fixed. The nature of the 'moral hazard' faced by the guarantor becomes apparent in this set up, since standard comparative statics results show that increases in d and increases in τ lead to increases in the value of the guarantee to the benefit of the owners of the bank and the detriment of the guarantor. In other words, if the risk of the banks assets increases or if the bank's leverage increases, equity holders benefit at the expense of the guarantor.[26]

Additional insights into the deficiencies of the deposit insurance scheme can be gained by exploiting this put option analogy. Since τ increases with T, the result that the value of the guarantee increases with τ can also be interpreted as the effect of an increase in the time until the option is exercised. Suppose that (1) the exercise date depends on the condition of the bank at an audit date, (2) exercise of the option can be forced based on the audit results, and (3) the audit data systematically bias asset values upward.[27] The result will be longer times to

[26] See Merton & Bodie [1992] for a further explication of this analytical framework.

[27] See Merton [1978] for an analysis of perpetual deposit insurance with random monitoring that can trigger exercise of the option.

exercise than would occur with exercise based on the bank's true condition. This increase in T results in a higher value for the guarantee since it increases the dispersion of the potential asset value outcomes with most of the positive effects accruing to the equity holders and all of the negative to the guarantor.[28]

To the extent that the guarantor does not have or does not exercise the authority to limit dividends, owner/manager perquisites, and other disbursements of the bank's assets, the proper analogy is to a put option without dividend protection.[29] In the absence of dividend protection, the holder of a put option who is also able to declare and receive the dividend (broadly construed) and who anticipates that the put may be exercised (i.e., in the case of deposit insurance, that the S&L will fail) has a strong incentive to increase his wealth at the expense of the writer of the put by declaring as large a dividend as possible prior to the exercise date. In other words, the insurance guarantor is faced with a serious agency problem. Note also that a delay in the exercise date, such as that caused by a false positive audit signal, allows an owner/manager more time to exploit the absence of dividend protection to the further disadvantage of the guarantor.

Another important insight into the operational deficiencies of the federal deposit insurance scheme may be gained by considering the effect of increases in the deposit-to-asset value ratio on the sensitivity of the put value to asset risk (i.e., the effect of an increase in d on $\partial g/\partial \sigma$). For a sufficiently low deposit-to-asset value ratio (high capital-to-asset ratio), the effect of increased asset volatility on the put value will be insignificant. As the deposit-to-asset value ratio increases toward one (the point of insolvency), the rate at which the put value increases with an increase in volatility becomes larger.[30] In other words, the lower the true net worth of an S&L, the larger is the incentive to undertake greater asset risk. As the true net worth approaches or falls below zero, the reluctance of risk-adverse owners and managers to 'bet the bank' or to exploit the lack of dividend protection or, most likely, to do both will diminish.

In evaluating supervisory actions preceding and during the S&L crisis, it is important to recognize that, if exercise of the put option (i.e., insolvency proceedings or bank reorganization) could be forced at asset value levels at or above the true insolvency point and if the full value of the assets could be realized during the resolution of that insolvency, the put value would be zero. Delays in forcing option exercise and inefficiencies in realizing asset values lead to higher costs for the guarantor.[31]

Finally, in considering the potential importance of moral hazard on the performance of S&Ls, it is useful to differentiate among these institutions on the basis of organization and control. S&Ls may be either mutually-owned or permanent stock organizations. In a mutual S&L, the net income after interest and taxes

[28] See Pyle [1986] for an analysis of the effects of biased audit values.

[29] See Cox & Rubinstein [1985, p. 150].

[30] Cox & Rubinstein [1985, p. 232].

[31] See Mullins & Pyle [1994] for an analysis of deposit insurance where there are significant liquidation costs.

accrues, in principle, to the depositors; in a permanent stock S&L it accrues to the shareholders. Consequently, it can be anticipated that the incentive to exploit the deposit insurance guarantee will be strongest in permanent stock firms.[32]

3.2. Adverse effects of deposit interest rate ceilings

The *Interest Rate Adjustment Act of 1966* temporarily protected S&Ls from the effects of secularly rising interest rates. Ultimately, this attempt at partial price control broke down and the interest cost for S&Ls rose sharply. In the interim, S&Ls attempted to circumvent the deposit interest rate ceilings by various forms of noninterest rate competition. Some of this competition took the form of variable costs for advertising, gifts to depositors and other incentives that were easily reduced when the ceilings were removed. Other noninterest rate responses involved increases in S&L service capacity and were less easily reversed. S&L offices per capita more than doubled between 1965 and 1982 (from 4.7 offices per 100,000 to 9.7 per 100,000). The number of S&L employees per capita also more than doubled. In constant dollar terms, assets per S&L office fell from $14.1 million to $10.3 million and assets per S&L employee from $1.33 million to $0.84 million. By 1982, S&L operating expenses per dollar of deposits had reached 177 basis points per dollar of deposits, an increase of more than 40% over the expense levels of 1965.[33]

Furthermore, during the period of interest rate ceilings, new competition for bank and S&L deposits developed in the form of money market mutual funds and other assets that fell outside the depository institutions regulatory purview. The import of these developments vis-a-vis the S&L crisis was two-fold. The increase in the S&L cost structure contributed to S&L losses and the reduction in their net worth. Perhaps more importantly, the increase in competition, whether from the proliferation of banking and thrift offices or from the growth of savings substitutes, reduced the value of a depository institution charter. When a bank or S&L charter has significant value, the potential loss of the charter due to bankruptcy is a counterbalance to the risk-taking incentives inherent in the federal deposit insurance system. Keeley [1990] presents empirical findings consistent with the view that some of the increase in bank and thrift risk and subsequent failures may be due to a decline in the value of bank and thrift charters associated with increased competition in the financial services industry.

By encouraging nonrate competition and the more rapid development of nonregulated substitutes for thrift deposits, deposit interest rate ceilings contributed to that decline in charter values and, therefore, to the depth of the S&L crisis. Perhaps the most significant consequence of the failed attempt to shelter S&Ls

[32] While the mutual versus permanent stock split may capture the major aspect of differences in the moral hazard incentive among S&Ls, this incentive may also depend on a number of other factors such as the concentration of stock ownership, management incentive systems, and board composition. See Hermalin & Wallace [1992] for a further discussion of these matters.

[33] The data on S&Ls in this and subsequent sections of the paper came from various issues of the *Savings and Loan Fact Book* (U.S. League of Savings Associations, Chicago) and its successor publication the *Savings Institutions Source Book*.

from market forces is that it left the industry weakened and ill-prepared to deal with the challenges and incentives of the subsequent deregulated and competitive environment. As shown above, financial theory predicts that economically insolvent institutions will be particularly apt to exploit the risk-taking incentives inherent in fixed price deposit insurance contracts.

3.3. *The effects of dysfunctional legislation and regulation*

By 1980, many S&Ls were facing a liquidity crisis due to the effects of deposit interest rate ceilings. In 1977, net new savings at FSLIC-insured institutions totalled \$32 billion. Under attack from money market mutual funds and other unregulated deposit substitutes, net new S&L deposits fell to less than half that amount in 1979 and to just over \$10 billion in 1980. The flight from S&L deposit classes still subject to binding interest rate ceilings was even more marked becoming negative from the second quarter of 1979 through the third quarter of 1980. At this rate of disintermediation, numerous S&Ls faced the prospect of selling illiquid assets at prices substantially below book to finance the cash withdrawals, an action that threatened to exhaust their book net worth and force insolvency proceedings.

The reduced ability of S&Ls to supply funds to residential mortgage markets became a matter of considerable concern to S&L regulators and the Congress. As Table 1 shows, S&L participation in mortgage markets in 1980 fell to about half of the average rate in the 1970s.

The initial Congressional response to this liquidity crisis was the *Depository Deregulation and Monetary Control Act* (*1980 Act*) passed in March 1980 which required all deposit interest rate ceilings to be eliminated by March 31, 1986. However, Congress failed to authorize any significant new deregulated deposit accounts for S&Ls. Predictably, these half-measures were inadequate and disintermediation accelerated. Net new savings at FSLIC-insured institutions were negative in each quarter from first quarter 1981 through the third quarter of 1982. In total, the net S&L deposit outflow during these seven quarters exceeded the net deposit inflows over the previous 10 quarters. This forced S&Ls, in aggregate, to be net sellers of mortgages during 1981 and 1982 (see Table 1). The deposit

Table 1

Annual growth rates for mortgages on residential properties, 1970–1982

Years	Growth in total loans outstanding (annual %)	Growth in loans outstanding at savings associations (annual %)	Growth in loans outstanding at all other institutions (annual %)
1970–1979	12.2	13.5	10.4
1979–1980	10.1	6.3	13.0
1980–1982	5.2	−2.0	9.9

Source: Savings Institutions Source Book 89, United States League of Savings Institutions, Chicago, 1990.

hemorrhaging at S&Ls was finally stopped with the passage of the *Garn-St Germain Act* (*1982 Act*) in December 1982. The *1982 Act* mandated the creation of a deposit account that would be competitive with money market mutual funds.

Solving this liquidity crisis put the S&L industry, now in far weaker condition, back into the negative earnings position that led to deposit interest rate ceilings in the first place. Aggregate reported profit margins (net income divided by total income) at FSLIC-insured savings institutions which had averaged 7.78% in the 1970s fell to 1.37% in 1980 and became negative in 1981 and 1982 (−6.96% and −5.49% respectively). Congress responded by authorizing new S&L asset powers. In the *1980 Act*, federal savings and loans were authorized to invest up to 20% of their assets in consumer loans, commercial paper, and corporate debt securities (including 'junk' bonds) and up to 3% in service corporations which could hold undeveloped land and other here-to-fore disallowed assets. The authority of S&Ls to make acquisition, development, and construction loans was expanded, geographical restrictions on real estate lending were removed, and permissible loan-to-value ratios were increased. The *Garn-St Germain Act of 1982* carried this expansion of federal S&L asset powers considerably farther permitting commercial mortgage and consumer lending to be as much as 40% and 30% of assets, respectively, and commercial loans and leases to be up to 10% of assets each. Some state authorities, notably those in California, Florida, and Texas, granted broader powers (e.g., unlimited assets in junk bonds) for similar investments by state-chartered institutions.

It was presumed by some authorities that these new powers would enhance the diversification of S&L asset portfolios and provide added earning capacity to help meet the increased S&L deposit costs. Providing these new asset powers, including the authorization of adjustable rate mortgages at federal S&Ls in 1981, was a belated recognition of the unsuitability of the earlier S&L asset/liability structure in a volatile interest rate environment. These new powers substantially increased the potential for risk-taking by insured institutions and the difficulty of monitoring their performance. If these new asset powers could have been accompanied by suitable monitoring and risk-control mechanisms and offered only to well-capitalized institutions, this change in asset powers would have been a far better response to the S&L earning crisis than the earlier, failed attempt to control liability costs through deposit interest rate ceilings. Given the actual conditions in the S&L industry in the early 1980s ... numerous economically insolvent institutions and low capital ratios in general plus grossly inadequate regulatory monitoring and risk-control[34] ... the application of financial first-principles that were well-known at the time, such as those presented in Section 3.1, would have led to predictions that the *1980* and *1982 Acts* would produce a

[34] Clearly, the new asset powers implied an increased need for the insurer to monitor the risk-taking and the economic net worth of the S&Ls. As Kane [1990, p. 100] has pointed out, 'Incredibly, examination and supervisory resources declined in 1983 and 1984, precisely when the economics of FSLIC's exposure to zombie risk taking was expanding and becoming harder to assess'. 'Zombies', for Kane, are economically insolvent institutions, support by the federal deposit guarantee, whose only hope of becoming profitable is to 'grow out of their problems'.

significant increase in S&L risk-taking, especially by the weakest institutions, and a corresponding increase in the unfunded liability of the insurance fund.

Other provisions of the *1980* and *1982 Acts* and subsequent regulatory changes exacerbated the problem by encouraging accounting practices and other forms of 'forbearance' designed to keep insolvent banks from being subjected to insolvency proceedings.[35] As seen in Section 3.1, the failure to close down an insolvent institution in a timely manner is equivalent to an increase in the exercise date of the put option with a concomitant increase in the guarantor's unfunded liability.[36]

A further provision of the *1980 Act*, the increase in the deposit insurance coverage from $40,000 to $100,000 per account, strengthened the ability of S&Ls to fund an expansion in the new asset categories. When combined with the introduction of money market certificates authorized by the *1982 Act*, the higher insurance coverage allowed efficient S&L funding using arms-length, brokered deposits. Given the S&L asset restrictions that prevailed prior to 1980, this would not have been a particularly significant development, at least in the short run, since most S&Ls would have found it difficult to use brokered funds to increase their residential mortgage lending rapidly. It has been argued that access to deposit brokerage and the ability to issue a market rate sensitive, insured liability 'leveled the playing field' between S&Ls and large banks for whom interest rate restrictions on large CDs were lifted in 1972. Since large bank depositors were protected by the 'too big to fail' practices of bank regulators, those large CDs paid rates close to a default-free rate and large quantities of funds could be raised outside a large bank's normal deposit base no matter what investment policy and capital ratio were being employed. Insured, brokered deposits gave S&Ls of any size access to similar, nonlocal funding sources.

Similarly, the introduction of new asset powers without the enhanced opportunity to raise large quantities of arms-length, insured deposits would have been of far less significance. Separately, neither the increased insurance coverage nor the new federal and state S&L asset powers need to have seriously increased the insolvency of the FSLIC insurance fund; together they were a lethal combination. As Table 2 shows, the combination of brokered deposits and new asset powers resulted in a rapid growth in S&L assets after 1980 (82% of that growth occurred after 1982) with almost half of the new funds having been invested in nontraditional asset classes. Furthermore, an indeterminate fraction of the new investment that is classified as mortgage lending in Table 2 was placed in mortgage loans other than the residential mortgages traditionally held by S&Ls, in nonlocal mortgages, and in mortgage loans with higher loan-to-value ratios, all of which increased the likelihood of less efficient, higher-risk lending by individual S&Ls.

The most important concern about this rapid and significant use of the new asset powers may have been more a question inefficient investing than of the inherent riskiness of the resulting portfolio of assets held by S&Ls. The idea that adding

[35] See Barth [1991, pp. 133–141] for a concise history of regulatory capital requirements at savings and loan associations.

[36] See Horvitz [1989] for a further discussion of forbearance and its costs.

Table 2

Change in assets at FSLIC-insured savings institutions 1975–1985

Years	Change in mortgage loans & mortgage-backed securities millions of $ (% of total change)	Change in all other loans millions of $ (% of total change)	Change in total loans outstanding millions of $ (% of total change)
1975–1980	249,733 (86%)	40,634 (14%)	290,367 (100%)
1980–1985	238,834 (53%)	210,552 (47%)	449,386 (100%)

Source: Savings Institutions Source Book 89, United States League of Savings Institutions, Chicago, 1990.

new asset classes to the set authorized for S&Ls improved the available risk-return frontier in the risk dimension has considerable merit. It is far less clear that it did so in the return dimension. The S&Ls that exploited their new powers extensively were, largely, marginal entrants into existing markets.[37] Despite the reduction in costs of noninterest competition that followed the elimination of deposit interest rate ceilings, operating expense as a fraction of total assets at FSLIC-insured savings institutions rose from 125 basis points in 1979 to 197 basis points in 1985. The diversification power of a class of assets was an insufficient basis for introducing that asset class into the asset mix of an institution receiving deposit guarantees. As long as the new asset investment strategies had the potential to generate sufficiently attractive positive outcomes, an insured institution, especially one with little or nothing to lose, has an incentive to undertake them even when they have a negative present value.

Another prediction of option-theoretic deposit insurance analysis is that put option contracts without dividend protection are subject to exploitation by the holder of the put. In the case of S&Ls, some this exploitation appears to have stepped over the line of legal propriety. The extent to which fraudulent practices contributed to the crisis is debated.[38] However, it should be emphasized that exploitation of the lack of effective 'dividend' protection in the deposit insurance contract also involved legal actions. For example, owner-managers pursuing high-risk strategies had a very strong incentive to pay themselves above market salaries and owners, in general, had strong incentives to declare dividends rather than to build-up the institution's capital or loan loss reserves.

3.4. Empirical evidence on S&L insolvency

There have been a number of investigations of the causes of the massive S&L insolvencies, including the studies by Barth, Brumbaugh, Sauerhaft & Wang

[37] See Gennotte [1990] for a model of bank competition with deposit insurance in which banks with comparative advantage in lending choose safe strategies and banks with greater investment costs choose riskier strategies.

[38] See Barth [1991, p. 44] and references he cites.

[1985], Benston & Carhill [1992], Pizzo, Fricker & Muolo [1991] and Williams, De Silva, Koehn & Ornstein [1991]. Hermalin & Wallace [1993] have carried out a very careful study in which they seek to explain an S&L's efficiency and then use those measures of efficiency and other factors as predictors of insolvency. All of these studies are generally supportive of the implications of the option-theoretic model of deposit insurance and its incentives. Because of their care with the data and their attention to econometric details in hypothesis testing, the Hermalin–Wallace study provides particularly compelling evidence cited extensively below.

Hermalin & Wallace begin by studying the efficiency of S&Ls in 1987 using a nonparametric analysis of production based on Varian [1984]. They found that the lines of business (i.e., types of investments) undertaken by an S&L had significant effects on the efficiency with which that firm operated and that inefficiency led to insolvency.[39] In particular, greater investment shares in service corporations[40], mortgages on commercial real estate and raw land, and in their own real capital (offices, furniture, and land) were all found to be negatively related to S&L efficiency while residential mortgage lending was positively related to efficiency. In other words, S&Ls that continued to emphasize traditional lines of business operated more efficiently than those who moved more aggressively into the deregulated lines. Controlling for the lines of business pursued, their study also shows that stock ownership and the proportion of brokered deposits employed were both positively related to S&L efficiency. However, the direct effect of each of these two variables (i.e. the effect *without* line of business controls) was strongly negative; stock firms were less efficient than mutual firms and firms which used brokered deposits heavily were less efficient than those which did not. An implication of these results is that stock ownership (presumably through better control of owner/manager agency problems) and brokered deposits (through their relative efficiency in raising funds) were per se efficient, but more likely to be associated with the adoption of the less efficient, deregulated lines of business.

A second set of findings in the Hermalin–Wallace study addresses the determinants of the types of assets held by S&Ls. These assets may be divided into three groups: deregulated lines of business (service corporations, commercial mortgages, and nonmortgage lending), hedging instruments (futures, options, and other derivatives), and traditional investments (residential mortgages and mortgage backed securities). They found that S&Ls that grew rapidly from 1982 to 1986 (presumably a set highly correlated with those which used brokered deposits extensively), those that were stock organizations, those with lower tangible net worth in 1982, and those located in California, Florida, or Texas[41] tended to emphasize the less efficient, deregulated lines of business and to de-emphasize

[39] The Hermalin–Wallace findings cited in this section were all significant at the 10% level or better and most were significant at the 1% level or better.

[40] Subsidiary corporations in which the primary assets were junk bonds or equity participations in real assets.

[41] Recall that these three states allowed the broadest use of deregulated assets by state-chartered institutions.

the use of hedging instruments (presumably risk-reducing) and investment in residential mortgages.

The third aspect of the Hermalin–Wallace study is an analysis of S&L insolvency in the period from 1987 to 1990 as a function of prevailing conditions, investment strategies, and efficiency. Insolvency in 1987–1990 was found to be strongly related to S&L inefficiency as of 1986. Controlling for this inefficiency and some other prevailing conditions (e.g. total assets), they found that greater 1982 tangible net worth led to a lower likelihood of insolvency, a finding consistent with the option-theoretic prediction on the effect of solvency on the incentive to exploited the deposit insurance contract. S&Ls that emphasized residential mortgage lending and the use of hedging instruments were less likely to become insolvent and those that emphasized commercial real estate lending were more likely to fail. The coefficients for investment in service corporations and nonmortgage lending, given the institution's overall efficiency, were insignificantly different from zero suggesting that inefficiency in these investment classes was more important than their inherent risks as a determinant of which firms became insolvent. Given the firm's investment strategy and its overall efficiency, S&Ls located in the California, Florida, or Texas were more likely to fail while stock firms and those which employed more brokered deposits were, statistically, no more likely to fail than mutual firms and those which did not rely heavily on brokered funds.

In interpreting the Hermalin–Wallace results on the effects of investment strategies, stock ownership, and the use of brokered deposits on insolvency, it is important to remember that stock ownership and the use of brokered deposits significantly increased the likelihood that an S&L would engage in the deregulated lines of business, that emphasis on those investments tended to make S&Ls less efficient, and that less efficient firms were more likely to fail.

Finally, the larger its investment in real capital (offices, furniture, etc.) the more likely an S&L failed, presumably an indication of the perverse agency incentives induced by the lack of effective 'dividend' protection in the deposit insurance contract.

4. Concluding remarks

The thesis of this essay has been that the U.S. Savings and Loan crisis of the late 1980s and early 1990s was caused and exacerbated by

1) a flaw in the structure of S&Ls that predisposed them to economic insolvency given rising interest rates,

2) the use of an incentive-incompatible deposit insurance scheme and its exploitation by S&Ls (especially permanent stock companies) that became poorly capitalized as a result of 1), and

3) legislative and regulatory actions to avoid recognizing the economic insolvency of numerous firms and the general under-capitalization of the industry, actions which in many cases were dysfunctional in the context of the existing deposit insurance contract.

Evidence on the determinants of efficiency and insolvency in S&Ls are strikingly supportive of this thesis and the option-theoretic model used in its development.

Acknowledgements

The work on this paper was supported by the Haas School of Business. The paper was completed while the author was visiting at the Banca d'Italia, Roma. The support of these institutions is gratefully acknowledged. The ideas expressed are solely the responsibility of the author.

References

Barth, J.R. (1991). *The Great Savings and Loan Debacle*, The AEI Press, Washington, D.C.

Barth, J.R., and R.D. Brumbaugh, Jr. (1992). Depository institution failures and failure costs: The role of moral-hazard and agency problems, working paper presented at the Conf. on Rebuilding Public Confidence through Financial Reform, Ohio State University

Barth, J.R., R.D. Brumbaugh, D. Sauerhaft and G.H.K., Wang (1985). Thrift institution failures: Causes and policy issues, in: *Proc. Conf. on Bank Structure and Performance*, Federal Reserve Bank of Chicago.

Benston, G., and M. Carhill (1992). The thrift disaster: Tests of moral hazard, deregulation, and other hypotheses, unpublished mimeo, Emory University.

Bhattacharya, S., and A.V., Thakor (1991). Contemporary banking theory, discussion paper #504, Graduate School of Business, Indiana University, Bloomington, IN.

Black, F., and M. Scholes (1973). The pricing of options and corporate liabilities. *J. Polit. Econ.* 81, 637–659.

Brumbaugh, R.D., Jr. (1988). *Thrifts Under Siege*, Balinger Publishing Company, Cambridge, MA.

Cootner, P. (1969). The liquidity of the savings and loan industry, in: *Study of the Savings and Loan Industry*, Federal Home Loan Bank, Washington, D.C.

Cox, J.C., and Rubinstein, M. (1985). *Options Markets*, Prentice-Hall, Englewood Cliffs, N.J.

Diamond, D. (1984). Financial intermediation and delegated monitoring. *Rev. Econ. Studies* 51, 393–414

Diamond, D., and P. Dybvig (1983). Bank runs, deposit insurance, and liquidity. *J. Polit. Econ.* 91, 401–419

Emerson, G. (1934). Guaranty of deposits under the Banking Act of 1933. *Q. J. Econ.* 48, 229–244.

Ewalt, J.H. (1962). *A Business Reborn*, American Savings and Loan Institution Press, Chicago, IL.

Federal Deposit Insurance Corporation (1950, 1952). *Annual Report*, FDIC.

Gennotte, G. (1990). Deposit insurance and bank competition, finance working paper, IBER, University of California, Berkeley, CA.

Gennotte, G., and D. Pyle (1991). Capital controls and bank risk. *J. Banking Finance* 15, 805–824.

Gibson, W.E. (1972). Deposit insurance in the United States: Evaluation and reform. *J. Financ. Quant. Anal.* 7, 1575–1594.

Grossman, R.S. (1992). Deposit insurance, regulation, and moral hazard in the thrift industry: Evidence from the 1930s. *Am. Econ. Rev.* 82, 800–822.

Hermalin, B., and N. Wallace (1993). The determinants of efficiency and solvency in savings and loans, working paper, Haas School of Business, University of California, Berkeley, CA.

Hermalin, B., and N. Wallace (1992). Organization, control, and the performance of savings and loans, working paper, Haas School of Business, University of California, Berkeley, CA.

Homer, S. (1977). *A History of Interest Rates*, 2nd edition, Rutgers University Press, New Brunswick, N.J.

Horvitz, P.M. (1975). Failures of large banks: Implications for deposit insurance and banking supervision. *J. Financ. Quant. Anal.* 10, 589–601.

Horvitz, P.M. (1989). The FSUC crisis and the southwest plan. *Am. Econ. Rev.* 79, 146–150.

Kane, E.J. (1985). *The Gathering Crisis in Federal Deposit Insurance*, MIT Press, MA.

Kane, E.J. (1989). Changing incentives facing financial services regulators. *J. Financ. Services Res.* 2, 265–274.

Kane, E.J. (1990). *The S&L Insurance Mess: How Did It Happen?*, The Urban Institute Press, Washington, D.C.

Keeley, M.C. (1990). Deposit insurance, risk, and market power in banking. *Am. Econ. Rev.* 80, 1183–1200.

Leland, H.E., and D.H. Pyle (1977). Informational asymmetries, financial structure, and financial intermediation. *J. Finance* 32, 371–387.

Lieber, P. (1931). The commercial and financial future of america, in: H.M. Bodfish (ed.), *History of Building And Loan in the United States*, U.S. Building and Loan League, Chicago, IL.

Mayer, T. (1965). A Graduated deposit insurance plan. *Rev. Econ. Stat.* 47, 114–116.

Mayers, D., and C.L. Smith, Jr. (1982). Toward a positive theory of insurance, in: *Monograph Series in Finance and Economics*, Graduate School of Business Administration, New York University, New York, NY.

Merton, R.C. (1977). An analytic derivation of the cost of deposit insurance and loan guarantees: An application of modern option pricing theory. *J. Banking Finance* 1, 3–11.

Merton, R.C. (1978). On the cost of deposit insurance when there are surveillance costs. *J. Bus.* 51, 439–452.

Merton, R.C., and Z. Bodie (1992). On the management of deposit insurance and other guarantees, working paper #92-081, Harvard Business School

Morton, J.E. (1956). *Urban Mortgage Lending: Comparative Markets and Experience*, Princeton University Press, Princeton, NJ.

Mullins, H., and D.H. Pyle (1994). Liquidation costs and risk-based capital, *J. Banking and Finance* 18, 113–138.

Office of Thrift Supervision (1992). Supplemental 1st Quarter 1992 Data, Washington, D.C.

Prather, W.C. (1970). *Savings Accounts*, American Savings and Loan Institution Press, Chicago, IL.

Pizzo, S., M. Fricker and P. Muolo (1991). *Inside Job*, Harper-Collins Publishers, New York, NY.

Pyle, D.H. (1984). Deregulation and deposit insurance reform. *Econ. Rev.* Spring, Federal Reserve Bank of San Francisco, 5–15.

Pyle, D.H. (1986). Capital regulation and deposit insurance. *J. Banking Finance* 10, 189–201.

Schwartz, E., and G.M. Vasconcellos, eds. (1989). *Restructuring the Thrift Industry: What Can We Learn from the British and Canadian Models?*, Martindale Center for the Study of Private Enterprise, Lehigh University, Bethlehem, PA.

Scott, K.W., and T. Mayer (1971). Risk and regulation in banking: Some proposals for deposit insurance. *Stanford Law Rev.* 23, 537–582.

Tobin, J. (1989). Deposit insurance must go. *Wall Street Journal*, November 22.

U.S. Congressional Budget Office (1991). *The Economic and Budget Outlook: An Update*, August.

U.S. General Accounting Office (various years). Resolving the savings and loan crisis: Billions more and additional reforms needed, GAO/T-AFMD-90-15.

United States League of Savings Institutions (1990). *Savings Institutions Sourcebook*, Chicago, IL.

Varian, H. (1984). The nonparametric approach to production analysis. *Econometrica* 52, 579–597.

Williams, M.A. (1991). Why did do many savings and loans go bankrupt? *Econ. Lett.*, 36, 61–66.

Biographical Information

Franklin ALLEN is Nippon Life Professor of Finance and Economics at the Wharton School of the University of Pennsylvania. He is currently Executive Editor of the *Review of Financial Studies*. He was formerly Vice Dean and Director of Wharton Doctoral Programs. He received his doctorate from Oxford University. Dr. Allen's main areas of interest are corporate finance, in the *American Economic Review, Econometrica, Economic Journal, European Economic Review, Journal of Finance, Journal of Financial Economics, Journal of Financial Intermediation, Journal of Economic Theory, Review of Economic Studies, Review of Financial Studies* and the *Rand Journal of Economics*. (Chapters 22 and 25).

Linda CANINA is an Assistant Professor of Finance at the Cornell University School of Hotel Administration, where she has been since 1993. She holds a Ph.D. in Finance from the New York University Leonard N. Stern School of Business. She has published in academic journals, in the area of options. Other research include empirical asset pricing. (Chapter 10).

Peter CARR is a Professor of Finance, who has been at Cornell University's Johnson Graduate School of Management, since receiving his Ph.D. in Finance from UCLA in 1989. He has published articles in *The Journal of Finance*, the *Review of Financial Studies*, and various other finance journals. He is currently an Associate Editor for *Management Science*. His research interests are primarily in the field of derivative securities, especially American-style and exotic derivatives. He consults for several firms and has given numerous talks at both practitioner and academic conferences. (Chapter 7).

Joseph A. CHERIAN received his B.Sc. degree in Electrical Engineering from Massachusetts Institute of Technology, his M.Sc. in Finance from Cornell University, and a Ph.D. degree in Finance from Cornell University. He currently teaches Finance at the graduate level at the School of Management, Boston University. Dr. Cherian has also lectured at the graduate level at the Johnson Graduate School of Management at Cornell University. He has published in both academic as well as practitioner journals and has served as a reviewer for various journals, including the *Journal of Economic Theory* and *Journal of Financial Intermediation*. He has also served as a consultant for various organizations on the pricing and hedging of derivative products, specifically equity and interest rate sensitive options and futures. His current research interests include interest rate derivatives, the use of non-linear filtering methods in optimal portfolio selection, and issues in financial market manipulation. (Chapter 20).

Gregory CONNOR received a Bachelor's degree in economics from Georgetown University (1975). He then worked for two years as a research assistant in the Division of Research and Statistics at the Board of Governors of the Federal Reserve System, in Washington D.C. This was followed by a return to school for a Master's (1978) and Ph.D. (1982) in economics at Yale University. He taught in the Departments of Finance at Northwestern University (1981–1985) and University of California Berkeley (1985–1994). During his time at Berkeley, he spent 18 months as a visiting faculty member in the Department of Banking and Finance at University College, Dublin in Ireland. He is currently Director of Research – Europe at BARRA International, working in BARRA's London office. (Chapter 4).

George M. CONSTANTINIDES is the Leon Carroll Marshall Professor of Finance at the Graduate School of Business, the University of Chicago. He holds degrees from Oxford University and Indiana University. He previously taught at the GSIA, Carnegie–Mellon University and visited the GSB, Harvard University as a Marvin Bower fellow. He is a founding member of the Society for Financial Studies and served as president and vice president of the Society. He is a research associate of the National Bureau of Economic research. He served as director of the American Finance Association and the Western Finance Association and as member of the Interim Governing Board of the University of Cyprus. He is a director/trustee of a number of DFA funds and trusts, member of the Merrill Lynch Academic Advisory Council and member of the Athens LBA Academic Council. His current research interests are on asset pricing, fixed income securities and derivative securities. (Chapter 1.)

Kent D. DANIEL is an Assistant Professor of Finance at the Graduate School of Business at the University of Chicago. He holds a B.S. degree in Physics from the California Institute of Technology, and an M.B.A. and Ph.D. in Finance from the Anderson Graduate School of Management at UCLA. His research interests are in the areas of corporate finance, econometrics and the formation of asset prices. (Chapter 23).

Werner F.M. De BONDT is Frank Graner Professor of Investment Management in the School of Business at the University of Wisconsin-Madison. He received his Ph.D. in Business Administration from Cornell University in 1985. As a native of Belgium, Werner De Bondt also studied at universities in Antwerp and Louvain. Over the years, he has been a Visiting Professor at Cornell University, the Catholic University of Louvain (Belgium), and Erasmus University Rotterdam (The Netherlands) (Chapter 13).

David EASLEY is a Professor of Economics at Cornell University where he is currently Director of the Center for Analytic Economics. He has also been on the faculty at the California Institute of Technology and Cambridge University. His research interests include market microstructure, evolution in markets and choice under uncertainty. He is an Associate Editor of *Econometrica* and the *Journal of Economic Theory*. (Chapter 12).

B. ESPEN ECKBO is Professor of Finance at the Faculty of Commerce and Business Administration, University of British Columbia, Canada, where he has been since his Ph.D. graduation from the University of Rochester in 1981. His main research interests are in the areas of mergers and acquisitions, investment banking, and the interface between corporate finance and industrial economics. He currently serves on seven editorial boards and, with more than 30 publications, is a frequent contributor in top finance journals. In 1987 he received the prestigious Batterymarch Fellowship, and Canadian Economics Association's Harry G. Johnson (best paper) Prize. He has won numerous research grants, most recently a three-year, $200, 000 grant from the Norwegian Research Council to study the economics of insider trading on the Oslo Stock Exchange. (Chapter 31).

Wayne FERSON holds the Pigott-PACCAR Professorship in Finance at the University of Washington, where he has taught investments and financial economics at the undergraduate through Ph.D. levels since 1992. He was formerly a faculty member at the University of Chicago, the Wharton School at the University of Pennsylvania, and a visiting faculty member of the Graduate School of Business at Stanford University. He holds the Ph.D. degree in Finance and the Masters degree in Economics from Stanford University, and the Masters of Business Administration and an undergraduate degree in Engineering from Southern Methodist University.

Professor Ferson is an internationally recognized expert on the empirical analysis of asset pricing models, with more than two dozen published papers in that area. His research focuses on asset pricing models, the predictability of security returns, the relation of security prices to economic variables, and the evaluation of investment performance. He has published his research in most of the leading finance journals, including the *Journal of Finance*, the *Journal of Financial Economics*, the *Journal of Political Economy*, the *Review of Financial Studies*, and others. He regularly presents his research findings at leading universities and conferences in the U.S. and abroad. He has served as a Director of the Western Finance Association and as a member of the editorial boards of the *Journal of Financial and Quantitative Analysis*, *Management Science*, the *Review of Financial Studies*, and the *Review of Quantitative Finance and Accounting*. He serves as a referee for many of the top journals in finance and as a program committee member for the leading professional associations.

Born in 1951, Professor Ferson is a U.S. Citizen raised in Massachusetts, Texas and New York. He is married with two step sons. His avocations include hiking, in-line skating, skiing, travel and dining. He is a private pilot, with an instrument rating. (Chapter 5).

Stephen FIGLEWSKI is a Professor of Finance and Yamaichi Faculty Fellow at the New York University Leonard N. Stern School of Business, where he has been since 1976. He holds a B.A. degree in Economics from Princeton and a Ph.D. in Economics from the Massachusetts Institute of Technology. He has published extensively in academic journals, especially in the area of financial futures and options. He is the founding Editor of *The Journal of Derivatives* and an Associate Editor for several other journals. He was also a senior editor and author for the book "Financial Options: From Theory to Practice".

In addition to his academic career, Professor Figlewski has also worked on Wall Street as a Vice President at the First Boston Corporation, in charge of research on equity derivative products, and he has been a member of the New York Futures Exchange and a Competitive Options Trader at the New York Stock Exchange, trading for his own account as a market maker in stock index futures and options. (Chapter 10).

Mark GRINBLATT is an Associate Professor at UCLA's Anderson School, where he has held an appointment since 1981. He held a visiting position at the Wharton School from 1987–1989 and worked as a Vice President for Salomon Brothers, Inc. from 1989–1990. Dr. Grinblatt received a Ph.D. in Economics from Yale University in 1982 and a B.A. in Economics and Mathematics from the University of Michigan in 1977. He currently serves as an Associate Editor of the *Journal of Financial and Quantitative Analysis* and as a Director on the board of Salomon Swapco, Inc. As an author of over 20 papers published in finance and economics journals, he has written extensively on the topic of performance evaluation. His past research, both theoretical and empirical, has also explored asset pricing, rational expectations equilibria, corporate finance, derivatives valuation, and agency theory. In addition to pursuing his current research interests in security design, derivatives, and LDC debt, Dr. Grinblatt is currently working with Sheridan Titman on a financial theory textbook for MBA's, "Financial Theory and Corporate Strategy", to be published by Irwin in the near future. (Chapter 19).

Nils H. HAKANSSON was born in Sweden and received his Ph.D. from UCLA in 1966. He is a former member of the faculty at UCLA as well as at Yale University and is currently the Sylvan C. Coleman Professor of Finance and Accounting at the University of California, Berkeley.

Professor Hakansson is a Certified Public Accountant and spent three years with Arthur Young & Company. He has twice been a Visiting Scholar at Bell Laboratories in New Jersey and was, in 1975, the Hoover Fellow at the University of New South Wales in Sydney and, in 1982, the Chevron Fellow at Simon Fraser University in British Columbia. In 1984, Professor Hakansson was a Special Visiting Professor at the Stockholm School of Economics, where he was also awarded an honorary doctorate in economics. He is listed in *Who's Who in Economics*, is a Fellow of Accounting Researchers International Association, a member of the Financial Economists Roundtable, and a member of the board of directors of several companies and foundations. (Chapter 3).

Donald B. HAUSCH is Associate Professor of Managerial Economics in the School of Business of the University of Wisconsin-Madison. He received his B.Sc. in Mathematics and M.Sc. in Management Science from the University of British Columbia and his Ph.D. in Managerial

Economics and Decision Sciences from the J.L. Kellogg Graduate School of Management at Northwestern University. He has held a visiting position at Dartmouth College and served as an Associate Editor of *Management Science*. His research interests are in market efficiency, auctions and competitive bidding, financial signalling, and the economics of organizations. He has co-authored and co-edited three books and has published papers in *Review of Financial Studies*, *Journal of Applied Corporate Finance*, *Rand Journal of Economics*, *Economic Theory*, *Journal of Business*, *Management Science*, *Interfaces*, and other journals. (Chapter 18).

Gabriel HAWAWINI is Yamaichi Professor of Finance and former Director General of the Euro–Asia Centre and Associate Dean of INSEAD, the European Institute of Business Administration (1988–1994). He is a Chemical Engineer by training and received his Doctorate in Economics and Finance from New York University (1977). Before joining INSEAD, he taught at New York University, the City University of New York and Columbia University (1974–1982). In 1982 he received the "Baruch College Presidential Award for Distinguished Faculty Scholarship". During the 1987–1988 academic year he was Visiting Professor of Finance at the Wharton School of the University of Pennsylvania where he received the "Helen Kardon Moss Anvil Award for Excellence in Teaching". Gabriel Hawawini is a past Vice President of the French Finance Association and the author of ten books and over sixty research papers. His recent publications are in the areas of financial-asset valuation, portfolio management and the structure of the financial-services industry in the U.S., Europe and Asia. His most recent book *Mergers and Acquisitions in the US Banking Industry*, has been published by North-Holland (1991). (Chapter 17.)

David HIRSHLEIFER is a Professor of Finance at the University of michigan Business School. He has published papers on varied topics, including the effects of managerial self-interest on corporate investment decisions; strategies for bidder and target firms in corporate takeover contests; how risk can be controlled using futures markets; how futures prices are determined; security analysis and trading strategies of institutional stock market investors; and the role of information in fads and fashions. He is currently serving as Editor of the *Review of Financial Studies*, Co-editor of the *Journal of Economics and Management Strategy*, Associate Editor of the *Journal of Financial Intermediation*, and Associate Editor of the *Journal of Corporate Finance*. He is collaborating with J. Fred Weston on a revision of *Mergers, Restructuring, and Corporate Control*. (Chapter 26).

Roger G. IBBOTSON is a Professor of Finance at Yale School of Management. He is also President of Ibbotson Associates, Inc. an investment consulting firm in Chicago and New Haven. Professor Ibbotson is co-author (with Rex Sinquefield) of *Stocks, Bonds, Bills, and Inflation* and co-author (with Gary Brinson) of *Global Investments*, McGraw-Hill. He has also written numerous scholarly articles. He previously taught at the University of Chicago, where he was Executive Director of the Center for Research in Security Prices. He received a B.S. from Purdue University, an M.B.A. from Indiana University, and a Ph.D. from the University of Chicago. (Chapter 30).

Robert JARROW is the Ronald P. and Susan E. Lynch Professor of Investment Management at the Johnson Graduate School of Management, Cornell University. He is a graduate of Duke University, Dartmouth College and the Massachusetts Institute of Technology. Professor Jarrow is renowned for his pioneering work on the Heath–Jarrow–Morton model for pricing interest rate derivatives. His current research interests include the pricing of exotic interest rate options and other derivative securities as well as investment management theory. His publications include two books, "Options Pricing" and "Finance Theory", as well as over 50 publications in leading finance and economic journals. Professor Jarrow is currently Co-editor of *Mathematical Finance* and an Associate Editor of the *Review of Financial Studies*, the *Journal of Financial and Quantitative Analysis*, and the *Review of Derivatives Research*. He is also a Managing Director and the Director of Research at Kamakura Corporation. (Chapter 7, 8, 20).

Donald B. KEIM is Professor of Finance at the Wharton School of the University of Pennsylvania. He received his Ph.D. in Finance and Economics from the University of Chicago. His research has dealt with the relation between stock returns and predetermined variables (market capitalization, earnings/price ratios and calendar turning points), testing asset pricing models, and the junk bond market. Current research projects are concerned with the price impact of block trades, the costs associated with trading common stocks, and the behavior of real estate-related common stocks. (Chapter 17).

Allan W. KLEIDON is Vice President of Cornerstone Research, and a Consulting Professor of Law (in Finance) at the School of Law, Stanford University. He received his Ph.D. and M.B.A. degrees from the University of Chicago, and B.Com. (Hons.) and LL.B. (Hons.) degrees from the University of Queensland, Australia. Dr. Kleidon joined Cornerstone Research from the Graduate School of Business, Stanford University, and has taught at the University of California at Berkeley, the University of Chicago and the University of Queensland, and continues to teach courses at Stanford. He has served as Associate Editor of the *Journal of Finance* and the *Journal of Financial Economics*. Dr. Kleidon has worked with Cornerstone Research providing expert testimony on securities valuation, securities markets, industry and damages analysis. His current research focuses on the structure and performance of securities markets, including the performance of markets under such stresses as the Crash of October 1987. (Chapter 16).

Robert A. KORAJCZYK is the Harry G. Guthmann Distinguished Professor of Finance and Chairman of the Department of Finance at the Kellogg Graduate School of Management, Northwestern University. He holds a B.A. in Mathematics (1976), an M.B.A. in Finance and Econometrics (1977), and a Ph.D. in Finance (1983) from the University of Chicago. He joined the faculty at Northwestern University in 1982 and has additionally held appointments at the University of Chicago (Visiting Associate Professor, 1989–1990, and Lecturer, 1981–1982). He is an Editor of the *Review of Financial Studies*, Associate Editor of the *Journal of Financial and Quantitative Analysis* and the *Journal of Empirical Finance*, and past Associate Editor of the *Review of Financial Studies*, *Journal of Business & Economic Statistics*, and *Review of Quantitative Finance and Accounting*. (Chapter 4).

Stephen F. LEROY is Carlson Professor of Finance at the Curtis L. Carlson School of Management, University of Minnesota. His prior affiliations were with the Department of Economics, University of California, Santa Barbara; the Federal Reserve Board; and the Federal Reserve Bank of Kansas City. He has visited at the California Institute of Technology, the University of Chicago, the University of California, Davis and the University of California, Berkeley. (Chapter 14).

Vojislav MAKSIMOVIC is at the College of Business and Management at the University of Maryland, College Park. He received his B.Sc. (Econ) and M.Sc. degrees in Mathematical Economics and Econometrics from the London School of Economics and his Ph.D. degree in Business Economics from Harvard University. He was previously on the faculty at the University of British Columbia. His principal research interests are in the interactions between financial and product markets. (Chapter 27).

A.G. MALLIARIS is the Walter F. Mullady Sr. Professor of Business Administration at Loyola University Chicago. He graduated from the Athens School of Economics and Business in 1965 and worked for one year as a research assistant at the Center of Planning and Economic Research in Athens. From 1966 to 1972 he studied Economics and Mathematics at the University of Oklahoma where he received the Ph.D. in Economics. From 1972 to 1976 he did post graduate studies in Mathematics and Economics at the University of Chicago. He has authored and co-authored numerous articles in professional journals such as *The Society of Industrial and Applied Mathematics Review*, *Mathematics of Operations Research*, *Review of Economic Studies*, *Journal of Financial and Quantitative Analysis*, *Review of Quantitative Finance and Accounting*, *Journal of Futures Markets* and others. He has also co-authored with William A. Brock two books on "Stochastic Methods in Economics and Finance" and "Differential Equations, Stability and Chaos in Dynamic Economics". He specializes in financial economics. (Chapter 1).

Terry A. MARSH has M.B.A. and Ph.D. degrees from the University of Chicago, and a Bachelor of Commerce with First Class Honors and University Medal from the University of Queensland (Australia). He was an Assistant and Associate Professor of Finance at M.I.T. from 1981–1985 is currently an Associate Professor of Finance at U.C. Berkeley. He was Chairman of the Finance Group from 1987–1990. He has been a Batterymarch Fellow in 1985, a National Fellow at the Hoover Institution, Stanford University in 1986, a member of the Presidential Task Force on Market Mechanisms ("Brady Commission") in 1987–1988, and a Visiting Professor and Yamaichi Fellow at the University of Tokyo, Department of Economics, in Fall 1994. He is a Fellow, CPA, Australian Society of Accountants. He has consulted for the New York Stock Exchange, the American Stock Exchange, the Options Clearing Corporation, the Industrial Bank of Japan, and New Japan Securities, is a member of the boards of the Buchanan Fund and Rubicon Capital, and is a founder and principal of Quantal International Inc. (Chapter 9).

Ronald W. MASULIS is the Frank K. Houston Professor of Finance at the Owen Graduate School of Management, Vanderbilt University. He earned his M.B.A. and Ph.D. degrees at the University of Chicago, with specializations in Finance and Economics. He conducts research in the fields of corporate finance, market microstructure, financial institutions, and most recently international finance. His research on capital structure changes and the security issuance process is widely referenced. Professor Masulis has taught at University of California, Los Angeles; the Australian Graduate School of Management; the european Institute of Business Administration; formerly James M. Collins Professor of Finance and Executive Director of the Center for the Study of Financial Institutions and Markets, Southern Methodist University. He is the author of *The Debt-Equity Choice*, which reviews the theoretical and empirical literature on capital structure. His research is published in the *Journal of Financial Economics*, *Journal of Finance*, *Review of Financial Studies*, *Journal of Financial and Quantitative Analysis*, *Journal of Monetary Economics*, *Journal of Accounting and Economics*, *Journal of Business and Economics Statistics*, and *Journal of Empirical Finance*. He has served on the board of directors of the American Finance Association and the executive committee of the Western Finance Association; was an Economic Fellow with Securities and Exchange Commission; a Visiting Scholar at the Federal Home Loan Bank Board; and a Financial Economist at the FSLIC. He has served as Associate Editor of the leading journals in the field and currently serves on the editorial boards of *Journal of Finance*, *Journal of Financial and Quantitative Analysis*, *Journal of Corporate Finance*, and *Journal of Financial Research*. (Chapter 31).

Roni MICHAELY is an Assistant Professor of Finance at Cornell University, Johnson Graduate School of Management. He received his doctorate from New York University. Dr. Michaely's main areas of interest concern the interaction between capital market imperfections, corporate policy, prices, and investors' behavior in financial markets. He has published articles in the *Review of Financial Studies*, *Journal of Finance*, and *Journal of Financial and Quantitative Analysis*. (Chapter 25).

John M. MULVEY is Professor of Operations Research at Princeton University. His specialty is the application of optimization techniques to financial planning problems. Over the past decade, he has implemented planning systems for several companies, including pacific Mutual, American Express, Towers Perrin, and Proprietary Financial Products. These systems integrate asset and liability decisions in order to maximize an investor's wealth over time. He holds a B.S. (1969) in Engineering and an M.S. (1969) in Computer Science from the University of Illinois, Urbana, and received an MS (1974) and a Ph.D. (1975) from UCLA in Management. He taught for three years at Harvard University (Business School) before moving to Princeton in 1978. He has consulted widely in business and industry (Office of Tax Analysis at the Treasury Department, Joint Chiefs of Staff at the Defense Department, IBM, TRW, and SAI). He has edited three books and has published close to 100 scholarly papers. (Chapter 15).

Vasant NAIK is Associate Professor of Finance at the Faculty of Commerce and Business Administration of the University of British Columbia. He received his Ph.D. from University of California, Berkeley in 1988. The areas of his specialization include the theory of asset pricing, valuation of contingent claims, the term structure of interest rates and portfolio theory. (Chapter 2).

Maureen O'HARA is the Robert W. Purcell Professor of Finance at the Johnson Graduate School of Management at Cornell University. She has also taught at the London Business School and the University of California at Los Angeles. She received the Young Scholar Recognition Award from the American Association of University Women in 1986. She is currently Vice President of the Western Finance Association and a Director of the American Finance Association. She is a Co-editor of the *Journal of Financial Intermediation* and is an Associate Editor of numerous finance journals. Her numerous publications include the book "Market Microstructure Theory". (Chapter 12).

David H. PYLE is Visiting Professor of Finance at the London Business School and Booth Professor of Banking & Finance (emeritus) at the Haas School of Business, University of California, Berkeley. He has published a number of articles on deposit insurance and bank regulation in economics and finance journals. Dr. Pyle has served as a Senior Advisor to the U.S. Comptroller of the Currency and as a Visiting Research Scholar at the Banca d'Italia and the Federal Reserve Bank of San Francisco. He is a past President of the Western Finance Association and an External Examiner for the Chinese University of Hong Kong. (Chapter 33).

Jay R. RITTER is the Fred S. Bailey Memorial Professor of Finance at the University of Illinois at Urbana-Champaign. He holds a Ph.D. in Economics and Finance from the University of Chicago (1981), and has previously taught at the Wharton School, the University of Michigan, and the M.I.T. Sloan School of Management. Prof. Ritter's publications include "The Long-Run Performance of Initial Public Offerings" in the March 1991 *Journal of Finance*, which won the Smith Breeden Award for the best article in the *Journal of Finance* during 1991, and "The New Issues Puzzle", with Tim Loughran, in the March 1995 *Journal of Finance*. He is a Director of the American Finance Association and an Associate Editor of the *Journal of Financial Economics*, the *Journal of Financial Research*, and the *Journal of Finance*. (Chapter 30).

Lemma W. SENBET (Ph.D. 1975) is the William E. Mayer Chair Professor of Finance at the University of Maryland. Previously he held two endowed chairs at the University of Wisconsin-Madison as the Charles Albright Professor of Finance (1987–1990) and as Dikson-Bascom Professor (1983–1987). As an invited Visiting Professor, Professor Senbet taught at the University of California – Berkeley (1984–1985) and at Northwestern University (1980–1981). He was also Distinguished Research Visitor at the London School of Economics in June 1994.

Professor Senbet is internationally recognized for his extensive contributions to corporate and international finance published in leading academic journals, and he has received numerous honors and research awards for his work. The 1986 survey ranked him third among world-wide contributing authors to the *Journal of Finance*, the premier journal in the field, for the period 1976–1985. He has been en elected member of the prestigious Board of Directors of the American Finance Association and past President of the Western Finance Association. Professor Senbet has served on numerous editorial boards of the leading journals in finance, including the *Journal of Finance*, *Journal of Financial and Quantitative Analysis*, and *Journal of Banking and Finance*.

Professor Senbet has been a consultant for the World Bank and government agencies in USA, Canada, and Africa on issues relating to corporate financial incentives, pricing of country funds, and financial reform. An Ethiopian by birth, he was awarded the 1970 Chancellor's Gold Medal as outstanding graduate of Haile Selassi I University (received from the Emperor). Professor Senbet has chaired numerous national and international programs, delivered invited and keynote speeches, and served on numerous panels at international forums around the United States, Europe, the Pacific-Basin, and Africa, including at the Third African–African American Summit (Dakar, 1995).

He has also served as a resource person for the African Economic Research Consortium (1994–1995) and for the Governors' Forum (a forum of governors of central banks from East and Southern Africa, London, 1995).

Professor Senbet has produced a string of doctoral graduates and has placed them in faculty positions at such major research universities as Carnegie Mellon, Dartmouth, Vanderbilt, and Florida. He is a recipient of the 1994 Allen Krowe Award for Teaching Excellence at the University of Maryland Business School. (Chapter 28).

James K. SEWARD is an Associate Professor of Business Administration at the Amos tuck School of Business Administration at Dartmouth College. His undergraduate degree in Business Administration is from Georgetown University; his Ph.D. in Finance is from the University of Wisconsin-Madison. He currently teaches courses in corporate finance, financial management and corporate restructuring and reorganization. His research interests include voluntary and distressed corporate restructurings, the use of equity-linked securities by corporations and the medium of exchange in corporate takeovers. Professor Seward has taught overseas in graduate and executive programs at The International University of Japan and The Helsinki School of Business and Economics. His articles have appeared in leading academic journals such as the *Journal of Finance*, *Journal of Financial Economics*, *Review of Financial Studies*, *Academy of Management Review* and *Journal of Economics and Management Strategy*. He has also been involved in consulting projects and management education with institutions such as the Wisconsin Public Service Commission, the New York State Public Service Commission, Arthur Andersen and Co., boston Consulting Group, Citicorp, Alex Brown & Sons, US West and Westinghouse. He has also worked previously in corporate finance with the Washington Gas Light Company and Marsh & McLennan. (Chapter 28).

Gordon A. SICK is a Professor of Finance at the University of Calgary. In the past, he has held faculty positions at the Yale School of Management, the University of British Columbia and the University of Alberta. In the field of real options his research is particularly oriented toward implementing models in the resource industries and the real estate industry. He also publishes articles on other aspects of capital budgeting, including certainty-equivalent valuation and the effects of corporate and personal taxation on valuation (interest tax shields). He has also published papers on security market seasonalities and bank cost analysis. He has been an Associate Editor of *Management Science* since 1982. He has served as a Director of the Western Finance Association and the Financial Management Association. (Chapter 21).

Douglas G. STEIGERWALD is Professor of Economics at the University of California, Santa Barbara. His principle research interests are in empirical finance and nonparametric time-series analysis. His published work includes articles in *Econometrica*, *Journal of Econometrics*, *Econometric Theory*, *Journal of the American Statistical Association*, *Review of Economic Studies*, and *Journal of Empirical Finance*. (Chapter 14).

René M. STULZ is the Ralph Kurtz Chair in Finance at the Ohio State University. He previously taught at the University of Rochester and held visiting appointments at the Massachusetts Institute of Technology and the University of Chicago. He received his Ph.D. from the Massachusetts Institute of Technology.

René M. Stulz is currently the Editor of the *Journal of Finance*. He was formerly an Editor of the *Journal of Financial Economics*. He is also Associate Editor of several other journals. Further, he is a member of the Asset Pricing and Corporate Finance Programs of the National Bureau of Economic Research.

He has published more than forty papers in finance and economics journals, including the *Journal of Political Economy*, the *Journal of Financial Economics*, the *Journal of Finance*, and the *Journal of Monetary Economics*. His research has addressed issues in international finance, corporate finance and investments.

His current research focuses on the relation between corporate performance and corporate diversification, on testing and developing the implications of agency costs of managerial discretion for corporate finance, Japanese corporate finance, international portfolio choice, and understanding cross-country covariances. He is also working on a book titled "Financial Engineering and Risk Management".

René M. Stulz teaches in executive development programs in the U.S. and in Europe. He has also served as a consultant for several major U.S. corporations. (Chapter 6).

Peter SWOBODA is Professor of Industrial Operations (including Finance) at the Karl Franzens University of Graz, Austria. He received his Ph.D. and Habilitation degrees at the Wirtschaftsuniversität (University of Business and Economics) of Vienna. He was previously Visiting Associate Professor at the University of Illinois in Champaign-Urbana, Professor of Business Administration at the Johann Wolfgang Goethe University of Frankfurt and full member of the Austrian Academy of Sciences, Vienna. His research interests are in the areas of finance, capital investments and the regulation of utilities. His numerous publications include two books on corporate finance and capital investments. He is a past president of the European Finance Association and organized the meeting of this organization in 1980 in Graz. Since 1989 he acts as a consultant for the Austrian government with respect to the regulation of the major Austrian electric utilities. (Chapter 24.)

Anjan THAKOR is NBD Professor of Finance and Chairman of the Finance Department at the School of Business, Indiana University. He has also served on the faculties of Northwestern University and UCLA.

Thakor obtained his Ph.D. in Finance from Northwestern University in August 1979. His research and teaching interests are in corporate finance and financial intermediation. He has published over 70 research papers and monographs on a variety of issues, including regulation of financial institutions, deposit insurance, loan commitments, securitization, credit rationing, security design, capital structure, dividend policy and stock repurchases, and corporate capital allocation decisions. His papers have been published in various academic journals, including *The American Economic Review*, *The Review of Economic Studies*, *The Journal of Finance*, *The Review of Financial Studies*, *The Journal of Economic Theory* and *The Journal of Financial Intermediation*. He also co-authored a textbook "Contemporary Financial Intermediation", with Stuart Greenbaum that was recently published by Dryden Press.

Thakor is and Editor of *The Journal of Financial Intermediation*, and Associate Editor of *The Journal of Banking and Finance*, *The Journal of Financial Research*, *Financial Management*, and *The Journal of Small Business Finance*. He has taught at the undergraduate, M.B.A. and Ph.D. levels and has won teaching awards. He is experienced in executive education and corporate consultancy. (Chapter 32).

Rex THOMPSON is Chairman of the Department of Finance and the Caruth Professor of Finance at the Cox School of Business, Southern Methodist University, Dallas Texas, 75275. He received his M.B.A. in 1975 and Ph.D. in 1978 from the University of Rochester. Starting as an Assistant Professor at Carnegie-Mellon University (1977–1981), he traveled to the University of British Columbia (1982–1986), and finally to the Wharton School (1986–1988) before moving to Cox. He has also had visiting appointments at the University of Washington (1981) and UBC (1991). Thompson's research and teaching interests are in capital market theory and evidence, corporate finance, and empirical methodology in finance and accounting. (Chapter 29).

Sheridan TITMAN currently holds the John J. Collins, S.J. Chair in Finance at Boston College. He has a B.S. from the University of Colorado and an M.S. and Ph.D. from Carnegie Mellon University. Professor Titman taught at UCLA for over ten years where in addition to his teaching and research activities he served as the department chair for the finance group and as the Vice Chairman of the UCLA management school faculty. Between 1992 and 1994 Professor Titman served on the faculty of the School of Business and Management at the Hong Kong University of Science and Technology where he was the Vice Chairman of the faculty and the Chairman of the faculty appointments committee for this new business school. In the 1988–1989 academic year Professor Titman worked in Washington D.C. as the special assistant to Assistant Secretary of the Treasury for Economic Policy. His duties in this position included policy analysis of proposed legislation related to the stock and future markets, leveraged buyouts and takeovers. Professor Titman's research interests include accounting, real estate and portfolio theory. He has published extensively in all these areas and serves on the board of a number of finance and real estate journals. He is a post Director of the American Finance Association and a current Director of the Asia Pacific Finance Association (Chapter 19).

Walter N. TOROUS is a member of the Finance faculty at UCLA's Anderson School. He received his undergraduate degree in Mathematics from the University of Waterloo and his Ph.D. degree in economics from the University of Pennsylvania. His research interests include empirical methods in financial economics. He has previously consulted with the U.S. Department of Housing and Urban Development and the Federal Home Loan Mortgage Corporation. (Chapter 11.)

Andrew WINTON is an Assistant Professor of Finance at the Kellogg Graduate School of Management of Northwestern University. Before entering academia, he was an asset/liability Management Officer at CoreStates Financial Corp in Philadelphia. He received an A.B. degree in Mathematics from Princeton University and M.B.A. and Ph.D. degrees in Finance from the University of Pennsylvania. Dr. Winton's research interests include financial contracting and security design, financial intermediation, and corporate finance. Dr. Winton has published articles in the *Journal of Finance*, *Review of Financial Studies*, and *Journal of Financial Intermediation*. (Chapter 22).

Josef ZECHNER holds a Finance Chair at the University of Vienna. He was previously a member of the Finance Department at the University of British Columbia and has held a research scholar position at the Stanford Graduate School of Business. His research interests are in the area of corporate finance, particularly applied to optimal choices of firms' financial structures. He has published numerous papers in top finance and economics journals and presented invited lectures in many research seminars and at international conferences. He is on the executive committee of the European Finance Association and program chair for the EFA conference in 1997. (Chapter 24.)

William T. ZIEMBA is the Alumni Professor of Management Science in the Faculty of Commerce and Business Administration at the University of British Columbia, Vancouver, Canada where he has taught since 1968. He has been a Visiting Professor at the University of California, Berkeley (where he received his Ph.D.), Stanford, UCLA, London School of Economics, University of Warwick, and the University of Tsukuba and will visit the University of Chicago in 1996. His research is in the areas of security market anomalies, worldwide asset management, portfolio analysis, financial modeling, Japanese financial markets and stochastic programming. He is the author of fifteen books and over a hundred research papers. His research papers have appeared in *Management Science*, *Mathematics of Operations Research*, *Operations Research*, *Interfaces*, *Stochastics*, *European Journal of Operational Research*, *Mathematical Programming*, *American Economic Review*, *Journal of Economic Perspectives*, *Journal of Finance*, *Bell Journal of Economics*, *JFQA*, *Economics Letters*, *OR Letters*, *Journal of Business*, *Journal of Portfolio Management*, *Financial Analysts Journal*, *Review of Futures Markets*, *Philosophical Transactions of the Royal Society*, *Applied Mathematical Finance*, *International Journal of Financial Analysis*, *Finanzmarket and Portfolio Management* and other journals and books. In May 1995 he organized research programs on Worldwide Security Market Anomalies and Worldwide Asset and Liability Allocation for the Program in Financial Mathematics at the Isaac Newton Institute, University of Cambridge and is co-editing volumes on these topics for the Cambridge University Press. He was the Departmental Editor for Finance of Management Science form 1982–1992 and has served on the TIMS Council and ORSA-TIMS publication committee. He is a former trustee of the UBC pension plan. Since 1989 he has been a consultant on worldwide asset allocation strategies to the Research Department of the Frank Russell Company in Tacoma, Washington, one of the world's leading pension fund consulting organizations. He helped Russell design the Russell–Yasuda asset-liability management model which has been used successfully since 1991 by Yasuda–Kasai, one of the largest insurance companies in Japan. That project was awarded second prize in the 1993 Franz Edelman Practice of Management Science competition. He has organized the finance sessions at eight ORSA-TIMS, International TIMS and INFORMS meetings and is the organizing chair of the International Conference on Stochastic programming to be held in Vancouver in August 1998. (Chapters 3, 15 and 18).

Subject Index

Handbooks in Operations Research and Management Science Contents of Previous Volumes

Volume 1. Optimization

Edited by G.L. Nemhauser, A.H.G. Rinnooy Kan and M.J. Todd

1989. xiv + 709 pp. ISBN 0-444-87284-1

Volume 2. Stochastic Models

Edited by D.P. Heyman and M.J. Sobel

1990. xv + 725 pp. ISBN 0-444-87473-9

Volume 3. Computing

Edited by E.G. Coffman, Jr., J.K. Lenstra and A.H.G. Rinnooy Kan

1992. x + 682 pp. ISBN 0-444-88097-6

Volume 4. Logistics of Production and Inventory

Edited by S.C. Graves, A.H.G. Rinnooy Kan and P.H. Zipkin

1993. xiii + 760 pp. ISBN 0-444-87472-0

9. Sequencing and Scheduling: Algorithms and Complexity, *by* E.L. Lawler, J.K. Lenstra, A.H.G. Rinnooy Kan and D.B. Shmoys
10. Hierarchical Production Planning, *by* G.R. Bitran and D. Tirupati
11. Requirements Planning, *by* K.R. Baker
12. The Just-in-Time System, *by* H. Groenevelt
13. Scientific Quality Management and Management Science, *by* P.J. Kolesar
14. Developments in Manufacturing Technology and Economic Evaluation Models, *by* C.H. Fine

Volume 5. Marketing

Edited by J. Eliashberg and G.L. Lilien

1993. xiv + 894 pp. ISBN 0-444-88957-4

1. Mathematical Marketing Models: Some Historic Perspectives and Future Projections, *by* J. Eliashberg and G.L. Lilien
2. Explanatory and Predictive Models of Consumer Behavior, *by* J.H. Roberts and G.L. Lilien
3. Mathematical Models of Group Choice and Negotiations, *by* K.P. Corfman and S. Gupta
4. Competitive Marketing Strategies: Game-Theoretic Models, *by* K.S. Moorthy
5. Non-Spatial Tree Models for the Assessment of Competitive Market Structure: An Integrated Review of the Marketing and Psychometric Literature, *by* W.S. DeSarbo, A.K. Manrai and L.A. Manrai
6. Market-Share Models, *by* L.G. Cooper
7. Pretest Market Forecasting, *by* G.L. Urban
8. New-Product Diffusion Models, *by* V. Mahajan, E. Muller and F.M. Bass
9. Econometric and Time-Series Market Response Models, *by* D.M. Hanssens and L.J. Parsons
10. Conjoint Analysis with Product-Positioning Applications, *by* P.E. Green and A.M. Krieger
11. Pricing Models in Marketing, *by* V.R. Rao
12. Sales Promotion Models, *by* R.C. Blattberg and S.A. Neslin
13. Salesforce Compensation: A Review of MS/OR Advances, *by* A.T. Coughlan
14. Salesforce Operations, *by* M.B. Vandenbosch and C.B. Weinberg
15. Marketing-Mix Models, *by* H. Gatignon
16. Marketing Decision Models: From Linear Programs to Knowledge-Based Systems, *by* A. Rangaswamy
17. Marketing Strategy Models, *by* Y. Wind and G.L. Lilien
18. Marketing–Production Joint Decision-Making, *by* J. Eliashberg and R. Steinberg

Volume 6. Operations Research and the Public Sector
Edited by S.M. Pollock, M.H. Rothkopf and A. Barnett
1994. xv + 723 pp. ISBN 0-444-89204-4

Volume 7. Network Models
Edited by M.O. Ball, T.L. Magnanti, C.L. Monma and G.L. Nemhauser
1995. xii + 758 pp. ISBN 0-444-89292-3

Volume 8. Network Routing

Edited by M.O. Ball, T.L. Magnanti, C.L. Monma and G.L. Nemhauser

1995. x + 785 pp. ISBN 0-444-82141-4